PRINCIPLES OF
MARKETING
A GLOBAL PERSPECTIVE

Philip **Kotler**

Gary **Armstrong**

Swee Hoon **Ang**

Siew Meng **Leong**

Chin Tiong **Tan**

Oliver **Yau** Hon-Ming

Prentice Hall
is an imprint of

Singapore   London   New York   Toronto   Sydney   Tokyo   Madrid
Mexico City   Munich   Paris   Capetown   Hong Kong   Montreal

Published in 2009 by
Prentice Hall
Pearson Education South Asia Pte Ltd
23/25 First Lok Yang Road, Jurong
Singapore 629733

Pearson Education offices in Asia: Bangkok, Beijing, Hong Kong, Jakarta, Kuala Lumpur, Manila, New Delhi, Seoul, Singapore, Taipei, Tokyo

Authorized adaptation from the United States edition, entitled PRINCIPLES OF MARKETING, 12th edition, ISBN: 9780132390026 by KOTLER, PHILIP AND ARMSTRONG, GARY, published by Pearson Education, Inc., publishing as Prentice Hall, Copyright © 2008

ASIA adaptation edition published by PEARSON EDUCATION SOUTH ASIA PTE LTD., Copyright © 2009

Printed in Singapore

4   3   2
12   11   10   09

ISBN 13   978-981-06-7952-1
ISBN 10   981-06-7952-1

Prentice Hall
is an imprint of

www.pearsoned-asia.com

ABOUT THE AUTHORS

PHILIP KOTLER is the S. C. Johnson & Son Distinguished Professor of International Marketing at the Kellogg Graduate School of Management, Northwestern University. He received his master's degree at the University of Chicago and his Ph.D. at M.I.T., both in economics. Dr. Kotler is the author of Marketing Management (Prentice Hall), now in its twelfth edition and the world's most widely used marketing textbook in graduate schools of business worldwide. He has authored dozens of other successful books and has written more than 100 articles in leading journals. He is the only three-time winner of the coveted Alpha Kappa Psi award for the best annual article in the Journal of Marketing.

Professor Kotler was named the first recipient of two major awards: the *Distinguished Marketing Educator of the Year Award* given by the American Marketing Association and the *Philip Kotler Award for Excellence in Health Care Marketing* presented by the Academy for Health Care Services Marketing. His numerous other major honors include the Sales and Marketing Executives International *Marketing Educator of the Year Award*; The European Association of Marketing Consultants and Trainers *Marketing Excellence Award*; the *Charles Coolidge Parlin Marketing Research Award*; and the *Paul D. Converse Award*, given by the American Marketing Association to honor "outstanding contributions to science in marketing." In a recent Financial Times poll of 1,000 senior executives across the world, Professor Kotler was ranked as the fourth "most influential business writer/guru" of the twenty-first century.

Dr. Kotler has served as chairman of the College of Marketing of the Institute of Management Sciences, a director of the American Marketing Association, and a trustee of the Marketing Science Institute. He has consulted with many major U.S. and international companies in the areas of marketing strategy and planning, marketing organization, and international marketing. He has traveled extensively throughout Europe, Asia, and South America, advising companies and governments about global marketing practices and opportunities.

GARY ARMSTRONG is the Crist W. Blackwell Distinguished Professor of Undergraduate Education in the Kenan-Flagler Business School at the University of North Carolina at Chapel Hill. He holds undergraduate and master's degrees in business from Wayne State University in Detroit, and he received his Ph.D. in marketing from Northwestern University. Dr. Armstrong has contributed numerous articles to leading business journals. As a consultant and researcher, he has worked with many companies on marketing research, sales management, and marketing strategy.

But Professor Armstrong's first love is teaching. His Blackwell Distinguished Professorship is the only permanent endowed professorship for distinguished undergraduate teaching at the University of North Carolina at Chapel Hill. He has been very active in the teaching and administration of Kenan-Flagler's undergraduate program. His administrative posts have included Chair of Marketing, Associate Director of the Undergraduate Business Program, Director of the Business Honors Program, and many others. He works closely with business student groups and has received several campuswide and Business School teaching awards. He is the only repeat recipient of school's highly regarded Award for Excellence in Undergraduate Teaching, which he has received three times. Professor Armstrong recently received the UNC Board of Governors Award for Excellence in Teaching, the highest teaching honor bestowed by the sixteen-campus University of North Carolina system.

SWEE HOON ANG is an Associate Professor at the NUS Business School, National University of Singapore. She received her Ph.D. from the University of British Columbia. She was a Visiting Professor at the University of California, Berkeley, Helsinki School of Economics and Business Administration, and the China-Europe International Business School. She is also a co-author of *Surviving the New Millennium and Principles of Marketing: An Asian Casebook*. In addition, she has written numerous articles for journals and conferences, including *Journal of Advertising, Marketing Letters, Long Range Planning, Journal of Business Ethics, Psycholoᵒ–ᵒgy & Marketing, and Journal of Cross-Cultural Psychology*. Her research and teaching interests are in Asian advertising and consumer behavior. She has consulted for such companies as Glaxo-Wellcome Pharmaceuticals, Johnson & Johnson Medical, Nokia, and PSA Corporation.

SIEW MENG LEONG is a Professor at the NUS Business School, National University of Singapore. He received his MBA and Ph.D. from the University of Wisconsin, Madison. He is a co-author of *Marketing in the New Asia and Strategic Marketing Cases for 21st Century Asia*. He has published in *Journal of Consumer Research, Journal of Marketing, Journal of Marketing Research, Journal of International Business Studies, Marketing Letters*, and other international journals and conference proceedings. His research focuses on consumer behavior, sales management, and marketing research. Professor Leong is editor of the *Asian Journal of Marketing*, an advisory board member of *Behavioral Marketing Abstracts*, and an editorial board member of *International Journal of Research in Marketing, Academy of Marketing Science Review*, and *Journal of Marketing Communications*. He was an advisory council member of the Association for Consumer Research and now serves on the Academic Standards Council of u21 Pedagogica. He has consulted for such clients as Citibank, DuPont, Philips, and Singapore Pools.

CHIN TIONG TAN is Provost at the Singapore Management University. He received his Ph.D. from Pennsylvania State University. He has taught at the Helsinki School of Economics and Business Administration and the University of Witwatersrand, and was a Visiting Scholar at the Stanford Business School. He is a co-author of *Asia's Tao of Business and New Asian Emperors*. He has published in *Journal of Consumer Research, Journal of International Business Studies, Journal of Business* and *Industrial Marketing, International Marketing Review, European Journal of Marketing*, and other international journals and conference proceedings. Professor Tan sits on the boards of several companies and committees of government agencies. He is academic advisor to the Singapore Airlines' Management Development Center, and has consulted for companies like Acer Computer, Altron Group, Inchcape, and Singapore Telecom.

OLIVER YAU HON-MING is Chair Professor of Marketing and Director of the Unit for Chinese Management Development, Faculty of Business at the City University of Hong Kong (CityU). He holds an International Teacher's Certificate from CESA (now HEC), France, and a Ph.D. degree in marketing from the Management Centre, Bradford University, England.

He has held teaching and research positions in four continents, including South America, Australia, Europe and Asia. Before he joined CityU, he was with the Chinese University of Hong Kong, University of Queensland, and the University of Southern Queensland, Australia. He was appointed as a visiting or consulting professor by more than 10 major universities in Mainland China, Australia, Taiwan, and England.

He has published over 200 articles in refereed international journals and conferences, including the *Journal of International Business Studies*, *Journal of International Marketing*, *Journal of Business Ethics*, *Journal of Business Research*, and the *European Journal of Marketing*. He has also published more than 30 books in both Chinese and English. Being a renowned consultant in services and marketing research, he has assisted over 50 companies in various countries by conducting surveys and providing consulting and training services.

He is now a member of the editorial board for more than 10 international journals. He was the Chairman of the Southeast Asia Region of the Academy of International Business (AIBSEAR) and Honorary President of the Hong Kong Institute of Marketing. Currently, he is the advisor of the Hong Kong Professional Validation Council of Hong Kong Industries, and also an adviser of the Academy of Chinese Marketing.

BRIEF CONTENTS

CONTENTS

MESSAGE
from the Authors

Welcome to *Principles of Marketing: A Global Perspective!* With this textbook, we work to bring you the freshest and most authoritative insights into the fascinating world of marketing. As we present this new edition, we want to again thank you and other marketing students and professors who have used our text. You've been our inspiration.

The goal of every Asian marketer is to create more value for customers. So it makes sense that our goal for this edition is to create more value for you—our customer. How does this text bring you more value? First, it builds on a unique, integrative, and intuitive marketing framework: Simply put, marketing is the art and science of creating value for customers to capture value *from* customers in return. Marketers lead the way in developing and managing profitable, value-based customer relationships. We introduce this customer-value framework in the first two chapters and then build upon it throughout the book.

Beyond the strengthened customer-relationships framework, we emphasize four additional customer-value themes. First, we expand our emphasis on *building strong brands* and *brand value*. After all, customer value and profitable customer relationships are built upon strong brands. Second, we focus on the importance of *measuring and managing return on marketing*—of capturing value in return for the customer value that the company creates. Third, we present all of the latest developments in the marketing technologies that are rapidly changing how marketers create and communicate customer value. Finally, we emphasize the importance of *socially responsible marketing around the globe*. As the world becomes an increasingly smaller place, Asian marketers must be good at marketing their brands globally and in socially responsible ways that create long-term value to society as a whole.

In addition to providing all the latest marketing thinking, to add even more value, we've worked to make learning about and teaching marketing easier and more exciting for both students and instructors. This textbook presents marketing in a complete yet practical, exciting, and easy-to-digest way. For example, to help bring marketing to life, we've filled the text with interesting examples and stories about real companies and their marketing practices. Moreover, the integrated, cutting-edge teaching and learning package lets you customize your learning and teaching experience. We highlight the second edition's many new features and enhancements in the pages that follow.

So, this textbook *creates more value for you*—more value in the content, more value in the supplements, more value in learning, and more value in YOUR classroom. We think that it's the best edition yet. We hope that you'll find *Principles of Marketing: A Global Perspective* the very best text from which to learn about and teach marketing.

Sincerely,

Philip Kotler
Northwestern University

Gary Armstrong
University of North Carolina–Chapel Hill

Swee Hoon Ang
National University of Singapore

Siew Meng Leong
National University of Singapore

Chin Tiong Tan
Singapore Management University

Oliver Yau Hon-Ming
City University of Hong Kong

ABOUT THIS BOOK

You will find that we have:

- Selected a good mix of international and Asian cases and vignettes to give your students a stronger understanding of global marketing.

- Made the text more concise and upped the use of visual aids to make learning easier.

- Refreshed our coverage on contemporary marketing issues with new and updated material.

- Improved the instructor's resources to help you with your lesson planning and preparation.

A Good Mix of International and Asian Cases and Vignettes

The cases and examples in *Principles of Marketing: A Global Perspective* are carefully selected to give your students a comprehensive understanding of marketing in today's globally connected way.

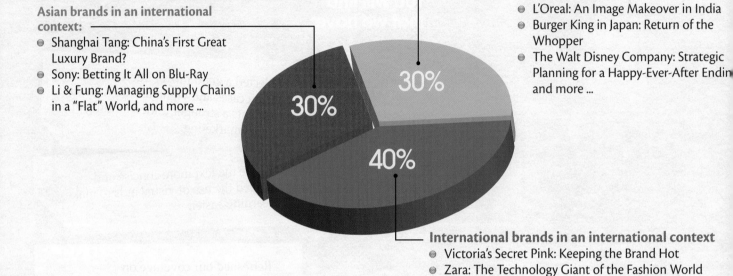

Asian brands in an international context:
- Shanghai Tang: China's First Great Luxury Brand?
- Sony: Betting It All on Blu-Ray
- Li & Fung: Managing Supply Chains in a "Flat" World, and more ...

International brands in an Asian context
- L'Oreal: An Image Makeover in India
- Burger King in Japan: Return of the Whopper
- The Walt Disney Company: Strategic Planning for a Happy-Ever-After Ending and more ...

International brands in an international context
- Victoria's Secret Pink: Keeping the Brand Hot
- Zara: The Technology Giant of the Fashion World
- The Ritz-Carlton: Taking Care of Those Who Take Care of Customers, and more ...

These cases and examples are presented in each chapter as one of the following:

Opening Cases

These opening cases set the stage for each chapter and use examples of well-known brands that your students can identify with in order to ease them into the topic.

Case Contexts

This icon appears at the start of all cases. It indicates the context of the case study.

Real Marketing

Give your students a taste of the real world marketing with these specially written case studies that highlight marketing practices around the world.

Use of recognizable brand names and contexts

Grab your students' attention with recognizable brands and companies throughout the text, which help them relate easily to marketing concepts and topics taught.

Company Cases

Wrap up the chapter effectively with Company Cases. These in-depth studies, together with the engaging discussion questions at the end of the case, hone students' critical thinking through applying marketing principles to real companies in real situations.

Concise with Engaging Visuals

➤ *Principles of Marketing: A Global Perspective* makes learning from the text easier for Asian students, who may not be native speakers of English. The effective use of visual learning aids also enables students to obtain a firm grasp of concepts quickly and is an attractive tool for revision.

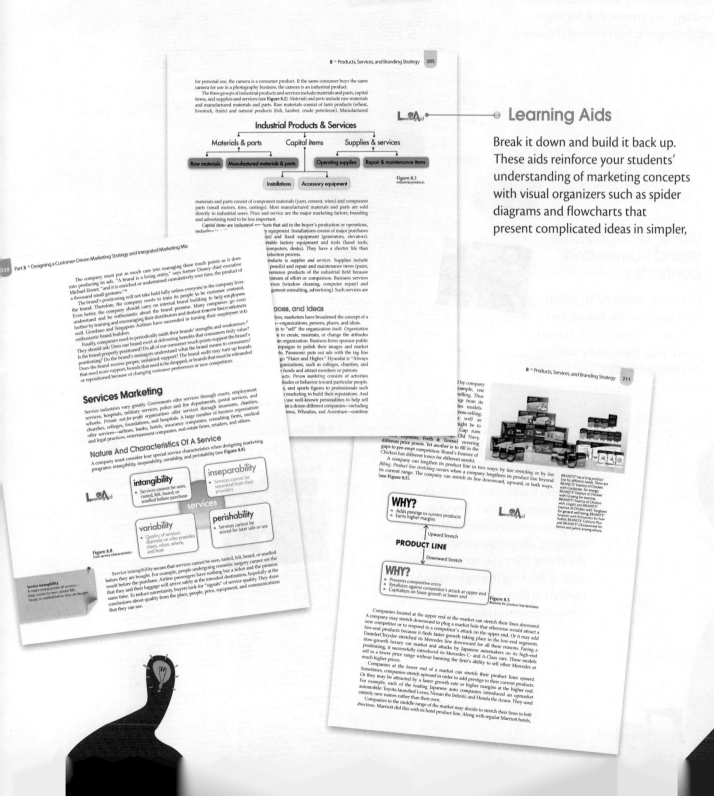

Learning Aids

Break it down and build it back up. These aids reinforce your students' understanding of marketing concepts with visual organizers such as spider diagrams and flowcharts that present complicated ideas in simpler,

Concise Language

An effort has been made to keep the text concise and readable. This means that it is now easier and faster for your students to access important marketing principles and concepts.

Lively Visual

Exciting color visuals bring the study of marketing to life and motivate your student to learn.

Coverage on Contemporary Marketing Issues

Keep your students at the front of the pack in today's ever-changing marketing environment. In today's globally-connected world, it is even more important for them to keep abreast of must-know contemporary marketing issues and be critical thinkers of issues that affect them.

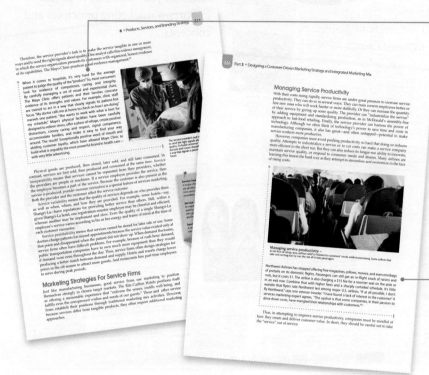

Vignettes

Help your students stay current in the world of marketing. These in-text vignettes present students with up-to-date perspectives in contemporary marketing.

Focus on Technology

Enable your students to better harness the emerging marketing technologies of this digital age. These application exercises provide students with valuable discussion on the development and effective use of these technologies

Focus on Ethics

It's not easy being a marketer with good morals. Equip your students with the mindset to deal with ethical challenges and dilemmas by exploring these difficult issues through the use of situational descriptions and analysis. Questions are provided to guide students in their quest for what's right or wrong.

Improved Instructor's Support

 A comprehensive range of resources is available to help you with effective course preparation and lesson planning.

● Instructor's Manual

The instructor's manual for *Principles of Marketing: A Global Perspective* provides learning objectives, chapter overviews and detailed lecture outlines, as well as additional student projects and interactive assignments.

● Slides

The teaching slides are now more visually arresting, and bring together the basic marketing outlines and key points in a convenient package design for easy customization and sharing.

● Test Item File

Creating customized tests for your students is a breeze with this test bank of over 3,000 multiple choice, true/false, short answer and essay questions. Each chapter also has a section dedicated to 10 continuing, real-world, small business cases.

● Image Bank

You can use illustrations and images from the bank to create the materials they require or to add an exciting visual dimension to your lessons.

● Advertising Bank

A collection of print and television commercials is available in a CD for use in your lessons. Add some spice to lessons and keep students interested by showing great examples of quality advertising.

PREFACE

Creating More Value for You!

The goal of *Principles of Marketing: A Global Perspective* is to introduce new marketing students to the fascinating world of global marketing in an innovative yet practical and enjoyable way. Like any good marketer, we're out to create more value for you, our customer. We've pored over every page, table, figure, fact, and example in an effort to make this the best text from which to learn about and teach marketing.

Global marketing is all about creating customer value and building profitable customer relationships. It starts with understanding consumer needs and wants, deciding which target markets the organization can serve best, and developing a compelling value proposition by which the organization can win, keep, and grow targeted consumers. If an organization does these things well, it will reap the rewards in terms of market share, profits, and customer equity.

Marketing is much more than just an isolated business function—it is a philosophy that guides the entire organization. The marketing department cannot create customer value and build profitable customer relationships by itself. This is a companywide undertaking that involves broad decisions about who the company wants as its customers, which needs to satisfy, what products and services to offer, what prices to set, what communications to send, and what partnerships to develop. Marketing must work closely with other company departments and with other organizations throughout its entire value-delivery system to delight customers by creating superior customer value.

Marketing: Creating Customer Value and Relationships

From beginning to end, *Principles of Marketing: A Global Perspective* develops an innovative customer-value and customer-relationships framework that captures the essence of today's marketing.

Five Major Value Themes

Principles of Marketing: A Global Perspective builds on five major value themes:

- **Creating value for customers to capture value from customers in return.** Asian marketers must be good at creating customer value and managing customer relationships. They must attract targeted customers with strong value propositions. Then, they must keep and grow customers by delivering superior customer value and effectively managing the company-customer interface. Outstanding marketing companies in Asia understand the marketplace and customer needs, design value-creating marketing strategies, develop integrated marketing programs that deliver customer value and delight, and build strong customer relationships. In return, they capture value from customers in the form of sales, profits, and customer loyalty. This innovative customer-value framework is introduced at the start of Chapter 1 in a five-step marketing process model, which details how marketing creates customer value and captures value in return. The framework is carefully explained in the first two chapters, providing students with a solid foundation. The framework is then integrated throughout the remainder of the text.

- **Building and managing strong, value-creating brands.** Well-positioned brands with strong brand equity provide the basis upon which to build customer value and profitable customer relationships. Asian marketers must position their brands powerfully and manage them well.

- **Managing return on marketing to recapture value.** To capture value from customers in return, marketing managers in Asia must be good at measuring and managing the return on their marketing investments. They must ensure that their marketing dollars are being well spent. In the past, many marketers spent freely on big, expensive marketing programs, often without thinking carefully about the financial and customer response returns on their spending. But all that is changing rapidly. Measuring and managing return on marketing investments has become an important part of strategic marketing decision making.

- **Harnessing new marketing technologies.** New digital and other high-tech marketing developments are dramatically changing how Asian marketers create and communication customer value. Marketers in Asia must know how to leverage new computer, information, communication, and distribution technologies to connect more effectively with customers and marketing partners in this digital age.

- **Marketing in a socially responsible way around the globe.** As technological developments make the world an increasingly smaller place, Asian marketers must be good at marketing their brands globally and in socially responsible ways that create not just short-term value for individual customers but also long-term value for society as a whole.

Important Changes and Additions

Principles of Marketing: A Global Perspective follows on from *Principles of Marketing: An Asian Perspective* to reflect the major trends and forces impacting marketing in this era of customer value and relationships. We've thoroughly revised the text, and here are just some of the major changes you'll find in this edition.

- This new edition builds on and extends the innovative customer-value framework from previous editions. No other marketing text presents such a clear and comprehensive customer-value approach.

- The integrated marketing communications chapters have been completely restructured to reflect sweeping shifts in how today's marketers communicate value to customers.

  - A newly revised Chapter 14—Communicating Customer Value—addresses today's **shifting integrated marketing communications model.** It tells how marketers are now adding a host new-age media—everything from interactive TV and the Internet to iPods and cell phones to reach targeted customers with more personalized messages.
  - Advertising and public relations are now combined in Chapter 15, which includes important new discussions on the merging of advertising and entertainment to break through the clutter, return on advertising, and other important topics. A restructured Chapter 16 now combines personal selling and sales promotion.
  - The new Chapter 17—**Direct and Online Marketing**—provides focused new coverage of direct marketing and its fastest-growing arm, marketing on the Internet. The new chapter includes a section on new digital direct-marketing technologies, such as mobile phone marketing, podcasts and vodcasts, and interactive TV.

- We've revised the pricing discussions in Chapter 10—Pricing: Understanding and Capturing Customer Value. It now focuses on **customer-value-based pricing**—on understanding and capturing customer value as the basis for setting and adjusting prices. The revised chapter includes new discussions of "good-value" and "value-added" pricing strategies, dynamic pricing, and competitive pricing considerations.

- In line with the text's emphasis on **measuring and managing return on marketing,** we've added a new Appendix 2: Marketing by the Numbers. This comprehensive new appendix introduces students to the marketing financial analysis that helps to guide, assess, and support marketing decisions in this age of marketing accountability. The Return on Marketing section in Chapter 2 has also been revised, and we've added return on advertising and return on selling discussions in later chapters.

- Chapter 9 contains a new section on managing new-product development, covering new **customer-driven, team-based, holistic new-product development** approaches.
- Chapter 5 (Consumer Behavior) provides a new discussion on **"online social networks"** that tells how marketers are tapping digital online networks such as YouTube, MySpace, and others to build stronger relationships between their brands and customers.

Principles of Marketing: A Global Perspective also includes new and expanded material on a wide range of other topics, including managing customer relationships and CRM, brand strategy and positioning, SWOT analysis, data mining and data networks, ethnographic consumer research, marketing and diversity, generational marketing, buzz marketing, services marketing, supplier satisfaction and partnering, environmental sustainability, cause-related marketing, socially responsible marketing, global marketing strategies, and much, much more.

Countless new examples have been added within the running text. All tables, examples, and references throughout the text have been thoroughly updated. *Principles of Marketing: A Global Perspective* contains mostly new photos and advertisements that illustrate key points and make the text more effective and appealing. All new or revised company cases and many new video cases help to bring the real world directly into the classroom. The text even has a new look, with freshly designed figures. We don't think you'll find a fresher, more current, or more approachable text anywhere.

Real Value through Real Marketing

Principles of Marketing: A Global Perspective features in-depth, real-world examples and stories that show concepts in action and reveal the drama of modern marketing. In this edition, chapter-opening vignettes and Real Marketing highlights have been updated or replaced to provide fresh and relevant insights into actual marketing practices. Learn how:

- Formula 1 creates avidly loyal fans by selling not car racing but a high-octane, totally involving experience
- Nike's "Just do it!" marketing strategy has matured as this venerable market leader has moved from maverick to mainstream
- Harrah's, the world's largest casino operator, maintains a vast customer database and uses CRM to manage day-to-day customer relationships and build customer loyalty
- Toyota targets Generation Y consumers with its Scion model
- Triumph International creates value via customer-centered service innovation
- Li & Fung manages supply chains for its multinational clients in a "flat" world
- Dove creates a broader and healthier view of beauty with its Campaign for Real Beauty campaign featuring candid and confident images of real women of all types

These and countless other examples and illustrations throughout each chapter reinforce key concepts and bring marketing to life.

Valuable Learning Aids

A wealth of chapter-opening, within-chapter, and end-of-chapter learning devices help students to learn, link, and apply major concepts:

- *Previewing the Concepts.* A section at the beginning of each chapter briefly previews chapter concepts, links them with previous chapter concepts, outlines chapter learning objectives, and introduces the chapter-opening vignette.

- *Chapter-opening marketing stories*. Each chapter begins with an engaging, deeply developed marketing story that introduces the chapter material and sparks student interest.
- *Real Marketing highlights*. In every chapter, these highlights provide an in-depth look at the actual marketing practices of large and small companies.
- *Reviewing the Concepts*. A summary at the end of each chapter reviews major chapter concepts and chapter objectives.
- *Reviewing the Key Terms*. Key terms are highlighted within the text, clearly defined in the margins of the pages in which they first appear, and listed at the end of each chapter.
- *Discussing the Concepts and Applying the Concepts*. Each chapter contains a set of discussion questions and application exercises covering major chapter concepts.
- *Visual Learning Aids*. You will see these icons frequently in each chapter, indicating where a useful figure or illustration is located. These learning aids will help you in illustrating or summarizing important marketing concepts to your students.
- *Case Study Icons*. At the start of each case study in the textbook, we've provided a case study context icon that shows you where the case study takes place, whether it is an international company functioning in an international or Asian context, or an Asian company operating in an international or Asian context.
- *Focus on Technology*. Application exercises at the end of each chapter provide discussion on important and emerging marketing technologies in this digital age.
- *Focus on Ethics*. Situation descriptions and questions highlight important issues in marketing ethics at the end of each chapter.
- *Company Cases*. All new or revised company cases for class or written discussion are provided at the end of each chapter. These cases challenge students to apply marketing principles to real companies in real situations.
- *Video Case*. Short vignettes and discussion questions appear at the end of every chapter, to be used with the set of 4- to 7-minute videos that accompany this edition.
- *Marketing Plan appendix*. Appendix 1 contains a sample marketing plan that helps students to apply important marketing planning concepts.
- *Marketing by the Numbers appendix*. A new Appendix 2 introduces students to the marketing financial analysis that helps to guide, assess, and support marketing decisions.

More than ever before, *Principles of Marketing: A Global Perspective* creates value for you—it gives you all you need to know about marketing in an effective and enjoyable total learning package!

A Valuable Supplements Package

A successful marketing course requires more than a well-written book. Today's classroom requires a dedicated teacher and a fully integrated teaching system. A total package of teaching supplements extends this edition's emphasis on creating value for both the student and instructor. The following aids support *Principles of Marketing: A Global Perspective*, and can be found on its Companion Website at *www.pearsoned-asia.com/kotler.*

Instructor's Manual with Video Case Notes

The instructor's handbook for this text provides suggestions for using features and elements of the text. This Instructor's Manual includes a chapter overview, objectives, a detailed lecture outline (incorporating key terms, text art, chapter objectives, and references to various pedagogical elements), and support for end-of-chapter material. Also included within each chapter is a section that offers barriers to effective learning, student projects/assignments, as well as an outside example, all of which provide a springboard for innovative learning experiences in the classroom. Video Case Notes, offering a brief summary of each segment, along with answers to the case questions in the text, as well as teaching ideas on how to present the material in class are also offered in the Instructor's Manual.

Test Item File

Featuring more than 3,000 questions, 175 questions per chapter, this Test Item File has been written specifically for this edition. Each chapter consists of multiple-choice, true/false, short-answer, and essay questions, with difficulty level provided for each question. New to this edition is the introduction of small-business cases, offering ten essay questions per chapter. Additionally, the questions are offered in two categories—General Concept and Application. The application questions provide real-life situations that take students beyond basic chapter concepts and vocabulary and ask them to apply their newly learned marketing skills. Available in both Microsoft Word and TestGen formats for PC and Mac.

PowerPoints

This set of PowerPoint presentations are now more visually arresting and include basic outlines and key points from each chapter, plus advertisements and art from the text, and images not included in the text. Instructors can further customize this presentation using the image library featured on the Instructor's Resource Center on CD-ROM.

Custom Videos

The video library features 20 exciting segments for this edition. All segments are available from the IRC on CD-ROM. Here are just a few of the videos offered:

- GE and pricing strategies
- Harley-Davidson and how brand image is managed through global marketing strategies
- NineMSN and its strategies in direct marketing
- American Express and the modern marketing environment
- The NFL and the importance of social responsibility
- Eaton's approach to B2B issues, including buyer behavior
- Hasbro's views on distribution channels and logistics management
- Wild Planet's strategies in the consumer markets

Image and Ad Bank

Access many of the images and illustrations featured in the text though the banks, which are ideal for PowerPoint customization. Instructors will also be furnished with a CD of print ads and TV commercials on request.

ACKNOWLEDGMENTS

No book is the work only of its authors. Our thanks go to our colleagues at Northwestern University, the University of North Carolina at Chapel Hill, National University of Singapore, Singapore Management University, and City University of Hong Kong for their support and encouragement.

Special thanks go to Ada Lau, Dr Raymond Chow of The Open University of Hong Kong, and Dr John Leung of City University of Hong Kong for their assistance in adapting several case studies for Chapters 13, 14, 15, 16, and 19.

The staff at Prentice Hall Singapore deserve mention for their role in shaping this book. We appreciate the efforts of Peggy Su, who worked on the supplements to this text. We are also indebted to the following instructors for their thoughtful inputs.

Dr. Malliga Marimuthu, School of Management, Universiti Sains Malaysia
Leo Leung, Department of Marketing and International Business, Lingnan University

We are grateful to the following individuals and their companies and advertising agencies for providing us permission to use some of the materials for this book:

AirAsia
Bandai America
Bartle Bogle Hegarty Singapore
Billabong – Peter Thew, Sharmin Lee
Essilor – Sim Peng Tak
Lawrence Ang Swee Leng
QB House
Seng Choon Farm Pte Ltd

Singapore Airlines – Grace Chak, Vernon Lim
Singapore Zoo – Fanny Lai, Frederic Eng
The Nielsen Corporation
Young & Rubicam Singapore

Last but certainly not least, we owe our overriding debt to our families who continue to support and inspire us. To them, we dedicate this book.

Philip Kotler   *Gary Armstrong*
Swee Hoon Ang   *Siew Meng Leong*
Chin Tiong Tan   *Oliver Yau Hon-Ming*

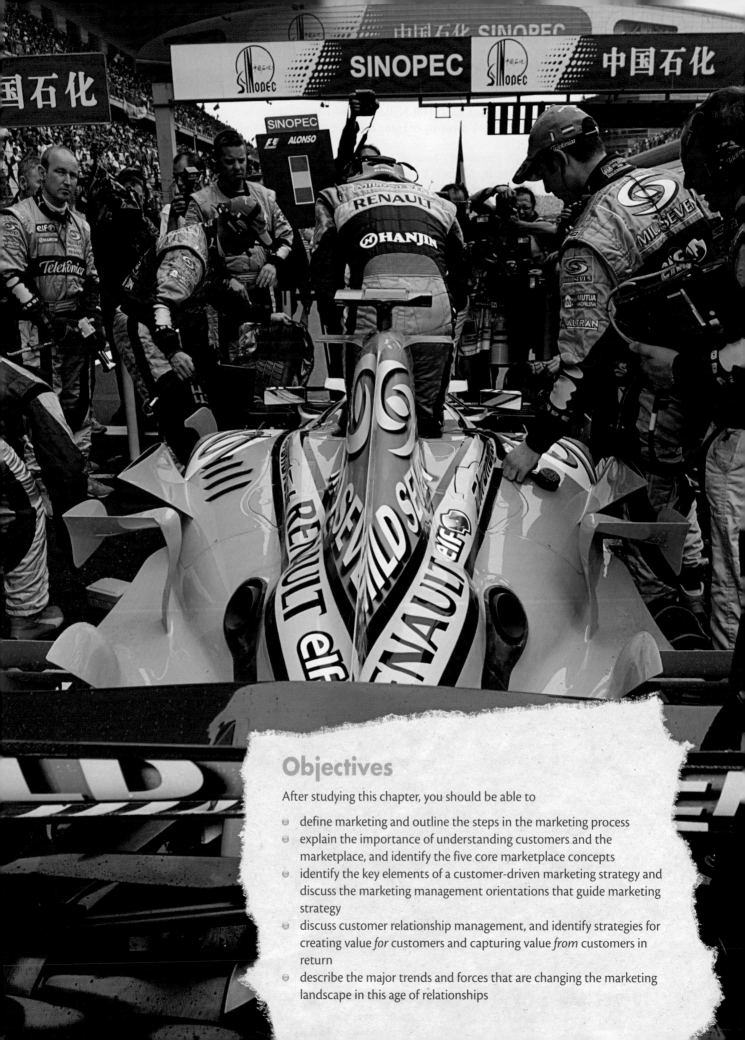

Objectives

After studying this chapter, you should be able to

- define marketing and outline the steps in the marketing process
- explain the importance of understanding customers and the marketplace, and identify the five core marketplace concepts
- identify the key elements of a customer-driven marketing strategy and discuss the marketing management orientations that guide marketing strategy
- discuss customer relationship management, and identify strategies for creating value *for* customers and capturing value *from* customers in return
- describe the major trends and forces that are changing the marketing landscape in this age of relationships

CHAPTER 1

MARKETING: Managing Profitable Customer Relationships

Previewing the Concepts

Welcome to the exciting world of marketing. In this chapter, we will introduce you to the basic marketing concepts. We'll start with a simple question: What *is* marketing? Marketing is managing profitable customer relationships. The aim of marketing is to create value for customers and to capture value in return. Chapter 1 is organized around five steps in the marketing process—from understanding customer needs, to designing customer-driven marketing strategies and programs, to building customer relationships and capturing value for the firm.

To set the stage, let's first look at Formula 1. In recent years, Formula 1 has swiftly evolved from a predominantly European sporting pastime into an international marketing phenomenon. How? By creating high-octane value for its millions of fans. In return, Formula 1 captures value from these fans, both for itself and for its many sponsors. Read on and see how Formula 1 does it.

Formula 1 (or F1) comprises a series of races called Grand Prix held usually on purpose-built circuits, and in a few cases, on closed city streets. The "formula" is a set of rules which all participants and cars must meet. But F1 is much, much more. In fact, it's a marketing phenomenon. For fans, Formula 1 is a lot more than auto races. It's a high-octane, totally involving experience.

F1 is a massive television event. According to Formula Global Broadcast 2006, F1 has 580 million unique viewers across 185 countries. The cars race at speeds often exceeding 320 kph. Europe is F1's traditional center and remains its leading market. However, F1 races are now conducted worldwide, with new races in Bahrain, China, Malaysia, and Turkey. Constructor teams include European powerhouses like Ferrari and BMW as well as newer Japanese entrants such as Honda and Toyota. Drivers on the F1 circuit include Spain's Fernando Alonso, Britain's Lewis Hamilton, Germany's Ralf Schumacher, and Japan's Takuma Sato.

F1's success results from creating lasting customer relationships. Some 91 percent of F1 fans are male, with just over 30 percent aged between 25 and 34. The majority are managers, professionals, technical specialists, and students. For fans, the F1 relationship develops through a careful blend of live racing events, abundant media coverage, and compelling Web sites.

Each year, fans can experience the adrenalin-charged, heart-stopping excitement of F1 racing firsthand by attending the races around the world. Fans can book their race tickets, flights, hotels, ground transportation, and other options on the official F1 Web site, *www.formula1.com.* At the races, fans watch the cars roar around the track, meet the drivers, and swap stories with other F1 enthusiasts. Fans, such as Ferrari's *tivosi*, arrive decked in their team colors, with many waving giant flags of their race teams.

Corporate sponsors entertain their guests and customers as well. For example, buyers of a Mercedes Benz car in Malaysia were invited to meet a McLaren Mercedes team driver at an autograph session. Other goodies included F1 Platinum grandstand tickets, limited edition Mercedes-Benz F1 merchandise, and an invitation to a welcome party at the Sepang track where the race was held. DaimlerChrysler Malaysia's VP of sales and marketing said the whole F1 experience was something "money cannot buy."

Can't make it to the track? F1 can be seen live or tape delayed in almost every country globally. Well-orchestrated coverage and in-car cameras put fans in the middle of the action, giving them vicarious thrills that keep them glued to the screen.

The F1 experience is also delivered through its engaging Web site, which serves up a glut of information and entertainment—in-depth news, driver bios, background information, photo gallery, and merchandise. True die-hard fans can register for its Live Timing system, which streams real-time data directly from F1 Management's technical facility at the race track. It displays information supplied by the teams from the practice, qualifying, and actual race sessions of the grand prix. The main timing screen contains position, lap times, sector times, and full text commentary. There is also a weather screen displaying data for ambient and track temperature, humidity, wind speed and direction, air pressure, and rainfall as well as a lap chart graphically depicting how each driver is fairing over the course of the race.

In addition, unofficial Web sites such as _www.planetf1.com_, _www.f1-live.com_, and _www.itv-f1.com_ as well as team Web sites like _www.Toyota-f1.com_ supplement the official one. For example, planetf1 contains a forum for fans, access to a betting Web site, and organizes fantasy F1 leagues. Media coverage is also abundant. Press reports highlight the race, personality, and business perspectives of F1 almost daily throughout the season. As Michael Payne, organizer of a sports marketing conference held in conjunction with the second Shanghai Grand Prix, remarked, "Formula 1 has a very strong technological image and leadership no other sport really has. If you want global exposure and awareness, Formula 1 is probably unique in that it is in 150 countries almost every other week for nine months."

But a big part of the F1 experience is the feeling that the sport, itself, is about aspiration, glitz, and glamor. Fans who drive at mundane speeds in their daily lives witness the fastest cars in the world piloted by the best drivers around demanding circuits. There is also the thrill of daring overtaking maneuvers, pit lane incidents, and spectacular race crashes. Add to that the celebrity quotient of attendees who regularly include movie and rock stars, business icons, fashion and sports luminaries, as well as settings exemplified by the harbor front, yacht-laden surroundings of Monaco, and a colorful and vibrant mix of fun, pleasure, and buzz is created. There is also night racing on Singapore streets.

Ultimately, fan enthusiasm translates into financial success for F1 Management, which owns F1's television rights, sells merchandise, and grants races at new circuits, F1 sponsors, constructors, and event hosts. Bernie Ecclestone, F1 Management's owner, is believed to have a personal fortune of $4 billion. F1's international profile and popularity lead to high investments from sponsors. Asian brands like Red Bull and Panasonic sponsor race teams, while Asian companies like Petronas, Sinopec, Fuji Television, and Singapore Telecommunications provide title sponsorship to races held in their countries. Constructors also benefit. For example, Honda used F1 to develop its technology, and leveraged its enhanced brand image obtained via F1 in hiring better graduates. Countries which invest in F1 spend money on building the needed infrastructure to earn tourism revenue and generate employment. F1 Malaysia brought in $175 million, while F1 Shanghai created 1,000 jobs directly and generated over 3,000 jobs indirectly.

Clearly, F1 is a premier marketing organization which knows how to create customer value that translates into deep and lasting customer relationships. F1 gives its fans and sponsors what they want. In turn, it is rewarded with their deep loyalty and the promise of lasting profits.

Marketing is all around you: Even in markets such as this in Vietnam, marketing is at work. The fruit seller has to understand her market, distribute her fruits at the right place, sell them at the right price, and be alert of who else are selling fruits or possible substitutes. She has to make sure that she offers superior customer value.

Today's successful companies have one thing in common: They are strongly customer focused and heavily committed to marketing. These companies share a passion for satisfying customer needs in well-defined target markets. They motivate everyone in the organization to help build lasting customer relationships through superior customer value and satisfaction. As Wal-Mart founder Sam Walton once asserted: "There is only one boss. The customer. And he can fire everybody in the company from the chairman on down, simply by spending his money somewhere else."

What Is Marketing?

Marketing deals with customers. It is managing profitable customer relationships. The twofold goal of marketing is to:

- attract new customers by promising superior value, and
- keep and grow current customers by delivering satisfaction.

At Disney theme parks, "imagineers" work wonders in their quest to "make a dream come true today." Dell leads the personal computer industry by consistently making good on its promise to "be direct." It makes it easy for customers to custom-design their own computers and have them delivered quickly to their doorsteps or desktops. These and other highly successful companies know that if they take care of their customers, market share and profits will follow.

Marketing is all around you. You see marketing in wet markets, small shops, and large shopping malls. You see marketing in the advertisements that fill your TV screen or enliven your Web pages. At home, at school, where you work, and where you play, you see marketing in almost everything you do. Yet, there is much more to marketing than meets the consumer's casual eye. Behind it is a massive network of people and activities competing for your attention and purchases.

Marketing Defined

What *is* marketing? Marketing is more than selling and advertising. It involves *satisfying customer needs.* The marketer needs to understand consumer needs; develop products and services that provide superior customer value; and price, distribute, and promote them effectively. Hence, **marketing** is the process by which companies create value for customers and build strong customer relationships to capture value from customers in return.[1]

Marketing
The process by which companies create value for customers and build strong customer relationships in order to capture value from customers in return.

The Marketing Process

Figure 1.1 presents a simple five-step model of the marketing process. In the first four steps, companies work to understand consumers, create customer value, and build strong customer relationships. In the final step, companies reap the rewards of creating superior customer value. By creating value *for* consumers, they in turn capture value *from* consumers in the form of sales, profits, and long-term customer equity.

In this and the next chapter, we will examine the steps of this simple model of marketing. In this chapter, we will review each step but focus more on the customer relationship steps—understanding customers, building customer relationships, and capturing value from customers. In Chapter 2, we'll discuss further the second and third steps—designing marketing strategies and constructing marketing programs.

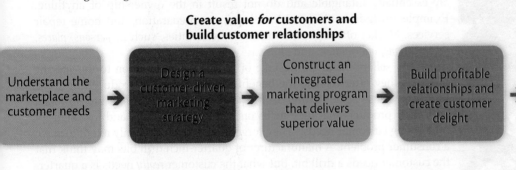

Figure 1.1
A simple model of the marketing process

Understanding the Marketplace and Customer Needs

As a first step, marketers need to understand customer needs and wants and the marketplace within which they operate. We will discuss five core customer and marketplace concepts:

- needs, wants, and demands;
- marketing offerings (products, services, and experiences);
- value and satisfaction;
- exchanges and relationships; and
- markets.

Customer Needs, Wants, and Demands

The most basic concept underlying marketing is that of human needs. Human **needs** are states of felt deprivation. They include basic *physical* needs for food, clothing, warmth, and safety; *social* needs for belonging and affection; and *individual* needs for knowledge and self-expression. For instance, a survey showed that as Chinese become increasingly cash rich and time poor, they want convenience without compromising their health.[2]

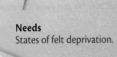
Needs
States of felt deprivation.

Wants
The form human needs take as shaped by culture and individual personality.

Demands
Human wants that are backed by buying power.

Market offering
Some combination of products, services, information, or experiences offered to a market to satisfy a need or want.

Marketing myopia
The mistake of paying more attention to the specific products a company offers than to the benefits and experiences produced by these products.

Wants are the form human needs take as they are shaped by culture and individual personality. An American *needs* food but *wants* a Big Mac, french fries, and a soft drink. A person in Japan *needs* food but *wants* rice, sashimi, and green tea. Wants are shaped by one's society and are described in terms of objects that will satisfy needs. When backed by buying power, wants become **demands**. Given their wants and resources, people demand products with benefits that add up to the most value and satisfaction.

Outstanding marketing companies conduct marketing research to learn about and understand their customers' needs, wants, and demands. For example, Harley-Davidson's chairman regularly mounts his Harley and rides with customers to get feedback and ideas.

Nissan conducted focus group interviews when they developed their pickup truck, Titan. It observed how truck drivers were frustrated when they had to struggle securing items in the truck bed. This led to Nissan designing the truck bed with a set of channels that enable flexible tie down. Nissan also followed some truck owners during their weekend personal trips. It was while watching people trying to load bags into their trucks and being trapped repeatedly between the doors that led Nissan to develop 180-degree swinging doors.[3]

Market offerings are not limited to physical products: Bangkok's famed floating market is a strong attraction for tourists worldwide.

Market Offerings—Products, Services, and Experiences

Consumers' needs and wants are fulfilled through a **market offering**—some combination of products, services, information, or experiences offered to a market to satisfy a need or want. Market offerings are not limited to physical *products*. They also include *services*, activities or benefits offered for sale that are essentially intangible and do not result in the ownership of anything. Examples include banking, airline, hotel, tax preparation, and home repair services. Market offerings also include other entities, such as *persons*, *places*, *organizations*, *information*, and *ideas*.

Many sellers make the mistake of paying more attention to the specific products they offer than to the benefits and experiences produced by these products. These sellers suffer from **marketing myopia**. They are so taken with their products that they focus only on existing wants and lose sight of underlying customer needs.[4] They forget that a product is only a tool to solve a consumer problem. A manufacturer of quarter-inch drill bits may think that the customer needs a drill bit. But what the customer *really* needs is a quarter-inch hole. These sellers will have trouble if a new product comes along that serves the customer's need better or less expensively. The customer will have the same *need* but will *want* the new product. **Figure 1.2** summarizes how to avoid marketing myopia.

Smart marketers look beyond the attributes of the products and services they sell. By orchestrating several services and products, they create *brand experiences* for consumers. For example, Walt Disney World is an experience; so is a stay at the Shangri-la Hotel. And you don't just watch a Formula 1 race; you immerse yourself in the Formula 1 experience.

Figure 1.2
Avoid marketing myopia by focusing on product benefits and customer needs

| **Look beyond** | Product attributes and existing customer wants | **to** | Product benefits and experiences, and customer's needs | **and** | Offer superior customer value |

Customer Value and Satisfaction

Consumers usually face a broad array of products and services that might satisfy a given need. How do they choose among these many market offerings? Customers form expectations about the value and satisfaction that various market offerings will deliver and buy accordingly. Satisfied customers buy again and tell others about their good experiences. Dissatisfied customers often switch to competitors and disparage the product to others.

Exchanges and Relationships

Marketing occurs when people decide to satisfy needs and wants through exchange relationships. **Exchange** is the act of obtaining a desired object from someone by offering something in return. In the broadest sense, the marketer tries to bring about a response to some market offering. The response may be more than buying or trading products and services. A political candidate, for instance, wants votes, a church wants membership, an orchestra wants an audience, and a social action group wants idea acceptance.

Marketing consists of actions taken to build and maintain desirable exchange *relationships* with target audiences involving a product, service, idea, or other object. Beyond simply attracting new customers and creating transactions, the goal is to retain customers and grow their business with the company. Marketers want to build strong relationships by consistently delivering superior customer value.

Markets

The concepts of exchange and relationships lead to the concept of a market. A **market** is the set of actual and potential buyers of a product. These buyers share a particular need or want that can be satisfied through exchange relationships.

Marketing means managing markets to bring about profitable customer relationships. Sellers must search for buyers, identify their needs, design good market offerings, set prices for them, promote them, and store and deliver them. Activities such as product development, research, communication, distribution, pricing, and service are core marketing activities.

Figure 1.3 shows the main elements in a modern marketing system. Marketing involves serving a market of final consumers in the face of competitors. The company and the competitors send their respective offers and messages to consumers. These are affected by major environmental forces (demographic, economic, physical, technological, political/legal, and social/cultural).

> **Exchange**
> The act of obtaining a desired object from someone by offering something in return.
>
> **Market**
> The set of all actual and potential buyers of a product or service.

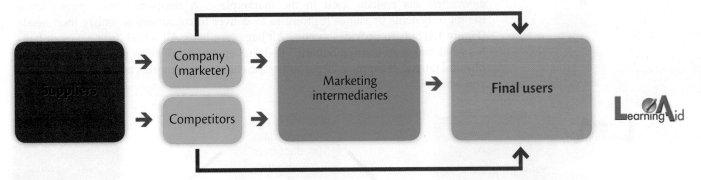

Figure 1.3
Elements of a modern marketing system

Each party in the system adds value for the next level. The arrows represent relationships that must be developed and managed. Thus, a company's success at building profitable relationships depends not only on its own actions but also on how well the entire system serves the needs of final consumers. Toyota cannot deliver high quality to car buyers unless its dealers provide outstanding sales and service.

Designing a Customer-Driven Marketing Strategy

Marketing management
The art and science of choosing target markets and building profitable relationships with them.

Once it fully understands consumers and the marketplace, marketing management can design a customer-driven marketing strategy. We define **marketing management** as the art and science of choosing target markets and building profitable relationships with them. The marketing manager's aim is to find, attract, keep, and grow target customers by creating, delivering, and communicating superior customer value.

To design a winning marketing strategy, the marketing manager must answer two important questions:

- What customers will we serve (what's our target market)?
- How can we serve these customers best (what's our value proposition)?

Selecting Customers to Serve

The company must first decide *who* it will serve. It does this by dividing the market into segments of customers (*market segmentation*) and selecting which segments it will go after (*target marketing*). Marketing managers know that they cannot serve all customers in every way. By trying to serve all customers, they may not serve any customers well. Instead, the company wants to select only customers that it can serve well and profitably. For example, The Oriental Hotel profitably targets affluent professionals; while Holiday Inn profitably targets families with more modest means.

Some marketers may even seek *fewer* customers and reduced demand. For example, many power companies have trouble meeting demand during peak usage periods. Companies may then practice *demarketing* to reduce the number of customers or to shift their demand temporarily or permanently. For instance, to reduce demand for space on congested expressways in Asia, some governments encourage carpooling or impose tolls.

Choosing a Value Proposition

The company must also decide how it will serve targeted customers—how it will *differentiate and position* itself in the marketplace. A company's *value proposition* is the set of benefits or values it promises to deliver to consumers to satisfy their needs. (**Figure 1.4**) Subaru provides safety: "Air bags save lives. All-wheel drive saves air bags. It's what makes a Subaru a Subaru." Red Bull energy drink helps you fight mental and physical fatigue. It captures 70 percent of the energy drink market by promising "It gives you wiiings!"

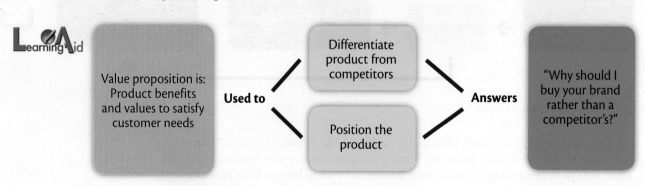

Figure 1.4
What is a value proposition?

Such value propositions differentiate one brand from another. They answer the customer's question "Why should I buy your brand rather than a competitor's?" Companies must design strong value propositions that give them the greatest advantage in their target markets.

Marketing Management Orientations

Marketing management wants to design strategies that will build profitable relationships with target consumers. But what *philosophy* should guide these marketing strategies? What weight should be given to the interests of customers, the organization, and society?

There are five alternative concepts under which organizations design and carry out their marketing strategies: the *production, product, selling, marketing,* and *societal marketing concepts.*

The Production Concept

The **production concept** holds that consumers will favor products that are available and highly affordable. Therefore, management should focus on improving production and distribution efficiency. The production concept is a useful philosophy in some situations. For example, computer maker Lenovo dominates the highly competitive, price-sensitive Chinese PC market through low labor costs, high production efficiency, and mass distribution. However, although useful in some situations, the production concept can lead to marketing short-sightedness. Companies adopting this orientation run a major risk of focusing too narrowly on their own operations and losing sight of the real objective—satisfying customer needs and building customer relationships.

The Product Concept

The **product concept** holds that consumers will favor products that offer the most in quality, performance, and innovative features. Under this concept, marketing strategy focuses on making continuous product improvements. Product quality and improvement are important parts of most marketing strategies. However, focusing *only* on the company's products can also lead to marketing myopia. For example, some manufacturers believe that if they can "build a better mousetrap, the world will beat a path to their door." But they are often rudely shocked. Buyers may well be looking for a better solution to a mouse problem but not necessarily for a better mousetrap. The better solution might be a chemical spray, an exterminating service, or something that works better than a mousetrap. Further, a better mousetrap will not sell unless the manufacturer designs, packages, and prices it attractively; places it in convenient distribution channels; brings it to the attention of people who need it; and convinces buyers that it is a better product.

The Selling Concept

Many companies follow the **selling concept**, which holds that consumers will not buy enough of the firm's products unless it undertakes a large-scale selling and promotion effort. The concept is typically practiced with unsought goods—those that buyers do not normally think of buying, such as insurance or blood donations. These industries must track down prospects and sell them on product benefits. Such aggressive selling, however, carries high risks. It focuses on creating sales transactions rather than on building long-term, profitable customer relationships. The aim often is to sell what the company makes rather than making what the market wants. It assumes that customers who are coaxed into buying the product will like it. Or, if they don't like it, they will possibly forget their disappointment and buy it again later. These are usually poor assumptions.

The Marketing Concept

The **marketing concept** holds that achieving organizational goals depends on knowing the needs and wants of target markets and delivering the desired satisfactions better than competitors do. Under the marketing concept, customer focus and value are the *paths* to sales and profits. Instead of a product-centered "make and sell" philosophy, the marketing concept is a customer-centered "sense and respond" philosophy. The job is not to find the right customers for your product, but to find the right products for your

Value propositions – Red Bull Energy Drink "vitalizes both body and mind. It Gives You Wiiings."

Production concept
The idea that consumers will favor products that are available and highly affordable and that the organization should therefore focus on improving production and distribution efficiency.

Product concept
The idea that consumers will favor products that offer the most quality, performance, and features and that the organization should therefore devote its energy to making continuous product improvements.

Selling concept
The idea that consumers will not buy enough of the firm's products unless it undertakes a large-scale selling and promotion effort.

Marketing concept
The marketing management philosophy that achieving organizational goals depends on knowing the needs and wants of target markets and delivering the desired satisfactions better than competitors do.

customers. McDonald's, for instance, customized its menu to suit the Chinese taste buds. Diners can choose from green pea pies, rice burgers, and a mint-flavored soda called Blue Haven alongside their staple Big Mac and fries.[5]

Figure 1.5 contrasts the selling concept and the marketing concept. The selling concept takes an *inside-out* perspective. It starts with the factory, focuses on the company's existing products, and calls for heavy selling and promotion to obtain profitable sales. It focuses primarily on customer conquest—getting short-term sales with little concern about who buys or why.

Implementing the marketing concept often means more than responding to customers' stated desires and obvious needs. *Customer-driven* companies research current customers deeply to learn about their desires, gather new product and service ideas, and test proposed product improvements. Such customer-driven marketing usually works well when a clear need exists and when customers know what they want.

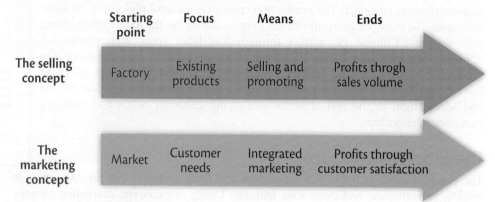

Figure 1.5
The selling and marketing concepts contrasted

In many cases, however, customers *don't* know what they want or even what is possible. For example, even 20 years ago, how many consumers would have thought to ask for now-commonplace products such as mobile phones, notebook computers, iPods, digital cameras, 24-hour online buying, and satellite navigation systems in their cars? Such situations call for *customer-driving* marketing—understanding customer needs even better than customers themselves do and creating products and services that meet existing and latent needs, now and in the future. **Figure 1.6** contrasts customer-driven and customer-driving marketing.

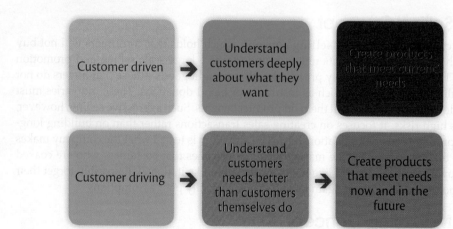

Figure 1.6
Customer driven versus customer driving marketing.

The Societal Marketing Concept

The **societal marketing concept** questions whether the pure marketing concept overlooks possible conflicts between consumer short-run wants and consumer long-run welfare. Is a firm that satisfies the immediate needs and wants of target markets always doing what's best for consumers in the long run? The societal marketing concept holds that marketing strategy should deliver value to customers in a way that maintains or improves both the consumer's and the society's well-being.

Consider the fast-food industry. You may view today's giant fast-food chains as offering tasty and convenient food at reasonable prices. Yet many consumer nutritionists and environmental groups have voiced strong concerns. They point to McDonald's, Burger King, and Fat Burger who still cook their fried foods in oils that are high in artery-clogging trans fats. Such unhealthy fare, the critics claim, is leading consumers to eat too much of the wrong foods, contributing to a national obesity epidemic. What's more, the products are wrapped in convenient packaging, but this leads to waste and pollution. Thus, in satisfying short-term consumer wants, the highly successful fast-food chains may be harming consumer health and causing environmental problems in the long run.[6]

As **Figure 1.7** shows, companies should balance three considerations in setting their marketing strategies: company profits, consumer wants, *and* society's interests. Johnson & Johnson does this well. Its concern for societal interests is summarized in a company document called "Our Credo," which stresses honesty, integrity, and putting people before profits. Under this credo, Johnson & Johnson would rather take a big loss than ship a bad batch of one of its products.

> **Societal marketing concept**
> A principle of enlightened marketing that holds that a company should make good marketing decisions by considering consumers' wants, the company's requirements, consumers' long-run interests, and society's long-run interests.

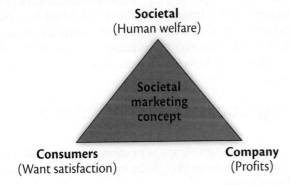

Figure 1.7
Three considerations underlying the societal marketing concept

Consider the tampering case in which people died from swallowing cyanide-laced capsules of Tylenol, a Johnson & Johnson brand. Although Johnson & Johnson believed that the pills had been altered in only a few stores, not in the factory, it quickly recalled its product and launched an information campaign to instruct and reassure consumers. However, in the long run, the company's swift recall of Tylenol strengthened consumer confidence and loyalty. Today, Tylenol remains a leading brand of pain reliever.

Preparing an Integrated Marketing Plan and Program

The company's marketing strategy outlines which customers the company will serve and how it will create value for these customers. Next, the marketer develops an integrated marketing program that delivers the intended value to target customers. The marketing program builds customer relationships by transforming the marketing strategy into action. It consists of the firm's *marketing mix*, the set of marketing tools the firm uses to implement its marketing strategy.

Our Credo

We believe our first responsibility is to the doctors, nurses and patients, to mothers and fathers and all others who use our products and services. In meeting their needs everything we do must be of high quality. We must constantly strive to reduce our costs in order to maintain reasonable prices. Customers' orders must be serviced promptly and accurately. Our suppliers and distributors must have an opportunity to make a fair profit.

We are responsible to our employees, the men and women who work with us throughout the world. Everyone must be considered as an individual. We must respect their dignity and recognize their merit. They must have a sense of security in their jobs. Compensation must be fair and adequate, and working conditions clean, orderly and safe. We must be mindful of ways to help our employees fulfil their family responsibilities. Employees must feel free to make suggestions and complaints. There must be equal opportunity for employment, development and advancement for those qualified. We must provide competent management, and their actions must be just and ethical.

We are responsible to the communities in which we live and work and to the world community as well. We must be good citizens — support good works and charities and bear our fair share of taxes. We must encourage civic improvements and better health and education. We must maintain in good order the property we are privileged to use, protecting the environment and natural resources.

Our final responsibility is to our stockholders. Business must make a sound profit. We must experiment with new ideas. Research must be carried on, innovative programs developed and mistakes paid for. New equipment must be purchased, new facilities provided and new products launched. Reserves must be created to provide for adverse times. When we operate according to these principles, the stockholders should realize a fair return.

Johnson & Johnson

The societal marketing concept –
Johnson & Johnson's Credo emphasizes people before profits. Johnson & Johnson's quick product recall following a tragic Tylenol tampering incident some years ago cost the company $100 million in earnings but strengthened consumer confidence and loyalty.

The major marketing mix tools are classified into four broad groups, called the *four Ps* of marketing: product, price, place, and promotion. To deliver on its value proposition, the firm must:

- create a need-satisfying market offering (product);
- decide how much it will charge for the offer (price);
- decide how it will make the offer available to target consumers (place); and
- communicate with target customers about the offer and persuade them of its merits (promotion).

The firm must blend all of these marketing mix tools into a comprehensive, *integrated marketing program* that communicates and delivers the intended value to chosen customers.

Building Customer Relationships

The first three steps in the marketing process—understanding the marketplace and customer needs, designing a customer-driven marketing strategy, and constructing marketing programs—all lead up to the fourth and most important step: building profitable customer relationships.

Customer Relationship Management

Customer relationship management (CRM) is perhaps the most important concept of modern marketing. More than managing detailed information about individual customers and managing customer "touch points" to maximize customer loyalty, **customer relationship management** involves building and maintaining profitable customer relationships by delivering superior customer value and satisfaction. It deals with all aspects of acquiring, keeping, and growing customers.

Relationship Building Blocks: Customer Value and Satisfaction

The key to building lasting customer relationships is to create superior customer value and satisfaction. Satisfied customers are more likely to be loyal customers and to give the company a larger share of their business.

Customer value

Customers often face a bewildering array of products and services from which to choose. A customer buys from the firm that offers the highest **customer perceived value**—the customer's evaluation of the difference between all the benefits and all the costs of a market offering relative to those of competing offers. **Figure 1.8** shows a customer's perception of value.

For example, Toyota Prius hybrid automobile owners gain a number of benefits. The most obvious benefit is fuel efficiency. However, by purchasing a Prius, the owners

Customer relationship management
The overall process of building and maintaining profitable customer relationships by delivering superior customer value and satisfaction.

Customer perceived value
The customer's evaluation of the difference between all the benefits and all the costs of a market offering relative to those of competing offers.

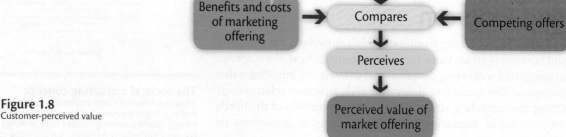

Figure 1.8
Customer-perceived value

also may receive some status and image values. Driving a Prius makes owners feel and appear more environmentally responsible. When deciding whether to purchase a Prius, customers will weigh these and other perceived values of owning the car against the money, effort, and psychic costs of acquiring it. Moreover, they will compare the value of owning a Prius against that of owning another hybrid or nonhybrid brand. They will select the brand that gives them the greatest perceived value.

Customers often do not judge product values and costs accurately or objectively. They act on *perceived* value. For example, is the Prius really the most economical choice? In reality, it might take years to save enough in reduced fuel costs to offset the car's higher sticker price. However, Prius buyers perceive that they are getting real value. A survey of the ownership experiences of 69,000 new car buyers showed that the Prius was rated as most "delightful" in terms of fuel economy, and that Prius owners perceived more overall value for their money than buyers of any other hybrid car.[7]

Customer satisfaction

Customer satisfaction depends on the product's perceived performance relative to a buyer's expectations. If the product's performance falls short of expectations, the customer is dissatisfied. If performance matches expectations, the customer is satisfied. If performance exceeds expectations, the customer is highly satisfied or delighted.

Outstanding marketing companies go out of their way to keep important customers satisfied. Most studies show that higher levels of customer satisfaction lead to greater customer loyalty, which in turn results in better company performance. Smart companies aim to *delight* customers by promising only what they can deliver, then delivering *more* than they promise. Delighted customers not only make repeat purchases, they become "customer evangelists" who tell others about their good experiences with the product.

For example, Samsung found that technology has lost its "wow" factor among consumers. Consumers are getting familiar with digital technology and view it as an appliance rather than something innovative. There is also technological parity and competitors have similar features, making it difficult for Samsung to be distinctive based on technology alone. Samsung then focused on the delight factor—what can digital technology bring to consumer's lives? Three areas were identified that would serve to delight consumers. In terms of design and style, Samsung produces products that would fit into a decorating scheme. It also focused on image as Samsung observed that consumers delight in expressing themselves with mobile devices that draw attention to themselves. Lastly, Samsung ensured that its consumers have a total brand experience where Samsung products enhance their lives. In short, since technology cannot deliver the delight factor, Samsung focused less on the details of the technology inside and more on what the technology produces on the outside—the experience.

> **Customer satisfaction**
> The extent to which a product's perceived performance matches a buyer's expectations.

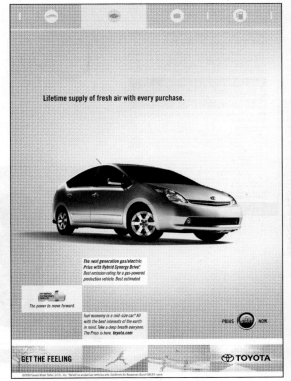

Lifetime supply of fresh air with every purchase.

The next generation gas/electric Prius with Hybrid Synergy Drive.™ Best emission rating for a gas-powered production vehicle. Best estimated

HYBRID SYNERGY DRIVE
The power to move forward.

fuel economy in a mid-size car.* All with the best interests of the earth in mind. Take a deep breath everyone. The Prius is here. toyota.com

GET THE FEELING   PRIUS START NOW.   TOYOTA

Perceived customer value – When deciding whether to purchase a Prius, customers will weigh its benefits against the benefits of owning another hybrid or non-hybrid brand.

Customer satisfaction: Samsung delights its customers by focusing on its design and style, image, a total brand experience. It enhances its image by being a sponsor of the Olympic Games and offers customers a total brand experience by sponsoring e-lounges at Hong Kong International Airport.

It also developed a brand personality to enrich the technology experience, moving from a high-tech to personal-tech experience.[8]

Delighting customers, with exceptional value and service is more than a set of policies or actions—it is a companywide attitude, an important part of the overall company culture.

However, although the customer-centered firm seeks to deliver high customer satisfaction relative to competitors, it does not attempt to *maximize* customer satisfaction. A company can always increase customer satisfaction by lowering its price or increasing its services. But this may result in lower profits. Thus, the purpose of marketing is to generate customer value profitably. This requires a very delicate balance.

Customer Relationship Levels and Tools

Companies can build customer relationships at many levels. At one extreme, a company with many low-margin customers may seek to develop *basic relationships* with them. For example, Procter & Gamble creates relationships through brand-building advertising, sales promotions, and a Web site. At the other extreme, in markets with few customers and high margins, sellers want to create *full partnerships* with key customers. For example, P&G customer teams work closely with its large retailers. In between these two extreme situations, other levels of customer relationships are appropriate.

Today, most leading companies are developing customer loyalty and retention programs. Beyond offering consistently high value and satisfaction, marketers can use specific marketing tools to develop stronger bonds with consumers. For example, many companies offer *frequency marketing programs* that reward customers who buy frequently or in large amounts. Airlines offer frequent-flyer programs and hotels give room upgrades to their frequent guests. Oil companies like Caltex, Shell, and ExxonMobil offer loyalty programs where bonus points can be redeemed for various rewards.[9]

Other companies sponsor *club marketing programs* that offer members special benefits and create member communities. For example, Harley-Davidson sponsors the Harley Owners Group (H.O.G.), which gives Harley riders "an organized way to share their passion and show their pride." H.O.G membership benefits include two magazines (*Hog Tales* and *Enthusiast*), a *H.O.G. Touring Handbook*, a roadside assistance program, a specially designed insurance program, theft reward service, a travel center, and a "Fly & Ride" program enabling members to rent Harleys while on vacation. The worldwide club now numbers more than 1,500 local chapters and over one million members.[10]

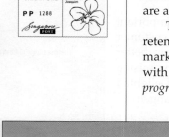

Relationship building tools –
Petrol companies such as ESSO created reward programs to develop customer loyalty and retain customers.

To build customer relationships, companies can add structural ties as well as financial and social benefits. A business marketer might supply customers with special equipment or online linkages that help them manage their orders, payroll, or inventory. For example, a pharmaceutical wholesaler may set up a supply management online system to help retail pharmacy customers manage their inventories, order entry, and shelf space.

The Changing Nature of Customer Relationships

Today's companies are building more direct and lasting relationships with more carefully selected customers. Here are some important trends in the way companies are relating to their customers.

Relating with More Carefully Selected Customers

Most companies are targeting fewer, more profitable customers. Called *selective relationship management*, many companies use customer profitability analysis to weed out losing customers and target winning ones. Attractive offers are created to capture the profitable customers and earn their loyalty.

Relating for the Long Term

Beyond designing strategies to *attract* new customers and create *transactions* with them, firms are using customer relationship management to *retain* current customers and build profitable, long-term *relationships* with them.

Why the new emphasis on retaining and growing customers? In the past, growing markets and an upbeat economy meant a plentiful supply of new customers. However, companies today face some new marketing realities. Changing demographics, more sophisticated competitors, and overcapacity in many industries mean that there are fewer customers to go around. As a result, the costs of attracting new consumers are rising. In fact, on average, it can cost five to ten times as much to attract a new customer as it does to keep a current customer satisfied.

Relating Directly

Direct marketing is booming. Consumers can buy virtually any product without going to a store—by telephone, mail-order catalogs, and online. Business purchasing agents routinely shop on the Web for items ranging from standard office supplies to high-priced, high-tech computer equipment.

Some companies sell *only* via direct channels—firms such as Dell and Amazon.com. Other companies use direct connections to supplement their other communications and distribution channels. For example, Sony sells PlayStation consoles and game cartridges through retailers, supported by millions of dollars of mass-media advertising. However, Sony uses its *www.PlayStation.com* Web site to build relationships with game players of all ages. The site offers information about the latest games, news about events and promotions, game guides and support, and even online forums in which game players can swap tips and stories.

Partner Relationship Management

Marketers must work closely with a variety of marketing partners. In addition to being good at *customer relationship management*, marketers must also be good at **partner relationship management**. Major changes are occurring in how marketers partner with others inside and outside the company to jointly bring more value to customers. **Figure 1.9** shows the internal and external partners that marketers work with.

Partner relationship management
Working closely with partners in other company departments and outside the company to jointly bring greater value to customers.

Partners Inside the Company

Traditionally, marketers have been charged with understanding customers and representing customer needs to different company departments. However, in today's more connected world, marketing no longer has sole ownership of customer interactions. Every functional area can interact with customers, especially electronically. The new thinking is that every employee must be customer focused. David Packard, late cofounder of Hewlett-Packard, wisely said, "Marketing is far too important to be left only to the marketing department."[11]

Today, rather than letting each department go its own way, firms are linking all departments to create customer value. Rather than assigning only sales and marketing people to customers, they are forming cross-functional customer teams. For example, Procter & Gamble assigns "customer development teams" to each of its major retailer accounts. These teams—consisting of sales and marketing people, operations specialists, market and financial analysts, and others—coordinate the efforts of many P&G departments toward helping the retailer be more successful.

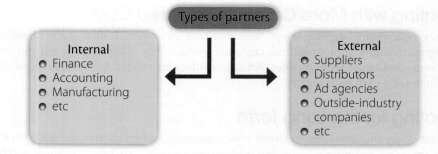

Figure 1.9
Internal and external partners that marketers need to work with

Marketing Partners Outside the Firm

Changes are also occurring in how marketers connect with their suppliers, channel partners, and even competitors. Most companies today are networked companies, relying heavily on partnerships with other firms.

Marketing channels consist of distributors, retailers, and others who connect the company to its buyers. The *supply chain* describes a longer channel, stretching from raw materials to components to final products that are carried to final buyers. For example, the supply chain for personal computers consists of suppliers of computer chips and other components, the computer manufacturer, and the distributors, retailers, and others who sell the computers.

Through *supply chain management*, companies are strengthening their connections with partners along the supply chain. They know that success at building customer relationships also rests on how well their entire supply chain performs against competitors' supply chains. These companies don't just treat suppliers as vendors and distributors as customers. They treat both as partners in delivering customer value. On the one hand, for example, Lexus works closely with carefully selected suppliers to improve quality and operations efficiency. On the other hand, it works with its franchise dealers to provide top-grade sales and service support that will bring customers in the door and keep them coming back.

Beyond managing the supply chain, companies are also discovering that they need *strategic* partners if they hope to be effective. *Strategic alliances* are booming across almost all industries and services. For example, Dell joins forces with software creators such as Oracle and Microsoft to help boost business sales of its servers and their software. In view of China's explosive growth in auto sales, McDonald's has partnered with Sinopec, a state-owned oil company, to give it right of first refusal on locating its restaurants at any of Sinopec's 30,000 petrol stations.[12]

Lexus works closely with its franchise dealers such as Borneo Motors in Singapore to provide top-grade sales and service support.

Capturing Value from Customers

The first four steps in the marketing process involve building customer relationships by creating and delivering superior customer value. The final step involves capturing value in return, in the form of current and future sales, market share, and profits. By creating superior customer value, the firm creates highly satisfied customers who stay loyal and buy more. This, in turn, means greater long-run returns for the firm. Here, we discuss the outcomes of creating customer value: customer loyalty and retention, share of market and share of customer, and customer equity.

Creating Customer Loyalty and Retention

Good customer relationship management creates customer delight. In turn, delighted customers remain loyal and talk favorably to others about the company and its products. Thus, the aim of customer relationship management is to create not just customer satisfaction, but customer delight.[13]

Companies are realizing that losing a customer means losing more than a single sale. It means losing **customer lifetime value**—the entire stream of purchases that the customer would make over a lifetime of patronage. For example, Lexus estimates that a single satisfied and loyal customer is worth $600,000 in lifetime sales. Thus, working to retain and grow customers makes good economic sense.

In fact, a company can lose money on a specific transaction but still benefit greatly from a long-term relationship. This means that companies must aim high in building customer relationships. Customer delight creates an emotional relationship with a product or service, not just a rational preference (see **Real Marketing**).

Growing Share of Customer

Good customer relationship management can also help marketers to increase their **share of customer**—the share they get of the customer's purchasing in their product categories. Thus, banks want to increase "share of wallet." Supermarkets and restaurants want to get more "share of stomach." Airlines want greater "share of travel."

To increase share of customer, firms can offer greater variety to current customers. Or they can train employees to cross-sell and up-sell in order to market more products and services to existing customers. For example, Amazon.com is highly skilled at leveraging relationships with its 50 million customers to increase its share of each customer's purchases. Originally an online bookseller, Amazon.com now offers customers music, videos, gifts, toys, consumer electronics, office products, home improvement items, lawn and garden products, apparel and accessories, jewelry, and an online auction. In addition, based on each customer's purchase history, the company recommends related products that might be of interest. In this way, Amazon.com captures a greater share of each customer's spending budget.

Building Customer Equity

What Is Customer Equity?

The ultimate aim of customer relationship management is to produce high *customer equity*.[14] **Customer equity** is the combined discounted customer lifetime values of all of the company's current and potential customers. Clearly, the more loyal the firm's profitable customers, the higher the firm's customer equity. Customer equity may be a better measure of a firm's performance than current sales or market share. Whereas sales and market share reflect the past, customer equity suggests the future.

Building the Right Relationships with the Right Customers

Companies should manage customer equity carefully. They should view customers as assets that need to be managed and maximized. But not all customers, not even all loyal customers, are good investments. Surprisingly, some loyal customers can be unprofitable, and some disloyal customers can be profitable.

The company can classify customers according to their potential profitability and manage its relationships with them accordingly. **Figure 1.10** classifies customers into one of four relationship groups, according to their profitability and projected loyalty.[15] Each group requires a different relationship management strategy.

- "Strangers" show low profitability and little projected loyalty. There is little fit between the company's offerings and their needs. The relationship management strategy for these customers is simple: Don't invest anything in them.
- "Butterflies" are profitable but not loyal. There is a good fit between the company's offerings and their needs. However, like real butterflies, we can enjoy them for only a short while and then they're gone. An example is stock market investors who trade shares often and in large amounts, but who enjoy hunting for the best deals without building a regular relationship with any single brokerage company.

Customer lifetime value
The value of the entire stream of purchases that a customer would make over a lifetime of patronage.

Share of customer
The portion of the customer's purchasing that a company gets in its product categories.

Customer equity
The total combined customer lifetime values of all of the company's customers.

REAL MARKETING

Private Banking in Asia: Building the Right Relationships with the Right Customers

One of the most significant business opportunities in Asia derives from the region's growing affluence. According to a report by Merrill Lynch and research firm Cap Gemini, there were 2.3 million individuals with a minimum net worth of $1 million in 2004, with their total wealth growing 8.5 percent to $7.2 trillion. To capture this growing market of high net-worth individuals, private bankers are aggressively expanding their budgets for Asia-focused initiatives.

Unlike the inherited old money that has traditionally comprised the clientele of private bankers in the West, Asian clients consisted mainly of entrepreneurs, with the remainder largely made up of professionals such as CEOs, doctors and lawyers. Having earned their wealth, these individuals are active in the investment process. They are inclined to have a hands-on approach in managing their funds and tend to be more demanding of their

private bankers. Entrepreneur clients also require services related to their businesses like monetizing their assets. They are also more savvy and are willing to invest in less conventional financial products such as hedge funds and private equity.

There is also a growing awareness of succession planning that has led to a higher demand for trust and estate planning services in the region. As Christine Ong, country head of UBS Singapore, notes, "The family is an important value in the Asian psyche, and inter-generational wealth transfer is a key focus." Thus, private banks have been splashing out on specially designed wealth-transfer programs for the baby boomer generation of ultra-high net worth clients.

For example, Credit Suisse sponsored a lavish three-day program tailored for its Asian private banking clients at the Ritz Carlton Bali Resort & Spa. Apart from the

airfare, all other expenses from seminars, airport transfers, and accommodation to activities such as wine tasting and watch appreciation were borne by the bank. This Family Legacy Program attracted 23 participants from two generations of 12 families. The bank chose "a location where the families would spend quality time together ... in a relaxed environment," said Dr Francois Monnet, its head of private banking for Southeast Asian and Australasia. Aside from workshops on estate and succession planning, and business and family governance structures, the program included a real-life case study session about the Eu Yan Sang family. Richard Eu, group CEO of the traditional Chinese medicine company, fielded questions from participants on the family's experience with wealth transfer. Activities like "whodunit," run by professional actors, had participants working together in teams to solve a

Efforts to convert butterflies into loyal customers are rarely successful. Instead, the company should enjoy the butterflies for the moment. It should use promotional blitzes to attract them, create satisfying and profitable transactions with them, and then cease investing in them until the next time around.

- "True friends" are both profitable and loyal. There is a strong fit between their needs and the company's offerings. The firm wants to make continuous relationship investments to delight these customers and nurture, retain, and grow them. It wants to turn true friends into "true believers," who come back regularly and tell others about their good experiences with the company.

- "Barnacles" are highly loyal but not very profitable. There is a limited fit between their needs and the company's offerings. An example is smaller bank customers who bank regularly but do not generate enough returns to cover the costs of maintaining their accounts. Like barnacles on the hull of a ship, they create drag. Barnacles are perhaps the most problematic customers. The company might be able to improve their profitability by selling them more, raising their fees, or reducing service to them. However, if they cannot be made profitable, they should be "fired."

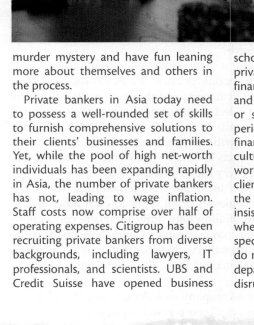

There is a growing awareness of succession planning that has led to higher demand for trust and estate plannning servicecs in Asia.

murder mystery and have fun leaning more about themselves and others in the process.

Private bankers in Asia today need to possess a well-rounded set of skills to furnish comprehensive solutions to their clients' businesses and families. Yet, while the pool of high net-worth individuals has been expanding rapidly in Asia, the number of private bankers has not, leading to wage inflation. Staff costs now comprise over half of operating expenses. Citigroup has been recruiting private bankers from diverse backgrounds, including lawyers, IT professionals, and scientists. UBS and Credit Suisse have opened business schools in Singapore to train would-be private bankers. To retain talent, some financial institutions offer commissions and bonuses paid over several years or stock options with longer vesting periods. Others rely more on non-financial attractions like corporate culture, workplace environment, and work/private life balance. To prevent clients following private bankers when the latter switch jobs, some banks insist that private bankers never meet when clients alone, but with a product specialist or adviser. Even when clients do not move with their private banker, departures usually cause massive disruptions in client service for banks.

It takes time, money, and people to build the right relationships with the right customers.

Sources:
Grace Ng, "Private Banks Send Families on Holiday to Plan Transfer," *The Straits Times* (Singapore), November 19, 2007, p. H22; Chow Penn Nee, "Banking on Asia's New Wealth," *TODAY* (Singapore), January 7, 2006; "Relationship Managers Wanted," *International Herald Tribune*, December 22, 2005.

The point here is an important one: Different types of customers require different relationship management strategies. The goal is to build the right relationships with the right customers.

	Short-term customers	Long-term customers
High profitability	**Butterflies** Good fit between company's offerings and customer's needs; high profit potential	**True Friends** Good fit between companys offerings and customer's needs; highest profit potential
Low profitability	**Strangers** Little fit between company's offerings and customer's needs; lowest profit potential	**Barnacles** Limited fit between company's offerings and customer's needs; low profit potential

Potential profitability →

Projected loyalty

Figure 1.10
Customer relationship groups
Source: Reprinted by permission of *Harvard Business Review*. Adapted from "Mismanagement of Customer Loyalty" by Werner Relnartz and V. Kumar, July 2002, p. 93. Copyright © by the president and fellows of Harvard College; all rights reserved.

The New Marketing Landscape

In this section, we examine the major trends and forces that are changing the marketing landscape and challenging marketing strategy. We look at four major developments: the new digital age, rapid globalization, the call for more ethics and social responsibility, and the growth in not-for-profit marketing.

The New Digital Age

Internet
A vast public web of computer networks that connects users of all types all around the world to each other and to an amazingly large information repository.

The technology boom has created exciting new ways to learn about and track customers and to create products and services tailored to individual customer needs. Technology is also helping companies to distribute products more efficiently and effectively. And it's helping them to communicate with customers in large groups or one-to-one.

Through videoconferencing, marketing researchers at a company's headquarters in New York can look in on focus groups in Shanghai or Paris without ever stepping onto a plane. With only a few clicks of a mouse button, a direct marketer can tap into online data services to learn anything from what car you drive to what you read to what flavor of ice cream you prefer. Or, using today's powerful computers, marketers can create their own detailed customer databases and use them to target individual customers with offers designed to meet their specific needs.

Technology has also brought a new wave of communication and advertising tools—ranging from mobile phones, iPods, DVRs, Web sites, and interactive TV to video kiosks at airports and shopping malls. Marketers can use these tools to zero in on selected customers with carefully targeted messages. Through the Internet, customers can learn about, design, order, and pay for products and services, without ever leaving home. From virtual reality displays that test new products to online virtual stores that sell them, the technology boom is affecting every aspect of marketing.

Technology has brought a new wave of marketing tools.

Perhaps the most dramatic new technology is the **Internet**. Today, the Internet links individuals and businesses of all types to each other and to information all around the world. It allows anytime, anywhere connections to information, entertainment, and communication. Companies are using the Internet to build closer relationships with customers and marketing partners. Beyond competing in traditional market*places*, they now have access to exciting new market*spaces*.

These days, it's hard to find a company that doesn't use the Web in a significant way. Most traditional "brick-and-mortar" companies have now become "click-and-mortar" companies. They have ventured online to attract new customers and build stronger relationships with existing ones. The Internet also spawned an entirely new breed of "click-only" companies—the so-called "dot-coms." Today, online consumer buying is growing at a healthy rate. Business-to-business e-commerce is also booming. It seems that almost every business has set up shop on the Web. Giants such as Sony, GE, Microsoft, Dell, Li & Fung and many others have moved quickly to exploit the B-to-B power of the Internet.

Rapid Globalization

In an increasingly smaller world, many marketers are now connected *globally* with their customers and marketing partners. Almost every company is touched in some way by global competition. American firms have been challenged at home by the skillful marketing of European and Asian multinationals. Companies such as Toyota, Siemens, Nestlé, Sony, Nintendo, and Samsung have often outperformed their U.S. competitors in American markets. Similarly, U.S. companies in a wide range of industries have developed truly global operations, making and selling their products worldwide. Coca-Cola offers a mind-boggling 400 different brands in more than 200 countries. It introduced Coke Zero in Singapore in 2008. Even MTV has joined the elite of global brands, delivering localized versions of its pulse-thumping fare to teens in 419 million homes in 164 countries around the globe.[16]

Many companies have developed truly global operations. Coca-Cola offers more than 400 different brands in more than 200 countries including BPM energy drink in Ireland, bitter Mare Rosso in Spain, Sprite Ice Cube in Belgium, Fanta in Chile, and NaturAqua in Hungary.

Today, companies are not only trying to sell more of their locally produced goods in international markets, they also are buying more supplies and components abroad. For example, Isaac Mizrahi, one of America's top fashion designers, may choose cloth woven from Australian wool with designs printed in Italy. He will design a dress and e-mail the drawing to a Hong Kong agent, who will place the order with a Chinese factory. Finished dresses will be airfreighted to New York, where they will be redistributed to department and specialty stores around the country.

Thus, managers in countries around the world are increasingly taking a global, not just local, view of the company's industry, competitors, and opportunities. They are asking: What is global marketing? How does it differ from domestic marketing? How do global competitors and forces affect our business? To what extent should we "go global"?

The Call for More Ethics and Social Responsibility

Marketers are reexamining their relationships with social values and responsibilities and with the very Earth that sustains us. As the worldwide consumerism and environmentalism movements mature, today's marketers are being called upon to take greater responsibility for the social and environmental impact of their actions. Few companies can ignore the renewed and very demanding environmental movement.

The social-responsibility and environmental movements will place even stricter demands on companies in the future. Some companies resist these movements, budging only when forced by legislation or organized consumer outcries. More forward-looking companies, however, readily accept their responsibilities to the world around them. They view socially responsible actions as an opportunity to do well by doing good. They seek ways to profit by serving the best long-run interests of their customers and communities.

The Growth of Not-for-Profit Marketing

In the past, marketing has been most widely applied in the for-profit business sector. In recent years, however, marketing also has become a major part of the strategies of many not-for-profit organizations, such as colleges, hospitals, museums, zoos, symphony orchestras, and even churches. Similarly, private colleges are using marketing to compete for students and funds. Many performing arts groups face huge operating deficits that they must cover by more aggressive donor marketing. Finally, many long-standing not-for-profit organizations—the YMCA and the Salvation Army—have lost members and are now modernizing their missions and "products" to attract more members and donors.

Government agencies have also shown an increased interest in marketing. For example, the Singapore government designs *social marketing campaigns* to encourage family growth and concern for the environment or to discourage smoking, excessive drinking, and drug use.

Not-for-profit marketing—
The Singapore Zoo aggressively markets its attractions to what might be its most important customer segment—children of all ages.

So, What Is Marketing? Pulling It All Together

At the start of this chapter, Figure 1.1 presented a simple model of the marketing process. Now that we've discussed all of the steps in the process, **Figure 1.11** presents an expanded model that will help you pull it all together. What is marketing? Simply put, marketing is the process of building profitable customer relationships by creating value for customers and capturing value in return.

The first four steps of the marketing process focus on creating value for customers. The company first gains a full understanding of the marketplace by researching customer needs and managing marketing information. It then designs a customer-driven marketing strategy based on the answers to two simple questions. The first question is "What consumers will we serve?" (market segmentation and targeting). Good marketing companies know that they cannot serve all customers in every way. Instead, they need to focus their resources on the customers they can serve best and most profitably. The second marketing strategy question is "How can we best serve targeted customers?" (differentiation and positioning). Here, the marketer outlines a value proposition that spells out what values the company will deliver in order to win target customers.

With its marketing strategy decided, the company now constructs an integrated marketing program—consisting of a blend of the four marketing mix elements, or the four Ps—that transforms the marketing strategy into real value for customers. The company develops product offers and creates strong brand identities for them. It prices these offers to create real customer value and distributes the offers to make them available to target consumers. Finally, the company designs promotion programs that communicate the value proposition to target consumers and persuade them to act on the market offering.

Perhaps the most important step in the marketing process involves building value-laden, profitable relationships with target customers. Throughout the process, marketers practice customer relationship management to create customer satisfaction and delight. In creating customer value and relationships, the company must work closely with marketing partners both inside the company and throughout the marketing system. Thus,

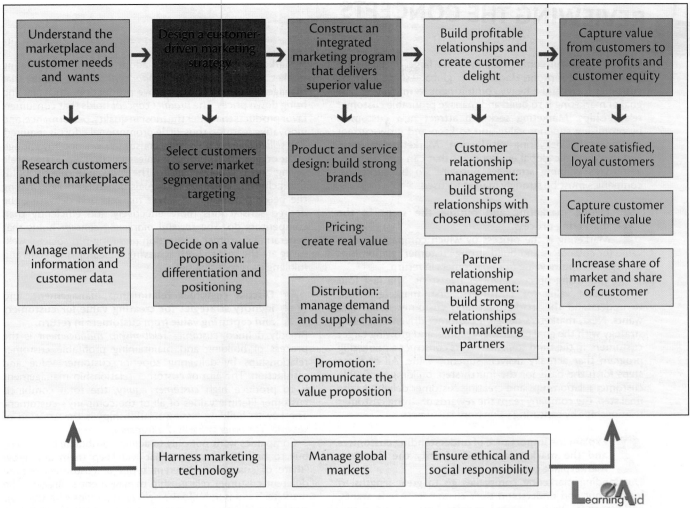

Understand the marketplace and customer needs and wants	Design a customer-driven marketing strategy	Construct an integrated marketing program that delivers superior value	Build profitable relationships and create customer delight	Capture value from customers to create profits and customer equity
Research customers and the marketplace	Select customers to serve: market segmentation and targeting	Product and service design: build strong brands	Customer relationship management: build strong relationships with chosen customers	Create satisfied, loyal customers
Manage marketing information and customer data	Decide on a value proposition: differentiation and positioning	Pricing: create real value		Capture customer lifetime value
		Distribution: manage demand and supply chains	Partner relationship management: build strong relationships with marketing partners	Increase share of market and share of customer
		Promotion: communicate the value proposition		

Harness marketing technology

Manage global markets

Ensure ethical and social responsibility

Figure 1.11
An expanded model of the marketing process

beyond practicing good customer relationship management, firms must also practice good partner relationship management.

The first four steps in the marketing process create value *for* customers. In the final step, the company reaps the rewards of its strong customer relationships by capturing value *from* customers. Delivering superior customer value creates highly satisfied customers who will buy more and will buy again. This helps the company to capture customer lifetime value and greater share of customer. The result is increased long-term customer equity for the firm.

Finally, in the face of today's changing marketing landscape, companies must take into account three additional factors. In building customer and partner relationships, they must harness marketing technology, take advantage of global opportunities, and ensure that they act in an ethical and socially responsible way.

Figure 1.11 provides a good roadmap to future chapters of the text. Chapters 1 and 2 introduce the marketing process, with a focus on building customer relationships and capturing value from customers. Chapters 3, 4, 5, and 6 address the first step of the marketing process—understanding the marketing environment, managing marketing information, and understanding consumer and business buyer behavior. In Chapter 7, we look more deeply into the two major marketing strategy decisions: selecting which customers to serve (segmentation and targeting) and deciding on a value proposition (differentiation and positioning). Chapters 8 through 17 discuss the marketing mix variables, one by one. Chapter 18 sums up customer-driven marketing strategy and creating competitive advantage in the marketplace. Then, the final two chapters examine special marketing considerations: global marketing and marketing ethics and social responsibility.

REVIEWING THE CONCEPTS

Today's successful companies—whether large or small, for-profit or not-for-profit, domestic or global—share a strong customer focus and a heavy commitment to marketing. The goal of marketing is to build and manage profitable customer relationships. Marketing seeks to attract new customers by promising superior value and to keep and grow current customers by delivering satisfaction. Marketing operates within a dynamic global environment that can quickly make yesterday's winning strategies obsolete. To be successful, companies must be strongly market focused.

1 **Define marketing and outline the steps in the marketing process.**
Marketing is the process by which companies create value for customers and build strong customer relationships in order to capture value from customers in return.

The marketing process involves five steps. The first four steps create value for customers. First, marketers need to understand the marketplace and customer needs and wants. Next, marketers design a customer-driven marketing strategy with the goal of getting, keeping, and growing target customers. In the third step, marketers construct a marketing program that actually delivers superior value. All of these steps form the basis for the fourth step, building profitable customer relationships and creating customer delight. In the final step, the company reaps the rewards of strong customer relationships by capturing value from customers.

2 **Explain the importance of understanding customers and the marketplace, and identify the five core marketplace concepts.**
Outstanding marketing companies go to great lengths to learn about and understand their customers' needs, wants, and demands. This understanding helps them to design want-satisfying market offerings and build value-laden customer relationships by which they can capture customer lifetime value and greater share of customer. The result is increased long-term customer equity for the firm.

The core marketplace concepts are needs, wants, and demands; market offerings (products, services, and experiences); value and satisfaction; exchange and relationships; and markets. Wants are the form taken by human needs when shaped by culture and individual personality. When backed by buying power, wants become demands. Companies address needs by putting forth a value proposition, a set of benefits that they promise to consumers to satisfy their needs. The value proposition is fulfilled through a market offering that delivers customer value and satisfaction, resulting in long-term exchange relationships with customers.

3 **Identify the key elements of a customer-driven marketing strategy and discuss marketing management orientations that guide marketing strategy.**
To design a winning marketing strategy, the company must first decide who it will serve. It does this by dividing the market into segments of customers (*market segmentation*) and selecting which segments it will cultivate (*target marketing*). Next, the company must decide how it will serve targeted customers (how it will *differentiate and position* itself in the marketplace).

Marketing management can adopt one of five competing market orientations. The *production concept* holds that management's task is to improve production efficiency and bring down prices. The *product concept* holds that consumers favor products that offer the most in quality, performance, and innovative features; thus, little promotional effort is required. The *selling concept* holds that consumers will not buy enough of the organization's products unless it undertakes a large-scale selling and promotion effort. The *marketing concept* holds that achieving organizational goals depends on determining the needs and wants of target markets and delivering the desired satisfactions more effectively and efficiently than competitors do. The *societal marketing concept* holds that generating customer satisfaction *and* long-run societal well-being are the keys to both achieving the company's goals and fulfilling its responsibilities.

4 **Discuss customer relationship management, and identify strategies for creating value *for* customers and capturing value *from* customers in return.**
Broadly defined, *customer relationship management* is the process of building and maintaining profitable customer relationships by delivering superior customer value and satisfaction. The aim of customer relationship management is to produce high *customer equity*, the total combined customer lifetime values of all of the company's customers. The key to building lasting relationships is the creation of superior *customer value* and *satisfaction*.

Companies want not only to acquire profitable customers, but to build relationships that will keep them and grow "share of customer." Different types of customers require different customer relationship management strategies. The marketer's aim is to build the *right relationships* with the *right customers*. In return for creating value *for* targeted customers, the company captures value *from* customers in the form of profits and customer equity.

In building customer relationships, good marketers realize that they cannot go it alone. They must work closely with marketing partners inside and outside the company. In addition to being good at customer relationship management, they must also be good at *partner relationship management*.

5 **Describe the major trends and forces that are changing the marketing landscape in this new age of relationships.**
As the world spins on, dramatic changes are occurring in the marketing arena. The boom in computer, telecommunications, information, transportation, and other technologies has created exciting new ways to learn about and track customers and to create products and services tailored to individual customer needs.

In an increasingly smaller world, many marketers are now connected *globally* with their customers and marketing partners. Today, almost every company, large or small, is touched in some way by global competition. Today's marketers are also reexamining their ethical and societal responsibilities. Marketers are being called upon to take greater responsibility for the social and environmental impact of their actions. Finally, in the past, marketing has been most widely applied in the for-profit business sector. In recent years, however, marketing also has become a major part of the strategies of many not-for-profit organizations, such as colleges, hospitals, museums, zoos, symphony orchestras, and even churches.

Pulling it all together, as discussed throughout the chapter, the major new developments in marketing can be summed

up in a single word: *relationships*. Today, marketers of all kinds are taking advantage of new opportunities for building relationships with their customers, their marketing partners, and the world around them.

REVIEWING THE KEY TERMS

Customer equity 17
Customer lifetime value 17
Customer perceived value 12
Customer relationship management 12
Customer satisfaction 13
Demands 6
Exchange 7
Internet 20
Market 7
Marketing 5
Marketing concept 9

Marketing management 8
Marketing myopia 6
Market offering 6
Needs 5
Partner relationship management 15
Product concept 9
Production concept 9
Selling concept 9
Share of customer 17
Societal marketing concept 11
Wants 5

DISCUSSING THE CONCEPTS

1. You can define marketing and its functions in many ways. In your own words, explain marketing to someone who has not yet read this chapter.

2. What is the difference between a need, a want, and a demand? Describe the need versus the want for the following products: Gatorade, Nike, iPod.

3. What are the five different marketing management orientations? Which orientation do you believe your university follows when marketing its undergraduate program?

4. Customer value is consumers' evaluation of the difference between total benefits and total costs. When a consumer orders a T-shirt from an online retailer, what are the total benefits and total costs?

5. What is customer equity? How can a company increase its customer equity?

6. How has the Internet changed consumers? Marketers?

APPLYING THE CONCEPTS

1. When companies have close competitors, they try to choose value propositions that will differentiate them from others in the market. Choose three fast-food restaurants and describe their value propositions. Are they strongly differentiating themselves?

2. What are the four customer relationship groups? Is there a way marketers can move a Stranger to a True Friend? Explain how Apple and BMW would move their Strangers to True Friends.

3. A cell phone company spends $148.50 in total costs to acquire a new user. On average, this new user spends $60 a month for calling and related services, and the cell phone company generates an 18 percent profit margin in each of the 25 months that the user is expected to stay with the service. What is the Customer Lifetime Value of this user to the cell phone company?

FOCUS ON TECHNOLOGY

Visit www.oddcast.com and you will find animated characters that interact with customers on various linked sponsor Web sites. The characters, referred to as VHosts, help customers navigate the site and find important information. A VHost can be set up to speak any one of 64 languages and to have a variety of facial characteristics, skin tones, and hair styles. More than 5,000 companies currently use Oddcast's technology, including major brands such as ESPN and L'Oréal.

1. What is the appeal of the VHost for a marketer?
2. What might be a concern for the marketer?
3. After visiting the site, as a consumer, what are your thoughts regarding the VHosts?
4. What specific target markets might benefit most from a VHost?

FOCUS ON ETHICS

In this digital age, marketers have more thorough data and can use the data for very precise market targeting. In fact, the U.S. military has developed a database of millions of high school and college students for recruiting. With the database, the military can more effectively target potential recruits. In addition to names and addresses, the data for each young person includes such things as favorite subjects, grade point averages, and consumer purchases. Currently, more than 100 groups, including the American Civil Liberties Union and Rock the Vote are demanding that the database be abandoned and that the military not continue to collect this information for marketing purposes.

1. Do you think the military has a right to improve its recruiting through a more elaborate database of their potential "customers"?
2. Do you think the database is an invasion of privacy?
3. How else might the military improve its recruiting?

See: "Military Database of Potential Recruits Rankles Privacy Groups," *Advertising Age*, October 31, 2005, p. 9.

VIDEO CASE

Dunkin' Donuts

For more than 50 years, Dunkin' Donuts has offered customers throughout the U. S., and around the world, a consistent experience—the same donuts, the same coffee, the same store décor—each time a customer drops in. Although the chain now offers iced coffee, breakfast sandwiches, smoothies, gourmet cookies, and Dunkin' Dawgs in addition to the old standbys, devoted customers argue that it's the coffee that sets Dunkin' Donuts apart. To keep customers coming back, the chain still relies on the recipe that founder Bill Rosenberg crafted more than 50 years ago.

The company is so concerned about offering a consistent, high-quality cup of coffee that managers in Dunkin' Donut's "Tree-to-Cup" program monitor the progress of its coffee beans from the farm to the restaurant. The result? Dunkin' Donuts sells more cups of coffee than any other retailer in the

U. S.—30 cups a second, nearly one billion cups each year. Building on that success, the company plans to more than triple its current number of stores, amassing 15,000 franchises by the year 2015.

After viewing the video featuring Dunkin' Donuts, answer the following questions about managing profitable customer relationships.

1. How does Dunkin' Donuts build long-term customer relationships?
2. What is Dunkin' Donuts' value proposition?
3. How is Dunkin' Donuts growing its share of customers?

 **COMPANY CASE**

Build-A-Bear: Build-A-Memory

When Maxine Clark founded Build-A-Bear Workshop in 1996, many critics thought that she was making a very poor business decision. Yet, by 2005, one retail consultancy named Build-A-Bear one of the five hottest retailers in the U.S. and the company ranked number 25 on *BusinessWeek's* Hot Growth list of fast-expanding small companies. Maxine Clark won Fast Company's Customer-Centered Leader Award. How does a small startup company achieve such accolades?

The Product

On paper, it all looks simple. Maxine Clark opened the first company store in 1996. Since then, the company has opened more than 200 stores and has custom-made more than 30 million teddy bears and other stuffed animals. Annual revenues reached $474 million for 2007 and are growing at a steady and predictable 20 percent annually. Annual sales per square foot are $600, roughly double the average for U.S. mall stores. The company plans to open approximately 30 new stores each year in the U.S. and Canada and to franchise an additional 20 stores per year internationally. Its stores are now located in 20 countries, including such Asian nations as India, Japan, Singapore, South Korea, Taiwan, and Thailand. Moreover, the company's Internet sales at buildabear.com are exploding.

Such success comes not from the tangible object that children clutch as they leave a store. It comes from what Build-A-Bear is really selling: the experience of participating in the creation of personalized entertainment.

When children enter a Build-A-Bear store, they step into a fantasy world organized around a child-friendly assembly line comprising clearly labeled work stations. The process begins at the "Choose Me" station where customers select an unstuffed animal from a bin. At the "Stuff Me" station, the animal literally comes to life. A friendly employee inserts a metal tube into the animal, extending from a large tumbler full of "fluff." The child operates a foot pedal that blows in the stuffing. She or he (25 percent of Build-A-Bear customers are boys) decides just how full the animal should be. Other stations include "Hear Me" (where customers decide whether or not to include a "voice box"), "Stitch Me" (where the child stitches the animal shut), "Fluff Me" (where the child can give the animal a blow-dry spa treatment), "Dress Me" (filled with accessories galore), and "Name Me" (where a birth certificate is created with the child-selected name).

Unlike most retail stores, waiting in line behind other customers is not an unpleasant activity. In fact, because the process is much of the fun, waiting actually enhances the experience. By the time children leave the store, they have a product unlike any they've ever bought or received. They have a product that they have created. More than just a stuffed animal that they can have and hold, it's entrenched with the memory created on their visit to the store.

Parents love Build-A-Bear too. The cost of the experience starts as low as $10. Although options and accessories can push that price up, the average bear leaves the store costing around $25. Many parents consider this a bargain when they see how each of those dollars translates into their child's delight.

Why the Concept Works

An observer might assume that Build-A-Bear is competing with other toy companies, or with other makers of stuffed animals. However, Maxine Clark disagrees. "Our concept is based on customization," says Clark. "Most things today are high-tech and hard-touch. We are soft-touch. We don't think of ourselves as a toy store—we think of ourselves as an experience." Clark points out that, unlike the rest of the toy industry, Build-A-Bear sales do not peak during the holiday season, but are evenly distributed throughout the year.

Product personalization has long been popular in various industries. Nike and Levi's allow customers to customize products through their Web site. Dell has achieved leadership by doing the same. One research analyst has stated that the customization feature is so satisfying, it "builds fiercely loyal customers."

Although not very common in the toy industry, Maxine Clark asserts that personalization is emerging because it lets customers be creative and express themselves. It provides far more value for the customer than they receive from mass-produced products. "It's empowerment—it lets the customer do something in their control," she adds. Build-A-Bear has capitalized on this concept by not just allowing for customization, but by making it a key driver of customer value. The extensive customer involvement in the personalization process is more of the "product" than the resulting item.

Although Build-A-Bear has performed impressively,

some analysts question whether or not it is just another toy industry fad, comparing the brand to Beanie Babies and Cabbage Patch Kids. Maxine Clark has considered this, and she is confident that the Build-A-Bear product and experience will evolve as quickly as the fickle tastes of children. Although some outfits and accessories might be trendy (the company added Spiderman costumes to the bear-size clothing line at the peak of the movie's popularity), accessories assortments are changed 11 times each year.

Knowing the Customer

Maxine Clark believes her success derives from more than just business skills relating to strategy development and implementation. She attributes it to "never forgetting what it's like to be a customer." Given that Clark has no children of her own, this is an amazing feat indeed. Clark has employed both low-tech and high-tech methods for making Build-A-Bear a truly customer-centric organization.

To put herself in the customer's shoes, Clark walks where they walk. Every week, she visits two or three of the more than 200 Build-A-Bear stores. Aside from seeing how the stores are running operationally, she uses the opportunity to interact with her customer base by chatting with preteens and parents. She actually puts herself on the front line, assisting employees in serving customers. She even hands out business cards.

As a result, Clark receives thousands of e-mails each week, and she's added to the buddy lists of preteens all over the world. Clark tries to respond to as many of those messages as possible via her BlackBerry. Also, to capitalize on these

customer communications, she has created what she calls the "Virtual Cub Advisory Council," a panel of children on her e-mail list. And what does Clark get in return from all this high-tech communication? "Ideas," she says. "I used to feel like I had to come up with all the ideas myself, but it's so much easier relying on my customers for help."

From the location of stores to accessories that could be added to the Build-A-Bear line, Build-A-Bear actually puts customer ideas into practice. As the ideas come in, Clark polls the Cub Council to get real-time feedback from customers throughout the areas where the company does business. Miniscooters, mascot bears at professional sports venues, and sequined purses are all ideas generated by customers that have become very successful additions.

The future holds great potential as more ideas are being considered and implemented. Soon, Build-A-Bear Workshops will house in-store galleries of bear-sized furniture designed by kids for kids. The company will add NASCAR to the sports licensing agreements that it currently has with the NBA, MLB, NHL, and NFL. And Clark will give much more attention to a new line of stores called "Friends 2B Made," a concept built around the personalization of dolls rather than stuffed animals.

Although Maxine Clark may communicate with only a fraction of her customers, she sees this as the basis for a personal connection with all customers. "With each child that enters our store, we have an opportunity to build a lasting memory," she says. "Any business can think that way, whether you're selling a screw, a bar of soap, or a bear."

Questions For Discussion

1. Give examples of needs, wants, and demands that Build-A-Bear customers demonstrate, differentiating each of these three concepts. What are the implications of each on Build-A-Bear's actions?
2. Detail all facets of Build-A-Bear's product. What is being exchanged in a Build-A-Bear transaction?
3. Which of the five marketing management concepts best describes Build-A-Bear Workshop?
4. Discuss the value that Build-A-Bear creates for its customers.
5. Is Build-A-Bear likely to be successful in continuing to build customer relationships? Why or why not?

Sources:
Parija Bhatnagar, "The Next Hot Retailers?" *CNNMoney.com*, January 9, 2006; Lucas Conley, "Customer-Centered Leader: Maxine Clark," *Fast Company*, October 2005, p. 54; Ray Allegrezza, "Kids Today," *Kids Today*, April 1, 2006, p. 10; "The Mini-Me School of Marketing," *Brand Strategy*, November 2, 2005, p. 12; Michael O'Rourke, "Build-a-Bear Assembles Dreams," *San Antonio Express-News*, February 4, 2006, p. 1E; Dody Tsiantar, "Not Your Average Bear," *Time*, July 3, 2005; Roger Crockett, "Build-A-Bear Workshop: Retailing Gets Interactive with Toys Designed by Tots," *BusinessWeek*, June 6, 2005, p. 77; "Build-A-Bear Workshop, Inc. Reports Strong Sales and Net Income Growth in Fiscal 2005 Fourth Quarter and Full Year," press release through *Business Wire*, February 16, 2006; and "Build-A-Bear workshop, Inc. Reports Fiscal 2007," www.franchising.com, February 14, 2008.

Objectives

After studying this chapter, you should be able to

- explain companywide strategic planning and its four steps
- discuss how to design business portfolios and develop growth strategies
- explain marketing's role in strategic planning and how marketing works with its partners to create and deliver customer value
- describe the elements of a customer-driven marketing strategy and mix, and the forces that influence it
- list the marketing management functions, including the elements of a marketing plan, and discuss the importance of measuring and managing return on marketing investment

CHAPTER 2

COMPANY AND MARKETING STRATEGY: Partnering to Build Customer Relationships

Previewing the Concepts

In the first chapter, we explored the marketing process by which companies create value for consumers to capture value in return. In this chapter, we examine steps two and three of the marketing process—designing customer-driven marketing strategies and constructing marketing programs. To begin, we look at the organization's overall strategic planning. Next, we discuss how marketers, guided by the strategic plan, work closely with others inside and outside the firm to serve customers. We then examine marketing strategy and planning—how marketers choose target markets, position their market offerings, develop a marketing mix, and manage their marketing programs. Finally, we look at the important step of measuring and managing return on marketing investment.

Let's look first at Nike. During the past several decades, Nike has changed the rules of sports marketing strategy. In the process, it has built the Nike swoosh into one of the world's best-known brand symbols. But the Nike we know today is far different from the brash young start-up company of 40 years ago. As Nike has grown and matured, its marketing strategy has matured as well. To stay on top in the intensely competitive sports apparel business, Nike will have to keep finding fresh ways to bring value to its customers.

The Nike "swoosh" is everywhere! Through innovative marketing, Nike has built the swoosh into one of the best-known brand symbols on earth. But 40-some years ago, when young accountant Phil Knight and college track coach Bill Bowerman cofounded the company, Nike was just a brash, young upstart in the athletic footwear industry.

In those early days, Knight and Bowerman ran Nike by gut feel. In 1964, they each contributed $500 to start Blue Ribbon Sports. In 1970, Bowerman developed up a new sneaker tread by stuffing a piece of rubber into his wife's waffle iron. The Waffle Trainer quickly became the best-selling training shoe in the U.S. In 1972, the company became Nike, named after the Greek goddess of victory. The swoosh was designed by a graduate student for $35. By 1979, Nike owned 50 percent of the U.S. running shoe market. It all seemed easy then. Running was in, sneakers were hot, and Nike had the right stuff.

During the 1980s, Nike revolutionized sports marketing. To build its brand image and market share, Nike spent lavishly on big-name endorsements, splashy promotional events, and in-your-face "Just Do It" ads. Beyond promotional hype, Nike's initial success resulted from the technical superiority of its running and basketball shoes. To this day, Nike leads the industry in R & D spending.

But Nike customers didn't just wear their Nikes, they *experienced* them. As stated on its Web page (www.nike.com),  "Nike has always known the truth—it's not so much the shoes but where they take you." Beyond shoes, apparel, and equipment, Nike marketed a way of life, a sports culture, a just-do-it attitude. Phil Knight once said, "Basically, our culture and our style is to be a rebel." The company was built on a genuine passion for sports, a disregard for convention, and a belief in hard work and serious sports performance.

Throughout the 1980s and 1990s, Nike sprinted ahead of its competition. Between 1988 and 1997, Nike's revenues grew at an annual rate of 21 percent; while annual return to investors averaged 47 percent. Nike leveraged its brand strength, moving aggressively into new product categories such as sunglasses, soccer balls, batting gloves, and hockey sticks. Nike invaded a dozen new sports, including baseball, golf, ice and street hockey, skateboarding, wall climbing, and hiking. It penetrated new markets worldwide. Nike Asia Pacific has been in operation since 1977, when it began selling footwear in the region. In 1997, two major customer service centers opened outside Seoul and Tokyo, and China became both a source country and a vital market for Nike. The Asia Pacific is Nike's third largest region in terms of revenue, and number one in terms of manufacturing. Almost half of Nike's sales in the region are from footwear, with the remainder from apparel and equipment.

However, Nike's sales slipped in the late 1990s. A "brown shoe" craze for hiking and outdoor shoe styles ate into the athletic sneaker business. Moreover, Nike's creative juices seemed to run dry. Mundane new sneaker designs collected dust on retailer shelves as buyers seeking a new look switched to competing brands. To aggravate matters, Nike was fighting off allegations that it was overcommercializing sports and exploiting child labor in Asian sweatshops.

But Nike's biggest obstacle may have been its own incredible success. The brand appeared to suffer from big-brand backlash, and the swoosh may have become too common to be cool. As sales moved past the $10 billion mark, Nike moved from maverick to mainstream. Instead of antiestablishment, Nike *was* the establishment. Once the brat of sports marketing, Nike now had to grow up and act its age.

And grow up it has. In recent years, Nike's marketing strategy has matured. The company still spends hundreds of millions of dollars each year on very creative advertising, innovative brand-building promotions, and big-name endorsers. For example, Nike signed basketball phenom LeBron James to a $90 million endorsement contract a few years back.

But Nike has toned down its antiestablishment attitude—its marketing is a bit less edgy. The company is now devoting much more attention to marketing details. "Gone are the days when Nike execs, working on little more than hunches, would do just about anything and spend just about any amount in the quest for publicity and market share," says one Nike observer. "More and more, Nike is searching for the right balance between its creative and its business sides, relying on a newfound financial and managerial discipline to drive growth."

The new Nike has returned to basics—focusing on innovation, methodically assessing new market opportunities, developing new product lines, and reworking its information and distribution systems. The old Nike also stumbled with its acquisitions, trying to force its own marketing culture onto them. The new Nike has learned to give its acquired brands some independence. As a result, acquisitions such as Cole Haan dress shoes, Converse retro-style sneakers, and Bauer in-line and hockey skates now account for over 13 percent of Nike's revenues and a quarter of its sales growth. The old Nike had difficulty going global. At the new Nike, over half of sales now come from rapidly growing international markets. However, there are still the occasional international marketing missteps. In 2004, a Chinese print ad depicting LeBron James beating cartoon martial arts masters offended authorities, who called the ad blasphemous and an insult to national dignity. While it was initially withdrawn, the ad was later reinstated in 2007.

Overall, the new, more-mature Nike is once again achieving stunning results. In the past five years, Nike's sales have grown more than 50 percent to almost $15 billion; profits have more than doubled. To stay on top, however, Nike must keep its marketing strategy fresh, finding new ways to deliver the kind of innovation and value that built the brand so powerfully in the past. Says Knight, "Now that we've [grown so large], there's a fine line between being a rebel and being a bully. [To our customers,] we have to be beautiful as well as big."[1]

Marketing strategies and programs are guided by broader, companywide strategic plans. Thus, to understand the role of marketing, we must first understand the organization's overall strategic planning process. Like Nike, all companies must look ahead and develop long-term strategies to meet the changing conditions in their industries and to ensure long-term survival.

Companywide Strategic Planning: Defining Marketing's Role

Each company must find the game plan for long-run survival and growth that makes the most sense given its specific situation, opportunities, objectives, and resources. This is the focus of **strategic planning**—the process of developing and maintaining a strategic fit between the organization's goals and capabilities and its changing marketing opportunities.

At the corporate level, the company starts the strategic planning process by defining its overall purpose and mission (see **Figure 2.1**). This mission is then turned into detailed supporting objectives that guide the whole company. Next, headquarters decides what portfolio of businesses and products is best for the company and how much support to give each one. In turn, each business and product develops detailed marketing and

Strategic planning
The process of developing and maintaining a strategic fit between the organization's goals and capabilities and its changing marketing opportunities.

other departmental plans that support the companywide plan. Thus, marketing planning occurs at the business-unit, product, and market levels. It supports company strategic planning with more detailed plans for specific marketing opportunities.[2]

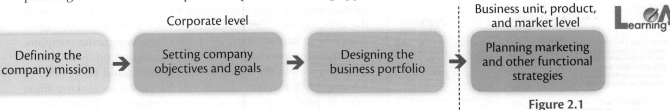

Corporate level

Business unit, product, and market level

Learningid

| Defining the company mission | → | Setting company objectives and goals | → | Designing the business portfolio | → | Planning marketing and other functional strategies |

Figure 2.1
Steps in strategic planning

Defining a Market-Oriented Mission

A **mission statement** is a statement of the organization's purpose—what it wants to accomplish in the larger environment. A clear mission statement acts as an "invisible hand" that guides people in the organization and answers questions such as: What is our business? Who is the customer? What do consumers value? What *should* our business be?

Some companies define their missions myopically in product or technology terms ("We make and sell furniture" or "We are a chemical-processing firm"). But mission statements should be *market oriented* and defined in terms of customer needs. Products and technologies eventually become outdated, but basic market needs may last forever.

A market-oriented mission statement defines the business in terms of satisfying basic customer needs. For example, Nike isn't just a shoe and apparel manufacturer—it wants "to bring inspiration and innovation to every athlete* in the world. (*If you have a body, you are an athlete.)" Likewise, eBay's mission isn't simply to hold online auctions and trading. Its mission is "to provide a global trading platform where practically anyone can trade practically anything—you can get *it* on eBay." It wants to be a unique Web community in which people can shop around, have fun, and get to know each other, for example, by chatting at the eBay Cafe. **Table 2.1** provides several other examples of product-oriented versus market-oriented business definitions,[3] while **Figure 2.2** summarizes characteristics of a good mission statement.

Mission statement
A statement of the organization's purpose—what it wants to accomplish in the larger environment.

Mission statements – eBay's mission is "to provide a global trading platform where practically anyone can trade practically anything—you can get *it* on eBay."

Table 2.1 Market-Oriented Business Definitions

Company	Product-Oriented Definition	Market-Oriented Definition
Amazon.com	We sell books, videos, CDs, toys, consumer electronics, hardware, housewares, and other products.	We make the Internet buying experience fast, easy, and enjoyable—we're the place where you can find and discover anything you want to buy online.
Disney	We run theme parks.	We create fantasies—a place where America still works the way it's supposed to.
eBay	We hold online auctions.	We provide a global marketplace where practically anyone can trade practically anything—a unique Web community in which people can shop around, have fun, and get to know each other.
Shiseido	We make cosmetics.	We sell lifestyle and self-expression; success and status; memories, hopes, and dreams.
Ritz-Carlton Hotels	We rent rooms.	We create the Ritz-Carlton experience—one that enlivens the senses, instills well-being, and fulfills even the unexpressed wishes and needs of our guests.
Wal-Mart	We run discount stores.	We deliver low prices every day and give ordinary folks the chance to buy the same things as rich people.

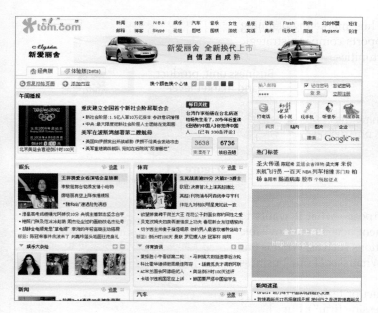

Missions should fit the *market environment*. Thus, with the growing digital influence, Sony has set forth to integrate computers with its entertainment products and yet provide a human touch in these products. Hong Kong's tom.com, with the dot-com bust, redefined its mission from a strictly online company to become more of an Old Economy media company. The organization should also base its mission on its *distinctive competencies*. Finally, mission statements should be *motivating*. A company's mission should not be stated as making more sales or profits—profits are only a reward for undertaking a useful activity. A company's employees need to feel that their work is significant and that it contributes to people's lives. Thus, Samsung's mission statement incorporates the notion of improving society: "We will devote our people and technology to create superior products and services, thereby contributing to a better global society."

Hong Kong's tom.com redefined its mission from a strictly online company to become more of an old Economy media company. (*www.tom.com*)

Mission statements should •·····

Figure 2.2
Characteristics of a good mission statement

Setting Company Objectives and Goals

The company needs to turn its mission into detailed supporting objectives for each level of management. Each manager should have objectives and be responsible for reaching them. For example, Monsanto operates in the agricultural biotechnology business. It defines its mission as "improving the future of farming … improving the future of food … abundantly and safely." It seeks to help feed the world's exploding population while at the same time sustaining the environment. Monsanto ads ask us to "Imagine innovative agriculture that creates incredible things today."

This mission leads to a hierarchy of objectives, including business objectives and marketing objectives. Monsanto's overall objective is to build profitable customer relationships by developing better agricultural products and getting them to market faster at lower costs. It does this by researching products that safely help crops produce more nutrition and higher yields without chemical spraying. But research is expensive and requires improved profits to plow back into research programs. So improving profits becomes another major Monsanto objective. Profits can be improved by increasing sales or reducing costs. Sales can be increased by improving the company's share of the U.S. market, by entering new foreign markets, or both. These goals then become the company's current marketing objectives.[4]

Marketing strategies and programs must be developed to support these marketing objectives. To increase its U.S. market share, Monsanto might increase its products' availability and promotion. To enter new foreign markets, the company may cut prices and target large farms abroad. These are its broad marketing strategies. Each broad marketing strategy must then be defined in greater detail. For example, increasing the product's promotion may require more salespeople and more advertising; if so, both requirements need to be spelled out. In this way, the firm's mission is translated into a set of objectives for the current period.

Designing the Business Portfolio

Guided by the company's mission statement and objectives, management now must plan its **business portfolio**—the collection of businesses and products that make up the company. The best business portfolio is the one that best fits the company's strengths and weaknesses to opportunities in the environment. Business portfolio planning involves two steps:

- Analyzing its current business portfolio and deciding which businesses should receive more, less, or no investment.
- Shaping the future portfolio by developing strategies for growth and downsizing.

Business portfolio
The collection of businesses and products that make up the company.

Analyzing the Current Business Portfolio

The major activity in strategic planning is business portfolio analysis, whereby management evaluates the products and businesses making up the company. The company will want to put strong resources into its more profitable businesses and phase down or drop its weaker ones.

Management's first step is to identify the key businesses making up the company. These can be called the strategic business units. A *strategic business unit* (SBU) is a unit of the company that has a separate mission and objectives and that can be planned independently from other company businesses. An SBU can be a company division, a product line within a division, or sometimes a single product or brand.

The next step in business portfolio analysis calls for management to assess the attractiveness of its various SBUs and decide how much support each deserves. It is usually a good idea to focus on adding products and businesses that fit closely with the firm's core philosophy and competencies.

The purpose of strategic planning is to find ways in which the company can best use its strengths to take advantage of attractive opportunities in the environment. Most standard portfolio-analysis methods evaluate SBUs on two important dimensions (1) the attractiveness of the SBU's market or industry and (2) the strength of the SBU's position in that market or industry. The best-known portfolio-planning method was developed by the Boston Consulting Group, a leading management consulting firm.[5]

Monsanto defines its mission as "improving the future of farming ... improving the future of food ... abundantly and safely." Its ads ask us to "Imagine innovative agriculture that creates incredible things today." This mission leads to specific business and marketing objectives.

The Boston Consulting Group approach

Using the Boston Consulting Group (BCG) approach, a company classifies all its SBUs according to the **growth-share matrix** shown in **Figure 2.3**. On the vertical axis, *market growth rate* provides a measure of market attractiveness. On the horizontal axis, *relative market share* serves as a measure of company strength in the market. The growth-share matrix defines four types of SBUs:

Growth-share matrix
A portfolio-planning method that evaluates a company's strategic business units in terms of their market growth rate and relative market share. SBUs are classified as stars, cash cows, question marks, or dogs.

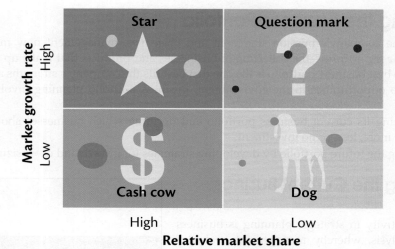

Figure 2.3
The BCG growth-share matrix

Stars

Stars are high-growth, high-share businesses or products. They often need heavy investment to finance their rapid growth. Eventually their growth will slow down, and they will turn into cash cows.

Cash cows

Cash cows are low-growth, high-share businesses or products. These established and successful SBUs need less investment to hold their market share. Thus, they produce a lot of cash that the company uses to pay its bills and to support other SBUs that need investment.

Question marks

Question marks are low-share business units in high-growth markets. They require a lot of cash to hold their share, let alone increase it. Management needs to think hard about which question marks it should try to build into stars and which should be phased out.

Dogs

Dogs are low-growth, low-share businesses and products. They may generate enough cash to maintain themselves but do not promise to be large sources of cash.

The ten circles in the growth-share matrix represent a company's ten current SBUs. The company has two stars, two cash cows, three question marks, and three dogs. The areas of the circles are proportional to the SBU's dollar sales. This company is in fair shape, although not in good shape. It wants to invest in the more promising question marks to make them stars and to maintain the stars so that they will become cash cows as their markets mature. Fortunately, it has two good-sized cash cows. Income from these cash cows will help finance the company's question marks, stars, and dogs. The company should take some decisive action concerning its dogs and its question marks. The picture would be worse if the company had no stars, if it had too many dogs, or if it had only one weak cash cow.

Once it has classified its SBUs, the company must determine what role each will play in the future. One of four strategies can be pursued for each SBU. The company can invest more in the business unit to *build* its share. Or it can invest just enough to *hold* the SBU's share at the current level. It can *harvest* the SBU, milking its short-term cash flow regardless of the long-term effect. Finally, the company can *divest* the SBU by selling it or phasing it out and using the resources elsewhere.

As time passes, SBUs change their positions in the growth-share matrix. Each SBU has a life cycle. Many SBUs start out as question marks and move into the star category if they succeed. They later become cash cows as market growth falls, then finally die off or turn into dogs toward the end of their life cycle. The company needs to add new products and units continuously so that some of them will become stars and, eventually, cash cows that will help finance other SBUs.

Problems with matrix approaches

The BCG and other formal methods revolutionized strategic planning. However, such centralized approaches have limitations. They can be difficult, time consuming, and costly to implement. Management may find it difficult to define SBUs and measure market share and growth. In addition, these approaches focus on classifying *current* businesses but provide little advice for *future* planning.

Formal planning approaches can also place too much emphasis on market-share growth or growth through entry into attractive new markets. Using these approaches, many companies plunged into unrelated and new high-growth businesses that they did not know how to manage—with very bad results. At the same time, these companies were often too quick to abandon, sell, or milk to death their healthy mature businesses. As a result, many companies that diversified too broadly in the past have narrowed their focus and gotten back to the basics of serving one or a few industries that they know best.

Because of such problems, many companies have dropped formal matrix methods in favor of more customized approaches that are better suited to their specific situations. Moreover, unlike former strategic-planning efforts, which rested mostly in the hands of senior managers at company headquarters, today's strategic planning has been decentralized. Increasingly, companies are placing responsibility for strategic planning in the hands of cross-functional teams of divisional managers who are close to their markets.

For example, consider The Walt Disney Company. Most people think of Disney as theme parks and wholesome family entertainment. But in the mid-1980s, Disney set up a powerful, centralized strategic planning group to guide the company's direction and growth. Over the next two decades, the strategic planning group turned The Walt Disney Company into a huge but diverse collection of media and entertainment businesses. The newly transformed company proved hard to manage and performed unevenly. Recently, Disney's chief executive disbanded the centralized strategic planning unit, decentralizing its functions to divisional managers (see **Real Marketing**).

Developing Strategies for Growth and Downsizing

Beyond evaluating current businesses, designing the business portfolio involves finding businesses and products the company should consider in the future. Companies need profitable growth if they are to compete more effectively, satisfy their stakeholders, and attract top talent.

Marketing has the main responsibility for achieving profitable growth for the company. Marketing must identify, evaluate, and select market opportunities and lay down strategies for capturing them. One useful device for identifying growth opportunities is the **product/market expansion grid**, shown in **Figure 2.3**.[6] We apply it here to Starbucks:

Product/market expansion grid
A portfolio-planning tool for identifying company growth opportunities through market penetration, market development, product development, or diversification.

	Existing products	New products
Existing markets	Market penetration	Product development
New markets	Market development	Diversification

Figure 2.4
The product/market expansion grid

REAL MARKETING

The Walt Disney Company: Strategic Planning for a Happy-Ever-After Ending

When you think of The Walt Disney Company, you probably think first of theme parks and animated films. Since the release of its first Mickey Mouse cartoon over 75 years ago, Disney has grown to become the undisputed master of family entertainment. From pioneering films such as *Snow White and the Seven Dwarfs*, *Fantasia*, and *Pinocchio* to more recent movies such as *Monsters, Inc.*, *Finding Nemo*, *The Incredibles*, *Valiant*, and *Cars*, Disney has brought pure magic to audiences worldwide.

Perhaps nowhere is the Disney magic more apparent than at its theme parks. Each year, some 43 million people flock to The Walt Disney World Resort alone, making it the world's top tourist attraction. Why? Part of the answer lies in its many attractions. The resort's four major theme parks—Magic Kingdom, Epcot, Disney-MGM Studios, and Disney's Animal Kingdom—brim with such attractions as the Twilight Zone Tower of Terror, Soarin' Over California, the Kilimanjaro Safaris, and Big Thunder Mountain Railroad.

But the real "Disney Magic" lies in the company's obsessive dedication to its mission to "make people happy" and to "make a dream come true." Disney goes to extremes to fulfill guests' expectations. Its theme parks are so highly regarded for outstanding customer service that many leading corporations send managers to Disney University to learn how Disney does it. However, theme parks and resorts account for only about 25 percent of today's Disney empire; movies and entertainment make up another 28 percent. The rest comes from a diverse portfolio of businesses acquired by Disney over the past two decades.

The Walt Disney Company has become a real study in strategic planning. In 1985, Disney's then CEO, Michael Eisner, set up a high-powered, centralized strategic planning unit, to source and nurture new growth opportunities and set the company's strategic path. Throughout the late 1980s and the 1990s, the group engineered a series of major acquisitions, including that of Capital Cities/ABC, which almost doubled Disney's size.

By the early 2000s, the group had transformed The Walt Disney Company into a $30 billion international media and entertainment giant. The company now owns all or part of hundreds of companies and divisions, organized into four major business groups:

Studio Entertainment: Four television production companies, eight movie and theatrical production companies, and a distribution company (including Walt Disney Pictures, Touchstone Pictures, Miramax Films, and Buena Vista Theatrical Productions); and four music labels (Walt Disney Records, Hollywood Records, Buena Vista Records, and Lyric Street Records).

Media Networks: A major broadcast television network (ABC, plus ten company-owned television stations); a dozen cable television networks (including the Disney Channel, Toon Dis-ney, ESPN, the History Channel, E! Entertainment, and ABC Family); three radio networks (ESPN Radio, ABC Radio, and Disney Radio, plus over 70 radio stations); and the Walt Disney Internet Group (19 Internet sites including Disney Online, Disney's Daily Blast, ABC.com, ESPN.com, Family.com, NASCAR.com, and NBA.com).

Consumer Products: Three Disney Merchandise Licensing divisions; four Disney Publishing divisions; the Baby Einstein Company (developmental media for infants); four Disney Retail groups (including Disney Stores Worldwide and Disney Direct Marketing); and Buena Vista Games (Disney content for the interactive gaming community).

Parks and Resorts: Eleven parks and 35 resort hotels on three continents (including Disneyland Resort Paris, Tokyo Disney Resort, and Hong Kong Disneyland); Disney Cruise Line; Disney Vacation Club; and ESPN Zone.

However, managing this diverse portfolio of businesses has become a major challenge for Disney. During the last half of the 1980s, the smaller, more focused Disney had annual average

For more than 75 years, The Walt Disney Company has been the undisputed master of family entertainment. But it will take masterful strategic planning—along with some big doses of the famed "Disney Magic"—to give the modern Disney a happy-ever-after ending.

revenue and net income growth of 23 percent and 50 percent respectively. In contrast, at least until recently, the larger, more complex Disney struggled for consistent profitability and growth.

Disney's centralized strategic planning group was frequently blamed for this uneven performance. Many critics assert that the company has grown too large, too diverse, and too distant from the core strengths that made it so successful. The strategic planning group also reviewed and often rejected the strategies proposed by Disney's business unit managers. The group even came to be called by some "the business prevention department."

In 2004, disagreements over Disney's long-term strategic direction resulted in Eisner's ouster. Tellingly, soon after replacing Eisner, new CEO Robert Iger disbanded the centralized strategic planning group, returning most of its functions to Disney's division managers. Iger believed that the individual business units, which are closer to their markets, can better plan growth strategies than the centralized unit. Iger is also expected to take a fresh look at Disney's disparate portfolio of businesses.

Thus, for Disney, bigger isn't necessarily better. More decentralized strategic planning seems to make better sense. Creating the right blend of businesses for the new Magic Kingdom won't be easy. It will take masterful strategic planning—along with some of the famed "Disney magic"—to give the modern Disney story a happy-ever-after ending.

Sources:

Merissa Marr, "Disney Cuts Strategic-Planning Unit," *Wall Street Journal*, March 28, 2005, p. A3; Jacqueline Doherty, "Better Days for Disney," *Barron's*, March 21, 2005, p. 14; Laura M. Holson, "Disney Intends to Overhaul Planning Unit," *New York Times*, March 26, 2005, p. C2; Robert Niles, "Disney Slams Universal in 2005 Theme Park Attendance," December 27, 2005, accessed at www.themeparkinsider.com/flume/200512/2/; Juliana Koranteng, "Parks Persist in the Face of Calamity," *Amusement Business*, January 2006, pp. 6-7; "The Walt Disney Company," *Hoover Company* Records, June 15, 2006, p. 11603; and information from www.disney.go.com, November 2006.

Strategies for growth –
To maintain its phenomenal growth in an increasingly overcaffeinated marketplace, Starbucks has brewed up an ambitious multipronged growth strategy

More than 20 years ago, Howard Schultz hit on the idea of bringing a European-style coffeehouse to America. People needed to slow down, he believed—to "smell the coffee" and enjoy life a little more. The result was Starbucks. This coffeehouse doesn't sell just coffee, it sells *The Starbucks Experience*. "There's the Starbucks ambience," notes an analyst, "The music. The comfy velvety chairs. The smells. The hissing steam." Says Starbucks Chairman Schultz, "We aren't in the coffee business, serving people. We are in the people business, serving coffee." People around the globe now flock to Starbucks, making it a powerhouse premium brand. Some 35 million customers now visit the company's more than 11,000 stores worldwide each week. Starbucks gives customers what it calls a "third place"—away from home and away from work.

Growth is the engine that keeps Starbucks perking—the company targets (and regularly achieves) jaw-dropping revenue growth exceeding 20 percent each year. Starbucks' success, however, has drawn a full litter of copycats, ranging from direct competitors such as Coffee Bean & Tea Leaf to fast-food merchants (such as McDonald's McCafé) and even discounters (Wal-Mart's Kicks Coffee). To maintain its phenomenal growth in an increasingly overcaffeinated marketplace, Starbucks must brew up an ambitious, multipronged growth strategy.

Market penetration
A strategy for company growth by increasing sales of current products to current market segments without changing the product.

Market development
A strategy for company growth by identifying and developing new market segments for current company products.

Product development
A strategy for company growth by offering modified or new products to current market segments.

Diversification
A strategy for company growth through starting up or acquiring businesses outside the company's current products and markets.

First, Starbucks management might consider whether the company can achieve deeper **market penetration**—making more sales to current customers without changing its products. It might add new stores in current market areas to make it easier for more customers to visit. In fact, Starbucks is adding an average of 34 stores a week, 52 weeks a year—its ultimate goal is 30,000 stores worldwide. Improvements in advertising, prices, service, menu selection, or store design might encourage customers to stop by more often, stay longer, or to buy more during each visit. For example, in the U.S., Starbucks has added drive-through windows to many of its stores. A Starbucks Card lets customers prepay for coffee and snacks or give the gift of Starbucks to family and friends. And to get customers to hang around longer, Starbucks offers wireless Internet access in most of its stores.

Second, Starbucks management might consider possibilities for **market development**—identifying and developing new markets for its current products. For instance, managers could review new *demographic markets*. Perhaps new groups—such as seniors or ethnic groups—could be encouraged to visit Starbucks coffee shops for the first time or to buy more from them. Managers also could review new *geographical markets*. Starbucks is expanding rapidly in new global markets. In 1996, Starbucks had only 11 coffeehouses outside North America. It now has more than 3,000, with plenty of room to grow. "We're just scratching the surface in China," says Starbucks's CEO. "We have 150 stores and the potential for more than 2,000 there."

Third, management could consider **product development**—offering modified or new products to current markets. For example, Starbucks has introduced new reduced-calorie options, such as Frappuccino Light Blended Beverages. It also added Chantico, an indulgent chocolate beverage, to its menu to draw in more non-coffee drinkers. To capture consumers who brew their coffee at home, Starbucks has also pushed into America's supermarket aisles. It has a co-branding deal with Kraft, under which Starbucks roasts and packages its coffee and Kraft markets and distributes it. And the company is forging ahead into new consumer categories. For example, it has brought out a line of Starbucks coffee liqueurs.

Fourth, Starbucks might consider **diversification**—starting up or buying businesses outside of its current products and markets. For example, in 1999, Starbucks purchased Hear Music, which was so successful that it spurred the creation of the new Starbucks entertainment division. Beginning with just selling and playing compilation CDs, Hear Music now has its own XM Satellite Radio station. It is also installing kiosks (called Media Bars) in select Starbucks stores that let customers download music and burn their own CDs while sipping their lattes. As a next step, Starbucks is investing in Hear Music retail outlets, which will be music stores first and coffee shops second.

In a more extreme diversification, Starbucks has partnered with Lion's Gate to coproduce movies and then market them in Starbucks coffee houses. Starbucks supported the partnership's first film, *Akeelah and the Bee*, by sprinkling flashcards around the stores, stamping the movie's logo on its coffee cups, and placing spelling-bee caliber words on the store chalkboards. This new venture has left some analysts asking whether Starbucks is diversifying too broadly, at the risk of losing its market focus. They are asking, "What do movies have to do with Starbucks coffee and the Starbucks experience?"[7]

Companies must not only develop strategies for growing their business portfolios but also strategies for **downsizing** them. The market environment might change, making some of the company's products or markets less profitable. The firm may have grown too fast or entered areas where it lacks experience. This can occur when a firm enters too many foreign markets without the proper research or when a company introduces new products that do not offer superior customer value. Finally, some products or business units simply age and die. When a firm finds brands or businesses that are unprofitable or that no longer fit its overall strategy, it must carefully prune, harvest, or divest them. Weak businesses usually require a disproportionate amount of management attention. Managers should focus on promising growth opportunities, not spend energy trying to salvage fading ones.

Planning Marketing: Partnering to Build Customer Relationships

After the company's strategic plan is established, more detailed planning for each business unit takes place. The major functional departments in each unit—marketing, finance, accounting, purchasing, operations, information systems, human resources, and others—must work together to accomplish strategic objectives.

Marketing plays a key role in the company's strategic planning in several ways. First, marketing provides a guiding *philosophy*—the marketing concept—that suggests that company strategy should revolve around building profitable relationships with important consumer groups. Second, marketing provides *inputs* to strategic planners by helping to identify attractive market opportunities and by assessing the firm's potential to take advantage of them. Finally, within individual business units, marketing designs *strategies* for reaching the unit's objectives. Once the unit's objectives are set, marketing's task is to help carry them out profitably.

Customer value and satisfaction are important ingredients in the marketer's formula for success. However, as we noted in Chapter 1, marketers alone cannot produce superior value for customers. Although it plays a leading role, marketing can be only a partner in attracting, keeping, and growing customers. In addition to *customer relationship management*, marketers must also practice *partner relationship management*. They must work closely with partners in other company departments to form an effective *value chain* that serves the customer. Moreover, they must partner effectively with other companies in the marketing system to form a competitively superior *value-delivery network*. We now take a closer look at the concepts of a company value chain and value-delivery network.

Partnering with Other Company Departments

Each company department can be thought of as a link in the company's **value chain**.[8] That is, each department carries out value-creating activities to design, produce, market, deliver, and support the firm's products. The firm's success depends not only on how well each department performs its work but also on how well the activities of various departments are coordinated.

For example, Wal-Mart's goal is to create customer value and satisfaction by providing shoppers with the products they want at the lowest possible prices. Marketers at Wal-Mart play an important role. They learn what customers need and stock the stores' shelves with the desired products at unbeatable low prices. They prepare advertising

Downsizing
Reducing the business portfolio by eliminating products of business units that are not profitable or that no longer fit the company's overall strategy.

Product development –
Starbucks has introduced to current markets modified or new products like the Frappucino Light Blended Beverage, a new reduced calorie option.

Value chain
The series of departments that carry out value-creating activities to design, produce, market, deliver, and support a firm's products.

The value chain – Wal-Mart's ability to offer the right products at low prices depends on the contributions of people in all of the company's departments— marketing, purchasing, information systems, and operations.

and merchandising programs and assist shoppers with customer service. Through these and other activities, Wal-Mart's marketers help deliver value to customers.

However, the marketing department needs help from the company's other departments. Wal-Mart's ability to offer the right products at low prices depends on the purchasing department's skill in developing the needed suppliers and buying from them at low cost. Wal-Mart's information technology department must provide fast and accurate information about which products are selling in each store. And its operations people must provide effective, low-cost merchandise handling.

A company's value chain is only as strong as its weakest link. Success depends on how well each department performs its work of adding customer value and on how well the activities of various departments are coordinated. At Wal-Mart, if purchasing can't wring the lowest prices from suppliers, or if operations can't distribute merchandise at the lowest costs, then marketing can't deliver on its promise of lowest prices. Marketing managers need to work closely with managers of other functions to develop a system of functional plans under which the different departments can work together to accomplish the company's overall strategic objectives.

Partnering with Others in the Marketing System

In its quest to create customer value, the firm needs to look beyond its own value chain and into the value chains of its suppliers, distributors, and, ultimately, customers. Consider McDonald's. Its nearly 32,000 restaurants worldwide serve more than 50 million customers daily, capturing more than a 40 percent share of the burger market.[9] People do not swarm to McDonald's only because they love the chain's hamburgers. In fact, consumers typically rank McDonald's behind Burger King and Wendy's in taste. Consumers flock to the McDonald's system, not just to its food products. Throughout the world, McDonald's finely-tuned system delivers a high standard of what the company calls QSCV—quality, service, cleanliness, and value. McDonald's is effective only to the extent that it successfully partners with its franchisees, suppliers, and others to jointly deliver exceptionally high customer value.

More companies today are partnering with the other members of the supply chain to improve the performance of the customer **value-delivery network**. For example, Toyota knows the importance of building close relationships with its suppliers. In fact, it even includes the phrase "achieve supplier satisfaction" in its mission statement.

Consumers go to McDonald's not because of its food but because it offers QSCV—quality, service, cleanliness, and value.

Value-delivery network
The network made up of the company, suppliers, distributors, and ultimately customers who "partner" with each other to improve the performance of the entire system.

Achieving satisfying supplier relationships has been a cornerstone of Toyota's stunning success. U.S. competitors often alienate their suppliers through self-serving, heavy-handed dealings. "The [U.S. automakers] set annual cost-reduction targets [for the parts they buy]," says one supplier. "To realize those targets, they'll do anything." Says another, "[Ford] seems to send its people to "hate school" so that they learn how to hate suppliers." By contrast, in survey after survey, auto suppliers rate Toyota as their most preferred customer. Rather than bullying suppliers, Toyota partners with them and helps them to meet its very high expectations. It learns about their businesses, conducts joint improvement activities, helps train their employees, gives daily performance feedback, and actively seeks out supplier concerns. Says one delighted Toyota supplier, "Toyota helped us dramatically improve our production system. We started by making one component, and as we improved, [Toyota] rewarded us with orders for more components. Toyota is our best customer."

Such high supplier satisfaction means that Toyota can rely on suppliers to help it improve its own quality, reduce costs, and develop new products quickly. For example, when Toyota launched a program to reduce prices by 30 percent on 170 parts that it would buy for its next generation of cars, suppliers didn't complain. Instead, they pitched in, trusting that Toyota would help them achieve the targeted reductions, in turn making them more competitive and profitable in the future. In all, creating satisfied suppliers helps Toyota to produce lower-cost, higher-quality cars, which in turn results in more satisfied customers.[10]

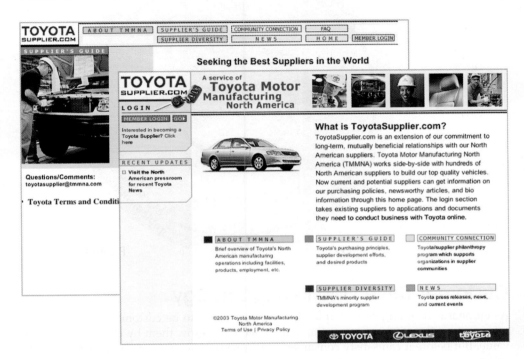

Toyota partners with its suppliers and helps them meet its very high expectations. Creating satisfied suppliers helps Toyota produce lower-cost, higher-quality cars, which in turn results in more satisfied customers.

Increasingly, competition no longer takes place between individual competitors. Rather, it takes place between the entire value-delivery networks created by these competitors. Thus, Toyota's performance against Ford depends on the quality of Toyota's overall value-delivery network versus Ford's. Even if Toyota makes the best cars, it might lose in the marketplace if Ford's dealer network provides more customer-satisfying sales and service.

Marketing Strategy and the Marketing Mix

The strategic plan defines the company's overall mission and objectives. Marketing's role and activities are shown in **Figure 2.5**, which summarizes the major activities involved in managing a customer-driven marketing strategy and the marketing mix.

Consumers stand in the center. The goal is to create value for customers and build strong and profitable customer relationships. Next comes **marketing strategy**—the marketing logic by which the company hopes to create this customer value and achieve these profitable relationships. The company decides which customers it will serve (segmentation and targeting) and how it will serve them (differentiation and positioning). It identifies the total market, then divides it into smaller segments, selects the most promising segments, and focuses on serving and satisfying customers in these segments.

Guided by marketing strategy, the company designs an integrated marketing mix made up of factors under its control—product, price, place, and promotion (the four Ps). To find the best marketing strategy and mix, the company engages in marketing analysis,

Marketing strategy
The marketing logic by which the business unit hopes to achieve its marketing objectives.

planning, implementation, and control. Through these activities, the company watches and adapts to the actors and forces in the marketing environment. We will now look briefly at each activity.

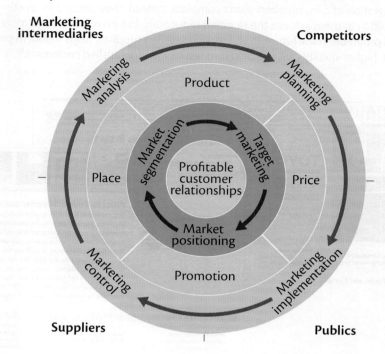

Figure 2.5
Managing marketing strategy and the marketing mix

Customer-Driven Marketing Strategy

As emphasized throughout Chapter 1, companies need to be customer centered. They must win customers from competitors, then keep and grow them by delivering greater value. But before it can satisfy consumers, a company must first understand their needs and wants. Thus, sound marketing requires a careful customer analysis.

Companies cannot profitably serve all consumers in a given market—at least not all consumers in the same way. There are too many different kinds of consumers with too many different kinds of needs. Thus, each company must divide up the total market, choose the best segments, and design strategies for profitably serving chosen segments. This process involves *market segmentation, target marketing, differentiation*, and *market positioning*.

Market Segmentation

The market consists of many types of customers, products, and needs. The marketer has to determine which segments offer the best opportunities. Consumers can be grouped and served in various ways based on geographic, demographic, psychographic, and behavioral factors. The process of dividing a market into distinct groups of buyers who have different needs, characteristics, or behaviors, who might require separate products or marketing programs is called **market segmentation**.

Every market has segments, but not all ways of segmenting a market are equally useful. For example, Panadol would gain little by distinguishing between low-income and high-income pain reliever users if both respond the same way to marketing efforts. A **market segment** consists of consumers who respond in a similar way to a given set of marketing efforts. In the car market, for example, consumers who want the biggest, most comfortable car regardless of price make up one market segment. Consumers who care mainly about price and operating economy make up another segment. It would be difficult to make one car model that was the first choice of consumers in both segments.

Market segmentation is about capturing buyers who have different needs, characteristics, and behaviors. Not every buyer will pick the same product or brand.

Market Targeting

After a company has defined the market segments, it can enter one or many of these segments. **Market targeting** involves evaluating each market segment's attractiveness and selecting one or more segments to enter. A company should target segments in which it can profitably generate the greatest customer value and sustain it over time.

A company with limited resources might decide to serve only one or a few special segments or "market niches." Such "nichers" specialize in serving customer segments that major competitors overlook or ignore. For example, Ferrari sells only 1,500 of its very high-performance cars in the U.S. each year, but at very high prices—from an eye-opening $287,020 for its Ferrari Superamerica model to an absolutely astonishing $2 million for its FXX super sports car, which can be driven only on race tracks.

Alternatively, a company might choose to serve several related segments—perhaps those with different kinds of customers but with the same basic wants. Yakult, the Japanese health drink, targets kids, teens, and adults with the same healthy lifestyle-themed products—regular Yakult, Yakult Light, and recently for the more sporty segment, Yakult Thorpedo. The latter was in collaboration with Olympic swimmer, Ian Thorpe. Or a large company might decide to offer a complete range of products to serve all market segments. Most companies enter a new market by serving a single segment, and if this proves successful, they add segments. Large companies eventually seek full market coverage to suit every "person, purse, and personality." The leading company normally has different products designed to meet the special needs of each segment.

Market Differentiation and Positioning

After a company has decided which market segments to enter, it must decide how it will differentiate its market offering for each targeted segment and what positions it wants to occupy in those segments. A product's *position* is the place the product occupies relative to competitors in consumers' minds. Marketers want to develop unique market positions for their products. If a product is perceived to be exactly like others on the market, consumers would have no reason to buy it.

Positioning is arranging for a product to occupy a clear, distinctive, and desirable place relative to competing products in the minds of target consumers. As one positioning expert puts it, positioning is "how you differentiate your product or company—why a shopper will pay a little more for your brand."[11] Thus, marketers plan positions that distinguish their products from competing brands and give them the greatest advantage in their target markets.

BMW makes "the ultimate driving machine"; Ford is "built for the road ahead"; and Kia promises "the power to surprise." While Nokia "connects people," Motorola has a phone for each personality. Such deceptively simple statements form the backbone of a product's marketing strategy.

In positioning its product, the company first identifies possible customer value differences that provide competitive advantages upon which to build the position. The company can offer greater customer value either by charging lower prices than competitors do or by offering more benefits to justify higher prices. But if the company promises greater value, it must then deliver that greater value. Thus, effective positioning begins with **differentiation**—differentiating the company's market offering so that it gives consumers more value. Once the company has chosen a desired position, it must deliver and communicate that position to target consumers. The company's entire marketing program should support the chosen positioning strategy.

Market targeting
The process of evaluating each market segment's attractiveness and selecting one or more segments to enter.

Yakult introduced the Thorpedo to appeal to the sports enthusiasts and fans of Olympic gold swimming medalist, Ian Thorpe.

Positioning
Arranging for a product to occupy a clear, distinctive, and desirable place relative to competing products in the minds of target consumers.

Differentiation
Actually differentiating the market offering to create superior customer value.

Motorola differentiates itself by having different mobile phone models for different personalities. This phone model was advertised in Hong Kong to appeal to the rebellious teenage girl.

Developing an Integrated Marketing Mix

After deciding on its overall marketing strategy, the company is ready to begin planning the details of the marketing mix, one of the major concepts in modern marketing. The **marketing mix** is the set of controllable, tactical marketing tools that the firm blends to produce the response it wants in the target market. It is also known as "four Ps": product, price, place, and promotion. **Figure 2.6** shows the marketing tools under each P.

Product means the goods-and-services combination the company offers to the target market. Thus, a Hyundai Sonata consists of nuts and bolts, spark plugs, pistons, headlights, and thousands of other parts. Hyundai offers several Sonata models and dozens of optional features, and a warranty.

Price is the amount of money customers have to pay to obtain the product. Hyundai calculates suggested retail prices that its dealers might charge for each Sonata. Hyundai dealers negotiate the price with each customer, offering discounts, trade-in allowances, and credit terms.

Place includes company activities that make the product available to target consumers. Hyundai partners with dealerships that sell the company's many different models. The dealers keep an inventory of Hyundai automobiles, demonstrate them to potential buyers, negotiate prices, close sales, and service the cars after the sale.

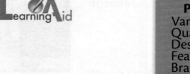

Product
Variety
Quality
Design
Features
Brand name
Packaging
Services

Price
List price
Discounts
Allowances
Payment period
Credit terms

Target customers
Intended positioning

Promotion
Advertising
Personal selling
Sales promotion
Public relations

Place
Channels
Coverage
Assortments
Locations
Inventory
Transportation
Logistics

Figure 2.6
The four P's of the marketing mix

Promotion means activities that communicate the merits of the product and persuade target customers to buy it. Suppose Hyundai Motor Company spends $2 billion each year on advertising to tell consumers about the company and its many products. Dealership salespeople assist potential buyers and persuade them that Hyundai is the best car for them.

An effective marketing program blends all of the marketing mix elements into an integrated marketing program designed to achieve the company's marketing objectives by delivering value to consumers. The marketing mix constitutes the company's tactical tool kit for establishing strong positioning in target markets.

One concern of the four Ps concept is that it takes the seller's view of the market, not the buyer's view. From the buyer's viewpoint, the four Ps might be better described as the four Cs:[12]

4Ps	4Cs
Product	Customer solution
Price	Customer cost
Place	Convenience
Promotion	Communication

Marketing mix
The set of controllable tactical marketing tools—product, price, place, and promotion—that the firm blends to produce the response it wants in the target market.

Thus, while marketers see themselves as selling products, customers see themselves as buying value or solutions to their problems. And customers are interested in more than just the price; they are interested in the total costs of obtaining, using, and disposing of a product. Customers want the product and service to be as conveniently available as possible. Finally, they want two-way communication. Marketers would do well to think through the four Cs first and then build the four Ps on that platform.

Managing the Marketing Effort

In addition to being good at the marketing in marketing management, companies also need to pay attention to the management. Managing the marketing process requires the four marketing management functions shown in **Figure 2.7**—*analysis, planning, implementation,* and *control.*

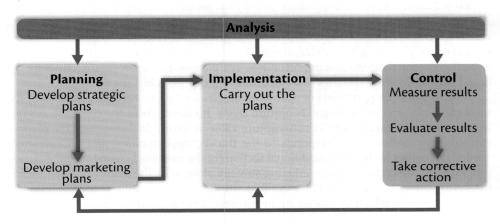

Figure 2.7
Marketing analysis, planning, implementation, and control

Marketing Analysis

Managing the marketing function begins with a complete analysis of the company's situation. The marketer should conduct a **SWOT analysis**, by which it evaluates the company's overall strengths (S), weaknesses (W), opportunities (O), and threats (T) (see **Figure 2.8**). Strengths include internal capabilities, resources, and positive situational factors that may help the company to serve its customers and achieve its objectives. Weaknesses include internal limitations and negative situational factors that may interfere with the company's performance. Opportunities are favorable factors or trends in the external environment that the company may be able to exploit to its advantage. And threats are unfavorable external factors or trends that may present challenges to performance.

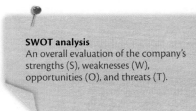

SWOT analysis
An overall evaluation of the company's strengths (S), weaknesses (W), opportunities (O), and threats (T).

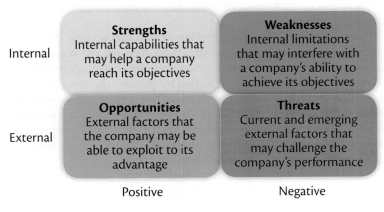

Figure 2.8
SWOT analysis

The company must analyze its markets and marketing environment to find attractive opportunities and identify environmental threats. It must analyze company strengths and weaknesses as well as current and possible marketing actions to determine which opportunities it can best pursue. The goal is to match the company's strengths to attractive opportunities in the environment, while eliminating or overcoming the weaknesses and minimizing the threats. Marketing analysis provides inputs to each of the other marketing management functions. We discuss marketing analysis more fully in Chapter 3.

Marketing Planning

Through strategic planning, the company decides what it wants to do with each business unit. Marketing planning involves deciding on marketing strategies that will help the company attain its overall strategic objectives. A detailed marketing plan is needed for each business, product, or brand. What does a marketing plan look like? Our discussion focuses on product or brand marketing plans.

Table 2.2 outlines the major sections of a typical product or brand marketing plan. (See **Appendix 1** for a sample marketing plan.) The plan begins with an executive summary, which quickly overviews major assessments, goals, and recommendations. The main section of the plan presents a detailed SWOT analysis of the current marketing situation as well as potential threats and opportunities. The plan next states major objectives for the brand and outlines the specifics of a marketing strategy for achieving them.

A *marketing strategy* consists of specific strategies for target markets, positioning, the marketing mix, and marketing expenditure levels. It outlines how the company intends to create value for target customers to capture value in return. In this section, the planner explains how each strategy responds to the threats, opportunities, and critical issues spelled out earlier in the plan. Additional sections of the marketing plan lay out an action program for implementing the marketing strategy along with the details of a supporting marketing budget. The last section outlines the controls that will be used to monitor progress, measure return on marketing investment, and take corrective action.

Marketing Implementation

A brilliant marketing strategy counts for little if the company fails to implement it properly. **Marketing implementation** is the process that turns marketing plans into marketing actions to accomplish strategic marketing objectives. Whereas marketing planning addresses the what and why of marketing activities, implementation addresses the *who, where, when,* and *how*.

Many managers think that "doing things right" (implementation) is as important as, or even more important than, "doing the right things" (strategy). Both are critical to success, and companies can gain competitive advantages through effective implementation. One firm can have essentially the same strategy as another, yet win in the marketplace through faster or better execution. Still, implementation is difficult—it is often easier to think up good marketing strategies than it is to carry them out.

Successful marketing implementation depends on how well the company blends its people, organizational structure, decision and reward systems, and company culture into a cohesive action program that supports its strategies. At all levels, the company must be staffed by people who have the needed skills, motivation, and personal characteristics. The company's formal organization structure plays an important role in implementing marketing strategy; so do its decision and reward systems. For example, if a company's compensation system rewards managers for short-run profit results, they will have little incentive to work toward long-run market-building objectives.

Finally, to be successfully implemented, the firm's marketing strategies must fit with its company culture, the system of values and beliefs shared by people in the organization. Research in Asia found that Chinese and Indian companies seemed to be positioned well to be globally competitive given their entrepreneurial corporate cultures. In contrast, the consensus culture of Japanese businesses may hinder their future growth.

Marketing implementation
The process that turns marketing strategies and plans into marketing actions in order to accomplish strategic marketing objectives.

Marketers must continually plan their analysis, implementation, and control activities.

Table 2.2   Contents of a Marketing Plan

Section	Purpose
Executive summary	Presents a brief summary of the main goals and recommendations of the plan for management review, helping top management to find the plan's major points quickly. A table of contents should follow the executive summary.
Current marketing situation	Describes the target market and company's position in it, including information about the market, product performance, competition, and distribution. This section includes: ● A *market description* that defines the market and major segments, then reviews customer needs and factors in the marketing environment that may affect customer purchasing. ● A *product review* that shows sales, prices, and gross margins of the major products in the product line. ● A review of *competition* that identifies major competitors and assesses their market positions and strategies for product quality, pricing, distribution, and promotion. ● A review of *distribution* that evaluates recent sales trends and other developments in major distribution channels.
Threats and opportunities analysis	Assesses major threats and opportunities that the product might face, helping management to anticipate important positive or negative developments that might have an impact on the firm and its strategies.
Objectives and issues	States the marketing objectives that the company would like to attain during the plan's term and discusses key issues that will affect their attainment. For example, if the goal is to achieve a 15 percent market share, this section looks at how this goal might be achieved.
Marketing strategy	Outlines the broad marketing logic by which the business unit hopes to achieve its marketing objectives and the specifics of target markets, positioning, and marketing expenditure levels. How will the company create value for customers in order to capture value from customers in return? This section also outlines specific strategies for each marketing mix element and explains how each responds to the threats, opportunities, and critical issues spelled out earlier in the plan.
Action programs	Spells out how marketing strategies will be turned into specific action programs that answer the following questions: *What* will be done? *When* will it be done? *Who* will do it? *How* much will it cost?
Budgets	Details a supporting marketing budget that is essentially a projected profit-and-loss statement. It shows expected revenues (forecasted number of units sold and the average net price) and expected costs (of production, distribution, and marketing). The difference is the projected profit. Once approved by higher management, the budget becomes the basis for materials buying, production scheduling, personnel planning, and marketing operations.
Controls	Outlines the control that will be used to monitor progress and allow higher management to review implementation results and spot products that are not meeting their goals. It includes measures of return on marketing investment.

Reflecting their unique history of melding Asian and European values, Hong Kong firms did not have a clear profile of corporate culture.[13]

Marketing Department Organization

The company must design a marketing organization that can carry out marketing strategies and plans. If the company is very small, one person might do all of the research, selling, advertising, customer service, and other marketing work. As the company expands, a marketing department emerges to plan and carry out marketing activities. In large companies, this department contains many specialists. Thus, GE and Microsoft have product and market managers, sales managers and salespeople, market researchers, advertising experts, and many other specialists. To head up such large marketing organizations, many companies have created a chief marketing officer (or CMO) position.

Modern marketing departments can be arranged in several ways. The most common form of marketing organization is the functional organization. Under this organization, different marketing activities are headed by a functional specialist—a sales manager, advertising manager, marketing research manager, customer service manager, or new-product manager. A company that sells across the country or internationally often uses a geographic organization. Its sales and marketing people are assigned to specific countries, regions, and districts. Geographic organization allows salespeople to settle into a territory, get to know their customers, and work with a minimum of travel time and cost.

Companies with many very different products or brands often create a product management organization. Using this approach, a product manager develops and implements a complete strategy and marketing program for a specific product or brand. Product management first appeared at Procter & Gamble in 1929. A new company soap, Camay, was not doing well, and a young P&G executive was assigned to give his exclusive attention to developing and promoting this product. He was successful, and the company soon added other product managers.[14] Since then, many firms, especially consumer products companies, have set up product management organizations.

For companies that sell one product line to many different types of markets and customers that have different needs and preferences, a *market* or *customer management organization* might be best. A market management organization is similar to the product management organization. Market managers are responsible for developing marketing strategies and plans for their specific markets or customers. This system's main advantage is that the company is organized around the needs of specific customer segments.

Large companies that produce many different products flowing into many different geographic and customer markets usually employ some *combination* of the functional, geographic, product, and market organization forms. This ensures that each function, product, and market receives its share of management attention. However, it can also add costly layers of management and reduce organizational flexibility. Still, the benefits of organizational specialization usually outweigh the drawbacks.

Marketing Control

Because many surprises occur during the implementation of marketing plans, the marketing department must practice constant marketing control. **Marketing control** involves evaluating the results of marketing strategies and plans and taking corrective action to ensure that objectives are attained. There are four steps involved. Management first sets specific marketing goals. It then measures its performance in the marketplace and evaluates the causes of any differences between expected and actual performance. Finally, management takes corrective action to close the gaps between its goals and its performance. This may require changing the action programs or even changing the goals.

Operating control involves checking ongoing performance against the annual plan and taking corrective action when necessary. Its purpose is to ensure that the company achieves the sales, profits, and other goals set out in its annual plan. It also involves determining the profitability of different products, territories, markets, and channels.

Strategic control involves looking at whether the company's basic strategies are well matched to its opportunities. Marketing strategies and programs can quickly become outdated, and each company should periodically reassess its overall approach to the marketplace. A major tool for such strategic control is a marketing audit. The **marketing audit** is a comprehensive, systematic, independent, and periodic examination of a company's environment, objectives, strategies, and activities to determine problem areas and opportunities. The audit provides good input for a plan of action to improve the company's marketing performance.[15]

Organizing the marketing department can be arranged in several ways—the functional, geographic, product management, and customer management organization.

Marketing control
The process of measuring and evaluating the results of marketing strategies and plans and taking corrective action to ensure that objectives are achieved.

Marketing audit
A comprehensive, systematic, independent, and periodic examination of a company's environment, objectives, strategies, and activities to determine problem areas and opportunities and to recommend a plan of action to improve the company's marketing performance.

The marketing audit covers *all* major marketing areas of a business, not just a few trouble spots. It assesses the marketing environment, marketing strategy, marketing organization, marketing systems, marketing mix, and marketing productivity and profitability. The audit is normally conducted by an objective and experienced outside party. Based on the findings, management then decides which actions make sense and how and when to implement them.

Measuring and Managing Return on Marketing Investment

Marketing managers must ensure that their marketing dollars are being well spent. Hence, better measures of return on marketing investment are developed. **Return on marketing investment** (or *marketing ROI*) is the net return from a marketing investment divided by the costs of the marketing investment. It measures the profits generated by investments in marketing activities.

Marketing returns can be difficult to measure. In measuring financial ROI, both the *R* and the *I* are uniformly measured in dollars. But there is as of yet no consistent definition of marketing ROI. Instead, a company can assess return on marketing in terms of standard marketing performance measures, such as brand awareness, sales, or market share. Campbell Soup uses sales and share data to evaluate specific advertising campaigns. For example, analysis revealed that its Soup at Hand advertising campaign, which depicted real-life scenarios of consumers using the portable soup, nearly doubled both the product's trial rate and repeat use rate after the first year.[16]

Many companies are assembling such measures into *marketing dashboards*—meaningful sets of marketing performance measures in a single display used to monitor strategic marketing performance. Just as automobile dashboards present drivers with details on how their cars are performing, the marketing dashboard gives marketers the detailed measures they need to assess and adjust their marketing strategies.[17]

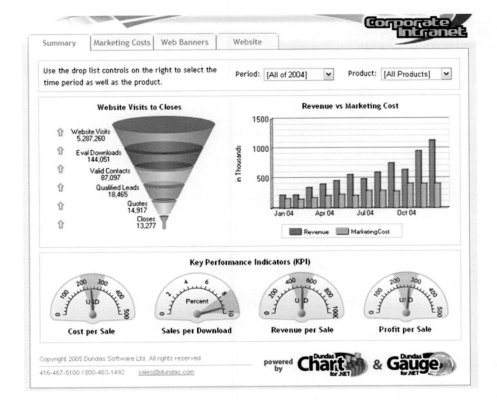

Marketing dashboards use a single display to monitor strategic marketing performance. Courtesy of Dundas Data Visualization. (www.dundas.com)

Increasingly, however, marketers are using customer-centered measures of marketing impact, such as customer acquisition, customer retention, and customer lifetime value. **Figure 2.9** views marketing expenditures as investments that produce returns in the form of more profitable customer relationships.[18] Marketing investments result in improved customer value and satisfaction, which in turn increases customer attraction and retention. This increases individual customer lifetime values and the firm's overall customer equity. Increased customer equity, in relation to the cost of the marketing investments, determines return on marketing investment.

Regardless of how it's defined or measured, the return on marketing investment concept is here to stay. "Marketing ROI is at the heart of every business," says an AT&T marketing executive. "[We've added another P to the marketing mix]—for *profit* and *loss* or *performance*. We absolutely have to … quantify the impact of marketing on the business. You can't improve what you can't measure."[19]

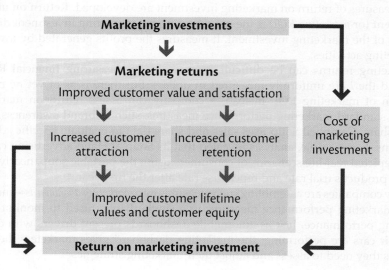

Figure 2.9
Return on marketing
Source: Adapted from Roland T. Rust, Katherine N. Lemon, and Valerie A. Zeithamal, "Return on Marketing: Using Consumer Equity to Focus Marketing Strategy," *Journal of Marketing*, January 2004, p. 112.

REVIEWING THE CONCEPTS

In Chapter 1, we defined *marketing* and outlined the steps in the marketing process. In this chapter, we examined companywide strategic planning and marketing's role in the organization. Then, we looked more deeply into marketing strategy and the marketing mix and reviewed the major marketing management functions. So you've now had a pretty good overview of the fundamentals of modern marketing. In future chapters, we'll expand on these fundamentals.

1 Explain companywide strategic planning and its four steps.

Strategic planning sets the stage for the rest of the company's planning. Marketing contributes to strategic planning, and the overall plan defines marketing's role in the company. Although formal planning offers a variety of benefits to companies, not all companies use it or use it well.

Strategic planning involves developing a strategy for long-run survival and growth. It consists of four steps: defining the company's mission, setting objectives and goals, designing a business portfolio, and developing functional plans. *Defining a clear company mission* begins with drafting a formal mission statement, which should be market oriented, realistic, specific, motivating, and consistent with the market environment. The mission is then transformed into detailed *supporting goals and objectives* to guide the entire company. Based on those goals and objectives, headquarters designs a *business portfolio*, deciding which businesses and products should receive more or fewer resources. In turn, each business and product unit must develop *detailed marketing plans* in line with the companywide plan.

2 Discuss how to design business portfolios and develop strategies for growth and downsizing.

Guided by the company's mission statement and objectives, management plans its *business portfolio*, or the collection of businesses and products that make up the company. The firm wants to produce a business portfolio that best fits its strengths and weaknesses to opportunities in the environment. To do this, it must analyze and adjust its *current* business portfolio and develop growth and downsizing strategies for adjusting the *future portfolio*. The company might use a formal portfolio-planning method. But many companies are now designing more customized portfolio-planning approaches that better suit their unique situations. The *product/market expansion grid* suggests four possible growth paths: market penetration, market development, product development, and diversification.

3 Assess marketing's role in strategic planning and explain how marketers partner with others inside and outside the firm to build profitable customer relationships.

Under the strategic plan, the major functional departments—marketing, finance, accounting, purchasing, operations, information systems, human resources, and others—must work together to accomplish strategic objectives. Marketing plays a key role in the company's strategic planning by providing a *marketing-concept philosophy* and *inputs* regarding attractive market opportunities. Within individual business units, marketing designs *strategies* for reaching the unit's objectives and helps to carry them out profitably.

Marketers alone cannot produce superior value for customers. A company's success depends on how well each department performs its customer value-adding activities and how well the departments work together to serve the customer. Thus, marketers must practice *partner relationship management*. They must work closely with partners in other company departments to form an effective *value chain* that serves the customer. And they must partner effectively with other companies in the marketing system to form a competitively superior *value-delivery network*.

4 Describe the elements of a customer-driven marketing strategy and mix, and the forces that influence it.

Consumer value and relationships are at the center of marketing strategy and programs. Through market segmentation, market targeting, differentiation, and market positioning, the company divides the total market into smaller segments, selects segments it can best serve, and decides how it wants to bring value to target consumers. It then designs an *integrated marketing mix* to produce the response it wants in the target market. The marketing mix consists of product, price, place, and promotion decisions.

5 List the marketing management functions, including the elements of a marketing plan, and discuss the importance of measuring and managing return on marketing.

To find the best strategy and mix and to put them into action, the company engages in marketing analysis, planning, implementation, and control. The main components of a *marketing plan* are the executive summary, current marketing situation, threats and opportunities, objectives and issues, marketing strategies, action programs, budgets, and controls. To plan good strategies is often easier than to carry them out. To be successful, companies must also be effective at *implementation*—turning marketing strategies into marketing actions.

Much of the responsibility for implementation goes to the company's marketing department. Marketing departments can be organized in one or a combination of ways: *functional marketing organization, geographic organization, product management organization, or market management organization*. In this age of customer relationships, more and more companies are now changing their organizational focus from product or territory management to customer relationship management. Marketing organizations carry out *marketing control*, both operating control and strategic control. They use *marketing audits* to determine marketing opportunities and problems and to recommend short-run and long-run actions to improve overall marketing performance.

Marketing managers must ensure that their marketing dollars are being well spent. Today's marketers face growing pressures to show that they are adding value in line with their costs. In response, marketers are developing better measures of *return on marketing investment*. Increasingly, they are using customer-centered measures of marketing impact as a key input into their strategic decision making.

REVIEWING THE KEY TERMS

Business portfolio 35
Differentiation 45
Diversification 40
Downsizing 41
Growth-share matrix 35
Market development 40
Market penetration 40
Market segment 44
Market segmentation 44
Market targeting 45
Marketing audit 50
Marketing control 50
Marketing implementation 48

Marketing mix 46
Marketing strategy 43
Mission statement 33
Positioning 45
Product development 40
Product/market expansion grid 37
Return on marketing investment (or marketing ROI) 51
Strategic planning 32
SWOT analysis 47
Value chain 41
Value-delivery network 42

DISCUSSING THE CONCEPTS

1. There are four major steps in strategic planning. Why is it important for a marketer to perform these steps in order?

2. The BCG growth-share matrix identifies four classifications of SBUs: stars, cash cows, question marks, and dogs. Briefly discuss why management may find it difficult to dispose of a "question mark."

3. Discuss the differences between the four growth strategies identified in the product/market expansion grid. Which option would a smaller company be pursuing if it decided to enter an existing market served by many large, well-known competitors? Assume that the product being introduced by this smaller company is a new

offering for the organization, but that this new product offers a number of unique features.

4. Does the "4 Ps" marketing mix framework do an adequate job of describing marketer responsibilities in preparing and managing marketing programs? Why? Do you see any issues with this framework in relation to service products?

5. What is the importance of marketing implementation? How might a company have excellent planning and poor implementation?

6. What is return on marketing investment? Why is it difficult to measure?

APPLYING THE CONCEPTS

1. In a small group, discuss whether the following statement from Samsung meets the five criteria of a good mission statement: "We will devote our people and technology to create superior products and services, thereby contributing to a better global society."

2. A company's value chain and value-delivery network are critical to its success. Describe how Reebok relies on its value chain. Sketch Reebok's value-delivery network and highlight the importance of each member in the network.

3. Discount retailers sell merchandise at lower prices with lower margins and higher volumes. Based on your experience with two such retailers in your country and visits to each of their Web sites, describe how they differ in their market segmentation, target marketing, and market positioning strategies.

FOCUS ON TECHNOLOGY

Visit the Web sites of several car manufacturers and you will see the technological innovations and additions offered in today's vehicles. From navigation systems to audio enhancements and DVD systems, these technologies are enhancing today's cars. Microsoft, known mostly for its computer operating systems, has been working with Fiat to develop a new "infotainment" system known as Blue&Me. Currently offered only in limited Fiat models, the system integrates mobile phones, MP3 players, and an Internet connection through controls on the steering wheel. The new technology will also contain a navigation system, weather and traffic forecasts, and antitheft devices.

1. According to the product/market expansion grid, which strategy best describes Microsoft's expansion into automobile applications?

2. Why is Fiat an important member of Microsoft's value-delivery network?

3. Describe why this advanced technology is important to Fiat in terms of positioning its products.

FOCUS ON ETHICS

Tyson Foods Inc. has been a leading provider of poultry products for more than 60 years. Its corporate mission statement includes a set of core values that clearly state the importance of being a faith-friendly company and honoring God. Internally, Tyson connects with its employees and has placed 128 part-time chaplains in 78 plants across the United States. But Tyson also wants to send its faith-friendly message to consumers. To reinforce its "Powered by Tyson" campaign, it has recently begun to offer free downloadable prayer books on its Web site. According to Tyson, it provides these books to help consumers discover (or rediscover) the joy and power of saying a word of thanks at mealtime.

1. What do you think of Tyson's strategy to offer the downloadable booklets? Is there a reason to believe it is embracing religion only to make increased profit?

2. In your opinion, does religion belong in a corporate mission statement? Why or why not?

3. Many consumers see chicken as a commodity product with no real difference between brands. Does this strategy make you more or less likely to buy Tyson over another brand?

VIDEO CASE

Harley-Davidson

Few brands engender such intense loyalty as that found in the hearts of Harley-Davidson owners. Why? Because the company's marketers spend a great deal of time thinking about customers. They want to know who their customers are, how they think and feel, and why they buy a Harley. That attention to detail has helped build Harley-Davidson into a $5 billion company with more than 900,000 Harley Owners Group (HOG) members and 1,200 dealerships worldwide.

Harley sells much more than motorcycles. The company sells a feeling of independence, individualism, and freedom. To support that lifestyle, Harley-Davidson offers clothes and accessories both for riders and those who simply like to associate with the brand. Harley further extends the brand experience by offering travel adventures. Through Harley's

Web site, customers can book a trip to Milwaukee to visit the Harley factory in the company's hometown or turn a Las Vegas vacation into "an authentic Harley-Davidson adventure."

After viewing the video featuring Harley-Davidson, answer the following questions about marketing strategy.

1. List several products that are included in Harley-Davidson's business portfolio. Analyze the portfolio using the Boston Consulting Group growth-share matrix.

2. Which strategies in the product/market expansion grid is Harley-Davidson using to grow sales and profits?

3. List some of the members of Harley's value-delivery network.

COMPANY CASE

Red Bull: Charging into the Future

Chaleo Yoovidhya, 75, a retiring Thai chemist, is responsible for concocting a caffeine-rich energy drink, Red Bull. For 20 years, Red Bull was popular with Thai truck drivers and rice farmers to keep them awake while working long hours. Now, some 1.6 billion cans of this non-alcoholic drink are consumed annually by trendy youngsters worldwide. How this happened is a story of marketing success. How Red Bull can maintain its competitive advantage will be one great marketing challenge.

Background

Dietrich Mateschitz, a toothpaste salesperson from Austria, discovered Red Bull on a visit to Bangkok. The firm he worked for had a franchise agreement with Yoovidhya's family business, TC Pharmaceutical Industries. His Thai business partners introduced him to a sweet, syrupy tonic drink with the uninspiring name of Krating Daeng, Thai for Red Bull. Mateschitz not only liked the drink ("one glass and my jet lag was gone," he recalls), but he also saw the potential for fashionable energy drinks among a new generation in Europe. He persuaded Yoovidhya and his son Chalerm to form a separate joint venture in Austria, Red Bull GmbH, in 1984. It took another three years to adapt the blue-collar drink to appeal to a completely different market—initially, skiers and mountain snowboarders. Mateschitz made the drink more refreshing by adding carbon dioxide, while retaining the original Thai ingredients of B-vitamins, caffeine, sugar, and the amino acid taurine.

By 1993, some 35 million cans of Red Bull were sold annually, a figure that doubled, then quadrupled, as distribution spread across Europe. Red Bull pursued a subtle promotion campaign that cost little in cash

but secured a lot of cult kudos. "We didn't bring the product to the people," Mateschitz says. "We brought people to the product. We made it available and those who loved our style come to us." These consumers included all-night disco dancers, cosmopolitan college students cramming for exams, and energy-burning sports enthusiasts across Europe and North America. Its distinctive packaging, 8.3 ounce silver-and-blue cans with two bulls about to head-butt each other, contain a promise of improved performance, "especially during times of increased stress or strain." Evidence of the drink's cult status can be found on the Internet, where such vintage Red Bull merchandise as jackets, logo stickers, Thai boxing shorts, and coolers are auctioned on eBay.

As part of its promotion efforts, Red Bull supports over 240 athletes worldwide, mainly in a diverse range of extreme sports, including kiteboarding, windsurfing, motorcross, freeskiing, triathlon, mountain biking, hang gliding, cliff diving, beach volleyball, inline skating, and paragliding. Red Bull also sponsors athletes of some conventional sports like swimming, golf, and sailing. It also engages in event marketing. For example, Red Bull Flugtag (German for "Flying Day") has been organized in Austria, Ireland, New Zealand, and the U.S., among other countries. In this competition in creativity, the amateur who can design and fly hand-made machines furthest wins. While no records are broken, the event draws numerous observers for its unparalleled showmanship of outrageous aircraft.

However, Red Bull's events are perceived to be hardly marketed. Take, for example, its kiteboarding expedition to Cuba. Kiteboarding blends elements of windsurfing and wakeboarding. Red Bull funded an effort to kiteboard to a nation that is subject to a U.S. trade embargo. Yet, the event had no advance press release. Nor was there a Red Bull tent to attract local news crews or hand out free samples to curious onlookers.

Such efforts are consistent with the findings of a recent survey of British marketers which dubbed Red Bull a "non-marketed brand" phenomenon during the 1990s. "Stealth" is most popularly used to describe Red Bull's marketing strategy. When it entered the U.S., it did not roll out a big, splashy ad campaign or buy massive coast-to-coast distribution. Instead, Red Bull used "street teams" to spread the word to important, trend setting Generation Y types. Carefully winning over these hip influentials set off a grass roots marketing wave. Red Bull also deploys "mobile energy teams" to hand out free samples at places where people might need an energy boost such as in gyms, office buildings, and construction sites.

Red Bull's mystique has been cited by many marketing experts. Marc Gobe, author of *Emotional Branding* and head of his own brand consultancy, notes that "Extreme sports deliver on the need to vibrate. In a way, Red Bull is one of the first products that … delivers on that energy." Gobe thinks Red Bull's cans are "sexy," with their small size implying that they pack an extra wallop. He deems Red Bull the "anti-brand."

Red Bull now holds 70 percent of the worldwide energy drink market. In the U.S., it is ranked among the top ten carbonated soft drinks. A December 7, 2001 editorial in *Beverage Digest* noted the buzz generated by Red Bull at U.S. convenience stores. Most notably, the brand commands a huge price premium. Its average price was $69.45 per 288-ounce case, compared to $9.41 for Coke Classic, $9.30 for Pepsi, $13.21 for Mountain Dew Code Red, and $13.08 for Cherry Coke. Red Bull is one of only ten Asian brands outside Japan that have achieved global success. In 2003, it launched both Mateschitz and Yoovidhya into the *Forbes* billionaire list. The company now employs over 1,200 employees globally.

Red Bull's success comes despite several health blips. France banned Red Bull for a time in the 1990s on the grounds that it was a dangerous stimulant. The Swedish and Malaysian governments issued a health warning when a woman in Sweden died after allegedly mixing vodka with Red Bull. The brand also overcame rumors circulated on the Internet in 2000 alleging that it contained an artificial stimulant linked to the formation of brain tumors and that it was made from bull testicles.

What Next?

Red Bull's enviable position is changing. Mateschitz concedes that the first generation of drinkers he wooed is now aging. "We need to get a new generation of 16-year-olds on board every year," he says. To this end, Red Bull is investing over $400 million in marketing and sports sponsorships. Its cartoon TV commercials (among them, Adam and Eve, Father, and Dracula) demonstrate Red Bull's stimulating effect on body and mind in a spirited, fresh, ironic, and witty way. Each ends with the tagline, "Red Bull gives you wiings." Among Red Bull's major sponsorship thrusts is the Sauber Formula One Motor Racing team. Other partners include the Malaysian gas company Petronas and Swiss bank Credit Suisse.

Red Bull is also cognizant of increased competition from companies like Coca-Cola, Pepsi Cola, and Anheuser Busch. Having seen the success of Red Bull, each is entering the market with its own brands. Among them are Gatorade, which introduced an energy drink version, PowerAde by Coca-Cola, and All Sport by Pepsi Cola. The U.S. market is a particularly important, and fertile, battle ground. If Americans can be induced to drink just half the quantity currently consumed in Ireland—11 cans per capita per year—Red Bull would sell more than a billion cans annually in the U.S. Hence, according to *Brandweek*, Red Bull spent $100 million in the U.S. alone in 2000.

Red Bull is also increasing its distribution coverage. In Great Britain, where it holds an 80 percent market share, the company will be distributing through vending machines. Red Bull may also be purchased at and delivered directly from Internet sites like www.coffeeforless.com, www.slimstore.com, and www.easycoffee.com. At www.downwindsports.com, Red Bull is offered at a special case pricing of $43.

Finally, Red Bull is also launching additional product variants. It marketed Red Bull Sugar Free as its first brand extension in the U.S. using the same packaging but a different sweetener. Also marketed is Red Bull Energy Supplement, the original Thai edition. It comes packaged in a 150ml glass bottle and is labeled as a liquid vitamin supplement.

Questions For Discussion

1. How do you think Red Bull would write its mission statement? How would you write it?
2. Has Red Bull identified the best target market for its product? What other market segments might the firm target?
3. How has the company positioned Red Bull for its chosen target market? Could it position the product in other ways?
4. Describe the current marketing mix for Red Bull. Do you recommend any changes to it?
5. Who is Red Bull's competition?
6. Would you change Red Bull's marketing strategy? If so, how? What kinds of control procedures would you establish for this strategy?
7. What marketing lessons can be drawn from Red Bull's experience for other small Asian businesses?

Sources:
Graham Lees, "Charging Ahead," *Asia Inc.*, November 2003, p. 31; www.beverage-digest.com/editorial;www.kidsworld.com/site/p192.htm; www.bevnet.com/reviews/redbull; www.snopes2.com/toxins/redbull.htm; "The Marketing of Red Bull," www.robwalker.net; www.redbull.com; www.redbullflugtagtexas.com; www.sauber.ch; and www.just-drinks.com; all accessed online on December, 2003.

it's what i **eat** and what i **do**™

i'm lovin' it™

Objectives

After studying this chapter, you should be able to

- describe the environmental forces that affect the company's ability to serve its customers
- explain how changes in the demographic and economic environments affect marketing decisions
- identify the major trends in the firm's natural and technological environments
- explain the key changes in the political and cultural environments
- discuss how companies can react to the marketing environment

CHAPTER 3

THE MARKETING ENVIRONMENT

Previewing the Concepts

In Part 1 (Chapters 1 and 2), you learned about the basic concepts of marketing and the steps in the marketing process for building profitable relationships with targeted consumers. In Part 2, we'll look deeper into the first step of the marketing process—understanding the marketplace and customer needs and wants. In this chapter, you'll discover that marketing operates in a complex and changing environment. Other *actors* in this environment—suppliers, intermediaries, customers, competitors, publics, and others—may work with or against the company. Major environmental *forces*—demographic, economic, natural, technological, political, and cultural—shape marketing opportunities, pose threats, and affect the company's ability to serve customers and develop lasting relationships with them. To understand marketing, and to develop effective marketing strategies, you must first understand the environment in which marketing operates.

First, we'll look at McDonald's. Over 50 years ago, Ray Kroc spotted an important shift in consumer lifestyles and bought a small chain of restaurants. He built that chain into the vast McDonald's fast-food empire. But although the shifting marketing environment brought opportunities for McDonald's, it has also created challenges.

In 1955, Ray Kroc, a 52-year-old salesman of milk-shake mixing machines, bought a string of seven restaurants owned by Richard and Maurice McDonald for $2.7 million. Kroc saw the McDonald brothers' fast-food concept as a perfect fit for America's increasingly on-the-go, time-squeezed, family-oriented lifestyles. The rest, as they say, is history.

McDonald's grew quickly to become the world's largest fast-feeder. Its more than 31,800 restaurants worldwide now serve 50 million customers each day, with system-wide sales of almost $60 billion annually. By making fast food for families, the Golden Arches are one of the world's most familiar symbols. Other than Santa Claus, no character in the world is more recognizable than Ronald McDonald. Anthropologists have examined the impact of McDonald's in East Asia. When it opened in Hong Kong in 1975, McDonald's was the first restaurant to consistently offer clean bathrooms, driving customers to demand the same from other food establishments. McDonald's also influenced the easing or elimination of the Japanese taboo of eating while walking.

But just as the changing marketplace has provided opportunities for McDonald's, it has also presented challenges. By early in this decade, sales growth at McDonald's slumped, and its market share fell by over 3 percent between 1997 and 2003. In 2002, the company posted its first-ever quarterly loss.

What happened? McDonald's seemed a bit out of step with the times as consumers were looking for fresher, better-tasting food and more upscale atmospheres. Result? McDonald's was losing share to "fast-casual" restaurants. New competitors such as Panera Bread and Cosi were offering more imaginative meals in more fashionable surroundings. And for consumers who'd rather "eat-out-in," supermarkets offered pre-prepared, ready-to-serve gourmet meals to go.

Consumers were also seeking healthier eating options. Fast-food patrons complained about too few healthy menu choices. As the market leader, McDonald's bore the brunt of much of this criticism. Reacting to these challenges, McDonald's announced a turnaround plan in early 2003— the "Plan to Win"—to better align the company with the new marketplace realities. The plan included the following initiatives:

Back to Basics—McDonald's began refocusing on what made it successful: consistent products and reliable service. It began pouring money back into existing stores, speeding up service, training employees, and monitoring restaurants to make sure they stay bright and clean. It's also "re-imaging" its restaurants, with clean, simple, more modern interiors and amenities such as wireless Internet access. McDonald's now promises to be a "forever young" brand.

If You Can't Lick 'Em, Join 'Em—To find new ways to compete better with the new breed of fast-casual competitors, and to expand its customer base, McDonald's has experimented with new restaurant and delivery concepts. For example, it has tested upscale McCafé coffee shops, which offer leather seating, knowledgeable staff, and espresso in porcelain cups, along with made-to-order drinks, gourmet sandwiches, and Internet access. The McCafé concept originated in Australia. Replicating the success of its pizza rivals, McDonald's also has a home delivery service, McDelivery, in Singapore. China's growing use of personal vehicles has led McDonald's to team up with Chinese oil company Sinopec in opening numerous drive-through outlets. More outlets are now offering 24-hour service.

*"It's what i **eat** and what i **do**… i'm lovin' it"*—McDonald's recently unveiled a major multifaceted education campaign to help consumers better understand the keys to living balanced, active lifestyles. The "it's what i **eat** and what i **do**… i'm lovin' it" theme underscores the important interplay between eating right and staying active. The company assembled a Global Advisory Council of outside experts in nutrition, wellness, and activity to provide input on its menu choice and variety, education outreach, and promoting physical fitness. A trimmer, fitter Ronald McDonald is now Chief Happiness Officer, a global ambassador of fun, fitness, and children's well-being. McDonald's has also refreshed its GoActive.com Web site, which offers tips on how to lead a balanced active lifestyle as well as a Family Fitness Tool Kit. In Singapore, it launched Veg Out Day, the first day of every month when customers are encouraged to eat more fruits and vegetables.

Improving the Fare—McDonald's has worked to provide more choice and variety on its menu. For example, it offers Chicken McNuggets made with white meat, Corn Cup, and a line of Premium Salads. Within a year of introducing its Premium Salads, McDonald's became the world's largest salad seller. McDonald's is well-known for localizing its menu worldwide. McDonald's India reformulated some of its products using spices favored by locals, including the McVeggie Burger, the McAloo Tiki Burger, and the Veg Pizza McPuff. Even its McShakes are eggless to suit vegetarian diets.

McDonald's efforts to realign itself with the changing marketing environment appear to be paying off. By almost any measure, the fast-food giant is back in shape. Since announcing its Plan to Win, McDonald's has increased its sales by 33 percent and profits have tripled. It looks like customers and stockholders alike are humming the chain's catchy jingle, "I'm lovin' it." A former McDonald's CEO summed it up this way: "Ray Kroc used to say he didn't know what we would be selling in the year 2000, but whatever it was we would be selling the most of it. He recognized early on that consumer needs change and we want to change with them."[1]

Marketing environment
The actors and forces outside marketing that affect marketing management's ability to build and maintain successful relationships with target customers.

Microenvironment
The actors close to the company that affect its ability to serve its customers—the company, suppliers, marketing intermediaries, customer markets, competitors, and publics.

Macroenvironment
The larger societal forces that affect the microenvironment—demographic, economic, natural, technological, political, and cultural forces.

Marketers need to be good at building relationships with customers, others in the company, and external partners. To do this effectively, they must understand the major environmental forces that surround these relationships. A company's **marketing environment** consists of the actors and forces outside marketing that affect marketing management's ability to build and maintain successful relationships with target customers. Successful companies know the vital importance of constantly watching and adapting to the changing environment.

As the environment changes, marketers must be the trend trackers to tap on opportunities. They have disciplined methods—marketing research and marketing intelligence—for collecting information about the marketing environment. They also spend more time in the customer and competitor environments. By carefully studying the environment, marketers can adapt their strategies to meet new marketplace challenges and opportunities.

The marketing environment is made up of a *microenvironment* and a *macroenvironment*. The **microenvironment** consists of the actors close to the company that affect its ability to serve its customers—the company, suppliers, marketing intermediaries, customer markets, competitors, and publics. The **macroenvironment** consists of the larger societal forces that affect the microenvironment—demographic, economic, natural, technological, political, and cultural forces. We look first at the company's microenvironment.

The Company's Microenvironment

Figure 3.1 shows the major actors in the marketer's microenvironment.

The Company

In designing marketing plans, marketing management takes other company groups into account—groups such as top management, finance, research and development (R&D), purchasing, operations, and accounting. These groups form the internal environment. Top management sets the company's mission, objectives, broad strategies, and policies. Marketing managers make decisions within the strategies and plans made by top management. As discussed in Chapter 2, marketing managers must work closely with other company departments to provide superior customer value and satisfaction.

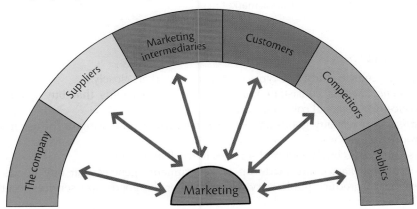

Figure 3.1
Actors in the microenvironment

Suppliers

Suppliers form an important link in the company's overall customer value delivery system. They provide the resources needed by the company to produce its goods and services. Marketing managers must watch supply availability as supply shortages or delays, labor strikes, and other events can cost sales in the short run and damage customer satisfaction in the long run. Marketing managers also monitor the price trends of their key inputs. Rising supply costs may force price increases that can harm the company's sales volume.

Marketing intermediaries
Firms that help the company to promote, sell, and distribute its goods to final buyers. They include resellers, physical distribution firms, marketing service agencies, and financial intermediaries.

Marketing Intermediaries

Marketing intermediaries help the company to promote, sell, and distribute its products to final buyers. They include resellers, physical distribution firms, marketing services agencies, and financial intermediaries.

- *Resellers* are distribution channel firms that help the company find customers or make sales to them. These include wholesalers and retailers, who buy and resell merchandise. Some are small while others are large such as Wal-Mart, Carrefour, and Giant. These large organizations have enough power to dictate terms or sometimes, even shut the manufacturer out of large markets.
- *Physical distribution firms* help the company to stock and move goods from their points of origin to their destinations. Working with warehouse and transportation firms, a company must determine the best ways to store and ship goods, balancing factors such as cost, delivery, speed, and safety.
- *Marketing services agencies* are the marketing research firms, advertising agencies, media firms, and marketing consulting firms that help the company target and promote its products to the right markets.
- *Financial intermediaries* include banks, credit companies, insurance companies, and other businesses that help finance transactions or insure against the risks associated with the buying and selling of goods.

Carrefour opened its first hypermarket in Tokyo, Japan, in 2000. It is a key player in entering the Asian market.

Marketers recognize the importance of working with their intermediaries as partners rather than as channels through which they sell their products. For example, when Coca-Cola signs on as the exclusive beverage provider for a fast-food chain, such as McDonald's or Subway, it provides much more than just soft drinks. It also pledges powerful marketing support.

Coca-Cola assigns cross-functional teams dedicated to understanding the finer points of each retail partner's business. It conducts a staggering amount of research on beverage consumers and shares these insights with its partners. It analyzes the demographics of U.S. zip code areas and helps partners to determine which Coke brands are preferred in their areas. Coca-Cola has even studied the design of drive-through menu boards to better understand which layouts, fonts, letter sizes, colors, and visuals induce consumers to order more food and drink. Such intense partnering efforts have made Coca-Cola a run-away leader in the U.S. fountain soft drink market.[2]

Partnering with marketing intermediaries—Coca-Cola provides Subway with much more than just soft drinks. It also pledges powerful marketing support. (*www.coca-cola.com*)

Customers

The company needs to study five types of customer markets closely.

- *Consumer markets* consist of individuals and households that buy goods and services for personal consumption.
- *Business markets* buy goods and services for further processing or for use in their production process.
- *Reseller markets* buy goods and services to resell at a profit.
- *Government markets* are made up of government agencies that buy goods and services to produce public services or transfer the goods and services to others who need them.
- *International markets* consist of these buyers in other countries, including consumers, producers, resellers, and governments.

Each market type has special characteristics that call for careful study by the seller.

Competitors

The marketing concept states that to be successful, a company must provide greater customer value and satisfaction than its competitors do. Thus, marketers must do more than adapt to the needs of target consumers. They also must gain strategic advantage by positioning their offerings strongly against competitors' offerings in the minds of consumers.

No single competitive marketing strategy is best for all companies. Each firm should consider its own size and industry position compared to those of its competitors. Large firms with dominant positions in an industry can use certain strategies that smaller firms cannot afford. Small firms can develop strategies that give them better rates of return than large firms enjoy.

Publics

Public
Any group that has an actual or potential interest in or impact on an organization's ability to achieve its objectives.

The company's marketing environment also includes various publics. A **public** is any group that has an actual or potential interest in or impact on an organization's ability to achieve its objectives. We can identify seven types of publics.

- *Financial publics* influence the company's ability to obtain funds. Banks, investment houses, and stockholders are the major financial publics.
- *Media publics* carry news, features, and editorial opinions. They include newspapers, magazines, and radio and television stations.
- *Government publics.* Management must take government developments into account. Marketers must often consult the company's lawyers on issues of product safety, truth in advertising, and other matters.

- *Citizen-action publics.* A company's marketing decisions may be questioned by consumer organizations, environmental groups, minority groups, and others. Its public relations department can help it stay in touch with consumer and citizen groups.
- *Local publics* include neighborhood residents and community organizations. Large companies usually appoint a community relations officer to deal with the community, attend meetings, answer questions, and contribute to worthwhile causes.
- *General public.* A company needs to be concerned about the general public's attitude toward its products and activities. The public's image of the company affects its buying.
- *Internal publics* include workers, managers, volunteers, and the board of directors. Large companies use newsletters and other means to inform and motivate their internal publics. When employees feel good about their company, this positive attitude spills over to external publics.

The Company's Macroenvironment

The company and all of the other actors operate in a larger macroenvironment of forces that shape opportunities and pose threats to the company. **Figure 3.2** shows the six major forces in the company's macroenvironment.

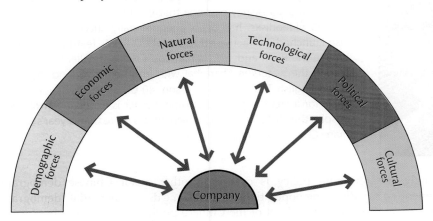

Figure 3.2
Major forces in the company's macroenvironment

Demographic Environment

Demography is the study of human populations in terms of size, density, location, age, gender, race, occupation, and other statistics. The demographic environment is of major interest to marketers because it involves people, and people make up markets. The world population is growing at an explosive rate. It now exceeds 6.5 billion people and will exceed 8.1 billion by the year 2030.[3] The world's large and highly diverse population poses both opportunities and challenges. **Figure 3.3** shows factors in the demographic environment that influence

Changes in the world demographic environment have major implications for business. Consider China. More than 25 years ago, the Chinese government passed regulations limiting families to one child each to curb its population. Result? Chinese children—known as "little emperors and empresses"—are being showered with attention and luxuries under what's known as the "six-pocket syndrome." As many as six adults—two parents and four doting grandparents—may be indulging the whims of each "only child." Parents in the average Beijing household now spend about 40 percent of their income on their cherished only child. This trend has created huge market opportunities for educational products.

Demography
The study of human populations in terms of size, density, location, age, gender, race, occupation, and other statistics.

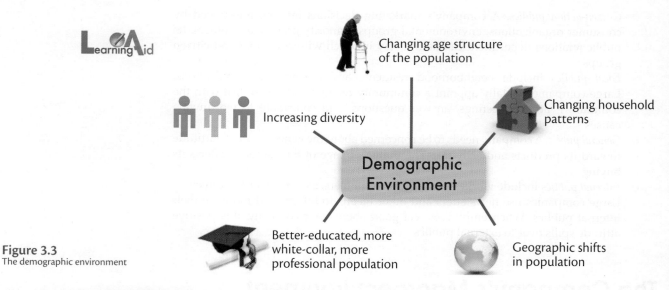

Figure 3.3
The demographic environment

Demographic Environment

- Changing age structure of the population
- Increasing diversity
- Changing household patterns
- Better-educated, more white-collar, more professional population
- Geographic shifts in population

Demographics and business—
Chinese regulations limiting families to one child have resulted in what's been known as the "six-pocket syndrome." Chinese children are being showered with attention and luxuries, creating opportunities for marketers.

In China's increasingly competitive society, parents are desperate to give their children an early edge. That's creating opportunities for companies marketing educational offerings aimed at kids. Disney, for example, is moving full speed into educational products. Magic English, a $225 Disney package that includes workbooks, flash cards, and 26 videodisks, has been phenomenally successful. Disney has also launched interactive educational CD-ROMs featuring the likes of Winnie the Pooh and *101 Dalmations'* Cruella DeVille. Time Warner is testing the waters in Shanghai with an interactive language course called English Time. The 200-lesson, 40-CD set takes as long as four years for a child to complete. Time Warner is expecting strong sales, despite the $3,300 price tag, which equals more than a year's salary for many Chinese parents.[4]

Interestingly, the one-child policy is creating another major Chinese demographic development—a rapidly aging population. In what some deem a potential "demographic earthquake," an estimated 58 percent of the Chinese population will be over age 40 by 2024. Moreover, close to 75 percent of all Chinese households will be childless, either because they chose to have no children or because their only child has left the nest. The result is an aging society that will need to be more self-reliant, which in turn will cause a large growth in service markets such as senior education, leisure clubs, and nursing homes.[5]

Thus, marketers keep close track of demographic trends and developments in their markets, both at home and abroad. They track changing age and family structures, geographic population shifts, educational characteristics, and population diversity.

Changing Age Structure of the Population

In general, the three largest age groups are the baby boomers, Generation X, and Generation Y.

The Baby Boomers

Baby boomers
The 78 million people born during the baby boom following World War II and lasting until the early 1960s.

These are people born post-World War II between 1946 and 1964. The **baby boomers** are one of the most powerful forces shaping the marketing environment in the U.S. and other developed economies. They have presented a moving target, creating new markets as they grew from infancy to mature years.

Baby boomers cut across all walks of life. But marketers typically have paid the most attention to the smaller upper crust of boomer generation—its more educated, mobile, and wealthy segments. The youngest boomers are now in their early forties; the oldest are entering their sixties. The maturing boomers are rethinking the purpose and value of their work, responsibilities, and relationships. As they reach their peak earning and spending years, the boomers constitute a lucrative market for new housing and home remodeling, financial services, travel and entertainment, eating out, health and fitness products, and just about everything else. Boomers are also likely to postpone retirement. Rather than viewing themselves as phasing out, they see themselves as entering new life phases. Perhaps no one is targeting the baby boomers more fervently than the financial services industry. Aging boomers are transferring their retirement nest eggs and other savings into new investments, and need money management advice.

However, not all boomers are an easy sell. They may have more money but they are also likely to be careful with it. In China, the over-60s have suffered through war and the Cultural Revolution. They tend to have little desire for consumer goods and do not like to indulge in themselves. Thus, one way to interest them is to play on financial security as many insurers are doing, or on general worries about safety.[6]

Generation X

This is the generation of people born between 1965 and 1976. They are called **Generation X** because they lie in the shadow of the boomers and lack obvious distinguishing characteristics. Others call them the "generation caught in the middle" (between the larger baby boomers and later Generation Ys).

The Generation Xers are defined as much by their shared experiences as by their age. Increasing higher employment for their mothers made them the first generation of latchkey kids. They care about the environment and respond favorably to socially responsible companies. Although they seek success, they are less materialistic; they prize experience, not acquisition. They are cautious romantics who want a better quality of life and are more interested in job satisfaction than in sacrificing personal happiness and growth for promotion. For many Gen Xers that are parents, family comes first, career second.[7]

As a result, the Gen Xers are a more skeptical bunch. "Marketing to Gen Xers is difficult," says one marketer, "and it's all about word of mouth. You can't tell them you're good, and they have zero interest in a slick brochure that says so …. They have a lot of 'filters' in place." Another marketer agrees, "Sixty-three percent of this group will research products before they consider a purchase. [They are also] creating extensive communities to exchange information. Even though nary a handshake occurs, the information swap is trusted and thus is more powerful than any marketing pitch ever could be."[8]

Generation Y

The **Generation Y** (also called echo boomers) are born between 1977 and 1994. These are children of the baby boomers. The echo boom has created a large teen and young adult market.

Generation Y oldsters have now graduated from college and are moving up in their careers. Like the trailing edge of the Generation Xers ahead of them, one distinguishing characteristic of Generation Y is their utter fluency and comfort with computer, digital, and Internet technology. In the U.S., some 87 percent of teens use the Internet, up 24 percent over the past four years. More than half of the 87 percent go online every day, and 84 percent of teens own at least one networked device, such as a mobile phone, Blackberry, or computer. In all, they are an impatient, now-oriented bunch.[9]

Generation Y represents an attractive target for marketers. However, reaching this message-saturated segment effectively requires creative marketing approaches. For example, the popularity of action sports with Gen Yers has provided creative marketing opportunities for products ranging from clothes to video games, movies, and beverages.

The automobile industry is also aggressively targeting this future generation of car buyers. Toyota created a completely new brand—the Scion—targeted to Gen Yers (see **Real Marketing**). Scion and other automakers are using a variety of programs and pitches to lure Generation Y as they move into their key car-buying years.[10]

Generation X
The 45 million people born between 1965 and 1976 in the "birth dearth" following the baby boom.

Generation Y
The 72 million children of the baby boomers, born between 1977 and 1994.

Generation Xers like the young parents shown here tend to value quality of life and family more.

Targeting at the Generation Y who are into action sports, Billabong uses its champion skaters in various countries to endorse its products. This one features Firdaus, a Billabong skater in Singapore. He won the Asian X Games and Xtreme Singapore Circuit in 2007.

Toyota had an unusual virtual promotion of its small, boxy Scion: It paid for the car's product placement in Whyville.net, an online interactive community populated almost entirely by 8- to 15-year-olds. Never mind that they cannot actually buy the car. Toyota is counting on Whyvillians to do two things—influence their parents' car purchases and maybe grow up with some Toyota brand loyalty. It may appear counterintuitive, but Toyota says the promotion is working. Ten days into the campaign, visitors to the site had used the word "Scion" in online chats more than 78,000 times; hundreds of virtual Scions were purchased, using "clams," the currency of Whyville; and the community meeting place, "Club Scion," was visited 33,741 times. These online Scion owners customized their cars, drove around the virtual Whyville, and picked up their Scion-less friends for a ride.

Generational marketing

Do marketers need to create separate products and marketing programs for each generation? Some experts warn that marketers must be careful about turning off one generation each time they craft a product or message that appeals effectively to another. Others caution that each generation spans decades of time and many socioeconomic levels. For example, marketers often split the baby boomers into three smaller groups—leading boomers, core boomers, and trailing boomers—each with its own beliefs and behaviors. Similarly, they split Generation Y into Gen Y adults and Gen Y teens. Thus, marketers need to form more precise age-specific segments within each group. More important, defining people by their birth date may be less effective than segmenting them by their lifestyle or life stage.

Geographic Shifts in Population

In 2008, the world will, for the first time, have most of its population living in towns and cities than in the rural areas. In Asia, there is a migration from the rural to the urban cities, although much of the shift is to outlying areas around mega-cities and medium-sized towns rather than major cities.[11] In China, the migration of workforces and subsequent rise in income levels have seen a proliferation of the number of urban households. Between 1950 and 2005, Shanghai saw its population grow by 7.3 million. For the same period, smaller cities such as Nanjing have seen their population increased more than 10-fold, while the population of Urumqi in the far west Xinjiang province has increased six-fold. A major trend emerging from this urban migration is a growing number of single-person households as families separate to take advantage of opportunities outside their home town and young people choose to leave home earlier.[12]

A Better-Educated, More White-Collar, More Professional Population

The world population is becoming better educated. The rising number of educated people will increase the demand for quality products, books, magazines, travel, personal computers, and Internet services. The workforce also is becoming more white-collar. In Japan, 99 percent of the population is literate, although the rate is much lower in the less developed countries and rural communities in Asia.

Increasing Diversity

Countries vary in their ethnic and racial makeup. At one extreme is Japan, where almost everyone is Japanese. At the other extreme is the U.S., with people from virtually all nations. Marketers are facing increasingly diverse markets, both at home and abroad as their operations become more international in scope. In Asia, for instance, some banks have introduced Islamic banking to cater to the Muslim market where the notion of interest earned and charged are considered incongruent with their faith.

Increasing diversity – The growth in Islamic banking caters to the Muslim market where the nation of interest earned and charged are considered incongruent with their faith.

Economic Environment

Markets require buying power as well as people. The **economic environment** consists of factors that affect consumer purchasing power and spending patterns (see **Figure 3.4**). Nations vary greatly in their levels and distribution of income. Some countries have *subsistence economies*—they consume most of their own agricultural and industrial output. These countries offer few market opportunities. At the other extreme are *industrial economies*, which constitute rich markets for many different kinds of goods. Marketers must pay close attention to major trends and consumer spending patterns both across and within their world markets.

Economic environment
Factors that affect consumer buying power and spending patterns.

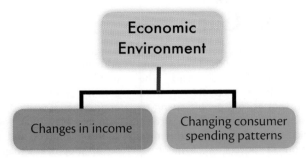

Figure 3.4
The economic environment

Changes in Income

The recession of the late 1990s and early 2000s that saw consumers seeking value products have given way to increased consumption since 2006. For instance, Vietnam's booming economy has spawned young adults keen on spending than saving.[13]

> Vietnam's dynamic young population are making up for lost time. They crowd shopping malls, snapping up Western jeans, slinky dresses, cosmetics, iPods, and DVDs. They head for cineplexes and throng downtown nightclubs and coffeeshops. Often, Vietnam's newly-liberated young professional women are the ones who set the pace. In Hanoi, Ho Chi Minh City, and Danang, they zip by on pink Piaggio motorbikes with Nokia mobile phones cupped to their ears as they head off to check out the latest fashion. Saving is for the old. Says a 27-year-old bank accountant, "Young people have more money and they mostly spend it on things that can show how stylish they are. They like to show off." Price is often less a factor than the desire to get the latest model from a top brand.

Rising affluence – For many Vietnamese youths new-found wealth means price is less a factor than the desire to get the latest model from a top brand.

Marketers should pay attention to *income distribution* as well as average income. At the top are *upper-class* consumers, whose spending patterns are not affected by current economic events and who are a major market for luxury goods. There is a comfortable *middle class* that is somewhat careful about its spending but can still afford the good life some of the time. The *working class* must stick close to the basics of food, clothing, and shelter and must try hard to save. Finally, the *underclass* (persons on welfare and many retirees) must count their pennies when making even the most basic purchases.

This distribution of income has created a tiered market. Many companies—such as Takashimaya—aggressively target the affluent. Others—such as the $1.99 stores—target those with more modest means. Still other companies tailor their marketing offers across a range of markets, from the affluent to the less affluent. For example, Levi-Strauss currently markets several different jeans lines. There is the low-priced Signature line, moderately priced Red Tab line, boutique lines such as Levi's [Capital E] and Warhol Factory X Levi's.[14]

REAL MARKETING

Toyota's Scion: Targeting Gen Y without Shouting "Buy This Car"

In the late 1990s, as Toyota's management team peered through the corporate windshield, it took great pride in the company's accomplishments in the U.S. market. Riding a wave of loyal baby boomers who had grown up with its Toyota and Lexus models, the company had become one of the nation's most powerful automobile brands.

However, as the baby boomers aged, the average age of the Toyota customer had risen as well. The median Toyota buyer was 49; the median Lexus buyer, 54. Too few younger customers were lining up to buy Toyotas. Gen Yers by the millions were now reaching driving age, and Toyota wasn't speaking their language. In fact, Toyota's strong reputation among the baby boomers for quality, efficiency, and value had translated to more youthful consumers as, well, "stodgy." Toyota tried to appeal to Gen Y with three vehicles in its Genesis Project: the frumpy Echo, an edgy Celica, and a pricey but impractical MR2 Spider. Each had failed to score with young people.

So, in the early 2000s, Toyota went back to the drawing board. The challenge was to keep Gen Y from seeing Toyota as "old people trying to make a young person's car." Success depended on understanding this new generation of buyers, a segment of strangers to most car marketers. "They demand authenticity, respect for their time, and products built just for them," observed a senior Toyota executive. "They are in their early 20s, new to us, and have changed every category they have touched so far. It's the most diverse generation ever seen."

The search for a new, more youthful model began in Toyota's own driveway. Following orders to "loosen up," Toyota engineers in Japan had designed and successfully introduced a boxy microvan, the bB, and a five-door hatchback, the "ist" (pronounced "east"). The company decided to rename these vehicles and introduce them in the United States. Thus was born Toyota's Gen Y brand, the Scion (Sigh-un). Soon after, Toyota launched the Scion tC coupe, which

adds more power and driving pleasure. In the Scion, Toyota created not just a new car brand, but new marketing approaches as well.

In late May 2003, young Toyota reps sporting goatees and sunglasses have set up shop near a major intersection in San Francisco's Haight-Ashbury district. Standing under banners heralding the new Scion brand, with hip-hop music blaring in the background, the reps encourage young passersby to test drive two new models, the Scion xA hatchback and the Scion xB van.

This was the opening round in a campaign to finally solve the Gen Y riddle. It signaled the most unorthodox new-car campaign in the company's 70-year history—one that was edgy, urban, and underground. To speak to Gen Y, Toyota employed guerrilla tactics. Its young marketing team put up posters with slogans such as "No Clone Zone" and "Ban Normality," even projecting those slogans onto buildings at night. It held "ride-and-drive" events to generate spontaneous test-drives by

To target Gen Yers with their "built-just-for-them" preferences, Toyota positioned the Scion on personalization. "Personalization begins here—what moves you?"

taking its cars to potential customers instead of waiting for them to find their way to showrooms. It put brochures in alternative publications such as *Urb* and *Tokion*, and sponsored events at venues ranging from hip-hop nightclubs and urban pubs to library lawns.

Toyota assigned Ahmed and Brian Bolain, two young members of its product development staff, to head the U.S. promotional campaign. Understanding the "built-just-for-them" preferences of the Gen Y target market, Ahmed and Bolain decided to position the Scion on *personalization*. They appealed to the new youth-culture club of "tuners," young fans of tricked-out vehicles (such as BMW's wildly successful Mini Cooper) who wanted to customize their cars from bumper to bumper. "We saw that the tuner phenomenon was really spreading, and took that idea of customization to a totally different level," Ahmed notes. "It comes back to that thing of rational versus emotional," observes Bolain. "Scion buyers have all the rational demands of a Toyota buyer, but they also want more fun, personality, and character."

So, along with all of the traditional Toyota features—like lots of airbags, remote keyless entry, and a 160-watt Pioneer stereo with MP3 capability—the Scion offers lots of room for individual self-expression. The staff worked with after-market auto-parts suppliers to develop specially designed Scion add-ons. To create their own one-of-a-kind cars, customers can select from 40 different accessory products, such as LED interior lighting and illuminated cup holders, wake-the-dead stereo systems, and stiffer shocks. As Bolain points out, "[We wanted the Scion to be a] blank canvas on which the consumer can make the car what they would like it to be."

Toyota dealers who agree to sell Scions provide special areas in their showrooms where customers can relax, check out the cars, and create their own customized Scions on computers linked to Scion's Web site. Scion buyers do, indeed, customize their cars. The Scion xA and Scion xB start at "no haggle" prices around $13,000 and $14,000, respectively. But 48 percent of Scion buyers spend another $1,000 to $3,000 to customize their cars. Two-thirds of buyers use the Scion Web site to configure the car they want before ever walking into the dealership.

How is Toyota's Scion strategy working? The California launch was so successful that Toyota quickly rolled out the Scion across the U.S., finishing the process in June 2004. Scion blew past its first-year, 60,000-unit sales target by mid-2004, selling 100,000 units for the year. Toyota sold nearly 160,000 Scions in 2005 and sales remain brisk. Most important, the Scion is bringing a new generation of buyers into the Toyota family. Eighty percent of Scion buyers have never before owned a Toyota. The average age of a Scion buyer is 31, the youngest in the automotive industry. This may be overstated, given that many parents are buying the car for their kids.

However, success brings new challenges. For example, according to an industry analyst, Gen Y consumers "disdain commercialism and don't really want 'their brand' to be discovered." To maintain its appeal to these young buyers, as the brand becomes more mainstream, Scion will have to keep its models and messages fresh and honest. Says VP Jim Farley, "We want to [reach out to youthful buyers] without shouting 'Buy This Car.'"

Sources:

Quotes from Lillie Guyer, "Scion Connects in Out-of-Way Places," *Advertising Age*, February 21, 2005, p. 38. Also see Brett Corbin, "Toyota's Scion Line Banks on Tech-Savvy Younger Drivers," *Business First*, June 18, 2004, p. 11; Nick Kurczewski, "Who's Your Daddy? Staid Toyota Gets a Hip Implant," *New York Times*, July 25, 2004, p. 12; Patrick Paternie, "Driven by Personality," *Los Angeles Times*, January 6, 2005, p. E34; Karl Greenberg, "Dawn Ahmed," *Brandweek*, April 11, 2005, p. 33; Chris Woodyard, "Outside-the-Box Scion Scores Big with Young Drivers," May 3, 2005, accessed at www.detnews.com/2005/autosinsider/0505/03/1auto-170121.htm; Mark Rechtin, "Scion's Delimma: Be Hip—But Avoid the Mainstream," *Automotive News*, May 22, 2006, pp. 42-45; and Julie Bosman, "Hey, Kid, You Want to Buy A Scion?" *New York Times*, June 14, 2006, p. C2.

Changing Consumer Spending Patterns

Food, housing, and transportation use up the most household income. However, consumers at different income levels have different spending patterns. As family income rises, the percentage spent on food declines, the percentage spent on housing remains about constant (except for such utilities as gas, electricity, and public services, which decrease), and both the percentage spent on most other categories and that devoted to savings increase.

Changes in major economic variables such as income, cost of living, interest rates, and savings and borrowing patterns have a large impact on the marketplace. Companies watch these variables by using economic forecasting. Businesses do not have to be wiped out by an economic downturn or caught short in a boom. With adequate warning, they can take advantage of changes in the economic environment.

Natural Environment

Natural environment
Natural resources that are needed as inputs by marketers or that are affected by marketing activities.

The **natural environment** involves the natural resources that are needed as inputs by marketers or that are affected by marketing activities. Environmental concerns have grown. In many cities around the world, air and water pollution have reached dangerous levels. World concern continues to mount about the possibilities of global warming.

Figure 3.5
The natural environment

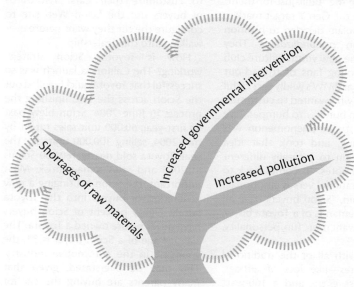

Natural Environment

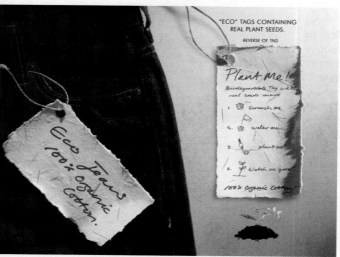

In response to ecological concerns, Levi Strauss and Co. has designed the Levi's® Eco jeans made of 100% organic cotton. The product tag is made of 100% recycled paper. (www.levistrauss.com)

Marketers should be aware of several trends in the natural environment (see **Figure 3.5**). The first involves growing *shortages of raw materials*. Air pollution chokes many of the world's large cities, and water shortages are already a big problem in some parts of the world. Renewable resources, such as forests and food, also have to be used wisely. Nonrenewable resources, such as oil, coal, and various minerals, pose a serious problem. Firms making products that require these scarce resources face large cost increases, even if the materials remain available.

A second environmental trend is *increased pollution*. Industry will almost always damage the quality of the natural environment. Consider the disposal of chemical and nuclear wastes; the quantity of chemical pollutants in the soil and food supply; and the littering of the environment with nonbiodegradable bottles, plastics, and other packaging materials.

A third trend is *increased government intervention* in natural resource management. The governments of different countries vary in their concern and efforts to promote a clean environment. Some, like the German government, vigorously pursue environmental quality. Others, especially many poorer nations, do little about pollution, largely because they lack the needed funds or political will.

Concern for the natural environment has spawned the green movement. Today, enlightened companies develop *environmentally sustainable* strategies and practices. They are responding to consumer demands with more environmentally responsible products. For example, GE is using its "ecomagination" to create products for a better world—cleaner aircraft engines, cleaner locomotives, cleaner fuel technologies. Levi Strauss and Co. has Eco jeans made from organic cotton.

Other companies are developing recyclable or biodegradable packaging, recycled materials and components, better pollution controls, and more energy-efficient operations. For example, HP is pushing legislation to force recycling of old TVs, computers, and other electronic gear:[15]

Computer manufacturers such as HP and Apple are now more active in recycling old gear.

HP wants your old PCs back. Teaming up with greens and retailers, Hewlett-Packard took on IBM, Apple Computer, and several major TV manufacturers, which were resisting recycling programs because of the costs. Aided by HP's energetic lobbying, the greens persuaded state lawmakers to adopt a landmark program that forces electronics companies to foot the bill for recycling their old equipment. With HP's help, the movement to recycle electronic refuse, or "e-waste," is now spreading across the nation. HP's efforts have made it the darling of environmentalists, but its agenda isn't entirely altruistic. Take-back laws play to the company's strategic strengths. For decades the computer maker has invested in recycling systems, giving it a head start against competitors. Last year, HP recycled more than 70,000 tons of products, the equivalent of about 10 percent of company sales. And it collected more than 2.5 million units of hardware to be refurbished for resale or donation. No other electronics maker has a recycling and resale program on this scale.

Thus, companies are recognizing the link between a healthy ecology and a healthy economy. They are learning that environmentally responsible actions can also be good business.

Technological Environment

The **technological environment** is perhaps the most dramatic force shaping our destiny. Technology has released such wonders as antibiotics, robotic surgery, miniaturized electronics, laptop computers, and the Internet. It also has released such horrors as nuclear missiles, chemical weapons, and assault rifles. It has released such mixed blessings as the automobile, television, and credit cards.

Technological environment
Forces that create new technologies, creating new product and market opportunities.

Our attitude toward technology depends on whether we are more impressed with its wonders or its blunders. For example, what would you think about having tiny little transmitters implanted in the products you buy that would allow tracking products from their point of production through use and disposal? On the one hand, it would provide many advantages to both buyers and sellers. On the other hand, it could be a bit scary. These tiny radio-frequency identification (RFID) transmitters—or "smart chips"— can be embedded in the products you buy. Beyond benefits to consumers, the RFID chips also give producers and retailers an amazing new way to track their products electronically—anywhere in the world, anytime, automatically—from factories, to warehouses, to retail shelves, to recycling centers. Procter & Gamble plans to have the chips on products in broad distribution as soon as 2008. And at the request of mega-retailers such as Wal-Mart, suppliers have begun placing RFID tags on selected products.[16]

RFID tags give producers and retailers a new way to track their product electronically.

Figure 3.6 highlights trends in the technological environment that may affect marketing. New technologies create new markets and opportunities. They replace older technology. Companies that do not keep up will soon find their products outdated and miss new product and market opportunities. Thus, marketers should watch the technological environment closely.

TECHNOLOGICAL ENVIRONMENT

- New markets and opportunities
- Safety of new, complex products and technology
- Higher research costs
- Longer times between ideas and product introduction

Figure 3.6
The technological environment

As products and technology become more complex, the public needs to know that these are safe. Thus, government agencies investigate and ban potentially unsafe products. Such regulations have resulted in much higher research costs and in longer times between new-product ideas and their introduction. Marketers should be aware of these regulations when applying new technologies and developing new products.

Political Environment

Marketing decisions are strongly affected by developments in the political environment. The **political environment** consists of laws, government agencies, and pressure groups that influence or limit various organizations and individuals in a given society (see **Figure 3.7**).

Political environment
Laws, government agencies, and pressure groups that influence and limit various organizations and individuals in a given society.

POLITICAL ENVIRONMENT

- Increasing legislation
- Changing government agency enforcement

- More socially responsible behavior
- More cause-related marketing

Figure 3.7
The political environment

Legislation Regulating Business

Business legislation has three main purposes: to protect companies from unfair competition, to protect consumer from unfair business practices, and to protect the interests of society from unbridled business behavior.

In terms of company protection, regulations on counterfeiting are particularly pertinent for Asian businesses. Asian exporters are expected to face tougher European Union customs controls. Popular counterfeited brands include Christian Dior, Louis Vuitton, Timberland, and Rolex. At Beijing's Silk Market and Bangkok's MBK market, counterfeit products are easily obtained. Although the production and sale of counterfeits is illegal, the rules against purchasing them are vague. While it is technically illegal to buy counterfeits, it is not a crime if a buyer is not aware or claims not to know the items are fake, or is not buying them for trade or business.

The popularity of counterfeit brands in Asia has proven to be a growing problem for companies. Purses and bags like these are easily available in markets in Asia.

Even Disneyland is not spared from being counterfeited. At Shijingshan Amusement Park, Beijing, its ad says Disneyland is too far. Solution? Build a counterfeit Disneyland complete with Cinderella's castle and mascots dressed as Mickey, Snow White, and other copyrighted characters. Disney has filed a case at the World Trade Organization. However, many Chinese do not see using these characters as a big problem. They do not think it should only be Disney's right. Such a view and the lax law enforcement have seen the counterfeit goods industry become a key part of the Chinese economy.[17]

The second purpose of government regulation is to *protect consumers* from unfair business practices. Some firms, if left alone, would make shoddy products, invade consumer privacy, tell lies in their advertising, and deceive consumers through their packaging and pricing. Thailand requires food processors selling national brands to also market low-price brands so that low-income consumers can find economy brands.

The third purpose of government regulation is to *protect the interests of society* against unrestrained business behavior. Profitable business activity does not always create a better quality of life. Regulation arises to ensure that firms take responsibility for the social costs of their production or products.

Increased Emphasis on Ethics and Socially Responsible Actions

Written regulations cannot possibly cover all potential marketing abuses, and existing laws are often difficult to enforce. However, beyond written laws and regulations, business is also governed by social codes and rules of professional ethics.

Socially responsible behavior

Enlightened companies encourage their managers to look beyond what the regulatory system allows and simply "do the right thing." These socially responsible firms actively seek out ways to protect the long-run interests of their consumers and the environment.

The recent rash of business scandals and increased concerns about the environment have created fresh interest in the issues of ethics and social responsibility. Almost every aspect of marketing involves such issues. Unfortunately, because these issues usually involve conflicting interests, well-meaning people can honestly disagree about the right course of action in a given situation. Thus, many industrial and professional trade associations have suggested codes of ethics. And more companies are now developing policies, guidelines, and other responses to complex social responsibility issues.

The boom in Internet marketing has created a new set of social and ethical issues. Critics worry most about online privacy issues. There has been an explosion in the amount of personal digital data available. Users, themselves, supply some of it. They voluntarily place highly private information on social networking sites such as MySpace or on genealogy sites, which are easily searched by anyone with a PC.

Users often voluntarily place information about themselves on social networking sites such as MySpace and Facebook, which are easily searched by anyone with a PC.

However, much of the information is systematically developed by businesses seeking to learn more about their customers, often without consumers realizing that they are under the microscope. Legitimate businesses plant cookies on consumers' PCs and collect, analyze, and share digital consumer information from every mouse click consumers make at their Web sites. Critics are concerned that companies may now know *too* much, and that some companies might use digital data to take unfair advantage of consumers. Although most companies fully disclose their Internet privacy policies, and most work to use data to benefit their customers, abuses do occur. As a result, consumer advocates and policymakers are taking action to protect consumer privacy.

Milk can rebuild what the tsunami has destroyed in Aceh Indonesia.

Spread the goodness with MARIGOLD UHT Milk. For every empty pack you bring, we'll make a donation to help homeless tsunami victims build a stronger foundation. For more details, visit foodkit.org.sg today.

MARIGOLD
For health. For life.

Marigold launched a campaign to help the tsunami victims in Aceh, Indonesia. For every empty pack of Marigold UHT Milk brought to Marigold, it will make a donation to help the homeless tsunami victims. (www.mdi.com.sg)

Cultural environment
Institutions and other forces that affect society's basic values, perceptions, preferences, and behaviors.

Cause-related marketing

To exercise their social responsibility and build more positive images, many companies are linking themselves to worthwhile causes. Cause-related marketing has become a primary form of corporate giving. It lets companies "do well by doing good" by linking purchases of the company's products or services with fund-raising for worthwhile causes or charitable organizations. During the tsunamic disaster in Asia, companies such as McDonald's and Marigold raised funds to provide relief to those affected.

Cause-related marketing has stirred some controversy. Critics worry that cause-related marketing is more a strategy for selling than a strategy for giving—that "cause-related" marketing is really "cause-exploitative" marketing. Thus, companies using cause-related marketing might find themselves walking a fine line between increased sales and an improved image, and facing charges of exploitation.

Cultural Environment

The **cultural environment** is made up of institutions and other forces that affect a society's basic values, perceptions, preferences, and behaviors. People grow up in a particular society that shapes their basic beliefs and values. They absorb a worldview that defines their relationships with others. The following cultural characteristics can affect marketing decision making.

Persistence of Cultural Values

People in a given society hold many beliefs and values. Their core beliefs and values have a high degree of persistence. For example, most people believe in working, getting married, giving to charity, and being honest. These beliefs shape more specific attitudes and behaviors found in everyday life. *Core* beliefs and values are passed on from parents to children and are reinforced by schools, religious organizations, businesses, and governments. For instance, Starbucks created a storm when it opened a café in Beijing's Forbidden City. A renewed sensitivity to their heritage led consumers to protest that Starbucks had nothing to do with Chinese tradition and that a tea shop would be more appropriate. Starbucks has since closed this outlet.

Secondary beliefs and values are more open to change. Believing in marriage is a core belief; believing that people should get married early in life is a secondary belief. Marketers have some chance of changing secondary values but little chance of changing core values. For example, family-planning marketers could argue more effectively that people should get married later in life than that they should not get married at all.

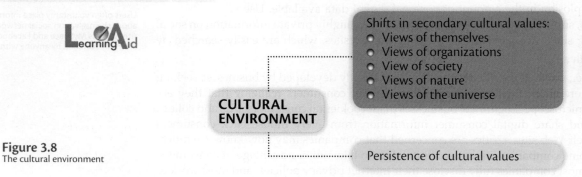

Shifts in secondary cultural values:
- Views of themselves
- Views of organizations
- View of society
- Views of nature
- Views of the universe

CULTURAL ENVIRONMENT

Persistence of cultural values

Figure 3.8
The cultural environment

Shifts in Secondary Cultural Values

Although core values are fairly persistent, cultural swings do take place. Consider the impact of popular music groups, movie personalities, and other celebrities on young people's hairstyling and clothing norms. Marketers want to predict cultural shifts in order to spot new opportunities or threats.

The major cultural values of a society are expressed in people's views of themselves and others, as well as in their views of organizations, society, nature, and the universe.

People's views of themselves

People vary in their emphasis on serving themselves versus serving others. Some people seek personal pleasure, wanting fun, change, and escape. Others seek self-realization through religion, recreation, or the avid pursuit of careers or other life goals. People use products, brands, and services as a means of self-expression, and they buy products and services that match their views of themselves. Marketers can target their products and services based on such self-views. Take the example of Levi's in Japan.

> Levi's found that Japanese teenagers were cynical of advertising and may perceive Levi's jeans as just another pair of jeans. Levi's thus launched its Engineered Jeans with Japanese pop star Takuya Kimura. This was followed by a campaign involving Japanese teenagers expressing their creativity, individuality, and originality. A photocopier, big enough to accommodate a human being, was used. Pop stars and Levi's customers were invited to hop onto the copier and create their own completely original poster ad. Each printout became an instant point-of-sale poster expressing the customer's and Levi's view of themselves as original and unique. The campaign was a success as Levi's brand image as an "individual" rose from 29 to 44 percent over the campaign period.

People's views of others

How people view others and hence, how others view you also influences consumption. As a collectivistic culture, Asian consumers tend to be particularly susceptible to such external influences. In Korea, keeping up with the Joneses is a serious business.

Asian consumers tend to be particularly susceptible to external influences. In Korea, keeping up with the Joneses is a serious business, and a child's first birthday is a major celebration.

> In Seoul, a child's first birthday is too important to be celebrated at home. Instead, a party at a five-star restaurant is organized with each guest receiving an expensive door gift. The bill for the birthday bash may cost up to half a year's earnings. The lack of money does not deter many Koreans from trying to keep up with the Kims. It illustrates the Korean obsession for dressing up, looking good, and giving the impression of being well off. There is also the obsession with "saving face." Businesses have exploited this obsession with stores selling second-hand luxury goods and renting out expensive gowns and luxury bags. For those who may fret over a small turnout at a social occasion, there are companies that rent out "friends" who show up and sit at tables. At one such wedding dinner, the groom's father hired 20 "guests" to avert the humiliation of a low turnout.[18]

People's views of organizations

People vary in their attitudes toward corporations, government agencies, trade unions, universities, and other organizations. By and large, people are willing to work for major organizations and expect them, in turn, to carry out society's work. Many people today see work not as a source of satisfaction but as a means to earn money to enjoy their non-work hours. This trend suggests that organizations need to find new ways to win consumer and employee confidence.

People's views of society

People vary in their attitudes toward their society; patriots defend it, reformers want to change it, malcontents want to leave it. People's orientation to their society influences their consumption patterns and attitudes toward the marketplace. For instance, American patriotism surged following the September 11th terrorist attacks and the Iraq war.

People's views of nature

People vary in their attitudes toward the natural world. Some feel ruled by it, others feel in harmony with it, and still others seek to master it. A long-term trend has been people's growing mastery over nature through technology and the belief that nature is bountiful. More recently, however, people have recognized that nature is finite and fragile, that it can be destroyed or spoiled by human activities. Business has responded by offering more products and services catering to such interests. For example, food producers have found fast-growing markets for natural and organic foods. In Asia where there are frequent food scares such as contaminated baby foods to pesticides in apples, some Chinese have turned to organically grown food.

People's views of the universe

Finally, people vary in their beliefs about the origin of the universe and their place in it. Although most Asians practice religion, religious conviction and practice have been dropping off gradually through the years. There is also a renewed interest in spirituality, perhaps as a part of a broader search for a new inner purpose. People have been moving away from materialism and dog-eat-dog ambition to seek more permanent values—family, community, earth, faith—and a more certain grasp of right and wrong.

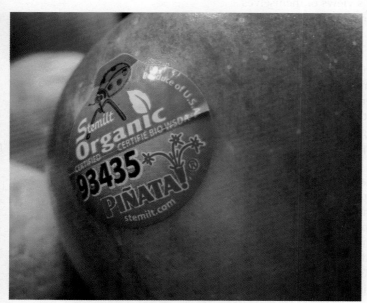

People's views of nature – Organically grown products including rice cakes, tea, chili, fruit, vegetables, and meat are slowly becoming popular in Asia.

Responding to the Marketing Environment

Someone once observed, "There are three kinds of companies: those who make things happen, those who watch things happen, and those who wonder what's happened."[19] Many companies view the marketing environment as an uncontrollable element to which they must react and adapt. They passively accept the marketing environment and do not try to change it. They analyze the environmental forces and design strategies that will help the company avoid the threats and take advantage of the opportunities the environment provides.

Other companies take a *proactive* stance toward the marketing environment. Rather than simply watching and reacting, these firms take aggressive actions to affect the publics and forces in their marketing environment. Such companies hire lobbyists to influence legislation affecting their industries and stage media events to gain favorable press coverage. They run advertorials (ads expressing editorial points of view) to shape public opinion. They press lawsuits and file complaints with regulators to keep competitors in line, and they form contractual agreements to better control their distribution channels.

By taking action, companies can often overcome seemingly uncontrollable environmental events. For example, whereas some companies view the ceaseless online rumor mill as something over which they have no control, others work proactively to prevent or counter negative word of mouth:[20]

One e-mail said that a former government lawyer knew a guy whose dog had to be put to sleep because he walked on a floor cleaned with Procter & Gamble's Swiffer WetJet, licked his paws and developed liver disease. Although the claim was proven false by toxicologists, it has been neither quick nor easy for P&G to squelch the story. But P&G learned long ago that it was best to face a false rumor head-on. Years before, P&G endured a nasty rumor that the stars-and-moon trademark the company then displayed on its packaging was linked with Satanism. The rumor was disseminated through fliers and, much later, e-mails. P&G officials were even claimed to have appeared on TV talk shows confirming the rumor. Rather than letting the rumor lie, P&G reacted strongly by soliciting support from a range of religious leaders as well as from its employees, who worked to convince members of their own churches that the rumors were false. It publicized letters from the TV networks saying that no P&G executives had appeared on the TV shows. Once P&G identified people it said had spread the rumor—some of whom it said worked for competitors—it pressed charges to get them to confess and stop distributing the information. Some did confess, and litigation is still pending against others.

Some companies view the rumor mill as something they cannot control, while others, like Procter & Gamble, work proactively to prevent or counter negative word of mouth.

Marketing management cannot always control environmental forces. In many cases, it must settle for simply watching and reacting to the environment. For example, a company would have little success trying to influence geographic population shifts, the economic environment, or major cultural values. But whenever possible, smart marketing managers will take a *proactive* rather than *reactive* approach to the marketing environment.

REVIEWING THE CONCEPTS

In this chapter and the next two chapters, you'll examine the environments of marketing and how companies analyze these environments to better understand the marketplace and consumers. Companies must constantly watch and manage the *marketing environment* in order to seek opportunities and ward off threats. The marketing environment consists of all the actors and forces influencing the company's ability to transact business effectively with its target market.

1 Describe the environmental forces that affect the company's ability to serve its customers.

The company's *microenvironment* consists of other actors close to the company that combine to form the company's value delivery network or that affect its ability to serve its customers. It includes the company's *internal environment*—its several departments and management levels—as it influences marketing decision making. *Marketing-channel firms*—suppliers and marketing intermediaries, including resellers, physical distribution firms, marketing services agencies, and financial intermediaries—cooperate to create customer value. Five types of customer *markets* include consumer, business, reseller, government, and international markets. *Competitors* vie with the company in an effort to serve customers better. Finally, various *publics* have an actual or potential interest in or impact on the company's ability to meet its objectives.

The *macroenvironment* consists of larger societal forces that affect the entire microenvironment. The six forces making up the company's macroenvironment include demographic, economic, natural, technological, political, and cultural forces. These forces shape opportunities and pose threats to the company.

2 Explain how changes in the demographic and economic environments affect marketing decisions.

Demography is the study of the characteristics of human populations. Today's *demographic environment* shows a changing age structure, shifting family profiles, geographic population shifts, a better-educated and more white-collar population, and increasing diversity. The *economic environment* consists of factors that affect buying power and patterns. The economic environment is characterized by more consumer concern for value and shifting consumer spending patterns. Today's squeezed consumers are seeking greater value—just the right combination of good quality and service at a fair price. The distribution of income also is shifting. The rich have grown richer, the middle class has shrunk, and the poor have remained poor, leading to a two-tiered market. Many companies now tailor their marketing offers to two different markets—the affluent and the less affluent.

3 Identify the major trends in the firm's natural and technological environments.

The *natural environment* shows three major trends: shortages of certain raw materials, higher pollution levels, and more government intervention in natural resource management. Environmental concerns create marketing opportunities for alert companies. The *technological environment* creates both opportunities and challenges. Companies that fail to keep up with technological change will miss out on new product and marketing opportunities.

4 **Explain the key changes in the political and cultural environments.**

The *political environment* consists of laws, agencies, and groups that influence or limit marketing actions. The political environment has undergone three changes that affect marketing worldwide: increasing legislation regulating business, strong government agency enforcement, and greater emphasis on ethics and socially responsible actions. The *cultural environment* is made up of institutions and forces that affect a society's values, perceptions, preferences, and behaviors. The environment shows trends toward digital "cocooning," a lessening trust of institutions, increasing patriotism, greater appreciation for nature, a new spiritualism, and the search for more meaningful and enduring values.

5 **Discuss how companies can react to the marketing environment.**

Companies can passively accept the marketing environment as an uncontrollable element to which they must adapt, avoiding threats and taking advantage of opportunities as they arise. Or they can take a *proactive* stance, working to change the environment rather than simply reacting to it. Whenever possible, companies should try to be proactive rather than reactive.

REVIEWING THE KEY TERMS

Baby boomers 64
Cultural environment 74
Demography 63
Economic environment 67
Generation X 65
Generation Y 65
Macroenvironment 60
Marketing environment 60

Marketing intermediaries 61
Microenvironment 60
Natural environment 70
Political environment 72
Public 62
Technological environment 71

DISCUSSING THE CONCEPTS

1. Assume you are a marketing manager for an automobile company. Your job is to reposition an SUV model that was once identified as a "fuel guzzler." The model now comes with a superefficient, nonpolluting hybrid engine. Which of the seven types of publics discussed in the chapter would have the greatest impact on your plans to the more fuel-efficient model?

2. What leading demographic factors must an Internet portal consider when marketing its products? Why is each factor important?

3. In response to the depletion of non-renewable resources, some Asian agri-businesses like Wilmar have begun producing biofuels derived from palm oil and the like. On the other hand, several of these firms have also been criticized for degrading the environment using slash-and-burn techniques in clearing land for their plantations. Discuss how forces in the natural environment have shaped these agri-businesses and how they can respond going forward.

4. Is it a certainty that a company will lose out on new opportunities if it does not keep up with new technology? Explain. Can you think of an industry segment where technology may not play an important role?

5. What can a mobile phones marketer do to take a more proactive approach to the changes in the marketing environment? Discuss specific forces, including macroenvironmental and microenvironmental forces.

6. Asian culture has been affected by products from Hollywood, including movies and television shows. Choose an American television show airing over a local station and explain how it might affect the cultural environment in your country.portal consider when marketing its products? Why is each factor important?

APPLYING THE CONCEPTS

1. Go to www.shonenjump.com and you will see a Web site devoted to Japanese anime and manga. In fact, these products are gaining in popularity. What environmental forces are involved in the increased demand for this Japanese entertainment?

2. Most well-known cause-related marketing campaigns are launched by companies with substantial resources. In a small group, discuss how smaller companies with more limited resources can implement successful cause-related marketing efforts. How can such organizations help the charities with which they partner while successfully promoting their own products and services?

FOCUS ON TECHNOLOGY

Television shows over the mobile phone. Crazy? In the U.S., "mobisodes," two-minute TV episodes, are being produced exclusively for mobile phones. Services such as Verizon's Vcast let subscribers watch TV or stream content for a monthly fee. Their target? The younger segment of the Generation Y demographic—the growing 57 percent of U.S. teens aged 13 to 17 who now own mobile phones. This group displays the most intense connectivity to their phones and the most interest in new features.

1. Explain why younger Gen Yers might be more likely to adapt new mobile phone technologies as compared to other demographic groups.

2. What other macroenvironmental and microenvironmental forces might affect the growth of mobile TV?

3. How can other marketers use mobile marketing to communicate with and promote to consumers?

FOCUS ON ETHICS

In July 2007, Philip Morris launched a Marlboro cigarette flavored with cloves in Indonesia, seeking to boost sales in the world's fifth largest tobacco market behind China, the U.S., Russia, and Japan. Almost two-thirds of adult males in this country of 230 million smoke, and growing numbers of females are joining them. Ninety percent of Indonesian smokers choose cigarettes blended with cloves called *kretek*. Their distinctive sweet aroma permeates cafes, offices, and public spaces across Indonesia. Philip Morris' move underscores the importance of Indonesia and other overseas markets as government bans and increased awareness of the health risks of smoking have hit sales in Europe and the U.S. "A Marlboro *kretek* makes sense," says Martin King, president director of local cigarette manufacturer Sampoerna, which Philip Morris bought in 2006. "What consumers are telling us

is that they like Marlboro … but they also want *kretek*." The Marlboro Mix 9 is the strongest Marlboro currently on the market, packing 1.8 milligrams of nicotine and 30 milligrams of tar. This is comparable to other full-strength *kretek* sold in Indonesia, and twice as much as regular Marlboros sold elsewhere in the world. King notes that no cigarettes were safe, but there was no evidence that *kretek* were more dangerous than regular cigarettes. King was confident Mix 9 would sell well, even though some 500 new brands were launched in Indonesia in 2006.[21]

1. What prominent environmental forces come into play in this situation?

2. Evaluate Philip Morris' launch of the Mix 9 in Indonesia from a commercial and an ethical perspective.

VIDEO CASE

American Express

Understanding consumers and their needs can be a challenge. As the American population diversifies, and as consumers redefine their values and preferences, marketers work to provide relevant products and services that meet consumers' changing needs and wants. For American Express, keeping up with environmental shifts translates into creating new marketing offers. American Express issued its first charge card in 1958. Within five years, it had more than one million cards in use. Eight years later, the company introduced the American Express Gold Card.

The company now offers more than 20 consumer cards and 14 small-business cards, in addition to its customizable corporate cards. Some cards target very specific consumers. For example, the IN:CHICAGO, IN:NYC, and IN:LA cards offer cardholders special perks, including saving 10 percent at select retailers, spas, and nightclubs; skipping lines at some of these cities' hottest clubs; access to select VIP rooms; and savings on concert tickets. By targeting such specific consumers, American Express builds strong relationships with the right customers.

After viewing the video featuring American Express, answer the following questions about the marketing environment.

1. Visit the American Express Web site (*www.americanexpress.com*) to learn more about the different cards that American Express offers. Select three of the macroenvironmental forces discussed in the chapter. How do the different card options reflect the changes in those forces?

2. What sections of the Web site reflect American Express's efforts to deal with the various publics in its microenvironment?

3. Is American Express taking a proactive approach to managing its marketing environment? How?

COMPANY CASE

Toyota Prius: Leading a Wave of Hybrids

Americans love their cars. In a country where SUVs sell briskly and the biggest sport is stockcar racing, you wouldn't expect a small, hybrid, sluggish vehicle to sell well. Despite such expectations, Honda successfully introduced the Insight in 1999 as a 2000 model. Toyota closely followed, bringing the 2001 Prius to market one year later. Introducing a fuel sipper in a market where vehicle size and horsepower reigned led one Toyota executive to profess, "Frankly, it was one of the biggest crapshoots I've ever been involved in." Considering these issues, it is nothing short of amazing that a mere five years later, the Prius is such a runaway success that former Toyota Motor Sales U.S.A. President Jim Press dubbed it "the hottest car we've ever had."

The Nuts and Bolts of the Prius

Like other hybrids currently available or in development, the Prius (pronounced PREE-us, not PRY-us) combines a gas engine with an electric motor. Different hybrid vehicles employ this combination of power sources in different ways to boost both fuel efficiency and power. The Prius runs on only the electric motor when starting up and under initial acceleration. At roughly 15 mph, the gas engine kicks in. This means that the auto gets power from only the battery at low speeds, and from both the gas engine and electric motor during heavy acceleration. Once up to speed, the gas engine sends power directly to the wheels and, through the generator, to the electric motor or battery. When braking, energy from the slowing wheels—energy that is wasted in a conventional car—is sent back through the electric motor to charge the battery. At a stop, the gas engine shuts off, saving fuel. When starting up and operating at low speeds, the auto does not make noise, which seems eerie to some drivers and to pedestrians who don't hear it coming!

The original Prius was a small, cramped compact with a dull design. It had 114 horsepower—70 from its four-cylinder gas engine and 44 from the electric motor. It went from 0 to 60 in a woeful 14.5 seconds. But it got 42 miles per gallon. Although the second-generation Prius, introduced as a 2004 model, benefited from a modest power increase, the car was still hardly a muscle car. But there were countless other improvements. The sleek, Asian-inspired design was much better looking than the first-generation Prius and came in seven colors. The interior was roomy and practical, with plenty of rear legroom and gobs of storage space.

The new Prius also provided expensive touches typically found only in luxury vehicles. A single push button brought the car to life. A seven-inch energy monitor touch screen displayed fuel consumption, outside temperature, and battery charge level. It also indicated when the car was running on gas, electricity, regenerated energy, or a combination of these. Multiple screens within the monitor also provided controls for air conditioning, audio, and a satellite navigation system. But perhaps the most important improvement was an increase in fuel efficiency to a claimed 60 miles per gallon in city driving.

A Runaway Success

Apparently, consumers liked the improvements. In its inaugural year, the Prius saw moderate sales of just over 15,000 units—not bad considering Toyota put minimal promotional effort into the new vehicle. But for 2005, more than 107,000 Priuses were sold in the U.S. alone, making it Toyota's third-best-selling passenger car following the Camry and Corolla. Perhaps more significantly, Toyota announced that as of April 2006, the Prius had achieved a major milestone, having sold over 500,000 units worldwide.

The rapid increase in demand for the Prius has created a rare automotive phenomenon. During a period when most automotive companies have offered substantial incentives to move vehicles, many Toyota dealers have had no problem getting premiums of up to $5,000 over sticker price for the Prius. By June 2004, waiting lists for the Prius stretched to six months or more. At one point, spots on dealers' waiting lists were being auctioned on eBay for $500. By 2006, the Prius had become the "hottest" car in the U.S., based on industry metrics of time spent on dealer lots, sales incentives, and average sale price relative to sticker price. In fact, demand for new Priuses is currently so strong, that the price of a used 2005 Prius with 20,000 miles is $25,970, more than $4,500 higher than the original sticker price.

There are many reasons for the success of the Prius. For starters, Toyota's targeting strategy has been spot-on from the beginning. It focused first on early adopters, techies who were attracted by the car's advanced technology. Such buyers not only bought the car, but found ways to modify it by hacking into the Prius's computer system. Soon, owners were sharing their hacking secrets through chat rooms such as Priusenvy.com, boasting such modifications as using the dashboard display screen to play video games, show files from a laptop, watch TV, and look at images taken by a rear-view camera. One savvy owner found a way to plug the Prius into a wall socket and boost fuel efficiency to as much as 100 miles per gallon.

By 2004, Toyota had skimmed off the market of techies and adopters. It knew that the second-generation Prius needed to appeal to a wider market. Toyota anticipated that environmentally conscious consumers as well as those desiring more fuel efficiency would be drawn to the vehicle. To launch the new Prius, Toyota spent more than $40 million spread over media in consumer-oriented magazines and TV. Toyota hit the nail right on the head. In the summer of 2004, gasoline prices began to rise—going to over $2 a gallon in some locations. By the summer of 2005, gas prices had skyrocketed to over $3 a gallon. Result? Buyers moved toward smaller SUVs, cars, and hybrids while sales of full-sized SUVs such as the Ford Expedition, Chevy Tahoe, and Hummer H2 fell significantly.

In addition to Toyota's effective targeting tactics, various external incentives have helped to spur Prius sales. For example, some states allow single-occupant hybrids in HOV (High Occupancy Vehicle) lanes. Some cities provide free parking for hybrids. But the biggest incentives contribute real dollars toward the price of the Prius, making it more affordable. Currently, the federal government gives a tax break of up to $3,150. This relief will expire in 2007, but there are various efforts to extend tax incentives for the Prius and other hybrid vehicles.

Some state governments are also offering tax incentives over and above any federal relief. The most generous is Colorado, giving a tax credit of up to $3,434. If this isn't enough, employees of certain companies can cash in for even more. Eco-friendly Timberland contributes $3,000 as well as preferred parking spaces, while Google gives employees $5,000 toward hybrids such as the Prius.

Fueling the Hybrid Craze

Although Honda's Insight was the first to market in the U.S., its sales have been miniscule compared to the Prius. Thus, after the 2006 model year, Honda will drop the Insight. Although Toyota's Japanese rival has had much better results with its Civic hybrid, its sales goal of 25,000 units for 2006 is less than one-fourth of the Prius's anticipated sales. The overall category of gas-electric vehicles in the U.S. appears to be hotter than ever, with unit sales up 140 percent from 2004 to 2005, to a total of 205,749 units. The Prius alone commands over 50 percent of the market and is largely responsible for category growth.

It appears that consumers like their green cars very green. Whereas sales of the ultra-high-mileage Prius and Civic have grown significantly each year since their introductions, less efficient (and more expensive) hybrid models such as the Honda Accord, Toyota Highlander, Ford Escape, and Mercury Mariner have had flat or even declining sales. Some analysts believe it is because consumers are doing the math and realizing that even with better fuel efficiency, they may not save money with a hybrid. In fact, a widely publicized report by *Consumer Reports* revealed that of six hybrid models studied, the Prius and the Civic were the only two to recover the price premium and save consumers money after five years and 75,000 miles.

However, although car makers are scaling back on some models, almost every one of them wants a piece of the growing pie. Ford blames the lack of success with the Escape and Mariner on a boggled promotional effort. With a lofty goal of producing 250,000 hybrids per year by 2010, it plans to put more money into campaigns for its existing models as well as introduce new models. General Motors also has big plans, beginning with the Saturn Vue Greenline, which will have the advantage of a low $2,000 price tag for the hybrid option. GM plans to extend the Saturn hybrid line to almost every vehicle in the lineup. It also plans to introduce hybrids in other divisions, including full-size trucks and SUVs. And while Subaru, Nissan, Hyundai, and Honda are all promoting upcoming hybrid models, Audi, BMW, and numerous others are busy developing hybrid vehicles of their own.

Even with all the activity from these automotive brands, Toyota is currently the clear leader in hybrid sales and will likely be for some time to come. 2006 Prius sales have actually dropped, but only because the company has dedicated production capacity to the 2006 Camry hybrid. The supply limitation has made demand for the Prius stronger than ever. In the past, Toyota Vice Chairman Fujio Cho had asserted that the company would not open a second plant for the production of hybrids, but he has quickly changed his tune. "[Given] the way American consumers have snapped up the [Prius]," he says, "I have been urging the company, almost as a matter of strategy, to produce [it] in the U.S." Given that Toyota plans to offer hybrid versions for all vehicle classes and quadruple worldwide hybrid sales to one million vehicles by 2012, it would seem that Mr. Cho's statement is conservative.

Questions For Discussion

1. What microenvironmental factors affected the introduction and relaunch of the Toyota Prius? How well has Toyota dealt with these factors?

2. Outline the major macroenvironmental factors—demographic, economic, natural, technological, political, and cultural—that affected the introduction and relaunch of the Toyota Prius. How well has Toyota dealt with each of these factors?

3. Evaluate Toyota's marketing strategy so far. What has Toyota done well? How might it improve its strategy?

4. GM's marketing director for new ventures, Ken Stewart, says, "If you want to get a lot of hybrids on the road, you put them in vehicles that people are buying now." This tends to summarize the U.S. automakers' approach to hybrids. Would you agree with Mr. Stewart? Why or why not?

Sources:

David Kushner, "How to Hack a Hybrid," *Business 2.0 Magazine*, July 13, 2006; "Toyota Prius Reaches Sales Milestone," *Car and Driver*, June 9, 2006, accessed online at www.caranddriver. com; Thane Peterson, "Harnessing Hybrid Tax Credits," *Business Week*, June 8, 2006, accessed at www.businessweek.com; Norihiko Shirouzu, "Toyota Seeks to Improve Prius and Plans to Produce Car in U.S.," *Wall Street Journal*, May 22, 2006, p. A2; Peter Valdes-Dapena, "Mad Market for Used Fuel Sippers," *CNNMoney.com*, May 18, 2006; John D. Stoll and Gina Chon, "Consumer Drive for Hybrid Autos Is Slowing Down," *Wall Street Journal*, April 7, 2006, p. A2; Matt Nauman, "Hybrid Sales Growth Slowing," *San Jose Mercury News*, April 14, 2006; "Toyota to Offer Hybrids for All Vehicle Classes by 2012," *The Wall Street Journal*, April 1, 2006, accessed at www.wsj.com; Peter Valdes-Dapena, "Toyota Tops Hottest Cars in America," *CNNMoney. com*, March 18, 2006; David Kiley and David Welch, "Invasion of the Hybrids," *Business Week*, January 10, 2006, accessed at www.businessweek.com; "Testing Toyota's Hybrid Car," *GP*, June 7, 2004; Gary S. Vasilash, "Is Toyota Prius the Most Important 2004 Model?" *Motor Trend*, November 11, 2003, accessed online at www.motortrend.com.

Objectives

After reading this chapter, you should be able to

- explain the importance of information to the company and its understanding of the marketplace
- define the marketing information system and discuss its parts
- outline the steps in the marketing research process
- explain how companies analyze and distribute marketing information
- discuss the special issues some marketing researchers face, including public policy and ethics issues

CHAPTER 4

MANAGING MARKETING INFORMATION

Previewing the Concepts

In the previous chapter, you learned about the complex and changing marketing environment. In this chapter, we'll discuss how marketers go about understanding the marketplace and consumers. We'll look at how companies develop and manage information about important marketplace elements—about customers, competitors, products, and marketing programs. We'll examine marketing information systems designed to give managers the right information, in the right form, at the right time to help them make better marketing decisions. We'll also take a close look at the marketing research process and at some special marketing research considerations. To succeed in today's marketplace, companies must know how to manage loads of marketing information effectively.

We'll start the chapter with a story about Coach, a company known for its classic, high-quality leather handbags and accessories. Coach seemed to get along fine in the mature and stable handbag industry without much marketing research. But when consumer needs and preferences shifted and sales slowed, all that changed. Read on to see how Coach used exhaustive marketing research to give itself an extreme strategic makeover.

Coach first opened its doors in 1941 as a family-owned, leather-goods workshop. Over the next 50 years, the company developed a strong following for its classically styled, high-quality leather handbags and accessories.

In its early years, Coach didn't seem to need much marketing research to understand its customers. For most buyers, handbags were largely functional, used for carrying keys, a wallet, and cosmetics. Women typically bought only two purses a year—one for everyday use and one for special occasions. The everyday handbag lasted a long time and styles changed infrequently.

Coach thus offered basic handbag designs in understated colors, black and brown. The classic bag's only ornamentation was a small gold latch and a small leather tag embossed with the Coach name. Over the years, with their understated styling and quality image, Coach handbags earned a reputation as classy but "traditional sturdy standbys." Conservative professionals, who liked the look, quality, and value of Coach's handbags, became the company's loyal core customers. Coach cruised along comfortably.

However, by the mid-1990s, Coach's world had changed dramatically and sales started to slow. As more women entered the workforce, they needed different types of bags. These increasingly influential women fueled the "mass luxury movement." They wanted the designer brands that only affluent women could afford. They also wanted more stylish and colorful bags. High-end designers such

as Prada, Fendi, Gucci, and Chanel were responding to these trends. Many of these designer bags sold for over $1,000, some for as much as $3,000. By comparison, Coach's traditional styles began to look downright plain.

It was time for an extreme makeover. To gain a better understanding of the new handbag buyer, Coach conducted marketing research. "Coach started thinking like a consumer-products company," says an analyst, "relentlessly testing the market to see what holes it could fill." Based on extensive marketing research, Coach overhauled its strategy. In the process, it helped engineer a shift in the way women shop for handbags.

Consumer research revealed that even Coach's conservative customers wanted more fashionable handbags. So, in early 2001, the company launched its "Signature" collection, stylish and colorful bags made of leather and fabric and covered in the letter *C*. Coach designers even began to use adjectives such as *sexy, fun, sophisticated, playful, grounded, luxurious,* and *quality driven* to describe Coach's customers and the company itself.

Another finding showed that women were carrying small Coach cosmetic cases inside their larger handbags to hold such essentials as keys and cell phones. However, when crammed into larger bags, these smaller cases made the larger bags appear bulky. Coach thus designed the "wristlet," a zippered bag with a looped strap, which a woman could either dangle from her wrist or clip inside a larger bag. Coach introduced the new product at prices as low as $38. In only the first 10 months, women snapped up more than 100,000 wristlets. By 2004, Coach was selling more than a million wristlets a year in 75 styles.

Other research revealed that women were increasingly interested in nonleather bags. It also faced the problem that customers did most of their handbag shopping only during the holiday season. To address these issues, the company developed its "Hamptons Weekend" line, stylish fabric bags designed for summer weekend use. The new Coach line featured an easily foldable shape, hot colors, and a durable, water-resistant material befitting a "relaxed-but-sophisticated" lifestyle. The new bags flew off the shelves at Coach's retail stores.

Now, research found that more women are now mixing formal clothing, stilettos, and diamonds with blue jeans and other casual clothes. This suggests an opportunity to get women to use formal accessories—including evening bags—during daylight hours. So Coach has introduced the "Madison" collection, sleek satin or bejeweled versions of its more traditional purses. Ads for the line show a casually dressed woman carrying a Madison bag in daylight, while also carrying a larger, casual tote bag.

Through research, Coach also identified Japan as a major market for its products. The company estimated that the premium handbag segment in Japan is twice (at $6 billion) the size of the U.S., despite having a population less than half of the U.S. Young (25-30 year old), single, fashion

conscious women willing to pay 60 percent more than their U.S. counterparts for similar products form Coach's primary target demographic in Japan. This segment has also been entering the workforce in large numbers, growing from 49 percent workforce participation in 1980 to 71 percent in 2004. Many of these consumers still live with their parents, earn an average salary of $28,000, and have discretionary income to indulge in Western luxury goods with a far greater appetite than U.S. women. Coach is now one of the fastest growing imported handbag and accessory brands in Japan. The company operates 118 department store shop-in-shop locations in Japan, its second largest market after the U.S. As in the U.S., Coach products are also sold through catalogs distributed in its Japanese stores.

Thus, Coach watches its customers closely, looking for trends that might suggest new market voids to fill. Last year alone, Coach spent $3 million on marketing research, interviewing 14,000 women about everything from lifestyles to purse styles to strap lengths. According to a Coach executive, everything Coach does is thoroughly "girlfriend tested, down to the last stitch."

Such exhaustive marketing research has more than paid for itself. The company's sales, profits, and share price are now soaring. Coach has achieved double-digit sales and earnings growth every year since 2000. Revenue in 2007 was $2.6 billion, a 28 percent increase over 2006, while profits stood at $663.7 million, a 34 percent increase over the previous year.[1]

Marketing information system (MIS)
People, equipment, and procedures to gather, sort, analyze, evaluate, and distribute needed, timely, and accurate information to marketing decision makers.

Information overload –
"In this oh-so-overwhelming information age, it's all too easy to be buried, burdened, and burned out by data overload."

To produce superior customer value and satisfaction, companies need information at almost every turn. As the Coach story highlights, good products and marketing programs begin with solid information on consumer needs and wants. Companies also need an abundance of information on competitors, resellers, and other actors and forces in the marketplace.

A **marketing information system (MIS)** consists of people, equipment, and procedures to gather, sort, analyze, evaluate, and distribute needed, timely, and accurate information to marketing decision makers. **Figure 4.1** shows that the MIS begins and ends with information users—marketing managers, internal and external partners, and others who need marketing information.

- It interacts with these information users to *assess information needs*.
- It *develops needed information* from internal company databases, marketing intelligence activities, and marketing research.
- It *helps users to analyze information* to put it in the right form for making marketing decisions and managing customer relationships.
- It *distributes* the marketing information and helps managers *use* it in their decision making.

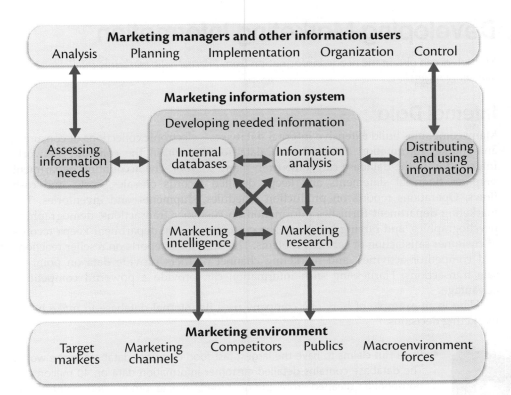

Figure 4.1
The marketing information system

Assessing Marketing Information Needs

The marketing information system primarily serves the company's marketing and other managers. However, it may also provide information to external partners, such as suppliers, resellers, or marketing services agencies. For example, Dell creates tailored Premium Pages for large customers, giving them access to product design, order status, and product support and service information.

A good marketing information system balances the information users would *like* to have against what they really *need* and what is *feasible* to offer. The company begins by interviewing managers to find out what information they would like. There are several issues to consider when developing the MIS:

- *Amount of information:* Too much information can be as harmful as too little. Managers may omit things they ought to know, or they may not know to ask for some types of information they should have. Hence, the MIS must monitor the marketing environment to provide decision makers with information they should have to make key marketing decisions.

- *Availability of information:* Sometimes the company cannot provide the needed information, either because it is not available or because of MIS limitations. For example, a brand manager might want to know how competitors will change their advertising budgets next year and how these changes will affect industry market shares. The information on planned budgets probably is not available. Even if it is, the company's MIS may not be advanced enough to forecast resulting changes in market shares.

- *Costs:* The costs of obtaining, processing, storing, and delivering information can mount quickly. Marketers should not assume that additional information will always be worth obtaining. Rather, they should weigh carefully the costs of getting more information against the benefits resulting from it.

Assessing marketing information needs –
Dell's Premium Pages are tailored for customers. It gives them access to product design, order status, and product support and service information. (www.dell.com)

Developing Marketing Information

Marketers can obtain the needed information from *internal data, marketing intelligence,* and *marketing research.*

Internal Data

Internal databases
Electronic collections of consumer and market information obtained from data sources within the company network.

Many companies build extensive **internal databases**—electronic collections of consumer and market information obtained from data sources within the company network. Information in the database can come from many sources. The accounting department prepares financial statements and keeps detailed records of sales, costs, and cash flows. Operations reports on production schedules, shipments, and inventories. The marketing department furnishes information on customer transactions, demographics, psychographics, and buying behavior. The customer service department keeps records of customer satisfaction or service problems. The sales force reports on reseller reactions and competitor activities, and marketing channel partners provide data on point-of-sale transactions. Harnessing such information can provide a powerful competitive advantage.

Here is an example of how one company uses its internal database to make better marketing decisions:

Internal database –
Pizza Hut can slice and dice its extensive customer database by favorite toppings, what you ordered last, and whether you buy a salad with your cheese and pepperoni pizza. It can target coupon offers to specific households based on past buying behaviors and preferences. (*www.pizzahut.com*)

> Pizza Hut claims to have the largest fast-food customer database in the world. The database contains detailed customer information data on 40 million U.S. households, gleaned from phone orders, online orders, and point-of-sale transactions at its more than 7,500 restaurants around the nation. The company can slice and dice the data by favorite toppings, what you ordered last, and whether you buy a salad with your cheese and pepperoni pizza. Pizza Hut also tracks in real time what commercials people are watching and responding to. It then uses all this data to enhance customer relationships. For example, it can target coupon offers to specific households based on past buying behaviors and preferences.[2]

Internal databases usually can be accessed more quickly and cheaply than other information sources, but they also present some problems. Because internal information was often collected for other purposes, it may be incomplete or in the wrong form for making marketing decisions. For example, sales and cost data used by the accounting department for preparing financial statements must be adapted for use in evaluating the value of specific customer segment, sales force, or channel performance. Data also ages quickly; keeping the database current requires a major effort. In addition, a large company produces mountains of information, which must be well integrated and readily accessible so that managers can find it easily and use it effectively.

Marketing Intelligence

Marketing intelligence
The systematic collection and analysis of publicly available information about competitors and developments in the marketing environment.

Marketing intelligence is the systematic collection and analysis of publicly available information about competitors and developments in the marketplace. The goal of marketing intelligence is to improve strategic decision making, assess and track competitors' actions, and provide early warning of opportunities and threats.

Competitive intelligence can be collected from people inside the company—executives, engineers and scientists, purchasing agents, and the sales force. The company can also obtain important intelligence information from suppliers, resellers, and key customers. Or it can observe competitors and monitor their published information. It can buy and analyze competitors' products, monitor their sales, check for new patents, and examine various types of physical evidence. For example, one company regularly checks out competitors' parking lots—full lots might indicate plenty of work and prosperity; half-full lots might suggest hard times.

Some companies have even gone through their competitors' garbage, which is legally considered abandoned property once it leaves the premises. Procter & Gamble admitted to "dumpster diving" at rival Unilever's headquarters. "P&G got its mitts on just about every iota of info there was to be had about Unilever's [hair care] brands," notes an analyst. However, when news of the questionable tactics reached top P&G managers, they were shocked. They immediately stopped the project and voluntarily set up negotiations with Unilever to right whatever competitive wrongs had been done. Although P&G claims it broke no laws, the company reported that the dumpster raids "violated our strict guidelines regarding our business policies."[3]

Competitors often reveal intelligence information through their annual reports, business publications, trade show exhibits, press releases, advertisements, and Web pages. The Internet is proving to be a vast new source of competitor-supplied information. Using Internet search engines, marketers can search specific competitor names, events, or trends and see what turns up. Moreover, most companies place information on their Web sites, providing details to attract customers, partners, suppliers, investors, or franchisees. This can provide useful information about competitors' strategies, markets, new products, facilities, and other happenings.

Something as simple as a competitor's job postings can be very revealing. For example, while poking around on Google's company Web site, Microsoft's Bill Gates came across a help-wanted page describing all of the jobs available at Google. To his surprise, he noted that Google was looking for engineers with backgrounds that had nothing to do with its Web-search business but everything to do with Microsoft's core software businesses. Forewarned that Google might be preparing to become more than just a search engine company, Gates e-mailed a handful of Microsoft executives, saying, in effect, "We have to watch these guys. It looks like they are building something to compete with us." Notes a marketing intelligence consultant, companies "are often surprised that there's so much out there to know. They're busy with their day-to-day operations and they don't realize how much information can be obtained with a few strategic keystrokes."[4]

The intelligence game goes both ways. Facing determined marketing intelligence efforts by competitors, most companies are now taking steps to protect their own information. For example, Unilever conducts widespread competitive intelligence training. Employees are taught not just how to collect intelligence information but also how to protect company information from competitors. Unilever even performs random checks on internal security. Says a former staffer, "At one [internal marketing] conference, we were set up when an actor was employed to infiltrate the group. The idea was to see who spoke to him, how much they told him, and how long it took to realize that no one knew him. He ended up being there for a long time."[5]

Marketing intelligence –
Procter & Gamble admitted to "dumpster diving" at rival Unilever's Helene Curtis headquarters. When P&G's top management learned of the questionable practice, it stopped the project, voluntarily informed Unilever, and set up talks to right whatever competitive wrongs had been done.

Marketing Research

Sometimes, marketers need formal studies of specific situations. For example, Tiger Beer wants to know whether its use of Jessica Alba was effective in its advertising. Or Samsung wants to know how many and what kinds of people will buy its next-generation plasma televisions. In such situations, managers will need marketing research.

Marketing research is the systematic design, collection, analysis, and reporting of data relevant to a specific marketing situation facing an organization. Companies use marketing research in a wide variety of situations. For example, marketing research can help marketers understand customer satisfaction and purchase behavior. It can help them to assess market potential and market share or to measure the effectiveness of pricing, product, distribution, and promotion activities.

Marketing research
The systematic design, collection, analysis, and reporting of data relevant to a specific marketing situation facing an organization.

The marketing research process has four steps (see **Figure 4.2**): defining the problem and research objectives, developing the research plan, implementing the research plan, and interpreting and reporting the findings.

Figure 4.2
The marketing research process

| Defining the problem and research objectives | → | Developing the research plan for collecting information | → | Implementing the research plan— collecting and analyzing the data | → | Interpreting and reporting the findings |

Defining the Problem and Research Objectives

Marketing managers and researchers must work closely together to define the problem and agree on research objectives. After the problem has been defined carefully, the research objectives are set. Together, the statement of the problem and research objectives guides the entire research process.

A marketing research project might have one of three types of objectives:

- The objective of **exploratory research** is to gather preliminary information that will help define the problem and suggest hypotheses.
- The objective of **descriptive research** is to describe things, such as the market potential for a product or the demographics and attitudes of consumers who buy the product.
- The objective of **causal research** is to test hypotheses about cause-and-effect relationships. For example, would a 10 percent decrease in tuition fees at a private college result in an enrollment increase sufficient to offset the reduced tuition?

Managers often start with exploratory research and later follow with descriptive or causal research.

Developing the Research Plan

Next, the researchers must:

- Determine the exact information needed;
- Develop a plan for gathering it efficiently; and
- Present the plan to management.

The research plan outlines sources of existing data and spells out the specific research approaches, contact methods, sampling plans, and instruments that researchers will use to gather new data.

Research objectives must be translated into specific information needs. For example, suppose Maggi Instant Noodles decides to conduct research on how consumers would react to the introduction of new heat-and-go microwavable cups for its new line of flavors. This research might call for the following specific information:

- The demographic, economic, and lifestyle characteristics of current Maggie Instant Noodle users. (Busy working couples might find the convenience of the new packaging worth the price; families with children might want to pay less and wash the bowls.)
- Consumer-usage patterns for Maggie Instant Noodles and related products: how much they eat, where, and when. (The new packaging might be ideal for adults eating lunch on the go, but less convenient for parents feeding lunch to several children.)
- Retailer reactions to the new packaging. (Failure to get retailer support could hurt sales of the new package.)
- Forecasts of sales of both new and current packages. (Will the new packaging create new sales or simply take sales from the current packaging? Will the package increase Maggi's profits?)

Maggi's managers will need these and many other types of information to decide whether to introduce the new packaging.

Exploratory research
Marketing research to gather preliminary information that will help define problems and suggest hypotheses.

Descriptive research
Marketing research to better describe marketing problems, situations, or markets, such as the market potential for a product or the demographics and attitudes of consumers.

Causal research
Marketing research to test hypotheses about cause-and-effect relationships.

The research plan should be presented in a *written proposal*. A written proposal is especially important when the research project is large and complex or when an outside firm carries it out. The proposal should cover the management problems addressed and the research objectives, the information to be obtained, and the way the results will help management decision making. The proposal also should include research costs.

To meet the manager's information needs, the research plan can call for gathering secondary data, primary data, or both. **Secondary data** consist of information that already exists somewhere, having been collected for another purpose. **Primary data** consist of information collected for the specific purpose at hand.

Secondary data
Information that already exists somewhere, having been collected for another purpose.

Primary data
Information collected for the specific purpose at hand.

Gathering Secondary Data

Researchers usually start by gathering secondary data. The company's internal database provides a good starting point. However, the company can also tap a wide assortment of external information sources, including commercial data services and government sources (see **Table 4.1**).

Companies can buy secondary data reports from outside suppliers. For example, The Nielsen Corporation sells buyer data from a panel of 125,000 households in two dozen countries, with measures of trial and repeat purchasing, brand loyalty, and buyer demographics.[6]

Table 4.1 Selected External Information Sources

For business data:

The Nielsen Corporation (*www.acnielsen.com*) provides supermarket scanner data on sales, market share, and retail prices; data on household purchasing; and data on television audiences.
J.D. Power and Associates (*www.jdpower.com*) provides information from independent consumer surveys of product and service quality, customer satisfaction, and buyer behavior.
Dun & Bradstreet (*www.dnb.com*) maintains a database containing information on more than 50 million individual companies around the globe.
comScore Networks (*www.comscore.com*) provides consumer behavior information and geodemographic analysis of Internet and digital media users around the world.
Thomson Dialog (*www.dialog.com*) offers access to more than 900 databases containing publications, reports, newsletters, and directories covering dozens of industries.
LexisNexis (*www.lexisnexis.com*) features articles from business, consumer, and marketing publications plus tracking of firms, industries, trends, and promotion techniques.
Factiva (*www.factiva.com*) specializes in in-depth financial, historical, and operational information on public and private companies.
Hoover's, Inc. (*www.hoovers.com*) provides business descriptions, financial overviews, and news about major companies around the world.
CNN (*www.cnn.com*) reports U.S. and global news and covers the markets and news-making companies in detail.

For Government data:

United Nations (Statistical Indicators for Asia and the Pacific and other publications)
Data books of various countries and cities
Annual Survey of Manufacturers; Census of Population; Census of Retail Trade, under various titles depending on country

For Internet data:

ClickZ Stats/CyberAtlas (*www.clickz.com/stats*) brings together a wealth of information about the Internet and its users, from consumers to e-commerce.
Interactive Advertising Bureau (*www.iab.net*) covers statistics about advertising on the Internet.
Jupiter Research (*www.jupiterresearch.com*) monitors Web traffic and ranks the most popular sites.

Using commercial **online databases**, marketing researchers can conduct their own searches of secondary data sources. General database services such as dialog, ProQuest, and LexisNexis put an incredible wealth of information at the keyboards of marketing decision makers. Beyond commercial Web sites offering information for a fee, almost every

Online databases
Computerized collections of information availale from online commercial sources or via the Internet.

Gathering secondary data –
Companies can buy secondary reports from outside suppliers such as The Nielsen Corporation. AC Nielsen is a marketing intelligence service of The Nielsen company. Image courtesy of The Nielsen Corporation. (*www.nielsen.com*)

industry association, government agency, business publication, and news medium offers free information to those tenacious enough to find their Web sites. There are so many Web sites offering data that finding the right ones can become an almost overwhelming task.

There are advantages to secondary data:

- They can be obtained more quickly and at a lower cost than primary data.
- They can sometimes provide data an individual company cannot collect on its own—information that either is not directly available or would be too expensive to collect. For example, it would be too expensive for Maggi to conduct a continuing retail store audit to find out about the market shares, prices, and displays of competitors' brands. But it can buy from ACNielsen information based on scanner data.

Secondary data can also present problems:

- The needed information may not exist. For example, Maggi will not find existing information about consumer reactions to new packaging that it has not yet placed on the market.
- Even when data can be found, they might not be very usable. The researcher must evaluate secondary information carefully to make certain it is *relevant* (fits research project needs), *accurate* (reliably collected and reported), *current* (up-to-date enough for current decisions), and *impartial* (objectively collected and reported).

Primary Data Collection

In most cases, the company must also collect primary data. It needs to make sure that the data will be relevant, accurate, current, and unbiased. **Table 4.2** shows that designing a plan for primary data collection calls for a number of decisions on *research approaches*, *contact methods*, *sampling plan*, and *research instruments*.

Research Approaches

Research approaches for gathering primary data include observation, surveys, and experiments. Here, we discuss each one in turn.

Observational research

> **Observational research**
> The gathering of primary data by observing relevant people, actions, and situations.

Observational research involves gathering primary data by observing relevant people, actions, and situations. For example, a bank might evaluate possible new branch locations by checking traffic patterns, neighborhood conditions, and the location of competing branches.

Researchers often observe consumer behavior to glean insights they can't obtain by simply asking customers questions. For instance, Fisher-Price set up an observation lab in which it can observe the reactions of little tots to new toys. The Fisher-Price Play Lab is a sunny, toy-strewn space where lucky kids get to test Fisher-Price prototypes, under the watchful eyes of designers who hope to learn what will get kids worked up into a new-toy frenzy.

Observational research can obtain information that people are unwilling or unable to provide. In some cases, observation may be the only way to obtain the needed information. In contrast, some things simply cannot be observed, such as feelings, attitudes and motives,

Observational research –
Fisher-Price set up an observation lab in which it could observe the reactions of little tots to new toys. (*www.fisher-price.com*)

or private behavior. Long-term or infrequent behavior is also difficult to observe. Because of these limitations, researchers often use observation along with other data collection methods.

Some companies also use **ethnographic research**. Ethnographic research involves sending trained observers to watch and interact with consumers in their "natural habitat." Consider this example:[7]

Ethnographic research
A form of observational research that involves sending trained observers to watch and interact with consumers in their "natural habitat."

Table 4.2 Planning Primary Data Collection

Research Approaches	Contact Methods	Sampling Plan	Research Instruments
Observation	Mail	Sampling unit	Questionnaire
Survey	Telephone	Sample size	Mechanical instruments
Experiment	Personal	Sampling procedure	
	Online		

Marriott hired design firm IDEO to help it take a fresh look at business travel and to rethink the hotel experience for an increasingly important customer: the young, tech-savvy road warrior. Rather than doing the usual customer surveys or focus group research, IDEO dispatched a team of consultants, including a designer, anthropologist, writer, and architect, on a six-week trip to mingle with customers and get an up-close and personal view of them. The group hung out in hotel lobbies, cafés, and bars and asked guests to graph what they were doing hour by hour.

They learned that hotels are not generally good at serving small groups of business travelers. Hotel lobbies tend to be dark and better suited for killing time than conducting casual business. Marriott lacked places where guests could comfortably combine work with pleasure outside their rooms. One IDEO consultant recalls watching a female business traveler drinking wine in the lobby while trying not to spill it on papers spread out on a desk. The result: Marriott reinvented the lobbies of its Marriott and Renaissance Hotels, creating a "social zone," with small tables, brighter lights, and wireless Web access, that is better suited to meetings. Another area allows solo travelers to work or unwind in larger, quiet, semiprivate spaces where they won't have to worry about spilling coffee on their laptops or papers.

Ethnographic research – Based on ethnographic research findings. Marriott reinvented the lobbies of its hotels to create a social zone better suited to meetings.

Ethnographic research often yields the details that do not emerge from traditional research questionnaires or focus groups. It provides a richer understanding of consumers than traditional research. Although companies are still using focus groups, surveys, and demographic data to glean insights into the consumer's mind, close observation allows companies to zero in on their customers' unarticulated desires.[8]

Survey research

Survey research, the most widely used method for primary data collection, is best suited for gathering *descriptive* information. A company that wants to know about people's knowledge, attitudes, preferences, or buying behavior can often find out by asking them directly.

Survey research
Gathering primary data by asking people questions about their knowledge, attitudes, preferences, and buying behavior.

The major advantage of survey research is its flexibility—it can be used to obtain many different kinds of information in many different situations. However, survey research also presents some problems. Sometimes people are unable to answer survey questions because they cannot remember or have never thought about what they do and why. People may be unwilling to respond to unknown interviewers or about things they consider private. Respondents may answer survey questions even when they do not know the answer to appear smarter or more informed. Or they may try to help the interviewer by giving pleasing answers. Finally, busy people may not take the time, or they might resent the intrusion into their privacy.

Experimental research

> **Experimental research**
> Gathering primary data by selecting matched groups of subjects, giving them different treatments, controlling related factors, and checking for differences in group responses.

Whereas observation is best suited for exploratory research and surveys for descriptive research, **experimental research** is best suited for gathering *causal* information. Experiments involve selecting matched groups of subjects, giving them different treatments, controlling unrelated factors, and checking for differences in group responses. Thus, experimental research tries to explain cause-and-effect relationships.

For example, before adding a new sandwich to its menu, McDonald's might use experiments to test the effects on sales of two different prices it might charge. It could introduce the new sandwich at one price in one city and at another price in another city. If the cities are similar, and if all other marketing efforts for the sandwich are the same, then differences in sales in the two cities could be related to the price charged.

Contact Methods

Information can be collected by mail, telephone, personal interview, or online. **Table 4.3** shows the strengths and weaknesses of each of these contact methods.

Table 4.3 Strengths and Weaknesses of Contact Methods

	Mail	*Telephone*	*Personal*	*Online*
Flexibility	Poor	Good	Excellent	Good
Quantity of data that can be collected	Good	Fair	Excellent	Good
Control of interviewer effects	Excellent	Fair	Poor	Fair
Control of sample	Fair	Excellent	Good	Excellent
Speed of data collection	Poor	Excellent	Good	Excellent
Response rate	Fair	Good	Good	Good
Cost	Good	Fair	Poor	Excellent

Source: Adapted with permission of the authors, Donald S. Tull and Del I. Hawkins, *Marketing Research: Measurement and Method*, 7th ed. (New York: Macmillan Publishing Company, 1993).

Mail, telephone, and personal interviewing

Mail questionnaires can be used to collect large amounts of information at a low cost per respondent. Respondents may give more honest answers to more personal questions on a mail questionnaire than to an unknown interviewer in person or over the phone. Also, no interviewer is involved to bias the respondent's answers.

However, mail questionnaires are not very flexible—all respondents answer the same questions in a fixed order. Mail surveys usually take longer to complete, and the response rate—the number of people returning completed questionnaires—is often very low. Finally, the researcher often has little control over the mail questionnaire sample. Even with a good mailing list, it is hard to control *who* at the mailing address fills out the questionnaire.

Telephone interviewing is one of the best methods for gathering information quickly, and it provides greater flexibility than mail questionnaires. Interviewers can explain difficult questions and, depending on the answers they receive, skip some questions or probe on others. Response rates tend to be higher than with mail questionnaires, and interviewers can ask to speak to respondents with the desired characteristics or even by name.

However, with telephone interviewing, the cost per respondent is higher than with mail questionnaires. Also, people may not want to discuss personal questions with an interviewer. The method introduces interviewer bias—the way interviewers talk, how they ask questions, and other differences may affect respondents' answers. Finally, different interviewers may interpret and record responses differently, and under time pressures some interviewers might even cheat by recording answers without asking questions.

Personal interviewing takes two forms—individual and group interviewing. *Individual interviewing* involves talking with people in their homes or offices, on the street, or in shopping malls. Such interviewing is flexible. Trained interviewers can guide interviews, explain difficult questions, and explore issues as the situation requires. They can show subjects actual products, advertisements, or packages and observe reactions and behavior. However, individual personal interviews may cost three to four times as much as telephone interviews.

Group interviewing consists of inviting six to ten people to meet with a trained moderator to talk about a product, service, or organization. Participants normally are paid a small sum for attending. The moderator encourages free and easy discussion, hoping that group interactions will bring out actual feelings and thoughts. At the same time, the moderator "focuses" the discussion—hence the name **focus group interviewing**.

Researchers and marketers watch the focus group discussions from behind one-way glass, and comments are recorded in writing or on video for later study. Today, focus group researchers can even use videoconferencing and Internet technology to connect marketers in distant locations with live focus group action. Using cameras and two-way sound systems, marketing executives in a far-off boardroom can look in and listen, using remote controls to zoom in on faces and pan the focus group at will.

Focus group interviewing – A trained moderator encourages free and easy discussion and guides the participants to discuss about the research topic.

Focus group interviewing has become one of the major marketing research tools for gaining insights into consumer thoughts and feelings. However, focus group studies present some challenges. They usually employ small samples to keep time and costs down, and it may be hard to generalize from the results. Moreover, consumers in focus groups are not always open and honest in front of other people. There may be some peer pressure in focus groups that gets in the way of finding the truth about real behavior and intentions.[9]

Focus group interviewing
Personal interviewing that involves inviting six to ten people to gather for a few hours with a trained interviewer to talk about a product, service, or organization. The interviewer "focuses" the group discussion on important issues.

Thus, although focus groups are still widely used, many researchers are tinkering with focus group design. For example, at Yahoo!, "immersion groups" are used where Yahoo! product designers talk informally to four or five people, without a focus group moderator present. That way, rather than just seeing videos of consumers reacting to a moderator, Yahoo! staffers can work directly with select customers to design new products and programs.[10]

Other researchers are changing the environments in which they conduct focus groups. To help consumers relax and to elicit more authentic responses, they use settings that are more comfortable and more relevant to the products being researched. For example, they might conduct focus groups for cooking products in a kitchen setting, or focus groups for home furnishings in a living room setting.

Online marketing research

Advances in communication technologies have resulted in a number of high-tech contact methods. The latest technology to hit marketing research is the Internet. Increasingly, marketing researchers are collecting primary data through **online marketing research**—*Internet surveys, online panels, experiments,* and *online focus groups*.

Online research can take many forms. A company can include a questionnaire on its Web site and offer incentives for completing it. Or it can use e-mail, Web links, or Web pop-ups to invite people to answer questions and possibly win a prize. The company can sponsor a chat room and introduce questions from time to time or conduct live discussions or online focus groups. A company can learn about the behavior of online customers by following their click streams as they visit the Web site and move to other sites. A company can experiment with different prices, use different headlines, or offer different product features on different Web sites or at different times to learn the relative effectiveness of its offerings. It can float "trial balloons" to quickly test new product concepts.

Online marketing research
Collecting primary data through Internet surveys and online focus groups.

Web research offers some advantages over traditional surveys and focus groups. The most obvious advantages are speed and low costs. Online focus groups require some advance scheduling, but results are practically instantaneous.[11]

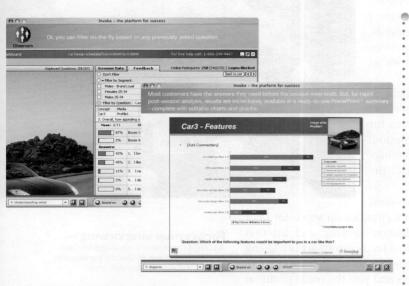

Looking for better methods of predicting consumer acceptance to potential new products, Pepsi recently turned to Invoke Solutions, an online consumer research company, which maintained several instant-message-style online panels of 80 to 100 people. Using the panels, Pepsi delved into attitudes among Gen Xers toward drinking mineral water. In just a few hours, the beverage marketer was able to gather and process detailed feedback from hundreds of consumers. At first, Pepsi marketers were jazzed that the group liked the idea of high levels of mineral content in water. But after further exchanges with the online panel, Pepsi beverage scientists on the scene squelched higher mineral levels; that would require adding sugar, which consumers didn't want, to make the taste acceptable. Using the online panels, "conclusions that could take three to four months to sort out through regular focus groups … got settled in a few hours," says an Invoke executive.

Online research companies –
Invoke Solutions provides a variety of online marketing research tools, from online interactive qual-quant research sessions to mobile phone SMS-based surveys with interactive reporting. (*www.invokesolutions.com*)

Internet research is also relatively low in cost. Participants can dial in for a focus group from anywhere in the world, eliminating travel, lodging, and facility costs. For surveys, the Internet eliminates most of the postage, phone, labor, and printing costs associated with other approaches. As a result, an Internet survey may be only 10 to 20 percent as expensive as mail, telephone, or personal surveys. Moreover, sample size has little influence on costs. Once the questionnaire is set up, there's little difference in cost between 10 and 10,000 respondents on the Web.

Online surveys and focus groups are also excellent for reaching the hard-to-reach—the often-elusive teen, single, affluent, and well-educated audiences. It's also good for reaching working mothers and other people who lead busy lives. They respond to it in their own space and at their own convenience. The Internet also works well for bringing together people from different areas, especially those in higher-income groups who can't spare the time to travel to a central site.

Using the Internet to conduct marketing research does have some drawbacks. For one, restricted Internet access can make it difficult to get a broad cross section of the market. Another major problem is controlling who's in the sample. Without seeing the respondents, it's difficult to know who they really are.

Even when you reach the right respondents, online surveys and focus groups can lack the dynamics of more personal approaches. The online world is devoid of the eye contact, body language, and direct personal interactions found in traditional focus group research. And the Internet format—running, typed commentary and online "emoticons" (punctuation marks that express emotion, such as :-) to signify happiness)—greatly restricts respondent expressiveness. Although the impersonal nature of the Internet may shield people from excessive peer pressure, it also prevents people from interacting with each other and getting excited about a concept.

To overcome such sample and response problems, many online research firms use opt-in communities and respondent panels. For example, online research firm Greenfield Online provides access to 12 million opt-in panel members in more than 40 countries. Advances in technology—such as the integration of animation, streaming audio and video, and virtual environments—also help to overcome online research dynamics limitations.

Perhaps the most explosive issue facing online researchers concerns consumer privacy. Some fear that unethical researchers will use the e-mail addresses and confidential responses gathered through surveys to sell products after the research is completed. They are concerned about the use of electronic agents (such as Spambots or Trojans) that collect personal information without the respondents' consent. Failure to address such privacy issues could result in angry, less-cooperative consumers and increased government intervention. Despite these concerns, most industry insiders predict healthy growth for online marketing research.[12]

Sampling Plan

Marketing researchers usually draw conclusions about large groups of consumers by studying a small sample of the total consumer population. A **sample** is a segment of the population selected for marketing research to represent the population as a whole. Ideally, the sample should be representative so that the researcher can make accurate estimates of the thoughts and behaviors of the larger population.

Designing the sample requires three decisions. (see **Figure 4.3**) First, *who* is to be surveyed (what *sampling unit*)? For example, to study the decision-making process for a family automobile purchase, should the researcher interview the husband, wife, other family members, dealership salespeople, or all of these? The researcher must determine what information is needed and who is most likely to have it.

> **Sample**
> A segment of the population selected for marketing research to represent the population as a whole.

Sampling Plan Decisions

Who is to be surveyed? (Sampling unit)	How many people should be surveyed? (Sample size)	How should the people be chosen? (Sampling procedure)

Figure 4.3
Decisions made in a sampling plan

Table 4.4 Types of Samples

PROBABILITY SAMPLE	
Simple random sample	Every member of the population has a known and equal chance of selection.
Stratified random sample	The population is divided into mutually exclusive groups (such as age groups), and random samples are drawn from each group.
Cluster (area) sample	The population is divided into mutually exclusive groups (such as blocks), and the researcher draws a sample of the groups to interview.
NONPROBABILITY SAMPLE	
Convenience sample	The researcher selects the easiest population members from which to obtain information.
Judgment sample	The researcher uses his or her judgment to select population members who are good prospects for accurate information.
Quota sample	The researcher finds and interviews a prescribed number of people in each of several categories.

Second, *how many* people should be surveyed (what *sample size*)? Large samples give more reliable results than small samples. However, larger samples usually cost more, and it is not necessary to sample the entire target market or even a large portion to get reliable results. If well chosen, samples of less than 1 percent of a population can often give good reliability.

Third, *how* should the people in the sample be *chosen* (what *sampling procedure*)? **Table 4.4** describes different kinds of samples. Using *probability samples*, each population member has a known chance of being included in the sample, and researchers can calculate confidence limits for sampling error. But when probability sampling costs too much or takes too much time, marketing researchers often take *nonprobability samples*, even though their sampling error cannot be measured. These varied ways of drawing samples have different costs and time limitations as well as different accuracy and statistical properties. Which method is best depends on the needs of the research project.

Research Instruments

In collecting primary data, marketing researchers have a choice of two main research instruments—the *questionnaire* and *mechanical devices*. The *questionnaire* is by far the most common instrument, whether administered in person, by phone, or online.

Questionnaires are very flexible—there are many ways to ask questions. *Closed-end questions* include all the possible answers, and subjects make choices among them. Examples include multiple-choice questions and scale questions. *Open-end questions* allow respondents to answer in their own words. In a survey of airline users, Cathay Pacific might simply ask, "What is your opinion of Cathay Pacific?" Or it might ask people to complete a sentence: "When I choose an airline, the most important consideration is …" These and other kinds of open-end questions often reveal more than closed-end questions because respondents are not limited in their answers. Open-end questions are especially useful in exploratory research, when the researcher is trying to find out *what* people think but not measuring *how many* people think in a certain way. Closed-end questions, on the other hand, provide answers that are easier to interpret and tabulate.

Researchers should also use care in the *wording* and *ordering* of questions. They should use simple, direct, unbiased wording. Questions should be arranged in a logical order. The first question should create interest if possible, and difficult or personal questions should be asked last so that respondents do not become defensive. A carelessly prepared questionnaire usually contains many errors (see **Table 4.5**).

Although questionnaires are the most common research instrument, researchers also use *mechanical instruments* to monitor consumer behavior. Nielsen Media Research attaches *people meters* to television sets in selected homes to record who watches which programs. Retailers use *checkout scanners* to record shoppers' purchases.

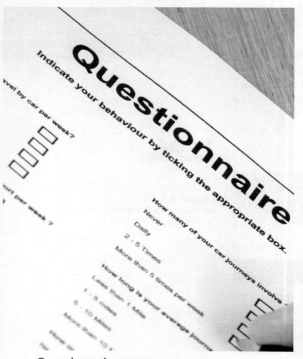

Questionnaire – Closed-end questions are easier to answer and to tabulate results from.

Table 4.5 A "Questionable Questionnaire"

Suppose that a director of a student exchange program has prepared the following questionnaire to use in interviewing the parents of prospective applicants. How would you assess each question?

1. What is your income to the nearest hundred dollars? *People don't usually know their income to the nearest hundred dollars, nor do they want to reveal their income that closely. Moreover, a researcher should never open a questionnaire with such a personal question.*

2. Are you a strong or weak supporter of overseas student exchange programs for your children? *What do "strong" and "weak" mean?*

3. Do your children behave themselves well in student exchange programs overseas? Yes ( ) No ( ) *"Behave" is a relative term. Further, are* yes *and* no *the best response options for this question? Besides, will people answer this honestly and objectively? Why ask the question in the first place?*

4. How many overseas schools mailed or e-mailed information to you last year? This year? *Who can remember this?*

5. What are the most salient and determinant attributes in your evaluation of overseas student exchange programs? *What are salient and determinant attributes? Don't use big words on me!*

6. Do you think it is right to deprive your child of the opportunity to grow into a mature person through the experience of overseas student exchange programs? *A loaded question. Given the bias, how can any parent answer yes?*

Other mechanical devices measure subjects' physical responses. For example, advertisers use eye cameras to study viewers' eye movements while watching ads—at what points their eyes focus first and how long they linger on any given ad component. IBM's BlueEyes human recognition technology goes even further.

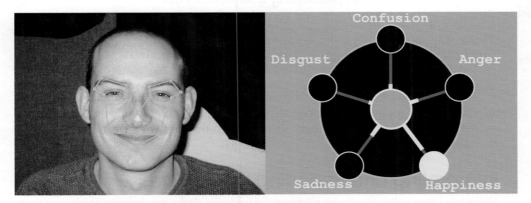

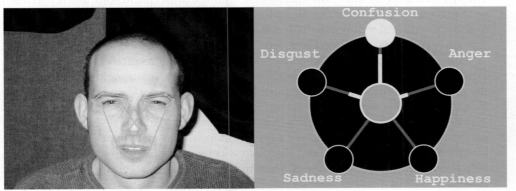

Mechanical measures of consumer response –
New technologies can record and interpret human facial expressions. In the not-too-distant future, marketers may be using machines that "know how you feel" to not just gauge customers' physical reactions, but to respond to them as well. (*www.almaden. ibm.com/cs/BlueEyes/index.html*)

BlueEyes uses sensing technology to identify and interpret user reactions. The technology was originally created to help users to interact more easily with a computer. For example, IBM is perfecting an "emotion mouse" that will figure out computer users' emotional states by measuring pulse, temperature, movement, and galvanic skin response. Another BlueEyes technology records and interprets human facial reactions by tracking pupil, eyebrow, and mouth movement. BlueEyes offers a host of potential marketing uses. Some retailers are using the technology to study customers and their responses. In the not-too-distant future, more than just measuring customers' physical reactions, marketers will be able to respond to them as well. An example: creating marketing machines that "know how you feel." Sensing through an emotion mouse that a Web shopper is frustrated, an Internet marketer offers a different screen display. An elderly man squints at a bank's ATM screen and the font size doubles almost instantly. A woman at a shopping center kiosk smiles at a travel ad, prompting the device to print out a travel discount coupon. Several users at another kiosk frown at a racy ad, leading a store to pull it. In the future, ordinary household devices—such as televisions, refrigerators, and ovens—may be able to do their jobs when we look at them and speak to them.[13]

Implementing the Research Plan

The researcher next puts the marketing research plan into action. This involves collecting, processing, and analyzing the information. Data collection can be carried out by the company's marketing research staff or by outside firms. The data collection phase of the marketing research process is generally the most expensive and the most subject to error. Researchers should watch closely to make sure that the plan is implemented correctly (see **Figure 4.4**). They must guard against problems with contacting respondents, with respondents who refuse to cooperate or who give biased answers, and with interviewers who make mistakes or take shortcuts.

Figure 4.4
Issues to consider when implementing a research plan

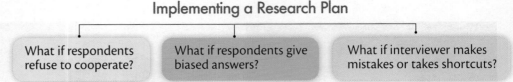

Researchers must also process and analyze the collected data to isolate important information and findings. They need to check data for accuracy and completeness and code it for analysis. The researchers then tabulate the results and compute statistical measures.

Interpreting and Reporting the Findings

The market researcher must now interpret the findings, draw conclusions, and report them to management. The researcher should not try to overwhelm managers with numbers and fancy statistical techniques. Rather, the researcher should present important findings that are useful in the major decisions faced by management.

However, interpretation should not be left only to the researchers. They are often experts in research design and statistics, but the marketing manager knows more about the problem and the decisions that must be made. The best research means little if the manager blindly accepts faulty interpretations from the researcher. Similarly, managers may be biased—they might tend to accept research results that show what they expected and to reject those that they did not expect or hope for. In many cases, findings can be interpreted in different ways, and discussions between researchers and managers will help point to the best interpretations. Thus, managers and researchers must work together closely when interpreting research results, and both must share responsibility for the research process and resulting decisions.

Analyzing Marketing Information

Information gathered in internal databases and through marketing intelligence and marketing research usually requires more analysis. And managers may need help applying the information to their marketing decisions. This help may include advanced statistical analysis to learn more about the relationships within a set of data. Such analysis allows managers to go beyond means and standard deviations in the data and to answer questions about markets, marketing activities, and outcomes.

Information analysis might also involve a collection of analytical models that will help marketers make better decisions. Each model represents some real system, process, or outcome. These models can help answer the questions of *what if* and *which is best*. Marketing scientists have developed numerous models to help marketing managers make better marketing mix decisions, design sales territories and sales call plans, select sites for retail outlets, develop optimal advertising mixes, and forecast new-product sales.

Customer Relationship Management (CRM)

The question of how best to analyze and use individual customer data presents special problems. Most companies are awash in information about their customers. In fact, smart companies capture information at every possible customer *touch point*. These touch points include customer purchases, sales force contacts, service and support calls, Web site visits, satisfaction surveys, credit and payment interactions, market research studies—every contact between the customer and the company.

The trouble is that this information is usually scattered widely across the organization. It is buried deep in the separate databases and records of different company departments. To overcome such problems, many companies are now turning to **customer relationship management (CRM)** to manage detailed information about individual customers and carefully manage customer "touch points" in order to maximize customer loyalty.

CRM consists of sophisticated software and analytical tools that integrate customer information from all sources, analyze it in depth, and apply the results to build stronger customer relationships. CRM integrates everything that a company's sales, service, and marketing teams know about individual customers to provide a 360-degree view of the customer relationship.

CRM analysts develop *data warehouses* and use sophisticated *data mining* techniques to unearth the riches hidden in customer data. A data warehouse is a companywide electronic database of finely detailed customer information that needs to be sifted through for gems. The purpose of a data warehouse is not just to gather information, but to pull it together into a central, accessible location. Then, once the data warehouse brings the data together, the company uses high-powered data mining techniques to sift through the data and dig out interesting findings about customers.

By using CRM to understand customers better, companies can provide higher levels of customer service and develop deeper customer relationships. They can use CRM to pinpoint high-value customers, target them more effectively, cross-sell the company's products, and create offers tailored to specific customer requirements. For example, Harrah's Entertainment, the world's largest casino operator, maintains a vast customer database and uses its CRM system to manage day-to-day relationships with important customers at its 43 casinos worldwide (see **Real Marketing**).

CRM benefits don't come without cost or risk, not only in collecting the original customer data but also in maintaining and mining it (see **Figure 4.5**). The most common CRM mistake is to view CRM only as a technology and software solution. But technology alone cannot build profitable customer relationships. Instead, CRM is just one part of an effective overall *customer relationship management strategy*. "Focus on the R," advises an expert. "Remember, a relationship is what CRM is all about."[14]

Customer relationship management (CRM)
Managing detailed information about individual customers and carefully managing customer "touch points" in order to maximize customer loyalty.

CRM – SAS customer intelligence software helps companies keep a profitable, loyal, customer base by leveraging customer information and developing targeted, personalized responses to customer needs. (*www.sas.com*)

Customer Relationship Management

+ Pros	**– Cons**
○ Understand customer better	○ Viewed only as a technology and software solution
○ Pinpoint high-value customers	
○ Cross-sell company's products	
○ Create tailor-made offerings	

Figure 4.5
Pros and cons of customer relationship management

When it works, the benefits of CRM can far outweigh the costs and risks. Based on a study by SAP, customers using its mySAP CRM software reported an average 10 percent increase in customer retention and a 30 percent increase in sales leads. Overall, 90 percent of the companies surveyed increased in value from use of the software and reported an attractive return on investment. The study's conclusion: "CRM pays off." Companies are looking for ways to bring disparate sources of customer information together, and then get it to all the customer touch points.[15]

REAL MARKETING

Harrah's Hits the CRM Jackpot

After casino operator Harrah's Entertainment recently acquired Caesars Entertainment, revenues soared to $7.1 billion from its 43 properties worldwide. The Harrah's portfolio includes such star-studded casino and gaming brands as Harrah's, Caesars, Horseshoe, Bally's, Flamingo, Showboat, and The World Series of Poker.

With rapidly increasing sales and profits, Harrah's stock is worth nearly two-and-a-half times its value five years ago. Why has Harrah's been so successful? In physical terms, all casinos are pretty much alike. Most customers can't distinguish one company's slot machines, game tables, restaurants, and hotel rooms from another's. What sets Harrah's apart is the way it relates to its customers and creates customer loyalty. During the past decade, Harrah's has become *the* model for good CRM and customer-loyalty management.

Central to Harrah's CRM strategy is its pioneering card-based Total Rewards program, the gaming industry's first and, by far, most successful loyalty program. Total Rewards members receive points based on the amount they spend at Harrah's facilities. They can then redeem the points for a variety of perks, such as cash, food, merchandise, rooms, and hotel show tickets. Total Rewards forms the basis for a two-part CRM process. First, the company uses Total Rewards to collect information about its customers. Then, it mines this information to identify important customers and finely tunes its market offerings to their specific needs.

Customer relationship management: Harrah's CRM system helps the company to focus its branding, marketing, and service development strategies on the needs of its most important customers. "We're trying to figure out which products sell, and we're trying to increase our customer loyalty."

Harrah's maintains a vast customer database. Over 80 percent of Harrah's 40 million customers worldwide use a Total Rewards card. Information from every swipe of every card at each of Harrah's casinos zips off to a central computer in Memphis, Tennessee. Harrah's current data warehouse can store up to 30 terabytes (30 trillion bytes) of data, roughly three times the volume of data contained in the U.S. Library of Congress. Amazingly, Harrah's is rapidly reaching full information capacity and plans to double its data storage capabilities.

Analyzing all this information gives Harrah's detailed insights into casino operations. For example, "visualization software" can generate a dynamic "heat map" of a casino floor, with machines glowing red when at peak activity, then turning blue and then white as the action moves elsewhere. More important, the information provides insights into the characteristics and behavior of individual customers—who they are, how often they visit, how long they stay, and how much they gamble and entertain.

From its Total Rewards data, Harrah's has learned that 26 percent of its customers produce 82 percent of revenues. These best customers aren't the "high-rollers" that have long been the focus of the industry. Rather, they are ordinary people from all walks of life—middle-aged and retired teachers, bankers, and doctors who have discretionary income and time. Such customers often visit casinos for an evening, rather than staying overnight at the hotel, and they are more likely to play at the slots than at tables. What motivates them is mostly the intense anticipation and excitement of gambling itself.

Using such insights, Harrah's focuses its marketing and service development strategies on the needs of its best customers. For example, the company's advertising reflects the feeling of exuberance that target customers seek. The data insights also help Harrah's do a better job of managing day-to-day customer relationships. After a day's gaming, by the next morning, it knows which customers should be rewarded with free show tickets, dinner vouchers, or room upgrades.

Harrah's is now starting to process customer information in real time, from the moment customers swipe their rewards cards, creating the ideal link between data and the customer experience. Harrah's chief information officer calls this "operational CRM." He explains, "(T)he hotel clerk can see your history and determine whether you should get a room upgrade, based on booking levels in the hotel at that time and on your past level of play. A person might walk up to you while you're playing and offer you $5 to play more slots, or a free meal, or maybe just wish you a happy birthday."

Harrah's CRM and customer-loyalty efforts are paying off. The company has found that whereas customer spending decreases by 10 percent based on an unhappy casino experience, it increases by 24 percent with a happy experience. Its Total Rewards customers appear to be happier. Compared with nonmembers, members visit Harrah's casinos more frequently, stay longer, and spend more of their gambling and entertainment dollars in Harrah's rather than in rival casinos. Since setting up Total Rewards, Harrah's share of customers' average annual gambling budgets has risen 20 percent, and revenue from customers gambling at Harrah's rather than their "home casino" has increased 18 percent.

Harrah's CEO Gary Loveman calls Total Rewards "the vertebrae of our business" and says, "it touches, in some form or fashion, 85 percent of our revenue." He says that Harrah's "customer-loyalty strategy [and] relationship marketing … are constantly bringing us closer to our customers so we better understand their preferences, and from that understanding we are able to improve the entertainment experiences we offer." Ka-ching! Through smart CRM investments, Harrah's has hit the customer-loyalty jackpot.

Sources:

Quotes and other information from Phil Bligh and Doug Turk, "Cashing In on Customer Loyalty," *Customer Relationship Management*, June 1, 2004, p. 48; Thomas Hoffman, "Harrah's Bets on Loyalty Program in Caesars Deal," *Computerworld*, June 27, 2005, p. 10; Daniel Lyons, "Too Much Information," *Forbes*, December 13, 2004, p. 110; Suzette Parmley, "When Its Customers Return, a Casino Always Wins," *Philadelphia Inquirer*, April 15, 2005; Kai Ryssdal and Andrew Park, "Harrah's Database of Gamblers," transcript from *Marketplace*, August 4, 2005; Neal A. Martin, "A Tempting Wager," *Barron's*, April 10, 2006, pp. 28–30; John S. Webster, "Harrah's CTO Tim Stanley Plays 'Operational CRM,'" June 7, 2006, accessed at www.computerworld.com; and Harrah's annual reports and other information accessed at http://investor.harrahs.com/phoenix.zhtml?c=84772&p=irol-reportsAnnual, August 2006.

Distributing and Using Marketing Information

Marketing information has no value until it is used to make better marketing decisions. Thus, the marketing information system must make the information readily available to the managers and others who make marketing decisions or deal with customers. In some cases, this means providing managers with regular performance reports, intelligence updates, and reports on the results of research studies.

But marketing managers may also need nonroutine information for special situations and on-the-spot decisions. For example, a sales manager having trouble with a large customer may want a summary of the account's sales and profitability over the past year. Or a retail store manager who has run out of a best-selling product may want to know the current inventory levels in the chain's other stores. Increasingly, therefore, information distribution involves entering information into databases and making it available in a timely, user-friendly way.

Many firms use a company *intranet* to facilitate this process. The intranet provides ready access to research information, stored reports, shared work documents, contact information for employees and other stakeholders, and more. For example, some firms are able to integrate incoming customer service calls with up-to-date database information about customers' background and past purchases. By accessing this information on the intranet while speaking with the customer, their service representatives can get a well-rounded picture of each customer.

In addition, companies are increasingly allowing key customers and value-network members to access account, product, and other data on demand through *extranets*. Suppliers, customers, resellers, and select other network members may access a company's extranet to update their accounts, arrange purchases, and check orders against inventories to improve customer service.

Using extranet for better customer service — TAL Apparel uses its comprehensive extranet to receive direct orders from clients like JC Penney and to generate priority production orders if inventory is insufficient. (http://www1.talgroup.com)

● Hong Kong's TAL Apparel has developed comprehensive electronic linkages with major clients like JC Penney (JCP). It receives orders direct from each JCP store and an automated system for collecting goods to meet orders received. For orders that cannot be filled from inventory, priority production orders are generated. TAL then packages goods individually for each JCP outlet and notifies JCP the packing and shipping information. Both companies have access to each other's information systems to assist in demand planning. TAL also manages JCP's stores' inventories by analyzing their point-of-sale data.[16]

Today's marketing managers can gain direct access to the information system at any time and from virtually any location. They can tap into the system while working at a home office, from a hotel room, or from the local Starbuck's through a wireless network. Such systems allow managers to get the information they need directly and quickly and to tailor it to their own needs.

Other Marketing Information Considerations

This section discusses marketing information in two special contexts: marketing research in small businesses and nonprofit organizations and international marketing research. Finally, we look at public policy and ethics issues in marketing research.

Marketing Research in Small Businesses and Nonprofit Organizations

Just like larger firms, small organizations need market information. Start-up businesses need information about their industries, competitors, potential customers, and reactions to new market offers. Existing small businesses must track changes in customer needs and wants, reactions to new products, and changes in the competitive environment.

Managers of small businesses and nonprofit organizations often think that marketing research can be done only by experts in large companies with big research budgets. True, large-scale research studies are beyond the budgets of most small businesses. However, many of the marketing research techniques discussed in this chapter also can be used by smaller organizations in a less formal manner and at little or no expense.

Managers of small businesses and nonprofit organizations can obtain good marketing information simply by *observing* things around them. For example, retailers can evaluate new locations by observing vehicle and pedestrian traffic. They can monitor competitor advertising by collecting ads from local media. They can evaluate their customer mix by recording how many and what kinds of customers shop in the store at different times. In addition, many small business managers routinely visit their rivals and socialize with competitors to gain insights.

Managers can conduct informal *surveys* using small convenience samples. The director of an art museum can learn what patrons think about new exhibits by conducting informal focus groups—inviting small groups to lunch and having discussions on topics of interest. Retail salespeople can talk with customers visiting the store; hospital officials can interview patients. Restaurant managers might make random phone calls during slack hours to interview consumers about where they eat out and what they think of various restaurants in the area.

Managers also can conduct their own simple *experiments*. For example, by changing the themes in regular fund-raising mailings and watching the results, a nonprofit manager can find out much about which marketing strategies work best. By varying newspaper advertisements, a store manager can learn the effects of things such as ad size and position, price coupons, and media used.

Small organizations can obtain most of the secondary data available to large businesses. The business sections at local libraries can also be a good source of information. Local newspapers often provide information on local shoppers and their buying patterns. Finally, small businesses can collect a considerable amount of information at very little cost on the Internet. They can scour competitor and customer Web sites and use Internet search engines to research specific companies and issues.

Informal observational research – Observing vehicle and pedestrian traffic can help retailers to determine a shop's new location.

International Marketing Research

International marketing researchers follow the same steps as domestic researchers, from defining the research problem and developing a research plan to interpreting and reporting the results. However, these researchers often face more and different problems. Whereas domestic researchers deal with fairly homogenous markets within a single country, international researchers deal with diverse markets in many different countries. These markets often vary greatly in their levels of economic development, cultures and customs, and buying patterns.

In many foreign markets, the international researcher may have a difficult time finding good secondary data. Whereas U.S. marketing researchers can obtain reliable secondary data from dozens of domestic research services, many countries have almost no research services at all. For example, secondary data on less economically developed Asian countries is nonexistent, unreliable, or very costly to collect. Many Asian countries estimate their population by asking local authorities to estimate local population; they will get pure guesses or just extrapolations of past numbers. China relies on birth registration

Secondary data from Asia –
Population figures are often inaccurate in less economically developed Asian countries, where children are not always registered with the population census.

records for population sizes. However, in rural areas, many families have several children and do not register their younger children with the population census.

Because of the scarcity of good secondary data, international researchers often must collect their own primary data. Yet, collection of primary data is also saddled with problems. For example, they may find it difficult simply to develop good samples in emerging Asian markets. Although researchers in developed countries can use current telephone directories, census tract data, and any of several sources of socioeconomic data to construct samples, such information is largely lacking in such countries. Survey research also suffers from a lack of sampling lists and few or unqualified interviewers.

Researchers must be aware of the cultural variations in Asian countries. For example, it may be decided that the wife be interviewed. However, in some Muslim countries, men have several wives. Which one is to be interviewed? The Japanese desire not to contradict makes for more "yea-saying" and upward social bias than in a Western culture.

Language is the most obvious challenge. For example, questionnaires must be prepared in one language and then translated into the languages of each country researched. Responses then must be translated back into the original language for analysis and interpretation. This adds to research costs and increases the risks of error. Translating a questionnaire from one language to another is anything but easy. Many idioms, phrases, and statements mean different things in different cultures.

Consumers in different countries also vary in their attitudes toward marketing research. People in one country may be very willing to respond; in other countries, nonresponse can be a major problem. Customs in some countries may prohibit people from talking with strangers. In certain cultures, research questions often are considered too personal. For example, in most Muslim countries, mixed-gender focus groups are taboo, as is videotaping female-only focus groups.

Even when respondents are *willing* to respond, they may not be *able* to because of high functional illiteracy rates. And middle-class people in developing countries often make false claims to appear well-off. For example, in a study of tea consumption in India, over 70 percent of middle-income respondents claimed that they used one of several national brands. However, the researchers had good reason to doubt these results—more than 60 percent of the tea sold in India is unbranded generic tea.

Moreover, reaching respondents is often not so easy in less developed Asian markets. The researcher cannot send a mailed questionnaire because of low population literacy or poor postal services; and telephone interviews are infeasible where telephone ownership or service is poor. This means that researchers must rely primarily on personal interviewing, focus-group interviewing, and observational research to arrive at a fair picture of the marketplace. While they can gain a lot of insight into the market from these methods, they cannot know how representative the findings are.

Asian countries also vary in their research capabilities. Hong Kong, Japan, the Philippines, and Singapore have fairly advanced research industries; while those in China, India, and Indonesia are more limited though improving. Some of the largest international research services do operate in many countries. For example, The Nielsen Corporation has offices in more than 100 countries. And 67 percent of the revenues of the world's 25 largest marketing research firms come from outside their home countries.[17]

Despite these problems, the recent growth of international marketing has resulted in a rapid increase in the use of international marketing research. Global companies have little choice but to conduct such research. Although the costs and problems associated with international research may be high, the costs of not doing it—in terms of missed opportunities and mistakes—might be even higher. Once recognized, many of the problems associated with international marketing research can be overcome or avoided.

Public Policy and Ethics in Marketing Research

Most marketing research benefits both the sponsoring company and its consumers. However, the misuse of marketing research can also harm or annoy consumers. Two major public policy and ethics issues in marketing research are intrusions on consumer privacy and the misuse of research findings.

Intrusions on Consumer Privacy

Some consumers fear that researchers might use sophisticated techniques to probe our deepest feelings or peek over our shoulders and then use this knowledge to manipulate our buying. Or they worry that marketers are building huge databases full of personal information about customers.

Other consumers may have been taken in by previous "research surveys" that actually turned out to be attempts to sell them something. Still other consumers confuse legitimate marketing research studies with telemarketing efforts and say "no" before the interviewer can even begin. Most, however, simply resent the intrusion. They dislike mail, telephone, or Web surveys that are too long or too personal or that interrupt them at inconvenient times.

Intrusions on consumer privacy – Consumers may confuse legitimate marketing research studies with telemarketing efforts.

Increasing consumer resentment has become a major problem for the research industry. One recent survey found that 70 percent of Americans say that companies have too much of consumers' personal information, and 76 percent feel that their privacy has been compromised if a company uses the collected personal information to sell them products. These concerns have led to lower survey response rates in recent years.[18]

American Express, which deals with a considerable volume of consumer information, has long taken privacy issues seriously. The company developed a set of formal privacy principles and became one of the first companies to post privacy policies on its Web site. Its online Internet privacy statement tells customers in clear terms what information American Express collects and how it uses it, how it safeguards the information, and how it uses the information to market to its customers (with instructions on how to opt out).

In the end, if researchers provide value in exchange for information, customers will gladly provide it. For example, Amazon.com's customers do not mind if the firm builds a database of products they buy to provide future product recommendations. This saves time and provides value. The best approach is for researchers to ask only for the information they need, to use it responsibly to provide customer value, and to avoid sharing information without the customer's permission.

Misuse of Research Findings

Some research studies appear to be little more than vehicles for pitching the sponsor's products. In some cases, the research surveys appear to have been designed just to produce the intended effect. Few advertisers openly rig their research designs or blatantly misrepresent the findings; most abuses tend to be subtle "stretches." Consider the following example. A study by Chrysler contends that Americans overwhelmingly prefer Chrysler to Toyota after test-driving both. However, the study included just 100 people in each of two tests. More importantly, none of the people surveyed owned a foreign car brand, so they appear to be favorably predisposed to U.S. brands.[19]

Thus, subtle manipulations of the study's sample or the choice or wording of questions can greatly affect the conclusions reached.

REVIEWING THE CONCEPTS

In today's complex and rapidly changing marketplace, marketing managers need more and better information to make effective and timely decisions. This greater need for information has been matched by the explosion of information technologies for supplying information. Using today's new technologies, companies can now obtain great quantities of information, sometimes even too much. Yet marketers often complain that they lack enough of the *right* kind of information or have an excess of the *wrong* kind. In response, many companies are now studying their managers' information needs and designing information systems to help managers develop and manage market and customer information.

1 Explain the importance of information to the company and its understanding of the marketplace.

The marketing process starts with a complete understanding of the marketplace and consumer needs and wants. Thus, the company needs sound information in order to produce superior value and satisfaction for customers. The company also requires information on competitors, resellers, and other actors and forces in the marketplace. Increasingly, marketers are viewing information not only as an input for making better decisions but also as an important strategic asset and marketing tool.

2 Define the marketing information system and discuss its parts.

The *marketing information system (MIS)* consists of people, equipment, and procedures to gather, sort, analyze, evaluate, and distribute needed, timely, and accurate information to marketing decision makers. A well-designed information system begins and ends with users.

The MIS first *assesses information needs.* The marketing information system primarily serves the company's marketing and other managers, but it may also provide information to external partners. Then, the MIS *develops information* from internal databases, marketing intelligence activities, and marketing research. *Internal databases* provide information on the company's own operations and departments. Such data can be obtained quickly and cheaply but often needs to be adapted for marketing decisions. *Marketing intelligence* activities supply everyday information about developments in the external marketing environment. *Market research* consists of collecting information relevant to a specific marketing problem faced by the company. Lastly, the MIS *distributes information* gathered from these sources to the right managers in the right form and at the right time.

3 Outline the steps in the marketing research process.

The first step in the marketing research process involves *defining the problem and setting the research objectives,* which may be exploratory, descriptive, or causal research. The second step consists of *developing a research plan* for collecting data from primary and secondary sources. The third step calls for *implementing the marketing research plan* by gathering, processing, and analyzing the information.

The fourth step consists of *interpreting and reporting the findings.* Additional information analysis helps marketing managers apply the information and provides them with sophisticated statistical procedures and models from which to develop more rigorous findings.

Both *internal* and *external* secondary data sources often provide information more quickly and at a lower cost than primary data sources, and they can sometimes yield information that a company cannot collect by itself. However, needed information might not exist in secondary sources. Researchers must also evaluate secondary information to ensure that it is *relevant, accurate, current,* and *impartial.* Primary research must also be evaluated for these features. Each primary data collection method—*observational, survey,* and *experimental*—has its own advantages and disadvantages. Each of the various primary research contact methods—mail, telephone, personal interview, and online—also has its own advantages and drawbacks. Similarly, each contact method has its pluses and minuses.

4 Explain how companies analyze and distribute marketing information.

Information gathered in internal databases and through marketing intelligence and marketing research usually requires more analysis. This may include advanced statistical analysis or the application of analytical models that will help marketers make better decisions. To analyze individual customer data, many companies have now acquired or developed special software and analysis techniques—called *customer relationship management (CRM)*—that integrate, analyze, and apply the mountains of individual customer data contained in their databases.

Marketing information has no value until it is used to make better marketing decisions. Thus, the marketing information system must make the information available to the managers and others who make marketing decisions or deal with customers. In some cases, this means providing regular reports and updates; in other cases it means making nonroutine information available for special situations and on-the-spot decisions. Many firms use company intranets and extranets to facilitate this process. Thanks to modern technology, today's marketing managers can gain direct access to the information system at any time and from virtually any location.

5 Discuss the special issues some marketing researchers face, including public policy and ethics issues.

Some marketers face special marketing research situations, such as those conducting research in small business, nonprofit, or international situations. Marketing research can be conducted effectively by small businesses and nonprofit organizations with limited budgets. International marketing researchers follow the same steps as domestic researchers but often face more and different problems. All organizations need to respond responsibly to major public policy and ethical issues surrounding marketing research, including issues of intrusions on consumer privacy and misuse of research findings.

REVIEWING THE KEY TERMS

Causal research 90
Customer relationship management (CRM) 101
Descriptive research 90
Ethnographic research 93
Experimental research 94
Exploratory research 90
Focus group interviewing 95
Internal databases 88
Marketing information system (MIS) 86
Marketing intelligence 88
Marketing research 89

Observational research 92
Online databases 91
Online marketing research 95
Primary data 91
Sample 97
Secondary data 91
Survey research 93

DISCUSSING THE CONCEPTS

1. Figure 4.1 describes four marketing information system activities for developing information. In groups of four, determine how these activities would apply to Reebok developing the information it needs to market a new running shoe.

2. Assume that you are a regional marketing manager for a cellular phone company. List at least three different sources of internal data and discuss how these data would help you create cellular services that provide greater customer value and satisfaction.

3. Marketing research over the Internet has increased significantly in the past decade. Outline the strengths and weaknesses of marketing research conducted online.

4. According to the text, "The most common cause of CRM failures is that companies mistakenly view CRM only as a technology and software solution." What does this statement mean?

5. How does your college use an intranet to help its students access data?

6. Small businesses and nonprofit organizations often lack the resources to conduct extensive market research. Assume that you are the director of fundraising for a small nonprofit organization that focuses on a social issue. List three ways, using limited resources, that you could gather information about your primary donor group.

APPLYING THE CONCEPTS

1. Imagine you are an owner of a small children's retail clothing store that specializes in upscale girls' fashions from sizes 2 to 6. You have found a potential clothing line but you are unsure whether the line will generate the sales needed to be profitable. Which type of research methodology (exploratory, descriptive, or causal) is best suited to solve your research objective? Why?

2. It has been argued that research data can be manipulated to support any conclusion. Assume you are attending a meeting where a research project for a new product in

a new market is being presented. List five questions that you would ask to test the interpretation and objectivity of the findings being presented.

3. Visit *zoomerang.com* or another free online Web survey site. Using the tools at the site, design a short five-question survey on the dining services for your university. Send the survey to six friends and look at the results. What did you think of the online survey method?

FOCUS ON **TECHNOLOGY**

Several companies offer technology that assists marketers in observational research. These techniques include cameras to monitor a shopper's movements, Web-tracking software to follow a visitor's click stream, and mechanisms to monitor the movement of a consumer's eyeballs. Visit eyetracking.com to learn more about eye-tracking devices. A visit to the "solutions" area of the Web site provides many examples of consumer marketing solutions, including television commercials, Web site branding, and package design. Eye-tracking measurements can help a television advertiser know whether the brand is noticed and, amazingly, report on whether the viewer's emotional reaction to the ad was pleasing or aversive.

1. What can marketers learn from eye-tracking technology in areas other than television advertising?

2. How can marketers use this technology to improve their marketing?

3. What might be some weaknesses with this technology?

 FOCUS ON **ETHICS**

In 2001, Procter & Gamble (P&G) created Tremor, a network of approximately 280,000 young consumers ages 13-19. Tremor uses these teens, identified as being very connected to and influential with others, to spread word of mouth regarding not just its own products but also those of companies as diverse as Coca-Cola and Toyota. Tremor does not pay the teens. Nor does it tell them what to say about specific products. But it does provide them with extensive free samples and the knowledge that their input will be important to marketing decisions.

1. How might P&G identify, attract, and then qualify teens to be members of Tremor?

2. What do you think of using teens to spread word of mouth about products and brands? Are there any ethics issues?

 VIDEO **CASE**

Burke

For more than 75 years, Burke has been helping marketers to understand the marketplace and build stronger relationships with customers. As a full-service, custom marketing research firm, the company helps its clients better understand everything from how consumers make purchase decisions to what drives customer loyalty. In the beginning in 1931, researchers with Burke went door to door to gather information. Today, the company uses a rich array of avenues to reach consumers, including telephone and Web interviewing, direct mail, and online surveys.

Burke helps marketers discover information about customers, competitors, products, and marketing programs. But more than just gathering information, Burke's services help clients use the information. With sophisticated computer analysis, Burke offers the right information, in the right form, at the right time to help them make better marketing decisions.

After viewing the video featuring Burke, answer the following questions about marketing research.

1. What process does Burke use to define the research question?

2. How does Burke's process for marketing research compare to the steps outlined in the chapter?

3. How does Burke help clients build strong relationships with customers?

Harley Davidson: Improving Quality

As part of its ongoing process to "improve anything that can be improved," Harley Davidson conducts periodic customer surveys. One such survey in Singapore several years ago employed the questionnaire shown in Exhibit 1. Respondents of the survey were to be given a 10 percent discount voucher and could win mystery gifts. The survey comprised 10 questions relating to various aspects of Harley Davidson's marketing efforts. Aside from these questions, respondents also furnish background information pertaining to their bike ownership, age, nationality, occupation, and income. They also provided their names, addresses, residential and office telephone numbers, date of birth, and identification source (e.g., passport number).

Exhibit 1

CUSTOMER SURVEY QUESTIONNAIRE

1. What comes to your mind when you think of Harley-Davidson?

   - ❏ It's about burly guys who are perpetually drunk.
   - ❏ It's about rich guys who are never drunk.
   - ❏ It's about cool bikes, I'll get one in the future.
   - ❏ It's about expensive bikes, and I won't ever get one.
   - ❏ It's about great clothes, I'd wear 'em everyday if I have 'em.
   - ❏ It's about cool clothes, but not suitable/too expensive for me.
   - ❏ Don't know what it is.

2. Where have you heard about Harley from?

   - ❏ TV/Radio
   - ❏ Papers/magazines
   - ❏ My friends/colleagues
   - ❏ The boutique
   - ❏ Others, please specify: _____

3. What do you think of our past/present ads?

   - ❏ Informative
   - ❏ Cool
   - ❏ Doesn't say much
   - ❏ Wrong image for me
   - ❏ Haven't seen much of them
   - ❏ Where's the bike?
   - ❏ Other comments: _____

4a. What do you hope to see in future ads?

   - ❏ Bikes
   - ❏ Sex appeal
   - ❏ Lots of leather
   - ❏ Lots of clothes
   - ❏ All of the above
   - ❏ Comments: _____

4b. Do you like seeing Harley-Davidson sponsoring more

   - ❏ Concerts
   - ❏ Fashion Shows
   - ❏ Local TV shows
   - ❏ Local Celebrities
   - ❏ Others, please specify: _____

5. You've seen our boutiques. What attracts you the most?

☐ The brand image
☐ The bike parked out front
☐ The helpful sales staff within
☐ The great looking products

☐ The music and/or jukebox
☐ I'm a Harley fan – I go there regularly
☐ Other comments: _____
_____

6. When you're in there, what do you buy?

☐ Nothing. I just browse
☐ Jeans
☐ Apparel, especially the T-shirts

☐ Apparel, for my kids
☐ Boots
☐ Others: _____
_____

7. How much would you spend in a Harley-Davidson boutique?

☐ $100 and above
☐ Above $50
☐ Below $50
☐ $20 and more
☐ Nothing

8. How much are you willing to spend, say, on a

T-shirt	
Pair of boots	
Jeans	
Jacket	

9. What do you think of Harley's other cool stuff

	Will Buy	Will Browse	Will not Buy/Browse
Caps	☐	☐	☐
Shades	☐	☐	☐
Pewter Mementoes	☐	☐	☐
Stationery Items	☐	☐	☐

10. Do you think Harley Davidson motor clothes are affordable?

☐ Yes   ☐ No.   If not, what kind of clothes do you go for _____
_____

Questions For Discussion

1. Analyze Harley Davidson's customer survey. What information is it trying to gather? What are its research objectives?

2. What recommendations would you make to Harley Davidson with regard to contact method and sampling plan for data collection using this questionnaire?

3. How can the data collected from this questionnaire be analyzed to obtain useful insights for Harley Davidson management?

4. In addition to or instead of the survey, what other means could Harley Davidson use to gather customer information?

Objectives

After studying this chapter, you should be able to

- define the consumer market and construct a simple model of consumer buyer behavior
- name the four major factors that influence consumer buyer behavior
- list and define the major types of buying decision behavior and the stages in the buyer decision process
- describe the adoption and diffusion process for new products

CHAPTER 5

CONSUMER MARKETS AND CONSUMER BUYER BEHAVIOR

Previewing the Concepts

In the previous chapter, you studied how marketers obtain, analyze, and use information to understand the marketplace and assess marketing programs. In this and the next chapter, we'll continue with a closer look at the most important element of the marketplace—customers. The aim of marketing is to affect how customers think about and behave toward the organization and its market offerings. In this chapter, we will look at *final consumer* buying influences and processes. You'll see that understanding buyer behavior is an essential but very difficult task.

To get a better sense of the importance of understanding consumer behavior, let's look first at Hello Kitty, the best-known of the fictional characters marketed by Japanese company Sanrio. Who buys Hello Kitty merchandise? What moves them?

Hello Kitty was born on November 1, 1974 in suburban Cambridge, England. A bright and kind-hearted kitten with no mouth, Kitty now lives with her twin sister Mimmy in London. Weighing the equivalent of three apples, Kitty is good at baking cookies, making pancakes for her friends, Origami, shopping for and with friends, buying things, and tennis. Her hobbies include traveling, music, reading, making new friends, and going on adventures. Her friends include a rabbit, a sheep, a raccoon, and a mouse. Kitty's significant other is Dear Daniel.

Hello Kitty is the best-known of the many fictional characters marketed by Japanese company Sanrio. Kitty's creator, Sanrio founder and president Shintaro Tsuji, researched his son's elementary school friends to determine which animal they liked most. Dog was the top choice followed by cat. Since the dog market was occupied by Snoopy, Tsuji branded a cat, choosing a simple greeting, Hello Kitty, as its name.

The original Kitty first appeared on a small purse in 1974. Initially targeting Japanese pre-adolescent females, Hello Kitty is now a $1.8 billion global marketing phenomenon, appealing to kids, teens, and women who like the sweet, cute, and feminine image. It is estimated that Sanrio has licensed the feline moniker to between 12,000 to 15,000 products. One can virtually live in a Hello Kitty world: Wake up in a Hello Kitty bedroom, have breakfast made with Hello Kitty appliances, work from a Hello Kitty computer on a Hello Kitty desk, relax in front of a Hello Kitty TV set, ride a Hello Kitty scooter to the beach, and ride a Hello

Kitty surfboard in a Hello Kitty wetsuit. There are many stores selling only Hello Kitty merchandise. The little cat has been featured on a MasterCard debit card to teach young girls how to shop and use a debit card.

Several Hello Kitty anime targeting young children have also been produced by Sanrio. In Japan, Hello Kitty and her friends starred in the TV series *Hello Kitty's Paradise*. In the U.S., *Hello Kitty and Friends* aired on CBS and on the Toon Disney cable station. There are also two Hello Kitty theme parks, Puroland and Harmonyland.

Moreover, Hello Kitty has been licensed to other marketers for their promotions. Notably, McDonald's launched a series of Kitty collectibles in several Asian markets in 2000. For example, Singapore customers could purchase the dolls when they bought Extra Value Meals. Demand was unprecedented. Some 250,000 people stood in endless lines for the dolls. Fights broke out and police were brought in to contain the crowd. Thousands of hamburgers were reportedly discarded uneaten by consumers more intent on acquiring the dolls.

Hello Kitty's global appeal is underscored by her selection as child ambassador for UNICEF in the U.S. since 1983, and in Japan since 1984. Why this appeal? Some argue that since Hello Kitty is Western, and she sells in Japan. Others assert that as she is Japanese, and she sells in the West. When introduced in Japan, Hello Kitty was initially positioned as a foreign product, a cat living in London. Says Kitty designer Yuko Yamaguchi, "When Kitty-chan was born, it was rare in those days for Japanese to go abroad. So people yearned for products with English associations. There was an idea that if Kitty–chan spoke English, she would be very fashionable."

The long-drawn Japanese recession also provided impetus for Hello Kitty. Remarked one focus group researcher, "In a recession, you think back to when you were young. Instead of thinking about the grim economic situation, you buy a Hello Kitty refrigerator." Sanrio ascribes Kitty's popularity with high-school girls, young female office workers, and housewives to their need to feel nostalgic during an age of uncertainty. Kitty's soft, round, toothless, clawless, and mute character also inspires a certain protectiveness and affection among women.

However, as the Japanese market became more mature, and Hello Kitty expanded to Western markets, some adaptations were necessary. For example, the American market does not share the same value of cuteness as the Japanese. This meant designing two Kittys. Recalls Yamaguchi, "Purple and pink were very strong colors in the U.S. Blue, yellow, and red were taboo. There were also motifs that were taboo in the U.S. When there is a rainstorm, Kitty-chan has an umbrella and a flower, and beside Kitty-chan is a snail. In the U.S., that was not accepted, and there was a request to eliminate the snail."

Hello Kitty's allure may also draw from the trend toward things Japanese. David McCaughan, Asia-Pacific consumer insights director for McCann-Erickson, notes that Tokyo is one of the world's hippest places. Sara Howard, houseware buyer for Urban Outfitters, remarked, "Japanese style is unique, decorative, and fun, and has become a fashion statement. Girls go for the cutest Hello Kitty characters, emblazoning everything from books to cell phone holders …"

Trend spotter Faith Popcorn explains that Hello Kitty's appeal to corporate women is a "wink on pink. It's like saying women can't be contained. We can wear monochromatic Armani suits and whip out Hello Kitty notepads at a moment's notice." In essence, it represents girl power. One cultural reference attesting to this appears in the hit TV series *Grey's Anatomy*. When Izzy wears Hello Kitty panties in one episode, she is greeted by fellow surgical intern Meredith with, "Hello Kitty."

American celebrities have also contributed to the character's popularity. Ricky Martin, Mariah Carey, Cameron Diaz, Heidi Klum, Steven Tyler, Christina Aguilera, Carmen Electra, as well as Paris and Nicky Hilton have all been spotted with Hello Kitty merchandise. Singer Lisa Loeb, who is marketing the pink Hello Kitty guitar, has admitted to being a fan and has dedicated an album to Hello Kitty called *Hello Lisa*.

Hello Kitty has also joined forces with famous Japanese singer Ayumi Hamasaki to produce products with Japanese jewelry and accessory designer Ash & Diamonds and Panasonic. For example, the Panasonic collaboration involves a line of Lumix cameras with Hello Kitty's image and Hamasaki's insignia. It appears only to be available to Hamasaki's fan club members.

Despite Hello Kitty's success, the future is challenging for Sanrio. The threat of counterfeits is ever present in the region. Markets are maturing, and Hello Kitty may be over-exposed. Asian-American culture magazine Giant Robot once described Sanrio, with its aggressive licensing practices, as a "corporate whore." Then there is competition from Pokemon, Tamagotchi, Winnie the Pooh, and other Disney characters. Still, an inside joke among Sanrio employees is, "Our Kitty is a cat, and their Mickey is a mouse … who's going to win is rather obvious.[1]

Consumer buyer behavior
The buying behavior of final consumers—individuals and households who buy goods and services for personal consumption.

Consumer market
All the individuals and households who buy or acquire goods and services for personal consumption.

The Hello Kitty example shows that many different factors affect consumer buyer behavior. Buyer behavior is never simple, yet understanding it is the essential task of marketing management. **Consumer buyer behavior** refers to the buying behavior of final consumers—individuals and households who buy goods and services for personal consumption. These final consumers combine to make up the **consumer market.** The world consumer market consists of more than 6.5 *billion* people who annually consume an estimated $61 trillion worth of goods and services.[2] In Asia alone, there are 3.5 billion Chinese, Indians, Indonesians, Japanese, and Koreans representing more than half of the world's population. With the economic recovery and boom, Asia is regarded as the most attractive consumer market in the world.

Such consumers vary tremendously in age, income, education level, and tastes. They also buy an incredible variety of goods and services. How these diverse consumers relate with each other and with other elements of the world around them impact their choices among various products, services, and companies. Here we examine the fascinating array of factors that affect consumer behavior.

Model of Consumer Behavior

Consumers make many buying decisions every day. Marketers can study actual consumer purchases to find out what they buy, where, and how much. But learning about the *whys* of consumer buying behavior is not so easy—the answers are often locked deep within the consumer's mind.

The challenge for marketers is to understand the consumer's mind to answer the question: How do consumers respond to various marketing efforts the company might use? The starting point is the stimulus response model of buyer behavior shown in **Figure 5.1.** This figure shows that marketing and other stimuli enter the consumer's "black box" and produce certain responses. Marketers must figure out what is in the buyer's black box.

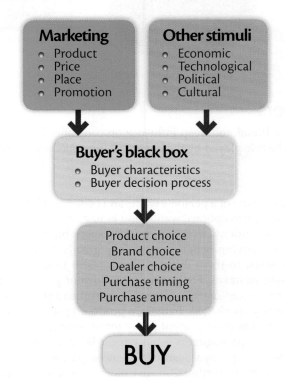

Figure 5.1
Model of buyer behavior

Marketing stimuli consist of the Four Ps: product, price, place, and promotion. Other stimuli include major forces and events in the buyer's environment: economic, technological, political, and cultural. All these inputs enter the buyer's black box, where they are turned into a set of observable buyer responses: product choice, brand choice, dealer choice, purchase timing, and purchase amount.

The marketer wants to understand how the stimuli are changed into responses inside the consumer's black box, which has two parts. First, the buyer's characteristics influence how he or she perceives and reacts to the stimuli. Second, the buyer's decision process itself affects the buyer's behavior. We look first at buyer characteristics as they affect buyer behavior and then discuss the buyer decision process.

Characteristics Affecting Consumer Behavior

Consumer purchases are influenced strongly by cultural, social, personal, and psychological characteristics, shown in **Figure 5.2.** For the most part, marketers cannot control such factors, but they must take them into account.

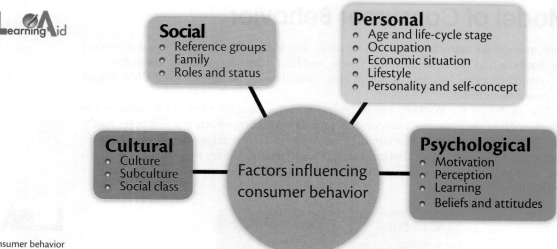

Figure 5.2
Factors influencing consumer behavior

Cultural Factors

Cultural factors exert a broad and deep influence on consumer behavior. The marketer needs to understand the role played by the buyer's *culture*, *subculture*, and *social class*.

Culture

Culture
The set of basic values, perceptions, wants, and behaviors learned by a member of society from family and other important institutions.

Culture is the most basic cause of a person's wants and behavior. Growing up in a society, a child learns basic values, perceptions, wants, and behaviors from the family and other important institutions. Every group or society has a culture, and cultural influences on buying behavior may vary greatly from country to country. Failure to adjust to these differences can result in ineffective marketing or embarrassing mistakes. For example, the idea of product packaging differs greatly across Asian markets. Japanese consumers pay a lot of attention to how a product is packaged. To them, a product's package is both a part of the product as well as an important proxy for its quality. Hence, in the Japanese culture, product packaging is usually regarded as an art. It is not unusual to have products (e.g., soya bean curd) whose packaging costs more than its product content. In contrast, most Chinese consumers regard a product's packaging as merely serving a protective function. They regard the extra effort and cost in packaging as unnecessary and wasteful. To them, the more a product's cost goes into a product, the more it signifies a higher price value return for their purchase.

Marketers are always trying to spot *cultural shifts* to discover new products that might be wanted. For example, the cultural shift toward greater concern about health and fitness has created a huge industry for health-and-fitness services, exercise equipment and clothing, more-natural foods, and a variety of diets.

Culture – Product packaging in Japan is an art; here, a box of cookies wrapped first in decorative paper, then with a sheer piece of cloth.

Subculture

Subculture
A group of people with shared value systems based on common life experiences and situations.

Each culture contains smaller **subcultures**, or groups of people with shared value systems based on common life experiences and situations. Subcultures include nationalities, religions, racial groups, and geographic regions. Many subcultures make up important market segments, and marketers often design products and marketing programs tailored to their needs.

While Japan is typically regarded as being culturally homogenous, there exist subcultures unique from the mainstream. For example, one subculture is interested in cosplay—the act of dressing up in and playing the role of one's favorite inspired Japanese personality. Members acquire clothes to dress like gothic Lolitas, dominatrices, or leather-jacketed Elvis Presleys.

Similarly, although there are common cultural traditions such as *ài miàn zi* (sensitivity to face) in China, there are regional subcultures reflected in varied business practices. Beijing is China's political capital, and many Chinese say that Beijingers are pure "political animals." Shanghainese tend to treat Westerners more equally and conform to international standards more readily than most other parts of China. Cantonese businesspeople are usually welcoming to outsiders. Northeasterners are said to have a reputation of a "tiger-like spirit." They are short-fused and have a propensity for big and quick deals. Sichuanese are known for their honesty and sincerity. Wenzhounese are known for their business acumen.[3]

Social Class

Social classes are society's relatively permanent and ordered divisions whose members share similar values, interests, and behaviors. Social class is not determined by a single factor, such as income, but is measured as a combination of occupation, income, education, wealth, and other variables. In some traditional social systems, such as India's caste system, members of different classes are designated for certain roles, making social mobility difficult.

Marketers are interested in social class because people within a given social class tend to exhibit similar buying behavior. Social classes show distinct product and brand preferences in areas such as clothing, home furnishings, leisure activity, and automobiles. Those in the upper middle prefer red wine and patronize Western restaurants, while those in the working class may drink local beer and dine at sidewalk foodstalls. Swiss luxury watchmaker Audemars Piguet positions its exclusive watches for a high end audience. It sponsors the Audemars Piguet Queen Elizabeth II Cup, a prestigious horse racing event in Hong Kong.

Social Factors

A consumer's behavior is also influenced by social factors, such as the consumer's *small groups*, *family*, and *social roles* and *status*.

Groups

A person's behavior is influenced by many small **groups**. Groups that have a direct influence and to which a person belongs are called membership groups. In contrast, reference groups serve as direct (face-to-face) or indirect points of comparison or reference in forming a person's attitudes or behavior. People often are influenced by reference groups to which they do not belong. For example, an aspirational group is one to which the individual wishes to belong, as when a young girl learning ballet hopes to someday emulate Zhang Ziyi and be a famous actress.

Marketers try to identify the reference groups of their target markets. Reference groups expose a person to new behaviors and lifestyles, influence the person's attitudes and self-concept, and create pressures to conform that may affect the person's product and brand choices. The importance of group influence varies across products and brands. It tends to be strongest when the product is visible to others whom the buyer respects.

Manufacturers of products and brands subjected to strong group influence must reach out to **opinion leaders**—people within a reference group who, because of special skills, knowledge, personality, or other characteristics, exert social influence on others. They are also referred to as the *influentials* or *leading adopters*. These consumers "drive trends, influence mass opinion and, most importantly, sell a great many products," says one expert. They often use their big circle of acquaintances to "spread their knowledge on what's good and what's bad."[4]

Marketers often try to identify opinion leaders for their products and direct marketing efforts toward them. They use *buzz marketing* by enlisting or even creating opinion leaders to spread the word about their brands. For example, Tremor and Vocalpoint, separate marketing arms of Procter & Gamble, have enlisted armies of buzzers to create word of mouth, not just for P&G products but for those of other client companies as well.

The cosplay subculture – Japanese girls dressed as sweet young girls in their role-playing cosplay hobby.

Social class
Relatively permanent and ordered divisions in a society whose members share similar values, interests, and behaviors.

Group
Two or more people who interact to accomplish individual or mutual goals.

Opinion leader
Person within a reference group who, because of special skills, knowledge, personality, or other characteristics, exerts social influence on others.

Social class – Audemars Piguet is an exclusive watch brand. It sponsors the prestigious horse racing event, Queen Elizabeth II Cup in Hong Kong, which targets the elites in society. (_www.hkjc.com.english/special/apqe/apqeii_index.htm_)

Another type of social interaction is online *social networking*—carried out over Internet media ranging from blogs to social networking sites such as MySpace.com and Facebook. com. This new form of high-tech buzz has big implications for marketers.

Social networking sites –
MySpace and Facebook are highly popular. Marketers need to harness their power to build closer customer relationships. (_www. myspace.com_ and _www.facebook.com_)

> Personal connections—forged through words, pictures, video, and audio posted just for the [heck] of it—are the life of the new Web, bringing together the estimated 60 million bloggers, [an unbelievable] 72 million MySpace. com users, and millions more on single-use social networks where people share one category of stuff, like Flickr (photos), Del.icio.us (links), Digg (news stories), Wikipedia (encyclopedia articles), and YouTube (video)… It's hard to overstate the coming impact of these new network technologies on business: They hatch trends and build immense waves of interest in specific products. They serve [up] giant, targeted audiences to advertisers. They edge out old media with the loving labor of amateurs. They effortlessly provide hyperdetailed data to marketers. If your customers are satisfied, networks can help build fanatical loyalty; if not, they'll amplify every complaint until you do something about it. [The new social networking technologies] provide an authentic, peer-to-peer channel of communication that is far more credible than any corporate flackery.

Marketers are working to harness the power of these new social networks to promote their products and build closer customer relationships. For example, when Volkswagen set up a MySpace.com site for Helga, the German-accented, dominatrix-type blonde who appears in its controversial Volkswagen GTI ads, tens of thousands of fans signed up as "friends."[5] And companies regularly post ads or custom videos on video-sharing sites such as YouTube.

> When Adidas recently reintroduced its adicolor shoe, a customizable white-on-white sneaker with a set of seven color markers, it signed on seven top creative directors to develop innovative videos designed especially for downloading to iPods and other handhelds. The directors were given complete creative control to interpret their assigned color as they saw fit. "The directors that we chose we feel have a good deal of underground street cred," says an Adidas marketing executive. The project was not tied specifically to the product. Rather, the directors were asked to "celebrate color, customization, and personal expression." The diverse set of short films was then released, one film a week, via e-mail and sites such as YouTube. The films drew more than 2.1 million viewers within three weeks, 20 million within the first two months, and the numbers were growing exponentially with each new release.[6]

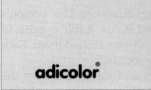 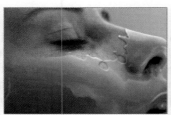  

Social networking – Adidas harnessed the power of social networks to reintroduce its customizable adicolor shoe. It developed innovative downloadable videos that celebrate color and personal expression—here in pink—and then released them through e-mail and social networking sites like YouTube.

However, marketers need to be careful when tapping into online social networking. Ultimately, the users control the content, and online network marketing attempts can easily backfire. For example, when Chevrolet launched a Web contest inviting people to create their own ads for its Chevy Tahoe, it quickly lost control. Says one observer, "the entries that got passed around, blogged about, and eventually covered in the mainstream media were all about the SUV's abysmal gas mileage and melting polar ice caps." One user-generated ad proclaimed, "Like this snowy wilderness? Better get your fill of it now. Then say hello to global warming." Another concluded, "$70 to fill up the tank, which will last less than 400 miles. Chevy Tahoe."[7]

Family

Family members can strongly influence buyer behavior. The family is the most important consumer buying organization in society, and it has been researched extensively. Marketers are interested in the roles and influence of the husband, wife, and children on the purchase of different products and services.

Husband-wife involvement varies widely by product category and by stage in the buying process. Buying roles change with evolving consumer lifestyles. The wife traditionally has been the main purchasing agent for the family in the areas of food, household products, and clothing. But with more women holding jobs outside the home and the willingness of husbands to do more of the family's purchasing, buying roles and lifestyles have changed.

Such changes suggest that marketers in industries that have sold their products to only men or only women are now courting the opposite sex. For example, after realizing that women today account for 50 percent of all technology purchases, Dell has stepped up its efforts to woo women buyers.[8]

Managers from Dell's marketing and public relations staff met earlier this year with editors and sales reps at a dozen publications. Their mission wasn't too surprising: Get editors to print more about Dell's computers, televisions, and pocketPCs. It was the choice of magazines that was unusual, including Oprah Winfrey's *O at Home*, *Ladies' Home Journal*, and *CosmoGIRL*—not exactly publications on the company's regular radar screen. In barely six months, though, Dell's laser printer, plasma TV, and notebook computer were featured as must-haves in gift guides in shelter magazines *Real Simple* and *O at Home*. And in an issue, *CosmoGIRL* gave Dell's Inspiron 700m, less-than-2 kg notebook a "kiss of approval." Why the new emphasis on women buyers? Dell realized that women are its fastest-growing customer group and a key to its growth strategy, especially as it branches out to TVs and MP3 players. Its own research shows that women make up half of its buyers and are as likely as men to prefer buying PCs online. So besides the women's magazines, Dell is running ads on women-centric cable-TV channels.

Children may also have a strong influence on family buying decisions. For example, one study found that kids significantly influence family decisions about where they take vacations and what cars and mobile phones they buy.[9] As children are highly regarded in Asian cultures, it is not uncommon for Asian parents to willingly sacrifice their comfort for their children's well-being. Hence, spending on child-related welfare, education, and development ranks highly in many Asian families.

Family buying influences – In Asia, parentalism suggests that much is spent on children. Especially in smaller families, children are doted upon.

Roles and Status

A person belongs to many groups—family, clubs, and organizations. The person's position in each group can be defined in terms of both role and status. A role consists of the activities people are expected to perform according to the persons around them. Each role carries a status reflecting the general esteem given to it by society.

People usually choose products appropriate to their roles and status. Consider the various roles a working mother plays. In her company, she plays the role of a brand manager; in her family, she plays the role of wife and mother; at her favorite sporting events, she plays the role of avid fan. As a brand manager, she will buy the kind of clothing that reflects her role and status in her company.

Personal Factors

A buyer's decisions also are influenced by personal characteristics such as the buyer's *age and life-cycle stage, occupation, economic situation, lifestyle,* and *personality and self-concept.*

Age and Life-Cycle Stage

People change the goods and services they buy over their lifetimes. Tastes in food, clothes, furniture, and recreation are often age related. Buying is also shaped by the stage of the family life cycle—the stages through which families might pass as they mature over time. Marketers often define their target markets in terms of life-cycle stage and develop appropriate products and marketing plans for each stage.

Traditional family life-cycle stages include young singles and married couples with children. Today, however, marketers are increasingly catering to a growing number of alternative, nontraditional stages such as unmarried couples, singles marrying later in life, childless couples, same-sex couples, single parents, extended parents (those with young adult children returning home), and others.

RBC Royal Bank has identified five life-stage segments. The *youth* segment includes customers younger than 18. *Getting Started* consists of customers aged 18 to 35 who are going through first experiences, such as graduation, first credit card, first car, first loan, marriage, and first child. *Builders,* customers aged 35 to 50, are in their peak earning years. As they build careers and family, they tend to borrow more than they invest. *Accumulators,* aged 50 to 60, worry about saving for retirement and investing wisely. Finally, *Preservers,* customers over 60, want to maximize their retirement income to maintain a desired lifestyle. RBC markets different services to the different segments. For example, with *Builders,* who face many expenses, it emphasizes loans and debt-load management services.[10]

Occupation

A person's occupation affects the goods and services bought. Bluecollar workers tend to buy more rugged work clothes, whereas executives buy more business suits. Marketers try to identify the occupational groups that have an above-average interest in their products and services.

Economic Situation

A person's economic situation will affect product choice. Marketers of income-sensitive goods watch trends in personal income, savings, and interest rates. If economic indicators point to a recession, marketers can take steps to redesign, reposition, and reprice their products closely. Some marketers target consumers who have lots of money and resources, charging prices to match. For example, Rolex positions its luxury watches as "a tribute to elegance, an object of passion, a symbol for all time." Other marketers target consumers with more modest means. Timex makes more affordable watches that "take a licking and keep on ticking."

Lifestyle

People coming from the same subculture, social class, and occupation may have quite different lifestyles. **Lifestyle** is a person's pattern of living as expressed in his or her psychographics. It involves measuring consumers' major AIO dimensions—activities (work, hobbies, shopping, sports, social events), interests (food, fashion, family, recreation), and opinions (about themselves, social issues, business, products). Lifestyle captures something more than the person's social class or personality. It profiles a person's whole pattern of acting and interacting in the world.

Lifestyle
A person's pattern of living as expressed in his or her activities, interests, and opinions.

Lifestyle – These billboard ads in Hong Kong illustrate how ads are positioned to appeal to sporty young women, as well as youths seeking individual expression and creativity.

Several research firms have developed lifestyle classifications. The one most widely used is SRI Consulting Business Intelligence's VALS™ typology (see **Figure 5.3**). VALS classifies people by psychological characteristics and four demographics that correlate with purchase behavior—how they spend their time and money. It divides consumers into eight groups based on two major dimensions: primary motivation and resources. *Primary motivations* include ideals, achievement, and self-expression. According to SRI-BI, consumers who are primarily motivated by *ideals* are guided by knowledge and principles. Consumers who are primarily motivated by *achievement* look for products and services that demonstrate success to their peers. Consumers who are primarily motivated by *self-expression* desire social or physical activity, variety, and risk.

Consumers within each orientation are further classified into those with high resources and those with low resources, depending on whether they have high or low levels of income, education, health, self-confidence, energy, and other factors. Consumers with either very high or very low levels of resources are classified without regard to their primary motivations (Innovators, Survivors). Innovators are people with so many resources that they exhibit all three primary motivations in varying degrees. In contrast, Survivors are people with so few resources that they do not show a strong primary motivation. They must focus on meeting needs rather than fulfilling desires.

Personality and Self-Concept

Each person's distinct personality influences his or her buying behavior. **Personality** refers to the unique psychological characteristics that lead to relatively consistent and lasting responses to one's own environment. Personality is usually described in terms of traits such as self-confidence, dominance, sociability, autonomy, defensiveness, adaptability, and aggressiveness. Personality can be useful in analyzing consumer behavior

Personality
The unique psychological characteristics that lead to relatively consistent and lasting responses to one's own environment.

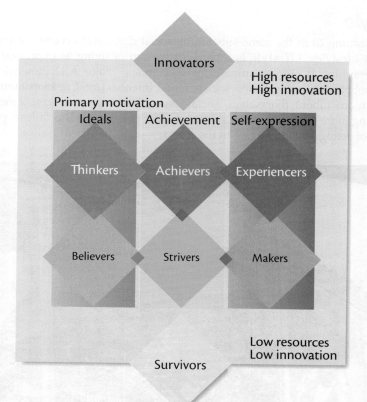

Figure 5.3
VALS™ lifestyle classifications

for certain product or brand choices. For example, coffee marketers have discovered that heavy coffee drinkers tend to be high on sociability. Thus, to attract customers, Starbucks and other coffeehouses create environments in which people can relax and socialize over a cup of steaming coffee.

The idea is that brands also have personalities, and that consumers are likely to choose brands with personalities that match their own. A **brand personality** is the specific mix of human traits that may be attributed to a particular brand. A study among Chinese youths found that Nike was perceived as having the "coolest" personality (30 percent of the votes), followed by Sony and Adidas. However, 51 percent of Chinese youths did not think that China had any cool brand.[11]

One researcher identified five brand personality traits:[12]

- Sincerity (down-to-earth, honest, wholesome, and cheerful)
- Excitement (daring, spirited, imaginative, and up-to-date)
- Competence (reliable, intelligent, and successful)
- Sophistication (upper class and charming)
- Ruggedness (outdoorsy and tough)

Several well-known brands were found to be strongly associated with one particular trait: Levi's with "ruggedness," MTV with "excitement," CNN with "competence," and Campbell with "sincerity." Hence, these brands will attract persons who are high on the same personality traits.

Many marketers use a concept related to personality—a person's *self-concept* (also called *self-image*). The basic self-concept premise is that people's possessions contribute to and reflect their identities; that is, "we are what we have." Thus, to understand consumer behavior, the marketer must first understand the relationship between consumer self-concept and possessions.

Apple applies this concept in a series of ads that characterize two people as computers—one guy plays the part of an Apple Mac and the other plays a PC. "Hello, I'm a Mac," says the guy on the right, who's younger and dressed in jeans. "And I'm a PC," says the one on the left, who's wearing dweeby glasses and a jacket and tie. The two men discuss

Brand personality
The specific mix of human traits that may be attributed to a particular brand.

the relative advantages of Macs versus PCs, with the Mac coming out on top. The ad presents the Mac brand personality as young, laid back, and hip. The PC is portrayed as buttoned down, corporate, and a bit dorky. The message? If you see yourself as young and with it, you need a Mac.[13]

Psychological Factors

A person's buying choices are further influenced by four major psychological factors: *motivation, perception, learning,* and *beliefs and attitudes.*

Motivation

A person has many needs at any given time. Some are biological, arising from states of tension such as hunger, thirst, or discomfort. Others are psychological, arising from the need for recognition, esteem, or belonging. A need becomes a motive when it is aroused to a sufficient level of intensity. A **motive** (or drive) is a need that is sufficiently pressing to direct the person to seek satisfaction. Psychologists have developed theories of human motivation. Two—the theories of Sigmund Freud and Abraham Maslow—are now discussed.

Sigmund Freud assumed that people are largely unconscious about the real psychological forces shaping their behavior. He saw the person as growing up and repressing many urges. These urges are never eliminated or under perfect control; they emerge in dreams, in slips of the tongue, in neurotic and obsessive behavior, or ultimately in psychoses. Freud's theory suggests that a person's buying decisions are affected by subconscious motives that even the buyer may not fully understand. Thus, an aging baby boomer who buys a sporty BMW 330Ci convertible might explain that he simply likes the feel of the wind in his thinning hair. At a deeper level, he may be trying to impress others with his success. At a still deeper level, he may be buying the car to feel young and independent again.

To probe consumers' hidden, subconscious motivations, qualitative research is used. Motivation researchers use a variety of probing techniques to uncover underlying emotions and attitudes toward brands and buying situations. These range from sentence completion, word association, and inkblot or cartoon interpretation tests, to having consumers form daydreams and fantasies about brands or buying situations. One writer offers the following tongue-in-cheek summary of a motivation research session:[14]

Good morning, ladies and gentlemen. We've called you here today for a little consumer research. Now, lie down on the couch, toss your inhibitions out the window, and let's try a little free association. First, think about brands as if they were your *friends.* Imagine your shampoo as an animal. Go on, don't be shy. Would it be a panda or a lion? A snake or a wooly worm? Next, let's sit up and pull out our magic markers. Draw a picture of a typical cake-mix user. Would she wear an apron or a negligee? A business suit or a can-can dress?

One company asks consumers to describe their favorite brands as animals or cars to assess the prestige associated with various brands. Still others rely on hypnosis, dream therapy, or soft lights and mood music to plumb the murky depths of consumer psyches.

Another motivation theory is by Abraham Maslow. He sought to explain why people are driven by particular needs at particular times. Why does one person spend much time and energy on personal safety and another on gaining the esteem of others? Maslow's answer is that human needs are arranged in a hierarchy, as shown in **Figure 5.4**, from the most pressing at the bottom to the least pressing at the top.[15] They include *physiological* needs, *safety* needs, *social* needs, *esteem* needs, and *self-actualization* needs.

Brand personality – What is Pepsi's personality? Happy? (*www.pepsithai.com*)

Motive (or drive)
A need that is sufficiently pressing to direct the person to seek satisfaction of the need.

Subconscious motivations – Inkblot interpretation tests are sometimes used to study consumers' subconscious emotion and attitudes towards brands and buying situations.

A person tries to satisfy the most important need first. When that need is satisfied, it will stop being a motivator and the person will then try to satisfy the next most important need. For example, starving people (physiological need) will not take an interest in the latest happenings in the art world (self-actualization needs), nor in how they are seen or esteemed by others (social or esteem needs), nor even in whether they are breathing clean air (safety needs). But as each important need is satisfied, the next most important need will come into play.

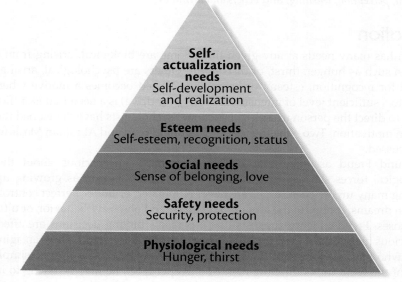

Figure 5.4
Maslow's hierarchy of needs

Perception

A motivated person is ready to act. How the person acts is influenced by his or her own perception of the situation. All of us learn by the flow of information through our five senses: sight, hearing, smell, touch, and taste. However, each of us receives, organizes, and interprets this sensory information in an individual way. **Perception** is the process by which people select, organize, and interpret information to form a meaningful picture of the world.

> **Perception**
> The process by which people select, organize, and interpret information to form a meaningful picture of the world.

People can form different perceptions of the same stimulus because of three perceptual processes: selective attention, selective distortion, and selective retention. People are exposed to a great amount of stimuli every day, for example, an estimated 3,000 to 5,000 ad messages daily.[16] It is impossible for a person to pay attention to all these stimuli. *Selective attention*—the tendency for people to screen out most of the information to which they are exposed—means that marketers must work especially hard to attract the consumer's attention.

Even noticed stimuli do not always come across in the intended way. Each person fits incoming information into an existing mind-set. *Selective distortion* describes the tendency of people to interpret information in a way that will support what they already believe. For example, if you distrust a company, you might perceive even honest ads from the company as questionable. Selective distortion means that marketers must try to understand

Selective perception – It's impossible for people to pay attention to the thousands of ads they're exposed to every day, so they screen most of them out.

the mind-sets of consumers and how these will affect interpretations of advertising and sales information.

People also will forget much of what they learn. They tend to retain information that supports their attitudes and beliefs. Because of *selective retention*, consumers are likely to remember good points made about a brand they favor and to forget good points made about competing brands. Because of selective exposure, distortion, and retention, marketers must work hard to get their messages through. This fact explains why marketers use so much drama and repetition in sending messages to their market.

Interpretation – When Marigold introduced its strawberry-flavored milk, its ads were designed to capture the audience's attention and interpretation. The strawberries are prominently placed and shaped as a cow's face in one and as a cow's udder in the other to suggest that the milk is strawberry flavored. (www.mdi.com.sg)

Learning

When people act, they learn. **Learning** describes changes in an individual's behavior arising from experience. Learning theorists say that most human behavior is learned. Learning occurs through the interplay of drives, stimuli, cues, responses, and reinforcement.

A *drive* is a strong internal stimulus that calls for action. A drive becomes a motive when it is directed toward a particular *stimulus object*. For example, a person's drive for self-actualization might motivate him or her to look into buying a digital camera. The consumer's response to the idea of buying a camera is conditioned by the surrounding cues. *Cues* are minor stimuli that determine when, where, and how the person responds. For example, the person might spot several camera brands in a shop window, hear of a special sale price, or discuss cameras with a friend. These are all cues that might influence a consumer's *response* to his or her interest in buying the product.

Suppose the consumer buys a Nikon digital camera. If the experience is rewarding, the consumer will probably use the camera more and more, and his or her response will be *reinforced*. Then, the next time the consumer shops for a camera, or for binoculars or some similar product, the probability is greater that he or she will buy a Nikon product. The practical significance of learning theory for marketers is that they can build up demand for a product by associating it with strong drives, using motivating cues, and providing positive reinforcement.

Beliefs and Attitudes

Through doing and learning, people acquire beliefs and attitudes. These, in turn, influence their buying behavior. A **belief** is a descriptive thought that a person has about something. Beliefs may be based on real knowledge, opinion, or faith and may or may not carry an emotional charge. Marketers are interested in the beliefs that people formulate about specific products and services, because these beliefs make up product and brand

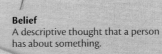

Learning
Changes in an individual's behavior arising from experience.

Belief
A descriptive thought that a person has about something.

images that affect buying behavior. If some of the beliefs are wrong and prevent purchase, the marketer will want to launch a campaign to correct them.

People have attitudes regarding religion, politics, clothes, music, food, and almost everything else. **Attitude** describes a person's relatively consistent evaluations, feelings, and tendencies toward an object or idea. Attitudes put people into a frame of mind of liking or disliking things, of moving toward or away from them. Our digital camera buyer may hold attitudes such as "Buy the best," "The Japanese make the best electronics products in the world," and "Creativity and self-expression are among the most important things in life." If so, the Nikon camera would fit well into the consumer's existing attitudes.

Attitudes are difficult to change. A person's attitudes fit into a pattern, and to change one attitude may require difficult adjustments in many others. Thus, a company should usually try to fit its products into existing attitudes rather than attempt to change attitudes. Of course, there are exceptions in which the cost of trying to change attitudes may pay off handsomely:

> By 1994, milk consumption had been in decline for 20 years. The general perception was that milk was unhealthy, outdated, just for kids, or good only with cookies and cake. To counter these notions, the National Fluid Milk Processors Education Program (MilkPEP) in the U.S. began an ad campaign featuring milk be-mustached celebrities and the tag line Got Milk? The campaign has not only been wildly popular, it has been successful as well—not only did it stop the decline, milk consumption actually increased. The campaign is still running. Although initially the target market was women in their 20s, the campaign has been expanded to other target markets and has gained cult status with teens, much to their parents' delight. Teens collect the print ads featuring celebrities ranging from music stars Kelly Clarkson and Beyoncé, to actors such as Jackie Chan and Zhang Ziyi, to sports idols such as Venus and Serena Williams. Building on this popularity with teens, the industry set up a Web site (www.whymilk.com) where young people can make their own mustache, check out the latest Got Milk? ads, or get facts about "everything you ever need to know about milk." The industry also promotes milk to them through grassroots marketing efforts. It recently launched an online promotion searching for the 50 healthiest student bodies in the U.S. People who enter their school can win prizes from various sponsors and a grant to support fitness and nutrition programs in the winner's school.[17]

Attitude
A person's relatively consistent evaluations, feelings, and tendencies toward an object or idea.

Attitudes are difficult to change. Despite this, National Fluid Milk Processor's wildly popular milk moustache campaign succeeded in changing attitudes toward milk. (www.whymilk.com)

Figure 5.5
Four types of buying behavior
Source: Adapted from Henry Assael, *Consumer Behavior and Marketing Action* (Boston: Kent Publishing Company 1987), p. 87. Copyright © 1987 by Wadsworth, Inc. Printed by permission of Kent Publishing Company, a division of Wadsworth, Inc.

Types of Buying Decision Behavior

Buying behavior differs greatly for a tube of toothpaste, an iPod, financial services, and a new car. More complex decisions usually involve more buying participants and more buyer deliberation. **Figure 5.5** shows types of consumer buying behavior based on the degree of buyer involvement and the degree of differences among brands.

	High involvement	Low involvement
Significant differences between brands	Complex buying behavior	Variety-seeking buying behavior
Few differences between brands	Dissonance-reducing buying behavior	Habitual buying behavior

Complex Buying Behavior

Consumers undertake **complex buying behavior** when they are highly involved in a purchase and perceive significant differences among brands. Consumers may be highly involved when the product is expensive, risky, purchased infrequently, and highly self-expressive. Typically, the consumer has much to learn about the product category. For example, a PC buyer may not know what attributes to consider.

This buyer will pass through a learning process, first developing beliefs about the product, then attitudes, and then making a thoughtful purchase choice. Marketers of high-involvement products must understand the information-gathering and evaluation behavior of high-involvement consumers. They need to help buyers learn about the attributes and their relative importance. They need to differentiate their brand's features, perhaps by describing the brand's benefits using print media with long copy. They must motivate store salespeople and the buyer's acquaintances to influence the final brand choice.

Dissonance-Reducing Buying Behavior

Dissonance-reducing buying behavior occurs when consumers are highly involved with an expensive, infrequent, or risky purchase, but see little difference among brands. For example, consumers buying a camera may face a high-involvement decision because cameras are expensive and self-expressive. Yet buyers may consider most camera brands in a given price range to be the same. In this case, because perceived brand differences are not large, buyers may shop around to learn what is available, but buy relatively quickly. They may respond primarily to a good price or to purchase convenience.

After the purchase, consumers might experience *postpurchase dissonance* (after-sale discomfort) when they notice certain disadvantages of the purchased camera brand or hear favorable things about brands not purchased. To counter such dissonance, the marketer's after-sale communications should provide evidence and support to help consumers feel good about their brand choices.

Habitual Buying Behavior

Habitual buying behavior occurs under conditions of low consumer involvement and little significant brand difference (see **Figure 5.6**). For example, take salt. Consumers have little involvement in this product category—they simply go to the store and reach for a brand. If they keep reaching for the same brand, it is out of habit rather than strong brand loyalty. Consumers appear to have low involvement with most low-cost, frequently purchased products.

Complex buying behavior
Consumer buying behavior in situations characterized by high consumer involvement in a purchase and significant perceived differences among brands.

Dissonance-reducing buying behavior
Consumer buying behavior in situations characterized by high involvement but few perceived differences among brands.

Habitual buying behavior
Consumer buying behavior in situations characterized by low consumer involvement and few significant perceived brand differences.

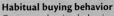

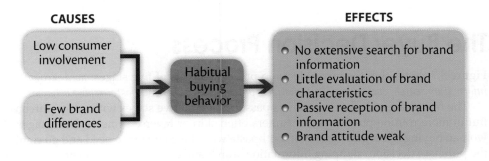

Figure 5.6
Causes and effects of habitual buying hehavior

In such cases, consumers do not search extensively for information about the brands, evaluate brand characteristics, and make weighty decisions about which brands to buy. Instead, they passively receive information as they watch television or read magazines. Ad repetition creates *brand familiarity* rather than *brand conviction*. Consumers do not form strong attitudes toward a brand; they select the brand because it is familiar. Because they are not highly involved with the product, consumers may not evaluate the choice even

Variety seeking – Consumers are spoilt for choice in the soda drink market. Brand switching may occur because consumers want to try another brand out of boredom or simply to try something different, rather than because of dissatisfaction.

Variety-seeking buying behavior
Consumer buying behavior in situations characterized by low consumer involvement but significant perceived brand differences.

after purchase. Thus, the buying process involves brand beliefs formed by passive learning, followed by purchase behavior, which may or may not be followed by evaluation.

Because buyers are not highly committed to any brands, marketers of low-involvement products with few brand differences often use price and sales promotions to stimulate product trial. In advertising for a low-involvement product, ad copy should stress only a few key points. Visual symbols and imagery are important because they can be remembered easily and associated with the brand. Ad campaigns should include high repetition of short-duration messages. Television is usually more effective than print media because it is a low-involvement medium suitable for passive learning. Advertising planning should be based on classical conditioning theory, in which buyers learn to identify a certain product by a symbol repeatedly attached to it. Below is an example of classical conditioning at work in China.

KFC entered China five years ahead of McDonald's. At one time, KFC had more outlets and more per head spending than McDonald's. One senior executive at McDonald's decided to personally find out the reasons for that. He stood at KFC's entrance and asked the incoming consumers a simple question, "Why don't you go to McDonald's?" To his surprise, many replied, "They don't sell chicken there." Recognizing consumers' strong preference for chicken over beef, McDonald's in China started to reduce its association with hamburgers and feature chicken more prominently in their menus.

Variety-Seeking Buying Behavior

Consumers undertake **variety-seeking buying behavior** in situations characterized by low consumer involvement but significant perceived brand differences. In such cases, consumers often do a lot of brand switching. For example, when buying soda drinks, a consumer may hold some beliefs, choose a soda drink without much evaluation, and then evaluate that brand during consumption. But the next time, the consumer might pick another brand out of boredom or simply to try something different. Brand switching occurs for the sake of variety rather than because of dissatisfaction.

In such product categories, the marketing strategy may differ for the market leader and minor brands. The market leader will try to encourage habitual buying behavior by:
- dominating shelf space, keeping shelves fully stocked, and
- running frequent reminder advertising.

Challenger firms will encourage variety seeking by:
- offering lower prices, special deals, coupons and free samples, and
- advertising reasons for trying something new.

The Buyer Decision Process

Figure 5.7 shows that the buyer decision process consists of five stages: *need recognition, information search, evaluation of alternatives, purchase decision,* and *postpurchase behavior*.[18]

The figure suggests that consumers pass through all five stages with every purchase. But in more routine purchases, consumers often skip or reverse some of these stages. A woman buying her regular brand of toothpaste would recognize the need and go right to the purchase decision, skipping information search and evaluation. However, we use the model in **Figure 5.7** because it shows all the considerations that arise when a consumer faces a new and complex purchase situation.

Figure 5.7
Buying decision process

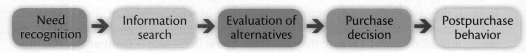

Need Recognition

The buying process starts with **need recognition**—the buyer recognizes a problem or need. The need can be triggered by *internal stimuli* when one of the person's normal needs—hunger, thirst, sex—rises to a level high enough to become a drive. A need can also be triggered by *external stimuli*. For example, an advertisement or a discussion with a friend might get you thinking about buying a new car. At this stage, the marketer should find out what kinds of needs or problems arise, what brought them about, and how they led the consumer to this particular product.

Need recognition
The first stage of the buyer decision process, in which the consumer recognizes a problem or need.

In Asia's transitional economies led by China and India, one can easily find shopping streets in residential and commercial areas in its cities. There, entrepreneurial owners put on the most aggressive and interesting displays of point-of-purchase promotions to remind shoppers of their consumption needs. In these shopping streets, large display signs, music, lighting, smell from restaurants and leather goods stores, together with sales pitches made through loudspeakers and accompanied by product demonstrations make up the typical retailing scene seen every evening after dinner. These small private entrepreneurs make every effort to catch the attention of passers-by.

Marketing stimuli –
A shopping mall in China filled with advertisements fighting for consumers' attention.

Information Search

An interested consumer may or may not search for more information. The amount of **information search** you do depends on the strength of your drive, the amount of information you start with, the ease of obtaining more information, the value you place on additional information, and the satisfaction you get from searching.

Consumers can obtain information from several sources (see **Figure 5.8**). These include *personal sources* (family, friends, neighbors, acquaintances), *commercial sources* (advertising, salespeople, Web sites, dealers, packaging, displays), *public sources* (mass media, consumer-rating organizations, Internet searches), and *experiential sources* (handling, examining, using the product). The relative influence of these information sources varies with the product and the buyer. Generally, the consumer receives the most information about a product from commercial sources—those controlled by the marketer. The most effective sources, however, tend to be personal. Commercial sources normally *inform* the buyer, but personal sources *legitimize* or *evaluate* products for the buyer.

Information search
The stage of the buyer decision process in which the consumer is aroused to search for more information; the consumer may simply have heightened attention or may go into active information search.

	Personal	**Commercial**	**Public**	**Experiential**
Sources of information	• Family • Friends • Neighbours • Acquaintances	• Advertising • Salespeople • Web sites • Dealers • Packaging • Display	• Mass media • Consumer-rating organizations • Internet searches	• Personal handling, examining, and use of brand
Role of information	Legitimize Evaluate	Inform	Inform	Evaluate

Figure 5.8
Sources of information

Evaluation of Alternatives

How does the consumer choose among the alternative brands? The marketer needs to know about **alternative evaluation**—that is, how the consumer processes information to arrive at brand choices. Unfortunately, consumers do not use a simple and single evaluation process in all buying situations. Instead, several evaluation processes are at work.

In some cases, consumers use careful calculations and logical thinking. At other times, the same consumers do little or no evaluating; instead they buy on impulse and rely on intuition. Sometimes consumers make buying decisions on their own; sometimes they turn to friends, consumer guides, or salespeople for buying advice.

Suppose you've narrowed your car choices to three brands. And suppose that you are primarily interested in four attributes—styling, operating economy, warranty, and price. By this time, you've probably formed beliefs about how each brand rates on each attribute. Clearly, if one car rated best on all the attributes, we could predict that you would choose it. However, the brands will no doubt vary in appeal. You might base your buying decision on only one attribute, and your choice would be easy to predict. If you wanted styling above everything else, you would buy the car that you think has the best styling. But most buyers consider several attributes, each with different importance. If we knew the importance that you assigned to each of the four attributes, we could predict your car choice more reliably.

Asian consumers are known to love to shop in the narrow, crowded shopping streets as well as in modern shopping malls. When they shop, they subconsciously use a number of criteria to evaluate product quality. While consumers from Western developed countries like to shop in a relaxed, non-crowded environment, Asian consumers take crowdedness as a sign of good product quality and more importantly, of good value. The crowded setting also helps to excite potential consumers and encourage them to shorten the evaluation process and move on to the purchase decision stage.

Alternative evaluation
The stage of the buyer decision process in which the consumer uses information to evaluate alternative brands in the choice set.

Need recognition –
This inventive ad from The LEGO Company triggers consumers to think about where the first little block might lead—"imagine..." (www.lego.com)

Purchase Decision

Generally, the consumer's **purchase decision** will be to buy the most preferred brand, but two factors can come between the purchase *intention* and the purchase *decision*. The first factor is the *attitudes of others*. If someone important to you thinks that you should buy the lowest-priced car, then the chances of your buying a more expensive car are reduced.

The second factor is *unexpected situational factors*. The consumer may form a purchase intention based on factors such as expected income, expected price, and expected product benefits. However, unexpected events may change the purchase intention. For example, the economy might take a turn for the worse or a close competitor might drop its price. Thus, preferences and even purchase intentions do not always result in actual purchase choice.

Purchase decision
The buyer's decision about which brand to purchase.

Postpurchase behavior
The stage of the buyer decision process in which the consumers takes further action after purchase, base on their satisfaction or dissaisfaction.

Postpurchase Behavior

The marketer's job does not end when the product is bought. After purchasing the product, the consumer will be satisfied or dissatisfied and will engage in **postpurchase behavior** of interest to the marketer. What determines whether the buyer is satisfied or dissatisfied with a purchase? The answer lies in the relationship between the *consumer's expectations* and the product's *perceived performance*.

- If the product falls short of expectations, the consumer is disappointed.
- If it meets expectations, the consumer is satisfied.
- If it exceeds expectations, the consumer is delighted.

The larger the gap between expectations and performance, the greater the consumer's dissatisfaction. This suggests that sellers should promise only what their brands can deliver so that buyers are satisfied. Some sellers might even understate product performance levels to boost later consumer satisfaction. For example, Boeing's salespeople tend to be conservative when they estimate the potential benefits of their aircraft. They almost always underestimate fuel efficiency—they promise a 5 percent savings that turns out to be 8 percent. Customers are delighted with better-than-expected performance; they buy again and tell other potential customers that Boeing lives up to its promises.

Almost all major purchases result in **cognitive dissonance**, or discomfort caused by postpurchase conflict. After the purchase, consumers are satisfied with the benefits of the chosen brand and are glad to avoid the drawbacks of the brands not bought. However, every purchase involves compromise. Consumers feel uneasy about acquiring the drawbacks of the chosen brand and about losing the benefits of the brands not purchased. Thus, consumers feel at least some postpurchase dissonance for every purchase.[19]

> **Cognitive dissonance**
> Buyer discomfort caused by postpurchase conflict.

Why is it so important to satisfy the customer? Customer satisfaction is a key to building profitable relationships with consumers—to keeping and growing consumers and reaping their customer lifetime value. **Figure 5.9** shows the importance of customer satisfaction. Satisfied customers buy a product again, talk favorably to others about the product, pay less attention to competing brands and advertising, and buy other products from the company. Many marketers go beyond merely *meeting* the expectations of customers—they aim to *delight* the customer (see **Real Marketing**).

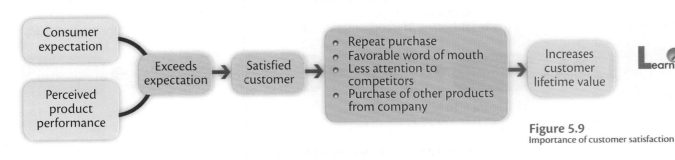

Figure 5.9
Importance of customer satisfaction

A dissatisfied consumer responds differently. Bad word of mouth often travels farther and faster than good word of mouth. It can quickly damage consumer attitudes about a company and its products. But companies cannot simply rely on dissatisfied customers to volunteer their complaints when they are dissatisfied. Most unhappy customers never tell the company about their problem. Therefore, a company should measure customer satisfaction regularly. It should set up systems that *encourage* customers to complain. In this way, the company can learn how well it is doing and how it can improve.

By studying the overall buyer decision, marketers may be able to find ways to help consumers move through it. For example, if consumers are not buying a new product because they do not see a need for it, marketing might launch advertising messages that trigger the need and show how the product solves customers' problems. If customers know about the product but are not buying because they hold unfavorable attitudes toward it, the marketer must find ways either to change the product or change consumer perceptions.

> **Cognitive dissonance –**
> Consumers are satisfied with the benefits of their choice, but also feel uneasy about losing the benefits of the brand not purchased.

The Buyer Decision Process for New Products

We now look at how buyers approach the purchase of new products. A **new product** is a good, service, or idea that is perceived by some potential customers as new. It may have been around for a while, but our interest is in how consumers learn about products for the first time and make decisions on whether to adopt them. We define the **adoption process** as "the mental process through which an individual passes from first learning about an innovation to final adoption," and *adoption* as the decision by an individual to become a regular user of the product.[20]

Stages in the Adoption Process

Consumers go through five stages in the process of adopting a new product: (see Figure 5.10)

- *Awareness:* The consumer becomes aware of the new product, but lacks information about it.
- *Interest:* The consumer seeks information about the new product.
- *Evaluation:* The consumer considers whether trying the new product makes sense.
- *Trial:* The consumer tries the new product on a small scale to improve his or her estimate of its value.
- *Adoption:* The consumer decides to make full and regular use of the new product.

Figure 5.10
Stages in the adoption process

This model suggests that the new-product marketer should think about how to help consumers move through these stages. A luxury car producer might find that many potential customers know about and are interested in its new model but aren't buying because of uncertainty about the model's benefits and the high price. The producer could launch a "take one home for the weekend" promotion to high-value prospects to move them into the trial process and lead them to purchase.

Individual Differences in Innovativeness

People differ greatly in their readiness to try new products. In each product area, there are "consumption pioneers" and early adopters. Other individuals adopt new products much later. People can be classified into the adopter categories shown in **Figure 5.11** After a slow start, an increasing number of people adopt the new product. The number of adopters reaches a peak and then drops off as fewer nonadopters remain. Innovators are defined as the first 2.5 percent of the buyers to adopt a new idea (those beyond two standard deviations from mean adoption time); the early adopters are the next 13.5 percent (between one and two standard deviations); and so forth.

The five adopter groups have differing values:

- Innovators are venturesome—they try new ideas at some risk.
- Early adopters are guided by respect—they are opinion leaders in their communities and adopt new ideas early but carefully.
- Early majority are deliberate—although they rarely are leaders, they adopt new ideas before the average person.
- Late majority are skeptical—they adopt an innovation only after a majority of people have tried it.
- Laggards are tradition bound—they are suspicious of changes and adopt the innovation only when it has become something of a tradition itself.

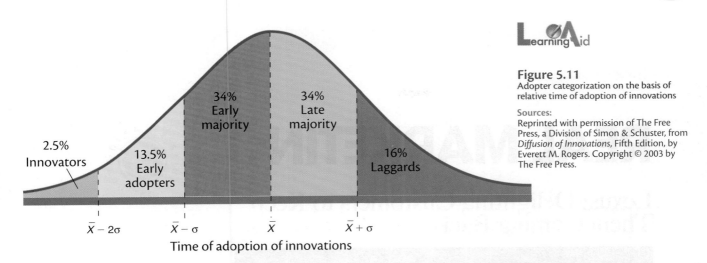

Figure 5.11
Adopter categorization on the basis of relative time of adoption of innovations

Sources:
Reprinted with permission of The Free Press, a Division of Simon & Schuster, from *Diffusion of Innovations*, Fifth Edition, by Everett M. Rogers. Copyright © 2003 by The Free Press.

This adopter classification suggests that an innovating firm should research the characteristics of innovators and early adopters and direct market to them. In general, innovators tend to be relatively younger, better educated, and higher in income than later adopters and nonadopters. They are more receptive to unfamiliar things, rely more on their own values and judgment, and are more willing to take risks. They are less brand loyal and more likely to take advantage of special promotions such as discounts, coupons, and samples.

Influence of Product Characteristics on Rate of Adoption

The characteristics of the new product affect its rate of adoption. Some products catch on almost overnight (iPod), whereas others take a long time to gain acceptance (HDTV). Five characteristics are especially important in influencing an innovation's rate of adoption. For example, consider the characteristics of HDTV in relation to the rate of adoption:

- *Relative advantage:* the degree to which the innovation appears superior to existing products. The greater the perceived relative advantage of using HDTV—say, in picture quality and ease of viewing—the sooner HDTVs will be adopted.
- *Compatibility:* the degree to which the innovation fits the values and experiences of potential consumers. HDTV, for example, is highly compatible with the lifestyles found in upper middle-class homes. However, it is not yet completely compatible with the programming and broadcasting systems currently available to consumers.
- *Complexity:* the degree to which the innovation is difficult to understand or use. HDTVs are not very complex and, therefore, once more programming is available and prices come down, will take less time to penetrate homes than more complex innovations.
- *Divisibility:* the degree to which the innovation may be tried on a limited basis. HDTVs are still relatively expensive. This will slow the rate of adoption.
- *Communicability:* the degree to which the results of using the innovation can be observed or described to others. Because HDTV lends itself to demonstration and description, its use will spread faster among consumers.

Other characteristics influence the rate of adoption, such as initial and ongoing costs, risk and uncertainty, and social approval. The new-product marketer must research all these factors when developing the new product and its marketing program.

Influencing rate of adoption –
Essilor introduced the Varilux Physio 3-in-1 progressive lens in Singapore in 2007. It has the relative advantage of smooth transition from distance vision through intermediate to near vision. It is also compatible with the target market's lifestyle by having no visible line dividing the power increase. Its ads communicate the benefits of this new lens. (*www.essilor.com.sg/consumer/products/aarilux/varilux.htm*)

REAL MARKETING

Lexus: Delighting Customers to Keep Them Coming Back

Delighting customers – Lexus and its dealers—such as Park Place Lexus—go to almost any extreme to take care of customers. "They don't cut corners here," says a Park Place salesperson. "It's like walking into a Ritz-Carlton."

Close your eyes and picture a typical car dealership. Not impressed? Talk to an American friend who owns a Lexus, and you'll no doubt get a very different picture. The typical Lexus dealership in the U.S. is ... well, anything but typical. And some Lexus dealers will go to almost any extreme to take care of customers and keep them coming back:

Jordan Case has big plans for the ongoing expansion of his business. He's already put in wireless Internet access. He's adding a café. And he's installing a putting green for customers who want to hone their golf skills while waiting for

service. Case isn't the manager of a swank hotel or restaurant. He's the president of Park Place Lexus, an auto dealership with two locations in the Dallas area, and he takes pride that his dealership is, well, the anti-dealership. "Buying a car doesn't rank up there with the top five things you like to do," Case says. "So we try to make the experience different." In addition to the café, putting green, and Internet access, customer perks include free car washes and portable DVD players with movies loaned to waiting service clients.

These ideas sprung from constant customer feedback, including a focus

group of more than 20 Lexus and non-Lexus customers who vetoed some ideas (while-you-wait manicures got a thumbs down) and helped gauge expectations in other areas (wait times for receiving newly bought cars should be only two minutes, they said). Says a Park Place salesperson, "The dealer spends an exorbitant amount of money on renovations, and there are fresh flowers everywhere. It's like walking into a Ritz-Carlton. Last year, Park Place Lexus's passion for customer service earned it a Malcolm Baldrige National Quality Award, a business-excellence honor bestowed by the U.S. government."

Lexus knows that good marketing doesn't stop with making the sale. Keeping customers happy *after* the sale is the key to building lasting relationships. Dealers across the country have a common goal: to delight customers and keep them coming back. Lexus believes that if you "delight the customer, and continue to delight the customer, you will have a customer for life." And Lexus understands just how valuable a customer can be—it estimates that the average lifetime value of a Lexus customer is $600,000.

Despite the amenities, few Lexus customers spend much time hanging around the dealership. Lexus knows that the best dealership visit is the one that you don't have to make at all. So it builds customer-pleasing cars to start with—high-quality cars that need little servicing. In its "Lexus Covenant," the company vows that it will make "the finest cars ever built." In survey after industry survey, Lexus rates at or near the top in quality. Last year's J.D. Powers Initial Quality Study rated Lexus highest in 6 of 19 model segments. Other than the Toyota brand, which topped four categories, no other brand led in more than one segment. Lexus has had the study's top-rated vehicle in five of the last six years.

Still, when a car does need to be serviced, Lexus goes out of its way to make it easy and painless. Most dealers will even pick up the car and then return it when the maintenance is finished. And the car comes back spotless, thanks to a complimentary cleaning to remove bugs and road grime from the exterior and smudges from the leather interior. You might even be surprised to find that they've touched up a door ding to help restore the car to its fresh-from-the-factory luster.

And when a customer does bring a car in, Lexus repairs it right the first time, on time. Dealers know that their well-heeled customers have money, "but what they don't have is time." So some dealers are testing a system that uses three technicians instead of one for 35,000-mile service checkups. The new system will cut a customer's wait in half. "I'm not in the car business," says one dealer. "I'm in the service business."

According to its Web site, Lexus set out to "revolutionize the automotive experience with a passionate commitment to the finest products, supported by dealers who create the most satisfying ownership experience the world has ever seen. We vow to value the customer as an important individual. To do things right the first time. And to always exceed expectations." Jordan Case of Park Place Lexus fully embraces this philosophy: "You've got to do it right, on time, and make people feel like they are the only one in the room."

At Lexus, exceeding customer expectations sometimes means fulfilling even seemingly outrageous customer requests. Dave Wilson, owner of several Lexus dealerships in Southern California, tells of a letter he received from an angry Lexus owner who spent $374 to repair her car at his dealership. She'd owned four prior Lexus vehicles without a single problem. She said in her letter that she resented paying to fix her current one. Turns out, she thought they were maintenance free—as in get in and drive ... and drive and drive. "She didn't think she had to do anything to her Lexus," says Wilson. "She had 60,000 miles on it, and never had the oil changed." Wilson sent back her $374.

By all accounts, Lexus has lived up to its ambitious customer satisfaction promise. It has created what appear to be the world's most satisfied car owners. Lexus regularly tops not just the J.D. Power quality ratings but also its customer-satisfaction ratings, and not just in the U. S., but worldwide. In 2004, in the United Kingdom, Lexus achieved the highest J.D. Power customer-satisfaction score ever in the rating's 12-year history. Customer satisfaction translates into sales and customer loyalty. In 2006, for the sixth straight year, Lexus was the top selling luxury car in the U.S. Similarly, in Japan, Lexus was ranked highest in satisfying customers with the dealer service experience in 2007. And once a Lexus customer, always a Lexus customer—Lexus retains 84 percent of customers who've gone to the dealership for service.

Sources:

The Park Place Lexus example is adapted from Julia Chang, "At Your Service," *Sales & Marketing Management*, June 2006, pp. 42–43. Other information and quotes from Steve Finlay, "At Least She Put Fuel in It," *Ward's Dealer Business*, August 1, 2003; "Lexus Roars for Loyal Customers," *B&T Magazine*, November 27, 2003; Jeremy W. Peters, "Lexus Tops Owners Survey for Fifth Year," *New York Times*, May 19, 2005, p. C10; "Porsche Tops Quality Survey: Toyota, Lexus Top Most Vehicle Segments in Revised J.D. Power Initial Quality Study," June 8, 2006, accessed at www.cnn.com/2006/AUTOS/06/07/jdpower_iqs/index.html; "Lexus Covenant," accessed at www.lexus.com/about/corporate/covenant.html, December 2006; "Lexus Ranks Highest in Customer Satisfaction with Dealer Service in Japan, J.D. Power Asia Pacific Reports," accessed at www.autospectator.com, May 2008.

Consumer Behavior Across International Borders

For companies operating in many countries, understanding and serving the needs of consumers can be daunting. Although consumers in different countries may have some things in common, their values, attitudes, and behaviors often vary greatly. International marketers must understand such differences and adjust their products and marketing programs accordingly.

Sometimes the differences are obvious. For example, in the U.S., where most people eat cereal regularly for breakfast, Kellogg focuses its marketing on persuading consumers to select a Kellogg brand rather than a competitor's brand. In France, however, where most people prefer croissants and coffee or no breakfast at all, Kellogg's advertising attempts to convince people that they should eat cereal for breakfast. Its packaging includes step-by-step instructions on how to prepare cereal. In India, where many consumers eat heavy, fried breakfasts or skip the meal altogether, Kellogg's advertising attempts to convince buyers to switch to a lighter, more nutritious breakfast diet. Kellogg also found that Indians who eat cereal like it with hot milk and lots of sugar.

In India, many people tend to prefer heavy, fried breakfasts or to skip the meal altogether. Kellogg's challenge is to convince them to swich to a lighter, more nutritious breakfast diet.

Often, differences across international markets are more subtle. They may result from physical differences in consumers and their environments. For example, Remington makes smaller electric shavers to fit the smaller hands of Japanese consumers. Other differences result from varying customs. In Japan, for example, where humility and deference are considered great virtues, pushy, hard-hitting sales approaches are considered offensive. Failing to understand such differences in customs and behaviors from one country to another can spell disaster for a marketer's international products and programs.

Marketers must decide on the degree to which they will adapt their products and marketing programs to meet the unique cultures and needs of consumers in various markets. They want to standardize their offerings to simplify operations and take advantage of cost economies. However, adapting marketing efforts within each country results in products and programs that better satisfy the needs of local consumers. The question of whether to adapt or standardize the marketing mix across international markets has created a lively debate in recent years. We will revisit this question in Chapter 19.

REVIEWING THE CONCEPTS

The Chinese consumer market consists of over 1.33 billion making it one of the most attractive consumer markets in the world. The world consumer market consists of more than 6.5 *billion* people. Consumers around the world vary greatly in age, income, education level, and tastes. Understanding how these differences affect *consumer buying behavior* is one of the biggest challenges marketers face.

1 Define the consumer market and construct a simple model of consumer buyer behavior.

The *consumer market* consists of all the individuals and households who buy or acquire goods and services for personal consumption. The simplest model of consumer buyer behavior is the stimulus-response model. According to this model, marketing stimuli (the four Ps) and other major forces (economic, technological, political, cultural) enter the consumer's "black box" and produce certain responses. Once in the black box, these inputs produce observable buyer responses, such as product choice, brand choice, purchase timing, and purchase amount.

2 Name the four major factors that influence consumer buyer behavior.

Consumer buyer behavior is influenced by four key sets of buyer characteristics: cultural, social, personal, and psychological. Although many of these factors cannot be influenced by the marketer, they can be useful in identifying interested buyers and in shaping products and appeals to serve consumer needs better. *Culture* is the most basic determinant of a person's wants and behavior. It includes the basic values, perceptions, preferences, and behaviors that a person learns from family and other important institutions. *Subcultures* are "cultures within cultures" that have distinct values and lifestyles and can be based on anything from age to ethnicity. People with different cultural and subcultural characteristics have different product and brand preferences. As a result, marketers may want to focus their marketing programs on the special needs of certain groups.

Social factors also influence a buyer's behavior. A person's *reference groups*—family, friends, social organizations, professional associations—strongly affect product and brand choices. The buyer's age, life-cycle stage, occupation, economic circumstances, lifestyle, personality, and other *personal characteristics* influence his or her buying decisions. Consumer *lifestyles*—the whole pattern of acting and interacting in the world—are also an important influence on purchase decisions. Finally, consumer buying behavior is influenced by four major *psychological factors*—motivation, perception, learning, and beliefs and attitudes. Each of these factors provides a different perspective for understanding the workings of the buyer's black box.

3 List and define the major types of buying decision behavior and stages in the buyer decision process.

Buying behavior may vary greatly across different types of products and buying decisions. Consumers undertake *complex buying behavior* when they are highly involved in a purchase and perceive significant differences among brands. *Dissonance-reducing behavior* occurs when consumers are higher involved but see little difference among brands. *Habitual buying behavior* occurs under conditions of low involvement and little significant brand difference. In situations characterized by low involvement but significant perceived brand differences, consumers engage in *variety-seeking buying behavior*.

When making a purchase, the buyer goes through a decision process consisting of *need recognition, information search, evaluation of alternatives, purchase decision*, and *postpurchase behavior*. The marketer's job is to understand the buyer's behavior at each stage and the influences that are operating. During *need recognition*, the consumer recognizes a problem or need that could be satisfied by a product or service in the market. Once the need is recognized, the consumer is aroused to seek more information and moves into the *information search* stage. With information in hand, the consumer proceeds to *alternative evaluation*, during which the information is used to evaluate brands in the choice set. From there, the consumer makes a *purchase decision* and actually buys the product. In the final stage of the buyer decision process, *postpurchase behavior*, the consumer takes action based on satisfaction or dissatisfaction.

4 Describe the adoption and diffusion process for new products.

The product adoption process is comprised of five stages: awareness, interest, evaluation, trial, and adoption. Initially, the consumer must become aware of the new product. *Awareness* leads to *interest*, and the consumer seeks information about the new product. Once information has been gathered, the consumer enters the *evaluation* stage and considers buying the new product. Next, in the *trial* stage, the consumer tries the product on a small scale to improve his or her estimate of its value. If the consumer is satisfied with the product, he or she enters the *adoption* stage, deciding to use the new product fully and regularly.

With regard to diffusion of new products, consumers respond at different rates, depending on the consumer's characteristics and the product's characteristics. Consumers may be innovators, early adopters, early majority, late majority, or laggards. *Innovators* are willing to try risky new ideas; *early adopters*—often community opinion leaders—accept new ideas early but carefully; the *early majority*—rarely leaders—decide deliberately to try new ideas, doing so before the average person does; the *late majority* try an innovation only after a majority of people have adopted it; whereas *laggards* adopt an innovation only after it has become a tradition itself. Manufacturers try to bring their new products to the attention of potential early adopters, especially those who are opinion leaders.

REVIEWING THE KEY TERMS

Adoption process 134
Alternative evaluation 132
Attitude 128
Belief 127
Brand personality 124
Cognitive dissonance 133
Complex buying behavior 129
Consumer buyer behavior 116
Consumer market 116
Culture 118
Dissonance-reducing buying behavior 129
Group 119
Habitual buying behavior 129
Information search 131

Learning 127
Lifestyle 123
Motive (or drive) 125
Need recognition 131
New product 134
Opinion leader 119
Perception 126
Personality 123
Postpurchase behavior 132
Purchase decision 132
Social class 119
Subculture 118
Variety-seeking buying behavior 130

DISCUSSING THE CONCEPTS

1. According to the model of consumer behavior, the buyer's black box consists of buyer characteristics and decision processes. Explain why the text calls this a black box.
2. Explain the cultural, social, and personal characteristics that affect people when they choose a restaurant at which to celebrate their birthdays.
3. A bank used SRI's Consulting Business Intelligence Values and Lifestyles (VALS) research to profile customer segments that did not use any automated or electronic services. Based on your knowledge of this lifestyle classification system, speculate what might be the primary and secondary VALS type for this customer segment.

4. The marketing manager for a sushi chain says, "We believe our customers exhibit high-involvement buying behaviors." Do you agree? Why or why not?
5. Form small groups and discuss how a consumer goes through the buyer decision process when choosing a college.
6. According to Figure 5.8, which adopter category is just now buying 'a' digital camera? Which group is now adding HDTV? Which category describes you? Why?

APPLYING THE CONCEPTS

1. Soft drink marketers spend about large amounts on television advertising each year. From a consumer behavior perspective, why is this important?
2. You are the marketing manager for a small software company that has developed new and novel spam-blocking software. You are charged with selecting the target market for the product launch. How would you use Roger's *Diffusion of Innovations* framework to help you with this decision? What are some of the likely characteristics of this customer group?

3. The chapter defines "alternative evaluation" as "how the consumer processes information to arrive at brand choices." Suppose that, as discussed in the chapter, you have narrowed your choice of new cars to brand A, B, or C. You have finalized the four most important new-car attributes and their weights and have created the evaluation [matrix]. Which new-car brand will you likely select?

Attributes	Importance Weight	New Car Alternatives		
		Brand A	Brand B	Brand C
Styling	0.5	3	7	4
Operating Economy	0.2	6	5	7
Warranty	0.1	5	5	6
Price	0.2	8	7	8

FOCUS ON TECHNOLOGY

Many Internet sites use collaborative filtering technology to assist consumers in decision making. The process begins by *collaborating* the purchasing or product rating behavior of a vast group of consumers. Then, the technology filters this information to offer recommendations to a single user based on individual search, rating, or purchasing behavior. Originated by Amazon.com for book recommendations, the technology is now used by many marketers, including iTunes and Netflix.

1. At which step of the consumer behavior decision process does collaborative filtering most help the consumer?

2. What are the drawbacks of collaborative filtering?

3. How could your college use this technology to help its consumers?

FOCUS ON ETHICS

Many countries are facing an obesity epidemic. Studies show that 66 percent of American adults and 17 percent of children and teens are overweight or obese. In India, 55 percent of women between 20 and 69 years old are overweight. The number of obese Chinese has doubled to 60 million between 1992 and 2002, while some 200 million are at least overweight. Among Chinese children, the obesity rate has reached 8.1 percent. This weight increase comes despite repeated medical studies showing that excess weight brings increased risks for heart disease, diabetes, and other maladies, even cancer.

1. Who is to blame for the obesity problem? Self-indulgent consumers who just can't say no to fat burgers, sugar-laden confectionary, and other tempting treats? Or greedy food marketers who are cashing in on vulnerable consumers?

2. The debate extends to the marketing of fast food and soft drinks in school cafeterias to cereal, cookies, and other "not-so-good-for-you" products targeted toward kids and teens. Why are these consumers considered especially vulnerable to seductive or misleading marketing pitches?

3. How should food marketers respond to these criticisms?

Wild Planet

Chances are that when you hear the term *socially responsible business*, a handful of companies leap to mind, companies such as Ben & Jerry's and The Body Shop. Although these companies and their founders led the revolution for socially responsible business, a new generation of activist entrepreneurs has now taken up the reins. Today, socially responsible businesses and their founders not only have a passion to do good, they also have the know-how to connect with consumers.

For example, Wild Planet markets high-quality, nonsexist, nonviolent toys that encourage kids to be imaginative and creative and to explore the world around them. But Wild Planet sells more than just toys. It sells positive play experiences. To better understand those experiences, the company conducts a tremendous amount of consumer research to delve into consumer buyer behavior. Wild Planet even created a Toy

Opinion Panel to evaluate current products and develop new product ideas. The panel helps Wild Planet to understand why parents and kids buy the toys they buy.

After viewing the video featuring Wild Planet, answer the following questions about consumer buyer behavior.

1. Which of the four sets of factors affecting consumer behavior do you believe most strongly affect consumers' choices to buy toys from Wild Planet?

2. What demographic segment of consumers is Wild Planet targeting?

3. Visit the Wild Planet Web site at *www.wildplanet.com* to learn more about the company. How does the Web site help consumers through the buyer decision process?

 **COMPANY CASE**

Victoria's Secret Pink: Keeping the Brand Hot

When most people think of Victoria's Secret, they think of lingerie. Indeed, it has done a very good job of developing this association by placing images of supermodels donning its signature bras, panties, and "sleepwear" in everything from standard broadcast and print advertising to the controversial prime-time television fashion shows that the company airs each year. Such promotional tactics have paid off for Victoria's Secret which continues to achieve healthy sales and profit growth.

How does a successful company ensure that its hot sales don't cool off? One approach is to sell more to existing customers. Another is to find new customers. Victoria's Secret is doing plenty of both. One key component in its quest to find new customers is the launch and growth of its new brand, Pink.

Expanding the Target Market

Victoria's Secret launched its line of Pink products in 50 test markets in 2003. Based on very positive initial results, the company expanded the subbrand quickly across the U.S. With the Pink introduction, Victoria's Secret hoped to add a new segment to its base: young, hip, and fashionable customers. "Young" in this case means 18 to 30 years of age. More specifically, Pink is geared toward undergraduates. According to company spokesman Anthony Hebron, "It's what you see around the dorm. It's the fun, playful stuff she needs, but is still fashionable."

The company classifies the Pink product line as "loungewear," a very broad term that includes sweatpants, T-shirts, pajamas, bras and panties, pillows and bedding, and even dog accessories. In keeping with the "young and fun" image, the product line includes bright colors (Pink is not a misnomer) and often incorporates stripes and polka-dots. The garments feature comfortable cuts and mostly soft cotton fabrics. To keep things fresh for the younger segment, stores introduce new Pink products every three or four weeks.

According to those at Victoria's Secret, in sharp contrast to the sexy nature of the core brand, Pink is positioned as cute and playful. "It's spirited and collegiate. It's not necessarily sexy—it's not sexy at all—but young, hip, and casual. It's fashion forward and accessible," said Mary Beth Wood, a spokeswoman for Victoria's Secret. The Pink line does include underwear that some might consider to be on par with standard Victoria's Secret items. But management is quick to point out that the designs such as heart-covered thongs are more cute than racy. Displays of Pink merchandise often incorporate stuffed animals, and many articles display Pink's trademark mascot, a pink dog.

Pink is currently a store-within-a-store concept. According to Les Wexner, chairman and chief executive of parent company Limited Brands, the company intended this from the beginning. "Two years ago, we did not believe Pink was a stand-alone concept, and I'm still not sure that it is, but it's possible." But with Pink sales expected to reach $700 million for 2006, the company is giving far more serious consideration to opening freestanding Pink lifestyle shops in several markets by early 2007.

To aid in Pink's expansion, Victoria's Secret has enlisted PR firm Alison Brod. Although the company plans to stay committed to fashion-advertising vehicles such as Vogue and Lucky, it also plans to expand its promotional campaigns to include nontraditional avenues. Lisette Sand-Freedman, VP of fashion and lifestyle for Alison Brod, indicates that it "will seek different arenas to be in, ways to get the word out," focusing on "more lifestyle angles and bigger campaigns." The company will also leverage the star power of trend-setting young Hollywood personalities such as Lindsay Lohan and Sophia Bush. This will be accomplished through formal product placements and through the placement of Pink products in the personal wardrobes of celebrities.

A Key Driver of Victoria's Secret's Future Growth

Victoria's Secret has been a huge part of the success of the Limited Brands portfolio (which includes Bath & Body Works, Express, and Limited stores). It accounts for more than 1,000 of the parent company's 3,559 stores and more than half of total sales.

But Wexner is not content to let the chain rest. He says, "We can double the Victoria's Secret business in the next five years." This would mean increasing sales from $5 billion to $10 billion. The umbrella strategy for achieving this growth is to continually broaden the customer base. This will include a focus on new and emerging lines, such as IPEX and Angels Secret Embrace (bras), Intimissimi (a line of Italian lingerie for women and men appealing to younger customers), and Sexy Sport (a collection of sports bras, yoga pants, tennis apparel, and dancewear).

Pink is a key component of this strategy. Aside being available in all its stores, Victoria's Secret has opened several Pink stores since 2004 including locations in San Francisco, Detroit, and Birmingham. Pink stores are featured with everything pink from blankets to chairs to dressing rooms, and from floors to walls. Pink also has its own Web site, _www.VSPink.com_, which contains an online store as well as various promotions such as "The World's PJ Party" in Chicago. The Web site also contains pages featuring a Pink lifestyle, including Pink celebrities, Pink Horoscopes, Pink on Campus, Pink fashion shows, and Pink back-to-school Must Haves.

Broadening the customer base... too far?

Although Victoria's Secret's introduction and expansion of Pink seems well founded, it has raised some eyebrows. As young and cute Pink's line has expanded rapidly, the brand's appeal has gone beyond that of its intended target market. Some women much older than 30 have shown an interest (an over-40 Courtney Cox Arquette was photographed wearing Pink sweats). But stronger interest is being shown by girls younger than 18. Girls as young as 11 are visiting Victoria's Secret stores to buy Pink items, with and without their mothers.

Two such 11-year-olds, Lily Feingold and Brittany Garrison, were interviewed while shopping at a Victoria's Secret store with Lily's mother. They confessed that Victoria's Secret was one of their favorite stores. Passing up cotton lounge pants because each already had multiple pairs, both girls bought $68 pairs of sweatpants with the "Pink" label emblazoned on the derriere. The girls denied buying the items because they wanted to seem more grown up, instead saying that they simply liked the clothes.

Victoria's Secret executives say that they are not targeting girls younger than 18. But regardless of Victoria's Secret's intentions, Pink is fast becoming popular among teens and "tweens," loosely defined by a range of about 8 to 14 years old. Most experts agree that by the time children reach 10, they are rejecting childlike images and aspiring to more mature things associated with being a teenager. Called "age compression," it explains the trend toward preteens leaving their childhoods earlier and giving up traditional toys for more mature interests, such as cell phones, consumer electronics, and fashion products.

Tweens are growing in size and purchase power. The 33 million teens (ages 12 to 19) in the U.S. spend more than $175 billion annually (over 60 percent have jobs), and the 25 million tweens spend $51 billion annually, a number that continues to increase. But even more telling is the $170 billion per year that is spent by parents and other family members directly for the younger consumers who may not have as much income as their older siblings. Although boys are a part of this group, it is widely recognized that girls account for the majority of dollars spent. With this kind of purchase power behind them, as they find revenue for their older target markets leveling off, marketers everywhere are focusing on the teen and tween segments.

Although executives at Victoria's Secret deny targeting the youth of America, experts disagree. David Morrison, president of marketing research agency TwentySomething, says he is not surprised that Victoria's Secret denies marketing to teens and preteens. "If Victoria's Secret is blatantly catering to seventh and eighth graders, that might be considered exploitative." Morrison also acknowledges that the age group is drawn to the relative maturity and sophistication of the Pink label.

Natalie Weathers, assistant professor of fashion-industry management at Philadelphia University, says that Victoria's Secret is capitalizing on a trend known as coshopping—mothers and tweens shopping together. "They are advising their daughters about their purchases, and their daughters are advising them," she said. This type of activity may have been strange 20 years ago, but according to Weathers, the preteens of today are more savvy and, therefore, more likely to be shopping partners for moms. "They are not little girls, and they aren't teenagers, but they have a lot of access to sophisticated information about what the media says is beautiful, what is pretty, what is hot and stylish and cool. They are very visually literate."

In general, introducing a brand to younger consumers is considered a sound strategy for growth and for creating long-term relationships. It's generally not considered controversial to engender aspirational motives in young consumers through an entry-level product line. But many critics have questioned the aspirations engendered in tweens as they identify with Pink because of what they are aspiring to. A creative director for ad agencies in New York, Timothy Matz, calls Pink "beginner-level lingerie." Matz does not question the practice of gateway marketing (getting customers to use the brand at an earlier age). But he admits that a "gateway" to a sexy lingerie shop may make parents nervous. "Being a 45-year-old dad, do I want my 10-year-old going to Victoria's Secret?"

Thus far, Victoria's Secret has avoided the negative reactions of the masses who opposed Abercrombie & Fitch's blatant marketing of thong underwear to preteens. Perhaps that's because it adamantly professes its exclusive focus on young adults. Nonetheless, many question Victoria's Secret's appeal to the preadult crowd, whether intentional or unintentional. Big tobacco companies have been under fire for years for using childlike imagery to draw the interest of youth to an adult product. Is Pink the Joe Camel of early adolescent sexuality? Are Pink's extreme low-rise string bikini panties the gateway drug to pushup teddies and Pleasure State Geisha thongs? Can Pink take off in more conservative parts of the world like Asia? These are questions that Victoria's Secret may have to address more directly in the near future.

Questions For Discussion

1. Analyze the buyer decision process of a typical Pink customer.
2. Apply the concept of aspirational groups to Victoria's Secret Pink line. Should marketers have boundaries with regard to this concept?
3. Explain how both positive and negative consumer attitudes toward a brand like Pink develop. How might someone's attitude toward Pink change?
4. What role does Pink appear to be playing in the self-concept of preteens, teens, and young adults?
5. How well would Pink be received in Asia? Why?

Sources:
Alycia De Mesa, "Marketing and Tweens," *BusinessWeek Online*, October 12, 2005; Fae Goodman, "Lingerie Is Luscious and Lovely—For Grown-Ups," *Chicago Sun Times*, February 19, 2006, p. B02; Vivian McInerny, "Pink Casual Loungewear Brand Nicely Colors Teen Girls' World," *The Oregonian*, May 7, 2006, p. O13; Randy Schmelzer, "Victoria's Secret Has Designs on Putting Everyone in the Pink," *PR Week*, March 13, 2006, p. 3; Jeffrey Sheben, "Victoria's Secret to Expand," *Columbus Dispatch*, May 18, 2006, p. 01B; Jane M. Von Bergen, "Victoria's Secret? Kids," *Philadelphia Inquirer*, December 22, 2005.

Objectives

After studying this chapter, you should be able to

- define the business market and explain how business markets differ from consumer markets
- identify the major factors that influence business buyer behavior
- list and define the steps in the business buying decision process
- appreciate the role of the Internet on e-procurement
- compare the institutional and government markets and explain how institutional and government buyers make their buying decisions

CHAPTER 6

BUSINESS MARKETS AND BUSINESS BUYER BEHAVIOR

Previewing the Concepts

In the previous chapter, you studied *final consumer* buying behavior and factors that influence it. In this chapter, we'll do the same for *business customers*—those that buy goods and services for use in producing their own products and services or for resale to others.

To start, let's look at IKEA, the world's largest furniture retailer. While IKEA sells to retail customers, it must work closely with its business partners such as its suppliers to succeed. IKEA doesn't just buy from its suppliers, it involves them deeply in the process of delivering a stylish and affordable lifestyle to IKEA's final customers.

I KEA, the world's largest furniture retailer, is the quintessential global cult brand. Over 410 million shoppers flocked to the Scandinavian retailer's 230-odd huge stores in 35 countries, generating more than $26 billion in sales in 2007. Most of the shoppers are loyal IKEA customers—many are avid apostles. All are drawn to the IKEA lifestyle, one built around trendy but simple and practical furniture at affordable prices. According to *BusinessWeek:*

> Perhaps more than any other company in the world, IKEA has become a curator of people's lifestyles, if not their lives. At a time when consumers face so many choices for everything they buy, IKEA provides a one-stop sanctuary for coolness. IKEA is far more than a furniture merchant. It sells a lifestyle that customers around the world embrace as a signal that they've arrived, that they have good taste and recognize value. "If it wasn't for IKEA," writes British design magazine *Icon*, "most people would have no access to affordable contemporary design."

As the world's Ambassador of Kul (Swedish for fun), IKEA is growing at a healthy clip. Sales have leapt 31 percent in just the past two years. IKEA plans to open new megastores worldwide, including Western China, Japan, and the U.S. Its biggest obstacle to growth isn't opening new stores and attracting customers, but finding enough of the right kinds of *suppliers* to help design and produce its products. IKEA currently relies on about 1,800 suppliers in over 50 countries to stock its shelves. If IKEA continues at its current rate of growth, it will need to double its supply network by 2010. "We can't increase by more than 20 stores a year because supply is the bottleneck," says IKEA's country manager for Russia.

Creating beautiful, durable furniture at low prices is no easy proposition. It calls for a resolute focus on design and an obsession for low costs. IKEA knows that it can't do it alone. Instead, it must develop close partnerships with suppliers worldwide who can help it develop simple new designs and keep costs down. Here's how the company describes its approach, and the importance of suppliers:

> First, we do our part. Our designers work with manufacturers to find smart ways to make furniture using existing production processes. Then our buyers look all over the world for good suppliers with the most suitable raw materials. Next, we buy in bulk—on a global scale—so that we can get the best deals, and you can get the lowest price. Then you do your part. Using the IKEA catalog and visiting the store, you choose the furniture yourself and pick it up at the self-serve warehouse. Because most items are packed flat, you can get them home easily, and assemble them yourself. This means we don't charge you for things you can easily do on your own. So together we save money... for a better everyday life.

At IKEA, design is important. But no matter how good the design, a product won't find its way to the showroom unless it's also affordable. IKEA finds supply partners who can help it to create just the right product at just the right price. According to *BusinessWeek*, IKEA "once contracted with ski makers—experts in bent wood—to manufacture its Poang armchairs, and it has tapped makers of supermarket carts to turn out durable sofas."

The design process for a new IKEA product can take up to three years. IKEA's designers start with a basic customer value proposition. Then, they work closely with key suppliers to bring that proposition to market. Consider IKEA's Olle chair. Based on customer feedback, designer Evamaria Ronnegard set out to create a sturdy, durable kitchen chair that would fit into any décor, priced at $52. Once her initial design was completed and approved, IKEA's 45 trading offices searched the world and matched the Olle with a Chinese supplier, based on both design and cost efficiencies.

Together, Ronnegard and the Chinese supplier refined the design to improve the chair's function and reduce its costs. For example, the supplier modified the back leg angle to prevent the chair from tipping easily. This also reduced the thickness of the seat without compromising the chair's strength, reducing both costs and shipping weight. However, when she learned that the supplier planned to use traditional wood joinery methods to attach the chair back to the seat, Ronnegard intervened. That would require that the chair be shipped in a costly L-shape, which by itself would inflate the chair's retail price to $58. Ronnegard convinced the supplier to go with metal bolts instead. The back-and-forth design process worked well. IKEA introduced its still-popular Olle chair at the $52 target price. (Through continued design and manufacturing refinements, IKEA and its supplier have now reduced the price to just $29.)

Throughout the design and manufacturing process, Ronnegard was impressed by the depth of the supplier partnership. "My job really hit home when I got a call from the supplier in China, who had a question about some aspect of the chair," she recalls. "There he was, halfway around the world, and he was calling me about my chair." Now, Ronnegard is often on-site in China or India or Vietnam, working face to face with suppliers as they help to refine her designs.

Another benefit of close collaboration with suppliers is that they can often help IKEA to customize its designs to make them sell better in local markets. In China, for example, at the suggestion of a local supplier, IKEA stocked 250,000 plastic place mats commemorating the year of the rooster. The place mats sold out in only three weeks.

Thus, before IKEA can sell the billions of dollars worth of products its customer covet, it must first find suppliers who can help it design and make all those products. IKEA doesn't just rely on spot suppliers who might be available when needed. Instead, it has systematically developed a robust network of supplier-partners that reliably provide the more than 10,000 items it stocks. And more than just buying from suppliers, IKEA involves them deeply in designing and making stylish but affordable products to keep IKEA's customers coming back. Working together, IKEA and its suppliers have kept fans like Jen Segrest clamoring for more. Every piece of Jen's furniture is from IKEA—except for an end table, which she hates and will be replacing from IKEA, whose store requires a 10-hour round trip drive from her home.[1]

In one way or another, many companies sell to other organizations. IKEA's suppliers sell products to IKEA, which, in turn, sells them to its retail customers. Companies such as DuPont, Boeing, Panasonic, Samsung, Caterpillar, and countless other firms, sell *most* of their products to other businesses. Even consumer products companies, which make products used by final consumers, must first sell their products to other businesses. For example, Nestlé makes many familiar consumer brands—milk (Nespray, Neslac), beverages (Nescafé, Milo), water (Perrier), confectionary (KitKat, Smarties, Crunch), ice cream (Movenpick), and others. But to sell these products to consumers, Nestlé must first sell them to its wholesaler and retailer customers, who in turn serve the consumer market.

Business buyer behavior

The buying behavior of the organizations that buy goods and services for use in the production of other products and services or for the purpose of reselling or renting them to others at a profit.

Business buying process

The decision process by which business buyers determine which products and services their organizations need to purchase, and then find, evaluate, and choose among alternative suppliers and brands.

Business buyer behavior refers to the buying behavior of the organizations that buy goods and services for use in the production of its products and services. It also includes the behavior of retailing and wholesaling firms that acquire goods to resell or rent them to others at a profit. In the **business buying process**, business buyers determine which products and services their organizations need to purchase and then find, evaluate, and choose among alternative suppliers and brands. *Business-to-business (B-to-B) marketers* must do their best to understand business markets and business buyer behavior. Then, like businesses that sell to final buyers, they must build profitable relationships with business customers by creating superior customer value.

Business Markets

The business market is *huge*. In fact, business markets involve far more dollars and items than do consumer markets. In some ways, business markets are similar to consumer markets. Both involve people who assume buying roles and make purchase decisions to satisfy needs. However, business markets differ in many ways from consumer markets. The main differences, shown in **Table 6.1**, are in *market structure and demand*, the *nature of the buying unit*, and the *types of decisions and the decision process* involved.

Market Structure and Demand

The business marketer normally deals with *far fewer but far larger buyers* than the consumer marketer does. Even in large business markets, a few buyers often account for most of the purchasing. For example, when Goodyear sells replacement tires to final consumers, its potential market includes the owners of the millions of cars around the world. But Goodyear's fate in the business market depends on getting orders from one of only a handful of large automakers. Business customers also tend to be *more geographically concentrated*.

Business demand is **derived demand**—it ultimately derives from the demand for consumer goods. Hewlett-Packard and Dell buy Intel microprocessor chips because consumers buy personal computers. If consumer demand for PCs drops, so will the demand for computer chips.

Therefore, B-to-B marketers sometimes promote their products directly to final consumers to increase business demand. For example, Intel advertises heavily to personal computer buyers, selling them on the virtues of Intel microprocessors. The increased demand for Intel chips boosts demand for the PCs containing them, and both Intel and its business partners win.

Many business markets have *inelastic demand*; that is, total demand for many business products is not affected much by price changes, especially in the short run. A drop in the price of leather will not cause shoe manufacturers to buy much more leather unless it results in lower shoe prices that, in turn, will increase consumer demand for shoes.

Finally, business markets have more *fluctuating demand*. The demand for many business goods and services tends to change more—and more quickly—than the demand for consumer goods and services does. A small percentage increase in consumer demand can cause large increases in business demand.

Derived demand
Business demand that ultimately comes from (derives from) the demand for consumer goods.

Derived demand – Intel's long-running "Intel Inside" logo advertising campaign boosts demand for Intel chips and for the PCs containing them. Now, most computer markets feature a logo like this one in their ads.

Table 6.1 Characteristics of Business Markets

Marketing Structure and Demand
Business markets contain *fewer but larger buyers.*
Business buyer demand is *derived* from final consumer demand.
Demand in many business markets is *more inelastic*—not affected as much in the short run by price changes.
Demand in business markets *fluctuates more*, and more quickly.
Nature of the Buying Unit
Business purchases involve more buyers.
Business buying involves a more professional purchasing effort.
Types of Decisions and the Decision Process
Business buyers usually face more complex buying decisions.
The business buying process is more formalized.
In business buying, buyers and sellers work closely together and build long-term relationships.

Difference between a business market and a consumer market – The activity may be the same, but the scale of it varies.

Nature of the Buying Unit

Compared with consumer purchases, a business purchase usually involves *more decision participants* and a *more professional purchasing effort*. Often, business buying is done by trained purchasing agents. When the purchase is complex, several people will participate in the decision-making process.

Many companies are upgrading their purchasing functions to "supply management" or "supplier development" functions. As B-to-B marketers face a new breed of higher-level, better-trained supply managers, salespeople must be trained to deal with such buyers.

Types of Decisions and the Decision Process

Business buyers usually face *more complex* buying decisions than do consumer buyers. Purchases often involve large sums of money, complex technical and economic considerations, and interactions among many people at many levels of the buyer's organization. The business buying process also tends to be *more formalized* than the consumer buying process. Large business purchases usually call for detailed product specifications, written purchase orders, careful supplier searches, and formal approval.

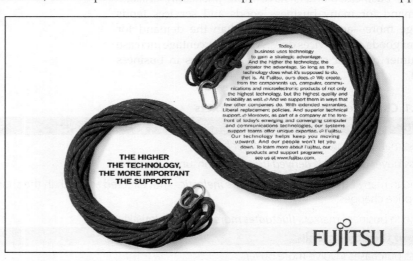

Business marketers work closely with their customers throughout the buying and consuming process – In this award-winning business-to-business ad, Fujitsu promises more than just high-tech products—"Our technology helps keep you moving upward. And our people won't let you down."

Finally, in the business buying process, the buyer and seller are often much *more dependent* on each other. B-to-B marketers work closely with their customers during all stages of the buying process—from helping customers define problems, to finding solutions, to supporting after sale operations. They often customize their offerings to individual customer needs. In the short run, sales go to suppliers who meet buyers' immediate product and service needs. In the long run, however, B-to-B marketers keep a customer's sales by meeting current needs *and* by partnering with customers to help them solve their problems.

When Unilever started operating in Vietnam, it grew its business by establishing strong partnerships with five key local suppliers. Initially, the suppliers lacked the financial resources, technology, quality control, safety, and environmental standards to meet Unilever's standards. Unilever offered financial support to upgrade equipment and provided extensive training programs on safety and environmental awareness. Technology transfers were made of machinery and formulations as well as quality assurance and analytical methods. As a result, Unilever's production lines were set up quickly, easily, and at lower costs, enabling the rapid launch of its products. With some of the production sites close to its customers, logistical complexities and transportation costs were reduced. Working with these suppliers, Unilever not only managed to achieve significant sales but also formed relationships with local people who understood the market in greater detail. This knowledge was vital in establishing its Vietnamese business.[2]

Over the years, relationships between customers and suppliers have been changing from being adversarial to close and cooperative. Many customer companies practice **supplier development**, systematically developing networks of supplier-partners to ensure an appropriate and dependable supply of products and materials that they will use in making their own products or resell to others. For example, Caterpillar no longer calls its buyers "purchasing agents"—they are managers of "purchasing and supplier development."

> **Supplier development**
> Systematic development of networks of supplier-partners to ensure an appropriate and dependable supply of products and materials for use in making products or reselling them to others.

Business Buyer Behavior

At the most basic level, marketers want to know how business buyers will respond to various marketing stimuli. Figure 6.1 shows a model of business buyer behavior. In this model, marketing and other stimuli affect the buying organization and produce certain buyer responses. As with consumer buying, the marketing stimuli for business buying consist of the Four Ps: product, price, place, and promotion. Other stimuli include major forces in the environment: economic, technological, political, cultural, and competitive. These stimuli enter the organization and are turned into buyer responses: product or service choice; supplier choice; order quantities; and delivery, service, and payment terms. In order to design good marketing mix strategies, the marketer must understand what happens within the organization to turn stimuli into purchase responses.[3]

Within the organization, buying activity consists of two major parts: the buying center, made up of all the people involved in the buying decision, and the buying decision process. The model shows that the buying center and the buying decision process are influenced by internal organizational, interpersonal, and individual factors as well as by external environmental factors.

The model in **Figure 6.1** suggests four questions about business buyer behavior:

- What buying decisions do business buyers make?
- Who participates in the buying process?
- What are the major influences on buyers?
- How do business buyers make their buying decisions?

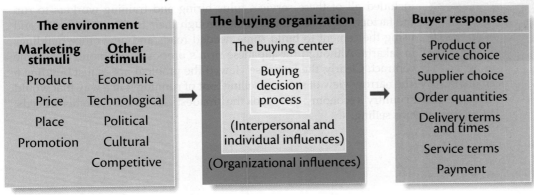

Figure 6.1
A model of business buyer behavior

Major Types of Buying Situations

Straight rebuy
A business buying situation in which the buyer routinely reorders something without any modifications.

Modified rebuy
A business buying situation in which the buyer wants to modify product specifications, prices, terms, or suppliers.

New task
A business buying situation in which the buyer purchases a product or service for the first time.

Systems selling
Buying a packaged solution to a problem from a single seller, thus avoiding all the separate decisions involved in a complex buying situation.

There are three major types of buying situations:[4]

- **Straight rebuy:** In this buying situation, the buyer reorders something without any modifications. It is usually handled on a routine basis by the purchasing department. Based on past buying satisfaction, the buyer simply chooses from the various suppliers on its list. "In" suppliers try to maintain product and service quality. They often propose automatic reordering systems so that the purchasing agent will save reordering time. "Out" suppliers try to find new ways to add value or exploit dissatisfaction so that the buyer will consider them.

- **Modified rebuy:** Here, the buyer wants to modify product specifications, prices, terms, or suppliers. The modified rebuy usually involves more decision participants than does the straight rebuy. The "in" suppliers may become nervous and feel pressured to put their best foot forward to protect an account. "Out" suppliers may see the modified rebuy situation as an opportunity to make a better offer and gain new business.

- **New-task situation:** This occurs when a company buys a product or service for the first time. In such cases, the greater the cost or risk, the larger the number of decision participants and the greater their efforts to collect information will be. The new-task situation is the marketer's greatest opportunity and challenge. The marketer not only tries to reach as many key buying influences as possible but also provides help and information.

The buyer makes the fewest decisions in the straight rebuy and the most in the new-task decision. In the new-task situation, the buyer must decide on product specifications, suppliers, price limits, payment terms, order quantities, delivery times, and service terms. The order of these decisions varies with each situation, and different decision participants influence each choice.

Many business buyers prefer to buy a packaged solution to a problem from a single seller. Instead of buying and putting all the components together, the buyer may ask sellers to supply the components *and* assemble the package or system. **Systems selling** is a two-step process. First, the supplier sells a group of interlocking products. For example, the supplier sells not only glue, but also applicators and dryers. Second, the supplier sells a system of production, inventory control, distribution, and other services to meet the buyer's need for a smooth-running operation. The sale often goes to the firm that provides the most complete system meeting the customer's needs. Thus, systems selling is often a key business marketing strategy for winning and holding accounts. Sellers increasingly have recognized that buyers like this method and have adopted systems selling as a marketing tool.

For example, the Indonesian government requested bids to build a cement factory near Jakarta. An American firm's proposal included choosing the site, designing the cement factory, hiring the construction crews, assembling the materials and equipment, and turning the finished factory over to the Indonesian government. A Japanese firm's proposal included all of these services, plus hiring and training workers to run the factory, exporting the cement through their trading companies, and using the cement to build some needed roads and new office buildings in Jakarta. Although the Japanese firm's proposal cost more, it won the contract. Clearly, the Japanese viewed the problem not as just building a cement factory (the narrow view of systems selling) but of running it in a way that would contribute to the country's economy. They took the broadest view of the customer's needs. This is true systems selling.[5]

Systems selling – It is about providing the most complete solution to the customer's needs.

Participants in the Business Buying Process

The decision-making unit of a buying organization is called its **buying center:** all the individuals and units that play a role in the purchase decision-making process. This group includes the actual users of the product or service, those who make the buying decision, those who influence the buying decision, those who do the actual buying, and those who control the buying information.

The buying center includes all members of the organization who play any of five roles in the purchase decision process.[6]

- **Users** are members of the organization who will use the product or service. In many cases, users initiate the buying proposal and help define product specifications.
- **Influencers** often help define specifications and also provide information for evaluating alternatives. Technical personnel are particularly important influencers.
- **Buyers** have formal authority to select the supplier and arrange terms of purchase. Buyers may help shape product specifications, but their major role is in selecting vendors and negotiating. In more complex purchases, buyers might include high-level officers participating in the negotiations.
- **Deciders** have formal or informal power to select or approve the final suppliers. In routine buying, the buyers are often the deciders, or at least the approvers.
- **Gatekeepers** control the flow of information to others. For example, purchasing agents often have authority to prevent salespersons from seeing users or deciders. Other gatekeepers include technical personnel and even personal secretaries.

The buying center concept presents a major marketing challenge. The business marketer must learn who participates in the decision, each participant's relative influence, and what evaluation criteria each decision participant uses.

Major Influences on Business Buyers

There are many factors influencing business buyers when they make their buying decisions. Some marketers assume that economic factors are the most important. They think buyers will favor the supplier who offers the lowest price or the best product or the most service. However, business buyers actually respond to both economic and personal factors.

Today, most B-to-B marketers recognize that emotion plays an important role in business buying decisions. For example, you might expect that an advertisement promoting large trucks to corporate fleet buyers would stress objective technical, performance, and economic factors. However, one ad for Volvo heavy-duty trucks shows two drivers arm-wrestling and claims, "It solves all your fleet problems. Except who gets to drive." It turns out that, in the face of an industry-wide driver shortage, the type of truck a fleet provides can help it to attract qualified drivers. The Volvo ad stresses the raw beauty of the truck and its comfort and roominess, features that make it more appealing to drivers. The ad concludes that Volvo trucks are "built to make fleets more profitable and drivers a lot more possessive."[7]

When suppliers' offers are very similar, business buyers have little basis for strictly rational choice. Because they can meet organizational goals with any supplier, buyers can allow personal factors to play a larger role in their decisions. However, when competing products differ greatly, business buyers are more accountable for their choice and tend to pay more attention to economic factors. **Figure 6.2** lists various groups of influences on business buyers—environmental, organizational, interpersonal, and individual.[8]

Buying center
All the individuals and units that play a role in the purchase decision-making process.

Users
Members of the buying organization who will actually use the purchased product or service.

Influencers
People in an organization's buying center who affect the buying decision; they often help define specifications and also provide information for evaluating alternatives.

Buyers
The people in the organization's buying center who make an actual purchase.

Deciders
People in the organization's buying center who have formal or informal power to select or approve the final suppliers.

Gatekeepers
People in the organization's buying center who control the flow of information to others.

INTRODUCING THE VOLVO 660. IT SOLVES ALL YOUR FLEET PROBLEMS. EXCEPT WHO GETS TO DRIVE.

May the best man win. We designed the new 660 to be the perfect fleet partner. Spacious and smooth handling. Efficient and easy to maintain. Built to make fleets more profitable and drivers a lot more possessive.

To find out how the Volvo 660 can help you be more successful, give us a call at 1-800-444-RSVP for a free video or visit www.volvotrucks.volvo.com.

VOLVO
Drive Smart.

Emotions play an important role in business buying –
This Volvo truck ad mentions objective factors, such as efficiency and ease of maintenance. But it stresses more emotional factors such as the raw beauty of the truck and its comfort and roominess, features that make "drivers a lot more possessive."

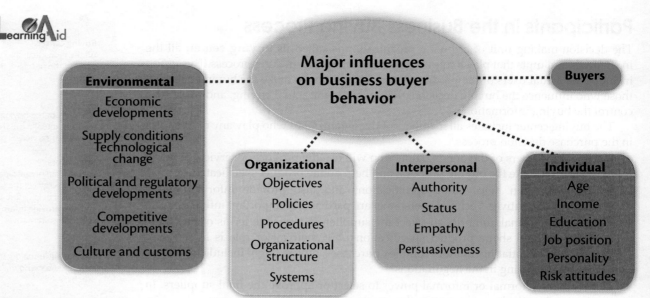

Figure 6.2
Major influences on business
buyer behavior

Environmental Factors

Business buyers are heavily influenced by factors in the current and expected *economic environment*, such as the level of primary demand, the economic outlook, and the cost of money. Another environmental factor is shortages in key materials. Many companies are more willing to buy and hold larger inventories of scarce materials to ensure adequate supply. Business buyers also are affected by technological, political, and competitive developments in the environment. Finally, culture and customs can strongly influence business buyer reactions to the marketer's behavior and strategies, especially in the international marketing environment (see **Real Marketing**). The business buyer must watch these factors, determine how they will affect the buyer, and try to turn these challenges into opportunities.

Organizational Factors

Each buying organization has its own objectives, policies, procedures, structure, and systems, and the business marketer must understand these factors well. Questions such as these arise: How many people are involved in the buying decision? Who are they? What are their evaluative criteria? What are the company's policies and limits on its buyers?

Interpersonal Factors

The buying center usually includes participants who influence each other, so *interpersonal factors* also influence the business buying process. However, it is often difficult to assess such interpersonal factors and group dynamics. Buying center participants do not wear tags that label them as "key decision maker" or "not influential." Nor do buying center participants with the highest rank always have the most influence. Participants may influence the buying decision because they control rewards and punishments, are well liked, have special expertise, or have a special relationship with other important participants. Interpersonal factors are often very subtle.

Individual Factors

Each participant in the business buying decision process brings in personal motives, perceptions, and preferences. These individual factors are affected by personal characteristics such as age, income, education, professional identification, personality, and attitudes toward risk. Also, buyers have different buying styles. Some may be technical types who make indepth analyses of competitive proposals before choosing a supplier. Other buyers may be intuitive negotiators who are adept at pitting the sellers against one another for the best deal.

The Business Buying Process

Figure 6.3 lists the eight stages of the business buying process.[9] Buyers who face a new-task buying situation usually go through all stages of the buying process. Buyers making modified or straight rebuys may skip some of the stages. We will examine these steps for the typical new-task buying situation.

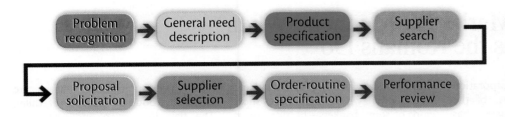

Figure 6.3
Stages of the business buying process

Problem Recognition

The buying process begins when someone in the company recognizes a problem or need that can be met by acquiring a specific product or service. **Problem recognition** can result from internal or external stimuli:

- *Internal stimuli*: The company may decide to launch a new product that requires new production equipment and materials. Or a machine may break down and need new parts. Perhaps a purchasing manager is unhappy with a current supplier's product quality, service, or prices.
- *External stimuli*: The buyer may get some new ideas at a trade show, see an ad, or receive a call from a salesperson who offers a better product or a lower price. In fact, in their advertising, business marketers often alert customers to potential problems and then show how their products provide solutions. For example, Kodak Health Imaging ads point out the complexities of hospital imaging and suggest that with Kodak, "complexity becomes clarity."

General Need Description

Having recognized a need, the buyer next prepares a **general need description** that describes the characteristics and quantity of the needed item. For standard items, this process presents few problems. For complex items, however, the buyer may need to work with others—engineers, users, consultants—to define the item. The team may want to rank the importance of reliability, durability, price, and other attributes desired in the item. In this phase, the alert business marketer can help the buyers define their needs and provide information about the value of different product characteristics.

Product Specification

The buying organization next develops the item's technical **product specifications**, often with the help of a value analysis engineering team. **Value analysis** is an approach to cost reduction in which components are studied carefully to determine if they can be redesigned, standardized, or made by less costly methods of production. The team decides on the best product characteristics and specifies them accordingly. Sellers, too, can use value analysis as a tool to help secure a new account. By showing buyers a better way to make an object, outside sellers can turn straight rebuy situations into new-task situations that give them a chance to obtain new business.

Supplier Search

The buyer now conducts a **supplier search** to find the best vendors. The buyer can compile a small list of qualified suppliers by reviewing trade directories, doing computer searches, or phoning other companies for recommendations. Today, more and more companies are turning to the Internet to find suppliers. For marketers, this has leveled

Problem recognition
The first stage of the business buying process in which someone in the company recognizes a problem or need that can be met by acquiring a good or a service.

General need description
The stage in the business buying process in which the company describes the general characteristics and quantity of a needed item.

Product specification
The stage of the business buying process in which the buying organization decides on and specifies the best technical product characteristics for a needed item.

Value analysis
An approach to cost reduction in which components are studied carefully to determine if they can be redesigned, standardized, or made by less costly methods of production.

Supplier search
The stage of the business buying process in which the buyer tries to find the best vendors.

REAL MARKETING

International Marketing Manners: When in Rome, Do as the Romans Do

Picture this: Blur King Corporation thinks it's time that the rest of the world enjoyed the fine products it has offered Asian consumers for generations. Accordingly, it sends Marketing Vice President Harry Lin to the Middle East, Europe, and the United States. Mr. Lin stops first in Saudi Arabia, where he coolly presents a potential client with a multimillion-dollar proposal in a classy pigskin binder.

In Milan, Harry wears his comfy short-sleeved shirt, khaki pants, and slip-ons for his appointment with the owner of an Italian packaging design firm. Everybody knows Italians are zany and laid back. In Germany, our hero whisks through a lavish, state-of-the-art marketing presentation, complete with flip charts and audiovisuals, and shows them that he *knows* how to make a buck.

Later, he swings through Paris. After securing a table at La Tour d'Argent, Harry greets his luncheon guest, the director of an industrial engineering firm

with, "Just call me Harry, Jacques." Next up is London, where Harry makes short work of some bankers—he rings them up on the phone.

Harry's final stop is New York, where he appears an hour late for his appointment. Putting on his best Harlem accent, Harry greets a potential client, who had recently relocated to the Big Apple from the Midwest, with a rousing, "What's happening, bro?"

A great tour, sure to generate a pile of orders, right? Wrong. Six months later, Blur King has nothing to show for the trip but a stack of bills. Abroad, they weren't wild about Harry.

This hypothetical case has been exaggerated for emphasis. Experts say success in international business has a lot to do with knowing the territory and its people.

Poor Harry tried, all right, but in all the wrong ways. To the Saudi Arabians, the pigskin binder would have been considered vile. Harry also goofed

when he assumed that Italians are like Hollywood's stereotypes of them. The flair for design and style that has characterized Italian culture for centuries is embodied in the business people of Milan and Rome. They dress beautifully and admire flair, but they blanch at garishness or impropriety in others' attire.

Harry's flashy presentation would likely have been a flop with the Germans, who dislike overstatement and showiness. According to one German expert, "I hugged an American woman at a business meeting last night. That would be normal in France, but [older] Germans still have difficulty [with the custom]." He says that calling secretaries by their first names would still be considered rude: "They have a right to be called by the surname. You'd certainly ask—and get—permission first." Germans address each other formally and correctly—someone with two doctorates (which is not uncommon) must be referred to as "Herr Doktor Doktor."

the playing field—the Internet gives smaller suppliers many of the same advantages as larger competitors.

The newer the buying task, and the more complex and costly the item, the greater the amount of time the buyer will spend searching for suppliers. The supplier's task is to get listed in major directories and build a good reputation in the marketplace. Salespeople should watch for companies in the process of searching for suppliers and make certain that their firm is considered.

Proposal Solicitation

Proposal solicitation
The stage of the business buying process in which the buyer invites qualified suppliers to submit proposals.

In the **proposal solicitation** stage of the business buying process, the buyer invites qualified suppliers to submit proposals. Some suppliers will send only a catalog or a salesperson. However, when the item is complex or expensive, the buyer will usually require detailed written proposals or formal presentations from each potential supplier.

A proper Frenchman neither likes instant familiarity—questions about family, church, or alma mater—nor refers to strangers by their first names. Explains an expert on French business practices, "It's considered poor taste. Even after months of business dealings, I'd wait for him or her to make the invitation [to use first names]... You are always right, in Europe, to say 'Mister.'"

The British do not, as a rule, make deals over the phone. And not all Americans from the Midwest appreciate an African American greeting, although most expect meetings to start punctually, given their monochronic time orientation.

Thus, to compete successfully in global markets, or even to deal effectively with international firms in their home markets, companies must help their managers to understand the needs, customs, and cultures of international business buyers. "When doing business in a foreign country and a foreign culture... assume nothing," advises an international business specialist. "Take

Companies must help their managers understand international customers and customs. For example, the Japanese consider the business card as an extension of self. They do not hand it to people, they present it.

nothing for granted. Turn every stone. Ask every question. Dig into every detail. Because cultures really are different, and those differences can have a major impact." So the old advice is still good advice: When in Rome, do as the Romans do.

Sources:

Portions adapted from Susan Harte, "When in Rome, You Should Learn to Do What the Romans Do," *The Atlanta Journal-Constitution*, January 22, 1990, pp. D1, D6. Additional examples can be found in David A. Ricks, *Blunders in International Business Around the World* (Malden, MA: Blackwell Publishing, 2000); Terri Morrison, Wayne A. Conway, and Joseph J. Douress, *Dun & Bradstreet's Guide to Doing Business* (Upper Saddle River, NJ: Prentice Hall, 2000); Jame K. Sebenius, "The Hidden Challenge of Cross-Border Negotiatons," *Harvard Business Review*, March 2002, pp. 76-85; Ross Thompson, "Lost in Translation," *Medical Marketing and Media*, March 2005, p. 82; and information accessed at www.executiveplanet.com, December 2006.

Business marketers must be skilled in researching, writing, and presenting proposals in response to buyer proposal solicitations. Proposals should be marketing documents, not just technical documents. Presentations should inspire confidence and make the marketer's company stand out from the competition.

Supplier Selection

The members of the buying center now review the proposals and select a supplier or suppliers. During **supplier selection**, the buying center often will draw up a list of the desired supplier attributes and their relative importance. In one survey, purchasing executives listed the following attributes as most important in influencing the relationship between supplier and customer: quality products and services, on-time delivery, ethical corporate behavior, honest communication, and competitive prices. Other important factors include repair and servicing capabilities, technical aid and advice, geographic location, performance history, and reputation.

Supplier selection
The stage of the business buying process in which the buyer reviews proposals and selects a supplier or suppliers.

Buyers may attempt to negotiate with preferred suppliers for better prices and terms before making the final selections. Buyers generally prefer multiple sources of supplies to avoid being totally dependent on one supplier and to allow comparisons of prices and performance of several suppliers over time. Supplier development managers want to develop a full network of supplier-partners that can help the company bring more value to its customers.

Order-Routine Specification

The buyer now prepares an **order-routine specification**. It includes the final order with the chosen supplier or suppliers and lists items such as technical specifications, quantity needed, expected time of delivery, return policies, and warranties. In the case of maintenance, repair, and operating items, buyers may use blanket contracts rather than periodic purchase orders. A blanket contract creates a long-term relationship in which the supplier promises to resupply the buyer as needed at agreed prices for a set time period.

Some large buyers practice *vendor-managed inventory*, in which they turn over ordering and inventory responsibilities to their suppliers. Under such systems, buyers share sales and inventory information directly with key suppliers. The suppliers then monitor inventories and replenish stock automatically as needed.

Performance Review

In this stage, the buyer reviews supplier performance. The buyer may contact users and ask them to rate their satisfaction. The **performance review** may lead the buyer to continue, modify, or drop the arrangement. The seller's job is to monitor the same factors used by the buyer to make sure that the seller is giving the expected satisfaction.

E-Procurement: Buying on the Internet

During the past few years, advances in information technology have changed the face of the B-to-B marketing process. Online purchasing, often called *e-procurement*, has grown rapidly.

Companies can do e-procurement in any of several ways. They can set up their own *company buying sites.* For example, GE operates a company trading site on which it posts its buying needs and invites bids, negotiates terms, and places orders. Or the company can create *extranet links* with key suppliers. For instance, they can create direct procurement accounts with suppliers such as Dell through which company buyers can purchase equipment, materials, and supplies.

B-to-B marketers can help customers who wish to purchase online by creating well-designed, easy-to-use Web sites. For example, *BtoB* magazine regularly rates Hewlett-Packard's B-to-B Web site among the very best.

> The HP site consists of some 1,900 site areas and 2.5 million pages. It integrates an enormous amount of product and company information, putting it within only a few mouse clicks of customers' computers. IT buying decision makers can enter the site, click directly into their customer segment—large enterprise business; small or medium business; or government, health, or educational institution—and quickly find product overviews, detailed technical information, and purchasing solutions.
>
> The site lets customers create customized catalogs for frequently purchased products, set up automatic approval routing for orders, and conduct end-to-end transaction processing. To build deeper, more personalized online relationships with customers, HP.com features flash demos

Order-routine specification
The stage of the business buying process in which the buyer writes the final order with the chosen supplier(s), listing the technical specifications, quantity needed, expected time of delivery, return policies, and warranties.

Performance review
The stage of the business buying process in which the buyer assesses the performance of the supplier and decides to continue, modify, or drop the arrangement.

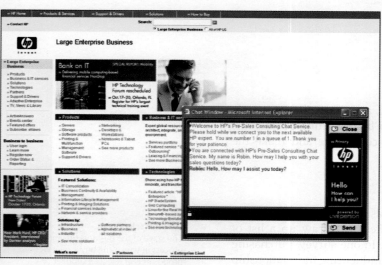

Company buying sites – To help customers who wish to purchase online, HP's Web site consists of some 1,500 site areas and 1 million pages. It provides product overviews, detailed technical information, purchasing solutions, e-newsletters, live chats with sales reps, online classes, and real-time customer support. (*www.hp.com*)

that show how to use the site, e-newsletters, live chats with sales reps, online classes, and real-time customer support. The site has really paid off. Roughly 55 percent the company's total sales now come from the Web site.[10]

E-procurement gives buyers access to new suppliers, lowers purchasing costs, and hastens order processing and delivery. In turn, business marketers can connect with customers online to share marketing information, sell products and services, provide customer support services, and maintain ongoing customer relationships.

Business-to-business e-procurement yields many benefits:

- It cuts transaction costs and results in more efficient purchasing for both buyers and suppliers. A Web-powered purchasing program eliminates the paperwork associated with traditional requisition and ordering procedures.

- It reduces the time between order and delivery. Time savings are particularly dramatic for companies with many overseas suppliers. Adaptec, a leading supplier of computer storage, used an extranet to tie all of its Taiwanese chip suppliers together in a kind of virtual family. Now messages from Adaptec flow in seconds from its headquarters to its Asian partners, and Adaptec has reduced the time between the order and delivery of its chips from as long as 16 weeks to just 55 days—the same turnaround time for companies that build their own chips.

- It frees purchasing people to focus on more-strategic issues. For many purchasing professionals, going online means reducing paperwork and spending more time managing inventory and working creatively with suppliers.

The rapidly expanding use of e-purchasing, however, also presents some problems. For example, at the same time that the Web makes it possible for suppliers and customers to share business data and even collaborate on product design, it can also erode decades-old customer-supplier relationships. Many firms are using the Web to search for better suppliers. Japan Airlines uses the Internet to post orders for in-flight materials such as plastic cups. On its Web site, it posts drawings and specifications that attracts proposals from any firm that comes across the site rather than just from Japanese suppliers whom the airlines want to deal with.

E-purchasing can also create potential security disasters. Although e-mail and home banking transactions can be protected through basic encryption, the secure environment that businesses need to carry out confidential interactions is often still lacking. Companies are spending millions for research on defensive strategies to keep away hackers. Cisco Systems, for example, specifies the types of routers, firewalls, and security procedures that its partners must use to safeguard extranet connections. It even sends its own security engineers to examine a partner's defenses and holds the partner liable for any security breach that originates from its computer.

Institutional and Government Markets

Much of the above discussion also applies to the buying practices of institutional and government organizations. However, these two nonbusiness markets have additional characteristics and needs. In this final section, we address the special features of institutional and government markets.

Institutional Markets

The **institutional market** consists of schools, hospitals, nursing homes, prisons, and other institutions that provide goods and services to people in their care. Institutions differ from one another in their sponsors and in their objectives. Each institution also has different buying needs and resources.

Many institutional markets are characterized by low budgets and captive patrons. For example, hospital patients have little choice but to eat whatever food the hospital supplies.

Institutional market
Schools, hospitals, nursing homes, prisons, and other institutions that provide goods and services to people in their care.

A hospital purchasing agent must decide on the quality of food to buy for patients. Because the food is provided as a part of a total service package, the buying objective is not profit. Nor is strict cost minimization the goal—patients receiving poor-quality food will complain to others and damage the hospital's reputation. Thus, the hospital purchasing agent must search for institutional-food vendors whose quality meets or exceeds a certain minimum standard and whose prices are low.

Many marketers set up separate divisions to meet the special characteristics and needs of institutional buyers. For example, Heinz produces, packages, and prices its ketchup and other condiments, canned soups, frozen desserts, pickles, and other products differently to better serve the requirements of hospitals, colleges, and other institutional markets.[11]

Institutional markets –
Heinz produces, packages, and prices its products differently to better serve the requirements of hospitals, colleges, and other institutional markets.

Government market
Governmental units—federal, state, and local—that purchase or rent goods and services for carrying out the main functions of government.

Government Markets

The **government market** offers large opportunities for many companies, both big and small. In most countries, government organizations are major buyers of goods and services. Government organizations typically require suppliers to submit bids, and normally they award the contract to the lowest bidder. In some cases, the government unit will make allowance for the supplier's superior quality or reputation for completing contracts on time. Governments will also buy on a negotiated contract basis, primarily in the case of complex projects involving major R&D costs and risks, and in cases where there is little competition.

Noneconomic criteria also play a growing role in government buying. Government organizations tend to favor domestic suppliers over foreign suppliers. For example, the Malaysian government's *bumiputra* ("son of the soil") policy favors suppliers whose owners are ethnic Malays. This has led to non-*bumi* firms partnering with *bumiputra*-owned enterprises when tendering for government projects. Approved Permits preferentially allow *bumiputra* to import vehicles.[12] In promoting domestic businesses, the Chinese government may favor local champions like Lenovo over foreign competitors.

Like consumer and business buyers, government buyers are affected by environmental, organizational, interpersonal, and individual factors. Transparency in government procurements vary from country to country. In countries where government buying is carefully watched by outside publics and spending decisions are subject to public review, government organizations require considerable paperwork from suppliers. Suppliers thus complain about excessive paperwork, bureaucracy, regulations, decision-making delays, and frequent shifts in procurement personnel. In other countries, close relationships with government officials overseeing procurement is often critical in winning contracts.

Many companies that sell to the government have not been very marketing oriented for a number of reasons. Total government spending is determined by elected officials rather than by any marketing effort to develop this market. Government buying has emphasized price, making suppliers invest their effort in technology to bring costs down. When the product's characteristics are specified carefully, product differentiation is not a marketing factor. Nor do advertising or personal selling matter much in winning bids on an open-bid basis.

Government organizations tend to favor domestic suppliers over foreign suppliers. Lenovo is a partner sponsor of the 2008 Beijing Olympics.

REVIEWING THE CONCEPTS

Business markets and consumer markets are alike in some key ways. For example, both include people in buying roles who make purchase decisions to satisfy needs. But business markets also differ in many ways from consumer markets. For one thing, the business market is *enormous*, far larger than the consumer market. Within the U.S. alone, the business market includes organizations that annually purchase trillions of dollars' worth of goods and services.

1 **Define the business market and explain how business markets differ from consumer markets.**

Business buyer behavior refers to the buying behavior of the organizations that buy goods and services for use in the production of other products and services that are sold, rented, or supplied to others. It also includes the behavior of retailing and wholesaling firms that acquire goods for the purpose of reselling or renting them to others at a profit.

As compared to consumer markets, business markets usually have fewer, larger buyers who are more geographically concentrated. Business demand is *derived*, largely *inelastic*, and more *fluctuating*. More buyers are usually involved in the business buying decision, and business buyers are better trained and more professional than are consumer buyers. In general, business purchasing decisions are more complex, and the buying process is more formal than consumer buying.

2 **Identify the major factors that influence busines buyer behavior.**

Business buyers make decisions that vary with the three types of *buying situations*: straight rebuys, modified rebuys, and new tasks. The decision-making unit of a buying organization—the *buying center*—can consist of many different persons playing many different roles. The business marketer needs to know the following: Who are the major buying center participants? In what decisions do they exercise influence and to what degree? What evaluation criteria does each decision participant use? The business marketer also needs to understand the major environmental, organizational, interpersonal, and individual influences on the buying process.

3 **List and define the steps in the business buying decision process.**

The *business buying decision process* itself can be quite involved, with eight basic stages: problem recognition, general need description, product specification, supplier search, proposal solicitation, supplier selection, order-routine specification, and performance review. Buyers who face a new-task buying situation usually go through all stages of the buying process. Buyers making modified or straight rebuys may skip some of the stages. Companies must manage the overall customer relationship, which often includes many different buying decisions in various stages of the buying decision process.

Recent advances in information technology have given birth to "e-procurement," by which business buyers are purchasing all kinds of products and services online. The Internet gives business buyers access to new suppliers, lowers purchasing costs, and hastens order processing and delivery. However, e-procurement can also erode customer-supplier relationships and create potential security problems. Still, business marketers are increasingly connecting with customers online to share marketing information, sell products and services, provide customer support services, and maintain ongoing customer relationships.

4 **Compare the institutional and government markets and explain how institutional and government buyers make their buying decisions.**

The *institutional market* consists of schools, hospitals, prisons, and other institutions that provide goods and services to people in their care. These markets are characterized by low budgets and captive patrons. The *government market*, which is vast, consists of government units that purchase or rent goods and services for carrying out the main functions of government.

Government buyers purchase products and services for defense, education, public welfare, and other public needs. Government buying practices are highly specialized and specified, with open bidding or negotiated contracts characterizing most of the buying. Suppliers need to be aware of environmental, organizational, interpersonal, and individual factors which may influence government procurement.

REVIEWING THE KEY TERMS

Business buyer behavior 146
Business buying process 146
Buyers 151
Buying center 151
Deciders 151
Derived demand 147
Gatekeepers 151
General need description 153
Government market 158
Influencers 151
Institutional market 157
Modified rebuy 150
New task 150

Order-routine specification 156
Performance review 156
Problem recognition 153
Product specification 153
Proposal solicitation 154
Straight rebuy 150
Supplier development 149
Supplier search 153
Supplier selection 155
Systems selling 150
Users 151
Value analysis 153

DISCUSSING THE CONCEPTS

1. How do the market structure and demand of the business markets for Intel's microprocessor chips differ from those of final consumer markets?

2. Discuss several ways in which a straight rebuy differs from a new-task situation.

3. In a buying center purchasing process, which buying center participant—a buyer, decider, gatekeeper, influencer, or user—is most likely to make each of the following statements?
   - "This bonding agent better be good, because I have to put this product together."
   - "I specified this bonding agent on another job, and it worked for them."
   - "Without an appointment, no sales rep gets in to see Mr. Chin."
   - "Okay, it's a deal—we'll buy it."
   - "I'll place the order first thing tomorrow."

4. Outline the major influences on business buyers. Why is it important for the business-to-business buyer to understand these major influences?

5. How does the business buying process differ from the consumer buying process?

6. Suppose that you own a small printing firm and have the opportunity to bid on a government contract that could bring a considerable amount of new business to your company. List three advantages and three disadvantages of working in a contract situation with the government.

APPLYING THE CONCEPTS

1. Burst-of-Energy is a food product positioned in the extreme sports market as a performance enhancer. A distributor of the product has seen an upward shift in the demand for the product (depicted in the figure at the right). The manufacturer has done nothing to generate this demand, but there have been a couple of reports that two popular celebrities were photographed with the product. Could something like this happen? Based on the figure, how would you characterize the demand for the product? Is it elastic or inelastic? Would you call this an example of fluctuating demand? Support your answers.

2. Assume that you own a market research consulting firm that specializes in conducting focus groups for food manufacturers. Your customers are marketing managers and market research managers at these large firms. Outline your business consumers' buying process and

explain how you can improve your chances of being hired at each step of the process.

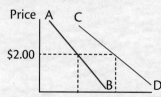

3. Form a small group and compare the similarities and differences between a buyer at a public hospital and a buyer at a for-profit hospital. Compare the buyers on the following four factors: environmental, organizational, interpersonal, and individual.

FOCUS ON TECHNOLOGY

Social networking is a hot topic in Internet marketing. Web sites including friendster.com and myspace.com are crowded meeting grounds for Web visitors who are hoping to get connected online. Social networking is also a growing technology for B-to-B interactions. From finding services, locating opportunities, even recruiting board members, these sites offer what business consumers need. InnerSell. com is a company that is using social networking to drive real business for clients by locating prospects. A sample scenario on InnerSell.com works like this:

a. An InnerSell.com member, who sells real estate, talks to a prospect or customer and learns that it has a need for $50,000 worth of photocopiers.

b. The member enters the need (lead) into InnerSell.com and sees a list of trusted photocopier vendors along with their ratings and their finder's fee.

c. The member views each vendor's ratings and selects two photocopier vendors who pay a 10 percent finder's fee.

d. The selected vendors receive an e-mail advising them that they've been chosen and instructing them to log into InnerSell.com to see the details of the opportunity.

e. When a selected vendor sees the lead, contacts the customer, and wins the business, it pays InnerSell.com its 10 percent finder's fee (in this case, $5,000).

f. InnerSell.com then passes $3,500 of the winning vendor's finder's fee to the member who entered the winning lead.

1. At what stage(s) of the business buying process does InnerSell.com operate?

2. What types of businesses is this best suited to serve?

3. What are some weaknesses with this technology?

FOCUS ON ETHICS

You are the senior buyer for a growing medical products company and an avid football fan. You have just opened an invitation to attend the World Cup tournament. The invitation is from a supplier company that has been trying to sell you its new line of products for the past year. The supplier will pay for everything—travel, room, meals—and you'll even get an opportunity to meet some of the players. You have read the newly released employee manual and there is no reference or rule that specifically states that an employee cannot accept a fully paid trip from a vendor, although there are some vague restrictions on lunches and dinners paid for by suppliers.

1. Do you accept or decline the invitation?

2. Just because it is not specifically mentioned in the employee manual, would you be acting ethically if you accepted?

3. Do you think the supplier will expect "special" treatment in the next buying situation?

4. How would other company employees interpret your acceptance of this invitation?

VIDEO CASE

Eaton

With nearly 60,000 employees doing business in 125 countries and sales of more than $11 billion, Eaton is one of the world's largest suppliers of diversified industrial goods. Eaton's products make cars more peppy, 18 wheelers safer to drive, and airliners more fuel efficient. So why haven't you heard of the company? Because Eaton sells its products not to end consumers but to other businesses.

At Eaton, B-to-B marketing means working closely with customers to develop a better product. Eaton partners its sophisticated, knowledgeable clients to create total solutions that meet their needs. It maps the decision-making process to better understand the concerns and interests of decision makers. Eaton's success depends on its ability to provide high-quality, dependable customer service and product

support. Through service and support, Eaton develops a clear understanding of consumer needs and builds stronger relationships with clients.

After viewing the video featuring Eaton, answer the following questions about business markets and business buyer behavior.

1. What is Eaton's value proposition?

2. To which decision makers does Eaton market its products and services?

3. How does Eaton add value to its products and services?

COMPANY CASE

Kodak: Changing the Picture

Memories

"You press the button—we do the rest." With that simple slogan, George Eastman unveiled the first Kodak camera in 1888. In 1900, Kodak launched its famous Brownie cameras, which it priced at $1.00, opening the photography market to millions. Throughout the 20th century, Kodak dominated the photography business. By 2000, Kodak was one of the most recognized and trusted brands in the world. Many people referred to the company as "Big Yellow." The company saw itself as being in the memory business, not in the photography business.

Going Negative

However, entering the new millennium, Kodak faced many challenges that would require it to rethink and perhaps redesign its business strategy. The company's stock price, which had reached a historic peak of $90 in 1997, had been plummeting, and Kodak had begun to lay off workers.

Several factors were causing Kodak's problems. First, although Kodak had been the first company to produce a digital camera in 1976, it had been reluctant to develop the technology. The core of Kodak's business strategy had always been the three-fold foundation of commercial and consumer photography: film, photo-developing chemicals, and light-sensitive paper. Kodak believed that consumers would be slow to adopt digital technology. But what held the company back even more was that a shift toward digital would to some extent have been a shift away from George Eastman's legacy. Thus, Kodak saw every digital camera consumers purchased as another nail in its coffin.

Second, despite Kodak's dominance in traditional photography, many competitors, especially Fuji, were exposing flaws in Kodak's marketing and stealing market share. Third, competition from an unexpected source—mobile phone manufacturers—surprised Kodak. Nokia introduced the first mobile phone with a built-in camera in November 2001. Although many people thought such phones would only be toys, consumers began snapping them up. By 2003, sales of camera phones doubled the sales of conventional digital cameras. Further, analysts predicted correctly that the number of mobile phones with cameras would increase dramatically during the early 2000s.

Finally, consumers who owned digital cameras or mobile-phone cameras were increasingly using their PCs and printers to download and print their own pictures, if they printed them at all. Analysts discovered that consumers printed only 2 percent of camera-phone pictures in the U.S., versus 10 percent in Japan.

The Proof Is in the Picture— Walgreens

Up through the 1980s, when consumers wanted to develop pictures, they took their film rolls to local drugstores, discount department stores, or photo shops. These stores sent the film to regional labs run by Kodak and others, which produced the prints and returned them to the store for pickup. This process took many days. Then, with the development of the self-contained photo lab, retailers could place a machine directly in their store that would do all the photo processing. These photo labs allowed the retailers to offer faster service—even one-hour service.

As consumers demanded more one-hour photo developing, Kodak agreed to help Walgreens, the largest drugstore chain in the U.S., set up a national one-hour photo business. Kodak had been the exclusive supplier of photo-developing services to Walgreens for years. In response to the request, Kodak provided minilabs, which it bought from a Swiss manufacturer that handled the photo developing on-site, collecting fees for leasing the equipment. Kodak even loaned Walgreens $31.6 million, interest free, to help it implement the system.

Problems developed, however, when the minilabs proved to be unreliable. They broke down up to 11 times a month due to paper jams and software glitches. It often took two to three days to get the machines serviced, and when they were, customers' film in the machines was exposed to light when service people opened the machines.

As a result, in 2001, Walgreens quietly began to install Fuji minilabs in some of its California stores. Unlike Kodak's, Fuji's machines allowed consumers to make prints from both traditional and digital cameras. Kodak began selling kits to allow its minilabs to handle digital prints, but Walgreens officials believed Kodak's prints were lower quality. By early 2004, Fuji had 1,500 minilabs in Walgreens' almost 4,300 outlets.

Kodak also approached Walgreens about developing a Walgreens Internet site that would allow consumers to upload digital photos over the Web. Kodak would then store images and allow customers to order prints, which would then be mailed to them. Walgreens did not like Kodak's proposal as it minimized the Walgreens role and allowed Kodak to keep the pictures on its site, gaining an advantage in future customer orders. Despite these concerns, Walgreens was about to sign a deal with Kodak when two top officials, who favored Kodak, retired. Walgreens then cancelled the deal and started developing its own Web site with Fuji, which was comfortable with a less prominent role. Walgreens launched its Web service in 2003, with Fuji carrying out the photo developing.

A New Development

Given all this, in early 2003, Kodak reevaluated its strategy. It recognized that the time had come to fully embrace the digital age. In September 2003, Kodak announced a historic shift in its strategy. It would now focus on digital imaging for consumers, businesses, and health care providers. The company would reduce its dependence on traditional film, boost investment in nonphotographic markets, and pursue digital markets, such as inkjet printers and high-end digital printing. These moves would put it in direct competition with entrenched players, such as HP, Canon, Seiko, Epson, and Xerox. It was a necessary but risky shift—at the time, traditional film and photography accounted for 70 percent of Kodak's revenue and all of its operating profits.

By 2004, Kodak had laid out a complete four-year restructuring plan. The plan was that Kodak's traditional business would progressively contribute less as a percentage of revenues and earnings while the digital business would contribute more. As a part of the shift in strategy, Kodak stopped selling reloadable film cameras in the U.S., Canada, and Europe. In 2005, Kodak focused intensely on further executing the strategic plan. CEO Antonio Perez even asserted, "Soon, I'm not going to be answering questions about film because I won't know. It will be too small for me to get involved."

CEO Perez made some dramatic moves. He divided the company into four units: imaging, commercial print, medical, and traditional film. To assist in phasing out the film business and to stop the "bleeding year after year," Kodak announced that it would shut down two-thirds of its manufacturing facilities and cut its employee base by more than one-third from 69,000 to 44,000.

In early 2006, Kodak launched various initiatives that would bolster its consumer business in digital imaging. At the same time, Perez realized that a key to the company's survival was to strengthen its commercial business. He poured resources into the commercial print and medical imaging units. These were areas with high growth potential and gave a promise of diversifying Kodak's revenue base. In the medical field alone, entire health care systems were transitioning from traditional to digital imaging. Perez anticipated that Kodak could reduce its health care division's dependency on X-ray film by playing a big role in the industry digitization.

But as 2006 unraveled, it seemed that Kodak's restructuring plan was doing the same. The first quarter of the year resulted in the sixth quarterly loss in a row. Though revenue rose slightly to $2.89 billion from $2.83 billion for the first quarter of 2005, Kodak had a net loss of $298 million, more than double the previous year's loss of $146 million. But Kodak lost more than money. After holding the leading revenue position in digital cameras for five straight quarters, the company's share dropped from 19.7 percent to 14.5 percent, leaving it at number three.

To make matters worse, the hopeful medical imaging unit was losing revenue and profit at a rapid pace, despite the efforts and resources to make the business thrive. After showcasing Kodak's medical imaging technology at the Winter Olympics in Torino, Perez surprisingly announced that he would consider selling the $2.7 billion Health Group to raise cash. "Our stated goal is to be among the top three in each of the businesses in which we compete," Perez said, underscoring the poor performance of the division.

While Kodak continued to struggle miserably, there were signs of life. The Graphic Communications Group was strong and growing. For the first time ever, digital imaging revenue surpassed that of traditional film at the end of 2005. Yet, according to one journalist, "one thing is as clear as a digital image: the concept of pressing a button and letting Kodak do the rest will have to take a dramatically different form if the company is to make it as a 21st century business."

Questions For Discussion

1. How are the market structure and demand, the nature of the buying unit, and the types of decisions and decision process different for Kodak's commercial markets relative to its consumer markets?

2. What examples of the major types of buying situations do you see in the case? Discuss the implications of each in terms of marketing strategy.

3. How might Kodak have made better use of the buying center concept to more effectively meet the needs of its commercial customers?

4. With respect to Kodak's industrial commercial customers, how is the buying process different for their current situation relative to their old business model?

5. What marketing recommendations would you make to Perez as he continues to try to turn things around at Kodak?

Sources:
Chris Noon, "Martha Stewart, Kodak in a Picture Perfect Deal," *Forbes*, June 27, 2006, accessed online at www.forbes.com; Danit Lidor, "Perez' Kodak Loses No. 1 U.S. Digital Camera Spot," *Forbes*, May 9, 2006, accessed online at www.forbes.com; Danit Lidor, "Kodak's Perez Eyes Medical Unit Sale after Glum Q1," *Forbes*, May 4, 2006, accessed online at www.forbes.com; Amy Yee, "Banishing the Negative: How Kodak Is Developing Its Blueprint for a Digital Transformation," *Financial Times*, January 26, 2006, p. 15; James Bandler, "Kodak Shifts Focus from Film, Betting Future on Digital Lines," *Wall Street Journal*, September 25, 2003, p. A1; James Bandler, "Ending Era, Kodak Will Stop Selling Most Film Cameras," *Wall Street Journal*, January 14, 2004; Andy Reinhardt, Hiroko Tashiro, and Ben Elgin, "The Camera Phone Revolution," *BusinessWeek*, April 12, 2004, p. 52.

Objectives

After studying this chapter, you should be able to

- define the four major steps in designing a customer-driven market strategy: market segmentation, market targeting, differentiation, and positioning
- list and discuss the major bases for segmenting consumer and business markets
- explain how companies identify attractive market segments and choose a market targeting strategy
- discuss how companies position their products for maximum competitive advantage in the marketplace

CHAPTER 7

CUSTOMER–DRIVEN MARKETING STRATEGY: Creating Value for Target Customers

Previewing The Concepts

So far, you've learned what marketing is and about the importance of understanding consumers and the marketplace environment. This chapter looks further into key customer-driven marketing strategy decisions—how to divide up markets into meaningful customer groups (*segmentation*), choose which customer groups to serve (*targeting*), create market offerings that best serve target customers (*differentiation*), and position the offerings in the minds of consumers (*positioning*). Then, the chapters that follow explore the tactical marketing tools—the Four Ps—by which marketers bring these strategies to life.

As an opening example of segmentation, targeting, differentiation, and positioning at work, let's look at Estée Lauder, the world's largest cosmetics and beauty company.

Estée Lauder is an expert in creating differentiated brands that serve the tastes of different market segments. Five of the top-ten best-selling prestige perfumes in the U.S. belong to Estée Lauder. So do eight of the top-ten prestige makeup brands. There's the original Estée Lauder brand, with its gold and blue packaging, which appeals to older baby boomers. Then there's Clinique, the company's most popular brand, perfect for the middle-aged mom with no time to waste and for younger women attracted to its classic free gift offers. For young, fashion-forward consumers, there's M.A.C., which provides makeup for clients like Pamela Anderson and Marilyn Manson. For eco-conscious consumers who want cosmetics made from nature ingredients, there's Origins. For New Age aromatherapy enthusiasts, there's upscale Aveda, with its salon, makeup, and lifestyle products. Aveda is based on the art and science of earthy origins and pure flower and plant essences, celebrating the connection between Mother Nature and human nature. And Prescriptives Custom Beauty "embraces all women, all skin types, and all ages with products that enhance the unique beauty of each individual." Its skin care range offers a customized regimen, while its Colorprint service identifies the color and foundation appropriate for every skin type.

Estée Lauder also markets fragrances and grooming products for men. Aramis was launched in 1964. It also became the first women's cosmetic company to introduce a second line for men with Lab Series, a separate line of skin supplies in 1976. Estée Lauder also markets lines under celebrities such as Donald Trump The Fragrance, Donna Karan, Michael Kors, and Tommy Hilfiger.

The company also targets the international market. Its first international account was in the London department store Harrods in 1960. The following year, Estée Lauder entered Hong Kong. In 1981, it achieved another breakthrough when its products became available in the then Soviet Union. Estée Lauder now sells its products in department stores across the world, as well as having a chain of freestanding retail outlets. It employs over 20,000 people, and in 2007, its sales topped $7 billion.[1]

Companies today recognize that they cannot appeal to all buyers in the marketplace, or at least not to all buyers in the same way. Buyers are too numerous, too widely scattered, and too varied in their needs and buying practices. Moreover, the companies themselves vary widely in their abilities to serve different segments of the market. Instead, like Estée Lauder, a company must identify the parts of the market that it can serve best and most profitably. It must design customer-driven marketing strategies that build the *right relationships* with the *right customers*.

Thus, most companies have moved away from mass marketing and toward target marketing—identifying market segments, selecting one or more of them, and developing products and marketing programs tailored to each. Instead of scattering their marketing efforts (the "shotgun" approach), firms are focusing on the buyers who have greater interest in the values they create best (the "rifle" approach).

Figure 7.1 shows the four major steps in designing a customer-driven marketing strategy. In the first two steps, the company selects the customers that it will serve. **Market segmentation** involves dividing a market into smaller groups of buyers with distinct needs, characteristics, or behaviors who might require separate products or marketing mixes. The company identifies different ways to segment the market and develops profiles of the resulting market segments. **Market targeting** (or **targeting**) consists of evaluating each market segment's attractiveness and select one or more market segments to enter.

In the final two steps, the company decides on a value proposition—on how it will create value for target customers. **Differentiation** involves actually differentiating the firm's market offering to create superior customer value. **Positioning** consists of arranging for a market offering to occupy a clear, distinctive, and desirable place relative to competing products in the minds of target consumers. We discuss each of these steps in turn.

Market segmentation
Dividing a market into smaller groups with distinct needs, characteristics, or behaviors who might require separate products or marketing mixes.

Market targeting
The process of evaluating each market segment's attractiveness and selecting one or more segments to enter.

Differentiation
Actually differentiating the firm's market offering to create superior customer value.

Positioning
Arranging for a product to occupy a clear, distinctive, and desirable place relative to competing products in the minds of target consumers.

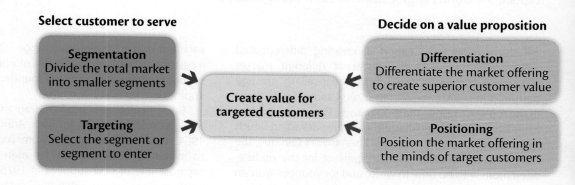

Figure 7.1
Steps in market segmentation, targeting, and positioning

Select customer to serve

Segmentation
Divide the total market into smaller segments

Targeting
Select the segment or segment to enter

Create value for targeted customers

Decide on a value proposition

Differentiation
Differentiate the market offering to create superior customer value

Positioning
Position the market offering in the minds of target customers

Market Segmentation

Markets consist of buyers, and buyers differ in one or more ways. They may differ in their wants, resources, locations, buying attitudes, and buying practices. Through market segmentation, companies divide large, heterogeneous markets into smaller segments that can be reached more efficiently and effectively with products and services that match their unique needs. In this section, we discuss four important segmentation topics:

- segmenting consumer markets
- segmenting business markets
- segmenting international markets
- requirements for effective segmentation

Segmenting Consumer Markets

There is no single way to segment a market. A marketer has to try different segmentation variables, alone and in combination, to find the best way to view the market structure. **Table 7.1** outlines the major variables that might be used in segmenting consumer markets. Here we look at the major geographic, demographic, psychographic, and behavioral variables.

Table 7.1 Major Segmentation Variables for Consumer Markets

Geographic	
World region or country	North America, Western Europe, Middle East, Pacific Rim, China, India, Canada, Mexico
Country region	North, South, East, West, Central
City or metro size	Under 5,000; 5,000–20,000; 20,000–50,000; 50,000–100,000; 100,000–250,000; 250,000–500,000; 500,000–1,000,000; 1,000,000–4,000,000; over 4,000,000
Density	Urban, suburban, rural
Climate	Northern, southern
Demographic	
Age	Under 6, 6–11, 12–19, 20–34, 35–49, 50–64, 65+
Gender	Male, female
Family size	1–2, 3–4, 5+
Family life cycle	Young, single; young, married, no children; young, married with children; older, married with children; older, married, no children; under 18; older, single; other
Income	Under $10,000; $10,000–$20,000; $20,000–$30,000; $30,000–$50,000; $50,000–$100,000; $100,000 and over
Occupation	Professional and technical; managers, officials, and proprietors; clerical; sales; craftspeople; supervisors; operatives; farmers; retired; students; homemakers; unemployed
Education	Grade school or less; some high school; high school graduate; some college; college graduate
Religion	Buddhist, Catholic, Hindu, Muslim, Protestant, other
Race	Chinese, Indian, Malay, other
Generation	Baby boomer, Generation X, Generation Y
Nationality	British, Chinese, French, German, Italian, Japanese
Psychographic	
Social class	Lower lowers, upper lowers, working class, middle class, upper middles, lower uppers, upper uppers
Lifestyle	Achievers, strivers, survivors
Personality	Compulsive, filial, gregarious, authoritarian, ambitious
Behavioral	
Occasions	Regular occasion; special occasion
Benefits	Quality, service, economy, convenience, speed
User status	Nonuser, ex-user, potential user, first-time user, regular user
User rates	Light user, medium user, heavy user
Loyalty status	None, medium, strong, absolute
Readiness stage	Unaware, aware, informed, interested, desirous, intending to buy
Attitude toward product	Enthusiastic, positive, indifferent, negative, hostile

Geographic Segmentation

Geographic segmentation calls for dividing the market into different geographical units such as nations, regions, states, counties, cities, or even neighborhoods. A company may decide to operate in one or a few geographical areas, or to operate in all areas but pay attention to geographical differences in needs and wants.

Many companies localize their products, advertising, promotion, and sales efforts to fit the needs of individual regions, cities, and even neighborhoods. For example, Coca-Cola developed four ready-to-drink canned coffees for the Japanese market, each targeted to a specific geographic region. Also, it found that with Japanese teenagers always on the go, they did not like to have Coke cans left open while they are talking

Geographic segmentation
Dividing a market into different geographical units such as nations, states, regions, counties, cities, or neighborhoods.

Geographic segmentation – Coke realized that Japanese teenagers did not like to leave their Coke cans open when they are talking on their mobile phones. The Coke can with a twisted cap that can be closed after opening was developed specifically for this market.

Demographic segmentation
Dividing a market into groups based on variables such as age, gender, family size, family life cycle, income, occupation, education, religion, race, generation, and nationality.

Age and life-cycle segmentation
Dividing a market into different age and life-cycle groups.

Gender segmentation
Dividing a market into different groups based on gender.

on their mobile phone. Hence, Coke introduced Coke cans with a twisted cap for the Japanese market. Procter & Gamble introduced Curry Pringles in England and Funky Soy Sauce Pringles in Asia to cater to different taste buds.[2]

Other companies are seeking to cultivate as-yet untapped geographic territory. For example, China's first-tier cities such as Shanghai and Shenzhen along its coast attract significant attention from many businesses. Some firms thus choose to venture further inland to tap the country's less developed regions. Consumer markets in second-tier Chinese cities like Xian and Chengdu in the West are also becoming more accessible to foreign companies as World Trade Organization commitments are phased in.[3]

In contrast, other businesses are developing stores in higher-density urban areas. For example, New Oriental Education & Technology, China's largest English-language and test preparation provider, concentrates on the country's larger cities to better tap soaring demand. It operates 128 schools and smaller learning centers in 34 cities, mainly in provincial capitals and larger cities. It believes that English learners and others who aim to study overseas will travel to its big-city schools even when they live in small towns as parents think the company's big-city centres are superior.[4]

Demographic Segmentation

Demographic segmentation divides the market into groups based on variables such as age, gender, family size, family life cycle, income, occupation, education, religion, race, generation, and nationality. Demographic factors are the most popular bases for segmenting customer groups. One reason is that consumer needs, wants, and usage rates often vary closely with demographic variables. Another is that demographic variables are easier to measure than most other types of variables. Even when market segments are first defined using other bases, such as benefits sought or behavior, their demographic characteristics must be known in order to assess the size of the target market and to reach it efficiently.

Age and life-cycle stage

Consumer needs and wants change with age. Some companies use **age and life-cycle segmentation**, offering different products or using different marketing approaches for different age and life-cycle groups. For example, Nintendo, known for its youth-oriented video games, has launched a subbrand, Touch Generations, which targets aging baby boomers. Touch Generations offers video games such as *Brain Training: How Old Is Your Brain?*, designed to exercise the mind to keep it young. The aim is to "lure in older nongamers by offering skill-building—or at least less violent, less fantasy-based—titles that might appeal to [older consumers] more than, say, *Grand Theft Auto* or *World of Warcraft*."[5]

Marketers must be careful to guard against stereotypes when using age and life-cycle segmentation. For example, while some 40-year-old couples are sending their children off to college, others are just beginning new families. Thus, age is often a poor predictor of a person's life cycle, health, work or family status, needs, and buying power. Companies marketing to mature consumers usually employ positive images and appeals. For example, Japan's baby food makers have targeted seniors given the country's rapidly ageing population. As elderly Japanese do not like admitting their age, discreet appeals are employed to reach them. Wakodo sells its elder food as "Fun Meals," while Q.P. labels its pouches "Food for Ages 0–100."

Gender

Gender segmentation has long been used in clothing, cosmetics, toiletries, and magazines. Of late, many mostly-women's cosmetics makers have begun marketing men's lines. For example, L'Oréal offers Men's Expert skin care products and a VIVE For Men grooming line. Ads proclaim, "Now L'Oréal Paris brings its grooming technology and expertise to men … because you're worth it too."

Nike has recently stepped up its efforts to capture the women's sports apparel market. It wasn't until 2000 that Nike made women's shoes using molds made from women's feet, rather than simply using a small man's foot mold. Since then, however, Nike has changed its approach to women. It has overhauled its women's apparel line—called Nikewomen—to create better fitting, more colorful, more fashionable workout clothes for women. Its revamped Nikewomen.com Web site now features the apparel, along with workout trend highlights. And Nike has been opening Nikewomen stores in several major cities.[6]

Income

Income segmentation has long been used by the marketers of products and services such as automobiles, clothing, cosmetics, financial services, and travel. Many companies target affluent consumers with luxury goods and convenience services. Credit-card companies offer super premium credit cards dripping with perks, such as VISA's Signature Card, MasterCard's World card, and American Express's super-elite Centurion card. Some cigarette manufacturers such as Luxury in Cambodia target the well-heeled and those aspiring to belong to the higher income bracket.

However, not all companies that use income segmentation target the affluent. Many retailers successfully target budget-conscious groups. In Hong Kong, there are discount garment shops, as well as food and grocery outlets, that cater to Filipino and Indonesian domestic helper market.

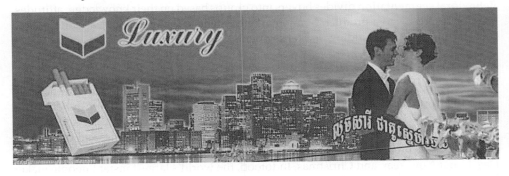

Gender segmentation – Nike stepped up its efforts to capture the women's sport apparel market by overhauling its women's apparel lines, revamping the Nikewomen.com Web site, and opening Nikewomen stores in several major cities. (www.Nikewomen.com)

Income segmentation
Dividing a market into different income groups.

Income segmentation – As the name suggests, Luxury cigarettes in Cambodia targets the higher income group.

Psychographic Segmentation

Psychographic segmentation divides buyers into different groups based on social class, lifestyle, or personality characteristics. People in the same demographic group can have very different psychographic makeups.

In Chapter 5, we discussed how the products people buy reflect their lifestyles. As a result, marketers often segment their markets by consumer lifestyles and base their marketing strategies on lifestyle appeals. For example, American Express promises "a card that fits your life." It's "My life. My card." campaign provides glimpses into the lifestyles of famous people with whom consumers might want to identify, from television personality Ellen DeGeneres to screen stars Robert DeNiro and Kate Winslet.

Marketers also have used *personality* variables to segment markets. For example, marketing for Honda motor scooters *appears* to target hip and trendy 22-year-olds. But it is *actually* aimed at a much broader personality group. One old ad, for example, showed a delighted child bouncing up and down on his bed while the announcer says, "You've been trying to get there all your life." The ad reminded viewers of the euphoric feelings they got when they broke away from authority and did things their parents told them not to do. Thus, Honda is appealing to the rebellious, independent kid in all of us. In fact, 22 percent of scooter riders are retirees. Competitor Vespa sells more than a quarter of its

Psychographic segmentation
Dividing a market into different groups based on social class, lifestyle or personality characteristic.

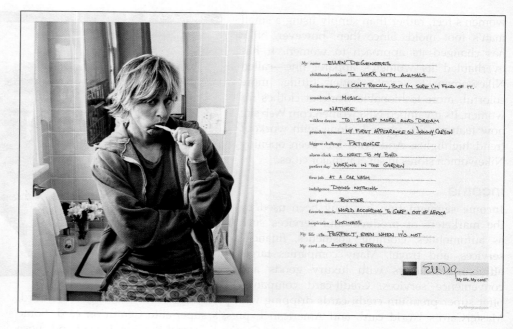

Psychographic segmentation – the American Express "My life. My card." campaign provides glimpses into the lifestyles of famous people with whom consumers identify, like Ellen DeGeneres here.

scooters to the over-50 set. "The older buyers are buying them for kicks," says one senior. "They never had the opportunity to do this as kids."[7]

Behavioral Segmentation

Behavioral segmentation divides buyers into groups based on their knowledge, attitudes, uses, or responses to a product. Many marketers believe that behavior variables are the best starting point for building market segments.

> **Behavioral segmentation**
> Dividing a market into groups based on consumer knowledge, attitude, use, or response to a product.

Occasions

Buyers can be grouped according to occasions when they get the idea to buy, actually make their purchase, or use the purchased item. **Occasion segmentation** can help firms build up product usage. Some holidays, such as Mother's Day and Father's Day, were originally promoted partly to increase the sale of candy, flowers, cards, and other gifts. Marketers also prepare special offers and ads for special occasions such as Valentine's Day, Lunar New Year, and Christmas. Indofood, the world's largest instant noodle maker by volume, practices occasion segmentation to create "aspirational noodle eaters." It promoted a special edition Valentine's Day box noodle set packed in a pink Chinese takeaway box with cartoon hearts for decoration. There are also "limited edition" Chinese New Year noodles, packed in auspicious red and gold, birthday noodles, and noodles for book launches. Indofood envisages other occasions like weddings, births, and college graduations to market its products.[8]

> **Occasion segmentation**
> Dividing a market into groups according to occasions when buyers get the idea to buy, actually make their purchase, or use the purchased item.

Benefits sought

A powerful form of segmentation is to group buyers according to the different benefits that they seek from the product. **Benefit segmentation** requires finding the major benefits people look for in the product class, the kinds of people who look for each benefit, and the major brands that deliver each benefit.

The Indonesian toothpaste market provides another illustration of benefit segmentation. Market leader Pepsodent, a Unilever brand, offers fluoride to keep teeth clean and healthy. Other brands like Close-Up, Ciptadent, and Formula aim to make your breath fresh, heal mouth ulcers, and prevent the mouth from getting dry. Kodomo produces fruit-tasting toothpaste for children. Miswak Utama launched Siwak, a brand containing

> **Benefit segmentation**
> Dividing a market into groups according to the different benefits that consumers seek from the product.

Salvadora Persica, an ingredient thought to be highly effective in tartar removal. Siwak targets Muslims who must clean their mouth before *solat*, the ritual prayers made five times a day. Thus, each segment seeks a different mix of benefits. The company must target the benefit segment or segments that it can serve best and most profitably using appeals that match each segment's benefit preferences.[9]

User status

Markets can be segmented into nonusers, ex-users, potential users, first-time users, and regular users of a product. For example, blood banks cannot rely only on regular donors. They must also recruit new first-time donors and remind ex-donors—each will require different marketing appeals.

Included in the potential user group are consumers facing life-stage changes—such as newlyweds and new parents—who can be turned into heavy users. For example, P&G acquires the names of parents to-be and showers them with product samples and ads for its Pampers and other baby products to capture a share of their future purchases. It invites them to visit Pampers.com and join MyPampers.com, giving them access to expert parenting advice, Parent Pages e-mail newsletters, and coupons and special offers.

Usage rate

Markets can also be segmented into light, medium, and heavy product users. Heavy users are often a small percentage of the market but account for a high percentage of total consumption. For example, Burger King targets what it calls "Super Fans," young (aged 18 to 34), Whopper-wolfing males who make up 18 percent of the chain's customers but account for almost half of all customer visits. They eat at Burger King an average of 16 times a month.[10] Burger King targets these Super Fans openly with ads that exalt monster burgers containing meat, cheese, and more meat and cheese that can turn "innies into outies." Its ad shows young Super Fans who are "too hungry to settle for chick food" rebel by burning their briefs, pushing a minivan off a bridge, chowing down on decadent Texas Double Whoppers, and proclaiming "Eat like a man, man!" Although such ads puzzled many a casual fast-food patron, they really pushed the hungry buttons of Burger King's heavy users.

Loyalty status

A market can also be segmented by consumer loyalty. Consumers can be loyal to brands (Kao), stores (Isetan), and companies (Toyota). Buyers can be divided into groups according to their degree of loyalty. Some consumers are completely loyal — they buy one brand all the time. For example, Apple has a small but almost cultlike following of loyal users:[11]

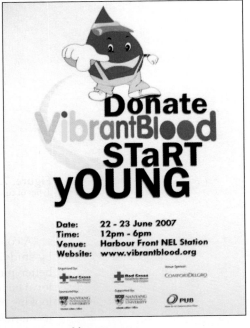

User status –
Blood banks use different marketing appeals to recruit new donors and to remind ex-donors.

Consumer loyalty –
"Macolytes"—fanatically loyal Apple users—helped keep Apple afloat during the lean years, and they are now at the forefront of Apple's burgeoning iPod and iTunes empire.

It's the "Cult of the Mac," and it's populated by "macolytes." Urbandictionary.com defines a macolyte as "One who is fanatically devoted to Apple products, especially the Macintosh computer. Also known as a Mac Zealot." Take Taylor Barcroft, who has spent the past 11 years traveling the country in an RV on a mission to be the Mac cult's ultimate "multimedia historical videographer." He goes to every Macworld Expo, huge trade shows centered on the Mac, as well as all kinds of other tech shows—and videotapes anything and everything Apple. He's accumulated more than 3,000 hours of footage. He's never been paid to do any of this, living off an inheritance. Barcroft owns 17 Macs. Such fanatically loyal users helped keep Apple afloat during the lean years, and are now at the forefront of Apple's burgeoning iPod-iTunes empire.

Other consumers are somewhat loyal—they are loyal to two or three brands of a given product or favor one brand while sometimes buying others. Still other buyers show no loyalty to any brand. They either want something different each time they buy or they buy whatever's on sale. (see **Figure 7.2**)

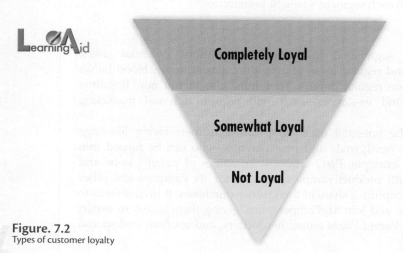

Figure. 7.2
Types of customer loyalty

A company can learn a lot by analyzing loyalty patterns in its market. It should start by studying its own loyal customers. For example, by studying "macolytes," Apple can better pinpoint its target market and develop marketing appeals. By studying its less loyal buyers, the company can detect which brands are most competitive with its own. By looking at customers who are shifting away from its brand, the company can learn about its marketing weaknesses.

Using Multiple Segmentation Bases

Marketers are increasingly using multiple segmentation bases in an effort to identify smaller, better-defined target groups. Thus, a bank may not only identify a group of wealthy retired adults but also, within that group, distinguish several segments based on their current income, assets, savings and risk preferences, housing, and lifestyles.

One example of multivariable segmentation is AC Nielsen's scheme to segment attitudes toward Internet usage and online purchasing among Malaysia's urban adult population. Based on ownership of home PCs, mobile phones, and PDAs, as well as satellite TV subscription, its research uncovered four better-defined segments. The eSavvy are mainly Chinese, young, and tended to come from high-income households. The Mobiles have an almost equal proportion of Chinese and Malays in their 20s and 30s, and from medium-income households. Also from medium-income households are the Home Bodies. They are mostly aged 15 to 20, followed by those in their 40s. The Not Interested are those in their 50s and largely Malay.[12]

Such segmentation provides a powerful tool for marketers. It helps companies identify and better understand key customer segments, target them more efficiently, and tailor market offerings and messages to their specific needs.

Segmenting Business Markets

Consumer and business marketers use many of the same variables to segment their markets. Business buyers can be segmented geographically, demographically (industry, company size), or by benefits sought, user status, usage rate, and loyalty status. Yet, business marketers also use some additional variables, such as *customer operating characteristics, purchasing approaches, situational factors, and personal characteristics*. By going after segments instead of the whole market, companies can deliver just the right value proposition to each segment served and capture more value in return.

Almost every company serves at least some business markets. For example, we've discussed American Express as the "My life. My card." company that offers credit cards to end consumers. But American Express also targets businesses in three segments—merchants, corporations, and small businesses. It has developed distinct marketing programs for each segment.

In the merchants segment, American Express focuses on convincing new merchants to accept the card and on managing relationships with those that already do. For larger corporate customers, the company offers a corporate card program, which includes extensive employee expense and travel management services. It also offers this segment a wide range of asset management, retirement planning, and financial education services.

Finally, for small business customers, American Express has created the OPEN: Small Business Network, "the one place that's all about small business." Small business cardholders can access the network for everything from account and expense management software to expert small business management advice and connecting with other small business owners to share ideas and get recommendations.[13]

Within a given target industry and customer size, the company can segment by purchase approaches and criteria. As in consumer segmentation, many marketers believe that buying behavior and benefits provide the best basis for segmenting business markets.

This helps you buy what your small business needs.

This lets you track, organize, categorize, subdivide, examine, break down, cross-reference, combine and archive online what your small business spends.

Now you can access the Expense Management Report and many other online tools. But only if you have the American Express® Business Card. The Card with the savings, rewards and services of OPEN: The Small Business Network℠ behind it. Apply now and get an instant decision. Visit OPEN.AMERICANEXPRESS.COM.

Segmenting business markets –
For small business customers, American Express has created the OPEN: Small Business Network, "the one place that's all about small business."

Segmenting International Markets

Although some large companies, such as Coca-Cola or Sony, sell products in more than 200 countries, most international firms focus on a smaller set. Operating in many countries presents new challenges. Different countries, even those that are close together, can vary greatly in their economic, cultural, and political makeup. Thus, just as they do within their domestic markets, international firms need to group their world markets into segments with distinct buying needs and behaviors.

Companies can segment international markets using one or a combination of several variables. They can segment by geographic location, grouping countries by regions such as Western Europe, North Asia, East Asia, or the Middle East. Geographic segmentation assumes that nations close to one another will have many common traits and behaviors. Although this is often the case, there are many exceptions. For example, although the U.S. and Canada have much in common, both differ culturally and economically from neighboring Mexico. Even within a region, consumers can differ widely. For example, Chinese consumers in Beijing are different from those in Shanghai or Hong Kong. Japanese consumers behave very differently from their Taiwanese counterparts.

World markets can also be segmented on the basis of economic factors. For example, countries might be grouped by population income levels or by their overall level of economic development. A country's economic structure shapes its population's product and service needs and, therefore, the marketing opportunities it offers. Countries can be segmented by *political and legal factors* such as the type and stability of government, receptivity to foreign firms, monetary regulations, and the amount of bureaucracy. Such factors can play a crucial role in a company's choice of which countries to enter and how. Cultural factors can also be used, grouping markets according to common languages, religions, values and attitudes, customs, and behavioral patterns.

Segmenting international markets based on geographic, economic, political, cultural, and other factors assumes that segments should consist of clusters of countries. However,

Intermarket segmentation –
Teens show surprising similarity no matter where they live—these teens could be from almost anywhere. Thus, many companies target teens with worldwide marketing campaigns.

Intermarket segmentation
Forming segments of consumers who have similar needs and buying behavior even though they are located in different countries.

many companies use a different approach called **intermarket segmentation**. They form segments of consumers who have similar needs and buying behavior even though they are located in different countries. For example, Mercedes-Benz targets the world's well-to-do, regardless of their country. And Swedish furniture giant IKEA targets the aspiring global middle class—it sells good-quality furniture that ordinary people worldwide can afford.

MTV targets the world's teenagers. The world's 1.2 billion teens have a lot in common: They study, shop, and sleep. They are exposed to many of the same major issues: love, crime, homelessness, ecology, and working parents. In many ways, they have more in common with each other than with their parents. "Last year I was in 17 different countries," says one expert, "and it's pretty difficult to find anything that is different, other than language, among a teenager in Japan, a teenager in the UK, and a teenager in China." Says another, "Global teens in Buenos Aires, Beijing, and Bangalore swing to the beat of MTV while sipping Coke." MTV bridges the gap between cultures, appealing to what teens around the world have in common. Sony, Adidas, Nike, and many other firms also actively target global teens. For example, Adidas's "Impossible Is Nothing" theme appeals to teens the world over.[14]

Requirements for Effective Segmentation

Clearly, there are many ways to segment a market, but not all segmentations are effective. To be useful, market segments must be:

- *Measurable*: The size, purchasing power, and profiles of the segments can be measured. Certain segmentation variables are difficult to measure. For example, there are millions of left handed people in the world. Yet, few products are targeted toward this left handed segment. The major problem may be that the segment is hard to identify an measure. There are no data on the demographics of lefties.

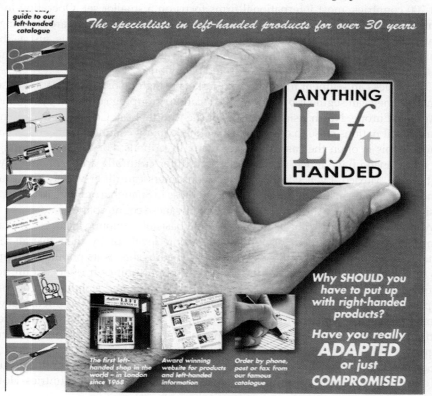

The "Leftie" segment can be hard to identify and measure. As a result, few companies tailor their offers to left-handers. However, some nichers such as Anything Left-Handed in the United Kingdom targets this segment.

- *Accessible*: The market segments can be effectively reached and served. Suppose a fragrance company finds that heavy users of its brand are single men and women who stay out late and socialize a lot. Unless this group lives or shops at certain places and is exposed to certain media, its members will be difficult to reach.
- *Substantial*: The market segments are large or profitable enough to serve. A segment should be the largest possible homogenous group worth pursuing with a tailored marketing program It would not pay, for example, for an automobile manufacturer to develop cars especially for people whose height is greater than seven feet.
- *Differentiable*: The segments are conceptually distinguishable and respond differently to different marketing mix elements and programs. If married and unmarried women respond similarly to a sale on perfume, they do not constitute separate segments.
- *Actionable*: Effective programs can be designed for attracting and serving the segments. For example, although one small airline identified seven market segments, its staff was too small to develop separate marketing programs for each segment.

Market Targeting

Market segmentation reveals the firm's market segment opportunities. The firm now must evaluate the various segments and decide how many and which segments it can serve best. We now look at how companies evaluate and select target segments.

Evaluating Market Segments

In evaluating different market segments, a firm must look at three factors:

- *Segment size and growth*: The company must collect and analyze data on current segment sales, growth rates, and expected profitability for various segments.
- *Segment structural attractiveness*: The company needs to examine major structural factors that affect long-run segment attractiveness.[15] For example, a segment is less attractive if it already contains many strong and aggressive competitors. The existence of many actual or potential substitute products may limit prices and the profits that can be earned in a segment. The relative power of buyers also affects segment attractiveness. Buyers with strong bargaining power relative to sellers will try to force prices down, demand more services, and set competitors against one another—all at the expense of seller profitability. Finally, a segment may be less attractive if it contains powerful suppliers who can control prices or reduce the quality or quantity of ordered goods and services.
- *Company objectives and resources*: Even if a segment has the right size and growth and is structurally attractive, the company must consider its own objectives and resources. Some attractive segments can be dismissed quickly because they do not mesh with the company's long-run objectives. Or the company may lack the skills and resources needed to succeed in an attractive segment. The company should enter only segments in which it can offer superior value and gain advantages over competitors.

Target market
A set of buyers sharing common needs or characteristics that the company decides to serve.

Selecting Target Market Segments

After evaluating different segments, the company must now decide which and how many segments it will target. A **target market** consists of a set of buyers who share common needs or characteristics that the company decides to serve.

Because buyers have unique needs and wants, a seller could potentially view each buyer as a separate target market. Ideally, a seller might design a separate marketing program for each buyer. However, most companies face larger numbers of smaller buyers and do not find individual targeting worthwhile. Instead, they look for broader segments of buyers. More generally, market targeting can be carried out at several different levels.

Figure 7.3 shows that companies can target very broadly (undifferentiated marketing), very narrowly (micromarketing), or somewhere in between (differentiated or concentrated marketing).

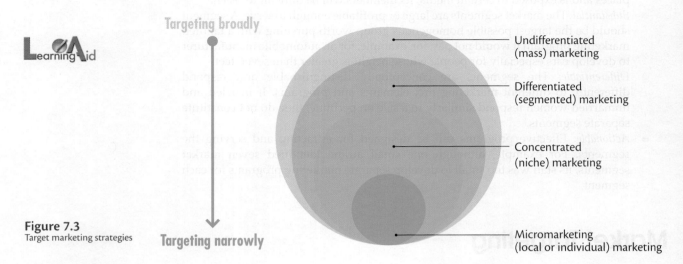

Learning **A**id

Targeting broadly

- Undifferentiated (mass) marketing
- Differentiated (segmented) marketing
- Concentrated (niche) marketing
- Micromarketing (local or individual) marketing

Targeting narrowly

Figure 7.3
Target marketing strategies

Undifferentiated (mass) marketing
A market-coverage strategy in which a firm decides to ignore market segment differences and go after the whole market with one offer.

Differentiated (segmented) marketing
A market-coverage strategy in which a firm decides to target several market segments and designs separate offers for each.

Undifferentiated Marketing

Using an **undifferentiated marketing** (or **mass-marketing**) strategy, a firm might decide to ignore market segment differences and target the whole market with one offer. This mass-marketing strategy focuses on what is common in the needs of consumers rather than on what is different. The company designs a product and a marketing program that will appeal to the largest number of buyers.

Most modern marketers have strong doubts about this strategy. Difficulties arise in developing a product or brand that will satisfy all consumers. Moreover, mass marketers often have trouble competing with more-focused firms that do a better job of satisfying the needs of specific segments and niches.

Differentiated Marketing

Using a **differentiated marketing** (or **segmented marketing**) strategy, a firm decides to target several market segments and designs separate offers for each. Toyota markets the full range of automobiles for different segments. For example, Yaris and Vios are subcompact brands for new car buyers, the midsize Corolla targets families, the upper midsize sedan Camry appeals to executives, while the Lexus luxury make represents its top end offering.

By offering product and marketing variations to segments, companies hope for higher sales and a stronger position within each market segment. Developing a stronger position within several segments creates more total sales than undifferentiated marketing across all segments. Estée Lauder's combined brands give it a much greater market share than any single brand could. The Estée Lauder and Clinique brands alone reap a combined 40 percent share of the prestige cosmetics market. Similarly, Procter & Gamble markets six different brands of laundry detergent which compete with each other on supermarket shelves. Together, these brands capture four times the market share of nearest rival Unilever in the U.S. (see **Real Marketing 7.1**).

But differentiated marketing also increases the costs of doing business. Developing separate marketing plans for the separate segments requires extra marketing research, forecasting, sales analysis, promotion planning, and channel management. Trying to reach different market segments with different advertising increases promotion costs. Thus, the company must weigh increased sales against increased costs when deciding on a differentiated marketing strategy.

Concentrated Marketing

A third market-coverage strategy, **concentrated marketing** (or **niche marketing**), is especially appealing when company resources are limited. Instead of going after a small share of a large market, the firm goes after a large share of one or a few smaller segments or niches. For example, Tetra sells 80 percent of the world's tropical fish food.

Innovation – From a nicher in the PC market, Apple invests in innovation that consumers want, resulting in the iPod and iTunes and capturing 70 percent of the music download market.

Through concentrated marketing, the firm achieves a strong market position because of its greater knowledge of consumer needs in the niches it serves and the special reputation it acquires. It can market more *effectively* by fine-tuning its products, prices, and programs to the needs of carefully defined segments. It can also market more *efficiently*, targeting its products or services, channels, and communications programs toward only consumers that it can serve best and most profitably.

Whereas segments are fairly large and attract several competitors, niches are smaller and may attract only one or a few competitors. Niching offers smaller companies anopportunity to compete by focusing their limited resources on serving niches that may be unimportant to or overlooked by larger competitors. Consider Apple Computer. Although it once enjoyed a better than 13 percent market share, Apple is now a PC market nicher, capturing less than 2 percent of the personal computer market worldwide. Rather than competing head-on with other PC makers as they slash prices and focus on volume, Apple invests in research and development, making it the industry trendsetter. For example, when the company introduced the iPod and iTunes, it captured more than 70 percent of the music download market. Such innovation has created a loyal base of consumers who are willing to pay more for Apple's cutting edge products.[16]

Many companies start as nichers to get a foothold against larger, more resourceful competitors, and then grow into broader competitors. For example, Air Asia began by serving intrastate, no-frills commuters in Malaysia but is now threatening former monopoly operator Malaysia Airlines and going international to such regional destinations as Thailand, Indonesia, Macau, Xiamen in China, Vietnam, Cambodia, Brunei, and Myanmar.

In contrast, as markets change, some megamarketers develop niche markets to create sales growth. For example, in recent years, Pepsi has introduced several niche products, such as Sierra Mist, Pepsi Twist, Mountain Dew Code Red, and Mountain Dew LiveWire. Initially, these brands combined accounted for barely 5 percent of Pepsi's overall soft-drink sales. However, Sierra Mist quickly blossomed and now is the number two lemon-lime soft drink behind Sprite, and Code Red and LiveWire have revitalized the Mountain Dew brand.

Today, the low cost of setting up shop on the Internet makes it even more profitable to serve

Niches – Air Asia started by serving Malaysia's intrastate market. As it grew, it is going international to such regional destination as Thailand, Vietnam and China.

- Kuala Lumpur *(LCC Terminal)*
- Johor Bahru *(Sultan Ismail Int. Airport)*
- Kuching *(Kuching Int. Airport)*
- Kota Kinabalu *(LCC Terminal)*
- Jakarta *(Soekarno Hatta Int. Airport)*
- Bangkok *(Suvarnabumi Airport)*

seemingly minuscule niches. Small businesses, in particular, are realizing riches from serving small niches on the Web. Here is a "Webpreneur" who achieved astonishing results:

> Sixty-three-year-old British artist Jacquie Lawson taught herself to use a computer only a few years ago. Last year, her business sold over $4 million worth of online cards. Lawson occupies a coveted niche in the electronic world: a profitable, subscription-based Web site (_www.jacquielawson.com_) where she sells her highly stylized e-cards without advertising. While Hallmark and American Greetings offer hundreds of e-cards for every occasion, Lawson only offers about 50, the majority of which she intricately designed herself. Revenue comes solely from members—81 percent from the U.S.—who pay $8 a year. Last year, membership

REAL MARKETING 7.1

Procter & Gamble: Competing with Itself—and Winning

Procter & Gamble is one of the world's premier consumer-goods companies. Some 99 percent of all U.S. households use at least one of P&G's over 300 brands, and the typical household regularly buys and uses from one to two dozen P&G brands.

P&G sells multiple brands of laundry detergent, bath soap, shampoo, dishwashing detergent, tissues and paper towels, deodorant, fabric softener, cosmetics, and disposable diapers worldwide. Moreover, P&G has many additional brands in each category for different international markets. For example, brands unique to Asia include Attento, Bonus, Cutie, Muse, Perla, Rejoice, and Whisper. A Touch of Sun, Hairpainting, Inner Science, and Ultress are offered in North America and Asia, while Loreto is marketed in Asia and Latin America. (see P&G's Web site at _www.pg.com_ for a full glimpse of the company's impressive lineup of brands.)

These P&G brands compete with one another on the same supermarket shelves. Why would P&G introduce several brands in one category instead of concentrating its resources on a single leading brand? The answer lies in the fact that different people want different mixes of benefits from the products

Differentiated marketing – Procter & Gamble markets six different laundry detergents, including Tide—each with multiple forms and formulations—that compete with each other on store shelves. Yet together, these multiple brands capture four times the market share of nearest rival Unilever.

they buy. Take laundry detergents as an example. People use laundry detergents to get their clothes clean. But they also want other things from their detergents—such as economy, strength or mildness, bleaching power, fabric softening, fresh smell, and lots of suds or only a few. We all want some of every one of these benefits from our detergent, but we may have different priorities for each benefit. To some people, cleaning and bleaching power are most important;

climbed from 300,000 to 500,000 and the membership renewal rate is close to 70 percent. Last December, Lawson's Web site attracted 22.7 million visitors, more than double that of closest rival AmericanGreetings.com. Lawson's success with a business model that has stumped many media giants speaks to both the Internet's egalitarian nature and her own stubborn belief that doing it her way is the right way.[17]

Concentrated marketing can be highly profitable. At the same time, it involves higher-than-normal risks. Companies that rely on one or a few segments for all of their business will suffer greatly if the segment turns sour. Or larger competitors may decide to enter the same segment with greater resources. For these reasons, many companies prefer to diversify in several market segments.

to others, fabric softening matters most; still others want a mild, fresh scented detergent. Thus, each segment of laundry detergent buyers seeks a special combination of benefits.

In Asia, Procter & Gamble has identified at least four important laundry detergent segments, along with numerous subsegments, and has developed a different brand designed to meet the special needs of each. The four brands are positioned for different segments as follows:

- *Tide* provides "fabric cleaning and care at its best." It's the all-purpose family detergent that "gets to the bottom of dirt and stains to help keep your whites white and your colors bright."

- *Cheer* is the "color expert." It helps protect against fading, color transfer, and fabric wear, with or without bleach.

- *Gain*, originally P&G's "enzyme" detergent, was repositioned as the detergent that gives you "great cleaning power and the smell that says clean." It "cleans and freshens like sunshine."

- *Dreft* is specially formulated "to help clean tough baby and toddler stains." It "rinses out thoroughly, leaving clothes soft next to a baby's delicate skin."

Within each segment, P&G has identified even narrower niches. For example, you can buy regular Tide (in powder or liquid form) or any or several formulations:

- *Tide Powder* helps keep everyday laundry clean and new. It comes in regular and such special scents as Tide Tropical Clean (a fresh tropical scent) and Tide Free ("has no scent at all leaves out the dyes or perfumes").

- *Tide Liquid* combines the great stain fighting qualities in Tide powder with the pretreating ease of a liquid detergent in various scents.

- *Tide* with Bleach helps to "clean even the dirtiest laundry without the damaging effects of chlorine bleach." Keeps "your family's whites white and colors bright."

- *Tide Liquid* with Bleach Alternative is the "smart alternative to chlorine bleach." It uses active enzymes in pretreating and washing to break down and remove the toughest stains while whitenin whites.

- *Tide with a Touch of Downy* provides "outstanding Tide clea with a touch of Downy softness and freshness."

- *Tide Coldwater* is specially formulated to help reduce your energy bills by delivering outstanding cleaning, even on the toughest stains, in cold water. Available in both liquid and powder formulas and in two scents.

- *Tide HE* is specially formulated to unlock the cleaning potential of high-efficiency washers and provides excellent cleaning with the right level of sudsing.

By segmenting the market and having several detergent brands, P&G has an attractive offering for consumers in all important preference groups. As a result, P&G is a major player in the global laundry detergen market.

More generally, P&G is a dominant force among consumer goods businesses. Despite its late entry into several Asian markets, the company now holds leadership positions in various product categories. For example, P&G entered Taiwan in 1985 when it launched Pampers as the market's first disposable diaper, and Head and Shoulders shampoo. Oil of Olay is now Taiwan's leading skin care series, while Pringles heads the potato chip category. P&G Taiwan was also the first to introduce worldwide such shampoo brands as B-5 Pantene Pro-V and Inner Science. The company was voted Commonwealth's most admired company in Taiwan for five consecutive years.

Sources:

See LeeAnn Prescott, "Case Study: Tide Boosts Traffic 9-Fold," *iMedia Connection*, November 30, 2005, accessed at www.imediaconnection.com; Doris de Guzman, "Household Products Struggle," *Chemical Market Reporter*, March 20–26, 2006, pp. 46–47; www.pgtaiwan.com.tw, December 2007; and information accessed at www.pg.com and www.tide.com, December 2006 and December 2007.

Micromarketing
The practice of tailoring products and marketing programs to the needs and wants of specific individuals and local customer groups—includes local marketing and individual marketing.

Local marketing
Tailoring brands and promotions to the needs and wants of local customer groups—cities, neighborhoods, and even specific stores.

Micromarketing

Differentiated and concentrated marketers tailor their offers and marketing programs to meet the needs of various market segments and niches. At the same time, however, they do not customize their offers to each individual customer. **Micromarketing** is the practice of tailoring products and marketing programs to suit the tastes of specific individuals and locations. Rather than seeing a customer in every individual, micromarketers see the individual in every customer. Micromarketing includes local marketing and individual marketing.

Local marketing

Local marketing involves tailoring brands and promotions to the needs and wants of local customer groups—cities, neighborhoods, and even specific stores. Kinokuniya, the Japanese bookstore chain, practices local marketing. In Singapore, its Bugis Junction branch taps into the high-volume youth clientele by carrying comics and books on travel and careers. In contrast, its Ngee Ann City flagship outlet offers upmarket lifestyle activities like tea-making demonstrations, reflecting Kinokuniya's focus on cultural books across different languages. Similarly, the 7-Eleven convenience chain is popular in Japan because it customizes its merchandise to match the locale.

Local marketing –
In Japan, the 7-Eleven chain customizes its merchandise to suit the locale's needs and wants.

Local marketing has some drawbacks. It can drive up manufacturing and marketing costs by reducing economies of scale. It can also create logistics problems as companies try to meet the varied requirements of different regional and local markets Further, a brand's overall image might be diluted if the product and message vary too much in different localities.

Still, as companies face increasingly fragmented markets, and as new supporting technologies develop, the advantages of local marketing often outweigh the drawbacks. Local marketing helps a company to market more effectively in the face of pronounced regional and local differences in demographics and lifestyles. It also meets the needs of the company's first-line customers—retailers—who prefer more fine-tuned product assortments for their neighborhoods.

Individual marketing
Tailoring products and marketing programs to the needs and preferences of individual customers—also labeled "markets-of-one marketing," "customized marketing," and "one-to-one marketing."

Individual marketing

In the extreme, micromarketing becomes **individual marketing**—tailoring products and marketing programs to the needs and preferences of individual customers. Individual marketing has also been labeled *one-to-one marketing*, *mass customization*, and *markets-of-one marketing*. (see **Figure 7.4**)

Figure 7.4
Mass production versus individual and self-marketing

THEN		NOW	
Mass Production ○ One size fits all ○ No human interaction	→	**Individual marketing** ○ Tailor-made to individual needs	**Self marketing** ○ Customer takes responsibility for what to buy

The widespread use of mass marketing has obscured the fact that for centuries consumers were served as individuals: The tailor custom-made the suit, the cobbler designed shoes for the individual, the cabinetmaker made furniture to order. Today, however, new technologies are permitting many companies to return to customized marketing. More powerful computers, detailed databases, robotic production and flexible manufacturing, and interactive communication media such as e-mail and the Internet—

all have combined to foster "mass customization." Mass customization is the process through which firms interact one-to-one with masses of customers to design products and services tailor-made to individual needs.[18]

Dell creates custom-configured computers. Visitors to Nike's NikeID Web site can personalize their sneakers by choosing from hundreds of colors and putting an embroidered word or phrase on the tongue. Companies selling all kinds of products—from computers, candy, clothing, and golf clubs to fire trucks—are customizing their offerings to the needs of individual buyers. Consider this example:

The LEGO Company recently launched LEGO Factory, a Web site (*LEGOFactory.com*) where LEGO fans can "design their own ultimate LEGO model, show it off, and bring it to life." Using free, downloadable Digital Designer software, customers can create any structure they can imagine. Then, if they decide to actually build their creation, the software, which keeps track of which pieces are required, sends the order to the LEGO warehouse. There, employees put all the pieces into a box, along with instructions, and ship it off. Customers can even design their own boxes. The software also lets proud users share their creations with others in the LEGO community, one of the traditional building blocks of the company's customer loyalty. The LEGO Factory Gallery features winning designs and lets users browse and order the inspired designs of others.[19]

Individual marketing – At the LEGO Factory Web site, fans can design their own ultimate LEGO model, show it off, and bring it to life. (*www.legofactory.com*)

Consumer goods marketers aren't the only ones going one-to-one. Business-to-business marketers are also finding new ways to customize their offerings. For example, John Deere manufactures seeding equipment that can be configured in more than two million versions to individual customer specifications. The seeders are produced one at a time, in any sequence, on a single production line.

The move toward individual marketing mirrors the trend in consumer *self-marketing*. Increasingly, individual customers are taking more responsibility for determining which products and brands to buy. Consider two business buyers with two different purchasing styles. The first sees several salespeople, each trying to persuade him to buy his or her product. The second sees no salespeople but rather logs onto the Internet. She searches for information on available products; interacts electronically with various suppliers, users, and product analysts; and then makes up her own mind about the best offer. The second purchasing agent has taken more responsibility for the buying process, and the marketer has had less influence over her buying decision.

As the trend toward more interactive dialogue and less advertising monologue continues, self-marketing will grow in importance. As more buyers look up consumer reports, join Internet product-discussion forums, and place orders via phone or online, marketers will need to influence the buying process in new ways. They will need to involve customers more in all phases of the product development and buying processes, increasing opportunities for buyers to practice self-marketing.

Choosing a Targeting Strategy

Companies need to consider many factors when choosing a market targeting strategy: (see **Figure 7.5**)

- *Company resources*: When the firm's resources are limited, concentrated marketing makes the most sense.
- *Product variability*: Undifferentiated marketing is more suited for uniform products such as grapefruit or steel. Products that can vary in design, such as cameras and automobiles, are more suited to differentiation or concentration.
- *Product's life-cycle stage*: When a firm introduces a new product, it may be practical

L⊘Aearning-Aid

		Concentrated marketing	Undifferentiated marketing	Differentiated marketing
Company resources	Finite	✔	✔	
	Vast			✔
Product variability	Limited		✔	
	High	✔		✔
Product life cycle stage	Introduction	✔	✔	
	Maturity			✔
Market variability	Low		✔	
	High			✔
Competitors' marketing strategies	Undifferentiated	✔		✔
	Differentiated		✖	✔

Figure 7.5
Factors influencing targeting strategy

to launch only one version, and undifferentiated marketing or concentrated marketing may make the most sense. In the mature stage of the product life cycle, however, differentiated marketing begins to make more sense.

● *Market variability*: If most buyers have the same tastes, buy the same amounts, and react the same way to marketing efforts, undifferentiated marketing is appropriate.

● *Competitors' marketing strategies*: When competitors use differentiated or concentrated marketing, adopting undifferentiated marketing can be suicidal. Conversely, when competitors use undifferentiated marketing, a firm can gain an advantage by using differentiated or concentrated marketing.

Socially Responsible Target Marketing

Smart targeting helps companies to be more efficient and effective by focusing on the segments that they can satisfy best and most profitably. Targeting also benefits consumers—companies reach specific groups of consumers with offers carefully tailored to satisfy their needs. However, target marketing sometimes generates controversy and concern. The biggest issues usually involve the targeting of vulnerable or disadvantaged consumers such as children with controversial or potentially harmful products. Some critics have even called for a complete ban on advertising to children.

Cigarette, beer, and fast-food marketers have also generated much controversy in recent years by their attempts to target the more vulnerable consumers. For example, McDonald's and other chains have drawn criticism for pitching their high-fat, salt-laden fare to low-income, urban residents who are much more likely to be heavy consumers than suburbanites are.

The meteoric growth of the Internet and other carefully targeted direct media has raised fresh concerns about potential targeting abuses. The Internet allows increasing refinement of audiences and, in turn, more precise targeting. This might help makers of questionable products or deceptive advertisers to more readily victimize the most vulnerable audiences. Unscrupulous marketers can now send tailor-made deceptive messages directly to the computers of millions of unsuspecting consumers.

Not all attempts to target children or other special segments draw such criticism. In fact, most provide benefits to targeted consumers. For example, Colgate makes a large selection of toothbrushes and toothpaste flavors and packages for children—from Colgate Barbie, Blues Clues, and SpongeBob SquarePants Sparkling Bubble Fruit toothpastes to Colgate LEGO BIONICLE and Bratz character toothbrushes. Such products help make tooth brushing more fun and get children to brush longer and more often.

Thus, in target marketing, the issue is not really who is targeted but rather how and for what. Controversies arise when marketers attempt to profit at the expense of targeted segments—when they unfairly target vulnerable segments or target them with questionable products or tactics. Socially responsible marketing calls for segmentation and targeting that serve not just the interests of the company but also the interests of those targeted.

Differentiation and Positioning

The company must also decide on a value proposition—on how it will create differentiated value for targeted segments and what positions it wants to occupy in those segments. A **product's position** is the way the product is *defined by consumers* on important attributes—the place the product occupies in consumers' minds relative to competing products. "Products are created in the factory, but brands are created in the mind," says a positioning expert.[20]

For example, in the automobile market, the Honda Fit is positioned on economy, Mercedes on luxury, and BMW on performance. Volvo positions powerfully on safety. And Toyota positions its fuel-efficient, hybrid Prius as a high-tech solution to the energy shortage. "How far will you go to save the planet?" it asks.

In the sports goods market, Nike and Adidas are positioned to appeal to the urban affluent. Both brands have substantial presence in China's prosperous cities and shopping districts. Mid-priced Li Ning, named after its founder who was a top national gymnast, offers the benefit of "brand nationalism"—for Chinese consumers who prefer to buy Chinese products when possible—as a unique positioning.

When seeking how to position a brand, marketers should bear in mind that consumers are overloaded with information about products and services. They cannot reevaluate products every time they make a buying decision. To simplify the buying process, consumers organize products, services, and companies into categories and "position" them in their minds. A product's position is the complex set of perceptions, impressions, and feelings that consumers have for the product compared with competing products.

Consumers position products with or without the help of marketers. But marketers do not want to leave their products' positions to chance. They must plan positions that will give their products the greatest advantage in selected target markets, and they must design marketing mixes to create these planned positions.

Positioning Maps

In planning their differentiation and positioning strategies, marketers often prepare *perceptual positioning maps*, which show consumer perceptions of their brands versus competing products on important buying dimensions. **Figure 7.6** shows a positioning map for the U.S. large luxury sport utility vehicle market.[21] The position of each circle on the map indicates the brand's perceived positioning on two dimensions—price and orientation (luxury versus performance). The size of each circle indicates the brand's relative market share. Thus, customers view the market-leading Cadillac Escalade as a moderately-priced large luxury SUV with a balance of luxury and performance.

The original Hummer H1 is positioned as a very high-performance SUV with a price tag to match. Hummer targets the current H1 Alpha toward a small segment of well-off rugged individualists. According to the H1 Web site, "The H1 was built around one central philosophy: function—the most functional off-road vehicle ever made available to the civilian market. The H1 Alpha not only sets you apart, but truly sets you free."

By contrast, although also oriented toward performance, the Hummer H2 is positioned as a more luxury-oriented and more reasonably priced luxury

Product position
The way the product is defined by consumers on important attributes—the place the product occupies in consumers' minds relative to competing products.

Positioning –
Mid-priced Li Ning's nationalistic positioning appeals to Chinese consumers who prefer to buy local brands.

中国国家跳水队：郭晶晶

SUV. The H2 is targeted toward a larger segment of urban and suburban professionals. "In a world where SUVs have begun to look like their owners, complete with love handles and mushy seats, the H2 proves that there is still one out there that can drop and give you 20," says the H2 Web site. The H2 "strikes a perfect balance between interior comfort, on-the-road capability, and off-road capability."

Choosing a Differentiation and Positioning Strategy

Some firms find it easy to choose a differentiation and their positioning strategy. For example, a firm well known for quality in certain segments will go for this position in a new segment if there are enough buyers seeking quality. But in many cases, two or more firms will go after the same position. Then, each will have to find other ways to set itself apart. Each firm must differentiate its offer by building a unique bundle of benefits that appeals to a substantial group within the segment.

The differentiation and positioning task consists of three steps:

- Identifying a set of possible customer value differences that provide competitive advantages upon which to build a position;
- Choosing the right competitive advantages, and selecting an overall positioning strategy; and
- Effectively communicating and delivering the chosen position to the market.

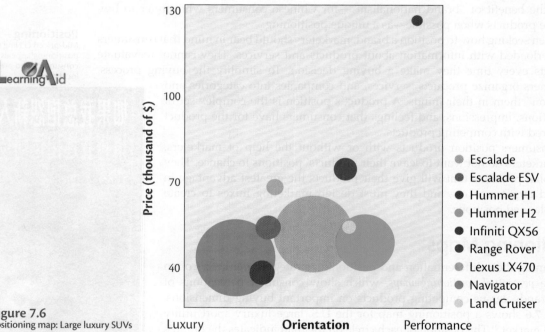

Figure 7.6
Positioning map: Large luxury SUVs

Identifying Possible Value Differences and Competitive Advantages

To build profitable relationships with target customers, marketers must understand customer needs better than competitors do and deliver more customer value. To the extent that a company can differentiate and position itself as providing superior value, it gains **competitive advantage**.

But solid positions cannot be built on empty promises. If a company positions its product as *offering* the best quality and service, it must actually differentiate the product so that it *delivers* the promised quality and service. Companies must do much more than simply shout out their positions in ad slogans and taglines. They must first live the

Competitive advantage
An advantage over competitors gained by offering consumers greater value, either through lower prices or by providing more benefits that justify higher prices.

slogan. For example, "The Friendly Skies" has been United Airlines' long-time tagline. Its customers thus expect friendly service from United staff, who must deliver this promise consistently in every encounter everywhere United flies.

To find points of differentiation, marketers must think through the customer's entire experience with the company's product or service. An alert company can find ways to differentiate itself at every customer contact point. In what specific ways can a company differentiate itself or its market offer? It can differentiate along the lines of product, services, channels, people, or image.

Product differentiation –
Seng Choon eggs are differentiated from others when it claims its eggs have less cholesterol.

- *Product differentiation* takes place along a continuum. At one extreme there are physical products that allow little variation: chicken, steel, aspirin. Yet even here some meaningful differentiation is possible. For example, Seng Choon eggs claims that its branded eggs have less cholesterol than other brands. At the other extreme are products that can be highly differentiated, such as automobiles, clothing, and furniture. Such products can be differentiated on features, performance, or style and design.

  Thus, Volvo provides new and better safety features; Whirlpool designs its dishwasher to run more quietly; Bose positions its speakers on their striking design and sound characteristics. Similarly, companies can differentiate their products on such attributes as consistency, durability, reliability, or repairability.

- *Services differentiation* occurs when the firm offers speedy, convenient, or careful delivery. Installation service can differentiate one company from another, as can repair services. Some companies gain service differentiation by providing customer training service or consulting services data, information systems, and advising services that buyers need. McKesson Corporation, a major drug wholesaler, consults with its 12,000 independent pharmacists to help them set up accounting, inventory, and computerized ordering systems. By helping its customers compete better, McKesson gains greater customer loyalty and sales.

- *Channel differentiation* allows firms to gain competitive advantage through the way they design their channel's coverage, expertise, and performance Amazon. com and Dell set themselves apart with their smooth-functioning direct channels. Caterpillar's success in the construction-equipment industry is based on superior channels. Its dealers worldwide are renowned for their first-rate service.

- *People differentiation* occurs when a firm can hire and train better people than their competitors do. Disney people are known to be friendly and upbeat. And Singapore Airlines enjoys an excellent reputation, largely because of the grace of its flight attendants. People differentiation requires that a company select its customer contact people carefully and train them well. For example, Disney trains its theme park people thoroughly to ensure that they are competent, courteous, and friendly from the hotel check-in agents, to the monorail drivers, to the ride attendants, to the people who sweep Main Street USA. Each employee is carefully trained to understand customers and to "make people happy."

People differentiation –
Singapore Airlines enjoys an excellent reputation, largely because of the grace of its flight attendants.

- *Image differentiation* occurs when buyers may perceive a difference even when competing offers look the same. A company or brand image should convey the product's distinctive benefits and positioning. Developing a strong and distinctive image calls for creativity and hard work. A company cannot develop an image in the public's mind overnight using only a few advertisements. If Ritz-Carlton means quality, this image must be supported by everything the company says and does.

Symbols—such as the McDonald's golden arches, the Nike swoosh, or Google's colorful logo—can provide strong company or brand recognition and image differentiation. The company might build a brand around a famous person, as Nike did with its Air Jordan basketball shoes and Tiger Woods golfing products. Some companies even become associated with colors, such as IBM (blue), UPS (brown), or Coca-Cola (red). The chosen symbols, characters, and other image elements must be communicated through advertising that conveys the company's or brand's personality.

Choosing the Right Competitive Advantages

Suppose a company is fortunate enough to discover several potential differentiations that provide competitive advantages. It now must choose the ones on which it will build its positioning strategy. It must decide how many differences to promote and *which ones*.

How many differences to promote

Many marketers think that companies should aggressively promote only one benefit to the target market. Ad man Rosser Reeves, for example, said a company should develop a *unique selling proposition* (USP) for each brand and stick to it. Each brand should pick an attribute and tout itself as "number one" on that attribute. Buyers tend to remember number one better, especially in this overcommunicated society. Thus, Crest toothpaste consistently promotes its anticavity protection and Wal-Mart promotes its always low prices.

Other marketers think that companies should position themselves on more than one differentiator. This may be necessary if two or more firms are claiming to be best on the same attribute. When the mass market is fragmenting into many small segments, companies are trying to broaden their positioning strategies to appeal to more segments. For example, Unilever introduced the first three-in-one bar soap—Lever 2000—offering cleansing, deodorizing, and moisturizing benefits. Clearly, many buyers want all three benefits. As companies increase the number of claims for their brands, they risk disbelief and a loss of clear positioning.

Which differences to promote

Not all brand differences are meaningful or worthwhile; not every difference makes a good differentiator. Each difference has the potential to create company costs as well as customer benefits. A difference is worth establishing to the extent that it satisfies the following criteria:

- *Important*: The difference delivers a highly valued benefit to target buyers.
- *Distinctive*: Competitors do not offer the difference, or the company can offer it in a more distinctive way.
- *Superior*: The difference is superior to other ways that customers might obtain the same benefit.
- *Communicable*: The difference is communicable and visible to buyers.
- *Preemptive*: Competitors cannot easily copy the difference.
- *Affordable*: Buyers can afford to pay for the difference.
- *Profitable*: The company can introduce the difference profitably.

Many companies have introduced differentiations that failed one or more of these tests. When the Westin Stamford Hotel in Singapore once advertised that it is the world's tallest hotel, it was a distinction that was not important to most tourists—in fact, it turned many off. Thus, choosing competitive advantages upon which to position a product or service can be difficult, yet such choices may be crucial to success.

Selecting an Overall Positioning Strategy

Value proposition
The full positioning of a brand—the full mix of benefits upon which it is positioned.

The full positioning of a brand is called the brand's **value proposition**—the full mix of benefits upon which the brand is differentiated and positioned. It is the answer to the customer's question "Why should I buy your brand?" Volvo's value proposition hinges on safety but also includes reliability, roominess, and styling, all for a price that is higher than average but seems fair for this mix of benefits.

Figure 7.7 shows possible value propositions upon which a company might position its products. In the figure, the five green cells represent winning value propositions— differentiation and positioning that gives the company competitive advantage. The blue cells, however, represent losing value propositions. The center yellow cell represents at best a marginal proposition. In the following sections, we discuss the five winning value propositions upon which companies can position their products: more for more, more for the same, the same for less, less for much less, and more for less.

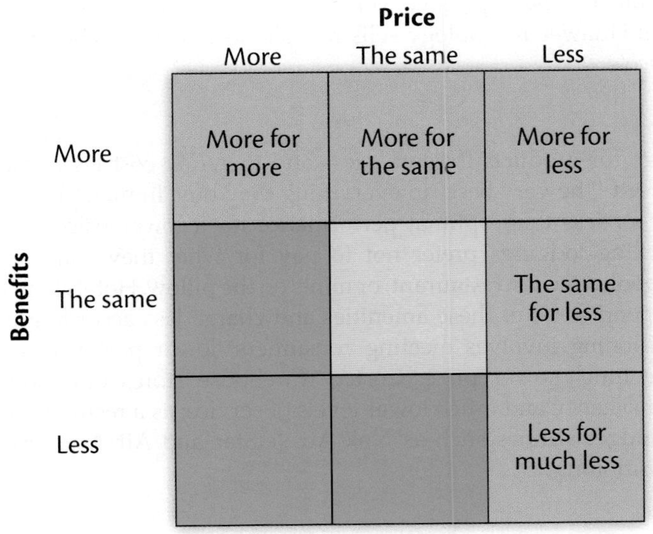

Price

	More	The same	Less
More	More for more	More for the same	More for less
The same			The same for less
Less			Less for much less

LearningAid

Figure 7.7
Possible value propositions

More for more

"More-for-more" positioning involves providing the most upscale product or service and charging a higher price to cover the higher costs. Ritz-Carlton Hotels, Mont Blanc writing instruments, Mercedes automobiles—each claims superior quality, craftsmanship, durability, performance, or style and charges a price to match. Not only is the market offering high in quality, it also gives prestige to the buyer. It symbolizes status and a loftier lifestyle. Often, the price difference exceeds the actual increment in quality.

Sellers offering "only the best" can be found in every product and service category, from hotels, restaurants, food, and fashion to cars and household appliances. Consumers are sometimes surprised, even delighted, when a new competitor enters a category with an unusually high-priced brand. Starbucks coffee entered as a very expensive brand in a largely commodity category.

In general, companies should be on the lookout for opportunities to introduce a "more-for-more" brand in any underdeveloped product or service category. Yet "more-for-more" brands can be vulnerable. They often invite imitators who claim the same quality but at a lower price. Luxury goods that sell well during good times may be at risk during economic downturns when buyers become more cautious in their spending.

More for the same

Companies can attack a competitor's more-for-more positioning by introducing a brand offering comparable quality but at a lower price. For example, Toyota introduced its Lexus line with a "more-for-the-same" value proposition versus Mercedes and BMW. Its first ad headline read: "Perhaps the first time in history that trading a $72,000 car for a $36,000 car could be considered trading up." It communicated the high quality of its new Lexus through rave reviews in car magazines and through a widely distributed videotape showing side-by-side comparisons of Lexus and Mercedes automobiles. It published surveys showing that Lexus dealers were providing customers with better sales and service experiences than were Mercedes dealerships. Many Mercedes owners switched to Lexus, and the Lexus repurchase rate has been 60 percent, twice the industry average.

The same for less

Offering "the same for less" can be a powerful value proposition—everyone likes a good deal. For example, Dell offers equivalent quality computers at a lower "price for performance." Discounts stores such as Wal-Mart also use this positioning. They offer many of the same brands as department stores and specialty stores but at deep discounts based on superior purchasing power and lower-cost operations. Other companies develop imitative but lower-priced brands in an effort to lure customers away from the market leader. For example, AMD makes less-expensive versions of Intel's market-leading microprocessor chips. China's Huawei Technology sells reliable, low-cost switches and routers which appear like Cisco's.

Less for much less

A market almost always exists for products that offer less and therefore cost less. Few people need, want, or can afford "the very best" in everything they buy. In many cases, consumers will gladly settle for less than optimal performance for a lower price. For example, many travelers seeking lodgings prefer not to pay for what they consider unnecessary extras, such as a pool, attached restaurant, or mints on the pillow. Hotel chains such as Ramada Limited suspend some of these amenities and charge less accordingly.

"Less-for-much-less" positioning involves meeting consumers' lower performance or quality requirements at a much lower price. Costco warehouse stores offer less merchandise selection and consistency and much lower levels of service; as a result, they charge rock-bottom prices. Budget airlines such as Nok Air, JetStar and Air Asia also practice less-for-much-less positioning.

More for less

Of course, the winning value proposition would be to offer "more for less." Many companies claim to do this. And, in the short run, some companies can actually achieve such lofty positions. But in the long run, companies will find it very difficult to sustain such best-of-both positioning. Offering more usually costs more, making it difficult to deliver on the "for-less" promise. Companies that try to deliver both may lose out to more focused competitors.

All said, each brand must adopt a positioning strategy designed to serve the needs and wants of its target markets. "More for more" will draw one target market, "less for much less" will draw another, and so on. Thus, in any market, there is usually room for many different companies, each successfully occupying different positions. The important thing is that each company must develop its own winning positioning strategy, one that makes it special to its target consumers.

Developing a Positioning Statement

Company and brand positioning should be summed up in a **positioning statement**. The statement should follow the form: To (target segment and need) our (brand) is (concept) that (point of difference).[22] For example: "*To busy, mobile professionals who need to always be in the loop, BlackBerry is a wireless connectivity solution that allows you to stay connected to data, people, and resources while on the go, easily and reliably—more so than competing technologies.*" Sometimes a positioning statement is more detailed:

Less for much less –
Nok Air's budget airline fares offer value-for-money positioning.

Positioning statement
A statement that summarizes company or brand positioning—it take its form: *To (target segment and next) our (brand) is (concept) that (point of difference).*

> To young, active soft-drink consumers who have little time for sleep, Mountain Dew is the soft drink that gives you more energy than any other brand because it has the highest level of caffeine. With Mountain Dew, you can stay alert and keep going even when you haven't been able to get a good night's sleep.

Note that the positioning first states the product's membership in a category (Mountain Dew is a soft drink) and then shows its point of difference from other members of the category (has more caffeine). Placing a brand in a specific category suggests similarities that it might share with other products in the category. But the case for the brand's superiority is made on its points of difference.

Communicating and Delivering the Chosen Position

Once it has chosen a position, the company must take strong steps to deliver and communicate the desired position to target consumers. All the company's marketing mix efforts must support the positioning strategy.

Positioning the company calls for concrete action, not just talk. If the company decides to build a position on better quality and service, it must first deliver that position. Designing the marketing mix—product, price, place, and promotion—involves working out the tactical details of the positioning strategy. (see **Figure 7.8**) Thus, a firm that seizes on a more-for-more position knows that it must produce high-quality products, charge a high price, distribute through high-quality dealers, and advertise in high-quality media. It must hire and train more service people, find retailers who have a good reputation for service, and develop sales and advertising messages that broadcast its superior service. This is the only way to build a consistent and believable more-for-more position.

Figure 7.8
A company's marketing mix efforts must support the positioning strategy

Companies often find it easier to come up with a good positioning strategy than to implement it. Establishing a position or changing one usually takes a long time. In contrast, positions that have taken years to build can quickly be lost. Once a company has built the desired position, it must take care to maintain the position through consistent performance and communication. It must closely monitor and adapt the position over time to match changes in consumer needs and competitors' strategies. However, the company should avoid abrupt changes that might confuse consumers. Instead, a product's position should evolve gradually as it adapts to the ever-changing marketing environment.

REAL MARKETING 7.2

Sentosa: Becoming Asia's Favorite Playground

In 1966, the island of Sentosa, off mainland Singapore, was selected to be developed into a holiday resort. However, flagging visitor numbers in the late 1990s led it to recognize that ther was a need to change the public's perceptions of the island. It was perceived, especially among locals, as an expensive place to visit with poor accessibility, aside from ferry and cable car services, with nothing much to see.

Framing a Stronger Value Proposition

A master plan of renewal was set in motion to revitalize the island, and to reposition and rebuild Sentosa as an attractive place to visit. Aspiring to be Asia's Favorite Playground, Sentosa sought to remove 'major barriers' deterring locals from visiting the island, whilst adding value to the offer. Several initiatives were executed to reposition Snetosa from an island resort to a full-fledged lersure waterfront precinct. These included:

- Island admission was revised down to an affordable S$3 to encourage frequent visits.
- Upgrading its attractions and infrastructure steadily with the introduction of new attractions such as Singapore's tallest observatory tower, the Sky Tower, and a state-of-the-art multi-sensory performance, *Songs of the Sea*.
- Improving facilities and F&B offerings along the three beaches on the island. Each respective beach was designed to cater to a different group of visitors. F&B offerings were also enhanced to deliver a wide range of options ranging from Italian fine dining to local food court fare.

TAKE A NEW LOOK

Pick up on all the fun
along our golden beaches

Looking for a family day out? There are 3.2 kilometres of fun for everyone along Sentosa's coastline. Whether you want to get active with roller-blading or a game of beach volleyball; or simply relax in one of the beach cafes or on the pontoons – you can do it all here! So, if you're looking to escape with the family, take a new look at Sentosa.
For more information, visit www.sentosa.com.sg

sentosa

- Upgrading the golf courses to attract more golf enthusiasts with two upgraded courses. One of which, the Serapong course, also hosted the prestigious Barclays Singapore Open in Asia.

- Making travel to the island easier with the launch of the Sentosa Express, a monrail system linking the mainland directly into Sentosa island.

The Communication Campaigns

Communication of the changes made was launched in phases. It was critical to recognize and segregate the different groups of target consumers. The three key segments are:

- Youths (15–24 years old)
- DINKS (Dual-income No Kids) / Professionals (25–34 years old)
- Families with young children aged 4–12 years old

A brand re-launch campaign (called "Take A New Look") was developed with the key objective of re-aligning people's perceptions of Sentosa. It was an invitational campaign with humility, asking consumers (primarily locals) to once again consider visiting Sentosa given its improved infrastructure and offerings.

Visitor numbers jumped from 4,151 million to 5,053 million between 2003 and 2004. More recently, the number of visitor arrivals from April 2007 to March 2008 was 6,125 million, an 8 percent increase over the same period in the previous year.

In 2005, a second phase, focusing on making sentosa a choice regular leisure destination by promoting return visits, was launched. Sub-brand campaigns

Adventure comes together at Sentosa

Discover your sentosa

for specific parts of Sentosa were developed. Siloso Beach and Imbiah Lookout are two locations targeting different audience segments, and each campaign showcased the cluster's unique selling points and encouraged visits.

A third phase, 'Discover Your Sentosa," campaign was launched. It reinforced the many various activities and experience that Sentosa has to offer, and invited both local and overseas visitors in discovering these for themselves and personalize their own experiences at Sentosa.

The master plans also reached out to corporate audiences to view Sentosa as a choice venue for business meetings and events. This was achievedd by showcasing the isalnd's quality facilities and infrastucture, such as the Sentosa Golf Club, the unique venues and hotels. Sentosa has since played host to a variety of events including Forbes Global CEO Conference and the forthcoming Volvo Ocean Race.

Looking Ahead

By 2010, developments to expand offerings both on and off the island will be near completion, including the highly-anticipated integrated resort, Resorts World at Sentosa. It will house Universal Studios Singapore, the region's first Universal Studios theme park, Marine Life Park, the world's largest oceanarium, and many more.

In the period leading up to 2010, the intention is to begin seeding the Asia's Favorite Playground proposition in the marketplace. By then, Sentosa looks forward to welcoming 15 milliion visitors in 2010. With its array of family-friendly attractions and completed developments, Sentosa is set to propel both itself and Singapore onto the global stage, becoming Asia's leading lifestyle and leisure destination by 2010, or simply Asia's Favorite Playground.

Sources:
Sentosa Development Corporation; Sentosa-Resorts World Joint Press Releases, March 1, 2007.

REVIEWING THE CONCEPTS

In this chapter, you've learned about the major elements of a customer-driven marketing strategy: segmentation, targeting, differentiation, and positioning. Marketers know that they cannot appeal to all buyers in their markets, or at least not to all buyers in the same way. Buyers are too numerous, too widely scattered, and too varied in their needs and buying practices. Therefore, most companies today practice target marketing—identifying market segments, selecting one or more of them, and developing products and marketing mixes tailored to each.

1 Define the major steps in designing a customer-driven marketing strategy: market segmentation, targeting, differentiation, and positioning.

Customer-driven marketing strategy begins with selecting which customers to serve and deciding on a value proposition that best serves the targeted customers. It consists of four steps. *Market segmentation* is the act of dividing a market into distinct groups of buyers with different needs, characteristics, or behaviors who might require separate products or marketing mixes. Once the groups have been identified, *market targeting* evaluates each market segment's attractiveness and selects one or more segments to serve. Market targeting consists of designing strategies to build *the right relationships* with *the right customers*. *Differentiation* involves actually differentiating the market offering to create superior customer value. *Positioning* consists of positioning the market offering in the minds of target customers.

2 List and discuss the major bases for segmenting consumer and business markets.

There is no single way to segment a market. Therefore, the marketer tries different variables to see which give the best segmentation opportunities. For consumer marketing, the major segmentation variables are geographic, demographic, psychographic, and behavioral. In *geographic segmentation*, the market is divided into different geographical units such as nations, regions, states, counties, cities, or neighborhoods. In *demographic segmentation*, the market is divided into groups based on demographic variables, including age, gender, family size, family life cycle, income, occupation, education, religion, race, generation, and nationality. In *psychographic segmentation*, the market is divided into different groups based on social class, lifestyle, or personality characteristics. In *behavioral segmentation*, the market is divided into groups based on consumers' knowledge, attitudes, uses, or responses to a product.

Business marketers use many of the same variables to segment their markets. But business markets also can be segmented by business consumer demographics (industry, company size), operating characteristics, purchasing approaches, situational factors, and personal characteristics. The effectiveness of segmentation analysis depends on finding segments that are *measurable*, *accessible*, *substantial*, *differentiable*, and *actionable*.

3 Explain how companies identify attractive market segments and choose a market targeting strategy.

To target the best market segments, the company first evaluates each segment's size and growth characteristics, structural attractiveness, and compatibility with company objectives and resources. It then chooses one of four market targeting strategies—ranging from very broad to very narrow targeting. The seller can ignore segment differences and target broadly using *undifferentiated* (or *mass*) *marketing*. This involves mass producing, mass distributing, and mass promoting about the same product in about the same way to all consumers. Or the seller can adopt *differentiated marketing*—developing different market offers for several segments. *Concentrated marketing* (or *niche marketing*) involves focusing on only one or a few market segments. Finally, micromarketing is the practice of tailoring products and marketing programs to suit the tastes of specific individuals and locations. Micromarketing includes *local marketing* and *individual marketing*. Which targeting strategy is best depends on company resources, product variability, product life-cycle stage, market variability, and competitive marketing strategies.

4 Discuss how companies differentiate and position their products for maximum competitive advantage in the marketplace.

Once a company has decided which segments to enter, it must decide on its *differentiation and positioning strategy*. The differentiation and positioning task consists of three steps: identifying a set of possible differentiations that create competitive advantage, choosing advantages upon which to build a position, choosing the right competitive advantages, and selecting an overall positioning strategy. The brand's full positioning is called its *value proposition*—the full mix of benefits upon which the brand is positioned. In general, companies can choose from one of five winning value propositions upon which to position their products: more for more, more for the same, the same for less, less for much less, or more for less. Company and brand positioning are summarized in positioning statements that state the target segment and need, positioning concept, and specific points of difference. The company must then effectively communicate and deliver the chosen position to the market.

REVIEWING THE KEY TERMS

Age and life-cycle segmentation 168
Behavioral segmentation 1702
Benefit segmentation 170
Competitive advantage 184
Concentrated (niche) marketing 177
Demographic segmentation 168
Differentiated (segmented) marketing 176
Differentiation 166
Gender segmentation 168

Geographic segmentation 167
Income segmentation 169
Individual marketing 180
Intermarket segmentation 174
Local marketing 180
Market segmentation 166
Market targeting 166
Micromarketing 180
Occasion segmentation 170

Positioning 166
Positioning statement 188
Product position 183
Psychographic segmentation 169
Target market 175
Undifferentiated (mass) marketing 176
Value proposition 186

DISCUSSING THE CONCEPTS

1. Explain which segmentation variables would be most important to marketers of the following products: vitamins, credit cards, coffee.

2. How can a company segment international markets for its products? How might Apple segment the international market for its iPod?

3. What is micromarketing? When should a company practice micromarketing?

4. The chapter discusses five requirements for effective segmentation. Suppose you are a product manager in regional fast-food restaurant company. You are listening to a presentation on a new rice burger idea (teriyaki chicken) and it is your turn to ask questions. Write five questions that you would ask the person presenting this product idea. Each question should be directed at one of the five segmentation requirements.

5. In the context of marketing, what does the term "product positioning" mean? Why is it so important?

6. Using the value propositions presented in **Figure 7.7**, describe the value proposition of Toys "R" Us. Is the Toys "R" Us value proposition clear? Is it appropriate?

APPLYING THE CONCEPTS

1. Apply lifestyle segmentation to each of the following retailers:
   a. Tiffany's   b. Giordano   c. Wal-Mart

2. You are a product manager of a financial services product that is being sold directly to consumers over the Internet. The most important measure to the company is customer acquisition cost—the cost associated with convincing a consumer to buy the service. You have been conducting tests with both a concentrated and undifferentiated segmentation strategy, and the results are presented here. Which strategy is the best? Why?

   Concentrated segmentation outcome
   - Purchased 10,000 very targeted exposures on Web sites such Yahoo Financial and keywords such as retirement, IRA, and ROTH.

   - Paid $80 per thousand exposures
   - Obtained 400 clicks to the site, 40 trials, and 20 repeat customers

   Undifferentiated segmentation outcome
   - Purchased 1,000,000 run-of-site exposures on Web sites
   - Paid $1.60 per thousand exposures
   - Obtained 2,000 clicks to the site, 100 trials, and 40 repeat customers

3. Form a small group and create an idea for a new reality television show. What competitive advantage does this show have over existing shows? How many and which differences would you promote? Develop a positioning statement for this television show.

FOCUS ON TECHNOLOGY

Marketers of technological products such as cell phones have become very focused on segmentation. They segment on benefits sought, allowing consumers to pick from many popular phone features including Bluetooth technology, camera, games, video screens, speakerphone, and voice dialing. Consumers make choices based on style and price, with most prices ranging from $20 to $800. To move style to the next level and to target the high-end consumer, Nokia offers Vertu, the luxury brand, which comes in platinum and gold. Vertu prices begin at around $5,000, with diamond-studded phones selling at more than $30,000. Visit Vertu on the Web at _www.vertu.com_ and compare this site to Nokia's general site at _www.nokia.com_.

1. Explain how the design of each Web site relates to positioning of the products featured.

2. What do you think of the Vertu luxury brand?

3. Nokia uses a different brand name for its luxury brands. Is this a good decision? How else might this product be marketed differently than other Nokia brands? Consider distribution and promotion.

FOCUS ON ETHICS

Pharmaceutical companies work very hard to get the word out to patients with specific illnesses when they have a new drug to treat that illness. People with a wide range of diseases have benefited from the advances in pharmaceutical research. But some are concerned by the way some companies market specific medications. Doctors worry about "disease-mongering," corporate-sponsored exaggeration of maladies that drives consumers to request and receive unnecessary medications. Diagnoses of rare diseases are soaring, and even mild cases of maladies are being treated with drugs.

Diseases cited include restless legs syndrome, social anxiety disorder, irritable bowel syndrome, and bipolar disorder. The drug makers say they are only trying to educate patients and that labels contain important information on the product. In addition, the pharmaceutical companies stress that the final decision for any medication is made by the doctor.

1. How do pharmaceutical marketers segment the market?

2. How do they position their medications?

3. Are these marketing strategies socially responsible?

See "Hey, You Don't Look So Good," _BusinessWeek_, May 8,

 VIDEO CASE

Procter & Gamble

Procter & Gamble has one of the world's largest and strongest brand portfolios, including such familiar brands Pampers, Tide, Ariel, Always, Pantene, Bounty, Folgers, Pringles, Charmin, Downy, Iams, Crest, Secret, and Olay. In fact, P&G offers seven shampoo brands, six detergent brands, and six soap brand in the U.S. In each of these categories, P&G's products compete against each other, in addition to products offered by other companies, for share of the customer's wallet.

How can a company with more than 300 brands sold in more than 140 countries maximize profits without cannibalizing its own sales? It all starts with a solid understanding of consumers and how a brand fits into consumers' lives. P&G believes that a brand must stand for something singular in a consumer's life. As a result, each brand is carefully positioned to target a very specific segment of the market. The result? P&G had nearly $57 billion in sales last year.

After viewing the video featuring Procter & Gamble, answer the following questions about segmentation, targeting, and positioning.

1. Visit the Procter & Gamble Web site, choose a specific product category, and review the brands in that category. How does P&G use positioning to differentiate the brands in the product category you selected?

2. What bases of segmentation does P&G use to differentiate the products in the category you selected?

3. How does P&G use its variety of brands to build relationships with the right customers?

🔊 COMPANY CASE

L'Oréal: An Image Makeover in India

When it first entered India in 1991, L'Oréal launched a shampoo called Garnier Ultra Doux. Following market leader Hindustan Lever, the brand was designed to appeal to the largest number of consumers possible. L'Oréal thought that Ultra Doux's combination of low price and natural ingredients would fit India's market, where women use plants and herbs as part of their beauty culture. To drive the price down even further than in Europe, L'Oréal simplified the shampoo's formula by eliminating some polymers, the molecular compounds that make hair stronger or shinier.

However, Ultra Doux was a failure. The shampoo offered no particular innovation compared to rival products from Hindustan Lever and Cavin Kare, a local company. L'Oréal struggled to persuade owners of local shops to stock it. "It was an absolute flop," says Alain Evrard, managing director for L'Oréal's Africa, Orient, and Pacific zone. Evrard decided to go upmarket, given Hindustan Lever's domination of the mass market. In a market where beauty products sell for less than a dollar, L'Oréal's products generally sell for three to 20 times as much. In shops across India, L'Oréal's offerings include a $5.60 Garnier Nutrisse hair dye, a $17 L'Oréal Paris face powder, and a $25 Vichy sunscreen. In contrast, Hindustan Lever sells a 70-cent bottle of body lotion and a 90-cent shampoo targeting the over 800 million people who live on less than $2 a day.

A New Consumer

Jaya Sethi says she is willing to spend. The office assistant in New Delhi recently bought two bottles of Nutrisse. She used to buy cheaper dyes made from henna plant extract, but says L'Oréal is "good quality" and "fun". Sethi represents India's emerging middle class, which Tata Consultancy Services estimates to be 200 million strong. Consumer attitudes began to shift by the mid-1990s as foreign brands like Tommy Hilfiger, Absolut, Mercedes, and Benetton moved in to capture a slice of the market. A spike in households with cable TV brought channels such as MTV and CNN into Indian living rooms.

The number of working women also rose. Between 1990 and 1995, 8.5 million women entered the Indian work force, according to the International Labor Organization, for a total of over 100 million women employed. In 2007, the figure swelled to 130 million, though millions more women also work in the informal economy, especially in the rural areas.

The cultural shift among working women in India formed the heart of the transformation in consume spending in the country. Decades of poverty instilled a strong sense of price consciousness in Indian women, which was passed from mother to daughter. But the generation that came of age during the market liberalization of the early 1990s is more willing to spend on luxuries, from bottled water to lipstick to eating out. "For these people, consumption is a way of life," says Neelah Hundekari, of management consultancy A.T. Kearney. One example is Aarti Sarin, a 30-year-old art gallery director in Delhi. She visits the hair salon of a five-star hotel weekly for a $15 head-oil massage, then tames her hair with a L'Oréal antifrizz treatment. Says Sarin, "A generation back, people weren't so bothered with healthy hair. But we're more out and about and we need to take care of it."

Indian working women like Sarin spend 23 percent more on cosmetics such as antiwrinkle cream and sunscreen than non-working women, according to a survey by The Future Group, which owns India's largest retailer, Pantaloon Retail. According to Euromonitor, the increase in foreign-style salons and international shampoos and dyes is expected to drive hair care sales to $1.33 billion in 2011 from $957 million in 2006.

L'Oréal Makeover

To better understand what products would best resonate with middle-class working women, L'Oréal's Evrard spoke to advertising executives, editors of fashion magazines, and local employees about their consumer habits, focusing on hair care. The breakthrough came when some employees complained that they and their peers were getting gray hair, despite being only in their 20s. At the time, Western-style, do-it-yourself hair-coloring kits barely existed in India. Women used henna and ammonia-based liquids and powders to cover their gray hair.

However, ammonia dried out their hair, while henna faded quickly. Moreover hair dye was one of the items Hindustan Lever didn't market.

So in late 1996, Evrard introduced L'Oréal Excellence Crème in India. Excellence Crème was one of L'Oréal's most innovative and pricey products in Europe. In cream form, dye is considered more gentle on hair than liquid products. In India, it costs $11 a bottle, about the same price as in France. Whereas it is a mass market item in Europe, L'Oréal positions it as a luxury purchase in India. L'Oréal hired Diana Hayden, Miss World 1997, as its first Indian advertising face. "For me, beauty starts with beautiful hair," Hayden cooed in one TV commercial.

However, securing distribution was a problem initially. Many shopkeepers still had unsold inventory of Ultra Doux and refused to carry another L'Oréal product. So L'Oréal hosted conferences for shopkeepers, showing them the difference between Excellence Crème and liquid or powder dyes from the local Godrej and Super Vasmol brands. It also designed incentives for shopkeepers who carried the products. It offered to help them clean spider webs out of their store windows and installed cardboard display cases of L'Oréal products. In the first year, 2,500 shops agreed to carry the product. Excellence Crème is now widely stocked across India.

L'Oréal also launched its salon business to reach more women. It introduced a line of hair dyes in 80 shades, from blonde to black, for use in salons. It set up a program to train hairdressers to use these products. By 2005, L'Oréal was training some 20,000 hairdressers a year. In 2006, it built its first-ever International Hairdressing Academy in Mumbai, where students learn more advanced techniques for hair cutting, coloring, and straightening, as well as basic hygiene rules.

A New L'Oréal

L'Oréal believes that creating a new high-end niche in the Indian hair care market helped restore its reputation. In 2004,

the company became profitable in India after 13 years of losses. Sales, which have doubled every two years since 2002, rose 40 percent in 2006 to $108 million, and are expected to hit $159 million in 2007. "We don't do poor products for poor people," says Evrard. L'Oréal's target segment, which it says comprises the 60 million urban middle-class men and women who earn over $275 monthly, is rising, and should reach 73 million in two years.

Yet, its success has allowed L'Oréal to re-enter the mass market dominated by Hindustan Lever. L'Oréal now offers a $2.70 hair dye called Color Naturals that can be spread over three applications and small packets of shampoo costing under $1 which compete directly with local brands. Color Naturals has since been rolled out in other emerging markets like Russia and the Middle East. L'Oréal's new $3.10 shampoo, Garnier Fructis' Long & Strong, is advertised across India on huge billboards showing a woman tugging on her braid, which is stretched across freeway overpasses and along the length of a bus. Archana Jain, a 40-year-old mother who shares a three-room apartment in Mumbai with eight relatives, still relies on home remedies for skin care, such as a mix of cream, turmeric, and gram flour to moisturize her face. However, she was inspired by the ads to start using the brand to wash her waist-length hair twice weekly. She hopes it will strengthen her hair, which she complains is weak. "It does good to my hair. It's used by everyone in the family," she says.

However, L'Oréal's competitors are encroaching on its territory. In 2004, Hindustan Lever entered the premium segment with Perfect Radiance face cream. At $5, it is seven times the price of its main Fair & Lovely line. Unlike L'Oréal's channels which are limited to urban areas, Hindustan Lever's distribution reaches the most remote areas of India, where the bulk of India's population lives. Prakash Jain sells about 45 boxes of L'Oréal's Color Naturals monthly at his pharmacy in Mumbai's Worli district. He says the more expensive lines, including L'Oréal's Excellence Crème, move more slowly: "Consumers have to think twice before buying it."

Questions For Discussion

1. Using the full spectrum of segmentation variables, describe how L'Oréal has segmented the Indian market.
2. What segment(s) is (are) L'Oréal now targeting? How is L'Oréal now positioning its products? How do these strategies differ from those employed by its competitors in India?
3. What role, if any, does social responsibility play in L'Oréal's targeting strategy in India?
4. Do you think that L'Oréal will accomplish its goals in India? Why or why not?
5. What segmentation, targeting, and positioning recommendations would you make to L'Oréal for future marketing efforts in India?

Source:
Christina Passariello, "L'Oréal Seeks Firmer Foundation in India by Targeting Middle Class," *Wall Street Journal*, July 13 –15, 2007, pp. 14 –15.

The Kelvinator brand of refrigerators from Electrolux was well known in India, but had been out of touch with consumer preferences. In 1997, it relaunched Kelvinator in India.

Objectives

After studying this chapter, you should be able to

- define product and the major classifications of products and services
- describe the decisions companies make regarding their individual products and services, product lines, and product mixes
- discuss branding strategy the decisions companies make in building and managing their brands
- identify the four characteristics that affect the marketing of a service and the additional marketing considerations that services require

CHAPTER 8

PRODUCT, SERVICES, AND BRANDING STRATEGY

Previewing the Concepts

Now that you've had a good look at marketing strategy, we'll take a deeper look at the marketing mix—the tactical tools that marketers use to implement their strategies. In this and the next chapter, we'll study how companies develop and manage products and brands. Then, in the chapters that follow, we'll look at pricing, distribution, and marketing communication tools.

The product is usually the first and most basic marketing consideration. To start things off, what is a product? Consider Kelvinator, a refrigerator brand marketed by Electrolux.

Kelvinator was the dominant brand in India until around 1992, with a market share of 22 percent. However, due to a major strike, increased competition, and uncertainty over the ownership of the brand, its share fell to 6 percent by 1997. Electrolux relaunched the brand in 1997, with the objective of arresting its decline and setting Kelvinator back on track for growth.

Market research found that the Kelvinator brand was well known in India but was out of touch with changed consumer preferences. The brand had not found a point of difference on which to compete. Its product range was limited. For example, there were no frost-free models. Kelvinator also enjoyed little trade support, resulting in poor distribution and in-store visibility.

Electrolux began by examining the generic role of refrigeration and how its multinational rivals positioned themselves. Electrolux discovered that its competitors were extremely Western-oriented, emphasizing the use of refrigerators for storage and to keep food fresher for longer. However, Electrolux found that fresh food was a daily habit among Indians, entailing daily trips to the neighborhood markets for many women. Keeping food fresh was not a priority for Indian women since they were going to buy fresh food the next day anyway. Closer analysis of Indian households revealed that most Indians needed a fridge for cooling, not storage.

Hence, Electrolux revitalized the Kelvinator brand based on the concept of "cool." Kelvinator was positioned as the fridge that "cools beyond the expected." A new range of models were launched that provided the benefit of rapid cooling. Improved distribution and better trade relations were also fostered. A creative marketing communications campaign was implemented that reinforced "The Coolest One" tagline. An amusing set of television commercials was aired. Print ads highlighted the features of Kelvinator, including its offering the most powerful compressor, the thickest insulation, and the fastest ice-making facility. Outdoor ads conveyed the consequences of the revitalized brand. "Summer? What Summer?", "12 months of Chill," and "Pull out your sweaters" were some featured headlines. Unusual point-of-sales materials such as chattering teeth were also employed which assured consumers that nothing cooled faster than "The Coolest One." A traveling road show, complete with a truck full of fridges, took the brand to rural India.

By 2003, intense competition led to price erosion. Kelvinator's market share grew to 18 percent. It also introduced new models including some from Electrolux's international portfolio[1].

This chapter begins with a simple question: What is a product? We will look at ways to classify products in consumer and business markets. Then we discuss the important decisions that marketers make regarding individual product lines, and product mixes. Next, we look into the critically important issue of how marketers build and manage brands. Finally, we examine the characteristics and marketing requirements of a special form of product—services.

What Is A Product?

A **product** is anything that can be offered to a market for attention, acquisition, use, or consumption that might satisfy a want or need. Products include more than just tangible goods. Broadly defined, products include physical objects, services, events, persons, places, organizations, ideas, or mixes of these entities. Throughout this text, we use the term *product* broadly to include any or all of these entities. Thus, an Apple iPod, a Toyota Camry, and a Caffé Mocha at Starbucks are products. But so are a Bali vacation, HSBC online investment services, and advice from your family doctor.

Because of their importance in the world economy, we give special attention to services. **Services** are a form of product that consists of activities, benefits, or satisfactions offered for sale that are essentially intangible and do not result in the ownership of anything. Examples are banking, hotel, airline, retail, tax preparation, and home-repair services.

Products, Services, and Experiences

Product is a key element in the overall *market offering*. A company's market offering often includes both tangible goods and services. Each component can be a minor or a major part of the total offer. At one extreme, the offer may consist of a pure tangible good, such as soap, toothpaste, or salt—no services accompany the product. At the other extreme are pure services, for which the offer consists primarily of a service. Examples include a doctor's exam or financial services. Between these two extremes, however, many goods-and-services combinations are possible.

As products and services become more commoditized, many companies are differentiating their offers by creating and managing customer experiences with their products or company. Companies that market experiences realize that customers are really buying much more than just products and services. They are buying what those offers will do for them.

Levels of Product and Services

Product planners need to think about products and services on three levels (see **Figure 8.1**).

Product
Anything that can be offered to a market for attention, acquisition, use, or consumption that might satisfy a want or need.

Service
Any activity or benefit that one party can offer to another that is essentially intangible and does not result in the ownership of anything.

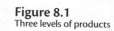

Figure 8.1
Three levels of products

When you buy an MP3 music player, you are buying more than the physical product. You are also buying the experience of using it, as well as the emotion associated with it.

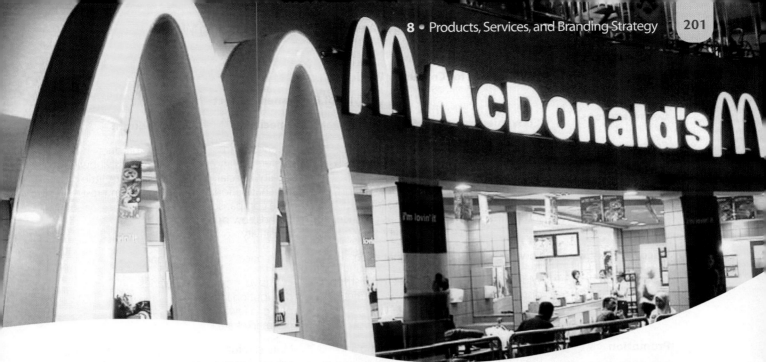

Each level adds more customer value. The three levels are:

- *Core benefit:* This is the most basic level. It addresses the question *What is the buyer really buying?* When designing products, marketers must first define the core, problem- solving benefits or services that consumers seek. A woman buying lipstick buys more than lip color. Charles Revson of Revlon saw this early: "In the factory, we make cosmetics; in the store, we sell hope." And people who buy a BlackBerry are buying more than a wireless mobile phone, e-mail and Web browsing device, or personal organizer. They are buying freedom and on-the go connectivity to people and resources.

- *Actual product:* At the second level, product planners develop product and service features, design, a quality level, a brand name, and packaging. For example, the BlackBerry is an actual product. Its name, parts, styling, features, packaging, and other attributes have all been combined carefully to deliver the core benefit of staying connected.

- *Augmented product:* Finally, product planners offer additional consumer services and benefits around the core benefit and actual product. BlackBerry offers more than just a communications device. It provides consumers with a complete solution to mobile connectivity problems. Thus, when consumers buy a BlackBerry, the company and its dealers also might give buyers a warranty on parts and workmanship, instructions on how to use the device, quick repair services when needed, and a toll-free telephone number and Web site to use if they have problems or questions.

> Keeping in touch with changing trends, McDonald's in Malaysia differentiates itself from other fast food restaurants by providing an atmosphere that encourages people, especially youngsters, to spend time there while enjoying the restaurant's food. (*www.mcdonalds.com.my*)

Core, actual, and augmented product –
People who buy a Blackberry are buying more than a wireless mobile phone, e-mail and Web-browsing device, or personal organizer. They are buying freedom and on-the-go connectivity to people and resources.

Product and Service Classifications

Products and services fall into two broad classes based on the types of consumers that use them—*consumer products* and *industrial products*. Broadly defined, products also include other marketable entities such as experiences, organizations, persons, places, and ideas.

Consumer Products

Consumer products are products and services bought by final consumers for personal consumption. Marketers usually classify these products and services further based on how consumers go about buying them. Consumer products include *convenience products*, *shopping products*, *specialty products*, and *unsought products*. These products differ in the ways consumers buy them and therefore in how they are marketed (**see Table 8.1**).

> **Consumer product**
> Product bought by final consumer for personal consumption.

Table 8.1 Marketing Considerations for Consumer Products

Marketing Considerations	Type of Consumer Product			
	Convenience	**Shopping**	**Specialty**	**Unsought**
Customer buying behavior	Frequent purchase, little planning, little comparison or shopping effort, low customer involvement	Less frequent purchase, much planning and shopping effort, comparison of brands on price, quality, style	Strong brand preference and loyalty, special purchase effort, little comparison of brands, low price sensitivity	Little product awareness, knowledge (or, if aware, little or even negative interest)
Price	Low price	Higher price	High price	Varies
Distribution	Widespread distribution, convenient locations	Selective distribution in fewer outlets	Exclusive distribution in only one or a few outlets per market area	Varies
Promotion	Mass promotion by the producer	Advertising and personal selling by both producer and resellers	More carefully targeted promotion by both producer and resellers	Aggressive advertising and personal selling by producer and resellers
Examples	Toothpaste, magazines, laundry detergent	Major appliances, televisions, furniture, clothing	Luxury goods, such as Rolex watches or fine crystal	Life insurance, Red Cross blood donations

Convenience products
Consumer product that the customer usually buys frequently, immediately, and with a minimum of comparison and buying effort.

Shopping product
Consumer good that the customer, in the process or selection and purchase, characteristically compares on such bases as suitability, quality, price, and style.

Specialty product
Consumer product with unique characteristics or brand identification for which a significant group of buyers is willing to make a special buy effort.

Unsought product
Consumer product that the consumer either does not know about or knows about but does not normally think of buying.

Industrial product
Product bought by individuals and organizations for further processing or for use in conducting a business.

Convenience products are consumer products and services that the customer usually buys frequently, immediately, and with a minimum of comparison and buying effort. Examples include soap, candy, newspapers, and fast food. Convenience products are usually low priced, and marketers place them in many locations to make them readily available when customers need them.

Shopping products are less frequently purchased consumer products and services that customers compare carefully on suitability, quality, price, and style. When buying shopping products and services, consumers spend much time and effort in gathering information and making comparisons. Examples include furniture, clothing, used cars, major appliances, and hotel and airline services. Marketers of shopping products usually distribute their products through fewer outlets but provide deeper sales support to help customers in their comparison efforts.

Specialty products are consumer products and services with unique characteristics or brand identification for which a significant group of buyers is willing to make a special purchase effort. Examples include specific brands and types of cars, high-priced photographic equipment, designer clothes, and the services of medical or legal specialists. A Lamborghini automobile, for example, is a specialty product because buyers are usually willing to travel great distances to buy one. Buyers normally do not compare specialty products. They invest only the time needed to reach dealers carrying the wanted products.

Unsought products are consumer products that the consumer either does not know about or knows about but does not normally think of buying. Most major new innovations are unsought until the consumer becomes aware of them through advertising. Classic examples of known but unsought products and services are life insurance, preplanned funeral services, and blood donations to the Red Cross. By their very nature, unsought products require a lot of advertising, personal selling, and other marketing efforts.

Industrial Products

Industrial products are those purchased for further processing or for use in conducting a business. Thus, the distinction between a consumer product and an industrial product is based on the purpose for which the product is bought. If a consumer buys a camera for personal use, the camera is a consumer product. If the same consumer buys the same camera for use in a photography business, the camera is an industrial product.

The three groups of industrial products and services include materials and parts, capital items, and supplies and services (see **Figure 8.2**). *Materials and parts* include raw materials and manufactured materials and parts. Raw materials consist of farm products (wheat, livestock, fruits) and natural products (fish, lumber, crude petroleum). Manufactured

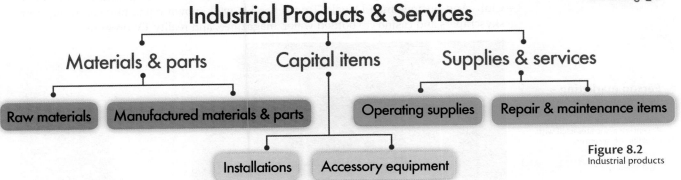

Industrial Products & Services

Figure 8.2
Industrial products

materials and parts consist of component materials (yarn, cement, wires) and component parts (small motors, tires, castings). Most manufactured materials and parts are sold directly to industrial users. Price and service are the major marketing factors; branding and advertising tend to be less important.

Capital items are industrial products that aid in the buyer's production or operations, including installations and accessory equipment. Installations consist of major purchases such as buildings (factories, offices) and fixed equipment (generators, elevators). Accessory equipment includes portable factory equipment and tools (hand tools, lift trucks) and office equipment (computers, desks). They have a shorter life than installations and simply aid in the production process.

The final group of industrial products is *supplies and services*. Supplies include operating supplies (lubricants, paper, pencils) and repair and maintenance items (paint, nails, brooms). Supplies are the convenience products of the industrial field because hey are usually purchased with a minimum of effort or comparison. Business services include maintenance and repair services (window cleaning, computer repair) and business advisory services (legal, management consulting, advertising). Such services are usually supplied under contract.

Organizations, Persons, Places, and Ideas

In addition to tangible products and services, marketers have broadened the concept of a product to include other market offerings—organizations, persons, places, and ideas.

Organizations often carry out activities to "sell" the organization itself. *Organization marketing* consists of activities undertaken to create, maintain, or change the attitudes and behavior of target consumers toward an organization. Business firms sponsor public relations or *corporate image advertising* campaigns to polish their images and market themselves to various publics. For example, Panasonic puts out ads with the tag line "Panasonic Ideas for Life." Haier wants to go "Haier and Higher." Hyundai is "Always There for You." Similarly, not-for-profit organizations, such as colleges, charities, and museums market their organizations to raise funds and attract members or patrons.

People can also be thought of as products. *Person marketing* consists of activities undertaken to create, maintain, or change attitudes or behavior toward particular people. People ranging from presidents, entertainers, and sports figures to professionals such as doctors, lawyers, and architects use person marketing to build their reputations. And businesses, charities, and other organizations use well-known personalities to help sell their products or causes. For example, more than a dozen different companies—including Nike, Apple, Tag Heuer, Buick, American Express, Wheaties, and Accenture—combine to pay more than $80 million a year to link themselves with golf superstar Tiger Woods. NBA star Yao Ming has been associated with companies like China Unicom, Sorrent, Apple, Visa, and Nike.

The skillful use of person marketing can turn a person's name into a powerhouse brand. The brand power of Oprah Winfrey's name has made her a billionaire: Oprah-branded products include her television show, TV and feature movies, *O, The Oprah Magazine*, Oprah's Angel Network, Oprah's Boutiques online shop, and Oprah's Book Club. And businessman Donald Trump has his well-known name on everything from skyscrapers and casinos to bottled water, magazines, and reality TV programs:

Person marketing –
Tiger Woods endorses Accenture. He symbolizes professionalism and drive, characteristics that Accenture associates itself with. Courtesy of Accenture.

distractions 0%

We know what it takes to be a Tiger.
To see insights from our research and experience, including our study of over 500 high performers, visit accenture.com/research

• Consulting • Technology • Outsourcing

accenture
High performance. Delivered.

Donald Trump has made and lost fortunes as a real-estate developer. But Trump's genius is in brand building, and he is the brand. Thanks to tireless self-promotion, "The Donald" has established the Trump brand as a symbol of quality, luxury, and success. What's the value of the Trump brand? Trump's name now adorns everything from magazines and bottled water (Trump Ice) to fashion (Donald J. Trump Signature Collection) and reality TV shows (*The Apprentice*). Trump does commercials for Verizon, was host of *Saturday Night Live*, and even unveiled a Trump Rewards Visa card, which rewards cardholders with casino discounts. Says a friend, "What's his greatest asset? It's his name. He's a skillful marketing person, and what he markets is his name."[3]

Place marketing –
Hong Kong and Shanghai are promoting themselves as "fun" and vibrant" cities to attract the creative elite.

Place marketing involves activities undertaken to create, maintain, or change attitudes or behavior toward particular places. Cities, states, regions, and nations compete to attract tourists, new residents, conventions, and company offices and factories. Take the case of Hong Kong and Shanghai in their rivalry as China's premier business center. They are learning that cities succeed by establishing themselves as fun places to live and attract the creative classes such as writers, musicians, and architects; and provide an environment for the elite to change society. Using cities such as London as reference points, Hong Kong and Shanghai observed that London's long-term planning has resulted in a surge in property prices, multinational investment, tourist income, and a flowering of the arts. As the Hong Kong-Shanghai rivalry goes beyond business to the arts, sports, lifestyle, entertainment, tourism, and convention business, each city took steps to change its image with greater emphasis on creativity. Shanghai, for instance, has invested $230 million in cultural complexes and will be holding the World Expo in 2010.[4]

Ideas can also be marketed. Here, we focus on the marketing of social ideas. This area has been called **social marketing**, defined by the Social Marketing Institute as the use of commercial marketing concepts and tools in programs designed to influence individuals' behavior to improve their well-being and that of society.[5]

Social marketing programs include public health campaigns to reduce smoking, alcoholism, drug abuse, and overeating. Other social marketing efforts include environmental campaigns to promote wilderness protection, clean air, and conservation. Still others address issues such as family planning, human rights, and racial equality. The Singapore government is well-known for its social marketing campaigns such as "Keep Singapore Clean, Green, and Mosquito Free," "Two (Children) Is Enough," "Have Three or More (Children) If You Can Afford It," "Speak Mandarin," "Towards a Nation of Non-Smokers," and "Singapore's OK."

Social marketing –
With smoking among female teens on the rise in Malaysia, its Ministry of Health started an anti-smoking campaign targeted at educating youths about the harms of smoking.
(*www.infosihat.gov.my/TakNak.html*)

> **Social marketing**
> The use of commercial marketing concepts and tools in programs designed to influence individuals' behavior to improve their well-being and that of society.

Product and Service Decisions

Marketers make product and service decisions at three levels: individual product decisions, product line decisions, and product mix decisions. We discuss each in turn.

Individual Product And Service Decisions

Figure 8.3 shows the important decisions in the development and marketing of individual products and services. We will focus on decisions about *product attributes, branding, packaging, labeling,* and *product support services.*

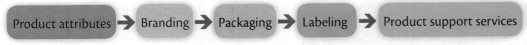

Product attributes → Branding → Packaging → Labeling → Product support services

Learning**A**id

Figure 8.3
Individual product decisions

Product and Service Attributes

Developing a product or service involves defining the benefits that it will offer. These benefits are communicated and delivered by product attributes such as *quality, features,* and *style and design.*

Product quality

Product quality is one of the marketer's major positioning tools. Quality has a direct impact on product or service performance; thus, it is closely linked to customer value and satisfaction. It concerns the product characteristics that can satisfy stated or implied customer needs. Similarly, Siemens defines quality this way: "Quality is when our customers come back and our products don't."[6]

Total quality management (TQM) is an approach in which all the company's people are involved in constantly improving the quality of products, services, and business processes. For most top companies, customer-driven quality has become a way of doing

> **Product quality**
> The characteristics of a product or service that bear on its ability to satisfy stated or implied customer needs.

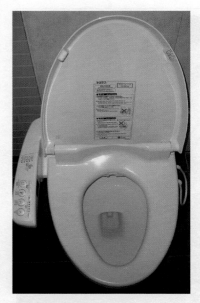

Product features –
In developing toilet seats, the Japanese have incorporated such features as a washing jet. Users can decide on the pressure and temperature of the water as well as whether they would like to have accompanying music.

business. Today, companies are taking a "return on quality" approach, viewing quality as an investment and holding quality efforts accountable for bottom-line results.[7]

Product quality has two dimensions—level and consistency. In developing a product, the marketer must first choose a *quality level* that will support the product's positioning. Here, product means *performance quality*—the ability of a product to perform its functions. For example, a Rolls-Royce provides higher performance quality than a Nissan: It has a smoother ride, provides more "creature comforts," and lasts longer. Companies rarely try to offer the highest possible performance quality level— few customers want or can afford the high levels of quality offered in products such as a Rolls-Royce automobile or a Patek Philippe watch. Instead, companies choose a quality level that matches target market needs and the quality levels of competing products.

High quality can also mean high levels of quality consistency. Here, product quality means conformance quality—freedom from defects and consistency in delivering a targeted level of performance. All companies should strive for high levels of conformance quality. In this sense, a Nissan can have just as much quality as a Rolls-Royce. Although a Nissan doesn't perform as well as a Rolls-Royce, it can as consistently deliver the quality that customers pay for and expect.

Product features

A product can be offered with varying features. A stripped-down model, one without any extras, is the starting point. The company can create higher-level models by adding more features. Features are a competitive tool for differentiating the company's product from competitors' products. Being the first producer to introduce a valued new feature is one of the most effective ways to compete. NTT DoCoMo has a reputation as being an innovator in camera phones.

How can a company identify new features and decide which ones to add to its product? The company should periodically survey buyers who have used the product and ask these questions: How do you like the product? Which specific features of the product do you like most? Which features could we add to improve the product? The company can then assess each feature's value to customers versus its cost to the company. Features that customers value highly in relation to costs should be added.

Product style and design

Product style and design –
Since 1960s, Sony's black & silver design elevated its image. The idea was to do away with excessive ornamentation and accentuate a powerful, high performance, professional feel through the use of simple, cool colors and materials.
(*www.sony.net/design*)

Another way to add customer value is through distinctive product style and design. Design is a larger concept than style. Style simply describes the appearance of a product. A sensational style may grab attention and produce pleasing aesthetics, but it does not necessarily make the product perform better. Unlike style, design is more than skin deep— it goes to the very heart of a product. Good design contributes to a product's usefulness as well as to its looks, while poor design can result in lost sales and embarrassment.

Branding

A **brand** is a name, term, sign, symbol, or design, or a combination of these, that identifies the maker or seller of a product or service. Consumers view a brand as an important part of a product, and branding can add value to a product. For example, most consumers would perceive a bottle of White Linen perfume as a high-quality, expensive product. But the same perfume in an unmarked bottle would likely be viewed as lower in quality, even if the fragrance was identical.

Branding has become so strong that today hardly anything goes unbranded. Salt is packaged in branded containers, common nuts and bolts are packaged with a distributor's

Brand
A name, term, sign, symbol, or design, or a combination of these that identifies the products or services of one seller or group of sellers and differentiates them from those of competitors.

label, and automobile parts—spark plugs, tires—bear brand names that differ from those of the automakers. Even fruits, vegetables, dairy products, and poultry are branded—Sunkist oranges, Dole pineapples, Del Monte bananas.

Branding helps buyers in many ways. (see **Figure 8.4**) Brand names help consumers identify products that might benefit them. Brands also say something about product

BRANDING

- Helps consumer identify products
- Says something about product quality
- Provides legal protection
- Helps segment the market
- Commands premium for better quality brands

Learning Aid

Figure 8.4
Advantages of branding

quality and consistency—buyers who always buy the same brand know that they will get the same features, benefits, and quality each time they buy. Branding also gives the seller several advantages. The brand name becomes the basis on which a whole story can be built around a product's special qualities. The seller's brand name and trademark provide legal protection for unique product features that otherwise might be copied by competitors. Branding helps the seller to segment markets. For example, P&G can offer Head & Shoulders, Pantene, and Rejoice and other shampoo brands, not just one general product for all consumers. And branding can also command a premium for the better quality brands. Farmers in China have branded their commodities so that consumers can identify them and pay a premium. The price of Dangyuan brand pears from Anhui province is 30 percent higher than brandless competitors.

Building and managing brands are perhaps the marketer's most important tasks. In China, about 200 to 300 milllion yuan ($24 to $36 million) is needed annually to establish a new name.[8] We will discuss branding strategy in more detail later in the chapter.

Packaging

Packaging involves designing and producing the container or wrapper for a product. Traditionally, the primary function of the package was to hold and protect the product. In recent times, however, numerous factors have made packaging an important marketing tool. Increased competition and clutter on retail store shelves means that packages must now perform many sales tasks—from attracting attention, to describing the product, to making the sale.

Companies are realizing the power of good packaging to create instant consumer recognition of the company or brand. For example, in an average supermarket, which stocks 15,000 to 17,000 items, the typical shopper passes by some 300 items per minute, and more than 60 percent of all purchases are made on impulse. In this highly competitive environment, the package may be the seller's last chance to influence buyers.

Innovative packaging can give a company an advantage over competitors and boost sales. Sometimes even seemingly small packaging improvements can make a big difference. For example, Heinz revolutionized the 170-year-old condiments industry by inverting the good old ketchup bottle, letting customers quickly squeeze out even the last bit of ketchup. In the year following the new bottle's debut, Heinz ketchup sales grew at three times the industry rate. It started a packaging trend that quickly spread to other categories.

Packaging plays an important role in East Asia. Superior packaging signals quality and makes imitation more difficult. Moreover, the East Asian preference for complexity of expression and decoration is evident in the display of multiple forms, shapes, and colors in packaging. For example, the color combination of red, black, and gold is particularly appealing in Korea. Further, East Asians value naturalism. Such objects as mountains and

Innovative packaging –
This can give a company an advantage over competitors and boost sales. When Heinz inverted the good old ketchup bottle, next-year sales grew at three times the industry rate.

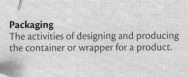

Packaging
The activities of designing and producing the container or wrapper for a product.

phoenixes are frequently found in Chinese advertising and packaging. In Japan, gardens, trees, and flowers are prime objects, while animals are emphasized in Southeast Asia.

Labeling

Labels range from simple tags attached to products to complex graphics that are part of the package. They perform several functions. At the very least, the label identifies the product or brand, such as the name Sunkist stamped on oranges. The label might also describe several things about the product—who made it, where it was made, when it was made, its contents, how it is to be used, and how to use it safely. Finally, the label might help to promote the product and support its positioning.

Product Support Services

Customer service is another element of product strategy. A company's offer usually includes some support services, which can be a minor or a major part of the total offering. For example, Samsung Asia launched Prestige Service to accompany its high-end products (plasma, projection, and LCD TVs, and Side-by-Side Refrigerator). Samsung promised quick repair through a one-day response service. Further, customers would be loaned a temporary set if it was unable to repair the product by the second day. Samsung also offered a free in-home product demonstration service and a 14-day exchange service.

The first step in providing such support services is to survey customers periodically to assess the value of current services and to obtain ideas for new ones. Once the company has assessed the value of various support services to customers, it must next assess the costs of providing these services. It can then develop a package of services that will both delight customers and yield profits to the company.

Many companies use a sophisticated mix of phone, e-mail, fax, Internet, and interactive voice and data technologies to provide support services that were not possible before. Consider the following examples:

> Some online merchants are watching where you surf, then opening a chat window on your screen to ask—just as they would in the store—if you have questions about the goods they see you eyeing. For example, at the Scion Web site, clicking on the Toyota Scion Chat button puts you in real-time touch with someone who can answer your questions or help you to design your personalized Scion.
>
> Hewlett-Packard sends pop-up chat boxes to visitors who are shopping on HP.com's pages for digital-photography products. If a shopper loiters a few minutes over some gear, up pops a photo of an attractive woman with the words, "Hello, need information? An HP live chat representative is standing by to assist you." Click on "Go" and type a question, and a "live" sales agent responds immediately. Since launching its pop-up chat feature, HP has seen a 65 percent surge in online questions.[9]

Product support services – Many companies are now using a sophisticated mix of interactive technologies to provide support services that were not possible before. For example, at the Scion Web site, clicking the Scion Chat button puts you in realtime touch with someone who can answer your questions or help you do design your own personalized Scion. (www.scion.com)

Product Line Decisions

A product strategy also calls for building a product line. A **product line** is a group of products that are closely related because they function in a similar manner, are sold to the same customer groups, are marketed through the same types of outlets, or fall within given price ranges. For example, Nike produces several lines of athletic shoes and apparel, and Citibank produces several lines of financial services.

The major product line decision involves product line length—the number of items in the product line. The line is too short if the manager can increase profits by adding items; the line is too long if the manager can increase profits by dropping items. Managers need to conduct a periodic product line analysis to assess each product item's sales and profits and to understand how each item contributes to the line's performance.

Product line
A group of products that are closely related because they function in a similar manner, are sold to the same customer groups, are marketed through the same types of outlets, or fall within given price ranges.

Product line length is influenced by company objectives and resources. For example, one objective might be to allow for upselling. Thus BMW wants to move customers up from its 3-series models to 5- and 7-series models. Another objective might be to allow cross-selling: Hewlett-Packard sells printers as well as cartridges. Still another objective might be to protect against economic swings: Gap runs several clothing-store chains (Gap, Old Navy, Banana Republic, Forth & Towne) covering different price points. Yet another is to fill in the gaps to pre-empt competition: Brand's Essence of Chicken has different tonics for different needs).

A company can lengthen its product line in two ways: by *line stretching* or by *line filling*. *Product line stretching* occurs when a company lengthens its product line beyond its current range. The company can stretch its line downward, upward, or both ways. (**see Figure 8.5**).

BRAND'S® has a long product line for different needs. There are BRAND'S® Essence of Chicken with Cordyceps for energy; BRAND'S® Essence of Chicken with Ginseng for stamina; BRAND'S® Essence of Chicken with Lingzhi and BRAND'S® Essence of Chicken with Tangkwei for general well being; BRAND'S® Sesamin with Schisandra for liver health; BRAND'S® Calcium Plus and BRAND'S® Glucosamine for bones and joints; among others.

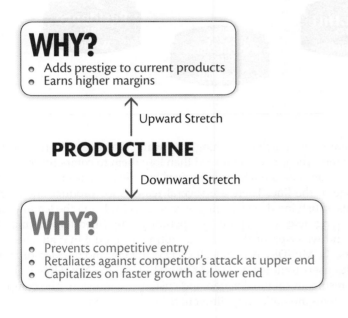

Figure 8.5
Reasons for product line decisions

Companies located at the upper end of the market can stretch their lines *downward*. A company may stretch downward to plug a market hole that otherwise would attract a new competitor or to respond to a competitor's attack on the upper end. Or it may add low-end products because it finds faster growth taking place in the low-end segments. DaimlerChrysler stretched its Mercedes line downward for all these reasons. Facing a slow-growth luxury car market and attacks by Japanese automakers on its high-end positioning, it successfully introduced its Mercedes C- and A-Class cars. These models sell in a lower price range without harming the firm's ability to sell other Mercedes at much higher prices.

Companies at the lower end of a market can stretch their product lines *upward*. Sometimes, companies stretch upward in order to add prestige to their current products. Or they may be attracted by a faster growth rate or higher margins at the higher end. For example, each of the leading Japanese auto companies introduced an upmarket automobile: Toyota launched Lexus; Nissan the Infiniti; and Honda the Acura. They used entirely new names rather than their own.

Companies in the middle range of the market may decide to stretch their lines in *both directions*. Marriott did this with its hotel product line. Along with regular Marriott hotels, it added new branded hotel lines to serve both the upper and lower ends of the market. In China, Renaissance Hotels & Resorts aims to attract and please top executives; Marriott, upper and middle managers. Marriott ExecuStay provides temporary housing for those relocating or away on long-term assignments of 30 days or longer.[10] The major risk with this strategy is that some travelers will trade down if they believe that the lower-price

Product line stretching– Marriott offers a full line of hotel brands, each aimed at a different target market.

Marriott hotels give them pretty much everything they want. However, Marriott would rather capture its customers who move downward than lose them to competitors.

An alternative to product line stretching is *product line filling*—adding more items within the present range of the line. There are several reasons for product line filling: reaching for extra profits, satisfying dealers, using excess capacity, being the leading full-line company, and plugging holes to keep out competitors. Sony filled its Walkman by adding solar-powered and water-proof Walkman, an ultralight model that attaches to a sweatband for exercisers, the MiniDisc Walkman, the CD Walkman, and the Memory Stick Walkman, which enables users to download tracks straight form the Net. However, line filling is overdone if it results in cannibalization and customer confusion. The company should ensure that new items are noticeably different from existing ones.

Product Mix Decisions

An organization with several product lines has a product mix. A **product mix** (or **product portfolio**) consists of all the product lines and items that a particular seller offers for sale. Colgate's product mix consists of four major product lines: oral care, personal care, home care, and pet nutrition. Each product line consists of several sublines. For example, the home care line consists of dishwashing, fabric conditioning, and household cleaning products. Each line and subline has many individual items. Altogether, Colgate's product mix includes hundreds of items.

A company's product mix has four important dimensions: width, length, depth, and consistency. Product mix *width* refers to the number of different product lines the company carries. For example, Colgate markets a fairly contained product mix, consisting of personal and home care products. By comparison, 3M markets more than 60,000 products and GE manufactures as many as 250,000 items, ranging from lightbulbs to jet engines.

Product mix *length* refers to the total number of items the company carries within its product lines. Colgate typically carries many brands within each line. For example, its personal care line includes Softsoap liquid soaps and body washes, Irish Spring bar

Product mix (or **product portfolio**) The set of all product lines and items that a particular seller offers for sale.

soaps, Speed Stick and Crystal Clean deodorants, and Skin Bracer and Afta aftershaves.

Product mix *depth* refers to the number of versions offered of each product in the line. Colgate toothpastes come in 11 varieties, ranging from Colgate Total, Colgate Tartar Control, Colgate 2in1, and Colgate Cavity Protection to Colgate Sensitive, Colgate Fresh Confidence, Colgate Max Fresh, Colgate Simply White, Colgate Sparkling White, Colgate Kids Toothpastes, and Colgate Baking Soda & Peroxide. Then, each variety comes in its own special forms and formulations. For example, you can buy Colgate Total in regular, mint fresh stripe, whitening paste and gel, advanced fresh gel, or 2in1 liquid gel versions.[11] Particular for food, product mix tends to be deeper because of varied cultural tastes.

Finally, the *consistency* of the product mix refers to how closely related the various product lines are in end use, production requirements, distribution channels, or some other way. Colgate's product lines are consistent insofar as they are consumer products that go through the same distribution channels. The lines are less consistent insofar as they perform different functions for buyers.

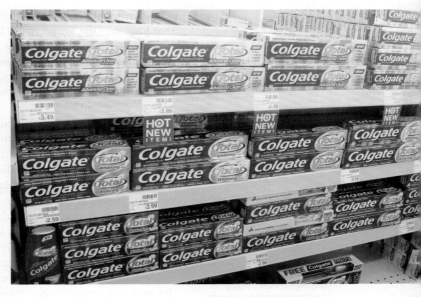

Product mix depth –
Colgate toothpastes come in many varieties.
(*www.colgate.com*)

These product mix dimensions provide the handles for defining the company's product strategy. The company can increase its business in four ways. It can add new product lines, widening its product mix. In this way, its new lines build on the company's reputation in its other lines. The company can lengthen its existing product lines to become a more full-line company. Or it can add more versions of each product and thus deepen its product mix. Finally, the company can pursue more product line consistency—or less—depending on whether it wants to have a strong reputation in a single field or in several fields.

Branding Strategy: Building Strong Brands

Some analysts see brands as *the* major enduring asset of a company, outlasting the company's specific products and facilities. A former CEO of McDonald's says: "If every asset we own, every building, and every piece of equipment were destroyed in a terrible natural disaster, we would be able to borrow all the money to replace it very quickly because of the value of our brand …. The brand is more valuable than the totality of all these assets."[12]

Thus, brands are powerful assets that must be carefully developed and managed. In this section, we examine the key strategies for building and managing brands.

Brand Equity

Brands are more than just names and symbols. They are a key element in the company's relationships with consumers. Brands represent consumers' perceptions and feelings about a product and its performance—everything that the product or service means to consumers.

The real value of a strong brand is its power to capture consumer preference and loyalty. Brands vary in the amount of power and value they have in the marketplace. Some brands—such as Coca-Cola, Sony, Nike, Harley-Davidson, Disney, and others— become larger-than-life icons that maintain their power in the market for years, even generations. These brands win in the marketplace not simply because they deliver unique benefits or reliable service. Rather, they succeed because they forge deep connections with customers.

A powerful brand has high *brand equity*. **Brand equity** is the positive differential effect that knowing the brand name has on customer response to the product or service. One measure of a brand's equity is the extent to which customers are willing to pay more for the brand. One study found that 72 percent of customers would pay a 20 percent premium for their brand of choice relative to the closest competing brand; 40 percent said they would pay a 50 percent premium. People who like Heinz are willing to pay a 100 percent premium.[13]

A brand with strong brand equity is a very valuable asset. *Brand valuation* is the process of estimating the total financial value of a brand. Measuring such value is difficult. However, according to one estimate, the brand value of Coca-Cola is $65 billion, Microsoft is $59 billion, and IBM is $57 billion. Other brands rating among the world's most valuable include GE, Intel, Nokia, Toyota, Disney, McDonald's, and Mercedes-Benz. Samsung is a rapid improver in the rankings.[14]

High brand equity provides a company with many competitive advantages. A powerful brand enjoys a high level of consumer brand awareness and loyalty. Because consumers expect stores to carry the brand, the company has more leverage in bargaining with resellers. Because the brand name carries high credibility, the company can more easily launch line and brand extensions. A powerful brand offers the company some defense against fierce price competition.

Brand valuation –
Samsung has shed its image as a low quality brand to one with inspiring designs and high quality.

Above all, however, a powerful brand forms the basis for building strong and profitable customer relationships. The fundamental asset underlying brand equity is customer equity—the value of the customer relationships that the brand creates. A powerful brand is important, but what it really represents is a profitable set of loyal customers. The proper focus of marketing is building customer equity, with brand management serving as a major marketing tool. Says one marketing expert, "Companies need to be thought of as portfolios of customers and not portfolios of products."[15]

Building Strong Brands

Branding poses challenging decisions to the marketer. **Figure 8.6** shows that the major brand strategy decisions involve brand positioning, brand name selection, brand sponsorship, and brand development.

Figure 8.6
Major brand strategy decisions

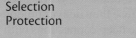

Brand Positioning	**Brand Name Selection**	**Brand Sponsorship**	**Brand Development**
○ Attributes ○ Benefits ○ Beliefs and values	○ Selection ○ Protection	○ Manufacturer's brand ○ Private brand ○ Licensing ○ Co-branding	○ Line extensions ○ Brand extensions ○ Multibrands ○ New brands

Brand Positioning

Marketers need to position their brands clearly in target customers' minds. They can position brands at any of three levels.[16] At the lowest level, they can position the brand on *product attributes*. Thus, The Body Shop marketers can talk about their products' natural, environmentally friendly ingredients, unique scents, and special textures. However, attributes are the least desirable level for brand positioning. Competitors can easily copy attributes. More important, customers are not interested in attributes as such; they are interested in what the attributes will do for them.

A brand can be better positioned by associating its name with a desirable benefit. Thus, The Body Shop can go beyond product ingredients and talk about the resulting beauty benefits, such as clearer skin from its Tea Tree Oil Facial Wash and sun-kissed cheeks from its Bronzing Powder. Some successful brands positioned on benefits are Volvo (safety), FedEx (guaranteed on-time delivery), Nike (performance), and Lexus (quality).

The strongest brands go beyond attribute or benefit positioning. They are positioned on strong *beliefs and values*. These brands pack an emotional wallop. Thus, The Body Shop can talk not just about environmentally friendly ingredients and skin-care benefits, but about how purchasing these products empowers its socially conscious customer to "make up your mind, not just your face."[17] Successful brands engage customers on a deep, emotional level. Brands such as Starbucks, Jollibee, and Godiva rely less on a product's tangible attributes and more on creating warmth, passion, and excitement surrounding a brand.

When positioning a brand, the marketer should establish a mission for the brand and a vision of what the brand must be and do. A brand is the company's promise to deliver a specific set of features, benefits, services, and experiences consistently to the buyers. The brand promise must be simple and honest. A motel, for example, offers clean rooms, low prices, and good service but does not promise expensive furniture or large bathrooms. In contrast, The Grand Hyatt offers luxurious rooms and a truly memorable experience but does not promise low prices.

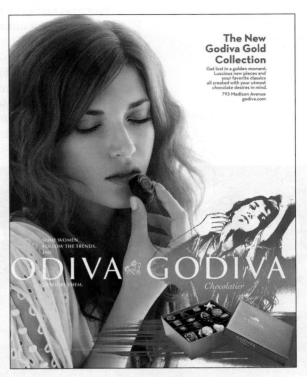

Brand positioning – The strongest brands go beyond attribute or benefit positioning. Godiva engages customers on a deeper level, touching universal emotions.

Brand Name Selection

A good name can add greatly to a product's success. However, finding the best brand name is a difficult task. It begins with a careful review of the product and its benefits, the target market, and proposed marketing strategies. After that, naming a brand becomes part science, part art, and a measure of instinct.

Desirable qualities for a brand name include the following:

- It should suggest something about the product's benefits and qualities. Examples: Walkman, SilkAir, OFF! bug spray.
- It should be easy to pronounce, recognize, and remember. Short names help. Examples: Kao, Za. However, longer ones can sometimes be effective. Examples: BRAND'S® Essence of Chicken, Teenage Mutant Ninja Turtles.
- The brand name should be distinctive. Examples: Qoo, Lexus, Kodak, Oracle.
- It should be extendable: Amazon.com began as an online bookseller but chose a name that allows expansion into other categories.
- The name should translate well into foreign languages. Suzuki sounds like "lose all your money" in Hokkien, a Chinese dialect. Hyatt does not translate easily and confers no meaning in China. So the company used the name "Yue" (悦) which means "Imperial," a character many rich Chinese aspire to be. It then came up with courtly variations to match its sub brands: "Kai Yue" (凯悦), "Jun Yue" (君悦), and "BoYue" (柏悦) for the Regency, Grand, and Park Hyatt respectively.[18]

One example of a company that exercised great consideration in its choice of a Chinese name is Omnicom. Frank Chen, CEO of Interbrand China said, "Omnicom is a great name in English, but difficult to pronounce for non-native English speakers." Hence, Interbrand searched for a Chinese name that would translate well across seven different Chinese dialects as well as capture the spirit of cooperation and the scale of Omnicom's business as implied by its English name. The result was "Hong Meng"(宏盟) which in English means "Magnificent Alliance."[19]

Once chosen, the brand name must be protected. A brand name cannot be registered if it infringes on existing brand names. In China, Starbucks successfully won the copyright battle against a Chinese chain, Shanghai Xingbake Coffee Company (上海星巴克咖啡馆), which copied its logo and name. "Xing Ba Ke" sounded phonetically similar to the pronunciation of Starbucks in Chinese. "Xing" means "star" in Chinese and "Ba Ke" is the phonetical equivalent of "bucks." Shanghai Xingbake's green and white logo was also very similar to the Starbucks design.[20]

Many firms try to build a brand name that will eventually become identified with the product category. Brand names such as Kleenex, Levi's, Scotch Tape, and Ziploc have succeeded in this way. However, their very success may threaten the company's rights to the name. Many originally protected brand names—such as cellophane, aspirin, nylon, kerosene, yo-yo, trampoline, escalator, and thermos—are now generic names that any seller can use. To protect their brands, marketers present them carefully using the word "brand" and the registered trademark symbol, as in "BAND-AID® Brand Adhesive Bandages."

Brand names –
A brand name cannot be registered if it infringes on existing brand names, such as the case between Starbucks and the Shanghai Xingbake Coffee Company.

Brand Sponsorship

A manufacturer has four sponsorship options. The product may be launched as a *manufacturer's brand* (or national brand), as when Hitachi and Apple sell their output under their own manufacturer's brand names. Or the manufacturer may sell to resellers who give it a **private brand** (also called a **store brand** or distributor brand). Although most manufacturers create their own brand names, others market *licensed brands*. Finally, two companies can join forces and co-brand a product.

Private brand (or **store brand**)
A brand created and owned by a reseller of a product or service.

Manufacturer's brands versus private brands

Manufacturers' brands have long dominated the retail scene. In recent times, however, an increasing number of retailers and wholesalers have created their own private brands (or store brands). Hong Kong's Watsons convenience store chain has branded bottled water, swabs, tissue paper, and other sundries under its own name. An ACNielsen survey found that 74 percent of Singaporeans polled found private brands extremely good value for money, while 55 percent found the quality to be at least on par with the big brands.[21]

In the so-called *battle of the brands* between manufacturers' and private brands, retailers have many advantages. They control what products they stock, where they go on the shelf, what prices they charge, and which ones they will feature in local circulars. Most retailers also charge manufacturers *slotting fees*—payments from the manufacturers before the retailers will accept new products and find "slots" for them on their shelves.

Private brands –
Watsons markets a wide range of products under its private brand.

Private brands can be hard to establish and costly to stock and promote. However, they also yield higher profit margins for the reseller. And they give resellers exclusive products that cannot be bought from competitors, resulting in greater store traffic and loyalty. Retailers price their store brands lower than comparable manufacturers' brands, thereby appealing to budget-conscious shoppers, especially in difficult economic times. Many large manufacturers such as Danone, maker of Evian, also make store brands.

To fend off private brands, leading brand marketers must invest in R&D to bring out new brands, new features, and continuous quality improvements. They must design strong advertising programs to maintain high awareness and preference. They must find ways to "partner" with major distributors in a search for distribution economies and improved joint performance.

Licensing

Most manufacturers take years and spend millions to create their own brand names. However, some companies license names or symbols previously created by other manufacturers, names of well-known celebrities, or characters from popular movies and books. For a fee, any of these can provide an instant and proven brand name.

Apparel and accessories sellers pay large royalties to adorn their products—from blouses to ties, and linens to luggage—with the names or initials of well-known fashion innovators such as Calvin Klein, Tommy Hilfiger, Gucci, or Armani. Sellers of children's products attach an almost endless list of character names to clothing, toys, school supplies, linens, dolls, lunch boxes, cereals, and other items. Licensed character names range from classics such as Hello Kitty and Disney to the more recent Powerpuff Girls and Harry Potter characters.

Co-branding

Although companies have been **co-branding** products for many years, there has been a recent resurgence in co-branded products. Co-branding occurs when two established brand names of different companies are used on the same product. For example, Bravo! Foods (which markets Slammers dairy brands) co-branded with MasterFoods (which markets M&Ms, Snickers, Starburst, and many other familiar candy brands) to create Starburst Slammers, 3 Musketeers Slammers, and Milky Way Slammers. American Express co-branded with Singapore Airlines to create a card for the latter's Singapore-based PPS Club members. In most co-branding situations, one company licenses another company's well-known brand to use in combination with its own.

Co-branding offers many advantages. Because each brand dominates in a different category, the combined brands create broader consumer appeal and greater brand equity. Co-branding also allows a company to expand its existing brand into a category it might otherwise have difficulty entering alone.

Co-branding also has limitations. Such relationships usually involve complex legal contracts and licenses. Co-branding partners must carefully coordinate their advertising, sales promotion, and other marketing efforts. Finally, when co-branding, each partner must trust the other will take good care of its brand. For example, consider the marriage between Kmart and the Martha Stewart Everyday housewares brand. When Kmart declared bankruptcy, it cast a shadow on the Martha Stewart brand. In turn, when Martha Stewart was convicted and jailed for illegal financial dealings, it created negative associations for Kmart. Kmart was further embarrassed when Martha Stewart recently struck a major licensing agreement with Macy's, announcing that it would separate from Kmart when the current contract ends in 2009. Thus, as one manager puts it, "Giving away your brand is a lot like giving away your child—you want to make sure everything is perfect."[22]

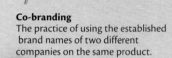

Co-branding
The practice of using the established brand names of two different companies on the same product.

Co-branding –
American Express and Singapore Airlines launched a credit card for SIA's Singapore-based PPS Club members. This card offers an attractive mileage earn rate, bonus miles for spending at selected merchants, and exclusive spa and golf privileges.

Brand Development

A company has four choices when it comes to developing brands (see **Figure 8.7**). It can introduce *line extensions, brand extensions, multibrands,* or *new brands*.

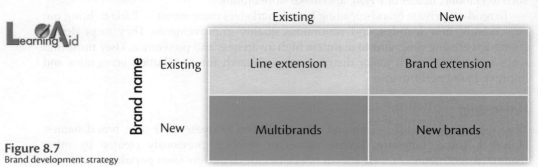

	Existing	New
Existing	Line extension	Brand extension
New	Multibrands	New brands

Figure 8.7
Brand development strategy

Line extensions

Line extensions occur when a company extends existing brand names to new forms, colors, sizes, ingredients, or flavors of an existing product category. The global Virgin brand, with its flamboyant owner and promoter, Richard Branson, seeks to nest all its brands under the global umbrella of the Virgin brand. The brand is built on "image, quality, and prominence." Yoplait introduced several line extensions, including new yogurt flavors, a yogurt smoothie, and a yogurt with added cholesterol reducers. The vast majority of all new-product activity consists of line extensions.

A company might introduce line extensions as a low-cost, low-risk way to introduce new products. Or it might want to meet consumer desires for variety, to use excess capacity, or simply to command more shelf space from resellers. However, line extensions involve some risks. An overextended brand name might lose its specific meaning, or heavily extended brands can cause consumer confusion or frustration.

Line extension –
There are many different types of Coca-Cola available. Visit *www.virtualvender.coca-cola.com* to find out which types are being sold in various regions around the world.

Want a Coke? Not so easy. Pick from more than 16 varieties. In zero-calorie versions alone, Coke comes in three subbrands—Diet Coke, Diet Coke with Splenda, and Coca-Cola Zero. Throw in the flavored and free versions—Diet Cherry Coke, Diet Coke with Lemon, Diet Coke with Lime, Diet Coke Black Cherry Vanilla, and Caffeine-Free Diet Coke—and you reach a dizzying nine diets from Coke. And that doesn't count "mid-calorie" Coca-Cola C2. Each subbrand has its own hype—Diet Coke tells you to "light it up," and Coke Zero allows you to "enjoy Coke-ness with zero calories." And Coca-Cola C2 has "1/2 the carbs, 1/2 the calories, all the great taste." But it's unlikely that many consumers fully appreciate the differences. Instead, the glut of extensions will likely cause what one expert calls "profusion confusion." Laments one Coke consumer, "How many versions of Diet Coke do they need?"[23]

Another risk is that sales of an extension may come at the expense of other items in the line. For example, the original Hershey's Kisses have now morphed into a full line of Kisses, including such morsels as Rich Dark Chocolate Hershey's Kisses, Hershey Kisses Filled with Caramel, Hershey Kisses Filled with Dulce de Leche, and a dozen others. Although all are doing well, the original Hershey's Kiss brand now seems like just another flavor. A line extension works best when it takes sales away from competing brands, not when it "cannibalizes" the company's other items.

Brand extensions

A **brand extension** extends a current brand name to new or modified products in a new category. For example, Kimberly-Clark extended its market-leading Huggies brand from disposable diapers to a full line of toiletries for tots, from shampoos, lotions, and diaper-rash ointments to baby wash, disposable washclothes, and disposable changing pads.

A brand extension gives a new product instant recognition and faster acceptance. It also saves the high advertising costs usually required to build a new brand name. At the same time, a brand extension strategy involves some risk. Brand extensions such as Bic pantyhose, Heinz pet food, and Clorox laundry detergent met early deaths. The extension may confuse the image of the main brand. And if a brand extension fails, it may harm consumer attitudes toward the other products carrying the same brand name.

Further, a brand name may not be appropriate to a particular new product, even if it is well made and satisfying—would you consider buying a Harley-Davidson cake-decorating kit or an Evian water-filled padded bra (both failed)? Companies that are tempted to transfer a brand name must research how well the brand's associations fit the new product.[24]

> **Brand extension**
> Extending an existing brand name to new product categories

Multibrands

Companies often introduce additional brands in the same category. Thus, Procter & Gamble markets many different brands in each of its product categories. Multibranding offers a way to establish different features and appeal to different buying motives. It also allows a company to lock up more reseller shelf space.

A major drawback of multibranding is that each brand might obtain only a small market share, and none may be very profitable. The company may end up spreading its resources over many brands instead of building a few brands to a highly profitable level. These companies should reduce the number of brands they sell in a given category and set up tighter screening procedures for new brands.

Multibrands – Procter & Gamble markets many different brands in each of its product categories, allowing them to establish different features and appeal to different buying motives. (_www.pg.com_)

New brands

A company might believe that the power of its existing brand name is waning and a new brand name is needed. Or it may create a new brand name when it enters a new product category for which none of the company's current brand names are appropriate. For example, Toyota created the separate Scion brand, targeted toward GenY consumers. Japan's Matsushita uses separate names for its different families of consumer electronics products: Panasonic, Technics, JVC, and Quasar, to name just a few.

As with _multibranding,_ offering too many new brands can result in a company spreading its resources too thin. And in some industries, such as consumer packaged goods, consumers and retailers have become concerned that there are already too many brands, with too few differences between them. Thus, Procter & Gamble, Frito-Lay, and other large consumer product marketers are now pursuing megabrand strategies—weeding out weaker brands and focusing their marketing dollars only on brands that can achieve the number-one or number-two market share positions in their categories.

Managing brands – Clothing label Giordano has earned a reputation for quality service by training its employees to be enthusiastic brand builders for the company. (_www.giordano.com.hk_)

Managing Brands

Companies must manage their brands carefully. First, the brand's positioning must be continuously communicated to consumers. Major brand marketers often spend huge amounts on advertising to create brand awareness and to build preference and loyalty. For example, Coca-Cola spends $317 million on its Coca-Cola and Diet Coke brands.[25]

Such advertising campaigns can help to create name recognition, brand knowledge, and maybe even some brand preference. However, brands are not maintained by advertising but by the _brand experience._ Today, customers come to know a brand through a wide range of contacts and touch points. These include advertising, but also personal experience with the brand, word of mouth, company Web pages, and many others

The company must put as much care into managing these touch points as it does into producing its ads. "A brand is a living entity," says former Disney chief executive Michael Eisner, "and it is enriched or undermined cumulatively over time, the product of a thousand small gestures."[26]

The brand's positioning will not take hold fully unless everyone in the company lives the brand. Therefore, the company needs to train its people to be customer centered. Even better, the company should carry on internal brand building to help employees understand and be enthusiastic about the brand promise. Many companies go even further by training and encouraging their distributors and dealers to serve their customers well. Giordano and Singapore Airlines have succeeded in turning their employees into enthusiastic brand builders.

Finally, companies need to periodically audit their brands' strengths and weaknesses.[27] They should ask: Does our brand excel at delivering benefits that consumers truly value? Is the brand properly positioned? Do all of our consumer touch points support the brand's positioning? Do the brand's managers understand what the brand means to consumers? Does the brand receive proper, sustained support? The brand audit may turn up brands that need more support, brands that need to be dropped, or brands that must be rebranded or repositioned because of changing customer preferences or new competitors.

Services Marketing

Service industries vary greatly. *Governments* offer services through courts, employment services, hospitals, military services, police and fire departments, postal services, and schools. *Private not-for-profit organizations* offer services through museums, charities, churches, colleges, foundations, and hospitals. A large number of *business organizations* offer services—airlines, banks, hotels, insurance companies, consulting firms, medical and legal practices, entertainment companies, real-estate firms, retailers, and others.

Nature And Characteristics Of A Service

A company must consider four special service characteristics when designing marketing programs: *intangibility, inseparability, variability,* and *perishability* (see **Figure 8.8**).

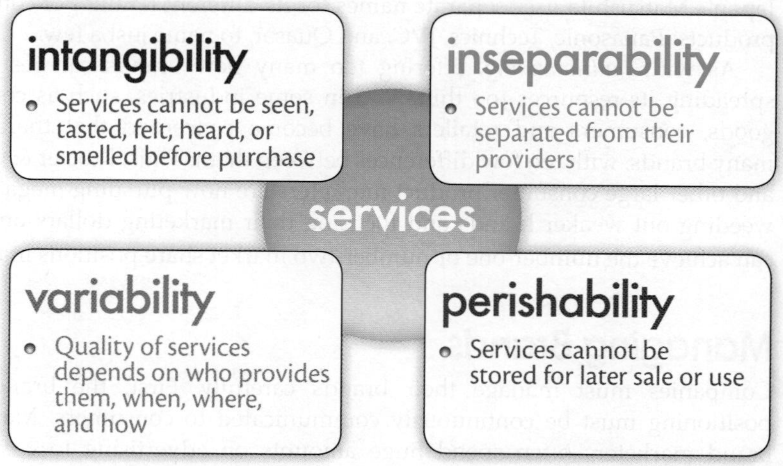

intangibility
- Services cannot be seen, tasted, felt, heard, or smelled before purchase

inseparability
- Services cannot be separated from their providers

services

variability
- Quality of services depends on who provides them, when, where, and how

perishability
- Services cannot be stored for later sale or use

Figure 8.8
Four service characteristics

Service intangibility
A major characteristic of services—they cannot be seen, tasted, felt, heard, or smelled before they are bought.

Service intangibility means that services cannot be seen, tasted, felt, heard, or smelled before they are bought. For example, people undergoing cosmetic surgery cannot see the result before the purchase. Airline passengers have nothing but a ticket and the promise that they and their luggage will arrive safely at the intended destination, hopefully at the same time. To reduce uncertainty, buyers look for "signals" of service quality. They draw conclusions about quality from the place, people, price, equipment, and communications that they can see.

Therefore, the service provider's task is to make the service tangible in one or more ways and to send the right signals about quality. One analyst calls this *evidence management*, in which the service organization presents its customers with organized, honest evidence of its capabilities. The Mayo Clinic practices good evidence management:[28]

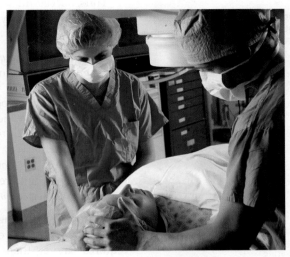

When it comes to hospitals, it's very hard for the average patient to judge the quality of the "product." So, most consumers look for evidence of competence, caring, and integrity. By carefully managing a set of visual and experiential clues, The Mayo Clinic offers patients and their families concrete evidence of its strengths and values. For example, clinic staff are trained to act in a way that clearly signals its patient-first focus. "My doctor calls me at home to check on how I am doing," marvels one patient. "She wants to work with what is best for my schedule." Mayo's physical facilities have been carefully designed to relieve stress, offer a place of refuge, create positive distractions, convey caring and respect, signal competence, accommodate families, and make it easy to find your way around. The result? Exceptionally positive word of mouth and abiding customer loyalty, which have allowed Mayo Clinic to build what is arguably the most powerful brand in health care—with very little advertising.

The service provider's task is to send the right signals about quality. To build customer loyalty, doctors and nurses should act in a way that signals a patient-first focus.

Physical goods are produced, then stored, later sold, and still later consumed. In contrast, services are first sold, then produced and consumed at the same time. **Service inseparability** means that services cannot be separated from their providers, whether the providers are people or machines. If a service employee provides the service, then the employee becomes a part of the service. Because the customer is also present as the service is produced, *provider-customer interaction* is a special feature of services marketing. Both the provider and the customer affect the service outcome.

Service variability means that the quality of services depends on who provides them as well as when, where, and how they are provided. For example, some hotels—say, Shangri-La—have reputations for providing better service than others. Still, within a given Shangri-La hotel, one registration-counter employee may be cheerful and efficient, whereas another may be unpleasant and slow. Even the quality of a single Shangri-La employee's service varies according to his or her energy and frame of mind at the time of each customer encounter.

Service perishability means that services cannot be stored for later sale or use. Some doctors charge patients for missed appointments because the service value existed only at that point and disappeared when the patient did not show up. When demand fluctuates, service firms often have difficult problems. For example, because of rush-hour demand, public transportation companies have to own much more equipment than they would if demand were even throughout the day. Thus, service firms often design strategies for producing a better match between demand and supply. Hotels and resorts charge lower prices in the off-season to attract more guests. And restaurants hire part-time employees to serve during peak periods.

Service inseparability
A major characteristic of services—they are produced and consumed at the same time and cannot be separated from their providers.

Service variability
A major characteristic of services—their quality may vary greatly, depending on who provides them and when, where, and how.

Service perishability
A major characteristic of services—they cannot be stored for later sale or use.

Marketing Strategies For Service Firms

Just like manufacturing businesses, good service firms use marketing to position themselves strongly in chosen target markets. The Ritz-Carlton Hotels positions itself as offering a memorable experience that "enlivens the senses, instills well-being, and fulfills even the unexpressed wishes and needs of our guests." These and other service firms establish their positions through traditional marketing mix activities. However, because services differ from tangible products, they often require additional marketing approaches.

The Service-Profit Chain

In a service business, the customer and front-line service employee *interact* to create the service. Effective interaction, in turn, depends on the skills of front-line service employees and on the support processes backing these employees.

Thus, successful service companies focus their attention on *both* their customers and their employees. They understand the **service-profit chain**, which links service firm profits with employee and customer satisfaction. This chain consists of five links:[28]

- *Internal service quality:* superior employee selection and training, a quality work environment, and strong support for those dealing with customers, which results in …
- *Satisfied and productive service employees:* more satisfied, loyal, and hardworking employees, which results in …
- *Greater service value:* more effective and efficient customer value creation and service delivery, which results in …
- *Satisfied and loyal customers:* satisfied customers who remain loyal, repeat purchase, and refer other customers, which results in …
- *Healthy service profits and growth:* superior service firm performance.

Therefore, reaching service profits and growth goals begins with taking care of those who take care of customers (see **Real Marketing**). Service marketing requires more than just traditional external marketing using the Four Ps. **Figure 8.9** shows that service marketing also requires *internal marketing* and *interactive marketing*. **Internal marketing** means that the service firm must orient and motivate its customer-contact employees and supporting-service people to work as a *team* to provide customer satisfaction. Marketers must get everyone in the organization to be customer centered. In fact, internal marketing must *precede* external marketing. For example, The Ritz-Carlton orients its employees carefully, instills in them a sense of pride, and motivates them by recognizing and rewarding outstanding service deeds.

Service-profit chain
The chain that links service firm profits with employee and customer satisfaction.

Internal marketing
Orienting and motivating customer-contact employees and the supporting service people to work as a team to provide customer satisfaction.

Figure 8.9
Three types of service marketing

Interactive marketing
Training service employees in the fine art of interacting with customers to satisfy their needs.

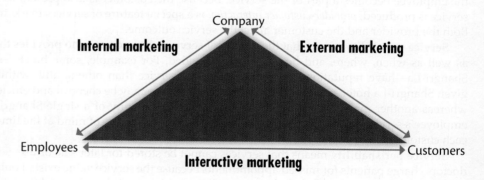

Interactive marketing means that service quality depends heavily on the quality of the buyer-seller interaction during the service encounter. In product marketing, product quality often depends little on how the product is obtained. But in services marketing, service quality depends on both the service deliverer and the quality of the delivery. Service marketers, therefore, have to master interactive marketing skills. Thus, Ritz-Carlton selects only "people who care about people" and instructs them carefully in the fine art of interacting with customers to satisfy their every need.

In today's marketplace, companies must know how to deliver interactions that are not only "high-touch" but also "high-tech." For example, customers can log onto the Charles Schwab Web site (_www.schwab.com_) and access account information, investment research, real-time quotes, after-hours trading, and the Schwab learning center. They can also participate in live online events and chat online with customer service representatives. Customers seeking more-personal interactions can contact service reps by phone or visit a local Schwab branch office. Thus, Schwab has mastered interactive marketing at all three levels—calls, clicks, *and* visits.

Today, as competition and costs increase, and as productivity and quality decrease, more service marketing sophistication is needed. Service companies face three major marketing tasks: They want to increase their *service differentiation, service quality,* and *service productivity.*

Managing Service Differentiation

In these days of intense price competition, service marketers often complain about the difficulty of differentiating their services from those of competitors. To the extent that customers view the services of different providers as similar, they care less about the provider than the price.

The solution to price competition is to develop a differentiated offer, delivery, and image. The *offer* can include innovative features that set one company's offer apart from competitors' offers. Some hotels offer car-rental, banking, and business-center services in their lobbies and free high-speed Internet connections in their rooms. Airlines differentiate their offers through frequent-flyer award programs and special services. For example, Economy Class passengers aboard Singapore Airlines enjoy audio-video on demand with more than 1,000 entertainment options. Singapore Airlines' new Business Class seat in the A380, A340-500 and B777-300ER is almost 50 percent wider than most products in this class. All passengers are offered World Gourmet Cuisine created by Singapore Airlines' International Culinary Panel, while First Class, Business Class, and Singapore Airlines Suites passengers enjoy soft furnishings designed exclusively for the airline by Givenchy.

Singapore Airlines offers all its passengers a wide variety of special services, ranging from more than 1,000 inflight entertainment options to gourmet cuisine prepared by world-class chefs.
(*www.singaporeair.com*)

Service companies can differentiate their service *delivery* by having more able and reliable customer-contact people, by developing a superior physical environment in which the service product is delivered or by designing a superior delivery process. For example, many grocery chains now offer online shopping and home delivery as a better way to shop than having to drive, park, wait in line, and tote groceries home.

Finally, service companies also can work on differentiating their *images* through symbols and branding. Well-known service symbols include Singapore Airlines' bird, Merrill Lynch's bull, and McDonald's Golden Arches.

Service symbols –
Among the well-known service symbols known globally is Merrill Lynch's bull.

Managing Service Quality

A service firm can differentiate itself by delivering consistently higher quality than its competitors do. Like manufacturers, most service industries have joined the customer-driven quality movement. And like product marketers, service providers need to identify what target customers expect concerning service quality.

Unfortunately, service quality is harder to define and judge than product quality. For instance, it is harder to agree on the quality of a haircut than on the quality of a hair dryer. Customer retention is perhaps the best measure of quality—a service firm's ability to hang onto its customers depends on how consistently it delivers value to them.

Top service companies set high service-quality standards. They watch service performance closely, both their own and that of competitors. They do not settle for merely good service; they aim for 100 percent defect-free service. A 98 percent performance standard may sound good, but using this standard, UPS would lose or misdirect 296,000 packages each day.[30]

Unlike product manufacturers who can adjust their machinery and inputs until everything is perfect, service quality will always vary, depending on the interactions between employees and customers. As hard as they try, even the best companies will have an occasional late delivery, burned steak, or grumpy employee. However, good *service recovery* can turn angry customers into loyal ones. In fact, good recovery can win more customer purchasing and loyalty than if things had gone well in the first place. Therefore,

REAL MARKETING

The Ritz-Carlton: Taking Care of Those Who Take Care of Customers

The Ritz-Carlton, a chain of luxury hotels renowned for outstanding service, caters to the top 5 percent of corporate and leisure travelers. The company's Credo sets lofty customer-service goals: "The Ritz-Carlton Hotel is a place where the genuine care and comfort of our guests is our highest mission.... The Ritz-Carlton experience enlivens the senses, instills well-being, and fulfills even the unexpressed wishes and needs of our guests."

The Credo is more than just words— The Ritz-Carlton delivers on its promises. Some 95 percent of departing guests report that they've had a truly memorable experience. In fact, at The Ritz-Carlton, exceptional service encounters have become almost commonplace. Take the experiences of Nancy and Harvey Heffner of Manhattan, who stayed at the Ritz-Carlton Naples, in Florida (recently rated the best hotel in the U.S. and fourth best in the world, by *Travel +*

Leisure magazine): "The hotel is elegant and beautiful," Mrs. Heffner said, "but more important is the beauty expressed by the staff. They can't do enough to please you." When the couple's son became sick last year in Naples, the hotel staff brought him hot tea with honey at all hours of the night, she said. When Mr. Heffner had to fly home on business for a day and his return flight was delayed, a driver for the hotel waited in the lobby most of the night.

Such personal, high-quality service has also made The Ritz-Carlton a favorite among conventioneers For six straight years, the luxury hotel topped *Business Travel New's* Top U.S. Hotel Chain Survey of business travel buyers. "They not only treat us like kings when we hold our top-level meetings in their hotels, but we just never get any complaints," comments one convention planner.

Since its incorporation in 1983, The Ritz-Carlton has received virtually every major award that the hospitality industry bestows. In addition, it's the only hotel company ever to win the prestigious Malcolm Baldrige National Quality Award and one of only two companies from any industry to win the award twice. The recent *Consumer Reports* Hotels issue ranked The Ritz-Carlton Hotel Company top luxury hotel company in all areas, including value, service, upkeep, and companies should take steps not only to provide good service every time but also to recover from service mistakes when they occur.

The first step is to *empower* front-line service employees—to give them the authority, responsibility, and incentives they need to recognize, care about, and tend to customer needs. At Marriott, for example, well-trained employees are given the authority to do whatever it takes, on the spot, to keep guests happy. They are also expected to help management ferret out the cause of guests' problems and to inform managers of ways to improve overall hotel service and guests' comfort.

problem resolution. More than 90 percent of The Ritz-Carlton's customers return. Despite its high room rates, the chain enjoys a 70 percent occupancy rate, almost nine points above the industry average.

Most of the responsibility for keeping guests satisfied falls on The Ritz–Carlton'scustomercontact employees. Thus, the hotel chain strives to "rigorously even fanatically—select and train employees, instill pride, and compensate generously," says an industry insider. "We want only people who care about people," notes the company's vice president of quality. Once selected, employees are given intensive customer training. New employees attend a two-day orientation, in which top management drums into them the 12 Ritz-Carlton "Service Values." Service Value number one: "I build strong relationships and create Ritz-Carlton guests for life."

Employees are taught to do everything they can never to lose a guest. "There's no negotiating at The Ritz-Carlton when it comes to solving customer problems," says the quality executive. Staffs learn that anyone who receives a customer complaint owns that complaint until it's resolved (Ritz-Carlton Service Value number six). They are trained to drop whatever they're doing to help a customer—whatever their department. The Ritz-Carlton employees are empowered to handle problems on the spot, without consulting higher-ups. Each employee can spend up to $2,000 to redress a guest grievance. And each is allowed to break from his or her routine

for as long as needed to make a guest happy. Thus, while competitors are still reading guest comment cards to learn about customer problems, The Ritz-Carlton has already resolved them.

The Ritz-Carlton instills a sense of pride in its employees. "You serve," they are told, "but you are not servants." The company motto states, "We are ladies and gentlemen serving ladies and gentlemen." Employees understand their role in The Ritz-Carlton's success. "We might not be able to afford a hotel like this," says employee Tammy Patton, "but we can make it so people who can afford it will want to keep coming here." As the general manager of The Ritz-Carlton Naples puts it, "When you invite guests to your house, you want everything to be perfect."

The Ritz-Carlton recognizes and rewards employees who perform outstanding service. Under its 5-Star Awards program, winners receive plaques at dinners celebrating their achievements. For on-the-spot recognition, managers award Gold Standard Coupons, redeemable for items in the gift shop and free weekend stays at the hotel. The Ritz-Carlton further motivates its employees with events such as Super Sports Day, an employee talent show, luncheons celebrating employment anniversaries and birthdays, a family picnic, and special themes in employee dining rooms. As a result, The Ritz-Carlton's employees appear to be just as satisfied as its customers. Employee turnover is under 25 percent a year, compared with 44 percent at other luxury hotels.

The Ritz-Carlton's success is based on a simple philosophy: To take care of customers, you must first take care of those who take care of customers. Satisfied employees deliver high service value, which then creates satisfied customers. Satisfied customers, in turn, create sales and profits for the company.

Sources:
Quotes and other information from Duff McDonald, "Roll Out the Blue Carpet," *Business 2.0*, May 2004, pp. 53–54; Marshall Krantz, "Buyers Say Four Seasons Is Most Luxurious," *Meeting News*, May 9, 2005, pp. 1–3; Edwin McDowell, "Ritz-Carlton's Keys to Good Service," New York Times, March 31, 1993, p. D1; "The Ritz-Carlton, Half Moon Bay," Successful Meetings, November 2001, p.40; Bruce Serlen, "Ritz Carlton Retains Hold on Corporate Deluxe Buyers," *Business Travel News*, February7, 2005, pp.15–17; Peter Sanders, "Takin' Off the Ritz—A Tad," *Wall Street Journal*, June 23, 2006, p. B1; and The Ritz Carlton Web site at www.ritzcarlton.com, August 2006.

Managing Service Productivity

With their costs rising rapidly, service firms are under great pressure to increase service productivity. They can do so in several ways. They can train current employees better or hire new ones who will work harder or more skillfully. Or they can increase the quantity of their service by giving up some quality. The provider can "industrialize the service" by adding equipment and standardizing production, as in McDonald's assembly-line approach to fast-food retailing. Finally, the service provider can harness the power of technology. Although we often think of technology's power to save time and costs in manufacturing companies, it also has great—and often untapped—potential to make service workers more productive.

However, companies must avoid pushing productivity so hard that doing so reduces quality. Attempts to industrialize a service or to cut costs can make a service company more efficient in the short run. But they can also reduce its longer-run ability to innovate, maintain service quality, or respond to consumer needs and desires. Many airlines are learning this lesson the hard way as they attempt to streamline and economize in the face of rising costs.

Managing service productivity –
In the face of rising costs, airlines need to balance its customers' needs while economizing. Some airlines that take cost-cutting too far run the risk of passengers.

Northwest Airlines has stopped offering free magazines, pillows, movies, and even minibags of pretzels on its domestic flights. Passengers can still get an in-flight snack of raisins and nuts, but it costs $1. The airline is also charging a $15 fee for a roomier seat on the aisle or in an exit row. Combine that with higher fares and a sharply curtailed schedule, it's little wonder that flyers rate Northwest last among major U.S. airlines. "If at all possible, I don't fly Northwest," says one veteran traveler. "I have found a lack of interest in the customer." A services marketing expert agrees, "The upshot is that some companies, in their passion to drive down costs, have mangled their relationships with customers."[31]

Thus, in attempting to improve service productivity, companies must be mindful of how they create and deliver customer value. In short, they should be careful not to take the "service" out of service.

REVIEWING THE CONCEPTS

A product is more than a simple set of tangible features. In fact, many market offerings consist of combinations of both tangible goods and services, ranging from pure tangible goods at one extreme to pure services at the other. Each product or service offered to customers can be viewed on three levels. The core product consists of the core problem-solving benefits that consumers seek when they buy a product. The actual product exists around the core and includes the quality level, features, design, brand name, and packaging. The augmented product is the actual product plus the various services and benefits offered with it, such as warranty, free delivery, installation, and maintenance.

1 Define product and the major classifications of products and services.

Broadly defined, a product is anything that can be offered to a market for attention, acquisition, use, or consumption that might satisfy a want or need. Products include physical objects but also services, events, persons, places, organizations, ideas, or mixes of these entities. Services are products that consist of activities, benefits, or satisfactions offered for sale that are essentially intangible, such asbanking, hotel, tax preparation, and home-repair services.

Products and services fall into two broad classes based on the types of consumers that use them. Consumer products—those bought by final consumers—are usually classified according to consumer shopping habits (convenience products, shopping products, specialty products, and unsought products). Industrial products—purchased for further processing or for use in conducting a business—include materials and parts, capital items, and supplies and services. Other marketable entities—such as organizations, persons, places, and ideas—can also be thought of as products.

2 Describe the decisions companies make regarding their individual products and services, product lines, and product mixes.

Individual product decisions involve product attributes, branding, packaging, labeling, and product support services. Product attribute decisions involve product quality, features, and style and design. Branding decisions include selecting a brand name and developing a brand strategy. Packaging provides many key benefits, such as protection, economy, convenience, and promotion. Package decisions often include designing labels, which identify, describe, and possibly promote the product. Companies also develop product support services that enhance customer service and satisfaction and safeguard against competitors.

Most companies produce a product line rather than a single product. A product line is a group of products that are related in function, customer-purchase needs, or distribution channels. Line stretching involves extending a line downward, upward, or in both directions to occupy a gap that might otherwise by filled by a competitor. In contrast, line filling involves adding items within the present range of the line. All product lines and items offered to customers by a particular seller make up the product mix. The mix can be described by four dimensions: width, length, depth, and consistency.

These dimensions are the tools for developing the company's product strategy.

3 Discuss branding strategy—the decisions companies make in building and managing their brands.

Some analysts see brands as the major enduring asset of a company. Brands are more than just names and symbols—they embody everything that the product or service means to consumers. Brand equity is the positive differential effect that knowing the brand name has on customer response to the product or service. A brand with strong brand equity is a very valuable asset.

In building brands, companies need to make decisions about brand positioning, brand name selection, brand sponsorship, and brand development. The most powerful brand positioning builds around strong consumer beliefs and values. Brand name selection involves finding the best brand name based on a careful review of product benefits, the target market, and proposed marketing strategies. A manufacturer has four brand sponsorship options: it can launch a manufacturer's brand (or national brand), sell to resellers who use a private brand, market licensed brands, or join forces with another company to co-brand a product. A company also has four choices when it comes to developing brands. It can introduce line extensions, brand extensions, multibrands, or new brands.

Companies must build and manage their brands carefully. The brand's positioning must be continuously communicated to consumers. Advertising can help. However, brands are not maintained by advertising but by the brand experience. Customers come to know a brand through a wide range of contacts and interactions. The company must put as much care into managing these touch points as it does into producing its ads. Thus, managing a company's brand assets can no longer be left only to brand managers. Some companies are now setting up brand asset management teams to manage their major brands. Finally, companies must periodically audit their brands' strengths and weaknesses. In some cases, brands may need to be repositioned because of changing customer preferences or new competitors.

4 Identify the four characteristics that affect the marketing of a service and the additional marketing considerations that services require.

Services are characterized by four key characteristics: they are intangible, inseparable, variable, and perishable. Each characteristic poses problems and marketing requirements. Marketers work to find ways to make the service more tangible, to increase the productivity of providers who are inseparable from their products, to standardize the quality in the face of variability, and to improve demand movements and supply capacities in the face of service perishability.

Good service companies focus attention on both customers and employees. They understand the service-profit chain, which links service firm profits with employee and customer satisfaction. Services marketing strategy calls not only for external marketing but also for internal marketing to motivate employees and interactive marketing to create service delivery skills among service providers. To succeed, service marketers must create competitive differentiation, offer high service quality, and find ways to increase service productivity.

REVIEWING THE KEY TERMS

Brand 206
Brand equity 212
Brand extension 217
Co-branding 215
Consumer product 200
Convenience product 202
Industrial product 202
Interactive marketing 220
Internal marketing 220
Line extension 215
Packaging 207
Private brand (or store brand) 214
Product 200

Product line 208
Product mix (or product portfolio) 210
Product quality 205
Service 200
Service inseparability 219
Service intangibility 218
Service perishability 219
Service-profit chain 220
Service variability 219
Shopping product 202
Social marketing 205
Specialty product 202
Unsought product 202

DISCUSSING THE CONCEPTS

1. Is Microsoft's Windows Vista operating software a product or a service? Describe the core, actual, and augmented levels of this software offering.

2. Classify the following consumer products as convenience, shopping, specialty, or unsought goods: a laptop computer, a surgeon, automobile tires.

3. What is a brand? Describe the value of branding for both the buyer and seller.

4. Brand positioning can occur on three levels. How is Giordano positioned on these three levels?

5. What are the four brand sponsorship options a manufacturer faces? How does a manufacturer decide which one makes the most sense for its products?

6. Merrill Lynch is one of the world's leading financial services and advisory companies (see www.ml.com) Do Merrill Lynch's financial advising activities meet the four special characteristics of a service? Explain.

APPLYING THE CONCEPTS

1. Using the six qualities that a good brand name should possess, create a brand name for a personal care product that has the following positioning statement: "Intended for X-Games sports participants and enthusiasts, _____ is a deodorant that combines effective odor protection with an enduring and seductive fragrance that will enhance your romantic fortunes."

2. You are the marketing director for an inline skate manufacturer that holds 45 percent of the men's 18 to 29 year-old segment. Using the four brand development strategies discussed in the chapter, give examples of products you could add to your brand.

3. Bumrungrad Hospital (www.bumrungrad.com) has been a leading private hospital in Bangkok, Thailand for many years. Describe how the service-profit chain is essential for this organization's success.

FOCUS ON TECHNOLOGY

For decades, consumers have dreamed of owning home robots. Industry uses many production-line robots, and many companies are now working on products for the consumer. Some basic products currently available for consumers include navigation systems, home security robots, cleaning tools such as robotic vacuums, and toys that provide some elementary robotic functions. Several companies are working on the next step—humanoid robots that can serve consumers. In designing these products, companies must determine what features are most desirable to consumers and the benefits their products can offer.

Two leading products are Honda's Asimo and Sony's QRIO. The products, both in the development stage, will offer companionship to humans. Honda's Asimo stands four feet tall and can walk smoothly on its two feet in any direction, including slopes and steps. It has voice and visual recognition, which allows it to greet people by name and follow basic

commands. In Japan, Asimo is now being used by museums as a guide and by some high-tech companies to greet visitors. It is not yet available for purchase in the U.S. Sony's QRIO has many of the same features. Like Honda, Sony is developing the product to make people's lives easier. In addition, Sony's wants to make life fun and happy and to provide a navigator as the world becomes more complex. See the corporate Web sites for more information on Asimo (*world.honda.com/ASIMO/*) and QRIO (*www.sony.net/SonyInfo/QRIO/*).

1. Explain the core, actual, and augmented levels of a home robot.

2. When these products are available, how might corporate branding and the brand name of the robot tie into the consumer's purchase decision? Would you keep or change the current names?

3. How must Honda and Sony consider services marketing when they eventually sell this product to end

FOCUS ON ETHICS

Under 21, with no income? You can now own a credit card in Singapore with a S$500 (US$330) credit limit. Following the easing of restrictions by the country's central bank in 2007, several banks have launched credit cards targeting young consumers. For example, Citibank's Clear Card targets the 450,000 people aged between 18 and 35, although applicants under 21 require parental consent. Its marketing director of credit cards said the limit set is a "good start for those who are new to credit."

To prevent debt building up, Citibank will deny access for first-time users who miss any minimum payment. It is also charging 28 percent annual interest on rollover balances, higher than the 24 percent on other cards. An annual fee of S$28 (US$19), or 5.6 percent of the credit limit, would also be imposed. To mitigate risk, Citibank put in place internal guidelines and credit assessments which could involve commonly used litigation or bankruptcy checks. So there is no need for income documents, said the bank. Profitability is expected to be limited. Citibank's country marketing director said the focus was to cultivate a long-term relationship with customers. Citibank may consider offering more products to 900,000 potential customers who earn below S$30,000 (US$20,000) a year.

Some question the marketing of such cards. Conservatives cite the wisdom of issuing a credit card to a jobless person and then hoping that he or his parents would exercise sufficient discipline to keep spending within affordable limits. They wonder how credit worthiness of young applicants could be assessed effectively if they had no jobs. They question whether the interest rate and annual fee charged was too high. Others asked if such cards were needed at all, pointing to the availability of ATM and supplementary credit cards, which were safer barriers against overspending. They feared that students may end up in debt before they graduated and young adults before they started a family.[32]

1. Explain the product line reasoning behind Citibank's adding credit cards targeting the young.

2. How could Citibank address the concerns raised about this initiative?

3. Local banks in Singapore such as OCBC and UOB have also launched such credit cards. OCBC targets tertiary students, while UOB extended its dining privileges and Smart Money program, which currently apply to existing cardholders, to individuals with incomes below S$30,000 (US$20,000). Compare their product strategy to Citibank's strategy.

VIDEO CASE

Accenture

Remember Andersen Consulting? One of the world's largest consulting firms, Andersen Consulting enjoyed tremendous name recognition and worked with some of the largest companies worldwide, including 87 of the Fortune Global 100. But, today, you're probably more familiar with the company's new name, Accenture. Accenture is a global management consulting, technology services, and outsourcing company. In 2001, a court ruling forced the company to change its name, jeopardizing the firm's brand equity. Rather than viewing the name change as a setback, Accenture's marketing executives used it as an opportunity to reposition the company and reintroduce it to customers.

The name Accenture, a combination of the words accent and future, was suggested by an Andersen employee and was received with considerable excitement by customers. Some

skeptics wondered about the effectiveness of a "made-up" name that had no real meaning. However, others saw it as an opportunity to start fresh and create new positioning with a name that carried no previous baggage. Today, Accenture's annual revenues total more than $15 billion. Perhaps more important, the new company enjoys the same or even more brand recognition and brand equity than it did under its old name.

After viewing the video featuring Accenture, answer the following questions about branding strategy.

1. How did Accenture transfer the brand equity from its original name, Andersen Consulting, to the new company name?

2. Evaluate the Accenture brand name using the six criteria detailed in the chapter.

3. How did Accenture use the requirement to rename the company as an opportunity to reposition itself?

⊞ COMPANY CASE

Shanghai Tang: China's First Great Luxury Brand?

One rainy October night in 2002 in a 1,300-year-old Confucian temple in Shanghai, journalists from three continents, local bigwigs, style-conscious Chinese yuppies (Chuppies), and three Chinese soccer stars gathered to watch a fashion show. Raphael le Masne de Chermont, CEO of the Chinese lifestyle brand Shanghai Tang, is unconcerned about the weather and its possibly detrimental effects on 46 expensive garments which were about to make their way down a slippery red lacquered catwalk. The lights go up, the beat of "Tainted Love" fills the temple, and the parade of Chinese models begins. On display is an array of sumptuous clothing: Brocaded parkas with fur trimmed hoods, a $49,000 chinchilla-lined silk coat, silk jackets topstitched in cloud patterns, tweed skirts festooned with crystals in a dragon-scale design, and cardigans embellished with jade. When the final outfit, a full-length shearling coat encrusted with Swarovski crystals, is shown, the crowd applauds de Chermont and his creative director Joanne Ooi. The glitzy event was a gamble for Shanghai Tang, which has had a rocky history since its launch.

Birth of a Brand

Shanghai Tang was founded in 1994 by British-educated David Tang in Hong Kong. It was a positioned originally as a custom-tailoring business leveraging on the talents of Shanghainese tailors. In 1996, anticipating a robust market selling Chinese souvenirs to well-heeled tourists attracted by the handover of the city to China, Tang expanded into ready-to-wear. At precisely 6.18pm on November 1997, a time chosen by a feng shui (geomancy) master, Shanghai Tang opened a palatial outlet on Madison Avenue in New York just opposite Barneys, welcoming the city's glitterati for a bash that featured roast suckling pig, lion dancers, and Fergie, the Duchess of York. It was such a hot ticket that many party goers couldn't get in, as the NYPD, citing New York's tough fire codes, turned them away.

However, the fashion world at the time seemed mystified about whether Tang was launching a new era of global fashion or peddling assorted Chinese merchandise. Nineteen months later, it was clear that Tang had miscalculated American's appetite for expensive Chinese fashion, silver rice bowls, and painted lanterns. "It was not the ideal way to start a business. But unlike Europe, America is tolerant of mistakes as long as you learn. And we have learned from this huge mistake. We needed to be more modern," concedes de Chermont.

The lessons from the New York disaster were clear: To compete in the high-end fashion business, you need a continuous array of fresh collections to keep customers coming back. Clothes must be wearable and relevant to modern lives, not costumey designs. And you need to know your market before you make a big real-estate bet, particularly in the most expensive cities in the world.

Shanghai Tang moved to a smaller outlet farther up Madison Avenue, and rethought its marketing strategy. Back in Hong Kong, mired in the Asian financial crisis, things weren't going well either. By the time de Chermont was hired in 2001, revenue stagnated. The SARS hit in 2002, effectively shutting down business in Hong Kong for six months.

Shanghai Tang also lost market share to rivals including Ooi, who opened her outlet across from its flagship store on Pedder Street in Hong Kong's Central District. China was chic, and international fashion editors loved *qi pao* dresses. "I thought I'd launch my own ready-to-wear line based on the idea of innovating this iconic symbol," said 37-year-old Singapore-born Ooi, an Asian American with a law degree. "To underscore my point, I even made one *qi pao* out of African kente cloth and put it in my window. I thought I would eat Shanghai Tang for lunch." However, personal problems led Ooi to seek a new life.

A Brand Reborn

Enter de Chermont, who met Ooi through a headhunter friend. Both realized they shared a passion for an authentic Chinese luxury brand and the need for constant innovation in the fashion industry. Ooi surveyed Shanghai Tang's outlets and concluded, "It's an overpriced Chinese emporium that has no credibility with local Chinese people, let alone with fashion people. Its very narrow market is high-end tourists. It's a once-in-a-lifetime destination shopping experience, a kind of fashion Disneyland. Plus, it's unwearable and eccentric." de Chermont offered her the job of marketing and creative director.

Both worked on repositioning Shanghai Tang. They believed the label had to be modern and relevant. It couldn't be kitschy. It had to be luxurious, since prestige is more important in the Asian market than creativity. They decided to focus on women's ready-to-wear, since that was likely to be the highest profile part of the line. For a year, they launched collections that over-corrected the problem. The clothes were fashion forward but still out of touch with the market. "The brand had no depth, no sincerity, no differentiation," Ooi concedes.

Then Ooi hit on an idea: Each collection would reflect a China-related theme. The fall/winter 2003 collection, inspired by the traditional costumes of a Chinese minority group called the Miao, came first. It outsold the two previous collections. A strategy was born. Ooi now roams China, visiting antique markets, art galleries, museums, and historic sites, making notes, sketches, and lists. She reads Chinese history and stays abreast of Chinese pop culture. Twice a year, she defines a theme for the next season's collection and emails the concept brief to 16 designers and consultants worldwide. It specifies the collection's intellectual underpinnings and suggests various elements to be incorporated into the design.

For example, the theme of the fall/winter 2005 collection, Beijing's Forbidden City, had design motifs which included elements such as symbols from the emperors' robes and embellishments fit for an imperial court. For the spring/ summer 2006 collection, the theme was contemporary Chinese art. Chinese artists were commissioned to create designs and students of China's most prestigious art academy created artworks based on fabrics from the collection. Ooi's role is to gather, distill, disseminate, and synthesize sketches from designers in Paris, London, New York, and China. "I allow the designers to pollinate themselves. The trick is to make it look like it all came from the same person," she says.

Local Dream, Global Ambition

As China enters the modern economic market, it has gone from being a low-cost producer to the purchaser of big name brands like Lenovo's acquisition of IBM's PC division. The third phase will be for China to create its own brands, becoming a center of design and innovation, capable of launching products that can compete in quality, style, and prestige with Western offerings. "The opportunity for Shanghai Tang right now is huge," says David Melancon, North American president of brand strategy firm FutureBrand. "They could be the first big luxury brand out of Asia." And in it, too. While the luxury market is already big at $168 billion a year, according to Bain & Co, and growing at 7 percent annually, it is developing even faster in China. By end-2004, there were over 236,000 mainland millionaires, compared to zero 25 years ago. Patrizio Bertelli, CEO of Prada, estimates that China could overtake the U.S. as a market for luxury goods by 2020.

The winds of fashion seem to be blowing in Shanghai Tang's direction. "Asian fusion is the top of the style wave," says Michael Silverstein of the Boston Consulting Group. That puts Shanghai Tang in a fashion sweet spot. "What Shanghai Tang does is translate two cultures," says de Chermont. Early signs show that the strategy is working. Shanghai Tang's New York store's revenues were up 50 percent in 2005. Overall, the company grew 40 percent in 2005, mostly in Asia, home to 70 percent of its stores. And it's profitable, though not quite yet in the U.S.

This success has led to more ambitious expansion plans away from its Asian stronghold. Shanghai Tang aims to launch five stores a year worldwide. As it emerges on the world stage, though, it must pull off a delicate balancing act: It must create a look that's both Chinese and international, authentic yet sophisticated enough for a global audience. Too much Asian kitsch, and it's dead.

Questions For Discussion

1. What are the core, actual, and augmented product benefits of Shanghai Tang?
2. What are the sources of brand equity for Shanghai Tang?
3. What targeting and positioning would you recommend for Shanghai Tang in the future?
4. Evaluate Shanghai Tang's global expansion plans.

Source:
Linda Tischler, "The Gucci Killers," *Fast Company*, January 2006, accessed on July 18, 2007 from www.fastcompany.com magazine/102/shanghai.

Objectives

After studying this chapter, you should be able to

- explain how companies find and develop new-product ideas
- list and define the steps in the new-product development process and the major considerations in managing this process
- describe the stages of the product life cycle
- describe how marketing strategies change during the product's life cycle
- discuss two additional product and services issues: socially responsible product decisions and international product and services marketing

NEW-PRODUCT DEVELOPMENT AND PRODUCT LIFE-CYCLE STRATEGIES

Previewing the Concepts

In the previous chapter, you learned how marketers manage individual brands and entire product mixes. In this chapter, we'll look into two additional product topics: developing new products and managing products through their life cycles. The first part of this chapter lays out a process for finding and growing successful new products. In the second part of the chapter, we will discuss the product life cycle. Finally, we'll look at social responsibility in product decisions and international product and services marketing.

For openers, consider Apple Computer. An early new-product innovator, Apple got off to a fast and impressive start. But only a decade later, as its creative fires cooled, Apple found itself on the brink of extinction. That set the stage for one of the most remarkable turnarounds in corporate history. Read on to see how Apple's cofounder, Steve Jobs, used lots of innovation and creative new products to first start the company and then to remake it again 20 years later.

From the start, the tale of Apple Computer has been one of dazzling creativity and customer-driven innovation. Under the leadership of its cofounder and creative genius, Steve Jobs, Apple's very first personal computers, introduced in the late 1970s, stood apart because of their user-friendly look and feel. The company's Macintosh computer, unveiled in 1984, and its LazerWriter printers, blazed new trails in desktop computing and publishing, making Apple an early industry leader in both innovation and market share.

But then things took an ugly turn for Apple. In 1985, after tumultuous struggles with the new president he'd hired only a year earlier, Steve Jobs left Apple. With Jobs gone, Apple's creative fires cooled. By the late 1980s, the company's fortunes dwindled as a new wave of PC machines, sporting Intel chips and Microsoft software, swept the market. By the mid-to late-1990s, Apple's sales had plunged to $5 billion, 50 percent off previous highs. And its once-commanding share of the PC market had dropped to a tiny two percent. Even the most ardent Apple fans—the "macolytes"—wavered, and the company's days seemed numbered.

Yet Apple has engineered a remarkable turnaround. Last year's sales soared to a record $16 billion, more than

double sales just two years earlier. Profits rose a stunning 20-fold in that same two-year period. Said one analyst, "Gadget geeks around the world have crowned Apple the keeper of all things cool."

What caused this breathtaking turnaround? Apple rediscovered the magic that had made the company so successful in the first place: customer driven creativity and new-product innovation. The remarkable makeover began with the return of Steve Jobs in 1997 Jobs' first task was to revitalize Apple's computer business. For starters, in 1998, Apple launched the iMac personal computer, which featured a sleek, egg-shaped monitor and hard drive, all in one unit, in a futuristic translucent turquoise casing. With its one-button Internet access, this machine was designed specifically for cruising the Internet (hence the "i" in "iMac"). The dramatic iMac won raves for design and lured buyers in droves. Within a year, it had sold more than a million units.

Jobs next unleashed Mac OS X, a ground-breaking new Apple operating system which served as the launching pad for a new generation of Apple computers and software products. Consider iLife, a bundle of programs that comes with every new iMac. It includes applications such as iMovie (for video editing), iDVD (for recording movies, digital-photo slide shows, and music onto TV-playable DVDs), iPhoto (for managing and touching up digital pictures), GarageBand (for making and mixing your own music), and iWork (for making presentations and newsletters).

The iMac and Mac OS X put Apple back on the map in personal computing. But Jobs knew that Apple, still a nicher claiming less than a 5 percent share of the U.S. market, would never catch up in computers with dominant competitors Dell and HP. Real growth would require even more creative thinking. And it just doesn't get much more creative than iPod and iTunes, innovations that would utterly change the way people acquire and listen to music.

A music buff himself, Jobs noticed that kids by the millions were using computers and CD writers to download digital songs from then-illegal online services, such as Napster, and then burning their own music CDs. He moved quickly to make CD burners standard equipment on all Macs. Then, to help users download music and manage their music databases, Apple's programmers created state-of-the-art jukebox software called iTunes.

Even before iTunes hit the streets, according to Apple watcher Brent Schendler, Jobs "recognized that although storing and playing music on your computer was pretty cool, wouldn't it be even cooler if there was a portable, Walkman-type player that could hold all your digital music so that you could listen to it anywhere?" Less than nine months later, Apple introduced the sleek and sexy iPod, a tiny computer with an amazing capacity to store digital music and an easy-to-use interface for managing and playing it. In another 18 months, the Apple iTunes Music Store opened on the Web, enabling consumers to legally download CDs and individual songs.

The results have been astonishing. The iPod ranks as one of the greatest consumer electronics hits of all time. By January of 2006, Apple had sold more than 50 million iPods, and more than one billion songs had been downloaded from the iTunes Music Store. "We had hoped to sell a million songs in the first six months, but we did that in the first six days," notes an Apple spokesman. And the iPod created a whole new market for downloadable videos, everything from music videos to television shows. Since the debut of the video iPod a year ago, users have downloaded more 35 million videos. Both iPod and the iTunes Music Store are capturing more than 75 percent shares of their respective markets.

Apple's success is attracting a horde of large, resourceful competitors. To stay ahead, the company must keep its eye on the consumer and continue to innovate. So, Apple isn't standing still. It recently introduced a line of new, easy-to-use wireless gadgets that link home and business computers, stereos, and other devices. Its .Mac (pronounced dot-Mac) online subscription service has signed up more than 600,000 members. Its iPhone (a combination of iPod and mobile phone) was introduced with much fanfare in 2007. Apple also opened more than 150 chic and gleaming Apple Stores. And observers see a host of new products: an iHome (a magical device that powers all your digital home entertainment devices) and an iPod on Wheels (a digital hub that integrates your iPod with your car's entertainment system).

For the second straight year, Apple was named the world's most innovative company in Boston Consulting Group's "Most Innovative Company" survey of 940 senior executives in 68 countries. Apple received 25 percent of the votes, twice the number of runner-up 3M and three times that of third-place Microsoft.

Thus, it seems Steve Jobs has transformed Apple from a failing niche computer maker to a major force in consumer electronics, digital music and video, and who knows what else in the future. And he's done it through innovation—by helping those around him to "Think Different" (Apple's motto) in their quest to bring value to customers. *Time magazine* sums it up this way:

> [Steve Jobs is] a marketing and creative genius with a rare ability to get inside the imaginations of consumers and understand what will captivate them. He is obsessed with the Apple user's experience… For every product his companies have released, it's clear that someone actually asked, How can we "think different" about this?… most of the company's products over the past three decades have had designs that are three steps ahead of the competition… Jobs has a drive and vision that renews itself… It leaves you waiting for his next move.[1]

As the Apple story suggests, a company must be good at developing and managing new products. Every product seems to go through a life cycle—it is born, goes through several phases, and eventually dies as newer products come along that better serve consumer needs. This product life cycle presents two major challenges:

- First, because all products eventually decline, a firm must be good at developing new products to replace aging ones (the challenge of *new-product development*).
- Second, the firm must be good at adapting its marketing strategies in the face of changing tastes, technologies, and competition as products pass through life-cycle stages (the challenge of *product life-cycle strategies*).

New-Product Development Strategy

Given the rapid changes in consumer tastes, technology, and competition, companies must develop a steady stream of new products and services. A firm can obtain new products in two ways. One is through *acquisition*—by buying a whole company, a patent, or a license to produce someone else's product. The other is through **new-product development** in the company's own research-and-development department. By new products we mean original products, product improvements, product modifications, and new brands that the firm develops through its own research-and-development efforts.

Yet, innovation can be very expensive and very risky. For example, Texas Instruments lost $660 million before withdrawing from the home computer business. New products face tough odds. Other costly product failures from sophisticated companies include New Coke (Coca-Cola Company) and Betamax videotape (Sony). Studies indicate that up to 90 percent of all new consumer products fail.

Why do so many new products fail? There are several reasons: Although an idea may be good, the company may overestimate market size. The actual product may be poorly designed. Or it might be incorrectly positioned, launched at the wrong time, priced too high, or poorly advertised. A high-level executive might push a favorite idea despite poor marketing research findings. Sometimes the costs of product development are higher than expected, and sometimes competitors fight back harder than expected.

> **New-product development**
> The development of original products, product improvements, product modifications, and new brands through the firm's own R&D efforts.

The Betamax videotape failed to capture market share and eventually lost to Sony's VHS in the videotape format war.

The New-Product Development Process

Companies must develop new products, but the odds weigh heavily against success. To create successful new products, a company must understand its consumers, markets, and competitors and develop products that deliver superior value to customers. It must carry out strong new-product planning and set up a systematic *new-product development process* for finding and growing new products. **Figure 9.1** shows the eight major steps in this process.

Idea generations → Idea screening → Concept development and testing → Marketing strategy development

Commercialization ← Test marketing ← Product development ← Business analysis

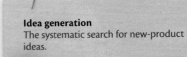

Figure 9.1
Major stages in new-product development

Idea Generation

New-product development starts with **idea generation**—the systematic search for new-product ideas. A company typically has to generate many ideas to find a few good ones. According to one management consultant, on average, companies "will run through 3,000 ideas before they hit a winner." For instance, one brainstorming session for Prudential Insurance Company came up with 1,500 ideas and only 12 were considered even usable.

Major sources of new-product ideas include internal sources and external sources such as customers, competitors, distributors and suppliers, and others (see **Figure 9.2**).

> **Idea generation**
> The systematic search for new-product ideas.

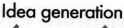

Idea generation

Internal Sources
- Top management
- Scientists
- Engineers
- Manufacturing staff
- Sales people

External Sources
- Customers
- Competitors
- Distributors and supplying
- Trade magazines, shows and seminars
- Ad agencies
- Design firms

Figure 9.2
Sources of new product ideas

Internal idea source –
The idea of an electronic pet came about when a Bandai staff noticed two trends—Japanese were inclined toward keeping small pets and love for electronic gadgets. She combined these two trends and created Tamagotchi. (*www.bandai.com*)

Internal Idea Sources

Using *internal sources*, the company can find new ideas by picking the brains of its executives, scientists, engineers, manufacturing staff, and salespeople. Some companies have developed successful "intrapreneurial" programs that encourage employees to think up and develop new-product ideas. For example, Hitachi has a shadow society called the *Henjinkai* (the oddball club) created to forge links among its researchers. Its more than 1,200 members, engineers with PhDs earned mostly after joining Hitachi, fraternize at technical conferences, swap ideas, and informally advise Hitachi's board on important technological developments.

> Samsung has built a special center to encourage and support new-product innovation internally—its Value Innovation Program (VIP) Center in Suwon, South Korea. The VIP Center is the ultimate round-the-clock idea factory in which company researchers, engineers, and designers co-mingle to come up with new-product ideas and processes. The invitation-only center features workrooms, dorm rooms, training rooms, a kitchen, and a basement filled with games, a gym, and a sauna. Almost every week, the center announces a "world's first" or "world's largest" innovation. Recent ideas sprouting from the VIP Center include a 102-inch plasma HDTV and a process to reduce material costs on a multifunction printer by 30 percent. The center has helped Samsung, once know as the maker of cheap knock-off products, become one of the world's most innovative and profitable consumer electronics companies.[2]

Everyone in the company can contribute good new-product ideas. In today's fast-moving and competitive environment, it is "everybody's business to come up with great ideas." Take the case of Tamagotchi, the electronic pet by Bandai. It came about not from the head of Bandai but from one of its market researchers. She noticed two trends—more Japanese were keeping small pets in their apartments and growing interest in electronic gadgets. The idea of an electronic pet was borne from the combination of these two trends.

Product ideas from customers –
Advice from 250 train-set enthusiasts resulted in the LEGO Santa Fe Super Chief set, a blockbuster new product that sold out in less than two weeks.

External Idea Sources

Good new-product ideas also come from *customers*. The company can analyze customer questions and complaints to find new products that better solve consumer problems. Or company engineers or salespeople can meet with and work alongside customers to get suggestions and ideas.

LEGO did just that when it invited 250 LEGO train-set enthusiasts to visit its New York office to assess new designs. The group gave LEGO lots of new ideas, and the company put them to good use. "We literally produced what they told us to produce," says a LEGO executive. The result was the

"Santa Fe Super Chief" set. Some 10,000 units were sold in less than two weeks with no additional marketing.[3]

Consumers often create new products and uses on their own, and companies can benefit by putting them on the market. For example, Haier, China's major appliance company, reported that in the 1990s, many of its customers in rural communities were using their washing machines to also clean vegetables. Such use clogged the machines, resulting in a deluge of complaints. Given its customers' unconventional usage of its washing machines, Haier redesigned the draining mechanism so that the machines could also wash vegetables without breaking down.

Companies must be careful not to rely too heavily on customer input when developing new products. For some products, especially highly technical ones, customers may not know what they need.

Beyond customers, companies can tap several other external sources. For example, *competitors* can be a good source of new-product ideas. Companies watch competitors' ads to get clues about their new products. They buy competing new products, take them apart to see how they work, analyze their sales, and decide whether they should bring out a new product of their own.

Distributors and suppliers can also contribute many good new-product ideas. Distributors are close to the market and can pass along information about consumer problems and new-product possibilities. Suppliers can tell the company about new concepts, techniques, and materials that can be used to develop new products. Other idea sources include trade magazines, shows, and seminars; government agencies; new-product consultants; advertising agencies; marketing research firms; university and commercial laboratories; and inventors.

Some companies seek the help of outside design firms for new-product ideas and design. For example, a design company helped Tupperware find a new-product solution to a common customer problem—organizing that closet full of randomly stacked plastic storage containers and matching the lids with the bases. From idea generation to final prototypes, the design company developed Tupperware's GoFlex series, flexible containers that can be collapsed, stacked, and stored flat with the lid attached. The new product received several design awards.[4]

Tupperware's GoFlex! series of collapsible containers was designed to solve the problem of storage and matching covers to the containers.

Idea Screening

The purpose of idea generation is to create a large number of ideas. The purpose of the succeeding stages is to *reduce* that number. The first idea-reducing stage is **idea screening**, which helps spot good ideas and drop poor ones as soon as possible. Product development costs rise greatly in later stages, so the company wants to go ahead only with the product ideas that will turn into profitable products.

Idea screening
Screening new-product ideas to spot good ideas and drop poor ones as soon as possible.

Many companies require their executives to write up new-product ideas on a standard form that can be reviewed by a new-product committee. The write-up describes the product, the target market, and the competition. It makes some rough estimates of market size, product price, development time and costs, manufacturing costs, and rate of return. The committee then evaluates the idea against a set of general criteria.

For example, at Kao Corporation, the large Japanese consumer products company, the new-product committee asks questions such as these: Is the product truly useful to consumers and society? Is it good for our company? Does it mesh well with our company's objectives and strategies? Do we have the people, skills, and resources to make it succeed?

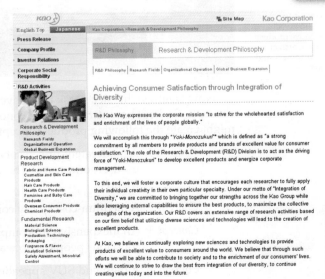

Idea screening – At Kao, new product ideas are carefully screened to ensure that they are in line with its corporate philosophy—products that enrich lives and satisfy customers. (www.kao.co.jp/en)

Does it deliver more value to customers than do competing products? Is it easy to advertise and distribute? Many companies have well-designed systems for rating and screening new-product ideas.

Concept Development and Testing

An attractive idea must be developed into a **product concept**. It is important to distinguish between a product idea, a product concept, and a product image. A *product idea* is an idea for a possible product that the company can see itself offering to the market. A *product concept* is a detailed version of the idea stated in meaningful consumer terms. A *product image* is the way consumers perceive an actual or potential product.

Concept Development

After more than a decade of development, DaimlerChrysler is beginning to commercialize its experimental fuel-cell-powered electric car. This car's nonpolluting fuel-cell system runs directly on hydrogen, which powers the fuel cell with only water as a by-product. It is highly fuel efficient and gives the new car an environmental advantage over even today's superefficient gasoline-electric hybrid cars.

DaimlerChrysler has released 30 "F-Cell" cars in California and 100 more worldwide for testing under varying weather conditions, traffic situations, and driving styles. Based on the Mercedes A-Class, the car accelerates from 0 to 60 in 16 seconds, reaches speeds of 85 miles per hour, and has a 100-mile driving range, giving it a huge edge over battery-powered electric cars that travel only about 80 miles before needing three to 12 hours of recharging.[5]

Product concept
A detailed version of the new-product idea stated in meaningful consumer terms.

DaimlerChrysler's task is to develop its fuel-cell-powered F-Cell car into alternative product concepts, find out how attractive each concept is to customers, and choose the best one.

Now DaimlerChrysler's task is to develop this new product into alternative product concepts, find out how attractive each concept is to customers, and choose the best one. It might create the following product concepts for the fuel-cell electric car:

Concept 1 A moderately-priced subcompact designed as a second family car to be used around town. The car is ideal for running errands and visiting friends.

Concept 2 A medium-cost sporty compact appealing to young people.

Concept 3 An inexpensive subcompact "green" car appealing to environmentally conscious people who want practical, low polluting transportation.

Concept 4 A high-end SUV appealing to those who love the space SUVs provide but lament its poor gas mileage.

Concept Testing

Concept testing calls for testing new-product concepts with groups of target consumers. The concepts may be presented to consumers symbolically or physically. Here, in words, is concept 3:

> An efficient, peppy, fun-to-drive, fuel-cell-powered electric subcompact car that seats four. This hydrogen-powered high-tech wonder provides practical and reliable transportation with virtually no pollution. It goes up to 85 miles per hour and, unlike battery-powered electric cars, it never needs recharging. It's priced, fully equipped, at $25,000.

For some concept tests, a word or picture description might be sufficient. However, a more concrete and physical presentation of the concept will increase the reliability of the concept test. After being exposed to the concept, consumers then may be asked to react to it by answering questions such as those in **Table 9.1.** The answers to such questions will help the company decide which concept has the strongest appeal. For example, the last question asks about the consumer's intention to buy. Suppose 10 percent of consumers say they "definitely" would buy, and another five percent say "probably." The company could project these figures to the full population in this target group to estimate sales volume. Even then, the estimate is uncertain because people do not always carry out their stated intentions.

Table 9.1 Questions for Fuel-Cell-Powered Electric Car Concept Test

1. Do you understand the concept of a fuel-cell-powered electric car?

2. Do you believe the claims about the car's performance?

3. What are the major benefits of the fuel-cell-powered electric car compared with a conventional car?

4. What are its advantages compared with a battery-powered electric car?

5. What improvements in the car's features would you suggest?

6. For what uses would you prefer a fuel-cell-powered electric car to a conventional car?

7. What would be a reasonable price to charge for the car?

8. Who would be involved in your decision to buy such a car? Who would drive it?

9. Would you buy such a car (definitely, probably, probably not, definitely not)?

Launched in 1996, M&M Mini's, in their handy plastic tube containers and sachets, proved to be popular with consumers.

Many firms routinely test new-product concepts with consumers before attempting to turn them into actual new products. For example, M&M Mini's, "teeny-tiny" M&Ms sold in a tube container, received a rare A+ concept rating, meaning that consumers thought it was an outstanding concept that they would try and buy.

Marketing Strategy Development

Suppose DaimlerChrysler finds that concept 3 for the fuel-cell-powered electric car tests best. The next step is **marketing strategy development**, designing an initial marketing strategy for introducing this car to the market.

The *marketing strategy statement* consists of three parts. The first part describes the target market; the planned product positioning; and the sales, market share, and profit goals for the first few years. Thus:

> The target market is younger, well-educated, moderate-to-high-income individuals, couples, or small families seeking practical, environmentally responsible transportation. The car will be positioned as more fun to drive and less polluting than today's internal combustion engine or hybrid cars. It is also less restricting than battery-powered electric cars, which must be recharged regularly. The company will aim to sell 100,000 cars in the first year, at a loss of not more than $15 million. In the second year, the company will aim for sales of 120,000 cars and a profit of $25 million.

The second part of the marketing strategy statement outlines the product's planned price, distribution, and marketing budget for the first year:

> The fuel-cell-powered electric car will be offered in three colors—green, white, and blue—and will have optional air-conditioning and power-drive features. It will sell at a retail price of $25,000—with 15 percent off the list price to dealers. Dealers who sell more than 10 cars per month will get an additional discount of five percent on each car sold that month. An advertising budget of $50 million will be split 50-50 between a national media campaign and local advertising. Advertising will emphasize the car's fun spirit and low emissions. During the first year, $100,000 will be spent on marketing research to find out who is buying the car and their satisfaction levels.

The third part of the marketing strategy statement describes the planned long-run sales, profit goals, and marketing mix strategy:

> DaimlerChrysler intends to capture a three percent long-run share of the total auto market and realize an after-tax return on investment of 15 percent. To achieve this, product quality will start high and be improved over time. Price will be raised in the second and third years if competition permits. The total advertising budget will be raised each year by about 10 percent. Marketing research will be reduced to $60,000 per year after the first year.

Business analysis
A review of the sales, costs, and profit projections for a new product to find out whether these factors satisfy the company's objectives.

Business Analysis

Once management has decided on its product concept and marketing strategy, it can evaluate the business attractiveness of the proposal. **Business analysis** involves a review of the sales, costs, and profit projections for a new product to find out whether they satisfy the company's objectives. If they do, the product can move to the product development stage.

To estimate sales, the company might look at the sales history of similar products and conduct surveys of market opinion. It can then estimate minimum and maximum sales to assess the range of risk. After preparing the sales forecast, management can estimate the expected costs and profits for the product, including marketing, R&D, operations, accounting, and finance costs. The company then uses the sales and costs figures to analyze the new product's financial attractiveness.

Estimating sales –
Companies look at the sales history of similar products and conduct surveys of market opinion.

Product development
Developing the product concept into a physical product to ensure that the product idea can be turned into a workable product.

Product Development

So far, the new-product concepts are word descriptions, drawings, or crude mock-ups. If the product concept passes the business test, it moves into **product development**. The physical product is created. The product development step, however, calls for a large jump in investment. It will show whether the product idea can be turned into a workable product.

The R&D department will develop and test one or more physical versions of the product concept. R&D hopes to design a prototype that will satisfy and excite consumers and that can be produced quickly at budgeted costs.

Often, products undergo rigorous tests to make sure that they perform safely and effectively or that consumers will find value in them. Here is an example of such product tests:[6]

> Behind a locked door in the basement of Louis Vuitton's elegant Paris headquarters, a mechanical arm hoists a brown-and-tan handbag a half-meter off the floor—then drops it. The bag, loaded with an 8-pound weight, will be lifted and dropped, over and over again, for four days. This is Vuitton's test laboratory, a high-tech torture chamber for its products. Another piece of lab equipment bombards handbags with ultraviolet rays to test resistance to fading. Still another tests zippers by tugging them open and shutting them 5,000 times. There's even a mechanized mannequin hand, with a Vuitton charm bracelet around its wrist, being shaken vigorously to make sure none of the charms fall off.

A new product must have the required functional features and also convey the intended psychological characteristics. The fuel-cell electric car, for example, should strike consumers as being well built, comfortable, and safe. Management must learn what makes consumers decide that a car is well built. To some consumers, this means that the car has "solid-sounding" doors. To others, it means that the car is able to withstand heavy impact in crash tests. Consumer tests are conducted in which consumers test-drive the car and rate its attributes.

Product development –
Products often undergo rigorous tests to ensure its quality so that consumers will find value in them.

Test Marketing

If the product passes concept and product tests, the next step is **test marketing**, the stage at which the product and marketing program are introduced into more realistic market settings. Test marketing gives the marketer experience with marketing the product before going to the great expense of full introduction. It lets the company test the product and its entire marketing program—positioning strategy, advertising, distribution, pricing, branding and packaging, and budget levels.

The amount of test marketing needed varies with each new product. Test marketing costs can be high, and it takes time that may allow competitors to gain advantages. When the costs of developing and introducing the product are low, or when management is already confident about the new product, the company may do little or no test marketing. Companies often do not test-market simple line extensions or copies of successful competitor products. However, when introducing a new product requires a big investment, or when management is not sure of the product or marketing program, a company may do more test marketing.

Test marketing
The stage of new-product development in which the product and marketing program are tested in more realistic market settings.

> In Singapore, Samsung conducted a phone trial called the "experience-centric" marketing exercise to get feedback on its new range of Ultra edition mobile phones. Consumers were allowed to try out the high range models for free over a one-month period. Instead of it being an isolated consumer occurrence, they also had the opportunity to share their experiences during the trial with an online community made up of users who were similarly involved in the trial. Samsung received feedback from the trial users on its Ultrablog Web site.

Getting customer's feedback –
Customers who tried Samsung's Ultra mobile phones provided feedback in its Ultrablog Web site. (*www.ultrablog.com.sg*)

P&G beat Clorox's new detergent to the U.S. market with Tide with Bleach, which quickly become the segment leader.

Although test-marketing costs can be high, they are often small when compared with the costs of making a major mistake. Still, test marketing doesn't guarantee success. For example, Procter & Gamble tested its Olay cosmetics for three years. Although market tests suggested the products would be successful, P&G pulled the plug shortly after their introductions.[7]

When using test marketing, consumer products companies usually choose one of three approaches—standard test markets, controlled test markets, or simulated test markets.

Standard Test Markets

Using standard test markets, the company finds a small number of representative test cities, conducts a full marketing campaign in these cities, and uses store audits, consumer and distributor surveys, and other measures to gauge product performance. The results are used to forecast national sales and profits, discover potential product problems, and fine-tune the marketing program.

Standard test markets have some drawbacks. They can be very costly and they may take a long time—some last as long as three to five years. Moreover, competitors can monitor test market results or interfere with them by cutting their prices in test areas, increasing their promotion, or even buying up the product being tested. Finally, test markets give competitors a look at the company's new product well before it is introduced. Thus, competitors may have time to develop defensive strategies, and may even beat the company's product to the market. For example, while Clorox was still test marketing its new detergent with bleach in selected markets, its competitor P&G launched Tide with Bleach nationally. Tide with Bleach quickly became the segment leader; Clorox later withdrew its detergent.

Controlled Test Markets

Several research firms keep controlled panels of stores that have agreed to carry new products for a fee. Controlled test marketing systems such as ACNielsen's Scantrack track individual consumer behavior for new products. There is a panel of shoppers who report all of their purchases by showing an identification card at check-out in participating stores and by using a handheld scanner at home to record purchases at nonparticipating stores. Detailed scanner information on each consumer's purchases is fed into a central computer, where it is combined with the consumer's demographic and TV viewing information and reported daily. Such panel purchasing data enables in-depth diagnostics not possible with retail point-of-sale data alone, including repeat purchase analysis, buyer demographics, and earlier, more accurate sales forecasts after just 12 to 24 weeks in market. Most importantly, the system allows companies to evaluate their specific marketing efforts.

Sample Lab, a Japanese store in the trendy district of Harajuku in Tokyo, offers free samples of a wide variety of products to its pre-registered customers in return for customer feedback on the products via mobile phone SMS surveys. (*www.samplelab.jp*)

Simulated Test Markets

Companies can also test new products in a simulated shopping environment. The company or research firm shows ads and promotions for a variety of products, including the new product being tested, to a sample of consumers. It gives consumers a small amount of money and invites them to a real or laboratory store where they may keep the money or use it to buy items. The researchers note how many consumers buy the new product and competing brands.

This simulation provides a measure of trial and the commercial's effectiveness against competing commercials. The researchers then ask consumers the reasons for their purchase or nonpurchase. Some weeks later, they interview the consumers by phone to determine product attitudes, usage, satisfaction, and repurchase intentions. Using sophisticated computer models, the researchers then project national sales from results of the simulated test market. Some marketers have used interesting new high-tech approaches to simulated test market research, such as virtual reality and the Internet.

Simulated test markets overcome some of the disadvantages of standard and controlled test markets. They usually cost much less, can be run in eight weeks, and keep the new product out of competitors' view. Yet, because of their small samples and simulated shopping environments, many marketers do not think that simulated test markets are as accurate or reliable as larger, real-world tests.

Still, simulated test markets are used widely, often as "pretest" markets. Because they are fast and inexpensive, they can be run to quickly assess a new product or its marketing program. If the pretest results are strongly positive, the product might be introduced without further testing. If the results are very poor, the product might be dropped or substantially redesigned and retested. If the results are promising but indefinite, the product and marketing program can be tested further in controlled or standard test markets.

Commercialization

Test marketing gives management the information needed to make a final decision about whether to launch the new product. If the company goes ahead with **commercialization**—introducing the new product into the market—it will face high costs. The company may have to build or rent a manufacturing facility. And, in the case of a major new consumer packaged good, it may spend millions of dollars for advertising, sales promotion, and other marketing efforts in the first year.

The company launching a new product must first decide on introduction timing. If DaimlerChrysler's new fuel-cell electric car will eat into the sales of the company's other cars, its introduction may be delayed. If the car can be improved further, or if the economy is down, the company may wait until the following year to launch it. However, if competitors are ready to introduce their own fuel-cell models, DaimlerChrysler may push to introduce the car sooner.

Commercialization
Introducing a new product into the market.

Next, the company must decide where to launch the new product— in a single location, a region, the national market, or the international market. Few companies have the confidence, capital, and capacity to launch new products into full national or international distribution. They will develop a planned market rollout over time. In particular, small companies may enter attractive cities or regions one at a time. Larger companies, however, may quickly introduce new models into several regions or into the full national market. For example, Procter & Gamble launched the Gillette Fusion razor in the U.S. with a full national blitz. Within the first week of launch, P&G had blanketed U.S. stores with some 180,000 Fusion displays. After three months, Fusion brand awareness exceeded 60 percent, and the new brand contributed to a 44 percent rise in overall U.S. sales of nondisposable razors.[8]

Companies with international distribution systems may introduce new products through global rollouts. P&G did this with its SpinBrush low-priced, battery-powered toothbrush. In a swift and successful global assault—its fastest global rollout ever—P&G quickly introduced the new product into 35 countries. Such rapid worldwide expansion overwhelmed rival Colgate's Actibrush brand. Within a year of its introduction, SpinBrush was outselling Actibrush by a margin of two to one.[9]

Commercialization –
Procter & Gamble introduced its new Gillette Fusion six-blade razor with an eye-popping $1 billion of global marketing support. It spent $300 million in the United States alone, complete with Super Bowl ads and star-studded launch spectaculars.

Managing New-Product Development

The new-product development process shown in **Figure 9.1** highlights the important activities needed to find, develop, and introduce new products. However, new-product development involves more than just going through a set of steps. Companies must take a holistic approach to managing this process. Successful new-product development requires a customer-centered, team-based, and systematic effort.

Customer-Centered New-Product Development

Above all else, new-product development must be customer centered. When looking for and developing new products, companies often rely too heavily on technical research in their R&D labs. But like everything else in marketing, successful new-product development begins with a thorough understanding of what consumers need and value. **Customer-centered new-product development** focuses on finding new ways to solve customer problems and create more customer-satisfying experiences.

One recent study found that the most successful new products are the ones that are differentiated, solve major customer problems, and offer a compelling customer value proposition.[10] Thus, innovative companies are getting out of the research lab and mingling with customers in the search for new customer value. Consider the following example:[11]

Customer-centered new-product development
New-product development that focuses on finding new ways to solve customer problems and create more customer-satisfying experiences.

> People at all levels of Procter & Gamble look for fresh ideas by tagging along with and talking to customers as they shop for and use the company's products. When one P&G team tackled the problem of "reinventing bathroom cleaning," it started by "listening with its eyes." The group spent many hours watching consumers clean their bathrooms. They focused on "extreme users," ranging from a professional house cleaner who scrubbed grout with his fingernail to four single guys whose idea of cleaning the bathroom was pushing a filthy towel around the floor with a big stick. If they could make both users happy, they figured they had a home run. One big idea—a cleaning tool on a removable stick that could both reach shower walls and get into crannies—got the green light quickly. Consumers loved the prototype, patched together with repurposed plastic, foam, and duct tape. Some refused to return it. The idea became P&G's highly successful Mr. Clean Magic Reach bathroom cleaning tool.

Thus, customer-centered new-product development begins and ends with solving customer problems. As one expert asks: "What is innovation after all, if not products and services that offer fresh thinking in a way that meets the needs of customers?"[12] **Real Marketing** examines service innovation via a customer-centered approach.

Team-based new-product development –
Departments work in cross-functional teams that stay with the new product from start to finish, allowing the team to work on resolving problems while moving on with development.

Team-Based New-Product Development

Good new-product development also requires a total-company, cross-functional effort. Some companies organize their new-product development process into the orderly sequence of steps shown in **Figure 9.1**, starting with idea generation and ending with commercialization. Under this *sequential product development* approach, one company department works individually to complete its stage of the process before passing the new product along to the next department and stage. This orderly, step-by-step process can help bring control to complex and risky projects. But it also can be dangerously slow. In fast-changing, highly competitive markets, such slow-but-sure product development can result in product failures, lost sales and profits, and crumbling market positions.

To get their new products to market more quickly, many companies use a **team-based new-product development** approach. Under this approach, company departments work closely together in cross-functional teams, overlapping the steps in the product development process to save time and increase effectiveness. Instead of passing the new product from department to department, the company assembles a team of people from various departments that stays with the new product from start to finish. Such teams usually include people from the marketing, finance, design, manufacturing, and legal

Team-based new-product development
An approach to developing new products in which various company departments work closely together, overlapping the steps in the product development process to save time and increase effectiveness.

departments, and even supplier and customer companies. In the sequential process, a bottleneck at one phase can seriously slow the entire project. In the simultaneous approach, if one functional area hits snags, it works to resolve them while the team moves on.

The team-based approach does have some limitations. For example, it sometimes creates more organizational tension and confusion than the more orderly sequential approach. However, in rapidly changing industries facing increasingly shorter product life cycles, the rewards of fast and flexible product development far exceed the risks. Companies that combine both a customer-centered approach with team-based new-product development gain a big competitive edge by getting the right new products to market faster.

Systematic New-Product Development

Finally, the new-product development process should be holistic and systematic rather than haphazard. Otherwise, few new ideas will surface, and many good ideas will sputter and die. To avoid these problems, a company can install an innovation management system to collect, review, evaluate, and manage new-product ideas.

The company can appoint a respected senior person to be the company's innovation manager. It can set up Web-based idea management software and encourage all company stakeholders—employees, suppliers, distributors, dealers—to become involved in finding and developing new products. It can assign a cross-functional innovation management committee to evaluate proposed new-product ideas and help bring good ideas to market. It can create recognition programs to reward those who contribute the best ideas.[13]

The innovation management system approach yields two favorable outcomes. First, it helps create an innovation-oriented company culture. It shows that top management supports, encourages, and rewards innovation. Second, it will yield a larger number of new-product ideas, among which will be found some especially good ones. The good new ideas will be more systematically developed, producing more new-product successes.

Thus, new-product success requires a holistic approach for finding new ways to create valued customer experiences, from generating and screening new-product ideas to creating and rolling out want-satisfying products to customers. It requires a whole-company commitment. At companies known for their new-product prowess—such as Apple, Google, 3M, Procter & Gamble, and Samsung—the culture encourages, supports, and rewards innovation. Consider 3M, which consistently rates among the world's most innovative companies:[14]

Innovation – At 3M, new products don't just happen. The company's entire culture encourages, supports, and rewards innovation. (*www.3m.com*)

You see the headline in every 3M ad: "Innovation Working for You." At 3M, innovation isn't just an advertising pitch. Throughout its history, 3M has been one of America's most innovative companies. The company markets more than 50,000 products, ranging from sandpaper, adhesives, and hundreds of sticky tapes to contact lenses, heart-lung machines, and futuristic synthetic ligaments. Each year, 3M invests $1.1 billion in research and launches more than 200 new products. 3M works hard to create an entrepreneurial culture that fosters innovation. For over a century, 3M's culture has encouraged employees to take risks and try new ideas. 3M knows that it must try thousands of new-product ideas to hit one big jackpot. Trying out lots of new ideas often means making mistakes, but 3M accepts blunders and dead ends as a normal part of creativity and innovation.

In fact, "blunders" have turned into some of 3M's most successful products. One example involves 3M scientist Spencer Silver. Silver started out to develop a superstrong adhesive. Instead, he came up with one that didn't stick very well at all. He sent the apparently useless substance on to other 3M researchers to see whether they could find something to do with it. Nothing happened for several years. Then Arthur Fry, another 3M scientist, had a problem—and an idea. As a choir member in a local church, Mr. Fry was having trouble marking places in his hymnal—the little scraps of paper he used kept falling out. He tried dabbing some of Mr. Silver's weak glue on one of the scraps. It stuck nicely and later peeled off without damaging the hymnal. Thus were born 3M's Post-It Notes, a product that is now one of the top selling office supply products in the world.

Product Life-Cycle Strategies

After launching the new product, management wants the product to enjoy a long and happy life. Although it does not expect the product to sell forever, the company wants to earn a decent profit to cover all the effort and risk that went into launching it. Management is aware that each product will have a life cycle, although its exact shape and length is not known in advance.

Figure 9.3 shows a typical **product life cycle (PLC)**, the course that a product's sales and profits take over its lifetime. The product life cycle has five distinct stages:

1. *Product development* begins when the company finds and develops a new product idea. During product development, sales are zero and the company's investment costs mount.

> **Product life cycle (PLC)**
> The course of a product's sales and profits over its lifetime. It involves five distinct stages: product development, introduction, growth, maturity, and decline.

REAL MARKETING

Triumph International: Customer-Centered Service Innnovation

Service innovation is rapidly emerging as 'The Next Big Thing' in the service industry. Already, MNCs like HP, Microsoft, and IBM have shifted their focus from product inventions to service innovation to grow their businesses. One company which has leveraged on service innovation to break into new markets is leading Swiss lingerie maker Triumph International.

As a premium lingerie brand, strong customer service is a crucial part of Triumph's competitive advantage. To sustain its competitiveness, Triumph participated in the Customer-Centric Initiative (CCI), a program launched by several Singapore government agencies in 2005. The CCI aimed to encourage businesses in Singapore to be more committed to service excellence and partially funded approved projects that involved the introduction of new service

At Triumph, male customers are given a hand in lingerie selection.

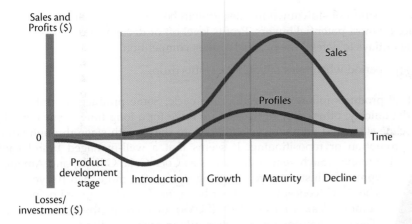

Figure 9.3
Sales and profits over the product's life
from inception to decline

2. *Introduction* is a period of slow sales growth as the product is introduced in the market. Profits are nonexistent in this stage because of the heavy expenses of product introduction.

3. *Growth* is a period of rapid market acceptance and increasing profits.

standards or led to an improvement in service leadership, service agility, and customer experience.

According to Ms Doy Teo, director of Triumph International (Singapore), "CCI has really helped us to understand our customers' evolving desires and uncover solutions that fit their lifestyle By innovating with the customer in mind and coming up with new service concepts, we add value to our business by retaining our existing customers and attracting new ones."

Since embarking on CCI, Triumph has successfully expanded its market to include a new segment which they had not previously targeted—men. Says Teo, "Men are usually shy when it comes to buying lingerie for their loved ones. To help them overcome this, Triumph started a 'Men Only' workshop where men can pick up tips on choosing lingerie. We also set aside two hours every last Friday of the month for men-only shopping sessions at one boutique."

Female customers have not been neglected. Besides school talks for young girls, Triumph has also conducted different workshops to cater to the various lifestyles of its

female customers, such as feng shui related seminars for women who want to enhance their fortune with the right lingerie as well as even 'Cleavage Creation' workshops.

These innovations derive from Triumph's mystery shopper scheme and customer satisfaction surveys, integral parts of its CCI implementation. Such feedback also resulted in Triumph creating special fitting rooms at several outlets to allow husbands, boyfriends, and girlfriends to join its customers during the selection and fitting process. Another finding revealed that Triumph sale staffs were constantly bogged down by administrative and operations tasks during peak hours. Triumph is now working with Singapore's national labor union, NTUC, to redesign jobs that will enable its counter staff to serve its customers better. For instance, Triumph is employing mature women in supporting roles as counter assistants.

Such customer-centric service innovations have led to an increase of up to 28 percent in sales at Triumph's Singapore outlets where CCI has been implemented. Its customer

compliment-to-complaint ratio has also improved to 11.84.

Triumph employees have also been enthusiastic about CCI. Ms Vivien Chong, its Singapore vice-president for human resource, states, "They don't enjoy a stagnant work environment and CCI helps to provide a dynamic culture. We have monthly meetings, for instance, where open discussions and feedback sessions are held. The ideas conceived by our employees have led to many service process improvements, and created a personalized and uplifting shopping experience for our customers." Indeed, Triumph will be conducting a worldwide study on consumer needs in 2008, and Singapore has been chosen as the Asian taskforce to develop a global retail process template for service.

Sources:
"Tap into New Markets through Service Innovation," *Business Times* (Singapore), December 4, 2007, p. 15; "Triumph Seduces New Customers with Innovative Services," Spring Singapore, www.spring.gov.sg, October 19, 2007 p.15; "Customer-Centric Initiative (CCI)," accessed at www.spring.gov.sg, December 6, 2007.

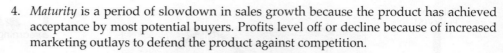

4. *Maturity* is a period of slowdown in sales growth because the product has achieved acceptance by most potential buyers. Profits level off or decline because of increased marketing outlays to defend the product against competition.

5. *Decline* is the period when sales fall off and profits drop.

Fads such as the Rubik's cube produce periods of unusually high sales driven by consumer enthusiasm and immediate product or brand popularity.

Not all products follow this product life cycle. Some products are introduced and die quickly; others stay in the mature stage for a long time. Some enter the decline stage and are then cycled back into the growth stage through strong promotion or repositioning. It seems that a well-managed brand could live forever. Such venerable brands as Coca-Cola, Gillette, and American Express, for instance, are still going strong after more than 100 years.

The PLC concept can describe a *product class* (gasoline-powered automobiles), a *product form* (SUVs), or a *brand* (the Toyota Camry). The PLC concept applies differently in each case. Product classes have the longest life cycles—the sales of many product classes stay in the mature stage for a long time. Product forms, in contrast, tend to have the standard PLC shape. Product forms such as "dial telephones" and "cassette tapes" passed through a regular history of introduction, rapid growth, maturity, and decline.

A specific brand's life cycle can change quickly because of changing competitive attacks and responses. For example, although laundry soaps (product class) and powdered detergents (product form) have enjoyed fairly long life cycles, the life cycles of specific brands have tended to be much shorter.

The PLC concept also can be applied to what are known as styles, fashions, and fads. Their special life cycles are shown in **Figure 9.4**. A **style** is a basic and distinctive mode of expression. For example, styles appear in homes (colonial, ranch), clothing (formal, casual), and art (surrealist, abstract). Once a style is invented, it may last for generations, passing in and out of vogue. A style has a cycle showing several periods of renewed interest. A **fashion** is a currently accepted or popular style in a given field. For example, the more formal "business attire" look of corporate dress of the 1980s and early 1990s gave way to the "business casual" look of today. Fashions tend to grow slowly, remain popular for a while, and then decline slowly. **Fads** are temporary periods of unusually high sales driven by consumer enthusiasm and immediate product or brand popularity.[15] Fads include the Rubik's Cube and low-carb diets.[16]

Style
A basic and distinctive mode of expression.

Fashion
A currently accepted or popular style in a given field.

Fad
A temporary period of unusually high sales driven by consumer enthusiasm and immediate product or brand popularity.

Figure 9.4
Styles, fashions, and fads

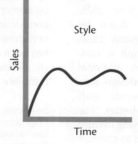
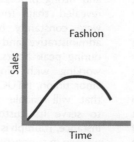
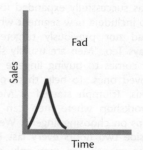

The PLC concept can be applied by marketers as a useful framework for describing how products and markets work. And when used carefully, the PLC concept can help in developing good marketing strategies for different stages of the product life cycle. But using the PLC concept for forecasting product performance or for developing marketing strategies presents some practical problems. For example, managers may have trouble identifying which stage of the PLC the product is in or pinpointing when the product moves into the next stage. They may also find it hard to determine the factors that affect the product's movement through the stages.

In practice, it is difficult to forecast the sales level at each PLC stage, the length of each stage, and the shape of the PLC curve. Using the PLC concept to develop marketing strategy also can be difficult because strategy is both a cause and a result of the product's life cycle. The product's current PLC position suggests the best marketing strategies, and the resulting marketing strategies affect product performance in later life-cycle stages.

Moreover, marketers should not blindly push products through the traditional stages of the product life cycle. Instead, marketers often defy the "rules" of the life cycle and position their products in unexpected ways to prolong their life.

We looked at the product development stage of the product life cycle in the first part of the chapter. We now look at strategies for each of the other life-cycle stages.

Table 9.2 summarizes the key characteristics of each stage of the product life cycle. The table also lists the marketing objectives and strategies for each stage.[17]

Table 9.2 Summary of Product Life-Cycle Characteristics, Objectives, and Strategies

Characteristics	Introduction	Growth	Maturity	Decline
Sales	Low sales	Rapidly rising sales	Peak sales	Declining sales
Costs	High cost per customer	Average cost per customer	Low cost per customer	Low cost per customer
Profits	Negative	Rising profits	High profits	Declining profits
Customers	Innovators	Early adopters	Middle majority	Laggards
Competitors	Few	Growing number	Stable number beginning to decline	Declining number
Marketing Objectives				
	Create product awareness and trial	Maximize market share	Maximize profit while defending market share	Reduce expenditure and milk the brand
Strategies				
Product	Offer a basic product	Offer product extensions, service, warranty	Diversify brand and models	Phase out weak items
Price	Use cost-plus	Price to penetrate market	Price to match or beat competitors	Cut price
Distribution	Build selective distribution	Build intensive distribution	Build more intensive distribution	Go selective: phase out unprofitable outlets
Advertising	Build product awareness among early adopters and dealers	Build awareness and interest in the mass market	Stress brand differences and benefits	Reduce to level needed to retain hardcore loyals
Sales Promotion	Use heavy sales promotion to entice trial	Reduce to take advantage of heavy consumer demand	Increase to encourage brand switching	Reduce to minimal level

Source: Philip Kotler, *Marketing Management*, 12th ed. (Upper Saddle River, NJ: Prentice Hall, 2006), p 332.

Introduction Stage

The **introduction stage** starts when the new product is first launched. Introduction takes time, and sales growth is apt to be slow. Well-known products such as instant coffee and frozen foods lingered for many years before they entered a stage of rapid growth.

In this stage, as compared to other stages, profits are negative or low because of the low sales and high distribution and promotion expenses. Much money is needed to attract distributors and build their inventories. Promotion spending is relatively high to inform consumers of the new product and get them to try it. Because the market is not generally ready for product refinements at this stage, the company and its few competitors produce basic versions of the product. These firms focus their selling on those buyers who are the most ready to buy.

A company, especially the *market pioneer*, must choose a launch strategy consistent with the intended product positioning. It should realize that the initial strategy is just the first step in a bigger marketing plan for the product's entire life cycle. If the pioneer chooses its launch strategy to make a "killing," it may be sacrificing long-run revenue for short-run gain. As the pioneer moves through later stages of the life cycle, it must continuously formulate new pricing, promotion, and other marketing strategies. It has the best chance of building and retaining market leadership if it plays its cards correctly from the start.

Growth Stage

If the new product satisfies the market, it will enter a **growth stage**, in which sales will start climbing quickly. The early adopters will continue to buy, and later buyers will start following their lead, especially if they hear favorable word of mouth. Attracted by the opportunities for profit, new competitors will enter the market. They will introduce new product features, and the market will expand. The increase in competitors leads to an increase in the number of distribution outlets, and sales jump to build reseller inventories. Prices remain where they are or fall slightly. Companies keep their promotion spending at the same or a slightly higher level. Educating the market remains a goal, but now the company must also meet the competition.

Profits increase during the growth stage, as promotion costs are spread over a large volume and as unit manufacturing costs fall. The firm uses several strategies to sustain rapid market growth as long as possible. It improves product quality and adds new product features and models. It enters new market segments and new distribution channels. It shifts some advertising from building product awareness to building product conviction and purchase, and it lowers prices at the right time to attract more buyers.

In the growth stage, the firm faces a trade-off between high market share and high current profit. By spending a lot of money on product improvement, promotion, and distribution, the company can capture a dominant position. In doing so, however, it gives up maximum current profit, which it hopes to make up in the next stage.

Maturity Stage

At some point, a product's sales growth will slow down, and the product will enter a maturity stage. This **maturity stage** normally lasts longer than the previous stages, and it poses strong challenges to marketing management.

Most products are in the maturity stage of the life cycle, and therefore most of marketing management deals with the mature product.

The slowdown in sales growth results in many producers with many products to sell. In turn, this overcapacity leads to greater competition. Competitors begin marking down prices, increasing their advertising and sales promotions, and upping their R&D

During the growth stage, competition becomes more intense. In Cambodia, there are many local and foreign beer companies such as Angkor Beer, Jade Beer, and Chang Beer. They see the growing beer consumption as attractive.

Introduction stage
The product life-cycle stage in which the new product is first distributed and made available for purchase.

Growth stage
The product life-cycle stage in which a product's sales start climbing quickly.

Maturity stage
The product life-cycle stage in which sales growth slows or levels off.

budgets to find better versions of the product. These steps lead to a drop in profit. Some of the weaker competitors start dropping out, and the industry eventually contains only well-established competitors.

Although many products in the mature stage appear to remain unchanged for long periods, most successful ones are actually evolving to meet changing consumer needs. Product managers should do more than simply ride along with or defend their mature products—a good offense is the best defense. They should consider modifying the market, product, and marketing mix.

In *modifying* the market, the company tries to increase the consumption of the current product. It may look for new users and new market segments.

The manager may also look for ways to increase usage among present customers. Amazon.com does this by sending permission-based e-mails to regular customers letting them know when their favorite authors or performers publish new books or CDs. The WD-40 Company has shown a real knack for expanding the market by finding new uses for its popular substance.

In 2000, the company launched a search to uncover 2,000 unique uses for WD-40. After receiving 300,000 individual submissions, it narrowed the list to the best 2,000 and posted it on the company's Web site. Some consumers suggest simple and practical uses. One teacher uses WD-40 to clean old chalkboards in her classroom. "Amazingly, the boards started coming to life again," she reports. "Not only were they restored, but years of masking and Scotch tape residue came off as well." Others, however, report some pretty unusual applications. One man uses WD-40 to polish his glass eye; another uses it to remove a prosthetic leg. And did you hear about the nude burglary suspect who had wedged himself in a vent at a café? The fire department extracted him with a large dose of WD-40. Then there's the college student who wrote to say that a friend's nightly amorous activities in the next room were causing everyone in his dorm to lose sleep—he solved the problem by treating the squeaky bedsprings with WD-40.[18]

Nip dirt and rust in the bud. For clean, smooth operation and perennial protection from the elements, spray your hand tools with WD-40® before and after each use.

wd40.com

The WD-40 Company's knack for finding new uses has made this popular substance one of the truly essential survival items in many homes.

The company might also try *modifying the product*—changing characteristics such as quality, features, style, or packaging to attract new users and to inspire more usage. It might improve the product's quality and performance—its durability, reliability, speed, taste. It can improve the product's styling and attractiveness. Thus, car manufacturers restyle their cars to attract buyers who want a new look. The makers of consumer food and household products introduce new flavors, colors, ingredients, or packages to revitalize consumer buying.

Or the company might add new features that expand the product's usefulness, safety, or convenience. For example, WD-40 introduced a new Smart Straw can featuring a permanently attached straw that never gets lost. And it brought out a No-Mess Pen, with a handy pen-shaped applicator that lets users "put WD-40 where you want it and nowhere else."

Finally, the company can try *modifying the marketing mix*—improving sales by changing one or more marketing mix elements. It can cut prices to attract new users and competitors' customers. It can launch a better advertising campaign or use aggressive sales promotions—trade deals, cents-off, premiums, and contests. In addition to pricing and promotion, the company can also move into larger market channels, using mass merchandisers, if these channels are growing. Finally, the company can offer new or improved services to buyers.

Decline Stage

Decline stage
The product life-cycle stage in which a product's sales decline.

The sales of most product forms and brands eventually dip. The decline may be slow, as in the case of oatmeal cereal, or rapid, as in the cases of cassette and VHS tapes. Sales may plunge to zero, or they may drop to a low level where they continue for many years. This is the **decline stage**.

Sales decline for many reasons, including technological advances, shifts in consumer tastes, and increased competition. As sales and profits decline, some firms withdraw from the market. Those remaining may prune their product offerings. They may drop smaller market segments and marginal trade channels, or they may cut the promotion budget and reduce their prices further.

Carrying a weak product can be very costly to a firm. A weak product may take up too much of management's time. It often requires frequent price and inventory adjustments. It requires advertising and sales-force attention that might be better used to make "healthy" products more profitable. A product's failing reputation can cause customer concerns about the company and its other products. The biggest cost may well lie in the future. Keeping weak products delays the search for replacements, creates a lopsided product mix, hurts current profits, and weakens the company's foothold on the future.

For these reasons, companies need to pay more attention to their aging products. The firm's first task is to identify those products in the decline stage by regularly reviewing sales, market shares, costs, and profit trends. Then, management must decide whether to maintain, harvest, or drop each of these declining products.

Management may decide to *maintain* its brand without change in the hope that competitors will leave the industry. For example, Procter & Gamble made good profits by remaining in the declining liquid soap business as others withdrew. Or management may decide to reposition or reinvigorate the brand in hopes of moving it back into the growth stage of the product life cycle. Procter & Gamble has done this with several brands, including Mr. Clean and Old Spice. Management may decide to harvest the product, which means reducing various costs (plant and equipment, maintenance, R&D, advertising, sales force) and hoping that sales hold up. If successful, harvesting will increase the company's profits in the short run. Or management may decide to drop the product from the line. It can sell it to another firm or simply liquidate it at salvage value. In recent years, Procter & Gamble has sold off a number of lesser or declining brands such as Jif peanut butter. If the company plans to find a buyer, it will not want to run down the product through harvesting.

Working at both ends of the product life-cycle –
Along with creating innovative new products, P&G has become adept at turning yesterday's faded favorites into today's hot new products. For example, its Mr. Clean brand has now muscled its way back into a market-leading position.

(image caption within ad) Cleans tables, chairs, stairs, you name it. Mr. Clean Magic Eraser. Cleans like magic.

Additional Product and Service Considerations

Here, we'll wrap up our discussion of products and services with two additional considerations: social responsibility in product decisions and issues of international product and service marketing.

Product Decisions and Social Responsibility

Product decisions have attracted much public attention. Marketers should carefully consider public policy issues and regulations involving acquiring or dropping products, patent protection, product quality and safety, and product warranties.

Regarding new products, the government may prevent companies from adding products through acquisitions if the effect threatens to lessen competition. Companies dropping products must be aware that they have legal obligations, written or implied, to their suppliers, dealers, and customers who have a stake in the dropped product.

Companies must also obey patent laws when developing new products. A company cannot make its product illegally similar to another company's established product.

Manufacturers must comply with specific laws regarding product quality and safety. Various acts provide for the inspection of sanitary conditions in the meat - and poultry-processing industries. If consumers have been injured by a product that has been designed defectively, they can sue manufacturers or dealers.

International Product and Services Marketing

International product and service marketers face special challenges. First, they must figure out what products and services to introduce and in which countries. Then, they must decide how much to standardize or adapt their products and services for world markets.

On the one hand, companies would like to standardize their offerings. Standardization helps a company to develop a consistent worldwide image. It also lowers the product design, manufacturing, and marketing costs of offering a large variety of products. On the other hand, markets and consumers around the world differ widely. Companies must usually respond to these differences by adapting their product offerings.

Packaging also presents new challenges for international marketers. Packaging issues can be subtle. For example, names, labels, and colors may not translate easily from one country to another. Yellow is a favored color in Thailand because it signifies royalty but may meet with disaster in Mexico, where a yellow flower symbolizes death or disrespect. Packaging may also need to be tailored to meet the physical characteristics of consumers in various parts of the world. For instance, soft drinks are sold in smaller cans in Japan to fit the smaller Japanese hand better. Thus, although product and package standardization can produce benefits, companies usually adapt their offerings to the unique needs of specific international markets.

Yellow is a favored color in Thailand where it signifies royalty and people wear it as a sign of respect for the king.

Service marketers also face special challenges when going global. Some service industries have a long history of international operations. For example, the commercial banking industry was one of the first to grow internationally. Banks had to provide global services to meet the foreign exchange and credit needs of their home country clients wanting to sell overseas.

Professional and business services industries such as accounting, management consulting, and advertising have also globalized. The international growth of these firms followed the globalization of the client companies they serve. For example, as more clients employ worldwide marketing and advertising strategies, advertising agencies have responded by globalizing their own operations. McCann Worldgroup, a large U.S.-based advertising and marketing services agency, operates in more than 130 countries. It serves international clients such as Coca-Cola, General Motors, ExxonMobil, Microsoft, MasterCard, Johnson & Johnson, and Unilever in markets ranging from the U.S. and Canada to Korea and Kazakhstan. Moreover, McCann Worldgroup is one company in the Interpublic Group of Companies, an immense, worldwide network of advertising and marketing services companies.[19]

Retailers are among the latest service businesses to go global. As their home markets become saturated, American retailers such as Wal-Mart are expanding into faster-growing markets abroad. For example, since 1991, Wal-Mart has entered 14 countries; its international division's sales grew more than 13 percent last year, skyrocketing to more than $90.6 billion in 2007. Foreign retailers are making similar moves. Asian shoppers can now buy American products in French-owned Carrefour stores. Carrefour, the world's second-largest retailer behind Wal-Mart, operates in more than 11,000 stores in more than 30 countries. It is the leading retailer in Europe, Brazil, and Argentina and the largest foreign retailer in China.[20]

The trend toward growth of global service companies will continue, especially in banking, airlines, telecommunications, and professional services. Today service firms are no longer simply following their manufacturing customers. Instead, they are taking the lead in international expansion.

REVIEWING THE CONCEPTS

A company's current products face limited life spans and must be replaced by newer products. But new products can fail—the risks of innovation are as great as the rewards. The key to successful innovation lies in a total-company effort, strong planning, and a systematic *new-product development process*.

1 Explain how companies find and develop new-product ideas.

Companies find and develop new-product ideas from a variety of sources. Many new-product ideas stem from internal sources. Companies conduct formal research and development, pick the brains of their employees, and brainstorm at executive meetings. Other *ideas* come from *external sources*. By conducting surveys and focus groups and analyzing *customer* questions and complaints, companies can generate new-product ideas that will meet specific consumer needs. Companies track *competitors'* offerings and inspect new products, dismantling them, analyzing their performance, and deciding whether to introduce a similar or improved product. *Distributors* and *suppliers* are close to the market and can pass along information about consumer problems and new-product possibilities.

2 List and define the steps in the new-product development process and the major considerations in managing this process.

The new-product development process consists of eight sequential stages. The process starts with *idea generation*. Next comes *idea screening*, which reduces the number of ideas based on the company's own criteria. Ideas that pass the screening stage continue through *product concept development*, in which a detailed version of the new-product idea is stated in meaningful consumer terms. In the next stage, *concept testing*, new-product concepts are tested with a group of target consumers to determine whether the concepts have strong consumer appeal. Strong concepts proceed to *marketing strategy development*, in which an initial marketing strategy for the new product is developed from the product concept. In the *business-analysis* stage, a review of the sales, costs, and profit projections for a new product is conducted to determine whether the new product is likely to satisfy the company's objectives. With positive results here, the ideas become more concrete through *product development* and *test marketing* and finally are launched during *commercialization*.

New-product development involves more than just going through a set of steps. Companies must take a systematic, holistic approach to managing this process. Successful new-product development requires a customer-centered, team-based, systematic effort.

3 Describe the stages of the product life cycle.

Each product has a *life cycle* marked by a changing set of problems and opportunities. The sales of the typical product follow an S-shaped curve made up of five stages. The cycle begins with the *product development* stage when the company finds and develops a new-product idea. The *introduction stage* is marked by slow growth and low profits as the product is distributed to the market. If successful, the product enters a growth stage, which offers rapid sales growth and increasing profits. Next comes a *maturity stage* when sales growth slows and profits stabilize. Finally, the product enters a *decline stage* in which sales and profits dwindle. The company's task during this stage is to recognize the decline and to decide whether it should maintain, harvest, or drop the product.

4 Describe how marketing strategies change during the product's life cycle.

In the *introduction stage*, the company must choose a launch strategy consistent with its intended product positioning. Much money is needed to attract distributors and build their inventories and to inform consumers of the new product and achieve trial. In the *growth stage*, companies continue to educate potential consumers and distributors. In addition, the company works to stay ahead of the competition and sustain rapid market growth by improving product quality, adding new product features and models, entering new market segments and distribution channels, shifting advertising from building product awareness to building product conviction and purchase, and lowering prices at the right time to attract new buyers.

In the *maturity stage*, companies continue to invest in maturing products and consider modifying the market, the product, and the marketing mix. When *modifying the market*, the company attempts to increase the consumption of the current product. When modifying the product, the company changes some of the product's characteristics—such as quality, features, or style—to attract new users or inspire more usage. When *modifying the marketing mix*, the company works to improve sales by changing one or more of the marketing-mix elements. Once the company recognizes that a product has entered the *decline stage*, management must decide whether to maintain the brand without change, hoping that competitors will drop out of the market; *harvest* the product, reducing costs and trying to maintain sales; or *drop* the product, selling it to another firm or liquidating it at salvage value.

5 Discuss two additional product issues: socially responsible product decisions and international product and services marketing.

Marketers must consider two additional product issues. The first is *social responsibility*. This includes public policy issues and regulations involving acquiring or dropping products, patent protection, product quality and safety, and product warranties. The second involves the special challenges facing international product and service marketers. International marketers must decide how much to standardize or adapt their offerings for world markets.

REVIEWING THE KEY TERMS

Business analysis 238
Commercialization 241
Concept testing 237
Customer-centered new-product development 242
Decline stage 250
Fad 246
Fashion 246
Growth stage 248
Idea generation 233
Idea screening 235
Introduction stage 248
Marketing strategy development 237

Maturity stage 248
New-product development 233
Product concept 236
Product development 288
Product life cycle (PLC) 244
Style 246
Team-based new-product development 242
Test marketing 239

DISCUSSING THE CONCEPTS

1. Why is concept testing important?

2. Under what conditions would you consider not test marketing a product? Describe a product or service that meets these no-need-to-test criteria.

3. Compare the sequential product development to the team-based approach. Is one approach better than the other? Explain.

4. Identify and discuss some potential problems with the product life cycle.

5. The chapter states that "In the growth stage of the product life cycle, the firm faces a trade-off between high market share and high current profit." Explain this statement.

6. What are some of the major reasons a product reaches the decline stage of the product life cycle? Explain.

APPLYING THE CONCEPTS

1. Form a small group. Generate ideas for a new consumer product that fills an existing need but does not currently exist. Select the one idea that you think is best. What process did your group use for idea generation and screening?

2. Write a marketing strategy statement for a new full functioning but folding bicycle.

3. You are a product manager in a firm that manufactures and markets a line of branded action figure toys. The branded toy line is five years old Annual sales and profits for this period are presented in the chart. Prepare a one-sentence strategy for each of the four Ps based on the brand's current product life-cycle position.

FOCUS ON TECHNOLOGY

There are over 250,000 deaths per year from sudden cardiac arrest in the U.S. Defibrillators are medical devices that are commonly used by firefighters and paramedics to treat victims of sudden cardiac arrest with an electrical charge that restarts their hearts. With more than 80 percent of sudden cardiac arrests occurring at home, and only five percent of victims receiving the lifesaving electrical charge, Philips is now marketing a portable consumer defibrillator called the HeartStart. The product, which is about the size of a handheld video game, can be operated by any individual and does not need a trained medical provider. Voice activation guides a consumer through each step, and smart technology gives specific instructions based on feedback to the main system. The FDA-approved product, priced at $1,495, is available online from amazon.com and drugstore.com. Visit *http://www.heartstart.com* for recent information on this new product.

1. Explain how this product might have moved through the stages of new-product development.

2. How might the marketing strategy for HeartStart change as it moves through the product life cycle?

 FOCUS ON ETHICS

Marks & Spencer (M&S), one of the largest retailers in the UK with over 400 stores, has embraced socially responsible fashion. Since March 2006, M&S began selling fair-trade-certified T-shirts. By July 2006, the line expanded to jeans, underwear, shorts, vests, and socks. The philosophy behind fair trade is to support the more than 100 million households worldwide who are involved in cotton production. These farmers, especially in poor countries, are vulnerable to lower cotton prices. In fact, a common reaction is for the farmers to use more pesticides to increase their yields, thus fueling an environmental issue in addition to a social issue. M&S brought its new products to consumers' attention with a look-behind-the-label campaign. According to the company, the new products are a reaction to consumers' questions about how cotton is produced and their realization of the social and environmental issues that are involved. According to a 2006 Yougov Brand Index poll, M&S's corporate reputation has risen since the new campaign began.

1. How did M&S conduct test marketing with the fair-trade certified clothing?

2. In what stage of the product life cycle are these trade certified clothing products?

3. Do you think the product life-cycle curve will follow the shape of a style, fashion, or fad?

See: Ellen Groves, "Fair Trade Fashion Takes Off in Europe," *Women's Wear Daily*, May 3, 2006, p. 6.

 VIDEO CASE

eGO Bikes

When it hit the market in 2002, the eGO was the first vehicle of its kind: an environmentally friendly, compact electric cycle. At the time, the product was so unique that the company had to develop new channels to distribute and sell it. Along with its cool, retro styling and innovative electrical design, the eGO Cycle costs less than half a cent per mile to drive. One model is even equipped with front and rear turn signals and a backlit speedometer for those who commute in heavy traffic.

Aside from being featured on national news broadcasts and in trade magazines, the eGO Cycle made Oprah Winfrey's list of favorite things and the Today Show's list for best Father's Day gifts. In addition, the company's Web site boasts testimonial after testimonial supporting the electric bike. Customers delight in using the bike for everything from commuting and running errands to enhancing business services. Says one thrilled owner, "This is the first bike I ever had that's built like a BMW!"

After viewing the video featuring eGO vehicles, answer the following questions about new-product development.

1. Describe eGO's design process. How is it similar to the process detailed in the chapter?

2. How did eGO manage its limited channel options to distribute the new product?

3. Visit eGO's Web site to learn more about products the company offers. What stage of the product life cycle is the eGO vehicle experiencing?

COMPANY CASE

Sony: Betting it All on Blu-Ray

The year was 1976. Sony was entering into a format war with other consumer electronics manufacturers. The victor would capture the prize of owning the consumer home video market. Wait a minute… is this 1976, or is it 2006? Actually, it could be either.

In 1976, Sony introduced the first VCR for home use. Called the Betamax, it was as big as a microwave oven and cost a whopping $1,295 (more than $6,000 in today's money). A year later, RCA was the first of many manufacturers to introduce a VCR using a different technology: VHS. In terms of image quality, Beta was considered superior to VHS. Sony also had the advantage of being first to market. But VHS machines were cheaper and allowed longer recording times (initially, four hours versus Beta's two hours). In addition, there were far more movies available for purchase or rent in VHS than in Beta. Ultimately, consumers decided that those features were more important. VHS quickly surpassed Beta in market share, eventually wiping out Beta entirely. In 1988, Sony surrendered by making the switch from Beta to VHS.

Two Modern Technologies: Blu-Ray versus HD DVD

Today, once again, Sony finds itself gearing up for a format war in the consumer home video market. This time, Sony will go to battle with Blu-ray technology, pitted against the HD DVD format. As in 1976, the two technologies will compete to dominate the home video market, now worth more than $24 billion.

Blu-ray was developed by a coalition that includes Sony, Hitachi, Pioneer, Philips, Panasonic, Samsung, LG, Sharp, Apple, HP, and other companies. HD DVD was developed by another coalition backed commercially by Toshiba, Sanyo, Kenwood, Intel, and NEC, among others. Although each of the technologies was developed by a coalition,

Sony and Toshiba appear to be the dominant players in their respective camps. And whereas Sony stood pretty much alone in pitting Beta against VHS, its Blu-ray forum has more corporate firepower in this battle.

In a situation where the differences between the two technologies seem critical, the formats are surprisingly similar. Both use physical discs identical in diameter and thickness to current DVD discs. This allows the developers of the new-generation players to make them backward compatible (able to play previous-generation DVDs). Additionally, each technology employs a blue laser of the same wave length, as well as similar video encoding and basic copyright protection features.

Will the Differences Matter?

Despite the similarities, the Blu-ray and HD DVD formats have notable differences. Interestingly, some of the key differences likely to affect the success of the two new DVD formats are the same features that differentiated Beta and VHS 30 years ago. Specifically, both sides are vying for image quality, disc capacity, price, and availability of content advantages. At least initially, Blu-ray captures the quality advantage in this race. However, both Blu-ray and HD DVD produce high-definition video far superior to current DVD images, and the quality difference between the two may be indistinguishable by the average human eye.

Although Blu-ray and HD DVD discs look identical, there are fundamental differences in the way the discs are put together. Blu-ray uses more layers of data encoding and can store more data on each layer. Thus, Blu-ray discs can store far more information—up to 200 gigabytes (GB) versus HD DVD's 90 GB. For home video, this means that a single Blu-ray disc can hold longer movies. "Capacity is always going to be your number-one concern," says Andy Parsons, spokesperson for Sony's coalition and senior vice president of advanced product development for Pioneer.

However, whereas capacity was critical in Beta versus VHS, many observers believe that it will be less of an issue today. Both Blu-ray and HD DVD discs will have more than enough capacity to hold a feature-length high-definition film. But Parsons is quick to point out that consumers really like the bonus features on DVDs, so much so that many titles now come in two–disc sets—one disc for the movie and the other for bonus features. Even so, given the compact size of modern discs, capacity may be less of an issue than it was when video tapes were the size of paperback books. Additionally, it has yet to be determined how many layers could be added to either technology, ultimately affecting data capacity.

Regardless of the capacity issue, price is critical. Toshiba introduced the first HD DVD players in April of 2006 at price points of $499 and $799. Pioneer introduced the first

Blu-ray machine in June of 2006 at a much higher price of $1,800. This price difference parallels that of Beta versus VHS in the 1970s. However, Parsons shares some insights on the implications of Toshiba's introductory strategy:

As part of a marketing strategy, certain companies such as Toshiba say, "Even though it costs us this much money to make this product, we're going to price it lower, even if it's below our factory cost, because taking that kind of loss up front might help to get the market populated with our product and help accelerate adoption." That kind of thinking is generally not very successful, because it ignores one very important element: You have to build awareness for the new technology before you can assume that price is an important or overriding factor.

This is why we have a natural curve with an early-adopter group of people who are very focused on technology and performance. Right now in this space, the big buzzword is 1080P progressive scan, 24 frames per second, full-resolution HD TV—this is the Holy Grail, because it's the closest you can get to a theater experience in terms of frame rates, and [it's] a hot button for people who are following this story at the consumer level.

Consumers interested in buying technology that gives them the best display or audio quality won't balk at the price. This is why our player is $1,800. We focused on getting 1080P, because that is something we knew would resonate with the initial target market, whereas the $499 strategy is probably going off in the wrong direction, because the folks who are really paying attention to this right now want the highest resolution.

Taking another cue from Beta versus VHS, the Blu-ray and HD DVD camps have fought to get the support of major movie studios. The idea is that the format offering more movies will have the advantage. As both technologies come to market, Blu-ray has signed seven studios; HD DVD has signed only three. Although most studios are backing only one technology at this point, Warner Bros. indicates that it will ultimately release movies in both formats. Other studios may well follow suit.

In the current format war, only time will tell if image quality, capacity, price, and content availability will have the same impact as they did 30 years ago. The HD DVD forum claims that new issues this time around will give its technology the advantage. For starters, manufacturing costs for Blu-ray will be significantly higher. (The Blu-ray camp counters that the cost difference is minimal and will likely disappear as volumes increase.) HD DVD software will also allow consumers to make copies of their discs to computer hard drives and portable devices. With its iHD technology, HD DVD discs promise greater interactivity by allowing for enhanced content and navigation, as well as fancy features such as picture-in-picture capability.

However, additional new issues could tilt the scales in favor of Blu-ray. Although Toshiba and HD DVD enjoy a brief first-to-market advantage, Blu-ray will likely experience a huge bump in market share when Sony introduces its PlayStation 3 gaming platform in late 2006. The PlayStation 3 not only uses Blu-ray technology for its game discs, it will be able to play all Blu-ray movies as well. This could put millions of Blu-ray players into homes very quickly via the video consoles.

Will the Point Be Moot?

Drawing comparisons to the Beta/VHS format war assumes that one of the two current competing formats will ultimately win and the other will die out. However, two other possibilities exist. First, both formats could succeed and do well. As both formats evolve, either of the two technologies could adopt features of the other. Additionally, at some point, hardware manufacturers may well release dual-format players, capable of playing both Blu-ray and HD DVD discs. Such a development could reduce the relevance of format labels.

Stephen Nickerson, senior vice president at Warner Home Video, believes that both formats could easily succeed. Although most analysts compare the DVD format war to the VCR format war, he suggests another analogy. "The [video] games industry since the early '90s has had two or three incompatible formats and it hasn't slowed the adoption of game platforms."

The other potential outcome is that both formats might fail. Ted Schadler, analyst with Forrester Research, says, "The irony of this format war is that it comes at the tail end of the century-long era of physical media. While a high-definition video format does bring benefits over today's standard-definition discs, in movies as in music, consumers are moving beyond shiny discs." Consumers have far more options than they used to, and the dust has yet to settle on which options will dominate for any given type of product.

For home video, more customers are choosing on-demand, nonphysical media, including online video and video-on-demand television. One in six cable subscribers has demonstrated significant interest in watching video-on-demand. As cable providers increase their video libraries and technologies improve, that number will only grow. Internet video is also spreading rapidly, with 46 percent of online consumers now watching movies via the Web. Additionally, with the success of the video iPod, major Hollywood studios aren't just considering which DVD formats to support. They're assessing how they can make money by selling movies directly to consumers in a file format that can be played on portable devices. According to Schadler, the device more consumers aged 12 to 21 now say they can't live without isn't their TV, it's their PC. Even Bill Gates has his doubts about the current DVD format war. "Understand that this is the last physical format there will ever be. Everything's going to be streamed directly or on a hard disk."

Although these predictions may very well be true, there is likely still plenty of steam left in the DVD market. Physical discs still hold many advantages over the nonphysical media. Even with the significant threat of VHS, Beta survived for eight years. And no format will last forever. In February 2008, Toshiba announced that it would reduce production of HD DVD players. It had lost the support of some main studies and retailers. Sony Blu-Ray has won the format war.

Questions For Discussion

1. Classify the high-definition DVD market using the product life-cycle framework. Based on this analysis, what objectives and strategies should Sony and the other competitors pursue? Are any of the competitors deviating from this formula?

2. As sales of the new DVD players increase, what will happen to the characteristics of the home video market and the strategies employed by Sony and other competitors?

3. Analyze the development of Blu-ray and HD DVD according to the stages of the new-product development process.

4. Who are the current combatants in the battle for the home video market? Who will they be in five years?

Sources:

Beth Snyder Bulik, "Marketing War Looms for Dueling DVD Formats," *Advertising Age*, April 10, 2006, p. 20; Gary Gentile, "Beta/VHS-Like Battle Shaping Up for New High Def DVDs," *Associated Press Worldstream*, January 6, 2006; Ann Steffora Mutschler, "The Convergence War," *Electronic Business*, May 1, 2006, p. 44; Sue Zeidler, "Hold On Tight; Going to the Store to Rent a DVD May Soon Be a Thing of the Past," *Calgary Sun*, p. 40; information on Beta and VHS accessed online at www totalrewind.org. "HD DVD Lost the War Against Blu-ray, Toshiba Gave Up," www.infoniac.com, February 19, 2008.

Objectives

After studying this chapter, you should be able to

- answer the question "What is price?" and discuss the importance of pricing in today's fast-changing environment
- discuss the importance of understanding customer value perceptions when setting prices
- discuss the importance of company and product costs in setting prices
- identify and define the other important internal and external factors affecting a firm's pricing decisions

CHAPTER 10

PRICING PRODUCTS: Understanding and Capturing Customer Value

Previewing the Concepts

Next, we look at a second major marketing mix tool—pricing. According to one pricing expert, pricing lets a company "get paid for the value it creates for customers."[1] Firms successful at creating customer value with the other marketing mix activities must still capture some of this value in the prices they earn. Yet, despite its importance, many firms do not handle pricing well. In this chapter, we'll look at internal and external considerations that affect pricing decisions and examine general pricing approaches. In the next chapter, we look into pricing strategies.

Pricing decisions can make or break a company. For openers, consider Steinway & Sons, makers of "the finest pianos in the world," with a price to match. Steinway's grand pianos can cost as much as $165,000.

A Steinway piano costs a lot. A Steinway grand piano typically runs from $40,000 to $165,000. The most popular model sells for around $72,000. For Steinway buyers, it seems the higher the prices, the better. High prices confirm that a Steinway is the best that money can buy—the epitome of handcrafted perfection. As important, the Steinway name is steeped in tradition. It evokes images of classical concert stages, sophisticated dinner parties, and the celebrities and performers who've owned and played Steinway pianos for over 150 years. Since its founding in 1853, the company's motto has been "The Instrument of the Immortals." When it comes to Steinway, price is nothing, the Steinway experience is everything.

Steinway & Sons makes pianos of very high quality. With 115 patents, it has done more than any other manufacturer to advance the art of piano building. Steinway pioneered the development of a one-piece piano rim produced from 17 laminations of veneer. It invented a process for bending a single 22-foot-long strip of these laminated sheets inside a massive piano-shaped vise. It's this strong frame that produces Steinway's distinctive clear tones. Steinway & Sons has continued perfecting this design. Today a Steinway piano's 243 tempered, hard-steel strings exert 35 tons of pressure—enough force to implode a three-bedroom house if the strings were strung between attic and cellar.

In addition to cutting-edge technology, Steinway & Sons uses only the finest materials to construct each piano. Rock maple, spruce, birch, poplar, and four other species of wood each play a crucial functional role in the physical and acoustical beauty of a Steinway.

The expansive wooden soundboard is made from select Alaskan Sitka spruce—one grade higher than aircraft grade. Through delicate handcraftsmanship, Steinway transforms these select materials into pianos of incomparable sound quality. It takes 450 skilled workers over a year to handcraft and assemble a Steinway piano from its 12,000 component parts. Each year, Steinway's factories in Astoria, New York, and Hamburg, Germany, craft approximately 5,000 pianos. By comparison, Yamaha produces 100,000 pianos per year.

Steinway buyers also get the Steinway mystique. Owning or playing a Steinway puts you in some very good company. Fully 98 percent of piano soloists with the world's major symphony orchestras prefer playing on a Steinway. Over 90 percent of the world's 1,300 concert pianists bear the title of Steinway Artist—an elite club of Steinway-owning professional musicians. Steinway customers include composers and professional musicians (from Van Cliburn to Billy Joel), upscale customers (from Lamar Alexander to Paula Zahn), and heads of state (the 25,000th Steinway was sold to Czar Alexander of Russia, and Piano No. 300,000 graces the East Room of the White House, replacing Piano No. 100,000, which is now in the Smithsonian).

Performers praise Steinway. "Steinway is the only piano on which the pianist can do everything he wants. And everything he dreams," declares premier pianist and conductor Vladimir Ashkenazy. Contemporary singer-songwriter Randy Newman says, "I have owned and played a Steinway all my life. It's the best Beethoven piano. The best Chopin piano. And the best Ray Charles piano. I like it, too." Whereas some people want a Porsche, others prefer a Steinway—both cost about the same, and both make a statement about their owners.

But Steinways aren't just for world-class pianists and the wealthy. Ninety-nine percent of all Steinway buyers are amateurs. "We see a lot of corporate executives and physicians buying Steinway grands," says a Steinway marketer. "But it is not unusual at all for a middle-income person to come in and buy a grand." Steinway offers a finance plan that lets cash-strapped enthusiasts pay for their grand piano over a 12-year period.

Even in the worst of times, Steinway & Sons has held true to its tradition and image—and to its premium prices. When its current owners bought the troubled company in 1984 from the Steinway family, they were burdened with 900 pianos of excess inventory. Rather than slashing prices and risk tarnishing the brand, managers restored the company's health by holding prices and renewing its commitment to quality. Steinway thus retained its cult-like following and continues to dominate its market. Despite its very high prices—or more likely because of them—Steinway enjoys a 95 percent market share in concert halls.

So, you won't find any weekend sales on Steinway pianos. Charging significantly higher prices continues to be a cornerstone of the company's "much more for much more" value proposition. High prices have been good for Steinway & Sons. Although the company accounts for only 3 percent of all U.S. pianos sold each year, it captures 25 percent of the industry's sales dollars and close to 35 percent of the profits.

To drive growth, Steinway has expanded its product range and started production and marketing in Asia. The company launched its lower-priced Boston and Essex lines featuring the tone and touch of its Steinway line. Designs are based on Steinway patents but the pianos are built in Asia using production-line assembly techniques. Manufactured at its Japanese factory, about 5,000 Boston pianos in nine versions are sold annually. The lowest-priced Essex line is built at Steinway's Korean and Chinese facilities. In Asia, Steinway showrooms, salons, and halls can be found in China, Japan, and Korea. The company also has Web sites for China and Japan.[2]

Companies today face a fierce and fast-changing pricing environment. Increasing customer price consciousness has made companies look for ways to slash prices. Yet, cutting prices unnecessarily can lead to lost profits and damaging price wars. It can signal to customers that the price is more important than the customer value a brand delivers. Instead, like Steinway & Sons, companies should sell value, not price. They should persuade customers that paying a higher price for the company's brand is justified by the greater value they gain. The challenge is to find the price that will let the company make a fair profit by getting paid for the customer value it creates.

In this chapter and the next, we focus on the process of setting prices. This chapter defines prices, looks at the factors marketers must consider when setting prices, and examines general pricing approaches. In the next chapter, we look at pricing strategies for new-product pricing, product mix pricing, price adjustments for buyer and situational factors, and price changes.

Price
The amount of money charged for a product or service, or the sum of the values that consumers exchange for the benefits of having or using the product or service.

What Is a Price?

In the narrowest sense, price is the amount of money charged for a product or service. It is the sum of all the values that customers give up to gain the benefits of having or using a product or service. It is one of the most important elements determining a firm's market share and profitability.

Price is the only element in the marketing mix that produces revenue; all other elements represent costs. Price is also one of the most flexible marketing mix elements. Unlike product features and channel commitments, prices can be changed quickly. At the same time, pricing is the number-one problem facing many marketing executives, and many companies do not handle pricing well. One frequent problem is that companies are too quick to reduce prices to get a sale rather than convincing buyers that their product's greater value is worth a higher price. Other common mistakes include pricing that is too cost- rather than customer-value oriented, and pricing that does not take the marketing mix into account.

Smart managers treat pricing as a key strategic tool for creating and capturing customer value. Prices have a direct impact on a firm's bottom line. More importantly, as a part of a company's overall value proposition, price plays a key role in creating customer value and building customer relationships.

Factors to Consider When Setting Prices

The price the company charges falls between one that is too high to produce any demand and one that is too low to produce a profit. **Figure 10.1** summarizes the major considerations in setting price. Customer perceptions of the product's value set the ceiling for prices. If customers perceive that the price is greater than the product's value, they will not buy the product. Product costs set the floor for prices. If the company prices the product below its costs, company profits will suffer. In setting its price between these two extremes, the company must consider a number of other internal and external factors, including its overall marketing strategy and mix, the nature of the market and demand, and competitors' strategies and prices.

Figure 10.1
Considerations in setting price

In the end, the customer will decide whether a product's price is right. Pricing decisions, like other marketing mix decisions, start with customer value. When customers buy a product, they exchange something of value (the price) to get something of value (the benefits of having or using the product). Effective, customer-oriented pricing involves understanding how much value consumers place on the benefits they receive from the product and setting a price that captures this value.

Value-Based Pricing

Good pricing begins with an understanding of the value that a product or service creates for customers. **Value-based** pricing uses buyers' perceptions of value, not the seller's cost, as the key to pricing. Value-based pricing means that the marketer cannot design a product and marketing program and then set the price. Price is considered along with the other marketing mix variables *before* the marketing program is set.

Figure 10.2 compares value-based pricing with cost-based pricing. Cost-based pricing is product driven. The company designs what it considers to be a good product, adds up the costs of making the product, and sets a price that covers costs plus a target profit. Marketing then convinces buyers that the product's value at that price justifies its purchase. If the price turns out to be too high, the company must settle for lower markups or lower sales, both resulting in less profit.

> **Value-based pricing**
> Setting prices based on buyers' perceptions of value rather than on the seller's cost.

Figure 10.2
Value-based pricing versus cost-based pricing

Source:
Thomas T. Nagle and Reed K.Holden, *The Strategy and Tactics of Pricing*, 3rd ed. (Upper Saddle River, NJ: Prentice Hall, 2002), p.4. Reproduced by permission of Pearson Education, Inc. Upper Saddle River, New Jersey

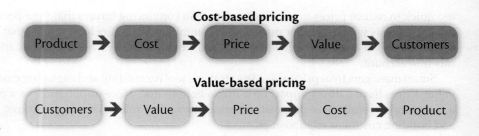

Cost-based pricing

Product → Cost → Price → Value → Customers

Value-based pricing

Customers → Value → Price → Cost → Product

Value-based pricing reverses this process. The company sets its target price based on customer perceptions of the product value. The targeted value and price then drive decisions about product design and what costs can be incurred. As a result, pricing begins with analyzing consumer needs and value perceptions, and price is set to match consumers' perceived value.

It's important to remember that "good value" is not the same as "low price." For example, prices for a Hermès Birkin Bag start at $6,000—a less expensive handbag might carry as much, but some consumers place great value on the intangibles they receive from a one-of-a kind handmade bag that has a year-long waiting list.

A company using value-based pricing must find out what value buyers assign to different competitive offers. However, companies often find it hard to measure the value customers will attach to its product. For example, calculating the cost of ingredients in a meal at a fancy restaurant is relatively easy. But assigning a value to other satisfactions such as taste, environment, relaxation, conversation, and status is challenging. Also, these values vary both for different consumers and different situations.

Sometimes, companies ask consumers how much they would pay for a basic product and for each benefit added to the offer. Or a company might conduct experiments to test the perceived value of different product offers. According to a Russian proverb, there are two fools in every market—one who asks too much and one who asks too little. If the seller charges more than the buyers' perceived value, the company's sales will suffer. If the seller charges less, its products sell very well. But they produce less revenue than they would if they were priced at the level of perceived value.

We now examine two types of value-based pricing: good-value pricing and value-added pricing.

Good-Value Pricing

During the past decade, marketers have noted a fundamental shift in consumer attitudes toward price and quality. Many companies have changed their pricing approaches to bring them into line with changing economic conditions and consumer price perceptions. More and more, marketers have adopted **good-value pricing** strategies—offering just the right combination of quality and good service at a fair price.

The waiting list for a Hermès Birkin bag ranges from anywhere between one to two years, and prices can reach six-digit sums if the bag is made of exotic animal skin. The exclusivity of the bag makes it even more valuable to consumers who are willing to fork out money to obtain one. (*www.hermes.com*)

Good-value pricing
Offering just the right combination of quality and good service at a fair price.

Wal-Mart is able to promise everyday low prices on everything it sells by having everyday low costs—something Kmart was unable to match. (www.walmart.com)

In many cases, this has involved introducing less-expensive versions of established, brand name products. Fast-food restaurants such as McDonald's offer "value menus." Armani offers the less-expensive, more casual Armani Exchange fashion line. In other cases, good-value pricing has involved redesigning existing brands to offer more quality for a given price or the same quality for less. For MNCs, offering good-value pricing does not necessarily mean matching local prices or even lower ones. The key is to make the product affordable to the majority of customers.

An important type of good-value pricing at the retail level is *everyday low pricing (EDLP)*. EDLP involves charging a constant, everyday low price with few or no temporary price discounts. In contrast, *high-low pricing* involves charging higher prices on an everyday basis but running frequent promotions to lower prices temporarily on selected items.

The king of EDLP is Wal-Mart. Except for a few sale items every month, Wal-Mart promises everyday low prices on everything it sells. In contrast, Kmart's recent attempts to match Wal-Mart's EDLP strategy failed. To offer everyday low prices, a company must first have everyday low costs.

Value-Added Pricing

In many business-to-business marketing situations, the challenge is to build the company's *pricing power*—its power to escape price competition and to justify higher prices and margins without losing market share. To retain pricing power, a firm must retain or build the value of its market offering.

To increase their pricing power, many companies adopt **value-added pricing** strategies. Rather than cutting prices to match competitors, they attach value-added features and services to differentiate their offers and thus support higher prices (see **Real Marketing**).

Company and Product Costs

Whereas customer-value perceptions set the price ceiling, costs set the floor for the price that the company can charge. **Cost-based pricing** involves setting prices based on the costs for producing, distributing, and selling the product plus a fair rate of return for its effort and risk. A company's costs may be an important element in its pricing strategy. Many companies, such as Air Asia, Carrefour, and Dell, work to become the "low-cost producers" in their industries. Companies with lower costs can set lower prices that result in greater sales and profits.

Types of Costs

A company's costs take two forms, fixed and variable. **Fixed costs** (also known as **overhead**) are costs that do not vary with production or sales level. For example, a company must pay each month's bills for rent, heat, interest, and executive salaries, whatever the company's output. **Variable costs** vary directly with the level of production. Each PC produced by Lenovo involves a cost of computer chips, wires, plastic, packaging, and other inputs. These costs tend to be the same for each unit produced. They are called variable because their total varies with the number of units produced. **Total costs** are the sum of the fixed and variable costs for any given level of production. Management wants to charge a price that will at least cover the total production costs at a given level of production.

The company must watch its costs carefully. If it costs the company more than it costs competitors to produce and sell its product, the company must charge a higher price or make less profit, putting it at a competitive disadvantage.

Costs at Different Levels of Production

To price wisely, management needs to know how its costs vary with different levels of production. For example, suppose Casio has built a plant to produce 1,000 calculators per day. **Figure 10.3A** shows the typical short-run average cost (SRAC) curve. It shows that the cost per calculator is high if Casio's factory produces only a few per day. But as production moves up to 1,000 calculators per day, average cost falls. This is because fixed costs are spread over more units, with each one bearing a smaller share of the fixed cost. Casio can try to produce more than 1,000 calculators per day, but average costs will increase because the plant becomes inefficient. Workers wait for machines, the machines break down more often, and workers get in each other's way.

Value-added pricing
Attaching value-added features and services to differentiate a company's offers and to support charging higher prices.

Cost-based pricing
Setting prices based on the costs for producing, distributing, and selling the product plus a fair rate of return for effort and risk.

Fixed costs (overhead)
Costs that do not vary with production or sales level.

Variable costs
Costs that vary directly with the level of production.

Total costs
The sum of the fixed and variable costs for any given level of production.

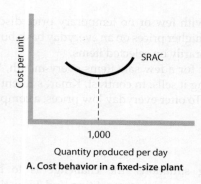

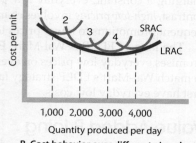

Figure 10.3
Cost per unit at different levels of production per period

A. Cost behavior in a fixed-size plant

Quantity produced per day

B. Cost behavior over different-size plants

Quantity produced per day

If Casio believed it could sell 2,000 calculators a day, it should consider building a larger plant. The plant would use more efficient machinery and work arrangements. Also, the unit cost of producing 2,000 calculators per day would be lower than the unit cost of producing 1,000 units per day, as shown in the long-run average cost (LRAC) curve (see **Figure 10.3B**). In fact, a 3,000-capacity plant would even be more efficient, according

REAL MARKETING

Pricing Power: The Value of Value Added

When a company finds its major competitors offering a similar product at a lower price, the natural tendency is to try to match or beat that price. Although the idea of undercutting competitors' prices and watching customers flock to you is tempting, there are dangers. Successive rounds of price-cutting can lead to price wars that erode the profit margins of all competitors in an industry. Or worse, discounting a product can cheapen it in the minds of customers, greatly reducing the seller's power to maintain profitable prices in the long term.

So, how can a company keep its pricing power when a competitor undercuts its price? Often, the best strategy is not to price below the competitor, but rather to price above and convince customers that the product is worth it. The company should ask, "What is the value of the product to the customer?" and then stand up for what the product is worth. In this way, the company shifts the focus from price to value.

Value added – Caterpillar offers its dealers a wide range of value-added services—from guaranteed parts delivery to investment management advice and equipment training. Such added value supports

But what if the company is operating in a "commodity" business, in which the products of all competitors seem pretty much alike? In such cases, the company must find ways to "decommoditize" its products—to create superior value for customers. It can do this by developing value-added features and services that differentiate its offer and justify higher prices and margins. Here are two examples of how suppliers are using value-added features and services to give them a competitive edge:

Caterpillar
Caterpillar charges premium prices for its heavy construction and mining equipment by convincing customers that its products and service justify every additional dollar. Caterpillar typically reaps a 20 to 30 percent price premium over competitors that can amount to an extra $200,000 or more for each truck.

When a large potential customer says, "I can get it for less from a competitor," the Caterpillar dealer doesn't discount the price. Instead, the dealer explains to Figure 10.3B. But a 4,000-daily production plant would be less efficient because of increasing diseconomies of scale—too many workers to manage, paperwork slowing things down, and so on. **Figure 10.3B** shows that a 3,000-daily production plant is the best size to build if demand is strong enough to support this level of production.

Costs as a Function of Production Experience

Suppose Casio runs a plant that produces 3,000 calculators per day. As Casio gains experience in producing calculators, it learns how to do it better. Workers learn shortcuts and become more familiar with their equipment. With practice, the work becomes better organized, and Casio finds better equipment and production processes. With higher volume, Casio becomes more efficient and gains economies of scale. As a result, average cost tends to fall with accumulated production experience. This is shown in **Figure 10.4**.[3] Thus, the average cost of producing the first 100,000 calculators is $10 per calculator. When the company has produced the first 200,000 calculators, the average cost has fallen to $9. After its accumulated production experience doubles again to 400,000, the average cost is $7. This drop in the average cost with accumulated production experience is called the **experience curve** (or the **learning curve**).

> **Experience curve (learning curve)**
> New-product development that focuses The drop in the average per-unit production cost that comes with accumulated production experience.

---

that, even at the higher price, Cat offers the best value. Caterpillar equipment is designed with modular components that can be removed and repaired quickly, minimizing machine downtime. Caterpillar dealers carry an extensive parts inventory and guarantee delivery within 48 hours anywhere worldwide, again minimizing downtime. Cat's products are designed to be rebuilt, providing a "second life" that competitors cannot match. As a result, Caterpillar used-equipment prices are often 20 percent to 30 percent higher. Beyond its high-quality equipment and maintenance, Caterpillar offers a wide range of value-adding services, from financing and insurance to equipment training and investment management advice.

In all, the dealer explains, even at the higher initial price, Caterpillar equipment delivers the lowest total cost per cubic yard of earth moved, ton of coal uncovered, or mile of road graded over the life of the product—guaranteed! Most customers seem to agree with Caterpillar's value proposition—themarket-leading company dominates its markets with a more than 37 percent worldwide market share. In the past two years, sales are up 60 percent and profits have rocketed 250 percent. Despite its higher prices, demand is so strong that

Caterpillar is having trouble making equipment fast enough to fill orders.

Pioneer Hi-Bred International
A major producer of commercial seeds and other agricultural products often thought of as commodities, DuPont subsidiary Pioneer Hi-Bred International (PHI) hardly acts like a commodity supplier. Its patented hybrid seeds yield 10 percent more crops than competitors' seeds. PHI's researchers harvest tens of thousands of test plots worldwide each year to perfect product yields and traits.

Beyond producing a superior product, PHI also provides a bundle of value-added services. For example, it equips its sales reps with laptop PCs and software that allow them to provide farmers with customized information and advice. The rep can plug in the type of hybrid that a farmer is using, along with information about pricing, acreage, and yield characteristics, and then advise the farmer on how to do a better job of farm management. The reps can also supply farmers with everything from agricultural research reports to assistance in comparison shopping. To add even more value, PHI offers farmers crop insurance, financing, and marketing services.

Backing its claim "We believe in customer success" with superior products and value-added services

gives PHI plenty of pricing power. Despite charging a significant price premium—or perhaps because of it—the company's share of the North American corn market has grown from 35 percent during the mid-1980s to its current level of 44 percent.

Sources:
William F. Kendy, "The Price Is Too High," *Selling Power*, April 2006, pp. 30–33; Ian Brat, "Caterpillar Posts 38% Profit Rise, Raises Outlook on Strong Demand," *Wall Street Journal*, July 22, 2006, p. A2; Michael Arndt, "Cat Claws Its Way into Services," *BusinessWeek*, December 5, 2005, pp.56–59; Erin Stout, "Keep Them Coming Back for More," *Sales & Marketing Management*, February 2002, pp. 51–52; "Global Construction & Farm Machinery: Industry Profile," *Datamonitor*, June 2006, accessed at www.datamonitor.com; and information accessed online at www.pioneer.com and www.caterpillar.com, December 2006.

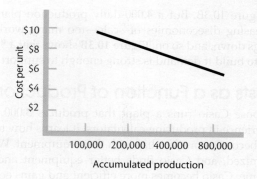

Figure 10.4
Cost per unit as a function of accumulated production: The experience curve

If a downward-sloping experience curve exists, this is highly significant for the company. Not only will the company's unit production cost fall, but it will fall faster if the company makes and sells more during a given time period. And to take advantage of the experience curve, Casio must get a large market share early in the product's life cycle. This suggests the following pricing strategy: Casio should price its calculators low; its sales will then increase, and its costs will decrease through gaining more experience, and then it can lower its prices further.

Some companies have built successful strategies around the experience curve. Bausch & Lomb solidified its position in the soft contact lens market by using computerized lens design and steadily expanding its one Soflens plant. As a result, its market share climbed steadily.

However, experience-curve pricing carries some major risks. The aggressive pricing might give the product a cheap image. The strategy also assumes that competitors are weak and not willing to fight it out by meeting the company's price cuts. Finally, while the company is building volume under one technology, a competitor may find a lower-cost technology that lets it start at prices lower than those of the market leader, who still operates on the old experience curve.

Cost-Based Pricing

The simplest pricing method is **cost-plus pricing**—adding a standard markup to the cost of the product. Construction companies, for example, submit job bids by estimating the total project cost and adding a standard markup for profit. Lawyers, accountants, and other professionals typically price by adding a standard markup to their costs. Some sellers tell their customers they will charge cost plus a specified markup; for example, aerospace companies price this way to the government.

To illustrate markup pricing:
Suppose a toaster manufacturer had the following costs and expected sales:

Variable cost	$10
Fixed costs	$300,000
Expected unit sales	50,000

Then the manufacturer's cost per toaster is given by:

$$\text{Unit Cost} = \text{Variable Cost} + \frac{\text{Fixed Cost}}{\text{Unit Sales}} = \$10 + \frac{\$300,000}{50,000} = \$16$$

Now suppose the manufacturer wants to earn a 20 percent markup on sales. The manufacturer's markup price is given by:[4]

$$\text{Markup Price} = \frac{\text{Unit Cost}}{(1 - \text{Desired Return on Sales})} = \frac{\$16}{1 - .2} = \$20$$

Cost-plus pricing
Adding a standard markup to the cost of the product.

The manufacturer would charge dealers $20 per toaster and make a profit of $4 per unit. The dealers, in turn, will mark up the toaster. If dealers want to earn 50 percent on the sales price, they will mark up the toaster to $40 ($20 + 50% of $40). This number is equivalent to a markup on cost of 100 percent ($20/$20).

Generally, using standard markups to set prices does not make sense. Any pricing method that ignores demand and competitor prices is not likely to lead to the best price. Such cost-plus pricing wrongly assumes that prices can be set without affecting sales volume. In our toaster example, suppose that consumers saw the $40 retail price as too high relative to competitors' prices, reducing demand to only 30,000 toasters instead of 50,000. Then the producer's unit cost would have been higher because the fixed costs are spread over fewer units, and the realized percentage markup on sales would have been lower. Markup pricing works only if that price actually brings in the expected level of sales.

Still, markup pricing remains popular for many reasons. First, sellers are more certain about costs than about demand. By tying the price to cost, sellers simplify pricing—they do not have to make frequent adjustments as demand changes. Second, when all firms in the industry use this pricing method, prices tend to be similar and price competition is thus minimized. Third, many people feel that cost-plus pricing is fairer to both buyers and sellers. Sellers earn a fair return on their investment but do not take advantage of buyers when buyers' demand becomes great.

Break-Even Analysis and Target Profit Pricing

Another cost-oriented pricing approach is **break-even pricing** (or a variation called **target profit pricing**). The firm tries to determine the price at which it will break even or make the target profit it is seeking. Such pricing is used by General Motors, which prices its automobiles to achieve a 15 to 20 percent profit on its investment. This pricing method is also used by public utilities, which are constrained to make a fair return on their investment.

Target pricing uses the concept of a break-even chart, which shows the total cost and total revenue expected at different sales volume levels **Figure 10.5** shows a break-even chart for the toaster manufacturer discussed here. Fixed costs are $300,000 regardless of sales volume. Variable costs are added to fixed costs to form total costs, which rise with volume. The total revenue curve starts at zero and rises with each unit sold. The slope of the total revenue curve reflects the price of $20 per unit.

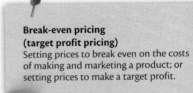

**Break-even pricing
(target profit pricing)**
Setting prices to break even on the costs of making and marketing a product; or setting prices to make a target profit.

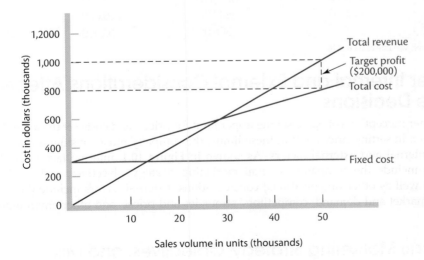

Figure 10.5
Break-even chart for determining target price

The total revenue and total cost curves cross at 30,000 units. This is the break-even volume. At $20, the company must sell at least 30,000 units to break even; that is, for total revenue to cover total cost. Break-even volume can be calculated using the following formula:

$$\text{Break-Even Volume} = \frac{\text{Unit Cost}}{\text{Price} - \text{Variable Cost}} = \frac{\$300,000}{\$20 - \$10} = 30,000$$

If the company wants to make a target profit, it must sell more than 30,000 units at $20 each. Suppose the toaster manufacturer has invested $1,000,000 in the business and wants to set the price to earn a 20 percent return, or $200,000. In that case, it must sell at least 50,000 units at $20 each. If the company charges a higher price, it will not need to sell as many toasters to achieve its target return. But the market may not buy even this lower volume at the higher price. Much depends on the price elasticity and competitors' prices.

The manufacturer should consider different prices and estimate break-even volumes, probable demand, and profits for each. This is done in **Table 10.1**. The table shows that as price increases, break-even volume drops (column 2). But as price increases, demand for the toasters also falls off (column 3). At the $14 price, because the manufacturer clears only $4 per toaster ($14 less $10 in variable costs), it must sell a very high volume to break even. Even though the low price attracts many buyers, demand still falls below the high break-even point, and the manufacturer loses money. At the other extreme, with a $22 price the manufacturer clears $12 per toaster and must sell only 25,000 units to break even. But at this high price, consumers buy too few toasters, and profits are negative. The table shows that a price of $18 yields the highest profits. Note that none of the prices produce the manufacturer's target profit of $200,000. To achieve this target return, the manufacturer will need to search for ways to lower fixed or variable costs, thus lowering the break-even volume.

Table 10.1 Break-Even Volume and Profits at Different Prices

(1) Price	(2) Unit Demand Needed to Break Even	(3) Expected Unit Demand at Given Price	(4) Total Revenue (1) × (3)	(5) Total Costs*	(6) Profit (4) – (5)
$14	75,000	71,000	$ 994,000	$1,010,000	–$16,000
16	50,000	67,000	1,072,000	970,000	102,000
18	37,500	60,000	1,080,000	900,000	180,000
20	30,000	42,000	840,000	720,000	120,000
22	25,000	23,000	506,000	530,000	–$24,000

* Assumes fixed costs of $300,000 and constant unit variable costs of $10.

Other Internal and External Considerations Affecting Price Decisions

Customer perceptions of value set the upper limit for prices, and costs set the lower limit. However, in setting prices within these limits, the company must consider a number of other internal and external factors. As shown in **Figure 10.1**, internal factors affecting pricing include the company's overall marketing strategy, objectives, and marketing mix, as well as other organizational considerations. External factors include the nature of the market and demand, competitors' strategies and prices, and other environmental factors.

Overall Marketing Strategy, Objectives, and Mix

Price is only one element of the company's broader marketing strategy. Thus, before setting price, the company must decide on its overall marketing strategy for the product or service. If the company has selected its target market and positioning carefully, then its marketing mix strategy, including price, will be fairly straightforward. For example, when Toyota developed its Lexus brand to compete with European luxury-performance cars in the higher-income segment, it charged a high price. In contrast, when it introduced its Yaris model—"the car that you can afford to drive is finally the car you actually want to drive"—this positioning required charging a low price. Thus, pricing strategy is largely determined by decisions on market positioning.

General pricing objectives might include survival, current profit maximization, market share leadership, or customer retention and relationship building (see **Figure 10.6**). At a more specific level, a company can set prices to attract new customers or to profitably retain existing ones. It can set prices low to prevent competition from entering the market or set prices at competitors' levels to stabilize the market. It can price to keep the loyalty and support of resellers or to avoid government intervention. Prices can be reduced temporarily to create excitement for a brand. Or one product may be priced to help the sales of other products in the company's line. Thus, pricing plays an important role in helping to accomplish the company's objectives at many levels.

- Attract new customers
- Profitability retain exisiting customers
- Prevent competition from entering market
- Stabilize the market
- Keep loyalty and support of resellers
- Avoid government intervention
- Help sales of ther products

Figure 10.6
Pricing objectives

Positioning on high price
— Porsche proudly advertises its curvacious Cayman as "Starting at $49,400."

vil on both shoulders.

lly dark intentions, the new Cayman just begs to be driven. Beneath sculpted s a 2.7-liter, 245-hp mid-mount engine yearning to run. Its rigid body ready to stantly to your will. Never has bad felt so good. Porsche. There is no substitute.

ew Cayman. Starting at $49,400.

PORSCHE

Price is only one of the marketing mix tools that a company uses to achieve its marketing objectives. Price decisions must be coordinated with product design, distribution, and promotion decisions to form a consistent and effective integrated marketing program Decisions made for other marketing mix variables may affect pricing decisions. For example, a decision to position the product on high-performance quality will mean that the seller must charge a higher price to cover higher costs. And producers whose resellers are expected to support and promote their products may have to build larger reseller margins into their prices.

Companies often position their products on price and then tailor other marketing mix decisions to the prices they want to charge. Here, price is a crucial product-positioning factor that defines the product's market, competition, and design. Many firms support such price-positioning strategies with a technique called **target costing**, a potent strategic weapon (see **Figure 10.7**). Target costing reverses the usual process of first designing a new product, determining its cost, and then asking, "Can we sell it for that?" Instead, it starts with an ideal selling price based on customer-value considerations and then targets costs that will ensure that the price is met.

Target costing
Pricing that starts with an ideal selling price, then targets costs that will ensure that the price is met.

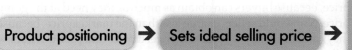

Product positioning → **Sets ideal selling price** →

Targets
- Market
- Competition
- Design

This ensures that costs allow price to be met.

Figure 10.7
Target costing

P&G used target costing to price and develop its highly successful Crest SpinBrush electric toothbrush:

● P&G usually prices its goods at a premium. But with Crest SpinBrush, P&G reversed its usual thinking. It started with an attractive low market price and then found a way to make a profit at that price. SpinBrush's inventors first came up with the idea of a low-priced electric toothbrush while walking through their local Wal-Mart, where they saw other electric toothbrushes priced at more than $50. These pricy brushes held only a fraction of the overall toothbrush market. A less-expensive electric toothbrush, the designers reasoned, would have huge potential. They decided on a target price of just $5, batteries included—only $1 more than the most expensive manual brushes—and set out to design a brush they could sell at that price. Every design element was carefully considered with the targeted price in mind. To meet the low price, P&G passed on the usual lavish new-product launch campaign. Instead, to give SpinBrush more point-of-sale impact, it relied on "Try Me" packaging that allowed consumers to turn the brush on in stores. Target cost pricing has made Crest SpinBrush one of P&G's most successful new products ever. It has become the best-selling toothbrush, manual or electric, in the U.S. with a more than 40 percent share of the electric toothbrush market.[5]

Other companies deemphasize price and use other marketing mix tools to create nonprice positions. Often, the best strategy is not to charge the lowest price, but to differentiate the marketing offer to make it worth a higher price. Some marketers even feature high prices as part of their positioning. For example, Grand Marnier offers a $225 bottle of Cuvée du Cent Cinquantenaire that's marketed with the tagline "Hard to find, impossible to pronounce, and prohibitively expensive."

Organizational Considerations

In small companies, prices are often set by top management rather than by the marketing or sales departments. In large companies, pricing is typically handled by divisional or product line managers. In industrial markets, salespeople may be allowed to negotiate with customers within certain price ranges. Even so, top management sets the pricing objectives and policies, and it often approves the prices proposed by lower level management or salespeople.

In industries in which pricing is a key factor (airlines, steel, railroads, oil companies), companies often have pricing departments to set the best prices or to help others in setting them.

The Market and Demand

Both consumer and industrial buyers balance the price of a product or service against the benefits of owning it. Thus, before setting prices, the marketer must understand the relationship between price and demand for its product.

Pricing in different types of markets

There are four types of markets, each presenting a different pricing challenge.

Differentiated offers –
L'Oréal differentiates its cosmetics from other brands through strong branding and advertising. It uses celebrities such as Gong Li to enhance its image and reduce the impact of price.
(*www.loreal.com*)

● *Pure competition:* This market consists of many buyers and sellers trading in a uniform commodity such as wheat, copper, or financial securities No single buyer or seller has much effect on the going market price. A seller cannot charge more than the going price, because buyers can obtain as much as they need at the going price. Nor would sellers charge less than the market price, because they can sell all they want at this price. If price and profits rise, new sellers can easily enter the market. In a purely competitive market, marketing research, product development, pricing, advertising,

and sales promotion play little or no role. Thus, sellers in these markets do not spend much time on marketing strategy.

● *Monopolistic competition:* This market consists of many buyers and sellers who trade over a range of prices rather than a single market price. A range of prices occurs because sellers an differentiate their offers to buyers. Either the physical product can be varied in quality, features, or style, or theaccompanying services can be varied. Buyers see differences in sellers' products and will pay different prices for them. Sellers try to develop differentiated offers for different customer segments and, in addition to price, freely use branding, advertising, and personal selling to set their offers apart. Thus, L'Oréal differentiates its cosmetics from dozens of other brands through strong branding and advertising, reducing the impact of price. Because there are many competitors in such markets, each firm is less affected by competitors' pricing strategies than in oligopolistic markets.

● *Oligopolistic competition:* This market consists of a few sellers who are highly sensitive to each other's pricing and marketing strategies. There are few sellers because it is difficult for new sellers to enter the market. Each seller is alert to competitors' strategies and moves. If VISA slashes its price by 10 percent, buyers will quickly switch to this supplier. The other credit card companies must respond by lowering their prices or increasing their services.

● *Pure monopoly:* This market consists of one seller. The seller may be a government monopoly (the postal service), a private regulated monopoly (a power company), or a private nonregulated monopoly (DuPont when it introduced nylon). Pricing is handled differently in each case. In a regulated monopoly, the government permits the company to set rates that will yield a "fair return." Nonregulated monopolies are free to price at what the market will bear. However, they do not always charge the full price for a number of reasons: a desire not to attract competition, a desire to penetrate the market faster with a low price, or a fear of government regulation.

Analyzing the price-demand relationship

Each price charged leads to a different level of demand. The relationship between the price charged and the resulting demand level is shown in the demand curve in **Figure 10.8**. The **demand curve** shows the number of units the market will buy in a given time period at different prices that might be charged. In the normal case, demand and price are inversely related; that is, the higher the price, the lower the demand. Thus, the company would sell less if it raised its price from P_1 to P_2. In short, consumers with limited budgets probably will buy less of something if its price is too high.

> **Demand curve**
> A curve that shows the number of units the market will buy in a given time period, at different prices that might be charged.

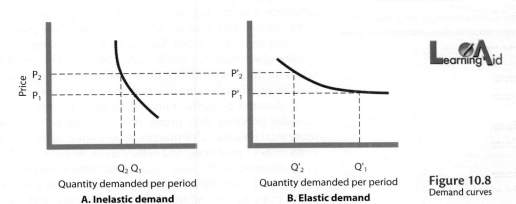

A. Inelastic demand   **B. Elastic demand**

Figure 10.8
Demand curves

In the case of prestige goods, the demand curve sometimes slopes upward. Consumers think that higher prices mean more quality. For example, Gibson Guitar Corporation once toyed with the idea of lowering its prices to compete more effectively with Japanese rivals such as Yamaha and Ibanez. Gibson found that its instruments didn't sell as well at lower prices. "We had an inverse [price-demand relationship]," noted Gibson's chief executive. "The more we charged, the more products we sold."

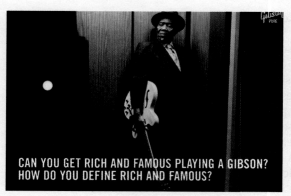

CAN YOU GET RICH AND FAMOUS PLAYING A GIBSON?
HOW DO YOU DEFINE RICH AND FAMOUS?

The demand curve sometimes slopes upward — Gibson was surprised to learn that its high-quality instruments didn't sell as well at lower prices.

At a time when other guitar manufacturers have chosen to build their instruments more quickly, cheaply, and in greater numbers, Gibson still promises guitars that "are made one-at-a-time, by hand. No shortcuts. No substitutions." Low prices are not consistent with "Gibson's century-old tradition of creating investment-quality instruments that represent the highest standards of imaginative design and masterful craftsmanship."[6] Still, if the company charges too high a price, the level of demand will be lower.

Most companies try to measure their demand curves by estimating demand at different prices. The type of market makes a difference. In a monopoly, the demand curve shows the total market demand resulting from different prices. If the company faces competition, its demand at different prices will depend on whether competitors' prices stay constant or change with the company's own prices.

Price elasticity of demand

Marketers also need to know **price elasticity**—how responsive demand will be to a change in price. Consider the two demand curves in **Figure 10.8**. In **Figure 10.8A**, a price increase from P_1 to P_2 leads to a relatively small drop in demand from Q_1 to Q_2. In **Figure 10.8B**, however, the same price increase leads to a large drop in demand from Q_1 to Q_2. If demand hardly changes with a small change in price, we say the demand is inelastic. If demand changes greatly, we say the demand is elastic. The price elasticity of demand is given by the following formula:

Price elasticity
A measure of the sensitivity of demand to changes in price.

$$\text{Price Elasticity of Demand} = \frac{\%\ \text{Change in Quantity Demanded}}{\%\ \text{Change in Price}}$$

Suppose demand falls by 10 percent when a seller raises its price by 2 percent. Price elasticity of demand is therefore –5 (the minus sign confirms the inverse relation between price and demand) and demand is elastic. If demand falls by 2 percent with a 2 percent increase in price, then elasticity is –1. In this case, the seller's total revenue stays the same: The seller sells fewer items but at a higher price that preserves the same total revenue. If demand falls by 1 percent when price is increased by 2 percent, then elasticity is –1/2 and demand is inelastic. The less elastic the demand, the more it pays for the seller to raise the price.

What determines the price elasticity of demand? Buyers are less price sensitive when the product they are buying is unique or when it is high in quality, prestige, or exclusiveness. They are also less price sensitive when substitute products are hard to find or when they cannot easily compare the quality of substitutes. Finally, buyers are less price sensitive when the total expenditure for a product is low relative to their income or when the cost is shared by another party.[7]

If demand is elastic rather than inelastic, sellers will consider lowering their prices. A lower price will produce more total revenue. This practice makes sense as long as the extra costs of producing and selling more do not exceed the extra revenue. At the same time, most firms want to avoid pricing that turns their products into commodities. Instant price comparisons afforded by the Internet and other technologies have increased consumer price sensitivity, turning products ranging from telephones and computers to new automobiles into commodities in consumers' eyes. Marketers need to work harder than ever to differentiate their offerings when a dozen competitors are selling virtually the same product at a comparable or lower price. Online travel agency ZUJI takes it one step further from allowing consumers to compare price points in air fares, by also offering "dynamically packaged" trips where travellers can customise various components according to their personal needs and budget.

Price elasticity – Instant price comparisons on the Internet provided by companies like ZUJI have increased consumer price sensitivity towards air tickets. (*www.zuji. com.sg*)

Competitors' Strategies and Prices

In setting its prices, the company must also consider competitors' costs, prices, and market offerings. Consumers will base their judgments of a product's value on the prices that competitors charge for similar products. A consumer who is thinking about buying a Canon digital camera will evaluate Canon's customer value and price against the value and prices of comparable products made by Nikon, Sony, Olympus, and others.

In addition, the company's pricing strategy may affect the nature of the competition it faces. If Canon follows a high-price, high-margin strategy, it may attract competition. A low-price, low-margin strategy, however, may stop competitors or drive them out of the market. Canon needs to benchmark its costs and value against competitors' costs and value. It can then use these benchmarks as a starting point for its own pricing.

In assessing competitors' pricing strategies, the company should ask several questions.

- *How does the company's market offering compare with competitors' offerings in terms of customer value?* If consumers perceive that the company's product or service provides greater value, the company can charge a higher price. If consumers perceive less value relative to competing products, the company must either charge a lower price or change customer perceptions to justify a higher price.

- *How strong are current competitors and what are their current pricing strategies?* If the company faces a host of smaller competitors charging high prices relative to the value they deliver, it might charge lower prices to drive weaker competitors out of the market. If the market is dominated by larger, low-price competitors, the company may decide to target unserved market niches with value-added products at higher prices. For example, if a local independent travel agency isn't likely to win a price war against ZUJI, it would be wiser for it to add special customer services and personal touches that justify its higher prices and margins.

- *How does the competitive landscape influence customer price sensitivity?*[8] For example, customers will be more price sensitive if they see few differences between competing products. They will buy whichever product costs the least. The more information customers have about competing products and prices before buying, the more price sensitive they will be. Easy product comparisons help customers to assess the value of different options and to decide what prices they are willing to pay. Finally, customers will be more price sensitive if they can switch easily from one product alternative to another.

What principle should guide decisions about what price to charge relative to those of competitors? The answer is simple in concept but often difficult in practice: No matter what price you charge—high, low, or in between—be certain to give customers superior value for that price.

Other External Factors

When setting prices, the company also must consider a number of other factors in its external environment. Economic conditions can have a strong impact on the firm's pricing strategies. Economic factors such as boom or recession, inflation, and interest rates affect pricing decisions because they affect both consumer perceptions of the product's price and value and the costs of producing a product.

The company must also consider what impact its prices will have on other parties in its environment. How will resellers react to various prices? The company should set prices that give resellers a fair profit, encourage their support, and help them to sell the product effectively. The government is another important external influence on pricing decisions. Finally, social concerns may have to be taken into account. In setting prices, a company's short-term sales, market share, and profit goals may have to be tempered by broader societal considerations.

REVIEWING THE CONCEPTS

Companies today face a fierce and fast-changing pricing environment. Firms successful at creating customer value with the other marketing mix activities must still capture some of this value in the prices they earn. This chapter looks at internal and external considerations that affect pricing decisions and examines general pricing approaches.

1 **Answer the question "What is price?" and discuss the importance of pricing in today's fast-changing environment.**

Price can be defined narrowly as the amount of money charged for a product or service. Or it can be defined more broadly as the sum of the values that consumers exchange for the benefits of having and using the product or service. The pricing challenge is to find the price that will let the company make a fair profit by getting paid for the customer value it creates.

Despite the increased role of nonprice factors in the modern marketing process, price remains an important element in the marketing mix. It is the only marketing mix element that produces revenue; all other elements represent costs. Price is also one of the most flexible elements of the marketing mix. Unlike product features and channel commitments, price can be raised or lowered quickly. Even so, many companies are not good at handling pricing—pricing decisions and price competition are major problems for many marketing executives. Pricing problems often arise because managers are too quick to reduce prices, prices are too cost oriented rather than customer-value oriented, or prices are not consistent with the rest of the marketing mix.

2 **Discuss the importance of understanding customer value perceptions when setting prices.**

Good pricing begins with a complete understanding of the value that a product or service creates for customers and setting a price that captures the value. Customer perceptions of the product's value set the ceiling for prices. If customers perceive that the price is greater than the product's value, they will not buy the product. *Value-based pricing* uses buyers' perceptions of value, not the seller's cost, as the key to pricing.

Companies can pursue either of two types of value-based pricing. *Good-value pricing* involves offering just the right combination of quality and good service at a fair price. Everyday low pricing (EDLP) is an example of this strategy. Value-added pricing involves attaching value-added features and services to differentiate the company's offers and support charging higher prices.

3 **Discuss the importance of company and product costs in setting prices.**

The price the company charges will fall somewhere between one that is too high to produce any demand and one that is too low to produce a profit. Whereas customer perceptions of value set the ceiling for prices, company and product costs set the floor. If the company prices the product below its costs, its profits will suffer. *Cost-based pricing* involves setting prices based on the costs for producing, distributing, and selling the product plus a fair rate of return for effort and risk.

Costs are an important consideration in setting prices. However, cost-based pricing is product driven rather than customer driven. The company designs what it considers to be a good product and sets a price that covers costs plus a target profit. If the price turns out to be too high, the company must settle for lower markups or lower sales, both resulting in disappointing profits. The company must watch its costs carefully. If it costs the company more than it costs competitors to produce and sell its product, the company must charge a higher price or make less profit, putting it at a competitive disadvantage.

Total costs are the sum of the fixed and variable costs for any given level of production. Management wants to charge a price that will at least cover the total costs at a given level of production. To price wisely, management also needs to know how its costs vary with different levels of production and accumulated production experience. Cost-based pricing approaches include *cost-plus pricing* and *break-even pricing* (or target profit pricing).

4 **Identify and define the other important external and internal factors affecting a firm's pricing decisions.**

Other *internal* factors that influence pricing decisions include the company's overall marketing strategy, objectives, mix, and organization for pricing. Price is only one element of the company's broader marketing strategy. If the company has selected its target market and positioning carefully, then its marketing mix strategy, including price, will be fairly straightforward. Some companies position their products on price and then tailor other marketing mix decisions to the prices they want to charge. Other companies deemphasize price and use other marketing mix tools to create *nonprice* positions.

Common pricing objectives might include survival, current profit maximization, market share leadership, or customer retention and relationship building. Price decisions must be coordinated with product design, distribution, and promotion decisions to form a consistent and effective marketing program. Finally, in order to coordinate pricing goals and decisions, management must decide who within the organization is responsible for setting price.

Other *external* pricing considerations include the nature of the market and demand, competitors' strategies and prices, and environmental factors such as the economy, reseller needs, and government actions. The seller's pricing freedom varies with different types of markets. Ultimately, the customer decides whether the company has set the right price. The customer weighs the price against the perceived values of using the product—if the price exceeds the sum of the values, consumers will not buy. So the company must understand concepts such as demand curves (the price-demand relationship) and price elasticity (consumer sensitivity to prices). Consumers also compare a product's price to the prices of competitors' products. A company therefore must learn the customer value and prices of competitors' offers.

REVIEWING THE KEY TERMS

Break-even pricing (target profit pricing) 267
Cost-based pricing 263
Cost-plus pricing 266
Demand curve 271
Experience curve (learning curve) 265
Fixed costs (overhead) 263
Good-value pricing 262

Price 260
Price elasticity 272
Target costing 269
Total costs 263
Value-added pricing 263
Value-based pricing 261
Variable costs 263

DISCUSSING THE CONCEPTS

1. The chapter points out that many companies do not handle pricing well. Beyond focusing too much on cost, what are some of the other difficulties that marketers have in setting prices?

2. What are the differences between cost-based and value-based pricing?

3. Four recent MBA graduates are starting their own financial services firm. They plan to promote a "good value" pricing strategy to their customers. Would you recommend this pricing strategy?

4. How would the risks of experience curve pricing apply to a new manufacturer of ink-jet printers?

5. Pricing is based on customer perceptions of value and costs in addition to other internal factors. Discuss these other internal factors and how they might affect the pricing of a new Sony MP3 player.

6. Explain why elasticity of demand is such an important concept to marketers who sell a "commodity" product.

APPLYING THE CONCEPTS

1. Visit U.S. News & World Report at _http://www.usnews. com/usnews/edu/college/rankingsbvrankindex_brief.php_ for a list of schools that offer the best value. How is value defined here? Is this a valid definition of value?

2. Given the following information, calculate the number of meals a restaurant would need to sell to break even:
   - Average meal price = $10.35
   - Meals sold = 8,560
   - Food = $27,653
   - Food labor = $18,386
   - Management = $4,855

   - Supplies = $3,133
   - Maintenance = $2,213
   - Marketing = $1,650
   - Insurance/legal = $1,904
   - Waste management = $988
   - Utilities = $3,159
   - Rent = $3,960

3. What does the following positioning statement suggest about the firm's marketing objectives, marketing-mix strategy, and costs? "No one beats our prices. We crush competition."

FOCUS ON TECHNOLOGY

Internet users have become used to receiving "for free" information. With some online revenues razor thin, many Internet operations are interested in moving to more of a "for fee" model. But customers resist paying and marketers are looking for creative ways to blend the models. Consider Google. To produce user fees, Google has supplemented its free search with a service called Google Answers (*www.google.answers.com*) from 2006. The service offers more than 500 carefully screened researchers to answer your questions.

The user pays a nonrefundable listing fee of $0.50 per question and sets a price that reflects how much he or she would pay for a well-researched answer. The user is charged this price only if the question is answered satisfactorily.

Google pays three-quarters of the revenue to the researcher who answers the question and keeps the other 25 percent. Fees start at $2.50 and average around the $75 point. A recent review of questions shows a $5 fee to answer a question on whether an artist is working on a new album and a fee of $150 to find the portion of the music industry's revenues derived from independent artists.

1. Is Google Answers using cost-based or value-based pricing? Explain.

2. What are Google's objectives with this product?

3. How will increased competition affect Google's marketing strategy for this product?

FOCUS ON ETHICS

Independent retailers have difficulty competing against megastores such as Wal-Mart. The larger retailers can usually offer lower prices due to operational efficiencies. They make up for their lower margins with much higher sales volumes. But what happens when one of these megaretailers prices items below its costs to compete with independent retailers?

Best Buy, long accused by independent music stores of using music as a loss leader, may have crossed the line into predatory pricing when it priced independent label CDs (indies) below its own wholesale cost. In 2006, Best Buy ran a promotion including a week-long sale on 20 indie titles at $7.99, about $2 below wholesale prices. Marketwide, indie CD sales soared during the week of the sale, up 65 percent from the previous week. The problem, according to the independent retailers, was that little of that surge came from independent stores. Music label executives claimed that they were unaware that Best Buy would be selling their CDs below the $9.99 wholesale price and were concerned about the future of the independent retailers.

1. How does the pricing of music CDs fit with Best Buy's broader marketing-mix strategy?

2. Comment on the elasticity of demand for indie music. Do you think Best Buy broke even on the music?

3. Was Best Buy's promotion legal? Was it ethical? Explain.

See: Todd Martens, "Best Buy Promo Raises Ire," *Billboard*, February 18, 2006, p. 10.

 VIDEO CASE

Song

Trying to replicate the success enjoyed by competitors such as Southwest and Jet Blue, Delta launched a new experiment: a separately branded airline called Song. The pricing strategy behind this low-cost airline involved more than simple discounting. Song implemented an upfront pricing structure that took the mystery out of buying airline tickets. In addition, the airline offered amenities such as healthy gourmet organic food, vibrant colors, leather seats, and in-flight satellite television. Song even enlisted designer Kate Spade to craft fashionable new uniforms for its flight attendants.

In the end, however, Delta could not sustain both Song and parent Delta Airlines. When Delta declared bankruptcy in late 2005, it announced that it would merge Song back into Delta, thereby reducing the costs of marketing two separate airlines. It would use Song airplanes for its own flights, but it would also incorporate Song's successes back into Delta's operations. According to Delta, "Song's ideas and innovations will continue to play a vital role in the refreshment and reinvigoration of the Delta product and experience." Delta plans to incorporate successful Song innovations, including zone boarding, faster aircraft turn times, all-leather seats, designer uniforms, improved food options, simplified fare structure, and upgraded online presence.

After viewing the video featuring Song Airlines, answer the following questions about pricing considerations and strategies.

1. How did Song lower fixed costs? How did the company lower variable costs?

2. Which of the external factors discussed in the text do you believe had the largest impact on Song's pricing decisions?

3. What pricing approach did Delta use when setting prices for passenger tickets on Song flights?

4. Can Delta successfully employ the lessons learned from Song?

COMPANY CASE

Burger King in Japan: Return of the Whopper

June 2007. Burger King, the world's number two hamburger chain, made its long-awaited return to Japan when it opened an outlet in Shinjuku located just beside McDonald's Japan HQ. By end-March 2008, Burger King plans to have eight restaurants in the Kanto area, mainly Tokyo. Following this, it plans to expand to Chiba, Sattana, Kanagawa, and then perhaps to Nagoya, Osaka, and Fukuoka. "Japan is a very important market for us, and one that we have great growth plans for in the future," said Burger King Chief Executive John Chidsey, in Tokyo for the countdown ceremony where a jazz band played. A giant firecracker went off and glittery streamers filled the air as the doors opened. It was all very different in 2001.

Then and Now

In 2001, Burger King pulled out of Japan after losing a price war with McDonald's and other fast-food chains. It had first entered Japan in 1996 and operated about 25 outlets in the Tokyo area before it quit. "At the time, price was the only factor for consumers in choosing a product," said its Japan president Shinichi Kasa. Kasa was hired by Burger King for its re-entry after having spent 29 years in McDonald's, where his last job was Chief Operating Officer. "Ten years ago, all companies in the food industry were doing big discount promotions. Not just hamburger outlets, but Yoshinoya, Mister Donut, everybody. Burger King came to Japan as

that was happening. Its prices were a little bit higher than its competitors. So were its food costs. Burger King didn't cut prices and suffered as a result," he continued.

However, Kasa believes that "times have changed, with consumers shifting from 'cheap is better' to a willingness to spend money for good quality products... This time the economy is different. It is showing signs of a recovery. All hamburger chains have started to sell higher-priced burgers costing more than 300 yen. There won't be another price war because customers are prepared to pay for quality burgers."

Burger King is banking on a new trend among some Japanese consumers favoring pricier, high-calorie meals. These Japanese have moved away from their healthy, traditional fish-and-rice diet toward more greasy and sweet food. Burger King's core product is the Whopper, which is the only burger whose beef patties are cooked by flame broiler. The size of the Whopper in Japan, as well as Burger King's other basic menu features, would be no different from anywhere else in the world. The Whopper, which Kasa believes "tastes better than any other burger," measures 13cm in diameter and weighs 113 grams. According to the company, the Whopper patty is 2.5 times heavier than the one used by McDonald's. For customers who desire an even bigger burger, there's the Double Whopper, which has two patties, or more for an additional fee. Burger King will also offer local items, although initially on a limited scale. The Whopper Teriyaki, a 5-inch, 4-ounce beef patty cooked in a sweet, spicy sauce and served on a sesame-seed bun with lettuce and tomato, is unique to Japan.

Burger King's regular Whopper is priced at 370 yen, while the Double Whopper goes for 520 yen. The standard set meal cost customers around 700 yen. Burger King's Whopper Teriyaki burger is priced at 390 yen. During its first Japanese foray, the Whopper was priced at 350 yen, and the Whopper with cheese 390 yen, both 20 yen less than their current prices. Then, the set meals featuring the leading products ranged from 650 yen to 690 yen.

Beef for the burgers comes from New Zealand and not the U.S. Peter Tan, president of Burger King Asia Pacific, said the decision to go with New Zealand beef was an economic one, and that the chain chooses different kinds of beef depending on its location. "We use different beef around the world. It really doesn't matter where the beef comes from," he said. McDonald's Japan uses Australian beef. Burger King will also offer seasonal items as well as a breakfast menu comprising of omelets, hash browns, and croissants. Chicken, onion rings, and salads are also expected to be popular menu items.

Aside from media interviews, Burger King has started advertising in some magazines. However, it plans to do TV commercials only after opening at least 100 restaurants, said Kasa. The chain also ran a radio campaign three days prior to its opening and distributed fliers for free Coke. Kasa plans to watch trends among Burger King's competitors and check out their menus, as well as those of family restaurants and gyudon outlets. "We will study the use of e-money for the future, as well as Internet access at our restaurants," he said.

Big Beef

Burger King's main rival in Japan is McDonald's, which operates 3,800 restaurants in the country. In April 2005, McDonald's had launched a 100-yen campaign by offering small drinks, cheese burgers, and chicken burgers for 100 yen each. It had succeeded in boosting customer numbers but suffered a double-digit drop in profits that year. While keeping those items at 100 yen, McDonald's raised prices in May 2006 by 10 yen to 50 yen on 60 percent of its entire product line to boost profits. The price increases resulted in a drop in customers for the next three months, but since then the number has been rising. The standard set at rival McDonald's is priced around 500 yen.

McDonald's spokesperson Kenji Kaniya said, "We didn't lose customers because we implemented various measures to meet diversifying customer demand." One example he cited was implementing a cook-to-order system at almost all its outlets. Costing the company nearly 15 billion yen, the system can provide customers with burgers and other items fresh from the stove in 35 to 50 seconds after the order is placed. Popular temporary items also attracted customers to McDonald's. These included the hit product Mega Mac. Priced at 350 yen, 3.32 million of four-beef patty offerings, nearly double the initial target, were sold in four days on its debut, outstripping demand. For a while, Mega Mac ads carried a notice that the burgers were not available, until the stock shortage was rectified. There are no plans to include the Mega Mac on its regular menu, although McDonald's did not deny the possibility. However, it does plan to offer a promotional item, the Mega Teriyaki burger, which will have two teriyaki port patties, at 330 yen.

Kaniya says that McDonald's now has 1,200 outlets, mostly with drive-throughs, that operate 24 hours, up from 25 outlets just a year ago. The move has proven highly popular in Japan. In contrast, Burger King's outlets will operate from 7 a.m. to 10 p.m. Chidsey acknowledged McDonald's remained Burger King's biggest rival, but said he wasn't worried about succeeding in Japan this time. "We think our flame-grilled food is superior to theirs, and quality at the end of the day is what the guest looks for. We think we will compete very well against McDonald's in this market."

Other Rivals

Aside from McDonald's, Burger King also faces competition from MOS Burger and Lotteria, both of whom are trying to arrest sales declines. MOS operates 1,461 outlets in Japan. Its set meal is priced between 600 yen to 700 yen. In April 2007, it offered discount coupons for the first time in its 35-year history, while launching its first campaign in June to reward customers who collect stamps with free burgers and gifts. Offering discounts is a turning point for MOS, which targets high-end customers. "We are losing customers... we have to try whatever we can to win them back," MOS president Atsushi Sakurada told a news conference in April.

Meanwhile, Lotteria, which operates roughly 600 outlets, is also trying to turn itself around. "Many people are familiar with the Lotteria brand, but there has been nothing distinctive about its shops or products," said its president Shingo Shinozaki. In 2006, Lotteria thus refurbished over 200 outlets, introduced new flagship produces based on its Straight Burger in May, and launched five new dessert items in March that used Lotte ice cream and chocolate. Lotteria is a subsidiary of Lotte and is under rehabilitation with the help of management consulting firm Revamp. Shinozaki said, "To make customers better aware of Lotteria's origins as an affiliate of Lotte, we thought providing good desserts will allow us to differentiate ourselves."

The Future

Interestingly, Burger King Japan is a joint venture between Lotte and Revamp and has an exclusive franchising contract to develop the chain there. Because it is tying up with different partners this time, Burger King Japan has little detailed information about what went wrong in the past, leaving the joint venture unable to analyze why it was forced to pull out. "Burger King is sure to have a tough time," said Seiichiro Samejima, a research analyst, citing intensifying competition among hamburger chains. "McDonald's is taking an all-around approach to increase the number of customers, while MOS Burger and Lotteria are trying various measures to win back those who have drifted away."

Burger King hopes to attract people in the 20s and 50s who love thick burgers. Shinichi Fujiki, 37, is an example. Wearing a paper crown as one of the first customers at the Toyko restaurant's opening, he said, "It feels more like you're eating a burger." Many hamburgers sold in Japan are small, with thin slices of meat. Fujiki frequented Burger King in the 1990s, said he missed it since it withdrew in 2001. Former customers with such deep-rooted loyalty are a natural target for Burger King. Similarly, 19-year-old university student Ryusuke Kimura said he developed a liking for Burger King during his travels abroad, but also frequents McDonald's and loves Japanese food too. However, Kimura notes that, "The Whopper is a bit different." Like Kimura, the Japanese thronging the opening were familiar with the Whopper, and shouted answers to a Burger King trivia quiz to win free T-shirts.

To survive, however, Burger King may also have to attract consumers who do not have a particular favorite hamburger shop. "I go to burger joints probably once a month," said Hiroshi Kawahata, a 35-year-old company employee, after buying a take-out lunch at a McDonald's near Burger King's Shinjuku outlet. Kawahata said he usually lunched at eateries other than hamburger chains. "Maybe I will go to the new Burger King if it's close to my office, maybe not," he added.

Questions For Discussion

1. How do Burger King's marketing objectives and its marketing mix strategy affect its pricing decisions?
2. Discuss factors that have affected the fast-food industry in Japan over time. How have these factors affected pricing decisions among hamburger chains?
3. How does the nature of the Japanese fast-food market and the demand for hamburgers affect Burger King's decisions?
4. What general pricing approaches have the hamburger chains in Japan pursued?
5. Do you think that Burger King will be able to succeed in Japan this time? What recommendations would you give to its management?

Sources:
"Burger King Back In Japan after 6-year Hiatus," *MSNBC.com*, June 8, 2007; "Return of the Whopper: Interview with Shinichi Kasa," *Japan Today*, May 17, 2007; Kahio Shimizu, "Burger King Stages Return under New Management, Realities," *The Japan Times*, June 7, 2007; all articles accessed online on July 24, 2007.

Objectives

After studying this chapter, you should be able to

- describe the major strategies for pricing imitative and new products
- explain how companies find a set of prices that maximize the profits from the total product mix
- discuss how companies adjust their prices to take into account different types of customers and situations
- discuss the key issues related to initiating and responding to price changes

CHAPTER 11

PRICING PRODUCTS: Pricing Strategies

Previewing the Concepts

In the last chapter, you explored the internal and external factors that affect a firm's pricing decisions and examined three general approaches to setting prices. In this chapter, we'll look at pricing strategies available to marketers—new-product pricing strategies, product mix pricing strategies, price-adjustment strategies, and price reaction strategies.

The airline industry is highly competitive. A major challenge for airlines is figuring out how to price their services in the face of fierce competition, high fuel costs, and disgruntled passengers. Some budget airlines like AirAsia appear to have thrived under such conditions.

Pricing strategies vary widely among airlines. Some airlines offer luxury and charge higher prices to match (Cathay Pacific, Singapore Airlines). More recently, however, such airlines have been attacked by competitors which offer no-frills flights and charge rock-bottom prices. A prime example of such budget airlines in the region is AirAsia.

AirAsia was launched as Asia's first low-fare, no-frills airline in 2002, with the mission to make travel so affordable that, according to its tagline, "now everyone can fly." Skeptics scoffed at the former insolvent subsidiary of a deeply indebted Malaysian conglomerate with two planes in its fleet and predicted that the airline would not survive more than six months. There were, after all, many barriers in the highly regulated and competitive airline industry. Moreover, a budget airline was a new concept in the region.

Few are laughing now. After only seven months in operation, the budget carrier repaid its $6.5 million debt. In 2007, AirAsia had profits of $157.8 million on revenues of $508 million. It carried 8.74 million passengers, up from 5.72 million in 2006. From its initial coverage of five Malaysian cities in 2002, AirAsia now flies to over 40 regional destinations in Malaysia, Thailand, Indonesia, Macau, China, the Philippines, Hong Kong, Singapore, Cambodia, Vietnam, and Myanmar using a fleet of 66 aircraft.

AirAsia targets passengers who can do without the frills of meals, frequent flyer miles, and airport lounges in exchange for fares up to 80 percent lower than other airlines. Passengers can purchase its Snack Attack in-flight line of snacks and drinks at affordable prices if they choose. The airline only flies two types of aircraft, the Airbus 320 and the Boeing 737, which reduces staff training, as well as operations and maintenance costs. It practices a turnaround time of 25 minutes which it claims is the fastest in the region, resulting in high aircraft utilization, lower costs, and greater airline and employee productivity.

Moreover, AirAsia provides convenient service. In August 2003, it became the first airline in the world to introduce SMS booking, where passengers can book their seats, check flight schedules, and obtain the latest updates on its promotions via their mobile phones. Aside from SMS, it also offers ticketless travel via phone and Internet reservations, thus saving the cost of printing and delivering tickets. It e-mails a booking number and a flight itinerary to its customers. AirAsia offers only economy class, with free seating and boarding that reduce boarding time. It prefers to use secondary airports as their procedures are less complicated. Intangibles such as reduced circling time and simpler baggage handling systems also contribute to lower-cost and more efficient operations.

AirAsia's fares are based on supply and demand, with prices generally increasing as seats are sold. Its system tries to predict how popular each flight will be, and the airline claims not to stipulate any restrictions to qualify for its cheapest fare. Fares include an online discount but exclude taxes and fees. No conditions are attached, although fares are non-refundable. Also, no changes in names, dates, or flights are permitted. AirAsia also introduced Go Holiday, a service where passengers can select flights and hotels of their choice online to create their own holiday package at an affordable price. Customers can also select various packages that come with recreational, relaxation, or rejuvenation aspects to suit their needs.

AirAsia's success has compelled full-service carriers to rethink their marketing strategy and encouraged other discount carriers to take to the sky. Arguably the most adversely affected has been Malaysian Airlines System (MAS), the country's flagship carrier, which has lost domestic market share to the budget carrier. With the liberalization of the lucrative Singapore-Kuala Lampur route, the fourth busiest in Asia, MAS now shares the route with AirAsia and other carriers including Singapore Airlines. Singapore Airlines also plays a role in the low-cost market segment through its investment in Tiger Airways. Tiger Airways recently established its first operating base outside Singapore in Melbourne, where it will base five of its Airbus A320 aircraft. It now boasts the widest Asia-Pacific network of any budget carrier and has been aggressively upsizing its fleet.

Another competitor is Australian low-cost carrier Jetstar, a subsidiary of Qantas. In 2007, Jetstar beat AirAsia to the long-haul punch by launching direct flights between Kuala Lumpur and Sydney for just $26 one-way. This special fare was available for only 34 hours for travel in September and February. Fly Asian Express, AirAsia's sister company, had planned to start long-haul services under the AirAsia X brand in July 2007, with Australia as a possible maiden destination. The launch was delayed to September the same year as it was difficult to obtain

suitable wide-body aircraft. Jetstar will price 15 to 20 percent below the average economy fare of full-service carriers. Jetstar operates two service classes on its Airbus A330-200s to be used on the Sydney-Kuala Lumpur route. Besides the $26 promotional fare, a "specially marketed" one-way fare of $143 for economy and $435 for starclass is being offered for a limited booking and travel period. As the load on Jetstar's six international services to Thailand, Indonesia, Vietnam, and Japan averages about 80 percent, it will take delivery of 15 new Boeing 787 Dreamliners in 2008. Jetstar can also accommodate disabled passengers and those with guide dogs, unlike other budget carriers such as AirAsia.

AirAsia is preparing to spread its wings to fly beyond the budget convention of no more than five hours to any destination. Its chairman, Tony Fernandes, expresses confidence that his long-haul venture will one day carry more passengers than Singapore Airlines.[1]

As the AirAsia example illustrates, pricing decisions are subject to a complex and fascinating array of company, environmental, and competitive forces. A company sets not a single price but a pricing structure that covers different items in its line. This pricing structure changes over time as products move through their life cycles. The company adjusts product prices to reflect changes in costs and demand and to account for variations in buyers and situations. As the competitive environment changes, the company considers when to initiate price changes and when to respond to them.

This chapter examines the major dynamic pricing strategies available to marketers. In turn, we look at new-product pricing strategies for products in the introductory stage of the product life cycle, product mix pricing strategies for related products in the product mix, price-adjustment strategies that account for customer differences and changing situations, and strategies for initiating and responding to price changes.[2]

New-Product Pricing Strategies

Pricing strategies usually change as the product passes through its life cycle. The introductory stage is especially challenging. Companies bringing out a new product face the challenge of setting prices for the first time. They can choose between two broad strategies: *market-skimming pricing* and *market-penetration pricing*. (see **Figure 11.1**)

Figure 11.1
New-product pricing strategies

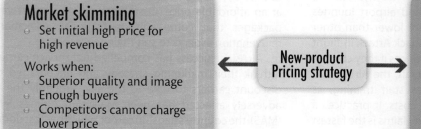

Market skimming
- Set initial high price for high revenue

Works when:
- Superior quality and image
- Enough buyers
- Competitors cannot charge lower price

New-product Pricing strategy

Market penetration
- Set initial low price for high market share

Works when:
- Price sensitive market
- Costs fall with large volume
- Competition kept out
- Low price can be maintained

Market-Skimming Pricing

Many companies that invent new products set high initial prices to "skim" revenues layer by layer from the market. Sony frequently uses this strategy, called **market-skimming pricing**. When Sony introduced the world's first high-definition television (HDTV) to the Japanese market in 1990, the high-tech sets cost $43,000. These televisions were purchased only by customers who could afford to pay a high price for the new technology. Sony rapidly reduced the price over the next several years to attract new buyers. By 1993 a 28-inch HDTV cost a Japanese buyer just over $6,000. In 2008, a Japanese consumer could buy a 40-inch HDTV for about $1,580, a price that many more customers could afford. An entry level HDTV set now sells for less than $500 in the U.S., and prices continue to fall. In this way, Sony skimmed the maximum amount of revenue from the various segments of the market.[3]

Market skimming makes sense only under certain conditions:

- The product's quality and image must support its higher price, and enough buyers must want the product at that price.
- The costs of producing a smaller volume cannot be so high that they cancel the advantage of charging more.
- Competitors should not be able to enter the market easily and undercut the high price.

In the mid-1980s, many MNCs entered China's home appliance market with expensive products. Microwave ovens cost more than $300, more than 80 percent of an ordinary Chinese worker's annual income at that time. Similarly, before 1996, when foreign brands controlled the large-screen TV market—19-inch TVs cost about 13,000 yuan, roughly three times the annual income of most Chinese. Such high-price strategies combined with a failure to monitor market trends prevented MNCs from capturing opportunities in rapidly growing mid- to low-end market segments.[4]

Market-Penetration Pricing

Rather than setting a high initial price to skim off small but profitable market segments, some companies use **market-penetration pricing**. They set a low initial price to penetrate the market—to attract a large number of buyers quickly and win a large market share. The high sales volume results in falling costs, allowing the company to cut its price even further.

- Chinese manufacturer, Galanz Enterprise, controls more than 60 percent of China's microwave market, while global giants such as Samsung, LG, and Matsushita are minor players. A senior executive at Galanz explained that its strategy is to use low prices to increase sales volume, which, because of economies of scale, enabled the firm to further lower its prices and gain more market share. Initially, LG controlled 25 percent of the market in Beijing and other northern markets, and 40 percent of the market in Tianjin. To compete with LG, Galanz cut its price by 40 percent, capturing 70 percent of the market share, while LG's share fell to 10 percent. LG regained some market share in northern China when Galanz diverted its attention from domestic to foreign markets. In response, Galanz again cut some of its prices by 40 percent. This enabled the company to control more than 50 percent of the market in areas where LG was strong.[5]

Market-skimming pricing
Setting a high price for a new product to skim maximum revenues layer by layer from the segments willing to pay the high price; the company makes fewer but more profitable sales.

Market-skimming pricing –
Sony priced its early HDTV's high, then reduced the prices gradually over the years to attract new buyers.
(*www.sony.com*)

Market-penetration pricing
Setting a low price for a new product to attract a large number of buyers and a large market share.

Several conditions must be met for this low-price strategy to work:

● The market must be highly price sensitive so that a low price produces more market growth.
● Production and distribution costs must fall as sales volume increases.
● The low price must help keep out the competition, and the penetration pricer must maintain its low-price position—otherwise, the price advantage may be only temporary. For example, Dell faced difficult times when IBM and other competitors established their own direct distribution channels. However, through its dedication to low production and distribution costs, Dell retained its price advantage and established itself as the industry's number-one PC maker.

● QB ("Quick Beauty") House, the barbershop chain, is a hit in Japan, Hong Kong, and Singapore. Founded in Japan, its business has thrived in a climate of falling prices. A typical Tokyo hairdresser charges 5,000 yen ($48) for men and a higher-end hairdresser charges double that. A large part of the cost goes to the hairdresser's wardrobe and premises. The rest goes to the rituals performed during a haircut—the consultation, the shoulder rub, and the hot towels. Not only does this add up the costs, but it also takes up a lot of time. At QB House, there is none of that, not even shampooing. A 1,000 yen ($10) haircut is offered. Says QB House's owner, Kazutaka Iwai, "We have turned barbershops from an emotional industry to a functional one." In Singapore, the chain has met with such success that it has attracted copycats. Faced with a possible economic slowdown, Singaporeans were more sensitive to high prices. In response, some local hair salons cut their prices to remain competitive.[6]

Market-peneration pricing –
Low initial prices help the company to attract a large number of buyers quickly and win a large market share. In Singapore, QB House met with so much success that it has attracted copycats.

Product Mix Pricing Strategies

The strategy for setting a product's price changes when the product is part of a product mix. In this case, the firm looks for a set of prices that maximizes the profits on the total product mix. Pricing is difficult because the various products have related demand and costs and face different degrees of competition. We now take a closer look at the five product mix pricing situations summarized in **Table 11.1**: *product line pricing, optional-product pricing, captive-product pricing, by-product pricing,* and *product bundle pricing.*

Table 11.1 Product Mix Pricing Strategies

Strategy	Description
Product line pricing	Setting price steps between product line items
Optional-product pricing	Pricing optional or accessory products sold with the main product
Captive-product pricing	Pricing products that must be used with the main product
By-product pricing	Pricing low-value by-products to get rid of them
Product bundle pricing	Pricing bundles of products sold together

Product Line Pricing

Companies usually develop product lines rather than single products. For example, Panasonic makes a line of TVs from standard tube TVs to LCD TVs, plasma TVs, and projection TVs. In **product line pricing**, management must decide on the price steps to set between the various products in a line.

The price steps should take into account cost differences between the products in the line, customer evaluations of their different features, and competitors' prices. In many industries, sellers use well-established *price points* for the products in their line. Thus, men's clothing stores might carry men's suits at three price levels: $185, $325, and $495. The customer will probably associate low-, average-, and high-quality suits with the three price points. Even if the three prices are raised a little, men normally will buy suits at their own preferred price points. The seller's task is to establish perceived quality differences that support the price differences.

India's Tata Group has a product line of cars—Indica, Indigo, and Nano—at various price points. While the Indica and Indigo are more expensive, in 2008, Tata introduced the world's cheapest car, Nano, priced at 100,000 Indian rupees ($2,500). The idea came about because its Chairman, Ratan Tata, felt it was dangerous to zip around in India on scooters. "There were three, four family members on a scooter with a kid standing in front, the guy driving and his wife setting side saddle holding a little kid," he said. So he set about thinking of a four-wheeled rural car. Costs were cut by packaging the car tightly and using less steel. Rata Tata believes that the Nano will cannibalize some of the existing low-end cars and two-wheelers. It may even take away some of the sales from its Indica model. Targeted at the second- and third-tier cities, affordable transport will be in demand. Other buyers of Nano are from the U.S. and Europe where people want a fun extra car. Those who need utilitarian transport and are not looking for creature comforts would also find the Tata appealing.[7]

Product line pricing –
The Tata Nano is aimed at people who need safer, utilitarian transport without playing for the creature comforts of a larger car.

> **Product line pricing**
> Setting the price steps between various products in a product line based on cost differences between the products, customer evaluations of different features, and competitors' prices.

Optional-Product Pricing

Many companies use **optional-product pricing**—offering to sell optional or accessory products along with their main product. For example, an iPod buyer can also choose from a bewildering array of accessories, everything from travel chargers and FM transmitters to external speakers and armband carrying cases. Refrigerators may come with optional ice makers.

Pricing these options is tricky. Automobile companies must decide which items to include in the base price and which to offer as options. Until recently, General Motors' pricing strategy was to advertise a stripped-down model at a base price to pull people into showrooms and then to devote most of the showroom space to showing option-loaded cars at higher prices. The economy model was stripped of so many comforts and conveniences that most buyers rejected it. Then, U.S. car makers followed the examples of the Japanese and German automakers and included in the sticker price many useful items previously sold only as options. Most advertised prices today represent well-equipped cars.

> **Optional-product pricing**
> The pricing of optional or accessary products along with a main product.
>
> **Captive-product pricing**
> Setting a price for products that must be used along with a main product, such as blades for a razor and cartridge for printers.

Captive-Product Pricing

Companies that make products that must be used along with a main product are using **captive-product pricing**. Examples of captive products are razor blade cartridges, video games, and printer cartridges. Producers of the main products (razors, video game consoles, and printers) often price them low and set high markups on the supplies. Thus, HP makes very low margins on its printers but very high margins on printer cartridges and other supplies. Sony and other video games makers sell game consoles at low prices and obtain the majority of their profits from the video games.

Two-part pricing –
Theme parks such as Disneyland charges a fixed fee for entrance and a variable usage fee for food and carnival games.

By-product pricing
Setting a price for by-products to make the main product's price more competitive.

Product bundle pricing
Combining several products and offering the bundle at a reduced price.

In the case of services, this strategy is called *two-part pricing*. The price of the service is broken into a *fixed fee* plus a *variable usage rate*. Thus, at Disneyland, you pay an entrance ticket plus additional fees for food and other in-park features such as the games. Theaters charge admission and then generate additional revenues from concessions. And mobile telecommunication companies charge a flat rate for a basic calling plan, then charge for minutes over what the plan allows. The service firm must decide how much to charge for the basic service and how much for the variable usage. The fixed amount should be low enough to induce usage of the service; profit can be made on the variable fees.

By-Product Pricing

In producing processed meats, petroleum and agricultural products, chemicals, and other products, there are often by-products. If the by-products have no value and if getting rid of them is costly, this will affect the pricing of the main product. Using **by-product pricing**, the manufacturer seeks a market for these by-products and accepts any price that covers more than the cost of storing and delivering them.

Product Bundle Pricing

Using **product bundle pricing**, sellers often combine several of their products and offer the bundle at a reduced price. For example, fast-food restaurants offer "value meal" by bundling a burger, fries, and a soft drink at a combo price. Resorts sell specially-priced vacation packages that include airfare, accommodations, meals, and entertainment. Cable companies bundle cable service, phone service, and high-speed Internet connections at a low combined price. Price bundling can promote the sales of products consumers might not otherwise buy, but the combined price must be low enough to get them to buy the bundle.[8]

Price-Adjustment Strategies

Companies usually adjust their basic prices to account for various customer differences and changing situations. Here we examine the seven price-adjustment strategies summarized in **Table 11.2**: *discount and allowance pricing, segmented pricing, psychological pricing, promotional pricing, geographical pricing, dynamic pricing,* and *international pricing*.

Table 11.2 Price-Adjustment Strategies

Strategy	Description
Discount and allowance pricing	Reducing prices to reward customer responses such as paying early or promoting the product
Segmented pricing	Adjusting prices to allow for differences in customers, products, or locations
Psychological pricing	Adjusting prices for psychological effect
Promotional pricing	Temporarily reducing prices to increase short-run sales
Geographical pricing	Adjusting prices to account for the geographic location of customers
Dynamic pricing	Adjusting prices continually to meet the characteristics and needs of individual customers and situations
International pricing	Adjusting prices for international markets

Discount and Allowance Pricing

Most companies adjust their basic price to reward customers for certain responses, such as early payment of bills, volume purchases, and off-season buying. These price adjustments—called *discounts and allowances*—can take many forms.

The many forms of **discounts** include a *cash discount*, a price reduction to buyers who pay their bills promptly. A typical example is "2/10, net 30," which means that although payment is due within 30 days, the buyer can deduct 2 percent if the bill is paid within 10 days. A *quantity discount* is a price reduction to buyers who buy large volumes. Such discounts provide an incentive to the customer to buy more from one given seller, rather than from many different sources.

A *functional discount* (also called a *trade discount*) is offered by the seller to trade-channel members who perform certain functions, such as selling, storing, and record keeping. A seasonal discount is a price reduction to buyers who buy merchandise or services out of season. For example, hotels and airlines typically offer seasonal discounts in their slower selling periods. Seasonal discounts allow the seller to keep production steady during an entire year.

Allowances are another type of reduction from the list price. For example, *trade-in allowances* are price reductions given for turning in an old item when buying a new one. Trade-in allowances are most common in the automobile industry but are also given for other durable goods such as mobile phones. *Promotional allowances* are payments or price reductions to reward dealers for participating in advertising and sales support programs.

Segmented Pricing

Companies often adjust their basic prices to allow for differences in customers, products, and locations. In **segmented pricing**, the company sells a product or service at two or more prices, even though the difference in prices is not based on differences in costs.

Segmented pricing takes several forms. Under customer-segment pricing, different customers pay different prices for the same product or service. Museums, for example, may charge a lower admission for students and senior citizens. Under product-form pricing, different versions of the product are priced differently but not according to differences in their costs. For instance, a 1-liter bottle of Evian mineral water may cost $1.59 at your local supermarket. But a 5-ounce aerosol can of Evian Brumisateur Mineral Water Spray sells for a suggested retail price of $11.39 at beauty boutiques and spas. The water is all from the same source in the French Alps, and the aerosol packaging costs little more than the plastic bottles. Yet you pay about 5 cents an ounce for one form and $2.28 an ounce for the other.

Using *location pricing*, a company charges different prices for different locations, even though the cost of offering each location is the same. For instance, theaters vary their seat prices because of audience preferences for certain locations, and universities charge higher tuition fees for foreign students. Finally, using *time pricing*, a firm varies its price by the season, the month, the day, and even the hour. Some telecommunication companies vary their prices by time of day and weekend versus weekday. Resorts give weekend and seasonal discounts. Airline fares vary depending on whether it was booked weeks in advance or at the last minute.

For segmented pricing to be an effective strategy, certain conditions must exist. The market must be segmentable, and the segments must show different degrees of demand. The costs of segmenting and watching the market cannot exceed the extra revenue obtained from the price difference. Most importantly, segmented prices should reflect real differences in customers' perceived value. Otherwise, in the long run, the practice will lead to customer resentment and ill will.

Discounts
A straight reduction in price on purchases during a stated period of time.

Allowance
Promotional money paid by manufacturers to retailers in return for an agreement to feature the manufacturer's products in some way.

Segmented pricing
Selling a product or service at two or more prices, where the difference in prices is not based on differences in costs.

Product-form pricing –
Evian water in a 1-liter bottle might cost you 5 cents an ounce at your local supermarket, whereas the same water might run $2.28 an ounce when sold in 5-ounce aerosol cans as Evian Brumisateur Mineral Water Spray moisturizer. (*www.evian.com*)

Psychological pricing
A pricing approach that considers the psychology of prices and not simply the economics; the price is used to say something about the product.

Psychological pricing –
What do the prices marked on this tag suggest about the product and buying solution?

Reference prices
Prices that buyers carry in their minds and refer to when they look at a given product.

Auspicious pricing –
"8" is an auspicious number to the Chinese. It sounds like prosperity. Hence, set dinners are priced at $288, $388, $888 to suggest good fortune for diners.

Psychological Pricing

Price says something about the product. For example, many consumers use price to judge quality. A $100 bottle of perfume may contain only $3 worth of scent, but some people are willing to pay the $100 because this price indicates something special.

In using **psychological pricing**, sellers consider the psychology of prices and not simply the economics. For example, consumers usually perceive higher-priced products as having higher quality. When they can judge the quality of a product by examining it or by calling on past experience with it, they use price less to judge quality. But when they cannot judge quality because they lack the information or skill, price becomes an important quality signal:

Some years ago, Heublein produced Smirnoff, then America's leading vodka brand. Smirnoff was attacked by another brand, Wolfschmidt, which claimed to have the same quality as Smirnoff but was priced at one dollar less per bottle. To hold on to market share, Heublein considered either lowering Smirnoff's price by one dollar or holding Smirnoff's price but increasing advertising and promotion expenditures. Either strategy would lead to lower profits and it seemed that Heublein faced a no-win situation. At this point, however, Heublein's marketers thought of a third strategy. They *raised* the price of Smirnoff by one dollar! Heublein then introduced a new brand, Relska, to compete with Wolfschmidt. Moreover, it introduced yet another brand, Popov, priced even lower than Wolfschmidt. This clever strategy positioned Smirnoff as the elite brand and Wolfschmidt as an ordinary brand, producing a large increase in Heublein's overall profits. The irony is that Heublein's three brands were pretty much the same in taste and manufacturing costs. Heublein knew that a product's price signals its quality. Using price as a signal, Heublein sold roughly the same product at three different quality positions.

Another aspect of psychological pricing is **reference prices**—prices that buyers carry in their minds and refer to when looking at a given product. The reference price might be formed by noting current prices, remembering past prices, or assessing the buying situation. Sellers can influence or use these consumers' reference prices when setting price. For example, a company could display its product next to more expensive ones to imply that it belongs in the same class. Department stores often sell women's clothing in separate departments differentiated by price: Clothing found in the more expensive department is assumed to be of better quality.

For most purchases, consumers don't have all the skill or information they need to figure out whether they are paying a good price. They don't have the time, ability, or inclination to research different brands or stores, compare prices, and get the best deals. Instead, they may rely on certain cues that signal whether a price is high or low. For example, the fact that a product is sold in a prestigious department store might signal that it's worth a higher price.

Interestingly, such pricing cues are often provided by sellers. A retailer might show a high manufacturer's suggested price next to the marked price, indicating that the product was originally priced much higher. Or the retailer might sell a selection of familiar products for which consumers have accurate price knowledge at very low prices, suggesting that the store's prices on other, less familiar products are low as well. The use of such pricing cues has become a common marketing practice (see **Real Marketing**).

Even small differences in price can signal product differences. Consider a stereo priced at $300 compared to one priced at $299.99. The actual price difference is only 1 cent, but the psychological difference can be much greater. For example, some consumers will see the $299.99 as a price in the $200 range rather than the $300 range. The $299.99 will more likely be seen as a bargain price, whereas the $300 price suggests more quality. Some psychologists argue that each digit has symbolic and visual qualities that should be considered in pricing. Thus, 8 is round and even and creates a soothing effect, whereas 7 is angular and creates a jarring effect.[9] For the Chinese, the digit 8 sounds like prosperity in Cantonese and Mandarin. Hence, 8 is used in pricing to suggest good fortune for potential customers.

Promotional Pricing

With **promotional pricing**, companies will temporarily price their products below list price and sometimes even below cost to create buying excitement and urgency. Promotional pricing takes several forms. Supermarkets and department stores will price a few products as loss leaders to attract customers to the store and hope that they will buy other items at normal markups. Sellers will also use special-event pricing in certain seasons to draw more customers. Thus, school shoes are promotionally priced before the school year begins to attract mothers and children to the stores.

Manufacturers sometimes offer cash rebates to consumers who buy the product from dealers within a specified time; the manufacturer sends the rebate directly to the customer. Rebates have been popular with automakers and producers of durable goods and small appliances, but they are also used with consumer packaged goods. Some manufacturers offer low-interest financing, longer warranties, or free maintenance to reduce the consumer's "price." This practice has become another favorite of the auto industry. Or, the seller may simply offer discounts from normal prices to increase sales and reduce inventories.

Promotional pricing, however, can have adverse effects:

- *Create "deal-prone" customers*: These customers wait until brands go on sale before buying them.
- *Erode brand equity*: Marketers sometimes use price promotions as a quick fix instead of sweating through the difficult process of developing effective longer-term strategies for building their brands.
- *Lead to industry price wars*: Such price wars usually play into the hands of only one or a few competitors—those with the most efficient operations For example, computer companies, including IBM and Hewlett Packard, showed strong profits as their new technologies were snapped up by eager consumers.

When the market cooled, however, many competitors began to unload PCs at discounted prices. In response, Dell, the industry's low-cost leader, started a brutal price war. Result? IBM sold off its PC unit to Lenovo, while HP PC profit margins average 3.9 percent compared to Dell's 6.4 percent. Dell has emerged atop the worldwide PC industry.[10]

The point is that promotional pricing can be an effective means of generating sales for some companies in certain circumstances. But it can be damaging if done too frequently.

Geographical Pricing

A company also must decide how to price its products for customers located in different parts of the country or world. Should the company risk losing the business of more-distant customers by charging them higher prices to cover the higher shipping costs? Or should the company charge all customers the same prices regardless of location? We will look at five **geographical pricing** strategies for the following hypothetical situation:

The Sawasdee Paper Company is located in Chiangmai and sells paper products to customers all over Thailand (see **Figure 11.2**). The cost of freight is high and affects the companies from whom customers buy their paper. Sawasdee wants to establish a geographical pricing policy. It is trying to determine how to price a $100 order to three specific customers: Customer A (Bangkok), Customer B (Phuket), and Customer C (Songkhla).

One option is for Sawasdee to ask each customer to pay the shipping cost from the Chiangmai factory to the customer's location. All three customers would pay the same factory price of $100, with Customer A paying, say, $10 for shipping; Customer B, $15; and Customer C, $25. Called **FOB-origin pricing**, this practice means that the goods are placed free on board (hence, FOB) a carrier. At that point the title and responsibility pass to the customer, who pays the freight from the factory to the destination. Because each customer picks up its own cost, supporters of FOB pricing feel that this is the fairest way to assess freight charges. The disadvantage, however, is that Sawasdee will be a high-cost firm to distant customers.

Uniform-delivered pricing is the opposite of FOB pricing. Here, the company charges the same price plus freight to all customers, regardless of their location. The freight charge is set at the average freight cost. Suppose this is $15. Uniform-delivered pricing therefore results in a higher charge to the Bangkok customer (who pays $15 freight instead of $10) and a lower charge to the Songkhla customer (who pays $15 instead of $25). Although the Bangkok customer would prefer to buy paper from another local paper company that uses FOB-origin pricing, Sawasdee has a better chance of winning over the Thai customer. Other advantages of uniform-delivered pricing are that it is fairly easy to administer and it lets the firm advertise its price nationally.

Zone pricing falls between FOB-origin pricing and uniform-delivered pricing. The company sets up two or more zones. All customers within a given zone pay a single total price; the more distant the zone, the higher the price. For example, Sawasdee might set up a North and charge $10 freight to all customers in this zone, a South Zone in which it

REAL MARKETING

Quick, What's a Good Price for ...? We'll Give You a Cue

Visit a supermarket and you're bombarded with price signs suggesting that you just can't beat this store's deals. You get lower prices with your frequent shopper card, if you buy in a large quantity, or if an item is on promotion. Then there are products sold at an "everyday low price."

But are they good prices? If you're like most shoppers, you don't really know. In a *Harvard Business Review* article, two pricing researchers conclude, "for most of the items they buy, consumers don't have an accurate sense of what the price should be." In fact, customers often don't even know what prices they're actually paying. In one study, researchers asked supermarket shoppers the price of an item just as they were putting it into their shopping carts. Fewer than half the shoppers gave the right answer.

To know for sure if you're paying the best price, you'd have to compare the marked price to past prices, prices of competing brands, and prices in other stores. For most purchases, consumers just don't bother. Instead, they rely on "the retailer to tell them if they're getting a good price," say the researchers.

"In subtle and not-so-subtle ways, retailers send signals [or pricing cues] to customers, telling them whether a given price is relatively high or low." In their article, the researchers outline the following common retailer pricing cues.

Sale Signs. The most straightforward retail pricing cue is a sale sign. It might take any of several familiar forms: "Sale!" "Reduced!" "New low price!" or "Now 2 for only...!" Such signs can be effective in signaling low prices to consumers and increasing sales for the retailer. The researchers' studies in retail stores and mail-order catalogs reveal that using the word "sale" beside a price (even without actually varying the price) can increase demand by over 50 percent. However, overuse or misuse of sales signs can damage both the seller's credibility and its sales. Unfortunately, some retailers don't always use such signs truthfully. Still, consumers trust sale signs. Why? "Because they are accurate most of the time," say the researchers. "And besides, customers are not that easily fooled." They quickly become suspicious when sale signs are used improperly.

Pricing cues such as sales signs and prices ending in 9 can be effective in signalling low prices to consumers and increasing sales for the retailer.

charges $15, and a West Zone in which it charges $25. In this way, the customers within a given price zone receive no price advantage from the company. For example, customers in Bangkok and Pattaya pay the same total price to Sawasdee. The complaint, however, is that the Bangkok customer is paying part of the Pattaya customer's freight cost.

Using **basing-point pricing**, the seller selects a given city as a "basing point" and charges all customers the freight cost from that city to the customer location, regardless of the city from which the goods are actually shipped. For example, Sawasdee might set Pattaya as the basing point and charge all customers $100 plus the freight from Pattaya to their locations. This means that a Bangkok customer pays the freight cost from Pattaya to Bangkok, even though the goods may be shipped from Bangkok. If all sellers used the same basing-point city, delivered prices would be the same for all customers and price competition would be eliminated. Industries such as sugar, cement, steel, and automobiles used basing-point pricing for years, but this method has become less popular today. Some

> **Basing-point pricing**
> A geographical pricing strategy in which the seller designates a city as a basing point and charges all customers the freight cost from that city to the customer.

Prices Ending in 9. Just like a sale sign, a 9 at the end of a price often signals a bargain. "In fact, this pricing tactic is so common," say the researchers, "you'd think customers would ignore it. Think again. Response to this pricing cue is remarkable." Normally, you'd expect that demand for an item would fall as the price goes up. Yet in one study involving women's clothing, raising the price of a dress from $34 to $39 *increased* demand by a third. By comparison, raising the price from $34 to $44 yielded no difference in demand.

But are prices ending in 9 accurate as pricing cues? "The answer varies," the researchers report. Some retailers, particularly for apparel items, do reserve prices that end in 9 for their discounted items. But at some stores, prices that end in 9 are a miscue—they are used on all products regardless of whether the items are discounted.

Signpost Pricing (or Loss-Leader Pricing). Unlike sale signs or prices that end in 9, signpost pricing is used on frequently purchased products about which consumers tend to have accurate price knowledge. For example, new parents usually know how much they should expect to pay for disposable diapers. Research suggests that customers use the prices of such "signpost" items to gauge a store's overall prices. If a store has a good price on Pampers, they reason, it probably also has good prices on other items.

Retailers have long known the importance of signpost pricing, often called "loss-leader pricing." They offer selected signpost items at or below cost to pull customers into the store, hoping to make money on the shopper's other purchases of higher-margin complementary products.

Pricing-Matching Guarantees. Another widely used retail pricing cue is price matching, whereby stores promise to meet or beat any competitor's price. Best Buy, for example, says "we'll meet or beat any local competitor's price, guaranteed!" If you find a better price within 30 days on something you bought at Best Buy, the retailer will refund the difference plus 10 percent.

Evidence suggests that customers perceive that stores offering price matching guarantees have overall lower prices than competing stores especially in markets where they perceive price comparisons to be relatively easy. But are such perceptions accurate? "The evidence is mixed," say the researchers. Consumers can usually be confident that they'll pay the lowest price on eligible items However, some manufacturers make it hard to take advantage of price matching policies by introducing "branded variants" slightly different versions of products with different model numbers for different retailers.

Used properly, pricing cues can help consumers. Careful buyers really can take advantage of signals such as sale signs, 9-endings, loss-leaders, and price guarantees to locate good deals. Used

improperly, however, these pricing cues can mislead consumers, tarnishing a brand and damaging customer relationships.

The researchers conclude: "Customers need price information, just as they need products. They look to retailers to provide both. Retailers must manage pricing cues in the same way that they manage quality... No retailer... interested in [building profitable long-term relationships with customers] would purposely offer a defective product. Similarly, no retailer who [values customers] would deceive them with inaccurate pricing cues. By reliably signaling which prices are low, companies can retain customers' trust—and [build more solid relationships]."

Sources:
Quotes and other information from Eric Anderson and Duncan Simester, "Mind Your Pricing Cues," *Harvard Business Review*, September 2003, pp. 96–103. Also see Joydeep Srivastava and Nicholas Lurie, "Price-Matching Guarantees as Signals of Low Store Prices Survey and Experimental Evidence," *Journal of Retailing*, volume 80, issue 2, 2004, pp. 117–128; Bruce McWilliams and Eiten Gerstner, "Offering Low Price Guarantees to Improve Customer Retention," *Journal of Retailing*, June 2006, pp. 105–113; Manoj Thomas and Vicki Morvitz, "Penny Wise and Pound Foolish: The Double-Digit Effect in Price Cognition," *Journal of Consumer Research*, June 2005, pp. 54–64; and Heyong Min Kim and Luke Kachersky, "Dimensions of Price Salience: A Conceptual Framework for Perceptions of Multi-Dimensional Prices," *Journal of Product and Brand Management*, 2006, vol. 15, no. 2, pp. 139–147.

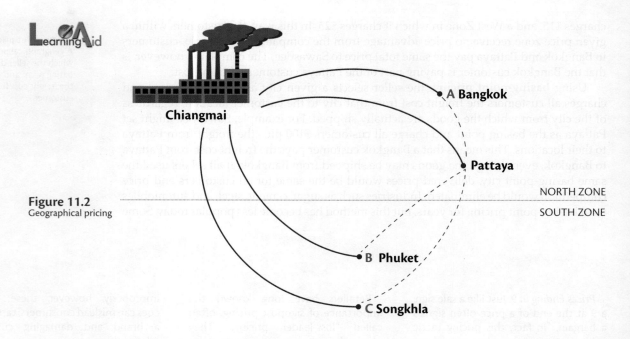

Figure 11.2
Geographical pricing

	A	**B**	**C**
FOB-origin pricing	$100 + $10	$100 + $15	$100 + $25
Uniform-delivered pricing	$100 + $15	$100 + $15	$100 + $15
Zone-pricing	$100 + $10	$100 + $15	
Basing-point pricing	$100 + cost of shipping from Pattaya		
Freight-absorption pricing	$100	$100	$100

companies set up multiple basing points to create more flexibility: They quote freight charges from the basing-point city nearest to the customer.

Finally, the seller who is anxious to do business with a certain customer or geographical area might use freight-absorption pricing. Using this strategy, the seller absorbs all or part of the actual freight charges to get the desired business. The seller might reason that if it can get more business, its average costs will fall and more than compensate for its extra freight cost. **Freight-absorption pricing** is used for market penetration and to hold on to increasingly competitive markets.

Dynamic Pricing

Some companies use **dynamic pricing**—adjusting prices continually to meet the characteristics and needs of individual customers and situations. For example, think about how the Internet has affected pricing. The Web allows for fluid pricing where a wide range of goods can be priced according to what the market will bear.

Dynamic pricing offers many advantages for marketers. For example, Internet sellers such as Amazon.com can mine their databases to gauge a specific shopper's desires, measure his or her means, instantaneously tailor products to fit that shopper's behavior, and price products accordingly.

Many direct marketers monitor inventories, costs, and demand at any given moment and adjust prices instantly. For example, Dell uses dynamic pricing to achieve real-time balancing of supply and demand for computer components:[11]

Freight-absorption pricing
A geographical pricing strategy in which the seller absorbs all or part of the freight charges to get the desired business.

Dynamic pricing
Adjusting prices continually to meet the characteristics and needs of individual customers and situations.

[Dell's] supply chain symphony—from my order over the phone to production to delivery to my house—is one of the wonders of the flat world… Demand shaping goes on constantly… It works like this: At 10 a.m. Austin time, Dell discovers that so many customers have ordered notebooks with 40-gigabyte hard drives since the morning that its supply chain will run short in two hours. That signal is automatically relayed to Dell's marketing department and to Dell.com and to all the Dell phone operators taking orders. If you happen to call to place your Dell order at 10:30 a.m., the Dell representative will say to you, "Tom, it's your lucky day! For the next hour we are offering 60-gigabyte hard drives with the notebook you want—for only $10 more than the 40-gigabyte drive. And if you act now, Dell will throw in a carrying case along with your purchase, because we so value you as a customer." In an hour or two, using such promotions, Dell can reshape the demand for any part of any notebook or desktop to correspond with the projected supply in its global supply chain. Today memory might be on sale, tomorrow it might be CD-ROMS.

Dynamic pricing –
Buyers benefit from the Web and dynamic pricing. Sites like Yahoo! Shopping give instant product and price comparisons from thousands of vendors, arming customers with price information they need to get the lowest prices.
(*www.shopping.yahoo.com*)

Buyers also benefit from the Web and dynamic pricing. A wealth of shopping bots—such as Yahoo! Shopping, Bizrate.com, NexTag.com, epinions.com, and PriceScan.com—offer instant product and price comparisons from thousands of vendors. Epinions.com, for instance, lets shoppers browse by category or search for specific products and brands. It then searches the Web and reports back links to sellers offering the best prices along with customer reviews. In addition to finding the best product and the vendor with the best price for that product, customers armed with price information can often negotiate lower prices.

Buyers can also negotiate prices at online auction sites and exchanges. Want to sell that mobile phone? Post it on eBay, the world's biggest online flea market. Want to name your own price for a hotel room or rental car? Visit Priceline.com or another reverse auction site. Dynamic pricing can also be controversial. Most customers would find it galling to learn that the person in the next seat on that flight from Jakarta to Phuket paid 20 percent less just because he or she happened to call at the right time or buy through the right sales channel. Amazon.com learned this some years ago when it experimented with lowering prices to new customers to woo their business. When regular customers learned through Internet chatter that they were paying generally higher prices than first-timers, they protested loudly. An embarrassed Amazon.com halted the experiments.

International Pricing

Companies that market their products internationally must decide what prices to charge in the different countries in which they operate. In some cases, a company can set a uniform worldwide price. For example, Boeing sells its jetliners at about the same price everywhere. However, most companies adjust their prices to reflect local market conditions and cost considerations.

The price that a company should charge in a specific country depends on many factors, including economic conditions, competitive situations, laws and regulations, and development of the wholesaling and retailing system. Consumer perceptions and preferences also may vary from country to country, calling for different prices. Or the company may have different marketing objectives in various world markets, which require changes in pricing strategy. For example, Samsung might introduce a new product into mature markets in highly developed countries with the goal of quickly gaining mass-market share—this would call for a penetration-pricing strategy. In contrast, it might enter a less developed market by targeting smaller, less price-sensitive segments; in this case, market-skimming pricing makes sense.

International pricing –
Companies that market products internationally must decide what prices to charge in the different countries. (*www.mcdonalds.com*)

Costs play an important role in setting international prices. Travelers abroad are often surprised to find that goods that are relatively inexpensive at home may carry outrageously higher price tags in other countries. A pair of Levi's selling for $30 in the U.S. might go for $63 in Tokyo, and $88 in Paris. Conversely, a Gucci handbag going for only $140 in Milan, Italy, might fetch $240 in the U.S. In some cases, such price escalation may result from differences in selling strategies or market conditions. In most instances, however, it is a result of the higher costs of selling in another country—the additional costs of product modifications, shipping and insurance, import tariffs and taxes, exchange-rate fluctuations, and physical distribution. Japan, for instance, has a complex distribution system that may increase cost.

Price Changes

After developing their pricing structures and strategies, companies often face situations in which they must initiate price changes or respond to price changes by competitors. (see **Figure 11.3**)

Initiating Price Changes

In some cases, the company may find it desirable to initiate either a price cut or a price increase. In both cases, it must anticipate possible buyer and competitor reactions.

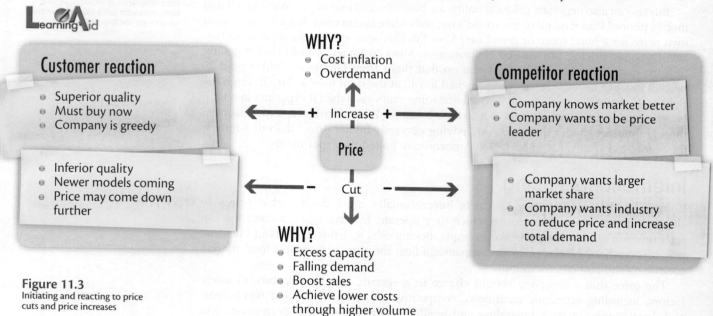

Figure 11.3
Initiating and reacting to price cuts and price increases

WHY?
- Cost inflation
- Overdemand

Customer reaction
- Superior quality
- Must buy now
- Company is greedy

- Inferior quality
- Newer models coming
- Price may come down further

Competitor reaction
- Company knows market better
- Company wants to be price leader

- Company wants larger market share
- Company wants industry to reduce price and increase total demand

Increase + → +
Price
Cut − → −

WHY?
- Excess capacity
- Falling demand
- Boost sales
- Achieve lower costs through higher volume

Initiating Price Cuts

Several situations may lead a firm to consider cutting its price. One such circumstance is excess capacity. Another is falling demand in the face of strong price competition. In such cases, the firm may aggressively cut prices to boost sales and share. But as the airline industry has learned, cutting prices in an industry loaded with excess capacity may lead to price wars as competitors try to hold on to market share.

A company may also cut prices in a drive to dominate the market through lower costs. Either the company starts with lower costs than its competitors, or it cuts prices in the hope of gaining market share that will further cut costs through larger volume. Dell used an aggressive low-cost, low-price strategy to become the market share leader in the competitive PC market. Asian companies, first from Japan, followed by those from Korea, then Taiwan, and now China have employed a similar approach in numerous markets.

Initiating Price Increases

A successful price increase can greatly increase profits. For example, if the company's profit margin is 3 percent of sales, a 1 percent price increase will increase profits by 33 percent if sales volume is unaffected. A major factor in price increases is cost inflation. Rising costs such as increases in Goods and Service Tax squeeze profit margins and lead companies to pass cost increases along to customers. Another factor leading to price increases is overdemand: When a company cannot supply all that its customers need, it may raise its prices, ration products to customers, or both.

When raising prices, the company must avoid being perceived as a price gouger. One way is to maintain a sense of fairness surrounding any price increase. Price increases should be supported by company communications telling customers why prices are being raised. Making low-visibility price moves first is also a good technique: Some examples include dropping discounts, increasing minimum order sizes, and curtailing production of low-margin products.

Wherever possible, the company should consider ways to meet higher costs or demand without raising prices. For example, it can consider more cost-effective ways to produce or distribute its products. It can shrink the product or substitute less expensive ingredients instead of raising the price. Or it can "unbundle" its market offering, removing features, packaging, or services and separately pricing elements that were formerly part of the offer. IBM, for example, now offers training and consulting as separately priced services.

Buyer Reactions to Price Changes

Customers do not always interpret price changes in a straightforward way. They may view a price cut in several ways. For example, what would you think if Panasonic suddenly cut its TV prices drastically? You might think that the TVs are about to be replaced by newer models or that they have some fault and are not selling well. You might believe that Panasonic's quality has been reduced. Or you might think that the price will come down even further and that it will pay to wait and see.

Similarly, a price increase, which would normally lower sales, may have some positive meanings for buyers. What would you think if Panasonic raised the price of its latest TV model? On the one hand, you might think that the item is very "hot" and may be unobtainable unless you buy it soon. Or you might think that the computer is an unusually good performer. On the other hand, you might think that Panasonic is greedy and charging what the traffic will bear.

Competitor Reactions to Price Changes

Competitors are most likely to react when the number of firms involved is small, when the product is uniform, and when the buyers are well informed about products and prices.

The competitor can interpret a company price cut in many ways. It might think the company is trying to grab a larger market share, or that it is doing poorly and trying to boost its sales. Or it might think that the company wants the whole industry to cut prices to increase total demand.

The company must guess each competitor's likely reaction. If all competitors behave alike, this amounts to analyzing only a typical competitor. In contrast, if the competitors do not behave alike, then separate analyses are necessary. However, if some competitors will match the price change, there is good reason to expect that the rest will also match it.

Responding to Price Changes

Here we reverse the question and ask how a firm should respond to a price change by a competitor. The firm needs to consider several issues: Why did the competitor change the price? Is the price change temporary or permanent? What will happen to the company's market share and profits if it does not respond? Are other competitors going to respond? Besides these issues, the company must also consider its own situation and strategy and possible customer reactions to price changes.

Figure 11.4 shows the ways a company might assess and respond to a competitor's price cut. Suppose the company learns that a competitor has cut its price and decides that this price cut is likely to harm company sales and profits. It might decide to hold its current price and profit margin. The company might believe that it will not lose too much market share, or that it would lose too much profit if it reduced its own price. Or it might decide that it should wait and respond when it has more information on the effects of the competitor's price change.

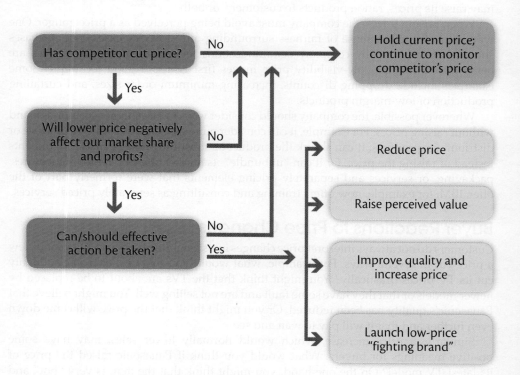

Figure 11.4
Assessing and responding to competitor price changes

If the company decides that effective action can and should be taken, it might make any of four responses. First, it could *reduce its price* to match the competitor's price. It may decide that the market is price sensitive and that it would lose too much market share to the lower-priced competitor. Cutting the price will reduce the company's profits in the short run. Some companies might also reduce their product quality, services, and marketing communications to retain profit margins, but this will ultimately hurt long-run market share. The company should try to maintain its quality as it cuts prices.

Alternatively, the company might maintain its price but raise the perceived value of its offer. It could improve its communications, stressing the relative value of its product over that of the lower-price competitor. The firm may find it cheaper to maintain price and spend money to improve its perceived value than to cut price and operate at a lower margin. Or, the company might *improve quality* and *increase price*, moving its brand into a higher price-value position. The higher quality creates greater customer value, which justifies the higher price. In turn, the higher price preserves the company's higher margins.

Finally, the company might launch a *low-price "fighting brand"*—adding a lower-price item to the line or creating a separate lower-price brand. This is necessary if the particular market segment being lost is price sensitive and will not respond to arguments of higher quality. Thus, when challenged on price by AirAsia and Jetstar, Singapore Airlines invested in low-fare Tiger Airways.

Public Policy and Pricing

Price competition is a core element of a free-market economy. In setting prices, companies may not usually free to charge whatever prices they wish. There may be laws governing the rules of fair play in pricing. In addition, companies must consider broader societal pricing concerns.

Figure 11.5 shows the major public policy issues in pricing. These include potentially damaging pricing practices within a given level of the channel (price-fixing and predatory pricing) and across levels of the channel (retail price maintenance, discriminatory pricing, and deceptive pricing).[12]

Low-price fighting brand –
In response to the entry of budget airlines such as AirAsia and Jetstar, Singapore Airlines invested in Tiger Airways. (*www.tigerairways.com*)

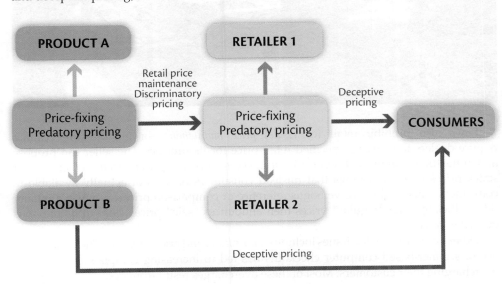

Figure 11.5
Public policy issues in pricing

Source:
Adapted with permission from Dbruv Grewel and Larry D. Compeau, "Pricing and Public Policy: A Research Agenda and Overview of Special Issue," *Journal of Public Policy and Marketing,* Spring 1999, pp. 3–10, Figure 1.

Pricing Within Channel Levels

Price-fixing occurs when sellers set prices after talking to competitors. Price-fixing is illegal. For example, Samsung and two other computer memory-chip makers agreed to pay $160 million to settle a suit alleging a four-year pricing-fixing conspiracy to artificially constrict the supply of D-Ram (dynamic random access memory) chips to computer makers such as Dell and Apple. This control of the supply helped keep prices artificially high, producing higher profits for the conspiring companies.

Sellers may also be prohibited from using *predatory pricing*—selling below cost with the intention of punishing a competitor or gaining higher long-run profits by putting competitors out of business. This protects small sellers from larger ones who might sell items below cost temporarily or in a specific locale to drive them out of business.

Pricing Across Channel Levels

Laws also exist to prevent unfair *price discrimination* by ensuring that sellers offer the same price terms to customers at a given level of trade. The seller can also discriminate in its pricing if the seller manufactures different qualities of the same product for different retailers. The seller must prove that these differences are proportional. Price differentials may also be used to "match competition" in "good faith," provided the price discrimination is temporary, localized, and defensive rather than offensive.

Deceptive pricing –
The widespread use of checkout scanners has led to increasing complaints of retailers overcharging their customers.

Laws also prohibit retail (or *resale*) *price maintenance*—a manufacturer cannot require dealers to charge a specified retail price for its product. The seller can propose a manufacturer's suggested retail price to dealers. *Deceptive pricing* occurs when a seller states prices or price savings that mislead consumers or are not actually available to consumers. This might involve bogus reference or comparison prices, as when a retailer sets artificially high "regular" prices then announces "sale" prices close to its previous everyday prices.

Other deceptive pricing issues include *scanner fraud* and *price confusion*. The widespread use of scanner-based computer checkouts has led to increasing complaints of retailers overcharging their customers. Most of these overcharges result from poor management—from a failure to enter current or sale prices into the system. Other cases, however, involve intentional overcharges. *Price confusion* results when firms employ pricing methods that make it difficult for consumers to understand just what price they are really paying. For example, consumers are sometimes misled regarding the real price of a home mortgage or car financing agreement. In other cases, important pricing details may be buried in the "fine print."

REVIEWING THE CONCEPTS

Pricing decisions are subject to an incredibly complex array of environmental and competitive forces. A company sets not a single price, but rather a *pricing structure* that covers different items in its line. This pricing structure changes over time as products move through their life cycles. The company adjusts product prices to reflect changes in costs and demand and to account for variations in buyers and situations. As the competitive environment changes, the company considers when to initiate price changes and when to respond to them.

1 Describe the major strategies for pricing imitative and new products.

Pricing is a dynamic process. Companies design a *pricing structure* that covers all their products. They change this structure over time and adjust it to account for different customers and situations. Pricing strategies usually change as a product passes through its life cycle. The company can decide on one of several price-quality strategies for introducing an imitative product, including premium pricing, economy pricing, good value, or overcharging. In pricing innovative new products, it can use *market-skimming pricing* by initially setting high prices to "skim" the maximum amount of revenue from various segments of the market. Or it can use *market-penetrating pricing* by setting a low initial price to penetrate the market deeply and win a large market share.

2 Explain how companies find a set of prices that maximizes the profits from the total product mix.

When the product is part of a product mix, the firm searches for a set of prices that will maximize the profits from the total mix. In *product line pricing*, the company decides on price steps for the entire set of products it offers. In addition, the company must set prices for *optional products* (optional or accessory products included with the main product), *captive products* (products that are required for use of the main product), *by-products* (waste or *residual products* produced when making the main product), and product bundles (combinations of products at a reduced price).

3 Discuss how companies adjust their prices to take into account different types of customers and situations.

Companies apply a variety of *price-adjustment strategies* to account for differences in consumer segments and situations. One is *discount and allowance pricing*, whereby the company establishes cash, quantity, functional, or seasonal discounts, or varying types of allowances. A second strategy is *segmented pricing*, where the company sells a product at two or more prices to accommodate different customers, product forms, locations, or times. Sometimes companies consider more than economics in their pricing decisions, using *psychological pricing* to better communicate a product's intended position. In *promotional pricing*, a company offers discounts or temporarily sells a product below list price as a special event, sometimes even selling below cost as a loss leader. Another approach is *geographical pricing*, whereby the company decides how to price to distant customers, choosing from such alternatives as FOB pricing, uniform-delivered pricing, zone pricing, basing-point pricing, and freight-absorption pricing. Finally, *international pricing* means that the company adjusts its price to meet different conditions and expectations in different world markets.

4 Discuss the key issues related to initiating and responding to price changes.

When a firm considers initiating a *price change*, it must consider customers' and competitors' reactions. There are different implications to *initiating price cuts* and *initiating price increases*. Buyer reactions to price changes are influenced by the meaning customers see in the price change. Competitors' reactions flow from a set reaction policy or a fresh analysis of each situation.

There are also many factors to consider in responding to a competitor's price changes. The company that faces a price change initiated by a competitor must try to understand the competitor's intent as well as the likely duration and impact of the change. If a swift reaction is desirable, the firm should preplan its reactions to different possible price actions by competitors. When facing a competitor's price change, the company might sit tight, reduce its own price, raise perceived quality, improve quality and raise price, or launch a fighting brand.

REVIEWING THE KEY TERMS

Allowance 287
Basing-point pricing 291
By-product pricing 286
Captive-product pricing 285
Discounts 287
Dynamic pricing 292
FOB-origin pricing 289
Freight-absorption pricing 292
Geographical pricing 289
Market-penetration pricing 283

Market-skimming pricing 283
Optional-product pricing 285
Product bundle pricing 286
Product line pricing 285
Promotional pricing 289
Psychological pricing 288
Reference prices 288
Segmented pricing 287
Uniform-delivered pricing 290
Zone pricing 290

DISCUSSING THE CONCEPTS

1. Why would Palm choose market-skimming pricing rather than market-penetration pricing for a new line of smartphones?

2. Why is product bundle pricing effective?

3. Psychological pricing is a pricing-adjustment strategy often used by retailers. Explain this pricing strategy. How it is tied to the concept of reference prices?

4. Discuss the difficulties an international company would encounter if it set a uniform worldwide price for a commodity-type product.

5. How might consumers react to a cruise line operator increasing the price for its five-day cruise from $700 per person to $1,000 per person? How might the operator reduce possible negative reactions?

6. Lawful price discrimination by sellers is a common practice. Discuss the conditions under which price discrimination practice becomes unlawful.

APPLYING THE CONCEPTS

1. Visit the Web sites of two wireless phone companies in your country. Compare their pricing strategies for cellular services. What types of product-mix and price-adjustment strategies do you observe?

2. Promotional pricing generates a sense of urgency and excitement. However, recognizing the dangers of this pricing approach, your boss has requested that you design an alternative pricing strategy that will generate the greater long-term sales and customer loyalty. What pricing strategy do you recommend? Will this strategy work as well as promotional pricing in the short term? Explain.

3. You are an owner of a small independent chain of coffee houses competing head-to-head with Starbucks. The retail price your customers pay for coffee is exactly the same as at Starbucks. The wholesale price you pay for roasted coffee beans has increased by 25 percent. You understand that you cannot absorb this increase and that it must be passed on to your customers. However, you are concerned about the consequences of an open price increase. Discuss three alternative price increase strategies that address your concerns.

FOCUS ON TECHNOLOGY

Space travel for the average person once seemed probable only in science fiction stories. But on April 28, 2001, the world saw its first true paying civilian astronaut when Dennis Tito, a California multimillionaire, became the first-ever space tourist. Tito traveled on a Russian Soyuz capsule and proved that an everyday citizen could endure this trip. Tito's trip, along with advances in rocket technology, accelerated the opportunities for space tourism. A pioneer in this area, Virgin Group founder Richard Branson has established Virgin Galactic, which will begin offering a fleet of space ships for travel into outer space. Virgin Galactic plans to build a $200-million spaceport on a 27-square-mile area in the southern New Mexico. Virgin Galactic is already collecting refundable deposits of $20,000 for the first year of travel. The deposits will be applied to the full fare of $200,000 for each trip into outer space. Visit *www.virgingalactic.com* to learn more about space tourism.

1. How should a company go about setting price for a new, high-technology product or service? What new-product pricing strategy is Virgin Galactic using for its space trips?

2. How might the entrance of a competitor affect the pricing?

3. How might Virgin Galactic bundle other products with space travel?

FOCUS ON ETHICS

Technology products, especially high-speed Internet delivery services, differ in their prices throughout the world. Such geographical price adjustments are often justified on the basis of increased communication costs in local markets. But in rare instances, prices are lowered in a country based on an initiative by corporate leaders, even if the country's infrastructure would support high prices. For example, in June 2006, Microsoft and South Africa's largest cellular operator, MTM, announced a project to offer cheap Internet connections throughout Africa. According to Microsoft cofounder and CEO Bill Gates, mobile connectivity is a key to growth in this country, and the current structure causes high prices in urban areas and makes connectivity prohibitive in rural areas. The Microsoft-MTM program offers affordable options for consumers who purchase Internet connectivity and a PC running Microsoft's Windows starter edition software.

1. What are the benefits of this program to Microsoft?

2. What do you think of this program? Does it present any ethical issues?

3. What pricing strategies from the chapter are involved in this initiative?

VIDEO CASE

GE

When you think of GE, you might think first of products such as appliances and light bulbs. But the giant $150 billion company also owns NBC, provides commercial and consumer financial services, develops and markets medical imaging equipment, and provides fundamental technology to build infrastructure in developing countries—all under its tagline "imagination at work."

Despite its growth and success, GE found its appliances business in decline several years ago. Prices were dropping and GE's brands stood largely undifferentiated. In response, GE applied its considerable marketing muscle to revamp, rebrand, and reprice its entire appliances line. Rather than accepting lower prices, GE invested heavily in new-product innovation to add more customer value that would support higher prices and margins. In addition to its core mass-market GE appliance brand, the company added the GE Monogram and GE Profile lines. GE Profile targeted the upper quartile of the market, offering "the marriage of style and innovation" with "the best in contemporary design matched with the latest kitchen technologies." GE Monogram targeted the ultrahigh end of the market, offering built-in products with "depth and breadth of design choices that allow you to customize your home and make it your own." The result? The average retail price paid for GE appliance products has increased more than 15 percent. At the same time, GE's appliances business has delivered five years of double-digit earnings growth.

After viewing the video featuring GE, answer the following questions about pricing strategies.

1. Which of the product-mix pricing strategies discussed in the book most closely describes GE's approach?

2. How did the new positioning statements for the Monogram and Profile lines affect pricing decisions?

3. Visit the Web site for GE's three appliance brands, GE, GE Profile, and GE Monogram. How do the sites support the positioning and pricing of the three brands?

🚃 COMPANY CASE

Toys 'R' Us: What Goes Around, Comes Around

Over three decades ago, Toys 'R' Us taught smaller independent toy retailers and department-store chains in its industry a hard pricing lesson, driving many of them to extinction. More recently, however, Toys 'R' Us has gotten a bitter taste of its own pricing medicine.

In the late 1970s, Toys 'R' Us emerged as a toy retailing "category killer," offering consumers a vast selection of toys at everyday low prices. The then-prevalent smaller toy stores, and toy sections of larger department stores, soon fell by the wayside because they couldn't match Toys 'R' Us's selection, convenience, and low prices. Throughout the 1980s and early 1990s, Toys 'R' Us grew explosively, grabbing as much as a 25 percent leading share of the U.S. toy market.

However, in the 1990s, Toys 'R' Us's heady success seemed to vanish with the emergence of Wal-Mart as a toy retailing force. Wal-Mart offered toy buyers an even more compelling value proposition. Like Toys 'R' Us, it offered good toy selection and convenience. But on toy prices, Wal-Mart offered not just everyday low prices, but rock-bottom prices.

Says one analyst, "With its mammoth stores, diverse array of products, and super efficient supply chain, Wal-Mart can provide consumers good quality, high levels of choice and convenience, and [incredibly low] prices." What's more, he continues, "Because it is a mass retailer with a broad, diverse inventory, Wal-Mart can afford to use toys as a loss-leader, losing money on toy purchases to lure in customers who then purchase higher-margin goods. Focused retailers such

as Toys 'R' Us just don't have that luxury." In 1998, Wal-Mart pushed Toys 'R' Us aside to become the largest toy seller in the U.S.

Toys 'R' Us fought back by trying to match Wal-Mart's super low prices, but with disastrous results. Consider this *Business Week* account of the 2003 Christmas season:

> He sings, he dances, he shakes it all about. For thousands of toddlers, Hokey Pokey Elmo was one of the great things about Christmas, 2003. But for Toys 'R' Us, Elmo was the fuzzy red embodiment of all that went wrong: He was just too cheap. In October, Wal-Mart stores surprised its competition by dropping Elmo's price from $25 to $19.50, $4.50 below what many retailers had paid for it. Within days, Toys 'R' Us dropped its price to $19.99. The price war dominoed all the way down the toy aisle. "Our choice was short-term profit vs. long-term market share; we chose to protect market share," says [former] CEO John Eyler, who thinks all stores could have sold out of the popular doll at $29.99.
>
> That's profit Toys 'R' Us couldn't afford to lose. The holiday season [its third disappointing one in a row] resulted in a five percent drop in sales at Toys 'R' Us stores open at least a year. Net income for the year fell 27 percent. Wal-Mart, on the other hand, [was] all smiles… CEO Lee Scott called 2003 "an excellent toy season" and toys "a very profitable category with a very strong gross margin." Clearly, Toys 'R' Us has little hope of competing on price with Wal-Mart.

By early 2005, Wal-Mart held a 25 percent share of the toy market; Toys 'R' Us's share had fallen to 15 percent. Later that year, new ownership took Toys 'R' Us private. Despite rumors that Toys 'R' Us would exit the toy business and focus on its growing and profitable Babies 'R' Us unit, the new owners vowed to remain a player in the toy industry.

However, Toys 'R' Us is implementing out a new strategy. Management has closed nearly 100 underperforming stores to cut costs, and is refocusing its marketing strategy. For example, the chain has retreated from cut-throat price wars that it simply can't win. Instead, it's dropping slow-selling products and emphasizing top-selling brands and higher-margin exclusive items, such as special Bratz or Barbie dolls sold only at its stores.

And to differentiate itself from Wal-Mart and Target, Toys 'R' Us is improving store atmosphere, shopper experiences, and customer service. It's cleaning up its stores, uncluttering its aisles, and hiring more helpful employees who can offer customers toy-buying advice. Says CEO Gerald Storch, "When you go to a large, multiproduct discount chain, you'll be lucky to find someone who can point you to the toy department or will even take you there, much less answer specific questions. When a customer comes in our store, our people can tell them what's a great toy for a 10-year-old boy for their birthday, because all we do is toys." Storch hopes that brighter, less-cluttered stores and better service will support higher prices and margins.

Still, Toys 'R' Us faces an uphill battle in its efforts to win back the now-price-sensitive toy buyers it helped to create decades ago. Consider this example.

> Aurore Boone of Alpharetta, Georgia, was recently at her local Wal-Mart checking out kids' bikes. She shops at Toys 'R' Us to see what's on the shelves, but of the roughly $500 she and her husband Mark spend on

toys a year, more than half goes to Wal-Mart, the rest to stores such as Target. It's cheaper, and she can do her other shopping there, too.

It isn't a matter of whether Toys 'R' Us can sell toys—with more than $11 billion in sales, the company remains one of the world's largest retailers. It's a matter of whether Toys 'R' Us can sell toys profitably (despite big sales, it's still posting losses). As Business Week concludes: "It's a harsh new world for Toys R' Us, which, as the industry's original 800-pound gorilla, wiped out legions of small toy stores in the 1960s and 1970s with its cut-price, no-frills, big-box outlets. Now, having taught consumers that toys should be cheap, the chain is finding that they learned the lesson all too well."

Questions For Discussion

1. Which, if any, of the pricing strategies discussed in the chapter are being applied by Toys 'R' Us? Could they adopt any other strategies?
2. Discuss buyer reactions to pricing strategies employed in the toy retailing industry. How can you explain these reactions?
3. Evaluate how Toys 'R' Us has responded to Wal-Mart's pricing strategy.
4. What recommendations would you make to the management of Toys 'R' Us going forward?

Sources:
Extracts and quotes from Nanette Byrnes, "Toys 'R' Us: Beaten at Its Own Game," *BusinessWeek*, March 29, 2004, pp. 89–90; and Jeffrey Gold, "Toys 'R' Us Is Due for a Makeover," *Raleigh News & Observer*, July 5, 2006, p. 8C. Also see Joan Verdon, "Toys 'R' Us Closes Deal to Go Private," *Knight Ridder Tribune Business News*, July 22, 2005, p. 1; and Doug DesJardins, "Babies 'R' Us Ready for Growth Spurt," *DSNRetailing Today*,

Objectives

After studying this chapter, you should be able to

- explain why companies use marketing channels and discuss the functions these channels perform
- discuss how channel members interact and how they organize to perform the work of the channel
- identify the major channel alternatives open to a company
- explain how companies select, motivate, and evaluate channel members
- discuss the nature and importance of marketing logistics and integrated supply chain management

CHAPTER 12

MARKETING CHANNELS AND SUPPLY CHAIN MANAGEMENT

Previewing the Concepts

We now arrive at the third marketing mix tool—distribution. Firms work with supply chain and marketing channels to create value for customers and build profitable customer relationships. As such, a firm's success depends not only on how well *it* performs but also on how well its *entire marketing channel* competes with competitors' channels. To be good at customer relationship management, a company must also be good at partner relationship management. The first part of this chapter explores the nature of marketing channels and the marketer's channel design and management decisions. We then examine physical distribution—or logistics. In the next chapter, we'll look at two major channel intermediaries—retailers and wholesalers.

We'll start with a look at Caterpillar. You might think that Caterpillar's success, and its ability to charge premium prices, rests on the quality of the heavy construction and mining equipment that it produces. But Caterpillar sees things differently. The company's dominance comes from its unparalleled distribution and customer support system—from the strong and caring partnerships that it has built with independent Caterpillar dealers. Read on and see why.

For over 70 years, Caterpillar has dominated the world's markets for heavy construction, mining, and logging equipment. Its familiar yellow tractors, crawlers, loaders, bulldozers, and trucks are a common sight at any construction area. Caterpillar sells more than 300 products in nearly 200 countries, with sales approaching $40 billion annually. Over the past two years, sales have grown 60 percent; profits have shot up 250 percent. The big Cat captures some 37 percent of the worldwide construction and farm equipment business, more than double that of number-two Komatsu. The waiting line for some of Caterpillar's biggest equipment is years long.

Many factors contribute to Caterpillar's enduring success—high-quality products, flexible and efficient manufacturing, and a steady stream of innovative new products. Yet these are not the most important reasons for Caterpillar's dominance. Instead, Caterpillar credits its focus on customers and its corps of 200 outstanding independent dealers worldwide, who do a superb job of taking care of every customer need. According to former Caterpillar CEO Donald Fites:

After the product leaves our door, the dealers take over. They are the ones on the front line. They're the ones who live with the product for its lifetime. They're

the ones customers see... They're out there making sure that when a machine is delivered, it's in the condition it's supposed to be in. They're out there training a customer's operators. They service a product frequently throughout its life, carefully monitoring a machine's health and scheduling repairs to prevent costly downtime. The customer... knows that there is a [$40-billion-plus] company called Caterpillar. But the dealers create the image of a company that doesn't just stand *behind* its products but *with* its products, anywhere in the world. Our dealers are the reason that our motto—Buy the Iron, Get the Company—is not an empty slogan.

"Buy the Iron, Get the Company"—that's a powerful value proposition. It means that when you buy Cat equipment, you become a member of the Caterpillar family. Caterpillar and its dealers work closely to find better ways to bring value to customers. Dealers play a vital role in almost every aspect of Caterpillar's operations, from product design and delivery, to product service and support, to market intelligence and customer feedback.

In the heavy-equipment industry, in which equipment downtime can mean big losses, Caterpillar's exceptional service gives it a huge advantage in winning and keeping customers. Consider Freeport-McMoRan, a Cat customer that operates one of the world's largest copper and gold mines. High in the mountains of Indonesia, the mine is accessible only by aerial cableway or helicopter. Freeport-McMoRan relies on more than 500 pieces of Caterpillar mining and construction equipment—worth several hundred million dollars—including loaders, tractors, and mammoth 240-ton, 2,000-plus-horsepower trucks. Many of these machines cost well over $1 million apiece. When equipment breaks down, Freeport-McMoRan loses money fast. Freeport-McMoRan gladly pays a premium price for machines and service it can count on. It knows that it can count on Caterpillar and its outstanding distribution network for superb support.

The close working relationship between Caterpillar and its dealers comes down to more than just formal contracts and business agreements. The powerful partnership rests on a handful of basic principles and practices:

- *Dealer profitability*: Caterpillar's rule: "Share the gain as well as the pain." When times are good, Caterpillar shares the bounty with its dealers rather than trying to grab all the riches for itself. When times are bad, Caterpillar protects its dealers. In the mid-1980s, facing a depressed global construction-equipment market and cutthroat competition, Caterpillar sheltered its dealers by absorbing much of the economic damage. It lost almost $1 billion in just three years but didn't lose a single dealer. In contrast, competitors' dealers struggled and many failed. As a result, Caterpillar emerged with its distribution system intact and its competitive position stronger than ever.

- *Extraordinary dealer support*: Nowhere is this support more apparent than in the company's parts delivery system, the fastest and most reliable in the industry. Caterpillar maintains 36 distribution centers and 1,500 service facilities worldwide, which stock 320,000 different parts and ship 84,000 items per day, every day. In turn, dealers have made huge investments in inventory, warehouses, fleets of trucks, service bays, diagnostic and service equipment, and information technology. Together, Caterpillar and its dealers guarantee parts delivery within 48 hours anywhere worldwide. The company ships 80 percent of parts orders immediately and 99 percent on the same day the order is received. In contrast, it's not unusual for competitors' customers to wait four or five days for a part.

- *Communications*: Caterpillar communicates with its dealers—fully, frequently, and honestly According to Fites, "There are no secrets between us and our dealers. We have the financial statements and key operating data of every dealer in the world… In addition, virtually all Caterpillar and dealer employees have real-time access to continually updated databases of service information, sales trends and forecasts, customer satisfaction surveys, and other critical data."

- *Dealer performance*: Caterpillar does all it can to ensure that its dealerships are run well. It closely monitors each dealership's sales, market position, service capability, financial situation, and other performance measures. It genuinely wants each dealer to succeed, and when it sees a problem, it jumps in to help. As a result, Caterpillar dealerships, many of which are family businesses, tend to be stable and profitable.

- *Personal relationships*: In addition to more formal business ties, Cat forms close personal ties with its dealers in a kind of family relationship. One Caterpillar executive relates the following example: "When I see Chappy Chapman, a retired executive vice-president,… he always asks about particular dealers or about their children, who may be running the business now. And every time I see those dealers, they inquire, 'How's Chappy?'… I consider the majority of dealers personal friends."

Thus, Caterpillar's superb distribution system serves as a major source of competitive advantage. The system is built on a firm base of mutual trust and shared dreams. Caterpillar and its dealers feel a deep pride in what they are accomplishing together. As Fites puts it, "There's a camaraderie among our dealers around the world that really makes it more than just a financial arrangement. They feel that what they're doing is good for the world because they are part of an organization that makes, sells, and tends to the machines that make the world work."[1]

Most firms cannot bring value to customers by themselves. Instead, they must work closely with other firms in a larger value delivery network.

Supply Chains and the Value Delivery Network

Producing a product or service and making it available to buyers requires building relationships not just with customers, but also with key suppliers and resellers in the company's supply chain. This supply chain consists of "upstream" and "downstream" partners. Upstream from the company is the set of firms that supply the raw materials, components, parts, information, finances, and expertise needed to create a product or service. Marketers, however, have traditionally focused on the "downstream" side of the supply chain—on the *marketing channels* or *distribution channels* that look forward toward the customer. Downstream marketing channel partners, such as wholesalers and retailers, form a vital connection between the firm and its customers.

As defined in Chapter 2, a **value delivery network** is made up of the company, suppliers, distributors, and ultimately customers who "partner" with each other to improve the performance of the entire system. For example, Palm, the leading manufacturer of handheld devices, manages a whole community of suppliers and assemblers of semiconductor components, plastic cases, LCD displays, and accessories. Its network also includes offline and online resellers, and 45,000 complementors who have created more than 5,000 applications for the Palm operating systems. All of these diverse partners must work effectively together to bring superior value to Palm's customers.

This chapter focuses on marketing channels—on the downstream side of the value delivery network. However, it is important to remember that this is only part of the full value network. To bring value to customers, companies need upstream supplier partners just as they need downstream channel partners.

The chapter examines four major questions concerning marketing channels: What is the nature of marketing channels and why are they important? How do channel firms interact and organize to do the work of the channel? What problems do companies face in designing and managing their channels? What role do physical distribution and supply chain management play in attracting and satisfying customers? In Chapter 13, we will look at marketing channel issues from the viewpoint of retailers and wholesalers.

The Nature and Importance of Marketing Channels

Few producers sell their goods directly to the final users. Instead, most use intermediaries to bring their products to market. They try to forge a **marketing channel** (or **distribution channel**)—a set of interdependent organizations that help make a product or service available for use or consumption by the consumer or business user.

A company's channel decisions directly affect every other marketing decision. Pricing depends on whether the company works with discount chains, uses high-quality specialty stores, or sells directly to consumers via the Web. The firm's sales force and communications decisions depend on how much persuasion, training, motivation, and support its channel partners need. Whether a company develops or acquires certain new

Value delivery network – Palm, Inc., manages a whole community of suppliers, assemblers, resellers, and complementors who must work effectively together to make life easier for Palm's customers. (*www.palm.com*)

Value delivery network
The network made up of the company, suppliers, distributors, and ultimately customers who "partner" with each other to improve the performance of the entire system.

Marketing channel (distribution channel)
A set of interdependent organizations that help make a product or service available for use or consumption by the consumer or business user.

Innovative marketing channels –
Calyx & Corolla sells fresh flowers and plants directly to consumers by phone and from its Web site, cutting a week or more off the time it takes flowers to reach consumers through conventional retail channels. (www.calyxflowers.com)

products may depend on how well those products fit the capabilities of its channel members.

Companies often pay too little attention to their distribution channels. In contrast, some companies have used imaginative distribution systems to gain a competitive advantage. FedEx's creative and imposing distribution system made it a leader in express delivery. Dell revolutionized its industry by selling personal computers directly to consumers rather than through retail stores. Amazon.com pioneered the sales of books and a wide range of other goods via the Internet.

Distribution channel decisions often involve long-term commitments to other firms. For example, companies such as Toyota or McDonald's can easily change their advertising, pricing, or promotion programs. They can scrap old products and introduce new ones as market tastes demand. But when they set up distribution channels through contracts with franchisees, independent dealers, or large retailers, they cannot readily replace these channels with company-owned stores or Web sites if conditions change. Therefore, management must design its channels carefully, with an eye on tomorrow's likely selling environment as well as today's.

How Channel Members Add Value

Why do producers give some of the selling job to channel partners? After all, doing so means giving up some control over how and to whom they sell their products. Producers use intermediaries because they create greater efficiency in making goods available to target markets. Through their contacts, experience, specialization, and scale of operation, intermediaries usually offer the firm more than it can achieve on its own.

Figure 12.1 shows how using intermediaries can provide economies. **Figure 12.1A** shows three manufacturers, each using direct marketing to reach three customers. This system requires nine different contacts. **Figure 12.1B** shows the three manufacturers working through one distributor, which contacts the three customers. This system requires only six contacts. In this way, intermediaries reduce the amount of work that must be done by both producers and consumers.

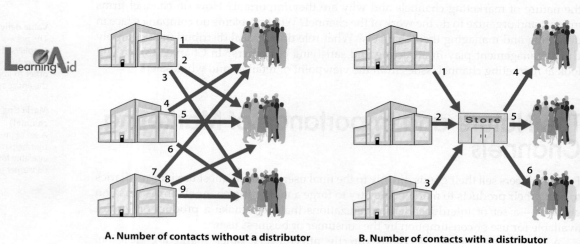

Figure 12.1
How using a marketing intermediary reduces the number of channel transactions

A. Number of contacts without a distributor
$M \times C = 3 \times 3 = 9$

B. Number of contacts with a distributor
$M + C = 3 + 3 = 6$

= Manufacturer   = Customer   Store = Distributor

From the economic system's point of view, the role of marketing intermediaries is to transform the assortments of products made by producers into the assortments wanted by consumers. Producers make narrow assortments of products in large quantities, but consumers want broad assortments of products in small quantities. Marketing channel members buy large quantities from many producers and break them down into the smaller quantities and broader assortments wanted by consumers.

For example, Kao makes millions of tubes of Bioré facial foam each day, but consumers buy only a tube at a time. So retailers such as Park n Save, Watsons, and Carrefour, buy Bioré facial foam by the truckload and stock it on their store's shelves. In turn, you can buy a single tube of Bioré facial foam, along with small quantities of toothpaste, shampoo, and other related products as you need them. Thus, intermediaries play an important role in matching supply and demand.

In making products and services available to consumers, channel members add value by bridging the major time, place, and possession gaps that separate goods and services from those who would use them. Members of the marketing channel perform many key functions. Some help to complete transactions:

- *Information*: Gathering and distributing marketing research and intelligence information about actors and forces in the marketing environment needed for planning and aiding exchange.
- *Promotion*: Developing and spreading persuasive communications about an offer.
- *Contact:* Finding and communicating with prospective buyers.
- *Matching*: Shaping and fitting the offer to the buyer's needs, including activities such as manufacturing, grading, assembling, and packaging.
- *Negotiation*: Reaching an agreement on price and other terms of the offer so that ownership or possession can be transferred.

Others help to fulfill the completed transactions:
- *Physical distribution*: Transporting and storing goods.
- *Financing*: Acquiring and using funds to cover the costs of the channel work.
- *Risk taking*: Assuming the risks of carrying out the channel work.

Number of Channel Levels

> **Channel level**
> A layer of intermediaries that performs some work in bringing the product and its ownership closer to the final buyer.

Each layer of marketing intermediaries that performs some work in bringing the product closer to the final buyer is a **channel level**. The number of *intermediary levels* indicates the length of a channel. **Figure 12.2A** shows several consumer distribution channels of

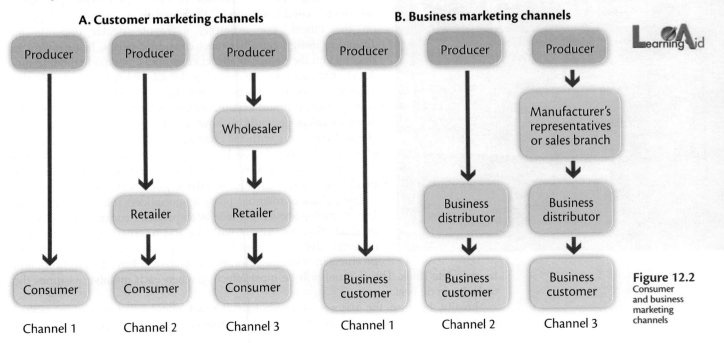

Figure 12.2
Consumer and business marketing channels

Direct marketing level
A marketing channel that has no intermediary levels.

Indirect marketing channel
Channel containing one or more intermediary levels.

different lengths. Channel 1, called a **direct marketing channel**, has no intermediary levels; the company sells directly to consumers. For example, Avon and Amway sell their products door-to-door, through home and office sales parties, and on the Web. The remaining channels in **Figure 12.2A** are **indirect marketing channels**, containing one or more intermediaries.

Figure 12.2B shows some common business distribution channels. The business marketer can use its own sales force to sell directly to business customers. Or it can sell to various types of intermediaries, who in turn sell to these customers. Consumer and business marketing channels with even more levels can sometimes be found, but less often. From the producer's point of view, the more levels means less control and greater channel complexity. Japan, for instance, has numerous layers of distribution and has one of the more complex distribution systems.

Direct marketing –
Amway sells its products through direct sales agents and retail stores in China. (www.amway.com.cn)

Channel Behavior and Organization

Distribution channels are complex behavioral systems in which people and companies interact to accomplish individual, company, and channel goals. Some channel systems consist of informal interactions among loosely organized firms. Others consist of formal interactions guided by strong organizational structures. Moreover, new types of intermediaries emerge and new channel systems evolve. Here we look at channel behavior and at how members organize to do the work of the channel.

Helping its dealers –
Toyota created Toyota City which showcases some of its past and present car models. Visitors can test drive some of the models. This helps to introduce the new models before customers visit its dealers. (www.toyota.co.jp/en/index.htm)

Channel Behavior

A marketing channel consists of firms that have partnered for their common good. Each channel member depends on the others. For example, a Toyota dealer depends on Toyota to design cars that meet consumer needs. In turn, Toyota depends on the dealer to attract consumers, persuade them to buy Toyota cars, and service cars after the sale. Each Toyota dealer also depends on other dealers to provide good sales and service that will uphold the brand's reputation. In fact, the success of individual Toyota dealers depends on how well the entire Toyota marketing channel competes with the channels of other auto manufacturers. One way that Toyota has helped its dealers is to set up a Toyota City showcase in Tokyo where its past and new car models are displayed. Visitors can also test drive some of the cars.

Each channel member plays a specialized role in the channel. For example, Samsung's role is to produce consumer electronics products that consumers will like and to create demand through national advertising. Best Denki's role is to display these Samsung products in convenient locations, to answer buyers' questions, and to complete sales. The channel will be most effective when each member assumes the tasks it can do best.

Ideally, because the success of individual channel members depends on overall channel success, all channel firms should work together smoothly. They should understand

and accept their roles, coordinate their activities, and cooperate to attain overall channel goals. Although channel members depend on one another, they often act alone in their own short-run best interests. They often disagree on who should do what and for what rewards. Such disagreements over goals, roles, and rewards generate **channel conflict**. There are two types of conflicts:

- *Horizontal conflict* occurs among firms at the same level of the channel. For instance, some Toyota dealers in one state might complain that dealers in another state steal sales from them by pricing too low or by advertising outside their assigned territories. Or Hilton Hotel franchisees might complain about other Hilton operators overcharging guests or giving poor service, hurting the overall Hilton image.
- *Vertical conflict*, conflicts between different levels of the same channel, is even more common. For example, United Airlines tried to stimulate sales by selling directly to consumers in Hong Kong—it gave significant mileage bonuses and price discounts directly to them without proper coordination with Hong Kong travel agents. The travel agents protested by refusing to sell United Airlines tickets. Seeing the dramatic decline in sales, United Airlines reverted to the previous agent distribution system.

Some conflict in the channel takes the form of healthy competition. Such competition can be good for the channel—without it, the channel could become passive and noninnovative. But severe or prolonged conflict can disrupt channel effectiveness and cause lasting harm to channel relationships as the following example illustrates:

After the Asian financial crisis, real estate developers suffered from a battered market with weak consumer and business demand. In Hong Kong, the powerful real estate developers tried to reduce their construction, development, and marketing costs by driving hard bargains with suppliers, law firms, and real estate agents. Some developed their own sales force instead of relying on agents, some negotiated with banks to cut mortgage rates, while others buy appliances in bulk for consumers. Their objective is clear—to try and maintain their profit and pass the costs to other members in the channel. By so doing, they create conflicts and mistrust among members in the channel that they had built up over the years. Many of the smaller players in the channel, dealers, and real estate agents included, were forced out and went bankrupt.[2]

Vertical Marketing Systems

For the channel to perform well, each channel member's role must be specified and channel conflict managed. The channel will perform better if it includes a firm, agency, or mechanism that provides leadership and has the power to assign roles and manage conflict.

Historically, *conventional distribution* channels lacked such leadership and power, often resulting in damaging conflict and poor performance. One of the biggest channel developments over the years has been the emergence of vertical marketing systems that provide channel leadership. **Figure 12.3** contrasts the two types of channel arrangements.

> **Channel conflict**
> Disagreement among marketing channel members on goals and roles—who should do what and for what rewards.

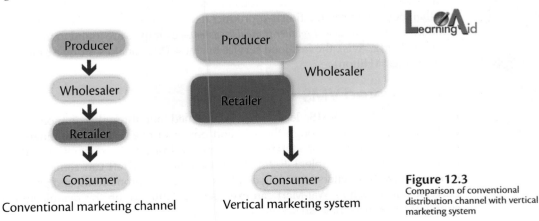

Conventional marketing channel

Vertical marketing system

Figure 12.3
Comparison of conventional distribution channel with vertical marketing system

Conventional distribution channel
A channel consisting of one or more independent producers, wholesalers, and retailers, each a separate business seeking to maximize its own profits even at the expense of profits for the sys-tem as a whole.

Vertical marketing system (VMS)
A distribution channel structure in which producers, wholesalers, and retailers act as a unified system. One channel member owns the others, has contracts with them, or has so much power that they all cooperate.

Corporate VMS
A vertical marketing system that combines successive stages of production and distribution under single ownership—channel leadership is established through common ownership.

A **conventional distribution channel** consists of one or more independent producers, wholesalers, and retailers. Each is a separate business seeking to maximize its own profits, sometimes at the expense of the system as a whole. No channel member has much control over the other members, and no formal means exists for assigning roles and resolving channel conflict.

In contrast, a **vertical marketing system (VMS)** consists of producers, wholesalers, and retailers acting as a unified system. One channel member owns the others, has contracts with them, or wields so much power that they must all cooperate. The VMS can be dominated by the producer, wholesaler, or retailer.

There are three major types of VMSs: *corporate, contractual, and administered.*

Corporate VMS

A **corporate VMS** integrates successive stages of production and distribution under single ownership. Coordination and conflict management are attained through regular organizational channels. For example, Italian eyewear maker Luxottica produces many famous eyewear brands—including Ray-Ban, Vogue, Anne Klein, Ferragamo, and Bvlgari. It then sells these brands through two of the world's largest optical chains, LensCrafters and Sunglass Hut, which it also owns.[3]

In the early 1990s, Japanese *keiretsus* were good examples of corporate VMSs. These large Japanese trading firms offer every type of service one can imagine. The managing director of Marenbanu once proudly said, "We have everything you need. If you need to build a bridge, we have engineering firms to design it for you. Our cement and steel factories will supply you the material needed. In case you lack money to finance it, we have banks to lend money to you."

However, a good corporate VMS has to be lean and economically efficient; otherwise, the damage of overexpansion and organization slack may turn the VMS into a white elephant. Throughout Asia, the corporate VMSs are common. In some ways, the South Korean big corporations and Chinese state-owned enterprises have similar set-ups. They need a good balance to achieve full vertical integrations with economic efficiencies.

Contractual VMS
A vertical marketing system in which independent firms at different levels of production and distribution join together through contracts to obtain more economies or sales impact than they could achieve alone.

Franchise organization
A contractual vertical marketing system in which a channel member, called a franchiser, links several stages in the production-distribution process.

Administered VMS
A vertical marketing system that coordinates successive stages of production and distribution, not through common ownership or contractual ties, but through the size and power of one of the parties.

Contractual VMS

A **contractual VMS** consists of independent firms at different levels of production and distribution who join together through contracts to obtain more economies or sales impact than each could achieve alone. Coordination and conflict management are attained through contractual agreements among channel members.

The **franchise organization** is the most common type of contractual relationship—a channel member called a *franchisor* links several stages in the production-distribution process. Almost every kind of business has been franchised—from hotels and fast-food restaurants to kindergartens and fitness centers.

There are three types of franchises. The first type is the *manufacturer-sponsored retailer franchise system*—for example, Toyota and its network of independent franchised dealers. The second type is the *manufacturer-sponsored wholesaler franchise system*—Coca-Cola licenses bottlers (wholesalers) in various markets who buy Coca-Cola syrup concentrate and then bottle and sell the finished product to retailers in local markets. The third type is the *service-firm-sponsored retailer franchise system*—examples are found in the auto-rental business (Hertz, Avis), the fast-food service business (McDonald's, Burger King), and the hotel business (Hilton).

Administered VMS

In an **administered VMS**, leadership is assumed not through common ownership or contractual ties but through the size and power of one or a few dominant channel members. Manufacturers of a top brand can obtain strong trade cooperation and support from resellers. For example, GE, Procter & Gamble, and Kraft can command unusual cooperation from resellers regarding displays, shelf space, promotions, and price policies. Large retailers such as Wal-Mart can exert strong influence on the manufacturers that supply the products they sell.

Horizontal Marketing Systems

Another channel development is the **horizontal marketing system**, in which two or more companies at one level join together to follow a new marketing opportunity. By working together, companies can combine their financial, production, or marketing resources to accomplish more than any one company could alone.

Companies might join forces with competitors or noncompetitors. They might work with each other on a temporary or permanent basis, or they may create a separate company. For example, Philips, the global appliance manufacturer, exchanged shares with TCL, a Chinese appliance manufacturer, so that Philips can use TCL's 2,000 distribution outlets throughout China. Or when McDonald's joined forces with Sinopec, China's largest gasoline retailer, to place restaurants at the latter's more than 30,000 gas stations. The move accelerates McDonald's expansion into China while at the same time pulls hungry motorists into Sinopec gas stations.[4]

Such channel arrangements also work well globally. For example, because of its excellent coverage of international markets, Coca-Cola and Nestlé formed a joint venture, Beverage Partners Worldwide, to market ready-to-drink coffees, teas, and flavored milks in more than 40 countries. Coke provides worldwide experience in marketing and distributing beverages, and Nestlé contributes two established brand names—Nescafé and Nestea.[5]

> **Horizontal marketing system**
> A channel arrangement in which two or more companies at one level join together to follow a new marketing opportunity.

Horizontal marketing systems – McDonald's recently joined forces with Sinopec, China's largest gasoline retailer, to place restaurants at its more than 30,000 gas stations. Here, the presidents of the two companies shake hands while announcing the partnership.

Multichannel Distribution Systems

In the past, many companies used a single channel to sell to a single market or market segment. Today, with the proliferation of customer segments and channel possibilities, more companies have adopted **multichannel distribution systems**—often called *hybrid marketing channels*. Such multichannel marketing occurs when a single firm sets up two or more marketing channels to reach one or more customer segments.

Figure 12.4 shows a multichannel distribution system. In the figure, the producer sells directly to consumer segment 1 using direct-mail catalogs, telemarketing, and the Internet and reaches consumer segment 2 through retailers. It sells indirectly to business segment 1 through distributors and dealers and to business segment 2 through its own sales force.

> **Multichannel distribution systems**
> A distribution system in which a single firm sets up two or more marketing channels to reach one or more customer segments.

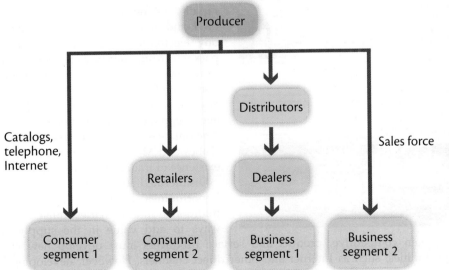

Figure 12.4
Multichannel distribution system

These days, almost every large company and many small ones distribute through multiple channels. HongKong Bank reaches customers by telephone, over the Internet, and through its branch offices. Hewlett-Packard (HP) uses multiple channels to serve dozens of segments and niches, ranging from large corporate and institutional buyers to small businesses to home office buyers. The HP sales force sells the company's information technology equipment and services to large and mid-size business customers. HP also sells through a network of distributors and value-added resellers, which sell HP computers, systems, and services to a variety of special business segments. Home office buyers can buy HP personal computers and printers from specialty computer stores or large retailers. Business, government, and home office buyers can buy directly from HP by phone or online from the company's Web site (*www.hp.com*).

Multichannel distribution systems offer many advantages to companies facing large and complex markets. With each new channel, the company expands its sales and market coverage and gains opportunities to tailor its products and services to the specific needs of diverse customer segments. But such multichannel systems are harder to control, and they generate conflict as more channels compete for customers and sales. For example, when HP began selling directly to customers through its own Web site, many of its retail dealers cried "unfair competition." Many salespeople felt that they were being undercut by the new "inside channels."

In most Asian markets, a multichannel distribution system is often employed by firms hoping to reach diverse customer segments. For example, the higher income earners as well as expatriates often shop at modern supermarkets in air-conditioned shopping centers. Many in the lower income group, however, may prefer to get better bargains at wet markets or small traditional retail stores.

Changing Channel Organization

Changes in technology and the explosive growth of direct and online marketing have affected the nature and design of marketing channels. One major trend is toward **disintermediation**. Disintermediation occurs when product or service producers cut out intermediaries and go directly to final buyers, or when radically new types of channel intermediaries displace traditional ones. For example, companies such as Dell and Singapore Airlines sell directly to final buyers, cutting retailers from their marketing channels.

Disintermediation
The cutting out of marketing channel intermediaries by product or service producers, or the displacement of traditional resellers by radical new types of intermediaries.

Disintermediation –
Besides selling tickets through travel agents and from its sales people, Singapore Airlines also sells its tickets through its Web site. (*www.singaporeair.com*)

In other cases, new forms of resellers are displacing traditional intermediaries. For example, online marketing is growing rapidly, taking business from traditional brick-and-mortar retailers. Consumers can buy electronics from sonystyle.com; tour packages from zuji.com; and books, videos, toys, jewelry, sports, consumer electronics, home and garden items, and almost anything else from Amazon.com; all without ever stepping into a traditional retail store. And online music download services such as iTunes and Musicmatch are threatening the existence of traditional music-store retailers.

Disintermediation presents problems and opportunities. To avoid being swept aside, traditional intermediaries must find new ways to add value in the supply chain. To remain competitive, product and service producers must develop new channel opportunities, such as Internet and other direct channels. However, developing these new channels often brings them into direct competition with their established channels, resulting in conflict.

To ease this problem, companies often look for ways to make going direct a plus for the entire channel. For example, Black & Decker knows that many customers would prefer to buy its power tools and outdoor power equipment online. But selling directly through its Web site would create conflicts with its retail partners. So, although Black & Decker's Web site provides detailed information about the company's products, you can't buy a Black & Decker cordless drill, laser level, leaf blower, or anything else there. Instead, the Black & Decker site refers you to resellers' Web sites and stores. Thus, Black & Decker's direct marketing helps both the company and its channel partners.

Avoiding disintermediation problems –
Black & Decker's Web site provides detailed information, but you can't buy any of the company's products there. Instead, Black & Decker refers you to resellers' Web sites and stores.
(*www.blackanddecker.com*)

Channel Design Decisions

In designing marketing channels, manufacturers struggle between what is ideal and what is practical. A new firm with limited capital usually starts by selling in a limited market area. If successful, the new firm can branch out to new markets through the existing intermediaries. In smaller markets, the firm might sell directly to retailers; in larger markets, it might sell through distributors. In one part of the country, it might grant exclusive franchises; in another, it might sell through all available outlets. Then, it might add a Web store that sells directly to hard-to-reach customers. In this way, channel systems often evolve to meet market opportunities and conditions.

For maximum effectiveness, however, channel analysis and decision making should be more purposeful. Designing a channel system calls for analyzing consumer needs, setting channel objectives, identifying major channel alternatives, and evaluating them (see **Figure 12.5**).

Analyzing Consumer Needs
- Consider what consumer
- Consider whether company has resources or skills to provide the needs
- Balance among consumer needs, feasibility and costs, and consumer price preferences

Setting Channel Objectives
- Decide which segments to serve and the best channels to use
- Evaluate the nature of the company, its products, its marketing intermediaries, its competitors, and the environment

Identifying Major Alternatives
- Consider type of intermediaries to use e.g. company sales force, manufacturer's agency and industrial distributors
- Consider number of intermediaries to use intensive, exclusive, or selective distribution
- Consider responsibilities of channel members regarding mega price policies, conditions of sale, territorial rights, and specific services to be performed by each party

Evaluating Major Alternatives
- Economy criteria: compare likely sales, costs, and profitability of different channel alternatives
- Control issues: give some control over the marketing of a product
- Adaptive criteria: keep the channel flexible enough to adapt to environmental changes

Figure 12.5
Designing a channel system

Designing the marketing channel –
Marketers need to know what target consumers want from the channel, for example, whether they prefer to buy in person or online?

Analyzing Consumer Needs

Designing the marketing channel starts with finding out what target consumers want from the channel. Do consumers want to buy from nearby locations or are they willing to travel to more distant centralized locations? Would they rather buy in person, over the phone, through the mail, or online? Do they value breadth of assortment or do they prefer specialization? The faster the delivery, the greater the assortment provided, and the more add-on services supplied, the greater the channel's service level.

Providing the fastest delivery, greatest assortment, and most services may not be possible or practical. The company and its channel members may not have the resources or skills needed to provide all the desired services. Also, providing higher levels of service results in higher costs for the channel and higher prices for consumers. The company must balance consumer needs not only against the feasibility and costs of meeting these needs but also against customer price preferences. The success of discount retailing shows that consumers will often accept lower service levels in exchange for lower prices.

Setting Channel Objectives

Companies should state their marketing channel objectives in terms of targeted levels of customer service. Usually, a company can identify several segments wanting different levels of service. The company should decide which segments to serve and the best channels to use in each case. In each segment, the company wants to minimize the total channel cost of meeting customer service requirements.

The company's channel objectives are also influenced by the nature of the company, its products, its marketing intermediaries, its competitors, and the environment. For example, the company's size and financial situation determine which marketing functions it can handle itself and which it must give to intermediaries. Companies selling perishable products may require more direct marketing to avoid delays and too much handling.

In some cases, a company may want to compete in or near the same outlets that carry competitors' products. In other cases, producers may avoid the channels used by competitors. Mary Kay Cosmetics, for example, sells direct to consumers through its corps of more than one million independent beauty consultants in 34 markets worldwide rather than going head-to-head with other cosmetics makers for scarce positions in retail stores.

Finally, environmental factors such as economic conditions and legal constraints may affect channel objectives and design. For example, in a depressed economy, producers want to distribute their goods in the most economical way, using shorter channels and dropping unneeded services that add to the final price of the goods.

Identifying Major Alternatives

When the company has defined its channel objectives, it should next identify its major channel alternatives in terms of *types* of intermediaries, the *number* of intermediaries, and the *responsibilities* of each channel member.

Types of Intermediaries

A firm should identify the types of channel members available to carry out its channel work. For example, suppose a manufacturer of test equipment has developed an audio device that detects poor mechanical connections in machines with moving parts. Company executives think this product would have a market in all industries in which electric, combustion, or steam engines are made or used. The company's current sales force is small, and the problem is how best to reach these different industries. The following channel alternatives might emerge:

- *Company sales force*: Expand the company's direct sales force. Assign outside sales people to territories and have them contact all prospects in the area, or develop separate company sales forces for different industries. Or, add an inside telesales operation in which telephone salespeople handle small or mid-size companies.

- *Manufacturer's agency*: Hire manufacturer's agents—independent firms whose sales forces handle related products from many companies—in different regions or industries to sell the new test equipment.
- *Industrial distributors*: Find distributors in the different regions or industries who will buy and carry the new line. Give them exclusive distribution, goodmargins, product training, and promotional support.

Number of Marketing Intermediaries

Companies must also determine the number of channel members to use at each level. Three strategies are available: intensive distribution, exclusive distribution, and selective distribution.

- **Intensive distribution** is a strategy in which producers stock their products in as many outlets as possible. Usually, these products are convenience products and common raw materials. These products must be available where and when consumers want them. For example, toothpaste, candy, and other similar items are sold in millions of outlets to provide maximum brand exposure and consumerconvenience. Kraft, Coca-Cola, Kimberly-Clark, and other consumer goods companies distribute their products in this way.
- **Exclusive distribution** occurs when producers give only a limited number of dealers the exclusive right to distribute its products in their territories. Exclusive distribution is often found in the distribution of luxury automobiles and prestige women's clothing. For example, Bentley dealers are few and far between even large cities may have only one dealer. By granting exclusive distribution, Bentley gains stronger distributor selling support and more control over dealer prices, promotion, credit, and services Exclusive distribution also enhances the car's image and allows for higher markups.
- **Selective distribution** occurs when producers use more than one, but fewer than all, of the intermediaries who are willing to carry a company's products. By using selective distribution, they can develop good working relationships with selected channel members and expect a better-than-average selling effort. Selective distribution gives producers good market coverage with more control and less cost than does intensive distribution.

Intensive distribution
Stocking the product in as many outlets as possible.

Exclusive distribution
Giving a limited number of dealers the exclusive right to distribute the company's products in their territories.

Selective distribution
The use of more than one, but fewer than all, of the intermediaries who are willing to carry the company's products.

Exclusive distribution –
Luxury car makers such as Bentley sell exclusively through a limited number of retailers. Such limited distribution enhances the car's image and generates stronger retail support.

Responsibilities of Channel Members

The producer and intermediaries need to agree on the terms and responsibilities of each channel member. They should agree on price policies, conditions of sale, territorial rights, and specific services to be performed by each party. The producer should establish a list price and a fair set of discounts for intermediaries. It must define each channel member's territory, and it should be careful about where it places new resellers.

Mutual services and duties need to be spelled out carefully, especially in franchise and exclusive distribution channels. For example, McDonald's provides franchisees with promotional support, a record-keeping system, training at Hamburger University, and general management assistance. In turn, franchisees must meet company standards for physical facilities, cooperate with new promotion programs, provide requested information, and buy specified food products.

Evaluating the Major Alternatives

Each alternative should be evaluated against economic, control, and adaptive criteria. Using *economic criteria*, a company compares the likely sales, costs, and profitability of different channel alternatives. What will the investment required by each channel alternative be, and what returns will result? The company must also consider *control issues*. Using intermediaries usually means giving them some control over the marketing of the product, and some intermediaries take more control than others. Finally, the company must apply *adaptive criteria*. Channels often involve long-term commitments, yet the company wants to keep the channel flexible so that it can adapt to environmental changes. Thus, a channel involving long-term commitments should be greatly superior on economic and control grounds.

Designing International Distribution Channels

International marketers face many additional complexities in designing their channels. Each country has its own unique distribution system that has evolved over time and changes very slowly. These channel systems can vary widely from country to country. Thus, global marketers must usually adapt their channel strategies to the existing structures within each country.

- In some markets, the distribution system is *complex* and *hard to penetrate*, consisting of many layers and large numbers of intermediaries. Consider Japan:

The Japanese distribution system stems from the early 17th century, when cottage industries and a fast growing urban population spawned a merchant class. Despite its economic achievements, the Japanese distribution system has remained remarkably faithful to its antique pattern. It encompasses a wide range of wholesalers and other agents, brokers, and retailers, differing more in number than in function form their American counterparts. There is a myriad of tiny retail shops, with many wholesalers supplying to them. These are layered tier after tier, many more than most U.S. executives would think necessary. For example, a bar of soap may move through three wholesalers plus a sales company after it leaves the manufacturer before it reaches the retail outlet. The distribution network reflects the traditionally closer ties among many Japanese companies. Much emphasis is placed on personal relationships. Although these channels appear inefficient and cumbersome, they seem to serve the Japanese customer well. Lacking storage space in their small homes, most Japanese homemakers shop several times a week and prefer convenient and more personal neighborhood shops.[6]

The Japanese distribution system –
It has remained remarkably traditional. A profusion of tiny retail shops are supplied by a large number of small wholesalers.

- In other markets, distribution systems in developing countries may be *scattered* and *inefficient*, or altogether lacking. For example, inadequate distribution systems in China have led most companies to profitably access only a small portion of its huge population located in the country's most affluent cities. "China is a very decentralized market," notes a China trade expert. "[It's] made up of two dozen distinct markets sprawling across 2,000 cities. Each has its own culture… It's like operating in an asteroid belt." China's distribution system is so fragmented that logistics costs amount to 15 percent of the nation's GDP, far higher than in most other countries. After 10 years of effort, even Wal-Mart executives admit that they have been unable to assemble an efficient supply chain in China.[7]

- Sometimes customs or *government regulation* can greatly restrict how a company distributes products in global markets. For example, it wasn't an inefficient distribution structure that caused problems for Avon in China. It was restrictive government regulations. Fearing the growth of multilevel marketing schemes, the Chinese government banned door-to-door selling in 1998. Forced to abandon its traditional direct marketing approach and trying to retail its products, Avon fell behind its more store-oriented competitors. The Chinese government has since given Avon permission to sell door to door, and the company has much catching up to do.[8]

International channel complexities –
Barred from door-to-door selling in China, Avon fell behind trying to sell through retail stores. Here, Chinese consumers buy Avon products from a supermarket in Shanghai. The Chinese government has since given Avon permission to sell door to door.

International marketers face a wide range of channel alternatives. Designing efficient and effective channel systems between and within various country markets poses a difficult challenge. We discuss international distribution decisions further in Chapter 19.

Channel Management Decisions

Once the company has reviewed its channel alternatives and decided on the best channel design, it must implement and manage the chosen channel. Channel management calls for selecting, managing, and motivating individual channel members and evaluating their performance over time. (see **Figure 12.6**)

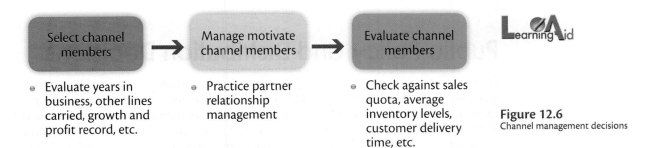

Figure 12.6
Channel management decisions

Selecting Channel Members

Producers vary in their ability to attract qualified marketing intermediaries. Some producers have no trouble signing up channel members. For example, when Toyota first introduced its Lexus line in the U.S., it had no trouble attracting new dealers. At the other extreme are producers who have to work hard to line up enough qualified intermediaries.

When selecting intermediaries, the company should determine what characteristics distinguish the better ones. It will want to evaluate each channel member's years in business, other lines carried, growth and profit record, cooperativeness, and reputation. If the intermediaries are sales agents, the company will want to evaluate the number and character of other lines carried and the size and quality of the sales force. If the intermediary is a retail store that wants exclusive or selective distribution, the company will want to evaluate the store's customers, location, and future growth potential.

Managing and Motivating Channel Members

Once selected, channel members must be continuously managed and motivated to do their best. Some companies practice strong *partner relationship management (PRM)* to forge long-term partnerships with channel members. This creates a marketing system that meets the needs of both the company *and* its marketing partners.

In managing its channels, a company must convince distributors that they can succeed better by working together as a part of a cohesive value delivery system. Thus, Procter & Gamble and Wal-Mart work together to create superior value for final consumers. They jointly plan merchandising goals and strategies, inventory levels, and advertising and promotion plans. In China, P&G recruited and helped develop a new breed of distributors. It trains these new distributors to set merchandising goals and strategies, inventory levels, and advertising and promotion plans.

Many companies are installing integrated high-tech partner relationship management systems to coordinate their whole-channel marketing efforts. Just as they use customer relationship management (CRM) software systems to help manage relationships with important customers, companies use PRM and supply chain management (SCM) software to help recruit, train, organize, manage, motivate, and evaluate relationships with channel partners.

Evaluating Channel Members

The producer must regularly check channel member performance against standards such as sales quotas, average inventory levels, customer delivery time, treatment of damaged and lost goods, cooperation in company promotion and training programs, and services to the customer. The company should recognize and reward intermediaries who are performing well and adding good value for consumers. Those who perform poorly should be assisted or, as a last resort, replaced. A company may periodically "requalify" its intermediaries and prune the weaker ones.

Finally, manufacturers need to be sensitive to their dealers. Those who treat their dealers poorly risk not only losing dealer support but also causing some legal problems. The next section describes various rights and duties pertaining to manufacturers and their channel members.

Public Policy and Distribution Decisions

For the most part, companies are legally free to develop whatever channel arrangements that suit them. Many producers and wholesalers like to develop exclusive channels for their products. In Asia, where counterfeit brands are common, the use of exclusive distributor rights enables a firm to better control its products in the marketplace. When the seller allows only certain outlets to carry its products, this strategy is called *exclusive distribution*. (see **Figure 12.7**) When the seller requires that these dealers not handle competitors' products, its strategy is called *exclusive dealing*. Both parties can benefit

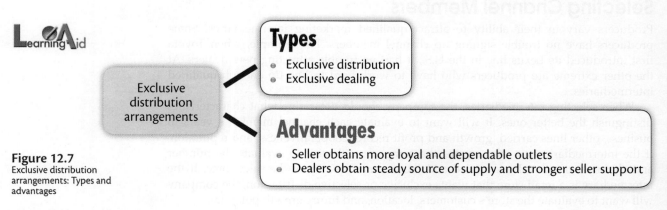

Figure 12.7
Exclusive distribution arrangements: Types and advantages

Exclusive distribution arrangements

Types
- Exclusive distribution
- Exclusive dealing

Advantages
- Seller obtains more loyal and dependable outlets
- Dealers obtain steady source of supply and stronger seller support

from exclusive arrangements: The seller obtains more loyal and dependable outlets, and the dealers obtain a steady source of supply and stronger seller support. But exclusive arrangements also exclude other producers from selling to these dealers.

Exclusive dealing often includes *exclusive territorial agreements*. The producer may agree not to sell to other dealers in a given area, or the buyer may agree to sell only in its own territory. The first practice is normal under franchise systems as a way to increase dealer enthusiasm and commitment. The second practice, whereby the producer tries to keep a dealer from selling outside its territory, has become a major legal issue.

Producers of a strong brand sometimes sell it to dealers only if the dealers will take some or all of the rest of the line. This is called full-line forcing. Such *tying agreements* are not necessarily illegal, but they tend to lessen competition substantially. The practice may prevent consumers from freely choosing among competing suppliers of these other brands.

Finally, producers are free to select their dealers, but their right to terminate dealers is somewhat restricted. In general, sellers can drop dealers "for cause." However, they cannot drop dealers if, for example, the dealers refuse to cooperate in a doubtful legal arrangement, such as exclusive dealing or tying agreements[9].

Marketing Logistics and Supply Chain Management

In a global marketplace, selling a product is sometimes easier than getting it to customers. Companies must decide on the best way to store, handle, and move their products and services so that they are available to customers in the right assortments, at the right time, and in the right place. Physical distribution and logistics effectiveness has a major impact on both customer satisfaction and company costs. Here we consider the nature and importance of logistics management in the supply chain, goals of the logistics system, major logistics functions, and the need for integrated supply chain management.

Nature and Importance of Marketing Logistics

Marketing logistics—also called **physical distribution**—involves planning, implementing, and controlling the physical flow of goods, services, and related information from points of origin to points of consumption to meet customer requirements at a profit. It involves getting the right product to the right customer in the right place at the right time. It starts with the marketplace and works backward to the factory, or even to sources of supply. Marketing logistics involves not only *outbound distribution* (moving products from the factory to resellers and ultimately to customers) but also *inbound distribution* (moving products and materials from suppliers to the factory) and *reverse distribution* (moving broken, unwanted, or excess products returned by consumers or resellers). That is, it involves entire **supply chain management**—managing upstream and downstream value-added flows of materials, final goods, and related information among suppliers, the company, resellers, and final consumers, as shown in **Figure 12.8**.

> **Marketing logistics (physical distribution)**
> The tasks involved in planning, implementing, and controlling the physical flow of materials, final goods, and related information from points of origin to points of consumption to meet customer requirements at a profit.
>
> **Supply chain management**
> Managing upstream and downstream value-added flows of materials, final goods, and related information among suppliers, the company, resellers, and final consumers.

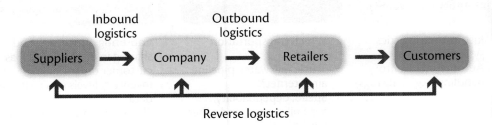

Figure 12.8
Supply chain management

The logistics manager's task is to coordinate activities of suppliers, purchasing agents, marketers, channel members, and customers. These activities include forecasting, information systems, purchasing, production planning, order processing, inventory, warehousing, and transportation planning.

Companies today are placing greater emphasis on logistics for several reasons:

- Companies can gain a powerful *competitive advantage* by using improved logistics to give customers better service or lower prices.
- Improved logistics can yield tremendous *cost savings* to both the company and its customers. As much as 20 percent of an average product's price is accounted for by shipping and transport alone.
- The explosion in *product variety* has created a need for improved logistic management. A hypermarket can carry more than 100,000 products, 30,000 of which are grocery products. Ordering, shipping, stocking, and controlling such a variety of products present a sizable logistics challenge.
- Improvements in information technology have created *opportunities* for major gains in distribution efficiency. Companies are using sophisticated supply chain management software, Web-based logistics systems, point-of sale scanners, uniform product codes, satellite tracking, and electronic transfer of order and payment data. Such technology lets them quickly and efficiently manage the flow of goods, information, and finances through the supply chain.

Goals of the Logistics System

The goal of marketing logistics is to provide a targeted level of customer service at the least cost. A company must first research the importance of various distribution services to customers and then set desired service levels for each segment. The objective is to maximize profits, not sales. Therefore, the company must weigh the benefits of providing higher levels of service against the costs. For example, Dell set up its China Customer Center (CCC) and applied its direct model to China. Products are made-to-order and upgraded systems delivered within a week. Technical-support telephone numbers provided immediate local-language assistance to customers. More generally, some companies offer less service than their competitors and charge a lower price. Other companies offer more service and charge higher prices to cover higher costs.

Major Logistics Functions

Given a set of logistics objectives, the company is ready to design a logistics system that will minimize the cost of attaining these objectives. The major logistics functions include *warehousing, inventory management, transportation,* and *logistics information management* (see **Figure 12.9**).

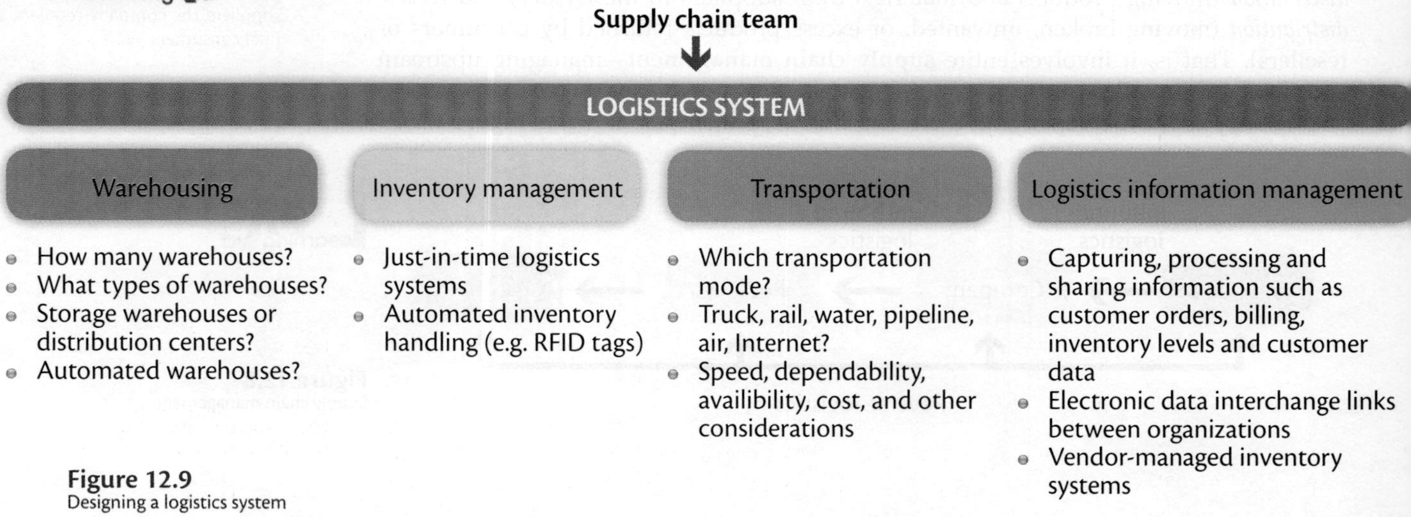

Supply chain team

↓

LOGISTICS SYSTEM			
Warehousing	**Inventory management**	**Transportation**	**Logistics information management**
• How many warehouses? • What types of warehouses? • Storage warehouses or distribution centers? • Automated warehouses?	• Just-in-time logistics systems • Automated inventory handling (e.g. RFID tags)	• Which transportation mode? • Truck, rail, water, pipeline, air, Internet? • Speed, dependability, availibility, cost, and other considerations	• Capturing, processing and sharing information such as customer orders, billing, inventory levels and customer data • Electronic data interchange links between organizations • Vendor-managed inventory systems

Figure 12.9
Designing a logistics system

Warehousing

Production and consumption cycles rarely match. Hence, most companies must store their tangible goods while they wait to be sold. For example, manufacturers of school books and apparel run their factories all year long and store up products for the heavy school reopening season. The storage function overcomes differences in needed quantities and timing, ensuring that products are available when customers are ready to buy them.

A company must decide on *how many* and *what types* of warehouses it needs and where they will be located. The company might use either *storage warehouses* or *distribution centers*. Storage warehouses store goods for moderate to long periods. **Distribution centers** are designed to move goods rather than just store them. They are large and highly automated warehouses designed to receive goods from various plants and suppliers, take orders, fill them efficiently, and deliver goods to customers as quickly as possible.

Warehousing has seen dramatic changes in technology in recent years. Older, multistoried warehouses with outdated materials-handling methods are being replaced by newer, single-storied *automated warehouses* with advanced, computer-controlled materials-handling systems requiring few employees. Computers and scanners read orders and direct lift trucks, electric hoists, or robots to gather goods, move them to loading docks, and issue invoices.

Distribution center
A large, highly automated warehouse designed to receive goods from various plants and suppliers, take orders, fill them efficiently, and deliver goods to customers as quickly as possible.

Inventory Management

Inventory management also affects customer satisfaction. Here, managers must maintain the delicate balance between carrying too little inventory and carrying too much. With too little stock, the firm risks not having products when customers want to buy. To remedy this, the firm may need costly emergency shipments or production. Carrying too much inventory results in higher-than-necessary inventory-carrying costs and stock obsolescence. Thus, in managing inventory, firms must balance the costs of carrying larger inventories against resulting sales and profits.

Many companies have greatly reduced their inventories and related costs through just-in-time logistics systems. With such systems, producers and retailers carry only small inventories of parts or merchandise, often only enough for a few days of operations. For example, Dell, a master just-in-time producer, carries just two to three days of inventory, whereas competitors might carry 40 days or even 60.[10] New stock arrives exactly when needed, rather than being stored in inventory until being used. Just-in-time systems require accurate forecasting along with fast, frequent, and flexible delivery so that new supplies will be available when needed. However, these systems result in substantial savings in inventory-carrying and handling costs.

Marketers are always looking for new ways to make inventory management more efficient. In the not-too-distant future, handling inventory might even become fully automated. For example, RFID or "smart tag" technology by which small transmitter chips are embedded in or placed on products and packaging may be used. "Smart" products could make the entire supply chain—which accounts for nearly 75 percent of a product's cost—intelligent and automated.

Companies using RFID would know, at any time, exactly where a product is located physically within the supply chain. "Smart shelves" would not only tell them when it's time to reorder, but would also place the order automatically with their suppliers. Such exciting new information technology applications will revolutionize distribution as we know it. Many large and resourceful marketing companies, such as Procter & Gamble, IBM, Wal-Mart, and Levi Strauss are investing heavily to make the full use of RFID technology a reality.[11]

Logistics technology –
In the not-too-distant future, RFID or "smart tag" technology could make the entire supply chain—which accounts for nearly 75 percent of a product's cost—intelligent and automated.

Transportation

The choice of transportation carriers affects the pricing of products, delivery performance, and condition of the goods when they arrive—all of which will affect customer satisfaction. In shipping goods to its warehouses, dealers, and customers, the company can choose among five main transportation modes: truck, rail, water, pipeline, and air, along with an alternative mode for digital products—the Internet.

Trucks are highly flexible in their routing and time schedules, and they can usually offer faster service than railroads. They are efficient for short hauls of high-value merchandise. Trucking firms have added many services in recent years. The more advanced carriers offer satellite tracking, 24-hour shipment information, logistics planning software, and "border ambassadors" who expedite cross-border shipping operations. In China, McKinsey observed that goods shipped by road are three times less likely to suffer damage than those shipped on trains. Much of the damage occurs during handling at either end, when the goods are transferred between trucks and rail car.[11]

Railroads, in general, are the conventional and most reliable carriers in Asia. They are one of the most cost-effective modes for shipping large amounts of bulk products—coal, sand, minerals, and farm and forest products—over long distances. In recent years, railroads have increased their customer services by designing new equipment to handle special categories of goods, providing flatcars for carrying truck trailers by rail (piggyback), and providing in-transit services such as the diversion of shipped goods to other destinations en route and the processing of goods en route.

Water carriers transport large amounts of goods by ships and barges on coastal and inland waterways. Although the cost of water transportation is very low for shipping bulky, low-value, nonperishable products such as sand, coal, grain, oil, and metallic ores, water transportation is the slowest mode and may be affected by the weather.

Railroads –
In Asia, railroads are one of the most cost-effective modes of shipping large amounts of bulk products such as coal.

Pipelines are a specialized means of shipping petroleum, natural gas, and chemicals from sources to markets. Most pipelines are used by their owners to ship their own products.

Air carrier is the least used transportation mode because of high airfreight rates. But airfreight is ideal when speed is needed or distant markets must be reached. Among the most frequently airfreighted products are perishables (fresh fish, cut flowers) and high-value, low-bulk items (technical instruments, jewelry). Companies find that airfreight also reduces inventory levels, packaging costs, and the number of warehouses needed.

The *Internet* carries digital products from producer to customer via satellite, cable modem, or telephone wire. Software firms, the media, music companies, and education all make use of the Internet to transport digital products. Although these firms primarily use traditional transportation to distribute CDs, newspapers, and more, the Internet holds the potential for lower product distribution costs. Whereas planes, trucks, and trains move freight and packages, digital technology moves information bits.

Intermodal transportation
Combining two or more modes of transportation.

Shippers also use **intermodal transportation**—combining two or more modes of transportation. *Piggyback* describes the use of rail and trucks; *fishyback*, water and trucks; *trainship*, water and rail; and *airtruck*, air and trucks. Combining modes provides advantages that no single mode can deliver. Each combination offers advantages to the shipper. For example, not only is piggyback cheaper than trucking alone but it also provides flexibility and convenience.

In choosing a transportation mode for a product, shippers must balance many considerations: speed, dependability, availability, cost, and others. Thus, if a shipper needs speed, air and truck are the prime choices. If the goal is low cost, then water or pipeline might be best.

Logistics Information Management

Companies manage their supply chains through information. Channel partners often link up to share information and to make better joint logistics decisions. From a logistics perspective, information flows such as customer orders, billing, inventory levels, and even customer data are closely linked to channel performance. The company wants to design a simple, accessible, fast, and accurate process for capturing, processing, and sharing channel information.

Information can be shared and managed in many ways—by mail or telephone, through salespeople, or through traditional or Internet-based *electronic data interchange (EDI)*, the computerized exchange of data between organizations. Wal-Mart, for example, maintains EDI links with almost all of its 91,000 suppliers. And where it once took eight weeks, using EDI, Krispy Kreme can now turn around 1,000 supplier invoices and process the checks in only a single week.[12]

In some cases, suppliers may be asked to generate orders and arrange deliveries for their customers. Many large retailers such as Wal-Mart work closely with major suppliers such as Procter & Gamble or Black & Decker to set up *vendor-managed inventory* (VMI) systems or *continuous inventory replenishment systems*. Using VMI, the customer shares real-time data on sales and current inventory levels with the supplier. The supplier then takes full responsibility for managing inventories and deliveries. Such systems require close cooperation between the buyer and seller.

Integrated Logistics Management

Today, more companies are adopting the concept of **integrated logistics management**. This concept recognizes that providing better customer service and trimming distribution costs require *teamwork*, both inside the company and among all the marketing channel organizations. Inside, the company's various departments must work closely together to maximize the company's own logistics performance. Outside, the company must integrate its logistics system with those of its suppliers and customers to maximize the performance of the entire distribution system.

> **Integrated logistics management**
> The logistics concept that emphasizes teamwork, both inside the company and among all the marketing channel organizations, to maximize the performance of the entire distribution system.

Cross-Functional Teamwork Inside the Company

In most companies, responsibility for various logistics activities is assigned to many different departments—marketing, sales, finance, operations, purchasing. Too often, each function tries to optimize its own logistics performance without regard for the activities of the other functions. However, transportation, inventory, warehousing, and order-processing activities interact, often in an inverse way. Lower inventory levels reduce inventory-carrying costs. But they may also reduce customer service and increase costs from stockouts, back orders, special production runs, and costly fast-freight shipments. Because distribution activities involve strong trade-offs, decisions by different functions must be coordinated to achieve better overall logistics performance.

Logistics managment – Lower inventory levels reduce inventory carrying costs, but they may also reduce customer services and increase costs from stockouts, back orders, and costly fast-freight shipments.

The goal of integrated supply chain management is to harmonize all of the company's logistics decisions. Close working relationships among departments can be achieved in several ways. Some companies have created permanent logistics committees, made up of managers responsible for different physical distribution activities. Companies can also create supply chain manager positions that link the logistics activities of functional areas. For example, Procter & Gamble has created supply managers, who manage all of the supply chain activities for each of its product categories. Many companies have a vice president of logistics with cross-functional authority. Finally, companies can employ sophisticated, systemwide supply chain management software, now available from wide range of software enterprises large and small, from SAP to RiverOne and Logility.[14] The important thing is that the company must coordinate its logistics and marketing activities to create high market satisfaction at a reasonable cost.

Building Logistics Partnerships

Companies must do more than improve their own logistics. They must also work with other channel partners to improve whole-channel distribution. The members of a marketing channel are linked closely in creating customer value and building customer relationships. One company's distribution system is another company's supply system. The success of each channel member depends on the performance of the entire supply chain. For example, IKEA can create its stylish but affordable furniture and deliver the "IKEA lifestyle" only if its entire supply chain—consisting of thousands of merchandise designers and suppliers, transport companies, warehouses, and service providers—operates at maximum efficiency and customer-focused effectiveness.

Smart companies coordinate their logistics strategies and forge strong partnerships with suppliers and customers to improve customer service and reduce channel costs. Many companies have created *cross-functional, cross-company teams*. For example, Procter & Gamble works closely with its counterparts to find ways to squeeze costs out of their distribution system. Working together benefits not only P&G and its distributors but also their final consumers. Similarly, Gap, Nike, and many global brands that source production capacity from Asian countries, particularly China, are investing huge amounts of executive time and money in their logistics systems to retain or improve their competitive advantage as their operations continue to grow.

Third-Party Logistics

Most big companies love to make and sell their products. But many do not like the associated logistics "grunt work." They detest the bundling, loading, unloading, sorting, storing, reloading, transporting, customs clearing, and tracking required to supply their

Logistics partnerships – IKEA's success is partly dependent on developing a partnership with its suppliers, transport companies, warehouses, and service providers.

REAL MARKETING

Li & Fung: Managing Supply Chains in a "Flat" World

Export trading company Li & Fung has the world's largest network of sourcing and manufacturing offices and is a leading supply chain manager for brands and retailers. Founded in Guangzhou in 1906, the company coordinates the manufacture and supply of time-sensitive consumer goods through a network of 66 offices in over 40 countries from its Hong Kong headquarters. According to its president, Bruce Rockowitz, "If you go to a mall in the U.S., 30 to 40 percent [of the vendors] would be a customer of Li & Fung. The consumer never really sees our name. We are behind a lot of things that you wear and see within your home."

Since it went public in 1992, Li & Fung has had a 22 percent compound annual growth rate, and between 1999 and 2006, its earnings have tripled. The company has a turnover of $8 billion, a market capital of $12 billion, and

Third-party logistics – Li & Fung customizes global supply chains for leading brands and retailers.

employs 12,000 people worldwide. While Li & Fung owns no factories, its global network of 10,000 suppliers enabled it to ship over two billion pieces to the world in 2006. According to its Web site, Li & Fung acts as an extension to its clients' businesses by managing every aspect of their global supply chains so that they can focus

on their customers. Li & Fung's clients include Avon, The Limited, Tesco, and Reebok.

A dedicated extranet links together the key components of the supply chain to provide tracking capabilities, streamline the flow of business information, and furnish more granular control of supply chain activities.

factories and to get products out to customers. Hence, they outsource some or all of their logistics to **third-party logistics (3PL) providers**.

These companies such as UPS Supply Chain Solutions, FedEx Logistics, or Li & Fung—help clients to tighten up sluggish, overstuffed supply chains, slash inventories, and get products to customers more quickly and reliably. For example, Li & Fung's Total Value-Added Package provides clients with a wide range of services from product design and development, through raw material and factory sourcing, production planning and management, as well as quality assurance and export documentation to shipping consolidation (see **Real Marketing**).

According to a recent survey of chief logistics executives at Fortune 500 companies, 82 percent of these companies use third-party logistics (also called *3PL, outsourced logistics, or contract logistics*) services.[15] Companies use third-party logistics providers for several reasons. First, because getting the product to market is their main focus, these providers can often do it more efficiently and at lower cost. Outsourcing typically results in 15 percent to 30 percent cost savings. Second, outsourcing logistics frees a company to focus more intensely on its core business. Finally, integrated logistics companies understand increasingly complex logistics environments. This can be especially helpful to companies attempting to expand their global market coverage. For example, companies distributing their products across China face a bewildering array of environmental challenges that affect logistics, including finding the best combination of land transport and packaging standards. By outsourcing its logistics, a company can gain a complete China distribution system without incurring the costs, delays, and risks associated with setting up its own system.

> **Third-party logistics (3PL) provider**
> An independent logistics provider that performs any or all of the functions required to get their client's product to market.

Internally, Li & Fung's global sourcing network leverages the capabilities of its intranet to ensure rapid dissemination of information worldwide. It leverages intimate market knowledge, experienced sourcing professionals, cutting-edge technology, and state-of-the-art information systems to ensure that all orders are delivered on time, on budget, and according the its customers' specifications.

For example, to fulfill an order of 10,000 garments from a European retailer, Li & Fung may buy yarn from Korea and have it woven and dyed in Taiwan. Then, based on quota considerations and labor conditions, it may ship these raw materials to manufacture the garments in five Thai factories. The completed garments are then assembled for quality control checks. Li & Fung then organizes export documentation and shipping. Effectively, Li & Fung is customizing the value chain to meet their customers' needs.

As chairman Victor Fung, who holds a doctorate in business and was a former faculty member of the Harvard Business School, says, "You see two retailers competing across the street. We see two supply chains ... years ago, the question was which factory should you ask to make a shirt. Today, you ask, where do we source the yarn? Where do you do the dyeing and weaving? Where do you do the cutting and trimming? Where do you do the sewing? The whole issue is how to break up the production process and then putting it all together again ... the glue that holds everything together ... is the Internet."

Rockowitz explains, "Today, countries are no longer really important, the world has become 'flat.' From a sourcing point of view ... you ... have to look at the whole world and find the best places ... The old supply chains used to deliver goods; the store would put the price tag on, put the hangers on, and add whatever they needed to add. Today, we ship everything almost store-ready. There is no work on the store's part. Same thing with packing—everything is prepacked ... We [also] plant a very small chip into the packages that are being shipped, or into the garments. This chip can tell you where the goods are—on the ship, at the store, etc—at any given moment."

To sustain its growth momentum, Rockowitz stressed the importance of reinvention at Li & Fung. "Every three years, we look at reinventing our company. We go through a year-long process of thinking up what we can change ... We want to throw everything out and start from scratch. We look ahead to paint a scenario, to anticipate how trade will be. Will there be recessions and other [problems]? We set high goals, and then we jump into the future and look back to see where the company can grow."

Still, Li & Fung remains faithful to its Asian roots. Chairman Fung states, "In many ways, we are an MNC but we see ourselves as an Asian-based MNC ... Our hardware and systems are Western. Our values are very Chinese. We value loyalty, we value long service, we value entrepreneurship."

Sources:
Joan Magretta, "Fast, Global, and Entrepreneurial: Supply Chain Management, Hong Kong Style: An Interview with Victor Fung," *Harvard Business Review*, (September–October 1998): 103–114; "Li & Fung's Bruce Rockowitz: Managing Supply Chains in a 'Flat' World," www.knowledgeatwharton.com, June 20, 2007; "A Business Family," *Business Times* (Singapore), July 2005; "Li & Fung,," Wikipedia, December 2007; and materials and information from www.lifung.com, December 2007.

REVIEWING THE CONCEPTS

Marketing channel decisions are among the most important decisions that management faces. A company's channel decisions directly affect every other marketing decision. Management must make channel decisions carefully, incorporating today's needs with tomorrow's likely selling environment. Some companies pay too little attention to their distribution channels, but others have used imaginative distribution systems to gain competitive advantage.

1 Explain why companies use marketing channels and discuss the functions these channels perform.

Most producers use intermediaries to bring their products to market. They try to forge a *marketing channel* (or *distribution channel*)—a set of interdependent organizations involved in the process of making a product or service available for use or consumption by the consumer or business user. Through their contacts, experience, specialization, and scale of operation, intermediaries usually offer the firm more than it can achieve on its own.

Marketing channels perform many key functions. Some help *complete* transactions by gathering and distributing *information* needed for planning and aiding exchange; by developing and spreading persuasive *communications* about an offer; by performing *contact* work—finding and communicating with prospective buyers; by *matching*—shaping and fitting the offer to the buyer's needs; and by entering into *negotiation* to reach an agreement on price and other terms of the offer so that ownership can be transferred. Other functions help to *fulfill* the completed transactions by offering *physical distribution*—transporting and storing goods; *financing*—acquiring and using funds to cover the costs of the channel work; and *risk taking*—assuming the risks of carrying out the channel work.

2 Discuss how channel members interact and how they organize to perform the work of the channel.

The channel will be most effective when each member is assigned the tasks it can do best. Ideally, because the success of individual channel members depends on overall channel success, all channel firms should work together smoothly. They should understand and accept their roles, coordinate their goals and activities, and cooperate to attain overall channel goals. By cooperating, they can more effectively sense, serve, and satisfy the target market. In a large company, the formal organization structure assigns roles and provides needed leadership. But in a distribution channel made up of independent firms, leadership and power are not formally set. Traditionally, distribution channels have lacked the leadership needed to assign roles and manage conflict. In recent years, however, new types of channel organizations have appeared that provide stronger leadership and improved performance.

3 Identify the major channel alternatives open to a company.

Each firm identifies alternative ways to reach its market. Available means vary from direct selling to using one, two, three, or more intermediary *channel levels*. Marketing channels face continuous and sometimes dramatic change. Three of the most important trends are the growth of *vertical, horizontal,* and *multichannel* marketing *systems*. These trends affect channel cooperation, conflict, and competition. *Channel design* begins with assessing customer channel service needs and company channel objectives and constraints. The company then identifies the major channel alternatives in terms of the *types* of intermediaries, the *number* of intermediaries, and the *channel responsibilities* of each. Each channel alternative must be evaluated according to economic, control, and adaptive criteria. Channel management calls for selecting qualified intermediaries and motivating them. Individual channel members must be evaluated regularly.

4 Explain how companies select, motivate, and evaluate channel members.

Producers vary in their ability to attract qualified marketing intermediaries. Some producers have no trouble signing up channel members. Others have to work hard to line up enough qualified intermediaries. When selecting intermediaries, the company should evaluate each channel member's qualifications and select those who best fit its channel objectives. Once selected, channel members must be continuously motivated to do their best. The company must sell not only *through* the intermediaries but *to* them. It should work to forge long-term partnerships with their channel partners to create a marketing system that meets the needs of both the manufacturer *and* the partners. The company must also regularly check channel member performance against established performance standards, rewarding intermediaries who are performing well and assisting or replacing weaker ones.

5 Discuss the nature and importance of marketing logistics and integrated supply chain management.

Just as firms are giving the marketing concept increased recognition, more business firms are paying attention to *marketing logistics* (or *physical distribution*). Logistics is an area of potentially high cost savings and improved customer satisfaction. Marketing logistics addresses not only *outbound distribution* but also *inbound distribution* and *reverse distribution*. That is, it involves entire *supply chain management*—managing value-added flows between suppliers, the company, resellers, and final users. No logistics system can both maximize customer service and minimize distribution costs. Instead, the goal of logistics management is to provide a *targeted* level of service at the least cost. The major logistics functions include *order processing, warehousing, inventory management,* and *transportation*.

The *integrated supply chain management* concept recognizes that improved logistics requires teamwork in the form of close working relationships across functional areas inside the company and across various organizations in the supply chain. Companies can achieve logistics harmony among functions by creating cross-functional logistics teams, integrative supply manager positions, and senior-level logistics executives with cross-functional authority. Channel partnerships can take the form of cross-company teams, shared projects, and information sharing systems. Today, some companies are outsourcing their logistics functions to third-party logistics (3PL) providers to save costs, increase efficiency, and gain faster and more effective access to global markets.

REVIEWING THE KEY TERMS

Administered VMS 312
Channel conflict 311
Channel level 309
Contractual VMS 312
Conventional distribution channel 312
Corporate VMS 312
Direct marketing channel 30
Disintermediation 314
Distribution center 323
Exclusive distribution 317
Franchise organization 312
Horizontal marketing system 313

Indirect marketing channel 310
Integrated logistics management 325
Intensive distribution 317
Intermodal transportation 324
Marketing channel (distribution channel) 307
Marketing logistics (physical distribution) 321
Multichannel distribution system 313
Selective distribution 317
Supply chain management 321
Third-party logistics (3PL) provider 327
Value delivery network 307
Vertical marketing system (VMS) 312

DISCUSSING THE CONCEPTS

1. What is the difference between a supply chain and a value-delivery network?

2. How might a distribution channel evolve from a conventional distribution channel to a vertical marketing system?

3. The chapter cites Hewlett-Packard as a company employing multichannel distribution. Discuss the pros and cons of choosing hybrid marketing channels.

4. What factors does a cosmetics company need to consider when designing its marketing channel for a new low-priced line of cosmetics?

5. Identify the primary challenges an organization faces in managing its channel members. What are some of the methods companies use to motivate channel partners?

6. Give three reasons why supply chain management is an important part of the value-delivery network.

APPLYING THE CONCEPTS

1. ExerWise, a new company marketing a high-end Ab Toner exercise machine, is considering direct marketing versus selling through a sporting-goods retailer. As the buyer for the retailer, explain the functions your retail chain can offer to ExerWise.

2. Assume you are selling fresh strawberries to a variety of retailers through a produce wholesale distributor Form a small group and have each member assume one of the following roles: berry farmer, wholesaler, and grocery

retailer. In your role, discuss three things that might have recently angered you about the other channel members. Take turns voicing your gripes and attempting to resolve the conflict.

3. Oracle offers software solutions for supply chain management. Go to Oracle's Web site at _www.oracle.com/applications/scm/index.html_ and explore its supply chain products. List five ways these products might help managers improve their supply chain management.

FOCUS ON TECHNOLOGY

RFID, radio frequency identification, is one of the most exciting recent technical innovations relating to a company's logistics operations. Applications involve placing small tags containing tiny electronic RFID chips on containers, pallets, cartons, or even individual products. The tags transmit a radio signal to readers, which translate and store the product-identification data. In the past, the costs of the RFID tags have been prohibitively expensive. However, thanks to improved semiconductor technology, chips can now be produced at reasonable prices. Improvements in software, telecommunications, and data sharing have all worked to move RFID to center stage for logistics managers. In fact, Wal-Mart, a pioneer in RFID application, has issued mandates to its suppliers that force them to begin using RFID tags on pallet shipments. As additional retailers adopt this technology and spread it through their value networks, analysts expect that RFID will become the standard for product identification.

1. What impact would RFID applications have on each of the major logistical functions?

2. What are the biggest current obstacles to adopting this technology?

3. How could RFID improve the customer experience?

FOCUS ON ETHICS

Slotting fees are a one-time fee paid by food manufacturers to retailers for allotting shelf space to a new product. The manufacturer buys the product's way into the marketing channel. The many critics of this system claim that grocery retailers have too much power in this situation. They also assert that the slotting fee system is unfair to small manufacturers who cannot afford such large fees. Slotting fees have been called everything from a bribe to a retailer's addiction, a questionable source of income that many retailers have come to rely on to survive. Retailers claim that they need the additional funds to offset the costs associated with new products. To stock a new product, they must shift other products on the shelf, move products in the warehouse, and update computer systems. In addition, retailers say they run the risk of costs associated with the potential failure of the product. In response to the cries of small manufacturers that these fees create unfair competition, retailers sometimes waive slotting fees for the smaller companies.

1. Assess slotting fees from the points of view of both the retailer and the producer. Which side do you support?

2. How might slotting fees affect a manufacturer's decision when selecting channel members?

3. Go to _www.ftc.gov/opa/2003/11/slottingallowance.htm_ to read about the FTC report on slotting fees. What did you learn from this report on slotting fees?

VIDEO CASE

Hasbro

It all started with GI Joe back in 1964. That was when Hasbro, now a $3 billion company operating in more than 100 countries, launched the now-legendary toy and pioneered the action figure category. Since then, the company has developed scores of new toys that are well known to children and adults around the world. Hasbro's brands include games such as Hungry Hungry Hippos, Parcheesi, Risk, Trouble, Scrabble, Outburst, Twister, Pictionary, Boggle, and Monopoly. The company also sells Tinkertoys, Lite-Brite, Transformers, Glowworms, Mr. Potato Head, VideoNow, and Play-Doh.

Today, to keep up with constantly changing trends in the marketplace, Hasbro develops almost 1,000 new products annually and launches nearly 80 percent of those products within a year's time. Getting all of those products to consumers requires a reliable and efficient supply chain and a well-tuned marketing channel. Hasbro's products can be found in toy stores, drugstores, wholesale stores, and even grocery stores. After viewing the video featuring Hasbro, answer the following questions about marketing channels and supply chain management.

1. What levels of distribution does Hasbro use? How does the company keep both mass merchandisers and other channels from competing directly with one another?

2. How does Hasbro use distribution channels to build stronger relationships with customers?

3. How does Hasbro partner with its channel members to deliver better value to consumers?

COMPANY CASE

Zara: The Technology Giant of the Fashion World

One global retailer is expanding at a dizzying pace for world domination of its industry. Having built its own state-of-the-art distribution network, the company is beating the competition in sales and profits, as well as speed of inventory management and turnover. We're talking about Zara, the flagship specialty chain of Spain-based clothing conglomerate, Inditex.

This dynamic retailer is known for selling stylish designs that resemble those of big-name fashion houses but at moderate prices. "We sell the latest trends at low prices, but our clients value our design, quality, and constant innovation," a company spokesman said. "That gives us the advantage even in highly competitive, developed markets." More interesting is the way that Zara achieves its mission.

Fast Fashion—The Newest Waves

A handful of European specialty clothing retailers are taking the fashion world by storm with a business model that has come to be known as "fast fashion." In short, these companies can recognize and respond to fashion trends very quickly, create products that mirror the trends, and get those products onto shelves much faster and more frequently than the industry norm. Fast-fashion retailers include Sweden's Hennes & Mauritz (H&M), Britain's Top Shop, and Spain's Mango. Although these companies are successfully employing the fast-fashion concept, Zara leads the pack on virtually every level.

For example, "fast" at Zara means that it can take a product from concept through design, manufacturing, and store shelf placement in as little as two weeks, much quicker than any of its fast-fashion competitors. For more mainstream clothing chains, such as Gap and Abercrombie and Fitch, the process takes months.

This gives Zara the advantage of virtually copying fashions from Vogue and having them on the streets in dozens of countries before the next issue of the magazine is published. When Spain's Crown Prince Felipe and Letizia Ortiz Rocasolano announced their engagement in 2003, the bride-to-be wore a stylish white trouser suit. European women loved it and within a few weeks, hundreds of them were wearing a nearly identical outfit they had purchased from Zara.

But Zara is more than just fast. It's also prolific. In a typical year, Zara launches about 19,000 new items. Compare that to the 2,000 to 4,000 items introduced by both H&M and Gap. In the fashion world, this difference is huge. Zara stores receive new merchandise two to three times each week, whereas most clothing retailers get large shipments on a seasonal basis, four to six times per year.

By introducing new products with frequency and in higher numbers, Zara produces smaller batches of items. Thus, it assumes less risk if an item doesn't sell well. But smaller batches also mean exclusivity, a unique benefit from a mass-market retailer that draws young fashionistas through Zara's doors. When items sell out, they are not restocked with another shipment. Instead, the next Zara shipment contains something new, something different. Popular items can appear and disappear within a week. Consumers know that if they like something, they must buy it or miss out. Customers are enticed to check out store stock more often, leading to very high levels of repeat patronage. But it also means that Zara doesn't need to follow the industry pattern of marking prices down as the season progresses. Thus, Zara reaps the benefit of prices that average much closer to the list price.

The Vertical Secret to Zara's Success

How does Zara achieve such responsiveness? The answer lies in its distribution system. In 1975, Amancio Ortega opened the first Zara store in Spain's remote northwest town of La Coruña, home to Zara's headquarters. Having already worked in the textile industry for two decades, his experience led him to design a system in which he could control every aspect of the supply chain, from design and production to distribution and retailing. He knew, for example, that in the textile business, the biggest markups were made by wholesalers and retailers. He was determined to maintain control over these activities. Ortega's original philosophy forms the heart of Zara's unique supply chain today. But it's Zara's high-tech information system that has taken vertical integration in the company to an unprecedented level. According to CEO Pablo Isla, "Our information system is absolutely avant-garde. It's what links the shop to our designers and our distribution system."

Zara's vertically-integrated system makes the starting point of a product concept hard to nail down. At Zara's headquarters, creative teams of over 300 professionals carry out the design process. But they act on information fed to them from the stores. This goes far beyond typical point-of-sales data. Store managers act as trend spotters. Every day they report hot fads to headquarters, enabling popular lines to be tweaked and slow movers to be whisked away within hours. If customers are asking for a rounded neck on a vest rather than a V neck, such an item can be in stores in seven to 10 days. This process would take traditional retailers months.

Managers also consult a personal digital assistant every evening to check what new designs are available and place their orders according to what they think will sell best to their customers. Thus, store managers help shape designs by ensuring that the creative teams have real-time information based on the observed tastes of actual consumers. Ortega refers to this as the democratization of fashion.

When it comes to sourcing, Zara's supply chain is unique as well. Current conventional wisdom calls for manufacturers in all industries to outsource their goods globally to the cheapest provider. Thus, most of Zara's competitors contract out their manufacturing work to low-wage countries, notably Asia. But Zara makes 40 percent of its own fabrics and produces more than half of its own clothes, rather than relying on suppliers. Even things that are farmed out are done locally to maximize time efficiency. Nearly all Zara clothes for its stores worldwide are produced in its remote Northeast corner of Spain.

As it completes designs, Zara cuts fabric in-house. It then sends the designs to one of several hundred local co-operatives for sewing, minimizing the time for raw material distribution. When items return to Zara's facilities, they are ironed by an assembly line of workers where each

worker specializes in a specific task (lapels, shoulders, and so on). Clothing items are wrapped in plastic and transported on conveyor belts to a group of giant warehouses.

Zara's warehouses are a vision of modern automation. Human labor is a rare sight in these cavernous buildings. Customized machines patterned after the equipment used by overnight parcel services process up to 80,000 items an hour. The computerized system sorts, packs, labels, and allocates clothing items to Zara's 1,000-plus stores. For stores within a 24-hour drive, Zara delivers goods by truck, whereas it ships merchandise via cargo jets to stores farther away.

Domestic Manufacturing Pays Off

Making speed the main goal of its supply chain has paid off for Inditex. In 2007, sales grew by 15 percent over the prior year to $14.6 billion (retail revenue growth worldwide averages single-digit increases). During the same period, profits soared by 25 percent to $1.9 billion. Zara, its biggest brand, is now ranked number 73 on Interbrand's list of top 100 most valuable worldwide brands. And Inditex wants more. International sales represent 2.5 percent of total sales. With more than one ribbon-cutting ceremony per day, Inditex wants to increase its number of stores from the current 3,691. Zara opened its first outlet in Shanghai in 2006, and now has some 40 stores from Bangkok to Tokyo. In 2008, it opened in Seoul, Korea bringing to 68 the number of cocuntries Zara is in.

European fast-fashion retailers have thus far expanded very cautiously in the U.S., Zara has only 19 stores stateside. But the threat has U.S. clothing retailers rethinking the models they have relied on for years. According to one analyst, the industry may soon experience a reversal from outsourcing to China to "Made in the U.S.A":

"U.S. retailers are finally looking at lost sales as lost revenue. They know that in order to capture maximum sales they need to turn their inventory much quicker. The disadvantage of importing from China is that it requires a longer lead time of between three to six months from the time an order is placed to when the inventory is stocked in stores. By then the trends may have changed and you're stuck with all the unsold inventory. If retailers want to refresh their merchandise quicker, they will have to consider sourcing at least some of the merchandise locally."

So being the fastest of the fast-fashion retailers has not only paid off for Zara, its model has reconfigured the fashion landscape everywhere. Zara has blazed a trail for cheaper fashion-led mass retailers, put the squeeze on mid-priced fashion, and forced luxury brands scrambling to find ways to set themselves apart from Zara's look-a-like designs.

Over-Reaching?

Not all are convinced about the Inditex story, however. As Zara ventures deeper into far-flung territories, it risks losing its speed advantage. With more stores in Asia and the U.S., replenishing its stores twice weekly from its Spanish base will be increasingly complex and expensive. The strains are already starting to show. Costs are climbing and growth in same-store sales is slowing. "The further away from Spain they move, the less competitive they will be," predicts

Harvard Business School professor Pankaj Ghemawat. "As long as Zara has one production and distribution base, its model is somewhat limited." So far Inditex has offset this problem by charging more for its goods as it gets farther from HQ. For instance, Zara's U.S. prices are some 65 percent higher than prices in Spain, estimates Lehman Brothers. Whether this can work in Asia, with its own competitively priced fast-fashion retailers like Giordano, remains to be seen.

Questions For Discussion

1. Sketch the supply chain for Zara from raw materials to consumer purchase.
2. Discuss the concepts of horizontal and vertical conflict as they relate to Zara.
3. Which type of vertical marketing system does Zara exhibit? List all the benefits that Zara receives by having adopted this system.
4. Does Zara incur disadvantages from its "fast-fashion" distribution system? Are these disadvantages offset by the advantages?
5. How does Zara add value for the customer through major logistics functions?
6. What recommendations would you make to Zara's management regarding its Asian expansion plans? How can it preserve its speed advantage without sacrificing its cost competitiveness in the region?

Sources:
"The Future of Fast Fashion," *The Economist*, June 18, 2005; Rachel Tiplady, "Zara: Taking the Lead in Fast Fashion," *BusinessWeek Online*, April 4, 2006; John Tagliabue, "A Rival to Gap that Operates Like Dell," *New York Times*, May 30, 2003, p. W1; Elizabeth Nash, "Dressed for Success," *The Independent*, March 31, 2006, p. 22; Parija Bhatnagar, "Is 'Made in U.S.A.' Back in Vogue?" www.CNNMoney.com, March 1, 2005; Sarah Mower, "The Zara Phenomenon," *The Evening Standard*, January 13, 2006, p. 30; "Fashion Conquistador," *BusinessWeek Online*, September 4, 2006; www.inditex.com, May 2008; "Spanish Fashion Hits Beijing," *China Daily*, February 2, 2007

Objectives

After studying this chapter, you should be able to

- explain the roles of retailers and wholesalers in the distribution channel
- describe the major types of retailers and give examples of each
- describe the major types of wholesalers and give examples of each
- explain the marketing decisions facing retailers and wholesalers

CHAPTER 13

RETAILING AND WHOLESALING

Previewing the Concepts

In the previous chapter, you learned the basics of distribution channel design and management. Now, we'll look more deeply into the two major intermediary channel functions, retailing and wholesaling. You already know something about retailing—you're served every day by retailers of all shapes and sizes. However, you probably know much less about the hoard of wholesalers that work behind the scenes. In this chapter, we'll examine the characteristics of different kinds of retailers and wholesalers, the marketing decisions they make, and trends for the future.

To start the tour, we'll look at Carrefour. In today's marketing world, almost every retailer, large or small, worries about competing with Wal-Mart, the world's largest retailer—the world's second-largest company. Few retailers can compete directly with Wal-Mart and survive. Yet, Carrefour is thriving in the shadow of the giant and has shown its success in China recently.

These days, Wal-Mart sells just about everything. That means that it competes ruthlessly with almost every other retailer, no matter what the product category. Wal-Mart outsells Toys "R" Us in the toy market and again sells half as many groceries as the leading groceries-only retailer, Kroger. It gives retailers big headaches in DVD and video sales, and puts a big dent in Best Buy's consumer electronics business. Almost every retailer, large or small, has its hands full devising strategies by which it can compete with Wal-Mart and survive.

So, how do you compete with a behemoth like Wal-Mart? The best answer: You don't—at least not directly. Perhaps the worst strategy is trying to out-Wal-Mart Wal-Mart. Instead of competing head-to-head, smart competitors choose their turf carefully.

In fact, this story isn't even about Wal-Mart—we'll cover that colossus later in the chapter. Instead, this is a story about Carrefour, a chain that's doing very well by carving out its own turf in the shadow of the giant.

Worldwide, Carrefour has over 12,500 stores as opposed to Wal-Mart's more than 6,500, and its annual sales total about 97.24 billion yuan (approximately $13.7 billion), compared to Wal-Mart's $312 billion in 2007.

Although it may not seem like a fair fight, Carrefour is thriving. It succeeds through careful positioning—specifically, by positioning away from Wal-Mart. Rather than pursuing mass-market sales volume and razor-thin margins, Carrefour targets a slightly different group of customers in four main grocery store formats: hypermarkets, supermarkets, discount stores, and convenience stores.

Carrefour's value proposition is summed up in its com-mitment to promoting local economic development.

Both online and in the flesh, a visit to Carrefour is more than just a shopping trip, it's an experience. And the experience is anything but what you'd find at Wal-Mart. While Wal-Mart makes customers feel at home, creating store environments that are inviting, fun, unique, informal, comfortable, attractive, nurturing, and educational, Carrefour lets you have the pleasure of shopping at a modern retail outlet. Its facility design can bring customers an unforgettable shopping experience. Let's look at the following:

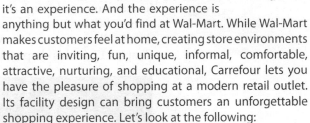

- separating the entrance and exit to allow customers the possibility of shopping their way through the entire store;
- dividing the store into distinctive areas according to product categories, to guide customer shopping;
- providing innovative facilities, such as safe non-staircase escalators and customer-oriented counters, to demonstrate its quality service; and
- focusing on atmospheric design which emphasizes store decoration, within-store sales promotion, point-of-purchase advertisements, and quality service from salespersons.

Carrefour customers therefore like the fact that the store's commitment to quality reaches far beyond what's on its shelves. It cares about the well-being and quality of life of everyone associated with the business, from customers and employees, to suppliers, to the broader communities in which it operates.

Like Wal-Mart, Carrefour in China is very much concerned with human resources management and tries hard to nurture the loyalty of its employees in order to encourage them to devote themselves to Carrefour's "good business". In this regard, Carrefour emphasizes the importance of the following practices within the organization:

- discipline;
- selection of quality staff;
- training;
- effective motivation programs; and
- staff empowerment.

Such commitment, along with strong targeting and positioning, has made Carrefour one of the leaders of China's growing retail sector. In China, its stores rang up an average of RMB 261 million in sales per store in 2007, an increase of 53 percent over 2006, and 8.9 percent higher than that of Wal-Mart. Whereas other retailers have faced limited sales and profit growth in the face of the withering Hua Lien Supermarket assault, Carrefour's sales and profits have achieved a growth of almost 12 percent over the last two years.

In China, Carrefour competes directly with the Wal-Mart stores. It matches Wal-Mart's massive economies of scale, incredible volume purchasing power, ultra efficient logistics, wide selection, and hard-to-beat prices. On top of this, it targets customers that Wal-Mart can't serve, offering them value that Wal-Mart doesn't deliver. By positioning away from Wal-Mart and other mainstream grocers, Carrefour has found its own very profitable place in the China market and in many markets in the world.

Retailing

Retailing
All activities involved in selling goods or services directly to final consumers for their personal, nonbusiness use.

Retailer
A business whose sales come primarily from retailing.

What is retailing? We all know that Wal-Mart, Carrefour, Sogo, and Target are retailers, but so are Avon representatives, Amazon.com, the local Holiday Inn, and a doctor seeing patients. **Retailing** includes all the activities involved in selling products or services directly to final consumers for their personal, nonbusiness use. Many institutions—manufacturers, wholesalers, and retailers—do retailing. But most retailing is done by **retailers**: businesses whose sales come *primarily* from retailing.

Although most retailing is done in retail stores, in recent years nonstore retailing has been growing much faster than has store retailing. *Nonstore retailing* includes selling to final consumers through direct mail, catalogs, telephone, the Internet, TV home-shopping shows, home and office parties, door-to-door contact, vending machines, and other direct-selling approaches. We discuss such direct-marketing approaches in detail in Chapter 17. In this chapter, we focus on store retailing.

Nonstore retailing –
The growth of nonstore retailing in recent years is espcially evident in Japn, where vending marchines are used to sell almost anything from drinks to cigarettes and instant noodles.

Types of Retailers

Retail stores come in all shapes and sizes, and new retail types keep emerging. The most important types of retail stores are described in **Table 13.1** and discussed in the following sections. They can be classified in terms of several characteristics, including *the amount of service* they offer, the breadth and depth of their *product lines*, the *relative prices* they charge, and how they are *organized*.

Amount of Service

Different products require different amounts of service, and customer service preferences vary. Retailers may offer one of three levels of service—self-service, limited service, and full service.

Self-service retailers serve customers who are willing to perform their own "locate-compare-select" process to save money. Self-service is the basis of all discount operations and is typically used by sellers of convenience goods (such as Circle K, Lawson, and 7-Eleven) and those of nationally branded, fast-moving shopping goods (such as Wal-Mart).

Table 13.1 Major Store Retailer Types

Specialty Stores: Carry a narrow product line with a deep assortment, such as apparel stores, sporting-goods stores, furniture stores, florists, and bookstores. A clothing store would be a *single-line* store, a women's clothing store would be a *limited-line* store, and a women's custom-shirt store would be a *superspecialty* store. For examples, Giordano is a single-line store, and Giordano Ladies is a limited-line store.

Department Stores: Carry several product lines—typically clothing, home furnishings, and household goods—with each line operated as a separate department managed by specialist buyers or merchandisers. Examples: Sogo, Shin Kong Mitsukoshi, Siam Paragon, Tangs, and Metrojaya.

Supermarkets: A relatively large, low-cost, low-margin, high-volume, self-service operation designed to serve the consumer's total needs for grocery and household products. Examples: Safeway, Wellcome, Hua Lien, Kimisawa Supermarket, and Giant.

Convenience Stores: Relatively small stores located near residential areas, open long hours seven days a week, and carrying a limited line of high-turnover convenience products at slightly higher prices. Examples: 7-Eleven, Family-mart, Lawson, Circle K, and Shell Select.

Discount Stores: Carry standard merchandise sold at lower prices with lower margins and higher volumes. Examples: Wal-Mart, Carrefour, The Store, and Daiso.

Off-Price Retailers: Sell merchandise bought at less-than-regular wholesale prices and sold at less than retail, often leftover goods, overruns, and irregulars obtained at reduced prices from manufacturers or other retailers. These include factory outlets owned and operated by manufacturers (examples: Esprit Outlet, Dickson Warehouse); *independent off-price retailers* owned and run by entrepreneurs or by divisions of larger retail corporations (example: Sogo Club); and warehouse (or wholesale) clubs selling a limited selection of brand-name groceries, appliances, clothing, and other goods at deep discounts to consumers who pay membership fees (examples: GrandMart, Metro Asia).

Superstores: Very large stores traditionally aimed at meeting consumers' total needs for routinely purchased food and nonfood items. Includes *category killers*, which carry a deep assortment in a particular category and have a knowledgeable staff (examples: Tokyu, eBay); *supercenters*, combined supermarket and discount stores (examples: Jual Murah, Big C); and hypermarkets with up to 220,000 square feet of space combining supermarket, discount, and warehouse retailing (examples: Carrefour, Pyrca, Giant).

Limited-service retailers, such as Sears and Sasa, provide more sales assistance because they carry more shopping goods about which customers need information. Their increased operating costs result in higher prices. In *full-service retailers*, such as specialty stores and first-class department stores, salespeople assist customers in every phase of the shopping process. Full-service stores usually carry more specialty goods for which customers like to be "waited on." They provide more services resulting in much higher operating costs, which are passed along to customers as higher prices. Some examples in Asia include

Specialty stores –
Some retailers carry narrow product lines with deep assortments within those lines, and niche stores such as these selling ceramic wares and plastic foods in Kappabashi, Tokyo are flourishing.

Specialty store
A retail store that carries a narrow product line with a deep assortment within that line.

Department store
A retail organization that carries a wide variety of product lines—each line is operated as a separate department managed by specialist buyers or merchandisers.

Supermarket
Large, low-cost, low-margin, high-volume, self-service store that carries a wide variety of grocery and household products.

Convenience store
A small store, located near a residential area, that is open long hours seven days a week and carries a limited line of high-turnover convenience goods.

Lane Crawford in Hong Kong, Mitsukoshi and Takashimaya in Japan, and Siam Paragon Department Store in Bangkok.

Product Line

Retailers also can be classified by the length and breadth of their product assortments. Some retailers, such as **specialty stores**, carry narrow product lines with deep assortments within those lines. Today, specialty stores are flourishing. The increasing use of market segmentation, market targeting, and product specialization has resulted in a greater need for stores that focus on specific products and segments. Just take a look at the sports gear shops in Mongkok, Hong Kong or the cooking utilities stores in Kappabashi, Tokyo.)

In contrast, **department stores** carry a wide variety of product lines. In recent years, department stores have added promotional pricing to counter the more efficient, lower-priced discounters. Others have stepped up the use of store brands and single-brand "designer shops" to compete with specialty stores. Still others are trying mail-order, telephone, and Web selling. For some, service remains the key differentiating factor. Retailers such as Sogo, Shin Kong Mitsukoshi, Lane Crawford, Takashimaya, Debenhams, and other high-end department stores are doing well by emphasizing high-quality service. In Hong Kong, sales from department stores amounted to HK$25.65 billion, constituting 10.36 percent of total retail sales in 2007.

Supermarkets are the most frequently shopped type of retail store. Today, however, they are facing slow sales growth because of slower population growth and an increase in competition from discount food stores and supercenters on the one hand, and upscale specialty food stores on the other. Supermarkets also have been hit hard by the rapid growth of out-of-home eating. In Hong Kong, sales from supermarkets and supermarket sections of department stores only achieved a growth rate of 3.4 percent over 2006, representing 13.62 percent of the total retail sales in 2007.

Many supermarkets are making improvements to attract more customers. In the battle for a "share of stomachs," many large supermarkets are moving upscale, providing improved store environments and higher-quality food offerings, such as from-scratch bakeries, gourmet deli counters, and fresh seafood departments. Others are cutting costs, establishing more efficient operations, and lowering prices in order to compete more effectively with food discounters. Finally, a few have added Web-based sales.

Convenience stores are small stores that carry a limited line of high-turnover convenience goods. After several years of stagnant sales, convenience stores are now experiencing healthy growth. Last year, U.S. convenience stores posted sales of $474 billion, a 20 percent increase over the previous year. More than 69 percent of convenience store revenues come from sales of gasoline; a majority of in-store sales are from tobacco products (38 percent) and beer and other beverages (25 percent).[1]

In recent years, convenience store chains have tried to expand beyond their primary operation of providing convenience goods such as sweets, bread, milk, and beverages so as to attract a wider target market. They are shedding the image of a "truck stop" where men go to buy beer, cigarettes, and magazines, and instead offer freshly prepared foods and cleaner, safer, more upscale environments. Consider this example:[2]

In Taiwan, 7-Eleven stores have undergone noticeable changes in providing services although customers may be still familiar with the stores and its muted orange-and-green color scheme. The aisles are wider, though, and the displays warmer in color. Chilling in the fridge are the Taiwanese beers and other beverages. Not far from the cashier is a cooker filled with tea-marinated eggs. An aisle away is a sausage machine with heated rollers and a boiler with seasoned turnips, fish balls, and beancurd in soup.

However, these changes are not those which have brought delight to the average Taiwanese's daily life. The convenience king, most commonly known for lowbrow yet popular features such as the Big Gulp and round-the-clock access to Twinkies, is moving away from the food chain in search of other sources of revenue. 7-Eleven is banking on some new services that compete more with post offices and express delivery companies than other traditional convenience stores. Customers can now pick up their products at 7-Eleven after they have bought their goods online. Or they can pay their bills over the counter at 7-Eleven. The transformation seems to be working very well, and the number of people using these services is increasing.

Convenience store makeover –
7-Eleven is shedding its "truck stop" image and transforming its stores to offer more upscale assortments and environments.

Superstores are much larger than regular supermarkets and offer a large assortment of routinely purchased food products, nonfood items, and services. Wal-Mart, Carrefour, Tesco, and other discount retailers offer *supercenters*, very large combination food and discount stores. Supercenters are growing rapidly in large cities in China. Wal-Mart now has almost 71 stores all over China, capturing more than 2.83 percent of the sales volume of the first 100 supercenters.3

Recent years have also seen the explosive growth of superstores that are actually giant specialty stores, the so-called **category killers**. They feature stores that carry a very deep assortment of a particular line, complete with knowledgeable staff at hand. Category killers are prevalent in a wide range of categories, including books, baby gear, toys, electronics, home-improvement products, linens and towels, party goods, sporting goods, and even pet supplies. Another superstore variation, a *hypermarket*, is a huge superstore, perhaps as large as six football fields. Although hypermarkets have been very successful in Europe and other world markets, they have met with little success in the United States and China, and Southeast Asia.

Finally, for some retailers, the product line is actually a service. Service retailers include hotels and motels, banks, airlines, colleges, hospitals, movie theaters, tennis clubs, bowling alleys, restaurants, repair services, hair salons, and dry cleaners. Service retailers in the U.S. are growing faster than product retailers.

Relative Prices

Retailers can also be classified according to the prices they charge (see **Table 13.1**). Most retailers charge regular prices and offer normal-quality goods and customer service. Others offer higher-quality goods and service at higher prices. The retailers that feature low prices are discount stores and "off-price" retailers.

A **discount store** sells standard merchandise at lower prices by accepting lower margins and selling higher volume. The early discount stores cut expenses by offering few services and operating in warehouselike facilities in low-rent, heavily traveled districts. Today's discounters have improved their store environments and increased their services,

Superstore
A store much larger than a regular supermarket that offers a large assortment of routinely purchased food products, nonfood items, and services.

Category killer
Giant specialty store that carries a very deep assortment of a particular line and is staffed by knowledgeable employees.

Discount store
A retail operation that sells standard merchandise at lower prices by accepting lower margins and selling at higher volume.

Off-price retailer
Retailer that buys at less-than-regular wholesale prices and sells at less than retail. Examples are factory outlets, independents, and warehouse clubs.

Independent off-price retailer
Off-price retailer that is either owned and run by entrepreneurs or is a division of a larger retail corporation.

while at the same time keeping prices low through lean, efficient operations. Leading discounters, such as Wal-Mart, now dominate the retail scene (see **Real Marketing 13.1**).

As the major discount stores traded up, a new wave of off-price retailers moved in to fill the ultralow-price, high-volume gap. Ordinary discounters buy at regular wholesale prices and accept lower margins to keep prices down. In contrast, off-price retailers buy at less-than-regular wholesale prices and charge consumers less than retail.

The three main types of off-price retailers are independents, *factory outlets,* and *warehouse clubs.* **Independent off-price retailers** are either owned and run by entrepreneurs or are divisions of larger retail corporations. Although many off-price operations are run by smaller independents, most large off-price retailer operations are owned by bigger retail chains.

REAL MARKETING 13.1

Wal-Mart: The World's Largest Retailer

Leading discounters, such as Wal-Mart, now dominate the retail scene. First and foremost, Wal-Mart is passionately dedicated to its value proposition of "Always Low Prices, Always!"

Wal-Mart is the world's largest retailer, and it's playing tag-team with ExxonMobil for the title of world's largest *company.* Wal-Mart is almost unimaginably big. It rang up an incredible $316 billion in sales last year—that's 1.7 times the sales of competitors Costco, Target, Sears/Kmart, JC Penney, and Kohl's *combined.*

Wal-Mart is the number-one seller in several categories of consumer products, including groceries, toys, CDs, and pet-care products. It sells more clothes than Gap and Limited combined and almost twice as many groceries as Kroger, the leading grocery-only food retailer. Incredibly, Wal-Mart sells 30 percent of the disposable diapers purchased in the United States each year, 30 percent of the hair-care products, 26 percent of the toothpaste, and 20 percent of the pet food. On average, some 130 million people visit Wal-Mart stores each week.

It's also hard to fathom Wal-Mart's impact on the U.S. economy. It's the nation's largest employer—one out of every 230 men, women, and children in the U.S. is a Wal-Mart associate. Its sales of $1.52 billion on one day in 2003 exceeded the GDPs of 26 countries. One study found that—through its own low prices and through its impact on

Factory outlets—producer-operated stores by firms—sometimes group together in *factory outlet malls* and *value-retail centers*, where dozens of outlet stores offer prices as low as 50 percent below retail on a wide range of items. Whereas outlet malls consist primarily of manufacturers' outlets, value-retail centers combine manufacturers' outlets with off-price retail stores and department store clearance outlets.

The malls now are moving upscale, and narrowing the gap between factory outlet and more traditional forms of retailers as discounts offered by outlets get smaller. However, a growing number of outlet malls now feature brands such as Coach, Polo, Ralph Lauren, Dolce & Gabbana, Giorgio Armani, Gucci, and Versace, causing department stores to protest to the manufacturers of these brands. Given their higher costs, the department stores must charge more than the off-price outlets. Manufacturers counter that they send last year's merchandise and seconds to the factory outlet malls, not the new merchandise that they supply to the department stores.

Factory outlet
Off-price retailing operation that is owned and operated by a manufacturer and that normally carries the manufacturer's surplus, discontinued, or irregular goods.

competitors' prices—Wal-Mart saved the American public $263 billion in 2004 alone—or $2,329 per household.

What are the secrets behind this spectacular success? First and foremost, Wal-Mart's mission is to "lower the world's cost of living." To accomplish this mission, Wal-Mart offers a broad selection of carefully selected goods at unbeatable prices. Says Wal-Mart's president and chief executive, "We're obsessed with delivering value to customers."

How does Wal-Mart make money with such low prices? Wal-Mart has the lowest cost structure in the industry. Low costs let the giant retailer charge lower prices but still reap higher profits. For example, grocery prices drop an average of 10 to 15 percent in markets Wal-Mart has entered, and Wal-Mart's food prices average 20 percent less than its grocery store rivals. Lower prices attract more shoppers, producing more sales, making the company more efficient, and enabling it to lower prices even more.

Wal-Mart's low costs result in part from superior management and sophisticated technology. Its Bentonville, Arkansas, headquarters contains a computer communications system that gives managers around the country instant access to sales and operating information. And its huge, fully automated distribution centers employ the latest technology to supply stores efficiently.

Wal-Mart is also known for the calculated way it wrings low prices from suppliers. "They are very, very focused people, and they use their buying power more forcefully than anyone else in America," says one supplier's sales executive after a visit to Wal-Mart's buying offices. Some critics argue that Wal-Mart squeezes its suppliers too hard, driving some out of business. Wal-Mart proponents counter, however, that it is simply acting in its customers' interests by forcing suppliers to be more efficient. "Wal-Mart is tough, but totally honest and straightforward in its dealings with vendors," says an industry consultant. "Wal-Mart has forced manufacturers to get their act together."

Despite its incredible success over the past four decades, some analysts see chinks in the seemingly invincible Wal-Mart's armor. "Many of its upscale customers ... come into the store for vegetables, cereal, detergent, and the like—but turn up their noses at higher margin items such as apparel and electronics," says an analyst.

So, to reignite growth and to extend its customer base by capturing a larger share-of-wallet from higher-income consumers, Wal-Mart recently began sprucing up its stores and adding new, higher-quality merchandise. Wal-Mart is also beefing up its spending on more stylish advertising.

However, in no way will Wal-Mart ever give up its core "Always Low Prices—*Always*" value proposition. And despite some growing pains, Wal-Mart appears well on its way to becoming the world's first trillion-dollar corporation. This leads some observers to wonder if an ever-larger Wal-Mart can retain its customer focus and positioning. The company's managers are betting on it. No matter where it operates, Wal-Mart's announced policy is to take care of customers "one store at a time." Says one top executive: "We'll be fine as long as we never lose our responsiveness to the consumer."

Sources:
Quotes and other information from Bill Saporito and Jerry Useem, "One Nation Under Wal-Mart," Fortune, March 3, 2003, pp. 65–78; Don Longo, "Wal-Mart on Its Way to Becoming the First Trillion Dollar Corporation," Retail Merchandiser, March 2005, p. 7; Pallavi Gogoi, "Wal-Mart Gets the Fashion Bug," BusinessWeek Online, October 7, 2006, accessed at www.businessweek.com; Luke Boggs, "Why I am Fighting for Wal-Mart," DSN Retailing Today, December 19, 2005, p. 11; "The Fortune 500," Fortune, April 17, 2006, pp. F1–F3; Theresa Howard, "Ads Try to Expand Customer Base," USA Today, February 21, 2006; Stuart Elliott and Michael Barbaro, "Wal-Mart on the Hunt for an Extreme Makeover," May 4, 2006, pp. C1, C13; Robert Berner, "Fashion Emergency at Wal-Mart," BusinessWeek, July 31, 2006, p. 67; and www.walmartstores.com January 2007.

Factory outlet malls –
These value-retail centers combine manufacturers' outlets with off-price retail stores and department store clearance outlets, and are popular with shoppers and tourists.

Warehouse club
Off-price retailer that sells a limited selection of brand name grocery items, appliances, clothing, and a hodgepodge of other goods at deep discounts to members who pay annual membership fees.

Chain stores
Two or more outlets that are commonly owned and controlled.

Warehouse clubs (or *wholesale clubs* or *membership warehouses*), such as Makro Asia in Thailand, Indonesia and China, operate in huge, warehouse like facilities and offer few frills. However, they do offer ultralow prices and surprise deals on selected branded merchandise.

Organizational Approach

Although many retail stores are independently owned, others band together under some form of corporate or contractual organization. The major types of retail organizations—*corporate chains, voluntary chains* and *retailer cooperatives, franchise organizations,* and *merchandising conglomerates*—are described in **Table 13.2**.

Chain stores are two or more outlets that are commonly owned and controlled. They have many advantages over independents. Their size allows them to buy in large quantities at lower prices and gain promotional economies. They can hire specialists to deal with areas such as pricing, promotion, merchandising, inventory control, and sales forecasting.

The great success of corporate chains caused many independents to band together in one of two forms of contractual associations. One is the *voluntary chain*—a wholesaler-sponsored group of independent retailers that engages in group buying and common merchandising—which we discussed in Chapter 12. The other type of contractual association is the *retailer cooperative*—a group of independent retailers that bands together to set up a jointly owned, central wholesale operation and conducts joint merchandising and promotion efforts. These organizations give independents the buying and promotion economies they need to meet the prices of corporate chains.

Table 13.2 Major Types of Retail Organizations

Type	Description	Examples
Corporate chain stores	Two of more outlets that are commonly owned and controlled employ central buying and merchandising. Corporate chains appear in all types of retailing, but they are strongest in department stores, food stores, drug stores, shoe stores, and women's clothing stores	Sears, Park-n-shop (grocery stores); Watsons, Cosmed (healthcare stores); Chow Sang Sang (Jwellery); Shell Select
Voluntary chains	Wholesaler-sponsored groups of independent retailers engaged in bulk buying and common merchandising	Independent Grocers Alliance (IGA), Do-it Best hardwares, Lukfook Jewellery
Retailer cooperatives	Groups of independent retailers who set up a central buying organization and conduct joint promotion efforts	Associated Grocers (groceries), Mitre 10 (hardware)
Franchise organizations	Contractual association between a franchiser (a manufacturer, wholesaler, or service organization) and franchisees (independent businesspeople who buy the right to own and operate one or more units in the franchise system). Franchise organizations are normally based on some unique product, service, or method of doing business, or on a trade name or patent, or on goodwill that the franchiser had developed.	McDonald's, Pizza Hut, Lukfook Jewellery, Circle K, 7-Eleven
Merchandising conglomerates	Free-form corporations that combine several diversified conglomerates retailing lines and forms under central ownership, along with some integration of their distribution and management functions	Limited Brands

Another form of contractual retail organization is a **franchise**. The main difference between franchise organizations and other contractual systems (voluntary chains and retail cooperatives) is that franchise systems are normally based on some unique product or service; on a method of doing business; or on the trade name, goodwill, or patent that the franchiser has developed. Franchising has been prominent in fast foods, health and fitness centers, haircutting, travel agencies, real estate, and dozens of other product and service areas.

Once considered upstarts among independent businesses, franchises now command 40 percent of all retail sales in China. These days, it is nearly impossible to stroll down a city block or drive on a suburban street without seeing a McDonald's, 7-Eleven, or Holiday Inn. One of the best-known and most successful franchisers, McDonald's, now has nearly 32,000 stores in 119 countries. It serves nearly 50 million customers a day and racks up more than $39 billion in annual systemwide sales. Some 58 percent of McDonald's restaurants worldwide are owned and operated by franchisees. Gaining fast is Subway Sandwiches and Salads, one of the fastest-growing franchises, with more than 26,000 shops in 85 countries, including over 20,000 in the United States.[4]

Finally, *merchandising conglomerates* are corporations that combine several different retailing forms under central ownership. An example is Li & Fung which operates Circle K, trendy private-label apparel Country Road, Calvin Klein Jeans, and Toys 'R' Us, etc. Such diversified retailing, similar to a multibranding strategy, provides superior management systems and economies that benefit all the separate retail operations.

Franchise
A contractual association between a manufacturer, wholesaler, or service organization (a franchiser) and independent businesspeople (franchisees) who buy the right to own and operate one or more units in the franchise system.

Retailer Marketing Decisions

Franchising –
These days, it's nearly impossible to stroll down a city block or drive on a suburban street without seeing Mcdonald's, Subway, or Holiday Inn.

Retailers are always searching for new marketing strategies to attract and hold customers. In the past, retailers attracted customers with unique product assortments and more or better services. Today, retail assortments and services are looking more and more alike, and it's now more difficult for any one retailer to offer exclusive merchandise.

Service differentiation among retailers has also eroded. Many department stores have trimmed their services, whereas discounters have increased theirs. Customers have become smarter and more price sensitive. For all these reasons, many retailers today are rethinking their marketing strategies.

As shown in **Figure 13.1**, retailers face major marketing decisions about their *target market* and *positioning*, *product assortment* and *services*, *price*, *promotion*, and *place*.

Figure 13.1
Retailer marketing decisions

Target Market and Positioning Decision

Retailers must first define their target markets and then decide how they will position themselves in these markets. Should the store focus on upscale, midscale, or downscale shoppers? Do target shoppers want variety, depth of assortment, convenience, or low prices? Until they define and profile their markets, retailers cannot make consistent decisions about product assortment, services, pricing, advertising, store décor, or any of the other decisions that must support their positions.

Too many retailers fail to define their target markets and positions clearly. They try to have "something for everyone" and end up satisfying no market well. In contrast, successful retailers define their target markets well and position themselves strongly. Even large stores such as Takashimaya, Wal-Mart, and Siam Paragon must define their major target customers so as to effectively design proper marketing strategies.

Product Assortment and Services Decision

Retailers must decide on three major product variables: *product assortment, services mix, and store atmosphere.*

The retailer's *product assortment* should differentiate the retailer while matching target shoppers' expectations. One strategy is to offer merchandise that no other competitor carries, such as private brands or national brands on which it holds exclusives. Another strategy is to feature blockbuster merchandising events—Bloomingdale's is known for running spectacular shows featuring goods from a certain country, such as India or China. Or the retailer can offer surprise merchandise, as when Costco offers surprise assortments of seconds, overstocks, and closeouts. Finally, the retailer can differentiate itself by offering a highly targeted product assortment—Lane Bryant carries plus-size clothing; Brookstone (*www.brookstone.com*) offers an unusual assortment of gadgets in what amounts to an adult toy store.

The *services mix* can also help set one retailer apart from another. For example, some retailers invite customers to ask questions or consult service representatives in person or via phone or keyboard.

The *store's atmosphere* is another element in the reseller's product arsenal. Every store has a physical layout that makes moving around in it either hard or easy. Each store has a "feel"; the retailer must design an atmosphere that suits the target market and moves customers to buy. One shopper sums up the Apple store atmosphere and experience this way:

It has become something of a second home to me—or, as I jokingly call it, "my temple." I've been known to spend hours at a time there. It seems a trifling thing that I can walk up to any terminal in the place during a… shopping break, log in to my e-mail account, and attend to my electronic correspondence. I am also able to freely Web-surf, instant-message, or do a bit of e-shopping (heck, even buy a new Mac or iPod on the online Apple Store). No one rushes or hassles me. It seems like a family room (albeit a gigantic one), with its comfortable theater seating in the back, its library-style shelves lined neatly with Mac software, books and magazines, its rows of flat-panel screens flashing Pixar trailers, its speaker-connected iPods cranking out catchy tunes, its low-to-the-ground kids' table and ball-shaped chairs for iMac gaming, and its Genius Bar, to which visitors could cozy up for guidance or troubleshooting with an Apple supergeek. That's why I sometimes don't want to leave. In fact, I wrote part of this essay on a MacBook laptop while reclining in one of those airport-style chairs. It's a testament to Apple's retail savvy that I felt totally at ease while typing away.[5]

Store atmosphere –
Apple stores are known for their shopper-friendly experiences, as customers can try out products or seek assistance from the Genius Bar.

It's no wonder that Apple stores "are full of shoppers," says the analyst. "The stores are attracting up to 10,000 visitors per week each, or 18.1 million visitors a year in total." By comparison, Gateway's more pedestrian retail stores pulled in an average of only 250 people a week.

Increasingly, retailers are turning their stores into theaters that transport customers into unusual, exciting shopping environments. For example, Borders uses atmospherics to turn shopping for books into entertainment. All of this confirms that retail stores are much more than simply assortments of goods. They are environments to be experienced by the people who shop in them.

Price Decision

A retailer's price policy must fit its target market and positioning, product and service assortment, and competition. Most retailers seek *either* high markups on lower volume (most specialty stores) or low markups on higher volume (mass merchandisers and discount stores). Retailers must also decide on the extent to which they will use sales and other price promotions. Some retailers compete instead on product and service quality rather than on price.

Promotion Decision

Retailers use any or all of the promotion tools—advertising, personal selling, sales promotion, public relations, and direct marketing—to reach consumers. They advertise in newspapers, magazines, radio, television, and on the Internet. Advertising may be supported by newspaper inserts and direct mail. Personal selling requires careful training of salespeople in how to greet customers, meet their needs, and handle their complaints. Sales promotions may include in-store demonstrations, displays, contests, and visiting celebrities. Public relations activities, such as press conferences and speeches, store openings, special events, newsletters, magazines, and public service activities, are always available to retailers. Most retailers have also set up Web sites, offering customers information and other features and often selling merchandise directly.

Place Decision

It's very important that retailers select locations that are accessible to the target market in areas that are consistent with the retailer's positioning. Small retailers may have to settle for whatever locations they can find or afford. Large retailers, however, usually employ specialists who select locations using advanced methods. They may also consider opening up more stores to gain a lion share of the market. Let us look at the following example and see how personal care retailers are reacting to a new entry in the market.

Promotion decision –
Retailers may use any or all of the promotion tools to reach consumers, such as this eye-catching display to promote a Chinese computer game.

In Taiwan, the sales for over-the-counter healthcare and cosmetic products reach $5 billion annually, with a growth of 11 percent in 2007. Its target customers are mainly females between 20 and 30 years of age. However, there is a trend towards customers of these products getting younger. The number of male customers is increasing as well. In 2007, in terms of sales, the ratio of male to female customers was three to seven.

Until recently, the market has been dominated by two major players, Watsons and Cosmed. Watsons is owned by Hutchinson-Wangpo Hong Kong, and Cosmed is owned by the President Group of Taiwan. In an effort to capture a share of the market, the Fuban group launched its first two chain stores called MoMo in Taipei in January 2008. Fuban plans to expand to 300 stores in three years' time.

In order to face the challenge from MoMo positively, Watsons and Cosmed have their own plans. Watsons does not intend to over-expand. It intends to use a product-differentiation strategy. Knowing that it has the advantage of having a strong and complete line of over-the-counter cosmetics, it will compete by introducing more European brands in healthcare and beauty. Cosmed is reacting to MoMo's challenges in a different manner by focusing on redesigning its existing logo and adding 40 stores to the current total of about 300 stores in the not-too-distant future.

Most stores today cluster together to increase their customer pulling power and to give consumers the convenience of one-stop shopping. *Central business* districts were the main form of retail cluster until the 1950s. When people began to move to the suburbs, however, these central business districts began to lose business. Downtown merchants opened branches in suburban shopping centers, and the decline of the central business districts continued. In recent years, many cities have joined with merchants to try to revive downtown shopping areas by building malls and providing underground parking.

A **shopping center** is a group of retail businesses planned, developed, owned, and managed as a unit. A *regional shopping center*, or *regional shopping mall*, the largest shopping center, contains from 40 to over 200 stores. A *community shopping center* contains between 15 and 40 retail stores. It normally contains a branch of a department store or variety store, a supermarket, specialty stores, professional offices, and sometimes a bank. Most shopping centers are *neighborhood shopping centers* or *strip malls* that generally contain between five and 15 stores. They are close and convenient for consumers. They usually contain a supermarket, perhaps a discount store, and several service stores.

A recent addition to the shopping center scene is the so-called power center. These huge unenclosed shopping centers consist of a long strip of retail stores, including large, freestanding anchors such as Wal-Mart. Each store has its own entrance with parking directly in front for shoppers who wish to visit only one store. Power centers have increased rapidly during the past few years to challenge traditional indoor malls.

However, despite the recent development of many new "megamalls" such as Pacific Place in Hong Kong, Taipei 101 in Taiwan, Pavilion in Kuala Lumpur, and Siam Paragon Shopping Centre in Bangkok, in some countries, there is an emerging trend towards smaller lifestyle centers. These lifestyle centers—smaller malls with upscale stores, convenient locations, and expensive atmospheres—are usually located near affluent residential neighborhoods and cater to the retail needs of consumers in their areas.

Despite the recent development of many new megamalls such as the Pavilion in Kuala Lumpur, in some countries there is an emerging trend towards smaller lifestyle centers such as the Dempsey Hill area in Singapore where smaller, upscale stores like Jones the Grocer are located.

Place decision –
It's very important that retailers select locations that are accessible to the target market in areas that are consistent with the retailer's positioning, such as these Watsons and Cosmed outlets in the trendy and popular Ximending area in Taipei.

Shopping center
A group of retail businesses planned, developed, owned, and managed as a unit.

The Future of Retailing

Retailers operate in a harsh and fast-changing environment, which offers threats as well as opportunities. For example, the industry suffers from chronic overcapacity, resulting in fierce competition for customer dollars. Consumer demographics, lifestyles, and shopping patterns are changing rapidly, as are retailing technologies. To be successful, then, retailers will need to choose target segments carefully and position themselves strongly. They will need to take the following retailing developments into account as they plan and execute their competitive strategies (see **Figure 13.2**).

Figure 13.2
The future of retailing

New Retail Forms and Shortening Retail Life Cycles

New retail forms continue to emerge to meet new situations and consumer needs, but the life cycle of new retail forms is getting shorter. Department stores took about 100 years to reach the mature stage of the life cycle; more recent forms, such as warehouse stores, reached maturity in about ten years.

Many retailing innovations are partially explained by the **wheel-of-retailing concept**.[6] According to this concept, many new types of retailing forms begin as low-margin, low-price, low-status operations. They challenge established retailers that have become "fat" by letting their costs and margins increase. The new retailers' success leads them to upgrade their facilities and offer more services. In turn, their costs increase, forcing them to increase their prices. Eventually, the new retailers become like the conventional retailers they replaced. The cycle begins again when still newer types of retailers evolve with lower costs and prices. The wheel of retailing concept seems to explain the initial success and later troubles of department stores, supermarkets, and discount stores.

Wheel-of-retailing concept
A concept of retailing that states that new types of retailers usually begin as low-margin, low-price, low-status operations but later evolve into higher-priced, higher-service operations, eventually becoming like the conventional retailers they replaced.

Growth of Nonstore Retailing

Consumers now have an array of alternatives, including mail-order, television, phone, and online shopping. They are increasingly avoiding the hassles and crowds at malls by doing more of their shopping by phone or computer. In fact, most store retailers have now developed direct-retailing channels.

Online retailing is the newest form of nonstore retailing. The dot-com meltdown of 2000 led experts to predict that e-tailing was destined to be little more than a tag-on to in-store retailing, but today's online retailing is alive, well, and growing. With easier-to-use Web sites, improved online service, and the increasing sophistication of search technologies, online business is booming.

In fact, online buying is growing at a much brisker pace than retail buying as a whole. Several large click-only retailers—Amazon.com, online auction site eBay, and others—are now making it big on the Web. At the other extreme, hordes of niche marketers are using the Web to reach new markets and expand their sales. Today's more sophisticated search engines (Google, Yahoo!) and comparison shopping sites (Shopping.com, Buy.com, Amazon.com, and others) put almost any e-tailer within a mouse click or two's reach of millions of customers.

Still, much of the anticipated growth in online sales will go to multichannel retailers—the click-and-brick marketers who can successfully merge the virtual and physical worlds. Consider the U.S. office-supply retailer Staples. Based on two years of research, Staples recently redesigned its Web site to extend its "Staples—That was easy" marketing promise to online shoppers. Sales through Staples.com jumped 27 percent last year, now accounting for almost one-quarter of Staples's revenues. But Staples online operations aren't robbing from store sales. For example, customers can buy conveniently online and then return unwanted or defective merchandise to their local Staples store. As a result, the average yearly spending of small-business customers jumps more than fourfold when they combine shopping online with shopping in the store.[7]

Online retailing – Today's online retailing is alive, well, and growing, especially for click-and-brick retailers like Staples. Its Web site (_www.staples.com_) now accounts for almost one-quarter of sales.

Retail Convergence

Today's retailers are increasingly selling the same products at the same prices to the same consumers in competition with a wider variety of other retailers. When it comes to brand-name appliances, department stores, discount stores, home improvement stores, off-price retailers, electronics superstores, and a slew of Web sites all compete for the same customers.

This merging of consumers, products, prices, and retailers is called retail convergence. Such convergence means greater competition for retailers and greater difficulty in differentiating offerings. Because of their bulk-buying power and high sales volume, chains can buy at lower costs and thrive on smaller margins. The arrival of a superstore can quickly force nearby independents out of business. However, many small, independent retailers are thriving. They are finding that sheer size and marketing muscle are often no match for the personal touch small stores can provide or the specialty merchandise niches that small stores fill.

The Rise of Megaretailers

Through their superior information systems and buying power, these giant retailers can offer better merchandise selections, good service, and strong price savings to consumers. As a result, they grow even larger by squeezing out their smaller, weaker competitors.

The megaretailers are also shifting the balance of power between retailers and producers. A relative handful of retailers now control access to enormous numbers of consumers, giving them the upper hand in their dealings with manufacturers. For example, in the U.S., Wal-Mart generates almost 20 percent of P&G's revenues. Wal-Mart can, and often does, use this power to wring concessions from P&G and other suppliers.[8]

Growing Importance of Retail Technology

Retail technologies are becoming critically important as competitive tools. Progressive retailers are using advanced information technology and software systems to produce better forecasts, control inventory costs, order electronically from suppliers, send information between stores, and even sell to customers within stores. They are adopting checkout scanning systems, online transaction processing, electronic data interchange, in-store television, and improved merchandise-handling systems.

Perhaps the most startling advances in retailing technology concern the ways in which today's retailers are connecting with customers. Many retailers now routinely use technologies such as touch-screen kiosks, customer-loyalty cards, electronic shelf labels and signs, handheld shopping assistants, smart cards, self-scanning systems, and virtual-reality displays. For example, in its new pilot stores, Skyphoto, a photo shop chain, uses technology to make shopping easier for its customers. Mr Ronald Chan, CEO of the SKYphoto Store describes one of his company's latest service offerings to its customers in Hong Kong:

Returning to Hong Kong from a sightseeing tour, you see a computerized kiosk in the arrival hall of Hong Kong Chek Lap Kok airport. You take out a SD card from your digital camera and insert it into the SD slot of a card reader next to the touch screen of the kiosk, which is located at an eye-catching point in the arrival hall. The card reader provides you with slots for all kinds of memory cards. Almost immediately, images of the pictures on the card appear on the screen. You take your time to select the pictures that you want to have developed by touching the images on the screen. For each picture that you select, you may touch a box on the screen to choose the size (e.g., 3R or 4R) and the number of prints that you want. Then the screen will show you a list of store locations where you can collect your prints and the earliest time you can collect them. If there is a SKYphoto store near your home, you may touch the appropriate boxes to indicate that you will pick up the prints there later. After an hour and a half, you arrive at the SKYphoto store near your home. The prints are now available for you to collect. Oh, what a wonderful day![9]

Retail technology – Many retailers now routinely use technologies such as touch-screen kiosks to make shopping easier for customers.

Global Expansion of Major Retailers

Retailers with unique formats and strong brand positioning are increasingly moving into other countries. Many are expanding internationally to escape mature and saturated home markets. Over the years, some big retailers—such as McDonald's, Gap and Toys 'R' Us—have become globally prominent as a result of their marketing prowess. Others are rapidly establishing a global presence. Wal-Mart operates more than 2,700 stores in 14 countries abroad, and its international division alone last year racked up sales of more than $67 billion, an increase of 11.4 percent over the previous year and 27 percent more than rival Target's total sales.[10]

However, most U.S. retailers are still significantly behind Europe and Asia when it comes to global expansion. Ten of the world's top 20 retailers are U.S. companies; but only two of these retailers have set up stores outside of North America (Wal-Mart and Costco). Of the ten non-U.S. retailers in the world's top 20, nine have stores in at least 10countries. Among foreign retailers that have gone global are France's Carrefour, Britain's Marks & Spencer, Italy's Benetton, Japan's Yaohan supermarkets, and Sweden's IKEA home furnishings stores.[11]

French discount retailer Carrefour, the world's second-largest retailer after Wal-Mart, has embarked on an aggressive mission to extend its role as a leading international retailer:

It leads Europe in supermarkets and the world in hypermarkets. Carrefour is outpacing Wal-Mart in several emerging markets, including South America, China, and the Pacific Rim. It's the leading retailer in Brazil and Argentina, where it operates close to 1,000 stores, compared to Wal-Mart's 300 units in those two countries. Carrefour has now become the largest foreign retailer in China, where it operates more than 112 stores versus Wal-Mart's 104.[12]

Table 13.3 summarizes some of the strategies used by Wal-Mart and Carrefour in China.

Wal-Mart	Carrefour
Low-cost	Specialist in bulk selling
Creating shopping environment	Experiential shopping
Satisfying services	Happy shopping
Low price everyday	It is nice to have low prices
Zero-cost promotion	Entertaining promotion
The best location strategy	Located-at-a-junction strategy
Employees as partner	Good Employees = Good Business

Retail Stores as "Communities" or "Hangouts"

With the rise in the number of people living alone, working at home, or living in isolated and sprawling suburbs, there has been a resurgence of establishments that also provide a place for people to get together. For example, today's bookstores have become part bookstore, part library, part living room, and part coffee house. On an early evening at your local Borders, you'll likely find students doing homework with friends in the coffee bar. Nearby, retirees sit in armchairs thumbing through books or magazines. Borders sells more than just books; it sells comfort, relaxation, and community.

And retailers don't create communities only in their brick-and-mortar stores. Many also build virtual communities on the Internet. For example, Nike not only creates community in its giant, interactive Niketown retail stores, but it also creates online gathering places:

In just over a decade, Nike's global soccer presence has grown dramatically today. So, when Nike discovered that rival Adidas had gotten the exclusive deal to broadcast ads in the United States during the 2006 World Cup, it partnered with Google and created Joga.com, a social networking site for soccer fans. Launched quietly in February 2006, the site became an instant hit—a bustling online soccer community. On Joga.com, fans can blog, create communities around favorite teams or players, organize pickup games, download videos, and rant about the encroaching commercialism of the game. Some of the most downloaded videos are clips containing Nike products.

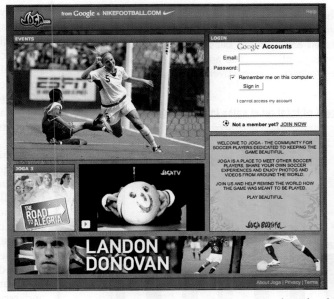

Nike creates community in its giant, interactive Niketown retail stores, but it also creates community in its online gathering place, Joga. com, a social networking site that allows soccer fans to blog, create communities around favorite teams or players, organize pickup games, download videos, and rant about the encroaching commercialism of the game.

REAL MARKETING 13.2

Retailing in China

Retailers in China have been enjoying a steady but rapid growth, with a marked increase in mergers and acquisitions. It is expected that foreign-owned retail companies will eventually control the regional markets.

From a macroeconomic perspective, there is a rising trend of mergers & acquisitions (M & A) in the China retail industry, where they have become a common phenomenon since 2006. With the opening up of China's retail a marked, foreigh-owned retail companies will continue to gain market share by means of M&A rather than from joint ventures with domestic retail companies. Retail business in municipalities and towns will soon become their target for mergers and acquisitions. It is expected that foreign-owned retail companies will eventually control the regional markets. This trend is not without any indications. The following are some major events in China's retail industry in 2007.

Since 2000, retailers in China have been enjoying a steady but rapid growth. In 2007, the total retail sales reached 8.92 trillion yuan, indicating an increase of 17.06 percent over 2006. The prospect of the retailing industry has been very encouraging. It is forecasted that the retail sales will reach 9.86 trillion yuan in 2008 and 11.24 trillion yuan in 2009 respectively (see **Figure 13.3**).

1: Carrefour in Chongqing

Between November 9 and 11, 2007, Carrefour in Chongqing held a series of promotions to celebrate the 10th anniversary of the chain's entry into Chongqing. In particular, it reduced the price of a brand of vegetable oil drastically, attracting a long queue of customers and causing a stampede in the store. The incident led to several deaths and injuries, and several similar incidents happened throughout 2007 in China.

The incident showed that consumers are eagerly looking for goods which are value-for-money during periods of high inflation. Inflation does not deter consumers' desire for high-end products, but it does make them more price-sensitive. They focus on products which offer the most value for money, so the high-end retail industry, which focuses on creating added value to products and services, still has a bright future. Instead, inflation would speed up the reform of the retail industry. The most significant reform caused by inflation is the emergence of low-price retailing and the rise of the supermarket.

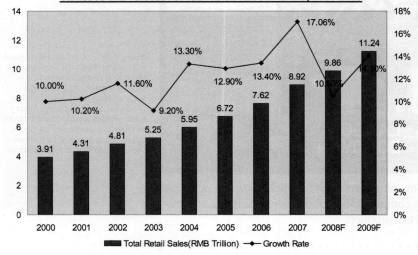

Figure 13.3

Statistics of total retail sales in China from 2000 to 2007 and forecasted sales for 2008 and 2009

2: Introduction of a new tax law and labor law

China's new Enterprise Income Tax Law was implemented on January 1, 2008. The tax rate for both domestic and foreign enterprises was standardized at 25 percent. At the industry level, it creates a fair competitive environment for enterprises. Some local enterprise managers may feel the pressure of competition as an unfavorable tax rate can no longer be used as an excuse for low profits. At the enterprise level, the new tax law is beneficial for all the retailing enterprises as it extends the criteria for tax deduction.

The new Labor Contract Law was implemented on the same day. For owners of retail firms, the new labor law is unwelcome news as it provides better protection to laborers or employees with regard to the issues of default penalty, duration of contract, compensation payments, probation period, and so on. Some of them panicked because an employee is automatically granted a permanent contact after serving a company for 10 years continuously. If their companies have been established for more than 10 years and have employees working for them for more than 10 years, it implies a huge amount of compensation. As such, the retail industry would have to draft a new contract to be signed by employees, and at the same time reduce the number of employees so as to avoid paying a abundant compensation in the future. This is evidenced by Carrefour which allegedly evades the new law by signing new contracts with employees.

3: Department stores returning to the merchandising system

Previously, Lane Crawford Department Store in Hong Kong had tried to extend its business to mainland China in terms of franchised outlets, but it was unsuccessful and thus retreated from the mainland market in early 2007. But in October 2007, taking advantage of China's surging economy, it made a comeback and opened a wholly-owned new branch in Beijing. It also announced plans to launch another store in Shanghai in the future. Another famous department store, Marks & Spencer, also announced the opening of its first store in Shanghai in 2008.

Both of these famous department stores adopt the merchandising system, which consists of merchandisers or buyers in various categories of merchandise such as fashion and toys, who have the responsibility and authority to source globally merchandise for the stores. Local department stores in mainland China tend to adopt an operation mode which is similar to renting out counters. Some have suggested that Chinese department stores should adopt the merchandising system so that they can strengthen their control over the range of products available to customers and establish their own brand value. The difficulties encountered implementing the merchandising system had previously deterred local department stores from adopting it, but Lane Crawford's comeback has once again raised their interest.

4: Wal-Mart's purchase of a local retailer

On February 27, 2007, Wal-Mart announced its purchase of 35 percent of the stock of a Chinese supermarket, Trust-Mart. The transaction, which amounted to $1 billion, was dubbed by the media as "the biggest purchase of the retail industry in China." The merger of these two supermarkets reflects a process of mutual learning for both parties. As the Chinese supermarket chain involved in the deal is similar to Carrefour in its marketing and operations, Wal-Mart will gain a better understanding of the operation system and procedures of one of its major rivals in China.

5: Home appliances store GOME's purchase of rival Dazhong

On December 12, 2007, GOME, one of the largest electrical appliances chain stores in China announced its purchase of its rival, Dazhong Electrics Co. The CEO of GOME said that together, GOME and Dazhong will become a world-class retailer brand aimed at providing high-quality services and expanding the number of stores. He hopes that GOME will be able to become the biggest international home appliances enterprise in the world by 2015.

Not only does Dazhong have an advantage in a high cash flow and its location, but its long history in Beijing has made its salespeople very familiar with the locals. The acquisition of Dazhong indicates that their suppliers can reduce their transaction cost as they now only need to negotiate with GOME. However, their bargaining power will be reduced when negotiating with GOME as GOME grows bigger.

6: Convenience stores: A merger between local giants

The advent of horizontal integration within the convenience store industry is at hand with the merger of China's two largest retail chains, Lianhua and Hualian, both based in Shanghai. Externally, mainland Chinese retailers are increasing their operation scale through M&As and forming alliances while internally, they are exploring new operation models.

M&As have happened frequently in the China's retail industry since 2006 and it has become a major measure for strategic investment in the retail industry. It has been forecasted that the M&A trend will keep its high frequency in the next three to five years, so one can expect great changes to take place in China's domestic retail market pattern.

Many suppliers have overlooked the potential of convenience stores. They may actually become the major shopping destination for the future generation of youths, enabling them to spend less time cooking.

7: A record single-day sales volume of 2 million yuan

Fashion retailers ZARA and H&M have broken the sales and profit growth records of China in the retail industry. ZARA opened in Shanghai and reached a single-day sales volume of 800,000 yuan, which matches the total sales volume of 80 local fashion stores. On April 12, 2007, Swedish fashion magnate H&M in Shanghai claimed that its first-day sales volume reached 2 million yuan.

8: Emergence of sporting goods superstores

Belle International Holdings Limited is the largest retailer of ladies footwear in China, Following its project to build a large-scale sports goods center, several other big brands in sporting goods are said to be emerging. This news largely suggests that China is moving into the age of superstores and chain stores in view of the upcoming Beijing Olympics.

9: Store management: An embarrassing situation for Carrefour

In 2006, Carrefour made a move to centralize its operations in China to avoid corruption. But in August 2007, the hypermarket was still found to have eight supervisors and meat buyers involved in bribery. The centralization and decentralization of operations, as well as prevention of corrupt practices of buying units and their supervisors, have generally been key issues of retail enterprises. Deciding on the most appropriate operation mode or system is still a question worth discussing in China.

10: Conflicts between retailers and suppliers

On June 5, 2007, a Chinese supplier accused a local retailer of being in arrears with payment for goods amounting to 16 million yuan and demanded payment at the retailer's headquarters. This incident triggered a debate about the strained relationship between suppliers and retailers in China. The fact remains that the incident is one of many. Calling for cooperation between retailers and suppliers is likely to be a new challenge in the face of prosperity in China's retail industry.

Sources:
Information from China Retail Industry Report (Merger & Reorganization), accessed at www.okokok.com.cn/abroad/Class105 Class117/200704/116785. html; China Chain store almanac 2007, Beijing: China Business Publishing Co. Ltd.; "Carrefour allegedly evades new labor contract law by signing new contracts with employees," accessed at http://chinareal news.typepad.com chinarealnews/2008/04/ carrefour-alleg html; information accessed at http//guide.ppsj.com.cn/art/6570/cxdxgmyx index1.html

Wholesaling

Wholesaling includes all activities involved in selling goods and services to those buying for resale or business use. We call those firms engaged primarily in wholesaling activities as **wholesalers**. Wholesalers buy mostly from producers and sell mostly to retailers, industrial consumers, and other wholesalers. As a result, many of the largest and most important wholesalers are largely unknown to final consumers.

Why are wholesalers important to sellers? Simply put, wholesalers add value by performing one or more of the following channel functions:

Wholesaling
All activities involved in selling goods and services to those buying for resale or business use.

Wholesaler
A firm engaged primarily in wholesaling activities.

- *Selling and promoting:* Wholesalers' sales forces help manufacturers reach many small customers at a low cost. The wholesaler has more contacts and is often more trusted by the buyer than the distant manufacturer.
- *Buying and assortment building:* Wholesalers can select items and build assortments needed by their customers, thereby saving the consumers much work.
- *Bulk-breaking:* Wholesalers save their customers money by buying in carload lots and breaking bulk (breaking large lots into small quantities).
- *Warehousing:* Wholesalers hold inventories, thereby reducing the inventory costs and risks of suppliers and customers.
- *Transportation:* Wholesalers can provide quicker delivery to buyers because they are closer than the producers.
- *Financing:* Wholesalers finance their customers by giving credit, and they finance their suppliers by ordering early and paying bills on time.
- *Risk bearing:* Wholesalers absorb risk by taking title and bearing the cost of theft, damage, spoilage, and obsolescence.
- *Market information:* Wholesalers give information to suppliers and customers about competitors, new products, and price developments.
- *Management services and advice:* Wholesalers often help retailers train their salesclerks, improve store layouts and displays, and set up accounting and inventory control systems.

Warehousing –
Wholesales hold inventories, therefore reducing the inventory costs and risks of suppliers and customers.

Types of Wholesalers

Wholesalers fall into three major groups (see **Table 13.4**): *merchant wholesalers, agents* and *brokers,* and *manufacturers' sales branches* and *offices.* **Merchant wholesalers** are the largest single group of wholesalers, accounting for roughly 50 percent of all wholesaling. Merchant wholesalers include two broad types: full-service wholesalers and limited-service wholesalers. *Full-service wholesalers* provide a full set of services, whereas the various limited-service wholesalers offer fewer services to their suppliers and customers. The several different types of *limited-service wholesalers* perform varied specialized functions in the distribution channel.

Brokers and *agents* differ from merchant wholesalers in two ways: They do not take title to goods, and they perform only a few functions. Like merchant wholesalers, they generally specialize by product line or customer type. A **broker** brings buyers and sellers together and assists in negotiation. **Agents** represent buyers or sellers on a more permanent basis. *Manufacturers' agents* (also called manufacturers' representatives) are the most common type of agent wholesaler. The third major type of wholesaling is that done in **manufacturers' sales branches and offices** by sellers or buyers themselves rather than through independent wholesalers.

Merchant wholesalers
Independently owned business that takes title to the merchandise it handles.

Broker
A wholesaler who does not take title to goods and whose function is to bring buyers and sellers together and assist in negotiation.

Agent
A wholesaler who represents buyers or sellers on a relatively permanent basis, performs only a few functions, and does not take title to goods

Manufacturers' sales branches and offices
Wholesaling by sellers or buyers themselves rather than through independent wholesalers.

Table 13.4 Major Types of Wholesalers

Type	Description
Merchant wholesalers	Independently owned businesses that take title to the merchandise they handle. In different trades they are called *jobbers,* distributors, or *mill supply houses.* They include full-service wholesalers and limited-service wholesalers.
Full-service wholesalers	Provide a full line of services: carrying stock, maintaining a sales force, offering credit, making deliveries, and providing management assistance. There are two types:
Wholesaler merchants	Sell primarily to retailers and provide a full range of services, *General merchandise wholesalers* carry several merchandise lines, whereas *general line wholesalers* carry one or two lines in great depth. *Specialty wholesalers specialize* in carrying only part of a line. Examples: health food wholesalers, seafood wholesalers.
Industrial distributors	Sell to manufacturers rather than to retailers. Provide several services, such as carrying stock, offering credit, and providing delivery. May carry a broad range of merchandise, a general line, or a specialty line.
Limited-service wholesalers	Offer fewer services than full-service wholesalers. Limited-service wholesalers are of several types:

Type	Description
Cash-and-carry wholesalers	Carry a limited line of fast-moving goods and sell to small retailers for cash. Normally do not deliver. Example: A small fish store retailer may drive to a cash-and-carry fish wholesaler, buy fish for cash, and bring the merchandise back to the store.
Truck wholesalers (or truck jobbers)	Perform primarily a selling and delivery function. Carry limited line of semiperishable merchandise (such as milk, bread, snack foods), which they sell for cash as they make their rounds to supermarkets, small groceries, hospitals, restaurants, factory cafeterias, and hotels.
Drop shippers	Do not carry inventory or handle the product. On receiving an order, they select a manufacturer, who ships the merchandise directly to the customer. The drop shipper assumes title and risk from the time the order is accepted to its delivery to the customer. They operate in bulk industries, such as coal, lumber, and heavy equipment.
Rack jobbers	Serve grocery and drug retailers, mostly in nonfood items. They send delivery trucks to stores, where the delivery people set up toys, paperbacks, hardware items, health and beauty aids, or other items. They price the goods, keep them fresh, set up point-of-purchase displays, and keep inventory records. Rack jobbers retain title to the goods and bill the retailers only for the goods sold to consumers.
Producers' cooperatives	Are owned by farmer members and assemble farm produce to sell in local markets. The co-op's profits are distributed to members at the end of the year. They often attempt to improve product quality and promote a co-op brand name, such as Sun Maid raisins or Sunkist oranges.
Mail-order wholesalers	Send catalogs to retail, industrial, and institutional customers featuring jewelry, cosmetics, specialty foods, and other small items. Maintain no outside sales force. Main customers are businesses in small outlying areas. Orders are filled and sent by mail, truck, or other transportation.
Brokers and agents	Do not take title to goods. Main function is to facilitate buying and selling, for which they earn a commission on the selling price. Generally specialize by product line or customer type.
Brokers	Chief function is bringing buyers and sellers together and assisting in negotiation. They are paid by the party who hired them and do not carry inventory, get involved in financing, or assume risk. Examples: food brokers, real estate brokers, insurance brokers, and security brokers.
Agents	Represent either buyers or sellers on a more permanent basis than brokers do. There are several types:
Manufacturers' agents	Represent two or more manufacturers of complementary lines. A formal written agreement with each manufacturer covers pricing, territories, order handling, delivery service and warranties, and commission rates. Often used in such lines as apparel, furniture, and electrical goods. Most manufacturers' agents are small businesses, with only a few skilled salespeople as employees. They are hired by small manufacturers who cannot afford their own field sales forces and by large manufacturers who use agents to open new territories or to cover territories that cannot support full-time salespeople.
Selling agents	Have contractual authority to sell a manufacturer's entire output. The manufacturer either is not interested in the selling function or feels unqualified. The selling agent serves as a sales department and has significant influence over prices, terms, and conditions of sale. Found in product areas such as textiles, industrial machinery and equipment, coal and coke, chemicals, and metals.

Type	Description
Purchasing agents	Generally have a long-term relationship with buyers and make purchases for them, often receiving, inspecting, warehousing, and shipping the merchandise to the buyers. They provide helpful market information to clients and help them obtain the best goods and prices available.
Commission merchants	Take physical possession of products and negotiate sales. Normally, they are not employed on a long-term basis. Used most often in agricultural marketing by farmers who do not want to sell their own output and do not belong to producers' cooperatives. The commission merchant takes a truckload of commodities to a central market, sells it for the best price, deducts a commission and expenses, and remits the balance to the producers.
Manufacturers' and retailers' branches and offices	Wholesaling operations conducted by sellers or buyers themselves rather than through independent wholesalers. Separate branches and offices can be dedicated to either sales or purchasing.
Sales branches and offices	Set up by manufacturers to improve inventory control, selling, and promotion. *Sales branches* carry inventory and are found in industries such as lumber and automotive equipment and parts. *Sales offices* do not carry inventory and are most prominent in dry-goods and notions industries.
Purchasing officers	Perform a role similar to that of brokers or agents but are part of the buyer's organization. Many retailers set up purchasing offices in major market centers such as Hong Kong, Tokyo, Shanghai and Taipei.

Wholesaler Marketing Decisions

Wholesalers now face growing competitive pressures, more demanding customers, new technologies, and more direct-buying programs on the part of large industrial, institutional, and retail buyers. As a result, they have taken a fresh look at their marketing strategies. As with retailers, their marketing decisions include choices of target markets, positioning, and the marketing mix—product assortments and services, price, promotion, and place (see **Figure 13.4**).

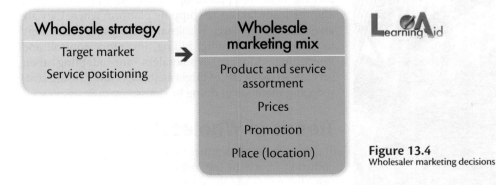

Figure 13.4
Wholesaler marketing decisions

Target Market and Positioning Decision

Like retailers, wholesalers must define their target markets and position themselves effectively. They can choose a target group by size of customer (only large retailers), type of customer (convenience stores only), need for service (customers who need credit), or other factors. Within the target group, they can identify the more profitable customers, design stronger offers, and build better relationships with them. They can propose automatic reordering systems, set up management-training and advising systems, or even sponsor a voluntary chain. They can discourage less profitable customers by requiring larger orders or adding service charges to smaller ones.

Marketing Mix Decisions

Like retailers, wholesalers must decide on product assortment and services, prices, promotion, and place. The wholesaler's "product" is the assortment of products and services that it offers. Wholesalers are under great pressure to carry a full line and to stock enough for immediate delivery. But this practice can damage profits. Wholesalers today are cutting down on the number of lines they carry, choosing to carry only the more profitable ones. Wholesalers are also rethinking which services count most in building strong customer relationships and which should be dropped or charged for. The key is to find the mix of services most valued by their target customers.

Price is also an important wholesaler decision. Wholesalers usually mark up the cost of goods by a standard percentage—say, 20 percent. Expenses may run 17 percent of the gross margin, leaving a profit margin of three percent. Wholesalers are trying new pricing approaches. They may cut their margin on some lines in order to win important new customers. They may ask suppliers for special price breaks when they can turn them into an increase in the supplier's sales. However, the amount of mark-up which varies from country to country tends to be smaller in Asian countries than in the U.S. and Europe. Mark-up by wholesalers is even smaller in Japan, due to long distribution channels, and in Hong Kong, due to keen competition.

Although *promotion* can be critical to wholesaler success, most wholesalers are not promotion minded. Their use of trade advertising, sales promotion, personal selling, and public relations is largely scattered and unplanned. Many still see selling as a single salesperson talking to a single customer instead of as a team effort to sell, build, and service major accounts. Wholesalers also need to adopt some of the nonpersonal promotion techniques used by retailers. They need to develop an overall promotion strategy and to make greater use of supplier promotion materials and programs.

Finally, *place* is important—wholesalers must choose their locations, facilities, and Web locations carefully. Wholesalers typically locate in low-rent, low-tax areas and tend

In recent years, wholesalers are reacting to rising costs by investing in automated warehouses and online ordering systems. The items are picked up by mechanical devices and automatically taken to a shipping platform where they are assembled.

to invest little money in their buildings, equipment, and systems. As a result, their materials-handling and order-processing systems are often outdated. In recent years, however, large and progressive wholesalers are reacting to rising costs by investing in automated warehouses and online ordering systems. Orders are fed from the retailer's system directly into the wholesaler's computer, and the items are picked up by mechanical devices and automatically taken to a shipping platform where they are assembled. Most large wholesalers are using technology to carry out accounting, billing, inventory control, and forecasting. Modern wholesalers are adapting their services to the needs of target customers and finding cost-reducing methods of doing business.

Trends in Wholesaling

Today's wholesalers remain vulnerable to one of the most enduring trends of the last decade—fierce resistance to price increases and the weeding out of suppliers who are not adding value based on cost and quality. Progressive wholesalers constantly watch for better ways to meet the changing needs of their suppliers and target customers, because in the long run, they must add value by increasing the efficiency and effectiveness of the entire marketing channel.

The distinction between large retailers and large wholesalers continues to blur. Many retailers now operate formats such as wholesale clubs and hypermarkets that perform many wholesale functions. In return, many large wholesalers are setting up their own retailing operations.

Wholesalers will continue to increase the services they provide to retailers—retail pricing, cooperative advertising, marketing and management information reports, accounting services, online transactions, and others. Rising costs on the one hand, and the demand for increased services on the other, will put the squeeze on wholesaler profits. Wholesalers who do not find efficient ways to deliver value to their customers will soon drop by the wayside. However, the increased use of computerized, automated, and Web-based systems will help wholesalers to contain the costs of ordering, shipping, and inventory holding, boosting their productivity.

Finally, facing slow growth in their domestic markets and such developments as China's entry into the World Trade Organization and hosting of the 2008 Olympic Games in Beijing, many large wholesalers are taking the opportunity to go global.

REVIEWING THE CONCEPTS

In this chapter, we looked at the nature and importance of retailing, major types of retailers, the decisions retailers make, and the future of retailing. We then examined these same topics for wholesalers.

1 Explain the roles of retailers and wholesalers in the distribution channel.

Retailing and wholesaling consist of many organizations bringing goods and services from the point of production to the point of use. *Retailing* includes all activities involved in selling goods or services directly to final consumers for their personal, nonbusiness use. *Wholesaling* includes all the activities involved in selling goods or services to those who are buying for the purpose of resale or for business use. Wholesalers perform many functions, including selling and promoting, buying and assortment building, bulk breaking, warehousing, transporting, financing, risk bearing, supplying market information, and providing management services and advice.

2 Describe the major types of retailers and give examples of each.

Retail stores come in all shapes and sizes, and new retail types keep emerging. Store retailers can be classified by the *amount of service* they provide (self-service, limited service, or full service), product line sold (specialty stores, department stores, supermarkets, convenience stores, superstores, and service businesses), and *relative prices* (discount stores and off-price retailers). Today, many retailers are banding together in corporate and contractual *retail organizations* (corporate chains, voluntary chains and retailer cooperatives, franchise organizations, and merchandising conglomerates).

3 Describe the major types of wholesalers and give examples of each.

Wholesalers fall into three groups. First, *merchant wholesalers* take possession of the goods. They include *full-service wholesalers* (wholesale merchants, industrial distributors) and *limited-service wholesalers* (cash-and-carry wholesalers, truck wholesalers, drop shippers, rack jobbers, producers' cooperatives, and mail-order wholesalers). Second, brokers and agents do not take possession of the goods but are paid a commission for aiding buying and selling. Finally, *manufacturers' sales branches and offices* are wholesaling operations conducted by nonwholesalers to bypass the wholesalers.

4 Explain the marketing decisions facing retailers and wholesalers.

Each retailer must make decisions about its target markets and positioning, product assortment and services, price, promotion, and place. Retailers need to choose target markets carefully and position themselves strongly. Today, wholesaling is holding its own in the economy. Progressive wholesalers are adapting their services to the needs of target customers and are seeking cost-reducing methods of doing business. Faced with slow growth in their domestic markets and developments such as the North American Free Trade Agreement, many large wholesalers are also now going global.

REVIEWING THE KEY TERMS

DISCUSSING THE CONCEPTS

1. Why have warehouse clubs grown in popularity over the past several years?

2. Describe the similarities and differences between corporate chain stores and franchise organizations.

3. Explain why it is important for retailers to define their target markets and to decide how they will position themselves in these markets. Give an example of a specialty retailer in the city that you are staying that has done this well.

4. What is the wheel-of-retailing concept? Does it apply to online retailing?

5. What is retail convergence? How has it helped or harmed small retailers?

6. What is the primary challenge facing a wholesaler who wishes to remain a viable part of the marketing channel? Explain.

7. What policy should Samsung set for selling High Resolution Digital Television (HDTV) and digital camera to off-price retailers?

8. Retailers are always searching for new marketing strategies to attract and retain customers. Using a top department store as an example, list and briefly describe the strategies this department store uses to differentiate itself from newly developed shopping malls.

9. Across Asian countries, given the emergence of supermarkets and major discount stores, the traditional markets, e.g. wet markets or food stalls (either on the streets or in government buildings), still prevail. Who are the target market segments of these traditional markets? How could these markets survive?

APPLYING THE CONCEPTS

1. Choose three retailers that you buy from often. Classify these retailers in terms of the characteristics presented in the chapter. Next, use Table 13.1 to categorize each retailer.

2. As virtual retailing is becoming more and more popular in some Asian countries,
    a. List some websites in your country that you think will be mostly frequented.
    b. What would be the target market segments of these websites?
    c. Suggest ways to attract more people to visit these websites.

3. Suppose that you are a manufacturer's agent for three lines of complementary women's apparel. Discuss what types of marketing mix decisions you will be making.

FOCUS ON TECHNOLOGY

Imagine having a friend who helps you with your grocery shopping by reminding you about how much you have spent, what you usually purchase, and what's on sale this week that you have purchased in the past. Stop & Shop Supermarket Company, the largest food retailer in New England, will soon introduce the Shopping Buddy.

According to the company, "Shopping Buddy can help you organize your shopping trip and save money! The Shopping Buddy is a small tablet that you activate with your Stop & Shop card. Once activated, the Shopping Buddy displays your personal savings coupons and shopping history by aisle, based on your location. It's easy to see the

things that you normally buy that are on sale in each aisle. You can also use Buddy to keep a running total of your current purchases, order deli without waiting in line, and scan and bag your items as you shop for quick checkout." Stop & Shop will soon be testing this new technology in 20 of its 360 stores.

1. What advantages does Stop & Shop gain by offering this technology?

2. What do you think of the Shopping Buddy concept? Would you use this technology?

3. Visit Stop & Shop at www.stopandshop.com. What other services does this retailer offer that differentiate its store from competitors' stores?

 ## FOCUS ON ETHICS

Purchase a television, computer, or other electronic device and you are bound to be asked whether you would like to purchase a service contract. Most large electronics retailers carefully train their salespeople and cashiers to ask this important question. In fact, some retailers urge their salespeople to exert strong sales pressure to sell these contracts. It's no wonder, because service contracts provide extremely high profits for the retailers, several times the profit margins realized from the equipment you are purchasing. But do you know when to say yes and when to pass on a contract? Most consumers are confused and will buy the contract because the price seems low in comparison to the

price of that new plasma television. Experts, such as those at Consumer Council of Hong Kong, Consumers' Foundation, and SPRING Singapore, generally recommend that buyers pass on these contracts. With increased product reliability and decreasing prices that make replacement more reasonable, such contracts are rarely worth the price. If most consumers do not need them, should retailers continue to offer and promote them?

1. Is it ethical for retailers to offer and strongly promote service contracts?

2. When should you purchase a service contract?

3. Why do retailers continue to offer these contracts, even under criticism from customer advocacy groups?

 ## VIDEO CASE

Wellbeing

In 2007, Dan Tan and Matt Lennox opened their first Wellbeing restaurant. Their goal was to offer consumers a healthy alternative to typical fast-food options. Working with fresh ingredients, bright and open stores, and a well-crafted, healthy menu, the new chain offered something new. "There are few truly healthy fast-food chains," says Tan. "People have been desperate for healthy options." So it came as no surprise that customers responded with enthusiasm to Wellbeing's new choices as they gobbled up sandwiches, salads, soups, juices, smoothies, and fruit salads. In only a few years, the chain has expanded to 18 stores and expects to nearly double that number in the next two years.

After viewing the video featuring Wellbeing, answer the following questions about retailing and wholesaling.

1. Categorize Wellbeing according to the four characteristics of retailers discussed in the chapter.

2. How is Wellbeing positioned in the marketplace? Which consumers does the chain target? Are its product assortment, pricing, promotion, and place decisions consistent with this targeting and positioning?

3. Which trend affecting the future of retailing do you think will most impact Wellbeing in the coming years?

COMPANY CASE

OldTown Café: A Timeless Meeting Place for Generations

In 2008, after seven years of successfully marketing White Coffee 3-in-1 and operating its food and beverage outlets, White Café is thinking about making some changes. Since 2005, the company has made two strategic moves. The first one was to expand its business locally by launching its first OldTown food and beverage outlet, the OldTown Café. This OldTown Café provides an ambience of warmth and camaraderie, making it a place where customers can meet and enjoy a cup of coffee. As the slogan of the company states, "the earliest … yet still the best," White Café was also devoted to encapsulating the brand's promise to deliver the best cup of coffee, while maintaining the authentic taste of the original white coffee, a tradition that is truly Malaysian. White Café calls it "the White Coffee Experience."

The second move was to grow by undertaking more organized export activities. It sought to develop global synergies and strategic partnerships that would increase and intensify the distribution network of OldTown White Coffee packs from Southeast Asia to the U.S. and Europe.

In 2008, three years after these moves, the company is now able to see fruitful results. The OldTown Café has grown into a full-fledged licensed chain which possesses over 83 outlets, and it plans to open three new outlets each month in Malaysia. Each of these outlets provides the White Coffee Experience together with appetizing Malaysian cuisine.

In terms of international marketing, the company has succeeded in exporting OldTown White Coffee packs to over 12 countries, including Japan, Hong Kong, Singapore, Indonesia, Canada, the U.S., and Taiwan. According to research conducted by AC Nielsen, not only did White Café become the market leader in the white coffee industry in Malaysia by capturing 35 percent of the market in 2006, but it also became the white coffee market leader in Hong Kong in 2007.

From An Idea To Reality

White Café Sdn Bhd, which owns the famous Ipoh White Coffee Brand, was founded in 1999 by a group of Ipohians in Malaysia. Long before that, back in 1958, the location was just an ordinary coffee shop called White Café. At that time, inspired with a vision and passion to make and serve fine coffee to customers, its owner created a formula for brewing white coffee from blended coffee beans and other ingredients. At White Café, he began to serve this unique white coffee to the neighborhood. The aroma of the white coffee soon gained popularity within the township and the news of its unique taste and smoothness spread from Ipoh to other towns in Malaysia. Eventually, customers from various towns would make special trips to Ipoh to savor the renowned White Coffee, making White Café a crowded and popular place.

A Milestone

The new company founded in 1999 still aspires to its original philosophy of "letting every customer enjoy a cup of authentic Malaysian Ipoh White Coffee anytime, anywhere." As such, it has been charged with a mission to continuously promote the unique Malaysian taste of its White Coffee (packs) through continuous improvement and innovation that exceeds customer expectations. However, with the influence of Western culture and the global economic development of the '90s, consumers in Asia, especially those of the younger generation, have the tendency to adopt a lifestyle which integrates practices from various cultures. In fact, many Southeast Asian economies, such as Malaysia, Singapore, and Hong Kong, are famous for being multicultural. For example, children in Malaysia grow up with the influence of four major cultures, namely, Malaysian, Chinese, Indian, and Islamic cultures. White Café understands the effect of culture on business operations. Starting in 1999, it attempted to create new experiences for customers through a combination of products and practices originating from different cultures, and turned OldTown F&B outlets into a place where everyone can enjoy authentic Malaysian Ipoh White Coffee as well as local dishes within a pleasant atmosphere that suits both young and old. Some changes in the elements of the marketing mix are described below.

The Product: Authentic Malaysia Café and Food

While OldTown focuses on promoting the authentic Malaysian coffee, which is a collective memory of many local Malaysians, it also serves typical Malaysian food such as nasi lemak, curry dishes, and Chinese noodles. To further realize the dream that everyone can enjoy their white coffee at home, OldTown developed the OldTown White Coffee Classic 3-in-1 instant coffee packs. To meet the needs of different customer segments, various products were extended. For example, OldTown White Coffee 3-in-1 without sugar was developed to meet the needs of more health-conscious consumers.

Old Town's White Coffee product lines:

Simply Pure White Coffee
- Old Town White OCffee – Enriched
- Old Town White Coffee – Original

Old Town Blends
- Old Town White Cofffee 3-in-1 Classic
- Old Town White Coffee 3-in-1 Natural Cane Sugar
- Old Town White Coffee 3-in-1 Hazelnut
- Old Town White Coffee 3-in-1 Ice Cold

The Distribution Channel

To reach out to customers proactively, White Café transformed itself into a franchising business in 1999 by standardizing its operations and products. With proper planning, outlets were established in Ipoh, Kuala Lumpur, and other large towns in Malaysia. In 2006, outlets of OldTown Café were established in countries outside Malaysia such as Taiwan and Indonesia. Partnerships were formed with renowned corporations like Malaysia Airlines.

The Atmosphere

The OldTown outlets are generally subdivided into sections. Chairs and tables are placed in the open area of the outlet without any fancy decorations or air conditioning. The uniqueness of this arrangement is that customers can enjoy the outdoor scenery and fresh air. More importantly, it brings back the coffee-tasting memories of the older generation. Once you enter the outlet, the atmosphere is different; classical-style ceiling fans are in place to ensure fresh air can be circulated effectively. The style of the layout still follows the original old town in Ipoh. However, the material of the furniture is much more modern. In other words, it retains the old town atmosphere but has more attractive decorations. In outlets with two levels, air-conditioners are installed on the top storey so one can enjoy the authentic coffee without suffering from Malaysia's hot weather—a welcome relief for professionals dressed in formal business attire.

The Service Delivery

To ensure high service quality, the service delivery process also follows modern practices. To minimize the language barrier, menus in fine print with pictures of food and beverages are placed on the table. Customers can choose whatever they want on the order forms. Instead of relying on the memory of the waiters, who in the past had to keep track of the orders of every table, orders are delivered based on the order forms. As a result, miscommunication is minimized and the reliability of the service improved. In addition, a more professional image is presented.

What is the Gateway to the Future?

Since 1999, the fact that OldTown Café has earned numerous awards signifies its continuous success. However, it is facing increasing competition from multinational brands such as Starbucks, which serves a variety of coffee drinks and has a pleasant atmosphere that can keep customers in the shop. OldTown Café is aware of the situation, and in early 2008, it plans to design new strategies to cope with the changing environment.

Questions For Discussion

1. Visit http://www.oldtown.com.my. Compare OldTown Café with Starbucks. What benefits can a customer receive from using OldTown Café? What are the disadvantages?
2. Using the various characteristics for classifying types of retailers, develop a profile of OldTown Café.
3. Who do these outlets target? How does OldTown Café position itself in this market?
4. Apply the wheel-of-retailing concept to the food and beverage industry, defining OldTown Café's role.
5. What does the future hold for OldTown Café in both the short-term and the long-term?

Source:
http://www.oldtown.com.my

Objectives

After studying this chapter, you should be able to

- discuss the process and advantages of integrated marketing communications in communicating customer value
- define the five promotion tools and discuss the factors that must be considered in shaping the overall promotion mix
- outline the steps in developing effective marketing communications
- explain the methods for setting the promotion budget and factors that affect the design of the promotion mix

CHAPTER 14

COMMUNICATING CUSTOMER VALUE: Integrated Marketing Communications Strategy

Previewing the Concepts

In this and the next three chapters, we'll examine the last of the marketing mix tools—promotion. Companies must do more than just create customer value. They must also use promotion to clearly and persuasively communicate that value. You'll find that promotion is not a single tool but rather a mix of several tools. Ideally, under the concept of integrated marketing communications, the company will carefully coordinate these promotion elements to deliver a clear, consistent, and compelling message about the organization and its products. We'll begin by introducing you to the various promotion mix tools. Next, we'll examine the rapidly changing communications environment and the need for integrated marketing communications. Finally, we'll discuss the steps in developing marketing communications and the promotion budgeting process. In the next three chapters, we'll visit the specific marketing communications tools.

To start this chapter, let's look behind the scenes at Mengniu Dairy, a renowned company in China, promoting its dairy products. As it turns out, Mengniu's success reflects the current trends in the fast-changing world of modern integrated marketing communications.

China Mengniu Dairy Company Limited manufactures and distributes dairy products in the People's Republic of China, including Hong Kong and Macau. Under the MENGNIU brand, the company manufactures dairy products, including liquid milk products, yogurt and milk beverages, ice cream, and other dairy products such as milk powder. In December 2007, the company operated 22 production bases with a combined annual production capacity of 4.78 million tons.[1] Mengniu's success can be largely attributed to its efforts to cultivate a brand image.

With rapid economic development and a surge in domestic consumption, the dairy industry in China has become the world's third largest milk producer and the largest emerging dairy market. Competition in traditional products continues to be keen, leading to an inevitable market consolidation. In this highly consolidated industry, only those major dairy players with a massive operating scale, supported by well-developed distribution networks, and who enjoy strong brand recognition, can survive.

Traditionally, the Chinese soft drinks market consists mainly of carbonated drinks, tea drinks, and sports drinks. Mengniu had to face the challenge of altering the consumers' preferences in taste and drinking habits. After several years of hard work, Mengniu managed to break into the market with its milk drinks with marked success.

2005 was an important year for Mengniu, in terms of business development, as it rolled out its massive integrated communication campaign that enhanced consumer awareness of its brand and products. Apart from buying prime-time slots on national television channels, the company also mounted a sponsorship—the "Mengniu Suan Suan Ru Super Girl Singing Contest," a nationwide singing competition for female contestants organized by Hunan TV.[2] It was generally described as the mainland Chinese version of Pop Idol and became one of the most popular entertainment shows in the country.

In order to further expand the market for milk drink products and establish a pioneering brand image, Mengniu realized that they had to do something innovative to gain the awareness and acceptance of the target consumer group (i.e. young females). In 2005, Mengniu decided to cooperate with Hunan TV by entering into sponsorship of the station's "Super Girl" singing contest, which turned out to be a great success in their integrated communication program. Mengniu's management believed that there were associations between the brand features of "Mengniu milk drink" (i.e., self-confident, young, lively, fashionable, and energetic) and those of "Super Girl." The "Super Girl" singing contest would undoubtedly draw great attention from society at large, and in particular draw the interest of females aged from 12 to 24, the target consumers of Mengniu milk drink, and so establish a leadership position and quickly dominate the fast-growing milk drink market.

This integrated communication campaign was carefully planned and executed, leading the direction and pace of media reports and aiming to establish a strong link between "Super Girl" and the Mengniu milk drink as a "Super Brand." In this context, a public relations program with more than 20 different themes was conducted and widely communicated through TV, radio, newspapers, magazines, and the Internet.[3]

The press was used for a large-scale promotion of the campaign and Mengniu milk drinks, the objective being to arouse the interest of young females, focusing not only on the competition, but also on the features and benefits of Mengniu products. Mainstream websites were also engaged to closely follow the whole campaign via a series of reports. The eye-catching interactive games "Look at

Mengniu again and again" and "Super FANS" were designed to stimulate interest and involve consumers.

On top of these activities, below-the-line promotions were also launched. Mengniu organized a series of roadshows in 32 selected cities that served as preliminary selections for "Super Girl." Mengniu sponsored winners of this round to attend the first round selection at the Hunan TV studio. At about the same time, Mengniu launched a prize-winning promotion in which customers who bought Mengniu milk drink products during the period would have a chance to win a two-day trip to Changsha to attend the final episode of the competition live at the Hunan TV studio.

The "Super Girl" 2005 season attracted more than 120,000 applicants during the preliminary selection rounds, which were held in the five provinces of Hunan, Sichuan, Guangdong, Henan, and Zhejiang. The final episode of the 2005 season was one of the most popular shows in Chinese broadcast history, drawing over 400 million viewers, more than the China Central Television New Year's Gala earlier that year.[4]

The campaign was a huge success for Mengniu, significantly boosting the popularity of the company, as well as its Suan Suan Ru series of products, among Chinese consumers. With millions of teenagers becoming crazy about the contest and almost all of the country talking about the event, Mengniu became more famous.[5] According to an ACNielsen survey conducted in 2007, the company held a 40.7 percent share of the liquid milk market in China in terms of sales revenue, and continued to champion the market in China.

The Promotion Mix

Promotion mix (marketing communications mix)
The specific blend of advertising, sales promotion, public relations, personal selling, and direct-marketing tools that the company uses to persuasively communicate customer value and build customer relationships.

Advertising
Any paid form of nonpersonal presentation and promotion of ideas, goods, or services by an identified sponsor.

Sales promotion
Short-term incentives to encourage the purchase or sale of a product or service.

Public relations
Building good relations with the company's various publics by obtaining favorable publicity, building up a good "corporate image," and handling or heading off unfavorable rumors, stories, and events.

A company's total **promotion mix**—also called its **marketing communications mix**—consists of the specific blend of advertising, sales promotion, public relations, personal selling, and direct-marketing tools that the company uses to persuasively communicate customer value and build customer relationships. Definitions of the five major promotion tools follow:[6]

Advertising: Any paid form of nonpersonal presentation and promotion of ideas, goods, or services by an identified sponsor.
Sales promotion: Short-term incentives to encourage the purchase or sale of a product or service.
Public relations: Building good relations with the company's various publics by obtaining favorable publicity, building up a good corporate image, and handling or heading off unfavorable rumors, stories, and events.
Personal selling: Personal presentation by the firm's sales force for the purpose of making sales and building customer relationships.
Direct marketing: Direct connections with carefully targeted individual consumers to both obtain an immediate response and cultivate lasting customer relationships—the use of direct mail, the telephone, direct-response television, e-mail, the Internet, and other tools to communicate directly with specific consumers.

Each category involves specific promotional tools used to communicate with consumers. For example, advertising includes broadcast, print, Internet, outdoor, and other forms. Sales promotion includes discounts, coupons, displays, and demonstrations. Personal selling includes sales presentations, trade shows, and incentive programs. Public relations includes press releases, sponsorships, special events, and Web pages. And direct marketing includes catalogs, telephone marketing, kiosks, the Internet, and more.

At the same time, marketing communication goes beyond these specific promotion tools. The product's design, its price, the shape and color of its package, and the stores that sell it—all communicate something to buyers. Thus, although the promotion mix is the company's primary communication activity, the entire marketing mix—promotion and product, price, and place—must be coordinated for greatest communication impact.

The entire marketing mix – Promotion, product, price, and place must be coordinated for greatest communication impact.

Integrated Marketing Communications

In past decades, marketers have perfected the art of mass marketing—selling highly standardized products to masses of customers. In the process, they have developed effective mass-media communications techniques to support these mass-marketing strategies. Large companies routinely invest millions or even billions of dollars in television, magazine, or other mass-media advertising, reaching tens of millions of customers with a single ad. Today, however, marketing managers face some new marketing communications realities.

The New Marketing Communications Landscape

Two major factors are changing the face of today's marketing communications. First, as mass markets have fragmented, marketers are shifting away from mass marketing. More and more, they are developing focused marketing programs designed to build closer relationships with customers in more narrowly defined micromarkets. Second, vast improvements in information technology are speeding the movement toward segmented marketing. With today's new information technologies, marketers can amass detailed customer information and keep closer track of customer needs.

Improved information technology has also caused striking changes in the ways in which companies and customers communicate with each other. The digital age has spawned a host of new information and communication tools—from mobile phones, iPods, and the Internet to satellite and cable television systems and digital video recorders (DVRs). The new technologies give companies exciting new media tools for interacting with targeted consumers. They also give consumers more control over the nature and timing of messages they choose to send and receive.

The Shifting Marketing Communications Model

The shift toward segmented marketing and the explosive developments in information and communications technology have had a dramatic impact on marketing communications. Just as mass marketing once gave rise to a new generation of mass-media communications, the shift toward targeted marketing and the changing communications environment are giving birth to a new marketing communications model. Although television, magazines, and other mass media remain very important, their dominance

Personal selling
Personal presentation by the firm's sales force for the purpose of making sales and building customer relationships.

Direct marketing
Direct connections with carefully targeted individual consumers to both obtain an immediate response and cultivate lasting customer relationships.

is now declining. Advertisers are now adding a broad selection of more specialized and highly targeted media to reach smaller customer segments with more personalized messages. The new media range from specialty magazines, cable television channels, and video on demand (VOD) to product placements in television programs and video games, Internet catalogs, e-mails, and podcasts. In all, companies are doing less *broadcasting* and more *narrowcasting*.

Some advertising industry experts even predict a doom-and-gloom "chaos scenario," in which the old mass-media communications model will collapse entirely. They believe that marketers will increasingly abandon traditional mass media in favor of "the glitzy promise of new digital technologies—from Web sites and e-mail to cell phone content and video on demand ... Fragmentation, the bane of network TV and mass marketers everywhere, will become the Holy Grail, the opportunity to reach—and have a conversation with—small clusters of consumers who are consuming not what is force-fed them, but exactly what they want."[7]

Just think about what's happening to television viewing these days. "Adjust your set," says one reporter, "television is changing as quickly as the channels. It's on cell phones. It's on digital music players. It's on almost anything with a screen. Shows can be seen at their regular times or when you want [with or without the commercials]. Some 'TV' programs aren't even on cable or network or satellite; they're being created just for Internet viewing."[8]

The growth of more specialized and highly targeted media has led to more narrowcasting as companies try to target niche markets.

Consumers, especially younger ones, appear to be turning away from the major television networks in favor of cable TV or altogether different media. According to a recent study in the U.S.:

Only one in four 12- to 34-year-olds can name all four major broadcast networks: ABC, NBC, CBS, and Fox. Teens may not be able to name the big four, but they know MTV, Cartoon Network, and Comedy Central. The most popular activity? That would be surfing the Internet, which 84 percent said they did during their free time. Hanging out with friends came in second at 76 percent, watching movies third at 71 percent, and TV viewing fourth at 69 percent.[9]

As a result, marketers are losing confidence in television advertising. As mass-media costs rise, audiences shrink, ad clutter increases, and more and more viewers use VOD and TiVo-like systems to skip past disruptive television commercials, many skeptics even predict the demise of the old mass-media mainstay—the 30-second television commercial. In a recent survey, 70 percent of major brand advertisers said that they believe DVRs and VOD will reduce or destroy the effectiveness of traditional 30-second commercials.[10]

Thus, many large advertisers are shifting their advertising budgets away from network television in favor of more targeted, cost-effective, interactive, and engaging media. "The ad industry's plotline used to be a lot simpler: Audiences are splintering off in dozens of

Audiences are splintering off in new directions and watching videos on new portable devices like the iPod and Playstation Portable.

new directions, watching TV shows on iPods, watching movies on videogame players, and listening to radio on the Internet," observes one analyst. So marketers must "start planning how to reach consumers in new and unexpected ways."[11]

Rather than a "chaos scenario, however, other industry insiders see a more gradual shift to the new marketing communications model. They note that broadcast television and other mass media still capture a lion's share of the promotion budgets of most major marketing firms, a fact that isn't likely to change quickly. Although some may question the future of the 30-second spot, it is still very much in use today. And although ad spending on the major TV networks decreased last year, cable ad spending increased 11 percent. Moreover, television offers many promotional opportunities beyond the 30-second commercial." One advertising expert advises:

"Because TV is at the forefront of 30 technological advances [such as DVRs and VOD], its audience will continue to increase. So if you think that TV is an aging dinosaur, or you're a national advertiser who is thinking of moving ad dollars away from TV, maybe you should think again."12

Thus, it seems likely that the new marketing communications model will consist of a gradually shifting mix of both traditional mass media and a wide array of exciting new, more targeted, more personalized media. Consider this example.

Jinmailang is a popular instant noodle brand in China. In its promotion campaigns, it uses a rich mix of media—conventional but clever magazine ads coupled with novel package design, quirky promotions, and voting activities on its Web site. The wise use of the media mix has helped Jinmailang move to the number two position in the instant noodle market in China with a market share of 16 percent in 2004."13

Jinmailang (China) promotion campaigns use a rich mix of media—conventional but clever magazine ads coupled with novel package design, quirky promotions, and voting activities on its Web site. (www.hualong.com)

The Need for Integrated Marketing Communications

The shift toward a richer mix of media and communication approaches poses a problem for marketers. Consumers today are bombarded by commercial messages from a broad range of sources. But consumers do not distinguish between message sources the way marketers do. In the consumer's mind, messages from different media and promotional approaches all become part of a single message about the company. Conflicting messages from these different sources can result in confused company images, brand positions, and customer relationships.

All too often, companies fail to integrate their various communications channels. The result is a hodgepodge of communications to consumers. Mass-media advertisements say one thing, while a price promotion sends a different signal, and a product label creates still another message. Company sales literature says something altogether different, and the company's Web site seems out of sync with everything else.

The problem is that these communications often come from different parts of the company. Advertising messages are planned and implemented by the advertising department or an advertising agency. Personal selling communications are developed by sales management. Other company specialists are responsible for public relations, sales promotion events, Internet marketing, and other forms of marketing communications.

However, whereas these companies have separated their communications tools, customers will not. According to one marketing communications expert:[14]

The truth is, most [consumers] will not compartmentalize their use of the [different media]. They will not say, "Hey, I am going off to do a bit of Web surfing. Burn my TV, throw out all my radios, cancel all my magazine subscriptions and, by the way, take out my telephone and do not deliver any mail anymore." It is not that kind of world for consumers, and it should not be that kind of world for marketers either.

Today, more companies are adopting the concept of **integrated marketing communications (IMC)**. Under this concept, as illustrated in **Figure 14.1**, the company carefully integrates its many communications channels to deliver a clear, consistent, and compelling message about the organization and its brands.[15]

IMC calls for recognizing all contact points where the customer may encounter the company and its brands (see **Figure 14.2**). Each *brand contact* will deliver a message, whether good, bad, or indifferent. The company wants to deliver a consistent and positive message with each contact. IMC leads to a total marketing communication strategy aimed

Integrated marketing communications (IMC)
Carefully integrating and coordinating the company's many communications channels to deliver a clear, consistent, and compelling message about the organization and its products.

Learning Aid

Carefully blended mix of promotion tools

Advertising ⟷ Personal selling

Consistent, clear and compelling company and brand messages

Sales promotion

Public relations

Direct marketing

Figure 14.1
Integrated marketing communications

at building strong customer relationships by showing how the company and its products can help customers solve their problems.

IMC ties together all of the company's messages and images. The company's television and print advertisements have the same message, look, and feel as its e-mail and personal selling communications. And its public relations materials project the same image as its Web site. For example, Ford recently created a nicely integrated promotion campaign for its Escape Hybrid model.

Learning Aid

INTEGRATED MARKETING COMMUNICATIONS (IMC) ●

Figure 14.2
Overview of the integrated marketing communications process

- Identify the target audience
- Recognize all contact points where the target audience may encounter the company and its brands
- Assess the influence each of these contact points will have at different stages of the buying process
- Tie together all of the company's messages and images (same message, look, and feel)
- Deliver a clear, consistent, and compelling message about the organization and its brands

Ford created a nicely integrated promotional campaign for its Escape Hybrid model, featuring Kermit the Frog in a Super Bowl and various print ads, as well as a special Web site that helped serious car buyers learn more about the benefits of the Escape Hybrid.

It kicked off the Escape Hybrid campaign with a blockbuster Super Bowl ad, in which Kermit the Frog lamented "It is not easy being green" before discovering that it really is easy being green with the Escape Hybrid. Ford followed up with print ads in major magazines, featuring Kermit and reinforcing the "I guess it is easy being green" theme. The Super Bowl and print ads helped to build consumer awareness and preference for the Escape Hybrid brand. But the ads also pointed viewers to a special Web site (_www.fordvehicles.com/suvs/escapehybrid_), which extended the Kermit theme with a number of relationship-building and sales-building features. Visitors to the site could view the Super Bowl commercial again and then watch a charming video on the making of the "Easy Being Green" commercial—narrated by Kermit, of course. The site also offered lots of help with very little hype to serious car buyers, letting them learn more about the benefits of the Escape Hybrid, build and price a model, and find a dealer online. Later, at the dealership, Ford salespeople communicated the "Easy Being Green" message in person while customers kicked the tyres and tested the Escape Hybrid's ride before deciding to purchase.

In the past, no one person or department was responsible for thinking through the communication roles of the various promotion tools and coordinating the promotion mix. To help implement integrated marketing communications, some companies appoint a marketing communications director who has overall responsibility for the company's communications efforts. This helps to produce better communications consistency and greater sales impact. It places the responsibility in someone's hands—where none existed before—to unify the company's image as it is shaped by thousands of company activities.

A View of the Communication Process

Integrated marketing communications involves identifying the target audience and shaping a well-coordinated promotional program to obtain the desired audience response. Too often, marketing communications focus on immediate awareness, image, or preference goals in the target market. But this approach to communication is too shortsighted. Today, marketers are moving toward viewing communications as *managing the customer relationship over time.*

Because customers differ, communications programs need to be developed for specific segments, niches, and even individuals. And, given the new interactive communications technologies, companies must ask not only, "How can we reach our customers?" but also, "How can we find ways to let our customers reach us?"

Thus, the communications process should start with an audit of all the potential contacts target customers may have with the company and its brands. For example, someone purchasing a new kitchen appliance may talk to others, see television ads, read articles and ads in newspapers and magazines, visit various Web sites, and check out appliances in one or more stores. The marketer needs to assess what influence each of these communications experiences will have at different stages of the buying process. This understanding will help marketers allocate their communication dollars more efficiently and effectively.

To communicate effectively, marketers need to understand how communication works. Communication involves the nine elements shown in **Figure 14.3**. Two of these elements are the major parties in a communication—the *sender* and the *receiver*. Another two are the major communication tools—the *message* and the *media*. Four more are major communication functions—*encoding, decoding, response,* and *feedback*. The last element is *noise* in the system. Definitions of these elements follow and are applied to an ad for Hewlett-Packard (HP) LaserJet color copiers.

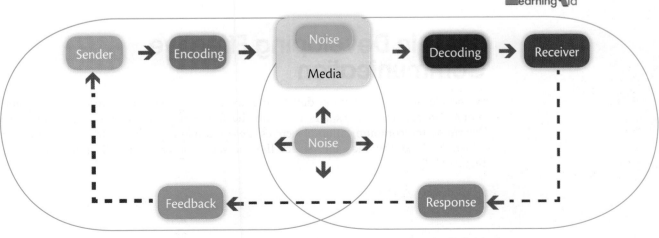

Figure 14.3
Elements in the communication process

- *Sender:* The party sending the message to another party—here, HP.
- *Encoding:* The process of putting thought into symbolic form—HP's advertising agency assembles words and illustrations into an advertisement that will convey the intended message.
- *Message:* The set of symbols that the sender transmits—the actual HP copier ad.
- *Media:* The communication channels through which the message moves from sender to receiver—in this case, the specific magazines that HP selects.
- *Decoding:* The process by which the receiver assigns meaning to the symbols encoded by the sender—a consumer reads the HP copier ad and interprets the words and illustrations it contains.
- *Receiver:* The party receiving the message sent by another party—the home office or business customer who reads the HP copier ad.
- *Response:* The reactions of the receiver after being exposed to the message—any of hundreds of possible responses, such as the consumer is more aware of the attributes of HP copiers, visits the HP Web site for more information, actually buys an HP copier, or does nothing.
- *Feedback:* The part of the receiver's response communicated back to the sender—HP research shows that consumers are struck by and remember the ad, or consumers write or call HP praising or criticizing the ad or HP's products.
- *Noise:* The unplanned static or distortion during the communication process, which results in the receiver's getting a different message than the one the sender sent—the consumer is distracted while reading the magazine and misses the HP ad or its key points.

For a message to be effective, the sender's encoding process must mesh with the receiver's decoding process. The best messages consist of words and other symbols that are familiar to the receiver. The more the sender's field of experience overlaps with that of the receiver, the more effective the message is likely to be. Marketing communicators may not always *share* their consumer's field of experience. For example, an advertising copywriter from one socioeconomic stratum might create ads for consumers from another stratum—say, wealthy business owners. However, to communicate effectively, the marketing communicator must *understand* the consumer's field of experience.

This model points out several key factors in good communication. Senders need to know what audiences they wish to reach and what responses they want. They must be good at encoding messages that take into account how the target audience decodes them. They must send messages through media that reach target audiences, and they must develop feedback channels so that they can assess the audience's response to the message.

Steps in Developing Effective Communication

We now examine the steps in developing an effective integrated communications and promotion program. Marketers must do the following: Identify the target audience; determine the communication objectives; design a message; choose the media through which to send the message; select the message source; and collect feedback (see **Figure 14.4**).

Steps In Developing Effective Communications

1. Identify the target audience.

2. Determine a message.
- Find out which buyer-readiness stage the target audience is at and to what stage it needs to be moved.

3. Design a message.
- What to say (message content)
    - i.   Rational appeal
    - ii. Emotional appeal
    - iii. Moral appeal
- How to say it (message structure and format)

4. Choose the media through which to send the message.
- Personal communication channels
    - i.   Word of mouth
    - ii. Buzz marketing
- Nonpersonal communication channels
    - i.   Major media
    - ii   Atmospheres
    - iii. Events

5. Choose the message source.
- Use highly credible or recognizable sources to promote or recommend the product to the target audience

6. Collect feedback
- Research the effect on the target audience.
    - i.   Do they remember the message?
    - ii. How many times did they see it?
    - iii. What points do they recall?
    - iv. How did they feel about the message?
    - v.   What are their past and present attitudes toward the product and company?
- Measure behavior resulting from the message
    - i.   How many people bought the product?
    - ii   How many people talked to others about it?
    - iii. How many people visited the store?

Figure 14.4
Steps in developing effective communication

Identifying the Target Audience

A marketing communicator starts with a clear target audience in mind. The audience may be potential buyers or current users, those who make the buying decision or those who influence it. The audience may be individuals, groups, special publics, or the general public. The target audience will heavily affect the communicator's decisions on *what* will be said, *how* it will be said, *when* it will be said, *where* it will be said, and *who* will say it.

Buyer-readiness stages
The stages consumers normally pass through on their way to purchase, including awareness, knowledge, liking, preference, conviction, and purchase.

Determining the Communication Objectives

Once the target audience has been defined, the marketers must decide what response they seek. Of course, in many cases, they will seek a purchase response. But a purchase results from a long consumer decision-making process. The marketing communicator needs to know where the target audience now stands and to what stage it needs to be moved. The target audience may be in any of six **buyer-readiness stages**, the stages consumers normally pass through on their way to making a purchase. These stages include *awareness, knowledge, liking, preference, conviction*, and *purchase* (see **Figure 14.5**).

Figure 14.5
Buyer-readiness stages

Awareness → Knowledge → Liking → Preference → Conviction → Purchase

The marketing communicator's target market may be totally unaware of the product, know only its name, or know only a few things about it. The communicator must first build *awareness* and *knowledge*. For example, when Jurong Point Shopping Centre in Singapore first introduced its promotion campaign, it used advertisements and press releases to create awareness and curiosity. When the shoppers arrived, big posters at the entrances welcomed them with instructions to participate in the promotion campaign and more information about the shopping center (see **Real Marketing 14.1**).

REAL MARKETING 14.1

Shopping Success Story:
Jurong Point Shopping Centre

The management of Jurong Point Shopping Centre made use of advertisements and press releases to promote the mall's opening. Today, it continues to hold regular events and promotions for its shoppers.

Assuming target consumers know about the product, how do they feel about it? Once potential buyers knew about the shopping center, marketers wanted to move them through successively stronger stages of feelings toward the shopping center. These stages included liking (having an inclination to the center), preference (preferring Jurong Point to other shopping centers), and conviction (believing that Jurong Point is the best shopping place for them). Jurong Point marketers used a combination of the promotion mix tools to create positive feelings and conviction. Advertising built an emotional brand connection. Press releases and other public relations activities stressed the shopping center's provision of an innovative shopping experience. Buyers were continuously informed of shopping events so that they could get the most out of their shopping at Jurong Point.

Finally, some members of the target market might be convinced about the product, but not quite get around to making the *purchase*. The communicator must lead these targeted shoppers to take the final step. Actions might include offering special promotional prices, rebates, or premiums. Salespeople might call or write to selected customers, inviting them to visit the dealership for a special showing. In Jurong Point's case, potential shoppers were provided SMS coupons so that they could try some of the products or services before they decided to buy more.

Of course, marketing communications alone cannot create positive feelings about a shopping center leading to purchases. The center itself must provide superior value for the shoppers. In fact, outstanding marketing communications can actually speed the demise of a poor product or service. The more quickly potential buyers learn about the poor product or services, the more quickly they become aware of its faults. Thus, good marketing communication calls for "good deeds followed by good words."

Jurong Point Shopping Centre is a leading retail mall situated in the western part of Singapore. It has a tenanted area of about 410,000 square feet housing more than 200 retailers, showcasing their products and services to an average of two million visitors a month. Opened in December 1995, Jurong Point provides shoppers with seven floors of shopping, dining, entertainment and services. Its mix of shops includes junior anchors and over 200 specialty shops/service providers, each contributing to a multi-faceted shopping experience.

To make shopping more fun and interesting, Jurong Point partnered with a mobile information service provider and various resident vendors at the mall to build an interactive mobile campaign that turned the Singapore shopping experience into something special for participating mobile users, where prizes could be won. The campaign led to an increase in the amount of revenue generated per mall visitor.

During the campaign, all visitors to the mall were greeted at each of Jurong Point's 14 entrances by big posters displaying clear instructions on how to participate. Shoppers were invited to send an SMS to the advertised number with the estimated number of hours they expected to spend in the mall. Upon registration, a welcome note was sent to the shopper's mobile phone, offering the option to create a personalized profile focusing on individual areas of interest, be it leisure, food, furniture, clothes, books, etc. For the duration of their stay in the mall, shoppers then periodically received relevant text messages on shopping events, promotions, money-off coupons, and incentives for entering a wide variety of competitions (all based on selected interests stored in their personalized profile).

The number of participating vendors grew very quickly following the launch of the campaign. This enabled the campaign to expand to include a whole host of promotions, from discounted books and beauty products to free beverages in onsite restaurants and competitions to win electrical goods.

Merchants enjoyed higher traffic from shoppers who received SMS coupons. User statistics were also analyzed for future promotional plans.

Sources:
"Singapore Shopping Success Story: Sybase 365", Sybase Inc., accessed at http://www.sybase.com/files/Success_Stories/Sybase365_ss_Singapore-021407.pdf; Tuna Newsletter, July 2007, accessed at http://www.tunamedia.com/tuna_English/pdf/TUNA%20Newseltter%20July.pdf

Designing a Message

Having defined the desired audience response, the communicator turns to developing an effective message. Ideally, the message should get *Attention*, hold *Interest*, arouse *Desire*, and obtain *Action* (a framework known as the *AIDA model*). In practice, few messages take the consumer all the way from awareness to purchase, but the AIDA framework suggests the desirable qualities of a good message.

When putting the message together, the marketing communicator must decide what to say (*message content*) and how to say it (*message structure* and *format*).

Message Content

The marketer has to figure out an appeal or theme that will produce the desired response. There are three types of appeals: rational, emotional, and moral. Rational appeals relate to the audience's self-interest. They show that the product will produce the desired benefits. Examples are messages showing a product's quality, economy, value, or performance. Thus, Panadol Nasal Clear runs a series of ads in Hong Kong, which inform customers about the pain reliever and why Panadol is the best choice. The ads promote "Runny nose cleared in a flash!"

Emotional appeals attempt to stir up either negative or positive emotions that can motivate purchase. Communicators may use positive emotional appeals such as love, pride, joy, harmony and humor. For example in China, advocates claim that auspicious messages attract more attention and create more liking and belief in the sponsor. Jinliufu (金六福), a famous Chinese liquor, does not have a distilling process which is different from its competitors. However, it has been capable in capturing a huge market share because of its brand name. The name Jinliufu in Chinese, when pronounced, sounds like "Having every good luck today" which serves as an emotional appeal to ordinary Chinese folk. Since the Chinese have always had a strong desire for good fortune, Jinliufu successfully stirs their emotion to seek "the liquor of a good day," especially to be used during daily rituals and festivals when they pray for prosperous days to come.

These days, it seems as though every company is using humor in its advertising, from consumer product firms such as Anheuser-Busch to the scholarly American Heritage Dictionary. Advertising in recent Super Bowls appears to reflect consumers' preferences for humor. For example, 14 of the top 15 most popular ads in USA Today's ad meter consumer rankings of 2006 Super Bowl advertisements used humor. Anheuser-Busch used humor to claim six of the top ten ad spots. Its Bud Light ads featured everything from young men worshiping a neighbor's rotating magic fridge stocked with Bud Light to an office manager who motivates employees by hiding bottles of Bud Light throughout the office.[16]

Humor in advertising – These days, it seems as though almost every company is using humor in its advertising, even the scholarly American Heritage Dictionary.

Properly used, humor can capture attention, make people feel good, and give a brand personality. Anheuser-Busch has used humor effectively for years, helping consumers relate to its brands. However, advertisers must be careful when using humor. Used poorly, it can detract from comprehension, wear out its welcome fast, overshadow the product, or even irritate consumers. For example, many consumers and ad critics took exception to some of the humor used in the 2004 Super Bowl ads, including Anheuser-Busch ads.

> Advertising professionals agreed that the quality of Super Bowl ads [in 2004] had declined, mostly from the use of "toilet bowl" humor that insulted viewers' intelligence. They pointed to Budweiser ads featuring a crotch-biting dog, a male monkey wooing a human female, and a gas-passing horse that spoiled a sleigh-ride date. Many critics and consumers complained that such ads showed that Budweiser was "reaching for the lowest common denominator in commercials aimed at the most frequent beer drinkers—men from 21 to 25 years old—resulting in a race to the bottom to fill commercials with bathroom humor, double entendres, crude sight gags and vulgarisms." As a result of such criticism, Anheuser-Busch [rethought] the tone and content of its ads for future Super Bowls. "We are taking a more cautious approach to our creative," says Anheuser-Busch president August Busch IV. "[Bud Light] is about fun, being with friends, and good times," says a senior Budweiser ad agency executive, "and we can do that within the boundaries of good taste."[17]

Communicators can also use negative emotional appeals, such as fear, guilt, and shame that get people to do things they should (brush their teeth, eat better, buy new tyres) or to stop doing things they shouldn't (smoke, drink too much, eat unhealthy foods). For example, an ad for TLC's show *Honey We're Killing the Kids* (a reality show that tries to get families to eat healthier) teaches "Life Lesson #74: Sometimes being their best friend is not being their best friend." And Etonic ads ask, "What would you do if you couldn't run?" They go on to note that Etonic athletic shoes are designed to avoid injuries—they're "built so you can last."

Moral appeals are directed to the audience's sense of what is "right" and "proper." They are often used to urge people to support social causes such as a cleaner environment, better race relations, equal rights for women, and aid to the disadvantaged. An example of a moral appeal is the Salvation Army headline, "While you're trying to figure out what to get the man who has everything, don't forget the man who has nothing."

Message Structure

Marketers must also decide how to handle three message structure issues. The first is whether to draw a conclusion or leave it to the audience. Research suggests that in many cases, rather than drawing a conclusion, the advertiser is better off asking questions and letting buyers come to their own conclusions. The second message structure issue is whether to present the strongest arguments first or last. Presenting them first gets strong attention but may lead to an anticlimactic ending.

The third message structure issue is whether to present a one-sided argument (mentioning only the product's strengths) or a two-sided argument (touting the product's strengths while also admitting its shortcomings). Usually, a one-sided argument is more effective in sales presentations—except when audiences are highly educated or likely to hear opposing claims, or when the communicator has a negative association to overcome. In this spirit, Heinz ran the message "Heinz Ketchup is slow good" and Listerine ran the message "Listerine tastes bad twice a day." In such cases, two-sided messages can enhance the advertiser's credibility and make buyers more resistant to competitor attacks.

Message Format

The marketing communicator also needs a strong *format* for the message. In a print ad, the communicator has to decide on the headline, copy, illustration, and color. To attract attention, advertisers can use novelty and contrast; eye-catching pictures and headlines; distinctive formats; message size and position; and color, shape, and movement. If the message is to be carried over the radio, the communicator has to choose words, sounds, and voices. The "sound" of an ad promoting banking services should be different from one promoting an iPod.

CAROUSEL. FOR SERIOUS FOOD LOVERS.

Indulge in your passion for food at Carousel – Singapore's only restaurant to offer a stunning variety of cuisine and four distinct dining atmospheres, all under one roof. Call (65) 6589 7799 for reservations.

Royal Plaza on Scotts, 25 Scotts Road, Singapore 228220 www.royalplaza.com.sg Email: carousel@royalplaza.com.sg

To attract attention, advertisers can use novelty and contrast; eye-catching pictures and headlines; distinctive formats; message size and position; and color, shape, and movement.

If the message is to be carried on television or in person, then all these elements plus body language must be planned. Presenters plan every detail—their facial expressions, gestures, dress, posture, and hairstyles. If the message is carried on the product or its package, the communicator has to watch texture, scent, color, size, and shape. For example, age and other demographics affect the way in which consumers perceive and react to color. Here are examples:

● How do you sell margarine—stodgy, wholesome margarine—to today's kids? One answer: color. "We knew we wanted to introduce a color product. It has been a big trend with kids since the blue M&M," says a Parkay spokesperson. So Parkay tried out margarine in blue, pink, green, and purple. "When we tested four different colors in focus groups, kids had a blast." Electric blue and shocking pink margarine emerged as clear favorites. In contrast, as we get older, our eyes mature and our vision takes on a yellow cast. Color looks less bright to older people, so they gravitate to white and other bright tones. A recent survey found 10 percent of people 55 years and older want the brightness of a white car, compared with 4 percent of 21- to 34-year-olds and 2 percent of teens. Lexus, which skews toward older buyers, makes sure that 60 percent of its cars are light in color.[18]

Thus, in designing effective marketing communications, marketers must consider color and other seemingly unimportant details carefully.

Choosing Media

The communicator must now select *channels of communication*. There are two broad types of communication channels—personal and nonpersonal.

Personal Communication Channels

In **personal communication channels**, two or more people communicate directly with each other. They might communicate face to face, on the phone, through mail or e-mail, or even through an Internet "chat." Personal communication channels are effective because they allow for personal addressing and feedback.

Some personal communication channels are controlled directly by the company. For example, company salespeople contact target buyers. But other personal communications about the product may reach buyers through channels not directly controlled by the company. These channels might include independent experts—consumer advocates, online buying guides, and others—making statements to buyers. Or they might be neighbors, friends, family members, and associates talking to target buyers. This last channel, known as **word-of-mouth influence**, has considerable effect in many product areas.

Personal influence carries great weight for products that are expensive, risky, or highly visible. Consider the power of simple customer reviews on Amazon.com:

● It does not matter how loud or how often you tell consumers your "truth," few today are buying a big-ticket item before they know what existing users have to say about the product. This is a low-trust world. That is why "recommendation by a relative or friend" comes out on top in just about every survey of purchasing influences. A recent study found that more than 90 percent of customers trust "recommendations from consumers," whereas trust in ads runs from a high of about 40 percent to less than 10 percent. It is also a major reason for Amazon's success in growing sales per customer. Who has not made an Amazon purchase based on another customer's review or the "Customers who bought this also bought…" section? And it explains what a recent Shop.org survey found—that 96 percent of retailers find ratings and reviews to be an effective tactic in lifting online sales.[19]

Personal communication channels
Channels through which two or more people communicate directly with each other, including face to face, on the phone, through mail or e-mail, or even through an Internet "chat."

Word-of-mouth influence
Personal communication about a product between target buyers and neighbors, friends, family members, and associates.

Word-of-mouth influence has considerable effect in many areas as a personal communication channel.

Companies can take steps to put personal communication channels to work for them. For example, they can create opinion leaders for their brands—people whose opinions are sought by others—by supplying influencers with the product on attractive terms or by educating them so that they can inform others. **Buzz marketing** involves cultivating opinion leaders and getting them to spread information about a product or service to others in their communities. Consider BzzAgent, a Boston marketing firm that creates word-of-mouth campaigns for many of the country's best-known companies.

Buzz marketing
Cultivating opinion leaders and getting them to spread information about a product or service to others in their communities.

BzzAgent has assembled a nationwide volunteer army of 130,000 natural-born buzzers, and they will channel their chatter toward products and services they deem authentically worth talking about. "Our goal is to find a way to capture honest word of mouth," says David Baiter, BzzAgent's founder, "and to build a network that will turn passionate customers into brand evangelists." Once a client signs on, BzzAgent searches its database for "agents" matching the demographic and psychographic profile of target customers of the product or service. Selected volunteers receive a sample product and a training manual for buzz-creating strategies. These volunteers are not just mall rats on mobile phones. Some 65 percent are over 25, 60 percent are women, and two are Fortune 500 CEOs. They have buzzed products as diverse as Estee Lauder facial masks, Lee Jeans, Rock Bottom Restaurants, and The March of Dimes. In Alabama, BzzAgent ArnoldGinger123 buttonholed her probation officer to chat up a tush-flattering new brand of jeans. In Illinois, BzzAgent GeminiDreams spent a family Christmas party extolling the features of Monster.com's new networking site. And, in an especially moving final tribute in New Jersey, BzzAgent Karnj buzzed her grandpa into the great beyond with a round of Anheuser World Select beer at the old gent's wake. The service's appeal is its authenticity. "What I like is that BzzAgents are not scripted," says Steve Cook, vice president of worldwide strategic marketing at Coca-Cola. "[The company tells its agents,] 'Here is the information; if you believe in it, say whatever you think.' It is… genuine."[20]

Taking advantage of personal communications channels: BzzAgent's army of 130,000 natural-born buzzers creates word-of-mouth chatter for many of the world's best-known brands.

Nonpersonal Communication Channels

Nonpersonal communication channels are media that carry messages without personal contact or feedback. They include major media, atmospheres, and events. Major media include print media (newspapers, magazines, direct mail), broadcast media (radio, television), display media (billboards, signs, posters), and online media (e-mail, Web sites). *Atmospheres* are designed environments that create or reinforce the buyer's leanings toward buying a product. Thus, lawyers' offices and banks are designed to communicate confidence and other qualities that might be valued by clients. Events are staged occurrences that communicate messages to target audiences. For example, public relations departments arrange press conferences, grand openings, shows and exhibits, public tours, and other events. Shanghai Volkswagen's Family Olympic Campaign did this effectively (see **Real Marketing 14.2**).

Nonpersonal communication channels
Media that carry messages without personal contact or feedback, including major media, atmospheres, and events.

REAL MARKETING 14.2

Getting Into the Olympic Spirit: Shanghai Volkswagen

Shanghai Volkswagen is a significant partner at the 2008 Beijing Summer Olympics, and the company has put much effort into raising awareness for sports and the Olympics by organising events such as the Family Olympics.

Shanghai Volkswagen is currently the biggest joint venture in China and it is also the first car-making enterprise to enter the Chinese market. After running a business in China for more than 20 years, Shanghai Volkswagen has the biggest market share of the passenger vehicle industry with 2.5 million cars in China.

After Beijing's successful bid for the 2008 Olympics, Volkswagen Group became a partner in the 2008 Beijing Olympics. At the advent of the Olympics, it organized the "Shanghai Volkswagen Championship" Family Olympics as a vehicle to promote Volkswagen cars. The preliminary contests were held in Guangzhou, Shenzhen, Dongguan, and Foshan, while the final was held in Guangzhou. The contest included several indoor athletics events under the theme of passenger vehicles and the Olympics. The event focuses on the interaction

Marketers hire celebrities to deliver their messages: Tiger Woods lends his image to Nike, while Jackie Chan endorses everything from Visa to Chinese frozen foods.

Nonpersonal communication affects buyers directly. In addition, using mass media often affects buyers indirectly by causing more personal communication. Communications first flow from television, magazines, and other mass media to opinion leaders and then from these opinion leaders to others. Thus, opinion leaders step between the mass media and their audiences and carry messages to people who are less exposed to media. This suggests that mass communicators should aim their messages directly at opinion leaders, letting them carry the message to others.

Interestingly, marketers often use nonpersonal communications channels to replace or stimulate personal communications by embedding consumer endorsements or word-of-mouth testimonials in their ads and other promotions.

Selecting the Message Source

In either personal or nonpersonal communication, the message's impact on the target audience is also affected by how the audience views the communicator. Messages delivered by highly credible sources are more persuasive. Thus, many food companies promote between cars and people as well as on the combination of competition and entertainment. The purpose of the activity was to promote the sporting spirit.

The event was hosted by the South China Sales and Services Center of Shanghai Volkswagen and jointly organized by Shanghai Lanmeng Advertising Co. Ltd., Southern Metropolitan Daily, and the Sports Federation of Guangdong Province.

Research and analysis

As the cradle of numerous Olympic champions, the Guangdong area has always put great emphasis on sport. Sporting activities are therefore usually welcomed by people in this area. Clients of Shanghai Volkswagen completed a survey about their interest in the activity. The results show that most clients are willing to participate in the event because they treat it as a warm-up activity for the Beijing Olympics, as well as an opportunity to carry out a routine check-up on their cars. With the co-operation of dealers in different cities, activities with a unique local style are held. These include a Chinese martial arts show in Foshan, a donation

ceremony in Guangzhou School, and a sports apparatus donation ceremony in Dongguan Secondary School.

The partners and working groups

The collaborative partners in Guangzhou have played important roles in the organization of the event. They have provided all the necessary materials for the decoration of exhibition halls in different cities efficiently, once the designs were approved by the Shanghai headquarters.

Working groups are also set up to coordinate with the clients, advertising company, dealers, and government departments. Details of the event are also discussed and modified one week in advance to ensure its complete success.

The "Shanghai Volkswagen Championship" Family Olympics has gained extensive coverage in different media. There are more than 30 articles that cover the event in various printed media such as Guangzhou Daily, Foshan Daily, and Yangcheng Evening News. Internet media such as 21CN.com draw public attention by providing a specially designed Web page to report the event.

This event has received positive responses from different sectors and

also has the support of the Guangdong province government. High-ranking officials of Guangdong province attended the opening ceremony of the event. Shanghai Volkswagen has been praised for its commitment to public welfare, rather than merely concerning itself with the economic benefits to the company. Some experts in the industry noted that the event has successfully improved the brand image of Shanghai Volkswagen by highlighting its sincerity in contributing to society through providing an alternative way for citizens to participate in the Olympics. Public awareness and accessibility of the brand are significantly raised through various contests and activities, which indirectly promote sales.

Source:
Li, W. S., China Market Promotion Report, Beijing, Business Management Publisher, 2004, p. 85–90; online accessed at http://www.csvw.com/csvw/index.shtml

to doctors, dentists, and other health care providers to motivate these professionals to recommend their products to patients. And marketers hire celebrity endorsers—well-known athletes, actors, and even cartoon characters—to deliver their messages. Golfer Tiger Woods speaks for Nike, Buick, Accenture, and a dozen other brands. Movie star Jackie Chan vouches for Visa and Hong Kong Tourist Association. NASCAR superstar Jeff Gordon pitches everything from Ray-Ban sunglasses to Pepsi and Edy's ice cream. Chinese actress Gong Li lends her image to cosmetic brand L'Oréal.

But companies must be careful when selecting celebrities to represent their brands. Picking the wrong spokesperson or endorser can result in embarrassment and a tarnished image. Adidas experienced this when one half of popular Hong Kong singing duo Twins, Gillian Chung, appeared in erotic photos circulated on the Internet. H&M, Chanel, and Burberry had to publicly dismiss supermodel Kate Moss after she was reportedly photographed using cocaine. And Pepsi, McDonald's, Roots, and Ford faced embarrassment when gambling scandals threatened to dirty the squeaky-clean image of their spokesperson, hockey great Wayne Gretzky. "Arranged marriages between brands and celebrities are inherently risky," notes an expert. "Today it is standard practice to sign a celeb only after an extensive background check. But accidents still happen."[21]

After sending the message, the communicator must research its effect on the target audience by collecting feedback.

Collecting Feedback

After sending the message, the communicator must research its effect on the target audience. This involves asking the target audience members whether they remember the message, how many times they saw it, what points they recall, how they felt about the message, and their past and present attitudes toward the product and company. The communicator would also like to measure behavior resulting from the message—how many people bought a product, talked to others about it, or visited the store.

Feedback on marketing communications may suggest changes in the promotion program or in the product offer itself. For example, JetBlue Airways uses television and newspaper advertising to inform area consumers about the airline, its routes, and its fares. Suppose feedback research shows that 80 percent of all fliers in an area recall seeing the airline's ads and are aware of its flights and prices. Sixty percent of these aware fliers have flown JetBlue, but only 20 percent of those who tried it were satisfied. These results suggest that although promotion is creating *awareness*, the airline is not giving consumers the *satisfaction* they expect. Therefore, JetBlue needs to improve its service while staying with the successful communication program. In contrast, suppose the research shows that only 40 percent of area consumers are aware of the airline, only 30 percent of those aware have tried it, but 80 percent of those who have tried it return. In this case, JetBlue needs to strengthen its promotion program to take advantage of its power to create customer satisfaction.

Setting the Total Promotion Budget and Mix

We have looked at the steps in planning and sending communications to a target audience. But how does the company decide on the total *promotion budget* and its division among the major promotional tools to create the *promotion mix*? By what process does it blend the tools to create integrated marketing communications? We now look at these questions.

Setting the Total Promotion Budget

One of the hardest marketing decisions facing a company is how much to spend on promotion. John Wanamaker, the U.S. department store magnate, once said, "I know that half of my advertising is wasted, but I don't know which half. I spent $2 million for advertising, and I don't know if that is half enough or twice too much." Thus, it is not surprising that industries and companies vary widely in how much they spend on promotion. Promotion spending may be 10 to 12 percent of sales for consumer packaged goods and less than one percent for industrial machinery products. Within a given industry, both low and high spenders can be found.[22]

How does a company decide on its promotion budget? We look at four common methods used to set the total budget for advertising: the *affordable method*, the *percentage-of-sales method*, the *competitive-parity method*, and the *objective-and-task method*.[23]

Affordable Method

Some companies use the **affordable method**: They set the promotion budget at the level they think the company can afford. Small businesses often use this method, reasoning

Affordable method
Setting the promotion budget at the level management thinks the company can afford.

that the company cannot spend more on advertising than it has. They start with total revenues, deduct operating expenses and capital outlays, and then devote some portion of the remaining funds to advertising.

Unfortunately, this method of setting budgets completely ignores the effects of promotion on sales. It tends to place promotion last among spending priorities, even in situations in which advertising is critical to the firm's success. It leads to an uncertain annual promotion budget, which makes long-range market planning difficult. Although the affordable method can result in overspending on advertising, it more often results in underspending.

Percentage-of-Sales Method

Other companies use the **percentage-of-sales method**, setting their promotion budget at a certain percentage of current or forecasted sales. Or they budget a percentage of the unit sales price. The percentage-of-sales method has advantages. It is simple to use and helps management think about the relationships between promotion spending, selling price, and profit per unit.

Despite these claimed advantages, however, the percentage-of-sales method has little to justify it. It wrongly views sales as the cause of promotion rather than as the result. Although studies have found a positive correlation between promotional spending and brand strength, this relationship often turns out to be effect and cause, not cause and effect. Stronger brands with higher sales can afford the biggest ad budgets.

Thus, the percentage-of-sales budget is based on availability of funds rather than on opportunities. It may prevent the increased spending sometimes needed to turn around falling sales. Because the budget varies with year-to-year sales, long-range planning is difficult. Finally, the method does not provide any basis for choosing a specific percentage, except what has been done in the past or what competitors are doing.

Competitive-Parity Method

Still other companies use the **competitive-parity method**, setting their promotion budgets to match competitors' outlays. They monitor competitors' advertising or get industry promotion spending estimates from publications or trade associations, and then they set their budgets based on the industry average.

Two arguments support this method. First, competitors' budgets represent the collective wisdom of the industry. Second, spending what competitors spend helps prevent promotion wars. Unfortunately, neither argument is valid. There are no grounds for believing that the competition has a better idea of what a company should be spending on promotion than does the company itself. Companies differ greatly, and each has its own special promotion needs. Finally, there is no evidence that budgets based on competitive parity prevent promotion wars.

Objective-and-Task Method

The most logical budget-setting method is the **objective-and-task method**, whereby the company sets its promotion budget based on what it wants to accomplish with promotion. This budgeting method entails (1) defining specific promotion objectives, (2) determining the tasks needed to achieve these objectives, and (3) estimating the costs of performing these tasks. The sum of these costs is the proposed promotion budget.

The advantage of the objective-and-task method is that it forces management to spell out its assumptions about the relationship between dollars spent and promotion results. But it is also the most difficult method to use. Often, it is hard to figure out which specific tasks will achieve stated objectives. For example, suppose Sony wants 95 percent awareness for its latest camcorder model during the six-month introductory period. What specific advertising messages and media schedules should Sony use to attain this objective? How much would these messages and media schedules cost? Sony management must consider such questions, even though they are hard to answer.

Percentage-of-sales method
Setting the promotion budget at a certain percentage of current or forecasted sales or as a percentage of the unit sales price.

Competitive-parity method
Setting the promotion budget to match competitors' outlays.

Objective-and-task method
Developing the promotion budget by (1) defining specific objectives; (2) determining the tasks that must be performed to achieve these objectives; and (3) estimating the costs of performing these tasks. The sum of these costs is the proposed promotion budget.

Shaping the Overall Promotion Mix

The concept of integrated marketing communications suggests that the company must blend the promotion tools carefully into a coordinated promotion mix. But how does the company determine what mix of promotion tools it will use? Companies within the same industry differ greatly in the design of their promotion mixes. For example, Mary Kay spends most of its promotion funds on personal selling and direct marketing, whereas SKII spends heavily on consumer advertising. HP relies on advertising and promotion to retailers, whereas Dell uses more direct marketing. We now look at factors that influence the marketer's choice of promotion tools.

The Nature of Each Promotion Tool

Each promotion tool has unique characteristics and costs. Marketers must understand these characteristics in shaping the promotion mix (see **Table 14.1**).

Promotion mix –
Companies within the same industry may use different mixes. Mary Kay relies heavily on personal selling and direct marketing; CoverGirl devotes significant resources to advertising.

Advertising

Advertising can reach masses of geographically dispersed buyers at a low cost per exposure, and it enables the seller to repeat a message many times. For example, television advertising can reach huge audiences. An estimated 141 million Americans tuned in to at least part of the most recent Super Bowl; about 38 million people watched at least part

Table 14.1 Nature of Each Promotion Tool

	Pluses	Minuses
Advertising	• Can reach masses of geographically dispersed buyers at a low cost per exposure • Enables the seller to repeat a message many times • Consumers tend to view advertised products as more legitimate • Very expressive and allows the company to dramatize its products	• Impersonal • One-way communication • Costly
Personal selling	• Effective in building up buyers' preferences, convictions, and actions • Allows personal interaction • Allows all kinds of customer relationships to develop • Buyer usually feels a greater need to listen and respond	• Requires a longer-term commitment • Most expensive promotion tool
Sales promotion	• Attract consumer attention • Offer strong incentives to purchase • Can be used to dramatize product offers and to boost sagging sales • Invite and reward quick customer response	• Effects are short-lived • Not as effective in building long-run brand preference and customer relationships
Public relations	• Very believable • Can reach prospects who avoid salespeople and advertisements • Can dramatize a company or a product	
Direct marketing	• Nonpublic • Immediate • Customized • Interactive • Well suited to highly targeted marketing efforts and building one-to-one customer relationships	

of the last Academy Awards broadcast; and 33.6 million fans tuned in to watch the debut episode of the fourth season of *American Idol*. For companies that want to reach a mass audience, TV is the place to be.[24]

Beyond its reach, large-scale advertising says something positive about the seller's size, popularity, and success. Because of advertising's public nature, consumers tend to view advertised products as more legitimate. Advertising is also very expressive—it allows the company to dramatize its products through the artful use of visuals, print, sound, and color. On the one hand, advertising can be used to build up a long-term image for a product (such as Coca-Cola ads). On the other hand, advertising can trigger quick sales (as when Kohl's advertises weekend specials).

Advertising also has some shortcomings. Although it reaches many people quickly, advertising is impersonal and cannot be as directly persuasive as can company salespeople. For the most part, advertising can carry on only a one-way communication with the audience, and the audience does not feel that it has to pay attention or respond. In addition, advertising can be very costly. Although some advertising forms, such as newspaper and radio advertising, can be done on smaller budgets, other forms, such as network TV advertising, require very large budgets.

Personal selling

Personal selling is the most effective tool at certain stages of the buying process, particularly in building up buyers' preferences, convictions, and actions. It involves personal interaction between two or more people, so each person can observe the other's needs and characteristics and make quick adjustments. Personal selling also allows all kinds of customer relationships to spring up, ranging from matter-of-fact selling relationships to personal friendships. An effective salesperson keeps the customer's interests at heart in order to build a long-term relationship by solving customer problems. Finally, with personal selling, the buyer usually feels a greater need to listen and respond, even if the response is a polite "No thank you."

Personal selling is the most effective tool at certain stages of the buying process, particularly in building up buyers' preferences, convictions, and actions.

These unique qualities come at a cost, however. A sales force requires a longer-term commitment than does advertising—advertising can be turned on and off, but sales force size is harder to change. Personal selling is also the company's most expensive promotion tool, costing companies $329 on average per sales call. In some industries, the average cost of a sales call reaches $452.[25] U.S. firms spend up to three times as much on personal selling as they do on advertising.

Sales promotion

Sales promotion includes a wide assortment of tools—coupons, contests, cents-off deals, premiums, and others—all of which have many unique qualities. They attract consumer attention, offer strong incentives to purchase, and can be used to dramatize product offers and to boost sagging sales. Sales promotions invite and reward quick response—whereas advertising says, "Buy our product," sales promotion says, "Buy it now." Sales promotion effects are often short-lived, however, and often are not as effective as advertising or personal selling in building long-run brand preference and customer relationships.

Public relations

Public relations is very believable—news stories, features, sponsorships, and events seem more real and believable to readers than ads do. Public relations can also reach many prospects who avoid salespeople and advertisements—the message gets to the buyers as "news" rather than as a sales-directed communication. And, as with advertising, public relations can dramatize a company or product. Marketers tend to underuse public relations or to use it as an afterthought. Yet a well-thought-out public relations campaign used with other promotion mix elements can be very effective and economical.

Push strategy
A promotion strategy that calls for using the sales force and trade promotion to push the product through channels. The producer promotes the product to channel members to induce them to carry the product and to promote it to final consumers.

Pull strategy
A promotion strategy that calls for spending a lot on advertising and consumer promotion to induce final consumers to buy the product. If the pull strategy is effective, consumers will then demand the product from channel members, who will in turn demand it from producers.

Direct marketing

Although there are many forms of direct marketing—direct mail and catalogs, telephone marketing, online marketing, and others—they all share four distinctive characteristics. Direct marketing is *nonpublic*: The message is normally directed to a specific person. Direct marketing is *immediate* and *customized*: Messages can be prepared very quickly and can be tailored to appeal to specific consumers. Finally, direct marketing is interactive: It allows a dialog between the marketing team and the consumer, and messages can be altered depending on the consumer's response. Thus, direct marketing is well suited to highly targeted marketing efforts and to building one-to-one customer relationships.

Promotion Mix Strategies

Marketers can choose from two basic promotion mix strategies—push promotion or pull promotion. **Figure 14.6** contrasts the two strategies. The relative emphasis on the specific promotion tools differs for push and pull strategies. A **push strategy** involves "pushing" the product through marketing channels to final consumers. The producer directs its marketing activities (primarily personal selling and trade promotion) toward channel members to induce them to carry the product and to promote it to final consumers.

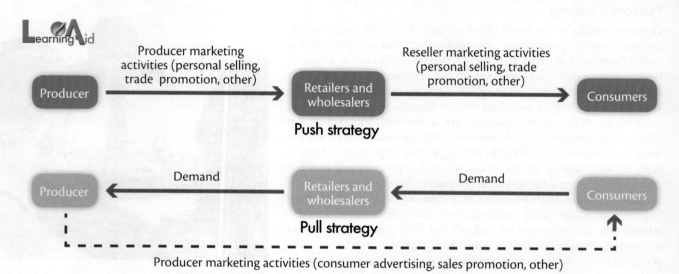

Figure 14.6
Push versus pull promotion strategy

Using a **pull strategy**, the producer directs its marketing activities (primarily advertising and consumer promotion) toward final consumers to induce them to buy the product. If the pull strategy is effective, consumers will then demand the product from channel members, who will in turn demand it from producers. Thus, under a pull strategy, consumer demand "pulls" the product through the channels.

Some industrial goods companies use only push strategies; some direct-marketing companies use only pull strategies. However, most large companies use some combination of both. For example, Kraft uses mass-media advertising and consumer promotions to pull its products and a large sales force and trade promotions to push its products through the channels. In recent years, consumer goods companies have been decreasing the pull portions of their mixes in favor of more push. This has caused concern that they may be driving short-run sales at the expense of long-term brand equity (see **Real Marketing 14.3**).

Companies consider many factors when designing their promotion mix strategies, including type of product/market and the product life-cycle stage. For example, the importance of different promotion tools varies between consumer and business markets. Business-to-consumer (B2C) companies usually "pull" more, putting more of their funds into advertising, followed by sales promotion, personal selling, and then public relations. In contrast, business-to-business (B2B) marketers tend to "push" more, putting more of their funds into personal selling, followed by sales promotion, advertising, and public relations. In general, personal selling is used more heavily with expensive and risky goods and in markets with fewer and larger sellers.

The effects of different promotion tools also vary with stages of the product life cycle. In the introduction stage, advertising and public relations are good for producing high awareness, and sales promotion is useful in promoting early trial. Personal selling must be used to get the trade to carry the product. In the growth stage, advertising and public relations continue to be powerful influences, whereas sales promotion can be reduced because fewer incentives are needed. In the mature stage, sales promotion again becomes important relative to advertising. Buyers know the brands, and advertising is needed only to remind them of the product. In the decline stage, advertising is kept at a reminder level, public relations is dropped, and salespeople give the product only a little attention. Sales promotion, however, might continue to be strong.

Integrating the Promotion Mix

Having set the promotion budget and mix, the company must now take steps to see that all of the promotion mix elements are smoothly integrated. Here is a checklist for integrating the firm's marketing communications.[26]

- Analyze trends—internal and external—that can affect the company's ability to do business. Look for areas where communications can help the most. Determine the strengths and weaknesses of each communications function. Develop a combination of promotional tactics based on these strengths and weaknesses.
- Audit the pockets of communications spending throughout the organization. Itemize the communications budgets and tasks and consolidate these into a single budgeting process. Reassess all communications expenditures by product, promotional tool, stage of the life cycle, and observed effect.
- Identify all customer touch points for the company and its brands. Work to ensure that communications at each touch point are consistent with the overall communications strategy and that communications efforts are occurring when, where, and how customers want them.
- Team up in communications planning. Engage all communications functions in joint planning. Include customers, suppliers, and other stakeholders at every stage of communications planning.
- Create compatible themes, tones, and quality across all communications media. Make sure each element carries the company's unique primary messages and selling points. This consistency achieves greater impact and prevents the unnecessary duplication of work across functions.
- Create performance measures that are shared by all communications elements. Develop systems to evaluate the combined impact of all communications activities.
- Appoint a director responsible for the company's persuasive communications efforts. This move encourages efficiency by centralizing planning and creating shared performance measures.

Socially Responsible Marketing Communication

In shaping its promotion mix, a company must be aware of the large body of legal and ethical issues surrounding marketing communications. Most marketers work hard to communicate openly and honestly with consumers and resellers. Still, abuses may occur, and public policy makers have developed a substantial body of laws and regulations to govern advertising, sales promotion, personal selling, and direct-marketing activities. In this section, we discuss issues regarding advertising, sales promotion, and personal selling. We discuss issues regarding direct marketing in Chapter 17.

Advertising and Sales Promotion

By law, companies must avoid false or deceptive advertising. Advertisers must not make false claims, such as suggesting that a product cures something when it does not. They must avoid ads that have the capacity to deceive, even though no one actually may be deceived. An automobile cannot be advertised as getting 32 miles per gallon unless it does so under typical conditions, and a diet bread cannot be advertised as having fewer calories simply because its slices are thinner.

By law, companies must avoid false claims and ads that have the capacity to deceive, even though no one actually may be deceived.

REAL MARKETING 14.3

Are Consumer Goods Companies Too Pushy?

Too pushy? Some categories tend to self-destruct by always being on sale. For example, when automakers get promotion happy, the market just sits back and waits for a deal while the car companies lose money on profit-eating incentives

Consumer packaged-goods companies such as Procter & Gamble, Master Kang, Kellogg, and President grew enormously by using mostly pull promotion strategies. They used massive doses of national advertising to differentiate their products, gain market share, and build brand equity and customer loyalty. But during the past few decades, such companies have gotten more "pushy," deemphasizing national advertising and putting more of their marketing budgets into trade and consumer sales promotions.

General trade promotions (trade allowances, displays, cooperative advertising, and slotting fees aimed at retailers) now account for 58 percent of total marketing spending by consumer product companies. That represents a six-percentage-point increase in trade spending in just the past eight years. Consumer promotions (coupons, discounts, premiums) account for another 16 percent of the typical marketing budget. That leaves less than 26 percent of total marketing spending for mass-media advertising, down from 42 percent 20 years ago.

Why have these companies shifted so heavily toward push strategies? One reason is that mass-media campaigns have become more expensive and less effective in recent years. Network television costs have risen sharply, while audiences have fallen off, making national advertising less cost effective. Companies are also tailoring their marketing programs more narrowly, making national advertising less suitable than localized retailer promotions. And in these days of brand extensions and me-too products, companies sometimes have trouble finding meaningful product differences to feature in advertising. So they have differentiated their products through price reductions, premium offers, coupons, and other push techniques.

Sellers must avoid bait-and-switch advertising that attracts buyers under false pretenses. For example, a large retailer advertised a sewing machine at $179. However, when consumers tried to buy the advertised machine, the seller downplayed its features, placed faulty machines on showroom floors, understated the machine's performance, and took other actions in an attempt to switch buyers to a more expensive machine. Such actions are both unethical and illegal.

A company's trade promotion activities also are closely regulated. For example, in the U.S., under the Robinson-Patman Act, sellers cannot favor certain customers through their use of trade promotions. They must make promotional allowances and services available to all resellers on proportionately equal terms.

Beyond simply avoiding legal pitfalls, such as deceptive or bait-and-switch advertising, companies can use advertising and other forms of promotion to encourage and promote

Another factor speeding the shift from pull to push has been the growing strength of retailers. Big retailers such as Wal-Mart, Target, Parknshop, and Safeway now have the power to demand and get what they want—and what they want is more push. Whereas advertising bypasses them on its way to the masses, push promotion benefits them directly. Thus, producers must often use push just to obtain good shelf space and other support from important retailers.

However, many marketers are concerned that the reckless use of push will lead to fierce price competition and a never-ending spiral of price slashing and deal making. If used improperly, push promotion can mortgage a brand's future for short-term gains. Sales promotion buys short-run reseller support and consumer sales, but advertising builds long-run brand equity and consumer preference. By robbing the media advertising budget to pay for more sales promotion, companies might win the battle for short-run earnings but lose the war for long-run brand equity, consumer loyalty, and market share. In fact, some analysts blame the shift away from advertising dollars for a recent two-decade-long drop in the percentage of consumers who buy only well-known brands.

Of special concern is the overuse of price promotions. The regular use of price as a selling tool can destroy brand equity by encouraging consumers to seek value though price rather than through the benefits of the brand. For example, one recent study showed that decreased TV spending and increased

trade promotions for Diet Coke and Coca-Cola Classic over a five-year period eroded equity for both brands, while at the same time increasing consumer price and promotion sensitivity.

In cases where price is a key part of the brand's positioning, featuring price makes sense. But for brands where price does not underlie value, "price promotions are really desperate acts by brands that have their backs against the wall," says one marketing executive. "Generally speaking, it is better to stick to your guns with price and invest in advertising to drive sales."

Jack Trout, a well-known marketing consultant, cautions that some categories tend to self-destruct by always being on sale. Furniture, automobile tyres, airline tickets, and many other categories of goods are rarely sold at anything near list price. And when automakers get rebate happy, the market just sits back and waits for a deal while the car companies lose money on profit-eating incentives. For example, in 2004, General Motors doled out billions of dollars in sales incentives—discounted prices, rebates, and low-cost financing—to move cars out of its showrooms. "While pinching pennies on its $3.5 billion media-buying budget," says an industry expert, "it's giving away $17 billion in incentives—undermining its brand-building efforts." Such promotion tactics have done little to win profits or customer loyalty over the years. Last year, GM lost a staggering $10.5 billion, and its domestic market share has dwindled to less than 25 percent, down from 44.5 percent in 1980.

Trout offers several "Commandments of Discounting," such as "Thou shalt not offer discounts because everyone else does," "Thou shalt be creative with your discounting," "Thou shalt put time limits on the deal," and "Thou shalt stop discounting as soon as you can."

Thus, many consumer companies are now rethinking their promotion strategies and reversing the trend by shifting their promotion budgets back toward advertising. They realize that it is not a question of sales promotion versus advertising, or of push versus pull. Success lies in finding the best mix of the two: consistent advertising to build long-run brand value and consumer preference, and sales promotion to create short-run trade support and consumer excitement. The company needs to blend both push and pull elements into an integrated marketing communications program that meets immediate consumer and retailer needs as well as long-run strategic needs.

Sources:
Promotion spending statistics from 2005 Trade Promotion Spending & Merchandising Industry Study (Cannondale Associates, Wilton, CT, May 2006), p. 13. Other information from Jack Trout, "Prices: Simple Guidelines to Get Them Right," Journal of Business Strategy, November-December 1998, pp. 13–16; Alan Mitchell, "When Push Comes to Shove, It is All About Pull," Marketing Week, January 9, 2003, pp. 26–27; E. Craig Stacey, "Abandon TV at Your Own Risk," Advertising Age, June 7, 2004, p. 32; Jean Halliday, "GM Bleeds as Incentives Undermine Brand Value," Advertising Age, March 21, 2005, pp. 1, 37; and "General Motors Corporation," Hoover's Company Records, May 15, 2006, p. 10640.

socially responsible programs and actions. For example, Caterpillar is one of several companies and environmental groups forming the Tropical Forest Foundation, which is working to save the great Amazon rain forest. Caterpillar promotes the cause through advertising and pages on its Web site. Similarly, Mont Blanc supports the National Arts Education Initiative in its efforts to raise awareness about the need for arts education in schools. Its ads state: "Time is precious. Use it wisely. To invest in our future, we must nurture our children's fantasies and inspire their creativity." And for more than a decade, Avon has sponsored the Avon Breast Cancer Crusade, dedicated to funding access to care and finding a cure for breast cancer. Through advertising and a variety of promotions—such as the Avon Walk for Breast Cancer, charity cruises, and the sale of pink ribbon products—Avon's crusade has raised more the $400 million for this worthwhile cause.[27]

Personal Selling

A company's salespeople must follow the rules of "fair competition." Most states have enacted deceptive sales acts that spell out what is not allowed. For example, salespeople may not lie to consumers or mislead them about the advantages of buying a product. To avoid bait-and-switch practices, salespeople's statements must match advertising claims.

Different rules apply to consumers who are called on at home versus those who go to a store in search of a product. Because people called on at home may be taken by surprise and may be especially vulnerable to high-pressure selling techniques, the Federal Trade Commission (FTC) has adopted a *three-day cooling-off rule* to give special protection to customers who are not seeking products. Under this rule, customers who agree in their own homes to buy something costing more than $25 have 72 hours in which to cancel a contract or return merchandise and get their money back, no questions asked.

Much personal selling involves business-to-business trade. In selling to businesses, salespeople may not offer bribes to purchasing agents or to others who can influence a sale. They may not obtain or use technical or trade secrets of competitors through bribery or industrial espionage. Finally, salespeople must not disparage competitors or competing products by suggesting things that are not true.[28]

REVIEWING THE CONCEPTS

In this chapter, you have learned how companies use integrated marketing communications (IMC) to communicate customer value. Modern marketing calls for more than just creating customer value by developing a good product, pricing it attractively, and making it available to target customers. Companies also must clearly and persuasively *communicate* that value to current and prospective customers. To do this, they must blend five promotion mix tools, guided by a well-designed and implemented integrated marketing communications strategy.

1 Discuss the process and advantages of integrated marketing communications in communicating customer value.

Recent shifts toward targeted or one-to-one marketing, coupled with advances in information and communication technology, have had a dramatic impact on marketing communications. As marketing communicators adopt richer but more fragmented media and promotion mixes to reach their diverse markets, they risk creating a communications hodgepodge for consumers. To prevent this, more companies are adopting the concept of *integrated marketing communications (IMC)*. Guided by an overall IMC strategy, the company works out the roles that the various promotional tools will play and the extent to which each will be used. It carefully coordinates the promotional activities and the timing of when major campaigns take place. Finally, to help implement its integrated marketing strategy, the company appoints a marketing communications director who has overall responsibility for the company's communications efforts.

2 Define the five promotion tools and discuss factors that must be considered in shaping the overall promotion mix.

A company's total *promotion mix*—also called its *marketing communications mix*—consists of the specific blend of *advertising, personal selling, sales promotion, public relations*, and *direct-marketing* tools that the company uses to persuasively communicate customer value and build customer relationships. Advertising includes any paid form of nonpersonal presentation and promotion of ideas, goods, or services by an identified sponsor. In contrast, public relations focuses on building good relations with the company's various publics by obtaining favorable

unpaid publicity. Personal selling is any form of personal presentation by the firm's sales force for the purpose of making sales and building customer relationships. Firms use sales promotion to provide short-term incentives to encourage the purchase or sale of a product or service. Finally, firms seeking immediate response from targeted individual customers use nonpersonal direct-marketing tools to communicate with customers.

3 Outline the steps in developing effective marketing communications.

In preparing marketing communications, the communicator's first task is to *identify the target audience* and its characteristics. Next, the communicator must determine the *communication objectives* and define the response sought, whether it be *awareness, knowledge, liking, preference, conviction*, or *purchase*. Then a *message* should be constructed with an effective content and structure. *Media* must be selected, both for personal and nonpersonal communication. The communicator must find highly credible sources to deliver messages. Finally, the communicator must collect *feedback* by watching how much of the market becomes aware, tries the product, and is satisfied in the process.

4 Explain the methods for setting the promotion budget and factors that affect the design of the promotion mix.

The company must decide how much to spend for promotion. The most popular approaches are to spend what the company can afford, to use a percentage of sales, to base promotion on competitors' spending, or to base it on an analysis and costing of the communication objectives and tasks.

The company divides the *promotion budget* among the major tools to create the *promotion mix*. Companies can pursue a *push* or a *pull* promotional strategy, or a combination of the two. The best specific blend of promotion tools depends on the type of product/market, the buyer's readiness stage, and the product life-cycle stage.

People at all levels of the organization must be aware of the many legal and ethical issues surrounding marketing communications. Companies must communicate openly, honestly, and agreeably with their customers and resellers.

REVIEWING THE KEY TERMS

Advertising 368
Affordable method 384
Buyer-readiness stages 376
Buzz marketing 381
Competitive-parity method 385
Direct marketing 369
Integrated marketing communications (IMC) 371
Nonpersonal communication channels 381
Objective-and-task method 3853

Percentage-of-sales method 385
Personal communication channels 380
Personal selling 369
Promotion mix (marketing communications mix) 368
Public relations 368
Pull strategy 388
Push strategy 388
Sales promotion 368
Word-of-mouth influence 380

DISCUSSING THE CONCEPTS

1. Many companies are adopting the Integrated Marketing Communication concept. Discuss two major problems that this marketing communications philosophy is designed to remedy.

2. Outline the nine elements of the communications process. Why do marketers need to understand these elements?

3. Why does the marketing communicator need to know the target market's readiness stage? Give an example of an ad targeting each stage.

4. Why might the AIG choose a rational appeal for its life insurance products targeted to 28- to 38-year-old males? Why might it choose a humor appeal?

5. Explain how a brand manager for Colgate toothpaste might use each of the common methods for setting total advertising budgets.

6. Name five types of sales that urgently need to have a cooling-off period in your country.

APPLYING THE CONCEPTS

1. Find and describe examples of advertisements or promotions that are examples of narrowcasting, nontraditional advertising, and innovative media technologies.

2. In your judgment who would be the best and the worst celebrity endorsers for each of these products/services: BMW, Dell, the 2008 Beijing Olympic.

3. Assume that Energizer is introducing a new line of batteries that provide a longer life than its existing Titanium models. The brand manager for the new line believes most of the promotion budget should be spent on consumer and trade promotions, but the assistant brand manager thinks that the promotion mix should emphasize television advertising. Partner with another student. Play the roles of the brand manager and assistant brand manager and debate their opposing views on advertising versus promotion.

FOCUS ON TECHNOLOGY

As network television viewership declines and fragments, many large advertisers are looking for alternative media. In fact, the 18- to 34-year-old male target market has reduced its hours watching television in favor of video gaming. According to Nielson Entertainment, consumers in this segment watch 9.8 hours of television a week versus 12.5 hours a week playing video games. Until recently, video game advertising posed many challenges for advertisers, including long lead times, technological issues, and the inability to change the advertising message packaged in the game.

Today, with more video games played on the Internet, in-game advertising has exploded. Companies such as Double Fusion (www.doublefusion.com) now offer dynamic, real-time advertising for online gamers. They state that this ultimate "lean-forward" environment offers unique opportunities for marketers. Advertisers can now rotate their advertising during the gaming experience, and they can use online metrics to track the advertising impressions they generate. Software giant Microsoft recently purchased Massive Inc., a pioneer of in-game advertising and is expected to take a lead in this field. The question remains as to how receptive gamers will be to such advertising. Massive hopes to enhance game realism by integrating brands into game items such as soda cans, pizza boxes, billboards, and televisions.

1. How can marketers use in-game advertising to practice IMC?

2. What might Double Fusion mean by a "lean-forward" environment? How might such an environment appeal to marketers when considering buyer-readiness stages?

3. What social responsibility concerns might in-game advertising raise?

FOCUS ON ETHICS

Interference Inc. (www.interferenceinc.com) offers guerrilla marketing approaches that enable brands to communicate with target consumers through guerrilla intercept, street teams, stunt and publicity events, and other high-impact creative executions. The company's case studies include many promotions for the Discovery Channel, including a promotion for Discovery's Nefertiti special. The Nefertiti promotion, which included 27 actors in three major cities dressed in historically accurate 12th-century BC Egyptian costume, was credited with helping the show exceed its national ratings goal. But a recent promotion by Sony Ericsson caught the attention of marketing critics. In the promotion, Sony Ericsson used actor couples pretending to be tourists visiting popular locations to promote a new mobile phone. The couples asked passersby to take their pictures with the new mobile phone's camera. Sony Ericsson also used actors posing as patrons to visit popular bars and strike up conversations that introduced the new phone to unsuspecting other patrons.

1. Why do you think guerrilla marketing is so effective?

2. What do you think of the Nefertiti guerrilla marketing tactics?

3. Do you consider the Sony Ericsson campaign to be ethical? Explain your opinion.

VIDEO CASE

Motorola

When you think of Motorola, what comes to mind? A sleek RAZR phone? Or maybe it is the impossibly thin SLVR, a cell phone, camera, and MP3 player all in one. Not so long ago, the Motorola brand was not quite so cutting edge. Competitors, such as Nextel, offered products that were more advanced and better designed. So Motorola redesigned it is products and hired Ogilvy & Mather, a global communications firm, to redefine and reposition the Motorola brand. Centered on a core, universal idea—"intelligence everywhere"—the "Moto" campaign hopes to enliven Motorola's image. Rather than convincing consumers by making direct appeals to sign contracts and buy phones, the campaign relies on a simple tagline—Moto—that Motorola hopes consumers will associate with edgy innovation.

More than just ads, the campaign reaches out to consumers through a variety of media. Ogilvy calls it "360-degree brand stewardship." In addition to print, radio, and television ads, the agency crafted interactive e-mails and helped design Motorola's Web site to convey the same lifestyle and value messages that consumers found in print and television ads. The result? Motorola, once seen as stodgy and out of date, is now a hip company with high-tech, sexy phones and annual U.S. sales of more than $31.3 billion.

After watching the video featuring Motorola, answer the following questions about integrated marketing communications.

1. How did Ogilvy & Mather apply the concepts of integrated marketing communications to build Motorola's communications strategy? What was the goal of the campaign that resulted?

2. What were Motorola's communication objectives?

3. How did Motorola's budget for the Moto campaign influence its development and success?

▤ COMPANY CASE

Neptunus Group

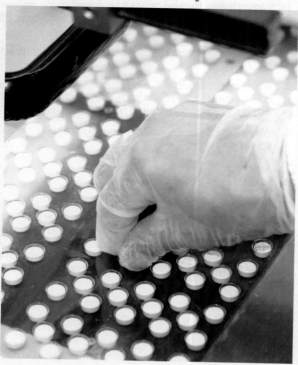

Neptunus Group, established in 1989 and headquartered in Shenzhen, China, is a large-scale integrated enterprise with total assets of over 7 billion yuan. The company produces approximately 400 types of chemical pharmaceuticals, biological pharmaceuticals, traditional Chinese medicines (TCM), and healthcare products. As of December 31, 2006, the company had six wholly owned subsidiaries, three partially owned subsidiaries, and five pharmaceutical manufacture bases. Its R&D capabilities, manufacturing system, marketing network, and logistics support is strong, and its social resources are abundant, making it one of the top players in China's pharmaceutical industry and a well-known brand in the market.

The healthcare market in China is rapidly expanding as the purchasing power of consumers grows, and has been undergoing complex and intensive transformation. China is currently the seventh largest healthcare market in the world. By 2010, it is expected to become the fifth largest with pharmaceutical sales of $24 billion.

For many years, the company has placed the Neptunus brand on the front line to promote their technological innovation and product development capabilities. They realize that success depends on their ability to establish effective advertising, marketing, and promotional programs; to be responsive to competitive pressures; and to drive demand from the target market.

At the turn of the century, Neptunus began to set the direction for their branding strategy. In 2000, the company undertook an intensive objective diagnosis of the brand. In late 2000, Neptunus announced their "21st Century Neptunus Branding Strategy Implementation Plan" wherein the core brand value was established and the strategic aim of developing Neptunus into a strong brand in the healthcare market was set. In 2001, a massive brand communication plan designed to promote their brand and corporate image was launched.

In early 2001, riding on the crest of the CCTV Spring Festival Event Program, Neptunus instigated a large-scale TV commercial promoting Neptunus Endophy, the flagship line of their over-the-counter (OTC) anti-cold drugs. This was followed by other commercials for Neptunus KingDrink and Neptunus Ginkgo, superlative items in their healthcare line and TCM. While each of these commercials spotlighted different products, they all carried the central theme of "Neptunus—Health enhances the future." This new brand advertising campaign focused on healthcare consumers' evolving needs in the area of lifetime wellness and how Neptunus as an organization can deliver to meet those needs. The campaign centered on the concept of "total health"; that is, helping individuals to be healthy at every stage of their lives. "Neptunus—Health enhances the future" was the catch phrase that described the many benefits available to Neptunus members and local communities to help them better manage their health.

During this period, the intensity of ad coverage reached 300 exposures per day nationwide. At the same time, a widespread dealer loading program was started with almost 50,000 drug stores all over China stacked with Neptunus OTC, healthcare, and prescription lines of products. This massive brand building advertising campaign not only pushed up sales of Neptunus OTC, healthcare products, and TCM, but also increased sales of their prescription drugs.

Advertising of pharmaceutical products in China is highly regulated. Consumers typically become familiar with a medicine through advertising and word-of-mouth. With increased restrictions on advertising of pharmaceutical products, pharmaceutical product manufacturers are expected to increasingly rely on more creative marketing strategies to build brand familiarity among the general public. Manufacturers of pharmaceutical products began to redirect their advertising expenditures into promoting their OTC and healthcare products, hoping that sales of these non-prescription drugs would help to increase sales of prescription drugs. The Neptunus brand building advertising campaign successfully increased consumers' awareness and acceptance of the Neptunus brand, and preference for their products.

Some proclaim that advertising, as a vehicle for brand building, is ineffectual. Perhaps, Neptunus is an exception. The Neptunus Group was named one of the Mundell 500 Asia's Most Influential Brands 2007, and ranked as number four in the pharmaceutical industry in Asia, and number one in China. They were also awarded the title of "The Most Valuable Chinese Brand 2007 (Pharmaceuticals)" by WBL (World Brand Lab) with a brand value of 12.275 billion yuan.

Questions For Discussion

1. What were Neptunus' communication objectives in 2000 for its target audience?
2. With its focus on the "total health," how did Neptunus go near to its customers? What are the implications of this?
3. Visit Neptunus' Web site (*http://www.neptunus.com*) and analyze the design of its Web site's message, including content, structure, and format. What can you conclude from this analysis? Is it effective?
4. According to this case, what had not been done by Neptunus in terms of elements of integrated marketing communications mentioned in this chapter?
5. What other recommendations would you make to Neptunus to help them improve the integration of Neptunus' promotion mix?

Sources:
Neptunus homepage: http://www.neptunus.com ; "The greatest life-science developments of 2004", accessed at http://wistechnology.com/articles/1445/?id=1445; R.D. Rusch (2003), "Is advertising effective in brand building?" accessed at http://www.brandchannel.com/features_effect.asp?pf_id=139; China Most Worth Pharmaceutical Brand 2007, accessed at http://www.healthoo.com/EN/200707/EN_20070724153441_325088.asp

Objectives

After studying this chapter, you should be able to

- define the roles of advertising in the promotion mix
- describe the major decisions involved in developing an advertising program
- define the role of public relations in the promotion mix
- explain how companies use public relations to communicate with and influence important publics

ADVERTISING AND PUBLIC RELATIONS

Previewing the Concepts

Now that we have looked at overall integrated marketing communications planning, let's dig more deeply into the specific marketing communications tools. In this chapter, we will explore advertising and public relations. Advertising involves communicating the company's or brand's value proposition by using paid media to inform, persuade, and remind consumers. Public relations involves building good relations with various company publics—from consumers and the general public to the media, investor, donor, and government publics. As with all of the promotion mix tools, advertising and public relations must be blended into the overall integrated marketing communications program. In the next two chapters, we will discuss the remaining promotion mix tools: personal selling, sales promotion, and direct marketing.

Let's start by examining some outstanding advertising. Until about three years ago, ABSOLUT was a little-known brand in the spirits industry in China. But now, thanks in large part to an industry-changing advertising campaign featuring the importance of culture in creativity, ABSOLUT has grown to become a major industry player. Here is the story.

A BSOLUT belongs to V&S Absolut Spirits a subsidiary of Vin & Spirit Group AB founded in 1917. V&S is a Swedish-owned corporation with extensive international operations. Based in Stockholm, Sweden, it operates in 12 countries and handles spirit distribution in 126 markets.

ABSOLUT is the biggest brand of V&S. Being the world's fourth largest premium spirit and number two brand of premium vodka globally, its global sales has reached more than 10 million nine-liter cases (89 million liters) in 2007, of which about 64 percent is in the U. S.

Since its launch in 1979, ABSOLUT has enjoyed a considerable growth rate worldwide of almost 1,000-fold in terms of volume over 30 years. In Åhus, a town in southern Sweden, some 500,000 bottles of ABSOLUT are produced every day from winter wheat, which gives the vodka a smooth grain character. Every year, approximately 80,000 tons of wheat are used to produce ABSOLUT by a unique process which removes all impurities by going through continuously numerous distillations.

ABSOLUT was first launched in the U. S. in 1979. At that time, Smirnoff had a solid position as market leader in the vodka category. No imported vodka in the United States had ever achieved any significant sales when faced with Smirnoff's dominance. ABSOLUT decided to position their product as "the Chivas Regal of vodkas" and adopted a premium-priced product strategy that later became the guiding principle for all its promotional activities.

However, the battle for the U. S. market was not an easy one. Gunnar Broman, the Swedish ad man who represented ABSOLUT, had to campaign endlessly for the unusual "less clear" bottle which was thought to be "too invisible," "too chubby," "too short," "too much like a blood plasma bottle" and most insultingly, "too much like a receptacle for urine samples." Luckily, the bottle has now turned out to be incredibly popular.

ABSOLUT also experienced a hard time finding distributors in the U. S. No distributor dared to try on a Swedish vodka. Finally a minor distributor, Carillon Importers, decided to take the product on, but it insisted on using its own advertising agency, instead of Swedish ad agency Carlsson & Broman.

Since then, ABSOLUT's sales have been growing in the U.S. before it looks to China as a potential market. According to Euromonitor, in 2005, the market reached 407.9 million liters and $10.93 billion in sales, enjoying a growth rate of 6.1 percent over 2004.

Growing the China Market

V&S has multiple strategic focuses. On one hand, it seeks to expand its territory globally, but at the same time, it also attempts to maintain strong local distribution in specific European markets and to enhance its strong base in the Nordic countries.

However, V&S has not been satisfied with these focuses since the U. S. and other mature Western markets provide relatively slow growth rates. Like many global marketers, ABSOLUT is looking to China as a potential growth engine. Although the vodka market in China is still small, with 507,900 liters sold in 2004 and sales of $19 million, these figures indicate a growth rate of 14 percent over 2003, as compared to 6 percent in the U. S. According to Euromonitor International, ABSOLUT, with a market share of 34 percent by volume, leads the vodka market in China as compared with 27 percent for Smirnoff in 2004.

ABSOLUT's Chinese campaigns

ABSOLUT is well known for its creative advertisements. On February 14, 2005, V&S announced an ad campaign called "ABSOLUT New Year," which reaffirmed its commitment to increase its dominance as the premium spirits brand in mainland China. Although ABSOLUT claims itself to be the leader in the Chinese premium spirits market, a vast majority of Chinese who are used to local spirits such as Motia and Wulianyi did not know ABSOLUT well. ABSOLUT New Year, which was launched during the Lunar New Year festive season, served as a trail-blazing event to forge closer relationships with ABSOLUT's consumers.

The theme of ABSOLUT New Year is "fortune and blessing," and consists of three sections specially designed for a mainland Chinese audience. The first section includes print advertisements featuring an ABSOLUT bottle emblazoned with a Chinese character, fu (福), specially written by a famous calligrapher, Mrs. Tong Yang-tse. The meaning of the character fu, which means fortune and blessing, is consistent with the campaign's theme. More interestingly, the ABSOLUT bottle is placed upside down in the ad; in Chinese culture, the inverted character fu means the arrival of fortune and blessing. "The idea of turning the character fu upside-down is for readers to upend the ad to get the double meaning of the symbol," an executive of ABSOLUT says.

The second section was a billboard featuring the character-bedecked bottle to appear in Xintiandi Plaza in Shanghai. The billboard was also installed with a street-level control button that when pressed by a passerby, would rotate the bottle. Similar promotions were conducted in bars, restaurants, and liquor stores. The third section was a new Web site which attracted visitors with a variety of entertainment such as videos with creative graphics and music.

"Absolut's previous Chinese ads, which featured scenes from a Chinese city, were not very different from the Western versions, but the new effort is meant to tap directly into Chinese culture," says Peter Wijk, director of marketing and communications for the Asia-Pacific region at V&S Absolut Spirits. "The campaign is obviously very Chinese," he said, adding that non-Chinese people would not understand it. "This is a way for us to celebrate the Chinese New Year with the Chinese, and be very relevant with that culture."

ABSOLUT's attempt to celebrating the Chinese New Year has become one of its most aggressive integrated advertising and marketing campaigns in China to date.

Advertising

Advertising
Any paid form of nonpersonal presentation and promotion of ideas, goods, or services by an identified sponsor.

Advertising can be traced back to the very beginnings of recorded history. Archaeologists working in the countries around the Mediterranean Sea have dug up signs announcing various events and offers. The Romans painted walls to announce gladiator fights, and the Phoenicians painted pictures promoting their wares on large rocks along parade routes. During the Golden Age in Greece, town criers announced the sale of cattle, crafted items, and even cosmetics. Modern advertising, however, is a far cry from these early efforts. U.S. advertisers now run up an estimated annual advertising bill of more than $271 billion; worldwide ad spending exceeds an estimated $604 billion. Procter & Gamble, the world's largest advertiser, last year spent almost $4.6 billion on U.S. advertising and more than $7.9 billion worldwide.[1]

Although advertising is used mostly by business firms, a wide range of not-for-profit organizations, professionals, and social agencies also use advertising to promote their causes to various target publics. Advertising is a good way to inform and persuade, whether the purpose is to sell Coca-Cola worldwide or to get consumers in a developing nation to use birth control.

Marketing management must make four important decisions when developing an advertising program (see **Figure 15.1**): *setting advertising objectives, setting the advertising budget, developing advertising strategy (message decisions and media decisions), and evaluating advertising campaigns.*

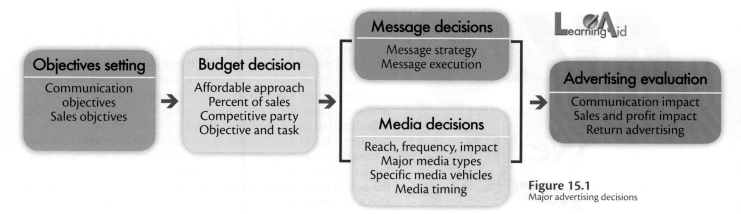

Figure 15.1
Major advertising decisions

Setting Advertising Objectives

The first step is to set *advertising objectives*. These objectives should be based on past decisions about the target market, positioning, and the marketing mix, which define the job that advertising must do in the total marketing program. The overall advertising objective is to help build customer relationships by communicating customer value. Here, we discuss specific advertising objectives.

An **advertising objective** is a specific communication *task* to be accomplished with a specific *target* audience during a specific period of *time*. Advertising objectives can be classified by primary purpose—whether the aim is to *inform*, *persuade*, or *remind*. **Table 15.1** lists examples of each of these specific objectives.

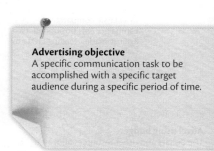

Advertising objective
A specific communication task to be accomplished with a specific target audience during a specific period of time.

Table 15.1 Possible Advertising Objectives

Informative Advertising	
Communicating customer value	Informing the market of a price change
Telling the market about a new product	Describing available services
Explaining how the product works	Correcting false impressions
Suggesting new uses for a product	Building a brand and company image

Persuasive Advertising	
Building brand preference	Persuading customers to purchase now
Encouraging switching to your brand	Persuading customers to receive a sales
Changing customer's perception of product attributes	Call convincing customers to tell others about the brand

Reminder Advertising	
Maintaining customer relationships	Reminding consumers where to buy the product
Reminding consumers that the product may off-seasons	Keeping the brand in customer's minds during be needed in the near future

Informative advertising is used heavily when introducing a new product category. In this case, the objective is to build primary demand. Thus, early producers of DVD players first had to inform consumers of the image quality and convenience benefits of the new product. *Persuasive advertising* becomes more important as competition increases. Here, the company's objective is to build selective demand. For example, once DVD players became established, Sony began trying to persuade consumers that its brand offered the best quality for their money.

Some persuasive advertising has become *comparative advertising*, in which a company directly or indirectly compares its brand with one or more other brands. Comparative advertising has been used for products ranging from soft drinks, beer, and pain relievers to computers, batteries, car rentals, and credit cards. For example, in its classic comparative campaign, Avis positioned itself against market-leading Hertz by claiming, "We try harder."

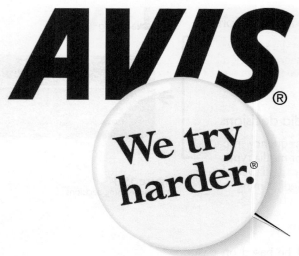

In a classic comparative campaign, Avis positioned itself against market-leading Hertz by claiming, "We try harder." (*www.avis.com*)

Advertising budget
The dollars and other resources allocated to a product or company advertising program.

Advertising strategy
The strategy by which the company accomplishes its advertising objectives. It consists of two major elements: creating advertising messages and selecting advertising media.

Reminder advertising is important for mature products—it helps to maintain customer relationships and keep consumers thinking about the product. Expensive Coca-Cola television ads primarily build and maintain the Coca-Cola brand relationship rather than informing or persuading customers to buy in the short run.

Advertising's goal is to move consumers through the buyer-readiness stages discussed in the previous chapter. Some advertising is designed to move people to immediate action. However, many of the other ads focus on building or strengthening long-term customer relationships. For example, a Nike television ad in which well-known athletes "just do it" never directly asks for a sale. Instead, the goal is to somehow change the way the customers think or feel about the brand.

Setting the Advertising Budget

After determining its advertising objectives, the company next sets its **advertising budget** for each product. Four commonly used methods for setting promotion budgets are discussed in Chapter 14. Here we discuss some specific factors that should be considered when setting the advertising budget.

A brand's advertising budget often depends on its stage in the product life cycle. For example, new products typically need large advertising budgets to build awareness and to gain consumer trial. In contrast, mature brands usually require lower budgets as a ratio to sales. Market share also impacts the amount of advertising needed: Because building the market or taking market share from competitors requires larger advertising spending than does simply maintaining current share, low-share brands usually need more advertising spending as a percentage of sales. Also, brands in a market with many competitors and high advertising clutter must be advertised more heavily to be noticed above the noise in the market. Undifferentiated brands—those that closely resemble other brands in their product class (soft drinks, laundry detergents)—may require heavy advertising to set them apart. When the product differs greatly from competitors, advertising can be used to point out the differences to consumers.

Setting the advertising budget is no easy task. Some critics charge that large consumer packaged-goods firms tend to spend too much on advertising and business-to-business marketers generally underspend on advertising. They claim that, on the one hand, the large consumer companies use lots of image advertising without really knowing its effects. They overspend as a form of "insurance" against not spending enough. On the other hand, business advertisers tend to rely too heavily on their sales forces to bring in orders. They underestimate the power of company and product image in preselling to industrial customers. Thus, they do not spend enough on advertising to build customer awareness and knowledge.

Companies such as Coca-Cola and 3 Hong Kong, a leading network provider in Hong Kong, have built sophisticated statistical models to determine the relationship between promotional spending and brand sales and to help determine the "optimal investment" across various media. However, because so many factors, some controllable and others not, affect advertising effectiveness, measuring the results of advertising spending remains an inexact science. In most cases, managers must rely on large doses of judgment along with more quantitative analysis when setting advertising budgets.[2]

Developing Advertising Strategy

Advertising strategy consists of two major elements: creating advertising *messages* and selecting advertising *media* (see **Figure 15.2**). Today, media fragmentation, soaring media costs, and more-focused target marketing strategies have promoted the importance of the media-planning function. More and more, advertisers are orchestrating a closer harmony between their messages and the media that deliver them.

Advertising strategy

Creating advertising messages	Selecting advertisement media
◔ Breaking through clutter	◔ Deciding on reach, frequency, and impact
◔ Message strategy	◔ Choosing among major media types
◔ Message execution	◔ Deciding on media timing

Figure 15.2
Developing advertising
strategy

◔ A long-simmering advertising debate is boiling anew: Should the people who create clever commercials work more closely with the people who decide where those same commercials appear? It used to be that creative executives who crafted commercials were the top dogs of the industry. Media buyers and planners played a less glamorous role, deciding which TV network or magazine an advertiser should use and then buying the time or space needed. Many large agency holding companies have widened the creative-media gap by separating their media planning and buying functions into separate divisions. More recently, however, the fragmentation of audiences among a growing array of new-media technologies is forcing marketers to put more emphasis on narrowly targeted media. As a result, the decision about which medium to use for an ad campaign—Web site, video on demand, broadcast or cable television, or e-mail—is now sometimes more critical than the creative elements of the campaign.

Some companies have long recognized the importance of tight media-creative partnerships. For example, for more than 25 years, Absolut created a wonderful assortment of creative ads that were tightly targeted to the audiences of the media in which they appeared. "Absolut Singapore" ads shows a clean bottle with a white handkerchief to convey Singapore's clean city image. At a time of soaring media costs and cluttered communication channels, a closer cooperation between creative and media people has paid off handsomely for Absolut. Largely as a result of its breakthrough advertising, Absolut is in many Asian consumers' "evoke set" of vodkas.

**Media-creative
partnerships –**
In its now classic campaign,
Absolut Vodka developed a
wonderful assortment of creative
ads that were tightly targeted to
the audiences of the media in
which they appeared.

ABSOLUT HONG KONG.   ABSOLUT SINGAPORE.   ABSOLUT BEIJING.

Creating the Advertising Message

No matter how big the budget, advertising can succeed only if advertisements gain attention and communicate well. Good advertising messages are especially important in today's costly and cluttered advertising environment. One expert estimates that the average person is exposed to some 3,000 ad messages a day. Another puts the number at an eye-popping 5,000 ads a day.[3]

Breaking through the clutter

If all this advertising clutter bothers some consumers, it also causes big problems for advertisers. Take the situation facing network television advertisers in the U. S. They pay an average of $338,000 to make a single 30-second commercial. Then, each time they

Advertising clutter – If advertising clutter bothers some consumers, it also causes big problems for advertisers. They might pay $1 million or more for 30 seconds of advertising time during a popular prime-time TV program like the final episode of American Idol, then have their ads sandwiched in with a glut of other commercials, announcements, and network promotions.

show it, they regularly pay $300,000 or more for 30 seconds of advertising time during a popular prime-time program. They pay even more if it is an especially popular program such as *American Idol* (as much as $705,000), *Desperate Housewives* ($560,000), *CSI* ($478,000), or a mega event such as the *American Idol* season finale ($1.3 million) or the Super Bowl ($2.5 million per 30 seconds!).[4]

Then, their ads are sandwiched in with other commercials, announcements, and network promotions. Such clutter in television and other ad media has created an increasingly hostile advertising environment. According to one recent study, 65 percent of Americans say they are "constantly bombarded with too much" advertising and about two-thirds say that their view of advertising is "much more negative than just a few years ago."[5]

With the growth in cable and satellite TV, the Internet, video on demand (VOD), and DVD rentals, today's viewers have many more options. Digital technology has also armed consumers with an arsenal of weapons for choosing what they watch or do not watch. Increasingly, consumers are choosing *not* to watch ads. They can fast-forward through commercials in recorded programs. With the remote control, they mute the sound during a commercial or "zip" around the channels to see what else is on. A recent study found that 40 percent of all television viewers now switch channels when the commercial break starts.[6]

Advertisers can no longer force-feed their ad messages to consumers through traditional media, a result of the rapid growth of digital video recorder systems like TiVo.

Adding to the problem is the rapid growth of TiVo-style DVR (digital video recorder) systems. One ad agency executive calls DVR systems "electronic weed whackers." "In time, the number of people using them to obliterate commercials will totally erode faith in the 30-second commercial," he declares. Similarly, the number of VOD viewers is expected to quadruple during the next five years. These viewers will be able to watch programming on their own time terms, with or without commercials.[7]

Thus, advertisers can no longer force-feed the same old ad messages to captive consumers through traditional media. Today's advertising messages must be better planned, more imaginative, more entertaining, and more rewarding to consumers. "Interruption or disruption as the fundamental premise of marketing" no longer works, says one advertising executive. "You have to create content that is interesting, useful, or entertaining enough to invite [consumers]." According to another, advertisers must now "draw people in. Tell a story. Encourage them to engage in it, and reward them when they do. If you do it right, they will want to see your ads again and again."[8]

Message strategy

The first step in creating effective advertising messages is to plan a message strategy—to decide what general message will be communicated to consumers. The purpose of advertising is to get consumers to think about or react to the product or company in a certain way. People will react only if they believe that they will benefit from doing so. Thus, developing an effective message strategy begins with identifying customer benefits that can be used as advertising appeals. Ideally, advertising message strategy will follow directly from the company's broader positioning and customer value strategies.

Message strategy statements tend to be plain, straightforward outlines of benefits and positioning points that the advertiser wants to stress. The advertiser must next develop a compelling **creative concept**—or "*big idea*"—that will bring the message strategy to life in a distinctive and memorable way. At this stage, simple message ideas become great ad campaigns. Usually, a copywriter and art director will team up to generate many creative concepts, hoping that one of these concepts will turn out to be the big idea. The creative concept may emerge as a visualization, a phrase, or a combination of the two.

The creative concept will guide the choice of specific appeals to be used in an advertising campaign. *Advertising appeals* should have three characteristics: First, they should be *meaningful*, pointing out benefits that make the product more desirable or interesting to consumers. Second, appeals must be *believable*—consumers must believe that the product or service will deliver the promised benefits.

However, the most meaningful and believable benefits may not be the best ones to feature. Appeals should also be *distinctive*—they should tell how the product is better than the competing brands. For example, the most meaningful benefit of owning a wristwatch is that it keeps accurate time, yet few watch ads feature this benefit. Instead, based on the distinctive benefits they offer, watch advertisers might select any of a number of advertising themes. For years, Timex has been the affordable watch that "Takes a lickin' and keeps on tickin'." In contrast, Swatch has featured style and fashion, whereas Rolex stresses luxury and status.

Procter & Gamble produced a series of 90-second advertising sitcoms called "At the Poocherellas," shown on Nick at Night, featuring a family of dogs and promoting its Febreze brand. Each mini episode includes the expected commercial break, which lasts just long enough to say, "Febreze, it is fresh." "We do not really think of this as advertising," says a media executive. "We create an environment where a brand's character and equity live in a show."

Branded entertainment (or *brand integrations*) involves making the brand an inseparable part of some other form of entertainment. The most common form of branded entertainment is product placements—imbedding brands as props within other programming. In all, advertisers paid an estimated $1.2 billion on product placements last year, up 30 percent from the previous year. The nature of the placement can vary widely. It might be a brief glimpse of a Starbucks coffee cup sitting on a table on HBO's Entourage or the judges on *American Idol* drinking out of Coca-Cola cups. Or it might involve scripting products into the theme of the program. For example, the boss of *The Office* frequents Chili's restaurant and orders his "awesome blossom, extra awesome"—in one episode, he even broke into the restaurant's catchy "baby back ribs" jingle while entertaining a client there.

Costs of product placements range widely. "A car manufacturer might be willing to pay $100,000 to $150,000 to show the mirror turns upside down," says one expert. "Going in and completely crafting a whole segment from scratch where the brand is a key player could be a million bucks." For example, blue-chip companies such as Procter & Gamble, General Motors, Staples, Unilever, and Burger King paid $1 to $4 million per episode to integrate their brands into the reality show, *The Apprentice*.

Perhaps no company has gotten more mileage out of such brand integrations than GM's Pontiac division. It all started with an extraordinary giveaway on a popular talk show:

● When *The Oprah Winfrey Show* opened its 19th season with a "Wildest Dreams" theme, Oprah electrified the studio audience by giving every one of the 276 people in attendance a new, fully loaded Pontiac G6 sedan worth $28,400. The Oprah giveaway set a new benchmark in the field of branded entertainment. It cost Pontiac about $8 million but generated an estimated $20 million in unpaid media coverage and favorable PR.

Creative concept
The compelling "big idea" that will bring the advertising message strategy to life in a distinctive and memorable way.

For years, Timex has marketed itself as the affordable watch that "Takes a lickin' and keeps on tickin'."

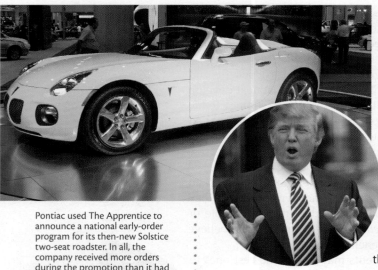

Pontiac used The Apprentice to announce a national early-order program for its then-new Solstice two-seat roadster. In all, the company received more orders during the promotion than it had planned to build for the entire year.

Pontiac followed quickly with another stunningly successful placement, this time on *The Apprentice*. Generally viewed as the most successful *Apprentice* brand integration ever, Pontiac used the show to announce a national early-order program for its then-new Solstice two-seat roadster. In a show that included photo shoots of the sleek new car and discussions of Solstice benefits, *Apprentice* teams pulled all-nighters to create Solstice promotion brochures. The result: Pontiac's Web site traffic skyrocketed 1,400 percent the night the episode aired, and some 41,000 people registered online for a chance to place an early order. Expecting to sell 1,000 cars within ten days, Pontiac blew by that goal in just 41 minutes after the cars went on sale the next day. In all, Pontiac chalked up 7,116 orders during the promotion, more Solstices than it planned to build for the entire year.

Originally created with TV in mind, branded entertainment has spread quickly into other sectors of the entertainment industry. It is widely used in movies—think about Ray Ban sunglasses in *Men in Black*, or the *Land Rover LR3 in Mission*: Impossible III. And when DreamWorks built the terminal for its movie *The Terminal*, along with United Airlines, more than 35 companies chipped in millions to build real stores—Brookstone, Discovery Store, Borders Books, Paul Mitchell—as well as a working food court with a Starbucks, Baskin-Robbins, Burger King, and Baja Fresh. If you look carefully, you will also see subtle and not-so-subtle product placements in online video games, magazines, Internet sites, and just about anything else—from comic books to Broadway musicals. For example, the script for *Sweet Charity* was revised to fit Jose Cuervo's Gran Centenario tequila into a scene.

So, **Madison & Vine** is the new meeting place for the advertising and entertainment industries. When done right, advertainment and branded entertainment can pay big dividends. However, experts caution that Madison & Vine can also be a dangerous crossing. They worry that making ads too entertaining might detract from the seller's brand message—consumers will remember the clever ad but forget the brand or advertiser. And they note that the intersection is getting pretty congested. With all these new ad formats and product placements, Madison & Vine threatens to create even more of the very clutter that it is designed to break through.

They also worry about potential customer resentment and backlash. Some TV shows outright bristle with product placements. A heavily branded show like American Idol contains, on average, more than 36 product placement shots per hour. During the fall season last year, the ten prime-time TV shows with the most placements included 9,019 "brand shout-outs," up from 5,821 the year before. At what point will consumers decide that the intersection of Madison & Vine is just too congested and take yet a different route?

Message execution

The advertiser now must turn the big idea into an actual ad execution that will capture the target market's attention and interest. The creative team must find the best approach, style, tone, words, and format for executing the message. Any message can be presented in different **execution styles**, such as the following:

- Slice of life: This style shows one or more "typical" people using the product in a normal setting. For example, two mothers at a picnic discuss the nutritional benefits of Skippy peanut butter.

Madison & Vine
A term that has come to represent the merging of advertising and entertainment in an effort to break through the clutter and create new avenues for reaching consumers with more engaging messages.

Execution style
The approach, style, tone, words, and format used for executing an advertising message.

- *Lifestyle:* This style shows how a product fits in with a particular lifestyle.
- *Fantasy:* This style creates a fantasy around the product or its use. For instance, many ads are built around dream themes.
- *Mood or image:* This style builds a mood or image around the product or service, such as beauty, love, or serenity. Few claims are made about the product except through suggestion. For example, ads for Singapore Airlines feature soft lighting and refined flight attendants pampering relaxed and happy customers.
- *Musical:* This style shows people or cartoon characters singing about the product. For example, one of the most famous ads in history was a Coca-Cola ad built around the song "I would Like to Teach the World to Sing."
- *Personality symbol:* This style creates a character that represents the product. The character might be animated (the jolly Green Giant, McDull the Pig [Hong Kong], Garfield the Cat) or real (the Marlboro man, Aaron Kwok, a Hong Kong celebrity in the Pepsi Coke ads).
- *Technical expertise:* This style shows the company's expertise in making the product. Thus, BBK (Bu Bu Gao, a top Chinese appliance manufacturer that makes DVD players) used Arnold Schwarzenegger in its ads to promote BBK's expertise as "Truth without Lies" (a concept borrowed from Schwarzenegger's movie True Lies).
- *Scientific evidence:* This style presents survey or scientific evidence that the brand is better or better liked than one or more other brands. For years, Crest toothpaste has used scientific evidence to convince buyers that Crest is better than other brands at fighting cavities.
- *Testimonial evidence or endorsement:* This style features a highly believable or likable source endorsing the product. It could be ordinary people saying how much they like a given product (see **Real Marketing 15.1**)

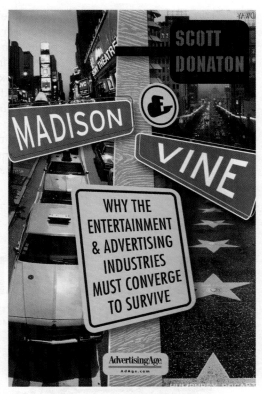

In today's cluttered advertising environment, advertisers and agencies in the U.S. must find new ways to engage ad-weary consumers with more compelling messages. The answer? Entertainment!

The advertiser also must choose a tone for the ad. Procter & Gamble always uses a positive tone: Its ads say something very positive about its products. P&G usually avoids humor that might take attention away from the message. In contrast, many advertisers now use edgy humor to break through the commercial clutter.

The advertiser must use memorable and attention-getting words in the ad. For example, rather than claiming simply that "a BMW is a well-engineered automobile," BMW uses more creative and higher-impact phrasing: "The ultimate driving machine." Haagen-Dazs is more than "a good-tasting luxury ice-cream," it is "Our passport to indulgence: passion in a touch, perfection in a cup, summer in a spoon, one perfect moment."

Finally, *format* elements make a difference in an ad's impact as well as in its cost. A small change in ad design can make a big difference in its effect. In a print ad, the *illustration* is the first thing the reader notices—it must be strong enough to draw attention. Next, the *headline* must effectively entice the right people to read the copy. Finally, the copy—the main block of text in the ad—must be simple but strong and convincing. Moreover, these three elements must effectively work *together* to persuasively present customer value.

Selecting Advertising Media

The major steps in **advertising media** selection are (1) deciding on *reach, frequency*, and *impact*; (2) choosing among major *media types*; (3) selecting specific *media vehicles*; and (4) deciding on *media timing*.

Deciding on reach, frequency, and impact

To select media, the advertiser must decide on the reach and frequency needed to achieve advertising objectives. *Reach* is a measure of the *percentage* of people in the target market

Advertising media
The vehicles through which advertising messages are delivered to their intended audiences.

who are exposed to the ad campaign during a given period of time. For example, the advertiser might try to reach 70 percent of the target market during the first three months of the campaign. *Frequency* is a measure of how many *times* the average person in the target market is exposed to the message. For example, the advertiser might want an average exposure frequency of three.

But advertisers want to do more than just reach a given number of consumers a specific number of times. The advertiser also must decide on the desired *media impact*—the *qualitative value* of a message exposure through a given medium. For example, the same message in one newspaper (say, the *South China Morning Post* or *Far East Economic Review*) may be more believable than in another (say, *Apple Daily*). For products that need to be demonstrated, messages on television may have more impact than messages on radio

REAL MARKETING 15.1

Mission Hills Golf Club: Teeing Off with Tiger

Mission Hills is the world's largest golf facility, with 12 golf courses, and is the only golf cup in China recognized by the U.S. PGA and Tournament Players Clubs.

Located at Shenzhen, Mission Hills Golf Club (hereafter called Mission Hills), China, was founded in 1994. With ten golf courses open and two more nearing completion, Mission Hills is the largest golf complex in the world, according to the Guinness Book of World Records in 2007. Among numerous golf courses in China, Mission Hills is the only golf club in China recognized by the U.S. PGA and the Tournament Players Clubs.

Mission Hills covers an area of 15 square kilometers leaving plenty of room for more a golf accessories shop, an outdoor kids' playground, and 51 tennis courts. The $625 million development also includes six driving ranges and the 300,000-square-foot main clubhouse, and the Mission Hills complex which features four spas, a 315-room five-star hotel and two luxury residential communities, plus, not surprisingly,

ample conference and function space for conventions and business events.

The Club boasts 12 signature courses designed by golf legends from five different continents. Each course is reflective of the designers' style, offering unique risk/reward challenges to the player.

Tiger Woods China Challenge

Hosting major tournaments is a regular activity at Mission Hills, China. It started with the first international golf tournament in China back in 1995, the 41st World Cup of Golf, and subsequently, the Tiger Woods China Challenge in 2001 and the first two editions of the Dynasty Cup in 2003 and 2005.

In November 2001, Tiger Woods made his first visit to Mission Hills, inaugurating a new era in the development of golf in China with his championship presence. As part of Woods' historic China tour, Mission Hills hosted a variety of golf and charitable events at the time. A golf clinic, in addition to the 18-hole tournament, was held on the first day of his visit while there was a professionals-vs-amateurs event on the second day. Woods was also invited to launch the First Tee Foundation, a program first founded because television uses sight *and* sound. Products for which consumers provide input on design or features might be better promoted at a Web site than in a direct mailing.

More generally, the advertiser wants to choose media that will *engage* consumers rather than simply reach them. For example, for television advertising, "how relevant a program is for its audience and where the ads are inserted are likely to be much more important than whether the program was a Nielsen winner" numbers-wise, says one expert. "This is about 'lean to' TV rather than 'lean back.'" Although Nielsen is beginning to measure levels of television *media engagement*, such measures are hard to come by for most media. "All the measurements we have now are media metrics: ratings, readership, listenership, click-through rates," says an executive of the Advertising Research Foundation, but engagement "happens inside the consumer, not inside the medium. What we need is a

Advertisers should choose media that will engage consumers rather than simply reach them. A program may have a large audience, but if the ad is irrelevant to its audience, then it will not be as effective.

in the U. S. which seeks to improve the affordability and accessibility of golf and facilities for young and economically disadvantaged players.

Promoting Mission Hills Golf Club
Sports marketing involves the broadest scope and also the highest degree of complexity when compared to marketing campaigns of other products and services. It usually requires cooperation among various industries while the sports marketing campaigns of these industries are interrelated. The success of the marketing campaign of Mission Hills highlights China's mature ability in complex sports event marketing. Some crucial factors of success are:

Tiger Woods as a celebrity
Positioning itself as a world-class golf resort, Mission Hills needed a spokesman to help raise its image to another new height. This person must have gained worldwide popularity and maintain a positive reputation among the general public. Being an international sports star because of his unprecedented achievements in golf, Tiger Woods has earned the respect and admiration of many wealthy golf-lovers. As such, "Woods" is a leading brand in the golf industry and the Tiger Woods China Challenge can be seen as a brand endorsement. Blending the Woods' positive public image with the luxurious designs of Mission Hills and its golf courses would attract a wave of golf players and spectators.

Cooperation among various stakeholders
Woods' visit to China continues to draws international attention. Its success depends very much on the cooperation and support from overseas media and sponsors. From a marketing perspective, the advertising, sales promotion, and the selection of contestants are also crucial to the success of the event. The organization of this event makes full use of integrated marketing communications. Considerable sums of money are spent by the organizing units to strengthen promotion during the contest. Also, the contest is broadcast on cable television channels that have Asia-wide coverage, such as ESPN and Star Sports. News about the event is broadcasted in 200 TV stations around the world. The extensive coverage of the news about the event creates a trend for sport activities and encourages consumption in the sports industry. This has provided a strong foundation for the future development of Mission Hills.

Looking forward the future
On its own, the Tiger Woods China Challenge does not bring any tangible profits to Mission Hills. However, the event itself is still highly regarded by people in the circle, who voted it a success. The Club believes that the event has paved the way for future returns. Under the large-scale coverage of the event by the media, golf has become a trend among China's upper class, and Mission Hills is their first choice. In addition, the prospect of commercial golf will be bright due to the increase of foreign-related commercial activities

after China's entry to the World Trade Organization.

The success of the Tiger Woods China Challenge has helped Mission Hills to gain experience for the upcoming sports events in the future and attract more sponsors through the improvement of brand image and influence in the industry.

Relevant figures from The Tiger Woods China Challenge
- Total audience: 10,000
- Number of VIPs: 2,000
- Typical background of VIPs: government officials, business partners, sponsors
- Number of tickets sold: 8,000
- Ticket price: HK$ or RMB 1,000 (members); HK$ or RMB 2,000 (general public)
- Sources of ticket buyers: Shenzhen, Guangzhou, Hong Kong
- Live broadcast: Phoenix Satellite TV—three hours; CCTV—two hours; ATV—four hours
- Number of press members: 200

Sources:
Tai-hong Lu (2002), *Marketing in China: 2002 Marketing Report*, Chengdu: Sichuan People Publishing Ltd, accessed at http://www.cybergolf.com/indexGenerator.asp?newsid=3256; http://english.peopledaily.com.cn/english/200110/07/eng20011007_81719.html; http://www.worldgolf.com/features/mission-hills-golf-club-inside-worlds-largest-golf-resort-5214.htm; http://www.missionhillsgroup.com/en/aboutus/mh/index.html.

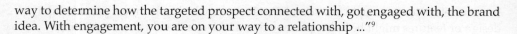

way to determine how the targeted prospect connected with, got engaged with, the brand idea. With engagement, you are on your way to a relationship ..."[9]

Choosing among major media types

The media planner must know the reach, frequency, and impact of each of the major media types. As summarized in **Table 15.2**, the major media types are television, newspapers, direct mail, magazines, radio, outdoor, and the Internet. Each medium has advantages and limitations. Media planners consider many factors when making their media choices. They want to choose media that will effectively and efficiently present the advertising message to target customers. Thus, they must consider each medium's impact, message effectiveness, and cost.

Table 15.2 Profiles of Major Media Types

Medium	Advantages	Limitations
Television	Good mass-marketing coverage; low cost per exposure; combines sight, sound, and motion; appealing to the senses	High absolute costs; high clutter; fleeting exposure; less audience selectivity
Newspapers	Flexibility; timeliness; good local market coverage; broad acceptability; high believability	Short life; poor reproduction quality; small pass-along audience
Direct mail	High audience selectivity; flexibility; no ad competition within the same medium; allows personalization	Relatively high cost per exposure, "junk mail"
Magazines	High geographic and demographic selectivity; credibility and prestige; high-quality reproduction; long life and good pass-along readership	Long ad purchase lead time; high cost; no guarantee of position
Radio	Good local acceptance; high geographic and demographic selectivity; low cost	Audio only, fleeting exposure; low attention ("the half-heard" medium); fragmented audiences
Outdoor	Flexibility; high repeat exposure; low cost; low message competition; good positional selectivity	Little audience selectivity; creative limitations
Internet	High selectivity; low cost; immediacy; interactive capabilities	Demographically skewed audience; relatively low impact; audience controls exposure

The mix of media must be reexamined regularly. For a long time, television and magazines dominated in the media mixes of national advertisers, with other media often neglected. However, as discussed in the previous chapter, the media mix appears to be shifting. As mass-media costs rise, audiences shrink, and exciting new digital media emerge, many advertisers are supplementing the traditional mass media with more specialized and highly targeted media that cost less, target more effectively, and engage consumers more fully.

For example, cable television and digital satellite systems are booming. Such systems allow narrow programming formats such as all sports, all news, nutrition, arts, home improvement and gardening, cooking, travel, history, finance, and others that target select groups.

Advertisers can take advantage of such "narrowcasting" to zoom in on special market segments rather than use the "one size fits all" approach offered by network broadcasting. Cable and satellite media seem to make good sense. But, increasingly, ads are popping up in far less likely places. In their efforts to find less costly and more highly targeted ways to reach consumers, advertisers have discovered a dazzling collection of "alternative media."

Another important trend affecting media selection is the rapid growth in the number of "media multitaskers," people who absorb more than one medium at a time:

It looks like people who are not satisfied with "just watching TV" are in good company. According to a recent survey, three-fourths of U.S. TV viewers read the newspaper while they watch TV, and two-thirds of them go online during their TV time. According to the study, 70 percent of media users say they at one time or another try to absorb two or more forms of media at once. What is more, if today's kids are any indication, media multitasking is on the rise. Americans aged eight to 18 are managing to cram an average 8.5 hours of media consumption into 6.5 hours. It is not uncommon to find a teenage boy chasing down photos of Keira Knightley on Google, IMing several friends at once, listening to a mix of music on iTunes, and talking on the cell phone to a friend all the while, in the midst of the multimedia chaos, trying to complete an essay he has got open in a Word file a few layers down on his desktop.[10]

Marketers have discoverd a dazzling array of "alternative media."

Media planners need to take such media interactions into account when selecting the types of media they will use.

Selecting specific media vehicles

The media planner now must choose the best media vehicles—specific media within each general media type. For example, television vehicles include Star TV and RoadShow (see **Real Marketing 15.2**). Magazine vehicles include *Time, Asia Inc.*, weekly TV guides, and *Cosmopolitan*.

Media planners must compute the cost per thousand persons reached by a vehicle. For example, if a full-page, four-color advertisement in the U.S. national edition of *Newsweek* costs $220,500 and *Newsweek's* readership is 3.1 million people, the cost of reaching each group of 1,000 persons is about $71. The same advertisement in *Business Week* may cost only $99,500 but reach only 971,000 persons—at a cost per thousand of about $102. The media planner ranks each magazine by cost per thousand and favors those magazines with the lower cost per thousand for reaching target consumers.[11]

The media planner must also consider the costs of producing ads for different media. Whereas newspaper ads may cost very little to produce, flashy television ads can be very costly.

In selecting specific media vehicles, the media planner must balance media costs against several media effectiveness factors. First, the planner should evaluate the media vehicle's audience quality. For a baby formula advertisement, for example, a family magazine would have a high exposure value; *Time* would have a low exposure value. Second, the media planner should consider *audience engagement*. Readers of *Vogue*, for example, typically pay more attention to ads than do Newsweek readers. Third, the planner should assess the vehicle's *editorial quality*—the *Wall Street Journal* and *South China Morning Post* are more believable and prestigious than the *Sun*.

Media multitasking –
According to a U.S. study, 70 percent of media users say that they try to absorb two or more forms of media at once.

Deciding on media timing

The advertiser must also decide how to schedule the advertising over the course of a year. Suppose sales of a product peak in December and drop in March. The firm can vary its advertising to follow the seasonal pattern, to oppose the seasonal pattern, or to be the same all year. Most firms do some seasonal advertising. For example, products suitable for personal gifts are heavily advertised before major holidays such as Christmas, Easter, Valentine's Day, and Chinese New Year.

Deciding on media timing –
Most companies advertised heavily before major holidays, such as this Coca-Cola poster to mark the Chinese New Year.

Return on advertising investment
The net return on advertising investment divided by the costs of the advertising investment.

Finally, the advertiser must choose the pattern of the ads. Continuity means scheduling ads evenly within a given period. *Pulsing* means scheduling ads unevenly over a given time period. Thus, 52 ads could either be scheduled at one per week during the year or pulsed in several bursts. The idea behind pulsing is to advertise heavily for a short period to build awareness that carries over to the next advertising period. Those who favor pulsing feel that it can be used to achieve the same impact as a steady schedule but at a much lower cost. However, some media planners believe that although pulsing achieves maximal awareness, it sacrifices depth of advertising communications.

Evaluating Advertising Effectiveness and Return on Advertising Investment

Advertising accountability and **return on advertising investment** have become hot issues for most companies. Increasingly, top management is asking: "How do we know that we are spending the right amount on advertising?" and "What return are we getting on our advertising investment?" According to a recent survey by the Association of National Advertisers (ANA) in the U. S., measuring advertising's efficiency and effectiveness is

REAL MARKETING 15.2

Taking the Show on the Road: RoadShow Media Ltd. in Hong Kong

The MMOB service is provided on most of the air-conditioned, double-deck KMB, Citybus, and New World First Bus buses in Hong Kong. There are now over 4,700 RoadShow MMOB buses operating throughout Hong Kong Island, Kowloon, and the New Territories.

In 1982, Mr. H M Yau and his friends from Jardine Matheson Holding Ltd. established a media sales company in Hong Kong, which engaged in outdoor and indoor advertising, aiming at passengers onboard public transportation such as Star Ferry and Yaumati Ferry, and customers visiting supermarkets.Kiosks—wooden boxes installed with a TV and a VHS player—were located at highly visible areas in piers and supermarkets, and continuously showed ads tailor-made for target customers as well as licensed short films for entertainment. After 18 months, the business was dissolved due to the lack of cooperation from ferry and supermarket owners.

Almost 20 years later, a company called Roadshow Media Ltd. appeared in Hong Kong in 2000. Its establishment the number-one issue in the minds of today's advertisers. In the survey, 61.5 percent of respondents said that it is important that they define, measure, and take action in the area of advertising accountability.[12]

Advertisers should regularly evaluate two types of advertising results: the communication effects and the sales and profit effects. Measuring the communication effects of an ad or ad campaign tells whether the ads and media are communicating the ad message well. Individual ads can be tested before or after they are run. Before an ad is placed, the advertiser can show it to consumers, ask how they like it, and measure message recall or attitude changes resulting from it. After an ad is run, the advertiser can measure how the ad affected consumer recall or product awareness, knowledge, and preference. Pre-and post-evaluations of communication effects can be made for entire advertising campaigns as well.

The sales and profits effects of advertising are often much harder to measure. For example, what sales and profits are produced by an ad campaign that increases brand awareness by 20 percent and brand preference by ten percent? Sales and profits are affected by many factors besides advertising—such as product features, price, and availability.

One way to measure the sales and profit effects of advertising is to compare past sales and profits with past advertising expenditures. Another way is through experiments. For example, to test the effects of different advertising spending levels, Coca-Cola could vary the amount it spends on advertising in different market areas and measure the differences in the resulting sales and profit levels. More complex experiments could be designed to include other variables, such as differences in the ads or media used.

was a spin-off from a listed company in Hong Kong, Kowloon Motor Bus Co. (1933) Ltd. It is a media sales company in Hong Kong, which provides RoadShow Multi-media On-board (MMOB) advertising services, which target passengers riding public transit vehicles in Hong Kong.

In fact, adopting the same concept from Mr. Yau and his friends in the 1980s, the MMOB service is provided on most of the air-conditioned, double-deck KMB, Citybus and New World First Bus buses in Hong Kong. A sticker with the RoadShow logo is displayed on the windshield of these buses to help passengers identify them. There are now over 4,700 RoadShow MMOB buses operating throughout Hong Kong Island, Kowloon, and the New Territories.

On each bus, MMOB is delivered through a series of four LCD monitors which are vibration-resistant and strategically located. Each monitor offers a 160-degree viewing angle with quality sound evenly distributed through a four-channel stereo system. Passengers on the bus can watch and listen comfortably to the programs produced by RoadShow from every seat.

RoadShow's programs are specifically tailor-made with the interest of transit vehicle passengers in mind. Two kinds of content are blended into programs: entertainment and infotainment. The former includes music videos, movie trailers, drama serials, animation, and travelogues, while the latter includes civic affairs information, community service messages, crime prevention tips, gourmet guides, health education, business and economic reviews, and news. Each one-hour program is telecast sixteen times per day.

Given the MMOB system, RoadShow is therefore able to offer a network of advertising sales platforms and sales expertise to help its clients to market their products and services to a mass audience through an advertising medium that also delivers high quality programs and infotainment for passengers everyday. Having no competitors, RoadShow enjoys a 100 percent market penetration in the transit vehicle market.

RoadShow has several sales teams which help design ad sales packages to accommodate respective needs of individual clients. The following is an example of an MMOB package.

Example of an MMOB Package

RoadShow Media Limited
Package No.: 2008/P07 Date: January 1, 2008

Package Details:
Campaign Period: three weeks (exact date to be confirmed)
Duration: 1.5 min
Telecast Pattern:
- Daily 16 x 1.5 min x 14 consecutive days x 1,000 MMOB buses
- (Upgrade to 1,600 MMOB buses) within the campaign period

Package Cost: HK$250,000

Source: http://www.roadshow.com.hk

Sources:
Accessed at http://www.roadshow.com.hk

However, because so many factors, some controllable and others not, affect advertising effectiveness, measuring the results of advertising spending remains an inexact science. "Marketers are tracking all kinds of data and they still cannot answer basic questions" about advertising accountability, says a marketing analyst, "because they do not have real models and metrics by which to make sense of it."[13] Thus, although the situation is improving as marketers seek more answers, managers often must rely on large doses of judgment along with quantitative analysis when assessing advertising performance.

Other Advertising Considerations

In developing advertising strategies and programs, the company must address two additional questions. First, how will the company organize its advertising function—who will perform which advertising tasks? Second, how will the company adapt its advertising strategies and programs to the complexities of international markets?

Organizing for Advertising

Advertising agency
A marketing services firm that assists companies in planning preparing, implementating, and evaluating all or portions of their advertising programs.

Different companies organize in different ways to handle advertising. In small companies, advertising might be handled by someone in the sales department. Large companies set up advertising departments whose job is to set the advertising budget, work with the ad agency, and handle other advertising not done by the agency. Most large companies use external advertising agencies because they offer several advantages.

How does an **advertising agency** work? Advertising agencies were started in the mid-to-late 1800s by salespeople and brokers who worked for the media and received a commission for selling advertising space to companies. As time passed, the salespeople began to help customers prepare their ads. Eventually, they formed agencies and grew closer to the advertisers than to the media. Today's agencies employ specialists who can often perform advertising tasks better than the company's own staff can. Agencies also bring an outside point of view to solving the company's problems, along with lots of experience from working with different clients and situations. So, today, even companies with strong advertising departments of their own use advertising agencies.

Ad agencies employ specialists such as art directors who can often perform advertising tasks better than the company's own staff can. They also bring an outside view to solving the company's problems.

Some ad agencies are huge—the largest U.S. agency, McCann Erickson Worldwide, has worldwide annual gross revenue of more than $1.4 billion. In recent years, many agencies have grown by gobbling up other agencies, thus creating huge agency holding companies. The largest of these agency "megagroups," WPP Group, includes several large advertising, public relations, and promotion agencies with combined worldwide revenues of almost $10.5 billion.[14] Most large advertising agencies have the staff and resources to handle all phases of an advertising campaign for their clients, from creating a marketing plan to developing ad campaigns and preparing, placing, and evaluating ads.

International Advertising Decisions

International advertisers face many complexities not encountered by domestic advertisers. The most basic issue concerns the degree to which global advertising should be adapted to the unique characteristics of various country markets. Some large advertisers have attempted to support their global brands with highly standardized worldwide advertising, with campaigns that work as well in Bangkok as they do in Baltimore. For example, Coca-Cola's Sprite brand uses standardized appeals to target the world's youth. Ads for Gillette's Venus razors are almost identical worldwide, with only minor adjustments to suit the local culture.

Standardization produces many benefits—lower advertising costs, greater global advertising coordination, and a more consistent worldwide image. But it also has

What is it about PINK
that makes you feel so good?

Introducing Passion Pink Venus®
From Gillette.

It shaves you so close, your skin stays smoother, longer.

Reveal the goddess in you.®
www.GilletteVenus.com

¿Qué tiene el ROSA
que te hace sentir tan bien?

Presentamos Venus® de Gillette en un
escandaloso nuevo color, Rosa Pasión.

Con una simple pasada, sentirás tu piel más suave que nunca.

Descubre la diosa que hay en ti.
www.GilletteVenus.com

Jamais le ROSE ne vous
a fait autant d'effet !

Découvrez Venus® Rose Passion
de Gillette.

Une peau d'une infinie douceur, en un clin d'œil.

Révélez la déesse qui est en vous.®
www.GilletteVenus.com

Standardized worldwide advertising –
Gillette's ads for its Gillette for Women Venus razors are almost identical worldwide, with only minor adjustments to suit the local culture.

drawbacks. Most importantly, it ignores the fact that country markets differ greatly in their cultures, demographics, and economic conditions. Thus, most international advertisers "think globally but act locally." They develop global advertising strategies that make their worldwide advertising efforts more efficient and consistent. Then they adapt their advertising programs to make them more responsive to consumer needs and expectations within local markets. For example, Coca-Cola has a pool of different commercials that can be used in or adapted to several different international markets. Some can be used with only minor changes—such as language—in several different countries. Local and regional managers decide which commercials work best for which markets.

Global advertisers face several special problems. For instance, advertising media costs and availability differ vastly from country to country. Countries also differ in the extent to which they regulate advertising practices. Many countries have extensive systems of laws restricting how much a company can spend on advertising, the media used, the nature of advertising claims, and other aspects of the advertising program. Such restrictions often require advertisers to adapt their campaigns from country to country.

For example, alcoholic products cannot be advertised in India or in Muslim countries. In many countries, Sweden and Norway, for example, food ads are banned from kids' TV. To play it safe, McDonald's advertises itself as a family restaurant in Sweden. Comparative ads, while acceptable and even common in the U. S. and Canada, are less commonly used in the United Kingdom, unacceptable in Japan, and illegal in India and Brazil. China bans sending e-mail for advertising purposes to people without their permission, and all advertising e-mail that is sent must be titled "advertisement."

China also has restrictive censorship rules for TV and radio advertising; for example, the words the best are banned, as are ads that "violate social customs" or present women in "improper ways." Development of the advertising industry has encountered numerous stumbling blocks. **Real Marketing 15.3** provides you with a list of issues faced by the industry as well as its future outlook.

McDonald's once avoided government sanctions there by publicly apologizing for an ad that crossed cultural norms by showing a customer begging for a discount. Similarly, Coca-Cola's Indian subsidiary was forced to end a promotion that offered prizes, such as a trip to Hollywood, because it violated India's established trade practices by encouraging customers to buy in order to "gamble."[15]

Thus, although advertisers may develop global strategies to guide their overall advertising efforts, specific advertising programs must usually be adapted to meet local cultures and customs, media characteristics, and advertising regulations.

Public Relations

Public relations (PR)
Building good relations with the company's various publics by obtaining favorable publicity, building a good corporate image, and handling or heading off unfavorable rumors, stories, and events.

Another major mass-promotion tool is **public relations (PR)**—building good relationships with the company's various publics by obtaining favorable publicity, building a good corporate image, and handling or diffusing unfavorable rumors, stories, and events. Public relations departments may perform any or all of the following functions:[16]

- *Press relations or press agency*: Creating and placing newsworthy information in the news media to attract attention to a person, product, or service

REAL MARKETING 15.3

Advertising Issues in China

international in • asia

Soaring and excessive demand for advertising slots in local media has led to major local media virtually monopolizing the market and the prices of advertising slots soaring sky high.

As China's economic growth continues to rocket upwards, its advertising industry has struggled to develop evenly across regions and media. Several infrastructural factors and practices have become stumbling blocks affecting the development of the industry. Where will it go from here?

Imbalanced structure
Advertising revenue varies widely across different districts in China. The advertising revenue in Beijing, Shanghai, and Guangdong accounts for almost half of the national advertising revenue and the proportion is still increasing. For example, it moved from 48 percent in 1993 to 52 percent in 1995. The imbalanced market is caused by differences in the degree of economic development, market maturity, and distribution of media in each district.

Imbalanced demand for media
The extremely uneven distribution of advertising revenues in different media shows that some major media, televison in particular, are facing excess demand for advertising slots, making the prices soar drastically. For example, the bidding price for advertising slots on China Central Television (CCTV) has soared from 50 million yuan to 2.4 billion yuan within three years. On the other hand, some media face the issue of not having enough advertising revenue to survive. Even within the same television stations, the distribution of advertising revenue across various channels or time slots has been extremely uneven.

Different behavior of advertisers
In mainland China, companies that put most emphasis on advertising are typically foreign-invested or joint- venture companies, while local companies account for only a small proportion of the total advertising revenue.

Disparity of strength among agencies
Since McCann Erickson, the first joint venture advertising agency was established in mainland China in 1992, international advertising agencies have gained significant ground in the mainland advertising market. Between 1994 and 1995, the growth rate of advertising revenue of foreign-invested advertising agencies was 172.2 percent, while that of the local companies was only 51.7 percent. According to a survey conducted in Beijing among 20 advertising companies, the per capita turnover of joint venture advertising agencies was 2.94 million yuan, while that of local agencies was 0.96 million yuan. The survey also indicated that international advertising agencies enjoy outstanding achievements in attracting local clients.

Irregularities affecting the development of advertising industry
The advertising rates of mainland Chinese media are unique in that they are usually classified into three categories: local enterprise, joint venture, and foreign-invested enterprise. In addition, these advertising charges are adjusted frequently and usually at short notice. Some media even require advertising agencies to make prepayment.

Providing commissions is a common practice adopted by both mainland

- *Product publicity*: Publicizing specific products
- *Public affairs*: Building and maintaining national or local community relations
- *Lobbying*: Building and maintaining relations with legislators and government officials to influence legislation and regulation
- *Investor relations*: Maintaining relationships with shareholders and others in the financial community
- *Development*: Public relations with donors or members of nonprofit organizations to gain financial or volunteer support

advertising agencies and local media in order to attract clients. This creates an unfair business environment for the industry, probably worsens the quality of advertisements, and dampens the development of the advertising industry in China.

Soaring and excessive demand for advertising slots in local media has led to major local media virtually monopolizing the market. For example, CCTV practices anonymous bidding for advertising slots in its channels since 1994, and there is no maximum bid limit. This has pushed the price of advertising slots sky high.

The high bidding price of advertising slots in CCTV is just one of the signs of irrational behavior in the advertising industry. As such, advertising is often considered as a kind of gamble. "First, the enterprises which made successful bids in CCTV advertising slots may sometimes record an increase in sales volume. Second, they may have a special preference for CCTV because of the immature market environment of the advertising industry. That is, they may not have many choices. Third, the intervention of local government has turned the competition within the advertising industry into a kind of political behavior," says an analyst in the advertising industry.

To maximize profit, many mainland media and enterprises have set up advertising companies to monopolize the advertising business. This has damaged the triad relationship among advertisers, advertising agents and the media.

Institutional irregularities are also a stumbling block for the advertising

industry. Some analysts have commented that the Advertisement Law of the People's Republic of China does not provide clear and consistent definitions for "illegal" and "indecent" advertisements. This makes self-regulation in the advertising industry very difficult, and leads to illegal and indecent advertisements becoming more common. In addition, the creditability and transparency of audience ratings or volume of circulation provided by local media is low due to the absence of a monitoring institution such as an Audit Bureau of Circulations.

In particular, the way that statistics are used by the advertising authorities in mainland China is not consistent with their international counterparts. This causes confusion when comparing advertising revenues across media. In China, the advertising revenue of agencies is counted as a single item in the total advertisement revenue for the industry, and it is the largest portion. However, this amount includes the media charge, which is already included in the media's advertising revenue. That is where the double counting occurs.

Future of the advertising industry in China

Compared with Hong Kong and Taiwan, the advertising industry of mainland China is still in its early infancy. Due to China's rapid economic growth, huge market potential, and a higher emphasis on advertising expenditures by local firms, the advertising industry is going to boom.

Because of the shortage of trained and experienced local staff, the

advertising industry is now operating ineffectively and inefficiently. As such, the quality of work produced by advertising companies is low. Furthermore, occasional interventions by the central government, in terms of macroeconomic controls, cause fluctuation and instability in advertising revenues. This is a major stumbling block in the development of the advertising industry.

"Adopting an agency system is the key for robust development in advertising industry," an analyst says. This can help with the convergence between mainland China's advertising industry and its international counterparts by eliminating chaotic and unfair practices in the market. The agency system would successfully remove the extreme power of local media due to monopolization, and help to establish a healthy and long-term relationship between advertising companies and their clients.

Facing keen competition with international counterparts, mainland China's advertising companies have an urgent need to enhance their capability by training local professionals for the industry. Although the popularity and availability of advertising courses in tertiary institutes has been increasing rapidly, the contents and teaching methods of these courses still need further improvement.

Public relations is used to promote products, people, places, ideas, activities, organizations, and even nations. Companies use public relations to build good relationships with consumers, investors, the media, and their communities. Trade associations have used public relations to rebuild interest in declining commodities such as eggs, apples, milk, and potatoes. Johnson & Johnson's masterly use of public relations played a major role in saving Tylenol from extinction after its product-tampering scare. Nations have used public relations to attract more tourists, foreign investment, and international support.

The Role and Impact of Public Relations

Public relations can have a strong impact on public awareness at a much lower cost than advertising can. The company does not pay for the space or time in the media. Rather, it pays for a staff to develop and circulate information and to manage events. If the company develops an interesting story or event, it could be picked up by several different media, having the same effect as advertising that would cost millions of dollars. And it would have more credibility than advertising.

Public relations results can sometimes be spectacular. Here is how a white liquor company, Swellfun, used public relations to turn a liquor introduction into a national event in China, all on a very small budget:

Here is the fifth major historical and cultural site in Chengdu, China, where the oldest distillery was located. As the clock crept past midnight on August 1, 2000, people in Guangzhou started to rush to buy Swellfun, a white liquor produced by Chengdu Swellfun Co., Ltd. One year after its launch, Swellfun successfully set up a sales network in various key cities in China and has become a leader in the white liquor market. Different from other famous liquor distilleries such as Maotai, Swellfun's success is attributable to the wise use of PR hype which turned it into a famous and prestigious brand in the liquor market.

Public relations – Chengdu Swellfun used public relations to great effect when it discovered a 600-year-old underground distillery in its own premises. It marketed itself as "the living relic" of the white liquor industry. (www.swellfun.com/tasteful/plane.html)

On establishing Chengdu Swellfun Co. Ltd. in 2000, a 600-year-old underground distillery for white liquor was discovered when renovating the old distillery in the Kamkuang district in Chengdu. Before the site was officially confirmed by the government as an ancient site to be protected, Swellfun announced the discovery and released information about the site to the public. It claimed to be "the number one site for Chinese white liquor" and "the living relic" of the white liquor industry. This created a huge sales response from the public.

Swellfun understood that to sustain its competitive advantages, it needed to do more than just empty talks. After the company approached government offices at various levels, the site was declared: a Major Site under Municipal and Provincial protection; one of the five Major Historical and Cultural Sites under State Protection in 2001; and one of the top ten Archaeological Discoveries of 1999 in 2002. Domestically, Swellfun was named as a "Famous Historical and Cultural Liquor of China" by China Food Industry Association, and "The Number One Liquor Distillery Site in China." Internationally, the site was listed as "The Oldest Distillery Site" in China by Shanghai Guinness Grand World in May 2001.

Along the same lines, Swellfun's package design also won the package design award at the Mobius Advertising Awards in 2001. Not only was it the first Chinese product to receive such an honor, it was the first time any Asian product package had received the prestigious award. "Blending both traditional and modern designs, Swellfun's liquor package exhibits a high level of elegance, dignity, and mystery of the oriental culture," said J. W. Anderson, founder and chairman of the Mobius awards.[17]

Despite its potential strengths, public relations is sometimes described as a marketing stepchild because of its often limited and scattered use. The PR staff is so busy dealing with various publics—stockholders, employees, legislators, the press—that PR programs to support product marketing objectives may be ignored. Marketing managers and PR practitioners do not always speak the same language. Many PR practitioners see their job as simply to communicate. In contrast, marketing managers tend to be much more interested in how advertising and public relations affect brand building, sales and profits, and customer relationships.

This situation is changing, however. Although public relations still captures only a small portion of the overall marketing budgets of most firms, it is playing an increasingly important brand-building role. Two well-known marketing consultants even go so far as to conclude that advertising does not build brands, PR does. In their book *The Fall of Advertising & the Rise of PR*, the consultants proclaim that the dominance of advertising is over and that public relations is quietly becoming the most powerful marketing communications tool:

The birth of a brand is usually accomplished with [public relations], not advertising. Our general rule is [PR] first, advertising second. [Public relations] is the nail, advertising the hammer. [PR] creates the credentials that provide the credibility for advertising … Anita Roddick built the Body Shop into a major brand with no advertising at all. Instead, she traveled the world on a relentless quest for publicity… Until recently Starbucks Coffee did not spend a hill of beans on advertising, either. In [ten] years, the company spent less than $10 million on advertising, a trivial amount for a brand that delivers annual sales of [in the billions]. Wal-Mart Stores became the world's largest retailer … with very little advertising … On the Internet, Amazon.com became a powerhouse brand with virtually no advertising.[18]

Although the book created much controversy, and most advertisers would not agree with a part of the title that says "fall of advertising", the point made is a good one. Advertising and public relations should work hand in hand to build and maintain brands.

Major Public Relations Tools

Public relations uses several tools (see **Figure 15.3**). One of the major tools is news. PR professionals find or create favorable news about the company and its products or people. Sometimes news stories occur naturally, and sometimes the PR person can suggest events

PR Tools
- News
- Speeches
- Special events
- Written materials
- Audio visual materials
- Corporate identity
- Public service activites
- Public service activites
- Buzz marketing

Figure 15.3
Major public relations tools

Public relations people also prepare written materials such as annual reports, brochures, articles, and company newsletters and magazines.

or activities that would create news. Speeches can also create product and company publicity. Increasingly, company executives must field questions from the media or give talks at trade associations or sales meetings, and these events can either build or hurt the company's image.

Another common PR tool is special events, ranging from news conferences, press tours, grand openings, and fireworks displays to laser shows, hot air balloon releases, multimedia presentations, star-studded spectaculars, or educational programs designed to reach and interest target publics.

Public relations people also prepare written materials to reach and influence their target markets. These materials include annual reports, brochures, articles, and company newsletters and magazines. *Audiovisual materials*, such as films, slide-and-sound programs, DVDs, and online videos are being used increasingly as communication tools. *Corporate identity materials* can also help create a corporate identity that the public immediately recognizes. Logos, stationery, brochures, signs, business forms, business cards, buildings, uniforms, and company cars and trucks—all become marketing tools when they are attractive, distinctive, and memorable. Finally, companies can improve public goodwill by contributing money and time to *public service activities*.

REVIEWING THE CONCEPTS

Companies must do more than make good products—they must inform consumers about product benefits and carefully position products in consumers' minds. To do this, they must master advertising and public relations.

1 Define the role of advertising in the promotion mix.

Advertising—the use of paid media by a seller to inform, persuade, and remind buyers about its products or organization—is an important promotion tool for communicating the value that marketers create for their customers. American marketers spend more than $264 billion each year on advertising, and worldwide ad spending exceeds $600 billion. Advertising takes many forms and has many uses. Although advertising is used mostly by business firms, a wide range of not-for-profit organizations, professionals, and social agencies also use advertising to promote their causes to various target publics. *Public relations*—gaining favorable publicity and creating a favorable company image—is the least used of the major promotion tools, although it has great potential for building consumer awareness and preference.

2 Describe the major decisions involved in developing an advertising program.

Advertising decision making involves decisions about the advertising objectives, the budget, the message, the media, and, finally, the evaluation of results. Advertisers should set clear target, task, and timing *objectives*, whether the aim is to inform, persuade, or remind buyers. Advertising's goal is to move consumers through the buyer-readiness stages discussed in the previous chapter. Some advertising is designed to move people to immediate action. However, many of the ads you see today focus on building or strengthening long-term customer relationships. The advertising *budget* can be based on sales, on competitors' spending, or on the objectives and tasks of the advertising program. The size and allocation of the budget depend on many factors.

Advertising strategy consists of two major elements: creating advertising *messages* and selecting advertising *media*. The message decision calls for planning a message strategy and executing it effectively. Good advertising messages are especially important in today's costly and cluttered advertising environment. Just to gain and hold attention, today's advertising messages must be better planned, more imaginative, more entertaining, and more rewarding to consumers. In fact, many marketers are now subscribing to a new merging of advertising and entertainment, dubbed "Madison & Vine." The *media decision* involves defining reach, frequency, and impact goals; choosing major media types; selecting media vehicles; and deciding on media timing. Message and media decisions must be closely coordinated for maximum campaign effectiveness.

Finally, *evaluation* calls for evaluating the communication and sales effects of advertising before, during, and after the advertising is placed. Advertising accountability has become a hot issue for most companies. Increasingly, top management is asking: "What return are we getting on our advertising investment?" and "How do we know that we are spending the right amount?" Other important advertising issues involve *organizing* for advertising and dealing with the complexities of international advertising.

3 Define the role of public relations in the promotion mix.

Public relations—gaining favorable publicity and creating a favorable company image—is the least used of the major promotion tools, although it has great potential for building consumer awareness and preference. Public relations is used to promote products, people, places, ideas, activities, organizations, and even nations. Companies use public relations to build good relationships with consumers, investors, the media, and their communities. Public relations can have a strong impact on public awareness at a much lower cost than advertising can, and its results can sometimes be spectacular. Although public relations captures only a small portion of the overall marketing budgets of most firms, it is playing an increasingly important brand-building role.

4 Explain how companies use public relations to communicate with their publics.

Companies use public relations to communicate with their publics by setting PR objectives, choosing PR messages and vehicles, implementing the PR plan, and evaluating PR results. To accomplish these goals, public relations professionals use several tools such as *news*, *speeches*, and *special events*. They also prepare *written*, *audiovisual*, and *corporate identity materials* and contribute money and time to *public service activities*. Buzz marketing is a form of public relations that gets consumers themselves to spread word-of-mouth information about the company and its brands. The Internet has also become a major public relations tool.

REVIEWING THE KEY TERMS

DISCUSSING THE CONCEPTS

1. What factors make management's task of setting advertising budgets difficult?

2. Why is it important that the advertising media and creative departments work closely together?

3. How do an advertisement's appeals differ from its execution style?

4. Evaluate why Maybelline New York might decide to remove all its advertising from MTV and instead place more advertising in Seventeen magazine.

5. Discuss three potential problems facing a pharmaceutical manufacturer who decides to advertise in Europe. Are these problems different from those the manufacturer would encounter when advertising in Asia?

6. Why is public relations sometimes referred to as a marketing stepchild? What can be done to correct this problem?

APPLYING THE CONCEPTS

1. Form a small group and choose three advertising media for a campaign to introduce a new line of men's personal care products under an Estee Lauder label.

2. Locate a magazine advertisement for a household cleaning product. Describe how the appeals in this ad display the three characteristics of a good advertising appeal.

3. How might Campbell Soup Company go about evaluating the effectiveness of an advertising campaign for a new "heat-and-drink" soup product?

FOCUS ON TECHNOLOGY

ALLERCA creates truly unique products—the world's first scientifically proven hypoallergenic cats (see them at www.allerca.com). Genetically engineered, the medium-sized ALLERCA GD cat weighs 10–15 pounds and is fully matured at age three. According to ALLERCA, the cats have long life expectancies and possess sweet and affectionate dispositions. For a price of about $3,000, you receive a 12-week-old kitten, complete with all shots and vaccinations, an embedded microchip identifier implant, and a one-year guarantee. Customers purchase kittens over the Internet and must pay approximately $1,000 for processing and transportation. The high shipping cost is because commercial air shipping is stressful to the animal; therefore, the kitten travels in a specialized private jet courier. According to

ALLERCA, the current waiting time for the ALLERCA GD kitten is approximately two years. Potential buyers may reduce their wait times to just a few months by paying $2,000 for one of the few kittens in the Premium Placement Program.

1. This product is sold over the Internet. How can ALLERCA use Internet advertising technologies to reach its target market? (Visit the Internet Advertising Bureau at www.iab.net to learn about recent technologies.)

2. What might be the main objectives of advertising and public relations for ALLERCA, and what factors will affect ALLERCA's decision about its advertising and PR budgets?

3. In addition to Internet marketing, what other advertising media and PR tools would you choose for promoting ALLERCA and its unique products?

FOCUS ON ETHICS

Splenda (sucralose) was introduced to the consumer market in 1999. It is now a common sweetener found in more than 3,500 food products. Splenda's advertising slogan is "made from sugar, so it tastes like sugar." Manufactured and marketed by packaged-goods giant Johnson & Johnson, Splenda now captures a substantial percentage of the artificial sweetener market and is beginning to cut into sugar's market share. But Splenda's campaign has attracted much attention from competitors, social advocacy groups, and nutritional experts. According to these groups, Splenda has clearly violated "truth in advertising" codes with its "made from sugar" slogan. Although currently produced from a sugar molecule, they claim, Splenda is an artificial sweetener that can be produced without sugar. In addition, the chemical name assigned to Splenda—sucralose—is misleading because it closely resembles the chemical name of sugar—sucrose.

The strongest opponent to the Splenda "made from sugar" campaign is The Sugar Association, which has launched a

large and expensive campaign of its own to educate the public and to expose Splenda's unethical behavior. The association's Web site (http://www.truthaboutsplenda.com) urges consumers to take action by contacting friends, sending letters to the FTC and the FDA, and sending letters of complaint directly to Johnson & Johnson. Another area of the Web site, labeled Fact vs. Fiction, highlights serious consumer misunderstandings that might result from Splenda's advertising. It describes in detail how Splenda is not natural sugar and notes that there exist no conclusive tests regarding the long-term safety of consuming Splenda.

1. What is the objective of Splenda's "made from sugar, so it tastes like sugar" message and campaign? Is this slogan an effective appeal?

2. What is the objective of The Sugar Association's communications campaign? Is that campaign effective?

3. Check the "truth in advertising" guidelines at the FTC Web site (www.ftc.gov/bcp/conline/pubs/buspubs/ad-faqs.htm). Has Splenda followed these rules?

DDB Worldwide

DDB Worldwide, a global communications firm, has crafted imaginative commercials and staged successful marketing events for megamarketers such as Ameriquest, Volkswagen, Budweiser, Pepsi, and Nike. Recently, DDB staged a live round of Monopoly on the streets of London to promote Milton Bradley's updated version of the classic game. Online players "bought" properties throughout the city and selected one of 18 London cabs to use as a playing piece. The cabs, tracked by GPS, tallied rent payments and receipts for each player as they moved about the streets. More than one million people played and the campaign garnered $3 million in free publicity. As a result, Monopoly: Here and Now was one of the best-selling games of the year.

With creativity and results like these, it is easy to understand why DDB is one of the world's most decorated agencies. DDB brought the same creativity to the challenge of

reinventing another classic, JC Penney. Relying on extensive consumer research, DDB crafted an ad campaign that built the JC Penney brand, connected with the retailer's core consumers, and brought customers back in droves.

After viewing the video featuring DDB Worldwide, answer the following questions about advertising and public relations.

1. What were DDB's advertising objectives for the JC Penney campaign?

2. How did DDB's consumer research affect the message strategy for the campaign? Does the major advertising appeal have the three characteristics discussed in the text? How did identifying JC Penney's core consumers affect DDB's message execution style?

3. Could JC Penney employ the "Madison & Vine" concept discussed in the chapter? How?

COMPANY CASE

Phoenix Satellite Television—The "Chinese CNN": The Use of Public Relations in Promotion

Phoenix Satellite Television Holdings Limited (Phoenix TV) was first established in 1996 in Hong Kong by Liu Chang Le. It is a public company in which STAR TV and Today's Asia Limited own 75 percent of the total shares as free shareholders and 16.4 percent are held by public investors.

The idea of establishing Phoenix came from Singapore, where about 74 percent of the population speak Chinese and 94 percent speak English. At that time, Singapore had two TV stations, one transmitting in English and one in Chinese. Although the English-language TV station provided better programs, its Chinese counterpart had

higher audience ratings and greater advertising revenues. This gave Liu the inspiration that although the Chinese people are spread out across the world and may use different languages to communicate in their daily life, the Chinese language remains closest to their hearts. In 1996, there was no global Chinese television medium. Phoenix was born in the belief that it could successfully fill this void with new television channels with quality programs targeted at the global Chinese market. "Phoenix TV is developing a global outlook and is independent of local political attachments," says Liu. This positioning has driven Phoenix TV toward meeting international standards by adopting a content orientation, an independent approach, and an expression style in the production of programs.

In 2008, Phoenix TV was operating five channels, each aiming at achieving a particular purpose, as shown in **Table 15.3**.

During these years, the Phoenix Chinese Channel alone has expanded to 53 countries and regions and has more than 20 million viewers worldwide, of which more than 63 percent are Chinese-speaking. In mainland China, it attracts 150 million viewers in 42 million households. The first three channels listed are broadcast via cable in Hong Kong, via satellite to Taiwan, mainland China, and other regions worldwide. However, Hong Kong audiences can only view Phoenix channels either using an installed satellite dish or via subscription cable TV.

Having said that, Hong Kong people are not greatly attracted to Phoenix TV, and this is for two reasons. First, they are generally less interested in political news than mainland or Taiwan audiences are, and second, Phoenix TV broadcasts in Standard Mandarin and not in Cantonese, which is the main dialect in Hong Kong. Phoenix TV has performed well

Table 15.3 The Five Channels of Phoenix TV

Name	Year of Launch	Operations
Phoenix Chinese Channel	1996	Long-term foreign broadcaster
Phoenix Movies Channel	1998	An encrypted pay-television service in China and worldwide
Phoenix InfoNews Channel	2001	24-hour news channel
Phoenix North America Chinese Channel	2001	Broadcast on EchoStar and DIRECTV satellite systems with the same programs as the Phoenix Chinese News and Entertaiment Channel
Phoenix Chinese News and Entertainment Channel	1996	24-hour channel broadcasting via satellite Eurobird D6 across Europe

in a number of ways. Internationally, in a survey conducted by *Fortune* magazine in 1999, it was voted one of the most reputable international brands among Chinese audiences. The advertising revenue of Phoenix has increased tenfold within five years, with an average annual growth rate of 81.15 percent.

Phoenix TV—The Chinese CNN

As the overseas media market in Standard Mandarin has grown to become a huge market, Phoenix TV has decided to call itself "the Chinese CNN" and shoulder the responsibility of serving the global Chinese community. The name Phoenix and the network logo each carry an indigenous meaning. A Chinese proverb says, "The Phoenix will only descend on treasured lands." Phoenix therefore means fortune or good luck. Its logo symbolizes the historical integration of the various ethnic communities in China. The logo also indicates Phoenix TV's endeavor to cater to the needs of the Chinese in various locations around the world and to spread the key cultural values of the Chinese nation. Every new member of staff at Phoenix TV is required to take a course called "phoenix studies" to learn the unique virtues of the creature known as the phoenix. The course aims to create a spirit of enterprise at Phoenix TV.

Marketing Strategies

Phoenix TV adopted several strategies to build up a reputable brand name among TV channels:

Listing. The first strategy was to become a listed company in the Hong Kong Growth Enterprise Market; this was achieved on June 30, 2000. Immediately after listing, a controversial documentary about the life of Zhang Xueliang was broadcast. The documentary aroused heated discussions in the Asia-Pacific and helped Phoenix TV create a reputation for being a vibrant medium.

Creating Star Presenters. Mr. Liu understands the importance of quality news anchors and talk show hosts to the success of Phoenix TV. He calls them star presenters, and most of them hold a degree in journalism, arts, or language studies. Compared with other channels in Asia, Phoenix has become well known as the producer of the greatest number of star presenters, such as Wu Xiaoli, Hu Yihu, Liu Hairuo, and Li Ao. To recognize their performance, Mr. Liu has launched a share-option scheme to motivate, reward, and retain them.

Forming international alliances. Phoenix is able to enter the overseas Chinese market and the mainstream European and American communities through cooperation with Murdoch and DIRECTV. Murdoch is the owner of News Corporation, with media interests in Europe and the U.S., while DIRECTV is the largest satellite TV platform in America.

Allowing international information flow. The Phoenix InfoNews Channel provides a platform for the Chinese media to express their viewpoints on international politics and economics, so that dependency on information provided by Western media can be halted.

Programs unique in style. Phoenix TV produces programs which are totally different in content and style from those produced by the mainland media. Its audacity and creativity help it to set new records in the history of the Chinese media.

Emphasis on news broadcasting. Phoenix TV's strategy of focusing on news broadcasting makes it distinct from its competitors in the mainland market. It also lets the locals understand that this strategy helps to end the monopoly of news broadcast by any one TV station.

Public Relations

Although various strategies have been developed and implemented, the company's strategy on public relations is regarded as the most successful one. Let's look at some public relations gimmicks used by Phoenix TV.

"Across China." This program was jointly produced by the China Intercontinental Communication Centre of the State Council Information Office and presented by the celebrated TV presenter, Wu Xiaoli. It helped Phoenix TV to make a successful entry to the mainland market. The theme of the program is to show today's China to the world by introducing the unique subcultures of various provinces, cities, and autonomous regions in mainland China. The program integrates beautifully the elements of entertainment, educational value, and culture. Government officials, particularly those from second-tier provinces, were invited to participate in the program as VIP guests. Since the promotion of second-tier provinces by the mass media is not a common practice, the invitation from Phoenix TV was well regarded by the governments of these provinces. Many of them sent high-ranking officials to appear in the program. Eventually, the program successfully drew the attention of local governments and acquired invaluable political assets by building up close relations with local administration.

Establishing relations with central government. Another PR strategy has been to establish indirect relations with the leaders of the Chinese government by letting Shanghai Industrial Holdings Limited (SIHL), a subsidiary of the Shanghai municipal government, become a strategic shareholder in Phoenix TV. As the chairperson of SIHL is the son of the former General Secretary of the communist party and President of the PRC, Jiang Zemin, Phoenix could be sure it would develop good relationships with the central government.

Independent views of reporting news. The third strategy is to ensure a neutral and empathic viewpoint in reporting news. News and programs regarding Sino-American relations, cross-strait relations, China's entry to WTO, and hosting the 2008 Olympics are regarded as "sensitive" and have to be handled carefully. Merely selecting and blindly following Western viewpoints would certainly damage the relationship with the Chinese government. Phoenix has therefore tried to ensure that TV programs are produced in a manner that takes the standpoint of the Chinese government into consideration, especially when Phoenix's viewpoint is not in line with that of the Chinese government.

Cooperating with other mass media in China. Phoenix TV understands that the importance of doing business in China is not to push its competitors out of the market, but to co-exist harmoniously with them. It therefore has cooperated with the mainland media as a working partner,

for example, in producing programs that involve large-scale interview activities. This not only serves to build up a good relationship with the other mass media, but also helps to expand its influence in mainland China. The above public relations strategy has successfully earned trust from, and established good relationships with, the Chinese government. In January 2003, the Phoenix InfoNews Channel was granted landing rights from the Chinese State Administration of Radio, Films, and Television (SARFT). These rights have enabled Phoenix to become one of the few non-government-related television broadcasters in mainland China that is permitted to broadcast information about events not covered by the government media, such as the Against Basic Law Article 23 rally on July 1, 2003 in Hong Kong.

Questions For Discussion

1. What is the strategy that has led to Phoenix TV's success in the global Chinese market?
2. Since American media are always proud of their professionalism in news reporting, do you consider Phoenix TV"s approach in reporting news unethical?
3. Visit Phoenix TV's Web site at www.phoenix.com. What are the strategies that you think Phoenix TV should adopt in the future?

Source:
Accessed at en.wikipedia.org/wiki/Phoenix Television; www.phoenix.com/; Lu Tai Hung, "Revelation of Marketing in China", Hong Kong: Hong Kong Economic Newspaper Ltd, 2002.

Objectives

After studying this chapter, you should be able to

- discuss the role of a company's salespeople in creating value for customers and building customer relationships
- identify and explain the six major sales force management steps
- discuss the personal selling process, distinguishing between transaction-oriented marketing and relationship marketing
- explain how sales promotion campaigns are developed and implemented

CHAPTER 16

PERSONAL SELLING AND SALES PROMOTION

Previewing the Concepts

In the previous two chapters, you learned about communicating customer value through integrated marketing communications (IMC) and about two elements of the promotion mix—advertising and public relations. In this chapter, we will look at two more IMC elements—personal selling and sales promotion. Personal selling is the interpersonal arm of marketing communications, in which the sales force interacts with customers and prospects to build relationships and make sales. Sales promotion consists of short-term incentives to encourage the purchase or sale of a product or service. As you read on, remember that although this chapter examines personal selling and sales promotion as separate tools, they must be carefully integrated with other elements of the promotion mix.

When someone says "salesperson," what image comes to mind? Perhaps you think about a stereotypical glad-hander who's out to lighten your wallet by selling you something you don't really need. Think again. Today, for most companies, personal selling plays an important role in building profitable customer relationships. Consider Prudential Assurance Company Ltd., an international company in Hong Kong whose customer-focused sales training strategy has helped it to grow rapidly in a changing and competitive business environment.

Prudential plc (UK) was established in London in 1848 as The Prudential Mutual Assurance, Investment and Loan Association. It is now an international retail financial group, providing retail financial services and fund management to over 20 million customers worldwide, with over US$510 billion of funds under management (as at June 20, 2007). According to *Fortune* Magazine on July 25, 2005, Prudential was the world's fifth largest life and health insurer (stock) in terms of revenue. It has also been granted AA+ rating from Standard & Poor's and Aa1 rating from Moody's for its robust financial foundation.

The Prudential Assurance Company Limited (PRU) was set up as a branch of Prudential plc (UK) in Hong Kong in 1964, offering a large range of insurance products to clients. With the corporate credo "Always Listening, Always Understanding", the Prudential Assurance Company offers general insurance, life insurance, group insurance protection, pensions, mandatory provident fund solutions, mutual funds, banking and investment management to Hong Kongers. It has been granted various industry awards for its outstanding business performance, such as the "Financial Planner Award (Insurance Category)," which was jointly organized by the *South China Morning Post* and the Institute of Financial Planners of Hong Kong in 2005 and 2006, and the "Outstanding Financial Planner Award" organized by the Hong Kong Institute of Bankers

(HKIB) in 2006. There are currently over 3,700 insurance consultants, financial planning managers, and staff in the Hong Kong branch of the Prudential to provide tailor-made insurance and financial services to their clients.

Academy of Financial Services (AFS)

With the continuous development of Hong Kong's economy, there are growing demands for high-quality and comprehensive financial management services, rather than just general insurance services. To capture the growing market, Prudential established the Academy of Financial Services (AFS) to recruit talent and provide training for candidates who are interested in joining the industry as salespersons for financial services. nurture future professional financial planners to provide clients with financial management services including protection, wealth accumulation and preservation, and retirement solutions.

ASF and the PRU Financial Planning Program were established in 2004, when 62 experienced consultants with professional qualifications such as Certified Financial Planner (CFPCM), Chartered Financial Practitioner (FChFP) and Registered Financial Consultant (RFC) were appointed as Financial Planners. There are currently over 250 Financial Planners in Prudential.

Prudential recruits approximately 100 new graduates from universities every year and helps them to develop their financial planning career. They are provided with a comprehensive and systematic training program which includes the Pre-contract Training Program, Rookies Development Program, and Three-tier Financial Planning Training. Individual branches may also have their own specially designed training programs such as the "mentor-mentee" scheme which allows new insurance consultants to gain experience through fieldwork observation.

Business Internship Program

Prudential launched the Business Internship Program for final year students of eight local universities, IED and IVE in 2001. The aims of this program are to provide a platform to recruit high caliber students who possess potential and interest in the industry, and to give students an overview of the business world through workshops and outbound training.

Pre-contract Training Program

This orientation program includes an IIQE (Insurance Intermediaries Qualifying Examination) Revision Course, a licensing course which is a prerequisite for every sales person in the insurance industry, and the "Prudential Vision," in which the elite from different industries are invited to share their stories of success with candidates.

Rookies' Development Program

Prudential provides various courses to rookies to nurture them as all-round sales people before they decide to pursue a role in sales management or as a consultant. The content of the courses includes insurance regulations, operational information, knowledge of company products, financial planning concepts, activity management, presentation skills, communication skills, and attitude training.

Three-tier Financial Planning Training

The financial planning training aims at producing three different calibers of salespersons. The first level of the training is for new insurance consultants, the second level for associate financial planners and the third level for full financial planners. Now let's look at what potential salespersons will learn at each level.

Level 1: Financial Planning Foundation

Courses at this level of training include Basic Retirement Planning, Wealth Planning in the Insurance Industry, a Retirement Products Presentation workshop, and Applications on Financial Planning-Related Information. After finishing the Rookies' Development Program and associated training, those consultants who have not yet gone through formal financial planning education programs and who aim at a higher level in their financial planning career can attend Core Training courses, to further their financial planning knowledge.

Level 2: Associate Financial Planner (AFP)

This level includes Professional Financial Planning Education and Business Requirements, Core Training, and the Retirement Specialist Program. Consultants who have passed at least two subjects in recognized financial planning education and have met the business performance requirements are granted a Level 2 certificate.

Level 3: Financial Planning Manager (FPM) and Senior Financial Planning Manager (SFPM)

Financial Planning Management (FPM or SFPM) targets professional financial planners who have already received a certain level of education in this field. To qualify at this top level and hold the title of Financial Planning Manager or Senior Financial Planning Manager, candidates must also have met particular business performance requirements.[1]

Personal Selling

Robert Louis Stevenson once noted that "everyone lives by selling something." Companies all around the world use sales forces to sell products and services to business customers and final consumers. But sales forces are also found in many other kinds of organizations. For example, colleges use recruiters to attract new students and churches use membership committees to attract new members. Museums and fine arts organizations use fund-raisers to contact donors and raise money. Even governments use sales forces. For instance, regional economic development agencies employ account executives to attract prospective investors. In the first part of this chapter, we examine personal selling's role in the organization, sales force management decisions, and the personal selling process.

The Nature of Personal Selling

Personal selling is one of the oldest professions in the world. The people who do the selling go by many names: salespeople, sales representatives, district managers, account

Personal selling
Personal presentation by the firm's sales force for the purpose of making sales and building customer relationships.

executives, sales consultants, sales engineers, agents, and account development reps to name just a few.

People hold many stereotypes of salespeople—including some unfavorable ones. Salespeople have been described as as loners, traveling their territories, trying to foist their wares on unsuspecting or unwilling buyers. However, modern salespeople are a far cry from these unfortunate stereotypes. Today, most salespeople are well-educated, well-trained professionals who work to build and maintain long-term customer relationships. They listen to their customers, assess customer needs, and organize the company's efforts to solve customer problems. Consider Boeing, the aerospace giant competing in the rough-and-tumble worldwide commercial aircraft market. It takes more than fast talk and a warm smile to sell expensive airplanes:

Selling high-tech aircraft at $100 million or more per order is complex and challenging. A single big sale can easily run into billions of dollars. Boeing salespeople head up an extensive team of company specialists—sales and service technicians, financial analysts, planners, engineers—all dedicated to finding ways to satisfy airline customer needs. The selling process is nerve-rackingly slow—it can take two or three years from the first sales presentation to the day the sale is announced. After getting the order, salespeople then must stay in almost constant touch to keep track of the account's equipment needs and to make certain the customer stays satisfied. Success depends on building solid, long-term relationships with customers, based on performance and trust. "When you buy an airplane, it is like getting married," says the head of Boeing's commercial airplane division. "It is a long-term relationship."[2]

Professional selling –
It takes more than fast talk and a warm smile to sell high-tech aircraft at $100 million or more per order. Success depends on building solid long-term relationships with customers.

Salesperson
An individual representing a company to customers by performing one or more of the following activities: prospecting, communicating, selling, servicing, information gathering, and relationship building.

The term **salesperson** covers a wide range of positions. At one extreme, a salesperson might be largely an *order taker*, such as the department store salesperson standing behind the counter. At the other extreme are *order getters*, whose positions demand *creative selling* and *relationship building* for products and services ranging from appliances, industrial equipment, and airplanes to insurance and information technology services. Here, we focus on the more creative types of selling and on the process of building and managing an effective sales force.

The Role of the Sales Force

Personal selling is the interpersonal arm of the promotion mix. Advertising consists largely of one-way, nonpersonal communication with target consumer groups. In contrast, personal selling involves two-way, personal communication between salespeople and individual customers—whether face to face, by telephone, through video or Web conferences, or by other means. Personal selling can be more effective than advertising in more complex selling situations. Salespeople can probe customers to learn more about their problems and then adjust the marketing offer and presentation to fit the special needs of each customer.

The role of personal selling varies from company to company. Some firms have no salespeople at all—for example, companies that sell only online or through catalogs, or companies that sell through manufacturer's reps, sales agents, or brokers. In most firms, however, the sales force plays a major role. In companies that sell business products and services, such as IBM, Huawei Technologies, and NEC, the company's salespeople work directly with customers. In consumer product companies such as Procter & Gamble, Sony, Meadi, and Nike, the sales force plays an important behind-the-scenes role. It works with wholesalers and retailers to gain their support and to help them be more effective in selling the company's products.

The sales force serves as a critical link between a company and its customers. In many cases, salespeople serve both masters—the seller and the buyer. First, they *represent the company to customers*. They find and develop new customers and communicate information about the company's products and services. They sell products by approaching customers, presenting their products, answering objections, negotiating prices and terms, and closing sales. In addition, salespeople provide customer service and carry out market research and intelligence work.

At the same time, salespeople *represent customers to the company*, acting inside the firm as "champions" of customers' interests and managing the buyer-seller relationship. Salespeople relay customer concerns about company products and actions back inside to those who can handle them. They learn about customer needs and work with other marketing and nonmarketing people in the company to develop greater customer value. The old view was that salespeople should worry about sales and the company should worry about profit. However, the current view holds that salespeople should be concerned with more than just producing *sales*—they should work with others in the company to produce *customer value* and *company profit*.

The sales force serves as a critical link between a company and its customers. They represent the company to customers, and vice versa.

Managing the Sales Force

Sales force management
The analysis, planning, implementation, and control of sales force activities. It includes designing sales force strategy and structure and recruiting, selecting, training, supervising, compensating, and evaluating the firm's salespeople.

We define **sales force management** as the analysis, planning, implementation, and control of sales force activities. It includes designing sales force strategy and structure and recruiting, selecting, training, compensating, supervising, and evaluating the firm's salespeople. These major sales force management decisions are shown in **Figure 16.1** and are discussed in the following sections.

L⊘A
earning Aid

Figure 16.1
Major steps in sales force management

Designing Sales Force Strategy and Structure

Marketing managers face several sales force strategy and design questions. How should salespeople and their tasks be structured? How big should the sales force be? Should salespeople sell alone or work in teams with other people in the company? Should they sell in the field or by telephone or on the Web?

Sales Force Structure

A company can divide sales responsibilities along any of several lines. The decision is simple if the company sells only one product line to one industry with customers in many locations. In that case the company would use a *territorial sales force structure*. However, if the company sells many products to many types of customers, it might need either a *product sales force structure*, a *customer sales force structure*, or a combination of the two.

Territorial sales force structure

In the **territorial sales force structure**, each salesperson is assigned to an exclusive geographic area and sells the company's full line of products or services to all customers in that territory. This organization clearly defines each salesperson's job and fixes accountability. It also increases the salesperson's desire to build local customer relationships that, in turn, improve selling effectiveness. Finally, because each salesperson travels within a limited geographic area, travel expenses are relatively small.

A territorial sales organization is often supported by many levels of sales management positions. For example, Campbell Soup uses a territorial structure in which each salesperson is responsible for selling all Campbell Soup products. Starting at the bottom of the organization, *sales merchandisers* report to *sales representatives*, who report to *retail supervisors*, who report to *directors of retail sales operations*, who report to *regional sales managers*. Regional sales managers, in turn, report to *general sales managers*, who report to a *vice president* and *general sales manager*.

> **Territorial sales force structure**
> A sales force organization that assigns each salesperson to an exclusive geographic territory in which that salesperson sells the company's full line.
>
> **Product sales force structure**
> A sales force organization under which salespeople specialize in selling only a portion of the company's products or lines.
>
> **Customer sales force structure**
> A sales force organization under which salespeople specialize in selling only to certain customers or industries.

Product sales force structure

Salespeople must know their products—especially when the products are numerous and complex. This need, together with the growth of product management, has led many companies to adopt a **product sales force structure**, in which the sales force sells along product lines. For example, Fuji uses different sales forces for its film products and its industrial products. The sales force for film products deals with simple products that are distributed intensively, whereas the sales force for industrial products deals with complex products that require technical understanding.

The product structure can lead to problems, however, if a single large customer buys many different company products. Several salespeople might end up calling on the same customer on the same day. This means that they travel over the same routes and wait to see the same customer's purchasing agents. These extra costs must be compared with the benefits of better product knowledge and attention to individual products.

Customer sales force structure

More and more companies are now using a **customer sales force structure**, in which they organize the sales force along customer or industry lines. Separate sales forces may be set up for different industries, for serving current customers versus finding new ones, and for major accounts versus regular accounts.

Organizing the sales force around customers can help a company become more customer focused and build closer relationships with important customers. For example, IBM shifted from a product-based structure to a customer-based one. Before the shift, droves of salespeople representing different IBM software, hardware, and services divisions might call on a single large client, creating confusion and frustration. Such large customers wanted a "single face," one point of contact for all its products and services. Following the restructuring, a single IBM "client executive" works with each large customer and manages a team of IBMers—product reps, systems engineers, consultant, and others—who work with the customer. The client executive becomes an expert in the customer's industry and owns the business relationship with the client. Such an intense focus on customers is widely credited for IBM's dramatic turnaround in recent years.

IBM's shift from a product-based structure to a customer-based one contributed to their dramatic turnaround in recent years.

Complex sales force structures

When a company sells a wide variety of products to many types of customers over a broad geographic area, it often combines several types of sales force structures. Salespeople can be specialized by customer and territory, by product and territory, by product and customer, or by territory, product, and customer. No single structure is best for all companies and situations. Each company should select a sales force structure that best serves the needs of its customers and fits its overall marketing strategy.

A good sales structure can mean the difference between success and failure. Companies should periodically review their sales force organizations to be certain that they serve the needs of the company and its customers. Over time, sales force structures can grow complex, inefficient, and unresponsive to customers' needs. This happened recently to technology giant Hewlett-Packard. To correct the the problem, the company's new CEO took dramatic steps to restructure HP's corporate sales forces (see **Real Marketing 16.1**).

Sales Force Size

Once the company has set its structure, it is ready to consider *sales force size*. Sales forces may range in size from only a few salespeople to tens of thousands. Some sales forces are huge—for example, American Express employs 23,500 U.S. salespeople, PepsiCo 36,000, and The Hartford Financial Services Group 100,000.[3] Salespeople constitute one of the company's most productive—and most expensive—assets. Therefore, increasing their number will increase both sales and costs.

Many companies use some form of *workload approach* to set sales force size. Using this approach, a company first groups accounts into different classes according to size, account status, or other factors related to the amount of effort required to maintain them. It then determines the number of salespeople needed to call on each class of accounts the desired number of times.

The company might think as follows: Suppose we have 1,000 Type-A accounts and 2,000 Type-B accounts. Type-A accounts require 36 calls a year and Type-B accounts require 12 calls a year. In this case, the sales force's workload—the number of calls it must make per year—is 60,000 calls [$(1,000 \times 36) + (2,000 \times 12) = 36,000 + 24,000 = 60,000$]. Suppose our average salesperson can make 1,000 calls a year. Thus, we need 60 salespeople ($60,000 \div 1,000$).[4]

Other Sales Force Strategy and Structure Issues

Sales management must also decide who will be involved in the selling effort and how various sales and sales support people will work together.

Outside and inside sales forces

Outside sales force (or field sales force)
Outside salespeople who travel to call on customers in the field.

Inside sales force
Inside salespeople who conduct business from their offices via telephone, the Internet, or visits from prospective buyers.

The company may have an **outside sales force** (or *field sales force*), an **inside sales force**, or both. Outside salespeople travel to call on customers in the field. Inside salespeople conduct business from their offices via telephone, the Internet, or visits from buyers.

Some inside salespeople provide support for the outside sales force, freeing them to spend more time selling to major accounts and finding new prospects. For example, *technical sales support people* provide technical information and answers to customers' questions. *Sales assistants* provide administrative backup for outside salespeople. They call ahead and confirm appointments, follow up on deliveries, and answer customers' questions when outside salespeople cannot be reached.

Other inside salespeople do more than just provide support. *Telemarketers* and *Web sellers* use the phone and Internet to find new leads and qualify prospects or to sell and service accounts directly. Telemarketing and Web selling can be very effective, less costly ways to sell to smaller, harder-to-reach customers. Depending on the complexity of the product and customer, for example, a telemarketer can make from 20 to 33 decision-maker contacts a day, compared to the average of four that an outside salesperson can make. And whereas an average business-to-business field sales call costs $329 or more, a routine industrial telemarketing call costs only about $5 and a complex call about $20.[5]

To sell its e-business solutions to small businesses, IBM is emphasizing its telemarketing effort. IBM's roughly 1,200 phone reps now generate 30 percent of IBM's revenues from small and midsize business. The reps focus on specific industries and each calls on as many as 300 accounts. They nurture client relationships, pitch IBM solutions, and, when needed, refer customers to product and service specialists within the call center or to resellers on their region.

Just as telemarketing is changing the way that many companies go to market, the Internet offers explosive potential for restructuring sales forces and conducting sales operations. More companies are now using the Internet to support their personal selling efforts—not just for selling, but for everything from training salespeople to conducting sales meetings and servicing accounts. For example, HSBC officers and clients can access a computer network called Hexagon to view account records, buy currencies, and obtain letters of credit. However establishing Web-based sales systems can be expensive. Such systems may also intimidate low-tech salespeople and are susceptible to server crashes or other network difficulties. Finally, in social oriented cultures where interpersonal relations are important, face-to-face sales interactions are still essential to closing sales and to building and maintaining customer relationships. Indeed, the practice of *guanxi* translates into large sales forces for maintaining contacts with clients.

Telemarketers use the phone to find new leads and qualify prospects or to sell and service accounts directly.

Team selling

As products become more complex, and as customers grow larger and more demanding, a single salesperson simply cannot handle all of a large customer's needs. Instead, most companies now use **team selling** to service large, complex accounts. Sales teams can unearth problems, solutions, and sales opportunities that no individual salesperson could. Such teams might include experts from any area or level of the selling firm—sales, marketing, technical and support services, R&D, engineering, operations, finance, and others. In team selling situations, the salesperson shifts from "soloist" to "orchestrator."

Often, the move to team selling mirrors similar charges in customers' buying organizations. As more businesses are using or are interested in using multifunctional buying teams, sellers have employed selling teams to sell effectively to buying teams. For example, Procter & Gamble (P&G) sales reps are organized into "customer business development (CBD) teams." Each CBD team is assigned to a major P&G customer. Teams consist of a customer business development manager, several account executives (each responsible for a specific category of P&G products), and specialists in marketing strategy, operations, information systems, logistics, and finance. Team selling does have some pitfalls. For example, selling teams can confuse or overwhelm customers who are used to working with only one salesperson. Salespeople who are used to having customers all to themselves may have trouble learning to work with and trust others on a team. Finally, difficulties in evaluating individual contributions to the team selling effort can create some sticky compensation issues.

Team selling
Using teams of people from sales, marketing, engineering, finance, technical support, and even upper management to service large, complex accounts.

Recruiting and Selecting Salespeople

At the heart of any successful sales force operation is the recruitment and selection of good salespeople. The performance difference between an average salesperson and a top salesperson can be substantial. In a typical sales force, the top 30 percent of the salespeople might bring in 60 percent of the sales. Thus, careful salesperson selection can greatly increase overall sales force performance. Beyond the differences in sales performance, poor selection results in costly turnover. When a salesperson quits, the costs of finding and training a new salesperson—plus the costs of lost sales—can be very high. Also, a sales force with many new people is less productive, and turnover disrupts important customer relationships.

What sets great salespeople apart from all the rest? In an effort to profile top sales performers, research from the Gallup Management Consulting Group, a division of the well-known Gallup polling organization, suggests that the best salespeople possess four key talents: intrinsic motivation, disciplined work style, the ability to close a sale, and perhaps most important, the ability to build relationships with customers.[6]

REAL MARKETING 16.1

Hewlett-Packard Overhauls Its Vast Corporate Sales Force

HP overhauled its vast sales force, reducing salesperson frustration and helping salespeople to create better value for customers.

Imagine this scenario: You need a new digital camera. You are not sure which one to buy or even what features you need. So you visit your nearest electronics superstore to talk with a salesperson. You walk through the camera section but can not find anyone to help you. When you finally find a salesperson, he yawns and tells you that he is responsible for selling all the products in the store, so he does not really know all that much about cameras—maybe you should talk to someone else. You finally find a camera-savvy salesperson. However, after answering a few questions, she disappears to handle some other task, handing you off to someone new. And the new salesperson seems to contradict what the first salesperson said, even quoting different prices on a couple of models you like.

As incredible as it seems, at least until recently, this is the kind of situation that many large business buyers faced when they attempted to buy from technology giant Hewlett-Packard. Before Mark Hurd took over as HP's new CEO in the spring of 2005, the company's revenues and

profits had flattened and its stock price had plummeted. To find out why, Hurd first talked directly with 400 corporate customers. Mostly what he heard was gripes about HP's corporate sales force.

Customers complained that they had to deal with too many salespeople, and that HP's confusing management layers made it hard to figure out whom to call. They had trouble tracking down HP sales representatives. And once found, the reps often came across as apathetic, leaving the customer to take the initiative. HP reps were responsible for a broad range of complex products, so they sometimes lacked the needed depth of knowledge on any subset of them. Customers grumbled that they received varying price quotes from different sales reps, and that it often took weeks for reps to respond to seemingly simple requests. In all, HP's corporate customers were frustrated, not a happy circumstance for a company that gets more than 70 percent of its revenues from businesses.

But customers were not the only ones frustrated by HP's unwieldy and unresponsive sales force structure. HP was organized into three main product divisions: the Personal Systems Group (PSG), the Technology Solutions Group (TSG), and the Image and Printing Group (IPG). However, these divisions had little control over the sales process. Instead, HP's corporate sales force was housed in a fourth division, the Customer Sales Group (CSG). All salespeople reported directly to the CSG and were responsible for selling products from all three

Super salespeople are motivated from within. "Different things drive different people—pride, happiness, money, you name it," says one expert. "But all great salespeople have one thing in common: an unrelenting drive to excel." Some salespeople are driven by money, a hunger for recognition, or the satisfaction of competing and winning. Others are driven by the desire to provide service and to build relationships. The best salespeople possess some of each of these motivating factors.

product divisions. To make matters worse, the CSG was bloated and underperforming. According to one reporter, "of the 17,000 people working in HP's corporate sales, only around 10,000 directly sold to customers. The rest were support staff or in management."

HP division executives were frustrated by the CSG structure. They complained that they had little or no direct control over the salespeople who sold their products. And multiple layers of management slowed sales force decision making and customer responsiveness. Finally, salespeople themselves were frustrated by the structure. They were not being given the time and support they needed to serve their customers well. Burdened with administrative tasks and bureaucratic red tape, they were spending less than a third of their time with customers. And they had to work through multiple layers of bureaucracy to get price quotes and sample products for customers. "The customer focus was lacking," says an HP sales vice president. "Trying to navigate inside HP was difficult. It was unacceptable."

As CEO Mark Hurd peeled back the layers, it became apparent that HP's organizational problems went deeper than the sales force. The entire company had become so centralized, with so many layers of management, that it was unresponsive and out of touch with customers. Thus began what one observer called "one of Hurd's biggest management challenges: overhauling HP's vast corporate sales force."

For starters, Hurd eliminated the CSG division, instead assigning salespeople directly to the three product divisions. He also did away with three layers of management and cut hundreds of unproductive sales workers. This move

gave divisional marketing and sales executives direct control over a leaner, more efficient sales process, resulting in speedier sales decisions and quicker market response.

Hurd also took steps to reduce salesperson and customer frustrations. Eliminating the CSG meant that each salesperson was responsible for selling a smaller number of products and was able to develop expertise in a specific product area. Hurd urged sales managers to cut back on salesperson administrative requirements and to improve sales support so that salespeople could spend more quality time with customers. As a result, salespeople now spend more than 40 percent of their time with customers, up from just 30 percent last year. And HP salespeople are noticing big changes in the sales support they receive:

Salesman Richard Ditucci began noticing some of the changes late last year. At the time, Ditucci was trying to sell computer servers to Staples. As part of the process, Staples had asked him to provide a sample server for the company to evaluate. In the past, such requests typically took two to three weeks to fulfill because of HP's bureaucracy. This time, Ditucci got the server he needed within three days. The quick turnaround helped him win the contract, valued at several million dollars.

To ensure that important customers are carefully tended to, HP assigned each salesperson three or fewer accounts. The top 2,000 accounts were assigned just one salesperson each—"so they will always know whom to contact." Customers are noticing differences in the attention that they get from HP salespeople:

Keith Morrow, chief information officer of convenience-store chain 7-Eleven, says his HP sales representative is now "here all the time," and has been more knowledgeable in pitching products tailored to his business. As a result, last October, 7-Eleven began deploying in its U.S. stores 10,000 HP pen pads—a mobile device that helps 7-Eleven workers on the sales floor.

So, HP's sales force restructuring appears to be paying off. Only one year after Mr. Hurd's arrival, HP is now a much leaner and more efficient sales organization. HP's earnings have improved over three consecutive quarters, stock prices are up by over 60 percent, and market share is improving against Dell and other competitors. More importantly, salespeople are happier and more productive, resulting in happier customers. CEO Hurd knows that there is still much more work to be done. But step by step, through restructuring, HP is fixing its sales force to create better value for its business customers. Now, if your local electronics superstore would only do the same for you ...

Sources:
Quotes and adapted examples from Pui-Wing Tam, "System Reboot: Hurd's Big Challenge at HP: Overhauling Corporate Sales," *Wall Street Journal*, April 3, 2006, p. A1. Other information from Steven Burke and Craig Zarley, "Tables Have Turned; HP Gaining Ground on Dell," *Computer Reseller News*, May 22, 2006, p. 15; Jeffrey Burt, "HP Gets a New Tune," *eWeek*, February 27, 2006, p. 11; "HP Restructures, Putting More Assignments In Play," *Adweek*, March 27, 2006, accessed at www.adweek.com; Craig Zarley and Robert Faletra, "Team Building," *Computer Reseller News*, April 24, 2006, p. 10; and Christopher Hosford, "Rebooting Hewlett-Packard," *Sales & Marketing Management*, July–August 2006, pp. 32–35.

A single salesperson can't handle all of a large customer's needs. Hence, companies now use team selling to service large, complex accounts.

Whatever their motivation, salespeople must also have a disciplined work style. If salespeople are not organized and focused, and if they do not work hard, they cannot meet the ever-increasing demands customers make these days. Great salespeople are tenacious about laying out detailed, organized plans, then following through in a timely, disciplined way.

Other skills mean little if a salesperson cannot close the sale. So what makes for a great closer? For one thing, it takes unyielding persistence. "Great closers are like great athletes," says one sales trainer. "They are not afraid to fail, and they do not give up until they close." Great closers also have a high level of self-confidence and believe that they are doing the right thing.

Perhaps most important in today's relationship-marketing environment, top salespeople are customer problem solvers and relationship builders. They instinctively understand their customers' needs. Talk to sales executives and they will describe top performers in these terms: Empathetic. Patient. Caring. Responsive. Good listeners. Honest. Top performers can put themselves on the buyer's side of the desk and see the world through their customers' eyes. They do not want just to be liked, they want to add value for their customers.

When recruiting, companies should analyze the sales job itself and the characteristics of its most successful salespeople to identify the traits needed by a successful salesperson in their industry. Then, it must recruit the right salespeople. The human resources department looks for applicants by getting names from current salespeople, using employment agencies, placing classified ads, searching the Web, and working through college placement services. Another source is to attract top salespeople from other companies. Proven salespeople need less training and can be immediately productive.

Great salespeople –
The best salespeople possess intrinsic motivation, disciplined work style, the ability to close a sale, and perhaps most important, the ability to build relationships with customers.

Recruiting will attract many applicants from whom the company must select the best. The selection procedure can vary from a single informal interview to lengthy testing and interviewing. Many companies give formal tests to sales applicants. Tests typically measure sales aptitude, analytical and organizational skills, personality traits, and other characteristics. But test scores provide only one piece of information in a set that includes personal characteristics, references, past employment history, and interviewer reactions.

Training Salespeople

New salespeople may spend anywhere from a few weeks or months to a year or more in training. In Asia, sales training is longer in MNCs than in local businesses. In addition to that, some companies provide continuing sales training via seminars, sales meetings, and the Web throughout the salesperson's career. The opening case in this chapter is a good example of this.

Training programs have several goals. First, salespeople need to know about customers and how to build relationships with them. So the training program must teach them about different types of customers and their needs, buying motives, and buying habits. And it must teach them how to sell effectively and train them in the basics of the selling process. Salespeople also need to know and identify with the company, its products, and its competitors. So an effective training program teaches them about the company's objectives, organization, and chief products and markets and about the strategies of major competitors.

Today, many companies are adding Web-based training to their sales training programs to cut training costs and make training more efficient. Cisco recently changed its training strategy by launching its Filed E-Learning Connection, an internal learning portal for its sales force. Today, Cisco has more than 9,000 learning resources online. Its online learning involves the blending of audio and video, live broadcasts of classes, and straight content. Online content can be conveniently turned into MP3 files, viewed on-screen, downloaded to the computer, or printed out in magazine form. Existing content is updated twice yearly, and new content is created in response to surveys of those out on the field. New sales hires can log on to FAST (Field, Acculturation, and Sales Training), which familiarizes them with Cisco's objectives and expectations. These changes have saved Cisco "several hundred thousand dollars," and the company has cut training-associated travel by 60 percent.

Sales training –
Some companies provide continuing sales training via seminars, sales meetings, and the Web throughout the salesperson's career.

Compensating Salespeople

To attract good salespeople, a company must have an appealing compensation plan. Compensation is made up of several elements—a fixed amount, a variable amount, expenses, and fringe benefits. The fixed amount, usually a salary, gives the salesperson some stable income. The variable amount, which might be commissions or bonuses based on sales performance, rewards the salesperson for greater effort and success.

Management must decide what *mix* of these compensation elements makes the most sense for each sales job. Different combinations of fixed and variable compensation give rise to four basic types of compensation plans—straight salary, straight commission, salary plus bonus, and salary plus commission. A study of sales force compensation plans showed that 70 percent of all companies surveyed use a combination of base salary and incentives. The average plan consisted of about 60 percent salary and 40 percent incentive pay.[7]

The sales force compensation plan can both motivate salespeople and direct their activities. Compensation should direct the sales force toward activities that are consistent with overall marketing objectives. **Table 16.1** illustrates how a company's compensation plan should reflect its overall marketing strategy. For example, if the strategy is to grow

Table 16.1 The Relationship between Overall Marketing Strategy and Sales Force Compensation

	Strategic Goal		
	To Gain Market	**To Solidify Market**	**To Maximize Profitability**
Ideal salesperson	• An independent self-starter	• A competitive problem solver	• A team player • A relationship manager
Sales focus	• Deal making • Sustained high effort	• Consultative selling	• Account penetration
Compensation role	• To capture accounts • To reward high performance	• To reward new and existing account sales	• To manage the product mix • To encourage team selling • To reward account management

Sources: Adapted from Sam T. Johnson, "Sales Compensation: In Search of a Better Solution," *Compensation & Benefits Review*, November–December 1993, p. 52. Copyright © 1998 American Management Association, NY, www.amanet.org. All rights reserved, used with permission.

rapidly and gain market share, the compensation plan might include a larger commission component, coupled with a new-account bonus to encourage high sales performance and new-account development. In contrast, if the goal is to maximize current account profitability, the compensation plan might contain a larger base-salary component with additional incentives for current account sales or customer satisfaction.

In fact, more and more companies are moving away from high commission plans that may drive salespeople to make short-term grabs for business. They worry that a salesperson who is pushing too hard to close a deal may ruin the customer relationship. Instead, companies are designing compensation plans that reward salespeople for building customer relationships and growing the long-run value of each customer.

Supervising and Motivating Salespeople

New salespeople need more than a territory, compensation, and training—they need supervision and motivation. The goal of *supervision* is to help salespeople "work smart" by doing the right things in the right ways. The goal of *motivation* is to encourage salespeople to "work hard" and energetically toward sales force goals.

Companies vary in how closely they supervise their salespeople. Many help their salespeople to identify target customers and set call norms. Some may also specify how much time the sales force should spend prospecting for new accounts and set other time management priorities. One tool is the weekly, monthly, or annual *call plan* that shows which customers and prospects to call on and which activities to carry out. Another tool is *time-and-duty analysis*. In addition to time spent selling, the salesperson spends time traveling, waiting, taking breaks, and doing administrative chores.

Figure 16.2 shows how salespeople spend their time. On average, active selling time accounts for only ten percent of total working time! If selling time could be raised from ten percent to 30 percent, this would triple the time spent selling.[8] Companies always are looking for ways to save time—simplifying record keeping, finding better sales call and routing plans, supplying more and better customer information, and using phones, e-mail, or video conferencing instead of traveling. Consider the changes Sanyo made to increase its sales force's face-to-face selling time.[9]

Figure 16.2
How salespeople spend their time

Source:
Proudfoot Consulting. Data used with permission

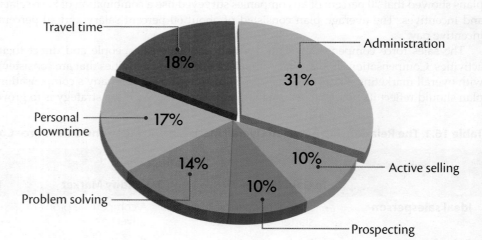

In the competitive Japanese electrical appliance industry, sales reps at Sanyo Life Electronics wanted instant access to detailed sales data to conduct their own analysis than to rely on week-old summary reports. A system was created that enabled the reps to obtain, manipulate, and analyze data on their accounts, and to create personalized sales information. Using this information, the reps could negotiate sales more effectively, while Sanyo could provide sales data electronically to distributors and retailers. Consequently, Sanyo closely tied its manufacturing schedules to intermediary needs and reduced its inventory costs.

Many firms have adopted *sales force automation systems*—computerized, digitized sales force operations that let salespeople work more effectively anytime, anywhere. Companies now routinely equip their salespeople with new-age technologies such as laptops, smart phones, wireless Web connections, Webcams for videoconferencing, and customer-contact and relationship management software. Armed with these technologies, salespeople can more effectively and efficiently profile customers and prospects, analyze and forecast sales, schedule sales calls, make presentations, prepare sales and expense reports, and manage account relationships. The result is better time management, improved customer service, lower sales costs, and higher sales performance.[10]

Perhaps the fastest-growing technology tool is the Internet. The Internet offers explosive potential for conducting sales operations and for interacting with and serving customers. More and more companies are now using the Internet to support their personal selling efforts—not just for selling, but for everything from training salespeople to conducting sales meetings and servicing accounts (see **Real Marketing 16.2**).

Beyond directing salespeople, sales managers must also motivate them. Some salespeople will do their best without any special urging from management. To them, selling may be the most fascinating job in the world. But selling can also be frustrating. Salespeople often work alone and they must sometimes travel away from home. They may face aggressive competing salespeople and difficult customers. Therefore, salespeople often need special encouragement to do their best.

Management can boost sales force morale and performance through its organizational climate, sales quotas, and positive incentives. *Organizational climate* describes the feeling that salespeople have about their opportunities, value, and rewards for a good performance. Some companies treat salespeople as if they are not very important, and performance suffers accordingly. Other companies treat their salespeople as valued contributors and allow virtually unlimited opportunity for income and promotion. Not surprisingly, these companies enjoy higher sales force

Sales force automation –
Many sales forces have gone high tech, equipping salespeople with everything from smartphones, wireless Web connections, and videoconferencing to customer-contact and relationship management software that helps them to be more effective and efficient.

performance and less turnover.

Many companies motivate their salespeople by setting **sales quotas**—standards stating the amount they should sell and how sales should be divided among the company's products. Compensation is often related to how well salespeople meet their quotas. Companies also use various *positive incentives* to increase sales force effort. *Sales meetings* provide social occasions, breaks from routine, chances to meet and talk with "company brass," and opportunities to air feelings and to identify with a larger group. Companies also sponsor *sales contests* to spur the sales force to make a selling effort above what would

Sales quota
A standard that states the amount a salesperson should sell and how sales should be divided among the company's products.

normally be expected. Other incentives include honors, merchandise and cash awards, trips, and profit-sharing plans. In all, American companies spend some $100 billion a year on incentive programs to motivate and reward sales-force performance.[11]

Evaluating Salespeople and Sales-Force Performance

We have thus far described how management communicates what salespeople should be doing and how it motivates them to do it. This process requires good feedback. And good feedback means getting regular information about salespeople to evaluate their performance.

Management gets information about its salespeople in several ways. The most important source is *sales reports,* including weekly or monthly work plans and longer-term territory marketing plans. Salespeople also write up their completed activities on *call reports* and turn in *expense reports* for which they are partly or wholly repaid. The company can also monitor the sales and profit performance of the salesperson's territory. Additional information comes from personal observation, customer surveys, and talks with other salespeople.

REAL MARKETING 16.2

Fotomax's Digital Kiosk: Digitally Removing The Salesperson?

Could salespersons for a photofinishing chain. like Fotomax be a thing of the past with increasing popularity of the digital kiosk?

Fotomax, established in 1982, has developed itself into one of the largest photofinishing chains in Hong Kong providing high-quality and advanced imaging services. The services of Fotomax range from photofinishing, digital imaging and digital-image gift items, to other imaging-related accessories. The company has 90 shops located in key areas in town, covering large-scale shopping malls, major commercial districts, and high-traffic shopping arcades in and along the MTR stations, providing a convenient and accessible service network.

Digital photography today reflects the rapidly changing nature of the photographic industry. More consumers now take photos with digital media than with film. As the market moves towards high-quality digital prints, the core business of Fotomax has undergone a transition from film to digital printing. More than 90 percent of its print orders derive from digital files rather than film. In pursuit of the digital-image market trend, Fotomax took the initiative of introducing Fotomax Digital Kiosks and mobile photo printing services in 2003, in order to enhance the convenience of digital output services for customers. Up to mid-2007, Fotomax had installed 188 digital kiosks in their photofinishing service chain.

The Fotomax Digital Kiosk service allows customers to process their digital images in store and can handle different types of digital image storage media and input from mobile phones as well as from digital cameras. This new digital kiosk provides customers with more convenience and a sense of control over their personal images, and

Using various sales force reports and other information, sales management evaluates members of the sales force. It evaluates salespeople on their ability to "plan their work and work their plan." Formal evaluation forces management to develop and communicate clear standards for judging performance. It also provides salespeople with constructive feedback and motivates them to perform well.

On a broader level, management should evaluate the performance of the sales force as a whole. Is the sales force accomplishing its customer relationship, sales, and profit objectives? Is it working well with other areas of the marketing and company organization? Are sales-force costs in line with outcomes? As with other marketing activities, the company wants to measure its *return on sales investment*.[12]

The Personal Selling Process

We now turn from designing and managing a sales force to the actual personal selling process. The **selling process** consists of several steps that the salesperson must master. These steps focus on the goal of getting new customers and obtaining orders from them. However, most salespeople spend much of their time maintaining existing accounts

Selling process
The steps that the salesperson follows when selling, which include prospecting and qualifying, preapproach, approach, presentation and demonstration, handling objections, closing, and follow-up.

allows customers to order digital prints themselves with just a few commands on a touch-screen monitor. The service offers greater capacity to customize, edit and order their prints, and meets the demands of a technologically savvy younger generation. The digital kiosk service has also reshaped the way people print pictures, and has become more an experience-driven activity than simply a means of obtaining prints.

With an improved customer experience, total sales and volumes of digital prints have continued to exhibit significant growth. Print orders received by Fotomax Digital Kiosks increased by 83.6 percent in 2006 and 50 percent in 2007 respectively, and have become the preferred method of photographic printing.

Customers can now benefit from the speed and convenience of these kiosks; in other words, a total self-service experience with no retailer assistance required. They can also obtain photographic prints and pay concurrently, resulting in a decreased waiting time.

Customer service has taken on more electronic characteristics, as exemplified by the digital kiosk system, and personal selling of this type of customer service has declined almost to zero. In the photofinishing service business, relationships with customers are built on trust, specifically the trust that the photo shops will deliver the prints to the customers on time, so that they will be able to share their cherished moments captured in pictures. Digital imaging has not altered the trust factor, but the reliance on a robotic kiosk to deliver the service could drastically change this relationship. Moreover, the need to deal with a variety of different customer demands leads to greater complexity and higher support costs. Yet, planning and implementing a customer relationship management application from the demand chain perspective is a complex and challenging undertaking for any service organization.

Within the demand chain, the core focus is on proactively uncovering customer pain, rather than strictly upon what the company has to offer. This should also be true for Fotomax if they want to maintain a leadership position in the photofinishing service market. A case in point is that, unless customers order their prints online, a multi-location order and pick up service is not yet available in the Fotomax photofinishing service outlets. This could become a major challenge when competitors develop worldwide coverage and add strategic value to this service. As a customer expressed it in a Web discussion blog:

"Is there any place in Hong Kong, preferably a chain store (or a place in Tsuen Wan), where I could upload my digital photos in Canada and then have my mother-in-law pick them up in Hong Kong? It has just occurred to me, why am I printing off photos here and then mailing them to Hong Kong? I should be able to do this all online and have her pick them up and save me the mailing cost."

Perhaps Fotomax should seriously look into this customer pain and proactively develop solutions to meet these needs.

Sources:
Company homepage, accessed at http://www.fotomax.com/; Company financial reports 2006 and 2007; GeoBaby.com, accessed at http://www.geobaby.com/forum/digital-photos-t119073.html

and building long-term customer *relationships*. We discuss the relationship aspect of the personal selling process in a later section.

Steps in the Selling Process

As shown in **Figure 16.3**, the selling process consists of seven steps: prospecting and qualifying, preapproach, approach, presentation and demonstration, handling objections, closing, and follow-up.

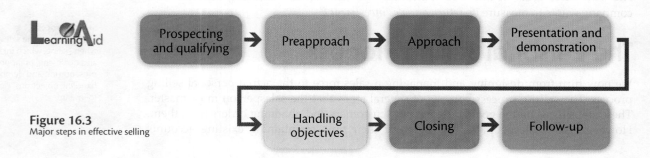

Figure 16.3
Major steps in effective selling

Prospecting and Qualifying

The first step in the selling process is **prospecting**—identifying qualified potential customers. Approaching the right potential customers is crucial to selling success. As one expert puts it: "If the sales force starts chasing anyone who is breathing and seems to have a budget, you risk accumulating a roster of expensive-to-serve, hard-to-satisfy customers who never respond to whatever value proposition you have." He continues, "The solution to this isn't rocket science. [You must] train salespeople to actively scout the right prospects." Another expert concludes: "Increasing your prospecting effectiveness is the fastest single way to boost your sales."[13]

The salesperson must often approach many prospects to get just a few sales. Although the company supplies some leads, salespeople need skill in finding their own. The best source is referrals. Salespeople can ask current customers for referrals and cultivate other referral sources, such as suppliers, dealers, noncompeting salespeople, and bankers. They can also search for prospects in directories or on the Web and track down leads using the telephone and direct mail. Or they can drop in unannounced on various offices (a practice known as "cold calling").

Salespeople also need to know how to *qualify* leads—that is, how to identify the good ones and screen out the poor ones. Prospects can be qualified by looking at their financial ability, volume of business, special needs, location, and possibilities for growth.

Preapproach

Before calling on a prospect, the salesperson should learn as much as possible about the organization (what it needs, who is involved in the buying) and its buyers (their characteristics and buying styles). This step is known as the **preapproach**. The salesperson can consult standard industry and online sources, acquaintances, and others to learn about the company. The salesperson should set *call objectives*, which may be to qualify the prospect, to gather information, or to make an immediate sale. Another task is to decide on the best approach, which might be a personal visit, a phone call, or a letter. The best timing should be considered carefully because many prospects are busiest at certain times. Finally, the salesperson should give thought to an overall sales strategy for the account.

Approach

During the **approach** step, the salesperson should know how to meet and greet the buyer and get the relationship off to a good start. This step involves the salesperson's appearance,

Prospecting
The step in the selling process in which the salesperson identifies qualified potential customers.

Preapproach
The step in the selling process in which the salesperson learns as much as possible about a prospective customer before making a sales call.

Approach
The step in the selling process in which the salesperson meets the customer for the first time.

opening lines, and the follow-up remarks. The opening lines should be positive to build goodwill from the beginning of the relationship. This opening might be followed by some key questions to learn more about the customer's needs or by showing a display or sample to attract the buyer's attention and curiosity. As in all stages of the selling process, listening to the customer is crucial.

Presentation and Demonstration

During the **presentation** step of the selling process, the salesperson tells the product "story" to the buyer, presenting customer benefits and showing how the product solves the customer's problems. The problem-solver salesperson fits better with today's marketing concept than does a hard-sell salesperson or the glad-handing extrovert. Buyers today want solutions; they want salespeople who listen to their concerns, understand their needs, and respond with the right products and services.

This *need-satisfaction approach* calls for good listening and problem-solving skills. A recent study revealed that 74 percent of 200 purchasers surveyed at companies in the U.S. said they would be much more likely to buy from a salesperson if the seller would simply listen to them. "To me, sales is listening to customers, finding out what they want, finding out what their concerns are, and then trying to fill them," notes one experienced salesperson. "It's no longer enough to have a good relationship with a client," says another. "You have to understand their problems. You have to feel their pain."[14]

The qualities that buyers *dislike most* in salespeople include being pushy, late, deceitful, and unprepared or disorganized. The qualities they *value most* include good listening, empathy, honesty, dependability, thoroughness, and follow-through. Great salespeople know how to sell, but more importantly they know how to listen and to build strong customer relationships. Says one professional, "Salespeople must have the right answers, certainly, but they also have to learn how to ask those questions and listen."[15]

Presentation
The step in the selling process in which the salesperson tells the "product story" to the buyer, highlighting customer benefits.

Today's advanced presentation technologies allow for full mutimedia presentations to only one or a few people. Online presentation technologies and hand-held and laptop computers with presentation software have replaced the old flipchart.

Handling Objections

Customers almost always have objections during the presentation or when asked to place an order. The problem can be either logical or psychological, and objections are often unspoken. In **handling objections**, the salesperson should use a positive approach, seek out hidden objections, ask the buyer to clarify any objections, take objections as opportunities to provide more information, and turn the objections into reasons for buying. Every salesperson needs training in the skills of handling objections.

Closing

After handling the prospect's objections, the salesperson now tries to close the sale. Some salespeople do not get around to **closing** or do not handle it well. They may lack confidence, feel guilty about asking for the order, or fail to recognize the right moment to close the sale. Salespeople should know how to recognize closing signals from the buyer, including physical actions, comments, and questions. For example, the customer might sit forward and nod approvingly or ask about prices and credit terms.

Salespeople can use one of several closing techniques. They can ask for the order, review points of agreement, offer to help write up the order, ask whether the buyer wants this model or that one, or note that the buyer will lose out if the order is not placed now. The salesperson may offer the buyer special reasons to close, such as a lower price or an extra quantity at no charge.

Handling objections
The step in the selling process in which the salesperson seeks out, clarifies, and overcomes customer objections to buying.

Closing
The step in the selling process in which the salesperson asks the customer for an order.

Follow-Up

The last step in the selling process—**follow-up**—is necessary if the salesperson wants to ensure customer satisfaction and repeat business. Right after closing, the salesperson should complete any details on delivery time, purchase terms, and other matters. The salesperson then should schedule a follow-up call when the initial order is received, to make sure there is proper installation, instruction, and servicing. This visit would reveal any problems, assure the buyer of the salesperson's interest, and reduce any buyer concerns that might have arisen since the sale.

Salespeople should be confident about closing the order, and follow up with the customer to ensure customer satisfaction and repeat business.

Personal Selling and Customer Relationship Management

The steps in the selling process as just described are *transaction oriented*—their aim is to help salespeople close a specific sale with a customer. But in most cases, the company is not simply seeking a sale: It has targeted a major customer that it would like to win and keep. The company would like to show that it has the capabilities to serve the customer over the long haul in a mutually profitable *relationship*. The sales force usually plays an important role in building and managing profitable customer relationships.

Today's large customers favor suppliers who can sell and deliver a coordinated set of products and services to many locations, and who can work closely with customer teams to improve products and processes. For these customers, the first sale is only the beginning of the relationship. Unfortunately, some companies ignore these relationship realities. They sell their products through separate sales forces, each working independently to close sales. Their technical people may not be willing to lend time to educate a customer. Their engineering, design, and manufacturing people may have the attitude that "it is our job to make good products and the salesperson's job to sell them to customers." Their salespeople focus on pushing products toward customers rather than listening to customers and providing solutions.

Other companies, however, recognize that winning and keeping accounts requires more than making good products and directing the sales force to close lots of sales. It requires listening to customers, understanding their needs, and carefully coordinating the whole company's efforts to create customer value and to build lasting relationships.

Sales Promotion

Personal selling and advertising often work closely with another promotion tool, sales promotion. **Sales promotion** consists of short-term incentives to encourage purchase or sales of a product or service, and includes a wide variety of promotional tools designed to stimulate earlier or stronger market responses. Whereas advertising offers reasons to buy a product or service, sales promotion offers reasons to buy *now*.

You may find a freestanding insert in the *Apple Daily* newspaper which contains a coupon offering HK$5 off a cup of cappuccino. The end of the aisle display in the ParknShop supermarket tempts you with a wall of Coca-Cola cases at a much discounted price. When you shop at the Nova Computer Centre opposite the Taipei Train Station for an Asus notebook, you get a free carrying case and a memory stick with 1GB memory. On a busy street in the old town of Shenzhen, you receive a promotion leaflet which offers you a dish of *dim sum* if you patronize a Cantonese restaurant nearby. Broadway, a renowned electronic appliance store in Hong Kong offers you a special discount on TV sets if you pay with a Hang Seng Bank credit card. And when you check your e-mail, a mailer from Amazon.com offers free shipping on your next purchase over $100.

Rapid Growth of Sales Promotion

Sales promotion tools are used by most organizations, including manufacturers, distributors, retailers, and not-for-profit institutions. They are targeted toward final buyers (*consumer promotions*), retailers and wholesalers (*trade promotions*), business customers (*business promotions*), and members of the sales force (*sales force promotions*). Today, in the average consumer packaged-goods company, sales promotion accounts for 74 percent of all marketing expenditures.[16]

Several factors have contributed to the rapid growth of sales promotion, particularly in consumer markets. First, inside the company, product managers face greater pressures to increase their current sales, and promotion is viewed as an effective short-run sales tool. Second, externally, the company faces more competition and competing brands are less differentiated. Increasingly, competitors are using sales promotion to help differentiate their offers. Third, advertising efficiency has declined because of rising costs, media clutter, and legal restraints. Finally, consumers have become more deal oriented, and ever-larger retailers are demanding more deals from manufacturers.

The growing use of sales promotion has resulted in *promotion clutter*, similar to advertising clutter. Consumers are increasingly tuning out promotions, weakening their ability to trigger immediate purchase. Manufacturers are now searching for ways to rise above the clutter, such as offering larger coupon values or creating more dramatic point-of-purchase displays.

Consumers are increasingly tuning out advertisement and promotions, weakening their ability to trigger immediate purchase. Manufacturers now have to search for ways to rise above the clutter.

In developing a sales promotion program, a company must first set sales promotion objectives and then select the best tools for accomplishing these objectives.

Sales Promotion Objectives

Sales promotion objectives vary widely. Sellers may use *consumer promotions* to urge short-term customer buying or to enhance long-term customer relationships. Objectives for *trade promotions* include getting retailers to carry new items and more inventory, buy ahead, or advertise the company's products and give them more shelf space. For the *sales force*, objectives include getting more sales force support for current or new products or getting salespeople to sign up new accounts.

Sales promotions are usually used together with advertising, personal selling, or other promotion mix tools. Consumer promotions must usually be advertised and can add excitement and pulling power to ads. Trade and sales force promotions support the firm's personal selling process.

In general, rather than creating only short-term sales or temporary brand switching, sales promotions should help to reinforce the product's position and build long-term *customer relationships*. If properly designed, every sales promotion tool has the potential to build both short-term excitement and long-term consumer relationships. Increasingly, marketers are avoiding "quick fix," price-only promotions in favor of promotions designed to build brand equity.

Examples include all the "frequency marketing programs" and loyalty clubs that have mushroomed in recent years. Most hotels, supermarkets, and airlines now offer frequent-guest/buyer/flyer programs offering rewards to regular customers. For example, the Friendship Shopping City in Dalian, China, is preparing to launch a new loyalty program that targets its wealthy customers. Members are entitled to have a VIP smartcard which has several functions. Cardholders may enjoy a special discount on almost all items in the store, and the smartcard contains a RFID system which allows the store to identify members as soon as they enter. Using this system, salespersons are promptly alerted upon each member's entrance into the store and can then swiftly get themselves ready to approach them.

Major Sales Promotion Tools

Many tools can be used to accomplish sales promotion objectives. Descriptions of the main consumer, trade, and business promotion tools follow.

Consumer Promotion Tools

The main **consumer promotion tools** include:

- *Samples,*
- *Coupons,*
- *Cash refunds,*
- *Price packs,*
- *Premiums,*
- *Advertising specialties,*
- *Patronage rewards,*
- *Point-of-purchase displays and demonstrations, and*
- *Contests, sweepstakes, and games.*

> **Consumer promotion tools**
> Sales promotion tools used to urge short-term customer buying or to enhance long-term customer relationships.

Sampling is the most effective—but most expensive—way to introduce a new product or to create new excitement for an existing one.

Samples are offers of a trial amount of a product. Sampling is the most effective—but most expensive—way to introduce a new product or to create new excitement for an existing one. Some samples are free; for others, the company charges a small amount to offset its cost. The sample might be delivered door-to-door, sent by mail, handed out in a store, attached to another product, or featured in an ad. Sometimes, samples are combined into sample packs, which can then be used to promote other products and services. Sampling can be a powerful promotional tool. For example, Procter & Gamble always gives away samples to potential consumers. Its road shows in the rural market in China have been successful in tempting consumers to switch to P&G products by trying its samples.[17]

Coupons are certificates that give buyers a saving when they purchase specified products. Most consumers love coupons. U.S. companies distributed 323 billion coupons last year with an average face value of $1.16. Consumers redeemed more than three billion of them for a total savings of about $3.47 billion.[18] Coupons can promote early trial of a new brand or stimulate sales of a mature brand. However, as a result of coupon clutter, redemption rates have been declining in recent years. Thus, most major consumer goods companies are issuing fewer coupons and targeting them more carefully.

Marketers are also cultivating new outlets for distributing coupons, such as supermarket shelf dispensers, electronic point-of-sale coupon printers, e-mail and online media, or even text-messaging systems. For example, text-message couponing is popular in Europe, India, and Japan, and it's slowly gaining popularity in the United States.

Cash refunds (or *rebates*) are like coupons except that the price reduction occurs after the purchase rather than at the retail outlet. The consumer sends a "proof of purchase" to the manufacturer, who then refunds part of the purchase price by mail.

Price packs (also called *cents-off deals*) offer consumers savings off the regular price of a product. The producer marks the reduced prices directly on the label or package. Price packs can be single packages sold at a reduced price (such as two for the price of one) or two related products banded together (such as a toothbrush and toothpaste). Price packs are very effective—even more so than coupons—in stimulating short-term sales.

Premiums are goods offered either free or at low cost as an incentive to buy a product, ranging from toys included with kids' products to phone cards and DVDs. A premium may come inside the package (in-pack), outside the package (on-pack), or through the mail. Kellogg often incorporates premiums with its cereals and related products. For instance, it recently offered a free *Cars* racer, based on characters from the Disney/Pixar movie, inside specially marked boxes of Apple Jacks. Customers who bought a pack of 12 Energizer batteries received a torch which was included with the package.

Advertising specialties, also called *promotional products,* are useful articles imprinted with an advertiser's name, logo, or message that are given as gifts to consumers. Typical items include T-shirts and other apparel, pens, coffee mugs, calendars, key rings, mouse pads, matches, tote bags, coolers, golf balls, and caps. Such items can be very effective. The "best of them stick around for months, subtly burning a brand name into a user's brain," notes a promotional products expert. In a recent study, 71 percent of all consumers surveyed had received at least one promotional product in the past 12 months. Seventy-six percent of those were able to recall the advertiser's name on the promotional product they received, compared to only 53.5 percent who could recall the name of an advertiser in a print publication they had read in the past week.[19]

New forms of coupons –
Text message couponing is gaining popularity. At the University of South Florida, local businesses can blast out text message coupons directly to interested students' cell phones via the university's MoBull Plus system.

Advertising specialties, also called promotional products, are useful articles imprinted with an advertiser's name, logo, or message that are given as gifts to consumers. They typically include items such as bumper stickers, stationary, mugs, keychains, and T-shirts.

Patronage rewards are cash or other awards offered for the regular use of a certain company's products or services. For example, airlines offer frequent flier plans, awarding points for miles traveled that can be turned in for free airline trips. And supermarkets issue frequent shopper cards that dole out a wealth of discounts at the checkout.

Point-of-purchase (POP) promotions include displays and demonstrations that take place at the point of sale. Think of your last visit to the local Wellcome, 7-Eleven, and Family Mart. Chances are good that you were tripping over aisle displays, promotional signs, "shelf talkers," or demonstrators offering free tastes of featured food products. Unfortunately, many retailers do not like to handle the hundreds of displays, signs, and posters they receive from manufacturers each year. Manufacturers have responded by offering better POP materials, offering to set them up, and tying them in with television, print, or online messages.

Contests, sweepstakes, and games give consumers the chance to win something, such as cash, trips, or goods, by luck or through extra effort. A *contest* calls for consumers to submit an entry—a jingle, guess, suggestion—to be judged by a panel that will select the best entries. A *sweepstakes* calls for consumers to submit their names for a drawing. A *game* presents consumers with something—bingo numbers, missing letters—every time they buy, which may or may not help them win a prize. A sales contest urges dealers or the sales force to increase their efforts, with prizes going to the top performers.

Trade Promotion Tools

Manufacturers direct more sales promotion dollars toward retailers and wholesalers (78 percent) than to final consumers (22 percent).[20] **Trade promotion tools** can persuade resellers to carry a brand, give it shelf space, promote it in advertising, and push it to consumers. Shelf space is so scarce these days that manufacturers often have to offer price-offs, allowances, buy-back guarantees, or free goods to retailers and wholesalers to get products on the shelf and, once there, to keep them on it.

Manufacturers use several trade promotion tools. Many of the tools used for consumer promotions—contests, premiums, displays—can also be used as trade promotions. Or the manufacturer may offer a straight *discount* off the list price on each case purchased during a stated period of time (also called a *price-off, off-invoice,* or *off-list*). Manufacturers also may offer an *allowance* (usually so much off per case) in return for the retailer's agreement to feature the manufacturer's products in some way. An advertising allowance compensates retailers for advertising the product. A display allowance compensates them for using special displays.

Manufacturers may offer *free goods*, which are extra cases of merchandise, to resellers who buy a certain quantity or who feature a certain flavor or size. They may offer *push money*—cash or gifts to dealers or their sales forces to "push" the manufacturer's goods. Manufacturers may give retailers free *specialty advertising items* that carry the company's name, such as pens, pencils, calendars, paperweights, matchbooks, memo pads, and yardsticks.

Business Promotion Tools

Companies spend billions of dollars each year on promotion to industrial customers. **Business promotion tools** are used to generate business leads, stimulate purchases, reward customers, and motivate salespeople. Business promotion includes many of the same tools used for consumer or trade promotions. Here, we focus on two additional major business promotion tools—conventions and trade shows, and sales contests.

Many companies and trade associations organize *conventions and trade shows* to promote their products. Firms selling to the industry show their products at the trade show. Vendors receive many benefits, such as opportunities to find new sales leads, contact customers, introduce new products, meet new customers, sell more to present customers, and educate customers with publications and audiovisual materials. Trade shows also help companies reach many prospects not reached through their sales forces.

Trade promotion tools
Sales promotion tools used to persuade resellers to carry a brand, give it shelf space, promote it in advertising, and push it to consumers.

Business promotion tools
Sales promotion tools used to generate business leads, stimulate purchases, reward customers, and motivate salespeople.

Some trade shows are huge. Each year, the Hong Kong Trade Development Council organizes nearly 30 world-class international trade fairs in Hong Kong—seven of which are the largest in Asia—attracting on average some 460,000 professional visitors. Along the same lines, at the BAUMA mining and construction equipment trade show in Munich, Germany, some 2,800 exhibitors from 47 countries presented their latest product innovations to more than 416,000 attendees from 171 countries.[21]

Some companies such as P&G may combine several components of sales promotion in a road show so as to create a large impact on a group of targeted audience (see **Company Case** at the end of the chapter).

Trade shows allow vendors to find new sales leads, contact customers, introduce new products, and educate customers with publications and audiovisual materials.

A *sales contest* is a contest for salespeople or dealers to motivate them to increase their sales performance over a given period. Sales contests motivate and recognize good company performers, who may receive trips, cash prizes, or other gifts. Some companies award points for performance, which the receipient can turn in for any of a variety of prizes. Sales contests work best when they are tied to measurable and achievable sales objectives (such as finding new accounts, reviving old accounts, or increasing account profitability).

Developing the Sales Promotion Program

Beyond selecting the types of promotions to use, marketers must make several other decisions in designing the full sales promotion program. First, they must decide on the *size of the incentive*. A certain minimum incentive is necessary if the promotion is to succeed; a larger incentive will produce more sales response. The marketer also must set *conditions for participation*. Incentives might be offered to everyone or only to select groups.

Marketers must decide how to *promote and distribute the promotion* program itself. A $2-off coupon could be given out in a package, at the store, via the Internet, or in an advertisement. Each distribution method involves a different level of reach and cost. Increasingly, marketers are blending several media formats into a total campaign concept. The *length of the promotion* is also important. If the sales promotion period is too short, many prospects (who may not be buying during that time) will miss it. If the promotion runs too long, the deal will lose some of its "act now" force.

Evaluation is also very important. Many companies fail to evaluate their sales promotion programs, and others evaluate them only superficially. Yet marketers should work to measure the returns on their sales promotion investments, just as they should seek to assess the returns on other marketing activities. The most common evaluation method is to compare sales before, during, and after a promotion. Marketers should ask: Did the promotion attract new customers or more purchasing from current customers? Can we hold onto these new customers and purchases? Will the long-run customer relationship and sales gains from the promotion justify its costs?

Clearly, sales promotion plays an important role in the total promotion mix. To use it well, the marketer must define the sales promotion objectives, select the best tools, design the sales promotion program, implement the program, and evaluate the results. Moreover, sales promotion must be coordinated carefully with other promotion mix elements within the overall integrated marketing communications program.

REAL MARKETING 16.3

Master Kong: One More Bottle! — A Sales Promotion Campaign

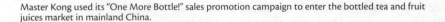

Master Kong used its "One More Bottle!" sales promotion campaign to enter the bottled tea and fruit juices market in mainland China.

Master Kong was founded in Taiwan in 1958. When it started, it was a small family business named Ting Hsin Oil. In 1992, the Group produced its first pack of instant noodles in mainland China, with the brand name of Master Kong. In Chinese, a "Master" is an expert and "Kong" means health. At that time, most instant noodle products in China contained a lot of preservatives. Master Kong's concept of selling healthy instant noodles was a revolutionary idea in China and its products were well received by the market.

Master Kong became a publicly listed company in Hong Kong in 1996 and has since done extremely well in the Chinese instant noodle and tea beverage markets. By 2006, the company had 36 production bases and 294 production lines. Today, Master Kong is the leading producer of instant noodles and tea in mainland China, with market shares of 43.3 percent and 53.6 percent respectively.

Industry Trend

The development of the beverage market in China went through four stages: carbonated drinks, mineral water, tea and then fruit juices. The tea market began in 1993 and increased rapidly in the early 2000s. By 2005, there were about 40 tea-producing firms with more than 100 brands in China.

Master Kong entered this market in 1996 with lemon tea and chrysanthemum tea, and by 2002 had gained a market share of 50 percent. Seeing that fruit juice drinks were gaining more popularity in China, the company launched a new fruit juice drink branded as "Fresh C Every Day" in early 2002. This achieved a market share of 17 percent by the end of that year.

"One more bottle!"

In 2002, Master Kong conducted an aggressive, large-scale sales promotion campaign for its tea and fruit juice products. Any of Master Kong's tea drinks and fruit juices in bottles that had labels stating "Open the bottle to get a surprise!", offered purchasers the chance of winning "One more bottle" if those same words were found on the inside of the bottle cap. Winners could exchange these bottle caps for a free second bottle at award claim posts.

Timing of the Promotion

Since the tea drink products were delivered onto the market in 1996, their consumption has grown rapidly. In recent years, tea drinks have seen sales increase by 300 percent each year, and have become the stars of the beverage market. At the same time, sales of fruit juice have increased at an even higher rate as fruit juice is considered healthy and more popular internationally. Master Kong chose a busy season during the high-growth period of tea and fruit drinks to launch its marketing campaign, so that the promotion could largely suppress their competitors' sales and deepen consumers' understanding of Master Kong's tea drink and fruit juice products.

Promotion Methods

Its "One more bottle!" promotion is a typical "win-upon-opening" lucky-draw strategy, which is one of the most frequently adopted in marketing fast-consumption goods such as food and beverages. Participants are not required to have special talents in such promotions and therefore they are more responsive and enthusiastic. Such lucky-draw type of activities have ten times more participants than those with a competitive nature. Consumers can redeem the prizes on the spot, saving the trouble of mailing back the winning proof as required by many other promotions. This can greatly stimulate buyers to consume the products immediately and repeatedly.

Promotion Awards

Master Kong's iced tea products are priced at CNY 3.5 per bottle. They are typical low-price products, therefore the award should also have a low price, but the possibility of winning should be high in order to spur consumers' interest in participating. Master Kong chose the same product as the award to winners. As a result, the promotion not only helped increase the loyalty of consumers, but also estranged competitors' products from the consumers. It really is a good "one stone-two birds" strategy.

Promotion Slogans

Master Kong chose "Open to get a surprise!" and "One more bottle!" as its promotion slogans. "One more bottle!" closely reflected the theme of the promotion and clearly indicated the awards. It also reminded the buyers to buy "One more bottle!" after finishing one.

Marketing Advertisement

To advertise and to inform potential consumers is a very important part of marketing, and it can affect the effectiveness of the marketing efforts. Firstly, in the "One more bottle!" promotion, all detailed promotion activity content such as procedure, prize and award claim issues was directly printed on the exterior of the product packages. Promotion slogans "Open to see a surprise!" and "One more bottle!" were highlighted with eye-catching large fonts. Secondly, they put advertisement posters and leaflets at as many award claim posts as possible. Thirdly, many parasols and dedicated showcases for the tea and juice beverages were designed, manufactured and installed in prominent places in retail stores. The combination of all the above methods achieved the aim of a multi-level and multi-angle marketing campaign.

Through this campaign, Master Kong successfully expanded its market share and further lifted its brand name. The company carefully controlled the prize-winning ratio in the promotion. The prize-winning ratio was up to 70 percent at the beginning, then it decreased steadily to below 10 percent, after which the campaign ended naturally.

Sources:
Quotes and adapted examples are from www.51cmc.com; Lu, T.H. & He, H.P. 2003. "How Master Kong conquered Chinese mainland market". In Lu, T.H. & He, H.P. (Eds.), Marketing in China (pp. 97–100). *Enterprise Management Press*; Qiu, W.S. 2004 "Why Xinwei failed in South China". Feb 10, 2004, accessed at www.51cmc.com.

REVIEWING THE CONCEPTS

This chapter is the third of four chapters covering the final marketing mix element—promotion. The two previous chapters dealt with overall integrated marketing communications and with advertising and public relations. This one investigates personal selling and sales promotion. Personal selling is the interpersonal arm of the communications mix. Sales promotion consists of short-term incentives to encourage the purchase or sale of a product or service.

1 Discuss the role of a company's salespeople in creating value for customers and building customer relationships.

Most companies use salespeople, and many companies assign them an important role in the marketing mix. For companies selling business products, the firm's salespeople work directly with customers. Often, the sales force is the customer's only direct contact with the company and therefore may be viewed by customers as representing the company itself. In contrast, for consumer product companies that sell through intermediaries, consumers usually do not meet salespeople or even know about them. The sales force works behind the scenes, dealing with wholesalers and retailers to obtain their support and helping them become effective in selling the firm's products.

As an element of the promotion mix, the sales force is very effective in achieving certain marketing objectives and carrying out such activities as prospecting, communicating, selling and servicing, and information gathering. But with companies becoming more market oriented, a customer-focused sales force also works to produce both *customer satisfaction* and *company profit*. The sales force plays a key role in developing and managing profitable *customer relationships*.

2 Identify and explain the six major sales force management steps.

High sales force costs necessitate an effective sales management process consisting of six steps: designing sales force strategy and structure, recruiting and selecting, training, compensating, supervising, and evaluating salespeople and sales force performance.

In designing a sales force, sales management must address strategy issues such as what type of sales force structure will work best (territorial, product, customer, or complex structure); how large the sales force should be; who will be involved in the selling effort; and how its various sales and sales support people will work together (inside or outside sales forces and team selling).

To hold down the high costs of hiring the wrong people, salespeople must be recruited and selected carefully. In recruiting salespeople, a company may look to job duties and the characteristics of its most successful salespeople to suggest the traits it wants in its salespeople. It must then look for applicants through recommendations of current salespeople, employment agencies, classified ads, and the Internet and by contacting college students. In the selection process, the procedure can vary from a single informal interview to lengthy testing and interviewing. After the selection process is complete, training programs familiarize new salespeople not only with the art of selling but also with the company's history, its products and policies, and the characteristics of its market and competitors.

The sales force compensation system helps to reward, motivate, and direct salespeople. In compensating salespeople, companies try to have an appealing plan, usually close to the going rate for the type of sales job and needed skills. In addition to compensation, all salespeople need supervision, and many need continuous encouragement because they must make many decisions and face many frustrations. Periodically, the company must evaluate their performance to help them do a better job. In evaluating salespeople, the company relies on getting regular information gathered through sales reports, personal observations, customers' letters and complaints, customer surveys, and conversations with other salespeople.

3 Discuss the personal selling process, distinguishing between transaction-oriented marketing and relationship marketing.

The art of selling involves a seven-step *selling process*: *prospecting and qualifying, preapproach, approach, presentation and demonstration, handling objections, closing,* and *follow-up*. These steps help marketers close a specific sale and as such are *transaction oriented*. However, a seller's dealings with customers should be guided by the larger concept of *relationship marketing*. The company's sales force should help to orchestrate a whole-company effort to develop profitable long-term relationships with key customers based on superior customer value and satisfaction.

4 Explain how sales promotion campaigns are developed and implemented.

Sales promotion campaigns call for setting sales promotions objectives (in general, sales promotions should be *consumer relationship building*); selecting tools; and developing and implementing the sales promotion program by using *consumer promotion tools* (coupons, cash refund offers, price packs, premiums, advertising specialties, patronage rewards, point-of-purchase promotions, and contests, sweepstakes, and games), *trade promotion tools* (discounts, allowances, free goods, and push money), and *business promotion tools* (conventions, trade shows, and sales contests) as well as deciding on such things as the size of the incentive, the conditions for participation, how to promote and distribute the promotion package, and the length of the promotion. After this process is completed, the company evaluates its sales promotion results.

REVIEWING THE KEY TERMS

DISCUSSING THE CONCEPTS

1. According to the chapter, salespeople serve "two masters." What does this mean? Is it a good or bad thing?

2. The chapter states that the ability to build relationships with customers is the most important of a salesperson's key talents. Do you agree? Explain.

3. DuPont sells thousands of industrial and consumer products throughout the world. It serves industries as diverse as aerospace, agriculture, and health care. Describe how DuPont can best structure its sales force.

4. A start-up manufacturer of low-carbohydrate muffins wants to sell its product in supermarkets all along the

East Coast. It has identified 400 large supermarket chains and 100 smaller chains. The large supermarket chains will require 30 calls per year and the smaller stores ten calls per year. An average salesperson can make 1,000 calls per year. Using the workload approach for setting sales force size, how many salespeople will this manufacturer need?

5. What are the main differences between sales otion and advertising?

6. Explain why there has been rapid growth in the use of sales promotions.

APPLYING THE CONCEPTS

1. Who in your class would make a good salesperson? Why?

2. Work in pairs to describe the stages in the selling process for a small company that sells cleaning services to owners of small businesses, such as hair salons, dentists' offices, and clothing stores. Role-play the actual selling process, from approach to close, with one team member acting as the salesperson. The other member of the team should act as a customer and raise at least three objections.

3. Suppose you are the marketing coordinator responsible for recommending the sales promotion plan for the market launch of a new brand of Red Bull energy drink sold in supermarkets. What promotional tools would you consider for this task? Explain.

FOCUS ON TECHNOLOGY

High-level salespeople need sophisticated tools to perform more effectively, especially when on the road. They need to gather customer contact information, check updated product inventories, and keep track of order information. Strong customer relationship management systems, such as those offered by SAP (www.sap.com), provide many features that empower the sales force. Visit SAP online to find information on the mySAP business suite and mySAP CRM. The Web site outlines the features of mySAP CRM, which benefit salespeople as follows:

- Sales planning and forecasting
- Territory management
- Account and contact management
- Lead and opportunity management
- Quotation and order management
- Contract management
- Incentive and commission management
- Time and travel management
- Sales analytics

1. Explain which SAP functions apply to sales force management and which tie in more to the salesperson's daily role with the customers.

2. Explain how these SAP functions fit into the personal selling process for an office furniture sales representative selling a new line of office chairs to an existing large customer.

3. Why would a company choose not to use SAP products?

FOCUS ON ETHICS

You are the senior sales manager for Johnson Manufacturing. Your company has developed a machine that makes electronic components faster and with a lower defect rate than your major competitor's machines. You call on Haywood Electronics, an important customer, to discuss its purchase of the new machine. Haywood's buyers have been very enthusiastic, but when you arrive, they want to discuss the results of some recent tests they've conducted. They show you output that shows that your competitor's new machine produces components at 1.2 times the rate of your machine with a .01 lower defect rate. Based on this research, they ask for a reduction on the price of your machine from $800,000 to $500,000. When you return to your company and talk to the vice president of manufacturing, she states that the test results are impossible and that the tests must have been faulty or the results intentionally falsified.

1. What actions would you take?

2. Why is it important that you be careful with your reaction to this situation?

3. Could such a situation really happen? Discuss.

VIDEO CASE

Nudie

All across the globe, consumers are seeking all-natural, wholesome foods. Even Wal-Mart, a low-price leader, carries organic and all-natural foods. Nudie, a quirky little company in Australia, makes its own contribution to the fast-growing natural foods market—all-natural fruit juices, fruit crushes, and smoothies that provide a day's fruit in every bottle. Amidst a sea of all-natural products, how did Nudie reach customers and encourage them to try its new products? Through a carefully designed program of personal selling and sales promotion.

Nudie uses well-crafted point-of-purchase displays and a devoted, motivated sales force to work with resellers to reach consumers. As a result, Nudie is the fastest-growing juice maker in Australia, attracting an ever-increasing number of highly devoted customers who love Nudie's products. Says one Nudie customer, "Don't be a prudie… get thee a Nudie." Says another, "Love and happiness are overrated. But Nudies make living worthwhile!"

After viewing the video featuring Nudie, answer the following questions about personal selling and sales promotion.

1. How does Nudie's process for selecting sales representatives compare to the process described in the text?

2. What sales promotion tools does Nudie employ to reach consumers and encourage sales?

3. Select a sales promotion tool not listed in your previous response. How could Nudie use that tool to further promote its products?

COMPANY CASE

Face-to-Face with P&G

Since establishing P&G China in 1988, Procter & Gamble has developed over a dozen joint ventures and fully owned factories to manufacture laundry detergents, cleaning products and personal care products. In just a few years, P&G became very successful in the major cities. Rejoice, Head & Shoulders, Pantene, Sassoon, Safeguard, Tide and Oil of Ulan, among others, have all become popular brands in the local market.

In China, the rural population, accounting for two thirds of the total population, contributes only one third of the country's total retail sales of consumer goods. The size of the opportunity was breathtaking. In a bid to sustain its enormous expansion, P&G soon began to push beyond China's costal regions and spend more time and effort selling its products to the untapped rural population in the interior.

Making inroads into the rural Chinese market can be more complicated than selling to the sophisticated city dwellers. On the one hand, Chinese consumers take advertising very literally. As most advertisements were designed to target the urban consumers, rural consumers might be alienated. On the other hand, most rural consumers still buy from tiny "mom-and-pop" stores where in-store promotions would be hard to come by.

In a remote villages' survey, P&G found, amazingly, that only a few village consumers recognized P&G products, and that their brand awareness was surprisingly low among P&G's target segment—housewives. These villages had also largely been unserved. Faced with this situation, P&G executives put their heads together and determined

that "seeing is believing" would be the solution—let them see it, touch it, try it and buy it. Instead of trying to create a consumer pull through advertising and other marketing communication tools, P&G moved themselves to where the customers were located.

In 1996, they launched the "P&G Road Show" campaign, which aimed to develop this high potential rural market. With this specific objective in mind, the P&G Road Show campaign was tailor-made to target the rural residents, get maximum visibility, create awareness, induce trial and enhance sales.

The road show toured around the outskirts of counties and visited even the remotest villages. Typically, the project team would first descend on the target villages, determine the market potential, search for the most appropriate sites for the road shows, and secure endorsement and support from the local authorities. Every show was carefully planned in terms of logistics and execution, with particular effort being made towards drawing a large crowd, promoting the brand and selling.

Drawing a large crowd

A beautifully decorated truck combined with television, sound effects, drums, flag-lines and a lottery were used to draw a large crowd. Drawing a crowd in the Chinese villages was not particularly difficult. As the villagers seldom have entertainment because of their remoteness and simple lifestyle, a preannouncement of the event and the arrival of the road show truck already drew hundreds of spectators. Not much effort would actually be needed to "fill the room" as a large crowd would just form out of curiosity.

Promoting the brand

A highly entertaining environment—a bit like a bazaar—was created that drew the attention and encouraged the interaction of the target audience. Many methods were used to raise the spirits, interest and involvement of the group: product pamphlets, small packets of product samples with simple guidelines explaining how to solve household cleaning problems, videos on P&G product commercials, speeches, prize-giving games, product demonstrations that dramatized the effect of P&G products, face-to-face promotions, lucky draws and so on. The theme "P&G—face to face with you" was brilliantly realized.

Promoting the brand

A highly entertaining environment—a bit like a bazaar—was created that drew the attention and encouraged the interaction of the target audience. Many methods were used to raise the spirits, interest and involvement of the group: product pamphlets, small packets of product samples with simple guidelines explaining how to solve household cleaning problems, videos on P&G product commercials, speeches, prize-giving games, product demonstrations that dramatized the effect of P&G products, face-to-face promotions, lucky draws and so on. The theme "P&G—face to face with you" was brilliantly realized.

Selling

Personal selling, discounted prices, free samples and product trials further enhanced consumers' awareness and acceptance of the P&G products. Later on, a "Movie at Night" program was added to the road show, which aimed to draw the villagers closer to P&G. Though they showed movies that would appeal to the villagers, they also showed P&G commercials during the intermission and continued with their personal selling efforts to drive immediate sales.

This road show proved to be a great springboard for the rural residents in China to adopt a modern lifestyle. The P&G Road Show campaign ran for four years, covering villages in 22 provinces and autonomous regions, and reaching over a billion of people in rural areas. This was an effective coverage of 75 percent and a product trial rate of 55 percent.

The last episode

A few days after the road show, a grocery store owner in a small village in Zhe Jiang Province responded as follows to an enquiry from a newspaper reporter: "After the truck went, no one could buy P&G products in the local stores. Even if they could find them, the prices would be much higher than those offered during the road show." "P&G still has a long way to go to reap the fruits of rural China," added the reporter.

Questions For Discussion

1. Classify P&G's promotion activities. What role has its road show played in the company's success or failures?
2. Why were advertising not used by P&G?
3. What are the key contents of P&G's road show? Do you think that it was a success? If yes, why?
4. Make recommendations for how P&G can further improve its road show strategy. How would you implement each recommendation?

Sources:

Ron Ho, "P&G (China)" accessed at http://www.greaterchinacrm.org:8080/eng/content_details.jsp?contentid=1171&subjectid=2; Dexter Roberts (2007), "Scrambling to Bring Crest to the Masses in China", BusinessWeek, accessed at http://www.businessweek.com/magazine/content/07_26/b4040058.htm; P&G Road Show, accessed at http://www.taqu.com/pinpaicehua/pinpaizhanlue/20070517/6287.html; P&G Road Show – Behind the Scene, accessed at http://www.globrand.com/2004/07/25/20040725-172124-1.shtml; P&G Road Show, accessed at http://www.taqu.com/pinpaicehua/pinpaizhanlue/20070517/6287.html; P&G Road Show, accessed at http://www.globrand.com/2007/06/13/20070613-111456-1.shtml

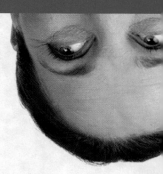

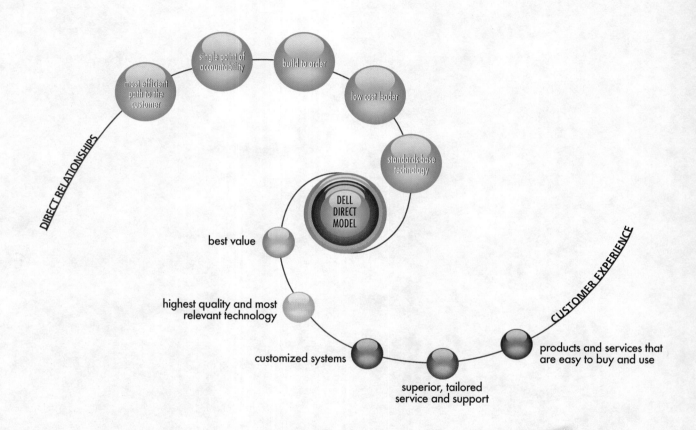

DIRECT RELATIONSHIPS

most efficient path to the customer

single point of accountability

build to order

low cost leader

standards-base technology

DELL DIRECT MODEL

best value

highest quality and most relevant technology

customized systems

superior, tailored service and support

products and services that are easy to buy and use

CUSTOMER EXPERIENCE

Beginning with the customer

Objectives

After studying this chapter, you should be able to

- define direct marketing and discuss its benefits to customers and companies
- identify and discuss the major forms of direct marketing
- explain how companies have responded to the Internet and other powerful new technologies with online marketing strategies
- discuss how companies go about conducting online marketing to profitably deliver more value to customers
- overview the public policy and ethical issues presented by direct marketing supply chain management

CHAPTER 17

DIRECT AND ONLINE MARKETING: Building Direct Customer Relationships

Previewing the Concepts

In the previous three chapters, you learned about communicating customer value through integrated marketing communication (IMC) and about four specific elements of the marketing communications mix—advertising, publicity, personal selling, and sales promotion. In this chapter, we'll look at the final IMC element, direct marketing, and at its fastest-growing form, online marketing. Direct marketing can be viewed as more than just a communications tool. In many ways it constitutes an overall marketing approach—a blend of communication and distribution channels all rolled into one. It has to be integrated with other elements of the promotion mix.

To set the stage, let's first look at Dell, the world's largest direct marketer of computer systems worldwide. The company owes its incredible success to what it calls the Dell Direct Model, which starts with direct customer relationships and ends with the Dell customer experience. Says one analyst, "There's no better way to make, sell, and deliver PCs than the way Dell does it, and nobody executes [the direct] model better than Dell."

When 19-year-old Michael Dell began selling personal computers out of his college dorm room in 1984, competitors and industry insiders scoffed at the concept of direct computer marketing. Yet young Michael proved the skeptics wrong. In little over two decades, he has turned his dorm-room mail-order business into a $56 billion computer empire. Dell is now the world's largest direct marketer of computer systems. It has produced a 10-year average annual return to investors of 39 percent, best among all Fortune 100 companies. Dell's shares have gained over 28,000 percent since its public offering fewer than 20 years ago.

The secret to Dell's stunning success is the company's direct model. Says Michael Dell, "There's no confusion about what the value proposition is, what the company offers, and why it's great for customers." Dell's direct-marketing approach delivers greater customer value through a winning combination of product customization, low prices, fast delivery, and award-winning customer service. A customer can call a Dell representative or log onto its Web site to order a fully customized, state-of-the-art PC to suit his or her special needs; and have it delivered to his or her doorstep within days—all at a price well below competitors' prices for a comparably performing PC. Dell backs its products with high-quality service and support.

As a result, Dell consistently ranks among the industry leaders in product reliability and service, and its customers are routinely among the industry's most satisfied.

Michael Dell's idea of serving individual buyers by letting them customize machines with the specific features they wanted at low prices also appeals strongly to corporate buyers. Dell can easily preconfigure each computer to precise requirements, preloading machines with a company's own software. It even undertakes such tedious tasks as pasting inventory tags onto each machine so that computers can be delivered directly to a given employee's desk. As a result, over 85 percent of Dell's sales come from business, government, and educational buyers.

The direct model results in more efficient selling and lower costs, which translate into lower prices for customers. "Nobody… makes [and markets] computer hardware more efficiently than Dell," says another analyst. Because Dell builds machines to order, it carries barely any inventory. Dealing one-to-one with customers helps the company react immediately to shifts in demand, so Dell doesn't get stuck with PCs no one wants. Finally, Dell has no dealers to pay. Thus, Dell's costs average 12 percent lower than those of its leading PC competitors.

As time is money, Dell is obsessed with "speed." According to one account, Dell squeezes "time out of every step in the process—from the moment an order is taken to the moment the cash is collected. [By selling direct, manufacturing to order, and] tapping credit cards and electronic payment, Dell converts the average sale to cash in less than 24 hours." By contrast, competitors selling through dealers might take 35 days or longer.

Such blazing speed results in more satisfied customers and still lower costs. For example, customers are often delighted to find their new computers arriving within as little as 36 hours of placing an order. And because Dell doesn't order parts until an order is booked, it can take advantage of ever-falling component costs. On average, its parts are 60 days newer than those in competing machines, and, hence, 60 days farther down the price curve. This gives Dell a 6 percent profit advantage from parts costs alone.

Competitors are no longer scoffing at Michael Dell's vision. In fact, competing and noncompeting companies alike are studying the Dell direct model closely. Still, the Dell direct model is facing challenges. Recent growth has slowed. The company admits that Dell isn't the high-flying growth company it once was. You can't expect a $56-billion-a-year giant to grow like a start-up. Some analysts suggest that Dell's vaunted direct model may not work as well for selling LCD TVs, handhelds, MP3 players, digital cameras, and other personal digital devices—products that consumers want to see and experience first-hand before buying. Thus, to continue growth in the face of fierce competition from HP, Acer, and Lenovo, Dell has expanded internationally, with the Asia Pacific being apriority focus. Dell first entered the region via Japan and Australia. Its direct sales operations now span 11 other markets: Brunei, China, Hong Kong, India, Korea, Macau, Malaysia, New Zealand, Singapore, Taiwan, and Thailand. In addition, 38 distributors serve another 31 markets.

At the heart of Dell's regional operations are two Asia Pacific Customer Centers (APCC) in Penang, Malaysia, and its China Customer Center (CCC) in Xiamen, China. Regional customers can order their computers directly from Dell. These facilities manufacture and ship the orders for receipt within seven to 10 working days. Customers can access a toll-free technical support hotline and benefit from Dell's on-site service programs. Its multilingual support engineers at the APCC and CCC resolve over 80 percent of all callers' technical issues over the phone. Dell's regional Web site, _www.dell.com/ap_, now supports 11 country-specific sites in four languages—Chinese, English, Korean, and Japanese. Sales in the Asia Pacific currently account for about 13 percent of Dell's global revenue. The region yields significant promise for Dell. Its third quarter 2007 growth in China was 28 percent, while in India it was 42 percent. According to the IDC, Dell is the number three vendor in the industry in the region in 2007. Dell aims to increase its presence to 1,000 cities in China from the present 45. The expansion will be achieved through increased direct sales as well as more partnerships. In fact, Dell plans to add retail stores to help bolster the consumer side of its business in general. Dell first started retailing PCs for the first time after 23 years in June 2007 at Wal-Mart stores. Its current retail partner in China is GOME Electrical Appliances, and it plans to sell PCs in France, Spain, and Belgium via Carrefour, the world's second largest retailer.

"It's hard to argue with success, and Michael Dell has been very successful ... he has built one of the world's hottest companies. In the process, he's become one of the world's richest men, amassing a personal fortune of more than $17 billion.[1]

Many marketing and promotion tools are developed in the context of mass marketing: targeting broad markets with standardized messages and offers distributed through intermediaries. Today, however, with the trend toward more narrowly targeted marketing, many companies are adopting direct marketing, either as a primary marketing approach or as a supplement to other approaches.

Direct marketing consists of direct connections with carefully targeted individual consumers to both obtain an immediate response and cultivate lasting customer relationships. Direct marketers communicate directly with customers, often on a one-to-one, interactive basis. Using detailed databases, they tailor their marketing offers and communications to the needs of narrowly defined segments or even individual buyers.

Beyond brand and relationship building, direct marketers usually seek a direct, immediate, and measurable consumer response. For example, Dell interacts directly with customers, by telephone or through its Web site, to design built-to-order systems that meet customers' individual needs. Buyers order directly from Dell, and Dell quickly and efficiently delivers the new computers to their homes or offices.

Direct marketing
Direct connections with carefully targeted individual consumers to obtain an immediate response and cultivate lasting customer relationships.

The New Direct-Marketing Model

Early direct marketers—catalog companies, direct mailers, and telemarketers—gathered customer names and sold goods mainly by mail and telephone. Today, however, with rapid advances in database technologies and new marketing media—especially the Internet—direct marketing has undergone a dramatic transformation.

In previous chapters, we've discussed direct marketing as direct distribution—as marketing channels that contain no intermediaries. We also include direct marketing as one element of the promotion mix—as an approach for communicating directly with consumers. In actuality, direct marketing is both these things.

Most companies still use direct marketing as a supplementary channel or medium for marketing their goods and messages. Thus, Lexus markets mostly through mass-media advertising and its high-quality dealer network but also supplements these channels with direct marketing. Its direct marketing includes promotional CDs and other materials mailed directly to prospective buyers, and a Web page (_www.lexus.com_) that provides consumers with information about various models, competitive comparisons, financing, and dealer locations. Similarly, some department stores sell the majority of their merchandise off their store shelves but also sell through direct mail and online catalogs.

However, for some companies today, direct marketing is more than just a supplementary channel or medium. For these companies, direct marketing—especially online marketing—constitutes a complete model for doing business. More than just another marketing channel or advertising medium, this new _direct model_ is rapidly changing the way companies think about building relationships with customers.

Rather than using direct marketing and the Internet only as supplemental approaches, firms employing the direct model use it as the _only_ approach. Companies such as Dell, Amazon.com, and eBay have built their entire approach to the marketplace around direct marketing.

Direct marketing – Companies such as Amazon.com and eBay have built their entireapproach around direct marketing. For example, personalized customer notifications via e-mail will alert customers to products they might be interested in. (_www.amazon.com_)

Growth and Benefits of Direct Marketing

Direct marketing has become the fastest-growing form of marketing. The Direct Marketing Association (DMA) estimates that direct marketing sales will grow 6.4 percent annually through 2009, compared with a projected 4.8 percent annual growth for total U.S. sales.[2]

Direct marketing continues to become more Web oriented, and Internet marketing is claiming a fast-growing share of direct marketing spending and sales. The Internet now accounts for only about 16 percent of direct marketing-driven sales. However, the DMA predicts that over the next five years Internet marketing expenditures will grow at a blistering 18 percent a year, three times faster than expenditures in other direct marketing media. Internet-driven sales will grow by 12.6 percent.

Whether employed as a complete business model or as a supplement to a broader integrated marketing mix, direct marketing brings many benefits to both buyers and sellers (see **Figure 17.1** and **Figure 17.2** respectively).

Figure 17.1
Benefits of direct marketing to buyers

Benefits to Buyers

For buyers, direct marketing is convenient, easy, and private. Direct marketers never close their doors, and customers don't have to battle traffic, find parking spaces, and trek through stores to find products. From the comfort of their homes or offices, they can browse catalogs or company Web sites at any time of the day or night. Business buyers can learn about products and services without tying up time with salespeople.

Direct marketing gives buyers ready access to a wealth of products. For example, unrestrained by physical boundaries, direct marketers can offer an almost unlimited selection to consumers almost anywhere in the world. For example, by making computers to order and selling directly, Dell can offer buyers thousands of self-designed PC configurations, many times the number offered by competitors who sell preconfigured PCs through retail stores. And just compare the huge selections offered by many Web merchants to the more meager assortments of their brick-and-mortar counterparts.

Direct marketing channels also give buyers access to a wealth of comparative information about companies, products, and competitors. Good catalogs or Web sites often provide more information in more useful forms than even the most helpful retail salesperson can. For example, the Amazon.com site offers more information than most of us can digest, ranging from top-10 product lists, extensive product descriptions, and expert and user product reviews to recommendations based on customers' previous purchases.

Finally, direct marketing is interactive and immediate—buyers can interact with sellers by phone or on the seller's Web site to create exactly the configuration of information, products, or services they desire, and then order them on the spot. Moreover, direct marketing gives consumers a greater measure of control. Consumers decide which catalogs they will browse and which Web sites they will visit.

However, some Asian consumers are not eager to dispense with the entertainment and social interaction related to shopping for the sake of convenience. For them, Web sites serve more as informational sources than shopping sites.

Benefits to Sellers

For sellers, direct marketing is a powerful tool for building customer relationships. Using database marketing, marketers can target small groups or individual consumers and promote their offers through personalized communications. Because of the one-to-one nature of direct marketing, companies can interact with customers by phone or online, learn more about their needs, and tailor products and services to specific customer tastes. In turn, customers can ask questions and volunteer feedback.

Sumitomo Mitsui Banking Corporation developed its Internet banking arm in the form of Japan Net Bank. Its system can copy transaction data from tellers and customers' responses from campaigns, and automatically collects the information using push technology so that market trends can be forecast as soon as possible. Thus, marketing results can be ascertained at a glance from the movement of the teller's transaction. From this same system, customer information analysis and segmentation can be easily carried out. Based on the results, different product and service information can be provided for each individual customer at the company's Web site Behavior analysis can also be done for each customer by time sequence through Web log mining, which tracks and analyzes customer "click streams" on the site. Besides such quick feedback, Japan Net Bank also offers "my m@il," a service that notifies customers to receive transaction details to a designated e-mail address. A customer can be notified when his salary has been deposited, a bank transfer has been completed, or when there are insufficient funds to cover an automatic debit for utility bill payment.[3]

Direct marketing –
Because of its one-to-one nature, companies can interact with customers by phone or online, learn about their needs, and tailor products and services to specific customer tastes.

Direct marketing also offers sellers a low-cost, efficient, speedy alternative for reaching their markets. Direct marketing has grown rapidly in business-to-business marketing, partly in response to the ever-increasing costs of marketing through the sales force. Such cost increases imply that personal sales calls should be made only when necessary and to high-potential customers and prospects. Lower-cost-per-contact media—such as telemarketing, direct mail, and company Web sites—often prove more cost effective. Similarly, online direct marketing results in lower costs, improved efficiencies, and speedier handling of channel and logistics functions, such as order processing, inventory handling, and delivery. Direct marketers such as Amazon.com or Dell also avoid the expense of maintaining a store and the related costs of rent, insurance, and utilities, passing the savings along to customers.

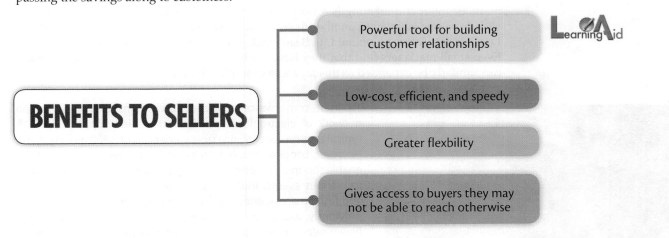

BENEFITS TO SELLERS

- Powerful tool for building customer relationships
- Low-cost, efficient, and speedy
- Greater flexbility
- Gives access to buyers they may not be able to reach otherwise

Figure 17.2
Benefits of direct marketing to sellers

By eliminating the need for physical branches, Japan Net Bank (_www.japannetbank. co.jp_) can provide services to customers with low service charges and high interest rates on deposits. It had 5,000 account applications on its opening day, increasing to 300,000 in seven months. Its strategy of using the Internet to minimize costs strikes well with customers who are sensitive about interest rates. Japan Net Bank's interest rates on deposits are about twice those offered by conventional financial institutions. There are no service charges for the first three cash transactions at its ATMs.

Direct marketing can also offer greater flexibility. It allows marketers to make ongoing adjustments to its prices and programs, or to make immediate and timely announcements and offers. For example, Southwest Airlines' DING! application takes advantage of the flexibility and immediacy of the Web to share low-fare offers directly with customers:[4]

When Jim Jacobs hears a "ding" coming from his desktop computer, he thinks about discount air fares like the $122 ticket he recently bought for a flight from Tampa to Baltimore on Southwest Airlines. Several times a day, Southwest sends Jacobs and hundreds of thousands of other computer users discounts through an application called DING! "If I move quickly," says Jacobs, a corporate telecommunications salesman who lives in Tampa, "I can usually save a lot of money." The fare to Baltimore underbid the airline's own Web site by $36, he says. DING! lets Southwest bypass the reservations system and pass bargain fares directly to interested customers. Eventually, DING! may even allow Southwest to customize fare offers based on each customer's unique characteristics

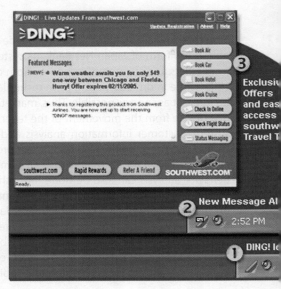

Sharing with customers – Southwest Airlines "DING!" application takes advantage of flexibility and immediacy of the Web to share low-fare offers directly with customers. (*www.southwest.com/ding*)

and travel preferences. For now, DING! gets a Southwest icon on the customer's desktop and lets the airline build relationships with customers by helping them to save money. Following its DING! launch in early 2005, Southwest experienced its two biggest online sales days ever. In the first 13 months, two million customers downloaded DING!and the program produced more than $80 million worth of fares.

Finally, direct marketing gives sellers access to buyers that they could not reach through other channels. Smaller firms can mail catalogs to customers outside their local markets. Internet marketing is a truly global medium that allows buyers and sellers to click from one country to another in seconds. A Web surfer from Hong Kong or Kuala Lumpur can access an online L.L. Bean catalog as easily as someone living in America. Even small marketers find that they have ready access to global markets. Local markets can similarly be expanded as this Japanese example illustrates.

Japanese convenience store chain Lawson installed a $57 million network of electronic shopping kiosks called Loppi in 1997. A typical Lawson convenience store carries about 2,800 grocery items. However, Loppi terminals installed in all of Lawson's 7,030 stores enable shoppers to select from nearly 3,000 items, including tickets for various events, music CDs, videos, game software, cosmetics and fashion accessories, and PCs and peripherals Whereas Lawson previously sold fresh flowers only in May, prior to Mother's Day, flower sales continue all year round thanks to Loppi. Lawson plans to develop an Internet based extension, a Web site tentatively called Lawson Digital Station, to integrate its Loppi touchscreen terminals. Users who order items through this Web site can visit any of Lawson's 24-hour stores to pick up their purchases. Lawson expects the new Internet shopping site to increase sales of its normal convenience store items through purchases by customers visiting its stores to pick up their Internet orders.[5]

Access to buyers – Lawson, Japan's second-largest convenience store, uses an electronic shopping network to expand the range of items that could be carried in a limited retail space, thereby generating more sales. (*www.lawson.com.jp/;oppi/index.html*)

Customer Databases and Direct Marketing

Effective direct marketing begins with a good customer database. A **customer database** is an organized collection of comprehensive data about individual customers or prospects, including geographic, demographic, psychographic, and behavioral data. A good customer database can be a potent relationship-building tool. The database gives companies "a snapshot of how customers look and behave."

Many companies confuse a customer database with a customer mailing list. A customer mailing list is simply a set of names, addresses, and telephone numbers. A customer database contains much more information. In consumer marketing, the customer database might contain a customer's demographics (age, income, family members, birthdays), psychographics (activities, interests, and opinions), and buying behavior (buying preferences and the recency, frequency, and monetary value—RFM—of past purchases). In business-to-business marketing, the customer profile might contain the products and services the customer has bought; past volumes and prices; key contacts (and their ages, birthdays, hobbies, and favorite foods); competing suppliers; status of current contracts; estimated customer spending for the next few years; and assessments of competitive strengths and weaknesses in selling and servicing the account.

Some of these databases are huge. For example, casino operator Harrah's Entertainment has built a customer database containing 30 terabytes worth of customer information. Yahoo! records every click made by every visitor, adding some 400 billion bytes of data per day to its database—the equivalent of 800,000 books. Wal-Mart captures data on every item, for every customer, for every store, everyday. Its database contains more than 570 terabytes of data—far greater than the storage horsepower of 100,000 personal computers.[6]

Companies use their databases in many ways:

- They use databases to locate good potential customers and to generate sales leads.
- They can mine their databases to learn about customers in detail, and then fine-tune their market offerings and communications to the special preferences and behaviors of target segments or individuals.

Like many other marketing tools, database marketing requires a special investment. Companies must invest in computer hardware, database software, analytical programs, communication links, and skilled personnel. The database system must be user-friendly and available to various marketing groups, including those in product and brand management, new-product development, advertising and promotion, direct mail, telemarketing, Web marketing, field sales, order fulfillment, and customer service. However, a well-managed database should lead to sales and customer-relationship gains that will more than cover its costs.

Forms of Direct Marketing

The major forms of direct marketing—as shown in **Figure 17.3**—include personal selling, direct-mail marketing, catalog marketing, telephone marketing, direct-response television marketing, kiosk marketing, new digital direct marketing technologies, and online marketing. We examined personal selling in depth in Chapter 16. Here, we examine the other direct-marketing forms.

Customer database
An organized collection of comprehensive data about individual customers or prospects, including geographic, demographic, psychographic, and behavioral data.

Customer database –
A customer profile might contain the products and services the customer has bought previously.

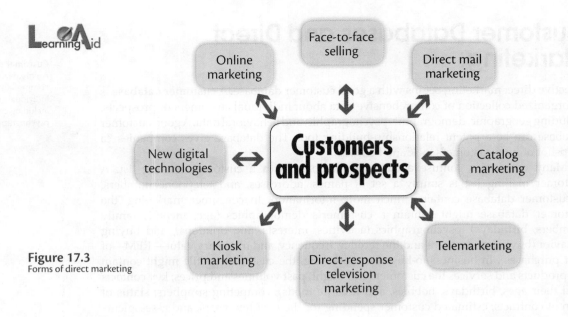

Figure 17.3
Forms of direct marketing

Direct-Mail Marketing

Direct-mail marketing
Direct marketing by sending an offer, announcement, reminder, or other item to a person at a particular address.

Direct-mail marketing involves sending an offer, announcement, reminder, or other item to a person at a particular address. Using highly selective mailing lists, direct marketers send out millions of mail pieces each year—letters, catalogs, ads, brochures, samples, CDs and DVDs, and other "salespeople with wings." Direct mail is by far the largest direct marketing medium.

Direct mail is well suited to direct, one-to-one communication. It permits high target-market selectivity, can be personalized, is flexible, and allows easy measurement of results. Although direct mail costs more than mass media such as television or magazines per thousand people reached, the people it reaches are much better prospects. Direct mail has proved successful in promoting products ranging from books, music, DVDs, and magazine subscriptions to insurance, gift items, clothing, gourmet foods, and industrial products.

Direct-mail –
The direct-mail industry constantly seeks new and creative methods and approaches to delivery the marketing message.

The direct-mail industry constantly seeks new methods and approaches. For example, CDs and DVDs are now among the fastest-growing direct-mail media. One study showed that including a CD or DVD in a marketing offer generates responses between 50 to 600 percent greater than traditional direct mail.[7] New forms of delivery have also become popular, such as fax mail, voice mail, and e-mail. Fax mail and voice mail are subject to the same do-not-call restrictions as telemarketing, so their use has been limited in recent years. However, e-mail is booming as a direct marketing tool. Today's e-mail messages have moved far beyond the drab text-only messages of old. The new breed of e-mail ad uses animation, interactive links, streaming video, and personalized audio messages to reach out and grab attention.

E-mail and other new forms deliver direct mail at incredible speeds compared to the post office's "snail mail" pace. Yet, much like mail delivered through traditional channels, they may be resented as "junk mail" or spam if sent to people who have no interest in them. For this reason, smart marketers are targeting their direct mail carefully so as not waste their money and recipients' time. They are designing permission-based programs, sending e-mail ads only to those who want to receive them. We will discuss e-mail marketing in more detail later in the chapter.

Catalog Marketing

Advances in technology, along with the move toward personalized, one-to-one marketing have resulted in exciting changes in **catalog marketing**. More and more catalogs are going digital. A variety of Web-only catalogers have emerged, and most print catalogers have added Web-based catalogs to their marketing mixes.

However, although the Internet has provided a new avenue for catalog sales, the printed catalogs still remain the primary medium. Research shows that print catalogs generate many of those online orders. Customers who receive print catalogs are more likely to buy online, and they spend 16 percent more than customers who did not receive catalogs.[8]

Catalogs can be an effective sales and relationship builder. A U.S. study found that a majority of women who receive catalogs are actively engaged with them.

> **Catalog marketing**
> Direct marketing through print, video, or electronic catalogs that are mailed to select customers, made available in stores, or presented online.

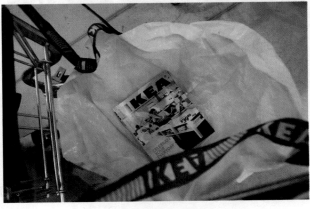

Print catalog –
Printed catalogs, such as this one from IKEA, are still the primary medium in catalog marketing.

Some 89 percent of the participants revealed that they do more than just browse through the catalogs they receive in the mail. They circle or "tab" the items that they want, fold over the corners of pages, and tear pages out. Some 69 percent save their catalogs to look through again. More than just a buying tool, many women view catalogs as a source of entertainment and inspiration. Women claim to love perusing catalogs almost like reading a woman's magazine, looking for ideas for everything from decorating, to fashion, to that extra special gift. More than one-third of women surveyed greet their catalogs with enthusiasm, stating they are the first things they look at when they get their mail. Some 75 percent of women find catalog browsing really enjoyable, fun, and relaxing, with 74 percent agreeing that they get excited when a new catalog arrives.[9]

Web-based catalogs present a number of benefits versus printed catalogs. They save on production, printing, and mailing costs. Whereas print-catalog space is limited, online catalogs can offer an almost unlimited amount of merchandise. Web catalogs also allow real-time merchandising: Products and features can be added or removed as needed, and prices can be adjusted instantly to match demand. Finally, online catalogs can be spiced up with interactive entertainment and promotional features, such as games, contests, and daily specials.

However, Web-based catalogs also present challenges. Whereas a print catalog is intrusive and creates its own attention, Web catalogs are passive and must be marketed. Attracting new customers is much more difficult for a Web catalog than for a print catalog. Thus, even catalogers who are sold on the Web are not likely to abandon their print catalogs.

Telephone Marketing

Telephone marketing involves using the telephone to sell directly to consumers and business customers. Marketers use *outbound* telephone marketing to sell directly to consumers and businesses. *Inbound* toll-free numbers are used to receive orders from television and print ads, direct mail, or catalogs.

> **Telephone marketing**
> Using the telephone to sell directly to customers.

Telephone marketing –
It has evolved over the years to focus more on managing existing customer relationships through "opt-in" calling systems.

Direct-response television marketing
Direct marketing via television, including direct-response television advertising (or infomercials) and home shopping channels.

Properly designed and targeted telemarketing provides many benefits, including purchasing convenience and increased product and service information. However, the explosion in unsolicited outbound telephone marketing over the years annoyed many consumers, who objected to the almost daily "junk phone calls." Thus, many of these marketers are shifting their call-center activity from making cold calls on often resentful customers to managing existing customer relationships. They are developing "opt-in" calling systems, in which they provide useful information and offers to customers who have invited the company to contact them by phone or e-mail. These "sales tactics have [produced] results as good—or even better—than telemarketing," declares one analyst. "The opt-in model is proving [more] valuable for marketers [than] the old invasive one."[10]

Telemarketing remains a major fundraising tool for nonprofits groups. However, many telemarketers are shifting to alternative methods for capturing new customers and sales, from direct mail, direct-response TV, and live-chat Web technology to sweepstakes that prompt customers to call in.

Direct-Response Television Marketing

Direct-response television marketing takes one of two major forms. The first is *direct-response television advertising* (DRTV). Direct marketers air television spots, often 60 or 120 seconds long, which persuasively describe a product and give customers a toll-free number or Web site for ordering. Television viewers also often encounter full 30-minute or longer advertising programs, or *infomercials*, for a single product. However, infomercials have been associated with somewhat questionable pitches for juicers and other kitchen gadgets, get-rich-quick schemes, and slimming programs. In the U.S., several large companies like Dell, Disney, Revlon, and IBM have begun using infomercials to sell their products, refer customers to retailers, send out product information, or attract buyers to their Web sites.

Direct-response TV commercials are usually cheaper to make and the media purchase is less costly. Moreover, unlike most media campaigns, direct-response ads always include a toll-free number or Web address, making it easier for marketers to track the impact of their pitches. "In a business environment where marketers are obsessed with return on investment," notes one such expert, "direct response is tailor-made—[marketers can] track phone calls and Web-site hits generated by the ads. [They can] use DRTV to build brand awareness while simultaneously generating leads and sales."[11]

Home shopping channels, another form of direct-response television marketing, are television programs or entire channels dedicated to selling goods and services. Some of these channels are popular in Korea and Taiwan. Program hosts chat with viewers by phone and offer products ranging from jewelry, lamps, collectible dolls, and clothing to power tools and consumer electronics. Viewers call a toll-free number or go online to order goods.

Despite their lowbrow images, home shopping channels have evolved into highly sophisticated, very successful marketing operations. Consider QVC:

QVC is one of the world's most successful and innovative retailers. The company is roughly twice as profitable as Amazon.com. Although it sells no advertising, it's the third-largest U.S. broadcaster in terms of revenue, and its sales and profits are larger than those of all other TV-based retailers combined. The company's Web site, QVC.com, is now the sixth-largest general merchandise Internet retailer. Prominent manufacturers such as Estee Lauder also sell via QVC. Dell sold $65 million worth of PCs in 24 hours on QVC in a 24-hour period. QVC has honed the art and science of TV retailing. Its producers react in real time, adjusting offers, camera angles, lighting, and dialog to maximize returns. QVC has set the benchmark for "retailment," the blending of retailing and entertainment. QVC staff call it the "backyard fence" sell, the feeling that the merchants are neighbors visiting. According to its president for U.S. commerce, "we aren't really in the business of selling." Instead, QVC uses products to build relationships with customers.[12]

Home shopping channels – QVC is more than just a place where little-known sellers hawk trinkets and trash at bare-bones prices. Behind the cameras, it's a sophisticated marketer with sales and profits larger than all other TV-based retailers combined.

Kiosk Marketing

As consumers become more and more comfortable with computer and digital technologies, many companies are placing information and ordering machines—called *kiosks* (in contrast to vending machines, which dispense actual products)—in stores, airports, and other locations. Kiosks are popping up everywhere, from self-service hotel and airline check-in devices to in-store ordering kiosks that let you order merchandise not carried in the store.

In-store Kodak, Fuji, and HP kiosks let customers transfer pictures from memory sticks, mobile phones, and other digital storage devices, edit them, and make high-quality color prints. Kiosks in some Hilton hotel lobbies let guests view their reservations, get room keys, view prearrival messages, check in and out, and even change seat assignments and print boarding passes for flights on any of 18 airlines.

Business marketers also use kiosks. For example, Dow Plastics places kiosks at trade shows to collect sales leads and to provide information on its products. The kiosk system reads customer data from encoded registration badges and produces technical data sheets that can be printed at the kiosk or faxed or mailed to the customer. The system has resulted in a 400 percent increase in qualified sales leads.[13]

Kiosk marketing – Kiosks allow customers to order merchandise not carried in the store. There are kiosks for photo printing and hotel and airline services. At Singapore Changi Airport, boarding passes can be dispensed from these kiosks for automatic check-ins.

New Digital Direct Marketing Technologies

Today, thanks to a wealth of new digital technologies, direct marketers can reach and interact with consumers just about anywhere, at anytime, about almost anything. Here, we look into several exciting new digital direct marketing technologies: mobile phone marketing, podcasts and vodcasts, and interactive TV (ITV).

Mobile Phone Marketing

According to one expert, "the cell phone, which makes on-the-go conversing so convenient, is morphing into a content device, a kind of digital Swiss Army knife with the capability of filling its owner's every spare minute with games, music, live and on-demand TV, Web browsing, and, oh yes, advertising."[14] A recent survey found that 89 percent of major brands will be marketed via mobile phones by 2008. More than half of those brands will likely spend up to 25 percent of their marketing budgets on mobile phone marketing.[15]

Marketers of all kinds are now integrating mobile phones into their direct marketing. Mobile phone promotions include everything from ring-tone give-aways, mobile games, and ad-supported content to text-in contests and sweepstakes. Perhaps nowhere is mobile phone marketing more advanced than in Japan.

Nami, a 37-year-old graphic designer in Tokyo, regularly uses her phone to send and receive e-mails on the go. Her 11-year-old daughter enjoys downloading wallpaper and animated trailers featuring Disney characters, and Nami's boyfriend relies on his phone's global positioning system to navigate Tokyo's labyrinth of streets. The family can also use mobilephones to buy a can of Coke from high-tech vending machines, receive e-coupons from neighborhood stores, and even have their fortunes told. Digital coupons are taking off, as are GPS-based promotions used by retailers to target people near their stores. Mobile-ad spending in Japan is expected to hit $680 million by 2009, up from just $158 million last year.

Japanese direct marketers are experimenting with new ways to use the mobile devices for brand building. Nestlé, for example, is trying out a new technology called Quick Response (QR) codes, which can be scanned like digital bar codes. QR codes on print and outdoor ads can be read by mobile phone cameras, which redirect the user's phone to a designated mobile URL site. Nestlé used QR codes in a campaign to launch a canned drink

Mobile phone marketing – To launch its Nescafé Shake canned drink in Japan, Nestlé used Quick Response codes, which can be scanned like UPC codes by a mobile phone, to direct consumers to marketing pitches for the new product.

called Nescafé Shake. It promoted Shake with two 15-minute short films that humorously communicated a sense of fun around the act of "shaking" with a story about a slacker kid who winds up with a dog's wagging tail on his behind. A QR code on promotional materials led mobile phone users to a mobile site where they could download the film as well as its original music as songs or ring tones. In the first three weeks after Nestlé's "Nonta's Tail" film debuted, 120,000 people visited the mobile site and another 550,000 watched the film on the Internet.[16]

Podcasts –
Marketers are increasingly integrating podcasts and vodcasts into their direct marketing programs to reach out to listeners, who tend to come from the higher-income bracket.

Podcasts and Vodcasts

Podcasting and vodcasting are the latest on-the-go, on-demand technologies. The name podcast derives from Apple's now-everywhere iPod. With podcasting, consumers can download audio files (podcasts) or video files (vodcasts) via the Internet to an iPod or other handheld device and then listen to or view them whenever and wherever they wish. They can search for podcast topics through sites such as iTunes or through podcast networks such as PodTrac, Podbridge, or PodShow. These days, you can download podcasts or vodcasts on an exploding array of topics, everything from your favorite radio show, a recent sit-com episode, or current sports features to the latest music video.

Podcast listeners tend to come from the higher-income bracket. To reach this segment, marketers are integrating podcasts and vodcasts into their direct marketing programs in the form of ad-supported podcasts, downloadable ads and informational features, and other promotions.

For example, Volvo sponsors podcasts on Autoblog and Absolut vodka buys ads on PodShow programs. Nestlé Purina publishes podcasts on animal training and behavioral issues. The Walt Disney World Resort offers weekly podcasts on a mix of topics, including behind-the-scenes tours, interviews, upcoming events, and news about new attractions.[17]

Honda recently offered a vodcast as part of a new ad campaign for its Honda Civic. The vodcast consists of a two-minute, "This is what a Honda feels like" ad, in which human voices replicate the sounds that passengers hear in a Honda Civic.

The vodcast also includes behind-the-scenes footage of the making of the ad. According to a Honda marketing executive, this dynamic new medium "is enabling people to experience what a Honda feels like from one of their most personal and closest touch points—their iPod."[18]

Interactive TV (ITV)

Interactive TV (ITV) lets viewers interact with television programming and advertising using their remote controls. In the past, ITV has been slow to catch on. However, satellite broadcasting systems can offer ITV capabilities.

Interactive TV gives marketers an opportunity to reach targeted audiences in an interactive, more involving way. For example, BMW recently ran interactive ads that allowed viewers to request catalogs and several screens worth of other information using their remotes. The number of requests exceeded BMW's expectations tenfold. Similarly, Sony uses ITV to interact with U.S. TiVo users:[19]

Sony is running ads for its Bravia flat-panel TVs that let viewers, if they have TiVo, choose among different endings, whether they're watching live TV or a recorded program. Five seconds into the commercial, two on-screen choices appear—one aimed at men and one at women. A menu of "male" endings revolves around picture quality and size, and the "female" options focus on the TV's aesthetics. Sony hopes that the interactive and entertaining ad will keep viewers involved. It's even hoping that by offering 12 possible endings for its ad, viewers will be curious enough to watch them all. "If you provide viewers with a worthwhile experience, they'll absolutely stay engaged," says an executive from the ad agency that created the Bravia campaign.

More broadly, TiVo plans to roll out what may sound like the ultimate in gall: ads on demand. It's not so crazy. Consumers about to spend big money on cars, travel, new kitchens, and the like have shown plenty of interest in watching video about the stuff they plan to buy. TiVo wants to offer that content more conveniently and on viewers' terms. TiVo's budding broadband link to the Net, which, among other things, connects a viewer's TiVo screen with their Yahoo! homepage, is seen as just the beginning of full-blown convergence between interactive TV and the Internet.

Interactive TV –
Users can interact with television programming and advertising using their remote controls.

Mobile phone marketing, podcasts and vodcasts, and interactive TV offer exciting direct marketing opportunities. But marketers must be careful to use these new direct marketing approaches wisely. As with other direct marketing forms, marketers who use them risk backlash from consumers who may resent such marketing as an invasion of their privacy. Marketers must target their direct marketing offers carefully, bringing real value to customers rather than making unwanted intrusions into their lives.

Online Marketing

As noted earlier, **online marketing** is the fastest-growing form of direct marketing. Recent technological advances have created a digital age. Widespread use of the Internet and other powerful new technologies are having a dramatic impact on both buyers and the marketers who serve them. In this section, we examine how marketing strategy and practice are changing to take advantage of today's Internet technologies.

Marketing and the Internet

Much of the world's business today is carried out over digital networks that connect people and companies. The **Internet**, a vast public web of computer networks, connects users of all types all around the world to each other and to an amazingly large information

Online marketing
Company efforts to market products and services and build customer relationships over the Internet.

Internet
A vast public web of computer networks that connects users of all types all around the world to each other and to an amazingly large "information repository."

repository. Internet usage continues to grow steadily. Worldwide, some 470 million people have Internet access.[20]

The Internet has given marketers a whole new way to create value for customers and build customer relationships. The Web has fundamentally changed customers' notions of convenience, speed, price, product information, and service. The amazing success of early *click-only* companies—Amazon.com, eBay, Expedia, and hundreds of others—caused existing *brick-and-mortar* manufacturers and retailers to reexamine how they served their markets. Now, almost all of these traditional companies have set up their own online sales and communications channels, becoming *click-and-mortar* competitors.

Online Marketing Domains

The four major online marketing domains are shown in **Figure 17.4.** They include B2C (business to consumer), B2B (business to business), C2C (consumer to consumer), and C2B (consumer to business).

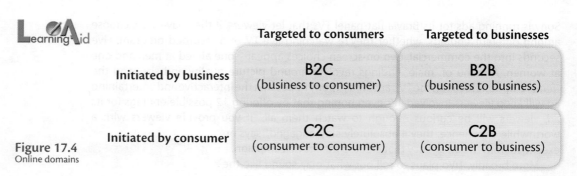

	Targeted to consumers	Targeted to businesses
Initiated by business	**B2C** (business to consumer)	**B2B** (business to business)
Initiated by consumer	**C2C** (consumer to consumer)	**C2B** (consumer to business)

Figure 17.4
Online domains

Business to Consumer (B2C)

Business-to-consumer (B2C) online marketing is the selling of goods and services online to final consumers. Today's consumers can buy almost anything online—from clothing, kitchen gadgets, and airline tickets to computers and cars. Online consumer buying continues to grow at a healthy rate.

Perhaps more importantly, the Internet now influences 27 percent of total retail sales—sales transacted online plus those carried out offline but encouraged by online research. By 2010, the Internet will influence a staggering 50 percent of total retail sales.[21] Thus, smart marketers are employing integrated multichannel strategies that use the Web to drive sales to other marketing channels.

People now go online to order a wide range of goods—clothing from Gap, books or electronics from Amazon.com, otah from savorydelights.com.sg, and hotel accommodation from asiahotels.com. As more and more people use the Web, the population of online consumers is becoming more mainstream and diverse. The Web now offers marketers a palette of different kinds of consumers seeking different kinds of online experiences.

However, Internet consumers still differ from traditional offline consumers in their approaches to buying and in their responses to marketing. In the Internet exchange process,

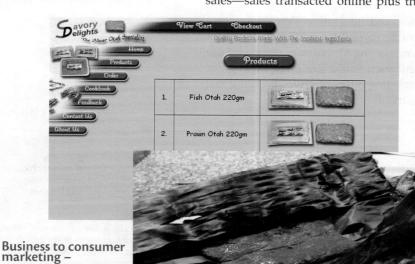

Business-to-consumer (B2C) online marketing
Selling goods and services online to final consumers.

Business to consumer marketing –
Singaporeans can order otah online and have it delivered to their doorstep. Otah is a local fish paste food.
(*www.savorydelights.com.sg*)

customer initiate and control the contact. Traditional marketing targets a somewhat passive audience. In contrast, online marketing targets people who actively select which Web sites they will visit and what marketing information they will receive about which products and under what conditions. Thus, the new world of online marketing requires new marketing approaches.

However, some Asian characteristics make Internet shopping unattractive. Take Hong Kong for instance. Given its compact urban geography, hardworking population, and low proportion (14 percent) of household car ownership, Hong Kong was thought to be suited for Internet grocery services. Thus, AdMart was started. However, it closed within 18 months. Several reasons accounted for this. Hong Kongers are not used to buying in bulk. Living space in Hong Kong is so cramped that few people have the cupboard space needed for bulk buying. Further, food shopping is an experience deeply ingrained in the Chinese culture where a maid or the wife is likely to visit the market twice a day so that both lunch and dinner will be made from the freshest ingredients. People like to feel the food, touch it, and squeeze it.[22]

Business to Business (B2B)

Business-to-business (B2B) online marketing involves B2B marketers using B2B Web sites, e-mail, online product catalogs, online trading networks, and other online resources to reach new business customers, serve current customers more effectively, and obtain buying efficiencies and better prices.

Most major B2B marketers offer product information, customer purchasing, and customer support services online. For example, corporate buyers can visit Sun Microsystems' Web site (_www.sun.com_), select detailed descriptions of Sun's products and solutions, request sales and service information, and interact with staff members. Some major companies conduct almost all of their business on the Web. Networking equipment and software maker Cisco Systems takes more than 80 percent of its orders over the Internet.

Beyond simply selling their products and services online, companies can use the Internet to build stronger relationships with important business customers. For example, Dell has set up customized Web sites for more than 113,000 business and institutional customers worldwide. These individualized Premier Dell.com sites help business customers to more efficiently manage all phases of their Dell computer buying and ownership. Each customer's Premier Dell.com Web site can include a customized online computer store, purchasing and asset management reports and tools, system-specific technical information, links to useful information throughout Dell's extensive Web site, and more. The site has all the information a customer needs to do business with Dell available in one place, 24 hours a day, seven days a week.[23]

Consumer to Consumer (C2C)

Much **consumer-to-consumer (C2C) online marketing** and communication occurs on the Web between interested parties over a wide range of products and subjects. In some cases, the Internet provides an excellent means by which consumers can buy or exchange goods or information directly with one another. For example, eBay, Amazon.com Auctions, Overstock.com, and other auction sites offer popular marketspaces for displaying and selling almost anything, from art and antiques, coins and stamps, and jewelry to computers and consumer electronics. In India, baazee.com is a popular site while taobao.com and paipai.com are popular in China.

EBay's C2C online trading community of more than 181 million registered users worldwide (greater than the combined populations of France, Spain, and Britain!) transacted some $40 billion in trades last year. On any given day, the company's Web site lists more than 16 million items up for auction in more than 45,000 categories. Based on its huge success in the C2C market, eBay has now attracted a large number of B2C sellers, ranging from small businesses peddling their regular wares to large businesses liquidating excess inventory at auction. In China, eBay marked its first foray into the B2C

Business-to-business (B2B) online marketing
Selling goods and services online to final consumers.

Consumer-to-consumer (C2C) online marketing
Online exchanges of goods and information between final consumers.

Using blogs as marketing tools –
Companies can advertise on an existing blog or influence content there, or set up their own blogs.

business with a strategic cooperation agreement with Yongle Electronic Appliance Store, one of the largest household appliance chain retailers.[24]

The popularity of C2C online marketing is set to boom in China. In 2007, China's C2C trade reached $5.55 billion, up from 90 percent compared to 2006, and is expected to exceed $9 billion in 2008. Web sites such as taobao.ccom and eBay are popular, with clothes and bags, IT products, and digital products being the most popularly bought online. With the number of Chinese netizens increasing rapidly, shopping online has become a part of more Chinese's daily life. It is estimated that by 2010, the registered customers in China's C2C online market will amount to 72 million, including 27 million active customers, and a trading volume of $15.7 billion. Like eBay, the success of taobao.com has spawned a new B2C business. Alibaba.com together with taobao.com has opened the Taobao Shopping Mall, a wholly new form of B2C. Not to be outdone, eBay China has also started its B2C business with flagship stores.[25]

In other cases, C2C involves interchanges of information through Internet forums that appeal to specific special-interest groups. Such activities may be organized for commercial or noncommercial purposes. An example is Web logs, or *blogs*, online journals where people post their thoughts, usually on a narrowly defined topic. Video blogs are termed *vlogs*. Today's blogosphere consists of more than 10 million blogs, with 40,000 new ones popping up every day.

Many marketers are now tapping into blogs as a medium for reaching carefully targeted consumers. One way is to advertise on an existing blog or to influence content there. For example, before GE announced a major energy-efficient technology initiative last year, GE executives met with major environmental bloggers to build support.

Other companies set up their own blogs. For example, Coca-Cola set up a blog to add an online community element to its sponsorship of the 2006 Winter Olympics. It enlisted a half-dozen college students from around the world to blog about their trips to the games. Coke paid to fly and accommodate students from China, Germany, Italy, Canada, and Australia, each of whom agreed to post conversations about the positive side of the games.[26]

As a marketing tool, blogs offer some advantages. They can offer a fresh, original, personal, and cheap way to reach today's fragmented audiences. For example, when Tiger Beer began organizing visual arts and music parties worldwide, it saw participants publicizing the events through photos on MySpace.com and videos on YouTube.com. Les Buckley, director of group commercial for Asia-Pacific Breweries, said, "The good thing is, it's genuine interest and there's authenticity. People much rather listen to the next-door neighbor than an advertiser."

However, the blogosphere is cluttered and difficult to control. "Blogs may help companies bond with consumers in exciting new ways, but they won't help them control the relationship," says a blog expert. When Chevy ran a contest to create an online commercial for its sports utility vehicle, the Tahoe, 16 percent of the 22,000 ads submitted were negative, some attacking the SUV's effect on climate change. As Web journals remain largely a C2C medium, citizen advertising can be a double-edged sword. "That isn't to suggest companies can't influence the relationship or leverage blogs to engage in a meaningful relationship," says the expert, "but the consumer will remain in control."[27]

In all, C2C means that online buyers don't just consume product information—increasingly, they create it. They join Internet interest groups to share information, with the result that "word of Web" is joining "word of mouth" as an important buying influence. As Michelle Kristula-Green, president of Leo Burnett Asia-Pacific notes, "If everyone can 'own' a radio or TV channel, why would they watch commercial TV, with its predetermined schedule of loud and contrived ads? Against this backdrop, marketers have to be willing to relinquish the control they think they have over their brands in the open marketplace of ideas." She added that some big brands like Kodak, Converse, and MasterCard are starting to "open themselves up to interpretation," with McDonald's even showcasing the faces and stories of its customers on its packaging. Kristula-Green concludes, "We've gone from monologue to dialogue. The future will be about customization and community … The challenge is to make brands feel more inclusive, to make creativity more personal, and to make it more contagious."[28]

Consumer to Business (C2B)

The final online marketing domain is **consumer-to-business (C2B) online marketing**. Thanks to the Internet, today's consumers are finding it easier to communicate with companies. Most companies now invite prospects and customers to send in suggestions and questions via company Web sites. Beyond this, rather than waiting for an invitation, consumers can search out sellers on the Web, learn about their offers, initiate purchases, and give feedback. Using the Web, consumers can even drive transactions with businesses, rather than the other way around. For example, using Priceline.com, would-be buyers can bid for airline tickets, hotel rooms, rental cars, cruises, and vacation packages, leaving the sellers to decide whether to accept their offers.

Priceline.com allows consumers to state the price that they would pay for various products and services. In Asia, Priceline has an airline and hotel booking service. Customers first provide their travel details (e.g., travel itinerary) and preferences (e.g., star rating of a hotel). Priceline then matches up the order with the 25 airlines and 8,000 hotels that it has signed up with to find those willing to accept the customer's price. It will revert to the customer within an hour, offering significant savings of up to 30 percent. In Hong Kong, Priceline also operates transaction counters in Park N Shop grocery stores, Watsons drug stores, and Fortress appliance stores where customers can buy and pick up tickets.

Consumer-to-business (C2B) online marketing
Online exchanges in which consumers search out sellers, learn about their offers, and initiate purchases, sometimes even driving transaction terms.

Consumer-to-business online marketing –
Consumers now search out sellers on the Web and initiate purchases. On Priceline, customers provide their travel details and the company matches it with the airlines and hotels it has signed up with. (*www.priceline.com*)

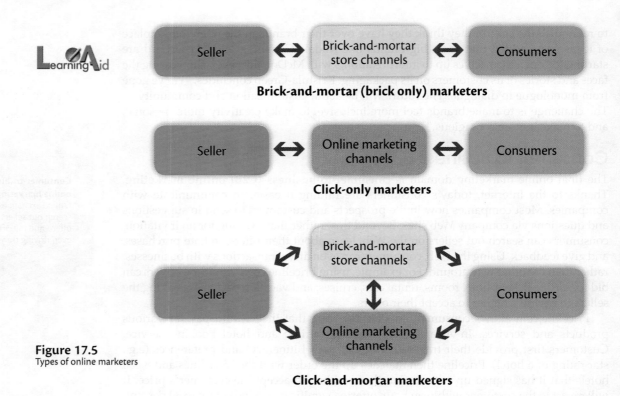

Figure 17.5
Types of online marketers

Types of Online Marketers

Companies of all types are now marketing online. In this section, we first discuss the different types of online marketers shown in **Figure 17.5.** Then, we examine how companies go about conducting online marketing.

Click-Only versus Click-and-Mortar Marketers

The Internet gave birth to a new species of marketers—the *click-only* dot-coms—which operate only online without any *brick-and-mortar* market presence. In addition, most traditional *brick-and-mortar* companies have now added online marketing operations, transforming themselves into *click-and-mortar* competitors.

Click-Only Companies

> **Click-only companies**
> The so-called dot-coms, which operate only online without any brick-and-mortar market presence.

Click-only companies come in many shapes and sizes. They include *e-tailers*, dot-coms that sell products and services directly to final buyers via the Internet. Examples include Amazon.com and Expedia. The click-only group also includes *shopping* or *price comparison sites*, such as Yahoo! Shopping and Bizrate.com, and gives instant product and price comparisons from thousands of vendors.

Internet service providers (ISPs) such as Pacific Net are click-only companies that provide Internet and e-mail connections for a fee. *Transaction sites,* such as eBay, take commissions for transactions conducted on their sites. Finally, various content sites, such as China's StockStar.com provide financial, news, research, and other information.

Search engines and *portals*, such as Baidu, Sina, Yahoo!, Google, and yam.com, which began as search engines, later added services such as news, weather, stock reports, entertainment, and storefronts, hoping to become the first port of entry to the Internet. In China, portal services NetEase, Sohu, and Sina were initially unprofitable but have since turned around. Instead of depending on ads pitched to China's 56 million people with PCs and Internet access, they have focused on selling online content to 200 million Chinese with mobile phones. They look for revenue streams such as short text messaging and online games (see **Real Marketing**). Similarly, in India, rediff.com is popular because it offers free e-mail while orkut.com, operated by Google, offers social networking.

Click-and-Mortar Companies

As the Internet grew, established brick-and-mortar companies realized that, to compete effectively with online competitors, they had to go online themselves. Thus, many one-time brick-and-mortar companies are now prospering as **click-and-mortar companies**.

By combining online marketing and established brick-and-mortar operations, the click-and-mortar retailers can also offer customers more options. For example, consumers can choose the convenience and assortment of 24-hour-a-day online shopping, the more personal and hands-on experience of in-store shopping, or both.

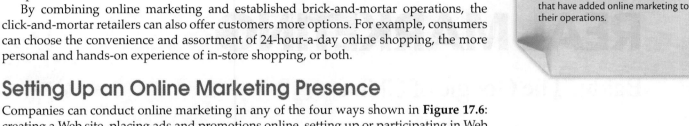

Click-and-mortar companies
Traditional brick-and-mortar companies that have added online marketing to their operations.

Setting Up an Online Marketing Presence

Companies can conduct online marketing in any of the four ways shown in **Figure 17.6**: creating a Web site, placing ads and promotions online, setting up or participating in Web communities, or using e-mail.

Figure 17.6
Setting up for online marketing

Creating a Web Site

For most companies, the first step in conducting online marketing is to create a Web site. However, beyond simply creating a Web site, marketers must design an attractive site and find ways to get consumers to visit the site, stay around, and come back often.

Types of Web Sites

Web sites vary greatly in purpose and content. The most basic type is a **corporate Web site**. These sites are designed to build customer goodwill and to supplement other sales channels, rather than to sell the company's products directly. They typically offer a rich variety of information and other features in an effort to answer customer questions, build closer customer relationships, and generate excitement about the company. For example, although you can buy ice cream and other items at the gift shop at Ben & Jerry's Web site (_benjerry.com_), the site's primary purpose is to enhance customer relationships. At the site, you can learn all about Ben & Jerry's company philosophy, products, and locations. Or you can visit the Fun Stuff area and send a free e-card to a friend, subscribe to the Chunk Mail newsletter, or while away time playing Scooper Challenge or Virtual Checkers.

Other companies create a **marketing Web site**. These sites engage consumers in an interaction that will move them closer to a direct purchase or other marketing outcome. For example, visitors to Sony's website (_SonyStyle.com_) can search through dozens of categories of Sony products, learn more about specific items, and read expert product reviews. They can check out the latest hot deals, place orders online, and pay by credit card, all with a few mouse clicks.

Corporate Web sites
A Web site designed to build customer goodwill and to supplement other sales channels, rather than to sell the company's products directly.

Marketing Web site
A Web site that engages consumers in interactions that will move them closer to a direct purchase or other marketing outcome.

REAL MARKETING

Baidu: The Google of China

In summer 1998, at a Silicon Valley picnic, Robin Li, a frustrated 30-year-old staff engineer at partly Disney-owned Infoseek, was introduced to John Wu, then head of Yahoo!'s search engine team. Wu was most impressed by Li's passion surrounding search, despite Disney's and Yahoo!'s fading commitment to its business prospects. In a colossal blunder, Yahoo! eventually outsourced its search functions to Google. In 1999, Li founded his own search company in China, naming it Baidu. Inspired by an 800-year-old poem, the name Baidu literally means hundreds of times, and represents the persistent search for the ideal.

Baidu started out offering search services to other Chinese portals before developing its own search engine. This shift was based on Li's observation of the success of Overture, a Californian company that sold advertising space correlated with search results. Unlike traditional online advertising services which charge by flat fee, Baidu has a pay-for-performance model. Thus, in September 2001, Baidu began its own site which looked almost exactly like Google's no-frills home page. Before Google did it, Baidu allowed advertisers to bid for ad space and then pay Baidu every time a customer clicked on an ad. Small and medium-size enterprises loved it, the site was deluged with traffic, and Baidu turned a profit in 2004.

In 2007 Baidu's annual revenue surged to $2.4 billion, registering a whopping 108 percent increase over 2006. And Baidu is doing what no other Internet company has been able to do: beat Google and Yahoo! in its home market. No mean feat,

considering China is the world's second largest online market, with 150 million users, slightly behind the U.S.'s 154 million. But those numbers represent 68 percent penetration in the U.S., and only slightly over 10 percent in China. How has Baidu captured 62 percent of China's online search market, compared to Google's 20 percent share?

The company's mission is to provide the best way for people to find information. Baidu focuses on what it knows best—Chinese language search. Applying avant-garde technology to the world's most ancient and complex language is a key competitive advantage. As stated in its IPO prospectus, Baidu believes that there are at least 38 ways of saying "I" in Chinese. Thus, it strives to master all the ways of addressing oneself in Chinese because its users depend on it to address every one of their daily queries. It asks itself: Have we collected all the Chinese Web pages they want to see? Are the pages current? Are the search results closely related to their queries? Did we return those results instantly?

Baidu constantly improves its products and services to enhance user experience. For example, it introduced "phonetic" or *pin yin* search which allows users to type in Chinese keywords using English alphabets. This feature is designed to skip the switching from English to Chinese inputting and for when the user is unsure of the written form of the keyword.

Baidu may also be better adept at affording Chinese users a more native experience. Eye-tracking research has indicated that North Americans tend to engage in "consideration set" scanning, scanning results in groups

of four or five at a time. In China, there appears to be no consistents patterns. Another difference is that North Americans scan and pick up word patterns immediately. However, as Chinese is a logographic language, where concepts take their final meaning from a group of combined symbols, it's much more difficult to scan information as quickly. Thus, the time spent on a page before the first click averaged eight to 10 seconds in North America, while that with Google China lasted about 30 seconds, and, with Baidu, over 55 seconds. On Google in the U.S. especially, a quick vertical scan will suffice to determine an item's relevance. However, in Baidu, a scan of an entire listing is needed.

Why? There appears to be no transparency on what's sponsored and what's not in Baidu. There are "preferred listings" heading the results which are paid listings cluttered with affiliates and spam. True organic listings are thus pushed down the page. For example, a Baidu search for the word "cancer" turned up ads for hospitals that paid for top spots in results rather than returning information on cancer itself. By North American standards, Baidu would not be a pleasant search experience. However, it's the preferred choice among Chinese users. Several reasons have been advanced to account for this preference.

First, Baidu allows censors to oversee its Web site, sealing its dominance with support from the Chinese government which regularly blocks Google there and imposes strict rules and censorship on other foreign Internet companies. Second, Baidu's media advertising positions the company as a suave Chinese native against the clueless foreigner (Google). East is Best. Third, Baidu's Web site is drawing millions of young Chinese eager to download music files (one of China's most popular online activities), create blogs, or search for pictures of China's "10 Most Beautiful Women."

More generally, Baidu may be attracting a different target segment than Western Internet companies because the Chinese are far more interested in entertainment than news, books, or car rental rates. Richard Ji, a Morgan Stanley analyst notes, "The fact is 70 percent of China's Internet users are under the age of 30. Most of them are single, only children. They're looking for entertainment." This may explain why China's dominant Internet companies are all entertainment focused, like Tencent (which hosts online communities and instant messaging), and Netease and Shanda (which are online gaming sites).

Still, Baidu faces numerous challenges, including lawsuits claiming that it violates copyright laws on music files. In a country rampant with click fraud, a Beijing hospital recently claimed that a Baidu affiliate kept clicking on its ads to fatten the fees that the hospital had to pay Baidu. Then there are Google and Yahoo!. Google plans to spend hundreds of millions of dollars to compete in China, funded partly from the $55 million it made from the sale of the Baidu stake it owned. It is building up a huge research team in Beijing near Baidu's HQ. Yahoo! has merged its Chinese operations with Chinese Internet company Alibaba.com, which analyst Ji claims to have the best sales force: "Baidu could get hurt on the technical side."

Baidu is not resting on its laurels. It recently announced a multi-year agreement with eBay China's subsidiary, EachNet. Under the agreement, Baidu will add PayPal Beibao to its paid search channel as the preferred online payment provider. It will promote the service

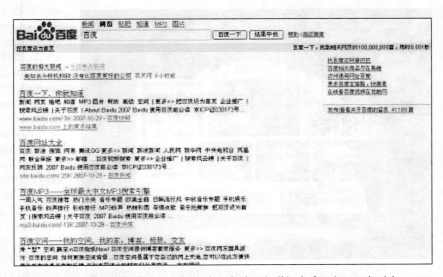

Search engine and portals: Baidu trumped Google and Yahoo! in China by focusing on what it knows best—Chinese language search.

as the preferred third-party solution on the Baidu Points platform and encourage SMEs to use it as their online payments processor. In return, Baidu will become the exclusive provider of text-based advertising on eBay EachNet. Baidu advertisers will thus have access to one of China's most robust online communities while enhancing the shopping experience of eBay EachNet buyers. The two companies will also integrate their respective toolbar features. The new co-branded toolbar will make it even easier for consumers to take advantage of both companies' offerings by providing users quick access to information wherever they are on the Web while leveraging each other's expertise in online protection. Baidu has also recently announced partnerships with Rock Music and EMI to launch an advertising-supported online music streaming service. In another strategic alliance, Microsoft will display Baidu's paid search listings on the search results pages of certain of its Web sites, including MSN Live, and other partners in China.

Baidu is also expanding overseas. In 2008, It launched Baidu Japan. The day after the launch, user traffic quadrupled. Baidu is investing $20 to

$25 million this year in this project.

Hence, Robin Li remains undaunted about the foreign challenge. "Our traffic keeps increasing. We're now the No. 1 Web site in China."

Sources:

David Barboza, "The Rise of Baidu (That's Chinese for Google)," www.nytimes.com, September 2006; "The Baidu Story," ir.baidu.com, July 25, 2007, "Baidu and eBay EachNet Expand Strategic Cooperation in China," ir.baidu.com, November 8, 2006; "Microsoft Teams Up with Baidu to Deliver Paid Search Listings in China," ir.baidu.com, December 14, 2006; "Baidu and Rock Music Announce Partnership to Stream Music Online," ir.baidu.com, July 4, 2007; "Baidu and EMI Launch Advertising-Supported Streaming Service," ir.baidu.com, January 16, 2007; Gord Hotchkiss, "Chinese Eye Tracking Study: Baidu Vs Google," searchengineland.com, June 15, 2007; "Financial Reports 2007," ir.baidu.com, May 2, 2008; "Baidu.com Q4 2007 Earnings Call Transcript," www.seekingalpha.com, February 14, 2008.

Designing effective Web sites

Creating a Web site is one thing; getting people to *visit* the site is another. To attract visitors, companies aggressively promote their Web sites in offline print and broadcast advertising and through ads and links on other sites. But today's Web users are quick to abandon any Web site that doesn't measure up. The key is to create enough value and excitement to get consumers who come to the site to stick around and come back again. This means that companies must constantly update their sites to keep them current, fresh, and useful.

Effective Web sites –
Applying the seven Cs of effective Web site design, is this a good site? (www.altoids.com)

For some types of products, attracting visitors is easy. Consumers buying new cars, computers, or financial services will be open to information and marketing initiatives from sellers. Marketers of lower-involvement products, however, may face a difficult challenge in attracting Web site visitors. If you're in the market for a computer and you see a banner ad that says, "The top 10 PCs under $800," you'll likely click on the banner. But what kind of ad would get you to visit a site like dentalfloss.com?

A key challenge is designing a Web site that is attractive on first view and interesting enough to encourage repeat visits. Many marketers create colorful, graphically sophisticated Web sites that combine text, sound, and animation to capture and hold attention (for examples, see www.looneytunes.com or www.nike.com). To attract new visitors and to encourage revisits, one expert suggests, online marketers should pay close attention to the seven Cs of effective Web site design:[29]

- *Context:* the site's layout and design.
- *Content:* the text, pictures, sound, and video that the Web site contains.
- *Community:* the ways that the site enables user-to-user communication.
- *Customization:* the site's ability to tailor itself to different users or to allow users to personalize the site.
- *Communication*: the ways the site enables site-to-user, user-to-site, or two way communication.
- *Connection:* the degree that the site is linked to other sites.
- *Commerce:* the site's capabilities to enable commercial transactions.

And to keep customers coming back to the site, companies need to embrace yet another "C"—constant change.

At the very least, a Web site should be easy to use, professional looking, and physically attractive. Ultimately, however, Web sites must also be *useful*. When it comes to Web surfing and shopping, most people prefer substance over style and function over flash. Thus, effective Web sites contain deep and useful information, interactive tools that help buyers find and evaluate products of interest, links to other related sites, changing promotional offers, and entertaining features that lend relevant excitement.

Placing Ads and Promotions Online

As consumers spend more and more time on the Internet, many companies are shifting more of their marketing dollars to **online advertising** to build their brands or to attract visitors to their Web sites. Online advertising is becoming a major medium. Here, we discuss forms of online advertising and promotion and their future.

Forms of online advertising

The major forms of online advertising include display ads, search-related ads, and online classifieds. Online display ads might appear anywhere on an Internet user's screen. The most common form is *banners*, banner-shaped ads found at the top, bottom, left, right, or

Online advertising
Advertising that appears while consumers are surfing the Web, including display ads (banners, interstitials,pop-ups) search-related ads, online classifieds, and other forms.

center of a Web page. For instance, a Web surfer looking up airline schedules or fares might encounter a flashing banner that screams, "Rent a car from Hertz and get up to two days free!" Clicking on the ad takes consumers to the Hertz Web site, where they can redeem the promotion.

Interstitials are online display ads that appear between screen changes on a Web site, especially while a new screen is loading. For example, when you visit some Web sites, you may see a 10-second ad for VISA or another sponsor before the homepage loads. *Pop-ups* are online ads that appear suddenly in a new window in front of the window being viewed. Such ads can multiply out of control, creating a major annoyance. As a result, Internet services and Web browser providers have developed applications that let users block most pop-ups. In response, many advertisers have developed pop-unders, new windows that evade pop-up blockers by appearing behind the page you're viewing.

Visit *www.advertisingcompetition.org/iac* for award-winning online advertising from recent years.

With the increase in broadband Internet access, some companies are developing exciting new *rich media* display ads, which incorporate animation, video, sound, and interactivity. Rich media ads attract and hold consumer attention better than traditional banner ads. They employ techniques such as float, fly, and snapback—animations that jump out and sail over the Web page before retreating to their original space. But many rich media ads do more than create a little bit of jumping animation. For example, to attract would-be commodity traders to its Web site, the Chicago Board of Trade runs a small rich media banner ad that explodes into a small site when the user's mouse rolls over it. The mouse-over site features free streaming quotes, sample research, and a virtual trading account, all of which would never fit into a traditional static ad.[30]

Another hot growth area for online advertising is *search-related ads* (or *contextual advertising*), in which text-based ads and links appear alongside search engine results on sites such as Google and Yahoo!. For example, search Google for "HDTV" and you'll see inconspicuous ads for 10 or more advertisers. Nearly all of Google's $6.1 billion in revenues come from ad sales. An advertiser buys search terms from the search site and pays only if consumers click through to its site. Search-related ads account for some 41 percent of all online advertising expenditures, more than any other category of online advertising.[31]

Search ads can be an effective way to link consumers to other forms of online promotion. For example, Honda used key word searches to lure Web surfers to a site promoting its Element truck:

Search-related ads account for some 41 percent of all online advertising expenditures – Honda used key word searches to lure Web surfers to a site promoting its Element truck. The site features the vehicle "talking" to sundry animals—a platypus, a possum, a burro, and a crab—in cartoony spots. (*www.elementandfriends.com*)

The Element campaign features the vehicle "talking" to sundry animals—a platypus, a possum, a burro, and a crab—in cartoony spots. Honda bought those keyword terms and uses search ads as invitations to "see the platypus in its Element." That link leads consumers to *elementandfriends.com*, which features Element ads and a related game. Honda also bought variants of "funny video" and "funny commercials," search terms that have demographic profiles compatible with likely Element buyers. In many cases, the search terms cost just 10 cents or 15 cents per click and drew about 40 percent of the Element's Web site traffic. "It seemed a little quirky, but the more you thought about it, the more it seemed to resonate well with the campaign," says Honda's senior manager of marketing. For its Ridgeline truck, which was advertised during the Super Bowl, Honda bought a "few thousand" search terms somehow related to the Super Bowl (as in "Super Bowl ad"). Those terms generated more than 3.5 million online impressions from just Yahoo! and Google on the day after the Super Bowl alone.[32]

Other forms of online promotion

Other forms of online promotions include content sponsorships, alliances and affiliate programs, and viral advertising.

Using *content sponsorships*, companies gain name exposure on the Internet by sponsoring special content on various Web sites, such as news or financial information or special-interest topics. Sponsorships are best placed in carefully targeted sites where they can offer relevant information or service to the audience.

Internet companies can also develop *alliances and affiliate programs*, in which they work with other companies, online and offline, to "promote each other." Amazon.com has more than 900,000 affiliates who post Amazon.com banners on their Web sites. And Yahoo!, whose ad revenue makes up 84 percent of its total worldwide revenue, has become a fertile ground for alliances with movie studios and TV production companies:

> In one episode of *The Apprentice*, teams created and marketed a new flavor of Ciao Bella Ice Cream. Although Ciao Bella had previously sold its ice creams in only 18 stores in the New York and San Francisco, Yahoo! convinced the manufacturer to place the new product in 760 stores around the country. An end-of-episode promotion urged viewers to visit Yahoo!'s local online search engine to look for the store nearest them. The product sold out by 5 P.M. the next day. And thanks to Yahoo!'s registration database, it was able to provide Ciao Bella with the demographic characteristics of respondents.[33]

Finally, online marketers use **viral marketing**, the Internet version of word-of-mouth marketing. Viral marketing involves creating a Web site, e-mail message, or other marketing event that is so infectious that customers will want to pass it along to their friends. Because customers pass the message or promotion along to others, viral marketing can be very inexpensive. And when the information comes from a friend, the recipient is much more likely to open and read it. Consider Burger King's now-classic Subservient Chicken viral campaign:

The Web site, *www.subservientchicken.com*, features a dingy living room, where the subservient chicken—someone in a giant chicken suit and a garter belt—hangs out in front of his Web cam and awaits your bidding. Type in commands, and the chicken does exactly what you ask. It will flap its wings, roll over, or jump up and down. It will also moon the viewer, dance the Electric Slide, or die. (Suggestions for lewd acts are met with a "naughty naughty" shake of the wing.) In other words, you can have your way with the chicken. Get it? Have it your way! The site promotes Burger King's TenderCrisp chicken and ties it into Burger King's successful "Have It Your Way" marketing campaign.

"As viral marketing goes, subservientchicken.com is a colossal success," says an advertising expert. "There is great overlap between Web regulars and Burger King's core audience." If nothing more, the site gets consumers to interact with the brand. And it gets them buzzing about Burger King's edgy new positioning. Burger King has never advertised the site. When it was first created, the ad agency e-mailed the URL to several people, asking them to send the link out to friends to test. From that single e-mail, without a peep of promotion, the Subservient Chicken site ended the day with one *million* total hits. It received 46 million hits in only the first week following its launch, 385 million in the first nine months. Says one Burger King ad director, the award-winning site helped "sell a lot, a lot, a lot of chicken sandwiches."[34]

Viral marketing
The internet version of word-of-mouth marketing—Web sites, email messages, or other marketing events that are so infectious that customers will want to pass them along to friends.

Viral marketing –
Burger King's colossally successful Subservient Chicken site gets consumers interacting with the brand and buzzing about its edgy new positioning.
(*www.subservientchicken.com*)

The future of online advertising

Although online advertising still accounts for only a minor portion of the total advertising and marketing expenditures of most companies, it is growing rapidly. Online advertising serves a useful purpose, especially as a supplement to other marketing efforts. As a result, it is playing an increasingly important role in the marketing mixes of many advertisers.

Creating or Participating in Web Communities

The popularity of blogs and other Web forums has resulted in a rash of commercially sponsored Web sites called **Web communities**, which take advantage of the C2C properties of the Internet. Such sites allow members to congregate online and exchange views on issues of common interest. They are the cyberspace equivalent to a Starbucks coffeehouse, a place where everybody knows your e-mail address.

Web communities
Web sites upon which members can congregate online and exchange views on issues of common interest.

Using E-Mail

E-mail has exploded onto the scene as an important online marketing tool. A recent study of ad, brand, and marketing managers found that nearly half of all the B2B and B2C companies surveyed use e-mail marketing to reach customers.

To compete effectively in this ever-more-cluttered e-mail environment, marketers are designing "enriched" e-mail messages—animated, interactive, and personalized messages full of streaming audio and video. Then, they are targeting these attention-grabbers more carefully to those who want them and will act upon them. Consider Nintendo, a natural for e-mail-based marketing:

> Young computer-savvy gaming fans actually look forward to Nintendo's monthly e-mail newsletter for gaming tips and for announcements of exciting new games. When the company launched its Star Fox Adventure game, it created an intensive e-mail campaign in the weeks before and after the product launch. The campaign included a variety of messages targeting potential customers. "Each message has a different look and feel, and … that builds excitement for Nintendo," notes an executive working on the account. The response? More than a third of all recipients opened the e-mails. And they did more than just glance at the messages: Click-through rates averaged more than 10 percent. Nearly two-thirds of those opening the message watched its 30-second streaming video in its entirety. Nintendo also gathered insightful customer data from the 20 percent of people who completed an embedded survey. Although the company feared that the barrage of messages might create "list fatigue" and irritate customers, the campaign received very few negative responses. The unsubscribe rate was under 1 percent.[35]

Spam
Unsolicited, unwanted commercial e-mail messages.

As with other types of online marketing, companies must be careful that they don't cause resentment among Internet users who are already overloaded with "junk e-mail." The explosion of **spam**—unsolicited, unwanted commercial e-mail messages that clog up our e-mail boxes—has produced consumer frustration and anger. E-mail marketers walk a fine line between adding value for consumers and being intrusive.

To avoid irritating consumers by sending unwanted marketing e-mail, companies should ask customers for permission to e-mail marketing pitches. They should also tell recipients how to "opt in" or "opt out" of e-mail promotions at any time. This approach, known as *permission-based marketing*, has become a standard model for e-mail marketing.

Consumer frustration –
Spam has produced consumer frustration and anger at the unsolicited, unwanted commercial e-mail messages that clog up e-mail boxes.

The Promise and Challenges of Online Marketing

Online marketing continues to offer both great promise and many challenges for the future. It will become a successful business model for some companies, Internet firms such as Amazon.com, eBay, and Google, and direct-marketing companies such as Dell. Michael Dell's goal is one day "to have all customers conduct all transactions on the Internet, globally." However, for most companies, online marketing will remain just one important approach to the marketplace that works alongside other approaches in a fully integrated marketing mix.

Integrated Direct Marketing

Too often, a company's different direct-marketing efforts are not well integrated with one another or with other elements of its marketing and promotion mixes. For example, a firm's media advertising may be handled by the advertising department working with a traditional advertising agency. Meanwhile, its direct-mail and catalog business may be handled by direct-marketing specialists, whereas its Web site is developed and operated by an outside Internet firm. Even within a given direct-marketing campaign, too many companies use only a "one-shot" effort to reach and sell a prospect or a single vehicle in multiple stages to trigger purchases.

A more powerful approach is **integrated direct marketing**, which involves using carefully coordinated multiple-media, multiple-stage campaigns (see **Figure 17.7**). Such campaigns can greatly improve response. Whereas a direct-mail piece alone might generate a 2 percent response, adding a Web site and toll-free phone number might raise the response rate by 50 percent. Then, a well-designed outbound e-mail campaign might lift response by an additional 500 percent. Suddenly, a 2 percent response has grown to 15 percent or more by adding interactive marketing channels to a regular mailing.

> **Integrated direct marketing**
> Direct-marketing campaigns that use multiple vehicles and multiple stages to improve response rates and profits.

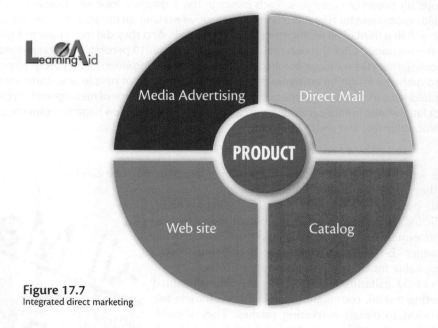

Figure 17.7
Integrated direct marketing

Integrating direct marketing channels with each other and with other media has become a top priority for marketers. For example, consider the integrated direct marketing efforts of professional services firm Ernst & Young:

Ernst & Young is taking a decidedly integrated approach with its online, e-mail, and other direct marketing. It integrates its e-mail efforts with other media, including direct mail, and tightly weaves both into interactive elements on the company's site. For example, a promotion for an annual conference it hosted in October for energy executives began much earlier in the year with a "save the date" e-mail to clients and prospects. That was followed up by a rich media e-mail. "We created these flash movies that we e-mailed them, and the call to action was embedded there," says an Ernst & Young marketing executive. "There was a link built in that brought them to the Web site to find out details about the conference." Next, to reinforce the online messages, the company sent out direct-mail invitations, which included a registration form as well as the Web address for those who chose to register online. To ensure that Ernst & Young's direct marketing messages are well integrated, representatives from each marketing discipline meet on a regular basis. "We all sit around the table and talk about what we've done, what's in process, and what we're planning," says the marketing executive. "The results rely on 'the whole thing.' Otherwise, it's like making a cake without putting in the flour."[36]

Public Policy Issues in Direct Marketing

The aggressive and sometimes shady tactics of a few direct marketers can bother or harm consumers. Abuses range from simple excesses that irritate consumers to instances of unfair practices or even outright deception and fraud. The direct marketing industry has also faced growing invasion-of-privacy concerns, and online marketers must deal with Internet security issues (see **Figure 17.8**).

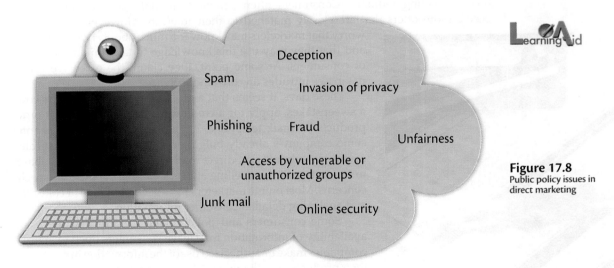

Figure 17.8
Public policy issues in direct marketing

Irritation, Unfairness, Deception, and Fraud

Most of us dislike direct-response TV commercials that are too loud, too long, and too insistent. Our mailboxes fill up with unwanted junk mail, our e-mail boxes fill up with unwanted spam, and our computer screens fill up with unwanted pop-up or pop-under ads.

Beyond irritating consumers, some direct marketers have been accused of taking unfair advantage of impulsive or less-sophisticated buyers. TV shopping channels and program-long "infomercials" targeting television-addicted shoppers seem to be the worst culprits. They feature smooth-talking hosts, elaborately staged demonstrations, claims of drastic price reductions, "while they last" time limitations, and unequaled ease of purchase to inflame buyers who have low sales resistance.

Phishing –
As many as half of all Internet users have received a phishing e-mail that tries to fool users into divulging their personal data.

Worse yet, so-called heat merchants design mailers and write copy intended to mislead buyers. Even well-known direct mailers have been accused of deceiving consumers. Fraudulent schemes, such as investment scams or phony collections for charity, have also multiplied in recent years. *Internet fraud*, including identity theft and financial scams, has become a serious problem.

One common form of Internet fraud is *phishing*, a type of identity theft that uses deceptive e-mails and fraudulent Web sites to fool users into divulging their personal data. According to one survey, half of all Internet users have received a phishing e-mail. Although many consumers are now aware of such schemes, phishing can be extremely costly to those caught in the Net. It also damages the brand identities of legitimate online marketers who have worked to build user confidence in Web and e-mail transactions.[37]

Many consumers also worry about *online security*. They fear that unscrupulous snoopers will eavesdrop on their online transactions or intercept their credit card numbers and make unauthorized purchases. In a recent survey, six out of 10 online shoppers were concerned enough about online security that they considered reducing the amount of their online holiday shopping.[38] Such concerns are costly for direct-marketing companies.

Another Internet marketing concern is that of *access* by *vulnerable* or *unauthorized groups*. For example, marketers of adult-oriented materials have found it difficult to restrict access by minors. In a more specific example, a while back, sellers using eBay found themselves the victims of a 14-year-old boy who'd bid on and purchased more than $3 million worth of high-priced antiques and rare artworks on the site. eBay has a strict policy against bidding by anyone under age 18 but works largely on the honor system. Unfortunately, this honor system did little to prevent the teenager from taking a cyberspace joyride.[39]

Invasion of Privacy

Invasion of privacy is perhaps the toughest public policy issue now confronting the direct-marketing industry. Consumers often benefit from database marketing—they receive more offers that are closely matched to their interests. However, many critics worry that marketers may know too much about consumers' lives and that they may use this knowledge to take unfair advantage of consumers. At some point, they claim, the extensive use of databases intrudes on consumer privacy.

Invasion of privacy –
Critics worry that the information collected from consumers through items such as credit card applications may be used by marketers privacy and take unfair advantage.

These days, it seems that almost every time consumers enter a sweepstakes, apply for a credit card, visit a Web site, or order products by mail, telephone, or the Internet, their names enter some company's already bulging database. Using sophisticated computer technologies, direct marketers can use these databases to "microtarget" their selling efforts. *Online privacy* causes special concerns. Most online marketers have become skilled at collecting and analyzing detailed consumer information.

Some consumers and policy makers worry that the ready availability of information may leave consumers open to abuse if companies make unauthorized use of the information in marketing their products or exchanging databases with other companies. For example, they ask, should a company such as American Express be allowed to make data on its millions of cardholders worldwide available to merchants who accept AmEx cards? Is it right for credit bureaus to compile and sell lists of people who have recently applied for credit cards—people who are considered prime direct-marketing targets because of their spending behavior? Or is it right for companies to sell the names and addresses of participants to their promotion contests?

In their drives to build databases, companies sometimes get carried away. For example, Microsoft caused substantial privacy concerns when one version of its Windows software used a "Registration Wizard" that snooped into users' computers. When users went online to register, without their knowledge, Microsoft "read" the configurations of their PCs to learn about the major software products they were running. Users protested loudly and Microsoft abandoned the practice.

REVIEWING THE CONCEPTS

Let's revisit this chapter's key concepts. This chapter is the last of four chapters covering the final marketing mix element—promotion. The previous chapters dealt with advertising, publicity, sales promotion, and personal selling. This one investigates direct and online marketing.

1 Define direct marketing and discuss its benefits to customers and companies.

Direct marketing consists of direct connections with carefully targeted individual consumers to both obtain an immediate response and cultivate lasting customer relationships. Using detailed databases, direct marketers tailor their offers and communications to the needs of narrowly defined segments or even individual buyers.

For buyers, direct marketing is convenient, easy to use, and private. It gives buyers ready access to a wealth of products and information, at home and around the globe. Direct marketing is also immediate and interactive, allowing buyers to create exactly the configuration of information, products, or services they desire, then order them on the spot. For sellers, direct marketing is a powerful tool for building customer relationships. Using database marketing, today's marketers can target small groups or individual consumers, tailor offers to individual needs, and promote these offers through personalized communications. It also offers them a low-cost, efficient alternative for reaching their markets. As a result of these advantages to both buyers and sellers, direct marketing has become the fastest-growing form of marketing.

2 Identify and discuss the major forms of direct marketing.

The main forms of direct marketing include personal selling, direct-mail marketing, catalog marketing, telephone marketing, direct-response television marketing, kiosk marketing, and online marketing. We discussed personal selling in the previous chapter.

Direct-mail marketing, the largest form of direct marketing, consists of the company sending an offer, announcement, reminder, or other item to a person at a specific address. Recently, new forms of "mail delivery" have become popular, such as e-mail marketing. Some marketers rely on catalog marketing—selling through catalogs mailed to a select list of customers, made available in stores, or accessed on the Web. Telephone marketing consists of using the telephone to sell directly to consumers. Direct-response television marketing has two forms: direct-response advertising (or infomercials) and home shopping channels. Kiosks are information and ordering machines that direct marketers place in stores, airports, and other locations. In recent years, a number of new digital direct marketing technologies have emerged, including mobile phone marketing, podcasts and vodcasts, and interactive TV. Online marketing involves online channels that digitally link sellers with consumers.

3 Explain how companies have responded to the Internet and other powerful new technologies with online marketing.

Online marketing is the fastest-growing form of direct marketing. The Internet enables consumers and companies to access and share huge amounts of information with just a few mouse clicks. In turn, the Internet has given marketers a whole new way to create value for customers and build customer relationships. It's hard to find a company today that doesn't have a substantial Web marketing presence.

Online consumer buying continues to grow at a healthy rate. Some 65 percent of American online users now use the Internet to shop. Perhaps more importantly, by 2010, the Internet will influence a staggering 50 percent of total retail sales. Thus, smart marketers are employing integrated multichannel strategies that use the Web to drive sales to other marketing channels.

4 Discuss how companies go about conducting online marketing to profitably deliver more value to customers.

Companies of all types are now engaged in online marketing. The Internet gave birth to the *click-only* dot-coms, which operate only online. In addition, many traditional brick-and-mortar companies have now added online marketing operations, transforming themselves into *click-and-mortar* competitors. Many click-and-mortar companies are now having more online success than their click-only competitors.

Companies can conduct online marketing in any of the four ways: creating a Web site, placing ads and promotions online, setting up or participating in Web communities, or using online e-mail. The first step typically is to set up a Web site. Beyond simply setting up a site, however, companies must make their sites engaging, easy to use, and useful in order to attract visitors, hold them, and bring them back again.

Online marketers can use various forms of online advertising to build their Internet brands or to attract visitors to their Web sites. Beyond online advertising, other forms of online promotion include online display advertising, search-related advertising, content sponsorships, alliances and affiliate programs, and viral marketing, the Internet version of word-of-mouth marketing. Online marketers can also participate in Web communities, which take advantage of the C2C properties of the Web. Finally, e-mail marketing has become a fast-growing tool for both B2C and B2B marketers. Whatever direct marketing tools they use, marketers must work hard to integrate them into a cohesive marketing effort.

5 Overview the public policy and ethical issues presented by direct marketing.

Direct marketers and their customers usually enjoy mutually rewarding relationships. Occasionally, however, direct marketing presents a darker side. The aggressive and sometimes shady tactics of a few direct marketers can bother or harm consumers, giving the entire industry a black eye. Abuses range from simple excesses that irritate consumers to instances of unfair practices or even outright deception and fraud. The direct-marketing industry has also faced growing concerns about invasion-of-privacy and Internet security issues. Such concerns call for strong action by marketers and public policy makers to curb direct-marketing abuses. In the end, most direct marketers want the same things that consumers want: honest and well-designed marketing offers targeted only toward consumers who will appreciate and respond to them.

REVIEWING THE KEY TERMS

Business-to-business (B2B) online marketing 475
Business-to-consumer (B2C) online marketing 474
Catalog marketing 469
Click-and-mortar companies 479
Click-only companies 478
Consumer-to-business (C2B) online marketing 477
Consumer-to-consumer (C2C) online marketing 475
Corporate Web site 479
Customer database 467
Direct-mail marketing 468
Direct marketing 462

Direct-response television marketing 470
Integrated direct marketing 486
Internet 473
Marketing Web site 479
Online advertising 482
Online marketing 473
Spam 485
Telephone marketing 469
Viral marketing 484
Web communities 485

DISCUSSING THE CONCEPTS

1. The Internet benefits both buyers and sellers in a number of ways. Using eBay as an example, describe the potential benefits gained by both the buyer and seller.

2. A local pest control company has contacted you for advice on setting up its customer database It needs this database for customer relationship management and for direct marketing of new products and services. Describe the qualities and features it must consider for an effective database.

3. Is it good marketing practice for a catalog mailer to continue sending catalogs after establishing a strong Web retail presence?

4. There is a Do-Not-Call Registry in the U.S. Should a similar one be started in your country? Should there be similar legislation banning unwanted e-mails?

5. Companies design Web sites for many purposes. What are the two basic types of Web sites and what are their purposes? Give an example of each.

6. What are the basic Internet security fears of consumers? Are these fears usually justified? Identify five actions a consumer can take to reduce the risk of Internet security problems.

APPLYING THE CONCEPTS

1. A small company that has developed an effective at-home hair-coloring system is considering using direct television. Would you recommend this medium? Why or why not?

2. Visit your favorite retail Web site and evaluate the site according to the seven Cs of effective Web site design.

3. Assume that you are a member of a marketing department for a click-only provider of financial services. Your company exchanges very personal and sensitive financial

information with each customer over the Internet on a daily basis. You have been asked by your boss to come up with a security idea that will be communicated in an ad. What primary message would you like to communicate to your customers in this ad?

FOCUS ON TECHNOLOGY

When marketers and engineers design new products, they rely heavily on input from consumers. At Massachusetts Institute of Technology, researchers are working on a multidisciplinary project known as the Virtual Customer Initiative. The purpose of the initiative is to improve the accuracy and usability of customer input by creating easy-to-use and effective Web-based tools. To see demonstrations of this technology, visit *http://conjoint.mit.edu/newdemo/* and click on the "Go" button in the box with a car, labeled "Web-Based Conjoint Analysis." Go through the entire demonstration for the crossover vehicle. The demonstrations show an application of a statistical technique called conjoint analysis. In simple terms, the objective of conjoint analysis

is to determine how a consumer makes trade-offs between different product features—to determine whether a consumer would trade, for instance, less passenger space for more cargo space.

1. What are the advantages and disadvantages of running this type of analysis as a Web-based system as opposed to having subjects come to a research lab and run through the study with a researcher?

2. In addition to cars and cameras, what are some other products that would benefit from this type of Web based analysis?

3. Why isn't this technology, and conjoint analysis in general, not more widely used?

FOCUS ON ETHICS

Technoethics, a recent field of study that examines ethical issues in technology, has recently been applied to many areas in Internet marketing. Blogs are an example of a growing Internet marketing technology that presents many ethical issues. For instance, is it ethical for a company to ask consumers to blog favorably about a product? Is it ethical for companies to pay these consumers to blog? Should a company fire an employee who blogs negative comments about it? Other technologies, created by leading Internet marketers to improve customer satisfaction on the Internet are also raising issues. Amazon.com has been criticized for its Wish List, which lets customers list books and other products they would like to receive from friends and family. What many consumers don't know is that the Wish List can be viewed by anyone, and that such wish list information can be used to create databases of everyone from gun owners to teenage girls. Take this one step further and consider Google's online mapping capabilities. By applying this technology to the wish list information, one could find the houses of wish listers interested in books on, say, terrorists.

Companies on the cutting edge of technology, such as Amazon.com, are constantly cited for having their updated technology fail on them. The popular online social network, MySpace, is currently suffering with a problem by which some users' sites have been rerouted to adult-content sites. LucasArts updated its Star Wars Galaxies programs and accidentally made it unplayable to players with disabilities, because it could no longer be played with one hand.

1. Is it ethical for an advertiser to pay a consumer to blog favorably about a product? To fire an employee presenting negative issues on his or her blog?

2. What can companies do to reduce the negative public relations effects of such technoethical issues?

3. What other examples have you heard or read about recently involving ethical issues with Web-based companies?

See: "The Technoethics Trap: As the Line between Right and Wrong Gets Blurrier, Even the Best Intentions Have a Way of Backfiring," *Inc.*, March 2006, pp. 69–70.

VIDEO CASE

NineMSN

Formed in 1997, NineMSN is a joint venture between Microsoft and Australia's leading media company, Publishing and Broadcasting Limited (PBL). The NineMSN site offers news and content from nine of Australia's largest media channels funneled through MSN's signature portal. Each month, more than 7.5 million people visit the NineMSN site for news, information, and communication services, including MSN Hotmail and MSN Messenger. That's 74 percent of all online Australians, and the number keeps growing.

NineMSN keeps users coming back by continually updating its content while maintaining a consistent, easy-to-use Web site that users can customize. Then, the portal

capitalizes on its steady stream of consumers by capturing demographic data and working with advertisers to build online marketing campaigns targeting the site's users.

After watching the video featuring NineMSN, answer the following questions about direct and online marketing.

1. How does NineMSN build and use its customer database?

2. Visit the NineMSN Web site, *www.ninemsn.com.au*, and evaluate the site based on the seven Cs of effective design discussed in the text.

3. What forms of online advertising and promotion do marketers use to reach NineMSN members through the Web site?

COMPANY CASE

Gems TV: Sparkle of Success

Gems TV is an integrated manufacturer and television home shopping retailer of colored gemstone jewelry. Its revenues have risen from $14.3 million in 2004 to $39.3 million in 2005, reaching $159.8 million in 2007. Likewise, it has gone from a loss of $200,000 in 2004 to net profits of $7.6 million in 2007 respectively. How has this Thailand-originated company become such a sparkling success over a short time period? Can Gems TV sustain its performance in future?

Human Beginnings

Gems TV's predecessor, Thaigem, was founded by Don Kogen. In 1989, Kogen, a 15-year-old American, arrived in Chanthaburi determined to learn about the gem business. The nearby Chanthaburi hills used to be studded with rubies and sapphires. When the mines dried up, the provincial town three hours southeast of Bangkok had a cosmopolitan community of artisans adept at cutting, polishing, and setting stones, and in altering hues by high heat treatments.

Although he spoke no Thai, Kogen became a gem selector, learning how to classify stones by quality and grade. He notes, "It was a perfect job because I learned what everything was worth, what it would sell in the market." Within three years, Kogen was doing low-level gem trading. Next, he ran a classified ad in *Lapidary Journal*, offering overseas retailers a simple photocopied catalog of gems for sale. In 1992, Kogen was among the first in town to upgrade to a fax machine. He was already turning a profit then based on the direct model Gems TV uses today, slicing away seven to nine layers of intermediaries that increase a gem's price from mine to jewelry store.

In August 1998, Kogen bought his first PC and became Chanthaburi's first Internet subscriber. He established the thaigem.com Web site that October, selling loose gemstones over the Internet. By 2003, the Thaigem Web

site claimed to be the vendor of 90 percent of the gems sold online worldwide. In May 2003, Thaigem opened its first gemstone jewelry workshop and began selling colored gemstone jewelry in addition to loose gems on its Web site, as well as on numerous other auction Internet sites including eBay and Amazon. Every piece of jewelry it sells is handcrafted in its low-cost Chanthaburi manufacturing facility. The company purchases cut gemstones for its jewelry both in Chanthaburi and through its overseas supply network in other major global gemstone markets including Brazil, China, East Africa, India, Madagascar, and Sri Lanka. In all, it purchases gemstones originating from 45 countries.

TV Home Shopping

Within three months of establishing its workshop, Thaigem was supplying jewelry to TV home shopping networks such as QVC, the Home Shopping Network, and Ideal Shopping UK. In addition, it also began supplying jewelry to a U.K. home shopping channel operated by Eagle Road, a U.K. TV home shopping company established by Steve Bennett, who also founded Software Warehouse and jungle.com. Eagle Road ran three home shopping channels, one of which used the "Snatch It" format that is currently the reverse auction system used by Gems TV. Gems TV was launched in October 2004 by Thaigem and Eagle Road on one of the latter's existing channels on Britain's BSkyB cable network. In May 2005, Eagle Road shut down the original Snatch It channel and launched Gems TV2 on BSkyB. Thaigem bought Eagle Road in June 2005 and has since used Gems TV as its corporate name. In October 2005, it expanded its broadcasts to ntl:Telewest in the U.K. BSkyB and ntl are the two key companies in the U.K. pay-TV market.

As of March 2006, Gems TV channels are broadcast to over 11 million homes in the U.K. BSkyB has 400 channels, of which 20 are for home shopping, while ntl has 160 total channels, of which 12 are for home shopping. Gems TV's direct competitors are Ideal World, QVC, and the Jewelry Channel. It has been estimated that the U.K. home shopping market will grow given its aging population's likely increased reliance on home delivery, the expansion of large companies like Tesco into all areas of retailing, and smaller companies targeting niches overlooked by the large home shopping companies.

It's All Game

Gems TV produces all its programming and broadcasts live 18 hours a day from 8 a.m. to 2 a.m. (U.K. time) everyday except Christmas Day. It adopts a reverse auction format in its TV programs which it feels provides viewers with an entertaining and interactive shopping experience. Short reverse auction games allow the company to showcase a wide variety of products and retain viewer attention. Its Snatch It game is meant to be more viewer friendly and effective than static presentations of traditional TV shopping. It believes the value of its program format lies in viewers staying tuned to wait for the outcome of a game or to wait for the next item to be put up for sale, although they may not be interested in the item currently being auctioned.

Essentially, before each game begins, the presenter will explain the attributes of the product such as its design and starting price, and disclose the number of pieces available for sale. When the game begins, viewers can begin placing orders (or bids) for the product at the starting price by phoning its call center or over its Gems TV Web site. During a game, the company constantly reduces the price of the product, and viewers can continue to bid for the product at the current price, until bids are received for all available pieces, at which point the game is stopped. The reverse auction format provides each customer with an incentive to bid the highest price he or she is willing to pay for a particular product or risk losing the product to other bidders. The game is not stopped until all pieces have been bid for. All participants who successfully placed an order during the game will pay the lowest price, which is the price at which the game is stopped.

Moreover, Gems TV provides customers with convenient access to purchase its products and with detailed information about gemstones and its jewelry manufacturing operations. Gems TV also sells jewelry through its own Web sites *gemstv.com* and *gemstv.co.uk*, in addition to its original *thaigem.com*. This online sales platform provides a vehicle for the company to sell inventory less suitable for sale via its TV channels. This assists in minimizing the need for inventory markdowns often required in retail store sales. Customers are also provided a 10-day guaranteed return period and a six-month warranty on Gems TV's products. The company furnishes its customers with recommended outlets for ring re-sizing and independent valuation services.

The Road Ahead

Gems TV went public in late 2006, raising $140.3 million. The added funds will be deployed to leverage its competitive strengths with the objective of expanding Gems TV's operations and enhancing its position in the jewelry home shopping industry.

To this end, Gems TV intends to replicate its successful U.K. sales format in other markets either organically or through joint ventures. Currently, it has expanded into the U.S., the world's largest home shopping market, and Germany. Gems TV signed an agreement with DirecTV in the U.S. to carry its TV programs, and a memorandum of understanding to supply jewelry to a German TV home shopping channel. Gems TV has also received approval for the Japanese government to be registered as a broadcaster for telecommunications services. Jason Choo, Gems TV's CEO, says, "Japan is the second largest jewelry market in the world and Japanese consumers are already very much used to shopping on TV, online, and on mobile phones. Receiving this approval to broadcast is a significant milestone in our growth plans." Gems TV is also exploring other distribution opportunities in Japan which are suited for jewelry products, such as mobile phones.

Gems TV will also continue to develop and improve its product offerings for its target markets, using its gemstone purchasing expertise to source gemstones at competitive prices and developing jewelry designs to suit particular consumer preferences in various markets. It also plans to explore opportunities to increase brand awareness and reach consumers via alternative channels. Gems TV will continue to focus on improving its customer experience by keeping its content new, innovative, and entertaining. It will produce new documentaries about its products, processes, and sources of gemstones, and refine customer service at each step of the sales process. Lastly, it aims to improve its profitability by exploiting its know-how, wide supply network, relatively low fixed-cost technology, and fulfillment infrastructure.

Questions For Discussion

1. Conduct a brief analysis of the marketing environment and the forces shaping the development of Gems TV from a predominantly online retailer of loose gemstones to a TV home shopping retailer of colored, handcrafted jewelry.
2. What general benefits does Gems TV afford to buyers? Which benefits are most important in terms of creating value?
3. As an integrated manufacturer and TV home shopping retailer of colored gemstones, what effects has Gems TV had on how gemstones are marketed compared to more traditional brick-and-mortar jewelry retailers?
4. Evaluate Gem TV's expansion strategies. What other recommendations can you make for improving Gem TV's future growth and success?

Sources:
GEM TV Holdings Limited, *IPO Prospectus*, November 3, 2006; "Gems TV Obtains Broadcasting Rights in Japan," Gems TV announcement on Singapore Exchange, April 27, 2007; "Use of Proceeds from Initial Public Offering of Ordinary Shares in the Capital of the Company," Gems TV announcement to Singapore Exchange, March 31, 2007; Susan Cunningham, "Sparkle of Success," *Asia Inc.*, December 2003, pp. 74-75; www.gemstv, May 3, 2008.

QB HOUSE
✂ 10 minutes Just Cut
TOKYO SINGAPORE

Objectives

After studying this chapter, you should be able to

- discuss the need to understand competitors as well as customers through competitor analysis
- explain the fundamentals of competitive marketing strategies based on creating value for customers
- illustrate the need for balancing customer and competitor orientations in becoming a truly market-centered organization

CHAPTER 18

CREATING COMPETITIVE ADVANTAGE

Previewing the Concepts

In previous chapters, you explored the basics of marketing. In this chapter, we pull all of the marketing basics together. Understanding customers is an important first step in developing profitable customer relationships, but it's not enough. To gain competitive advantage, companies must use this understanding to design market offers that deliver more value than the offers of *competitors* seeking to win the same customers. In this chapter, we look first at competitor analysis, the process companies use to identify and analyze competitors. Then, we examine competitive marketing strategies by which companies position themselves against competitors to gain the greatest possible competitive advantage.

First let's examine QB House. As you read about QB House, ask yourself: Just what *is* it about this company's marketing strategy that has made it Japan's largest chain of barber shops? Pursuing this strategy, can QB House become the Wal-Mart of the hairstyling industry?

Q B ("Quick Barber") House was founded in Japan in November 1996. It is a business that has thrived in an environment of falling prices. A typical Tokyo hairdresser (*biyoshi*) charges 5,000 yen ($43) for men, and a *karisuma* (charisma) *biyoshi* may easily charge double that. Much of the money goes toward the *biyoshi's* wardrobe and modish premises. Much of the rest goes in the hairstyling ritual: the wrapping in shrouds, the "consultation," the many hot flannels, and the shoulder rub.

QB House offers none of that. Not even a shampooing. No shaving, no telephones, no toilets, no reading materials, no water supply. No TV either, only background music via FM radio. Instead, a 1,000-yen ($8) no-frills haircut is marketed. "We have turned barbershops from an emotional industry to a functional one," says QB House's boss, Kazutaka Iwai. From the moment a customer takes his seat, the stylist goes at him with all the gusto of a husband with a new lawn mower. Iwai tells his staff that the barbershop chain's product is "not a haircut, but a shorter period of time." Customers are in and out in 10 minutes flat. The chain takes no appointments. Customers enter and insert the exact amount (no receptionist to help with change) or swipe their Suica smart cards used on Tokyo's commuter lines in a machine by the entrance for a queue ticket. The cut and air-washing begins immediately if the outlet's signal lamp glows green. A yellow signal means a 10-minute wait, and a red one for the maximum 15-minute wait.

QB stylists have their tools immediately on hand. Store layout is as ergonomically efficient as possible to minimize expensive time wasted walking from one spot to another in the course of a hairdresser's work. Mazda's design subsidiary created the layout for each hairdressing unit. There is a cupboard facing the barber's chair with a coat hangar and sufficient space to take a briefcase. The cupboard door closed to display a mirror in front of the customer. Each unit contains combs, towels, talcum powder, clippers and trimmers, sterilizing ethanol, trays, brushes, used towel and comb disposals, and a payment voucher box within easy reach of the barber.

Everything is sanitized. An alcohol-based hand cleaner is installed for customer and employee use. To expedite the brushing up and disposal of waste hair after cutting, QB fitted a compartment under the barber's chair into which hair was swept after each cutting, falling into a plastic bag which was easily collected for disposal when full. QB employs compact and powerful vacuum equipment to remove loose hair from the customer's neck, shoulders, and clothes. Customers get to keep the comb used on them.

QB also makes use of IT. A sensor on the door of each shop records the time of opening, and each barber has a smart card used to input his or her personal data and the number of customers served, so that wages, which can be related to throughput, can be computed automatically. Data are recorded to establish a market profile for each outlet. The gender and approximate age of each customer are entered into the database by staff, together with comments on the day's weather. All data are transferred to a data center. Consumption of supplies is directly related to customer throughput, and suppliers are automatically alerted through a data link when shop inventory drops to a certain level requiring replenishment.

QB House outlets are squeezed into corners of railway stations and shopping malls. Many are deliberately placed next to a public lavatory. The company found that such busy outlets had turnovers of 10 percent above the chain's average. After travelers or shoppers have relieved themselves, a quick look in the mirror evidently reinforces the desire for a haircut. The chain's nearly 340 outlets now cut almost 10 million heads of hair a year in Japan. It has expanded its operations to Singapore and Hong Kong. Margins in these cities are similar to Japan's; higher rents are offset by lower wages. China, with very cheap labor costs (and haircuts) does not interest the company. Iwai believes that the idea of quick, cheap haircuts can be extended further to other services: to massages, manicures, and even instant loans.[1]

Competitive advantage
An advantage over competitors gained by offering consumers greater value than competitors offer.

Competitor analysis
The process of identifying key competitors; assessing their objectives, strategies, strengths and weaknesses, and reaction patterns; and selecting which competitors to attack or avoid.

Competitive marketing strategies
Strategies that strongly position the company against competitors and that give the company the strongest possible strategic advantage.

Today's companies face their toughest competition ever. In previous chapters, we argued that to succeed in today's fiercely competitive marketplace, companies will have to move from a product-and-selling philosophy to a customer-and-marketing philosophy. John Chambers, CEO of Cisco Systems put it well: "Make your customer the center of your culture."

This chapter discusses how companies can outperform competitors to win, keep, and grow customers. To win in today's marketplace, companies must become adept not just in *managing products*, but in *managing customer relationships* in the face of determined competition. Understanding customers is crucial, but it's not enough. Building profitable customer relationships and gaining **competitive advantage** requires delivering *more* value and satisfaction to target consumers than *competitors* do.

In this chapter, we examine *competitive marketing strategies*—how companies analyze their competitors and develop successful, value-based strategies for building and maintaining profitable customer relationships. The first step is **competitor analysis**, the process of identifying, assessing, and selecting key competitors. The second step is developing **competitive marketing strategies** that strongly position the company against competitors and give it the greatest possible competitive advantage.

Competitor Analysis

To plan effective marketing strategies, the company needs to find out about its competitors. It must constantly compare its marketing strategies, products, prices, channels, and promotion with those of close competitors. In this way the company can find areas of potential competitive advantage and disadvantage. As shown in **Figure 18.1**, competitor analysis involves:

- Identifying and assessing competitors.
- Selecting which competitors to attack or avoid.

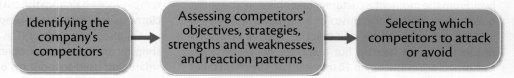

Figure 18.1
Steps in analyzing competitors

Identifying Competitors

At the narrowest level, a company can define its competitors as other companies offering similar products and services to the same customers at similar prices. Thus, Pepsi might view Coca-Cola as a major competitor, but not Tiger Beer or Qoo. Bookseller Kinokuniya might see Borders as a major competitor, but not Popular or Page One. Ritz-Carlton might see Four Seasons hotels as a major competitor, but not Holiday Inn Hotels.

But companies actually face a much wider range of competitors. The company might define competitors as all firms making the same product or class of products. Thus,

Ritz-Carlton would see itself as competing against all other hotels. Even more broadly, competitors might include all companies making products that supply the same service. Here Ritz-Carlton would see itself competing not only against other hotels but also against anyone who supplies rooms for weary travelers. Finally, and still more broadly, competitors might include all companies that compete for the same consumer dollars. Here Ritz-Carlton would see itself competing with travel and leisure services, from cruises and summer homes to vacations abroad.

Companies must avoid "competitor myopia." Latent competition can be more deadly than current ones. For example, for decades, Kodak held a comfortable lead in the photographic film business. It saw only Fuji as its major competitor in this market. However, in recent years, Kodak's major new competition has not come from Fuji and other film producers, but from Sony, Canon, and other digital camera makers, and from a host of digital image developers and online image-sharing services.

Competitor myopia –
A late entry into the digital imaging market, Kodak must continue to innovate and introduce new products that deliver on their promise to the consumer: "You press the button, we do the rest."

Because of its myopic focus on film, Kodak was late to enter the digital imaging market. It paid a heavy price. With digital cameras now outselling film cameras, and with film sales plummeting 20 percent every year, Kodak has faced major sales and profit setbacks, massive layoffs, and a 74 percent drop in its stock over the past five years. Kodak is now changing its focus to digital imaging, but the transformation will be difficult. The company has to "figure out not just how to convince consumers to buy its [digital] cameras and home printers but also how to become known as the most convenient and affordable way to process those images," says an industry analyst. "That means home and store printing as well as sending images over the Internet and cell phones."[2]

Companies can identify their competitors from the *industry* point of view. (see **Figure 18.2**) They might see themselves as being in the oil industry, the pharmaceutical industry, or the beverage industry. A company must understand the competitive patterns in its industry if it hopes to be an effective "player" in that industry. Companies can also identify competitors from a *market* point of view. Here they define competitors as companies that are trying to satisfy the same customer need or build relationships with the same customer group.

Ways to identify competition

Industry Perspective
○ What companies are in the same industry as you?

Example:
Pepsi's competitors are Coca-cola, 7 UP, A&W Root Beer, and other soft drink makers

Market Perspective
○ What companies satisfy the same customer needs as you?

Example:
Pepsi's competitors are all drinks that satisfy consumers' need for thirst quenching—bottled water, fruit juice, ice tea, and other drinks.

Figure 18.2
Perspectives in identifying competition

From an industry point of view, Pepsi might see its competition as Coca-Cola, 7UP, and other soft drink makers. From a market point of view, however, the customer really wants "thirst quenching." This need can be satisfied by bottled water, fruit juice, iced tea, or many other fluids. Similarly, Crayola crayons might define its competitors as other makers of crayons and children's drawing supplies. But from a market point of view, it would include all firms making recreational products for children.

In general, the market concept of competition opens the company's eyes to a broader set of actual and potential competitors. One approach is to profile the company's direct and indirect competitors by mapping the steps buyers take in obtaining and using the product. **Figure 18.3** illustrates a *competitor map* of Eastman Kodak in the digital imaging business.[3] In the center is a list of consumer activities: buying a camera, taking photos, creating digital photo albums, printing photos, and others. The first outer ring lists Kodak's main competitors with respect to each consumer activity: Canon and Sony for buying a camera, HP's Snapfish for sharing and printing photos, and so on. The second outer ring lists indirect competitors—Apple, Motorola, Microsoft, and others—who may become direct competitors. This type of analysis highlights both the competitive opportunities and the challenges a company faces.

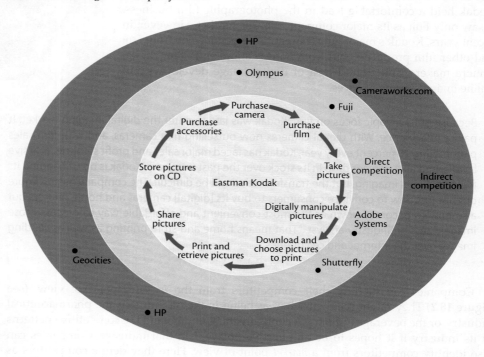

Figure 18.3
Competitor map
Source: Based on Jeffrey F. Rayport and Bernard J. Jaworski, *e-Commerce* (New York: McGraw-Hill, 2001), p. 53.

Assessing Competitors

Having identified the main competitors, marketing management now asks: What are competitors' objectives—what does each seek in the marketplace? What is each competitor's strategy? What are various competitor's strengths and weaknesses, and how will each react to actions the company might take?

Determining Competitors' Objectives

Each competitor has a mix of objectives. The company wants to know the relative importance that a competitor places on current profitability, market share growth, cash flow, technological leadership, service leadership, and other goals. Knowing a competitor's mix of objectives reveals whether the competitor is satisfied with its current situation and how it might react to different competitive actions. For example, a company that pursues low-cost leadership will react more strongly to a competitor's cost-reducing manufacturing breakthrough than to the same competitor's advertising increase.

A company also must monitor its competitors' objectives for various segments. If the company finds that a competitor has discovered a new segment, this might be an opportunity. If it finds that competitors plan new moves into segments now served by the company, it will be forewarned and, hopefully, forearmed.

Identifying Competitors' Strategies

The more that one firm's strategy resembles another firm's strategy, the more the two firms compete. In most industries, the competitors can be sorted into groups that pursue different strategies. A **strategic group** is a group of firms in an industry following the same or a similar strategy in a given target market. For example, in the television set industry, Sharp and Panasonic belong to the same strategic group. Each produces a full line of medium-price appliances supported by good service. In contrast, Pioneer belongs to a different strategic group. It produces a narrower line of high-quality appliances and charges a premium price.

Some important insights emerge from identifying strategic groups. For example, if a company enters one of the groups, the members of that group become its key competitors. Thus, if the company enters the first group, against Sharp and Panasonic, it can succeed only if it develops strategic advantages over these competitors.

Although competition is most intense within a strategic group, there is also rivalry among groups. First, some of the strategic groups may appeal to overlapping customer segments. For example, no matter what their strategy, all television set manufacturers will go after the apartment and homebuilders segment. Second, the customers may not see much difference in the offers of different groups—they may see little difference in quality between Panasonic and Pioneer. Finally, members of one strategic group might expand into new strategy segments.

The company needs to look at all of the dimensions that identify strategic groups within the industry. It must understand how each competitor delivers value to its customers. It needs to know each competitor's product quality, features, and mix; customer services; pricing policy; distribution coverage; sales force strategy; and advertising and sales promotion programs. And it must study the details of each competitor's R&D, manufacturing, purchasing, financial, and other strategies.

Assessing Competitors' Strengths and Weaknesses

Marketers need to assess each competitor's strengths and weaknesses carefully to answer the critical question: What can our competitors do? As a first step, companies can gather data on each competitor's goals, strategies, and performance over the past few years. Some of this information will be hard to obtain. For example, business-to-business marketers find it hard to estimate competitors' market shares because they do not have the same syndicated data services that are available to consumer packaged-goods companies.

Companies normally learn about their competitors' strengths and weaknesses through secondary data, personal experience, and word of mouth. They can also conduct primary marketing research with customers, suppliers, and dealers. Or they can **benchmark** themselves against other firms, comparing the company's products and processes to those of competitors or leading firms in other industries to find ways to improve quality and performance. Benchmarking has become a powerful tool for increasing a company's competitiveness.

Estimating Competitors' Reactions

Next, the company wants to know: What *will* our competitors do? A competitor's objectives, strategies, and strengths and weaknesses may explain its likely actions. They also suggest its likely reactions to company moves such as price cuts, promotion increases, or new-product introductions. In addition, each competitor has a certain philosophy of doing business, a certain internal culture and guiding beliefs. An understanding of a competitor's mentality helps marketing managers anticipate how the competitor will act or react.

Each competitor reacts differently. Some do not react quickly or strongly to a competitor's move. They may feel their customers are loyal; they may be slow in noticing the move; they may lack the funds to react. Some competitors react only to certain types of

Strategic group
A group of firms in an industry following the same or a similar strategy.

Strategic groups –
Pioneer belongs to the television set industry strategic group offering a narrow line of high-quality appliances supported by good service.

Benchmarking
The process of comparing the company's products and processes to those of competitors or leading firms in other industries to find ways to improve quality and performance.

Assessing competitors' strengths –
Trade shows like the annual Consumer Elecronics Show in the U.S. provide an arena for companies to 'check out' what their competitors are offering.

moves and not to others. Other competitors react swiftly and strongly to any action. Thus, Procter & Gamble does not let a new detergent come easily into the market. Many firms avoid direct competition with P&G and look for easier prey, knowing that P&G will react fiercely if challenged.

In some industries, competitors live in relative harmony; in others, they fight constantly. Knowing how major competitors react gives the company clues on how best to attack competitors or how best to defend the company's current positions.

Selecting Competitors to Attack and Avoid

A company has already largely selected its major competitors through prior decisions on customer targets, distribution channels, and marketing-mix strategy. Management now must decide which competitors to compete against most vigorously.

Strong or Weak Competitors

The company can focus on one of several classes of competitors. Most companies prefer to compete against *weak competitors*. This requires fewer resources and less time. But in the process, the firm may gain little. The firm can also compete with *strong competitors* to sharpen its abilities. Strong competitors also have some weaknesses, and succeeding against them often provides greater returns.

A useful tool for assessing competitor strengths and weaknesses is **customer value analysis**. The aim of customer value analysis is to determine the benefits that targeted customers value and how customers rate the relative value of various competitors' offers. In conducting a customer value analysis, the company first identifies the major attributes that customers value and the importance customers place on these attributes. Next, it assesses the company's and competitors' performance on the valued attributes.

The key to gaining competitive advantage is to take each customer segment and examine how the company's offer compares to that of its major competitor. If the company's offer delivers greater value by exceeding the competitor's offer on all important attributes, the company can charge a higher price and earn higher profits, or it can charge the same price and gain more market share. But if the company is seen as performing at a lower level than its major competitor on some important attributes, it must invest in strengthening those attributes or finding other important attributes where it can build a lead on the competitor.

Customer value analysis
Analysis conducted to determine what benefits target customers value and how they rate the relative value of various competitors' offers.

Close or Distant Competitors

Most companies will compete with *close competitors*—those that resemble them most—rather than *distant competitors*. Thus, Nike competes more against Adidas than against Timberland. And Lexus competes more with Mercedes rather than Hyundai or Daihatsu.

At the same time, the company may want to avoid trying to "destroy" a close competitor. For example, in the late 1970s, Bausch & Lomb moved aggressively against other soft lens manufacturers with great success. However, this forced weak competitors to sell out to larger firms such as Johnson & Johnson. As a result, Bausch & Lomb now faces much larger competitors—and it has suffered the consequences. Johnson & Johnson acquired Vistakon, a small nicher with only $20 million in annual sales. Backed by Johnson & Johnson's deep pockets, however, the small but nimble Vistakon developed and introduced its innovative Acuvue disposable lenses. With Vistakon leading the way, Johnson & Johnson is now the top U.S. contact lens maker with a 33 percent market share, and Bausch & Lomb lags in fourth place with a 13 percent share.[4] In this case, success in hurting a close rival brought in tougher competitors.

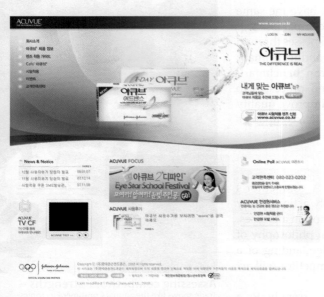

Competitive makeup – After driving smaller competitors from the market, Bausch & Lomb faces larger, more resourceful ones, such as Johnson & Johnson's Vistakon division. With Vistakon's Acuvue lenses lending the way, J&J is now the top U.S. contact lens maker. (www.acuvue.com)

"Good" or "Bad" Competitors

A company benefits from competitors. The existence of competitors results in several strategic benefits. Competitors may help increase total demand. They may share the costs of market and product development and help to legitimize new technologies. They may serve less-attractive segments or lead to more product differentiation.

However, a company may not view all of its competitors as beneficial. An industry often contains *"good" competitors* and *"bad" competitors*.[5] Good competitors play by the rules of the industry. Bad competitors, in contrast, break the rules. They try to buy share rather than earn it, take large risks, and play by their own rules. For example, Yahoo! Music Unlimited sees Napster, Rhapsody, AOL Music, Sony Connect, and most other digital music download services as good competitors. They share a common platform, so that music bought from any of these competitors can be played on almost any playback device. However, it sees Apple's iTunes Music Store as a bad competitor, one that plays by its own rules at the expense of the industry as a whole.

With the iPod, Apple created a closed system with mass appeal. iPods account for an estimated 73 percent of the 30 million MP3 players currently in use in the U.S. In 2003, when the iPod was the only game in town, Apple cut a deal with the Big Five record companies that locked up its device. The music companies wanted to sell songs on iTunes, but they were afraid of Internet piracy. So Apple promised to wrap their songs in its FairPlay software—the only copy-protection software that is iPod-compatible. Other digital music services such as Yahoo! Music Unlimited and Napster have since reached similar deals with the big record labels. But Apple refused to license FairPlay to them. So those companies turned to Microsoft for copy protection. That satisfied fearful music companies, but it means none of the songs sold by those services can be played on iPod. And music downloaded from iTunes will play *only* on an iPod, making it difficult for other MP3 players that support the Microsoft format to get a toehold. The situation has been a disaster for Apple's competitors. iTunes holds a commanding lead over its rivals, selling more than 75 percent of all digital music.[6]

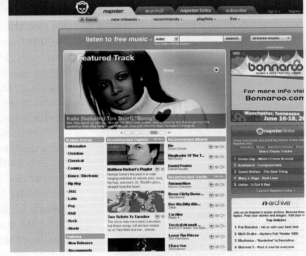

Good and bad competitors – Digital music download services such as Yahoo! Music Unlimited, Napster, and Rhapsody see Apple as a bad competitor. Music downloaded from their sites can't be played on the Apple's wildly popular iPod, and music from Apple's iTunes Music Store will play only on an iPod.

The implication is that "good" companies would like to shape an industry that consists of only well-behaved competitors. A company might be smart to support good competitors, aiming its attacks at bad competitors. Thus, Yahoo! Music Unlimited, Napster, and other digital music competitors will no doubt support one another in trying to break Apple's stranglehold on the market.

Designing a Competitive Intelligence System

We have described the main types of information that companies need about their competitors. This information must be collected, interpreted, distributed, and used. The cost in money and time of gathering competitive intelligence is high, and the company must design its competitive intelligence system in a cost-effective way.

The competitive intelligence system first identifies the vital types of competitive information and the best sources of this information. Then, the system continuously collects information from the field (sales force, channels, suppliers, market research firms, trade associations, Web sites) and from published data (government publications, speeches, articles). Next the system checks the information for validity and reliability, interprets it, and organizes it in an appropriate way. Finally, it sends key information to relevant decision makers and responds to inquiries from managers about competitors.

With this system, company managers will receive timely information about competitors in the form of phone calls, e-mails, bulletins, newsletters, and reports. In addition, managers can connect with the system when they need an interpretation of a competitor's sudden move, or when they want to know a competitor's weaknesses and strengths, or when they need to know how a competitor will respond to a planned company move.

Smaller companies that cannot afford to set up formal competitive intelligence offices can assign specific executives to watch specific competitors. Thus, a manager who used to work for a competitor might follow that competitor closely; he or she would be the "in-house expert" on that competitor. Any manager needing to know the thinking of a given competitor could contact the assigned in-house expert.

Competitive Strategies

Having identified and evaluated its major competitors, the company now must design broad competitive marketing strategies by which it can gain competitive advantage through superior customer value. But what broad marketing strategies might the company use? Which ones are best for a particular company, or for the company's different divisions and products?

Approaches to Marketing Strategy

No one strategy is best for all companies. Each company must determine what makes the most sense given its position in the industry and its objectives, opportunities, and resources. Even within a company, different strategies may be required for different businesses or products. Johnson & Johnson uses one marketing strategy for its leading brands in stable consumer markets—such as BAND-AIDs, Tylenol, or Johnson's baby products—and a different marketing strategy for its high-tech health care businesses and products—such as Monocryl surgical sutures or NeuFlex finger joint implants.

Companies also differ in how they approach the strategy-planning process. Many large firms develop formal competitive marketing strategies and implement them religiously. However, other companies develop strategies in a less formal and orderly fashion. Some companies, such as Harley-Davidson, Virgin Atlantic Airways, and BMW's MINI unit succeed by breaking many of the "rules" of marketing strategy. Such companies don't operate large marketing departments, conduct expensive marketing research, spell out elaborate competitive strategies, and spend huge sums on advertising. Instead, they sketch out strategies on the fly, stretch their limited resources, live close to their customers, and create more satisfying solutions to customer needs. They form buyer's clubs, use buzz marketing, and focus on winning customer loyalty. It seems that not all marketing must follow in the footsteps of marketing giants such as IBM and Procter & Gamble.

In fact, approaches to marketing strategy and practice often pass through three stages: entrepreneurial marketing, formulated marketing, and intrepreneurial marketing.[7]

Strategy-planning process – Some companies such as Virgin Atlantic Airways break many of the "rules" of marketing strategy and succeed. Here, the company uses air-sickness bags to highlight how the Virgin Atlantic experience will "rinse that bad taste of flying right out of your mouth."

- *Entrepreneurial marketing*: Most companies are started by individuals who live by their wits. They visualize an opportunity, construct flexible strategies on the backs of envelopes, and knock on every door to gain attention.
- *Formulated marketing*: As small companies achieve success, they inevitably move toward more-formulated marketing. They develop formal marketing strategies and adhere to them closely.
- *Intrepreneurial marketing*: Many large and mature companies get stuck in formulated marketing. They pore over the latest Nielsen numbers, scan market research reports, and try to fine-tune their competitive strategies and programs. These companies sometimes lose the marketing creativity and passion that they had at the start. They now need to reestablish within their companies the entrepreneurial spirit and actions that made them successful in the first place. They need to encourage more initiative and "intrepreneurship" at the local level. They need to refresh their marketing strategies and try new approaches. Their brand and product managers need to get out of the office, start living with their customers, and visualize new and creative ways to add value to their customers' lives.

Basic Competitive Strategies

Michael Porter suggested four basic competitive positioning strategies that companies can follow—three winning strategies and one losing one.[8] The three winning strategies include:

- *Overall cost leadership:* Here the company works hard to achieve the lowest production and distribution costs. Low costs let it price lower than its competitors and win a large market share. Dell and Wal-Mart are leading practitioners of this strategy.
- *Differentiation:* Here the company concentrates on creating a highly differentiated product line and marketing program so that it comes across as the class leader in the industry. Most customers would prefer to own this brand if its price is not too high. Apple and Caterpillar follow this strategy in computer and services and heavy construction equipment, respectively.
- *Focus:* Here the company focuses its effort on serving a few market segments well rather than going after the whole market. For example, Ritz-Carlton focuses on the top five percent of corporate and leisure travelers.

Companies that pursue a clear strategy—one of the above—will likely perform well. The firm that carries out that strategy best will make the most profits. But firms that do not pursue a clear strategy—*middle-of-the-roaders*—do the worst. Holiday Inn encountered difficult times because they did not stand out as the lowest in cost, highest in perceived value, or best in serving some market segment. Middle-of-the-roaders try to be good on all strategic counts, but end up being not very good at anything.

Michael Treacy and Fred Wiersema offered new classifications of competitive marketing strategies.[9] They suggested that companies gain leadership positions by delivering superior value to their customers. Companies can pursue any of three strategies—called *value disciplines*—for delivering superior customer value. These are:

- *Operational excellence:* The company provides superior value by leading its industry in price and convenience. It works to reduce costs and to create a lean and efficient value-delivery system. It serves customers who want reliable, good-quality products or services, but who want them cheaply and easily. Examples include Wal-Mart, AirAsia, and Dell.
- *Customer intimacy:* The company provides superior value by precisely segmenting its markets and tailoring its products or services to match exactly the needs of targeted customers. It specializes in satisfying unique customer needs through a close relationship with and intimate knowledge of the customer. It builds detailed customer databases for segmenting and targeting, and it empowers its marketing people to respond quickly to customer needs. Customer-intimate companies serve customers who are willing to pay a premium to get precisely what they want. They will do almost anything to build long-term customer loyalty and to capture customer lifetime value. Examples include Ritz-Carlton, Lexus, American Express, and British Airways (see **Real Marketing**).

Customer intimacy –
Companies provide superior value by tailoring its products or services to match exactly the needs of targeted customers.

- *Product leadership:* The company provides superior value by offering a continuous stream of leading-edge products or services. It aims to make its own and competing products obsolete. Product leaders are open to new ideas, relentlessly pursue new solutions, and work to get new products to market quickly. They serve customers who want state-of-the-art products and services, regardless of the costs in terms of price or inconvenience. Examples include Nokia and Microsoft.

REAL MARKETING

Marketing Upscale: Creating Customer Intimacy

Some companies go to extremes to coddle big spenders. From carmakers like Lexus and BMW, to hotels like Ritz-Carlton and Four Seasons, such companies give their well-heeled customers exactly what they need—and even more.

For example, concierge services are no longer the sole province of five-star hotels and fancy credit cards. They are starting to show up at airlines, retailers, and even electronic-goods makers. Sony Electronics, for instance, offers a service for its wealthiest customers, called Cierge, that provides a free personal shopper and early access to new gadgets, as well as "white-glove" help with the installation. (Translation: They will send someone over to set up the new gear.)

But when it comes to stalking the well-to-do, perhaps nowhere is the competition greater than in the credit-card industry. To rise above the credit-card clutter and to attract high-end card holders, the major credit-card companies have created a new top tier of superpremium cards—Visa's Signature card, MasterCard's World card, American Express's super-elite Centurion card. Affluent customers are extremely profitable. While premium cards represent only 1.5 percent of the consumer credit cards issued by Visa, MasterCard, and American Express, they account for 20 percent of the spending. And well-to-do cardholders tend to default a lot less, too.

Among premium cards, the American Express Centurion card is the "elite of the elite" for luxury card carriers. This mysterious black credit card is issued by invitation only, to customers who *spend* more than $150,000 a year on other AmEx cards and meet other not-so-clear requirements. Then, the select few who do receive the card pay a $2,500 annual fee for the privilege of carrying it.

But the prestigious Centurion card,

Targeting affluent consumers: Visa' Signature card zeros in on the "new affluent." It offers no preset spending limit, 24-hour concierge services, and loads of "upgrades, perks, and discounts... it's just not everywhere you want to be. It's everything you ever wanted."

Some companies successfully pursue more than one value discipline at the same time. For example, FedEx excels at both operational excellence and customer intimacy. However, such companies are rare—few firms can be the best at more than one of these disciplines. By trying to be *good at all* of the value disciplines, a company usually ends up being *best at none*.

Treacy and Wiersema found that leading companies focus on and excel at a single value discipline, while meeting industry standards on the other two. Such companies design their entire value delivery network to single-mindedly support the chosen discipline. For

in its elegant matte finish, comes with numerous perks. "A black card is plastic bling-bling," says an industry observer, "a way for celebrities, athletes, and major business people to express their status."

A T-shirt-and-jeans kind of guy, Peter H. Shankman certainly doesn't look like a high roller, but American Express knows better. After he was snubbed by salesmen at a Giorgio Armani boutique on Fifth Avenue in New York recently, the 31-year-old publicist saw "an unbelievable attitude reversal" at the cash register when he whipped out his black AmEx Centurion Card. In June, a RadioShack cashier refused the card, thinking it was a fake. "'Trust me,' I said. 'Run the card,'" recalls the chief executive of Geek Factory, a public-relations and marketing firm. "I could buy a Learjet with this thing."

An exaggeration, perhaps. But AmEx's little black card is coveted by big spenders. Some would-be customers go to absurd lengths to get what they see as a must-have status symbol. Hopefuls have written poems to plead their cases. "Every week I get phone calls or letters, often from prominent people, asking me for the card," says AmEx's head of consumer cards, Alfred F. Kelly Jr. AmEx deliberately builds an air of mystery around the sleek card, keeping secret such details as the number of cards in circulation. Analysts say AmEx earns back many times what it spends on

perks for black-card customers in both marketing buzz and fees.

Basic services on the Centurion card include a personal travel counselor and concierge, available 24/7. Beyond that, almost anything goes. Feel like shopping at Saks Fifth Avenue at midnight? No problem. Traveling abroad in first class? Take a pal—the extra ticket is free. The royal treatment often requires elaborate planning. One AmEx concierge arranged a bachelor party for 25, which involved a four-day trip that included 11 penthouse suites, travel by private jet, and a meet-and-greet with an owner of the Sacramento Kings basketball team. The tab was more than $300,000.

How did Shankman earn his card? All the travel and entertainment charges he racks up hosting his clients prompted AmEx to send it to him. It arrived with a 43-page manual. Recently, Shankman sought reservations for Spice Market, an often-overbooked restaurant in Manhattan, to impress a friend. He called his concierge. "Half an hour later it was done," says Shankman. Membership does have its privileges.

American Express seeks new Centurion cardholders discreetly. When it wanted to expand the elite list in Europe without attracting the ineligible, it mailed invitations to the top one percent of its platinum card holders. The mailing contained a card embedded in a glass paperweight with an invitation to

meet personally with American Express's European president.

So, how many people actually have a Centurion card? "About the same number of people who can afford a Mercedes Maybach," says Desiree Fish, a spokeswoman for American Express, referring to a luxury car that can list for more than $300,000. The best guess is that only about 5,000 people worldwide own a Centurion card.

Sources:

American Express example adapted from Mara Der Hovanesian, "This Black Card Gives You Carte Blanche," *Business Week*, August 9, 2004, p. 54. Quotes and other information from David Carr, "No Name, but Plenty of Bling-Bling for Show," *New York Times*, September 13, 2004, p. C11; Eleena de Lisser, "How to Get an Airline to Wait for Your Plumber—In Battle for Biggest Spenders, British Airways, Sony Rolls Out Hotel-Style 'Concierge' Service," *Wall Street Journal*, July 2, 2002, p. D1; James Tenser, "Cards Play Their Luxury Hand Right," *Advertising Age*, September 13, 2004, pp. S13–S14; Frederick H. Lowe, "Cards for the Rich: They're Different, Indeed," *Credit Card Management*, February 2005, pp. 18–22; Eric Dash, "New Spots for the Credit Card Companies Show Fierce Competition for the High-End Consumer," *New York Times*, May 11, 2005, p. C8; "The 10 Best DM Campaigns," *Campaign*, December 16, 2005, p. 38; and www.visa.com and www.mastercard.com, December 2006.

example, Wal-Mart knows that customer intimacy and product leadership are important. Compared with other discounters, it offers very good customer service and an excellent product assortment. Still, it purposely offers less customer service and less product depth than do high-end retailers which pursue customer intimacy. Instead, Wal-Mart focuses obsessively on operational excellence—on reducing costs and streamlining its order-to-delivery process in order to make it convenient for customers to buy just the right products at the lowest prices.

By the same token, Ritz-Carlton Hotels wants to be efficient and to employ the latest technologies. But what really sets the luxury hotel chain apart is its customer intimacy. Ritz-Carlton creates custom-designed experiences to coddle its customers:

> Check into any Ritz-Carlton Hotel around the world, and you'll be amazed at how well the hotel's employees anticipate your slightest need. Without ever asking, they seem to know that you want a nonsmoking room with a king-size bed, a nonallergenic pillow, and breakfast with decaffeinated coffee in your room. How does Ritz-Carlton work this magic? At the heart of the system is a huge customer database, which contains information gathered through the observations of hotel employees. Each day, hotel staffers—from those at the front desk to those in maintenance and housekeeping—discreetly record the unique habits, likes, and dislikes of each guest on small "guest preference pads." These observations are then transferred to a corporatewide "guest preference database." Every morning, a "guest historian" at each hotel reviews the files of all new arrivals who have previously stayed at a Ritz-Carlton and prepares a list of suggested extra touches that might delight each guest. Guests have responded strongly to such personalized service. Since inaugurating the guest-history system, Ritz-Carlton has boosted guest retention by 23 percent. An amazing 95 percent of departing guests report that their stay has been a truly memorable experience.

Classifying competitive strategies as value disciplines is appealing. It defines marketing strategy in terms of the single-minded pursuit of delivering superior value to customers. Each value discipline defines a specific way to build lasting customer relationships.

Competitive Positions

Firms competing in a given target market, at any point in time, differ in their objectives and resources. Some firms are large, others small. Some have many resources, others are strapped for funds. Some are mature and established, others new and fresh. Some strive for rapid market share growth, others for long-term profits. And the firms occupy different competitive positions in the target market.

We now examine competitive strategies based on the roles firms play in the target market—leader, challenger, follower, or nicher. Suppose that an industry contains the firms shown in **Figure 18.4.** Forty percent of the market is in the hands of the **market leader**, the firm with the largest market share. Another 30 percent is in the hands of **market challengers**, runner-up firms that are fighting hard to increase their market share. Another 20 percent is in the hands of **market followers**, other runner-up firms that want to hold their share without rocking the boat. The remaining 10 percent is in the hands of **market nichers**, firms that serve small segments not being pursued by other firms.

Market leader
The firm in an industry with the largest market share.

Market challenger
A runner-up firm that is fighting hard to increase its market share in an industry.

Market follower
A runner-up firm that wants to hold its share in an industry without rocking the boat.

Market nicher
A firm that serves small segments that the other firms in an industry overlook or ignore.

Figure 18.4
Hypothetical market structure

Market leader	Market challengers	Market followers	Market nichers
40%	30%	20%	10%

Table 18.1 shows specific marketing strategies that are available to market leaders, challengers, followers, and nichers.[10] Remember, however, that these classifications often do not apply to a whole company, but only to its position in a specific industry. Large companies such as GE, Microsoft, Procter & Gamble, or Disney might be leaders in some markets and nichers in others. For example, Procter & Gamble leads in many segments, such as laundry detergents and shampoo. But it challenges Unilever in the hand soaps and Kimberly-Clark in facial tissues. Such companies often use different strategies for different business units or products, depending on the competitive situations of each.

Market Leader Strategies

Most industries contain an acknowledged market leader. The leader has the largest market share and usually leads the other firms in price changes, new-product introductions, distribution coverage, and promotion spending. The leader may or may not be admired or respected, but other firms concede its dominance. Competitors focus on the leader as a company to challenge, imitate, or avoid. Some of the best-known market leaders are Toyota (automobile), Microsoft (computer software), IBM (information technology services and equipment), Caterpillar (earth-moving equipment), McDonald's (fast food), Adidas (athletic footwear), and Google (Internet search services).

A leader must constantly be on the watch. Other firms keep challenging its strengths or trying to take advantage of its weaknesses. The market leader can easily miss a turn in the market and plunge into second or third place. A product innovation may come along and hurt the leader (as when Apple developed the iPod and took the market lead from Sony's Walkman portable audio devices). The leader might grow arrogant or complacent and misjudge the competition (as when Nintendo underestimated Sony's PlayStation before regaining its leadership via the Wii). Or the leader might look old-fashioned against new and peppier rivals (as when Levi's lost serious ground to more current or stylish brands such as Tommy Hilfiger and Guess).

To remain number one, leading firms can take any of three actions:

- They can find ways to expand total demand.
- They can protect their current market share through good defensive and offensive actions.
- They can try to expand their market share further, even if market size remains constant.

Table 18.1 Strategies for Market Leaders, Challengers, Followers, and Nichers

Market Leader Strategies	Market Challenger Strategies	Market Follower Strategies	Market Nicher Strategies
Expand total market	*Full frontal attack*	*Follow closely*	*By customer, market, quality-price, service*
Protect market share	*Indirect attack*	*Follow at a distance*	*Multiple niching*
Expand market share			

Expanding the Total Demand

The leading firm normally gains the most when the total market expands. If drivers purchase more hybrid automobiles, Toyota stands to gain the most because it sells the nation's largest share of hybrids. If Toyota can convince more drivers that hybrid cars are both more economical and more environmentally friendly, it will benefit more than its competitors.

Market leaders can expand the market by developing new users, new uses, and more usage of its products. They usually can find *new users* in many places. For example, Shiseido might find new skincare users in its current markets by convincing women who do not use skincare to try it. It might find users in new demographic segments, such as by producing skincare for men. Or it might expand into new geographic segments, perhaps by selling its skincare products in other countries.

Marketers can expand markets by discovering and promoting *new uses* for the product. For example, Arm & Hammer baking soda, whose sales had flattened after 125 years, discovered that consumers were using baking soda as a refrigerator deodorizer. It launched a heavy advertising and publicity campaign focusing on this use and persuaded consumers in half of America's

New users – Shiseido has expanded into a new market—skincare products for men. (*www.shiseido.co.jp/men/html*)

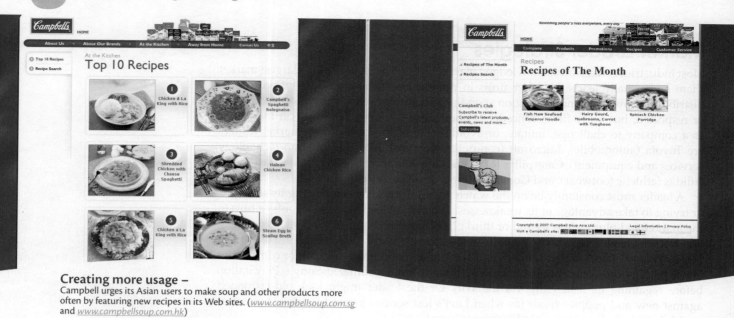

Creating more usage –
Campbell urges its Asian users to make soup and other products more often by featuring new recipes in its Web sites. (www.campbellsoup.com.sg and www.campbellsoup.com.hk)

homes to place an open box of baking soda in their refrigerators and to replace it every few months. Today, its Web site (www.armandhammer.com) features new uses—"Solutions for my home, my family, my body"—ranging from removing residue left behind by hair-styling products and sweetening garbage disposals, laundry hampers, refrigerators, and trash cans to creating a home spa in your bathroom.

Finally, market leaders can encourage *more usage* by convincing people to use the product more often or to use more per occasion. For example, Campbell urges Hong Kongers and Singaporeans to drink soup and other Campbell products more often by running ads containing new recipes. The Campbell's Kitchen section of the company's Web site (www.campbellsoup.com.hk) lets visitors search for or exchange recipes.

Protecting Market Share

While trying to expand total market size, the leading firm also must protect its current business against competitors' attacks. Dell must also constantly guard against Lenovo; Sony PlayStation against Nintendo and xBox; and McDonald's against Burger King.

What can the market leader do to protect its position? First, it must prevent or fix weaknesses that provide opportunities for competitors. It must always fulfill its value promise. Its prices must remain consistent with the value that customers see in the brand. It must work tirelessly to keep strong relationships with valued customers. The leader should "plug holes" so that competitors do not jump in.

But the best defense is a good offense, and the best response is *continuous innovation*. The leader refuses to be content with the way things are and leads the industry in new products, customer services, distribution effectiveness, and cost cutting. It keeps increasing its competitive effectiveness and value to customers.

To fortify its position as a premium airline, Singapore Airlines is the world's first commercial airline to fly the double-decker super-jumbo Airbus aircraft known as A380. The 471-seat juggernaut enables the airline to take a larger number of passengers on long-haul routes at a lower operating cost per seat. The services that Singapore Airlines intends to offer on these aircraft are aimed at giving an unprecedented flying experience, and setting new standards for the airline industry. Already, Singapore Airlines offers a new class on the A380—the Singapore Airlines Suites—and has been a pioneer in introducing innovative inflight entertainment services as multi-player electronic games including chess and *mahjong*.

And when attacked by challengers, the market leader reacts decisively. For example, consider NTT DoCoMo.

NTT DoCoMo dominated the Japanese mobile phone market when it rolled out i-mode that allowed users to e-mail, shop, and bank online through their mobile phones. DoCoMo had twice the market share of its next rival, KDDI. However, KDDI started to make inroads when DoCoMo's 3G offering was less than impressive. Consumers liked KDDI's slower but less buggy data offering called AU. They were impressed with its sleek handsets, longer-lasting batteries, and fun services such as easy video mail and song downloads. Not to be outdone, DoCoMo countered by expanding the network coverage of its 3G service—FOMA (Freedom of Mobile Multimedia Access). It also started offering a monthly fixed rate similar to KDDI's. This represents a major shift for DoCoMo, which grew its i-mode business by charging users based on the amount of data they send. DoCoMo also teamed up with Sony to offer phones with "smart cards" that allow users to use their phones to buy such items as train and cinema tickets or restaurant meals by passing the phone through a sensor device.

i-mode – Consumers can use their mobile phones to pay for items such as train and cinema tickets with smart card technology from DoCoMo and Sony. (*www.nttdocom.com/services/im/index.html*)

Expanding Market Share

Market leaders also can grow by increasing their market shares further. Studies have shown that, on average, profitability rises with increasing market share. Because of these findings, many companies have sought expanded market shares to improve profitability. GE, for example, declared that it wants to be at least number one or two in each of its markets or else get out. GE shed its computer, air-conditioning, small appliances, and television businesses because it could not achieve top-dog position in these industries.

However, some studies have found that many industries contain one or a few highly profitable large firms, several profitable and more focused firms, and a large number of medium-sized firms with poorer profit performance. It appears that profitability increases as a business gains share relative to competitors in its *served market*. For example, Lexus holds only a small share of the total car market, but it earns high profits because it is the leading brand in the luxury-performance car segment. And it has achieved this high share in its served market because it does other things right, such as producing high-quality products, creating good service experiences, and building close customer relationships.

Companies must not think, however, that gaining increased market share will automatically improve profitability. Much depends on their strategy for gaining increased share. There are many high-share companies with low profitability and many low-share companies with high profitability. The cost of buying higher market share may far exceed the returns. Higher shares tend to produce higher profits only when unit costs fall with increased market share, or when the company offers a superior-quality product and charges a premium price that more than covers the cost of offering higher quality.

Market Challenger Strategies

Firms that are second, third, or lower in an industry are sometimes quite large, such as Honda, Darlie, Avis, and Pepsi. These runner-up firms can adopt one of two competitive strategies: They can challenge the leader and other competitors in an aggressive bid for more market share (market challengers). Or they can play along with competitors and not rock the boat (market followers).

A market challenger must first define which competitors to challenge and its strategic objective. The challenger can attack the market leader, a high-risk but potentially high-gain strategy. Its goal might be to take over market leadership. Xerox assumed leadership of the copier market from 3M by developing a better copying process. Later, Canon took a large chunk of Xerox's market by launching desk copiers. Or the challenger's objective may simply be to wrest more market share. Although it might seem that the market leader has the most going for it, challengers often have what some strategists call a "second-mover advantage." The challenger observes what has made the leader successful and improves upon it.

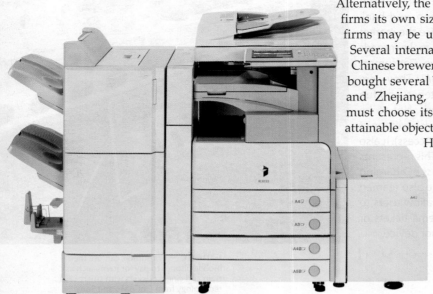

Market challenger strategies –
A market challenger can attack the market leader with the goal of taking over market leadership. Canon took a large chunk of Xerox's market by launching copiers developed with its original technologies.

Alternatively, the challenger can avoid the leader and instead challenge firms its own size, or smaller local and regional firms. These smaller firms may be underfinanced and not serving their customers well. Several international beer companies are buying stakes in regional Chinese breweries to penetrate the China market. Belgium's Interbrew bought several breweries near Shanghai to gain share in Guangdong and Zhejiang, two of China's richest provinces. The challenger must choose its opponents carefully and have a clearly defined and attainable objective.

How can the market challenger best attack the chosen competitor and achieve its strategic objectives? There are several strategies available:

- *Frontal attack:* It may launch a full frontal attack, matching the competitor's product, advertising, price, and distribution efforts. It attacks the competitor's strengths rather than its weaknesses. The outcome depends on who has the greater strength and endurance. If the market challenger has fewer resources than the competitor, a frontal attack makes little sense.

- *Indirect attack:* Rather than challenging head-on, the challenger can make an indirect attack on the competitor's weaknesses or on gaps in the competitor's market coverage. For example, budget airlines such as AirAsia and JetStar challenged large carriers by serving the overlooked short-haul, no-frills commuter segment at smaller airports. Such indirect challenges make good sense when the company has fewer resources than the competitor.

Market Follower Strategies

Not all runner-up companies want to challenge the market leader. Challenges are never taken lightly by the leader. If the challenger's lure is lower prices, improved service, or additional product features, the leader can quickly match these to defuse the attack. The leader probably has more staying power in an all-out battle for customers. Thus, many firms prefer to follow rather than challenge the leader.

Similarly, after years of challenging Procter & Gamble unsuccessfully in the U.S. laundry detergent market, Unilever recently decided to throw in the towel and become a follower instead. P&G captures 55 and 75 percent shares of the liquid and powder detergent markets, respectively, versus Unilever's 17 and 7 percent shares. P&G has outmuscled competitors on every front. For example, it batters competitors with a relentless stream of new and improved products. Recently, P&G spent more than $50 million introducing one new product alone, Tide with Downy. In response, Unilever has cut prices and promotion on its detergents to focus on profit rather than market share.[11]

A follower can gain many advantages. The market leader often bears the huge expenses of developing new products and markets, expanding distribution, and educating the market. By contrast, as with challengers, the market follower can learn from the leader's experience. It can copy or improve on the leader's products and programs, usually with much less investment. Although the follower will probably not overtake the leader, it often can be as profitable.

Following is not the same as being passive or a carbon copy of the leader. A market follower must know how to hold current customers and win a fair share of new ones. It must find the right balance between following closely enough to win customers from the market leader but following at enough of a distance to avoid retaliation. Each follower tries to bring distinctive advantages to its target market—location, services, financing. The follower is often a major target of attack by challengers. Therefore, the market follower must keep its manufacturing costs and prices low or its product quality and services high. It must also enter new markets as they open up.

Market Nicher Strategies

Almost every industry includes firms that specialize in serving market niches. Instead of pursuing the whole market, or even large segments, these firms target subsegments. Nichers are often smaller firms with limited resources. But smaller divisions of larger firms also may pursue niching strategies. Firms with low shares of the total market can be highly successful and profitable through smart niching. For example, McDonald's has a major competitor in Jollibee in the Philippines. In terms of global market share, Jollibee is dwarfed by the American giant. But in its niche, the Philippines, where it concentrated its limited resources, Jollibee owns a 75 percent share of the hamburger market by serving the unique tastes of local consumers. Sweet, spicy burgers and seasoned chicken and spaghetti with sweet sauce are offered with rice or noodles, not French fries. Its mascot, the Jolly Bee, epitomizes the Filipino spirit of lighthearted, everyday happiness. And Jollibee staff outsmiles those of McDonalds'.

Niching –
Jollibee is king of the burger market in the Philippines. The Jollibee burger is similar to "what a Filipino mother would cook at home." (_www.jollibee.com.ph_)

Why is niching profitable? The main reason is that the market nicher ends up knowing the target customer group so well that it meets their needs better than other firms that casually sell to that niche. As a result, the nicher can charge a substantial markup over costs because of the added value. Whereas the mass marketer achieves high volume, the nicher achieves high margins.

Nichers try to find one or more market niches that are safe and profitable. An ideal market niche is big enough to be profitable and has growth potential. It is one that the firm can serve effectively. Perhaps most importantly, the niche is of little interest to major competitors. And the firm can build the skills and customer goodwill to defend itself against a major competitor as the niche grows and becomes more attractive. Here's an example of a profitable nicher:

> • Logitech has become a $1.5 billion global success story by focusing on human interface devices—computer mice, game controllers, keyboards, PC video cameras, and others. It makes every variation of computer mouse imaginable. Over the years, Logitech has flooded the world with more than 500 million computer mice of all varieties, mice for left- and right-handed people, wireless mice, travel mice, mini mice, mice shaped like real mice for children, and 3-D mice that let the user appear to move behind screen objects. Breeding mice has been so successful that Logitech dominates the world mouse market, with giant Microsoft as its runner-up. Niching has been very good for Logitech.[12]

MOUSTERPIECE

When does technology become art? It happens when form is optimized and function is perfected. Introducing the world's most advanced mouse—the MX™ Revolution. Its MicroGear™ Precision Scroll Wheel helps you fly through even the longest documents with ease, while the precision of next-generation laser technology gives you unprecedented control. Learn about our family of wireless mice at Logitech.com

Logitech
Designed to move you™

Profitable niching –
Breeding mice has been so successful for Logitech that it dominates the world mouse market, with giant Microsoft as its runner–up. (_www.logitech.com_)

The key idea in niching is specialization. A market nicher can specialize along any of several markets, customer, product, or marketing mix lines. For example, it can specialize in serving one type of _end user_, as when a law firm specializes in the criminal, civil, or business law markets. The nicher can specialize in serving a given _customer-size_ group. Many nichers specialize in serving small and mid-size customers who are neglected by the majors.

Some nichers focus on one or a few _specific customers_, selling their entire output to a single company. Still other nichers specialize by _geographic market_, selling only in a certain locality, region, or area of the world. _Quality-price_ nichers operate at the low or high end of the market. For example, Hewlett-Packard specializes in the high-quality, high-price end of the hand-calculator market. Finally, _service_ nichers offer services not available from other firms.

Niching carries some major risks. For example, the market niche may dry up, or it might grow to the point that it attracts larger competitors. That is why many companies practice _multiple niching_. By developing two or more niches, a company increases its chances for survival. Even some large firms prefer a multiple niche strategy to serving the total market. For example, Alberto Culver has used a multiple niching strategy to grow profitably without incurring the wrath of a market leader. The company, known mainly for its Alberto VO5 hair products, has focused on acquiring a stable of smaller niche brands. It niches in hair, skin, and personal care products (e.g., Alberto VO5, St. Ives, TRESemme, and Consort men's hair products), beauty supplies retailing (Sally Beauty Supply stores), seasonings and sweeteners (Mrs. Dash, Baker's Joy), and home products (static-cling fighter Static Guard). Most of its brands are number one in their niches. Its CEO explains: "We know who we are and, perhaps more importantly, we know who we are not. We know that if we try to out-Procter Procter, we will fall flat on our face."[13]

Balancing Customer and Competitor Orientations

Whether a company is a market leader, challenger, follower, or nicher, it must watch its competitors closely and find the competitive marketing strategy that positions it most effectively. And it must continually adapt its strategies to the fast-changing competitive environment. This question now arises: Can the company spend *too* much time and energy tracking competitors, damaging its customer orientation? The answer is yes! A company can become so competitor centered that it loses its even more important focus on maintaining profitable customer relationships.

A **competitor-centered company** is one that spends most of its time tracking competitors' moves and market shares and trying to find strategies to counter them. This approach has some pluses and minuses. On the positive side, the company develops a fighter orientation, watches for weaknesses in its own position, and searches out competitors' weaknesses. On the negative side, the company becomes too reactive. Rather than carrying out its own customer relationship strategy, it bases its own moves on competitors' moves. As a result, it may end up simply matching or extending industry practices rather than seeking innovative new ways to create more value for customers.

A **customer-centered company**, by contrast, focuses more on customer developments in designing its strategies. Clearly, the customer-centered company is in a better position to identify new opportunities and set long-run strategies that make sense. By watching customer needs evolve, it can decide what customer groups and what emerging needs are the most important to serve. Then it can concentrate its resources on delivering superior value to target customers. In practice, today's companies must be **market-centered companies**, watching both their customers and their competitors. But they must not let competitor watching blind them to customer focusing.

Figure 18.5 shows that companies have moved through four orientations over the years. In the first stage, they were product oriented, paying little attention to either customers or competitors. In the second stage, they became customer oriented and started to pay attention to customers. In the third stage, when they started to pay attention to competitors, they became competitor oriented. Today, companies need to be market oriented, paying balanced attention to both customers and competitors. Rather than merely watching competitors and trying to beat them on current ways of doing business, they need to watch customers and find innovative ways to build profitable customer relationships by delivering more value than competitors do. As noted previously, marketing begins with a good understanding of consumers and the marketplace.

Competitor-centered company
A company whose moves are mainly based on competitors' actions and reactions.

Customer-centered company
A company that focuses on customer developments in designing its marketing strategies and on delivering superior value to its target customers.

Market-centered company
A company that pays balanced attention to both customers and competitors in designing its marketing strategies.

		Customer-centered	
		No	Yes
Competitor-centered	No	Product orientation	Customer orientation
	Yes	Competitor orientation	Market orientation

Figure 18.5
Evolving company orientations

REVIEWING THE CONCEPTS

Today's companies face their toughest competition ever. Understanding customers is an important first step in developing strong customer relationships, but it's not enough. To gain competitive advantage, companies must use this understanding to design market offers that deliver more value than the offers of *competitors* seeking to win over the same customers. This chapter examines how firms analyze their competitors and design effective competitive marketing strategies.

1 **Discuss the need to understand competitors as well as customers through competitor analysis.**

In order to prepare an effective marketing strategy, a company must consider its competitors as well as its customers. Building profitable customer relationships requires satisfying target consumer needs *better than competitors do*. A company must continuously analyze competitors and develop *competitive marketing strategies* that position it effectively against competitors and give it the strongest possible *competitive advantage*.

Competitor analysis first involves identifying the company's major competitors, using both an industry-based and a market-based analysis. The company then gathers information on competitors' objectives, strategies, strengths and weaknesses, and reaction patterns. With this information in hand, it can select competitors to attack or avoid. Competitive intelligence must be collected, interpreted, and distributed continuously. Company marketing managers should be able to obtain full and reliable information about any competitor affecting their decisions.

2 **Explain the fundamentals of competitive marketing strategies based on creating value for customers.**

Which *competitive marketing strategy* makes the most sense depends on the company's industry and on whether it is a market leader, challenger, follower, or nicher. A *market leader* must mount strategies to expand the total market, protect market share, and expand market share. A *market challenger* is a firm that tries aggressively to expand its market share by attacking the leader, other runner-up companies, or smaller firms in the industry. The challenger can select from a variety of direct or indirect attack strategies.

A *market follower* is a runner-up firm that chooses not to rock the boat, usually from fear that it stands to lose more than it might gain. But the follower is not without a strategy and seeks to use its particular skills to gain market growth. Some followers enjoy a higher rate of return than the leaders in their industry. A *market nicher* is a smaller firm that is unlikely to attract the attention of larger firms. Market nichers often become specialists in some end use, customer size, specific customer, geographic area, or service.

3 **Illustrate the need for balancing customer and competitor orientations in becoming a truly market-centered organization.**

A competitive orientation is important in today's markets, but companies should not overdo their focus on competitors. Companies are more likely to be hurt by emerging consumer needs and new competitors than by existing competitors. *Market-centered companies* that balance consumer and competitor considerations are practicing a true market orientation.

REVIEWING THE KEY TERMS

Benchmarking 499
Competitive advantage 496
Competitive marketing strategies 496
Competitor analysis 496
Competitor-centered company 512
Customer-centered company 512
Customer value analysis 500

Market-centered company 512
Market challenger 506
Market follower 506
Market leader 506
Market nicher 506
Strategic group 499

DISCUSSING THE CONCEPTS

1. Think of a discount retailer in your country that is attempting to identify its competitors but wants to avoid competitor myopia. Name some of its potential competitors from both an industry and market point of view.

2. Why is it important to understand competitor's objectives?

3. What is the difference between entrepreneurial, formulated, and intrepreneurial marketing? What are the advantages and disadvantages of each?

4. Apply Treacy and Wiersema's value disciplines to online search engines. Identify a company that competes according to each discipline.

5. What are the advantages and disadvantages of a market-nicher competitive strategy?

6. Why is it important for a company to maintain a balance between customer and competitor orientations?

APPLYING THE CONCEPTS

1. Form a small group and conduct a customer-value analysis for five local restaurants. Who are the strong and weak competitors? For the strong competitors, what are their vulnerabilities?

2. Dell is the leader in the notebook market, with HP threatening its market share. What are some potential market-leader strategies for Dell?

3. Tiffany & Co. is a high-profile firm in the luxury retail jewelry market. Visit _www.tiffany.com/about/Timeline.aspx_ and review the Tiffany historical timeline for important events. What is Tiffany & Co.'s dominant marketing strategy? Explain.

FOCUS ON TECHNOLOGY

In 1923, Arthur Charles Nielsen introduced consumer marketers to many innovative research methods and techniques. Today, ACNielsen provides market intelligence for most of the world's leading manufacturers and retailers. Its sister company, Nielsen Media Research, is the global leader in television audience measurement and provides the well-known television "Nielsen Ratings." Visit ACNielsen at _www.acnielsen.com_ to find its retail measurement services. The retail measurement service provides consolidated register scanner data from most retail channels, including supermarkets, drugstores, mass merchandisers, and warehouse clubs.

In addition to the register data, Nielsen also uses in-store observation to gather data on in-store promotions. Clients can download reports on a daily basis that track sales volume, selling price, observed promotion, and other data points. The information is provided on a company's own brands as well as competitive brands and is easily examined by brand, category, store, or market.

1. How can a marketer use this to analyze its competitors?
2. How might a market leader such as Procter & Gamble react to increased sales of a store's private brand?
3. What might be a disadvantage of using Nielsen data?

FOCUS ON ETHICS

Competitive intelligence offers strong advantages in the area of product development. Knowing the competitor's progress on products, processes, and technology is highly beneficial in competitive markets. A trade secret, information that creates value for a company because it remains a secret, often creates strong competitor curiosity. Companies sometimes go to great lengths to uncover such secrets. They develop creative techniques to access information, sometimes pushing legal and ethical boundaries. One widely used technique is observation. Observational methods include aerial photography of manufacturing plants, dumpster diving to analyze discarded products and materials, and plant tours.

One documented case involves a visit in the 1970s by Steve Jobs and other Apple executives to a Xerox research center. During the tour, Apple executives asked many probing questions about a new technology they observed. After leaving with some proprietary information, Apple subsequently hired some of the Xerox employees to further

develop the technology at Apple. Apple's behavior would not be considered illegal. According to The Uniform Trade Secrets Act (UTSA) of 1985, which attempts to offer some protection for trade secrets, legal protection does not hold if a company did not take reasonable attempts to protect its secrets.

1. Give some examples of the information that might be gleaned from aerial photography of a competitor's plant.
2. Google the Uniform Trade Secrets Act and scan its contents. What else do you observe about this legislation?
3. The Apple incident may not have been illegal, but was it unethical?

See: William Fitzpatrick, "Uncovering Trade Secrets: The Legal and Ethical Conundrum of Creative Competitive Intelligence," _S.A.M. Advanced Management Journal_, Summer 2003, p. 4; and Jim Dalrymple, "Apple Loses Rumor-Site Appeal," _MacWorld_, August 2006, Vol. 23, Issue 8, p. 18.

VIDEO CASE

Nike

Nike's mission statement is "to bring inspiration and innovation to every athlete in the world." That's a substantial goal—one goal made even more sizable when you consider that Nike believes that "if you have a body, you're an athlete." Despite the lofty nature of the mission, Nike has made considerable strides in its effort to fulfill it. The Nike swoosh is so ubiquitous in today's market that it may be difficult to believe the symbol appeared just 35 years ago. Since that time, Nike has become the largest sports and fitness company in the world, and 97 percent of Americans recognize the swoosh.

The Nike brand succeeds by staying true to its core values and delivering consistently high-quality, cutting-edge products that appeal to the athlete in all of us, building strong relationships with customers based on real value. By making innovation the centerpiece of its product development and

marketing strategy, the Nike brand has become the market leader, reaching millions of consumers around the globe and raking in annual revenues totaling $15 billion.

After viewing the video featuring Nike, answer the following questions about creating competitive advantage.

1. In the broadest sense, who are Nike's generic competitors? Who are Nike's direct competitors? What competitive strategy does Nike employ?
2. What market strategies does Nike rely on to maintain its market position? Identify a competitor pursuing a niche in Nike's market. How do the actions of that competitor benefit Nike? How do they challenge Nike's market share and positioning?
3. How does Nike use partnerships with professional athletes and teams to strengthen its relationships with consumers?

🎞 COMPANY CASE

Bose: Competing by Being Truly Different

In April of 2006, Forrester Research announced the results of its semiannual survey ranking consumer electronics and personal computer companies on consumer trust. Based on the opinions of over 4,700 customers regarding 22 of the best-known consumer technology brands, the company drew this conclusion: "Americans' trust in consumer technology companies is eroding."

Despite the decline in trust for most technology companies, Forrester found that consumer trust in the Bose Corporation was high. In fact, Bose far outscored all other companies in Forrester's survey. Forrester pointed out that these results were no fluke, noting that Bose has 10 million regular users but more than 17 million consumers who aspire to use the brand (compared to seven million for next-highest Apple).

These high levels of consumer trust result from philosophies that have guided Bose for more than 40 years. Although Bose pays attention on building revenue, profits, and stock price, they try to outdo the competition by differentiating product lines with features and attributes that other companies do not have. However, its true differentiation derives from the company's unique corporate philosophy.

The Bose Philosophy

Amar Bose, the company's founder and still its CEO, has been in charge from the start. In the 1950s, Bose was working on his third degree at the Massachusetts Institute of Technology. He studied various areas of electrical engineering and had a strong interest in music. When he purchased his first hi-fi system, Bose was very disappointed in the system's ability to reproduce realistic sound. So he set out to find his own solution. Thus began a stream of research that would ultimately lead to the founding of the Bose Corporation in 1964.

From those early days, Amar Bose worked around certain core principles that have guided his company's philosophy. In conducting his first and subsequent research on speakers and sound, he ignored existing technologies and started entirely from scratch. Says Bose president Bob Maresca: "We are not in it strictly to make money. Dr. Bose is extremely eclectic in his research interests. The business is almost a secondary consideration."

Hence, Amar Bose plows all of the privately held company's profits back into research. This practice reflects his belief in producing the highest-quality products. But he also does this because he can. Bose has been quoted many times saying, "if I worked for another company, I would have been fired a long time ago," since publicly held companies have numerous constraints that don't apply to his privately held company. Thus, Bose has vowed that he will never take the company public. "My real interest is research—that's the excitement—and I wouldn't have been able to do long-term projects with Wall Street breathing down my neck."

This commitment to research and development has led to the high level of trust that Bose customers have for the company. It also explains their almost cultlike loyalty. Customers know that Bose cares more about their best interests than about maximizing profits. Yet, for a company not driven by the bottom line, Bose does just fine. Analysts estimate that between 2004 and 2006, the company's revenues increased more than 38 percent, from $1.3 billion to over $1.8 billion. According to market information firm NPD Group, Bose leads the U.S. market in home speakers with a 12.6 percent share. Not only were home speakers the company's original product line, but they also remain one of its largest and most profitable endeavors.

Groundbreaking Products

Bose now has a breadth of product lines beyond its core home audio line. Additional lines target a variety of applications that have captured Amar Bose's creative attention over the years, including military, automotive, homebuilding/remodeling, aviation, test equipment, and professional and commercial sound systems. The following are just a few the products that illustrate the innovative breakthroughs produced by the company.

Speakers

Bose's first product, introduced 1965, was a speaker. Expecting to sell $1 million worth of speakers that first year, Bose made 60 but sold only 40. The original Bose speaker evolved into the 901 Direct/Reflecting speaker system launched in 1968. The speaker was so technologically advanced that the company still sells it today.

The system was designed around the concept that live sound reaches the human ear via direct as well as reflected channels (off walls, ceilings, and other objects). The configuration of the speakers was completely unorthodox. They were shaped like an eighth of a sphere and mounted facing into a room's corner. The speakers had no woofers or tweeters and were tiny compared to the high-end speakers of the day. The design came much closer to the essence and emotional impact of live music than anything else on the market and won immediate industry acclaim.

However, Bose had a hard time convincing customers of the merits of these innovative speakers. At a time when woofers, tweeters, and size were everything, the 901 series initially flopped. In 1968, a retail salesman explained to Amar Bose why the speakers weren't selling:

"I love your speaker but I cannot sell it because … I can't explain to anyone why the 901 doesn't have any woofers or tweeters. A man came in and saw the small size, and he started looking in the drawers for the speaker cabinets … he said, 'Where are you hiding the woofer?' I said to him, 'There is no woofer.' So he said, 'You're a liar,' and he walked out."

Bose eventually worked through the challenges of communicating the virtues of the 901 series to customers through innovative display and demonstration tactics. The product became so successful that Amar Bose now credits the 901 series for building the company.

The list of major speaker innovations at Bose is a long one. In 1975, the company introduced concertlike sound in the bookshelf-size 301 Direct/Reflecting speaker system. In 1984, it developed acoustic waveguide speaker technology, a technology found today in the award-winning Wave radio, Wave music system, and Acoustic Wave music system. In 1986, the company launched the Acoustimass system which enabled palm-size speakers to produce audio quality equivalent to that of high-end systems many times their size. The technological basis of the Acoustimass system is still in use in Bose products today.

Headphones

Bob Maresca recalls that, "Bose invested tens of millions of dollars over 19 years developing headset technology before making a profit. Now, headsets are a major part of the business." Initially, Bose focused on noise reduction technologies to make headphones for pilots that would block out the high level of noise interference from planes. Bose headphones combined both passive and active noise reduction methods. Passive methods involve physically blocking out noise with sound-deadening insulation. Active methods are much more complex, involving circuitry that samples ambient noise and then cancels it out by creating sound waves opposite to the "noise" waves. Bose quickly discovered that airline passengers could benefit as much as pilots from its headphone technology. Today, Bose sells its QuietComfort and Triport headphone lines for use in a variety of consumer applications.

Automotive Suspensions

Another major innovation at Bose has yet to be introduced. The company has been conducting research since 1980 on a product outside of its known areas of expertise: automotive suspensions. Amar Bose's interest in suspensions dates back to the 1950s when he bought both a Citroen DS-19 C and a Pontiac Bonneville, each riding on unconventional air suspension systems. Since that time, he's been obsessed with the engineering challenge of achieving good cornering capabilities without sacrificing a smooth ride. The Bose Corporation is now on the verge of introducing a suspension that it believes will accomplish this feat better than any system to date.

The basics of the system include an electromagnetic motor installed at each wheel. Based on inputs from road-sensing monitors, the motor can retract and extend almost instantaneously. If there is a bump in the road, the suspension reacts by "jumping" over it. If there is a pothole, the suspension allows the wheel to extend downward, but then retracts it quickly enough that the pothole is not felt. In addition to these comfort-producing capabilities, the wheel motors are strong enough to prevent the car from rolling and pitching during an aggressive maneuver.

The suspension system has been designed so that it can be bolted right onto the chassis of current production cars, thus minimizing both time and expense for manufacturers. Initially, the cost of the system will put it in the class of luxury automobiles. Currently, Bose is demonstrating the system only to a handful of companies, with the intention of partnering with one manufacturer before rolling it out to others. Eventually, Bose anticipates that wider adoption and higher volume will bring the price down to the point where the suspension could be found in all but the least expensive cars.

Global Expansion

Bose has also expanded its operations globally. In Asia, it has sales offices in China, Hong Kong, India, Vietnam, South Korea, Singapore, Taiwan, Thailand, Japan, Sri Lanka, Indonesia, and Bangladesh. Among its regional success stories is the design and installation of a sound system for the Shanghai Grand Prix. Bose loudspeakers were placed throughout the concourse and concession areas of the track such that over 150,000 spectators could enjoy the roar of the engines and still hear the announcements and music. Using its Modeler software and Auditioner systems, Bose could predict acoustic performance accurately and make precise decisions on speaker models, cluster positioning, and their aiming angles. "As F1 cars generate over 130dB of noise, sound systems must be powerful enough to compete and sophisticated enough to provide clear speech for the spectators," commented Ma Jun, assistant technical manager of Bose Greater China.

In New Delhi, Honeywell boasts one of the biggest Bose office sound system installations in India, including almost 200 separate loudspeakers. The diversity of business functions located in the building was reflected in the complexity of the sound system requirements. A multi-zone sound system was installed such that each zone could select one of six different channels of music and announcements could be made to one, some, or all zones depending on the message and its target audience. The sound system also functioned as an emergency notification system.

Still Going Strong

At an age when most people have long ago retired, 76-year-old Amar Bose works every day. "He's got more energy than an 18-year-old," says Maresca. "Every one of the naysayers only strengthens his resolve." This work ethic illustrates the passion of the man who has shaped one of today's most innovative and yet most trusted companies. His philosophies have produced Bose's long list of groundbreaking innovations. Even now, as the company prepares to enter the world of automotive suspensions, it continues to achieve success by following another one of Dr. Bose's basic philosophies: "The potential size of the market? We really have no idea. We just know that we have a technology that's so different and so much better that many people will want it."

Questions For Discussion

1. Based on the business philosophies of Amar Bose, how do you think the Bose Corporation goes about analyzing its competition?
2. Which of the text's three approaches to marketing strategy best describes Bose's approach?
3. Using the Michael Porter and Treacy and Wiersema frameworks presented in the text, which basic competitive marketing strategies does Bose pursue?
4. What is Bose's competitive position in its industry? Do its marketing strategies match this position?
5. In your opinion, is Bose a customer-centric company?
6. What do you think will happen when Amar Bose leaves the company?

Sources:

Brian Dumaine, "Amar Bose," *Fortune Small Business*, September 1, 2004, accessed online at www.money.cnn.com/magazines/fsb/; Olga Kharif, "Selling Sound: Bose Knows," *Business Week Online*, May 15, 2006, accessed online at www.businessweek.com; Mark Jewell, "Bose Tries to Shake Up Auto Industry," *Associated Press*, November 27, 2005; "Bose Introduces New QuietComfort 3 Acoustic Noise-Cancelling Headphones," *Business Wire*, June 8, 2006; "Forrester Research Reveals the Most Trusted Consumer Technology Brands," press release accessed online at www.forrester.com; also see "About Bose," accessed online at www.bose.com, June, 2006; "Shanghai Gets the Checkered Flag," and "Acoustic Bridges Across Space," www.bose.com accessed on July 30, 2007.

Objectives

After studying this chapter, you should be able to

- discuss how the international trade system and the economic, political-legal, and cultural environments affect a company's international marketing decisions
- describe three key approaches to entering international markets
- explain how companies adapt their marketing mixes for international markets
- identify the three major forms of international marketing organization

CHAPTER 19

THE GLOBAL MARKETPLACE

Previewing the Concepts

You've now learned the fundamentals of how companies develop competitive marketing strategies to create customer value and to build up long and lasting customer relationships. In this chapter, we extend these fundamentals to global marketing. We've visited global topics in each previous chapter—it's difficult to find an area of marketing that doesn't contain at least some international issues. Here, however, we'll focus on special considerations that companies face when they market their brands globally. Advances in communication, transportation, and other technologies have made the world a much smaller place. Today, almost every firm, large or small, faces international marketing issues. In this chapter, we will examine six major decisions marketers make in going global.

We will look at one of the world leaders in convenient foods and beverages PepsiCo's international marketing strategies with the focus in Asia Pacific markets, especially in China and Hong Kong. *Fortune* 500's 2006 Global 500 World's Largest Corporations analysis reported that PepsiCo's revenue reached over $35 billion with profits over $5.6 billion (38.4 percent increase from 2005) and 168,000 employees, while its major rival Coca-Cola's revenue reached $24 billion with profits over $5 billion (4.3 percent increase from 2005) and 71,000 employees[1]. Coca-Cola Enterprises ranked 354 and with $1.1 billion lost in profits.

Have you heard of the term **Cola Wars?** In the 1980s, Pepsi ran a series of advertisements that involved getting soft drink consumers to choose a better tasting "Coke"—Pepsi, not Coca-Cola. Pepsi ran the "blind taste tests" campaigns (getting consumers to choose the better tasting Coke from two unknown glasses of coke). They used a hidden camera to capture consumers' excited responses when the "Coke" they chose tasted bet0ter than the other one. In the campaign, more consumers chose Pepsi.

In the mid-1930s, Pepsi-Cola began selling its products outside the U.S. and Canada. Pepsi-Cola started its overseas business in the United Kingdom in 1936. Beginning in the 1950s, operations grew rapidly. PepsiCo was founded in 1965 through the merger of Pepsi-Cola and Frito-Lay. Tropicana was acquired in 1998 and PepsiCo merged with The Quaker Oats Company, including Gatorade, in 2001. Today, PepsiCo beverages are available in more than 200 countries and territories. Brands include Aquafina, Gatorade, and Tropicana. In addition to brands marketed in the U.S., PepsiCo International brands include Mirinda, 7UP, and many local brands.

One of the key factors behind why Pepsi entered the global marketplace was the support of top management. Ex-CEO Steve Reinemund fervently believed in what he refered to as the Six Ps: (1) Principles, his belief that leaders need a moral compass consistent with the goals of the organization; (2) Perspective, a vision that grows from a broader view of the world; (3) Passion, a commitment to what you do; (4) Perseverance, the ability to stick with it even when things are bad; (5)Performance, getting results and choosing others who do; (6) People, finding and keeping people who bring improvements to the organization.[2] These values became part of the company's vision. We will discuss the key approaches to entering international markets later in this chapter.

PepsiCo's business strategy involves building a long-term relationship between Pepsi and the consumer in the international marketplace. Before 2007, Pepsi focused a majority of its marketing efforts on attracting young people in growing markets such as China, India, and Eastern Europe. A large number of regional promotions were developed, while its rival Coca-Cola had found a successful formula to universally appealing advertising. Both PepsiCo and Coca-Cola are superb marketing companies. Their competition has caused the industry to grow worldwide. It is likely that continued growth will come more from increased total consumption rather than from stealing market share from each other, especially in China.

In January 2007, Mr. Harry Hui joined the PepsiCo International China Beverages business as Chief Marketing

Officer (CMO), bringing his broad creative and business capabilities to manage PepsiCo International's marketing and innovation agenda across the full portfolio of its beverage brands in China. The brands under his management include Pepsi-Cola (China's number one soft drink), Gatorade, Tropicana, Dole, 7UP, Mirinda, as well as other locally developed brands.

In a speech presented by Hui at the 2007 ad:tech conference in Beijing, he highlighted that there are now 200 million Chinese born after 1980, and by 2015 there will be 300 million[3]. As such, China is a huge market for the convenience foods and beverages business. However, China's media is increasingly fragmented: "There were at least 250 new media companies using many different tactics to promote Pepsi's products," according to Hui. For example, they are using outdoor signs, elevator televisions, lobby ad techniques, and even spaces behind the toilet bowl. Hui also commented that young Chinese consumers are the most experimental and the least brand-loyal. They are always willing to try something new because they are attracted by ads everywhere. China's young consumers are unique and many marketing campaigns that succeed in other regions do not resonate with them.

In 2007, PepsiCo's overall global strategy moved from being brand-centric to consumer-centric; projective to engaging; static to customized experiences; episodic contact to one where each message is a link to the next; and lastly, from unilateral to multilateral communication through virtual communities and community enabling. In China, PepsiCo concentrates on the use of music, sports, and interactive media to create emotion when communicating with consumers.

Create an Ad (Customer Centric and Interactive) In 2006, Pepsi ran a competition to get consumers to create a complete Pepsi commercial, called "Show Me Your Idea." The competition invited consumers to write a 200-word script featuring Taiwanese pop singer Jay Chou as the main character and to upload the scripts to Pepsi's Web site. Consumers sent their opinions and comments about the scripts and they also voted for the winner. A 28-year-old teacher from Zhejiang wrote the winning advertisement called "The Origin of Trading," which became the first Pepsi commercial to adopt creative ideas from consumers, and he won a prize of $125,000. The winner's ad was broadcast on national TV. During this campaign, PepsiCo received 28,000 scripts, and over five million people voted on the Web site.

Appearing on a Can (Static to Customized Experiences) Pepsi has turned their product cans and bottles into a national media platform by placing the picture of the contestant with the highest number of votes on the Pepsi can. Hui said, "We wanted to create YouTube on a can." Pepsi received three million photos, 7.5 million bulletin board messages, and 7.5 million votes. Pepsi has put 20 winners on their cans and bottles.

Global Marketing

McDonald's and many other American companies have made the world their market.

Today, the world is shrinking rapidly with the advent of faster communication, transportation, and financial flows. Products developed in one country—Gucci purses, Mont Blanc, McDonald's hamburgers, Japanese sushi, German BMWs, and Samsung mobile phones—are finding enthusiastic acceptance in other countries. We would not be surprised to hear about a German businessman wearing an Italian suit meeting an English friend at a Japanese restaurant who later returns home to drink Russian vodka and watch NBA on TV.

International trade is booming. Since 1969, the number of multinational corporations in the world has grown from 7,000 to more than 70,000. Some of these multinationals are true giants. In fact, of the largest 100 "economies" in the world, only 53 are countries. The remaining 47 are multinational corporations.

Since 2003, total world trade has been growing at 6 to 10 percent annually, while global gross domestic product has grown at only 2.5 to 4 percent annually. World trade of products and services was valued at over 12.4 trillion dollars in 2005, which accounted for about 28 percent of gross domestic product worldwide. This trade growth is most visible in developing countries, such as China, which saw their share in world exports rise sharply to 24 percent in 2005.[4] Many U.S. companies have long been successful at international marketing: Coca-Cola, McDonald's, Colgate, General Electric, Caterpillar, Boeing, and Motorola, and dozens of other American firms have made the world their market. And in Asia, names such as Sony, Toyota, Nestlé, Nokia, Mercedes, Panasonic, and Prudential have become household words. Other products and services that appear to be American or Japanese are in fact produced or owned by foreign companies such as Thailand, Singapore, and China.

But today global competition is intensifying. Foreign firms are expanding aggressively into new international markets, and home markets are no longer as rich in opportunity. Few industries are now safe from foreign competition. If companies delay taking steps toward internationalizing, they risk being shut out of growing markets in Western and Eastern Europe, China and the Pacific Rim, Russia, and elsewhere. Firms that stay at home to play it safe not only might lose their chances to enter other markets but also risk losing their home markets. Domestic companies that never thought about foreign competitors suddenly find these competitors in their own backyards.

Ironically, although the need for companies to go abroad is greater today than in the past, so are the risks. Companies that go global may face highly unstable governments and currencies, restrictive government policies and regulations, and high trade barriers. Corruption is also an increasing problem—officials in several countries often award business not to the best bidder but to the highest briber.

A **global firm** is one that, by operating in more than one country, gains marketing, production, R&D, and financial advantages that are not available to purely domestic competitors. The global company sees the world as one market. It minimizes the importance of national boundaries and develops "transnational" brands. It raises capital, obtains materials and components, and manufactures and markets its goods wherever it can do the best job. For example, Otis Elevator gets its elevators' door systems from France, small geared parts from Spain, electronics from Germany, and special motor drives from Japan. It uses the U.S. only for systems integration. The global firm takes the advantages of the sources to make their products / services within their cost budget, meet the local quality standards requirement and competitiveness in global markets.

This does not mean that small and medium-size firms must operate in a dozen countries to succeed. These firms can practice global niching. But the world is becoming smaller, and every company operating in a global industry—whether large or small—must assess and establish its place in world markets. The rapid move toward globalization means that all companies will have to answer some basic questions: What market position should we try to establish in our country, in our economic region, and globally? Who will our global competitors be, and what are their strategies and resources? Where should we produce or source our products? What strategic alliances should we form with other firms around the world?

As shown in **Figure 19.1**, a company faces six major decisions in international marketing. We will discuss each decision in detail in this chapter.

> **Global firm**
> A firm that, by operating in more than one country, gains R&D, production, marketing, and financial advantages in its costs and reputation that are not available to purely domestic competitors.

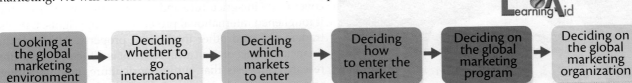

Figure 19.1
Major international marketing decisions

Looking at the Global Marketing Environment

Before deciding whether to operate internationally, a company must understand the international marketing environment. That environment has changed a great deal in the past two decades, creating both new opportunities and new problems.

The International Trade System

Companies looking abroad must start by understanding the international *trade system*. When selling to another country, a firm may face restrictions on trade between nations. Foreign governments may charge *tariffs*, taxes on certain imported products designed to raise revenue or to protect domestic firms. Or they may set *quotas*, limits on the amount of foreign imports that they will accept in certain product categories. The purpose of a quota is to conserve on foreign exchange and to protect local industry and employment. Firms may also face *exchange controls,* which limit the amount of foreign exchange and the exchange rate against other currencies. The company also may face *nontariff trade barriers,* such as biases against U.S. company bids or restrictive product standards that go against American product features:

> For years, Japan has successfully devised nontariff trade barriers to shut foreign products out of its domestic markets. One of the cleverest ways the Japanese have found to keep foreign manufacturers out is to plead "uniqueness." Japanese skin is different, the government argues, so foreign cosmetics companies must test their products in Japan before selling there. The Japanese say their stomachs are small and have room for only the *mikan,* the local tangerine, so imports of U.S. oranges are limited. Now the Japanese have come up with what may be the flakiest argument yet: Their snow is different, so ski equipment should be too.[5]

At the same time, certain forces *help* trade between nations. Examples include the General Agreement on Tariffs and Trade (GATT) and various regional free trade agreements.

The World Trade Organization and GATT

The General Agreement on Tariffs and Trade (GATT) is a 59-year-old treaty designed to promote world trade by reducing tariffs and other international trade barriers. Since the treaty's inception in 1947, member nations (currently numbering 149) have met in eight rounds of GATT negotiations to reassess trade barriers and set new rules for international trade. The first seven rounds of negotiations reduced the average worldwide tariffs on manufactured goods from 45 percent to just 5 percent.[6]

The most recently completed GATT negotiations, dubbed the Uruguay Round, dragged on for seven long years before concluding in 1993. The benefits of the Uruguay Round will be felt for many years as the accord promotes long-term global trade growth. It reduced the world's remaining merchandise tariffs by 30 percent. The agreement also extended GATT to cover trade in agriculture and a wide range of services, and it toughened international protection of copyrights, patents, trademarks, and other intellectual property. Although the financial impact of such an agreement is difficult to measure, research suggests that cutting agriculture, manufacturing, and services trade barriers by one-third would boost the world economy by $613 billion, the equivalent of adding another Australia to the world economy.[7]

Beyond reducing trade barriers and setting global standards for trade, the Uruguay Round set up the World Trade Organization (WTO) to enforce GATT rules. In general, the WTO acts as an umbrella organization, overseeing GATT, mediating global disputes, and imposing trade sanctions. The previous GATT organization never possessed such authorities. A new round of GATT negotiations, the Doha Round, began in Doha, Qatar, in late 2001 and was set to conclude in 2005, but the discussions continue.[8]

The WTO and GATT – The General Agreement on Tariffs and Trade (GATT) promotes world trade by reducing tariffs in other international trade barriers. The WTO oversees GATT, imposes trade sanctions, and mediates global disputes.

Regional Free Trade Zones

Certain countries have formed free trade *zones* or **economic communities**. These are groups of nations organized to work toward common goals in the regulation of international trade. One such community is the *European Union* (EU). Formed in 1957, the European Union set out to create a single European market by reducing barriers to the free flow of products, services, finances, and labor among member countries and developing policies on trade with nonmember nations. Today, the European Union represents one of the world's single largest markets. By 2007, it has 27 member countries containing close to half a billion consumers and accounting for more than 30 percent of the world's exports.[9]

European unification offers tremendous trade opportunities for U.S. and other non-European firms. However, it also poses threats. As a result of increased unification, European companies have grown bigger and more competitive. Perhaps an even greater concern, however, is that lower barriers *inside* Europe will create only thicker *outside* walls. Some observers envision a "Fortress Europe" that heaps favors on firms from EU countries but hinders outsiders by imposing obstacles.

Progress toward European unification has been slow—many doubt that complete unification will ever be achieved. In recent years, 12 member nations have taken a significant step toward unification by adopting the euro as a common currency. Many other countries are expected to follow within the next few years. Widespread adoption of the euro will decrease much of the currency risk associated with doing business in Europe, making member countries with previously weak currencies more attractive markets.[10]

However, even with the adoption of the euro, it is unlikely that the EU will ever go against 2,000 years of tradition and become the "United States of Europe." A community with two dozen different languages and cultures will always have difficulty coming together and acting as a single entity. For example, efforts to forge a single European constitution appear to have failed following French and Dutch "no" votes in mid-2005. And economic disputes between member nations have stalled long-term budget negotiations. Still, although only partly successful so far, unification has made Europe a global force with which to reckon, with a combined annual GDP of more than $12.1 trillion.[11]

In 1994, the *North American Free Trade Agreement (NAFTA)* established a free trade zone among the U.S., Mexico, and Canada. The agreement created a single market of 435 million people who produce and consume over $14.4 trillion worth of goods and services annually. As it is implemented over a 15-year period, NAFTA will eliminate all trade barriers and investment restrictions among the three countries. Thus far, the agreement has allowed trade between the countries to flourish. In the dozen years following its establishment, trade among the NAFTA nations has risen 173 percent. U.S. merchandise exports to NAFTA partners grew 133 percent, compared with exports to the rest of the world at 77 percent. Canada and Mexico are now the nation's first and second largest trading partners.[12]

Following the apparent success of NAFTA, in 2005 the Central American Free Trade Agreement (CAFTA) established a free trade zone between the U.S. and Costa Rica, the Dominican Republic, El Salvador, Guatemala, Honduras, and Nicaragua. And talks have been underway since 1994 to investigate establishing a Free Trade Area of the Americas (FTAA). This mammoth free trade zone would include 34 countries stretching from the Bering Strait to Cape Horn, with a population of 800 million and a combined gross domestic product of about $17 trillion.[13]

Other free trade areas have formed in Latin America and South America. For example,

Economic community
A group of nations organized to work toward common goals in the regulation of international trade.

Economic communities –
The European Union represents one of the world's single largest markets. Its current member countries contain more than half a billion consumers and account for 20 percent of the world's exports.

MERCOSUR links 10 Latin America and South America countries, and the Andean Community (CAN, for its Spanish initials) links five more. In late 2004, MERCOSUR and CAN agreed to unite, creating the South American Community of Nations (CSN), which will be modeled after the European Union. Complete integration between the two trade blocs is expected by 2007 and all tariffs between the nations are to be eliminated by 2019. With a population of more than 370 million, a combined economy of more than $2.8 trillion a year, and exports worth $181 billion, the CSN will make up the largest trading bloc after NAFTA and the European Union.[14]

Although the recent trend toward free trade zones has caused great excitement and new market opportunities, some see it as a mixed blessing. For example, in the U.S., unions fear that NAFTA will lead to an exodus of manufacturing jobs to Mexico, where wage rates are much lower. Environmentalists worry that companies that are unwilling to play by the strict rules of the U.S. Environmental Protection Agency will relocate in Mexico, where pollution regulation has been lax.[15]

Asian unification has been even slower. The Association of Southeast Asian Nations, known as ASEAN was established on August 8, 1967 originally by five original member countries: Indonesia, Malaysia, the Philippines, Singapore, and Thailand. ASEAN has been expanding in terms of its membership. Brunei Darussalam, Vietnam, and Cambodia joined the Association in 1984, 1995, and 1999 respectively while both Lao PDR and Myanmar became members in 1997. As of 2006, with a population of about 560 million, and a total area of 4.5 million square kilometers, the ASEAN region enjoys a combined gross domestic product of almost $ 1,100 billion, and a total trade of about $ 1,400 billion.[16]

ASEAN is a geo-political and economic organization of 10 countries in Southeast Asia. It aims to accelerate economic growth, social progress and cultural development, and to promote regional peace and stability in the region.

ASEAN has two key objectives: to accelerate economic growth, social progress and cultural development, and to promote regional peace and stability in the region. In order to achieve these two objectives, ASEAN has adopted a number of fundamental principles which emphasize very much non-interference, collaboration, cooperation, and mutual respect for rights, independence, equality, and national identity of all nations.

Each nation has unique features that must be understood. A nation's readiness for different products and services and its attractiveness as a market to foreign firms depend on its economic, political-legal, and cultural environments.

Economic Environment

The international marketer must study each country's economy. Two economic factors reflect the country's attractiveness as a market: the country's industrial structure and its income distribution. The country's industrial structure shapes its product and service needs, income levels, and employment levels. The four types of industrial structures are as follows:

- *Subsistence economies*: In a subsistence economy, the vast majority of people engage in simple agriculture. They consume most of their output and barter the rest for simple goods and services. They offer few market opportunities.
- *Raw material exporting economies*: These economies are rich in one or more natural resources but poor in other ways. Much of their revenue comes from exporting these resources. Examples are Chile (tin and copper), Democratic Republic of Congo (copper, cobalt, and coffee), and Saudi Arabia (oil). These countries are good markets for large equipment, tools and supplies, and trucks. If there are many foreign residents and a wealthy upper class, they are also a market for luxury goods.
- *Industrializing economies*: In an industrializing economy, manufacturing accounts for 10 to 20 percent of the country's economy. Examples include Egypt, India, and Russia. As manufacturing increases, the country needs more imports of raw textile materials, steel, and heavy machinery, and fewer imports of finished textiles, paper products, and automobiles. Industrialization typically creates a new rich upper class and a small but growing middle class, both demanding new types of imported goods.
- Industrial economies: Industrial economies are major exporters of manufactured

goods, services, and investment funds. They trade goods among themselves and also export them to other types of economies for raw materials and semi-finished goods. The varied manufacturing activities of these industrial nations and their large middle class make them rich markets for all sorts of goods.

The second economic factor is the country's income distribution. Industrialized nations may have low-, medium-, and high-income households. For example, there exists very low-income households in the U.S. In contrast, countries with subsistence economies may consist mostly of households with very low family incomes. Still other countries may have households with only either very low or very high incomes. However, even poor or developing economies may be attractive markets for all kinds of goods, including luxuries. For example, many luxury brand marketers are rushing to take advantage of China's rapidly developing consumer markets.[17] However, more than half of China's 1.3 billion consumers can barely afford rice, let alone luxuries. According to The World Bank, more than 400 million Chinese live on less than $2 a day.

Thus, country and regional economic environments will affect an international marketer's decisions about which global markets to enter and how.

Economic environment –
Many luxury brand marketers are rushing to take advantage of China's rapidly developing consumer markets.

Political-Legal Environment

Nations differ greatly in their political-legal environments. In considering whether to do business in a given country, a company should consider factors such as the country's attitudes toward international buying, government bureaucracy, political stability, and monetary regulations.

Some nations are very receptive to foreign firms; others are less accommodating. For example, India has tended to bother foreign businesses with import quotas, currency restrictions, and other limitations that make operating there a challenge. In contrast, neighboring Asian countries such as Singapore and Thailand court foreign investors and shower them with incentives and favorable operating conditions. Political stability is another issue. For example, governments of India and Thailand are notoriously unstable. India has elected 10 new governments and Thailand's government was occasionally overthrown in military coups over the past 20 years—increasing the risk of doing business there. Although most international marketers still find India's huge market attractive, the unstable political situation will affect how they handle business and financial matters.[18] Thailand, though in a better situation, is also considered unstable politically.

Companies must also consider a country's monetary regulations. Sellers want to take their profits in a currency of value to them. Ideally, the buyer can pay in the seller's currency or in other world currencies. Short of this, sellers might accept a blocked currency—one whose removal from the country is restricted by the buyer's government—if they can buy other goods in that country that they need themselves or can sell elsewhere for a needed currency. Besides currency limits, a changing exchange rate also creates high risks for the seller. Most international trade involves cash transactions. Yet many nations have too little hard currency to pay for their purchases from other countries. They may want to pay with other items instead of cash, which has led to a growing practice called **countertrade**.

Countertrade takes several forms: Barter involves the direct exchange of goods or services, as when Azerbaijan imported wheat from Romania in exchange for crude oil, and Vietnam exchanged rice for the Philippines' fertilizer and coconuts. Another form is compensation (or buyback), whereby the seller sells a plant, equipment, or technology

Countertrade can take place as barter, where goods or services are exchanged directly. For example, Vietnam exchanged rice for fertilizer and coconuts from the Philippines.

Countertrade
International trade involving the direct or indirect exchange of goods for other goods instead of cash.

to another country and agrees to take payment in the resulting products. Thus, Japan's Fukusuke Corporation sold knitting machines and raw textile materials to Shanghai's clothing manufacturer Chinatex in exchange for finished textiles produced on the machines. The most common form of countertrade is counter purchase, in which the seller receives full payment in cash but agrees to spend some of the money in the other country. For example, Boeing sells aircraft to India and agrees to buy Indian coffee, rice, castor oil, and other goods and sell them elsewhere.[19] Countertrade deals can be very complex. For example, in 1972 Pepsi obtained Western marketing rights to Stolichnaya vodka in the U.S. in exchange for Pepsi to be sold in Russia.[20]

Cultural Environment

Each country has its own folkways, norms, and taboos. When designing global marketing strategies, companies must understand how culture affects consumer reactions in each of its world markets. In turn, they must also understand how their strategies affect local cultures.

The Impact of Culture on Marketing Strategy

The seller must examine the ways consumers in different countries think about and use certain products before planning a marketing program. There are often surprises. For example, the average French man uses almost twice as many cosmetics and grooming aids as his wife. The Germans and the French eat more packaged, branded spaghetti than do Italians. Italian children like to eat chocolate bars between slices of bread as a snack.

Overlooking cultural difference can result in embarrassing mistakes. China imposed a nationwide ban on this "blasphemous" kung-fu-themed ad campaign featuring LeBron James crushing a number of culturally revered Chinese figures.

Women in Tanzania will not give their children eggs for fear of making them bald or impotent. The Chinese believe that drinking "hot Chinese tea" is better for health than "cold soft drinks". Companies that ignore cultural norms and differences can make some very expensive and embarrassing mistakes. Here are some examples:

- McDonald's and Coca-Cola managed to offend the entire Muslim world by putting the Saudi Arabian flag on their packaging. The flag's design includes a passage from the Koran (the sacred text of Islam), and Muslims feel very strongly that their Holy Writ should never be wadded up and tossed in the trash. Nike faced a similar situation in Arab countries when Muslims objected to a stylized "Air" logo on its shoes, which resembled "Allah" in Arabic script. Nike apologized for that as well and pulled the shoes from distribution.

Business norms and behavior also vary from country to country. Here are same examples:

- American executives like to get right down to business and engage in fast and tough face-to-face bargaining. However, Japanese and other Asian businesspeople often find this behavior offensive. They prefer to start with polite conversation, and they rarely say no in face-to-face conversations.
- Asians tend to sit or stand very close to one another when they queue or talk business—in fact, almost nose-to-nose. The Asian business executive tends to move closer as the American and Australian keep backing away. Both may end up being offended. Asian business executives need to be briefed on these kinds of factors before conducting business in another country.[21]
- Chinese businessmen like to hold a welcome banquet, especially for major overseas visitors, prior to a business meeting discussion. They believe it creates a "good" atmosphere for the discussion in the following meeting.

By the same token, companies that understand cultural nuances can use them to their advantage when positioning products internationally. Consider the following example:

> A television ad in India shows a mother lapsing into a daydream: Her young daughter is in a beauty contest dressed as Snow White, dancing on a stage. Her flowing gown is an immaculate white. The garments of the other contestants, who dance in the background, are a tad gray. Snow White, no surprise, wins the blue ribbon. The mother awakes to the laughter of her adoring family—and glances proudly at her Whirlpool White Magic washing machine. The TV spot is the product of 14 months of research by Whirlpool into the psyche of the Indian consumer. Among other things, [Whirlpool] learned that Indian homemakers prize hygiene and purity, which they associate with white. The trouble is, white garments often get discolored after frequent machine washing in local water. Besides appealing to this love of purity in its ads, Whirlpool custom-designed machines that are especially good with white fabrics. Whirlpool now is the leading brand in India's fast-growing market for fully automatic washing machines.[22]

Thus, understanding cultural traditions, preferences, and behaviors can help companies not only to avoid embarrassing mistakes but also to take advantage of cross-cultural opportunities.

The Impact of Marketing Strategy on Cultures

Whereas marketers worry about the impact of culture on their global marketing strategies, others may worry about the impact of marketing strategies on global cultures.

That is, exposing to American values and products erodes other cultures and as a result, countries around the globe are losing their individual cultural identities. They pointed out that teens in India watch MTV and ask their parents for more westernized clothes and other symbols of American pop culture and values. In China, most people never drank coffee before Starbucks entered the market. Now Chinese consumers rush to Starbucks stores "because it's a symbol of a new kind of lifestyle." Similarly, in China, where McDonald's operates 80 restaurants in Beijing alone, nearly half of all children identify the chain as a domestic brand.

Such concerns have sometimes led to a backlash against American globalization. Well-known U.S. brands have become the targets of boycotts and protests in some international markets. Companies such as McDonald's, which are symbols of American capitalism, has been singled out by antiglobalization protestors in hot spots all around the world, especially when anti-American sentiment peaks. McDonald's stores in Pakistan, India, and many other countries around the world were attacked right after U.S. armed forces invaded Afghanistan following the September 11 attacks.

Despite such problems, defenders of globalization argue that concerns of "Americanization" and the potential damage to American brands are overblown. U.S. brands are doing very well internationally. Recently, based on a study of 3,300 consumers in 41 countries, researchers concluded that consumers did not appear to translate anti-American sentiment into anti-brand sentiment.[23] However, a study in Hong Kong indicates otherwise—that the trend of translating into anti-brand sentiment is on the rise (reference). Consumers have become more aware if the global brands they bought were American. A French panelist called American brands "imperialistic threats that undermine French culture." A German told that Americans "want to impose their way on everybody."

Americanization – Social critics contend that large American multinationals aren't just "globalizing" their brands, they are "Americanizing" the world's cultures. In China, most people never drank coffee before Starbucks entered the market.

The consistent success of Ocean Park may be due to its adoption of a blend of both Chinese and Western cultures. Disneyland Hong Kong has had trouble competing with its more established local rival, and visitor attendance fell by 20 percent in the park's second year.

Defenders against American globalization also hold the view that globalization results in both-way cultural exchange—America gets as well as gives cultural influence.[24] However, they forget the fact that, as an economic superpower, the American culture has been the all-the-time winner in the cultural exchange process.

Therefore, the basic principle for companies to succeed abroad is to adapt to local cultural values and traditions rather than trying to force their own. Disneyland Paris flopped at first because it failed to take local cultural values and behaviors into account. According to a Euro Disney executive, "When we first launched, there was the belief that it was enough to be Disney. Now we realize that our guests need to be welcomed on the basis of their own culture and travel habits."[25] That realization has made Disneyland Paris the number one tourist attraction in Europe—even more popular than the Eiffel Tower. The newest attraction there is The Walt Disney Studios Park, a movie-themed park that blends Disney entertainment and attractions with the history and culture of European film. A show celebrating the history of animation features Disney characters speaking six different languages. Rides are narrated by foreign-born stars speaking in their native tongues.

Having said that, its Chinese counterpart Disneyland Hong Kong has not been as lucky. It failed to compete with its more established local rival, Ocean Park. Recently, the Themed Entertainment Association and Economic Research Associates published a report on the top 25 most popular theme parks in the world using the number of visitors as a performance index. Ocean Park was ranked 16th and Disneyland Hong Kong 21st. The success of Ocean Park may be due to its adoption of a blend of both the Chinese and Western cultures. As a result, Ocean Park has been able to attract more visitors than Disneyland Hong Kong, which only organizes special celebrations for local seasonal events on top of its original entertainment programs.[26]

Deciding Whether to Go Global

Not all companies need to venture into international markets to survive. For example, most local businesses need to market well only in the local marketplace. Operating domestically is easier and safer. Managers don't need to learn another country's language and laws. They don't need to deal with unstable currencies, face political and legal uncertainties, or redesign their products to suit different customer expectations. However, companies that operate in global industries, where their strategic positions in specific markets are affected strongly by their overall global positions, must compete on a regional or worldwide basis to succeed.

Any of several factors might draw a company into the international arena. Global competitors might attack the company's home market by offering better products or lower prices. The company might want to counterattack these competitors in their home markets to tie up their resources. Or the company's home market might be stagnant or shrinking, and foreign markets may present higher sales and profit opportunities. Or the company's customers might be expanding abroad and require international servicing. Before going abroad, the company must weigh several risks and answer many questions about its ability to operate globally. Can the company learn to understand the preferences and buyer behavior of consumers in other countries? Can it offer competitively attractive products? Will it be able to adapt to other countries' business cultures and deal effectively with foreign nationals? Do the company's managers have the necessary international experience? Has management considered the impact of regulations and the political environments of other countries?

Because of the difficulties of entering international markets, most companies do not act until some situation or event thrusts them into the global arena. Someone—a domestic exporter, a foreign importer, a foreign government—may ask the company to sell abroad. Or the company may be saddled with overcapacity and need to find additional markets for its goods.

Deciding Which Markets to Enter

Before going abroad, the company should try to define its international *marketing objectives and policies*. It should decide what volume of foreign sales it wants. Most companies start small when they go abroad. Some plan to stay small, seeing international sales as a small part of their business. Other companies have bigger plans, seeing international business as equal to or even more important than their domestic business.

The company also needs to choose in how many countries it wants to market. Companies must be careful not to spread themselves too thin or to expand beyond their capabilities by operating in too many countries too soon. Next, the company needs to decide on the types of countries to enter. A country's attractiveness depends on the product, geographical factors, income and population, political climate, and other factors. The seller may prefer certain country groups or parts of the world. In recent years, many major new markets have emerged, offering both substantial opportunities and daunting challenges.

Colgate's decision to enter the huge Chinese market seems fairly straightforward. Using aggressive promotional and education programs, Colgate has expanded its market share from 7 percent in 1995 to more than 35 percent today.

After listing possible international markets, the company must carefully evaluate each one. It must consider many factors. For example, Colgate's decision to enter the Chinese market seems fairly straightforward: China's huge population makes it the world's largest toothpaste market. And given that only 20 percent of China's rural dwellers now brush daily, this already huge market can grow even larger. Yet Colgate must still question whether market size alone is reason enough for investing heavily in China.

Colgate should ask some important questions: Will it be able to overcome cultural barriers and convince Chinese consumers to brush their teeth regularly? Does China provide for the needed production and distribution technologies? Can Colgate compete effectively with dozens of local competitors, a state-owned brand managed by Unilever, and P&G's Crest? Will the Chinese government remain stable and supportive? Colgate's current success in China suggests that it could answer yes to all of these questions. By expanding its product line and aggressively pursuing promotional and educational programs—from massive ad campaigns to visits to local schools to sponsoring oral care research—Colgate has expanded its market share from 7 percent in 1995 to more than 35 percent today.[27]

Possible global markets should be ranked on several factors, including market size, market growth, cost of doing business, competitive advantage, and risk level. The goal is to determine the potential of each market, using indicators such as those shown in **Table 19.1.** Then the marketer must decide which markets offer the greatest long-run return on investment.

Deciding How to Enter the Market

Once a company has decided to sell in a foreign country, it must determine the best mode of entry. Its choices are exporting, joint venturing, and direct investment. **Figure 19.2** shows three market entry strategies, along with the options each one offers. As the figure shows, each succeeding strategy involves more commitment and risk, but also more control and potential profits.

Table 19.1 Indicators of Market Potential

Demographic characteristics	*Sociocultural factors*
Education	Consumer lifestyles, beliefs, and values
Population size and growth	Business norms and approaches
Population age composition	Cultural and social norms
	Languages

Geographic characteristics	*Political and legal factors*
Climate	National priorities
Country size	Political stability
Population density—urban, rural	Government attitudes toward global trade
Transportation structure and market	Government bureaucracy
Accessibility	Monetary and trade regulations

Economic factors
GDP size and growth
Income distribution
Industrial infrastructure
Natural resources
Financial and human resources

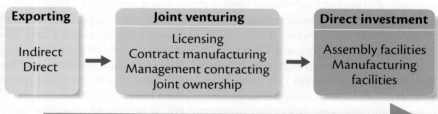

Figure 19.2
Market entry strategies

Exporting
Entering a foreign market by selling goods produced in the company's home country, often with little modification.

Exporting

The simplest way to enter a foreign market is through exporting. The company may passively export its surpluses from time to time, or it may make an active commitment to expand exports to a particular market. In either case, the company produces all its goods in its home country. It may or may not modify them for the export market. Exporting involves the least change in the company's product lines, organization, investments, or mission.

Companies typically start with indirect exporting, working through independent international marketing intermediaries. Indirect exporting involves less investment because the firm does not require an overseas marketing organization or network. It also involves less risk. International marketing intermediaries bring know-how and services to the relationship, so the seller normally makes fewer mistakes.

Sellers may eventually move into direct exporting, whereby they handle their own exports. The investment and risk are somewhat greater in this strategy, but so is the potential return. A company can conduct direct exporting in several ways: It can set up a domestic export department that carries out export activities. It can set up an overseas sales branch that handles sales, distribution, and perhaps promotion. The sales branch gives the seller more presence and program control in the foreign market and often serves as a display center and customer service center. The company can also send home-based salespeople abroad at certain times in order to find business. Finally, the company can do its exporting either through foreign-based distributors who buy and own the goods or through foreign-based agents who sell the goods on behalf of the company.

Joint Venturing

A second method of entering a foreign market is **joint venturing**—joining with foreign companies to produce or market products or services. Joint venturing differs from exporting in that the company joins with a host country partner to sell or market abroad. It differs from direct investment in that an association is formed with someone in the foreign country. There are four types of joint ventures: licensing, contract manufacturing, management contracting, and joint ownership.[28]

Licensing

Licensing is a simple way for a manufacturer to enter international marketing. The company enters into an agreement with a licensee in the foreign market. For a fee or royalty, the licensee buys the right to use the company's manufacturing process, trademark, patent, trade secret, or other item of value. The company thus gains entry into the market at little risk; the licensee gains production expertise or a well-known product or name without having to start from scratch.

Coca-Cola markets internationally by licensing bottlers around the world and supplying them with the syrup needed to produce the product. In Japan, Budweiser beer flows from Kirin breweries, Lady Borden ice cream is churned out at Meiji Milk Products dairies, and Marlboro cigarettes roll off production lines at Japan Tobacco, Inc. Tokyo Disneyland Resort is owned and operated by Oriental Land Company under license from The Walt Disney Company. The 45-year license gives Disney licensing fees plus 10 percent of admissions and 5 percent of food and merchandise sales.

Contract Manufacturing

Another option is **contract manufacturing**—the company contracts with manufacturers in the foreign market to produce its product or provide its service. Sears used this method in opening up department stores in Mexico and Spain, where it found qualified local manufacturers to produce many of the products it sells. The drawbacks of contract manufacturing are decreased control over the manufacturing process and loss of potential profits on manufacturing. The benefits are the chance to start faster, with less risk, and the later opportunity either to form a partnership with or to buy out the local manufacturer.

Management Contracting

Under **management contracting**, the domestic firm supplies management know-how to a foreign company that supplies the capital. The domestic firm exports management services rather than products. Hilton uses this arrangement in managing hotels around the world.

Management contracting is a low-risk method of getting into a foreign market, and it yields income from the beginning. The arrangement is even more attractive if the contracting firm has an option to buy some share in the managed company later on. The arrangement is not sensible, however, if the company can put its scarce management talent to better uses or if it can make greater profits by undertaking the whole venture. Management contracting also prevents the company from setting up its own operations for a period of time.

Joint venturing
Entering foreign markets by joining with foreign companies to produce or market a product or service.

Licensing
A method of entering a foreign market in which the company enters into an agreement with a licensee in the foreign market.

Contract manufacturing
A joint venture in which a company contracts with manufacturers in a foreign market to produce the product or provide its service.

Management contracting
A joint venture in which the domestic firm supplies the management know-how to a foreign company that supplies the capital.

Licensing – Tokyo Disneyland Resort is owned and operated by the Oriental Land Co. Ltd. (a Japanese development company), under license from The Walt Disney Company.

Joint Ownership

Joint ownership
A joint venture in which a company joins investors in a foreign market to create a local business in which the company shares joint ownership and control.

Joint ownership ventures consist of one company joining forces with foreign investors to create a local business in which they share joint ownership and control. A company may buy an interest in a local firm, or the two parties may form a new business venture. Joint ownership may be needed for economic or political reasons. The firm may lack the financial, physical, or managerial resources to undertake the venture alone. Or a foreign government may require joint ownership as a condition for entry. KFC entered Japan through a joint ownership venture with Japanese conglomerate Mitsubishi. KFC sought a good way to enter the large but difficult Japanese fast-food market. In turn, Mitsubishi, one of Japan's largest poultry producers, understood the Japanese culture and had money to invest. Together, they helped KFC succeed in the semi closed Japanese market. Surprisingly, with Mitsubishi's guidance, KFC developed decidedly un-Japanese positioning for its Japanese restaurants:

When KFC first entered Japan, the Japanese were uncomfortable with the idea of fast food and franchising. They saw fast food as artificial and unhealthy. To build trust, KFC Japan created ads depicting the most authentic version of Colonel Sanders' beginnings possible. The ads featured the quintessential southern mother and highlighted the KFC philosophy—the southern hospitality, old American tradition, and authentic home cooking. With "My Old Kentucky Home" by Stephen Foster playing in the background, the commercial showed Colonel Sanders' mother making and feeding her grandchildren KFC chicken made with 11 secret spices. It conjured up scenes of good home cookin' from the American South, positioning KFC as wholesome, aristocratic food. The campaign was hugely successful—in the end, the Japanese people could not get enough of this special American chicken. Most Japanese grew to know "My Old Kentucky Home" by heart. There are now more than 1,100 KFC locations in the country.[29]

Joint ownership – KFC entered Japan through a joint ownership venture with Japanese conglomerate Mitsubishi.

Joint ownership has certain drawbacks. The partners may disagree over investment, marketing, or other policies. Whereas many U.S. firms like to reinvest earnings for growth, local firms often prefer to take out these earnings; and whereas U.S. firms emphasize the role of marketing, local investors may rely on selling.

Direct Investment

Direct investment
Entering a foreign market by developing foreign-based assembly or manufacturing facilities.

The biggest involvement in a foreign market comes through **direct investment**—the development of foreign-based assembly or manufacturing facilities. If a company has gained experience in exporting and if the foreign market is large enough, foreign production facilities offer many advantages. The firm may have lower costs in the form of cheaper labor or raw materials, foreign government investment incentives, and freight savings. The firm may improve its image in the host country because it creates jobs. Generally, a firm develops a deeper relationship with government, customers, local suppliers, and distributors, allowing it to adapt its products to the local market better. Finally, the firm keeps full control over the investment and therefore can develop manufacturing and marketing policies that serve its long-term international objectives.

The main disadvantage of direct investment is that the firm faces many risks, such as restricted or devalued currencies, falling markets, or government changes. In some cases, a firm has no choice but to accept these risks if it wants to operate in the host country.

Deciding on the Global Marketing Program

Companies that operate in one or more foreign markets must decide how much, if at all, to adapt their marketing strategies and programs to local conditions. At one extreme are global companies that use a **standardized marketing mix**, selling largely the same products and using the same marketing approaches worldwide. At the other extreme is an **adapted marketing mix**. In this case, the producer adjusts the marketing mix elements to each target market, bearing more costs but hoping for a larger market share and return.

The question of whether to adapt or standardize the marketing strategy and program has been much debated in recent years. On the one hand, some global marketers believe that technology is making the world a smaller place and that consumer needs around the world are becoming more similar. This paves the way for "global brands" and standardized global marketing. Global branding and standardization, in turn, result in greater brand power and reduced costs from economies of scale.

On the other hand, the marketing concept holds that marketing programs will be more effective if tailored to the unique needs of each targeted customer group. If this concept applies within a country, it should apply even more in international markets. Despite global convergence, consumers in different countries still have widely varied cultural backgrounds. They still differ significantly in their needs and wants, spending power, product preferences, and shopping patterns. Because these differences are hard to change, most marketers adapt their products, prices, channels, and promotions to fit consumer desires in each country.

However, global standardization is not an all-or-nothing proposition but rather a matter of degree. Most international marketers suggest that companies should "think globally but act locally"—that they should seek a balance between standardization and adaptation. The corporate level gives global strategic direction; regional or local units focus on individual consumer differences across global markets. "It is often a mistake to set out to create a worldwide strategy," says one expert. "Better results come from strong regional [or local] strategies brought together into a global whole." Simon Clift, head of marketing for global consumer-goods giant Unilever, puts it this way: "We're trying to strike a balance between being mindlessly global and hopelessly local."[30]

McDonald's operates this way. It uses the same basic fast-food operating model in its restaurants around the world but adapts its menu to local tastes. In Korea it sells the Bulgogi Burger, a grilled pork patty on a bun with a garlicky soy sauce. In India, where cows are considered sacred, McDonald's serves McChicken, Filet-O-Fish, McVeggie (a vegetable burger), Pizza McPuffs, McAloo Tikki (a spiced-potato burger), and the Maharaja Mac—two all-chicken patties, special sauce, lettuce, cheese, pickles, onions on a sesame-seed bun. In Hong Kong, consumers tend to accept new things from both western and eastern countries (e.g. Japan, Korea, and Thailand), thus, McDonald's succeeds to switching their taste of hamburger from American style to Japanese style from time to time. Similarly, South Korean electronics and appliance powerhouse LG Electronics makes and markets its brands globally but carefully localizes its products to the needs of specific country markets. By acting locally, it succeeds globally (see **Real Marketing 19.1**).

Standardized marketing mix
An international marketing strategy for using basically the same product, advertising, distribution channels, and other marketing mix elements in all the company's international markets.

Adapted marketing mix
An international marketing strategy for adjusting the marketing mix elements to each international target market, bearing more costs but hoping for a larger market share and return.

Marketing mix adaptation – In India, McDonald's serves chicken, fish, and vegetable burgers, and the Maharaja Mac—two all-chicken patties, special sauce, lettuce, cheese, pickles, onions, on a sesame seed bun.

REAL MARKETING 19.1

LG Electronics: Thinking Locally, Succeeding Globally

By thinking locally, LG Electronics is succeeding globally. It makes a kimchi fridge for the Korean market, a shish kebab microwave for the Iranians, karaoke phones for the Russians, and gold-plated 71-inch flat-screen televisions for Middle Easterners with a taste for gilded opulence.

If you've got kimchi in your fridge, it's hard to keep it a secret. Made from fermented cabbage seasoned with garlic and chili, kimchi is served with most meals in Korea. But when it's stored inside a normal refrigerator, its pungent odor taints nearby foods. That's why, two decades ago, South Korean appliance manufacturer LG Electronics introduced the kimchi refrigerator, a product specifically designed to address the odor problem. Featuring a dedicated compartment that isolates smelly kimchi from other foods, the fridge gradually became a must-have in Korean homes, inspiring rivals such as Samsung to offer similar models. Kimchi refrigerators have become a fixture in 65 percent of Korean homes, and after facing down the competition, LG is the country's top-selling manufacturer.

The kimchi fridge has become a model for the approach that LG uses to expand into new global markets—a passionate focus on in-depth localization. LG insists on understanding and catering to the idiosyncrasies of local markets through in-country research, manufacturing, and marketing. Localization has been a key element of LG's successful global expansion. "Gone are the days where you could just roll out one product for the global market," explains LG's Middle East marketing director. "We speak to consumers individually."

LG certainly has been successful globally. The $47 billion electronics, telecommunications, and appliance powerhouse now operates in more than 39 countries, and 86 percent of its sales come from markets outside its home country. It's the world's top producer of air conditioners and one of the top three global players in washing machines, microwaves, and refrigerators. And LG is surging into high-tech digital markets—it's now the world's fourth-largest producer of mobile handsets and the second-largest mobile phone maker in the United States. Its mission is to "make customers happy" worldwide by creating products that change their lives, no matter where they live.

Nowhere is the success of LG's localization approach more evident than in India, where the company is now the clear leader in virtually every appliance and electronics category—from microwaves to televisions—despite having entered the market in 1997, two years after Samsung. With a population of more than one billion that spans several religions and languages, India functions like dozens of smaller regional markets. LG initially differentiated itself by introducing a line of health-oriented products, such as televisions that reduced eyestrain. By 1999, however, it had set up local research and design facilities, manufacturing plants, and a network of service centers.

To meet the needs of Indian consumers, LG rolled out refrigerators with larger vegetable- and water-storage compartments, surge-resistant power supplies, and brightly colored finishes that reflect local preferences (red in the south, green in Kashmir). Some of LG's Indian microwaves have dark-colored interiors to hide masala stains. In 1999, LG introduced a television for cricket fans that came with a built-in cricket video game. After research showed that many Indians use their TVs to listen to music as well, the company offered its Ballad television with extra loud sound. Over time, these efforts have paid off. LG dominates in India, with sales that are projected to reach $1.8 billion this year. In some categories, such as washing machines, LG's market share is more than twice that of its nearest competitor.

Localization helps LG gain traction in emerging markets, where consumers have few preexisting brand loyalties. In Iran, LG offers a microwave oven with a preset button for reheating shish kebabs—a favorite dish. LG now claims to command roughly 40 percent of the Iranian microwave market. Meanwhile, LG's Primian refrigerator includes a special compartment for storing dates, a Middle Eastern staple fruit that spoils easily.

Although not always huge sellers, LG's localized products clearly generate buzz. The company recently made headlines throughout the Middle East by unveiling a gold-plated 71-inch flat-screen television that sells for $80,000—a tribute to the region's famous affinity for gilded opulence. In Russia, LG's research revealed that many people entertain at home during the country's long winters, prompting the company to develop a karaoke phone that can be programmed with the top 100 Russian songs, whose lyrics scroll across the screen when they're played. Introduced in late 2004, the phone has been a hit, selling more than 220,000 handsets.

All this experience will be put to the test as LG moves to make its presence felt in China, the world's biggest consumer market, where major international brands must compete against domestic rivals such as Haier. Just as it did in India, LG is establishing extensive in-country facilities in China—from research to manufacturing to product marketing. LG opened research and development operations in Beijing in 2002 and has since ramped up its staff to more than 1,500. The company also reached out to local consumers by creating an "LG village," a high-profile initiative that transformed a decrepit agricultural community into a showcase for LG technologies. The efforts seem to be paying off: With help from such simple touches as making the exteriors of products red—a lucky color in China—LG raked in sales of $8 billion on the mainland last year.

Thus, from Korean kimchi to Indian cricket mania to Russian karaoke, LG's unrelenting commitment to localization is winning the company waves of new customers around the globe. By thinking locally, LG is succeeding globally.

Sources:
Adapted from Elizabeth Esfahani, "Thinking Locally, Succeeding Globally," Business 2.0, December 2005, pp. 96–98. Also see Evan Ramstas, "LG Electronics' Net Surges 91 Percent As Cell Phone Margins Improve," Wall Street Journal, January 25, 2006, p. B2; and information from www.lge.com, December 2006.

Product

Five strategies allow for adapting product and marketing communication strategies to a global market (see **Figure 19.3**).[31] We first discuss the three product strategies and then turn to the two communication strategies.

	Product		
Promotion	Don't change product	Adapt product	Develop new product
Don't change promotion	Straight extension	Product adaptation	Product invention
Adapt promotion	Communication adaptation	Dual adaptation	Product invention

Figure 19.3
Five global product and commuunications strategies

Straight product extension means marketing a product in a foreign market without any change. Top management tells its marketing people, "Take the product as it is and find customers for it." The first step, however, should be to find out whether foreign consumers use that product and what form they prefer.

Straight extension has been successful in some cases and disastrous in others. Kellogg cereals, Heineken beer, and Black & Decker tools are all sold successfully in about the same form around the world. But General Foods introduced its standard powdered Jell-O in the British market only to find that British consumers prefer a solid wafer or cake form. Likewise, Philips began to make a profit in Japan only after it reduced the size of its coffeemakers to fit into smaller Japanese kitchens and its shavers to fit smaller Japanese hands. Straight extension is tempting because it involves no additional product development costs, manufacturing changes, or new promotion. But it can be costly in the long run if products fail to satisfy foreign consumers.

Product adaptation involves changing the product to meet local conditions or wants. For example, Vidal Sassoon shampoos contain a single fragrance worldwide, but the amount of scent varies in each country: less in Japan, where subtle scents are preferred, and more in Europe. Gerber serves the Japanese baby food fare that might turn the stomachs of many Western consumers — local favorites include flounder and spinach stew, cod roe spaghetti, mugwort casserole, and sardines ground up in white radish sauce. Finnish mobile phone maker Nokia customizes its mobile phones for every major market. Developers build in rudimentary voice recognition for Asia where keyboards are a problem and raise the ring volume so phones can be heard on crowded Asian streets.

Product invention consists of creating something new for a specific country market. This strategy can take two forms. It might mean maintaining or reintroducing earlier product forms that happen to be well adapted to the needs of a given country. Or a company might create a new product to meet a need in a given country. For example, an enormous need exists for low-cost, high-protein foods in less developed countries. Companies such as Quaker Oats, and Monsanto are researching the nutrition needs of these countries, creating new foods, and developing advertising campaigns to gain product trial and acceptance. Product invention can be costly but the payoffs are worthwhile.

Promotion

Companies can either adopt the same communication strategy they used in the home market or change it for each local market. Consider advertising messages. Some global companies use a standardized advertising theme around the world. Of course, even in highly standardized communications campaigns, some small changes might be required to adjust for language and minor cultural differences. For example, to help communicate its global reach, IBM Global Services ran virtually identical "People Who Think. People Who Do. People Who Get It" ads in dozens of countries around the world. Of course, even in highly standardized promotion campaigns, some small changes might be required to adjust for language and minor cultural differences.

Straight product extension
Marketing a product in a foreign market without any change.

Product adaptation
Adapting a product to meet local conditions or wants in foreign markets.

Product invention
Creating new products or services for foreign markets.

Colors also are changed sometimes to avoid taboos in other countries. Purple is associated with death in most of Latin America, white is a mourning color in Japan, red is a lucky color in China, and green is associated with jungle sickness in Malaysia.[32] Even names must be changed. Kellogg had to rename Bran Buds cereal in Sweden, where the name roughly translates as "burned farmer." And in the Americas, Mitsubishi changed the Japanese name of its Pajero SUV to Montero—it seems that *pajero* in Spanish is a slang term for sexual self-gratification. (See **Real Marketing 19.2** for more on language blunders in international marketing.)[33]

Other companies follow a strategy of **communication adaptation**, fully adapting their advertising messages to local markets. Kellogg ads in the U.S. promote the taste and nutrition of Kellogg's cereals versus competitors' brands. In France, where consumers drink little milk and eat little for breakfast, Kellogg's ads must convince consumers that cereals are a tasty and healthful breakfast. In India, where many consumers eat heavy, fried breakfasts, Kellogg's advertising convinces buyers to switch to a lighter, more nutritious breakfast diet. Similarly, Coca-Cola sells its low-calorie beverage as Diet Coke in North America, the United Kingdom, and the Middle and Far East but as Light elsewhere. According to Diet Coke's global brand manager, in Spanish-speaking countries Coke Light ads "position the soft drink as an object of desire, rather than as a way to feel good about yourself, as Diet Coke is positioned in the U.S." This "desire positioning" plays off research showing that "Coca-Cola Light is seen in other parts of world as a vibrant brand that exudes a sexy confidence."[34]

Media also need to be adapted internationally because media availability varies from country to country. TV advertising time is very limited in Europe, for instance, ranging from four hours a day in France to none in Scandinavian countries. Advertisers must buy time months in advance, and they have little control over airtimes. Magazines also vary in effectiveness. For example, magazines are a major medium in Italy but a minor one in Austria. Newspapers are national in the United Kingdom but are only local in Spain.[35]

Colors are changed sometimes to avoid taboos in other countries. Red is a lucky color in China, and is commonly used in many aspects of Chinese life.

Communication adaptation
A global communication strategy of fully adapting advertising messages to local markets.

Price

Companies also face many problems in setting their international prices. For example, how might Black & Decker price its power tools globally? It could set a uniform price all around the world, but this amount would be too high a price in poor countries and not high enough in rich ones. It could charge what consumers in each country would bear, but this strategy ignores differences in the actual costs from country to country. Finally, the company could use a standard markup of its costs everywhere, but this approach might price Black & Decker out of the market in some countries where costs are high.

Regardless of how companies go about pricing their products, their foreign prices probably will be higher than their domestic prices for comparable products. A Gucci handbag may sell for $60 in Italy and $240 in the United States. Why? Gucci faces a price escalation problem. It must add the cost of transportation, tariffs, importer margin, wholesaler margin, and retailer margin to its factory price. Depending on these added costs, the product may need to sell for two to five times as much in another country to make the same profit. For example, a pair of Levi's jeans that sells for $30 in the U.S. typically fetches $63 in Tokyo and $88 in Paris. A DaimlerChrysler automobile priced at $10,000 in the U.S. might sell for more than $47,000 in South Korea.

Communication adaptation – Coca-Cola sells its low-calorie beverage as Diet Coke in North America, the United Kingdom, and the Middle and Far East but as Light elsewhere.

Another problem involves setting a price for goods that a company ships to its foreign subsidiaries. If the company charges a foreign subsidiary too much, it may end up paying higher tariff duties even while paying lower income taxes in that country. If the company

REAL MARKETING 19.2

Watch Your Language!

Global language barriers: Some standardized brand names do not translate well globally.

Many global companies have had difficulty crossing the language barrier, with results ranging from mild embarrassment to outright failure. Seemingly innocuous brand names and advertising phrases can take on unintended or hidden meanings when translated into other languages. Careless translations can make a marketer look downright foolish to foreign consumers.

The classic language blunders involve standardized brand names that do not translate well. When Coca-Cola first marketed Coke in China in the 1920s, it developed a group of Chinese characters that, when pronounced, sounded like the product name. Unfortunately, the characters actually translated as "bite the wax tadpole." Now, the characters on Chinese Coke bottles translate as "happiness in the mouth."

Several modern-day marketers have had similar problems when their brand names crashed into the language barrier. Chevy's Nova translated into Spanish as no va—"it doesn't go." GM changed the name to Caribe (Spanish for Caribbean) and sales increased. Rolls-Royce avoided the name Silver Mist in German markets, where mist means "manure." Sunbeam, however, entered the German market with its Mist Stick hair curling iron. As should have been expected, the Germans had little use for a "manure wand." IKEA marketed a children's workbench named FARTFULL (the word means "speedy" in Swedish)—it soon discontinued the product.

Interbrand of London, the firm that created household names such as Prozac and Acura, recently developed a brand-name "hall of shame" list, which contained these and other foreign brand names you are never likely to see inside the local Safeway: Krapp toilet paper (Denmark), Crapsy Fruit cereal (France), Poo curry powder (Argentina), and Pschitt lemonade (France).

charges its subsidiary too little, it can be charged with dumping. Dumping occurs when a company either charges less than its costs or less than it charges in its home market. Thus, Harley-Davidson accused Honda and Kawasaki of dumping motorcycles on the U.S. market. The U.S. International Trade Commission agreed and the Commerce Department imposed duties as high as 112.81 percent on shrimp imports from the offending countries.[36] Various governments are always watching for dumping abuses, and they often force companies to set the price charged by other competitors for the same or similar products.

Recent economic and technological forces have had an impact on global pricing. For example, in the European Union, the transition to the euro is reducing the amount of price differentiation. As consumers recognize price differentiation by country, companies are being forced to harmonize prices throughout the countries that have adopted the single currency. Companies and marketers that offer the most unique or necessary products or services will be least affected by such "price transparency."

Travelers often encounter well-intentioned advice from service firms that takes on meanings very different from those intended. The menu in one Swiss restaurant proudly stated, "Our wines leave you nothing to hope for." Signs in a Japanese hotel pronounced, "You are invited to take advantage of the chambermaid." At a laundry in Rome, it was, "Ladies, leave your clothes here and spend the afternoon having a good time."

Advertising themes often lose—or gain—something in the translation. The Coors beer slogan "get loose with Coors" in Spanish came out as "get the runs with Coors." Coca-Cola's "Coke adds life" theme in Japanese translated into "Coke brings your ancestors back from the dead." The milk industry learned too late that its American advertising question "Got Milk?" translated in Mexico as a more provocative "Are you lactating?" In Chinese, the KFC slogan "finger-lickin' good" came out as "eat your fingers off." And Frank Perdue's classic line, "It takes a tough man to make a tender chicken," took on added meaning in Spanish: "It takes an aroused man to make a chicken affectionate." Even when the language is the same, word usage may differ from country to country. Thus, the British ad line for Electrolux vacuum cleaners—"Nothing sucks like an Electrolux"—would capture few customers in the United States.

So, what can a company do to avoid such mistakes? One answer is to call in the experts. Brand consultancy Lexicon Branding has been dreaming up brand names for more than 20 years, including names like Dasani, Swiffer, and Blackberry. David Placek, Lexicon's founder and president acknowledges that "coming up with catchy product names is a lot harder than [you] might imagine, especially in this Global Age, when a word that might inspire admiration in one country can just as easily inspire red faces or unintended guffaws in another."

Lexicon maintains a global network of high-quality linguists from around the world that it calls GlobalTalk—"so we can call on them to evaluate words for language and cultural cues and miscues." Beyond screening out the bad names, the GlobalTalk network can also help find good ones. "We created the brand name Zima for Coors with help from the GlobalTalk network," says Placek. "I put out a message saying that we were looking for a name for a light alcoholic drink that would be cold, crisp, and refreshing. I got a fax in quickly from our Russian linguist saying that zima meant "winter" in Russian. I circled the word because I thought it was beautiful and unusual, and the client loved it. We sent it around the world to make sure that it didn't have a negative connotation anywhere, and it didn't."

Sources:
Lexicon example and quotes from "Naming Products Is No Game," BusinessWeek Online, April 9, 2004, accessed at www.businessweekonline.com. For the above and other examples, see David A. Ricks, "Perspectives: Translation Blunders in International Business," *Journal of Language for International Business*, 7:2, 1996, pp. 50–55; Sam Solley, "Developing a Name to Work Worldwide," *Marketing*, December 21, 2000, p. 27; Thomas T. Sermon, "Cutting Corners in Language Risky Business," *Marketing News*, April 23, 2001, p. 9; Martin Croft, "Mind Your Language," *Marketing*, June 19, 2003, pp. 35–39; Mark Lasswell, "Lost in Translation," *Business 2.0*, August 2004, pp. 68–70; "Lost in Translation," *Hispanic*, May 2005, p. 12; and "Striking a Chord in Tamil," *Businessline*, January 19, 2006, p. 1.

When the exchange rate of renminbi was lower than the Hong Kong dollar (e.g. HK$100: 105 yuan), there was an increase in the number of Hong Kong citizens visiting Shenzhen during the weekend for vacations. Now that the renminbi's rate is higher than the Hong Kong dollar (e.g. HK$100: 92 yuan), more "freewalk" travelers from many PRC provinces come to Hong Kong for shopping.

The Internet will also make global price differences more obvious. When firms sell their wares over the Internet, customers can to see how much products sell for in different countries. They might even be able to order a given product directly from the company location or dealer offering the lowest price. This will force companies toward more standardized international pricing.

International pricing – Twelve European Union countries have adopted the euro as a common currency creating "pricing transparency" and forcing companies to harmonize their prices throughout Europe.

Distribution Channels

The international company must take a **whole-channel view** of the problem of distributing products to final consumers. **Figure 19.4** shows the three major links between the seller and the final buyer. The first link, the seller's headquarters organization, supervises the channels and is part of the channel itself. The second link, channels between nations, moves the products to the borders of the foreign nations. The third link, channels within nations, moves the products from their foreign entry point to the final consumers. Some U.S. manufacturers may think their job is done once the product leaves their hands, but they would do well to pay more attention to its handling within foreign countries.

Figure 19.4
Whole-channel concept for international marketing

| Seller | → | Seller's headquarters organization for international marketing | → | Channels between nations | → | Channels within nations | → | Final user or buyer |

Channels of distribution within countries vary greatly from nation to nation. First, there are the large differences in the numbers and types of intermediaries serving each foreign market. For example, a U.S. company marketing in China must operate through a frustrating maze of state-controlled wholesalers and retailers. Chinese distributors often carry competitors' products and frequently refuse to share even basic sales and marketing information with their suppliers. Hustling for sales is an alien concept to Chinese distributors, who are used to selling all they can obtain. Working with or getting around this system sometimes requires much time and investment.

When Coke first entered China, for example, customers bicycled up to bottling plants to get their soft drinks. Many shopkeepers still don't have enough electricity to run soft drink coolers. Now, Coca-Cola has set up direct-distribution channels, investing heavily in refrigerators and trucks, and upgrading wiring so that more retailers can install coolers. The company has also built an army of more than 10,000 sales representatives that makes regular visits on resellers, often on foot or bicycle, to check on stocks and record sales. "Coke and its bottlers have been trying to map every supermarket, restaurant, barbershop, or market stall where a can of soda might be consumed," notes an industry observer. "Those data help Coke get closer to its customers, whether they are in large hypermarkets, Spartan noodle shops, or schools." Still, to reach the most isolated spots in the country, Coca-Cola relies on some pretty unlikely business partners—teams of delivery donkeys. "Massive advertising budgets can drum up demand," says another observer, "but if the distribution network doesn't exist properly or doesn't work, the potential of China's vast market cannot be realized."[37]

Another difference lies in *the size and character of retail units* abroad. Whereas large-scale retail chains dominate the U.S. scene, much retailing in other countries is done by many small, independent retailers. In India, millions of retailers operate tiny shops or sell in open markets. Their markups are high, but the actual price is lowered through haggling. Supermarkets could offer lower prices, but supermarkets are difficult to build and open because of many economic and cultural barriers. Incomes are low, and people prefer to shop daily for small amounts rather than weekly for large amounts. They also lack storage and refrigeration to keep food for several days. Packaging is not well developed because it would add too much to the cost. These factors have kept large-scale retailing from spreading rapidly in developing countries.

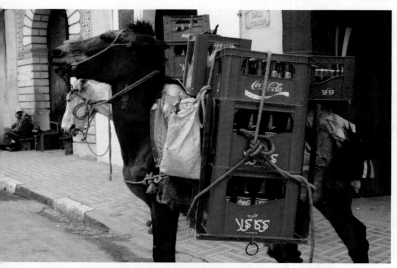

Distribution channels may vary greatly from nation to nation, as suggested by this picture of a "delivery donkey" delivering Coca-Cola in Morocco.

Deciding on the Global Marketing Organization

Companies manage their international marketing activities in at least three different ways: Most companies first organize an export department, then create an international division, and finally become a global organization.

A firm normally gets into international marketing by simply shipping out its goods. If its international sales expand, the company organizes an export department with a sales manager and a few assistants. As sales increase, the export department can expand to include various marketing services so that it can actively go after business. If the firm moves into joint ventures or direct investment, the export department will no longer be adequate. Many companies get involved in several international markets and ventures. A company may export to one country, license to another, have a joint ownership venture in a third, and own a subsidiary in a fourth. Sooner or later it will create international divisions or subsidiaries to handle all its international activity. International divisions are organized in a variety of ways. An international division's corporate staff consists of marketing, manufacturing, research, finance, planning, and personnel specialists. It plans for and provides services to various operating units, which can be organized in one of three ways. They can be geographical organizations, with country managers who are responsible for salespeople, sales branches, distributors, and licensees in their respective countries. Or the operating units can be world product groups, each responsible for worldwide sales of different product groups. Finally, operating units can be international subsidiaries, each responsible for its own sales and profits.

Many firms have passed beyond the international division stage and become truly global organizations. They stop thinking of themselves as national marketers who sell abroad and start thinking of themselves as global marketers. The top corporate management and staff plan worldwide manufacturing facilities, marketing policies, financial flows, and logistical systems. The global operating units report directly to the chief executive or executive committee of the organization, not to the head of an international division. Executives are trained in worldwide operations, not just domestic or international. The company recruits management from many countries, buys components and supplies where they cost the least, and invests where the expected returns are greatest.

Today, major companies must become more global if they hope to compete. As foreign companies successfully invade their domestic markets, companies must move more aggressively into foreign markets. They will have to change from companies that treat their international operations as secondary, to companies that view the entire world as a single borderless market.

REVIEWING THE CONCEPTS

In the past, U.S. companies paid little attention to international trade. If they could pick up some extra sales through exporting, that was fine. But the big market was at home, and it teemed with opportunities. Companies today can no longer afford to pay attention only to their domestic market, regardless of its size. Many industries are global industries, and firms that operate globally achieve lower costs and higher brand awareness. At the same time, global marketing is risky because of variable exchange rates, unstable governments, protectionist tariffs and trade barriers, and several other factors. Given the potential gains and risks of international marketing, companies need a systematic way to make their global marketing decisions.

1 **Discuss how the international trade system and the economic, political-legal, and cultural environments affect a company's international marketing decisions.**

A company must understand the global marketing environment, especially the international trade system. It must assess each foreign market's economic, political-legal, and cultural characteristics. The company must then decide whether it wants to go abroad and consider the potential risks and benefits. It must decide on the volume of international sales it wants, how many countries it wants to market in, and which specific markets it wants to enter. This decision calls for weighing the probable rate of return on investment against the level of risk.

2 **Describe three key approaches to entering international markets.**

The company must decide how to enter each chosen market—whether through *exporting*, *joint venturing*, or *direct investment*. Many companies start as exporters, move to joint ventures, and finally make a direct investment in foreign markets. In *exporting*, the company enters a foreign market by sending and selling products through international marketing intermediaries (indirect exporting) or the company's own department, branch, or sales representative or agents (direct exporting). When establishing a *joint venture*, a company enters foreign markets by joining with foreign companies to produce or market a product or service. In *licensing*, the company enters a foreign market by contracting with a licensee in the foreign market, offering the right to use a manufacturing process, trademark, patent, trade secret, or other item of value for a fee or royalty.

3 **Explain how companies adapt their marketing mixes for international markets.**

Companies must also decide how much their products, promotion, price, and channels should be adapted for each foreign market. At one extreme, global companies use a *standardized marketing* mix worldwide. Others use an *adapted marketing mix*, in which they adjust the marketing mix to each target market, bearing more costs but hoping for a larger market share and return.

4 **Identify the three major forms of international marketing organization.**

The company must develop an effective organization for international marketing. Most firms start with an *export department* and graduate to an *international division*. A few become *global organizations*, with worldwide marketing planned and managed by the top officers of the company. Global organizations view the entire world as a single, borderless market.

REVIEWING THE KEY TERMS

Adapted marketing mix 534
Communication adaptation 539
Contract manufacturing 533
Countertrade 527
Direct investment 534
Economic community 525
Exporting 532
Global firm 523
Joint ownership 534

Joint venturing 533
Licensing 533
Management contracting 533
Product adaptation 538
Product invention 538
Standardized marketing mix 534
Straight product extension 538
Whole-channel view 542

DISCUSSING THE CONCEPTS

1. What factors are contributing to the intensity of today's global competition?

2. Netflix, the world's largest online DVD movie rental service, currently operates only in the United States. What must Netflix consider when it decides whether to expand globally?

3. Red Bull markets its energy drink in about 75 countries. What must Red Bull consider when selecting which countries to enter?

4. Discuss the advantages and disadvantages of direct investment in a foreign market. Name two Asian markets in which a household appliance manufacturer would be interested in investing, and two foreign markets in which it would have no interest in investing. Discuss.

5. Assume your boss has asked you how your company should enter the Japanese, South Korean, and Vietnamese markets with a new line of women's athletic shoes. Would you recommend that the company standardize or adapt its marketing mix? Explain.

6. **Figure 19.4** shows a "whole-channel view" of international distribution. Would a company require the full range of international channel intermediaries discussed in the chapter?

APPLYING THE CONCEPTS

1. Visit the Web site of the Royal Thai Consulate-General in Hong Kong at _www.thai-consulate.org.hk_ . Discuss doing business in Thailand.

2. The U.S. restricts trade with North Korea. Visit the U.S. Department of the Treasury Web site at _www.ustreas.gov/ offices/enforcement/ofac_ to learn more about economic and trade sanctions. Click on the "Other Sanctions" link to learn more about the trade restrictions on North Korea. Is this restriction a tariff, quota, or embargo? To what extent does this trade restriction allow U.S. businesses to export their products to North Korea?

3. Form teams of four students and discuss how the following products might adapt their marketing mixes when entering the Chinese market.
   - Mrs. Field's cookies
   - Herbal Essences Conditioner
   - Ben and Jerry's ice cream

FOCUS ON TECHNOLOGY

GMI (Global Market Insight) is a leader in global market research. It offers an online global panel of more than five million members in 200 countries. Panelists speak more than 37 different languages and are available in the Americas, Europe, the Pacific Rim, and the Middle East. In addition to consumer markets, GMI provides access to hard-to-reach business consumers, including B2B specialty medical markets of physicians, nurses, and patients with a variety of chronic illnesses. GMI differentiates itself from competitors with claims that it has the highest standards of panel integrity. In addition to survey panelists, GMI assists with international mystery shoppers. Mystery shoppers, common in the retail and financial services industries, are individuals who are paid to visit retailers and pose as regular shoppers. After they visit, the mystery shoppers file reports on a variety of topics, which might include the politeness of the service representative, the appearance of the location, or customer waiting time.

1. What questions might Haier, a manufacturer of household electrical appliances, ask the members of the GMI household appliances panel when considering entry into the United States?

2. How might McDonald's use global mystery shoppers? Why would it prefer to use local shoppers rather than sending mystery shoppers from McDonald's U.S. home office?

3. Sign up to be a survey respondent at www.globaltestmarket.com. After going through the registration process, do you think that a rigid standard for its survey respondents should be used?

 FOCUS ON ETHICS

In Hong Kong , The Hong Kong Jockey Club is the authorized operator of horse racing, Mark Six lottery and betting on football matches held outside Hong Kong. The Club is the largest single taxpayer in Hong Kong, the company tax paid in the financial year 2006/07 was HK$12.64 billion or about 8.2 percent of all taxes collected by the Government's Inland Revenue Department.

In the 1970s, the growth of the sport's popularity was accompanied by an increase in illegal bookmaking. The government authorized the Club to operate off-course betting branches to tackle illegal gambling head-on. Since then, the Mark Six lottery and regulated football betting have also been introduced to combat illegal gambling. In 2003, the Club launched regulated football betting services with the same aim—to combat illegal gambling. Besides The Hong Kong Jockey Club, the government authority also offers betting licenses to the local Chinese traditional gambling houses for "Mah Jong" gambling. The government takes necessary action and control to combat illegal gambling within the Hong Kong territory. However, we believe that it hardly stops illegal betting by phone, online gambling and the "mobile" casino on the cruise which is operated just outside the Hong Kong sea boundary.

1. Should the Hong Kong government authorize the Club to set up the online casino for the citizens?

2. Would the Club give the awards to the person who provides the illegal gambling transaction information and would the police make use of those information to put the involved parties /person on official criminal charges?

 VIDEO CASE

Nivea

In 1911, Nivea introduced a revolutionary product, Nivea Crème, in a simple blue tin. Still in its signature blue tin, today the Crème is the centerpiece of a wide range of personal care products Nivea markets, including everything from soap, shampoo, and shaving products to baby care products, deodorant, and sunscreen. And despite its small beginnings, today the company's products are sold in more than 150 countries worldwide. Most Nivea consumers believe that the products they buy are produced and marketed locally. Why? Although Nivea looks for commonalities between consumers around the globe, the company's marketers also recognize the differences between consumers in different markets. So Nivea adapts its marketing mix to reach local consumers while keeping its message consistent everywhere products are sold. This globally consistent, locally customized marketing strategy has sold more than 11 billion tins of the traditional Nivea Crème. After viewing the video featuring Nivea, answer the following questions about the company and the global marketplace.

1. Which of the five strategies for adapting products and promotion for the global market does Nivea employ?

2. Visit Nivea's Web site, www.nivea.com, and tour the sites for several different countries. How does Nivea market its products differently in different countries? How does the company maintain the consistency of its brand?

COMPANY CASE

Internationalization of the Haier Group

The Haier group is located in Qingdao City, Shandong province, China. The former Haier Qingdao Refrigerator Factory was established in Qingdao in 1984. Zhang Ruimin was appointed Director and set up a new leadership team. The Qingdao Refrigerator Factory had 820 employees, producing 740 refrigerators a year with an annual sales revenue of 3.48 million yuan, fixed assets of 5 million yuan, and an annual loss of 1.47 million yuan.

One day at the Qingdao Refrigerator Factory, Zhang made a tough decision to personally destroy 76 defective refrigerators with a sledgehammer—to this day, the Group preserves the smashed refrigerators for their symbolic value in the Haier museum. He made the difficult decision to destroy the products produced by the factory workers with the aim of making the employees fully understand that poor quality would not be tolerated by the management. He reinforced the message with an aggressive Western-style quality control program.

At Haier, Zhang promoted a mix of international management principles and Chinese wisdom, with innovation and excellence as his cornerstones. In the past two decade under his supervision, the Haier Group has developed and undergone a period of rapid growth, internationalization, and globalization. (See **Figure 19.5** for a summary of Haier's development strategy.)

Development (1984-1991): Brand Building

The original Qingdao Refrigerator Factory was a small, ailing, collectively owned factory. When Zhang became director, he carried out an intensive restructuring in the

factory. Haier's brand products, refrigerators, freezers, and home air conditioners were launched. In 1989, the Haier Company Limited was established in Qingdao. Haier exported its first batch of refrigerators to Germany in 1990.

The Haier Group was formed in 1991 with the merger of the Qingdao General Refrigerator Factory and the Qingdao Air Conditioner General Factory. During these seven years, the Qingdao Refrigerator Factory adopted a new management concept, the "Haier culture"—Being comes from nothingness. The group implemented new quality improvement programs on the production line, in order to make their products competitive in the global marketplace. In 1988, their refrigerator products won the first National Quality Gold Medal in the Chinese refrigerator industry and received the UL (US) certification in the same year.

Rapid Growth (1991-1995): Diversification

In this period of rapid growth, Haier obtained its ISO 9001 certification in 1992. The Haier Refrigerator Company was listed on the Shanghai Stock Exchange (SHA:600690) in 1993. Haier refrigerators and other products entered the Middle East market in the same year. Haier launched its microwave ovens and top-loading washing machines on the market in 1995. In the same year, Haier merged with the Qingdao Red Star Appliance Co., Ltd. and began exporting products to the U.S., both in original equipment manufacturing (OEM) form and under Haier's brand name. At the same time, Haier established a local assembly plant in Southeast Asia to strengthen its overseas expansion plan.

International Growth (1995-1997): Internationalization

Haier's senior management's vision is to establish a good reputation for Haier brand products that will be well recognized by customers throughout the world. Even when Haier had become a national brand and achieved success in the domestic market, they considered themselves still far from their ultimate goal. Haier's senior management wanted Haier products to be sold in volume in all the major economic regions of the world. In 1996, Haier launched commercial air conditioners and front-loading washing machines. At that time, its annual production of washing machines reached one million units. In 1997, Haier started to produce television sets and dishwashers.

Haier has a development strategy: to set up a sound overseas distribution network and after-sales service to cope with their international growth. The company aims to build employee loyalty with the internationalization of the management system, to build customer loyalty with the internationalization of service, and to build international competence with the internationalization of the brand.

The 2010 Target—Global 500 (The World's Largest Corporations)

Today, the Haier Group has successfully climbed from being a small factory to become one of the world's largest home appliance manufacturers and one of China's top 100 electronics and IT companies. Haier has 240 subsidiary companies, 30 design centers, plants, and trade companies, and more than 50,000 employees throughout the world with a distribution network presence in over 100 countries. Haier specializes in technological research, manufacture, trading, and financial services.

The Haier Electronics Group Co. Ltd was listed on the main board of the Stock Exchange of Hong Kong (HKG:1169) in 2005. Haier's global revenue in 2006 was RMB107.5 billion ($13.8 billion). Haier's products range from refrigerators, freezers, household air conditioners, microwave ovens, washing machines, dishwashers, vacuum cleaners, water heaters, kitchenware, television sets, DVD players, commercial air conditioners, and mobile phones, to computers. Haier also achieved the number one place on the list of China's Most Valuable Brands in 2006, as determined by the World Brand Lab (WBL), with a brand value reaching RMB 63.989 billion; it was followed by Lenovo, China Mobile, CCTV, Chang Hong, Bank of Communications, GOME, China Life, CREC, and Sinochem. To study how Haier achieves its mission—globalized Haier—we need to look at the Haier Group's path to the world stage between 1998 and 2006 as one of the largest home appliance manufacturers.

Global Market Competition

Chinese brands are facing fierce global market competition. Haier has launched a global brand building strategy to strengthen the corporate culture, increase resources, and build up a worldwide reputation and worldwide distribution network systems, with the aim of gaining world recognition and sustainable product positioning in the global market.

In 1999, Haier set up its first overseas factory, the Haier America Refrigerator Corporation Ltd. in South Carolina and established its first overseas industrial complex: the Haier (America) Industrial Complex. In 2000, Haier (America) built its first "made in America" refrigerators, and a joint venture, Haier-CCT Holdings, was established in Qingdao and Hong Kong.

In addition to its core businesses, Haier started to produce mobile phones. Haier incorporated Ericsson Bluetooth technology into Haier household appliances and launched the "Patriot 1" MPEG-II decoding chip, China's first chip designed for use in super integrated digital TV circuits.

In 2001, Haier introduced dual-drive washing machine technology. To increase its overseas capacity, Haier set up a second factory in Pakistan and acquired a refrigerator plant in Italy, both also in 2001. For market exploration purposes, Haier products were introduced to the Australian and New Zealand markets, and trading companies were established in Malaysia and Thailand, in 2002. Another joint venture, the Sanyo-Haier company, was established in Japan in the same year.

Together with global expansion, Haier's development of technology is also a key to success. Haier's proposal for safe care water heater technology was an initiative accepted by the 66th IEC Conference in 2002. Haier Benfeng-brand slim mobile phones were launched in Beijing in 2003. Haier home computers were introduced to the French market in 2004. Haier introduced 'e-Home' products, including the first wireless networking digital home solution based on self-developed IP technology, in 2005. Haier's non-detergent powder washing machines were launched in Malaysia in 2006.

In summary, Haier's globalization strategies are: globalization of design, globalization of manufacturing capability globalization of marketing networks, globalization of sourcing, and globalization of capital operations.

Haier is one of China's most successful cases of a Chinese enterprise growing from a small factory into a large world corporation. Haier's successful pace is also proof of China's significant economic growth in the last two decades. Zhang Ruimin is now the Chairperson of the Board of Directors and CEO of the Haier Group. He is regarded as a role model for modern Chinese entrepreneurs, and his leadership philosophy and business acumen are widely admired, both in China and within the international business community. However, what will Haier's goal be for the coming decade? In addition, with Zhang approaching the age of 60, what are the succession plans for the positions of chairman and CEO of the Haier group? These are issues the company will need to deal with in order to continue its meteoric rise into the future.

Figure 19.5
Haier's Development Strategy (from The Haier Group's website: http://haier.com)

Questions For Discussion

1. Based on your remarks on your knowledge of "Deciding Whether to Go Global", "Deciding Which Market to Enter", and "Deciding How to Enter the Market", learned previously in this chapter, analyze why Haier built its first overseas factory and established its first overseas industrial complex in the U.S. in 1999?

2. Are you impressed by the "tough decision" Mr. Zhang made at the Qingdao Refrigerator Factory? Do you agree that it laid the foundation for the company culture, especially its quality concept, which contributed to the success of the Haier Group in later stages?

3. Based on what you learned in this chapter, discuss the difficulties encountered by a multinational company entering the China market, comparing them with those of the Haier Group entering any one of the Western markets.

4. Analyze Haier's global marketing strategy and compare it with one of the national rivals: Changhong, Konka, Lenovo, Midea, or TCL.

5. Analyze Haier's global marketing strategy, comparing it with an international rival such as Samsung.

Source:
Liu, R. "The Experience of Success," Shanghai, Shanghai Fast East Publisher. 1999, p. 359–414; accessed at http://haier.com.

Objectives

After studying this chapter, you should be able to

- identify the major social criticisms of marketing
- define *consumerism* and *environmentalism* and explain how they affect marketing strategies
- describe the principles of socially responsible marketing
- explain the role of ethics in marketing

CHAPTER 20

MARKETING ETHICS AND SOCIAL RESPONSIBILITY

Previewing the Concepts

In this final chapter, we'll focus on marketing as a social institution. First, we'll look at some common criticisms of marketing as it impacts individual consumers, other businesses, and society as a whole. Then, we'll examine consumerism, environmentalism, and other citizen and public actions to keep marketing in check. Finally, we'll see how companies can benefit from proactively pursuing socially responsible and ethical practices that bring value not just to individual customers, but to society as a whole.

First, let's visit the concept of social responsibility in business. Consider the Tata Group, India's largest conglomerate comprising 96 companies in seven business sectors, including engineering, materials, information technology, communications, automotives, chemicals, and energy. The group believes firmly that it can do well by doing good. Here's the story.

Tata chairman Ratan Tata oversees the Tata Group, India's largest conglomerate. With 246,000 employees, Tata Group's revenues amounted to $28.5 billion in 2007, the equivalent of about 2.8 percent of India's GDP. The Tata Group has operations in over 40 countries in six continents, and its 96 companies export products and services to 140 nations.

Tata's corporate slogan is "Improving the quality of life of the communities we serve." This mission dates to the group's founding in the 1870s by Ratan Tata's grandfather, Jamsetji, who was a pioneering philanthropist and fervent nationalist. Jamsetji Tata opened India's first textile mill, mainly to wean Indians from their industrial dependence on Britain. Tata offered worker benefits such as child care and pensions long before most Western companies. One of Jamsetji's sons financed a young Mahatma Gandhi while he fought for the rights of immigrant Indians in South Africa.

To this day, the Tata Group remains devoted to good works. Charitable trusts own two-thirds of the shares in its parent company Tata Sons. Many of the group's businesses fund grassroots anti-poverty projects that seem far removed from their core operations. Tata also has a reputation for being an honest company. It has avoided major business and political scandals, a remarkable record in a country where corruption is not uncommon. The group has sometimes lost deals because it would not pay bribes, according to chairman Ratan Tata. Ratan, who serves as the group's chief dealmaker, visionary, and spiritual cement, is a passionate promoter of corporate social responsibility. According to Ratan, the two major challenges confronting the Tata Group are, "Talent, and retaining our value system as we get bigger

and more diverse. We have to increase the management bandwidth, and with the same ethical standards."

Exemplifying these challenges is Tata Steel, the first company founded by Jamsetji Tata and one of the group's three most important companies, along with Tata Consulting Services and Tata Motors. In January 2007, acquired U.K. company Corus, one of the world's leading steel and aluminum producers. Tata Steel is currently the largest steel producer in India and the fifth largest in the world. A visit to Tata Steel's production base in Jamshedpur provides insights into the Tata Culture at its most generous. Named after the founder of the group and carved out of a jungle in the 1900s, Jamshedpur resembles a time capsule of a more paternalistic industrial age. Statues of Tata chairmen, some erected by grateful employees, are everywhere, testament to a unique cult of personality.

Jamshedpur's biggest employer is Tata Steel. Even though it now employs only 20,000 of the city's 700,000 residents, the company still provides Jamshedpur the most comprehensive social services of any Indian city. At a cost of $40 million a year, Tata Steel pays for water, schools, garbage removal, hospitals, and even rogue elephant hunters. However, in the early 1990s, India started opening to global competition. The 100-year-old company was saddled with antiquated plants, a bloated payroll, and "no market orientation… we were a good study in demise," recalls its managing director B. Muthuraman. Aside from a $2.5 billion plant modernization program, Tata Steel laid off 35,000 workers in 1999 to cut costs. Yet, it agreed to pay the workers' full salaries until the age of 60 and provide them lifelong health care. In contrast, rival Essar produces about half of Tata Steel's output with just 1,300 employees. One survey of Indian companies by *Business Today*, an Indian magazine, and consultancy Stern Stewart ranked Tata Steel 496th out of 500 Indian companies in terms of value created by management.

The Tata Group says it wants to "privatize" the services it provides, betraying its view of Tata being Jamshedpur's de facto government. However, former Tata Steel CEO Jamshed Irani insists that the welfare net "is what makes Tata great." Indeed, Tata Steel still spends millions annually on education, health, and agricultural development projects in 800 villages around Jamshedpur. For example, thanks to Tata funding, the 32 families in Sidhma Kudhar now have irrigation systems that allow them to grow rice crops and a variety of vegetables. The hillsides are covered with thousands of mahogany and teak seedlings as well as jatropha bushes for future income. Most children attend classes in the refurbished school, and the village has three TVs, powered by Tata solar units that also supply electricity for lights and clocks.

Ratan Tata defends this practice: "Yes, it's expensive to run Jamshedpur, and yes, we are scaling back our commitment there, but we are also proud that we've never had serious industrial problems. There has got to be a reason for that." At Tata, being loved may be more highly prized than being profitable.

Tata's largesse will be tested at its new acquisition Corus. The deal loads the Indian steelmaker with $7.4 billion in debt, and absorbing Corus' higher-cost operations will weaken margins. A key question concerns Corus' mills such as that in Port Talbot in Wales, which employs 3,000 workers. The union representing most Corus workers wants Tata Steel to invest an additional $600 million in Port Talbot for it to remain competitive without cutting jobs. A delegation of 20 Corus labor representatives visited Jamshedpur in April 2007 to meet the mill's new owners. However, Tata executives declined to give guarantees. "We were extremely impressed by their workforce and commitment to social responsibility," says Corus labor leader Michael Leahy. "But how will they be able to translate those principles into the British and European context? They couldn't answer that."[1]

Responsible marketers discover what consumers want and respond with market offerings that create value for buyers to capture value in return. The *marketing concept* is a philosophy of customer value and mutual gain. Its practice leads the economy by an invisible hand to satisfy the many and changing needs of millions of consumers.

However, not all marketers follow the marketing concept. In fact, some companies use questionable marketing practices, and some marketing actions that seem innocent in themselves strongly affect the larger society. Consider the sale of cigarettes. On the surface, companies should be free to sell cigarettes and smokers should be free to buy them. But this private transaction involves larger questions of public policy. For example, the smokers are harming their health and may be shortening their own lives. Smoking places a financial burden on the smoker's family and on society at large. Other people around smokers may suffer discomfort and harm from secondhand smoke. Finally, marketing cigarettes to adults might also influence young people to begin smoking. Thus, the marketing of tobacco products has sparked substantial debate and negotiation in recent years.

This chapter examines the social effects of private marketing practices. We examine several questions: What are the most frequent social criticisms of marketing? What steps have private citizens taken to curb marketing ills? What steps have legislators and government agencies taken to curb marketing ills? What steps have enlightened companies taken to carry out socially responsible and ethical marketing that creates value for both individual customers and society as a whole?

Social Criticisms of Marketing

Marketing receives much criticism. Some of this criticism is justified; much is not. Social critics claim that certain marketing practices hurt individual consumers, society as a whole, and other business firms.

Marketing's Impact on Individual Consumers

Consumers have many concerns about how well the marketing system serves their interests. They hold mixed or even slightly unfavorable attitudes toward marketing practices. Consumer advocates, government agencies, and other critics have accused marketing of harming consumers through high prices, deceptive practices, high-pressure selling, shoddy or unsafe products, planned obsolescence, and poor service to disadvantaged consumers (see **Figure 20.1**).

Figure 20.1
Impact of marketing on individual consumers

High Prices

Many critics charge that the marketing system causes prices to be higher than they would be under more "sensible" systems. They point to three factors—*high costs of distribution, high advertising and promotion costs*, and *excessive markups*.

High costs of distribution

A long-standing charge is that greedy intermediaries mark up prices beyond the value of their services. Critics charge that there are too many intermediaries, that intermediaries are inefficient, or that they provide unnecessary or duplicate services. As a result, distribution costs too much, and consumers pay for these excessive costs in the form of higher prices. How do resellers answer these charges? They argue that intermediaries do work that would otherwise have to be done by manufacturers or consumers. Markups reflect services that consumers themselves want—more convenience, larger stores and assortments, more service, longer store hours, return privileges, and others. In fact, they argue, where retail competition is so intense, margins are actually quite low. If some resellers try to charge too much relative to the value they add, other resellers will step in with lower prices. Low-price stores such as Wal-Mart and other discounters pressure their competitors to operate efficiently and keep their prices down.

High advertising and promotion costs

Modern marketing is also accused of pushing up prices to finance heavy advertising and sales promotion. For example, a few dozen tablets of a heavily promoted brand of pain reliever sell for the same price as 100 tablets of less-promoted brands. Differentiated products—cosmetics, detergents, toiletries—include promotion and packaging costs that can amount to 40 percent or more of the manufacturer's price to the retailer. Critics charge that much of the packaging and promotion adds only psychological value to the product rather than functional value.

Marketers respond that advertising adds to product costs. But it also adds value by informing potential buyers of the availability and merits of a brand. Brand name products may cost more, but branding gives buyers assurances of consistent quality. Moreover, consumers can usually buy functional versions of products at lower prices. However, they *want* and are *willing* to pay more for products that also provide psychological benefits—that make them feel wealthy, attractive, or special. Also, heavy advertising and promotion may be necessary for a firm to match competitors' efforts—the business would lose "share

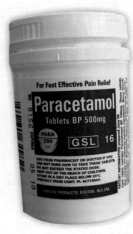

Promotional costs – Is there a difference between brands like Panadol or Tylenol and generic paracetamol? Critics charge that promotion adds only psychological value to the product rather than functional value.

of mind" if it did not match competitive spending. At the same time, companies are cost conscious about promotion and try to spend their money wisely.

Excessive markups

Critics also charge that some companies mark up goods excessively. They point to the drug industry, where a pill costing five cents to make may cost the consumer $2 to buy. They point to the pricing tactics of funeral homes that prey on the confused emotions of bereaved relatives and to the high charges for auto repair and other services.

Marketers respond that most businesses try to deal fairly with consumers because they want to build customer relationships and repeat business. Most consumer abuses are unintentional. When shady marketers take advantage of consumers, they should be reported to consumer protection associations. Marketers also respond that consumers often don't understand the reasons for high markups. For example, pharmaceutical markups must cover the costs of purchasing, promoting, and distributing existing medicines plus the high research and development costs of formulating and testing new medicines. As pharmaceuticals company GlaxoSmithKline states in its ads, "Today's medicines finance tomorrow's miracles."

Deceptive Practices

Marketers are sometimes accused of deceptive practices that lead consumers to believe they will get more value than they actually do. Deceptive practices fall into three groups: pricing, promotion, and packaging. *Deceptive pricing* includes practices such as falsely advertising "factory" or "wholesale" prices or a large price reduction from a phony high retail list price. *Deceptive promotion* includes practices such as misrepresenting the product's features or performance or luring the customers to the store for a bargain that is out of stock. *Deceptive packaging* includes exaggerating package contents through subtle design, using misleading labeling, or describing size in misleading terms.

To be sure, questionable marketing practices do occur. Consider the advertising of airline ticket prices:[2]

Deceptive practices –
Technically legal, ads like this one lure readers with promises of low, low prices. But watch out for the small print at the bottom—you will need a magnifying glass to figure out the actual ticket cost.

● When is $49 not $49? When it's the advertised price for an airline ticket. Consumers are lured by ads promising cheap tickets. But by the time you add in all the extras, that bargain ticket will cost nearly $200. Whatever happened to truth in advertising? Technically, the advertising is legal. But the average airline consumer needs a magnifying glass to get an idea of the actual ticket cost. For the cheap ticket, radio commercials warn that the discount price comes with conditions and fees. However, you must read the fine print across the bottom of a newspaper ad to discover the true cost. Excluded in the listed prices are government taxes and fees, passenger facility charges, and fuel-related surcharges, which can add up to another $150. Not quite the $49 in the big print at the top of the ad.

The toughest problem is defining what is "deceptive." For instance, an advertiser's claim that its powerful laundry detergent "makes your washing machine 10 feet tall," showing a surprised homemaker watching her appliance burst through her laundry room ceiling, isn't intended to be taken literally. Instead, the advertiser might claim, it is "puffery"—innocent exaggeration for effect. Advertising puffery and alluring imagery are bound to occur—and may even be desirable: "There is hardly a company that would not go down in ruin if it refused to provide fluff, because nobody will buy pure functionality... Worse, it denies ... people's honest needs and values. Without distortion, embellishment, and elaboration, life would be drab, dull, anguished, and at its existential worst."[3]

However, others claim that puffery and alluring imagery can harm consumers in subtle ways, and that consumers must be protected through education:

> The real danger to the public… comes not from outright lies—in most cases facts can ultimately be proven and mistakes corrected. But… advertising uses [the power of images and] emotional appeals to shift the viewer's focus away from facts. Viewers who do not take the trouble to distinguish between provable claims and pleasant but meaningless word play end up buying "the sizzle, not the steak" and often paying high prices. The best defense against misleading ads… is not tighter controls on [advertisers], but more education and more critical judgment among… consumers. Just as we train children to be wary of strangers offering candy, to count change at a store, and to kick the tires before buying a used car, we must make the effort to step back and judge the value of… advertisements, and then master the skills required to separate spin from substance.[4]

Marketers argue that most companies avoid deceptive practices because such practices harm their business in the long run. Profitable customer relationships are built upon a foundation of value and trust. If consumers do not get what they expect, they will switch to more reliable products. In addition, consumers usually protect themselves from deception. Most consumers recognize a marketer's selling intent and are careful when they buy, sometimes to the point of not believing completely true product claims.

High-Pressure Selling

Salespeople are sometimes accused of high-pressure selling that persuades people to buy goods they had no thought of buying. It is often said that insurance, time share facilities, and used cars are *sold*, not *bought*. Salespeople are trained to deliver smooth, canned talks to entice purchase. They sell hard because sales contests promise big prizes to those who sell the most.

But in most cases, marketers have little to gain from high-pressure selling. Such tactics may work in one-time selling situations for short-term gain. However, most selling involves building long-term relationships with valued customers. High-pressure or deceptive selling can do serious damage to such relationships. For example, imagine a Procter & Gamble account manager trying to pressure a Carrefour buyer, or a Lenovo salesperson trying to browbeat a GE information technology manager. It simply wouldn't work.

Shoddy, Harmful, or Unsafe Products

Another criticism concerns poor product quality or function. One complaint is that, too often, products are not made well and services are not performed well. A second complaint is that many products deliver little benefit, or that they might even be harmful.

Consider the obesity problem. Are fast-food chains partly to blame for overweight children? What should responsible food companies do about it? As with most social responsibility issues, there are no easy answers. McDonald's has worked to improve its fare and make its menu and its customers healthier. However, Hardee's has introduced a 1,410-calorie Monster Thickburger, and Burger King launched its Enormous Omelet breakfast sandwich, packing 47 grams of fat. Are these companies being socially irresponsible? Or are they simply serving customers choices they want?

A third complaint concerns product safety. Product safety has been a problem for several reasons, including company indifference, increased product complexity, and poor quality control. For example, Mattel recently recalled 1.5 million made-in-China toys worldwide which were reportedly coated in toxic lead paint. The toys included popular characters like Big Bird and Elmo from the hit TV series, *Sesame Street*. The incident was one of a host of recent product safety scares to have involved Chinese contract manufacturers. Other tainted Chinese-made products involved toothpaste, pet food, and seafood.[5]

The obesity debate –
Is Hardee's being socially irresponsible or simply practicing good marketing by giving customers a big juicy burger that clearly pings their taste buds? Judging by the nutrition calculator at its Web site, the company certainly isn't hiding the nutritional facts. (*www.hardees. com/nutrition.php*)

However, most manufacturers *want* to produce quality goods. The way a company deals with product quality and safety problems can damage or help its reputation. Companies selling poor-quality or unsafe products risk damaging conflicts with consumer groups and regulators. Moreover, unsafe products can result in product liability suits and large awards for damages.

More fundamentally, consumers who are unhappy with a firm's products may avoid future purchases and talk other consumers into doing the same. Similarly, principals of contract manufacturers may switch vendors. Thus, quality missteps can have severe consequences. Today's marketers know that customer-driven quality results in customer value and satisfaction, which in turn creates profitable customer relationships.

Planned Obsolescence

Critics also have charged that some producers follow a program of planned obsolescence, causing their products to become obsolete before they actually should need replacement. For example, consider printer companies and their toner cartridges:

> Refilled printer cartridges offer the same or improved performance for about half the price of a new one. Some companies offer toner cartridge refill services to businesses. You can refill most cartridges eight to 10 times—if you can find the right parts. However, printer companies would prefer to sell their cartridges rather than allow someone to refill an exhausted one for half the price. So they make it hard for refill operations by continually introducing new models and tweaking inkjet cartridges and laser toner containers. Refill parts manufacturers struggle to keep up with the printer companies that are working to thwart refill-enabling rollers, ribbons and other pieces. There is planned obsolescence. [6]

Planned obsolescence –
Printer companies continually introduce new cartridge models and tweak designs.

Critics charge that some producers continually change consumer concepts of acceptable styles to encourage more and earlier buying. An obvious example is constantly changing clothing fashions. Other producers are accused of holding back attractive functional features, then introducing them later to make older models obsolete. Critics claim that this occurs in the consumer electronics and computer industries. For example, Intel and Microsoft have been accused of holding back their next-generation computer chips and software until demand is exhausted for the current generation. Still other producers are accused of using materials and components that will break, wear, rust, or rot sooner than they should.

Marketers respond that consumers like style changes; they get tired of the old goods and want a new look in fashion or a new design in cars. No one has to buy the new look, and if too few people like it, it will simply fail. For most technical products, customers want the latest innovations, even if older models still work. Companies that withhold new features run the risk that competitors will introduce the new feature first and steal the market. For example, consider personal computers. Some consumers grumble that the consumer electronics industry's constant push to produce "faster, smaller, cheaper" models means that they must continually buy new machines just to keep up. Others, however, can hardly wait for the latest model to arrive.

Thus, most companies do not design their products to break down earlier, because they do not want to lose customers to other brands. Instead, they seek constant improvement to ensure that products will consistently meet or exceed customer expectations. Some of the planned obsolescence is the working of the competitive and technological forces in a free society—forces that lead to ever-improving goods and services.

Poor Service to Disadvantaged Consumers

Finally, the marketing system has been accused of serving disadvantaged consumers poorly. For example, home and auto insurers have been accused of assigning higher premiums to people with poor credit ratings. The insurers claim that individuals with bad credit tend to make more insurance claims, and that this justifies charging them higher premiums.

Marketing's Impact on Society

The marketing system has been accused of adding to several "evils" in society at large (see **Figure 20.2**). Advertising has been a special target.

Figure 20.2
Impact of marketing on society

False Wants and Too Much Materialism

Critics have charged that the marketing system emphasizes material possessions. People are judged by what they *own* rather than by who they *are*. Reflecting this drive for wealth and possessions are such catch phrases as "greed is good" and "shop till you drop." As Asian economies develop, newly affluent and face conscious consumers may be particularly susceptible to marketing efforts that emphasize material acquistions and ownership.

The critics do not view this interest in material things as a natural state of mind but as a matter of false wants created by marketing. Businesses stimulate people's desires for goods by using the mass media to create materialistic models of the good life. Thus, marketing is seen as creating false wants that benefit industry more than they benefit consumers.

However, these criticisms overstate the power of business to create needs. People have strong defenses against advertising and other marketing tools. Marketers are most effective when they appeal to existing wants rather than when they attempt to create new ones. Further, people seek information when making important purchases and often do not rely on single sources. Even minor purchases that may be affected by advertising messages lead to repeat purchases only if the product delivers the promised customer value. Finally, the high failure rate of new products shows that companies are not able to control demand.

On a deeper level, our wants and values are influenced not only by marketers but also by family, peer groups, religion, cultural background, and education. If consumers are highly materialistic, these values arose out of basic socialization processes that go much deeper than business and mass media could produce alone.

Too Few Social Goods

Business has been accused of overselling private goods at the expense of public goods. As private goods increase, they require more public services that are usually not forthcoming. For example, an increase in automobile ownership (private good) requires more highways, traffic control, parking spaces, and police services (public goods). The overselling of private goods results in "social costs." For cars, the social costs include traffic congestion, air pollution, gasoline shortages, and deaths and injuries from car accidents.

A way must be found to restore a balance between private and public goods. One option is to make producers bear the full social costs of their operations. The government can require automobile manufacturers to build cars with even more safety features, more efficient engines, and better pollution-control systems. Automakers will then raise their prices to cover extra costs. If buyers find the price of some cars too high, however, the producers of these cars will disappear. Demand will then move to those producers that can support the sum of the private and social costs.

Balancing private and public goods – In response to traffic congestion, Singapore has an electronic road pricing system where tolls are automatically deducted from prepaid cards placed in readers installed in all cars.

A second option is to make consumers pay the social costs. For example, many cities around the world are starting to charge "congestion tolls" in an effort to reduce traffic congestion. To unclog its streets, Singapore has an Electronic Road Pricing (ERP) system that automatically deducts toll from prepaid cards installed in all cars. Tolls charged are highest during peak hours and in the central city areas. Prospective car purchasers also need to bid for a Certificate of Entitlement—the right to buy a new car and drive it for 10 years.

Cultural Pollution

Critics charge the marketing system with creating *cultural pollution*. Our senses are constantly assaulted by marketing and advertising. Commercials interrupt serious programs; pages of ads obscure magazines; billboards mar beautiful scenery; spam fills our e-mail boxes. These interruptions continually pollute people's minds with messages of materialism, sex, power, or status.

Marketers answer the charges of "commercial noise" with these arguments: First, they hope that their ads reach primarily the target audience. But because of mass-communication channels, some ads are bound to reach people who have no interest in the product and are therefore bored or annoyed. People who buy magazines addressed to their interests—such as *Vogue* or *Fortune*—rarely complain about the ads because the magazines advertise products of interest.

Second, ads make much of television and radio free to users and keep down the costs of magazines and newspapers. Many people think commercials are a small price to pay for these benefits. Finally, today's consumers have alternatives. For example, they can zip and zap TV commercials or avoid them altogether on many cable or satellite channels. Thus, to hold consumer attention, advertisers are making their ads more entertaining and informative.

Too Much Political Power

Another criticism is that business wields too much political power. Advertisers are accused of holding too much power over the mass media, limiting media freedom to report independently and objectively. The critics ask: How can magazines afford to tell the truth about the low nutritional value of packaged foods when these magazines are being subsidized by such advertisers as General Foods, Kellogg's, Kraft, and General Mills? How can a TV network criticize the practices of the large auto companies when such companies invest billions of dollars a year in broadcast advertising?

As the media receive advertising revenues from more different advertisers, it is easier to resist the influence of one or a few of them. Too much business power tends to result in counterforces that check and offset these powerful interests.

Marketing's Impact on Other Businesses

Critics also charge that a company's marketing practices can harm other companies and reduce competition. Three problems are involved: acquisitions of competitors, marketing practices that create barriers to entry, and unfair competitive marketing practices.

- *Acquisition of competitors*: Critics claim that firms are harmed and competition reduced when companies expand by acquiring competitors rather than by developing their own new products. The large number of acquisitions and rapid pace of industry consolidation over the past decades have caused concern that vigorous young competitors will be absorbed and that competition will be reduced. In many industries—retailing, entertainment, financial services, utilities, transportation, automobiles, telecommunications, health care—the number of major competitors is shrinking.

  Acquisition is a complex subject. Acquisitions can sometimes be good for society. The acquiring company may gain economies of scale that lead to lower costs and lower prices. A well managed company may take over a poorly managed company and improve its efficiency. An industry that was not very competitive might become more competitive after the acquisition. But acquisitions can also be harmful and, therefore, are closely regulated by some governments.

- *Barriers to entry*: Critics have also charged that marketing practices bar new companies from entering an industry. Large marketing companies can use patents and heavy promotion spending, and they can tie up suppliers or dealers to keep out or drive out competitors. Some barriers are the natural result of the economic advantages of doing business on a large scale.

- *Unfair practices*: Some firms use unfair competitive marketing practices with the intention of hurting or destroying other firms. They may set their prices below costs, threaten to cut off business with suppliers, or discourage the buying of a competitor's products. Laws in various countries work to prevent such predatory competition. It is difficult, however, to prove that the intent or action was really predatory.

  Wal-Mart has been accused of using predatory pricing in selected market areas to drive smaller retailers out of business. However, whereas critics charge that Wal-Mart's actions are predatory, others question whether this is unfair competition or the healthy competition of a more efficient company against less efficient ones.[7]

Predatory business practices –
Wal-Mart has become a lightning rod for protests by citizens who worry that the mega-retailer's unfair practices will choke out local businesses. Wal-Mart defenders claim that it's more a matter of healthy competition of a more efficient company against less efficient ones.

Citizen and Public Actions to Regulate Marketing

Because some people view business as the cause of many economic and social ills, grassroots movements have arisen from time to time to keep business in line. The two major movements have been *consumerism* and *environmentalism*.

Consumerism

Consumers are now better educated, some products have become more complex and potentially hazardous, and some people are unhappy with institutions. Consumer groups have been organized and several consumer laws have been passed.

But what is the consumer movement? **Consumerism** is an organized movement of citizens and government agencies to improve the rights and power of buyers in relation to sellers. Traditional *sellers' rights* include:

- The right to introduce any product in any size and style, provided it is not hazardous to personal health or safety; or, if it is, to include proper warnings and controls.
- The right to charge any price for the product, provided no discrimination exists among similar kinds of buyers.
- The right to spend any amount to promote the product, provided it is not defined as unfair competition.
- The right to use any product message, provided it is not misleading or dishonest in content or execution.
- The right to use any buying incentive programs, provided they are not unfair or misleading.

Consumerism
An organized movement of citizens and government agencies to improve the rights and power of buyers in relation to sellers.

Traditional *buyers' rights* include (see **Figure 20.3**):
- The right not to buy a product that is offered for sale.
- The right to expect the product to be safe.
- The right to expect the product to perform as claimed.

Comparing these rights, many believe that the balance of power lies on the seller's side. True, the buyer can refuse to buy. But critics feel that the buyer has too little information, education, and protection to make wise decisions when facing sophisticated sellers. Consumer advocates call for the following additional consumer rights:
- The right to be well informed about important aspects of the product.
- The right to be protected against questionable products and marketing practices.
- The right to influence products and marketing practices in ways that will improve the "quality of life."

Buyers' Rights

- The right not to buy a product that is offered for sale
- The right to expect the product to be safe
- The right to expect the product to perform as claimed

- The right to be well-informed about important aspects of the product
- The right to be protected against questionable products and marketing practices
- The right to influence products and marketing practices in ways that will improve the "quality of life"

Figure 20.3
Buyers' rights

Each proposed right has led to more specific proposals by consumerists. The right to be informed includes the right to know the true interest on a loan (truth in lending), the true cost per unit of a brand (unit pricing), the ingredients in a product (ingredient labeling), the nutritional value of foods (nutritional labeling), product freshness (open dating), and the true benefits of a product (truth in advertising). Proposals related to consumer protection include strengthening consumer rights in cases of business fraud, requiring greater product safety, ensuring information privacy, and giving more power to government agencies. Proposals relating to quality of life include controlling the ingredients that go into certain products and packaging, reducing the level of advertising "noise," and putting consumer representatives on company boards to protect consumer interests.

Consumers have not only the *right* but also the *responsibility* to protect themselves instead of leaving this function to someone else. Consumers who believe they got a bad deal have several remedies available, including contacting the company or the media; contacting local consumer agencies; and going to small-claims courts.

Environmentalism

Environmentalism
An organized movement of concerned citizens and government agencies to protect and improve people's living environment.

Whereas consumerists consider whether the marketing system is efficiently serving consumer wants, environmentalists are concerned with marketing's effects on the environment and with the costs of serving consumer needs and wants. **Environmentalism** is an organized movement of concerned citizens, businesses, and government agencies to protect and improve people's living environment.

Environmentalists are not against marketing and consumption; they simply want people and organizations to operate with more care for the environment. The marketing system's goal, they assert, should not be to maximize consumption, consumer choice, or consumer satisfaction, but rather to maximize life quality. And "life quality" means not only the quantity and quality of consumer goods and services, but also the quality of the environment. Environmentalists want environmental costs included in both producer and consumer decision making.

Companies are now accepting more responsibility for protecting the environment. They are shifting from protest to prevention, and from regulation to responsibility. More companies are adopting policies of **environmental sustainability**. Simply put, environmental sustainability is about generating profits while helping to save the planet. Sustainability is a crucial but difficult societal goal.

Some companies have responded to consumer environmental concerns by doing only what is required to avert new regulations or to keep environmentalists quiet. Enlightened companies, however, are taking action not because someone is forcing them to, or to reap short-run profits, but because it is the right thing to do—for both the company and for the planet's environmental future.

Figure 20.4 shows a grid that companies can use to gauge their progress toward environmental sustainability. At the most basic level, a company can practice pollution prevention. This involves more than pollution control—cleaning up waste after it has been created. Pollution prevention means eliminating or minimizing waste before it is created. Companies emphasizing prevention have responded with "green marketing" programs—developing ecologically safer products, recyclable and biodegradable packaging, better pollution controls, and more energy-efficient operations.

Environmentalists gathered together to send a message out to companies that they are polluting the earth.

Tomorrow	**New environmental technology** Is the environmental performance of our products limited by our existing technology base? Is there potential to realize major improvements through new technology?	**Sustainability vision** Does our corporate vision direct us toward the solution of social and environmental problems? Does our vision guide the development of new technologies, markets, products, and processes?
Today	**Pollution prevention** Where are the most significant waste and emission streams from our current operations? Can we lower costs and risks by eliminating waste at the source or by using it as useful input?	**Product stewardship** What are the implications for product design and development if we assume responsibility for a product's entire life cycle? Can we add value or lower costs while simultaneously reducing the impact of our products?
	Internal	**External**

Figure 20.4
The environmental sustainability grid
Source: Reprinted by permission of Harvard Business Review. From "Beyond Greening: Strategy for a Sustainable World." by Stuart L. Hart, January–February 1997, p.74. Copyright © 1997 by the President and Fellows of Harvard College; all rights reserved.

For example, Sony has reduced the amount of heavy metals—such as lead, mercury, and cadmium—in its electronic products. Nike produces PVC-free shoes, recycles old sneakers, and educates young people about conservation, reuse, and recycling.[8]

At the next level, companies can practice *product stewardship*—minimizing not just pollution from production but all environmental impacts throughout the full product life cycle, and all the while reducing costs. Many companies are adopting *design for environment (DFE)* practices, which involve thinking ahead to design products that are easier to recover, reuse, or recycle. DFE not only helps to sustain the environment, it can be highly profitable for the company.

An example is Xerox Corporation's Equipment Remanufacture and Parts Reuse Program, which converts end-of-life office equipment into new products and parts. Equipment returned to Xerox can be remanufactured reusing 70 to 90 percent by weight of old machine components, while still meeting performance standards for equipment made with all new parts. The program creates benefits for both the environment and for the company. It prevents more than 120 million pounds of waste from entering landfills each year. And it reduces the amount of raw material and energy needed to produce new parts. Energy savings from parts reuse total an estimated 320,000 megawatt hours annually—enough energy to light more than 250,000 U.S. homes for the year.[9]

Environmental sustainability
A management approach that involves developing strategies that both sustain the environment and produce profits for the company.

At the third level, companies look to the future and plan for *new environmental technologies*. Many organizations that have made good sustainability headway are still limited by existing technologies. To develop fully sustainable strategies, they will need to develop new technologies. Wal-Mart has two experimental superstores designed to test dozens of environmentally friendly and energy-efficient technologies:[10]

A 143-foot-tall wind turbine stands outside a Wal-Mart Supercenter in Aurora, Colorado. On the outside, the store's facade features row upon row of windows to allow in as much natural light as possible. The landscaping uses native, drought-tolerant plants well adapted to the hot, dry Colorado summers, cutting down on watering, mowing, and the amount of fertilizer and other chemicals needed. Inside the store, an efficient high-output linear fluorescent lighting system saves enough electricity annually from this store alone to supply the needs of 52 single-family homes. The store's heating system burns recovered cooking oil from the deli's fryers. The oil is collected, mixed with waste engine oil from the store's Tire and Lube Express, and burned in the waste-oil boiler. All organic waste, including produce, meats, and paper, is placed in an organic waste compactor, which is then hauled off to a company that turns it into mulch for the garden.

These and dozens more technological touches make the supercenter a laboratory for efficient and Earth-friendly retail operations. In the long run, Wal-Mart's environmental goals are to use 100 percent renewable energy, to create zero waste, and to sell products that sustain its resources and environment.

New environmental technologies – Wal-Mart has opened two experimental superstores designed to test dozens of environmentally friendly and energy-efficient technologies. The façade of this store features rows and rows of windows to let in as much natural light as possible, and its "urban forest" landscaping uses native, well-adapted plants, cutting down on watering, mowing, and the amount of fertilizer and other chemicals needed.

Finally, companies can develop a *sustainability vision*, which serves as a guide to the future. It shows how the company's products and services, processes, and policies must evolve and what new technologies must be developed to get there. This vision of sustainability provides a framework for pollution control, product stewardship, and environmental technology.

Most companies today focus on the lower-left quadrant of the grid in **Figure 20.4**, investing most heavily in pollution prevention. Some forward-looking companies practice product stewardship and are developing new environmental technologies. Few companies have well-defined sustainability visions. However, emphasizing only one or a few quadrants in the environmental sustainability grid can be shortsighted. Investing only in the bottom half of the grid puts a company in a good position today but leaves it vulnerable in the future. In contrast, a heavy emphasis on the top half suggests that a company has good environmental vision but lacks the skills needed to implement it. Thus, companies should work at developing all four dimensions of environmental sustainability.

Environmentalism creates some special challenges for global marketers. As international trade barriers come down and global markets expand, environmental issues are having an ever-greater impact on international trade. In the U.S., for example, more than two dozen major pieces of environmental legislation have been enacted since 1970. The European Union has "end-of-life" regulations affecting automobiles and consumer electronics products. And the EU's Eco-Management and Audit Scheme provides guidelines for environmental self-regulation.[11]

However, environmental policies still vary widely from country to country. Countries such as Denmark, Germany, Japan, and the U.S. have fully developed environmental policies and high public expectations. But major countries such as China, India, Brazil, and Russia are in only the early stages of developing such policies. Moreover, environmental factors that motivate consumers in one country may have no impact on consumers in another. For example, PVC soft drink bottles cannot be used in Switzerland or Germany. However, they are preferred in France, which has an extensive recycling process for them. Thus, international companies have found it difficult to develop standard environmental practices that work around the world. Instead, they are creating general policies and then translating these policies into tailored programs that meet local regulations and expectations.

Public Actions to Regulate Marketing

Citizen concerns about marketing practices will usually lead to public attention and legislative proposals. New bills will be passed. The task is to translate these laws into the language that marketing executives understand as they make decisions about competitive relations, products, price, promotion, and channels of distribution. **Figure 20.5** illustrates the major legal issues facing marketing management.

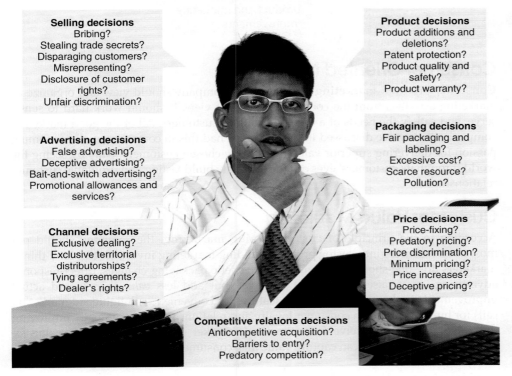

Selling decisions
Bribing?
Stealing trade secrets?
Disparaging customers?
Misrepresenting?
Disclosure of customer rights?
Unfair discrimination?

Advertising decisions
False advertising?
Deceptive advertising?
Bait-and-switch advertising?
Promotional allowances and services?

Channel decisions
Exclusive dealing?
Exclusive territorial distributorships?
Tying agreements?
Dealer's rights?

Product decisions
Product additions and deletions?
Patent protection?
Product quality and safety?
Product warranty?

Packaging decisions
Fair packaging and labeling?
Excessive cost?
Scarce resource?
Pollution?

Price decisions
Price-fixing?
Predatory pricing?
Price discrimination?
Minimum pricing?
Price increases?
Deceptive pricing?

Competitive relations decisions
Anticompetitive acquisition?
Barriers to entry?
Predatory competition?

Figure 20.5
Major marketing decision areas that may be called into question under the law

Business Actions toward Socially Responsible Marketing

Initially, many companies opposed consumerism and environmentalism. They thought the criticisms were either unfair or unimportant. But by now, many companies have grown to embrace the new consumer rights. They recognize the consumer's right to information and protection. Many of these companies have responded positively to consumerism and environmentalism as a way to create greater customer value and to strengthen customer relationships.

Enlightened Marketing

The philosophy of **enlightened marketing** holds that a company's marketing should support the best long-run performance of the marketing system. Enlightened marketing consists of five principles: *consumer-oriented marketing, customer-value marketing, innovative marketing, sense-of-mission marketing,* and *societal marketing* (see **Figure 20.6**).

Enlightened marketing
A marketing philosophy holding that a company's marketing should support the best long-run performance of the marketing system.

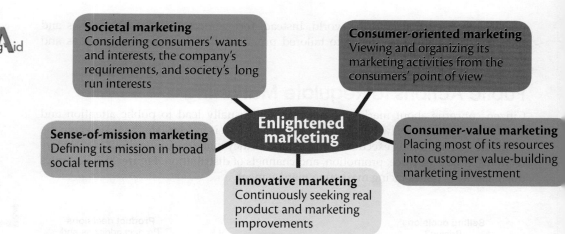

Societal marketing
Considering consumers' wants and interests, the company's requirements, and society's long run interests

Consumer-oriented marketing
Viewing and organizing its marketing activities from the consumers' point of view

Sense-of-mission marketing
Defining its mission in broad social terms

Enlightened marketing

Consumer-value marketing
Placing most of its resources into customer value-building marketing investment

Innovative marketing
Continuously seeking real product and marketing improvements

Figure 20.6
Principles of enlightened marketing

Consumer-oriented marketing
The philosophy of enlightened marketing that holds that the company should view and organize its marketing activities from the consumer's point of view.

Customer-value marketing
A principle of enlightened marketing that holds that a company should put most of its resources into customer value-building marketing investments.

Innovative marketing
A principle of enlightened marketing that requires that a company seek real product and marketing improvements.

Consumer-Oriented Marketing

Consumer-oriented marketing means that the company should view and organize its marketing activities from the consumer's point of view. It should work hard to sense, serve, and satisfy the needs of a defined group of customers. All of the good marketing companies that we've discussed in this text have had this in common: an all-consuming passion for delivering superior value to carefully chosen customers. Only by seeing the world through its customers' eyes can the company build lasting and profitable customer relationships.

Customer-Value Marketing

According to the principle of **customer-value marketing**, the company should put most of its resources into customer value-building marketing investments. Many things marketers do—one-shot sales promotions, cosmetic packaging changes, direct-response advertising—may raise sales in the short run but add less *value* than would actual improvements in the product's quality, features, or convenience. Enlightened marketing calls for building long-run consumer loyalty and relationships by continually improving the value consumers receive from the firm's market offering. By creating value *for* consumers, the company can capture value *from* consumers in return.

Innovative Marketing

The principle of **innovative marketing** requires that the company continuously seek real product and marketing improvements. The company that overlooks new and better ways to do things will eventually lose customers to another company that has found a better way. An excellent example of an innovative marketer is Samsung Electronics:

A dozen years ago, Samsung was a copycat consumer electronics brand you bought if you couldn't afford a Sony. But today, the brand holds a high-end, cutting-edge aura. In 1996, Samsung Electronics made an inspired decision. It turned its back on cheap knock-offs and set out to overtake rival Sony. The company hired a crop of fresh, young designers, who unleashed a torrent of sleek, bold, and beautiful products targeted to high-end users. Samsung called them "lifestyle works of art"—from brightly colored mobile phones and elegantly thin DVD players to flat-panel TV monitors that hung on walls like paintings. Every new product had to pass the "Wow!" test: If it didn't get a "Wow!" reaction during market testing, it went straight back to the design studio.

Samsung also changed its distribution to match its new caché. It initially abandoned low-end distributors such as Wal-Mart and Kmart, instead building strong relationships with specialty retailers such as Best Buy and Circuit City. Interbrand calculates that Samsung is the world's fastest growing brand over the past five years. It's the world leader in CDMA mobile phones and battling for the number two spot in total handsets sold. It's also number one worldwide in color TVs, flash memory, and LCD panels. "Samsung's performance continues to astound brand watchers," says one analyst. The company has become a model for others that "want to shift from being a cheap supplier to a global brand." Says a Samsung designer, "We're not el cheapo anymore."[12]

Sense-of-Mission Marketing

Sense-of-mission marketing means that the company should define its mission in broad *social* terms rather than narrow *product* terms. When a company defines a social mission, employees feel better about their work and have a clearer sense of direction. Brands linked with broader missions can serve the best long-run interests of both the brand and consumers. For example, Dove wants to do more than just sell its beauty-care products. It's on a mission to discover "real beauty" and to help women be happy just the way they are (see **Real Marketing**).

Some companies define their overall corporate missions in broad societal terms. For example, defined in narrow product terms, the mission of Unilever's Ben & Jerry's unit might be "to sell ice cream." However, Ben & Jerry's states its mission more broadly, as one of "linked prosperity," including product, economic, and social missions. From its beginnings, Ben & Jerry's championed a host of social and environmental causes, and it donated 7.5 percent of pretax profits to support worthy causes. It has since become the number two super premium ice cream brand in the U.S. However, having a "double bottom line" of values and profits is not easy. Ben & Jerry's appear to have, at times, focused too much on social issues at the expense of sound business management.

Such experiences taught the socially responsible business movement some hard lessons. The result is a new generation of activist entrepreneurs—not social activists with big hearts who hate capitalism, but well-trained business managers and company builders with a passion for a cause.

Societal Marketing

Following the principle of **societal marketing**, an enlightened company makes marketing decisions by considering consumers' wants and interests, the company's requirements, and society's long-run interests. The company is aware that neglecting consumer and societal long-run interests is a disservice to consumers and society. Alert companies view societal problems as opportunities.

A societally oriented marketer wants to design products that are not only pleasing but also beneficial. The difference is shown in **Figure 20.7.** Products can be classified according to their degree of immediate consumer satisfaction and long-run consumer benefit. **Deficient products**, such as bad-tasting and ineffective medicine, have neither immediate appeal nor long-run benefits. **Pleasing products** give high immediate satisfaction but may hurt consumers in the long run. Examples include cigarettes and junk food. **Salutary products** have low appeal but may benefit consumers in the long run; for instance, seat belts and air bags. **Desirable products** give both high immediate satisfaction and high long-run benefits, such as Philips Lighting's Earth Light compact fluorescent light bulb which provides good lighting while offering long life and energy savings. Toyota's hybrid Prius gives both a quiet ride and fuel efficiency.

Linked prosperity – Ben & Jerry's not only sells ice-cream, it also donates 7.5 percent of pretax profits to support worthy causes. (*www.benjerry.com*)

Sense-of-mission marketing
A principle of enlightened marketing that holds that a company should define its mission in broad social terms rather than narrow product terms.

Societal marketing
A principle of enlightened marketing that holds that a company should make marketing decisions by considering consumers' wants, the company's requirements, consumers' long-run interests, and society's long-run interests.

Deficient products
Products that have neither immediate appeal nor long-run benefits.

Pleasing products
Products that give high immediate satisfaction but may hurt consumers in the long run.

Salutary products
Products that have low appeal but may benefit consumers in the long run.

Desirable products
Products that give both high immediate satisfaction and high long-run benefits.

Immediate satisfaction

Long-run consumer benefit	Low	High
High	Salutary products	Desirable products
Low	Deficient products	Pleasing products

Figure 20.7
Societal classification of products

REAL MARKETING

Dove on a Mission: "Normal Is the New Beautiful"

How do you define beauty? Ads for cosmetics and beauty-care products in the latest fashion magazines depict beautiful models with incredibly lean, sexy figures and flawless features. They're one-of-a-kind supermodels, chosen to portray ideal beauty. The ads are meant to be aspirational. But real women, who compare themselves to these idealized images each day, too often come away feeling diminished by thoughts that they could never really look like that.

Unilever's Dove brand is on a mission to change all of this. Its Dove Campaign for Real Beauty hopes to do much more than just sell Dove beauty creams and lotions. It aims to change the traditional definition of beauty—to "offer in its place a broader, healthier, more democratic view of beauty." It tells women to be happy just the way they are. "In Dove ads," says one advertising expert, "normal is the new beautiful."

It all started with a Unilever study that examined the impact on women of a society that narrowly defines beauty by the images seen in entertainment, in advertising, and on fashion runways. The startling result: Only 2 percent of 3,300 women and girls surveyed in 10 countries considered themselves beautiful. Unilever's research revealed that among women ages 15 to 64 worldwide, 90 percent want to change at least one aspect of their physical appearance; 67 percent withdraw from life-engaging activities because they are uncomfortable with their looks. Unilever's conclusion: It's time to redefine beauty. "We believe that beauty comes in different shapes, sizes, and ages," says Dove marketing director

Philippe Harousseau. "Our mission is to make more women feel beautiful every day by broadening the definition of beauty."

Unilever launched the Dove Campaign for Real Beauty with ads that featured candid and confident images of real women of all types (not actresses or models) and headlines that prompted consumers to ponder their perceptions of beauty. Among others, it featured full-bodied women ("Oversized or Outstanding?"), older women ("Gray or Gorgeous?", "Wrinkled or Wonderful?"), and a heavily freckled woman ("Flawed or Flawless?"). In 2005, the campaign's popularity skyrocketed as Dove introduced six new "real beauties" of various ethnicities and proportions, in sizes ranging from 6 to 14. These women appeared in magazines and on billboards wearing nothing but their underwear and big smiles, with headlines proclaiming, "New Dove Firming: As Tested on Real Curves."

Similarly, Unilever found that few Asian women were more satisfied with their friendships, family relations, and health than with their own sense of beauty. The Dove campaign was

Unilever's Dove brand is on a mission. The Dove Campaign for Real Beauty aims to change the traditional definition of beauty. Visit *www.compaignforrealbeauty.com.sg* to find out more.

launched in 2005 across 11 Asian countries. It questions whether stereotype model attributes such as large eyes, youth, slimness, long hair, and flawless skin are required to be beautiful. Each ad presents an image of a woman whose appearance differs from the stereotypical physical ideal and asks the reader to judge the woman's looks. One ad showed Atsuko Honda, 57, of Tokyo and asked "Aging? Ageless? Will society ever accept that old can be beautiful too?" Another featured Naruechol Phanichjaroen, 32, of Bangkok, and asked "Flat? Flattering? Can you be sexy without being busty?"

As the campaign has taken off, so have sales of Dove products. And calls to Unilever's consumer call center have surged, as has traffic to the campaignforrealbeauty.com Web site. Women, girls, and even men praise Dove for addressing a too-long-ignored social issue. In addition to the positive reactions, however, the Dove Campaign for Real Beauty has also received criticism.

Critics point out that the "real women" in the Dove ads are still headturners, with smooth skin, straight teeth, and not an ounce of cellulite. Although these unretouched beauties are more realistic than supermodels, they still represent a lofty standard of beauty. Fans of the campaign counter that, compared with typical ad-industry portrayals, the Dove

women represent an image of beauty that is healthy, constructive, and much closer to reality. Other critics claim that the campaign is hypocritical, celebrating less-than-perfect bodies while at the same time selling products designed to restore them, such as firming lotions. "Any change in the culture of advertising that allows for a broader definition of beauty and encourages women to be more accepting and comfortable with their natural appearance is a step in the right direction," says noted psychologist and author Mary Pipher. "But embedded within this is a contradiction. They are still saying you have to use this product to be beautiful." Still, she concedes, "It's better than what we've had in the past." Still others criticize Unilever for capitalizing on women's low self-esteem just to make a buck. But the company responds that it has created much more than a series of ads. It's promoting a philosophy, one supported by a substantial advertising budget, the Dove Self-Esteem Fund, and a Web site full of resources designed to build the self-esteem of women and young girls.

To be sure, Unilever does have financial objectives for its Dove brand—most consumers understand and accept that fact. And if women are not buying the message of Dove about the nature of real beauty, then they aren't buying its products either. But the people behind the Dove brand and the Campaign for

Real Beauty have noble motives beyond sales and profits. According to Fernando Acosta, Dove vice president of brand development, the bold and compelling mission of the Dove brand to redefine beauty and reassure women rank well above issues of dollars and cents. "You should see the faces of the people working on this brand now," he says. "There is a real love for the brand."

Sources:
"Dove Ads with 'Real' Women Get Attention," *Associated Press Financial Wire*, July 29, 2005; Theresa Howard, "Ad Campaigns Tell Women to Celebrate How They Are," *USA Today*, August 7, 2005, accessed at www.usatoday.com; Pallavi Gogoi, "From Reality TV to Reality Ads," *BusinessWeek Online*, August 17, 2005, accessed at www.businessweek.com; "Positioning: Getting Comfy in Their Skin," *Brandweek*, December 19, 2005, p. 16; Patricia Odell, "Real Girls," *Promo*, March 1, 2006, p. 24; "Beyond Stereotypes: Rebuilding the Foundation of Beauty Beliefs," February 2006, accessed at www.campaignforrealbeauty.com; Jeani Read, "Women Modeling for Dove Love Challenging Skinny Stereotypes," *The Calgary Herald*, May 15, 2006, p. C3; and information found at www.campaignforrealbeauty.com, December 2006.

Companies should try to turn their products into desirable products. The challenge posed by pleasing products is that they sell very well but may end up hurting the consumer. The product opportunity, therefore, is to add long-run benefits without reducing the product's pleasing qualities. The challenge posed by salutary products is to add some pleasing qualities so that they will become more desirable in consumers' minds.

Marketing Ethics

Conscientious marketers face many moral dilemmas. The best thing to do is often unclear. Because not all managers have fine moral sensitivity, companies need to develop *corporate marketing ethics policies*—broad guidelines that everyone in the organization must follow. These policies should cover distributor relations, advertising standards, customer service, pricing, product development, and general ethical standards.

The finest guidelines cannot resolve all the difficult ethical situations the marketer faces. **Table 20.1** lists some difficult ethical situations marketers could face during their careers. If marketers choose immediate sales-producing actions in all these cases, their marketing behavior might well be described as immoral or even amoral. If they refuse to go along with *any* of the actions, they might be ineffective as marketing managers and unhappy because of the constant moral tension. Managers need a set of principles that will help them figure out the moral importance of each situation and decide how far they can go in good conscience.

But *what* principle should guide companies and marketing managers on issues of ethics and social responsibility? One philosophy is that such issues are decided by the free market and legal system. Under this principle, companies and their managers are not responsible for making moral judgments. Companies can in good conscience do whatever the market and legal systems allow.

A second philosophy puts responsibility not on the system but in the hands of individual companies and managers. This more enlightened philosophy suggests that a company should have a "social conscience." Companies and managers should apply high standards of ethics and morality when making corporate decisions, regardless of "what the system allows."

Each company and marketing manager must work out a philosophy of socially responsible and ethical behavior. Under the societal marketing concept, each manager must look beyond what is legal and develop standards based on personal integrity, corporate conscience, and long-run consumer welfare. A clear and responsible philosophy will help the company deal with knotty issues such as the one faced by 3M:

What information should be divulged? What kinds of information shouldn't? Companies need to develop corporate marketing ethics policies that everyone in the organization must follow.

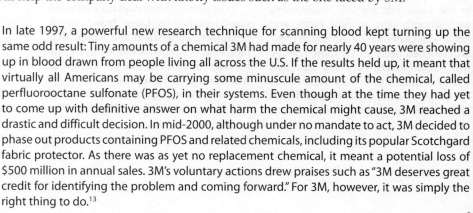

In late 1997, a powerful new research technique for scanning blood kept turning up the same odd result: Tiny amounts of a chemical 3M had made for nearly 40 years were showing up in blood drawn from people living all across the U.S. If the results held up, it meant that virtually all Americans may be carrying some minuscule amount of the chemical, called perfluorooctane sulfonate (PFOS), in their systems. Even though at the time they had yet to come up with definitive answer on what harm the chemical might cause, 3M reached a drastic and difficult decision. In mid-2000, although under no mandate to act, 3M decided to phase out products containing PFOS and related chemicals, including its popular Scotchgard fabric protector. As there was as yet no replacement chemical, it meant a potential loss of $500 million in annual sales. 3M's voluntary actions drew praises such as "3M deserves great credit for identifying the problem and coming forward." For 3M, however, it was simply the right thing to do.[13]

Table 20.1 Some Morally Difficult Situations in Marketing

1. You work for a cigarette company. Public policy debates over the past many years leave no doubt in your mind that cigarette smoking and cancer are closely linked. Although your company currently runs an "if you don't smoke, don't start" promotion campaign, you believe that other company promotions might encourage young (although legal age) nonsmokers to pick up the habit. What would you do?

2. Your R&D department has changed one of your products slightly. It is not really "new and improved," but you know that putting this statement on the package and in advertising will increase sales. What would you do?

3. You have been asked to add a stripped-down model to your line that could be advertised to pull customers into the store. The product won't be very good, but salespeople will be able to switch buyers up to higher-priced units. You are asked to give the green light for the stripped-down version. What would you do?

4. You are thinking of hiring a product manager who has just left a competitor's company. She would be more than happy to tell you all the competitor's plans for the coming year. What would you do?

5. One of your top dealers in an important territory recently has had family troubles, and his sales have slipped. It looks like it will take him a while to straighten out his family trouble. Meanwhile you are losing many sales. Legally, on performance grounds, you can terminate the dealer's franchise and replace him. What would you do?

6. You have a chance to win a big account that will mean a lot to you and your company. The purchasing agent hints that a "gift" would influence the decision. Your assistant recommends sending a fine color television set to the buyer's home. What would you do?

7. You have heard that a competitor has a new product feature that will make a big difference in sales. The competitor will demonstrate the feature in a private dealer meeting at the annual trade show. You can easily send an observer to this meeting to learn about the new feature. What would you do?

8. You have to choose between three ad campaigns outlined by your agency. The first (a) is a soft-sell, honest, straight-information campaign. The second (b) uses sex-loaded emotional appeals and exaggerates the product's benefits. The third (c) involves a noisy, somewhat irritating commercial that is sure to gain audience attention. Pretests show that the campaigns are effective in the following order: c, b, and a. What would you do?

9. You are interviewing a capable female applicant for a job as salesperson. She is better qualified than the men that you just interviewed. Nevertheless, you know that some of your important customers prefer dealing with men, and you will lose some sales if you hire her. What would you do?

As with environmentalism, the issue of ethics provides special challenges for international marketers. Business standards and practices vary a great deal from one country to the next. For example, whereas bribes and kickbacks are illegal for U.S. firms, they are standard business practice in many Asian and South American countries. One study found that companies from some nations were much more likely to use bribes when seeking contracts in emerging-market nations. The most flagrant bribe-paying firms were from Russia and China, with Taiwan and South Korea close behind. Other countries where corruption is common include Turkmenistan, Bangladesh, and Chad. The least corrupt were companies from Iceland, Finland, New Zealand, and Denmark.[14]

The question arises as to whether a company must lower its ethical standards to compete effectively in countries with lower standards. Ideally, companies should make a commitment to a common set of shared standards worldwide. For example, John Hancock Mutual Life Insurance Company operates successfully in Southeast Asia, an area that by Western standards has widespread questionable business and government practices. Despite warnings from locals that Hancock would have to bend its rules to succeed, the

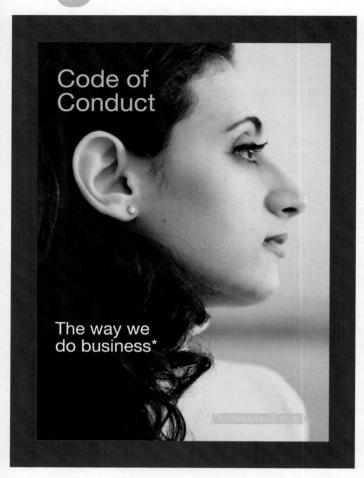

Code of Conduct

The way we do business*

Ethics programs –
PricewaterhouseCoopers established a comprehensive ethics program, which begins with a code of conduct, called "The Way We Do Business." Says PwC's CEO, "Ethics is in everything we say or do." (*www.pwc.com/ethics*)

company set out strict guidelines. "We told our people that we had the same ethical standards, same procedures, and same policies in these countries that we have in the U.S., and we do," says Hancock Chairman Stephen Brown. "We just felt that things like payoffs were wrong—and if we had to do business that way, we'd rather not do business." Hancock employees feel good about the consistent levels of ethics. "There may be countries where you have to do that kind of thing," says Brown. "We haven't found that country yet, and if we do, we won't do business there."[15]

Many industrial and professional associations have suggested codes of ethics, and many companies are now adopting their own codes. Companies are also developing programs to teach managers about important ethics issues and help them find the proper responses. They hold ethics workshops and seminars and set up ethics committees. Further, some major companies have appointed high-level ethics officers to champion ethics issues and to help resolve ethics problems and concerns facing employees.

PricewaterhouseCoopers (PwC) is a good example. In 2002, PwC established a global ethics office and comprehensive ethics program, headed by a high-level global ethics officer. The ethics program begins with a code of conduct, called "The Way We Do Business." PwC employees learn about the code of conduct and about how to handle thorny ethics issues in comprehensive ethics training programs, which start when the employee joins the company and continue through the employee's career. The program also includes an ethics help line and regular communications at all levels. "It is obviously not enough to distribute a document," says PwC's CEO, Samuel DiPiazza. "Ethics is in everything we say and do."[16]

Still, written codes and ethics programs do not ensure ethical behavior. Ethics and social responsibility require a total corporate commitment. They must be a component of the overall corporate culture. According to PwC's DiPiazza, "I see ethics as a mission-critical issue... deeply imbedded in who we are and what we do. It's just as important as our product development cycle or our distribution system... It's about creating a culture based on integrity and respect, not a culture based on dealing with the crisis of the day. We ask ourselves every day, 'Are we doing the right things?' "[17]

REVIEWING THE CONCEPTS

Well—here you are at the end of your introductory marketing travels! In this chapter, we've closed with many important concepts involving marketing's sweeping impact on individual consumers, other businesses, and society as a whole. You learned that responsible marketers discover what consumers want and respond with the right market offerings, priced to give good value to buyers and profit to the producer. A marketing system should deliver customer value and improve the quality of consumers' lives. In working to meet consumer needs, marketers may take some actions that are not to everyone's liking or benefit. Marketing managers should be aware of the main *criticisms of marketing.*

1 Identify the major social criticisms of marketing.

Marketing's *impact on individual consumer welfare* has been criticized for its high prices, deceptive practices, high-pressure selling, shoddy or unsafe products, planned obsolescence, and poor service to disadvantaged consumers. Marketing's *impact on society* has been criticized for creating false wants and too much materialism, too few social goods, cultural pollution, and too much political power. Critics have also criticized marketing's *impact on other businesses* for harming competitors and reducing competition through acquisitions, practices that create barriers to entry, and unfair competitive marketing practices. Some of these concerns are justified; some are not.

2 Define consumerism and environmentalism and explain how they affect marketing strategies.

Concerns about the marketing system have led to *citizen action movements. Consumerism* is an organized social movement intended to strengthen the rights and power of consumers relative to sellers. Alert marketers view it as an opportunity to serve consumers better by providing more consumer information, education, and protection. *Environmentalism* is an organized social movement seeking to minimize the harm done to the environment and quality of life by marketing practices. The first wave of modern environmentalism was driven by environmental groups and concerned consumers, whereas the second wave was driven by government, which passed laws and regulations governing industrial practices impacting the environment. The first two environmentalism waves are now merging into a third and stronger wave in which companies are accepting responsibility for doing no environmental harm. Companies now are adopting policies of *environmental sustainability*—developing strategies that both sustain the environment and produce profits for the company.

3 Describe the principles of socially responsible marketing.

Many companies originally opposed these social movements and laws, but most of them now recognize a need for positive consumer information, education, and protection. Some companies have followed a policy of *enlightened marketing*, which holds that a company's marketing should support the best long-run performance of the marketing system. Enlightened marketing consists of five principles: *consumer-oriented marketing, customer-value marketing, innovative marketing, sense-of-mission marketing,* and *societal marketing.*

4 Explain the role of ethics in marketing.

Increasingly, companies are responding to the need to provide company policies and guidelines to help their managers deal with questions of *marketing ethics.* Of course even the best guidelines cannot resolve all the difficult ethical decisions that individuals and firms must make. But there are some principles that marketers can choose from. One principle states that such issues should be decided by the free market and legal system. A second, and more enlightened principle, puts responsibility not on the system but in the hands of individual companies and managers. Each firm and marketing manager must work out a philosophy of socially responsible and ethical behavior. Under the societal marketing concept, managers must look beyond what is legal and allowable and develop standards based on personal integrity, corporate conscience, and long-term consumer welfare.

Because business standards and practices vary from country to country, the issue of ethics poses special challenges for international marketers. The growing consensus among today's marketers is that it is important to make a commitment to a common set of shared standards worldwide.

REVIEWING THE KEY TERMS

Consumerism 559
Consumer-oriented marketing 564
Customer-value marketing 564
Deficient products 565
Desirable products 565
Enlightened marketing 563
Environmentalism 560

Environmental sustainability 561
Innovative marketing 564
Pleasing products 565
Salutary products 565
Sense-of-mission marketing 565
Societal marketing 565

DISCUSSING THE CONCEPTS

1. In what ways do consumers believe that marketers make products more expensive to the end consumer?

2. What deceptive marketing practices have you witnessed personally? Are they price, promotion, product, or packaging based? Make a list and then briefly describe one incident in detail.

3. Review claims made by critics that marketing creates false wants and too much materialism, too few social goods, cultural pollution, and too much political power. Do you agree or disagree with these claims?

4. Can an organization be focused on both consumerism and environmentalism at the same time? Explain.

5. In what ways do companies benefit from practicing the philosophy of enlightened marketing?

6. Select three moral dilemmas from Table 20.1. Propose an ethical response for each dilemma.

APPLYING THE CONCEPTS

1. Visit _adage.com_ and click on the "why it matters" section on the left-hand column. Choose two reports at this site and discuss how they relate to the ethical and social responsibility topics in this chapter.

2. Recent public concerns over children and the Internet resulted in the Children's Online Privacy Protection Act (COPPA) in the U.S. Among other things, this act

requires Web sites that are visited by children under the age of 13 to post a privacy policy detailing any personally identifiable information collected from those children. Do some research and answer the question: What consumer need does COPPA meet?

3. Visit _adbuster.org_. What is the purpose of this Web site? Do you think it is effective with its message?

FOCUS ON TECHNOLOGY

Cause-related marketing and corporate philanthropy, companies donating a portion of their profits to charity, have been popular for some time. Meet Goodsearch.com, which harnesses the power of Internet technology to create a business model based on donations. A recent entry into the crowded search engine market dominated by Google and Yahoo!, Goodsearch differentiates itself on its ability to raise money for thousands of charities. Founded by a brother and sister who lost their mother to cancer, Goodsearch lets people use the power of Yahoo! search engine technology to search the Internet while donating money to charity. Searchers choose an existing charity on Goodsearch or add their own charity. Each time they search, 50 percent of the advertising revenues are donated to the charity. Each search earns about $0.01, so continued searching could reach the following totals in one year.

Charity Size	Number of Supporters	Average Searches per Day	Estimated Revenue/Year
Small	100	2	$730
Medium	1,000	2	$7,300
Large	10,000	2	$73,000

1. Were you aware of Goodsearch? If not, why have so few people heard of it?

2. Would you use this Web site? Discuss.

3. What search engine do you use? Why are you loyal to this search engine?

FOCUS ON ETHICS

In a commercial shown repeatedly over Chinese TV, cross-talk star Guo Degang is seen endorsing a "special Tibetan fat-eliminating tea." The promise of a slimmer figure ("Three boxes will flatten big stomachs!" was the product's tagline) and a celebrity endorsement made the tea a hot seller. Thousands of boxes retailing at 29 yuan ($3.85) flew off supermarket shelves. Sales exceeded $13 million in 2006. For his role, Guo pocketed $265,000.

However, in March 2007, a CCTV program on consumer rights featured the tea as among the dubious and substandard products and services it had uncovered. The tea was pulled from the market and Guo came under fire online for "irresponsible behavior." Netizens vilified him together with other celebrities who had fronted misleading ads.

According to the State Administration of Industry and Commerce, 2.5 million Chinese take incorrect medicine every year, deceived by misleading commercials. The authorities have stepped up efforts to prevent bogus ads from appearing on radio, TV, newspapers, and magazines. Still, consumers have increasingly called for a law that holds personalities appearing in an ad responsible for promoting problematic products. One victim said, "Stars should not abuse their fame. They should do background checks and not endorse products they themselves have not tried or are not sure about."

Defending himself on a blog, Guo reasoned that he was paid to do the tea ad and that if the product was not as advertised, the responsibility should lie with the company which paid him. He added that he himself had tried the tea and found it to be "pretty good." However, his defense cut no ice with some consumers who are suing him and the manufacturer of the tea.[18]

1. Should there be regulations against celebrities endorsing problematic products?

2. Should celebrities conduct background checks and not endorse products they have not tried or are uncertain about?

3. Should celebrities be held at a higher standard in product endorsements than other individuals such as product experts and satisfied customers of a brand?

VIDEO CASE

NFL

Think of the NFL and you might conjure up images of burly football players and adrenaline-filled stadiums. But the league offers fans much more than Sunday afternoons full of football. Players and teams alike consider football and community involvement to be the twin pillars of the NFL. Through more than 20 separate community programs, the NFL focuses considerable manpower on its efforts to give back to the community and encourage others to do the same. In addition, for more than 30 years the NFL has partnered with United Way. NFL teams and players support local United Way chapters by making personal appearances, participating in joint programs, and offering campaign contributions. The NFL and United Way have also created public service television ads featuring NFL stars volunteering in their communities—reading to children, playing shuffleboard with senior citizens, and working at local charities. In total, more than 1,000 such ads have aired during NFL games, making it the longest-running public service ad campaign in history.

It's clear that the partnership benefits United Way. With help from the NFL, United Way fundraising has skyrocketed from $800 million in 1974 to nearly $4 billion today. But the NFL benefits too. Working in the community makes players more accessible and helps to build stronger relationships with fans by connecting with them in their own backyards.

After viewing the video featuring the NFL, answer the following questions about marketing and social responsibility.

1. Why does the NFL partner with United Way? How, if at all, does that partnership impact your opinion of the league? How does it impact your interest in volunteering?

2. Make a list of social criticisms of the NFL. Then visit JoinTheTeam.com and read more about the NFL's outreach programs. Do these efforts alleviate any concerns you have about the league's negative impact on society?

3. By the text's definition, does the NFL practice "enlightened marketing"?

COMPANY CASE

Alibaba.com: Shark Attack

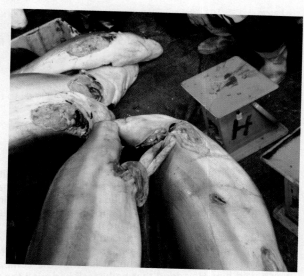

Patric Douglas runs a San Francisco company which offers shark diving for thrill-seekers. His customers go out on a boat, get into cages, are submerged beneath the ocean, and watch sharks swim by. His company, Mega Outdoor Adventures, takes about 500 people a year to the waters off Baja California to see all sorts of sharks, including great whites, tiger sharks, and whale sharks. Thanks to his shark-diving business, Douglas has also become an unlikely leader of a campaign targeting one of China's leading e-commerce companies, Alibaba.com, a business-to-business marketplace that is 40 percent owned by Yahoo!. Alibaba provides small and midsized companies in China the opportunity to find buyers and sellers overseas. And, among the numerous products displayed on its Web site are numerous types of shark fins, prized by many Chinese as the vital ingredient in shark fin soup. This delicacy is often offered at high-end Chinese restaurants in East Asia.

The Campaign

Harvesting shark fin can be a brutal practice. After finning, sharks are often tossed back into the ocean to sink to the bottom and die. Douglas and other activists say that shark populations worldwide are declining given the growing demand for the fins. "Something evil is going on here," he says. The shark fin trade "is decimating the oceans."

Thus, since 2006, Douglas and other activists have sent petitions with thousands of signatures to Alibaba demanding that founder, chairman, and CEO Jack Ma crack down on the shark fin merchants using its site. Alibaba, which has over 180 companies engaged in the buying

and selling of shark fins, is "the New York Stock Exchange of shark fins," says Douglas. Wolfgang Leander, director of shark preservation at the Ocean Realm Society, a Florida-based lobbying group, "They are offering the shark fin traders a very convenient platform to do business."

The Response

Alibaba denies any wrongdoing regarding shark fins. Its spokesperson Christina Splinder said, "We respect our members' rights to make their own decisions on issues of cultural tradition." Alibaba has a policy prohibiting Web site users from listing products taken from animals protected by local or international law such as the Convention on International Trade in Endangered Species of Wild Fauna and Flora (CITES), she says.

"We had an open dialogue with activists," she adds. "We took their suggestions and opinions on board and reviewed our policies… We decided that our current policy is the appropriate policy at this time." Trade in officially recognized endangered species "is strictly forbidden on Alibaba," says Splinder. "Our editing team will promptly remove listings if we become aware that listings are not CITES compliant." Sharks are not on the CITES protected list.

Not Enough Bite

Hence, activists contend that Alibaba uses a different standard than the CITES list. They argue that some of the shark fin merchants using the company's site are violating laws prohibiting over-fishing of sharks. "A vast proportion of this trade is actually done illegally," says Brian Darvell, a University of Hong Kong professor of dental material science. Darvell was active in a 2005 grassroots movement that successfully pressured Disney to drop shark fin soup from the menus at Hong Kong Disneyland hotels.

While the Hong Kong government says local buyers and sellers only deal in legitimately obtained shark fins, Darvell says that argument "is simply inconceivable. The volume is so great. We know that fishing occurs in areas that are supposed to be protected."

Interestingly, Alibaba's critics found an ally in Hong Kong's top shark fin traders group. Charlie Lim, general secretary of the Shark Fin and Marine Products Association in the city, says that cyberspace is a risky venue for shark fin merchants. "To buy shark's fin, you really need to look at the fins and check the quality," he says. "I presume only small or new companies would turn to the Internet. There might be a greater chance to be duped if everything is done online."

What Next?

Having made no progress with Alibaba, the activists pledge to continue lobbying. Yet, they are aware that they face a major hurdle in getting people to care about saving creatures that are hardly beloved by many. "Sharks aren't cuddly and cute," says Duncan Carson, a Madrid-based activist running the Web site stopsharkfinning.net. "So people aren't inclined to take notice."

For Yahoo!, the campaign against Alibaba by the world's shark activists is the latest in a string of China-related public relations challenges. In 2006, Yahoo! and other companies were condemned for their willingness to cooperate with the Chinese government in censoring the Internet in China. In May 2007, Shi Tao, a journalist currently imprisoned in China, sued Yahoo! in the U.S.

The problems haven't just been about free-speech issues. In April 2007, a Chinese court ruled against Yahoo! China (owned by Alibaba) in a lawsuit brought by the International Federation of the Phonographic Industry. The suit alleged that the company facilitated digital music piracy. Alibaba, widely rumored to be readying for an initial public offering, is appealing. Probably the last thing it wants is another black mark.

Questions For Discussion

1. Which of the textbook's criticisms of marketing's impact on consumers, if any, are evident in the Alibaba case?
2. Which of the criticisms of marketing's impact on society, if any, are evident in the Alibaba case?
3. Evaluate Alibaba's policy response to the shark fin activist community. Could it have done more? Why or why not?
4. What should the activists do next? Is theirs a lost environmental cause?
5. Visit stopsharkfinning.net. Is the production and marketing of shark fins socially, ethically, and environmentally responsible? How would you improve the situation?

Source:
Bruce Einhorn, "Sharks Circle China's Alibaba.com," *BusinessWeek Online Asia*, July 20, 2007.

MARKETING PLAN

The Marketing Plan: An Introduction

As a marketer, you'll need a good marketing plan to provide direction and focus for your brand, product, or company. With a detailed plan, any business will be better prepared to launch a new product or build sales for existing products. Nonprofit organizations also use marketing plans to guide their fundraising and outreach efforts. Even government agencies put together marketing plans for initiatives such as building public awareness of proper nutrition and stimulating area tourism.

The Purpose and Content of a Marketing Plan

Unlike a business plan, which offers a broad overview of the entire organization's mission, objectives, strategy, and resource allocation, a marketing plan has a more limited scope. It serves to document how the organization's strategic objectives will be achieved through specific marketing strategies and tactics, with the customer as the starting point. It is also linked to the plans of other departments within the organization. Suppose a marketing plan calls for selling 200,000 units annually. The production department must gear up to make that many units, the finance department must have funding available to cover the expenses, the human resources department must be ready to hire and train staff, and so on. Without the appropriate level of organizational support and resources, no marketing plan can succeed.

Although the exact length and layout will vary from company to company, a marketing plan usually contains the sections described in Chapter 2. Smaller businesses may create shorter or less formal marketing plans, whereas corporations frequently require highly structured marketing plans. To guide implementation effectively, every part of the plan must be described in considerable detail. Sometimes a company will post its marketing plan on an internal Web site, which allows managers and employees in different locations to consult specific sections and collaborate on additions or changes.

The Role of Research

Marketing plans are not created in a vacuum. To develop successful strategies and action programs, marketers need up-to-date information about the environment, the competition, and the market segments to be served. Often, analysis of internal data is the starting point for assessing the current marketing situation, supplemented by marketing intelligence and research investigating the overall market, the competition, key issues, and threats and opportunities issues. As the plan is put into effect, marketers use a variety of research techniques to measure progress toward objectives and identify areas for improvement if results fall short of projections. Finally, marketing research helps marketers learn more about their customers' requirements, expectations, perceptions, and satisfaction levels. This deeper understanding provides a foundation for building competitive advantage through well-informed segmenting, targeting, and positioning decisions. Thus, the marketing plan should outline what marketing research will be conducted and how the findings will be applied.

The Role of Relationships

The marketing plan shows how the company will establish and maintain profitable customer relationships. In the process, however, it also shapes a number of internal and external relationships. First, it affects how marketing personnel work with each other and with other departments to deliver value and satisfy customers. Second, it affects how the company works with suppliers, distributors, and strategic alliance partners to achieve the objectives listed in the plan. Third, it influences the company's dealings with other stakeholders, including government regulators, the media, and the community at large. All of these relationships are important to the organization's success, so they should be considered when a marketing plan is being developed.

From Marketing Plan to Marketing Action

Companies generally create yearly marketing plans, although some plans cover a longer period. Marketers start planning well in advance of the implementation date to allow time for marketing research, thorough analysis, management review, and coordination between departments. Then, after each action program begins, marketers monitor ongoing results, compare them with projections, analyze any differences, and take corrective steps as needed. Some marketers also prepare contingency plans for implementation if certain conditions emerge. Because of inevitable and sometimes unpredictable environmental changes, marketers must be ready to update and adapt marketing plans at any time.

For effective implementation and control, the marketing plan should define how progress toward objectives will be measured. Managers typically use budgets, schedules, and performance standards for monitoring and evaluating results. With budgets, they can compare planned expenditures with actual expenditures for a given week, month, or other period. Schedules allow management to see when tasks were supposed to be completed—and when they were actually completed. Performance standards track the outcomes of marketing programs to see whether the company is moving forward toward its objectives. Some examples of performance standards are: market share, sales volume, product profitability, and customer satisfaction.

Sample Marketing Plan for Sonic

This section takes you inside the sample marketing plan for Sonic, a hypothetical start-up company. The company's first product is the Sonic 1000, a multimedia personal digital assistant (PDA), also known as a handheld computer. Sonic will be competing with Palm, Hewlett-Packard, and other well-established PDA rivals in a crowded, fast-changing marketplace where enhanced cell phones and many other electronics devices have PDA functionality. The annotations explain more about what each section of the plan should contain and why.

Executive Summary

Executive summary
This section summarizes the main goals, recommendations, and points as an overview for senior managers who must read and approve the marketing plan. Generally, a table of contents follows this section for management convenience.

Sonic is preparing to launch a new multimedia PDA product, the Sonic 1000, in a maturing market. Despite the dominance of PDA leader Palm, we can compete because our product offers a unique combination of features at a value-added price. We are targeting specific segments in the consumer and business markets, taking advantage of opportunities indicated by higher demand for easy-to-use PDAs with expanded communications, entertainment, and storage functionality.

The primary marketing objective is to achieve first-year U.S. market share of 3 percent with unit sales of 240,000. The primary financial objectives are to achieve first-year sales revenues of $60 million, keep first-year losses to less than $10 million, and break even early in the second year.

Current Marketing Situation

Current marketing situation
In this section, marketing managers discuss the overall market, identify the market segments they will target, and provide information about the company's current situation.

Sonic, founded 18 months ago by two entrepreneurs with experience in the PC market, is about to enter the now-mature PDA market. Multifunction cell phones, e-mail devices, and wireless communication devices are increasingly popular today; forecasts suggest that annual sales of such devices will grow at more than 50 percent for the next three years. Competition is therefore more intense even as PDA demand flattens, industry consolidation continues, and pricing pressures squeeze profitability. Yet the worldwide

PDA market remains substantial, with annual sales of 10 to 15 million units. To gain market share in this dynamic environment, Sonic must carefully target specific segments with features that deliver benefits valued by each customer group.

Market Description

Sonic's market consists of consumers and business users who prefer to use a single device for communication, information storage and exchange, and entertainment on the go. Specific segments being targeted during the first year include professionals, corporations, students, entrepreneurs, and medical users. **Table A1.1** shows how the Sonic 1000 addresses the needs of targeted consumer and business segments.

PDA purchasers can choose between models based on several different operating systems, including systems from Palm, Microsoft, and Symbian, plus Linux variations. Sonic licenses a Linux-based system because it is somewhat less vulnerable to attack by hackers and viruses. With hard drives becoming commonplace in the PDA market, Sonic is equipping its first product with an ultrafast one-gigabyte hard drive for information and entertainment storage. Technology costs are decreasing even as capabilities are increasing, which makes value-priced models more appealing to consumers and to customers with older PDAs who want to trade up to newer, high-end multifunction units

Market description
By describing the targeted segments in detail, marketers provide context for the marketing strategies and detailed action programs discussed later in the plan.

Benefits and product features
Exhibit 1 clarifies the benefits that product features will deliver to satisfy the needs of customers in each targeted segment.

Table A1.1 Needs and Corresponding Features/Benefits of Sonic PDA

Targeted Segment	Customer Need	Corresponding Feature/Benefit
Professionals (consumer market)	• Stay in touch conveniently and securely while on the go • Perform many functions hands-free without carrying multiple gadgets	• Built-in mobile phone and push-to-talk to communicate anywhere at any time; wireless e-mail/Web access from anywhere; Linux-based operating system less vulnerable to hackers • Voice-activated applications are convenient; GPS function, camera add value
Students (consumer market)	• Perform many functions hands-free without carrying multiple gadgets • Express style and individuality	• Compatible with numerous applications and peripherals for convenient, cost-effective note taking and functionality • Wardrobe of PDA cases in different colors, patterns, and materials
Corporate users (business market)	• Security and adaptability for proprietary tasks • Obtain driving directions to business meetings	• Customizable to fit corporate tasks and networks; Linux-based operating system less vulnerable to hackers • Built-in GPS allows voice-activated access to directions and maps
Entrepreneurs (business market)	• Organize and access contacts, schedule details, business and financial files • Get in touch fast	• No-hands, wireless access to calendar, address book, information files for checking appointments and data, connecting with contacts • Push-to-talk instant calling speeds up communications
Medical users (business market)	• Update, access, and exchange medical records • Photograph medical situations to maintain a visual record	• No-hands, wireless recording and exchange of information to reduce paperwork and increase productivity • Built-in camera allows fast and easy photography, stores images for later retrieval

Product Review

Our first product, the Sonic PDA 1000, offers the following standard features with a Linux OS:

- Voice recognition for hands-free operation
- Built-in cell phone functionality and push-to-talk instant calling
- Digital music/video recording, downloading, and playback
- Wireless Web and e-mail, text messaging, instant messaging
- Organization functions, including calendar, address book, synchronization
- Global positioning system for directions and maps
- Connectors for multiple peripherals and applications
- One-gigabyte hard drive with expansion potential
- Interchangeable case wardrobe of different colors and patterns

First-year sales revenues are projected to be $60 million, based on sales of 240,000 Sonic 1000 units at a wholesale price of $250 each. During the second year, we plan to introduce the Sonic 2000, also with Linux OS, as a higher-end product offering the following standard features:

- Global phone and messaging compatibility
- Translation capabilities to send English text as Chinese text (other languages to be offered as add-on options)
- Integrated six-megapixel camera

Competitive Review

The emergence of new multifunction phones, marketed by mobile phone manufacturers and carriers, has pressured industry participants to continually add features and cut prices. Competition from specialized devices for text and e-mail messaging, such as BlackBerry devices, is a major factor as well. Key competitors include:

- *Palm.* The trendy Treo PDA-phone combos account for more than half of Palm's $1.6 billion in annual revenues. As the best-known maker of PDAs, Palm has achieved excellent distribution in multiple channels and has alliances with a number of mobile phone service carriers in the U.S. and Europe. Its latest models are available with either the Palm or the Windows operating system.
- *Hewlett-Packard.* HP is targeting business markets with its iPAQ Pocket PC devices, many with wireless capabilities to accommodate corporate users. For extra security, one model allows access by fingerprint match as well as by password. HP enjoys excellent distribution, and its products are priced from below $300 to more than $600.
- *Samsung.* Many of this manufacturer's products combine mobile phone capabilities with multifunction PDA features. Its i730, a smartphone based on the Windows operating system, provides wireless Web access and MP3 streaming and downloads, plays videos, and offers PDA functions such as address book, calendar, and speed dial.
- *RIM.* Research in Motion makes the lightweight BlackBerry wireless phone/PDA products that are popular among corporate users. Although legal entanglements have slightly slowed market-share momentum, RIM's continuous innovation and solid customer service support clearly strengthen its competitive standing.
- *Siemens.* This company's latest PDA-phone combinations have several distinctive features. For example, some models dial any phone number that the user writes on the screen with a stylus. Also, on some models, the keyboard slides out of the way when not in use. Siemens is a particularly formidable competitor in European markets.

Despite this strong competition, Sonic can carve out a definite image and gain recognition among the targeted segments. Our voice-recognition system for hands-off operation is a critical point of differentiation for competitive advantage. Also, offering GPS as a standard feature gives our product a competitive edge compared with PDAs in the same general price range. Moreover, our product runs the Linux OS, which is an appealing alternative for customers concerned about security. **Table A1.2** shows a selection of competitive PDA products and prices.

Table A1.2 Selected PDA Products and Pricing

Competitor	Model	Features	Price
Palm	Treo 700	PDA functions, camera and phone, streaming audio/video, music downloads, Bluetooth connection, high-resolution screen, model P runs Palm OS, model W runs Windows	$349.99
Hewlett- Packard	iPAQ hw6500	PDA functions, backlit keyboard, Bluetooth connection, GPS included, built-in camera, memory slot, wireless radio and messaging capabilities, Windows OS	$549
Samsung	i730 PDA phone	PDA functions, built-in mobile phone, Wi-Fi Web access, Bluetooth connection, slide-out keyboard, voice dialing, music streaming and downloads, video playback, Windows OS	$299.99
RIM	BlackBerry 8700c	PDA functions, wireless e-mail and phone functions, multimedia messaging, Bluetooth connection, ergonomic keyboard, light-sensing screen, lightweight (4.7 ounces)	$299.99
Siemens	SX66	PDA functions, Wi-Fi and phone functions, handwriting-recognition dialing, slide-out keyboard, Bluetooth connection, Windows OS, relatively heavy (7.4 ounces)	$499.99

Distribution Review

Sonic-branded products will be distributed through a network of retailers in the top 50 U.S. markets. Among the most important channel partners being contacted are:

- *Office supply superstores.* Office Max and Staples will both carry Sonic products in stores, in catalogs, and online.
- *Computer stores.* CompUSA will carry Sonic products.
- *Electronics specialty stores.* Circuit City and Best Buy will carry Sonic PDAs.
- *Online retailers.* Amazon.com will carry Sonic PDAs and, for a promotional fee, will give Sonic prominent placement on its home page during the introduction.

Distribution review
In this section, marketers list the most important channels, provide an overview of each channel arrangement, and mention any new developments or trends.

Although distribution will initially be restricted to the U.S. we plan to expand into Canada and beyond, according to demand. We will emphasize trade sales promotion in the first year.

Strengths, Weaknesses, Opportunities, and Threat Analysis

Sonic has several powerful strengths on which to build, but our major weakness is lack of brand awareness and image. The major opportunity is demand for multimedia PDAs that deliver a number of valued benefits, eliminating the need for customers to carry more than one device. We also face the threat of ever-higher competition from consumer electronics manufacturers, as well as downward pricing pressure. **Table A1.3** summarizes Sonic's main strengths, weaknesses, opportunities, and threats.

Table A1.3 Sonic's Strengths, Weaknesses, Opportunities, and Threats

Strengths	Weaknesses
● Innovative combination of functions operated hands-free in one portable device ● Value pricing ● Security due to Linux-based operating system	● Lack of brand awareness and image ● Heavier than most competing models
Opportunities	**Threats**
● Increased demand for multimedia models with diverse functions and benefits ● Lower technology costs	● Intense competition ● Downward pricing pressure ● Compressed product life

Strengths
Strengths are internal capabilities that can help the company reach its objectives.

Weaknesses
Weaknesses are internal elements that may interfere with the company's ability to achieve its objectives.

Opportunities
Opportunities are external elements that the company may be able to exploit to its advantage.

Threats
Threats are current or emerging external elements that may possibly challenge the company's performance.

Strengths

Sonic can build on three important strengths:

1. *Innovative product*. The Sonic 1000 combines a variety of features that would otherwise require customers to carry multiple devices; these include mobile phone and wireless e-mail functionality, GPS capability, and digital video music storage and playback—all with hands-free operation.
2. *Security*. Our PDA uses a Linux-based operating system that is less vulnerable to hackers and other security threats that can result in stolen or corrupted data.
3. *Pricing*. Our product is priced lower than competing multifunction models none of which offer the same bundle of features—which gives us an edge with price-conscious customers.

Weaknesses

By waiting to enter the PDA market until considerable consolidation of competitors has occurred, Sonic has learned from the successes and mistakes of others. Nonetheless, we have two main weaknesses:

1. *Lack of brand awareness*. Sonic has not yet established a brand or image in the marketplace, whereas Palm and others have strong brand recognition. We will address this area with promotion.
2. *Heavier weight*. The Sonic 1000 is slightly heavier than most competing models because it incorporates multiple features and a sizable hard drive. To counteract this weakness, we will emphasize our unique combination of features and our value-added pricing, two compelling competitive strengths.

Opportunities

Sonic can take advantage of two major market opportunities:

1. *Increasing demand for multimedia models with multiple functions*. The market for multimedia, multifunction devices is growing much faster than the market for single use devices. Customers are now accustomed to seeing users with PDAs in work and educational settings, which is boosting primary demand. Also, customers who bought entry-level models are replacing older models with more-advanced models.
2. *Lower technology costs*. Better technology is now available at a lower cost than ever before. Thus, Sonic can incorporate technically advanced features at a value-added price that allows for reasonable profits.

Threats

We face three main threats at the introduction of the Sonic 1000:

1. *Increased competition*. More companies are entering the U.S. PDA market with models that offer some but not all of the features and benefits provided by Sonic's PDA. Therefore, Sonic's marketing communications must stress our clear differentiation and value-added pricing.

2. *Downward pressure on pricing.* Increased competition and market-share strategies are pushing PDA prices down. Still, our objective of seeking a 10 percent profit on second year sales of the original model is realistic, given the lower margins in the PDA market.

3. *Compressed product life cycle.* PDAs have reached the maturity stage of their life cycle more quickly than earlier technology products. We have contingency plans to keep sales growing by adding new features, targeting additional segments, and adjusting prices.

Objectives and Issues

We have set aggressive but achievable objectives for the first and second years of market entry.

First-year Objectives

During the Sonic 1000's initial year on the market, we are aiming for a 3 percent share of the U.S. PDA market through unit sales volume of 240,000.

Second-year Objectives

Our second-year objectives are to achieve a 6 percent share based on sales of two models and to achieve break-even early in this period.

Issues

In relation to the product launch, our major issue is the ability to establish a well-regarded brand name linked to a meaningful positioning. We must invest heavily in marketing to create a memorable and distinctive brand image projecting innovation, quality, and value. We also must measure awareness and response so we can adjust our marketing efforts as necessary.

Marketing Strategy

Sonic's marketing strategy is based on a positioning of product differentiation. Our primary consumer target is middle- to upper-income professionals who need one portable device to coordinate their busy schedules, communicate with family and colleagues, get driving directions, and be entertained on the go. Our secondary consumer target is high school, college, and graduate students who want a multimedia device. This segment can be described demographically by age (16–30) and education status.

Our primary business target is mid- to large-sized corporations that want to help their managers and employees stay in touch and input or access critical data when out of the office. This segment consists of companies with more than $25 million in annual sales and more than 100 employees. A secondary business target is entrepreneurs and small-business owners. We are also targeting medical users who want to reduce paperwork and update or access patients' medical records.

Positioning

Using product differentiation, we are positioning the Sonic PDA as the most versatile, convenient, value-added model for personal and professional use. The marketing strategy will focus on the hands-free operation of multiple communication, entertainment, and information capabilities differentiating the Sonic 1000.

Product Strategy

The Sonic 1000, including all the features described in the earlier Product Review section, will be sold with a one-year warranty. We will introduce a more compact, powerful high-end model (the Sonic 2000) during the following year. Building the Sonic brand is an integral part of our product strategy. The brand and logo (Sonic's distinctive yellow thunderbolt) will be displayed on the product and its packaging and reinforced by its prominence in the introductory marketing campaign.

Objectives and issues
The company's objectives should be defined in specific terms so management can measure progress and, if needed, take corrective action to stay on track. This section describes any major issues that might affect the company's marketing strategy and implementation.

Positioning
A positioning built on meaningful differences, supported by appropriate strategy and implementation, can help the company build competitive advantage.

Pricing Strategy

The Sonic 1000 will be introduced at $250 wholesale/$350 estimated retail price per unit. We expect to lower the price of this first model when we expand the product line by launching the Sonic 2000, to be priced at $350 wholesale per unit. These prices reflect a strategy of (1) attracting desirable channel partners and (2) taking share from Palm and other established competitors.

Distribution Strategy

Our channel strategy is to use selective distribution, marketing Sonic PDAs through well-known stores and online retailers. During the first year, we will add channel partners until we have coverage in all major U.S. markets and the product is included in the major electronics catalogs and Web sites. We will also investigate distribution through mobile phone outlets maintained by major carriers such as Cingular Wireless. In support of our channel partners, Sonic will provide demonstration products, detailed specification handouts, and full-color photos and displays featuring the product. We will also arrange special trade terms for retailers that place volume orders.

Marketing Communications Strategy

By integrating all messages in all media, we will reinforce the brand name and the main points of product differentiation. Research about media consumption patterns will help our advertising agency choose appropriate media and timing to reach prospects before and during product introduction. Thereafter, advertising will appear on a pulsing basis to maintain brand awareness and communicate various differentiation messages. The agency will also coordinate public relations efforts to build the Sonic brand and support the differentiation message. To attract customer attention and encourage purchasing, we will offer as a limited-time premium a leather carry-case. To attract, retain, and motivate channel partners for a push strategy, we will use trade sales promotions and personal selling. Until the Sonic brand has been established, our communications will encourage purchases through channel partners rather than from our Web site.

Marketing Research

Using research, we are identifying the specific features and benefits that our target market segments value. Feedback from market tests, surveys, and focus groups will help us develop the Sonic 2000. We are also measuring and analyzing customers' attitudes toward competing brands and products. Brand awareness research will help us determine the effectiveness and efficiency of our messages and media. Finally, we will use customer satisfaction studies to gauge market reaction.

Marketing Organization

Sonic's chief marketing officer, Jane Melody, holds overall responsibility for all of the company's marketing activities. **Figure A1.1** shows the structure of the eight-person marketing organization. Sonic has hired Worldwide Marketing to handle national sales campaigns, trade and consumer sales promotions, and public relations efforts.

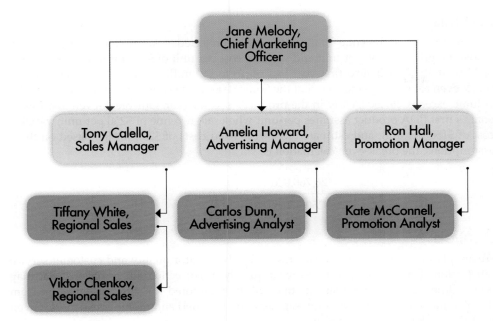

Figure A1.1
Sonic's marketing organization

Action Programs

The Sonic 1000 will be introduced in February. Following are summaries of the action programs we will use during the first six months of next year to achieve our stated objectives.

January We will initiate a $200,000 trade sales promotion campaign to educate dealers and generate excitement for the product launch in February. We will exhibit at the major consumer electronics trade shows, Webcast the product launch, and provide samples to selected product reviewers, opinion leaders, and celebrities as part of our public relations strategy. Our training staff will work with sales personnel at major retail chains to explain the Sonic 1000's features, benefits, and competitive advantages.

February We will start an integrated print/radio/Internet campaign targeting professionals and consumers. The campaign will show how many functions the Sonic PDA can perform and emphasize the convenience of a single, powerful handheld device. This multimedia campaign will be supported by point-of-sale signage as well as online-only specials.

March As the multimedia advertising campaign continues, we will add consumer sales promotion tactics such as giving away leather carry-cases as a premium. We will also distribute new point-of-purchase displays to support our retailers.

April We will hold a trade sales contest offering prizes for the salesperson and retail organization that sells the most Sonic PDAs during the four-week period.

May We plan to roll out a new national advertising campaign this month. The radio ads will feature celebrity voices telling their Sonic PDAs to perform functions such as initiating a phone call, sending an e-mail, playing a song or video, and so on. The print ads will show these celebrities holding their Sonic PDAs.

June Our radio campaign will add a new voice-over tag line promoting the Sonic 1000 as a graduation gift. We will also exhibit at the semiannual electronics trade show and provide channel partners with new competitive comparison handouts as a sales aid. In addition, we will tally and analyze the results of customer satisfaction surveys for use in future promotions and to provide feedback for product and marketing activities.

Action programs
Action programs should be coordinated with the resources and activities of other departments, including production, finance, purchasing, etc.

Budgets

Total first-year sales revenue for the Sonic 1000 is projected at $60 million, with an average wholesale price of $250 per unit and variable cost per unit of $150 for unit sales volume of 240,000. We anticipate a first-year loss of up to $10 million on the Sonic 1000 model. Break-even calculations indicate that the Sonic 1000 will become profitable after the sales volume exceeds 267,500, early in the product's second year. Our break-even analysis of Sonic's first PDA product assumes per-unit wholesale revenue of $250 per unit, variable cost of $150 per unit, and estimated first-year fixed costs of $26,750,000. Based on these assumptions, the break-even calculation is:

$$\frac{26,760,000}{\$250 - \$150} = 267,500 \text{ units}$$

Controls

We are planning tight control measures to closely monitor quality and customer service satisfaction. This will enable us to react quickly in correcting any problems that may occur. Other early warning signals that will be monitored for signs of deviation from the plan include monthly sales (by segment and channel) and monthly expenses. Given the PDA market's volatility, we are developing contingency plans to address fast-moving environmental changes such as new technology and new competition.

Marketing Plan Tools

Prentice Hall offers two valuable resources to assist you in developing a marketing plan:
- *The Marketing Plan Handbook* by Marian Burk Wood explains the process of creating a marketing plan, complete with detailed checklists and dozens of real-world examples.
- *Marketing Plan Pro* is an award-winning software package that includes sample plans, step-by-step guides, an introductory video, help wizards, and customizable charts for documenting a marketing plan.

Sources: Background information and market data adapted from "Palm 'Hiccup' Highlights EU Enviro Regulations," *RCR Wireless News*, July 10, 2006, p. 6; Arik Hesseldahl, "The Swarm of Killer PDAs," *BusinessWeek*, May 15, 2006, p. 100; Pui-Wing Tam, "The Hand-Helds Strike Back," *Wall Street Journal*, May 18, 2005, pp. D1, D6; Michael V. Copeland, Om Malik, and Rafe Needleman, "The Next Big Thing," *Business 2.0*, July 2003, pp. 62–69; "2005 PDA Shipments Set Record," *Business Communications Review*, April 2006, p. 6; "Smartphone Market Grows Fast Despite Challenges," *Appliance*, March 2006, p. 16; and Sean Ginevan, "A New PDA Is Born," *Network Computing*, July 6, 2006, p. 19.

MARKETING BY THE NUMBERS

Marketing decisions are coming under increasing scrutiny, and marketing managers must be accountable for the financial implications of their actions. This appendix provides a basic introduction to marketing financial analysis. Such analysis guides marketers in making sound marketing decisions and in assessing the outcomes of those decisions.

The appendix is built around a hypothetical manufacturer of high definition consumer electronics products—HDX-treme. This company is launching a new product, and we will discuss and analyze the various decisions HDX-treme's marketing managers must make before and after launch.

HDX-treme manufactures high-definition televisions for the consumer market. The company has concentrated on televisions but is now entering the accessories market. Specifically, the company is introducing a high-definition optical disc player (DVD) using the Blu-ray format.

The appendix is organized into three sections. The first section deals with the pricing considerations and break-even and margin analysis assessments that guide the introduction of HDX-treme's new-product launch. The second section begins with a discussion of estimating market potential and company sales. It then introduces the marketing budget, as illustrated through a pro forma profit-and-loss statement followed by the actual profit-and-loss statement. Next, the section discusses marketing performance measures, with a focus on helping marketing managers to better defend their decisions from a financial perspective. In the final section, we analyze the financial implications of various marketing tactics, such as increasing advertising expenditures, adding sales representatives to increase distribution, lowering price, or extending the product line.

At the end of each section, quantitative exercises provide you with an opportunity to apply the concepts you learned in that section to contexts beyond HDX-treme.

Pricing, Break-Even, and Margin Analysis

Pricing Considerations

Determining price is one of the most important marketing-mix decisions, and marketers have considerable leeway when setting prices. The limiting factors are demand and costs. Demand factors, such as buyer-perceived value, set the price ceiling. The company's costs set the price floor. In between these two factors, marketers must consider competitors' prices and other factors such as reseller requirements, government regulations, and company objectives.

Current competing high-definition DVD products in this relatively new product category were introduced in 2006 and sell at retail prices between $500 and $1,200. HDX-treme plans to introduce its new product at a lower price in order to expand the market and to gain market share rapidly. We first consider HDX-treme's pricing decision from a cost perspective. Then, we consider consumer value, the competitive environment, and reseller requirements.

Determining Costs

Recall from Chapter 10 that there are different types of costs. **Fixed costs** do not vary with production or sales level and include costs such as rent, interest, depreciation, and clerical and management salaries. Regardless of the level of output, the company must

Fixed costs
Costs that do not vary with production or sales level.

Variable costs
Costs that vary directly with the level of production.

Total costs
The sum of the fixed and variable costs for any given level of production.

pay these costs. Whereas total fixed costs remain constant as output increases, the fixed cost per unit (or average fixed cost) will decrease as output increases because the total fixed costs are spread across more units of output. **Variable costs** vary directly with the level of production and include costs related to the direct production of the product (such as costs of goods sold—COGS) and many of the marketing costs associated with selling it. Although these costs tend to be uniform for each unit produced, they are called variable because their total varies with the number of units produced. **Total costs** are the sum of the fixed and variable costs for any given level of production.

HDX-treme has invested $10 million in refurbishing an existing facility to manufacture the new DVD product. Once production begins, the company estimates that it will incur fixed costs of $20 million per year. The variable cost to produce each DVD player is estimated to be $250 and is expected to remain at that level for the output capacity of the facility.

Setting Price Based on Costs

Cost-plus pricing (or markup pricing)
Adding a standard markup to the cost of the product.

HDX-treme starts with the cost-based approach to pricing discussed in Chapter 10. Recall that the simplest method, **cost-plus pricing** (or **markup pricing**), simply adds a standard markup to the cost of the product. To use this method, however, HDX-treme must specify an expected unit sales so that total unit costs can be determined. Unit variable costs will remain constant regardless of the output, but *average unit fixed costs* will decrease as output increases.

To illustrate this method, suppose HDX-treme has fixed costs of $20 million, variable costs of $250 per unit, and expects unit sales of one million units. Thus, the cost per DVD player is given by:

$$\text{Unit cost} = \text{variable cost} + \frac{\text{fixed costs}}{\text{unit sales}} = \$250 + \frac{\$20{,}000{,}000}{1{,}000{,}000} = \$270$$

Relevant costs
Costs that will occur in the future and that will vary across the alternatives being considered.

Break-even price
The price at which total revenue equals total cost and profit is zero.

Note that we do not include the initial investment of $10 million in the total fixed cost figure. It is not considered a fixed cost because it is not a *relevant* cost. **Relevant costs** are those that will occur in the future and that will vary across the alternatives being considered. HDX-treme's investment to refurbish the manufacturing facility was a one-time cost that will not reoccur in the future. Such past costs are sunk costs and should not be considered in future analyses.

Also notice that if HDX-treme sells its DVD player for $270, the price is equal to the total cost per unit. This is the **break even price**—the price at which unit revenue (price) equals unit cost and profit is zero.

Suppose HDX-treme does not want to merely break even but rather wants to earn a 25 percent markup on sales. HDX-treme's markup price is:[1]

$$\text{Markup price} = \frac{\text{unit cost}}{(1 - \text{desired returned on sales})} = \frac{\$270}{1 - .25} = \$360$$

This is the price that HDX-treme would sell the DVD player to resellers such as wholesalers or retailers to earn a 25 percent profit on sales.

Return on investment (ROI) pricing (or target-return pricing)
A cost-based pricing method that determines price based on a specified rate of return on investment.

Another approach HDX-treme could use is called **return on investment (ROI) pricing** (or target-return pricing). In this case, the company would consider the initial $10 million investment, but only to determine the dollar profit goal. Suppose the company wants a 30 percent return on its investment. The price necessary to satisfy this requirement can be determined by:[2]

$$\text{ROI price} = \text{unit cost} + \frac{\text{ROI} \times \text{investment}}{\text{unit sales}} = \$270 + \frac{0.3 \times \$10{,}000{,}000}{1{,}000{,}000} = \$273$$

That is, if HDX-treme sells its DVD players for $273 each, it will realize a 30 percent return on its initial investment of $10 million.

In these pricing calculations, unit cost is a function of the expected sales, which were estimated to be one million units. But what if actual sales were lower? Then the unit cost would be higher because the fixed costs would be spread over fewer units, and the realized percentage markup on sales or ROI would be lower. Alternatively, if sales are higher than the estimated 1 million units, unit cost would be lower than $270, so a lower price would produce the desired markup on sales or ROI. It's important to note that these cost-based pricing methods are internally focused and do not consider demand, competitors' prices, or reseller requirements. Because HDX-treme will be selling these DVD players to consumers through wholesalers and retailers offering competing brands, the company must consider markup pricing from this perspective.

Setting Price Based on External Factors

Whereas costs determine the price floor, HDX-treme also must consider external factors when setting price. HDX-treme does not have the final say concerning the final price to consumers—retailers do. So it must start with its suggested retail price and work back. In doing so, HDX-treme must consider the markups required by resellers that sell the product to consumers.

In general, a dollar **markup** is the difference between a company's selling price for a product and its cost to manufacture or purchase it. For a retailer, then, the markup is the difference between the price it charges consumers and the cost the retailer must pay for the product. Thus, for any level of reseller:

Markup
The difference between a company's selling price for a product and its cost to manufacture or purchase it.

$$\text{Dollar markup} = \text{selling price} - \text{cost}$$

Markups are usually expressed as a percentage, and there are two different ways to compute markups—on *cost* or on *selling price*:

$$\text{Markup percentage on cost} = \frac{\text{dollar markup}}{\text{cost}}$$

$$\text{Markup percentage on selling price} = \frac{\text{dollar markup}}{\text{selling price}}$$

To apply reseller margin analysis, HDX-treme must first set the suggested retail price and then work back to the price at which it must sell the DVD player to a wholesaler. Suppose retailers expect a 30 percent margin and wholesalers want a 20 percent margin based on their respective selling prices. And suppose that HDX-treme sets a manufacturer's suggested retail price (MSRP) of $599.99 for its high-definition DVD player.

Recall that HDX-treme wants to expand the market by pricing low and generating market share quickly. HDX-treme selected the $599.99 MSRP because it is much lower than most competitors' prices, which can be as high as $1,200. And the company's research shows that it is below the threshold at which more consumers are willing to purchase the product. By using buyers' perceptions of value and not the seller's cost to determine the MSRP, HDX-treme is using **value-based pricing**. For simplicity, we will use an MSRP of $600 in further analyses.

Value-based pricing
Offering just the right combination of quality and good service at a fair price.

To determine the price HDX-treme will charge wholesalers, we must first subtract the retailer's margin from the retail price to determine the retailer's cost ($600 − ($600 × 0.30) = $420). The retailer's cost is the wholesaler's price, so HDX-treme next subtracts the wholesaler's margin ($420 − ($420 × 0.20) = $336). Thus, the **markup chain** representing the sequence of markups used by firms at each level in a channel for HDX-treme's new product is:

Markup chain
The sequence of markups used by firms at each level in a channel.

Suggested retail price:	$600
minus retail margin (30%):	− $180
Retailer's cost/wholesaler's price:	$420
minus wholesaler's margin (20%):	− $ 84
Wholesaler's cost/HDX-treme's price:	$336

By deducting the markups for each level in the markup chain, HDX-treme arrives at a price for the DVD player to wholesalers of $336.

Break-Even and Margin Analysis

The previous analyses derived a value-based price of $336 for HDX-treme's DVD player. Although this price is higher than the break-even price of $270 and covers costs, that price assumed a demand of one million units. But how many units and what level of dollar sales must HDX-treme achieve to break even at the $336 price? And what level of sales must be achieved to realize various profit goals? These questions can be answered through break-even and margin analysis.

Determining Break-Even Unit Volume and Dollar Sales

Based on an understanding of costs, consumer value, the competitive environment, and reseller requirements, HDX-treme has decided to set its price to wholesalers at $336. At that price, what sales level will be needed for HDX-treme to break even or make a profit? **Break-even analysis** determines the unit volume and dollar sales needed to be profitable given a particular price and cost structure. At the break-even point, total revenue equals total costs and profit is zero. Above this point, the company will make a profit; below it, the company will lose money. HDX-treme can calculate break-even volume using the following formula:[3]

$$\text{Break-even volume} = \frac{\text{fixed costs}}{\text{price} - \text{unit variable cost}}$$

The denominator (price – unit variable cost) is called **unit contribution** (sometimes called contribution margin). It represents the amount that each unit contributes to covering fixed costs. Break-even volume represents the level of output at which all (variable and fixed) costs are covered. In HDX-treme's case, break-even unit volume is:

$$\text{Break even volume} = \frac{\text{fixed cost}}{\text{price} - \text{variable cost}} = \frac{\$20,000,000}{\$336 - \$250} = 282.558.1 \text{ units}$$

Thus, at the given cost and pricing structure, HDX-treme will break even at 232,559 units.

To determine the break-even dollar sales, simply multiply unit break-even volume by the selling price:

$$\text{BE sales} = \text{BE}^{\text{vol}} \times \text{price} = 232,559 \text{ units} \times \$336 = \$78,139,824$$

Another way to calculate dollar break-even sales is to use the percentage contribution margin (hereafter referred to as **contribution margin**), which is the unit contribution divided by the selling price:

$$\text{Contribution margin} = \frac{\text{price} - \text{variable cost}}{\text{price}} = \frac{\$336 - \$250}{\$336} = 0.256 \text{ or } 25.6\%$$

Then,

$$\text{Break-even sales} = \frac{\text{fixed cost}}{\text{contribution margin}} = \frac{\$20,000,000}{0.256} = \$78,125,000$$

Note that the difference between the two break-even sales calculations is due to rounding.

Such break-even analysis helps HDX-treme by showing the unit volume needed to cover costs. If production capacity cannot attain this level of output, then the company should not launch this product. However, the unit break-even volume is well within HDX-treme's capacity. Of course, the bigger question concerns whether HDX-treme can sell this volume at the $336 price. We'll address that issue a little later.

Break-even analysis
Analysis to determine the unit volume and dollar sales needed to be profitable given a particular price and cost structure.

Unit contribution
The amount that each unit contributes to covering fixed costs—the difference between price and variable costs.

Contribution margin
The unit contribution divided by the selling price.

Understanding contribution margin is useful in other types of analyses as well, particularly if unit prices and unit variable costs are unknown or if a company (say, a retailer) sells many products at different prices and knows the percentage of total sales variable costs represent. Whereas unit contribution is the difference between unit price and unit variable costs, total contribution is the difference between total sales and total variable costs. The overall contribution margin can be calculated by:

$$\text{Contribution margin} = \frac{\text{total sales} - \text{total variable costs}}{\text{total sales}}$$

Regardless of the actual level of sales, if the company knows what percentage of sales is represented by variable costs, it can calculate contribution margin. For example, HDX-treme's unit variable cost is $250, or 74 percent of the selling price ($250 ÷ $336 = 0.74). That means for every $1 of sales revenue for HDX-treme, $0.74 represents variable costs, and the difference ($0.26) represents contribution to fixed costs. But even if the company doesn't know its unit price and unit variable cost, it can calculate the contribution margin from total sales and total variable costs or from knowledge of the total cost structure. It can set total sales equal to 100 percent regardless of the actual absolute amount and determine the contribution margin:

$$\text{Contribution margin} = \frac{100\% - 74\%}{100\%} = \frac{1 - 0.74}{1} = 1 - 0.74 = 0.26 \text{ or } 26\%$$

Note that this matches the percentage calculated from the unit price and unit variable cost information. This alternative calculation will be very useful later when analyzing various marketing decisions.

Determining "Breakeven" for Profit Goals

Although it is useful to know the break-even point, most companies are more interested in making a profit. Assume HDX-treme would like to realize a $5 million profit in the first year. How many DVD players must it sell at the $336 price to cover fixed costs and produce this profit? To determine this, HDX-treme can simply add the profit figure to fixed costs and again divide by the unit contribution to determine unit sales:[4]

$$\text{Unit volume} = \frac{\text{fixed cost} + \text{profit goal}}{\text{price} - \text{variable cost}} = \frac{\$20,000,000 + \$5,000,000}{\$336 - \$250} = 290,697.7 \text{ units}$$

Thus, to earn a $5 million profit, HDX-treme must sell 290,698 units. Multiply by price to determine dollar sales needed to achieve a $5 million profit:

$$\text{Dollar sales} = 290,698 \text{ units} \times \$336 = \$97,674,528$$

Or use the contribution margin:

$$\text{Sales} = \frac{\text{fixed cost} + \text{profit goal}}{\text{contribution margin}} = \frac{\$20,000,000 + \$5,000,000}{0.256} = \$97,656,250$$

Again, note that the difference between the two break-even sales calculations is due to rounding.

As we saw previously, a profit goal can also be stated as a return on investment goal. For example, recall that HDX-treme wants a 30 percent return on its $10 million investment. Thus, its absolute profit goal is $3 million ($10,000,000 × 0.30). This profit goal is treated the same way as in the previous example:[5]

$$\text{Unit volume} = \frac{\text{fixed cost} + \text{profit goal}}{\text{price} - \text{variable cost}} = \frac{\$20,000,000 + \$3,000,000}{\$226 - \$250} = 267,442 \text{ units}$$

$$\text{Dollar sales} = 267,442 \text{ units} \times \$336 = \$89,860,512$$

Or

$$\text{Dollar sales} = \frac{\text{fixed cost} + \text{profit goal}}{\text{contribution margin}} = \frac{\$20,000,000 + \$3,000,000}{0.256} = \$89,843,750$$

Finally, HDX-treme can express its profit goal as a percentage of sales, which we also saw in previous pricing analyses. Assume HDX-treme desires a 25 percent return on sales. To determine the unit and sales volume necessary to achieve this goal, the calculation is a little different from the previous two examples. In this case, we incorporate the profit goal into the unit contribution as an additional variable cost. Look at it this way: If 25% of each sale must go toward profits, that leaves only 75% of the selling price to cover fixed costs. Thus, the equation becomes:[6]

$$\text{Unit volume} = \frac{\text{fixed cost}}{\text{price} - \text{variable cost} - (0.25 \times \text{price})} \quad \text{or} \quad \frac{\text{fixed cost}}{(0.75 \times \text{price}) - \text{variable cost}}$$

So,

$$\text{Unit volume} = \frac{\$20,000,000}{(0.75 \times \$336) - \$250} = 10,000,000 \text{ units}$$

$$\text{Dollar sales necessary} = 10,000,000 \text{ units} \times \$336 = \$3,360,000,000$$

Thus, HDX-treme would need more than $3 billion in sales to realize a 25 percent return on sales given its current price and cost structure! Could it possibly achieve this level of sales? The major point is this: Although break-even analysis can be useful in determining the level of sales needed to cover costs or to achieve a stated profit goal, it does not tell the company whether it is *possible* to achieve that level of sales at the specified price. To address this issue, HDX-treme needs to estimate demand for this product.

Before moving on, however, let's stop here and practice applying the concepts covered so far. Now that you have seen pricing and break-even concepts in action as they related to HDX-treme's new DVD player, here are several exercises for you to apply what you have learned in other contexts.

Marketing by the Numbers Exercise Set One

Now that you've studied pricing, break-even, and margin analysis as they relate to HDX-treme's new-product launch, use the following exercises to apply these concepts in other contexts.

1.1   Sanborn, a manufacturer of electric roof vents, realizes a cost of $55 for every unit it produces. Its total fixed costs equal $2 million. If the company manufactures 500,000 units, compute the following:
   a.   unit cost
   b.   markup price if the company desires a 10 percent return on sales
   c.   ROI price if the company desires a 25 percent return on an investment of $1 million

1.2   An interior decorator purchases items to sell in her store. She purchases a lamp for $125 and sells it for $225. Determine the following:
   a. dollar markup
   b. markup percentage on cost
   c. markup percentage on selling price

1.3   A consumer purchases a toaster from a retailer for $60. The retailer's markup is 20 percent, and the wholesaler's markup is 15 percent, both based on selling price. For what price does the manufacturer sell the product to the wholesaler?

1.4   A vacuum manufacturer has a unit cost of $50 and wishes to achieve a margin of 30 percent based on selling price. If the manufacturer sells directly to a retailer who then adds a set margin of 40 percent based on selling price, determine the retail price charged to consumers.

1.5   Advanced Electronics manufactures DVDs and sells them directly to retailers who typically sell them for $20. Retailers take a 40 percent margin based on the retail selling price. Advanced's cost information is as follows:

DVD package and disc	$2.50/DVD
Royalties	$2.25/DVD
Advertising and promotion	$500,000
Overhead	$200,000

Calculate the following:
   a. contribution per unit and contribution margin
   b. break-even volume in DVD units and dollars
   c. volume in DVD units and dollar sales necessary if Advanced's profit goal is 20 perecnt profit on sales
   d. net profit if 5 million DVDs are sold

Demand Estimates, the Marketing Budget, and Marketing Performance Measures

Market Potential and Sales Estimates

HDX-treme has now calculated the sales needed to break even and to attain various profit goals on its DVD player. However, the company needs more information regarding demand to assess the feasibility of attaining the needed sales levels. This information is also needed for production and other decisions. For example, production schedules need to be developed and marketing tactics need to be planned.

The **total market demand** for a product or service is the total volume that would be bought by a defined consumer group in a defined geographic area in a defined time period in a defined marketing environment under a defined level and mix of industry marketing effort. Total market demand is not a fixed number but a function of the stated conditions. For example, next year's total market demand for high-definition DVD players will depend on how much Samsung, Sony, Pioneer, Toshiba, and other producers spend on marketing their brands. It also depends on many environmental factors, such as government regulations, economic conditions, and the level of consumer confidence in a given market. The upper limit of market demand is called **market potential**.

Total market demand
The total volume that would be bought by a defined consumer group in a defined geographic area in a defined time period in a defined marketing environment under a defined level and mix of industry marketing effort.

Market potential
The upper limit of market demand.

One general but practical method that HDX-treme might use for estimating total market demand uses three variables: (1) the number of prospective buyers, (2) the quantity purchased by an average buyer per year, and (3) the price of an average unit. Using these numbers, HDX-treme can estimate total market demand as follows:

$$Q = n \times q \times p$$

where

Q	=	total market demand
n	=	number of buyers in the market
q	=	quantity purchased by an average buyer per year
p	=	price of an average unit

A variation of this approach is the **chain ratio method**. This method involves multiplying a base number by a chain of adjusting percentages. For example, HDX-treme's high-definition DVD player is designed to play high-definition DVD movies on high-definition televisions. Thus, consumers who do not own a high-definition television will not likely purchase this player. Additionally, not all HDTV households will be willing and able to purchase the new high-definition DVD player. HDX-treme can estimate U.S. demand using a chain of calculations like the following:

Total number of U.S. households
- × The percentage of U.S. households owning a high-definition television
- × The percentage of these households willing and able to buy a high-definition DVD player

AC Nielsen, the television ratings company, estimates that there are more than 110 million TV households in the U.S.[7] The Consumer Electronics Association estimates that 38 percent of TV households will own HDTVs by the end of 2006.[8] However, HDX-treme's research indicates that only 44.5 percent of HDTV households possess the discretionary income needed and are willing to buy a high-definition DVD player. Then, the total number of households willing and able to purchase this product is:

110 million households × 0.38 × 0.445 = 18.6 million households

Because HDTVs are relatively new and expensive products, most households have only one of these televisions, and it's usually the household's primary television.[9] Thus, consumers who buy a high-definition DVD player will likely buy only one per household. Assuming the average retail price across all brands is $750 for this product, the estimate of total market demand is as follows:

18.6 million households × 1 DVD player per household × $750 = $14 billion

This simple chain of calculations gives HDX-treme only a rough estimate of potential demand. However, more detailed chains involving additional segments and other qualifying factors would yield more accurate and refined estimates. Still, these are only estimates of market potential. They rely heavily on assumptions regarding adjusting percentages, average quantity, and average price. Thus, HDX-treme must make certain that its assumptions are reasonable and defendable. As can be seen, the overall market potential in dollar sales can vary widely given the average price used. For this reason, HDX-treme will use unit sales potential to determine its sales estimate for next year. Market potential in terms of units is 18.6 million DVD players (18.6 million households × 1 DVD player per household).

Chain ratio method
Estimating market demand by multiplying a base number by a chain of adjusting percentages.

Assuming that HDX-treme wants to attain 2 percent market share (comparable to its share of the HDTV market) in the first year after launching this product, then it can forecast unit sales at 18.6 million units × 0.02 = 372,000 units. At a selling price of $336 per unit, this translates into sales of $124.99 million (372,000 units × $336 per unit). For simplicity, further analyses will use forecasted sales of $125 million.

This unit volume estimate is well within HDX-treme's production capacity and exceeds not only the break-even estimate (232,559 units) calculated earlier, but also the volume necessary to realize a $5 million profit (290,698 units) or a 30 percent return on

The Profit-and-Loss Statement and Marketing Budget

All marketing managers must account for the profit impact of their marketing strategies. A major tool for projecting such profit impact is a **pro forma** (or projected) **profit-and-loss statement** (also called an **income statement** or **operating statement**). A pro forma statement shows projected revenues less budgeted expenses and estimates the projected net profit for an organization, product, or brand during a specific planning period, typically a year. It includes direct product production costs, marketing expenses budgeted to attain a given sales forecast, and overhead expenses assigned to the organization or product. A profit-and-loss statement typically consists of several major components (see **Table A2.1**):

> **Pro forma** (or projected) **profit-and-loss statement** (or **income statement** or **operating statement**) A statement that shows projected revenues less budgeted expenses and estimates the projected net profit for an organization, product, or brand during a specific planning period, typically a year.

- *Net sales*—gross sales revenue minus returns and allowances (for example, trade, cash, quantity, and promotion allowances). HDX-treme's net sales for 2006 are estimated to be $125 million, as determined in the previous analysis.
- *Cost of goods sold* (sometimes called *cost of sales*)—the actual cost of the merchandise sold by a manufacturer or reseller. It includes the cost of inventory, purchases, and other costs associated with making the goods. HDX-treme's cost of goods sold is estimated to be 50 percent of net sales, or $62.5 million.
- *Gross margin* (*or gross profit*)—the difference between net sales and cost of goods sold. HDX-treme's gross margin is estimated to be $62.5 million.
- *Operating expenses*—the expenses incurred while doing business. These include all other expenses beyond the cost of goods sold that are necessary to conduct business. Operating expenses can be presented in total or broken down in detail. Here, HDX treme's estimated operating expenses include *marketing expenses* and *general and administrative expenses*.

Marketing expenses include sales expenses, promotion expenses, and distribution expenses. The new product will be sold through HDX-treme's sales force, so the company budgets $5 million for sales salaries. However, because sales representatives earn a 10 percent commission on sales, HDX-treme must also add a variable component to sales expenses of $12.5 million (10 percent of $125 million net sales), for a total budgeted sales expense of $17.5 million. HDX-treme sets its advertising and promotion to launch this product at $10 million. However, the company also budgets 4 precent of sales, or $5 million, for cooperative advertising allowances to retailers who promote HDX-treme's new product in their advertising. Thus, the total budgeted advertising and promotion expenses are $15 million ($10 million for advertising plus $5 million in co-op allowances). Finally, HDX-treme budgets 10 percent of net sales, or $12.5 million, for freight and delivery charges. In all, total marketing expenses are estimated to be $17.5 million + $15 million + $12.5 million = $45 million.

General and administrative expenses are estimated at $5 million, broken down into $2 million for managerial salaries and expenses for the marketing function and $3 million of indirect overhead allocated to this product by the corporate accountants (such as depreciation, interest, maintenance, and insurance). Total expenses for the year, then, are estimated to be $50 million ($45 million marketing expenses + $5 million in general and administrative expenses).

Table A2.1 Pro Forma Profit-and-Loss Statement for the 12-Month Period Ended December 31, 2006

			% of sales
Net Sales		$125,000,000	100%
Cost of Goods Sold		62,500,000	50%
Gross Margin		$ 62,500,000	50%
Marketing Expenses			
Sales expenses	$17,500,000		
Promotion expenses	15,000,000		
Freight	12,500,000	45,000,000	36%
General and Administrative Expenses			
Managerial salaries and expenses	$2,000,000		
Indirect overhead	3,000,000	5,000,000	4%
Net Profit Before Income Tax		$12,500,000	10%

- *Net profit before taxes*—profit earned after all costs are deducted. HDX-treme's estimated net profit before taxes is $12.5 million.

In all, as **Table A2.1** shows, HDX-treme expects to earn a profit on its new DVD player of $12.5 million in 2006. Also note that the percentage of sales that each component of the profit-and-loss statement represents is given in the right-hand column. These percentages are determined by dividing the cost figure by net sales (that is, marketing expenses represent 36 percent of net sales determined by $45 million ÷ $125 million). As can be seen, HDX-treme projects a net profit return on sales of 10 percent in the first year after launching this product.

Marketing Performance Measures

Now let's fast-forward a year. HDX-treme's high-definition DVD player has been on the market for one year and management wants to assess its sales and profit performance. One way to assess this performance is to compute performance ratios derived from HDX-treme's **profit-and-loss statement**.

Whereas the pro forma profit-and-loss statement shows projected financial performance, the statement given in **Table A2.2** shows HDX-treme's actual financial performance based on actual sales, cost of goods sold, and expenses during the past year. By comparing the profit-and-loss statement from one period to the next, HDX-treme can gauge performance against goals, spot favorable or unfavorable trends, and take appropriate corrective action.

The profit-and-loss statement shows that HDX-treme lost $1 million rather than making the $12.5 million profit projected in the pro forma statement. Why? One obvious reason is that net sales fell $25 million short of estimated sales. Lower sales translated into lower variable costs associated with marketing the product. However, both fixed costs and the cost of goods sold as a percentage of sales exceeded expectations. Hence, the product's contribution margin was 21 percent rather than the estimated 26 percent. That is, variable costs represented 79 percent of sales (55 percent for cost of goods sold, 10 percent for sales commissions, 10 percent for freight, and 4 percent for co-op allowances). Recall that contribution margin can be calculated by subtracting that fraction from one (1 − 0.79 = 0.21). Total fixed costs were $22 million, $2 million more than estimated. Thus, the sales that HDX-treme needed to break even given this cost structure can be calculated as:

$$\text{Break-even sales} = \frac{\text{fixed costs}}{\text{contribution margin}} = \frac{\$22,000,000}{0.21} = \$104,761,905$$

Profit-and-loss statement (or income statement or operating statement)
A statement that shows actual revenues less expenses and net profit for an organization, product, or brand during a specific planning period, typically a year.

If HDX-treme had achieved another $5 million in sales, it would have earned a profit.

Although HDX-treme's sales fell short of the forecasted sales, so did overall industry sales for this product. Overall industry sales were only $2.5 billion. That means that HDX-treme's market share was 4 percent ($100 million ÷ $2.5 billion = 0.04 = 4 percent), which was higher than forecasted. Thus, HDX-treme attained a higher-than-expected **market share** but the overall market sales were not as high as estimated.

Market share
Company sales divided by market sales.

Table A2.2 Profit-and-Loss Statement for the 12-Month Period Ended Dec 31, 2006

			% of sales
Net Sales		$100,000,000	100%
Cost of Goods Sold		55,000,000	55%
Gross Margin		$45,000,000	45%
Marketing Expenses			
Sales expenses	$15,000,000		
Promotion expenses	14,000,000		
Freight	10,000,000	39,000,000	39%
General and Administrative Expenses			
Managerial salaries and expenses	$2,000,000		
Indirect overhead	5,000,000	7,000,000	7%
Net Profit Before Income Tax		($1,000,000)	(−1%)

Analytic Ratios

The profit-and-loss statement provides the figures needed to compute some crucial **operating ratios**—the ratios of selected operating statement items to net sales. These ratios let marketers compare the firm's performance in one year to that in previous years (or with industry standards and competitors' performance in that year). The most commonly used operating ratios are the gross margin percentage, the net profit percentage, and the operating expense percentage. The inventory turnover rate and return on investment (ROI) are often used to measure managerial effectiveness and efficiency.

The **gross margin percentage** indicates the percentage of net sales remaining after cost of goods sold that can contribute to operating expenses and net profit before taxes. The higher this ratio, the more a firm has left to cover expenses and generate profit. HDX-treme's gross margin ratio was 45 percent:

Operating ratios
The ratios of selected operating statement items to net sales.

Gross margin percentage
The percentage of net sales remaining after cost of goods sold—calculated by dividing gross margin by net sales.

Net profit percentage
The percentage of each sales dollar going to profit—calculated by dividing net profits by net sales.

$$\text{Gross margin percentage} = \frac{\text{gross margin}}{\text{net sales}} = \frac{\$45,000,000}{\$100,000,000} = 0.45 = 45\%$$

Note that this percentage is lower than estimated, and this ratio is seen easily in the percentage of sales column in **Table A2.2**. Stating items in the profit-and-loss statement as a percent of sales allows managers to quickly spot abnormal changes in costs over time. If there was previous history for this product and this ratio was declining, management should examine it more closely to determine why it has decreased (that is, because of a decrease in sales volume or price, an increase in costs, or a combination of these). In HDX-treme's case, net sales were $25 million lower than estimated, and cost of goods sold was higher than estimated (55 percent rather than the estimated 50 percent).

The **net profit percentage** shows the percentage of each sales dollar going to profit. It is calculated by dividing net profits by net sales:

$$\text{Net profit percentage} = \frac{\text{net profit}}{\text{net sales}} = \frac{-\$1,000,000}{\$100,000,000} = -0.01 = -1.0\%$$

This ratio is easily seen in the percent of sales column. HDX-treme's DVD player generated negative profits in the first year, not a good situation given that before the product launch net profits before taxes were estimated at more than $12 million. Later in this appendix, we will discuss further analyses the marketing manager should conduct to defend the product.

The **operating expense percentage** indicates the portion of net sales going to operating expenses. Operating expenses include marketing and other expenses not directly related to marketing the product, such as indirect overhead assigned to this product. It is calculated by:

Operating expense percentage
The portion of net sales going to operating expenses—calculated by dividing total expenses by net sales.

$$\text{Operating expense percentage} = \frac{\text{total expenses}}{\text{net sales}} = \frac{\$46,000,000}{\$100,000,000} = 0.46 = 46\%$$

This ratio can also be quickly determined from the percent of sales column in the profit-and-loss statement by adding the percentages for marketing expenses and general and administrative expenses (39% + 7%). Thus, 46 cents of every sales dollar went for operations. Although HDX-treme wants this ratio to be as low as possible, and 46 percent is not an alarming amount, it is of concern if it is increasing over time or if a loss is realized.

Another useful ratio is the **inventory turnover rate** (also called *stockturn rate* for resellers). The inventory turnover rate is the number of times an inventory turns over or is sold during a specified time period (often one year). This rate tells how quickly a business is moving inventory through the organization. Higher rates indicate that lower investments in inventory are made, thus freeing up funds for other investments. It may be computed on a cost, selling price, or unit basis. The formula based on cost is:

Inventory turnover rate (or stockturn rate for resellers)
The number of times an inventory turns over or is sold during a specified time period (often one year)—calculated based on costs, selling price, or units.

$$\text{Inventory turnover rate} = \frac{\text{cost of goods sold}}{\text{average inventory at cost}}$$

Assuming HDX-treme's beginning and ending inventories were $30 million and $20 million, respectively, the inventory turnover rate is:

$$\text{Inventory turnover rate} = \frac{\$55,000,000}{(\$30,000,000 + \$20,000,000)/2} = \frac{\$55,000,000}{\$25,000,000} = 2.2$$

That is, HDX-treme's inventory turned over 2.2 times in 2006. Normally, the higher the turnover rate, the higher the management efficiency and company profitability. However, this rate should be compared to industry averages, competitors' rates, and past performance to determine if HDX-treme is doing well. A competitor with similar sales but a higher inventory turnover rate will have fewer resources tied up in inventory, allowing it to invest in other areas of the business.

Companies frequently use **return on investment (ROI)** to measure managerial effectiveness and efficiency. For HDX-treme, ROI is the ratio of net profits to total investment required to manufacture the new product. This investment includes capital investments in land, buildings, and equipment (here, the initial $10 million to refurbish the manufacturing facility) plus inventory costs (HDX-treme's average inventory totaled $25 million), for a total of $35 million. Thus, HDX-treme's ROI for the DVD player is:

Return on investment (ROI)
A measure of managerial effectiveness and efficiency—net profit before taxes divided by total investment.

$$\text{Return on investment} = \frac{\text{net profit before taxes}}{\text{investments}} = \frac{-\$1,000,000}{\$35,000,000} = -.0286 = -2.86\%$$

ROI is often used to compare alternatives, and a positive ROI is desired. The alternative with the highest ROI is preferred to other alternatives. HDX-treme needs to be concerned with the ROI realized. One obvious way HDX-treme can increase ROI is to increase net profit by reducing expenses. Another way is to reduce its investment, perhaps by investing less in inventory and turning it over more frequently.

Marketing Profitability Metrics

Given the above financial results, you may be thinking that HDX-treme should drop this new product. But what arguments can marketers make for keeping or dropping this product? The obvious arguments for dropping the product are that first-year sales were well below expected levels and the product lost money, resulting in a negative return on investment.

So what would happen if HDX-treme did drop this product? Surprisingly, if the company drops the product, the profits for the total organization will decrease by $4 million! How can that be? Marketing managers need to look closely at the numbers in the profit-and-loss statement to determine the net marketing contribution for this product. In HDX-treme's case, the *net marketing contribution* for the DVD player is $4 million, and if the company drops this product, that contribution will disappear as well. Let's look more closely at this concept to illustrate how marketing managers can better assess and defend their marketing strategies and programs.

Net Marketing Contribution

Net marketing contribution (NMC), along with other marketing metrics derived from it, measures marketing profitability. It includes only components of profitability that are controlled by marketing. Whereas the previous calculation of net profit before taxes from the profit-and-loss statement includes operating expenses not under marketing's control, NMC does not. Referring back to HDX-treme's profit-and-loss statement given in **Table A2.2**, we can calculate net marketing contribution for the DVD player as:

> **Net marketing contribution (NMC)**
> A measure of marketing profitability that includes only components of profitability controlled by marketing.

NMC = net sales – cost of goods sold – marketing expenses
= $100 million – $55 million – $41 million = $4 million

The marketing expenses include sales expenses ($15 million), promotion expenses ($14 million), freight expenses ($10 million), and the managerial salaries and expenses of the marketing function ($2 million), which total $41 million.

Thus, the DVD player actually contributed $4 million to HDX-treme's profits. It was the $5 million of indirect overhead allocated to this product that caused the negative profit. Further, the amount allocated was $2 million more than estimated in the pro forma profit-and-loss statement. Indeed, if only the estimated amount had been allocated, the product would have earned a *profit* of $1 million rather than losing $1 million. If HDX-treme drops the DVD player product, the $5 million in fixed overhead expenses will not disappear—it will simply have to be allocated elsewhere. However, the $4 million in net marketing contribution *will* disappear.

Marketing Return on Sales and Investment

To get an even deeper understanding of the profit impact of marketing strategy, we'll now examine two measures of marketing efficiency—*marketing return on sales* (marketing ROS) and marketing return on investment (marketing ROI).[10]

Marketing return on sales (or **marketing ROS**) shows the percent of net sales attributable to the net marketing contribution. For our DVD player, ROS is:

> **Marketing return on sales (or marketing ROS)**
> The percent of net sales attributable to the net marketing contribution—calculated by dividing net marketing contribution by net sales.

$$\text{Marketing ROS} = \frac{\text{net marketing contribution}}{\text{net sales}} = \frac{\$4,000,000}{\$100,000,000} = 0.04 = 4\%$$

Thus, out of every $100 of sales, the product returns $4 to HDX-treme's bottom line. A high marketing ROS is desirable. But to assess whether this is a good level of performance, HDX-treme must compare this figure to previous marketing ROS levels for the product, the ROSs of other products in the company's portfolio, and the ROSs of competing products.

Marketing return on investment (or marketing ROI)
A measure of the marketing productivity of a marketing investment—calculated by dividing net marketing contribution by marketing expenses.

Marketing return on investment (or **marketing ROI**) measures the marketing productivity of a marketing investment. In HDX-treme's case, the marketing investment is represented by $41 million of the total expenses. Thus, Marketing ROI is:

$$\text{Marketing ROI} = \frac{\text{net marketing contribution}}{\text{net sales}} = \frac{\$4,000,000}{\$41,000,000} = 0.0976 = 9.76\%$$

As with marketing ROS, a high value is desirable, but this figure should be compared with previous levels for the given product and with the marketing ROIs of competitors' products. Note from this equation that marketing ROI could be greater than 100 percent. This can be achieved by attaining a higher net marketing contribution and/or a lower total marketing expense.

In this section, we estimated market potential and sales, developed profit-and-loss statements, and examined financial measures of performance. In the next section, we discuss methods for analyzing the impact of various marketing tactics. However, before moving on to those analyses, here's another set of quantitative exercises to help you apply what you've learned to other situations.

Marketing by the Numbers Exercise Set Two

2.1   Determine the market potential for a product that has 50 million prospective buyers who purchase an average of 3 per year and price averages $25. How many units must a company sell if it desires a 10 percent share of this market?

2.2   Develop a profit-and-loss statement for the Westgate division of North Industries. This division manufactures light fixtures sold to consumers through home improvement and hardware stores. Cost of goods sold represents 40 percent of net sales. Marketing expenses include selling expenses, promotion expenses, and freight. Selling expenses include sales salaries totaling $3 million per year and sales commissions (5 percent of sales). The company spent $3 million on advertising last year, and freight costs were 10 percent of sales. Other costs include $2 million for managerial salaries and expenses for the marketing function and another $3 million for indirect overhead allocated to the division.

   a.   Develop the profit-and-loss statement if net sales were $20 million last year.
   b.   Develop the profit-and-loss statement if net sales were $40 million last year.
   c.   Calculate Westgate's break-even sales.

2.3   Using the profit-and-loss statement you developed in question 2.2b, and assuming that Westgate's beginning inventory was $11 million, ending inventory was $7 million, and total investment was $20 million including inventory, determine the following:

   a.   gross margin percentage
   b.   net profit percentage
   c.   operating expense percentage
   d.   inventory turnover rate
   e.   return on investment (ROI)
   f.   net marketing contribution
   g.   marketing return on sales (marketing ROS)
   h.   marketing return on investment (marketing ROI)
   i.   Is the Westgate division doing well? Explain your answer.

Financial Analysis of Marketing Tactics

Although the first-year profit performance for HDX-treme's DVD player was less than desired, management feels that this attractive market has excellent growth opportunities. Although the sales of HDX-treme's DVD player were lower than initially projected, they were not unreasonable given the size of the current market. Thus, HDX-treme wants to explore new marketing tactics to help grow the market for this product and increase sales for the company.

For example, the company could increase advertising to promote more awareness of the new DVD player and its category. It could add salespeople to secure greater product distribution. HDX-treme could decrease prices so that more consumers could afford its player. Finally, to expand the market, HDX-treme could introduce a lower-priced model in addition to the higher-priced original offering. Before pursuing any of these tactics, HDX-treme must analyze the financial implications of each.

Increase Advertising Expenditures

Although most consumers understand DVD players, they may not be aware of high-definition DVD players. Thus, HDX-treme is considering boosting its advertising to make more people aware of the benefits of high-definition DVD players in general and of its own brand in particular.

What if HDX-treme's marketers recommend increasing national advertising by 50 percent to $15 million (assume no change in the variable cooperative component of promotional expenditures)? This represents an increase in fixed costs of $5 million. What increase in sales will be needed to break even on this $5 million increase in fixed costs?

A quick way to answer this question is to divide the increase in fixed cost by the contribution margin, which we found in a previous analysis to be 21 percent:

$$\text{Increase in sales} = \frac{\text{increase in fixed cost}}{\text{contribution margin}} = \frac{\$5,000,000}{0.21} = \$23,809,524$$

Thus, a 50 percent increase in advertising expenditures must produce a sales increase of almost $24 million to just break even. That $24 million sales increase translates into an almost 1 percentage point increase in market share (1 percent of the $2.5 billion overall market equals $25 million). That is, to break even on the increased advertising expenditure, HDX-treme would have to increase its market share from 4 percent to 4.95 percent ($123,809,524 ÷ $2.5 billion = 0.0495 or 4.95 percent market share). All of this assumes that the total market will not grow, which might or might not be a reasonable assumption.

Increase Distribution Coverage

HDX-treme also wants to consider hiring more salespeople in order to call on new retailer accounts and increase distribution through more outlets. Even though HDX-treme sells directly to wholesalers, its sales representatives call on retail accounts to perform other functions in addition to selling, such as training retail salespeople. Currently, HDX-treme employs 60 sales reps who earn an average of $50,000 in salary plus 10 percent commission on sales. The DVD player is currently sold to consumers through 1,875 retail outlets. Suppose HDX-treme wants to increase that number of outlets to 2,500, an increase of 625 retail outlets. How many additional salespeople will HDX-treme need, and what sales will be necessary to break even on the increased cost?

One method for determining what size sales force HDX-treme will need is the **workload method**. The workload method uses the following formula to determine the salesforce size:

$$NS = \frac{NC \times FC \times LC}{TA}$$

where

NS	=	number of salespeople
NC	=	number of customers
FC	=	average frequency of customer calls per customer
LC	=	average length of customer call
TA	=	time an average salesperson has available for selling per year

Workload method
An approach to determining sales force size based on the workload required and the time available for selling.

HDX-treme's sales reps typically call on accounts an average of 20 times per year for about two hours per call. Although each sales rep works 2,000 hours per year (50 weeks per year × 40 hours per week), they spent about 15 hours per week on nonselling activities such as administrative duties and travel. Thus, the average annual available selling time per sales rep per year is 1,250 hours (50 weeks × 25 hours per week). We can now calculate how many sales reps HDX-treme will need to cover the anticipated 2,500 retail outlets:

$$NS = \frac{2,500 \times 20 \times 2}{1,250} = 80 \text{ salespeople}$$

Therefore, HDX-treme will need to hire 20 more salespeople. The cost to hire these reps will be $1 million (20 salespeople × $50,000 salary per sales person).

What increase in sales will be required to break even on this increase in fixed costs? The 10 percent commission is already accounted for in the contribution margin, so the contribution margin remains unchanged at 21 percent. Thus, the increase in sales needed to cover this increase in fixed costs can be calculated by:

$$\text{Increase in sales} = \frac{\text{increase in fixed cost}}{\text{contribution margin}} = \frac{\$1,000,000}{0.21} = \$4,761,905$$

That is, HDX-treme's sales must increase almost $5 million to break even on this tactic. So, how many new retail outlets will the company need to secure to achieve this sales increase? The average revenue generated per current outlet is $53,333 ($100 million in sales divided by 1,875 outlets). To achieve the nearly $5 million sales increase needed to break even, HDX-treme would need about 90 new outlets ($4,761,905 ÷ $53,333 = 89.3 outlets), or about 4.5 outlets per new rep. Given that current reps cover about 31 outlets apiece (1,875 outlets ÷ 60 reps), this seems very reasonable.

Decrease Price

HDX-treme is also considering lowering its price to increase sales revenue through increased volume. The company's research has shown that demand for most types of consumer electronics products is elastic—that is, the percentage increase in the quantity demanded is greater than the percentage decrease in price. It has also been found that when the price of HDTVs goes down, the quantity of DVD players demanded increases because they are complementary products.

What increase in sales would be necessary to break even on a 10 percent decrease in price? That is, what increase in sales will be needed to maintain the total contribution that HDX-treme realized at the higher price? The current total contribution can be determined by multiplying the contribution margin by total sales:[11]

$$\text{Current total contribution} = \text{contribution margin} \times \text{sales}$$
$$= .21 \times \$100 \text{ million} = \$21 \text{ million}$$

Price changes result in changes in unit contribution and contribution margin. Recall that the contribution margin of 21 percent was based on variable costs representing 79 percent of sales. Therefore, unit variable costs can be determined by multiplying the original price by this percentage: $336 × 0.79 = $265.44 per unit.

If price is decreased by 10 percent, the new price is $302.40. However, variable costs do not change just because price decreased, so the contribution and contribution margin decrease as follows:

	Old	New (reduced 10%)
Price	$336	$302.40
– Unit variable cost	$265.44	$265.44
= Unit contribution	$ 70.56	$ 36.96
Contribution margin	$ 70.56/$336 = 0.21 or 21%	$ 36.96/$302.40 = 0.12 or 12%

So a 10 percent reduction in price results in a decrease in the contribution margin from 21 percent to 12 percent.[12] To determine the sales level needed to break even on this price reduction, we calculate the level of sales that must be attained at the new contribution margin to achieve the original total contribution of $21 million:

New contribution margin × new sales level = original total contribution

So,

$$\text{New sales level} = \frac{\text{original contribution}}{\text{new contribution margin}} = \frac{\$21,000,000}{0.12} = \$175,000,000$$

Thus, sales must increase by $75 million ($175 million – $100 million) just to break even on a 10 percent price reduction. This means that HDX-treme must increase market share to 7 percent ($175 million ÷ $2.5 billion) to achieve the current level of profits (assuming no increase in the total market sales). The marketing manager must assess whether or not this is a reasonable goal.

Extend the Product Line

As a final option, HDX-treme is considering extending its DVD player product line by offering a lower-priced model. Of course, the new, lower-priced product would steal some sales from the higher-priced model. This is called **cannibalization**—the situation in which one product sold by a company takes a portion of its sales from other company products. If the new product has a lower contribution than the original product, the company's total contribution will decrease on the cannibalized sales. However, if the new product can generate enough new volume, it is worth considering.

To assess cannibalization, HDX-treme must look at the incremental contribution gained by having both products available. Recall in the previous analysis we determined that unit variable costs were $265.44 and unit contribution was just over $70. Assuming costs remain the same next year, HDX-treme can expect to realize a contribution per unit of approximately $70 for every unit of the original DVD player sold.

Assume that the first model high-definition DVD player offered by HDX-treme is called HD1 and the new, lower-priced model is called HD2. HD2 will retail for $400, and resellers will take the same markup percentages on price as they do with the higher-priced model. Therefore, HD2's price to wholesalers will be $224 as follows:

Retail price:	$400
minus retail margin (30%):	– $120
Retailer's cost/wholesaler's price:	$280
minus wholesaler's margin (20%):	– $ 56
Wholesaler's cost/HDX-treme's price	$224

If HD2's variable costs are estimated to be $174, then its contribution per unit will equal $50 ($224 – $174 = $50). That means for every unit that HD2 cannibalizes from HD1, HDX-treme will *lose* $20 in contribution toward fixed costs and profit (that is, contribution^{HD2} – contribution^{HD1} = $50 – $70 = –$20). You might conclude that HDX-treme should not pursue this tactic because it appears as though the company will be worse off if it introduces the lower-priced model. However, if HD2 captures enough *additional sales*, HDX-treme will be better off even though some HD1 sales are cannibalized. The company must examine what will happen to *total* contribution, which requires estimates of unit volume for both products.

Originally, HDX-treme estimated that next year's sales of HD1 would be 600,000 units. However, with the introduction of HD2, it now estimates that 200,000 of those sales will be cannibalized by the new model. If HDX-treme sells only 200,000 units of the new HD2 model (all cannibalized from HD1), the company would lose $4 million in total contribution (200,000 units × –$20 per cannibalized unit = –$4 million)—not a

Cannibalization
The situation in which one product sold by a company takes a portion ot its sales from other company products.

good outcome. However, HDX-treme estimates that HD2 will generate the 200,000 of cannibalized sales plus an *additional* 500,000 unit sales. Thus, the contribution on these additional HD2 units will be $25 million (i.e., 500,000 units × $50 per unit = $25 million). The net effect is that HDX-treme will gain $21 million in total contribution by introducing HD².

The following table compares HDX-treme's total contribution with and without the introduction of HD2:

	HD1 only	HD1 and HD2
HD1 contribution	600,000 units × $70 = $42,000,000	400,000 units × $70 = $28,000,000
HD2 contribution	0	700,000 units × $50 = $35,000,000
Total contribution	$42,000,000	$63,000,000

The difference in the total contribution is a net gain of $21 million ($63 million – $42 million). Based on this analysis, HDX-treme should introduce the HD2 model because it results in a positive incremental contribution. However, if fixed costs will increase by more than $21 million as a result of adding this model, then the net effect will be negative and HDX-treme should not pursue this tactic.

Now that you have seen these marketing tactic analysis concepts in action as they related to HDX-treme's new DVD player, here are several exercises for you to apply what you have learned in this section in other contexts.

Marketing by the Numbers Exercise Set Three

3.1 Kingsford, Inc. sells small plumbing components to consumers through retail outlets. Total industry sales for Kingsford's relevant market last year were $80 million, with Kingsford's sales representing 10 percent of that total. Contribution margin is 25 percent. Kingsford's sales force calls on retail outlets and each sales rep earns $45,000 per year plus 1 percent commission on all sales. Retailers receive a 40 percent margin on selling price and generate average revenue of $10,000 per outlet for Kingsford.

 a. The marketing manager has suggested increasing consumer advertising by $300,000. By how much would dollar sales need to increase to break even on this expenditure? What increase in overall market share does this represent?

 b. Another suggestion is to hire three more sales representatives to gain new consumer retail accounts. How many new retail outlets would be necessary to break even on the increased cost of adding three sales reps?

 c. A final suggestion is to make a 20 percent across-the-board price reduction. By how much would dollar sales need to increase to maintain Kingsford's current contribution? (See endnote 12 to calculate the new contribution margin.)

 d. Which suggestion do you think Kingsford should implement? Explain your recommendation.

3.2 PepsiCo sells its soft drinks in approximately 400,000 retail establishments, such as supermarkets, discount stores, and convenience stores. Sales representatives call on each retail account weekly, which means each account is called on by a sales rep 52 times per year. The average length of a sales call is 75 minutes (or 1.25 hours). An average salesperson works 2,000 hours per year (50 weeks per year × 40 hours per week), but each spends 10 hours a week on nonselling activities, such as administrative tasks and travel. How many sales people does PepsiCo need?

3.3 Hair Zone manufactures a brand of hair-styling gel. It is considering adding a modified version of the product—a foam that provides stronger hold. Hair Zone's variable costs and prices to wholesalers are:

	Current hair gel	New foam product
Unit selling price	2.00	2.25
Unit variable costs	.85	1.25

Hair Zone expects to sell 1 million units of the new styling foam in the first year after introduction, but it expects that 60 percent of those sales will come from buyers who normally purchase Hair Zone's styling gel. Hair Zone estimates that it would sell 1.5 million units of the gel if it did not introduce the foam. If the fixed cost of launching the new foam will be $100,000 during the first year, should Hair Zone add the new product to its line? Why or why not?

CAREERS IN MARKETING

Now that you have completed this course in marketing, you have a good idea of what the field entails. You may have decided you want to pursue a marketing career because it offers constant challenge, stimulating problems, the opportunity to work with people, and excellent advancement opportunities. But you still may not know which part of marketing best suits you—marketing is a very broad field offering a wide variety of career options.

This appendix helps you discover what types of marketing jobs best match your special skills and interests, shows you how to conduct the kind of job search that will get you the position you want in the company of your choice, describes marketing career paths open to you, and suggests other information resources.

Marketing Careers Today

The marketing field is booming. Marketing salaries may vary by company, position, and region, and salary figures change constantly. In general, entry-level marketing salaries usually are only slightly below those for engineering and chemistry but equal or exceed starting salaries in economics, finance, accounting, general business, and the liberal arts. Moreover, if you succeed in an entry-level marketing position, it's likely that you will be promoted quickly to higher levels of responsibility and salary. In addition, because of the consumer and product knowledge you will gain in these jobs, marketing positions provide excellent training for the highest levels in an organization.

Overall Marketing Facts and Trends

In conducting your job search, consider the following facts and trends that are changing the world of marketing.

Focus on customers: More and more, companies are realizing that they win in the marketplace only by creating superior value for customers. To capture value from customers, they must first find new and better ways to solve customer problems and improve customer brand experiences. This increasing focus on the customer puts marketers at the forefront in many of today's companies. As the primary customer-facing function, marketing's mission is to get all company departments to "think customer."

Technology: Technology is changing the way marketers work. For example, price coding allows instantaneous retail inventorying. Software for marketing training, forecasting, and other functions is changing the ways we market. And the Internet is creating new jobs and new recruiting rules. Consider the explosive growth in new media marketing. Whereas advertising firms have traditionally recruited "generalists" in account management, "generalist" has now taken on a whole new meaning—advertising account executives must now have both broad and specialized knowledge.

Diversity: The number of women and minorities in marketing continues to rise. Traditionally, women were mainly in retailing. However, women and minorities have now moved fully into all industries. They also are rising rapidly into marketing management. For example, women now outnumber men by nearly two to one as advertising account executives. As marketing becomes more global, the need for diversity in marketing positions will continue to increase, opening new opportunities.

Global: Companies such as Toyota, Samsung, Coca-Cola, McDonald's, and Procter & Gamble have become multinational, with manufacturing and marketing operations in hundreds of countries. Indeed, such companies often make more profit from sales overseas than from local markets. And it's not just the big companies that are involved in international marketing. Organizations of all sizes have moved into the global arena. Many new marketing opportunities and careers will be directly linked to the expanding global marketplace. The globalization of business also means that you will need more cultural, language, and people skills in the marketing world of the twenty-first century.

Not-for-profit organizations: Increasingly, colleges, arts organizations, libraries, hospitals, and other not-for-profit organizations are recognizing the need for effectively marketing their "products" and services to various publics. This awareness has led to new marketing positions—with these organizations hiring their own marketing directors and marketing vice presidents or using outside marketing specialists.

Looking for a Job in Today's Marketing World

To choose and find the right job, you will need to apply the marketing skills you've learned in this course, especially marketing analysis and planning. Follow these eight steps for marketing yourself: (1) Conduct a self-assessment and seek career counseling; (2) examine job descriptions; (3) explore the job market and assess opportunities; (4) develop search strategies; (5) prepare a résumé; (6) write a cover letter and assemble supporting documents; (7) interview for jobs; and (8) follow up.

Conduct a Self-Assessment and Seek Career Counseling

If you're having difficulty deciding what kind of marketing position is the best fit for you, start out by doing some self-testing or get some career counseling. Self-assessments require that you honestly and thoroughly evaluate your interests, strengths, and weaknesses. What do you do well (your best and favorite skills) and not so well? What are your favorite interests? What are your career goals? What makes you stand out from other job seekers?

The answers to such questions may suggest which marketing careers you should seek or avoid. For help in making an effective self-assessment, look at the following books in your local bookstore: Susan Johnston, *The Career Adventure: Your Guide to Personal Assessment, Career Exploration, and Decision Making*, 4th edition (Prentice Hall, 2006) and Richard Bolles, *What Color Is Your Parachute 2007?* (Ten Speed Press, 2006). Many Web sites also offer self-assessment tools, such as the Keirsey Temperament Theory and the Temperament Sorter, a free but broad assessment available at AdvisorTeam.com. For a more specific evaluation, CareerLeader.com offers a complete online business career self-assessment program designed by the Directors of MBA Career Development at Harvard Business School. You can use this for a fee. For help in finding a career counselor to guide you in making a career assessment, Richard Bolles' What Color Is Your Parachute 2007? contains a useful state-by-state sampling. CareerLeader.com also offers personal career counseling. (Some counselors can help you in your actual job search, too.)

You can also consult the career counseling, testing, and placement services at your college or university.

Examine Job Descriptions

After you have identified your skills, interests, and desires, you need to see which marketing positions are the best match for them. Two publications (available in your local library or online)—the *Occupation Outlook Handbook* (<u>www.bls.gov/oco</u>) and the *Dictionary of Occupational Titles* (<u>www.occupationalinfo.org</u>)—describe the duties involved in various occupations, the specific training and education needed, the availability of jobs in each field, possibilities for advancement, and probable earnings.

Your initial career shopping list should be broad and flexible. Look for different ways to achieve your objectives. For example, if you want a career in marketing management, consider the public as well as the private sector, and local and regional as well as national and international firms. Be open initially to exploring many options, then focus on specific industries and jobs, listing your basic goals as a way to guide your choices. Your list might include "a job in a start-up company, near a big city, doing new-product planning with a computer software firm."

Explore the Job Market and Assess Opportunities

At this stage, you need to look at the market and see what positions are actually available. You do not have to do this alone. Any of the following may assist you.

Career Development Centers

Your college's career development center is an excellent place to start. More and more, college career development centers are also going online.

In addition, find out everything you can about the companies that interest you by consulting business magazines, Web sites, annual reports, business reference books, faculty, career counselors, and others. Try to analyze the industry's and the company's future growth and profit potential, advancement opportunities, salary levels, entry positions, travel time, and other factors of significance to you.

Job Fairs

Career development centers often work with corporate recruiters to organize on-campus job fairs. You might also use the Internet to check on upcoming career fair in your region.

Networking and the Yellow Pages

Networking, or asking for job leads from friends, family, people in your community, and career centers, is one of the best ways to find a marketing job. A recent study estimated that 60.7 percent of jobs are found through networking. The idea is to spread your net wide, contacting anybody and everybody.

The phone book's yellow pages are another effective way to job search. Check out employers in your field of interest in whatever region you want to work, then call and ask if they are hiring for the position of your choice.

Cooperative Education and Internships

According to the National Association of Colleges and Employers 2004 Experimental Education Survey, employers on average give full-time employment offers to about 58 percent of students who have had internships with their companies. They give offers to more than 67 percent of the students that participate in co-ops with their organizations. Many company Internet sites have separate internship areas. If you know of a company for which you wish to work, go to that company's corporate Web site, enter the human resources area, and check for internships. If none are listed, try e-mailing the human resources department, asking if internships are offered.

The Internet

A constantly increasing number of sites on the Internet deal with job hunting. You can also use the Internet to make contacts with people who can help you gain information on companies and research companies that interest you.

Most companies have their own Web sites on which they post job listings. This may be helpful if you have a specific and fairly limited number of companies that you are keeping your eye on for job opportunities. But if this is not the case, remember that to find out what interesting marketing jobs the companies themselves are posting, you may need to visit hundreds of corporate sites.

Develop Search Strategies

Once you've decided which companies you are interested in, you need to contact them. One of the best ways is through on-campus interviews. But not every company you are interested in will visit your school. In such instances, you can write, e-mail, or phone the company directly or ask marketing professors or school alumni for contacts.

Prepare a Résumé

A résumé is a concise yet comprehensive written summary of your qualifications, including your academic, personal, and professional achievements, that showcases why you are the best candidate for the job. An employer will spend an average of only 15 to 20 seconds reviewing your résumé; therefore, you want to be sure that you prepare a good one.

In preparing your résumé, remember that all information on it must be accurate and complete. Résumés typically begin with the applicant's full name, telephone and fax numbers, and mail and e-mail addresses. A simple and direct statement of career objectives generally appears next, followed by work history and academic data (including awards and internships), and then by personal activities and experiences applicable to the job sought.

The résumé sometimes ends with a list of references the employer may contact (at other times, references may be listed separately). If your work or internship experience is limited, nonexistent, or irrelevant, then it is a good idea to emphasize your academic and nonacademic achievements, showing skills related to those required for excellent job performance.

There are three types of résumés. Reverse chronological résumés, which emphasize career growth, are organized in reverse chronological order, starting with your most recent job. They focus on job titles within organizations, describing the responsibilities required for each job. Functional résumés focus less on job titles and work history and more on assets and achievements. This format works best if your job history is scanty or discontinuous. Mixed, or combination, résumés take from each of the other two formats. First, the skills used for a specific job are listed, then the job title is stated. This format works best for applicants whose past jobs are in other fields or seemingly unrelated to the position.

Your local bookstore or library has many books that can assist you in developing your résumé. Popular guides are Brenda Greene, *Get the Interview Every Time : Fortune 500 Hiring Professionals' Tips for Writing Winning Resumes and Cover Letters* (Dearborn Trade, 2004) and Arthur Rosenberg and David Hizer, *The Résumé Handbook* (Adams Media Corporation, 2003). Computer software programs, such as RésuméMaker Career Edition, provide hundreds of sample résumés and ready-to-use phrases while guiding you through the résumé preparation process. America's Career InfoNet (*www.acinet.org/acinet/resume/resume_intro.asp*) offers a step-by-step résumé tutorial, and Monster.com (*www.resume.monster.com*) offers résumé advice and writing services. Finally, you can even create your own personalized online résumé at sites such as optimalresume.com.

Electronic Résumés

Use of the Internet as a tool in the job search process is increasing, so it's a good idea to have your résumé ready for the online environment. You can forward an electronic résumé to networking contacts or recruiting professionals through e-mail. You can also post it in online databases with the hope that employers and recruiters will find it.

Successful electronic résumés require a different strategy than paper résumés. For instance, when companies search résumé banks, they search key words and industry buzz words that describe a skill or core work required for each job, so nouns are much more important than verbs. Two good resources for preparing electronic résumés are Susan

Ireland's *Electronic Resume Guide* (http://susanireland.com/eresumeguide/) and *The Riley Guide* (www.rileyguide.com/eresume.html).

After you have written your electronic résumé, you need to post it. The following sites may be good locations to start: Monster.com (www.monster.com) and Yahoo! hotjobs (www.hotjobs.yahoo.com). However, use caution when posting your résumé on various sites. In this era of identity theft, you need to select sites with care so as to protect your privacy. Limit access to your personal contact information and don't use sites that offer to "blast" your résumé into cyberspace.

Résumé Tips

- Communicate your worth to potential employers in a concrete manner, citing examples whenever possible.
- Be concise and direct.
- Use active verbs to show you are a doer.
- Do not skimp on quality or use gimmicks. Spare no expense in presenting a professional résumé.
- Have someone critique your work. A single typo can eliminate you from being considered.
- Customize your résumé for specific employers. Emphasize your strengths as they pertain to your targeted job.
- Keep your résumé compact, usually one page.
- Format the text to be attractive, professional, and readable. Times New Roman is often the font of choice. Avoid too much "design" or gimmicky flourishes.

Write Cover Letter, Follow Up, and Assemble Supporting Documents

Cover Letter

You should include a cover letter informing the employer that a résumé is enclosed. But a cover letter does more than this. It also serves to summarize in one or two paragraphs the contents of the résumé and explains why you think you are the right person for the position. The goal is to persuade the employer to look at the more detailed résumé. A typical cover letter is organized as follows: (1) the name and position of the person you are contacting; (2) a statement identifying the position you are applying for, how you heard of the vacancy, and the reasons for your interest; (3) a summary of your qualifications for the job; (4) a description of what follow-ups you intend to make, such as phoning in two weeks to see if the résumé has been received; (5) an expression of gratitude for the opportunity of being a candidate for the job. America's Career InfoNet (www.acinet.org/acinet/resume/resume_intro.asp) offers a step-by-step tutorial on how to create a cover letter, and Susan Ireland's Web site contains more than 50 cover letter samples (http://susanireland.com/coverletterindex.htm).

Follow Up

Once you send your cover letter and résumé to perspective employers via the method they prefer—e-mail, their Web site, fax, or regular mail—it's often a good idea to follow up. In today's market, job seekers can't afford to wait for interviews to find them. A quality résumé and an attractive cover letter are crucial, but a proper follow-up may be the key to landing an interview. However, before you engage your potential employer, be sure to research the company. Knowing about the company and understanding its place in the industry will help you shine. When you place a call, send an e-mail, or mail a letter to a company contact, be sure to restate your interest in the position, check on the status of your résumé, and ask the employer about any questions they may have.

Letters of Recommendation

Letters of recommendation are written references by professors, former and current employers, and others that testify to your character, skills, and abilities. Some companies may request letters of recommendation, to be submitted either with the résumé or at the interview. Even if letters of recommendation aren't requested, it's a good idea to bring them with you to the interview. A good reference letter tells why you would be an excellent candidate for the position. In choosing someone to write a letter of recommendation, be confident that the person will give you a good reference. In addition, do not assume the person knows everything about you or the position you are seeking. Rather, provide the person with your résumé and other relevant data. As a courtesy, allow the reference writer at least a month to complete the letter and enclose a stamped, addressed envelope with your materials.

In the packet containing your résumé, cover letter, and letters of recommendation, you may also want to attach other relevant documents that support your candidacy, such as academic transcripts, graphics, portfolios, and samples of writing.

Interview for Jobs

As the old saying goes, "The résumé gets you the interview; the interview gets you the job." The job interview offers you an opportunity to gather more information about the organization, while at the same time allowing the organization to gather more information about you. You'll want to present your best self. The interview process consists of three parts: before the interview, the interview itself, and after the interview. If you pass through these stages successfully, you will be called back for the follow-up interview.

Before the Interview

In preparing for your interview, do the following:

1. Understand that interviewers have diverse styles, including the "chitchat," let's-get-to-know-each-other style; the interrogation style of question after question; and the tough-probing "why, why, why" style, among others. So be ready for anything.
2. With a friend, practice being interviewed and then ask for a critique. Or, videotape yourself in a practice interview so that you can critique your own performance. Your college placement service may also offer "mock" interviews to help you.
3. Prepare at least five good questions whose answers are not easily found in the company literature, such as "What is the future direction of the firm?" "How does the firm differentiate itself from competitors?" "Do you have a new-media division?"
4. Anticipate possible interview questions, such as "Why do you want to work for this company?" or "Why should we hire you?" Prepare solid answers before the interview. Have a clear idea of why you are interested in joining the company and the industry to which it belongs. (See Susan Ireland's site for additional interview questions: *http://susanireland.com/interviewwork.html*)
5. Avoid back-to-back interviews—they can be exhausting and it is unpredictable how long they will last.
6. Prepare relevant documents that support your candidacy, such as academic transcripts, letters of recommendation, graphics, portfolios, and samples of writing. Bring multiple copies to the interview.
7. Dress conservatively and professionally. Be neat and clean.
8. Arrive ten minutes early to collect your thoughts and review the major points you intend to cover. Check your name on the interview schedule, noting the name of the interviewer and the room number. Be courteous and polite to office staff.
9. Approach the interview enthusiastically. Let your personality shine through.

During the Interview

During the interview, do the following:

1. Shake hands firmly in greeting the interviewer. Introduce yourself, using the same form of address the interviewer uses. Focus on creating a good initial impression.
2. Keep your poise. Relax, smile when appropriate, and be upbeat throughout.
3. Maintain eye contact, good posture, and speak distinctly. Don't clasp your hands or fiddle with jewelry, hair, or clothing. Sit comfortably in your chair. Do not smoke, even if it's permitted.
4. Along with the copies of relevant documents that support your candidacy, carry extra copies of your résumé with you.
5. Have your story down pat. Present your selling points. Answer questions directly. Avoid either one-word or too-wordy answers.
6. Let the interviewer take the initiative but don't be passive. Find an opportunity to direct the conversation to things about yourself that you want the interviewer to hear.
7. To end on a high note, make your most important point or ask your most pertinent question during the last part of the interview.
8. Don't hesitate to "close." You might say, "I'm very interested in the position, and I have enjoyed this interview."
9. Obtain the interviewer's business card or address and phone number so that you can follow up later.

A tip for acing the interview: Before you open your mouth, find out what it's like to be a brand manager, sales representative, market researcher, advertising account executive, or other position for which you're interviewing. See if you can find a "mentor"—someone in a position similar to the one you're seeking, perhaps with another company. Talk with this mentor about the ins and outs of the job and industry.

After the Interview

After the interview, do the following:

1. After leaving the interview, record the key points that arose. Be sure to note who is to follow up and when a decision can be expected.
2. Analyze the interview objectively, including the questions asked, the answers to them, your overall interview presentation, and the interviewer's responses to specific points.
3. Immediately send a thank-you letter or e-mail, mentioning any additional items and your willingness to supply further information.
4. If you do not hear within the specified time, write, e-mail, or call the interviewer to determine your status.

Follow Up

If your first interview takes place off-site, such as at your college or at a job fair, and if you are successful with that initial interview, you will be invited to visit the organization. The in-company interview will probably run from several hours to an entire day. The organization will examine your interest, maturity, enthusiasm, assertiveness, logic, and company and functional knowledge. You should ask questions about issues of importance to you. Find out about the working environment, job role, responsibilities, opportunity for advancement, current industrial issues, and the company's personality. The company wants to discover if you are the right person for the job, whereas you want to find out if it is the right job for you. The key is to determine if the right fit exists between you and the company.

Marketing Jobs

This section describes some of the key marketing positions.

Advertising

Advertising is one of today's hottest fields in marketing. In fact, *Money* magazine lists a position in advertising as among the 50 best jobs in America.

Job Descriptions

Key advertising positions include copywriter, art director, production manager, account executive, and media planner/buyer.

- Copywriters write advertising copy and help find the concepts behind the written words and visual images of advertisements.
- Art directors, the other part of the creative team, help translate the copywriters' ideas into dramatic visuals called "layouts." Agency artists develop print layouts, package designs, television layouts (called "storyboards"), corporate logotypes, trademarks, and symbols.
- Production managers are responsible for physically creating ads, in-house or by contracting through outside production houses.
- Account development executives research and understand clients' markets and customers and help develop marketing and advertising strategies to impact them.
- Account executives serve as liaisons between clients and agencies. They coordinate the planning, creation, production, and implementation of an advertising campaign for the account.
- Account planners serve as the voice of the consumer in the agency. They research consumers to understand their needs and motivations as a basis for developing effective ad campaigns.
- Media planners (or buyers) determine the best mix of television, radio, newspaper, magazine, and other media for the advertising campaign.

Skills Needed, Career Paths, and Typical Salaries

Work in advertising requires strong people skills in order to interact closely with an often-difficult and demanding client base. In addition, advertising attracts people with high skills in planning, problem solving, creativity, communication, initiative, leadership, and presentation. Advertising involves working under high levels of stress and pressure created by unrelenting deadlines. Advertisers frequently have to work long hours to meet deadlines for a presentation. But work achievements are very apparent, with the results of creative strategies observed by thousands or even millions of people.

Because they are so sought after, positions in advertising sometimes require an MBA. But there are many jobs open for business, graphics arts, and liberal arts undergraduates. Advertising positions often serve as gateways to higher-level management. Moreover, with large advertising agencies opening offices all over the world, there is the possibility of eventually working on global campaigns.

Starting advertising salaries are relatively low compared to some other marketing jobs because of strong competition for entry-level advertising jobs. You may even want to consider working for free to break in. Compensation will increase quickly as you move into account executive or other management positions. For more facts and figures, see the Web pages of *Advertising Age*, a key ad industry publication (*www.adage.com*, click on the Job Bank button), and the American Association of Advertising Agencies (*www.aaaa.org*).

Brand and Product Management

Brand and product managers plan, direct, and control business and marketing efforts for their products. They are involved with research and development, packaging, manufacturing, sales and distribution, advertising, promotion, market research, and business analysis and forecasting.

Job Descriptions

A company's brand management team consists of people in several positions.

- Brand managers guide the development of marketing strategies for a specific brand.
- Assistant brand managers are responsible for certain strategic components of the brand.
- Product managers oversee several brands within a product line or product group.
- Product category managers direct multiple product lines in the product category.
- Market analysts research the market and provide important strategic information to the project managers.
- Project directors are responsible for collecting market information on a marketing or product project.
- Research directors oversee the planning, gathering, and analyzing of all organizational research.

Skills Needed, Career Paths, and Typical Salaries

Brand and product management requires high problem-solving, analytical, presentation, communication, and leadership skills, as well as the ability to work well in a team. Product management requires long hours and involves the high pressure of running large projects. In consumer goods companies, the newcomer—who usually needs an MBA—joins a brand team as an assistant and learns the ropes by doing numerical analyses and watching senior brand people. This person eventually heads the team and later moves on to manage a larger brand, then several brands.

Many industrial goods companies also have product managers. Product management is one of the best training grounds for future corporate officers. Product management also offers good opportunities to move into international marketing. Product managers command relatively high salaries. Because this job category encourages or requires a master's degree, starting pay tends to be higher than in other marketing categories such as advertising or retailing.

Sales and Sales Management

Sales and sales management opportunities exist in a wide range of profit and not-for-profit organizations and in product and service organizations, including financial, insurance, consulting, and government organizations.

Job Descriptions

Key jobs include consumer sales, industrial sales, national account manager, service support, sales trainers, sales management, and telesellers.

- Consumer sales involves selling consumer products and services through retailers.
- Industrial sales involves selling products and services to other businesses.
- National account managers (NAM) oversee a few very large accounts.
- Service support personnel support salespeople during and after the sale of a product.
- Sales trainers train new hires and provide refresher training for all sales personnel.
- Sales management includes a sequence of positions ranging from district manager to vice president of sales.
- The teleseller (not to be confused with the home consumer telemarketer) offers service and support to field salespeople.

Salespeople enjoy active professional lives, working outside the office and interacting with others. They manage their own time and activities. And successful salespeople can be very well paid. Competition for top jobs can be intense. Every sales job is different, but some positions involve extensive travel, long workdays, and working under pressure. You can also expect to be transferred more than once between company headquarters and regional offices. However, most companies are now working to bring good work-life balance to their salespeople and sales managers.

Skills Needed, Career Paths, and Typical Salaries

Selling is a people profession in which you will work with people every day, all day long. Besides people skills, sales professionals need sales and communication skills. Most sales positions also require high problem-solving, analytical, presentation, and leadership ability as well as creativity and initiative. Teamwork skills are increasingly important.

Career paths lead from salesperson to district, regional, and higher levels of sales management and, in many cases, to the top management of the firm. Today, most entry-level sales management positions require a college degree. Increasingly, people seeking selling jobs are acquiring sales experience in an internship capacity or from a part-time job before graduating. Sales positions are great springboards to leadership positions, with more CEOs starting in sales than in any other entry-level position. Possibly this explains why competition for top sales jobs is intense.

Starting base salaries in sales may be moderate, but compensation is often supplemented by significant commission, bonus, or other incentive plans. In addition, many sales jobs include a company car or car allowance. Successful salespeople are among most companies' highest paid employees.

Other Marketing Jobs

Retailing

Retailing provides an early opportunity to assume marketing responsibilities. Key jobs include store manager, regional manager, buyer, department manager, and salesperson. Store managers direct the management and operation of an individual store. Regional managers manage groups of stores across several states and report performance to headquarters. Buyers select and buy the merchandise that the store carries. The department manager acts as store manager of a department, such as clothing, but on the department level. The salesperson sells merchandise to retail customers. Retailing can involve relocation, but generally there is little travel, unless you are a buyer. Retailing requires high people and sales skills because retailers are constantly in contact with customers. Enthusiasm, willingness, and communication skills are very helpful for retailers, too.

Retailers work long hours, but their daily activities are often more structured than some types of marketing positions. Starting salaries in retailing tend to be low, but pay increases as you move into management or some retailing specialty job.

Marketing Research

Marketing researchers interact with managers to define problems and identify the information needed to resolve them. They design research projects, prepare questionnaires and samples, analyze data, prepare reports, and present their findings and recommendations to management. They must understand statistics, consumer behavior, psychology, and sociology. A master's degree helps. Career opportunities exist with manufacturers, retailers, some wholesalers, trade and industry associations, marketing research firms, advertising agencies, and governmental and private nonprofit agencies.

New-Product Planning

People interested in new-product planning can find opportunities in many types of organizations. They usually need a good background in marketing, marketing research, and sales forecasting; they need organizational skills to motivate and coordinate others; and they may need a technical background. Usually, these people work first in other marketing positions before joining the new-product department.

Marketing Logistics (Physical Distribution)

Marketing logistics, or physical distribution, is a large and dynamic field, with many career opportunities. Major transportation carriers, manufacturers, wholesalers, and retailers all employ logistics specialists. Increasingly, marketing teams include logistics specialists, and marketing managers' career paths include marketing logistics assignments. Coursework in quantitative methods, finance, accounting, and marketing will provide you with the necessary skills for entering the field.

Public Relations

Most organizations have a public relations staff to anticipate problems with various publics, handle complaints, deal with media, and build the corporate image. People interested in public relations should be able to speak and write clearly and persuasively, and they should have a background in journalism, communications, or the liberal arts. The challenges in this job are highly varied and very people oriented.

Not-for-Profit Services

The key jobs in nonprofits include marketing director, director of development, event coordinator, publication specialist, and intern/volunteers. The marketing director is in charge of all marketing activities for the organization. The director of development organizes, manages, and directs the fund-raising campaigns that keep a nonprofit in existence. An event coordinator directs all aspects of fund-raising events, from initial planning through implementation. The publication specialist oversees publications designed to promote awareness of the organization.

Although typically an unpaid position, the intern/volunteer performs various marketing functions, and this work can be an important step to gaining a full-time position. The nonprofit sector is typically not for someone who is money driven. Rather, most nonprofits look for people with a strong sense of community spirit and the desire to help others. So starting pay is usually lower than in other marketing fields. However, the bigger the nonprofit, the better your chance of rapidly increasing your income when moving into upper management.

Chapter 1

1. The American Marketing Association offers the following definition: "Marketing is an organizational function and a set of processes for creating, communicating, and delivering value to customers and for managing customer relationships in ways that benefit the organization and its stakeholders." Accessed at www.marketingpower.com/mg-dictionary-view1862.php?, December 2006.

2. China Trend Watch 2006, ACNielsen.

3. Martha Rogers, "Nissan Builds Relationships before Products," *Inside 1to1*, July 21, 2003.

4. See Theodore Levitt's classic article, "Marketing Myopia," *Harvard Business Review*, July–August 1960, pp. 45–56. For more recent discussions, see Yves Doz, Jose Santos, and Peter J. Williamson, "Marketing Myopia Re-Visited: Why Every Company Needs to Learn from the World," *Ivey Business Journal*, January–February 2004, p. 1; Lon Zimmerman, "Product Positioning Maps Secure Future," *Marketing News*, October 15, 2005, p. 47.

5. Mark Kleinman, "Great Haul of China's Burgers," *The West Australian*, November 25, 2006, p. 91.

6. See "America's Most Fattening Burger," Time, January 3, 2005, p. 186; "For the Health-Unconscious, Era of Mammoth Burger Is Here," *Wall Street Journal*, January 27, 2005, p. B.1; Jim Slater, "New Hardee's Sandwich Piles Meat on More Meat," *Associated Press Wire*, April 19, 2006; and Bruce Horowitz, "Wendy's Will Be 1st Fast Foodie with Healthier Oil," *USA Today*, June 8, 2006. p. 1B.

7. Paul A. Eisenstein, "Strategic Vision Puts Toyota, Honda on Top," October 10, 2005, accessed at www.thecarconnection.com; and Silvio Schindler, "Hybrids and Customers," *Automotive Design & Production*, June 2006, pp. 20–22.

8. John Quelch and Anna Harrington, "Samsung Electronics Company: Global Marketing Operations," Harvard Business School Case N2-504-051, 2004.

9. Colin Yong, "Playing the Loyalty Card," *Today (Weekend)*, August 12, 2006, p. 26.

10. Information about the Harley Owners Group accessed at www.hog.com, September 2006. For more on loyalty programs, see Joseph C. Nunes and Xavier Dreze, "Your Loyalty Program Is Betraying You," *Harvard Business Review*, April 2006, pp. 124–131.

11. Philip Kotler and Kevin Lane Keller, *Marketing Management*, 12th ed. (Upper Saddle River, NJ: Prentice Hall, 2006), p. 27.

12. Mark Kleinman, "Great Haul of China's Burgers," *The West Australian*, November 25, 2006, p. 91

13. For more discussion of customer delight and loyalty, see Barry Berman, "How to Delight Your Customers," *California Management Review*, Fall 2005, pp. 129–151; Clara Agustin and Jagdip Singh, "Curvilinear Effects of Consumer Loyalty Determinants in Relational Exchanges," *Journal of Marketing Research*, February 2005, pp. 96–108; Ben McConnell and Jackie Huba, "Learning to Leverage the Lunatic Fringe," *Point*, July–August, 2006, pp. 14–15; and Fred Reichheld, *The Ultimate Question: Driving Good Profits and True Growth* (Boston: Harvard Business School Publishing, 2006).

14. See Roland T. Rust, Valerie A. Zeithaml, and Katherine A. Lemon, *Driving Customer Equity* (New York: Free Press, 2000); Robert C. Blattberg, Gary Getz, Jacquelyn S. Thomas, *Customer Equity* (Boston, MA: Harvard Business School Press, 2001); Rust, Lemon, and Zeithaml, "Return on Marketing: Using Customer Equity to Focus Marketing Strategy," *Journal of Marketing*, January 2004, pp. 109–127; James D. Lenskold, "Customer-Centered Marketing ROI," *Marketing Management*, January/February 2004, pp. 26–32; Rust,. Zeithaml, and Lemon, "Customer-Centered Brand Management," *Harvard Business Review*, September 2004, p. 110; Don Peppers and Martha Rogers, "Hail to the Customer," *Sales & Marketing Management*, October 2005, pp. 49–51; and Allison Enright, "Serve Them Right," *Marketing News*, May 1, 2006, pp. 21–22.

15. Werner Reinartz and V. Kumar, "The Mismanagement of Customer Loyalty," *Harvard Business Review*, July 2002, pp. 86–94. For more on customer equity management, see Sunil Gupta, Donald R. Lehman, and Jennifer Ames Stuart, "Valuing Customers," *Journal of Marketing Research*, February 2004, pp. 7–18; Michael D. Johnson and Fred Selnes, "Customer Portfolio Management: Toward a Dynamic Theory of Exchange Relationships," *Journal of Marketing*, April 2004, pp. 1–17; Sunil Gupta and Donald R. Lehman, *Managing Customers as Investments* (Philadelphia: Wharton School Publishing, 2005); and Roland T. Rust, Katherine N. Lemon, and Das Narayandas, *Customer Equity Management* (Upper Saddle River, NJ: Prentice Hall, 2005).

16. Anver Versi, "MTV Rolls Out African Channel," *African Business*, January 2005, pp. 58–59; and Johnnie L. Roberts, "World Tour," *Newsweek*, June 6, 2005, pp. 34–35.

Chapter 2

1. Quotes and other information from Stanley Holmes, "The New Nike," *BusinessWeek*, September 20, 2004, pp. 78–86; "Nike, Inc.," *Hoover's Company Records*, May 15, 2006, p. 14254; Daniel Roth, "Can Nike Still Do It Without Phil Knight?" *Fortune*, April 4, 2005, pp. 59–68; Helen Jung, "Phil Knight's Charity Is Billion Dollar Secret," *The Oregonian*, December 25, 2005, accessed at www.oregonlive.com; Stanley Holmes, "Adidas' World Cup Shutout," *BusinessWeek*, April 3,

2006, pp. 104–106; www.wikipedia.com, November 2007; and www.nikebiz.com, November 2007.

2. For a more detailed discussion of corporate- and business-level strategic planning as they apply to marketing, see Philip Kotler and Kevin Lane Keller, *Marketing Management*, 12th ed. (Upper Saddle River, N.J.: Prentice Hall, 2006), Chapter 2.

3. Nike and eBay mission statements from www.nike.com/nikebiz/nikebiz.jhtml?page=4 and http://pages.ebay.com/aboutebay/thecompany/companyoverview.html, respectively, November 2006.

4. Monsanto Company Pledge Report, accessed at http://monsanto.com/monsanto/layout/our_pledge/default.asp, December 2006.

5. The following discussion is based in part on information found at www.bcg.com/this_is_BCG/mission/growth_share_matrix.html, December 2006. For more on strategic planning, see Anthony Lavia, "Strategic Planning in Times of Turmoil," *Business Communications Review*, March 2004, pp. 56–60; Rita Gunther McGrath and Ian C. MacMillan, "Market Busting," *Harvard Business Review*, March 2005, pp. 80–89; and Lloyd C. Harris and Emmanuel Ogbonna, "Initiating Strategic Planning," *Journal of Business Research*, January 2006, pp. 100–111.

6. H. Igor Ansoff, "Strategies for Diversification," *Harvard Business Review*, September-October 1957, pp. 113–124. Quotes and information in the Starbucks examples and in the growth discussion that follows are from Monica Soto Ouchi, "Starbucks Ratchets Up Growth Forecast," *Knight Ridder Tribune News*, October 15, 2004, p. 1; Patricia Sellers, "Starbucks: The Next Generation," *Fortune*, April 4, 2005, p. 30; Leon Lazaroff, "Starbucks Brews Up Successful Formula for Growth," *Chicago Tribune*, December 18, 2005; Kim Wright Wiley, "Taste of Success," *Sell-ing Power*, April 2006, pp. 51–54; Bruce Horovitz, "Starbucks Nation," USA Today, May 19, 2006, accessed at www.usatoday.com/money/industries/food/2006-05-18-starbucks-usat_x.htm; and the company fact sheet, annual report, and other information accessed at www.starbucks.com, July 2006.

7. T. L. Stanley, "Starbucks and Vine Changes the Rules," *Advertising Age*, April 3, 2006, pp. 3–4.

8. Michael E. Porter, *Competitive Advantage: Creating and Sustaining Superior Performance* (New York: Free Press, 1985); and Michael E. Porter, "What Is Strategy?" *Harvard Business Review*, November–December 1996, pp. 61–78. Also see Kim B. Clark, et al., *Harvard Business School on Managing the Value Chain* (Boston: Harvard Business School Press, 2000); "Buyer Value and the Value Chain," *Business Owner*, September-October 2003, p. 1; and "The Value Chain," accessed at www.quickmba.com/strategy/value-chain, December 2006.

9. McDonald's 2006 Fact Sheet, accessed at www.mcdonalds.com/corp/invest/pub/2006_fact_sheet.html, May 2006; "McDonald's Fetes 50th Birthday, Opens Anniversary Restaurant," *Knight Ridder Tribune Business News*, April 15, 2005, p. 1; and "McDonald's Corporation," *Hoover's Company Records*, June 15, 2006, p. 10974.

10. Quotes and other information from Jeffery K. Liker and Thomas Y. Choi, "Building Deep Supplier Relationships," *Harvard Business Review*, December 2004, pp. 104–113; Lindsey Chappell, "Toyota Aims to Satisfy Its Suppliers," *Automotive News*, February 21, 2005, p. 10; and www.toyotasupplier.com, December 2006.

11. Jack Trout, "Branding Can't Exist without Positioning," *Advertising Age*, March 14, 2005, p. 28.

12. The four Ps classification was first suggested by E. Jerome McCarthy, *Basic Marketing: A Managerial Approach* (Homewood, IL: Irwin, 1960). For the 4Cs, other proposed classifications, and more discussion, see Robert Lauterborn, "New Marketing Litany: 4P's Passé; C-Words Take Over," *Advertising Age*, October 1, 1990, p. 26; Don E. Schultz, "New Definition of Marketing Reinforces Idea of Integration," *Marketing News*, January 15, 2005, p. 8; and Phillip Kotler, "Alphabet Soup," *Marketing Management*, March–April 2006, p. 51.

13. Rohit Deshpande and John U. Farley, "Tigers and Dragons: Profiling High-Performance Asian Firms," MSI Report No. 01-101, 2001.

14. For more on brand and product management, see Kevin Lane Keller, *Strategic Brand Management*, 2nd ed. (Upper Saddle River, N.J.: Prentice Hall, 2003).

15. For details, see Kotler and Keller, *Marketing Management*, pp. 719–725. Also see Neil A. Morgan, Bruce H. Clark, and Rich Gooner, "Marketing Productivity, Marketing Audits, and Systems for Marketing Performance Assessment: Integrating Multiple Perspectives," *Journal of Marketing*, May 2002, pp. 363–375.

16. Matthew Creamer, "Shops Push Affinity, Referrals Over Sales," *Advertising Age*, June 20, 2005, p. S4.

17. For more discussion, see Michael Karuss, "Marketing Dashboards Drive Better Decisions," *Marketing News*, October 1, 2005, p. 7; Richard Karpinski, "Making the Most of a Marketing Dashboard," *BtoB*, March 13, 2006, p. 18; and Bruce H. Clark, Andrew V. Abela, and Tim Ambler, "Behind the Wheel," *Marketing Management*, May-June 2006, pp. 19–23.

18. For a full discussion of this model and details on customer-centered measures of return on marketing investment, see Roland T. Rust, Katherine N. Lemon, and Valarie A. Zeithaml, "Return on Marketing: Using Customer Equity to Focus Marketing Strategy," *Journal of Marketing*, January 2004, pp. 109–127; Roland T. Rust, Katherine N. Lemon, and Das Narayandas, *Customer Equity Management* (Upper Saddle River, NJ: Prentice Hall, 2005); and Allison Enright, "Serve Them Right," *Marketing News*, May 1, 2006, pp. 21–22.

19. Deborah L. Vence, "Return on Investment," *Marketing News*, October 15, 2005, pp. 13–14.

Chapter 3

1. John O'Connor, "Golden Arches Still Standing After 50 Years," *Knight Ridder Tribune Business News*, April 19, 2005, p. 1; Sherri Day, "After Years at Top, McDonald's Strives To Regain Ground," *New York Times*, March 3, 2003, p. A.1; Amy Garber, "Bistro Gourmet at McDonald's," *Nation's Restaurant News*, January 31, 2005, pp. 34–35; Michael V. Copeland, "Ronald Gets Back in Shape," *Business 2.0*, January/February 2005, pp. 46–47; *Kate MacArthur*, "McD's to Shops: Make 'Lovin' It' More than Tag," *Advertising Age*, March 13, 2006, p. 8; Pallavi Gogoi, "Mickey D's McMakeover," *BusinessWeek*, May 15, 2006, pp. 42–43; www.wikipedia.com, November 27, 2007; McDonald's India and Singapore Web sites, November 27, 2007; and financial information and other facts accessed at www.mcdonalds.com/corp/invest.html and http://mcdonalds.com/corp/about/factsheets.html, July 2006.

2. See Sarah Lorge, "The Coke Advantage," *Sales & Marketing Management*, December 1998, p. 17; Chad Terhune, "Coke Wins a 10-Year Contract From Subway, Ousting PepsiCo," *Wall Street Journal*, November 28, 2003, p. B.3; and "The Best in Foodservice Just Get Better," *Beverage Industry*, September 2004, pp. 15–16.

3. World POPClock, U.S. Census Bureau, accessed online at www.census.gov, July 2006. This Web site provides continuously updated projections of the U.S. and world populations.

4. Adapted from Frederik Balfour, "Educating the 'Little Emperors' There's a Big Market for Products That Help China's Coddled Kids Get Ahead," *BusinessWeek*, November 10, 2003, p. 22. Also see Clay Chandler, "Little Emperors," *Fortune*, October 4, 2004, pp. 138–150; and "Hothousing Little Tykes," *Beijing Review*, May 5, 2005, accessed at www.bjreview.com.cn/En-2005/05-18-e/china-5.htm.

5. See "China's Golden Oldies," *The Economist*, February 26, 2005, p. 74. See also "China Economy: How Do You Prepare for the Retirement of 1.3bn People?" *EIU ViewsWire*, March 27, 2006.

6. "China's Golden Oldies," *The Economist*, February 26, 2005, p. 374.

7. Scott Schroder and Warren Zeller, "Get to Know Gen X and Its Segments," *Multichannel News*, March 21, 2005, p. 55.

8. Quotes from "Mixed Success: One Who Targeted Gen X and Succeeded—Sort Of," *Journal of Financial Planning*, February 2004, p. 15; and Paul Greenberg, "Move Over, Baby Boomers; Gen Xers Want Far More Collaboration with Companies, Both As Consumers and Employees," *CIO*, March 1, 2006, p. 1.

9. Quote from Tobi Elkin, "Gen Y Quizzed about On-Demand," *Advertising Age*, February 14, 2003, p. 37. Teen statistics and other information from "Teens Forge Forward with Internet and Other New Technologies,"

Pew Internet & American Life Project, July 25, 2005, accessed at www.pewinternet.org; and Jessi Hempel, "The MySpace Generation," *BusinessWeek*, December 12, 2005, pp. 86–96.

10. Julie Bosman, "Hey, Kid, You Want to Buy A Scion?" *New York Times*, June 14, 2006, p. C2.

11. "Urban Boom: Next Year, City Dwellers Will Outnumber Rural Folk for First Time," *The Straits Times*, June 28, 2007, p. 21.

12. China Trend Watch 2006, ACNielsen.

13. Roger Mitton, "Young Vietnamese Bitten Hard by Consumer Bug," *The Straits Times*, March 26, 2007, p. 12.

14. "How Levi Strauss Rekindled the Allure of Brand America," *World Trade*, March 2005, p. 28; Levi Strauss Press Releases, accessed at www.levistrauss.com, May 27, 2006; and Levi's Web site at www.levis.com, July, 2006.

15. Adapted from Lorraine Woellert, "HP Wants Your Old PC Back," *BusinessWeek*, April 10, 2006, pp. 82–83. For more discussion, see the "Environmentalism" section in Chapter 20.

16. Jack Neff, "P&G Products to Wear Wire," *Advertising Age*, December 15, 2004, pp. 1, 32; "Gartner Says Worldwide RFID Spending to Surpass $3 Billion in 2010," *BusinessWire*, December 13, 2005; Renee Boucher, "Wal-Mart Forges Ahead with RFID," *eWeek*, March 6, 2006; Michael Garry, "Wal-Mart Expands RFID Program to Atlanta," *Supermarket News*, June 12, 2006, p. 24; and information accessed online at www.autoidlabs.org, August 2006.

17. "Fake Disney: This Isn't the Happiest Place on Earth," *The New Paper*, May 5, 2007, p. 16.

18. Tee Jong Lee, "Keeping Up with the Kims, Korean Style," *The Sunday Times*, September 10, 2006, p. 24.

19. See Philip Kotler, *Kotler on Marketing* (New York: Free Press, 1999), p. 3; and Kotler, *Marketing Insights from A to Z* (Hoboken, NJ: John Wiley & Sons, 2003), pp. 23–24.

20. Adapted from Jayne O'Donnell, "Online Rumor Mill Dogs Companies," *USA Today*, October 29, 2005, p. 3B.

21. Chris Brummit, "Clove-Flavored Marlboro Now in Indonesia," biz.yahoo.com/ap/070703/Indonesia_clove_marlboro.html?.v=3 accessed on July 3, 2007.

Chapter 4

1. Quotes and extracts from Ellen Byron, "Case by Case: How Coach Won a Rich Purse by Inventing New Uses for Bags," *Wall Street Journal*, November 17, 2004, p. A1. Other information from Pallavi Gogoi, "I Am Woman, Hear Me Shop," *BusinessWeek Online*, February 14, 2005; Gogoi, "How a Woman Spends Her Money,"

BusinessWeek Online, February 14, 2005; Lauren Foster, "How Coach Pulled into Luxury's Fast Lane," *Financial Times*, June 30, 2004, p. 12; Coach 2005 Annual Report, accessed at www.coach.com; Kate Betts, "It's All in the Bag," *Time*, March 20, 2006, p. 101; Vicki M. Young, "Coach: Jewelry Launch in the Works," *WWD*, April 26, 2006, p. 11; "Coach, Inc. Company Profile," Datamonitor, August 24, 2007; "Coach, Inc.," *Hoover's Company Records*, June 15, 2006, p. 101101; and Google Finance, accessed at http://finance.google.com/finance?q=NYSE:COH.

2. Jennifer Brown, "Pizza Hut Delivers Hot Results Using Data Warehousing," *Computing Canada*, October 17, 2003, p. 24; and "Pizza Hut, Inc.," *Hoover's Company Records*, May 15, 2006, p. 89521.

3. Andy Serwer, "P&G's Covert Operation," *Fortune*, September 17, 2001, pp. 42–44. Also see Andrew Crane, "In the Company of Spies: When Competitive Intelligence Gathering Becomes Industrial Espionage," *Business Horizons*, May–June 2005, pp. 233+; and Kate MacKenzie, "Employees May Be Opening the Door to Criminals," *Financial*, May 31, 2006, p. 4.

4. Fred Vogelstein and Peter Lewis, "Search and Destroy," *Fortune*, May 2, 2005.

5. James Curtis, "Behind Enemy Lines," *Marketing*, May 21, 2001, pp. 28–29. Also see Brian Caufield, "Know Your Enemy," *Business 2.0*, June 2004, p. 89; Michael Fielding, "Damage Control: Firms Must Plan for Counterintelligence," *Marketing News*, September 15, 2004, pp. 19–20; and Bill DeGenaro, "A Case for Business Counterintelligence," *Competitive Intelligence Magazine*, September–October 2005, pp. 5+.

6. For more on research firms that supply marketing information, see Jack Honomichl, "Honomichl 50," special section, *Marketing News*, June 15, 2006, pp. H1–H67. Other information from www.infores.com; www.smrb.com; www.nielsen.com; and http://www.yankelovich.com/products/monitor.aspx, September 2006.

7. Adapted from an example in Spencer E. Ante, "The Science of Desire," *BusinessWeek*, June 5, 2006, pp. 99–106.

8. Spencer E. Ante, "The Science of Desire," *BusinessWeek*, June 5, 2006, p. 100.

9. David Kiley, "Shoot the Focus Group," *BusinessWeek*, p. 120.

10. Ibid, p. 120.

11. Adapted from an example in David Kiley, "Shoot the Focus Group," *BusinessWeek*, November 14, 2005, pp. 120–121.

12. For more on Internet privacy, see James R. Hagerty and Dennis K. Berman, "Caught in the Net: New Battleground over Web Privacy," *Wall Street Journal*, August 27, 2004, p. A1; Alan R. Peslak, "Internet Privacy Policies," *Information Resources Management Journal*, January–March 2005, pp. 29+; and Larry Dobrow, "Privacy Issues Loom for Marketers," *Advertising Age*, March 13, 2006, p. S6.

13. See Gary H. Anthes, "Smile, You're on Candid Computer," *Computerworld*, December 3, 2001, p. 50; Claire Tristram, "Behind BlueEyes," *Technology Review*, May 2001, p. 32; and "Creating Computers That Know How You Feel," accessed at www.almaden.ibm.com/cs/BlueEyes/index.html, September 2006.

14. Michael Krauss, "At Many Firms, Technology Obscures CRM," *Marketing News*, March 18, 2002, p. 5. Also see Darrell K. Rigby and Dianne Ledingham, "CRM Done Right," *Harvard Business Review*, November 2004, p. 129; Barton Goldenberg, "Let's Keep to the High Road," *CRM Magazine*, March 2005, p. 22; and Sean Collins, Firish Nair, and Jeffrey Schumacher, "Reaching the Next Level of Performance," *Customer Relationship Management*, May 2006, p. 48.

15. See Robert McLuhan, "How to Reap the Benefits of CRM," *Marketing*, May 24, 2001, p. 35; Stewart Deck, "Data Mining," *Computerworld*, March 29, 1999, p. 76; Jason Compton, "CRM Gets Real," *Customer Relationship Management*, May 2004, pp. 11–12; Ellen Neuborne, "A Second Act of CRM," Inc., March 2005, p. 40; and "Value Added with mySAP CRM," accessed at www.sap.com/solutions/business-suite/crm/pdf/Misc_CRM_Study.pdf, June 2006.

16. See "Electronic Commerce in Hong Kong Reference Case: TAL Apparel Ltd," www.info.gov.hkdigital21/eng/commerce/refcase/tal.html.

17. Jack Honomichl, "Acquisitions Up, Growth Rate Varies," *Marketing News*, August 15, 2005, pp. H3–H4; Jack Honomichl, "Honomichl 50," special section, *Marketing News*, June 15, 2006, pp. H1–H67; and the ACNielsen International Research Web site, accessed at www.acnielsen.com/company/where.php, September 2006.

18. See "Too Much Information?" *Marketing Management*, January–February 2004, p. 4.

19. Cynthia Crossen, "Studies Galore Support Products and Positions, but Are They Reliable?" *Wall Street Journal*, November 14, 1991, pp. A1, A9. Also see Allan J. Kimmel, "Deception in Marketing Research and Practice: An Introduction," *Psychology and Marketing*, July 2001, pp. 657–661; and Alvin C. Burns and Ronald F. Bush, *Marketing Research* (Upper Saddle River, NJ: Prentice Hall, 2005), pp. 63–75.

Chapter 5

1. Swee Hoon Ang, "Hey Kitty Kitty," in *Marketing Management: An Asian Casebook*, Hellmut Schutte, Swee Hoon Ang, Siew Meng Leong, and Chin Tiong Tan, eds., Singapore: Prentice Hall, 2004, pp. 105–114; Swee Hoon Ang, "McDonald's Hello Kitty Promotion," in *Marketing*

Management: An Asian Casebook, Hellmut Schutte, Swee Hoon Ang, Siew Meng Leong, and Chin Tiong Tan, eds., Singapore: Prentice Hall, 2004, pp. 257–263;"Hello Kitty," www.wikipedia.com, November 2007.

2. GDP figures from The World Fact Book, July 11, 2006, accessed at www.cia.gov/cia/publications/factbook/geos/us.html. Population figures from the World POPClock, U.S. Census Bureau, www.census.gov, September 2006. This Web site provides continuously updated projections of the U.S. and world populations.

3. Min Chen (2004), "Common Culture, Diverse Styles," *The China Business Review*, September-October, pp. 53-59.

4. See Edward Keller and Jonathan Berry, *The Influentials* (New York, NY: The Free Press, 2003); John Battelle, "The Net of Influence," *Business 2.0*, March 2004, p. 70; Alicia Clegg, "Following the Leaders," *Marketing Week*, September 30, 2004, pp. 47–49; Ronald E. Goldsmith, "The Influentials," *Journal of Product & Brand Management*, 2005, pp. 371–372; Matthew Creamer, "Study: Go Traditional to Influence Influencers," *Advertising Age*, March 7, 2005, p. 8; and Dave Balter and Ed Keller, "In Search of True Marketplace Influencers," *Advertising Age*, December 5, 2005, p. 22.

5. Saul Hansell, "For MySpace, Making Friends Was Easy. Big Profit Is Tougher," *New York Times*, April 23, 2006, p. 3.1.

6. Quote and information from "Colored Vision Adidas Unleashes Seven-Film Mobile Media," *Boards*, May 2006, p. 15.

7. Quote from Anya Kamenetz, "The Network Unbound," *Fast Company*, pp. 73. Also see Julie Bosman, "Chevy Tries a Write-Your-Own-Ad Approach," *New York Times*, April 4, 2006, p. C1.

8. Adapted from Pallavi Gogoi, "Meet Jane Geek," *BusinessWeek*, November 28, 2005, pp. 94–95.

9. Kevin Downey, "What Children Teach Their Parents," *Broadcasting & Cable*, March 13, 2006, p. 26.

10. Alice Dragoon, "How to Do Customer Segmentation Right," *CIO*, October 1, 2005, p. 1.

11. Jeff Smith and Jean Wylie (2004), "China's Youth Define"Cool"," *The China Business Review*, July–August, pp. 30–34.

12. Jennifer Aaker, "Dimensions of Measuring Brand Personality," *Journal of Marketing Research*, August 1997, pp. 347–356. Also see Aaker, "The Malleable Self: The Role of Self Expression in Persuasion," *Journal of Marketing Research*, May 1999, pp. 45–57; and Audrey Azoulay and Jean-Noel Kapferer, "Do Brand Personality Scales Really Measure Brand Personality?" *Journal of Brand Management*, November 2003, p. 143.

13. Seth Stevenson, "Ad Report Card: Mac Attack," June 19, 2006, accessed at www.slate.com/id/2143810.

14. Annetta Miller and Dody Tsiantar, "Psyching Out Consumers," *Newsweek*, February 27, 1989, pp. 46–47. Also see Leon G. Schiffman and Leslie L. Kanuk, *Consumer Behavior*, 9th ed. (Upper Saddle River, NJ: 2007), chapter 4.

15. See Abraham. H. Maslow, "A Theory of Human Motivation," *Psychological Review*, 50 (1943), pp. 370–396. Also see Maslow, *Motivation and Personality*, 3rd ed. (New York: HarperCollins Publishers, 1987); and Barbara Marx Hubbard, "Seeking Our Future Potentials," *The Futurist*, May 1998, pp. 29–32.

16. Charles Pappas, "Ad Nauseam," *Advertising Age*, July 10, 2000, pp. 16–18. See also Mark Ritson, "Marketers Need to Find a Way to Control the Contagion of Clutter," *Marketing*, March 6, 2003, p. 16; and David H. Freedman, "The Future of Advertising Is Here," *Inc.*, August 2005, pp. 70–78.

17. Rebecca Flass, "'Got Milk?' Takes a Serious Look Inside the Body," *Adweek*, January 27, 2003, p. 5; Katie Koppenhoefer, "MilkPEP Ads Make Big Impact with Hispanics," press release, *International Dairy Foods Association*, March 3, 2003, accessed at www.idfa.org/news/gotmilk/2003/miklpepads.cfm; Jeff Manning and Kevin Lane Keller, "Got Advertising That Works?" *Marketing Management*, January–February 2004, pp. 16–20; and information from www.whymilk.com, November 2006.

18. For a deeper discussion of the buyer decision process, see Philip Kotler and Kevin Lane Keller, *Marketing Management*, 12th ed. (Upper Saddle River, NJ: 2006), pp. 191–203.

19. See Leon Festinger, *A Theory of Cognitive Dissonance* (Stanford, CA: Stanford University Press, 1957); Schiffman and Kanuk, *Consumer Behavior*, pp. 219–220; Patti Williams and Jennifer L. Aaker, "Can Mixed Emotions Peacefully Coexist?" *Journal of Consumer Research*, March 2002, pp. 636–649; Adam Ferrier, "Young Are Not Marketing Savvy; They're Suckers," *B&T Weekly*, October 22, 2004, p. 13; and "Cognitive Dissonance and the Stability of Service Quality Perceptions," *The Journal of Services Marketing*, 2004, p. 433+.

20. The following discussion draws from the work of Everett M. Rogers. See his *Diffusion of Innovations*, 5th ed. (New York: Free Press, 2003). Also see Eric Waarts, Yvonne M. van Everdingen, and Jos van Hillegersberg, "The Dynamics of Factors Affecting the Adoption of Innovations," *The Journal of Product Innovation Management*, November 2002, pp. 412–423; Chaun-Fong Shih and Alladi Venkatesh, "Beyond Adoption: Development and Application of a Use-Diffusion Model," *Journal of Marketing*, January 2004, pp. 59–72; and Richard R. Nelson, Alexander Peterhansl, and Bhaven Sampat, "Why and How Innovations Get Adopted: A Tale of Four Models," *Industrial and Corporate Change*, October 2004, pp. 679–699.

Chapter 6

1. Extracts, quotes, and other information from Kerry Capell, "How the Swedish Retailer Became a Global Cult Brand," *BusinessWeek*, November 14, 2005, p. 103; Shari Kulha, "Behind the Scenes at IKEA," *The Guardian*, September 29, 2005, p. 8; Greta Guest, "Inside IKEA's Formula for Global Success," *Detroit Free Press*, June 3, 2006; "Our Vision: A Better Everyday Life," accessed at www.ikea.com, December 2006; and "IKEA CEO: 2007 revenue approaching $26B," March 30, 2007, accessed at www.boston.com/news/world/europe/articles/2007/03/30.

2. "Vietnam: Building Partnerships and Suppliers," accessed online at www.unilever.com, February 2004.

3. For more discussion of business markets and business buyer behavior, see Das Narayandas, "Building Loyalty in Business Markets," *Harvard Business Review*, September 2005, pp. 131–139; and James C. Anderson, James A. Narus, and Wouter van Rossum, "Customer Value Propositions in Business Markets," *Harvard Business Review*, March 2006, pp. 91–99.

4. Patrick J. Robinson, Charles W. Faris, and Yoram Wind, *Industrial Buying Behavior and Creative Marketing* (Boston: Allyn & Bacon, 1967). Also see James C. Anderson and James A. Narus, *Business Market Management*, 2nd ed. (Upper Saddle River, NJ: 2004), chapter 3; and Philip Kotler and Kevin Lane Keller, *Marketing Management*, 12th ed. (Upper Saddle River, NJ: Prentice Hall, 2006), chapter 7.

5. See Philip Kotler, *Marketing Management*, 12th ed. (Upper Saddle River, NJ: Prentice Hall, 2006), pp. 213–214.

6. See Frederick E. Webster Jr. and Yoram Wind, *Organizational Buying Behavior* (Upper Saddle River, NJ: Prentice Hall, 1972), pp. 78–80. Also see James C. Anderson and James A. Narus, *Business Market Management: Understanding*, Creating and Delivering Value (Upper Saddle River, NJ: Prentice Hall, 2004), chapter 3.

7. For more discussion, see Stefan Wuyts and Inge Geyskens, "The Formation of Buyer-Seller Relationships: Detailed Contract Drafting and Close Partner Selection," *Harvard Business Review*, October 2005, pp. 103–117; and Robert McGarvey, "The Buyer's Emotional Side," *Selling Power*, April 2006, pp. 35–36.

8. See Frederick E. Webster, Jr., and Yoram Wind, *Organizational Buying Behavior*, pp. 33–37.

9. Robinson, Faris, and Wind, *Industrial Buying Behavior*, p. 14.

10. For this and other examples, see Kate Maddox, "#1 Hewlett-Packard Co.: www.hp.com," *BtoB*, August 11, 2003, p. 1; "Great Web Sites: www.hp.com," BtoB Online, September 13, 2004; and "10 Great Web Sites," BtoB Online, September 12, 2005; all accessed at www.btobonline.com.

11. H.J. Heinz Company Annual Report 2006, p. 20; accessed at http://heinz.com/2006annualreport/2006HeinzAR.pdf.

12. En.wikipedia.org/wiki/Bumiputra accessed on July 11, 2007.

Chapter 7

1. Nina Munk, "Why Women Find Lauder Mesmerizing," *Fortune*, May 25, 1998, pp. 97–106; Christine Bittar, "New Faces, Same Name," *Brandweek*, March 11, 2002, pp. 28–34; Robin Givhan, "Estee Lauder, Sending a Message in a Bottle," *Washington Post*, April 26, 2004, p. C.01; and information accessed at www.elcompanies.com, www.stila.com, and www.macmakeup.com, September 2006; www.prescriptives.com and en.wikipedia.org accessed on July 16, 2007.

2. For these and other examples, see Darell K. Rigby and Vijay Vishwanath, "Localization: The Revolution in Consumer Markets," *Harvard Business Review*, April 2006, pp. 82–92.

3. Catherine Gelb and Dennis Chen, "Going West: A Progress Report," *The China Business Review*, March–April 2004, pp. 8–23.

4. Jason Leow, "Educator Sticks to China's Cities," *Wall Street Journal*, July 13–15, 207, p. 6.

5. Reena Jana, "Nintendo's New Brand Game," June 22, 2006, accessed at www.businessweek.com/innovate/content/jun2006/id20060622_124931.htm?chan=search.

6. See Fara Warner, "Nike Changes Strategy on Women's Apparel," *New York Times*, May 16, 2005, accessed at www.nytimes.com; and Thomas J. Ryan, "Just Do It for Women," *SGB*, March 2006, pp. 25–26.

7. See Maureen Wallenfang, "Appleton, Wis.-Area Dealers See Increase in Moped Sales," *Knight Ridder Tribune Business News*, August 15, 2004, p. 1; Louise Lee, "Love Those Boomers," *BusinessWeek*, October 24, 2005, pp. 94–100; and Honda's Web site at www.powersports.honda.com/scooters/, September 2006.

8. Shawn Donnan, "Indofood Wants to Say It with Noodles," *Financial Times*, February 14, 2003, p. 27.

9. P.T. Data Consult, "Oligopoly in Toothpaste Market," *Indonesian Commercial Newsletter*, September 24, 2002.

10. Kate MacArthur, "BK Rebels Fall in Love with King," *Advertising Age*, May 1, 2006, pp. 1, 86.

11. Portions adapted from Alan T. Saracevic, "Author Plumbs Bottomless Depth of Mac Worship," December 12, 2004, accessed at www.sfgate.com. Definition from www.urbandictionary.com/define.php?term=Macolyte&r=d, September 2006.

12. "Malaysian Tech Advances Reaching 50%," *AC Nielsen Insights Asia Pacific*, August 2001, p. 2.

13. Information from http://home.americanexpress.com/home/mt_personal.shtml, August 2006.

14. See Arundhati Parmar, "Global Youth United," *Market-ing News*, October 28, 2002, pp. 1, 49; "'Impossible Is Nothing' Adidas Launches New Global Brand Advertising Campaign," accessed at www.adidas.com, February 5, 2004; "Teen Spirit," *Global Cosmetic Industry*, March 2004, p. 23; Johnnie L. Roberts, "World Tour," *Newsweek*, June 6, 2005, pp. 34–36; and the MTV Worldwide Web site, www.mtv.com/mtvinternational.

15. See Michael Porter, *Competitive Advantage* (New York: Free Press, 1985), pp. 4–8, 234–236. For more recent discussions, see Stanley Slater and Eric Olson, "A Fresh Look at Industry and Market Analysis," *Business Horizons*, January–February 2002, p. 15–22; Kenneth Sawka and Bill Fiora, "The Four Analytical Techniques Every Analyst Must Know: 2. Porter's Five Forces Analysis," *Competitive Intelligence Magazine*, May–June 2003, p. 57; and Philip Kotler and Kevin Lane Keller, *Marketing Management*, 12th ed. (Upper Saddle River, NJ: Prentice Hall, 2006), pp. 342–343.

16. Arik Hesseldahl, "Apple Set to Take Bigger Bite of the Market," *BusinessWeek Online*, June 16, 2006; and Mark Veverka, "Beyond the iPod: Mac Attack," *Barron's*, July 17, 2006, pp. 20–23.

17. Gwendolyn Bounds, "How an Artist Fell into a Profitable Online Card Business," *Wall Street Journal*, December 21, 2004, p. B1; and David Smith, "UK's Cottage Industry Beats US Internet Giants," *The Observer*, February 12, 2006, accessed at http://oberserver.guardian.co.uk.

18. For a good discussion of mass customization and relationship building, see Don Peppers and Martha Rogers, *Managing Customer Relationships: A Strategic Framework* (Hoboken, NJ: John Wiley & Sons, 2004), chapter 10.

19. Example adapted from Michael Prospero, "Lego's New Building Blocks," *Fast Company*, October 2005, p. 35; with information from http://factory.lego.com/, September 2006.

20. Jack Trout, "Branding Can't Exist without Positioning," *Advertising Age*, March 14, 2005, p. 28.

21. Adapted from a positioning map prepared by students Brian May, Josh Payne, Meredith Schakel, and Bryana Sterns, University of North Carolina, April 2003. SUV sales data furnished by WardsAuto.com, June 2006. Price data from www.edmunds.com, June 2006.

22. See Bobby J. Calder and Steven J. Reagan, "Brand Design," in Dawn Iacobucci, ed. *Kellogg on Marketing* (New York: John Wiley & Sons, 2001) p. 61. The Mountain Dew example is from Alice M. Tybout and Brian Sternthal, "Brand Positioning," in Iacobucci, ed., *Kellogg on Marketing*, p. 54.

Chapter 8

1. Adapted from Mark Blair, Richard Armstrong, and Mike Murphy, *The 360 Degree Brand in Asia*, (Singapore: Wiley, 2003), pp. 121-123. See also Sumali Moitra, "Electrolux Kelvinator Targets Number One Position," *The Times of India*, Sep 11, 2003.

2. See "The Celebrity 100," Forbes, accessed at www.forbes.com, July 2006; and Reed Tucker, "Tiger Woods," *Fortune*, October 17, 2005, p. 142.

3. See Daniel Roth, "The Trophy Life," Fortune, April 19, 2004, pp. 70–84; Ryan Underwood, "Bring on the Clown," *Fast Company*, January 2005, p. 28; "New Trump Products on the Market," *Knight Ridder Tribune Business News*, February 26, 2005, p. 1; and "He's Hired: Trump Gets into Jewelry Business," National-Jeweler.com, June 1, 2006.

4. Lo, KY, 'Hong Kong-Shanghai rivalry goes creative', *International Herald Tribune*, January 20 2005, p. 3.

5. Accessed online at www.social-marketing.org/aboutus.html, October 2006.

6. Quotes and definitions from Philip Kotler, *Kotler on Marketing* (New York: Free Press, 1999), p. 17; and www.asq.org, October 2006.

7. See Roland T. Rust, Christine Moorman, and Peter R. Dickson, "Getting Return on Quality: Revenue Expansion, Cost Reduction, or Both?" *Journal of Marketing*, October 2002, pp. 7–24; and Roland T. Rust, Katherine N. Lemon, and Valarie A. Zeithaml, "Return on Marketing: Using Customer Equity to Focus Marketing Strategy," *Journal of Marketing*, January 2004, p. 109.

8. Kai-Alexander Schievogt, "The Branding Revolution in China," *The China Business Review*, May-June 2000, pp. 52-57.

9. Example adapted from Michelle Higgins, "Pop-Up Sales Clerks: Web Sites Try the Hard Sell," Wall Street Journal, April 15, 2004, p. D.1. Also see Dawn Chmielewski, "Software That Makes Tech Support Smarter," *Knight Ridder Tribune Business News*, December 25, 2005, p. 1.

10. Information accessed online at www.marriott.com, October 2006.

11. Information about Colgate's product lines accessed at www.colgate.com/app/Colgate/US/Corp/Products.cvsp, August 2006.

12. See "McAtlas Shrugged," Foreign Policy, May–June 2001, pp. 26–37; and Philip Kotler and Kevin Lane Keller, *Marketing Management*, 12th ed. (Upper Saddle River, NJ: Prentice Hall, 2006), pp. 290–291.

13. David C. Bello and Morris. B. Holbrook, "Does an Absence of Brand Equity Generalize across Product Classes?" *Journal of Business Research*, October 1995, p. 125; and Scott Davis, *Brand Asset Management: Driving Profitable Growth through Your Brands* (San Francisco: Jossey-Bass, 2000). Also see Kevin Lane Keller, Building, *Measuring, and Managing Brand Equity*, 2nd ed. (Upper Saddle River, NJ: Prentice Hall, 2003), chapter 2; and Kusum Ailawadi, Donald R. Lehman, and Scott A. Neslin, "Revenue Premium as an Outcome Measure of Brand Equity," *Journal of Marketing*, October 2003, pp. 1–17.

14. "The 100 Top Brands," *BusinessWeek*, August 7, 2006, pp. 59–64. For another ranking, see Normandy Madden, "Hold the Phone," *Advertising Age*, April 10, 2006, pp. 4, 64.

15. Larry Selden and Yoko S. Selden, "Profitable Customer: Key to Great Brands," *Point*, July–August 2006, pp. 7–9. Also see Roland Rust, Katherine Lemon, and Valarie Zeithaml, "Return on Marketing: Using Customer Equity to Focus Marketing Strategy," *Journal of Marketing*, January 2004, p. 109; and Connie S. Olasz, "Marketing's Role in a Relationship Age," *Baylor Business Review*, Spring 2006, pp. 2–7.

16. See Scott Davis, *Brand Asset Management*, 2nd ed. (San Francisco: Jossey-Bass, 2002). For more on brand positioning, see Philip Kotler and Kevin Lane Keller, *Marketing Management*, 12th ed. (Upper Saddle River, NJ: Prentice Hall, 2006), chapter 10.

17. See Jacquelyn A. Ottman, Edwin R. Strattford, and Cathy L. Hartman, "Avoiding Green Marketing Myopia," *Environment*, June 2006, pp. 22–37.

18. 'For Global Hyatt Corp., success in the Middle Kingdom means peddling luxury to a rapidly emerging moneyed class', *Crain's Chicago Business*, Vol. 29 No. 26, 26 June, 2006, p. 20.

19. 'Omnicom and China's Tsinghua University join hands on naming project', *PR Newswire*, 6 April 2006, accessed on 13 July 2006, www.global.factiva.com.

20. The Straits Times 2006, 'Victory brew: Starbucks wins copyright battle in China', 3 January, p. 6.

21. Sandra Leong, "Win-Win Housebrands," *The Sunday Times*, August 27, 2006, p. L6.

22. Gabrielle Solomon, "Co-branding Alliances: Arranged Marriages Made by Marketers," *Fortune*, October 12, 1998, p. 188; and "Martha Stewart Upgrading from Kmart to Macys," *FinancialWire*, April 26, 2006, p. 1.

23. Based on information from Kate McArthur, "Cannibalization a Risk as Diet Coke Brand Tally Grows to Seven," *Advertising Age*, March 28, 2005, pp. 3, 123; "Coca-Cola Zero Pops into Stores Today," Atlanta Business Chronicle, June 13, 2005, accessed at http://atlanta. bizjournals.com/atlanta/stories/2005/06/13/daily7.html; and www2.coca-cola.com, July 2006.

24. For more on the use of line and brand extensions and consumer attitudes toward them, see Franziska Volckner and Henrik Sattler, "Drivers of Brand Extension Success," *Journal of Marketing*, April 2006, pp. 18–34; and Chris Pullig, Carolyn J. Simmons, and Richard G. Netemeyer, "Brand Dilution: When Do New Brands Hurt Existing Brands?" *Journal of Marketing*, April 2006, pp. 52–66.

25. "100 Leading National Advertisers," supplement to *Advertising Age*, June 26, 2006, pp. 29 and 96.

26. Stephen Cole, "Value of the Brand," *CA Magazine*, May 2005, pp. 39–40.

27. See Kevin Lane Keller, "The Brand Report Card," *Harvard Business Review*, January 2000, pp. 147–157; Keller, *Strategic Brand Management*, pp. 766–767; and David A. Aaker, "Even Brands Need Spring Cleaning," *Brandweek*, March 8, 2004, pp. 36–40.

28. Adapted from information in Leonard Berry and Neeli Bendapudi, "Clueing in Customers," *Harvard Business Review*, February 2003, pp. 100–106; with information accessed at www.mayoclinic.org, October 2006.

29. See James L. Heskett, W. Earl Sasser Jr., and Leonard A. Schlesinger, *The Service Profit Chain: How Leading Companies Link Profit and Growth to Loyalty, Satisfaction, and Value* (New York: Free Press, 1997); Heskett, Sasser, and Schlesinger, *The Value Profit Chain: Treat Employees Like Customers and Customers Like Employees* (New York: Free Press, 2003); and "Recovering from Service Failure," *Strategic Direction*, June 2006, pp. 37–40.

30. See "UPS Fact Sheet," accessed at http://pressroom.ups.com/mediakits/factsheet/0,2305,866,00.html, August 2006; and "Prescription Drug Trends," *Kaiser Family Foundation*, June 2006, accessed at www.kff.org/rxdrugs/upload/3057-05.pdf.

31. Brian Hindo, "Satisfacton Not Guaranteed," *BusinessWeek*, June 19, 2006, pp. 32–36.

32. Xin Yi Cheow, "A Credit Card for the Young," *TODAY (Singapore)*, July 19, 2007, p. 36; "Sze Hian Leong, "Students with a Debt Burden," *TODAY (Singapore)*, July 25, 2007, p. 24; Murali Sharma, "Students and Those Unemployed may not be Disciplined Enough to Control Spending," *TODAY (Singapore)*, July 25, 2007, p. 24; Penn Nee Chow, "Citibank Offers Credit Card for Low Earners," *Business Times (Singapore)*, July 19, 2007, p. 4.

Chapter 9

1. Quotes and other information in this Apple story from Terry Semel, "Steve Jobs: Perpetual Innovation Machine," *Time*, April 18, 2005, p. 78; Steve Maich, "Nowhere to Go But Down," *Maclean's*, May 9, 2005, p. 32; Brent Schlender, "How Big Can Apple Get," *Fortune*, February 21, 2005, pp. 67–76; Jim Dalrymple, "Apple's Uphill Climb," *Macworld*, June 2005, p. 16;

Paul Sloan and Paul Kaihla, "What's Next for Apple," *Business 2.0*, April 2005; Peter Burrows and Andrew Park, "Apple's Bold Swim Downstream," *BusinessWeek*, January 24, 2005, p. 32; Bruce Nussbaum, "Get Creative!" *BusinessWeek*, August 1, 2005, pp. 61–70; "The World's Most Innovative Companies," *BusinessWeek*, April 24, 2006, p. 62; "Apple Posts Record Earnings," *Apple Matters*, July 20, 2006; and Apple annual reports and other information accessed at www.apple.com, October 2006.

2. Based on material from Peter Lewis, "A Perpetual Crisis Machine," *Fortune*, September 19, 2005, pp. 58–67.

3. Based on quotes and information from Robert D. Hof, "The Power of Us," *BusinessWeek*, June 20, 2005, pp. 74–82. See also Robert Weisman, "Firms Turn R&D on Its Head, Looking Outside for Ideas," *Boston Globe*, May 14, 2006, p. E1.

4. Example from www.Frogdesign.com, accessed July 2006.

5. See "DaimlerChrysler Presents California with Three F-Cell Fuel Cell Vehicles," *Fuel Cell Today*, June 1, 2005, accessed at www.fuelcelltoday.com; Steven Ashley, "On the Road to Fuel-Cell Cars," *Scientific American*, March 1, 2005, p. 62; and Kathy Jackson, "Calif. Leads the Way in Fleet Fuel Cell Tests," *Automotive News*, June 5, 2006, p. 35.

6. Examples adapted from those found in Carol Matlack, "The Vuitton Machine," *BusinessWeek*, March 22, 2004, pp. 98–102; and Brendan Koerner, "For Every Sport, A Super Sock," *New York Times*, March 27, 2005, p. 3.2.

7. Jack Neff, "Is Testing the Answer?" *Advertising Age*, July 9, 2001, p. 13; and Dale Buss, "P&G's Rise," *Potentials*, January 2003, pp. 26–30. For more on test marketing, see Philip Kotler and Kevin Lane Keller, *Marketing Management*, 12th ed. (Upper Saddle River, NJ: Prentice Hall, 2006), pp. 653–655.

8. See William C. Symonds, "Gillette's New Edge," *BusinessWeek*, February 6, 2006, p. 44; and "Sales Are Razor Sharp," *Drug Store News*, April 10, 2006, p. 25.

9. See Jack Neff, "New SpinBrush Line Backed by $30 Million," *Advertising Age*, September 9, 2002, p. 36; and Jenn Abelson, "Firms Likely to Shed Some Products," *Knight Ridder Tribune Business News*, June 22, 2005, p.1.

10. Robert G. Cooper, "Formula for Success," *Marketing Management*, March–April 2006, pp. 19–23.

11. Examples adapted from information in Jennifer Reingold, "The Interpreter," *Fast Company*, June 2005, pp. 59–61; and Jonah Bloom, "Beth Has an Idea," *Point*, September 2005, pp. 9–14. Also see Paul Bennett, "Listening Lessons: Make Consumers Part of the Design Process by Tuning In," *Point*, March 2006, pp. 9–10; and Larry Selden and Ian C. MacMillan, "Manage Customer-Centric Innovation—Systematically," *Harvard Business Review*, April 2006, pp. 108–116.

12. Lawrence A. Crosby and Sheree L. Johnson, "Customer-Centric Innovation," *Marketing Management*, March–April 2006, pp. 12–13.

13. See Philip Kotler, *Kotler on Marketing* (New York, NY: The Free Press, 1999), pp. 43–44; Judy Lamont, "Idea Management: Everyone's an Innovator," KM World, November/December 2004, pp. 14–16; and J. Roland Ortt, "Innovation Management: Different Approaches to Cope with the Same Trends," *Management*, 2006, pp. 296–318.

14. See Tim Studt, "3M—Where Innovation Rules," *R&D*, April 2003, pp. 20–24; Tim Stevens, "3M Reinvents Its Innovation Process," *Research Technology Management*, March/April 2004, p. 3; Daniel Del Re, "Pushing Past Post-Its," *Business 2.0*, November 2005, pp. 54–56; and "Innovation at 3M," accessed at www.3m.com/about3m/innovation/index.jhtml, October 2006. Also see Blair Sheppard and Michael Canning, "Innovation Culture," *Leadership Excellence*, January 2006, p. 18.

15. This definition is based on one found in Bryan Lilly and Tammy R. Nelson, "Fads: Segmenting the Fad-Buyer Market," *Journal of Consumer Marketing*, vol. 20, no. 3, 2003, pp. 252–265.

16. See "Scooter Fad Fades, as Warehouses Fill and Profits Fall," *Wall Street Journal*, June 14, 2001, p. B4; Katya Kazakina, "Toy Story: Yo-Yos Make a Big Splash," *Wall Street Journal*, April 11, 2003, p. W–10; Robert Johnson, "A Fad's Father Seeks a Sequel," *New York Times*, May 30, 2004, p. 3.2; and Tom McGhee, "Spotting Trends, Eschewing Fads," *Denver Post*, May 29, 2006.

17. For a more comprehensive discussion of marketing strategies over the course of the product life cycle, see Philip Kotler and Kevin Lane Keller, *Marketing Management*, 12th ed. (Upper Saddle River, NJ: Prentice Hall, 2006), pp. 321–335.

18. These and other uses found in "Always Another Use," www.wd40.com/Brands/wd40.cfm, October 2006.

19. Information accessed online at www.interpublic.com and www.mccann.com, October 2006.

20. See "Wal-Mart International Operations," accessed at www.walmartstores.com, July 2006; "2005 Global Powers of Retailing," Stores, January 2005, accessed at www.stores.org; and information accessed at www.carrefour.com/english/groupecarrefour/profil.jsp, October 2006.

Chapter 10

1. Thomas T. Nagle and John E. Hogan, *The Strategy and Tactics of Pricing*, 4th ed. (Upper Saddle River, NJ: Prentice Hall, 2006), p. 1.

2. See Rosemary Barnes, "The Price of Perfection: Steinway Piano Commands a Premier Price," *Knight*

Ridder Tribune Business News, February 26, 2005, p. 1; Andy Serwer, "Happy Birthday Steinway," *Fortune*, March 17, 2003, p. 94; "Books and Arts: Making the Sound of Music; Piano Manufacturers," *The Economist*, June 7, 2003, p. 102; Brian T. Majeski, "The Steinway Story," *Music Trades*, September 2003, p. 18; "The Most Famous Name in Music," Music Trades, September 2003, p. 118–130; Stephan Wilkinson, "High-Strung. Powerful. Very Pricey," *Popular Science*, March 1, 2003, p. 32; "Steinway Musical Instruments, Inc.," *Hoover's Company Capsules*, Austin, July 2006, p. 48052; Michael Z. Wise, "Piano Versus Piano," *New York Times*, May 9, 2004; Lisa Gschwandtner, "Keys to Success," *Selling Power*, July–August 2006, p. 50; James Barron, *Piano: The Making of a Steinway Concert Grand* (New York: Times Books, 2006); "Steinway & Sons," *Wikipedia*, accessed on October 29, 2007; and quotes and information found at www.steinway.com, December 2006.

3. Here accumulated production is drawn on a semilog scale so that equal distances represent the same percentage increase in output.

4. The arithmetic of markups and margins is discussed in Appendix 2, "Marketing by the Numbers."

5. See Robert Berner, "Why P&G's Smile Is So Bright," *BusinessWeek*, August 12, 2002, pp. 58–60; Jack Neff, "Power Brushes a Hit at Every Level," *Advertising Age*, May 26, 2003, p. 10; Matt Phillips, "Sales of Toothbrushes Decline as Consumers Look to Electric Models," *Knight Ridder Tribune Business News*, November 12, 2004, p. 1; Robert Brenner and William C. Symonds, "Welcome to Procter & Gadget," *Business Week*, February 7, 2005, p. 76; and information accessed at www.spinbrush.com, August 2005.

6. Joshua Rosenbaum, "Guitar Maker Looks for a New Key," *Wall Street Journal*, February 11, 1998, p. B1; and information accessed online at www.gibson.com, October 2006.

7. See Nagle and Hogan, *The Strategy and Tactics of Pricing*, chapter 7.

8. See Robert J. Dolan, "Pricing: A Value-Based Approach," *Harvard Business School Publishing*, 9-500-071, November 3, 2003.

Chapter 11

1. Pauline Ng, "Jetstar Beats AirAsia with RM88 KL-Sydney Fare," *Business Times (Singapore)*, July 25, 2007, p. 17; Ven Sreenivasan, "Tiger Airways Paving Way for an IPO?" *Business Times (Singapore)*, July 10, 2007, p. 6; www.airasia.com, accessed on July 25, 2007; "Malaysian Airline Unions Oppose Early Launch of Singapore-KL Budget Flights," *TODAY (Singapore)*, July 27, p. 2; Liang Dingzi, "AirAsia Soaring into Turbulence?" *Today*, April 30, p. 12.

2. For comprehensive discussions of pricing strategies, see Thomas T. Nagle and John E. Hogan, *The Strategy and Tactics of Pricing*, 4th ed. (Upper Saddle River, NJ: Prentice Hall, 2006).

3. See Philip Kotler and Kevin Lane Keller, *Marketing Management*, 12th ed. (Upper Saddle River, NJ: Prentice Hall, 2006), p. 438; and Robert Evatt, "Video Fans Tuning in to HDTV Experience: Prices of High-Definition Television Sets Continue to Fall," *Tulsa World*, July 16, 2006, p. 1.

4. Roger Chen, "Price Wars," *The China Business Review*, September-October 2003, pp. 42-46.

5. Ibid.

6. "Japanese barbers, Ready at the Gate," www.economist.com, November 2, 2006,; "Singaporeans Turn to Cheap and Quick Haircuts Amid Slump," *Asian Economic News*, September 9, 2003.

7. "Making the World's Cheapest Car was very Lonely, " *The New Paper*, January 13, 2008, pp. 22–23.

8. See Nagle and Holden, *The Strategy and Tactics of Pricing*, pp. 244–247; Stefan Stremersch and Gerard J. Tellis, "Strategic Bundling of Products and Prices: A New Synthesis for Marketing," *Journal of Marketing Research*, January 2002, pp. 55–72; Chris Janiszewski and Marcus Cunha, Jr., "The Influence of Price Discount Framing on the Evaluation of a Product Bundle," *Journal of Marketing Research*, March 2004, pp. 534–546; and "Save a Bundle, Comcast Says," *Tacoma News Tribune*, July 25, 2006.

9. For more discussion, see Manoj Thomas and Vicki Morvitz, "Penny Wise and Pound Foolish: The Double-Digit Effect in Price Cognition," *Journal of Consumer Research*, June 2005, pp. 54–64; and Heyong Min Kim and Luke Kachersky, "Dimensions of Price Salience: A Conceptual Framework for Perceptions of Multi-Dimensional Prices," *Journal of Product and Brand Management*, 2006, vol. 15, no. 2, pp. 139–147.

10. See "Dell, the Conqueror," *BusinessWeek*, September 24, 2001, pp. 92–102; Andy Serwer, "Dell Does Domination," *Fortune*, January 21, 2002, pp. 70–75; and Pui-Wing Tam, "H-P Gains Applause as It Cedes PC Market Share to Dell," *Wall Street Journal*, January 18, 2005, p. C1; Andrea Orr, "Doors Closing on Creaky Gateway," *Daily Deal*, February 10, 2006; Richard Waters, "HP Sees Unexpected Jump in Profits for PCs Computer Technology," *Financial Times*, February 16, 2006, p. 25; and "The Merits of A Diverse Portfolio," *Business Today*, July 2, 2006, p. 10.

11. Thomas L. Friedman, *The World Is Flat: A Brief History of the Twenty-First Century* (New York: Farrar, Straus and Giroux, 2005), pp. 417–418.

12. For discussions of these issues, see Dhruv Grewel and Larry D. Compeau, "Pricing and Public Policy: A Research Agenda and Overview of Special Issue," *Journal of Public Policy and Marketing, Spring 1999,* pp. 3–10; and Michael V. Marn, Eric V. Roegner, and Craig C. Zawada, *The Price Advantage* (Hoboken, NJ: John Wiley & Sons, 2004), Appendix 2.

Chapter 12

1. Quotes and other information from Donald V. Fites, "Make Your Dealers Your Partners," *Harvard Business Review*, March-April 1996, pp. 84–95; Sandra Ward, "The Cat Comes Back," *Barron's*, February 25, 2002, pp. 21–24; Michael Arndt, "Cat Claws Its Way into Services," *BusinessWeek*, December 5, 2005, pp. 56–59; "Global Construction & Farm Machinery: Industry Profile," *Datamonitor*, June 2006, accessed at www.datamonitor.com; Iian Brat, "Caterpillar Posts 38% Profit Rise, Raises Outlook on Strong Demand," *Wall Street Journal*, July 22, 2006, p. A2; "Caterpillar, Inc.," *BusinessWeek*, April 3, 2006, p. 100; and information accessed at www.caterpillar.com, October 2006.

2. Mark L. Clifford, "Hong Kong's Real Estate Market Gets Worse," *BusinessWeek Online*, May 19, 2003; Philip Segal, "Hong Kong's Go-Go Real Estate Days are Gone," March 29, 2000, accessed online at www.thestreet.com/int/asia/908653.html.

3. Matthew Boyle, "Brand Killers," *Fortune*, August 11, 2003, pp. 89–100; and information accessed at www.giantfood.com and www.luxottica.com/english/profilo_aziendale/index_keyfacts.html, October 2006.

4. Andrew Yeh, "McDonald's Seeks Heavy Traffic Fast-Food Expansion," *Financial Times*, June 21, 2006, p. 12.

5. Information accessed at www.mind-advertising.com/ch/nestea_ch.htm and www.nestle.com/Our_Brands/Breakfast_Cereals/Overview/Breakfast+Cereals.htm, September 2006. Also see Andrew McMains, "Anomaly to Introduce Gold Peak Tea," July 25, 2006, accessed at www.adweek.com.

6. Warren J. Keegan, *Global Marketing Management* (Upper Saddle River, N.J.: Prentice Hall, 2002).

7. Quotes and information from Normandy Madden, "Two Chinas," *Advertising Age*, August 16, 2004, pp. 1, 22; Dana James, "Dark Clouds Should Part for International Marketers," *Marketing News*, January 7, 2002, pp. 9, 13; Russell Flannery, "Red Tape," *Forbes*, March 3, 2003, pp. 97–100; and Russell Flannery, "China: The Slow Boat," *Forbes*, April 12, 2004, p. 76.

8. Nanette Byrnes, "Avon Calls. China Opens the Door," *BusinessWeek Online*, February 28, 2006, p. 19.

9. For a full discussion of laws affecting marketing channels, see Anne Coughlin, Erin Anderson, Louis W. Stern, and Adel El-Ansary, *Marketing Channels*, 7th ed. (Upper Saddle River, NJ: Prentice Hall, 2006), chapter 10.

10. "Adding a Day to Dell," *Traffic World*, February 21, 2005, p1; William Hoffman, "Dell Ramps Up RFID," *Traffic World*, April 18, 2005, p. 1; and William Hofman, "Dell Beats the Clock," *Traffic World*, October 24, 2005, p. 1.

11. See Ann Bednarz, "IBM Has Some Tall RFID Plans," *Network World*, May 2, 2005, pp. 17–18; "RFID: From Potential to Reality," *Frozen Food Age*, April 2005, p. 40; Jack Neff, "P&G Products to Wear Wire," *Advertising Age*, December 15, 2004, pp. 1, 32; Tom Van Riper, "Retailers Eye RFID Technology to Make Shopping Easier," *Knight Ridder Tribune Business News*, May 23, 2005, p. 1; John S. McClenahen, "Wal-Mart's Big Gamble," *Industry Week*, April 2005, pp. 42–46; and Mark Roberti, "Using RFID at Item Level," *Chain Store Age*, July 2006, pp. 56–57.

12. European Intelligence Unit, *China Hand*, Chapter 11.

13. Ann Bednarz, "Internet EDI: Blending Old and New," *Network World*, February 23, 2004, pp. 29–31; Laurie Sullivan, "Hey, Wal-Mart, A New Case of Pampers Is on the Way," *InformationWeek*, January 23, 2006, p. 28; and Connie Robbins Gentry, "No More Holes at Krispy Kreme," *Chain Store Age*, July 2006, pp. 64–65.

14. See "Supply Chain Management Systems," *Logistics Today*, 2006, pp.34–42; and Sarah Murray and Andrew K. Reese, "The 2006 Supply & Demand Chain Executive 100," *Supply & Demand Chain Executive*, July 2006; accessed at www.sdcexec.com/article.asp?article_id=8812.

15. John Paul Quinn, "3PLs Hit Their Stride," *Logistics Management/Supply Chain Management Review*, July 2006, pp. 3T–8T.

Chapter 13

1. "Convenience Store Industry Sales Hit New Highs in 2005," April 5, 2006, accessed online at www.nacsonline.com/.

2. Adapted from Elizabeth Esfahani, "7-Eleven Gets Sophisticated," *Business 2.0*, January–February 2005, pp. 93–100. Also see Tatiana Serafin, "Smokes and Sandwiches," *Forbes*, February 13, 2006, p. 120.

3. Patricia Callahan and Ann Zimmerman, "Price War in Aisle 3—Wal-Mart Tops Grocery List with Supercenter Format," *Wall Street Journal*, May 27, 2003, p. B-1; Mike Troy, "What Setback? Supercenters Proliferate," *DSN Retailing Today*, May 17, 2004, p. 1; Elliot Zwiebach, "Wal-Mart's Next Weapon," *Supermarket News*, March 7, 2005, p. 14; Lucia Moses, "Supermarkets' Share Seen Fading," *Supermarket News*, February 6, 2006, p. 8; and Wal-Mart 2006 Annual Report, accessed at www.walmartstores.com.

4. See "Quick Franchise, Franchising, Facts and Statistics," accessed at www.azfranchises.com/franchisefacts.htm, September 2006; and information accessed at www.subway.com and www.mcdonalds.com/corp.html, November 2006.

5. Adapted from "At Home in the Apple Store: A Welcoming Temple to a Devout Member of the Cult," *Saint Paul Pioneer Press*, June 19, 2006.

6. See Malcolm P. McNair and Eleanor G. May, "The Next Revolution of the Retailing Wheel," *Harvard Business Review*, September–October 1978, pp. 81–91; Stephen Brown, "The Wheel of Retailing: Past and Future," *Journal of Retailing*, Summer 1990, pp. 143–147; Stephen Brown, "Variations on a Marketing Enigma: The Wheel of Retailing Theory," *Journal of Marketing Management*, 7, no. 2, 1991, pp. 131–155; Jennifer Negley, "Retrenching, Reinventing and Remaining Relevant," *Discount Store News*, April 5, 1999, p. 11; and Don E. Schultz, "Another Turn of the Wheel," *Marketing Management*, March-April 2002, pp. 8–9; and Carol Krol, "Staples Preps Easier E-Commerce Site," *BtoB*, March 14, 2005, pp. 3–4.

7. Joseph Pereira, "Staples Posts Strong Earnings on High-Margin Internet Sales," *Wall Street Journal*, March 5, 2004, p. A13; "The BusinessWeek 50: Staples, Inc.," *BusinessWeek*, April 3, 2006, p. 97; and information accessed online at www.staples.com, October 2006.

8. See "The Fortune 500," *Fortune*, April 17, 2006, p. F1.

9. SKYphoto, accessed at www.skyphoto.com.hk

10. "Wal-Mart International Operations," September 2006, accessed online at www.walmartstores.com.

11. See "2006 Global Powers of Retailing," *Stores*, January 2006, accessed at www.nxtbook.com/nxtbooks/nrfe/stores0106-globalretail/index.php.

12. Latest Counts of Wal-Mart, accessed at www.wal-martchina.com/news/stat.htm; Carrefour China, accessed at http://www.carrefour.com.cn/; see Dexter Roberts, Wendy Zellner, and Carol Matlack, "Let the Retail Wars Begin," *BusinessWeek*, January 17, 2005, pp. 44–45; "Carrefour: At the Intersection of Global," *DSN Retailing Today*, September 18, 2000, p. 16; "Top 250 Global Retailers," Stores, January 2006, accessed at www.nxtbook.com/nxtbooks/nrfe/stores0106-globalretail/index.php.; and information from www.walmartstores.com and www.carrefour.com, accessed October 2006.

Chapter 14

1. China Mengniu Dairy Company Limited annual report 2007, accessed at www.mengniuir.com/inve-f.asp

2. China Mengniu Dairy Company Limited annual report 2005, accessed at www.mengniuir.com/inve-f.asp

3. "Mengniu Milk Drink Super Girl," Push Marcom Group, accessed at www.prpush.com.cn/english/anli/4/2007322171837.htm

4. "Super Girl (contest)", Wikipedia, accessed at http://en.wikipedia.org/wiki/Super_Girl_(contest)

5. Han Lei (2006), "Brand matters for China's dairy giant", *Chinadaily*, 2006-09-02, accessed at www.chinadaily.com.cn/china/2006-09/02/content_727796.htm

6. The first four of these definitions are adapted from Peter D. Bennett, *The AMA Dictionary of Marketing Terms*, 2nd ed. (New York: McGraw-Hill, 1995). Other definitions can be found at www.marketingpower.com/live/mg-dictionary.php?, August 2006.

7. Bob Garfield, "The Chaos Scenario," *Advertising Age*, April 4, 2005, pp. 1, 57+; and "Readers Respond to 'Chaos Scenario'," *Advertising Age*, April 18, 2005, pp. 1+.

8. Chase Squires and Dave Gussow, "The Ways in which We Watch TV Are Changing Right Before Our Eyes," *St. Petersburg Times*, April 27, 2006.

9. Abbey Klaassen, "Study: Only One in Four Teens Can Name Broadcast Networks," *Advertising Age*, May 15, 2006.

10. Abbey Klaassen, "Marketers Lose Confidence in TV Advertising," *Advertising Age*, March 22, 2006, accessed at adage.com/mediaworks/article?article_id=107965.

11. Brian Steinberg and Suzanne Vranica, "As 30-Second Spot Fades, What Will Advertisers Do Next?" *Wall Street Journal*, January 3, 2006, p. A15.

12. Mike Shaw, "Direct Your Advertising Dollars Away from TV at Your Own Risk," *Advertising Age*, February 27, 2006, p. 29. Also see John Consoli, "2005 Spending Rose 4.2 Percent, Says Nielsen Monitor-Plus," *MediaWeek*, March 15, 2006, accessed at www.mediaweek.com; and Claire Atkinson, "Measured Network TV Ad Spending Fell Last Year," *Advertising Age*, March 6, 2006, accessed at www.adage.com.

13. Hung, M and Li, Wanlung, *Case of Advertising*, (Beijing: Renmin University Press, 2006), pp.324–329.

14. Don E. Schultz, "New Media, Old Problem: Keep Marcom Integrated," *Marketing News*, March 29, 1999, p. 11. Also see Don E. Schultz, Stanley I. Tannenbaum, and Robert F. Lauterborn, *Integrated Marketing Communications* (Chicago, IL: NTC, 1992); Claire Atkinson, "Integration Still a Pipe Dream for Many," *Advertising Age*, March 10, 2003, pp. 1, 47; and Randall Rothenberg, "Despite All the Talk, Ad and Media Shops Still Aren't Truly Integrated," *Advertising Age*, March 27, 2006, p. 24.

15. See Don E. Schultz and Philip J. Kitchen, *Communication Globally: An Integrated Marketing Approach* (New York: McGraw-Hill, 2000); and Don E. Schultz and Heidi Schultz, *IMC The Next Generation* (New York: McGraw-Hill, 2004).

16. See "Magic Fridge of Bud Lite Ices a Win," *USA Today*, February 6, 2006, p. 5B.

17. Quotes and other information found in Hillary Chura, "A Creative Low Point," *Advertising Age*, February 9, 2004, p. 49; Stuart Elliott, "Can Beer Ads Extol Great Taste in Good Taste?" *New York Times*, April 2004, p. C2; and Heather Landi, "Madison Avenue's Greatest Hits," *Beverage World*, December 15, 2005, pp. 28–29.

18. For these and other examples, see Pamela Paul, "Color by Numbers," *American Demographics*, February 2002, pp. 31–35; and Arundhati Parmar, "Marketers Ask: Hues on First?" *Marketing News*, February 15, 2004, pp. 8–10.

19. Jonah Bloom, "The Truth Is: Consumers Trust Fellow Buyers Before Marketers," *Advertising Age*, February 13, 2006, p. 25.

20. Example adapted from Linda Tischler, "What's the Buzz?" Fast Company, May 2004, p. 76; with information from Matthew Creamer, "BzzAgent Seeks to Turn Word of Mouth into a Saleable Medium," *Advertising Age*, February 2006, p. 12.

21. Eugenia Levenson, "When Celebrity Endorsements Attack," *Fortune*, October 17, 2005, p. 42; and Charlie Gillis, "Thee Shill of Victory," *Maclean's*, February 27, 2006, p. 40.

22. For more on advertising spending by company and industry, see the *Advertising Age*, "Ad to Sales Ratios 2005 Edition," March 1, 2006, accessed at http://adage.com/datacenter/article.php?article_id=106936.

23. For more on setting promotion budgets, see W. Ronald Lane, Karen Whitehill King, and J. Thomas Russell, *Kleppner's Advertising Procedure*, 16th ed. (Upper Saddle River, NJ: Prentice Hall, 2005), Chap. 6.

24. See David Barron, "TV Ratings Beat Last Year's," *Knight Ridder Tribune Business News*, February 7, 2006, p. 1; Nick Madigan and Rob Hiaasen, "Oscar Host Is One Tough Gig," *Knight Ridder Tribune Business News*, March 7, 2006, p. 1; and Lisa de Moraes, " 'American Idol' Belts Out a Huge Opening Number: 33.6 Million," *Washington Post*, January 20, 2006, p. C1.

25. Roy Chitwood, "Making the Most Out of Each Outside Sales Call," February 4, 2005, accessed at http://seattle.bizjournals.com/seattle/stories/2005/02/07/smallb3.html; and "The Cost of the Average Sales Call Today is More Than $400," *Business Wire*, February 28, 2006.

26. Based on Matthew P. Gonring, "Putting Integrated Marketing Communications to Work Today," *Public Relations Quarterly*, Fall 1994, pp. 45-48. Also see Philip Kotler, *Marketing Management*, 12th ed. (Upper Saddle River, NJ: Prentice Hall, 2006), pp. 558–561.

27. Information accessed at www.tropicalforest.foundation.org/about.html and www.avoncompany.com/women/avoncrusade/, August 2006.

28. For more on the legal aspects of promotion, see Lane, King, and Russell, Kleppner's Advertising Procedure, chapter 25; and William L. Cron and Thomas E. DeCarlo, *Dalrymple's Sales Management*, 9th ed. (New York: Wiley, 2006), chapter 10.

Chapter 15

1. For information on U.S. and international advertising spending, see Lisa Sanders, "Global Ad Spend to Rise to 6 Percent in 2006," *Advertising Age*, December 5, 2005, p. 1; and "100 Leading National Advertisers," *special issue of Advertising Age*, June 26, 2006.

2. For more on advertising budgets, see W. Ronald Lane, Karen Whitehill King, and J. Thomas Russell, *Kleppner's Advertising Procedure*, 16th ed. (Upper Saddle River, NJ: Prentice Hall, 2005), chapter 6.

3. Charles Pappas, "Ad Nauseam," *Advertising Age*, July 10, 2000, pp. 16–18; Mark Ritson, "Marketers Need to Find a Way to Control the Contagion of Clutter," *Marketing*, March 6, 2003, p. 16; and David H. Freedman, "The Future of Advertising Is here," *Inc.*, August 2005, pp. 70–78.

4. See Steve McClellan, "American Idol No. 1 with a $705k Bullet," *Mediaweek*, September 12, 2005, pp. 4–5; Abbey Klaassen and Claire Atkinson, "Super Bowl Spots Lose Their Luster," *Advertising Age*, February 13, 2006, p. 1; Roberta Bernstein, "Actors' Digital Destiny," *Adweek*, April 10, 2006, pp. 22–23; and Claire Atkinson, " 'Idol' Finale Hits $1.3M High Note," *Advertising Age*, April 17, 2006, pp. 1, 14.

5. Paul Holmes, "Programs that Demonstrate the Value of Public Relations," *Advertising Age*, January 24, 2005, pp. C12–C16; Gary Levin, "Ad Glut Turns Off Viewers," *USA Today*, October 11, 2005, accessed at www.usatoday.com; and John Consoli, "Broadcast, Cable Ad Clutter Continues to Rise," *MediaWeek*, May 4, 2006, accessed at www.mediaweek.com.

6. John Consoli, "Broadcast, Cable Ad Clutter Continues to Rise," *MediaWeek*, May 4, 2006, accessed at www.mediaweek.com.

7. Ronald Grover, "The Sound of Many Hands Zapping," *BusinessWeek*, May 22, 2006, p. 38; David Ki9ley, "Learning to Love the Dreader TiVo," *BusinessWeek*, April 17, 2006, p. 88; and Randall Stross, "Someone Has to Pay. But Who? And How?" *New York Times*, May 7, 2006, p. 3.3.

8. See Theresa Howard, " 'Viral' Advertising Spreads through Marketing Plans," *USA Today*, June 6, 2005, accessed at www.usatoday.com/money/advertising/2005-06-22-viral-usat_x.htm; and Steve McKee, Advertising: Less Is Much More," *BusinessWeek Online*, May 10, 2006, accessed at www.businessweek.com.

9. Stuart Elliot, "New Rules of Engagement," *New York Times*, March 21, 2006, p. C7; and Abbey Klaassen, "New Wins Early Battle in Viewer-Engagement War," *Advertising Age*, March 20, 2006, p. 10.

10. Adapted from information found in "Multi-Taskers," *Journal of Marketing Management*, May–June 2004, p. 6; "Kids Today: Media Multitaskers," March 9, 2005, accessed at www.cbsnews.com/stories/2005/03/09/tech/main678999.shtml; and Claudia Wallis, "The Multitasking Generation," *Time*, March 27, 2006, accessed at www.time.com.

11. *Newsweek* and *BusinessWeek* cost and circulation data accessed online at http://mediakit.businessweek.com and www.newsweekmediakit.com, August 2006.

12. Stuart Elliot, "How Effective Is This Ad, in Real Numbers? Beats Me," *New York Times*, July 20, 2005, p. C8.

13. Elliot, "How Effective Is This Ad, in Real Numbers? Beats Me," p. C8. Also see, Dan Lippe, "Media Scorecard: How ROI Adds Up," *Advertising Age*, June 20, 2005, p. S6; and Pat LaPointe, "For Better ROI, Think Sailing, Not Driving," *Brandweek*, January 30, 2006, pp. 17–18.

14. Information on advertising agency revenues from "Advertising Age's Special Agency Report," *Advertising Age*, May 1, 2006.

15. See Alexandra Jardine and Laurel Wentz, "It's a Fat World After All," *Advertising Age*, March 7, 2005, p. 3; George E. Belch and Michael A. Belch, *Advertising and Promotion*, (New York: McGraw-Hill/Irwin, 2004), pp. 666–668; Jonathan Cheng, "China Demands Concrete Proof of Ads," *Wall Street Journal*, July 8, 2005, p. B1; Cris Prystay, "India's Brewers Cleverly Dodge Alcohol-Ad Ban," *Wall Street Journal*, June 15, 2005, p. B1; and Dean Visser, "China Puts New Restrictions on Cell Phone, E-Mail Advertising," *Marketing News*, March 15, 2006, p. 23.

16. Adapted from Scott Cutlip, Allen Center, and Glen Broom, *Effective Public Relations*, 9th ed. (Upper Saddle River, NJ: Prentice Hall, 2006), chapter 1.

17. Chi-ying Siu, "Thirty Six Tactics of Marketing, (Beijing: Machinery Industry Publishers, 2007), pp. 44–45; accessed online at www.swelllfun.com

18. Al Ries and Laura Ries, "First Do Some Publicity," *Advertising Age*, February 8, 1999, p. 42. Also see Al Ries and Laura Ries, *The Fall of Advertising and the Rise of PR* (New York: HarperBusiness, 2002). For points and counterpoints and discussions of the role of public relations, see O. Burtch Drake, "'Fall' of Advertising? I Differ," *Advertising Age*, January 13, 2003, p. 23; Robert E. Brown, "Book Review: The Fall of Advertising & the Rise of PR," *Public Relations Review*, March 2003, pp. 91–93; Mark Cheshire, "Roundtable Discussion—Making & Moving the Message," *The Daily Record*, January 30, 2004, p. 1; and David Robinson. "Public Relations Comes of Age," *Business Horizons*, May–June 2006, pp. 247+.

Chapter 16

1. Information from company leaflets of Prudential

2. Quote from Laurence Zuckerman, "Selling Airplanes with a Smile," *New York Times*, February 17, 2002, p. 3.2. Also see Joann Muller, "7 Digital 7," *Forbes*, June 21, 2004, p. 117; and Perry Flint, "What Will They Do for an Encore?" *Air Transport World*, March 2006, pp. 22–25.

3. "Selling Power 500," accessed at www.sellingpower.com/sp500/index.asp, October 2006.

4. For more on this and other methods for determining sales force size, see William L. Cron and Thomas E. DeCarlo, *Sales Management*, 9th ed. (New York: John Wiley & Sons, 2006), pp. 84–85.

5. Roy Chitwood, "Making the Most Out of Each Outside Sales Call," February 4, 2005, accessed at http://seattle.bizjournals.com/seattle/stories/2005/02/07/smallb3.html; and "The Cost of the Average Sales Call Today is More Than $400," *Business Wire*, February 28, 2006.

6. Quotes and other information in this section on super salespeople are from Geoffrey Brewer, "Mind Reading: What Drives Top Salespeople to Greatness?" *Sales & Marketing Management*, May 1994, pp. 82–88; Andy Cohen, "The Traits of Great Sales Forces," *Sales & Marketing Management*, October 2000, pp. 67–72; Julia Chang, "Born to Sell?" *Sales & Marketing Management*, July 2003, pp. 34–38; Henry Canaday, "Recruiting the Right Stuff," *Selling Power*, April 2004, pp. 94–96. Also see Tom Andel, "How to Cultivate Sales Talent," *Official Board Markets*, April 23, 2005, pp. 14–16; and Kevin McDonald, "Therapist, Social Worker or Consultant?" *CRN*, December 2005–January 2006, p. 24.

7. See *Dartnell's 30th Sales Force Compensation Survey*, Dartnell Corporation, August 1999; and Galea "2006 Compensation Survey," *Sales & Marketing Management*, May 2006, pp. 30–35.

8. See Henry Canady, "How to Increase the Times Reps Spend Selling," *Selling Power*, March 2005, p. 112; George Reinfeld, "8 Tips to Help Control the Hand of Time," *Printing News*, January 9, 2006, p. 10; and David J. Cichelli, "Plugging Sales 'Time Leaks,'" *Sales & Marketing Management*, April 2006, p. 23.

9. See Gary H Anthes, "Portal Powers GE Sales," *Computerworld*, June 2, 2003, pp. 31–32. Also see Betsy Cummings, "Increasing Face Time," *Sales & Marketing Management*, January 2004, p. 12; and David J. Cichelli, "Plugging Sales 'Time Leaks,'" *Sales & Marketing Management*, April 2006, p. 23.

10. For extensive discussions of sales force automation, see the May 2005 issue of *Industrial Marketing Management*, which is devoted to the subject.

11. Irwin Speizer, "Incentives Catch on Overseas, But Value of Awards Can Too Easily Get Lost in Translation," *Workforce Management*, November 21, 2005.

12. For more on return on sales investment, see Tim Lukes and Jennifer Stanley, "Bringing Science to Sales," *Marketing Management*, September–October 2004, pp. 36–41.

13. Quotes from Bob Donath, "Delivering Value Starts with Proper Prospecting," *Marketing News*, November 10, 1997, p. 5; and Bill Brooks, "Power-Packed Prospecting Pointers," *Agency Sales*, March 2004, p. 37. See also the audio slide presentation by Mike Trigg and others, "Best Practices for Sales Prospecting," Salesforce.com User & Development Conference 2005, accessed at www.spoke.com/bestpractices, April 2006.

14. Quotes and other information from Dana Ray, "Are You Listening?" *Selling Power*, October 2004, pp. 24–27; Erin Stout, "Throwing the Right Pitch," *Sales & Marketing Management*, April 2001, pp. 61–63; Betsy Cummings, "Listening for Deals," *Sales & Marketing Management*, August 2005, p. 8; and William Kendy, "Learning to Listen," *Selling Power*, July–August 2006, p. 25. Also see Geoffrey James, "Solution Selling," *Selling Power*, May 2006, pp. 45–48.

15. Betsy Cummings, "Listening for Deals," *Sales & Marketing Management*, August 2005, p. 8.

16. *2005 Trade Promotion Spending & Merchandising Industry Study* (Cannondale Associates, Wilton, CT, May 2006), p. 13.

17. Chi-ying Siu, *Thirty Tactics in Marketing*, (Beijing: Machinery Industry Publisher, 2007), p. 70.

18. See Betsy Spethmann, "Clipping Slows," *Promo Magazine*, April 1, 2006; and Direct Marketing Association, "The DMA 2006 Statistical Fact Book," June 2006, p. 90.

19. See "Promotional Products—Impact, Exposure, and Influence" at Promotional Products Association International Web site, www.ppai.org, accessed May 2006; and Stacey Burling, "Your Logo Sells Here," *Philadelphia Enquirer*, May 31, 2006, accessed at www.philly.com/mld/philly/business/14702529.htm.

20. *2005 Trade Promotion Spending & Merchandising Industry Study* (Cannondale Associates, Wilton, CT, May 2006), p. 13.

21. See "Nearly Half a Million Attend Bauma Trade Show," *Pit & Quarry*, May 2004, p. 16; and "Record Breaking 2006 International CES Reflects Strength of Computer Technology Industry," press release at Consumer Electronics Association Web site, www.cesweb.org, January 8, 2006.

Chapter 17

1. Quotes and other information from Louise Lee, "It's Dell vs. The Dell Way," *BusinessWeek*, March 6, 2006, pp. 61–62; Andy Serwer, "Dell's Midlife Crisis," *Fortune*, November 28, 2005, pp. 147–152; Kathryn Jones, "The Dell Way," *Business 2.0*, February 2003, pp. 60–66; Serwer, "Dell Does Domination," *Fortune*, January 21, 2002, pp. 71–75; Serwer, "The Education of Michael Dell," *Fortune*, March 7, 2005, pp. 73–78; "Dell Inc.," *Hoover's Company Records*, Austin, May 1, 2006, p. 132692; "Top PC Venders by Market Share," Interactive Marketing & Media, *supplement to Advertising Age*, April 17, 2006, p. 50; Luisa Kroll and Allison Fass, "The World's Billionaires," *Forbes*, March 9, 2006, accessed at www.forbes.com/billionaires; Sophie Taylor, "Dell Eyes Smaller China Cities, Talks to Asian Retailers," investing.reuters.co.uk, November 30, 2007; "Dell at a Glance: Asia-Pacific/Japan Factsheet," www1.ap.dell.com, December 2007; and www.dell.com/us/en/gen/corporate/access_company_direct_model.htm, December 2006.

2. For these and other direct marketing statistics in this section, see Direct Marketing Association, "The DMA 2006 Statistical Fact Book," June 2006, pp. 249–250; *Direct Marketing Association*, "U.S. Direct Marketing Today: Economic Impact 2005," October, 2005, various pages; and a wealth of other information accessed at www.the-dma.org, September 2006.

3. "Fujitsu Customers—Case Studies," accessed online at http://crm.fujitsu.com/en/case_study/japan_net.htmol.

4. Portions adapted from Christopher Elliott, "Your Very Own Personal Air Fare," *New York Times*, August 9, 2005, p. C5. Also see "Southwest Airlines Makes DING! Available to MAC Users," *Telecomworldwire*, March 21, 2006, p. 1; and "What Is DING!?" accessed at www.southwest.com/ding/, September 2006.

5. William Auckerman, "Japan's Lawson Eyes Web Sales," www.internetnews.com, July 13, 1999.

6. Daniel Lyons, "Too Much Information," *Forbes*, December 13, 2004, p. 110; and Mike Freeman, "Data Company Helps Wal-Mart, Casinos, Airlines Analyze Data," *Knight Ridder Business Tribune News*, February 24, 2006, p. 1.

7. David Ranii, "Compact Discs, DVDs Get More Use as Promotional Tool," *Knight Ridder Tribune Business News*, May 5, 2004, p. 1.

8. Jim Emerson, "Print and the Internet Go Hand-in-Hand," *Printing News*, June 20, 2005, p. 2; and "Abacus Report: Web Sales Soon to Overtake Catalog Sales," August 3, 2005, accessed at http://multichannelmerchant.com/news/Abacus-trend-report-080305/.

9. Janie Curtis, "Catalogs as Portals: Why You Should Keep on Mailing," *Multichannel Merchant*, November 30, 2005, accessed at http://multichannelmerchant.com/news/catalogs_portal_1130/index.html.

10. Ira Teinowitz, "'Do Not Call' Does Not Hurt Direct Marketing," *Advertising Age*, April 11, 2005, p. 3.

11. Steve McLellan, "For a Whole New DRTV Experience, Call Now," *Adweek*, September 5, 2005, p. 10; and Jack Neff, "What Procter & Gamble Learned from Veg-O-Matic," p. 1.

12. Adapted from portions of Elizabeth Esfashani, "A Sales Channel They Can't Resist," *Business 2.0*, September 2005, pp. 91-96.

13. "Interactive: Ad Age Names Finalists," *Advertising Age*, February 27, 1995, pp. 12–14.

14. Alice Z. Cuneo, "Scramble for Content Drives Mobile," *Advertising Age*, October 24, 2005, p. S6.

15. "Mobile Marketing," *Marketing News*, April 1, 2006, p. 4.

16. Adapted from information found in Normandy Madden, "Cellphones Spawn New 'Fast' Promotions in Japan," *Advertising Age*, November 7, 2005, p. 14.

17. For these and other examples, see Karyn Strauss and Derek Gale, Hotels, March 2006, p. 22; and "Disneyland Offers Behind-the-Scenes Podcast," *Wireless News*, Febraury 19, 2006, p. 1.

18. Susie Haywood, "Honda Scores First with Civic 'Vodcast,'" *Revolution*, February 2006, p. 11.

19. Adapted from David Liley, "Learning to Love the Dreaded TiVo," *BusinessWeek*, April 17, 2006, p. 88. Also see Daisy Whitney, "Marketers Quick to Say 'Yes' to Opt-In TV Fare," *Advertising Age*, October 24, 2005, p. S4; and "Nickelodeon Runs SeaWord iTV Ads," *New Media Age*, April 27, 2006, p. 3.

20. For these and other statistics on Internet usage, see "United States: Average Web Usage," Nielsen/ NetRatings, April 2006, accessed at www.nielsen-netratings.com; Antony Bruno, "Web Adoption Slows, Broadband Grows," *Billboard*, April 15, 2006, p. 16; and Enid Burns, "Global Internet Adoption Slows While Involvement Deepens," *ClickZ Stats*, April 3, 2006, accessed at www.clickz.com.

21. "JupiterResearch Forecasts Online Retail Spending Will Reach $144 Billion in 2010, a CAGR of 12% from 2005," February 6, 2006, accessed at www.jupitermedia.com/ corporate/releases/06.02.06-new jupresearch.html.

22. Ron Gluckman, "Going Offline in Asia," accessed online at www.gluckman.com/E-ComAsia.htm.

23. Information for this example accessed at www.dell. com/html/us/segments/pub/premier/tutorial/ users_guide.html, September 2006.

24. See Kim Wright Wiley, "Meg Whitman: The $40 Billion eBay Sales Story," *Selling Power*, November–December, 2005, pp. 63–70; "eBay Inc.," *Hoover's Company Records*, May 1, 2006, p. 56307; and facts from eBay annual reports and other information accessed at www.ebay. com, September 2006.

25. "China Expects US$9.16 billion in C2C Trade in 2008," ww.chinadaily.com.sn, February 17, 2008; Huang Xin, "Online Shopping Gaining Popularity in China," www.

26. Gavin O'Malley, "Coca-Cola Sends Bloggers to Olympics," *MediaPost Publications*, February 10, 2006, accessed at http://publications.mediapost.com.

27. Pete Blackshaw, "Irrational Exuberance? I Hope We're Not Guilty," *Barcode Blog*, August 26, 2005, accessed at www.barcodefactory.com/wordpress/?p=72.

28. Derrick A. Paulo, "Citizen Advertising: The Next Big Thing?" *TODAY (Singapore)*, August 15, 2006, p. 31.

29. Jeffrey F. Rayport and Bernard J. Jaworski, *e-Commerce* (New York: McGraw-Hill, 2001), p. 116. Also see Goutam Chakraborty, "What Do Customers Consider Important in B2B Web sites?" *Journal of Advertising*, March 2003, p. 50; and "Looks Are Everything," *Marketing Management*, March/April 2006, p. 7.

30. Ellis Booker, "Vivid 'Experiences' as the New Frontier," *BtoB*, March 14, 2005, p. 14; and Karen J Bannan, "Rich Media Rule Book," *BtoB*, March 13, 2006, pp. 27–30.

31. See Mike Shields, "Google Faces New Rivals," August 22, 2005, accessed at www.mediaweek.com; and "Internet Advertising Revenues Grow 30% to a Record $12.5 Billion in '05," *Internet Advertising Bureau*, April 20, 2006, accessed at www.iab.net.

32. Adapted from Jon Fine, "Rise of the Lowly Search Ad," *BusinessWeek*, April 24, 2006, p. 24.

33. Kris Oser, "Video in Demand," *Advertising Age*, April 4, 2005, pp. S1–S5.

34. Adapted from information found in Bob Garfield, "War & Peace and Subservient Chicken," April 26, 2004, accessed at www.adage.com; Gregg Cebrzynski, "Burger King Says It's OK to Have Your Way with the Chicken," *Nation's Restaurant News*, May 10, 2004, p. 16; and Ryan Underwood, "Ruling the Roost," *Fast Company*, April 2005, pp. 70–78.

35. Heidi Anderson, "Nintendo Case Study: Rules Are Made to Be Broken," *E-Mail Marketing Case Studies*, March 6, 2003, accessed online at www.clickz.com.

36. Adapted from information found in Carol Krol, "E-Mail Marketing Gains Ground with Integration," *BtoB*, April 3, 2006, p. 1.

37. See Don Oldenburg, "Hook, Line and Sinker: Personalized Phishing Scams Use Customers' Names to Attract Attention," *Washington Post*, April 2, 2006, p. F05; and "How Not to Get Caught by a Phishing Scam," accessed at www.ftc.gov/bcp/online/pubs/ alerts/phishingalrt.htm, June 2006.

38. Rob McCann, "Concerns over Online Threats This Holiday Season," *ClickZ Stats*, November 24, 2004, accessed at www.clickz.com. Also see Ann E. Schlosser, Tiffany Barnett White, and Susan M. Lloyd, "Converting Web Site Visitors into Buyers: How Web Site Investment Increases Consumer Trusting Beliefs and Online Purchase Intentions," *Journal of Marketing*, April 2006, pp. 133–148.

oe.cn, February 25, 2007.

39. "14-Year-Old Bids over $3M for Items in eBay Auctions," *USA Today*, April 30, 1999, p. 10B.

Chapter 18

1. Miles Dodd, "QB House: 10 Minutes, Just Cut," in Hellmut Schutte, Swee Hoon Ang, Siew Meng Leong, and Chin Tiong Tan, *Marketing Management: An Asian Casebook*, Singapore: Prentice Hall, 2004, pp. 115–130; "Barbers at the Gate," *The Economist*, November 2, 2006; Lilya, "QB House in HK: 10-minute, no-frills haricut," *Subtle Shocks From Hong Kong*, September 8, 2005 accessed on subtleshocks.blogspot.com, July 30, 2007; Jacob Ward, "Should a Bank Be a Store?" *USBanker*, April 2004, pp. 36–40; "Washington Mutual, Inc." *Hoover's Company Records*, May 15, 2006, p. 15119; Mary McGarity, "WaMu's Back," *Mortgage Banking*, October 2005, pp. 104–113; and "The WaMu Difference," accessed at www.wamu.com/about, September 2006.

2. Leon Lazaroff, "Kodak Big Picture Focusing on Image Change," *Knight Ridder Tribune Business News*, January 26, 2006. Also see Brad Stone, "What's Kodak's Strategy?" *Newsweek*, January 16, 2006, p. 25.

3. Adapted from Jeffrey F. Rayport and Bernard J. Jaworski, *e-Commerce* (New York: McGraw-Hill, 2001), p. 53.

4. Johanna Bennett, "Turn Around, Bright Eyes," *Barron's*, May 16, 2005, p. 48.

5. See Michael Porter, *Competitive Advantage: Creating and Sustaining Superior Performance* (New York: Free Press, 1998), chap. 6.

6. Adapted from Devin Leonard, "The Player," *Fortune*, March 20, 2006, p. 54.

7. See Philip Kotler and Kevin Lane Keller, *Marketing Management*, 12th ed. (Upper Saddle River, NJ: Prentice Hall, 2006), pp. 13–14; Sam Hill and Glenn Rifkin, *Radical Marketing* (New York: HarperBusiness, 1999); Gerry Khermouch, "Keeping the Froth on Sam Adams," *BusinessWeek*, September 1, 2003, p. 54; and information accessed at www.bostonbeer.com, September 2006.

8. Michael E. Porter, *Competitive Strategy: Techniques for Analyzing Industries and Competitors* (New York: Free Press, 1980), chap. 2; and Porter, "What Is Strategy?" *Harvard Business Review*, November–December 1996, pp. 61–78. Also see Richard Allen and others, "A Comparison of Competitive Strategies in Japan and the United States," *S.A.M. Advanced Management Journal*, Winter 2006, pp. 24–36.

9. See Michael Treacy and Fred Wiersema, "Customer Intimacy and Other Value Disciplines," *Harvard Business Review*, January-February 1993, pp. 84–93; Michael Treacy and Mike Wiersema, *The Discipline of Market Leaders: Choose Your Customers, Narrow Your Focus, Dominate Your Market* (Perseus Press, 1997); Fred Wiersema, *Customer Intimacy: Pick Your Partners, Shape Your Culture, Win Together* (Knowledge Exchange, 1998); and Wiersema, *Double-Digit Growth: How Great Companies Achieve It—No Matter What* (Portfolio, 2003).

10. For more discussion, see Philip Kotler and Kevin Lane Keller, *Marketing Management*, 12th ed., chap. 11.

11. Jack Neff, "Unilever Cedes Laundry War," *Advertising Age*, May 27, 2002, pp. 1, 47; Veronica Mac Donald, "Soaps and Detergents: Going the World Over to Clean," *Chemical Week*, January 26, 2005, pp. 21–23; Jack Neff, "Unilever 3.0: CEO Not Afraid to Copy from P&G," *Advertising Age*, October 23, 2005, p. 8; and Kerri Walsh, "Brand Extensions Clean Up," *Chemical Week*, February 1, 2006, pp. 24+.

12. "Logitech Aims at Convergence for New Growth," *Wall Street Journal*, June 16, 2004, p. 1; Logitech Annual Report, www.logitech.com, April 1, 2006; and "Logitech International S.A.," *Hoover's Company Records*, June 1, 2006, p. 42459.

13. Jim Kirk, "Company Finds Itself, Finds Success: Alberto-Culver Adopts Strategy of Knowing Its Strengths and Promoting Small Brands, Rather Than Tackling Giants," *Chicago Tribune*, January 22, 1998, Business Section, p. 1; "Alberto-Culver Company," *Hoover's Company Records*, June 1, 2006, p. 10048; and www.alberto.com, September 2006.

Chapter 19

1. "Global 500 World's Largest Corporations Rankings," *Fortune 500 Vol. 156*, No. 2 July 23, 2007.

2. "PepsiCo CEO Steve Reinemund Shares Leadership Principles," *Texas Business Weekly*, February 21, 2005 accessed at http://media.www.texasbusinessweekly.com/media/storage/paper480/news/2005/02/21/News/Pepsico.Ceo.Steve.Reinemund.Shares.Leadership.Principles-874315.shtml

3. "Harry Hui: How Pepsi engages China's youth," accessed at www.thomascrampton.com/2007/10/16/harry-hui-how-pepsi-engages-chinas-youth

4. *Global Economic Prospects*, 2006, World Bank, June 3, 2005, accessed at www.worldbank.org; CIA, *The World Factbook*, accessed at www.cia.gov, June 2006; and WTO, "World Trade Picks Up in Mid-2005; But 2006 Picture Is Uncertain," *WTO press release*, April 11, 2006, accessed at www.wto.org/english/news_e/pres06_e/pr437_e.htm.

5. "The Unique Japanese," *Fortune*, November 24, 1986, p. 8. Also see James D. Southwick, "Addressing Market Access Barriers in Japan Through the WTO," *Law and Policy in International Business*, Spring 2000, pp. 923–976; U.S. Commercial Service, *Country Commercial Guide Japan*, FY 2005, chap. 5, accessed at www.buyusa.gov, June 18, 2005; and "Japan-U.S. Beef Row Tip of Iceberg: U.S. Lawmaker," *Jiji Press English News Service*, February 16, 2006, p.1.

6. "What Is the WTO?" accessed at www.wto.org/english/ thewto_e/whatis_e/whatis_e.htm, September 2006 .

7. See *WTO Annual Report 2005*, accessed at www.wto. org, September 2006; and World Trade Organization, "10 Benefits of the WTO Trading System," accessed at www.wto.org/english/thewto_e/whatis_e/whatis_ e.htm, September 2006.

8. "Finance and Economics: In the Rough; World Trade Talks," *Economist*, November 5, 2005, p. 102; and Peter Coy, "Why Free-Trade Talks Are in Free Fall," *BusinessWeek*, May 22, 2006, p. 44

9. "The European Union at a Glance," accessed online at http://europa.eu.int, September 2006; http:// en.wikipedia.org/wiki/European_Union

10. "Overviews of European Union Activities: Economic and Monetary Affairs," accessed at http://europa. eu.int/pol/emu/overview_en.htm, September 2006.

11. See "European Union's Heated Budget Negotiations Collapse," *New York Times*, June 18, 2005, p. A3; "Europe: Desperately Seeking a Policy; France and the European Union," *Economist*, January 21, 2006; CIA, *The World Factbook*, accessed at www.cia.gov, June 2006; and Vito Breda, "A European Constitution in a Multinatioal Europe or a Multinational Constitution for Europe?" *European Law Journal*, May 2006, pp. 330+.

12. Statistics and other information from "List of Countries by GDP," *Wikipedia*, accessed at http:// en.wikipedia.org/wiki/List_of_countries_by_GDP_ %28nominal%29, July 2006; "Area and Population of Countries," infoplease, accessed at www.infoplease. com/ipa/A0004379.html, July 2006; and "Trade Facts: NAFTA—A Strong Record of Success," Office of the United States Trade Representative, March 2006, accessed at www.ustr.gov/assets/Document_Library/ Fact_Sheets/2006/asset_upload_file242_9156.pdf.

13. See Angela Greiling Keane, "Counting on CAFTA," *Traffic World*, August 8, 2005, p. 1; Gilberto Meza, "Is the FTAA Floundering," *Business Mexico*, February 2005, pp. 46–48; Peter Robson, "Integrating the Americas: FTAA and Beyond," *Journal of Common Market Studies*," June 2005, p. 430; Diana Kinch, "Latin America: Mercosul Boosted," *Metal Bulletin Monthly*, February 2006, p. 1; "Foreign Trade Statistics," accessed at www. census.gov, June 2006; and Kevin Z. Jiang, "Americas: Trading Up?" *Harvard International Review*, Spring 2006, pp. 10–12.

14. Richard Lapper, "South American Unity Still a Distant Dream," *Financial Times*, December 9, 2004, accessed at www.news.ft.com; Alan Clendenning, "Venezuela's Entry May Shake Up Mercosur," *AP Financial Wire*, November 30, 2005, p. 1; and Mary Turck, "South American Community of Nations," Resource Center of the Americas.org, accessed at www.americas.org, September 2006.

15. See Shanti Gamper-Rabindran, "NAFTA and the Environment: What Can the Data Tell Us?" *Economic Development and Cultural Change*, April 2006, pp. 605–634.

16. Overview of ASEAN, accessed at www.aseansec. org/64.htm

17. Adapted from information found in Clay Chandler, "China Deluxe," *Fortune*, July 26, 2004, pp. 148–156. Also see "Selling to China's Rich and Not So Rich," *Strategic Directions*, June 2005, pp. 5–8; Lisa Movius, "Luxury's China Puzzle," *WWD*, June 15, 2005, p. 1; and Normandy Madden, "After Slow Start, Porsche Cranks Its Chinese Marketing Plan into Top Gear," *Advertising Age*, May 8, 2006, p. 28.

18. See Om Malik, "The New Land of Opportunity," *Business 2.0*, July 2004, pp. 72–79; and "India Economy: South Asia's Worst Business Environment," *EIU ViewsWire*, January 2006.

19. Ricky Griffin and Michael Pustay, *International Business*, 4th ed. (Upper Saddle River, NJ: Prentice Hall, 2005), pp. 522–523.

20. Dan West, "Countertrade—An Innovative Approach to Marketing," accessed at http://www.barternews.com/ approach_marketing.htm

21. For other examples and discussion, see www. executiveplanet.com, December 2006; *Dun & Bradstreet's Guide to Doing Business Around the World* (Upper Saddle River, NJ: Prentice Hall, 2000); Ellen Neuborne, "Bridging the Culture Gap," *Sales & Marketing Management*, July 2003, p. 22; Richard Pooley, "When Cultures Collide," *Management Services*, Spring 2005, pp. 28–31; and Helen Deresky, *International Management*, 5th ed. (Upper Saddle River, NJ: Prentice Hall, 2006).

22. Pete Engardio, Manjeet Kripalani, and Alysha Webb, "Smart Globalization," *BusinessWeek*, August 27, 2001, pp. 132–136.

23. Robert Berner and David Kiley, "Global Brands," *BusinessWeek*, August 1, 2005, pp. 86–94.

24. Portions adapted from information found in Mark Rice-Oxley, "In 2,000 Years, Will the World Remember Disney or Plato?" *Christian Science Monitor*, January 15, 2004, p. 16.

25. Paulo Prada and Bruce Orwall, "A Certain 'Je Ne Sais Quoi' at Disney's New Park—Movie-Themed Site Near Paris Is Multilingual, Serves Wine—and Better Sausage Variety," *Wall Street Journal*, March 12, 2002, p. B1. Also see "Euro Disney S. C. A.," *Hoover's Company Records*, June 15, 2006, p. 90721.

26. *Apple Daily*, Hong Kong, March 25, 2008, p. A4

27. See Jack Neff, "Submerged," *Advertising Age*, March 4, 2002, p. 14; Ann Chen and Vijay Vishwanath, "Expanding in China," *Harvard Business Review*, March 2005, pp. 19–21; and information accessed at www. colgate.com, September 2006.

28. For a good discussion of joint venturing, see James Bamford, David Ernst, and David G. Fubini, "Launching a World-Class Joint Venture," *Harvard Business Review*, February 2004, pp. 91–100.

29. See Cynthia Kemper, "KFC Tradition Sold Japan on Chicken," *Denver Post*, June 7, 1998, p. J4; Milford Prewitt, "Chains Look for Links Overseas," *Nation's Restaurant News*, February 18, 2002, pp. 1, 6; and Yum Brands, Inc. restaurant count, accessed at www.yum.com, September 2006.

30. Quotes from Pankaj Ghemawat, "Regional Strategies for Global Leadership," *Harvard Business Review*, December 2005, pp. 97–108; Douglas B. Holt, John A. Quelch, and Earl L. Taylor, "How Global Brands Compete," *Harvard Business Review*, September 2004, pp. 68–75; and Simon Sherwood, "Building an Advertising Factory," accessed at www.internationalist.com/commentary/commentary%2020+21%202-18.1.pdf, June 16, 2006.

31. Warren J. Keegan, *Global Marketing Management*, 7th ed. (Upper Saddle River, NJ: Prentice Hall, 2002), pp. 346–351. Also see Phillip Kotler and Kevin Lane Keller, *Marketing Management*, 12th ed. (Upper Saddle River, NJ: 2006), pp. 677–684.

32. For further information on color and culture see Mubeen M. Aslam, "Are You Selling the Right Colour? A Cross-Cultural Review of Colour as a Marketing Cue," *Journal of Marketing Communications*, March 2006, pp. 15–20.

33. See "Naming Products Is No Game," BusinessWeek Online, April 9, 2004, accessed at www.businessweek.com; and Ross Thomson, "Lost in Translation," *Medical Marketing and Media*, March 2005, p. 82.

34. Kate MacArthur, "Coca-Cola Light Employs Local Edge," *Advertising Age*, August 21, 2000, pp. 18–19; and "Case Studies: Coke Light Hottest Guy," Advantage Marketing, msn India, accessed at http://advantage.msn.co.in, March 15, 2004.

35. See Alicia Clegg, "One Ad One World?" *Marketing Week*, June 20, 2002, pp. 51–52; and George E. Belch and Michael A. Belch, Advertising and Promotion: An Integrated Marketing Communications Perspective, 7th ed. (New York, NY: McGraw Hill, 2007), Chapter 20.

36. Michael Schroeder, "The Economy: Shrimp Imports to U.S. May Face Antidumping Levy," *Wall Street Journal*, February 18, 2004, p. A.2; Woranuj Maneerungsee, "Shrimpers Suspect Rivals of Foul Play," *Knight Ridder Tribune Business News*, April 28, 2005, p. 1; and David Bierderman, "Tough Journey," *Journal of Commerce*, March 13, 2006, p. 1.

37. See Patrick Powers, "Distribution in China: The End of the Beginning," *China Business Review*, July–August, 2001, pp. 8–12; Drake Weisert, "Coca-Cola in China: Quenching the Thirst of a Billion," *China Business Review*, July-August 2001, pp. 52–55; Gabriel Kahn, "Coke Works Harder at Being the Real Thing in Hinterland," *Wall Street Journal*, November 26, 2002,

p. B1; Leslie Chang, Chad Terhune, and Betsy McKay, "A Global Journal Report; Rural Thing—Coke's Big Gamble in Asia," *Wall Street Journal*, August 11, 2004, p. A1; and Ann Chen and Vijay Vishwanath, "Expanding in China," *Harvard Business Review*, March 1, 2005.

Chapter 20

1. Pete Engardio, "The Last Rajah," *BusinessWeek*, August 13, 2007; Eric Ellis, "Tata Steels Itself for Change,' *Fortune*, April 21, 2002; and "Tata Group," www.wikipedia.com, December 2007.

2. Adapted from Kevin DeMarrais, "You Can't Believe Airlines' Ticket Ads," *Knight Ridder Tribune Business News*, April 2, 2006, p. 1.

3. Theodore Levitt, "The Morality (?) of Advertising," *Harvard Business Review*, July–August 1970, pp. 84–92. For counterpoints, see Heckman, "Don't Shoot the Messenger," pp. 1, 9.

4. Lane Jennings, "Hype, Spin, Puffery, and Lies: Should We Be Scared?" *The Futurist*, January–February 2004, p. 16. For recent examples of deceptive advertising, see "Mobile Providers Sued by New York City," *Telecomworldwire*, July 22, 2005, p. 1; Chad Bray, "Federated to Pay Civil Penalty," *Wall Street Journal*, March 15, 2006, p. B3; and "Pfizer Sues P&G Over Crest Ads," *Wall Street Journal*, March 6, 2006, p. 1.

5. Tracy Quek, "Mattel Recalls 1.5m Made-in-China Toys," *The Straits Times (Singapore)*, August 3, 2007, p. 4.

6. Adapted from information found in Mark Fagan, "Commodity Driven Market," *Lawrence Journal-World*, May 4, 2005, p. 1. Also see Clint Swett, "High Prices on Printer Cartridges Feeds Marketing for Alternative Industry," *Knight Ridder Tribune Business News*, February 15, 2006, p. 1.

7. For more discussion, see Jeremiah Mcwilliams, "Big-Box Retailer Takes Issue with Small Documentary," *Knight Ridder Tribune Business News*, November 15, 2005, p. 1; Nicole Kauffman, "Movie Paints a Dark Picture of Wal-Mart's Impact on Communities," *Knight Ridder Tribune Business News*, January 19, 2006, p. 1; and John Reid Blackwell, "Documentarian Defends Wal-Mart," *Knight Ridder Tribune Business News*, May 12, 2006, p. 1.

8. See "Sustainability Key to UPS Environmental Initiatives," UPS press release, accessed at www.pressroom.ups.com, July 2006.

9. Information from "Xerox Equipment Remanufacture and Parts Reuse," accessed at www.xerox.com, September 2006.

10. Adapted from information found in Joeseph Tarnowski, "Green Monster," *Progressive Grocer*, April 1, 2006, pp. 20–26.

11. See "EMAS: What's New?" accessed at http://europa.eu.int/comm/environment/emas, August 2005; "Special Report: Free Trade on Trial—Ten Years of NAFTA," *The Economist*, January 3, 2004, p. 13; Daniel J. Tschopp, "Corporate Social Responsibility: A Comparison between the United States and Europe," *Corporate Social-Responsibility and Environmental Management*, March 2005, pp. 55–59; and www.epa.gov, accessed September 2006.

12. Information and quotes from Andy Milligan, "Samsung Points the Way for Asian Firms in Global Brand Race," *Media*, August 8, 2003, p. 8; Gerry Khermouch, "The Best Global Brands," *BusinessWeek*, August 5, 2002, p. 92; Leslie P. Norton, "Value Brand," *Barron's*, September 22, 2003, p. 19; "Cult Brands," *BusinessWeek Online*, August 2, 2004, accessed at www.businessweek.com; Bill Breen, "The Seoul of Design," *Fast Company*, December 2005, pp. 91–98; and Samsung Annual Reports and other information accessed at www.samsung.com, September 2006.

13. Joseph Webber, "3M's Big Cleanup," *BusinessWeek*, June 5, 2000, pp. 96–98. Also see Kara Sissell, "3M Defends Timing of Scotchgard Phaseout," *Chemical Week*, April 11, 2001, p. 33; Peck Hwee Sim, "Ausimont Targets Former Scotchgard Markets," *Chemical Week*, August 7, 2002, p. 32; Jennifer Lee, "E.P.A. Orders Companies to Examine Effect of Chemicals," *New York Times*, April 15, 2003, p. F2; and Kara Sissell, "Swedish Officials Propose Global Ban on PFOS," *Chemical Week*, June 22, 2005, p. 35.

14. See "Transparency International Bribe Payers Index" and "Transparency International Corruption Perception Index," accessed at www.transparency.org, August 2006; "Minxin Pei, "The Dark Side of China's Rise," *Foreign Policy, March/April 2006*, pp. 32–40; and "Everybody's Doing It," *Middle East*, April 2006, pp. 20–21.

15. John F. McGee and P. Tanganath Nayak, "Leaders' Perspectives on Business Ethics," *Prizm*, Arthur D. Little, Inc., Cambridge, MA, first quarter 1994, pp. 71–72. Also see Adrian Henriques, "Good Decision—Bad Business?" *International Journal of Management & Decision Making*, 2005, p. 273; and Marylyn Carrigan, Svetla Marinova, and Isabelle Szmigin, "Ethics and International Marketing: Research Background and Challenges," *International Marketing Review*, 2005, pp. 481–494.

16. See Samuel A. DiPiazza, "Ethics in Action," *Executive Excellence*, January 2002, pp. 15–16; Samuel A. DiPiazza, Jr., "It's All Down to Personal Values," accessed online at www.pwcglobal.com, August 2003; and "Code of Conduct: The Way We Do Business," accessed at www.pwcglobal.com/gx/eng/ins-sol/spec-int/ethics/index.html, September 2006. PricewaterhouseCoopers (www.pwc.com) provides industry-focused assurance, tax, and advisory services to build public trust and enhance value for its clients and their stakeholders.

More than 130,000 people in 148 countries across its network share their thinking, experience, and solutions to develop fresh perspectives and practical advice. 'PricewaterhouseCoopers' refers to the network of member firms of PricwaterhouseCoopers International limited, each of which is a separate and independent legal entity.

17. DiPiazza, "Ethics in Action," p. 15.

18. Tracy Quek, "Celebrities Used to Sell Misleading Ads," *The Straits Times (Singapore)*, April 2, 2007, p. 7.

Appendix 2

1. This is derived by rearranging the following equation and solving for price: Percentage markup = (price − cost) ÷ price.

2. The equation is derived from the basic profit = total revenue − total cost equation. Profit is set to equal the return on investment times the investment (ROI × I), total revenue equals price times quantity (P × Q), and total costs equals quantity times unit cost (Q × UC): ROI × I = (P × Q) − (Q × UC). Solving for P gives P = ((ROI × I) ÷ Q) + UC.

3. The breakeven volume equation can also be derived from the basic profit = total revenue − total cost equation. At the breakeven point, profit is equal to zero, and it is best to separate fixed and variable costs: 0 = (P × Q) − TFC − (Q × UVC). Solving for Q gives Q = TFC ÷ (P − UVC).

4. As in the previous note, this equation is derived from the basic profit = total revenue − total cost equation. However, unlike the break-even calculation, in which profit was set to equal zero, we set the profit equal to the dollar profit goal: Dollar profit goal = (P × Q) − TFC − (Q × UVC). Solving for Q gives Q = (TFC + dollar profit goal) ÷ (P − UVC).

5. Again, using the basic profit equation, we set profit equal to ROI × I: ROI × I = (P × Q) − TFC − (Q × UVC). Solving for Q gives Q = (TFC + (ROI × I)) ÷ (P − UVC).

6. Again, using the basic profit equation, we set profit equal to 25 percent of sales, which is 0.25 × P × Q: 0.25 × P × Q = (P × Q) − TFC − (Q × UVC). Solving for Q gives Q = TFC ÷ (P − UVC − (0.25 × P)) or TFC ÷ ((0.75 × P) − UVC).

7. "Nielson Finds More TVs; Hispanics Top 11 Million," *Advertising Age*, August 29, 2005, p. 1.

8. Consumer Electronics Association available at www.ce.org, accessed July 25, 2006.

9. Daisy Whitney, "'06 HDTV Sales to Outpace Analog," *Television Week*, October 31, 2005, pp. 19–24.

10. See Roger J. Best, *Market-Based Management*, 4th ed. (Upper Saddle River, NJ: Prentice Hall, 2005).

11. Total contribution can also be determined from the unit contribution and unit volume: Total contribution = unit contribution × unit sales. Total units sold in 2006 were 297,619 units, which can be determined by dividing total sales by price per unit ($100 million ÷ $336). Total contribution = $70 contribution per unit × 297,619 units = $20,833,330 (difference due to rounding.

12. Recall that the contribution margin of 21 percent was based on variable costs representing 79 percent of sales. Therefore, if we do not know price, we can set it equal to $1.00. If price equals $1.00, 79 cents represents variable costs and 21 cents represents unit contribution. If price is decreased by 10 percent, the new price is $0.90. However, variable costs do not change just because price decreased, so the unit contribution and contribution margin decrease as follows:

	Old	New (reduced 10%
Price	$1.00	$0.90
– Unit variable cost	$0.79	$0.79
– Unit contribution	$0.21	$0.11
Contribution margin	$0.21 + $1.00 = 0.21 or 21%	$0.11 + $0.90 = 0.12 or 12%

Adapted marketing mix An international marketing strategy for adjusting the marketing mix elements to each international target market, bearing more costs but hoping for a larger market share and return.

Administered VMS A vertical marketing system that coordinates successive stages of production and distribution, not through common ownership or contractual ties, but through the size and power of one of the parties.

Adoption process The mental process through which an individual passes from first hearing about an innovation to final adoption.

Advertising Any paid form of nonpersonal presentation and promotion of ideas, goods, or services by an identified sponsor.

Advertising agency A marketing services firm that assists companies in planning, preparing, implementing, and evaluating all or portions of their advertising programs.

Advertising budget The dollars and other resources allocated to a product or company advertising program.

Advertising media The vehicles through which advertising messages are delivered to their intended audiences.

Advertising objective A specific communication task to be accomplished with a specific target audience during a specific period of time.

Advertising strategy The strategy by which the company accomplishes its advertising objectives. It consists of two major elements: creating advertising messages and selecting advertising media.

Affordable method Setting the promotion budget at the level management thinks the company can afford.

Age and life-cycle segmentation Dividing a market into different age and life-cycle groups.

Agent A wholesaler who represents buyers or sellers on a relatively permanent basis, performs only a few functions, and does not take title to goods.

Allowance Promotional money paid by manufacturers to retailers in return for an agreement to feature the manufacturer's products in some way.

Alternative evaluation The stage of the buyer decision process in which the consumer uses information to evaluate alternative brands in the choice set.

Approach The step in the selling process in which the salesperson meets the customer for the first time.

Attitude A person's relatively consistent evaluations, feelings, and tendencies toward an object or idea.

Baby boomers The 78 million people born during the baby boom following World War II and lasting until the early 1960s.

Basing-point pricing A geographical pricing strategy in which the seller designates some city as a basing point and charges all customers the freight cost from that city to the customer.

Behavioral segmentation Dividing a market into groups based on consumer knowledge, attitude, use, or response to a product.

Belief A descriptive thought that a person has about something.

Benchmarking The process of comparing the company's products and processes to those of competitors or leading firms in other industries to find ways to improve quality and performance.

Benefit segmentation Dividing a market into groups according to the different benefits that consumers seek from the product.

Brand A name, term, sign, symbol, or design, or a combination of these that identifies the products or services of one seller or group of sellers and differentiates them from those of competitors.

Brand equity The positive differential effect that knowing the brand name has on customer response to the product or service.

Brand extension Extending an existing brand name to new product categories.

Brand personality The specific mix of human traits that may be attributed to a particular brand.

Break-even pricing (target profit pricing) Setting prices to break even on the costs of making and marketing a product; or setting prices to make a target profit.

Broker A wholesaler who does not take title to goods and whose function is to bring buyers and sellers together and assist in negotiation.

Business analysis A review of the sales, costs, and profit projections for a new product to find out whether these factors satisfy the company's objectives.

Business buyer behavior The buying behavior of the organizations that buy goods and services for use in the production of other products and services or for the purpose of reselling or renting them to others at a profit.

Business buying process The decision process by which business buyers determine which products and services their organizations need to purchase, and then find, evaluate, and choose among alternative suppliers and brands.

Business portfolio The collection of businesses and products that make up the company.

Business promotion tools Sales promotion tools used to generate business leads, stimulate purchases, reward customers, and motivate salespeople.

Business-to-business (B2B) online marketing Using B2B Web sites, e-mail, online product catalogs, online trading networks, and other online resources to reach new business customers, serve current customers more effectively, and obtain buying efficiencies and better prices.

Business-to-consumer (B2C) online marketing Selling goods and services online to final consumers.

Buyer-readiness stages The stages consumers normally pass through on their way to purchase, including awareness, knowledge, liking, preference, conviction, and purchase.

Buyers The people in the organization's buying center who make an actual purchase.

Buying center All the individuals and units that play a role in the purchase decision-making process.

Buzz marketing Cultivating opinion leaders and getting them to spread information about a product or service to others in their communities.

By-product pricing Setting a price for by-products in order to make the main product's price more competitive.

Captive-product pricing Setting a price for products that must be used along with a main product, such as blades for a razor and film for a camera.

Catalog marketing Direct marketing through print, video, or electronic catalogs that are mailed to select customers, made available in stores, or presented online.

Category killer Giant specialty store that carries a very deep assortment of a particular line and is staffed by knowledgeable employees.

Causal research Marketing research to test hypotheses about cause-and-effect relationships.

Chain stores Two or more outlets that are commonly owned and controlled.

Channel conflict Disagreement among marketing channel members on goals and roles—who should do what and for what rewards.

Channel level A layer of intermediaries that performs some work in bringing the product and its ownership closer to the final buyer.

Click-and-mortar companies Traditional brick-and-mortar companies that have added online marketing to their operations.

Click-only companies The so-called dot-coms, which operate only online without any brick-and-mortar market presence.

Closing The step in the selling process in which the salesperson asks the customer for an order.

Co-branding The practice of using the established brand names of two different companies on the same product.

Cognitive dissonance Buyer discomfort caused by postpurchase conflict.

Commercialization Introducing a new product into the market.

Communication adaptation A global communication strategy of fully adapting advertising messages to local markets.

Competitive advantage An advantage over competitors gained by offering consumers greater value, either through lower prices or by providing more benefits that justify higher prices.

Competitive marketing strategies Strategies that strongly position the company against competitors and that give the company the strongest possible strategic advantage.

Competitive-parity method Setting the promotion budget to match competitors' outlays.

Competitor analysis The process of identifying key competitors; assessing their objectives, strategies, strengths and weaknesses, and reaction patterns; and selecting which competitors to attack or avoid.

Competitor-centered company A company whose moves are mainly based on competitors' actions and reactions.

Complex buying behavior Consumer buying behavior in situations characterized by high consumer involvement in a purchase and significant perceived differences among brands.

Concentrated (niche) marketing A market-coverage strategy in which a firm goes after a large share of one or a few segments or niches.

Concept testing Testing new-product concepts with a group of target consumers to find out if the concepts have strong consumer appeal.

Consumer buyer behavior The buying behavior of final consumers—individuals and households who buy goods and services for personal consumption.

Consumer market All the individuals and households who buy or acquire goods and services for personal consumption.

Consumer-oriented marketing The philosophy of enlightened marketing that holds that the company should view and organize its marketing activities from the consumer's point of view.

Consumer product Product bought by final consumer for personal consumption.

Consumer promotion tools Sales promotion tools used to urge short-term customer buying or to enhance long-term customer relationships.

Consumerism An organized movement of citizens and government agencies to improve the rights and power of buyers in relation to sellers.

Consumer-to-business (C2B) online marketing Online exchanges in which consumers search out sellers, learn about their offers, and initiate purchases, sometimes even driving transaction terms.

Consumer-to-consumer (C2C) online marketing Online exchanges of goods and information between final consumers.

Contract manufacturing A joint venture in which a company contracts with manufacturers in a foreign market to produce the product or provide its service.

Contractual VMS A vertical marketing system in which independent firms at different levels of production and distribution join together through contracts to obtain more economies or sales impact than they could achieve alone.

Convenience product Consumer product that the customer usually buys frequently, immediately, and with a minimum of comparison and buying effort.

Convenience store A small store, located near a residential area, that is open long hours seven days a week and carries a limited line of high-turnover convenience goods.

Conventional distribution channel A channel consisting of one or more independent producers, wholesalers, and retailers, each a separate business seeking to maximize its own profits even at the expense of profits for the system as a whole.

Corporate VMS A vertical marketing system that combines successive stages of production and distribution under single ownership—channel leadership is established through common ownership.

Corporate Web site A Web site designed to build customer goodwill and to supplement other sales channels, rather than to sell the company's products directly.

Cost-based pricing Setting prices based on the costs for producing, distributing, and selling the product plus a fair rate of return for effort and risk.

Cost-plus pricing Adding a standard markup to the cost of the product.

Countertrade International trade involving the direct or indirect exchange of goods for other goods instead of cash.

Creative concept The compelling "big idea" that will bring the advertising message strategy to life in a distinctive and memorable way.

Cultural environment Institutions and other forces that affect society's basic values, perceptions, preferences, and behaviors.

Culture The set of basic values, perceptions, wants, and behaviors learned by a member of society from family and other important institutions.

Customer-centered company A company that focuses on customer developments in designing its marketing strategies and on delivering superior value to its target customers.

Customer-centered new-product development New-product development that focuses on finding new ways to solve customer problems and create more customer-satisfying experiences.

Customer database An organized collection of comprehensive data about individual customers or prospects, including geographic, demographic, psychographic, and behavioral data.

Customer equity The total combined customer lifetime values of all of the company's customers.

Customer lifetime value The value of the entire stream of purchases that a customer would make over a lifetime of patronage.

Customer perceived value The customer's evaluation of the difference between all the benefits and all the costs of a market offering relative to those of competing offers.

Customer relationship management The overall process of building and maintaining profitable customer relationships by delivering superior customer value and satisfaction.

Customer relationship management (CRM) Managing detailed information about individual customers and carefully managing customer "touch points" in order to maximize customer loyalty.

Customer sales force structure A sales force organization under which salespeople specialize in selling only to certain customers or industries.

Customer satisfaction The extent to which a product's perceived performance matches a buyer's expectations.

Customer value analysis Analysis conducted to determine what benefits target customers value and how they rate the relative value of various competitors' offers.

Customer-value marketing A principle of enlightened marketing that holds that a company should put most of its resources into customer value-building marketing investments.

Deciders People in the organization's buying center who have formal or informal power to select or approve the final suppliers.

Decline stage The product life-cycle stage in which a product's sales decline.

Deficient products Products that have neither immediate appeal nor long-run benefits.

Demand curve A curve that shows the number of units the market will buy in a given time period, at different prices that might be charged.

Demands Human wants that are backed by buying power.

Demographic segmentation Dividing a market into groups based on variables such as age, gender, family size, family life cycle, income, occupation, education, religion, race, generation, and nationality.

Demography The study of human populations in terms of size, density, location, age, gender, race, occupation, and other statistics.

Department store A retail organization that carries a wide variety of product lines—each line is operated as a separate department managed by specialist buyers or merchandisers.

Derived demand Business demand that ultimately comes from (derives from) the demand for consumer goods.

Descriptive research Marketing research to better describe marketing problems, situations, or markets, such as the market potential for a product or the demographics and attitudes of consumers.

Desirable products Products that give both high immediate satisfaction and high long-run benefits.

Differentiated (segmented) marketing A market-coverage strategy in which a firm decides to target several market segments and designs separate offers for each.

Differentiation Actually differentiating the firm's market offering to create superior customer value.

Direct investment Entering a foreign market by developing foreign-based assembly or manufacturing facilities.

Direct marketing Direct connections with carefully targeted individual consumers to both obtain an immediate response and cultivate lasting customer relationships.

Direct marketing channel A marketing channel that has no intermediary levels.

Direct-mail marketing Direct marketing by sending an offer, announcement, reminder, or other item to a person at a particular address.

Direct-response television marketing Direct marketing via television, including direct-response television advertising (or infomercials) and home shopping channels.

Discount A straight reduction in price on purchases during a stated period of time.

Discount store A retail operation that sells standard merchandise at lower prices by accepting lower margins and selling at higher volume.

Disintermediation The cutting out of marketing channel intermediaries by product or service producers, or the displacement of traditional resellers by radical new types of intermediaries.

Dissonance-reducing buying behavior Consumer buying behavior in situations characterized by high involvement but few perceived differences among brands.

Distribution center A large, highly automated warehouse designed to receive goods from various plants and suppliers, take orders, fill them efficiently, and deliver goods to customers as quickly as possible.

Diversification A strategy for company growth through starting up or acquiring businesses outside the company's current products and markets.

Downsizing Reducing the business portfolio by eliminating products of business units that are not profitable or that no longer fit the company's overall strategy.

Dynamic pricing Adjusting prices continually to meet the characteristics and needs of individual customers and situations.

Economic community A group of nations organized to work toward common goals in the regulation of international trade.

Economic environment Factors that affect consumer buying power and spending patterns.

Engel's laws Differences noted over a century ago by Ernst Engel in how people shift their spending across food, housing, transportation, health care, and other goods and services categories as family income rises.

Enlightened marketing A marketing philosophy holding that a company's marketing should support the best long-run performance of the marketing system; its five principles include consumer-oriented marketing, customer-value marketing, innovative marketing, sense-of-mission marketing, and societal marketing.

Environmental sustainability A management approach that involves developing strategies that both sustain the environment and produce profits for the company.

Environmentalism An organized movement of concerned citizens and government agencies to protect and improve people's living environment.

Ethnographic research A form of observational research that involves sending trained observers to watch and interact with consumers in their "natural habitat."

Exchange The act of obtaining a desired object from someone by offering something in return.

Exclusive distribution Giving a limited number of dealers the exclusive right to distribute the company's products in their territories.

Execution style The approach, style, tone, words, and format used for executing an advertising message.

Experience curve (learning curve) The drop in the average per-unit production cost that comes with accumulated production experience.

Experimental research Gathering of primary data by selecting matched groups of subjects, giving them different treatments, controlling related factors, and checking for differences in group responses.

Exploratory research Marketing research to gather preliminary information that will help define problems and suggest hypotheses.

Exporting Entering a foreign market by selling goods produced in the company's home country, often with little modification.

Factory outlet Off-price retailing operation that is owned and operated by a manufacturer and that normally carries the manufacturer's surplus, discontinued, or irregular goods.

Fad A temporary period of unusually high sales driven by consumer enthusiasm and immediate product or brand popularity.

Fashion A currently accepted or popular style in a given field.

Fixed costs (overhead) Costs that do not vary with production or sales level.

FOB-origin pricing A geographical pricing strategy in which goods are placed free on board a carrier; the customer pays the freight from the factory to the destination.

Focus group interviewing Personal interviewing that involves inviting six to ten people to gather for a few hours with a trained interviewer to talk about a product, service, or organization. The interviewer "focuses" the group discussion on important issues.

Follow-up The last step in the selling process in which the salesperson follows up after the sale to ensure customer satisfaction and repeat business.

Franchise A contractual association between a manufacturer, wholesaler, or service organization (a franchiser) and independent businesspeople (franchisees) who buy the right to own and operate one or more units in the franchise system.

Franchise organization A contractual vertical marketing system in which a channel member, called a franchiser, links several stages in the production-distribution process.

Freight-absorption pricing A geographical pricing strategy in which the seller absorbs all or part of the freight charges in order to get the desired business.

Gatekeepers People in the organization's buying center who control the flow of information to others.

Gender segmentation Dividing a market into different groups based on gender.

General need description The stage in the business buying process in which the company describes the general characteristics and quantity of a needed item.

Generation X The 45 million people born between 1965 and 1976 in the "birth dearth" following the baby boom.

Generation Y The 72 million children of the baby boomers, born between 1977 and 1994.

Geographic segmentation Dividing a market into different geographical units such as nations, states, regions, counties, cities, or neighborhoods.

Geographical pricing Setting prices for customers located in different parts of the country or world.

Global firm A firm that, by operating in more than one country, gains R&D, production, marketing, and financial advantages in its costs and reputation that are not available to purely domestic competitors.

Good-value pricing Offering just the right combination of quality and good service at a fair price.

Government market Governmental units—federal, state, and local—that purchase or rent goods and services for carrying out the main functions of government.

Group Two or more people who interact to accomplish individual or mutual goals.

Growth-share matrix A portfolio-planning method that evaluates a company's strategic business units in terms of their market growth rate and relative market share. SBUs are classified as stars, cash cows, question marks, or dogs.

Growth stage The product life-cycle stage in which a product's sales start climbing quickly.

Habitual buying behavior Consumer buying behavior in situations characterized by low consumer involvement and few significant perceived brand differences.

Handling objections The step in the selling process in which the salesperson seeks out, clarifies, and overcomes customer objections to buying.

Horizontal marketing system A channel arrangement in which two or more companies at one level join together to follow a new marketing opportunity.

Idea generation The systematic search for new-product ideas.

Idea screening Screening new-product ideas in order to spot good ideas and drop poor ones as soon as possible.

Income segmentation Dividing a market into different income groups.

Independent off-price retailer Off-price retailer that is either owned and run by entrepreneurs or is a division of a larger retail corporation.

Indirect marketing channel Channel containing one or more intermediary levels.

Individual marketing Tailoring products and marketing programs to the needs and preferences of individual customers—also labeled "markets-of-one marketing," "customized marketing," and "one-to-one marketing."

Industrial product Product bought by individuals and organizations for further processing or for use in conducting a business.

Influencers People in an organization's buying center who affect the buying decision; they often help define specifications and also provide information for evaluating alternatives.

Information search The stage of the buyer decision process in which the consumer is aroused to search for more information; the consumer may simply have heightened attention or may go into active information search.

Innovative marketing A principle of enlightened marketing that requires that a company seek real product and marketing improvements.

Inside sales force Inside salespeople who conduct business from their offices via telephone, the Internet, or visits from prospective buyers.

Institutional market Schools, hospitals, nursing homes, prisons, and other institutions that provide goods and services to people in their care.

Integrated direct marketing Direct-marketing campaigns that use multiple vehicles and multiple stages to improve response rates and profits.

Integrated logistics management The logistics concept that emphasizes teamwork, both inside the company and among all the marketing channel organizations, to maximize the performance of the entire distribution system.

Integrated marketing communications (IMC) Carefully integrating and coordinating the company's many communications channels to deliver a clear, consistent, and compelling message about the organization and its products.

Intensive distribution Stocking the product in as many outlets as possible.

Interactive marketing Training service employees in the fine art of interacting with customers to satisfy their needs.

Intermarket segmentation Forming segments of consumers who have similar needs and buying behavior even though they are located in different countries.

Intermodal transportation Combining two or more modes of transportation.

Internal databases Electronic collections of consumer and market information obtained from data sources within the company network.

Internal marketing Orienting and motivating customer-contact employees and the supporting service people to work as a team to provide customer satisfaction.

Internet A vast public web of computer networks that connects users of all types all around the world to each other and to an amazingly large "information repository."

Introduction stage The product life-cycle stage in which the new product is first distributed and made available for purchase.

Joint ownership A joint venture in which a company joins investors in a foreign market to create a local business in which the company shares joint ownership and control.

Joint venturing Entering foreign markets by joining with foreign companies to produce or market a product or service.

Learning Changes in an individual's behavior arising from experience.

Licensing A method of entering a foreign market in which the company enters into an agreement with a licensee in the foreign market, offering the right to use a manufacturing process, trademark, patent, trade secret, or other item of value for a fee or royalty.

Lifestyle A person's pattern of living as expressed in his or her activities, interests, and opinions.

Line extension Extending an existing brand name to new forms, colors, sizes, ingredients, or flavors of an existing product category.

Local marketing Tailoring brands and promotions to the needs and wants of local customer groups—cities, neighborhoods, and even specific stores.

Macroenvironment The larger societal forces that affect the microenvironment—demographic, economic, natural, technological, political, and cultural forces.

Madison & Vine A term that has come to represent the merging of advertising and entertainment in an effort to break through the clutter and create new avenues for reaching consumers with more engaging messages.

Management contracting A joint venture in which the domestic firm supplies the management know-how to a foreign company that supplies the capital; the domestic firm exports management services rather than products.

Manufacturers' sales branches and offices Wholesaling by sellers or buyers themselves rather than through independent wholesalers.

Market The set of all actual and potential buyers of a product or service.

Market-centered company A company that pays balanced attention to both customers and competitors in designing its marketing strategies.

Market challenger A runner-up firm that is fighting hard to increase its market share in an industry.

Market development A strategy for company growth by identifying and developing new market segments for current company products.

Market follower A runner-up firm that wants to hold its share in an industry without rocking the boat.

Market leader The firm in an industry with the largest market share.

Market nicher A firm that serves small segments that the other firms in an industry overlook or ignore.

Market offering Some combination of products, services, information, or experiences offered to a market to satisfy a need or want.

Market penetration A strategy for company growth by increasing sales of current products to current market segments without changing the product.

Market-penetration pricing Setting a low price for a new product in order to attract a large number of buyers and a large market share.

Market segment A group of consumers who respond in a similar way to a given set of marketing efforts.

Market segmentation Dividing a market into distinct groups of buyers who have distinct needs, characteristics, or behavior and who might require separate products or marketing programs.

Market-skimming pricing Setting a high price for a new product to skim maximum revenues layer by layer from the segments willing to pay the high price; the company makes fewer but more profitable sales.

Market targeting The process of evaluating each market segment's attractiveness and selecting one or more segments to enter.

Marketing The process by which companies create value for customers and build strong customer relationships in order to capture value from customers in return.

Marketing audit A comprehensive, systematic, independent, and periodic examination of a company's environment, objectives, strategies, and activities to determine problem areas and opportunities and to recommend a plan of action to improve the company's marketing performance.

Marketing channel (distribution channel) A set of interdependent organizations that help make a product or service available for use or consumption by the consumer or business user.

Marketing concept The marketing management philosophy that achieving organizational goals depends on knowing the needs and wants of target markets and delivering the desired satisfactions better than competitors do.

Marketing control The process of measuring and evaluating the results of marketing strategies and plans and taking corrective action to ensure that objectives are achieved.

Marketing environment The actors and forces outside marketing that affect marketing management's ability to build and maintain successful relationships with target customers.

Marketing implementation The process that turns marketing strategies and plans into marketing actions in order to accomplish strategic marketing objectives.

Marketing information system (MIS) People, equipment, and procedures to gather, sort, analyze, evaluate, and distribute needed, timely, and accurate information to marketing decision makers.

Marketing intelligence The systematic collection and analysis of publicly available information about competitors and developments in the marketing environment.

Marketing intermediaries Firms that help the company to promote, sell, and distribute its goods to final buyers; they include resellers, physical distribution firms, marketing service agencies, and financial intermediaries.

Marketing logistics (physical distribution) The tasks involved in planning, implementing, and controlling the physical flow of materials, final goods, and related information from points of origin to points of consumption to meet customer requirements at a profit.

Marketing management The art and science of choosing target markets and building profitable relationships with them.

Marketing mix The set of controllable tactical marketing tools—product, price, place, and promotion—that the firm blends to produce the response it wants in the target market.

Marketing myopia The mistake of paying more attention to the specific products a company offers than to the benefits and experiences produced by these products.

Marketing research The systematic design, collection, analysis, and reporting of data relevant to a specific marketing situation facing an organization.

Marketing strategy development Designing an initial marketing strategy for a new product based on the product concept.

Marketing strategy The marketing logic by which the business unit hopes to achieve its marketing objectives.

Marketing Web site A Web site that engages consumers in interactions that will move them closer to a direct purchase or other marketing outcome.

Maturity stage The product life-cycle stage in which sales growth slows or levels off.

Merchant wholesaler Independently owned business that takes title to the merchandise it handles.

Microenvironment The actors close to the company that affect its ability to serve its customers—the company, suppliers, marketing intermediaries, customer markets, competitors, and publics.

Micromarketing The practice of tailoring products and marketing programs to the needs and wants of specific individuals and local customer groups—includes local marketing and individual marketing.

Mission statement A statement of the organization's purpose—what it wants to accomplish in the larger environment.

Modified rebuy A business buying situation in which the buyer wants to modify product specifications, prices, terms, or suppliers.

Motive (or drive) A need that is sufficiently pressing to direct the person to seek satisfaction of the need.

Multichannel distribution system A distribution system in which a single firm sets up two or more marketing channels to reach one or more customer segments.

Natural environment Natural resources that are needed as inputs by marketers or that are affected by marketing activities.

Need recognition The first stage of the buyer decision process, in which the consumer recognizes a problem or need.

Needs States of felt deprivation.

New product A good, service, or idea that is perceived by some potential customers as new.

New-product development The development of original products, product improvements, product modifications, and new brands through the firm's own R&D efforts.

New task A business buying situation in which the buyer purchases a product or service for the first time.

Nonpersonal communication channels Media that carry messages without personal contact or feedback, including major media, atmospheres, and events.

Objective-and-task method Developing the promotion budget by (1) defining specific objectives; (2) determining the tasks that must be performed to achieve these objectives; and (3) estimating the costs of performing these tasks. The sum of these costs is the proposed promotion budget.

Observational research The gathering of primary data by observing relevant people, actions, and situations.

Occasion segmentation Dividing a market into groups according to occasions when buyers get the idea to buy, actually make their purchase, or use the purchased item.

Off-price retailer Retailer that buys at less-than-regular wholesale prices and sells at less than retail. Examples are factory outlets, independents, and warehouse clubs.

Online advertising Advertising that appears while consumers are surfing the Web, including display ads (banners, interstitials, pop-ups), search-related ads, online classifieds, and other forms.

Online databases Computerized collections of information available from online commercial sources or via the Internet.

Online marketing Company efforts to market products and services and build customer relationships over the Internet.

Online marketing research Collecting primary data through Internet surveys and online focus groups.

Opinion leader Person within a reference group who, because of special skills, knowledge, personality, or other characteristics, exerts social influence on others.

Optional-product pricing The pricing of optional or accessory products along with a main product.

Order-routine specification The stage of the business buying process in which the buyer writes the final order with the chosen supplier(s), listing the technical specifications, quantity needed, expected time of delivery, return policies, and warranties.

Outside sales force (or field sales force) Outside salespeople who travel to call on customers in the field.

Packaging The activities of designing and producing the container or wrapper for a product.

Partner relationship management Working closely with partners in other company departments and outside the company to jointly bring greater value to customers.

Percentage-of-sales method Setting the promotion budget at a certain percentage of current or forecasted sales or as a percentage of the unit sales price.

Perception The process by which people select, organize, and interpret information to form a meaningful picture of the world.

Performance review The stage of the business buying process in which the buyer assesses the performance of the supplier and decides to continue, modify, or drop the arrangement.

Personal communication channels Channels through which two or more people communicate directly with each other, including face to face, on the phone, through mail or e-mail, or even through an Internet "chat."

Personal selling Personal presentation by the firm's sales force for the purpose of making sales and building customer relationships.

Personality The unique psychological characteristics that lead to relatively consistent and lasting responses to one's own environment.

Pleasing products Products that give high immediate satisfaction but may hurt consumers in the long run.

Political environment Laws, government agencies, and pressure groups that influence and limit various organizations and individuals in a given society.

Portfolio analysis The process by which management evaluates the products and businesses making up the company.

Positioning Arranging for a product to occupy a clear, distinctive, and desirable place relative to competing products in the minds of target consumers.

Positioning statement A statement that summarizes company or brand positioning—it takes this form: To (target segment and need) our (brand) is (concept) that (point of difference).

Postpurchase behavior The stage of the buyer decision process in which the consumers takes further action after purchase, based on their satisfaction or dissatisfaction.

Preapproach The step in the selling process in which the salesperson learns as much as possible about a prospective customer before making a sales call.

Presentation The step in the selling process in which the salesperson tells the "product story" to the buyer, highlighting customer benefits.

Price The amount of money charged for a product or service, or the sum of the values that consumers exchange for the benefits of having or using the product or service.

Price elasticity A measure of the sensitivity of demand to changes in price.

Primary data Information collected for the specific purpose at hand.

Private brand (or store brand) A brand created and owned by a reseller of a product or service.

Problem recognition The first stage of the business buying process in which someone in the company recognizes a problem or need that can be met by acquiring a good or a service.

Product Anything that can be offered to a market for attention, acquisition, use, or consumption that might satisfy a want or need.

Product adaptation Adapting a product to meet local conditions or wants in foreign markets.

Product bundle pricing Combining several products and offering the bundle at a reduced price.

Product concept A detailed version of the new-product idea stated in meaningful consumer terms.

Product concept The idea that consumers will favor products that offer the most quality, performance, and features and that the organization should therefore devote its energy to making continuous product improvements.

Product development A strategy for company growth by offering modified or new products to current market segments; developing the product concept into a physical product in order to ensure that the product idea can be turned into a workable product.

Product invention Creating new products or services for foreign markets.

Product life cycle (PLC) The course of a product's sales and profits over its lifetime. It involves five distinct stages:

product development, introduction, growth, maturity, and decline.

Product line A group of products that are closely related because they function in a similar manner, are sold to the same customer groups, are marketed through the same types of outlets, or fall within given price ranges.

Product line pricing Setting the price steps between various products in a product line based on cost differences between the products, customer evaluations of different features, and competitors' prices.

Product/market expansion grid A portfolio-planning tool for identifying company growth opportunities through market penetration, market development, product development, or diversification.

Product mix (or product portfolio) The set of all product lines and items that a particular seller offers for sale.

Product position The way the product is defined by consumers on important attributes—the place the product occupies in consumers' minds relative to competing products.

Product quality The characteristics of a product or service that bear on its ability to satisfy stated or implied customer needs.

Product sales force structure A sales force organization under which salespeople specialize in selling only a portion of the company's products or lines.

Product specification The stage of the business buying process in which the buying organization decides on and specifies the best technical product characteristics for a needed item.

Production concept The idea that consumers will favor products that are available and highly affordable and that the organization should therefore focus on improving production and distribution efficiency.

Promotion mix (marketing communications mix) The specific blend of advertising, sales promotion, public relations, personal selling, and direct-marketing tools that the company uses to persuasively communicate customer value and build customer relationships.

Promotional pricing Temporarily pricing products below the list price, and sometimes even below cost, to increase short-run sales.

Proposal solicitation The stage of the business buying process in which the buyer invites qualified suppliers to submit proposals.

Prospecting The step in the selling process in which the salesperson identifies qualified potential customers.

Psychographic segmentation Dividing a market into different groups based on social class, lifestyle, or personality characteristics.

Psychological pricing A pricing approach that considers the psychology of prices and not simply the economics; the price is used to say something about the product.

Public Any group that has an actual or potential interest in or impact on an organization's ability to achieve its objectives.

Public relations Building good relations with the company's various publics by obtaining favorable publicity, building a good corporate image, and handling or heading off unfavorable rumors, stories, and events.

Pull strategy A promotion strategy that calls for spending a lot on advertising and consumer promotion to induce final consumers to buy the product. If the pull strategy is effective, consumers will then demand the product from channel members, who will in turn demand it from producers.

Purchase decision The buyer's decision about which brand to purchase.

Push strategy A promotion strategy that calls for using the sales force and trade promotion to push the product through channels. The producer promotes the product to channel members to induce them to carry the product and to promote it to final consumers.

Reference prices Prices that buyers carry in their minds and refer to when they look at a given product.

Retailer A business whose sales come primarily from retailing.

Retailing All activities involved in selling goods or services directly to final consumers for their personal, nonbusiness use.

Return on advertising investment The net return on advertising investment divided by the costs of the advertising investment.

Return on marketing investment (or marketing ROI) The net return from a marketing investment divided by the costs of the marketing investment.

Sales force management The analysis, planning, implementation, and control of sales force activities. It includes designing sales force strategy and structure and recruiting, selecting, training, supervising, compensating, and evaluating the firm's salespeople.

Salesperson An individual representing a company to customers by performing one or more of the following activities: prospecting, communicating, selling, servicing, information gathering, and relationship building.

Sales promotion Short-term incentives to encourage the purchase or sale of a product or service.

Sales quota A standard that states the amount a salesperson should sell and how sales should be divided among the company's products.

Salutary products Products that have low appeal but may benefit consumers in the long run.

Sample A segment of the population selected for marketing research to represent the population as a whole.

Secondary data Information that already exists somewhere, having been collected for another purpose.

Segmented pricing Selling a product or service at two or more prices, where the difference in prices is not based on differences in costs.

Selective distribution The use of more than one, but fewer than all, of the intermediaries who are willing to carry the company's products.

Selling concept The idea that consumers will not buy enough of the firm's products unless it undertakes a large-scale selling and promotion effort.

Selling process The steps that the salesperson follows when selling, which include prospecting and qualifying,

preapproach, approach, presentation and demonstration, handling objections, closing, and follow-up.

Sense-of-mission marketing A principle of enlightened marketing that holds that a company should define its mission in broad social terms rather than narrow product terms.

Service Any activity or benefit that one party can offer to another that is essentially intangible and does not result in the ownership of anything.

Service inseparability A major characteristic of services—they are produced and consumed at the same time and cannot be separated from their providers.

Service intangibility A major characteristic of services—they cannot be seen, tasted, felt, heard, or smelled before they are bought.

Service perishability A major characteristic of services—they cannot be stored for later sale or use.

Service-profit chain The chain that links service firm profits with employee and customer satisfaction.

Service variability A major characteristic of services—their quality may vary greatly, depending on who provides them and when, where, and how.

Share of customer The portion of the customer's purchasing that a company gets in its product categories.

Shopping center A group of retail businesses planned, developed, owned, and managed as a unit.

Shopping product Consumer good that the customer, in the process of selection and purchase, characteristically compares on such bases as suitability, quality, price, and style.

Social class Relatively permanent and ordered divisions in a society whose members share similar values, interests, and behaviors.

Social marketing The use of commercial marketing concepts and tools in programs designed to influence individuals' behavior to improve their well-being and that of society.

Societal marketing A principle of enlightened marketing that holds that a company should make marketing

decisions by considering consumers' wants, the company's requirements, consumers' long-run interests, and society's long-run interests.

Societal marketing concept A principle of enlightened marketing that holds that a company should make good marketing decisions by considering consumers' wants, the company's requirements, consumers' long-run interests, and society's long-run interests.

Spam Unsolicited, unwanted commercial e-mail messages.

Specialty product Consumer product with unique characteristics or brand identification for which a significant group of buyers is willing to make a special purchase effort.

Specialty store A retail store that carries a narrow product line with a deep assortment within that line.

Standardized marketing mix An international marketing strategy for using basically the same product, advertising, distribution channels, and other elements of the marketing mix in all the company's international markets.

Straight product extension Marketing a product in a foreign market without any change.

Straight rebuy A business buying situation in which the buyer routinely reorders something without any modifications.

Strategic group A group of firms in an industry following the same or a similar strategy.

Strategic planning The process of developing and maintaining a strategic fit between the organization's goals and capabilities and its changing marketing opportunities.

Style A basic and distinctive mode of expression.

Subculture A group of people with shared value systems based on common life experiences and situations.

Supermarket Large, low-cost, low-margin, high-volume, self-service store that carries a wide variety of grocery and household products.

Superstore A store much larger than a regular supermarket that offers a large assortment of routinely purchased food products, nonfood items, and services.

Supplier development Systematic development of networks of supplier-partners to ensure an appropriate and dependable supply of products and materials for use in making products or reselling them to others.

Supplier search The stage of the business buying process in which the buyer tries to find the best vendors.

Supplier selection The stage of the business buying process in which the buyer reviews proposals and selects a supplier or suppliers.

Supply chain management Managing upstream and downstream value-added flows of materials, final goods, and related information among suppliers, the company, resellers, and final consumers.

Survey research Gathering of primary data by asking people questions about their knowledge, attitudes, preferences, and buying behavior.

SWOT analysis An overall evaluation of the company's strengths (S), weaknesses (W), opportunities (O), and threats (T).

Systems selling Buying a packaged solution to a problem from a single seller, thus avoiding all the separate decisions involved in a complex buying situation.

Target costing Pricing that starts with an ideal selling price, then targets costs that will ensure that the price is met.

Target market A set of buyers sharing common needs or characteristics that the company decides to serve.

Team-based new-product development An approach to developing new products in which various company departments work closely together, overlapping the steps in the product development process to save time and increase effectiveness.

Team selling Using teams of people from sales, marketing, engineering, finance, technical support, and even upper management to service large, complex accounts.

Technological environment Forces that create new technologies, creating new product and market opportunities.

Telephone marketing Using the telephone to sell directly to customers.

Territorial sales force structure A sales force organization that assigns each salesperson to an exclusive geographic territory in which that salesperson sells the company's full line.

Test marketing The stage of new-product development in which the product and marketing program are tested in more realistic market settings.

Third-party logistics (3PL) provider An independent logistics provider that performs any or all of the functions required to get their client's product to market.

Total costs The sum of the fixed and variable costs for any given level of production.

Trade promotion tools Sales promotion tools used to persuade resellers to carry a brand, give it shelf space, promote it in advertising, and push it to consumers.

Undifferentiated (mass) marketing A market-coverage strategy in which a firm decides to ignore market segment differences and go after the whole market with one offer.

Uniform-delivered pricing A geographical pricing strategy in which the company charges the same price plus freight to all customers, regardless of their location.

Unsought product Consumer product that the consumer either does not know about or knows about but does not normally think of buying.

Users Members of the buying organization who will actually use the purchased product or service.

Value-added pricing Attaching value-added features and services to differentiate a company's offers and to support charging higher prices.

Value analysis An approach to cost reduction in which components are studied carefully to determine if they can be redesigned, standardized, or made by less costly methods of production.

Value-based pricing Setting prices based on buyers' perceptions of value rather than on the seller's cost.

Value chain The series of departments that carry out value-creating activities to design, produce, market, deliver, and support a firm's products.

Value delivery network The network made up of the company, suppliers, distributors, and ultimately customers who "partner" with each other to improve the performance of the entire system.

Value proposition The full positioning of a brand—the full mix of benefits upon which it is positioned.

Variable costs Costs that vary directly with the level of production.

Variety-seeking buying behavior Consumer buying behavior in situations characterized by low consumer involvement but significant perceived brand differences.

Vertical marketing system (VMS) A distribution channel structure in which producers, wholesalers, and retailers act as a unified system. One channel member owns the others, has contracts with them, or has so much power that they all cooperate.

Viral marketing The Internet version of word-of-mouth marketing—Web sites, e-mail messages, or other marketing events that are so infectious that customers will want to pass them along to friends.

Wants The form human needs take as shaped by culture and individual personality.

Warehouse club Off-price retailer that sells a limited selection of brand name grocery items, appliances, clothing, and a hodgepodge of other goods at deep discounts to members who pay annual membership fees.

Web communities Web sites upon which members can congregate online and exchange views on issues of common interest.

Wheel-of-retailing concept A concept of retailing that states that new types of retailers usually begin as low-margin, low-price, low-status operations but later evolve into higher-priced, higher-service operations, eventually becoming like the conventional retailers they replaced.

Whole-channel view Designing international channels that take into account all the necessary links in distributing the seller's products to final buyers, including the seller's headquarters organization, channels among nations, and channels within nations.

Wholesaler A firm engaged primarily in wholesaling activities.

Wholesaling All activities involved in selling goods and services to those buying for resale or business use.

Word-of-mouth influence Personal communication about a product between target buyers and neighbors, friends, family members, and associates.

Zone pricing A geographical pricing strategy in which the company sets up two or more zones. All customers within a zone pay the same total price; the more distant the zone, the higher the price.

Subject